ARE 5 Review Manual

for the Architect Registration Exam

David Kent Ballast, FAIA, NCARB, CSI
Steven E. O'Hara, PE

Professional Publications, Inc. • Belmont, California

Benefit by Registering This Book with PPI

- Get book updates and corrections.
- Hear the latest exam news.
- Obtain exclusive exam tips and strategies.
- Receive special discounts.

Register your book at **ppi2pass.com/register**.

Report Errors and View Corrections for This Book

PPI is grateful to every reader who notifies us of a possible error. Your feedback allows us to improve the quality and accuracy of our products. You can report errata and view corrections at **ppi2pass.com/errata**.

ARE 5 REVIEW MANUAL

Release History

date	edition number	revision number	description
September 2016	1	1	New book.
February 2017	1	2	Minor corrections. Minor cover updates.

Printed in the United States of America.

PPI
1250 Fifth Avenue, Belmont, CA 94002
(650) 593-9119
ppi2pass.com

ISBN: 978-1-59126-515-3

Library of Congress Control Number: 2016946608

F E D C B A

DIVISIONS

TABLE OF CONTENTS

PREFACE AND ACKNOWLEDGMENTS

The *ARE 5 Review Manual* is written to give you a thorough review of the subjects most likely to appear on the Architect Registration Examination 5 (ARE 5). This book's organization is based on the structure of ARE 5, and the content reflects the most recent editions of a number of codes and standards, including

- 2007 AIA Contract Documents
- 2009 SectionFormat
- 2010 *Americans with Disabilities Act (ADA) Standards for Accessible Design*
- 2011 AISC *Steel Construction Manual*, 14th edition
- 2013 LEED Rating Systems
- 2014 ACI 318, *Building Code Requirements for Structural Concrete*
- 2014 *National Electrical Code* (NFPA 70)
- 2015 *International Building Code*
- 2015 *International Energy Conservation Code*
- 2015 *International Green Construction Code*
- 2015 *International Mechanical Code*
- 2015 *International Plumbing Code*
- 2015 *Life Safety Code* (NFPA 101)
- 2016 CSI MasterFormat

ARE 5 Review Manual includes subject areas that are new to the ARE with version 5. Recent developments in architecture and construction in a number of areas are covered, including

- building commissioning
- business development and operations
- concrete reinforcement
- conformance with sustainability requirements
- construction manager as advisor or constructor
- contract documents for sustainable projects
- contractor selection
- cost control
- curtain walls
- design-build project delivery
- elevator design
- environmental context
- ethical standards
- financial management
- human resources
- integrated project delivery
- integrating building systems
- mechanical rooms
- office organization
- paving
- planning construction documentation
- plenum requirements
- post-occupancy evaluation
- practice methodologies
- project delivery methods, execution, follow-up, planning, and management
- quality control
- supplemental contract documentation
- sustainable materials
- value engineering
- weather barriers
- wood framing

Many people have helped in the production of this book. We would like to thank Holly Williams Leppo, AIA, who reviewed the book for technical accuracy and offered many good suggestions for additions and improvements, as well as Gary E. Demele, FAIA, NCARB, and Bradley E. Saeger, AIA, who contributed and reviewed many of the example problems. We would also like to thank all the fine people at PPI including Steve Buehler, associate director of acquisitions; Matt Schneiderman, editorial project manager; Scott Marley, senior copy editor; Brian Gonzalez, Tyler Hayes, Richard Iriye, Ellen Nordman, Ceridwen Quattrin, and Ian A. Walker, copy editors and typesetters; Tom Bergstrom, cover designer and technical illustrator; Sam Webster, publishing systems manager; Cathy Schrott, production services manager; and Grace Wong, director of publishing services.

Although we had much help in preparing this new edition, the responsibility for any errors is our own. A current list of known errata for this book is maintained at **ppi2pass.com/errata**, and you can let us know of any errors you find at the same place. We greatly appreciate the time you take to help us keep this book accurate and up to date.

David Kent Ballast, FAIA, NCARB, CSI
Steven E. O'Hara, PE

INTRODUCTION

ABOUT THIS BOOK

ARE 5 Review Manual is tailored to the needs of those studying for version 5 of the Architect Registration Examination (ARE 5). Although there is no substitute for a good formal education and the broad-based experience provided by your internship with a practicing architect, this book will help direct your study efforts to help you pass the ARE 5.

ARE 5 Review Manual is organized into six divisions that correspond to the six divisions of the ARE.

- Division 1: Practice Management
- Division 2: Project Management
- Division 3: Programming & Analysis
- Division 4: Project Planning & Design
- Division 5: Project Development & Documentation
- Division 6: Construction & Evaluation

Each division of the book is divided into chapters that cover all the subject areas included in the corresponding ARE division.

Wherever practical, these subject areas are covered in the same order as they are listed in the exam specifications. To avoid repetition and make your review more efficient, however, this order is occasionally modified slightly so that related subject areas can be discussed together.

For example, according to NCARB's specifications, the first division of the ARE, "Practice Management," covers the following subject areas.

- Business Operations
- Finances, Risk & Development of Practice
- Practice-Wide Delivery of Services
- Practice Methodologies

Accordingly, Division 1 of this book, "Practice Management," contains these chapters.

- Business Operations
- Financial and Risk Management
- Delivery of Services

Development of practice is more closely connected with business operations than it is with financial and risk management, so development of practice is discussed as part of the "Business Operations" chapter. Similarly, the subject area of practice methodologies is closely related to that of delivery of services, so practice methodologies are discussed in the "Delivery of Services" chapter.

Even when the order is slightly different, all the subject areas listed in the exam specifications for a division of ARE 5 are covered within the corresponding division of the book.

In the ARE, there is considerable overlap among the various divisions and what you need to study to prepare for them. One subject area might be relevant to Divisions 1 and 2, another to Divisions 2, 3, and 6, and a third to Divisions 3, 4, and 5. For this reason, *ARE 5 Review Manual* covers topics from all six divisions in a single volume. Where appropriate, we've included cross references to material in other chapters that you may want to add to your review.

Scattered throughout the book are over 150 example questions. Some of these are multiple-choice questions like the ones on the exam; others are open-ended. These are meant to help you absorb the material, and many of them are easier than the questions on your exam are likely to be.

It is a very good idea, however, to practice on questions that are similar in format and difficulty to those on the exam. Practice problems and practice exams can be found in two companion books, *ARE 5 Practice Problems* and *ARE 5 Practice Exam*, respectively. Like *ARE 5 Review Manual*, each of these books covers all six divisions.

THE ARCHITECT REGISTRATION EXAMINATION

The Architect Registration Examination (ARE) is a uniform test administered to candidates who wish to become licensed architects after they have served their required internships. It is given throughout the United States, the U.S. territories, Canada, England, People's Republic of China, and United Arab Emirates. The ARE has been developed to protect the health, safety, and welfare of the public by testing a candidate's entry-level competence to practice architecture. Its content relates as closely as possible to situations encountered in practice. It tests for the kinds of knowledge, skills, and abilities required of an entry-level architect, with particular emphasis on those services that affect public health, safety, and welfare.

In order to accomplish these objectives, the exam tests for

- knowledge in specific subject areas
- the ability to make decisions
- the ability to consolidate and use information to solve a problem
- the ability to coordinate the activities of others on the building team

The ARE also includes professional practice and project management problems, and problems that are based on particular editions of codes.

The ARE is developed by the National Council of Architectural Registration Boards (NCARB) and is administered by Prometric. Prometric serves as NCARB's test center administration consultant and operates and maintains the test centers where the ARE is administered. Alpine Testing Solutions, Inc. serves as NCARB's test content and candidate management consultant for the ARE.

Although the responsibility for professional licensing rests with individual states, every state board requires successful completion of the ARE to achieve licensure. One of the primary reasons for a uniform test is to facilitate reciprocity—that is, to enable an architect to more easily gain a license to practice in states other than the one in which he or she was originally licensed.

The ARE is administered on and graded entirely by computer. All divisions of the exam are offered six days a week at a network of Prometric test centers. The results are scored by computer, and the results are forwarded to individual state boards of architecture, which process them and notify candidates. If a candidate fails a division, he or she must wait at least 60 days before retaking that division.

FIRST STEPS

As you begin to prepare for the exam, you should first obtain current copies of the *Your Guide to ARE 5.0 (ARE Guidelines)* and the *ARE 5.0 Test Specification* from NCARB. The *ARE Guidelines* give instructions on how to apply, pay for, and take the ARE, and other useful information. *ARE 5.0 Test Specification* describes the six divisions of the exam; for each division, it gives the major subject areas and what percentage of the questions in that division will come from each subject area. You can download PDF versions at the NCARB website, ncarb.org, or you can request printed copies through the contact information provided on that website.

The NCARB website also gives current information about the exam, education requirements, training, examination procedures, and NCARB reciprocity services. It includes sample scenarios of the computer-based examination process, examples of costs associated with taking the computer-based exam, and descriptions of new question types. The PPI website is also a good source of answers to frequently asked questions about the exam (**ppi2pass.com/arefaq**).

To register as an examinee, you should follow the registration requirements of the board in the state, province, or territory where you want to be registered. The exact requirements vary from one jurisdiction to another, so contact your local board. Links to state boards can be found at **ppi2pass.com/faqs/architecture-state-boards**.

As soon as NCARB has verified your qualifications, you can begin scheduling examinations. The exams are offered on a first come, first served basis and must be scheduled at least 72 hours in advance. See the *ARE Guidelines* for instructions on finding a current list of testing centers. You can take the exams at any location, even outside the state in which you intend to become registered.

You can schedule any division of the ARE at any time and may take the divisions in any order. Divisions can be taken one at a time, to spread out preparation time and exam costs, or they can be taken together in any combination. However, you must pass all six divisions of the ARE within a single five-year period. This period, or "rolling clock," begins on the date of the first division you pass. If you have not completed the ARE within five years, the divisions that you passed more than five years ago are no longer credited, and those division exams must be retaken. Your new five-year period begins on the date of the earliest division you passed within the most recent five years.

EXAMINATION FORMAT

The ARE is organized into six divisions that test various areas of architectural knowledge and problem-solving ability.

Practice Management

80 questions, 3.5 hours

Project Management

95 questions, 4 hours

Programming & Analysis

95 questions, 4 hours

Project Planning & Design

120 questions, 5 hours

Project Development & Documentation

120 questions, 5 hours

Construction & Evaluation

95 questions, 4 hours

Past experience suggests that there is quite a bit of overlap among these divisions. Problems that seem better suited to the Project Planning & Design division may show up on the Construction & Evaluation division, for example, and problems on architectural history and building regulations might show up anywhere. That is why it is important for you to have a comprehensive strategy for studying and taking the exams.

The ARE is a computer-based exam (CBT). There are six kinds of problems on the exam: multiple-choice, check-all-that-apply, quantitative fill-in-the-blank, drag-and-place, hot spot, and case study. Each division includes between 80 and 120 questions along with one or two case studies.

Each case study is a collection of questions that includes a description of a scenario with a related set of resource documents (e.g., drawings, specifications, code resources). Case studies require you to assess multiple pieces of information and make judgments based on the context provided.

Multiple-Choice Problems

There are several types of multiple-choice problems.

One type of multiple-choice problem is based on written, graphic, or photographic information. You will need to examine the information and select the correct answer from four given options. Some problems may require calculations. A second type of multiple-choice problem describes a situation that could be encountered in actual practice. Drawings, diagrams, photographs, forms, tables, or other data may also be given. The problem requires you to select the best answer from four options.

Keep in mind that multiple-choice problems often require you to do more than just select an answer based on memory. At times it will be necessary to combine several facts, analyze data, perform a calculation, or review a drawing. You will probably not need the entire time allotted for the multiple-choice sections. If you have time for more than one pass through the problems, you can make good use of it.

Check-All-That-Apply Problems

In this variation of a multiple-choice problem, six options are given, and you must choose all the correct options. The problem tells how many of the options are correct, from two to four. You must choose all the correct options to receive credit; partial credit is not given.

Fill-in-the-Blank Problems

In this type of problem, you must fill a blank with a number that you have derived from a table or a calculation.

Hot Spot Problems

Hot spot problems are used to assess visual judgment, evaluation, or prediction. Hot spot problems include the information needed to make a determination, along with an image (e.g., diagram, floor plan) and instructions on how to interact with the image. The problems will indicate that you should place a single target, also known as a *hot spot icon*, on the base image in the correct location or general area. On the exam, you will place the target on the image by moving the computer cursor to the correct location on the image and clicking on it. You will see crosshairs to help you position the point of click. You will be able to click on an alternate spot if you think your first choice is not correct. Your choice is not registered until you exit the problem. You can click anywhere within an acceptable area range and still be scored as correct.

Drag-and-Place Problems

Another ARE 5 problem type is drag-and-place. Whereas hot spot problems involve placing just one target on the base image, drag-and-place problems involve placing two to six design elements on the base image. Drag-and-place problems are used to assess visual judgment or evaluation with multiple pieces of information. The problem statement describes what information is to be used to make the determination, and provides instructions on how to interact with the image or graphic item.

A drag-and-place problem, for example, may require you to drag and place design elements such as walls or beams onto the base image. On the exam, you will use the computer cursor to place the elements on the image by clicking and holding elements and dragging and releasing the elements on the correct location on the image. Depending on the question, you may use an element more than once or not at all. This type of question also provides an acceptable area range for placing the elements. The range may be small for questions about a detail or large for something like a site plan.

Case Study Problems

Each division exam includes one to two case studies. Case studies are performance item types comprising a scenario, a set of related resource documents (for example, code resources, drawings, and specifications), and a set of case study-specific problems. During the exam, you will be able to click on browser-like tabs at the top of the computer screen and flip back and forth between the case study scenario and resource documents. The case studies will test your ability to examine and use multiple pieces of information to make decisions about scenarios that could be encountered in the practice of architecture.

Case study problems may be multiple-choice, check-all-that-apply, fill-in-the-blank, hot spot, or drag-and-place.

STUDY GUIDELINES

After many years of higher education, you probably have a good idea of the study method that works best for you. The trick is figuring out how to apply that to the ARE. Unlike many college courses, there is not a single textbook or set of class notes from which all the exam problems will be derived. The exams are very broad and draw problems from multiple areas of knowledge.

The first challenge, then, is figuring out what to study. The ARE is never quite the same exam twice. The field of knowledge tested is always the same, but the specific problems asked are drawn randomly from a large pool, and the problems will differ from one candidate to the next. For example, one division may contain many code-related problems for one candidate and only a few for the next. This makes preparing for the ARE a challenge.

Your method of studying for the ARE should be based on both the content and form of the exam as well as on your school and work experience. Because the exam covers such a broad range of content, it cannot possibly include every detail of practice. Rather, it tends to focus on what is considered entry-level knowledge and on knowledge that is important for the protection of the public's health, safety, and welfare. Other types of problems are asked, too, but these two kinds of knowledge should be the focus of your review schedule.

Your work experience should also help you determine what areas to study the most. If, for example, you have been working with construction documents for several years, you will probably need less review in that area than in others you have not had much experience with.

The *ARE 5 Review Manual* and its companion books are structured to help you focus on the topics that are more likely to be included in the exam in one form or another. Some subjects may seem familiar or may be easy to recall from memory, and others may seem completely foreign; the latter are the ones to give particular attention to. It may be wise to study additional sources on these subjects, take review seminars, or get special help from someone who is knowledgeable in the topic.

A typical candidate might spend about forty hours preparing for and taking each division exam. Some will need to study more, some less. Forty hours is about one week of studying eight hours a day, or two weeks of four hours a day, or a month of two hours a day, along with reasonable breaks and time to attend to other responsibilities. As you probably work full time and have other family and personal obligations, it is important to develop a realistic schedule and do your best to stick to it. The ARE is not the kind of exam you can cram for the night before. Also, since the fees are high and retaking a test is expensive, you will want to do your best and pass in as few tries as possible. If you allow enough time to study and you go into each exam well prepared, you will be better able to relax and concentrate on the problems.

The following steps may provide a useful structure for an exam study program.

Step 1: Start early. You cannot review for a test like the ARE by starting two weeks before the date.

Step 2: Start by reviewing the *ARE Guidelines* and the *ARE 5.0 Test Specification.*

Step 3: Go through the *ARE 5 Review Manual* quickly to get a feeling for the scope of the chapters and how the major topics are organized.

Step 4: Based on your review in Step 3 and on a realistic appraisal of your strong and weak areas, set priorities for study and determine which topics need more study time.

Step 5: Divide review subjects into manageable units and organize them into a sequence of study. It is generally best to start with the less familiar subjects. Based on the exam date and plans for beginning study, assign a time limit to each study unit. Your knowledge of a subject should determine the time devoted to it. You may want to devote an entire week to earthquake design if it is an unfamiliar subject, and only one day to timber design if it is a familiar one. In setting up a schedule, be realistic about other life commitments as well as your personal ability to concentrate on studying over extended periods of time.

Step 6: Begin studying, and stick with the schedule. Of course, this requires self-discipline. The job should be easier if you have started early and if you are following a realistic schedule that allows time for recreation and personal commitments.

Step 7: Stop studying new material a day or two before the exam. By this time, no amount of additional cramming will help. At the very least, spend the evening before the exam relaxing, and get plenty of sleep that night. On the morning of the exam, a light review of some of the areas you've already studied can be helpful.

There are many schools of thought on the best order for taking the divisions. One factor to consider is the 60-day waiting period before you can retake a particular division. It is never fun to predict what you might fail, but if you know that a specific division might give you trouble, consider taking that exam near the beginning. You might be pleasantly surprised when you receive your results, but if not, as you work through the rest of the exams, the clock will be ticking and you can schedule the retest as soon as 60 days in the future.

On the other hand, don't tackle *all* your weakest subjects first. Make one of your early exams one that you feel fairly confident about. It is nice to get off on the right foot with a PASS.

Here are some additional study tips.

- Learn concepts first, and then details later. For example, it is much better to understand the basic ideas and theories of waterproofing than it is to attempt to memorize all the specific waterproofing methods and their details. Once the concept is clear, the details are much easier to learn and to apply during the exam.

- Use the *ARE 5 Review Manual's* index to focus on particular subjects in which you feel weak or subjects that can apply to more than one division.
- Brush up on architectural history before taking any of the divisions. Know major buildings and their architects, particularly structures that are representative of an architect's philosophy (for example, Le Corbusier and the Villa Savoye) or that represent "firsts" or "turning points." These have a way of turning up in any of the divisions.
- Try to schedule your exams so that you will have enough time on exam day to get yourself ready, eat, and review a little. If you will have a long drive to the testing center, try to avoid having to drive during rush hour. Alternatively, plan to spend the night before in a hotel near the testing center.
- If you are planning to take more than one division at a time, do not overstudy any one portion of the exam. It is generally better to review the concepts than to try to become an overnight expert in one area. For example, you may need to know general facts about built-up sections (plate girders), but you will not need to know how to complete a detailed design of a built-up section.
- Even though you may have a good grasp of the information and knowledge in a particular subject area, be prepared to address problems on the material in a variety of forms and from different points of view. For example, you may have studied and know definitions of terms in a subject area, but you will also need to be able to apply that knowledge when a problem uses a term as part of a more complex situation.
- Solve as many sample problems as possible, including those in *ARE 5 Practice Problems, ARE 5 Practice Exam*, and any other books that are available.
- Take advantage of the community of intern architects going through this experience with you. Some local AIA chapters offer ARE preparation courses, or they may be able to help you organize a study group with other interns in your area. Visit website forums to discuss the exam with others who have taken it or are preparing to take it. Even though the particular problems on the ARE are different for each candidate, it is a good idea to get a feeling for the subject areas that previous candidates have found particularly troublesome.
- Try to relax as much as possible during study periods and during the exam itself. Worrying is counterproductive. If you have worked diligently in school, have obtained a wide range of experience during internship, and have started exam review early, then you will be in the best possible position to pass the ARE.

TAKING THE EXAM

What to Bring

Bring multiple forms of photo ID, including a government-issued photo ID, to the test site. It is neither necessary nor permitted to bring any reference materials or scratch paper into the test site. Pencils and scratch paper are provided by Prometrics and must be returned when leaving the exam room. Earplugs are also provided. Leave all your books and notes in the car. Most testing centers have lockers for your keys, small personal belongings, and cell phone. Do not bring a calculator into the test site. A calculator built into the testing software will be available in all divisions.

Arriving at the Testing Center

Allow plenty of time to get to the exam site to avoid transportation problems such as getting lost or stuck in traffic jams. If you can, arrive a little early, and take a little time in the parking lot to review one last time the formulas and other things you have decided to memorize. Then relax, take a few deep breaths, and walk to the exam site.

Once at the exam site, you will check in with the attendant, who will verify your identification. After you check in, you will be shown to your testing station.

When the exam begins, you will have an opportunity to click through a tutorial that explains how the computer program works. You will probably want to read through it for your first exam, but after that initial exam, you will know how the software works and you won't need the tutorial. Take a deep breath, organize your paper and pencils, and take advantage of the opportunity to dump all the facts floating around in your brain onto your scratch paper—write down as much as you can. This includes formulas, ratios ("if x increases, y decreases"), and so on—anything that you are trying desperately not to forget. If you can get all the things you've crammed at the last minute onto that paper, you will be able to think a little more clearly about the problems on the screen.

Exam Tips

Here are some tips for taking the exam.

- Go through the entire exam in one somewhat swift pass, answering the problems that you are sure about and marking the others so you can return to them later. If a problem requires calculations, skip it for now unless it is very simple. Then, go back to the beginning and work your way through the exam again, taking a little more time to read each problem and think through the answer.
- Another benefit of initially going through the entire exam is that occasionally there is information in one problem that may help you answer another problem somewhere else.
- If you are very unsure of a problem, pick your best guess, mark it, and move on. You will probably have time at the end of the test to go back and recheck these answers. But, remember, your first response is usually the best.
- Always answer all the problems. An unanswered problem is counted wrong, so even if you are just guessing, it is better to choose an answer and have a chance of being correct than to skip the problem and be certain of getting it wrong. When faced with four options, the old SAT strategy of eliminating the options that are definitely wrong and making your best guess among the two or three that remain applies to the ARE, too.
- Some problems may seem *too* simple. Although a few very easy and obvious problems are included on the ARE, more often the simplicity should serve as a red flag to warn you to reevaluate the problem. Look for an exception to a rule or for special circumstances that make the obvious, easy response incorrect.
- Watch out for absolute words in a problem, such as "always," "never," and "completely." These are often a clue that some little exception exists, turning what reads like a true statement into a false one or vice versa.
- Occasionally there may be a defective problem. This does not happen very often, but if it does, make the best choice possible under the circumstances. Flawed problems are usually discovered, and either they are not counted on the test or any one of the correct answers is credited.

AFTER THE EXAM

When you have clicked the button to end the test, the computer may prompt you to provide some demographic information about yourself, your education, and your experience. Then gather your belongings and turn in your scratch paper and materials—you must leave them with the proctor. For test security reasons, you cannot remove anything from the site.

If you should encounter any problems during the exam or have any concerns, be sure to report them to the test site administrator and to NCARB as soon as possible. If you wait longer than 15 days after your test, NCARB will not respond to your complaint. You must report your complaint immediately and directly to NCARB and copy your state registration board for any hope of assistance.

Then, it is all over but the wait for your results via email. How long it takes to get your scores will vary with the efficiency of your state registration board, which reviews the scores from NCARB before passing along the results. A wait of at least four weeks is typical.

CODES AND STANDARDS USED IN THIS BOOK

ACI 318-14: *Building Code Requirements for Structural Concrete*, 2014. American Concrete Institute, Farmington Hills, MI.

ADA Standards: *2010 Americans with Disabilities Act (ADA) Standards for Accessible Design*, U.S. Department of Justice, Washington, DC.

AIA: Contract Documents, 2007. American Institute of Architects, Washington, DC.

AISC: *Steel Construction Manual*, 14th ed, 2011. American Institute of Steel Construction, Chicago, IL.

ANSI/ASHRAE 62.1-2016: *Ventilation for Acceptable Indoor Air Quality*, 2016. American Society of Heating, Refrigerating and Air-Conditioning Engineers, Atlanta, GA.

ANSI/ASHRAE 62.2-2016: *Ventilation and Acceptable Indoor Air Quality in Low-Rise Residential Buildings*, 2016. American Society of Heating, Refrigerating and Air-Conditioning Engineers, Atlanta, GA.

ANSI/ASHRAE/IESNA 90.1-2013: *Energy Standard for Buildings Except Low-Rise Residential Buildings*, 2013. American Society of Heating, Refrigerating and Air-Conditioning Engineers, Atlanta, GA.

ANSI/BOMA Z65.1-2010: *Office Buildings: Standard Methods of Measurement*, 2010. Building Owners and Managers Association, Washington, DC.

ASCE/SEI 7-10: *Minimum Design Loads for Buildings and Other Structures*, 2010. American Society of Civil Engineers, Reston, VA.

CSI: MasterFormat, 2016. Construction Specifications Institute, Alexandria, VA.

CSI: SectionFormat, 2009. Construction Specifications Institute, Alexandria, VA.

IBC: *International Building Code*, 2015. International Code Council, Washington, DC.

ICC/ANSI A117.1-2009: *Accessible and Usable Buildings and Facilities*, 2009. International Code Council. Washington, DC.

IECC: *International Energy Conservation Code*, 2015. International Code Council, Washington, DC.

IgCC: *International Green Construction Code*, 2015. International Code Council, Washington, DC.

IMC: *International Mechanical Code*, 2015. International Code Council, Washington, DC.

IPC: *International Plumbing Code*, 2015. International Code Council, Washington, DC.

IRC: *International Residential Code*, 2015. International Code Council, Washington, DC.

LEED 2013: Leadership in Energy and Environmental Design (LEED) 2013 Green Building Rating System for New Construction. U.S. Green Building Council, Washington, DC.

NDS 2015: *National Design Specification (NDS) for Wood Construction*, 15th ed., 2015. American Wood Council, Leesburg, VA.

NEC (NFPA 70): *National Electrical Code*, 2014. National Fire Protection Association, Quincy, MA.

NFPA 101: *Life Safety Code*, 2015. National Fire Protection Association, Quincy, MA.

The Secretary of the Interior's Standards for Rehabilitation, 2010. *Code of Federal Regulations*, Title 36, Part 67.

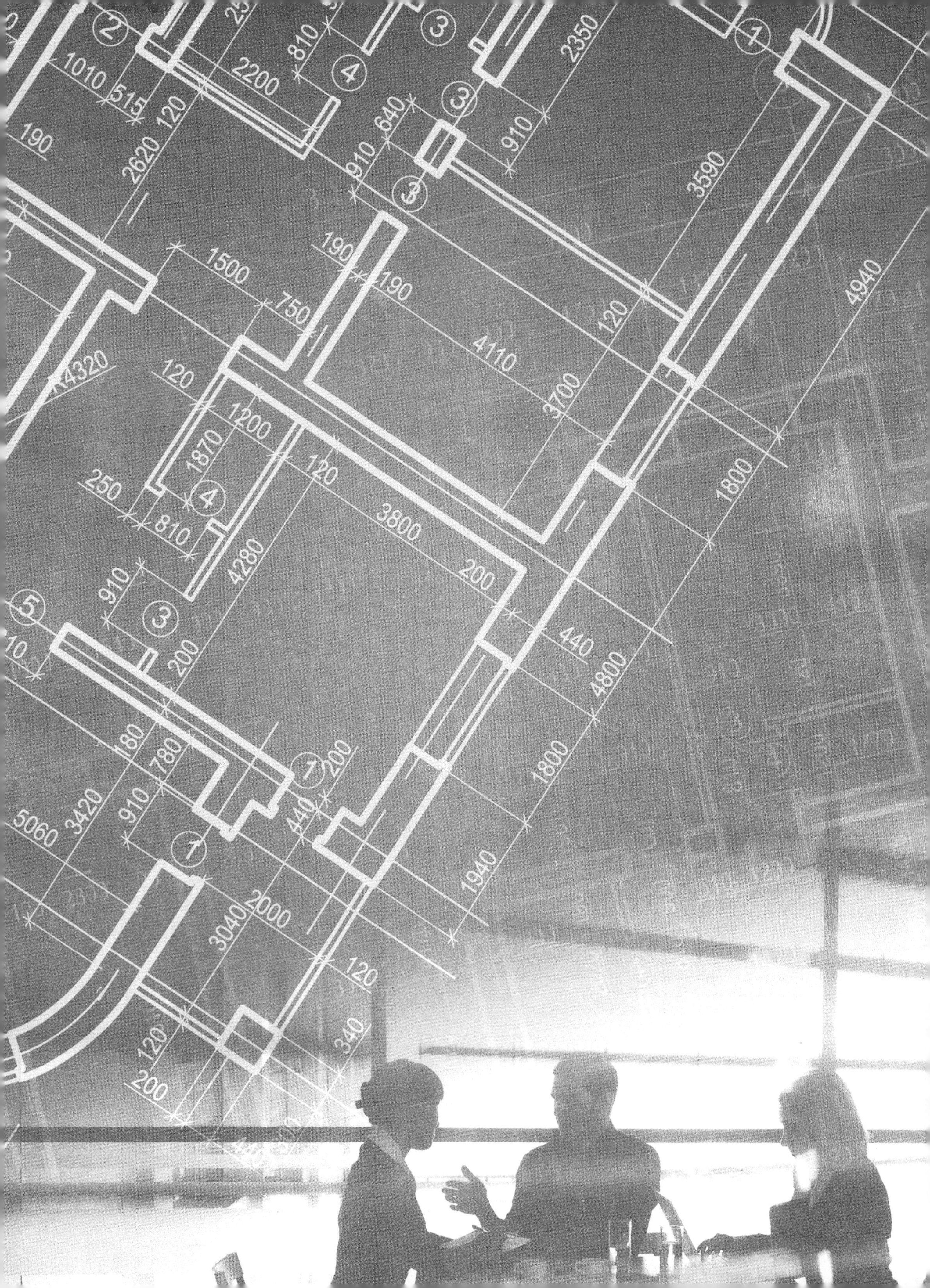

DIVISION 1: PRACTICE MANAGEMENT

1

BUSINESS OPERATIONS

For architectural firms, the subject of business operations includes

- *business organization:* the legal structure of an architectural firm
- *office organization:* the way the firm organizes to complete its work
- *ethical standards:* the accepted principles of correct professional conduct
- *human resources:* the practices and legal responsibilities pertaining to employing others
- *business development:* the use of marketing and public relations to increase business

These five subjects are discussed in this chapter. In addition, financial management and risk management are discussed in Chap. 2, and methods of service delivery and practice methodologies are discussed in Chap. 3.

BUSINESS ORGANIZATION

There are a number of different ways in which an architectural firm can be structured, and each structure has different legal and financial consequences.

- sole proprietorship
- general or limited partnership
- corporation
- limited liability company or limited liability partnership
- joint venture

Each has advantages and disadvantages and may be more or less appropriate depending on the number of people in the firm, the type of practice, the size of the business, the level of risk the owner or owners want to take, the laws of the state or states where the firm is doing business, and the requirements of the state licensing board or boards in regard to the participation of licensed architects in firm management.

Sole Proprietorship

The simplest business type is the *sole proprietorship*. In this structure, the business is owned by an individual. The business may operate under the owner's name or under a company name.

Setting up a sole proprietorship requires only a name and location for the business, company stationery, whatever electronic communications systems are needed, and the business licenses required by the local jurisdiction. If employees are hired, state and local requirements must also be met.

The advantages of a sole proprietorship include ease of setup, total management control by the owner, and possible tax advantages to the owner because business expenses and losses may be deducted from the gross income of the business. The main disadvantage is that the owner is personally liable for the company's debts and losses. If a client sues the company, the owner's personal income, personal property (possibly including property co-owned with a spouse), and other assets can be seized to pay any judgments.

Another possible disadvantage is that raising capital and establishing credit will depend entirely on the owner's personal credit rating and assets. Similarly, because success or failure depends mainly on the work and personal reputation of its owner, it may be difficult to sell even a successful sole proprietorship to others. When the owner stops practicing, the firm will usually cease to exist.

Partnerships

In a *general partnership*, two or more people, called *general partners*, share in the management, profits, and risks of the business. Income is shared among the general partners and is reported on personal tax forms. Each general partner is also personally liable for business debts and liabilities.

A *limited partnership* is similar, but has at least one general partner and at least one *limited partner.* As with a general partnership, the general partners invest in the business, manage it, and are financially responsible for it. The limited partners are investors who receive a portion of the profits, but who have no say in the management of the company and are liable only to the extent of their investment. The limited partnership has largely been superseded by the limited liability company, described later in this section.

A partnership is relatively easy to form. A partnership agreement is usually advisable. The additional requirements are similar to those of a sole proprietorship. Where a sole proprietorship depends mainly on a single person, a partnership brings together the skills of several people. Most partnerships are formed because each partner brings to the business a particular talent, such as business development, design ability, or technical knowledge.

The primary disadvantage of a partnership is that all the partners are responsible and liable for the actions of the others. As with a sole proprietorship, the personal assets of any of the partners are vulnerable to lawsuits and other claims. Income is taxed at individual rates, another disadvantage of the partnership form. On a personal level, the partners may eventually disagree on how to run the business. If one partner wants to withdraw, the partnership is usually dissolved.

Corporations

A *corporation*, sometimes called a *C corporation*, is an association of individuals that exists as a legal entity apart from its members. A corporation can be created only in accordance with statutory requirements. To form a corporation, formal articles of incorporation must be drawn up by an attorney and filed with the appropriate state office. The specific regulations and requirements are governed by state law.

Corporations have three levels of participants. Stockholders are owners of the corporation in proportion to the number of shares they own. They elect the directors. The directors have the fiduciary duty to act in the best interest of the stockholders and are responsible for broad policy decisions. The directors, in turn, elect the officers who carry out the day-to-day management of the corporation.

A corporation is financially and legally independent from its shareholders. Each shareholder is financially liable only for the amount of money he or she has invested in the corporation. If the corporation is sued, the personal assets of the shareholders are not at risk. This is the greatest advantage of the corporation. Additionally, a corporation has a continuity that is independent of any changes in shareholders, directors, and principals. It is also relatively easy to raise capital for corporations through the sale of stock.

Corporations are generally taxed at lower rates than individuals, which can result in considerable savings over a partnership or sole proprietorship. As the corporation and the shareholders are separate legal entities, however, they are also taxed separately, the corporation on its profits and the shareholders on their dividends. In this way, corporate income is, in effect, taxed twice.

The primary disadvantages of a corporation are the initial cost to establish the business and the continuing paperwork and formal requirements necessary to maintain it. These, however, are usually outweighed by the reduced liability and tax benefits.

Stockholders are owners of the corporation. Directors are responsible for broad policy decisions. Officers carry out the day-to-day managment of the corporation

An *S corporation* does not retain profits and pay out dividends in the usual manner. Instead, an S corporation chooses to allocate its income and losses directly to shareholders in proportion to their holdings. Shareholders report their shares of the business's income and losses on their personal federal tax returns and are assessed tax at their individual rates. This avoids the tax on corporate income, and can also be advantageous when the business loses money or when tax rates favor the individual over the corporation; in addition, an S corporation offers all the advantages of a standard corporation. S corporation status, however, is limited to *small business corporations* as defined in Chap. 1, Subsection S, of the *Internal Revenue Code.* To qualify for S corporation status, a corporation must be a domestic company with no more than 100 shareholders; there are other restrictions as well.

Many states allow the formation of a *professional corporation* for professionals such as architects, lawyers, doctors, accountants, and interior designers. This form of business is similar to other corporations except that liability for malpractice is generally limited to the person responsible for the act. However, each state has its own laws regarding the burden of liability in a professional corporation.

Limited Liability Companies and Limited Liability Partnerships

The *limited liability company* (LLC) and the *limited liability partnership* (LLP) are similar business structures that combine the advantages of a partnership or sole proprietorship with the limited liability of a corporation. Each is formed like a partnership. Those who invest are called members, and those who manage are called managers. Unlike a partnership, however, it is possible for a non-member to be a manager.

The main advantage to these types of organizations is that liability is limited to a member's investment; a member has no personal liability. An LLC is not a separate entity in the eyes of the federal government, so the business itself is not taxed. Accordingly, profits and losses are passed through the business to each member who must report a profit or loss on his or her personal federal tax return. However, some states may tax the LLC. In addition, members of an LLC are considered to be self-employed, so they must report and pay self-employment tax for Social Security and Medicare. In some cases, the members of an LLC can elect to be classified as an S corporation; the organization remains an LLC from a legal standpoint but is taxed as an S corporation. Generally, an LLC is easier to set up and operate than a corporation.

Joint Ventures

A *joint venture* is a temporary association of two or more persons or firms for the purpose of completing a specific project or achieving a specific goal. This business arrangement is typically used by architectural firms when a project is too large or complex to be completed by one firm alone, or when one firm needs the expertise in a particular area that another firm can offer. The joint venture is typically dissolved when the project is completed or the goal is reached.

A joint venture should be based on a formal, written agreement that describes the duties and responsibilities of each firm, how profits and losses will be divided, and how the work will be completed. The joint venture is treated like a partnership; it is not itself a legal entity independent from its members, and it cannot be sued as a corporation can. Depending on the laws in the state in which the joint venture operates, profits may be taxed as a partnership, or the individual members of the joint venture may be taxed separately.

Before a joint venture is formed, a *teaming agreement* (also called a *memorandum of understanding*) should be developed that defines the roles, responsibilities, and contractual relationships that will be established if the firms are awarded the project and the joint venture is formed. A teaming agreement is not a formal business organization, but it can be used to market the team and forms the basis of a joint venture. A teaming agreement can also be used if a firm wants to form a prime-consultant agreement.

Example 1.1

Three colleagues, who have worked together in a large firm serving institutional clients, have made the decision to start their own firm. One is a licensed architect and a great designer. The other two have experience in technical construction issues and are both excellent marketers. Their vision is to serve large institutional clients and grow the firm into providing service for international customers. Another goal of these owners is to protect their personal assets from potential lawsuits. What type of business organization would be best suited for the three firm owners to meet these goals?

(A) C corporation

(B) sole proprietorship

(C) S corporation

(D) general partnership

Solution

A sole proprietorship is a business owned by one person, not multiple owners. An S corporation is limited to small business corporations and would not allow for the growth anticipated by an international practice.

A general partnership requires each partner to be personally responsible for business debts and liabilities. A C corporation best meets the growth demands of the firm, while shielding the owners from personal liability.

The answer is (A).

Standard of Care

Whatever legal structure a firm takes, the architects in the firm must exercise an appropriate standard of care. *Standard of care* is a legal concept, defined as the level of skill and diligence that a reasonably prudent architect would exercise in the same community, in the same time frame, and given the same or similar facts and circumstances.

The law does not require perfection, but it does require the architect to practice with reasonable care. For example, if an architect designing a building in Florida did not incorporate hurricane-resistant detailing, he or she would most likely be found negligent because a reasonably prudent architect designing for the same location would do so. Of course, as with any legal issue, the final determination may be made in a court of law, with both sides arguing their cases and expert witnesses giving their opinions about the particular point of dispute.

"In the same time frame" is generally taken to mean at the time the project is designed or built, not at the time of the dispute. For example, a client may claim that the architect should have used a certain material to prevent damage to the building. But, if that material was not yet available or not yet tested at the time the project was designed, the architect is unlikely to be found negligent.

"The same or similar facts and circumstances" includes budget, scheduling, and the complexity of the project, among other matters. For example, a client might want a shorter construction time and agree to a fast-track delivery system using a construction manager. Then, after the project is completed with some increased costs due to the shortened schedule, the client may claim that the architect should have suggested a design-bid-build project delivery method to get a lower price. A court would probably hold that a prudent architect working under the same circumstances would also choose a fast-track delivery method, rendering the client's claim without merit.

An architect should be cautious about raising the standard of care. For example, the architect may agree to the inclusion of a statement in the contract that the architect should deliver the project "with the highest standards" or similar language. The architect may also raise the standard of care by promising or guaranteeing certain results or taking on responsibilities that are not part of the contract. In both cases, the architect's actions create a higher standard of care and can increase the architect's liability or even make the architect's work uninsurable.

Example 1.2

A firm has performed design construction administration services in the building of a new five-story library on the campus of a small college. After the owner moves in the equipment, furniture, and books, the floors of the library begins to deflect. When the books and equipment are removed, the floors return to their original position. A study commissioned by the owner and a careful review of the project documentation finds that the structural engineer included a dead load and a live load for the occupancy of the building in the floor calculations as required by code, but did not include concentrated loads for the shelving and books. Has the architect met the standard of care for this building?

(A) Yes, the owner is responsible for the loads imposed on the building by furniture, equipment, and books.

(B) No, the architect is obligated to meet the standard of care and include elements that meet the requirements for this type of building.

(C) Yes, the structural engineer, not the architect, is responsible for providing the proper calculations and design of the structural components of the building.

(D) No, the architect should have made calculations to check the work of the engineer.

Solution

The architect has not met the standard of care for this building. The firm's contract with the owner holds the architect responsible for the design of the building, including the work of the structural engineer and any structural load requirements.

The answer is (B).

OFFICE ORGANIZATION

Several aspects should be considered in the organization of an architectural office, including

- work organization
- support staff
- regulations governing architectural practice

Work Organization

A firm's staff can be organized in various ways in order to work on and complete projects. The most traditional structure is *departmental organization*, sometimes called *horizontal organization* or *flat organization*. In this structure, the staff is organized into departments, each of which specializes in a different function. There may be a marketing department, a design department, a specifications department, a contract documents department, and a construction administration department. Every department works on every project as needed, and a project moves from one department to another in its route from start to finish.

Departmental organization is very efficient, allowing a firm to standardize and fine-tune its processes, make full use of many types of specialists, and create economies of scale. However, it can also make a business inflexible and resistant to innovation and change. Keeping communication open among departments can be a challenge. It can be difficult for employees gain breadth of experience or to share knowledge outside their specialties.

A *studio organization*, sometimes called a *vertical organization* or *tall organization*, is organized around groups of employees called *studios*. Each studio is responsible for completing an entire project, from initial planning to production and construction administration. Within each studio, members must have among themselves the expertise needed to accomplish all or most of the work required for their project. Studios can be created and dissolved as the need arises, or they can remain intact and be assigned new projects based on their particular strengths and expertise. For example, a firm may have one studio for retail projects, another to do industrial work, and another to provide office planning.

The advantages of studio organization include close and immediate communication among members of the design team and the synergy that comes from sharing ideas and group problem solving. Studios also work well with a strong project manager system, in which the project manager has daily contact with the design and production teams as well as with the client. Sometimes studio organization is combined with one or more departments that provide very specialized work, such as specification writing.

Smaller firms may work on a very informal basis, where the principal or the partners complete the client contact and design work and then hand off the production and administration other employees.

Many firms, both large and small, outsource some of their work. *Outsourcing* is contracting with another company to do some of the work needed for a project. Among architectural firms, the production of construction documents and renderings is often outsourced. Outsourcing is discussed in greater detail in Chap. 3.

Outsourcing requires careful management and coordination, but it can be a way to manage a fluctuating workload without continually hiring and firing employees. Firms may outsource to either foreign or domestic companies.

Support Staff

Support staff includes employees other than the professional staff and senior management. The types and number of people needed on the support staff will vary with the size of the firm, but may include administrative assistants, receptionists, bookkeepers, marketing people, model builders, and technology assistants.

Regulations Governing Architectural Practice

All architectural businesses must conform to local, state, and federal laws and regulations, regardless of their size and organizational structure. Requirements for licensing and taxation vary widely from one local and state jurisdiction to another, but some of the more common requirements are listed here. Architects should research the particular requirements of their local and state licensing and taxing agencies. The various types of insurance that an architectural office should have are discussed in Chap. 2.

Business Licenses

Most local jurisdictions require every business to have a license, including those offering professional services. This license allows the business to practice, and it usually serves as the basis for taxation.

A corporation must be registered with the state in which it practices. Each corporation is issued a corporate identification number by a state agency, typically the secretary of state's office. In some states, a firm must make a filing with the state registration board and obtain a *certificate of authorization* (COA) in order to offer services to the public. For limited liability corporations and professional limited liability corporations, an LLC certificate or other type of business license may be required.

Taxes

All businesses must pay taxes. If a business has employees, it must withhold taxes for each employee and forward this money to the Internal Revenue Service (IRS). A business with employees must file IRS Form SS-4, Application for Employer Identification Number (EIN). This number is used in tax filings and other correspondence with the IRS. The business must submit a copy of Form W-4, Employee's Withholding Allowance Certificate, for each employee. This form, which is completed by the employee, indicates the number of deductions the employee is claiming.

At the beginning of each year, the business must supply each employee with Form W-2, Wage and Tax Statement, showing all wages paid in the previous year to the employee along with federal, state, city, and FICA taxes withheld.[1] The employer must send Form W-2 to each employee no later than January 31 each year for the employee's use in preparing personal taxes. Most states have similar requirements for filing state income taxes.

For sole proprietors and some partnerships, federal and state income tax must be filed as estimated taxes every quarter. In addition, sole proprietors and some partnerships must pay self-employment tax to cover Social Security and Medicare taxes.

Most local jurisdictions require every business to have a license, including those offering professional services.

Many states also apply a use tax on goods purchased from out of state, either for use by the business or for resale. The architect must file a use tax certificate and pay what amounts to a sales tax. Some states also charge a personal property tax on furniture and equipment that is used by the business.

An architectural firm may be subject to a variety of city taxes. These can include city income taxes, employment taxes, occupational privilege taxes, and use taxes. Property taxes are also assessed if the firm owns property.

---

[1]FICA is the Federal Insurance Contribution Act, more commonly known as Social Security.

Professional Licensing and Regulation

All states have laws regulating the practice of architecture. An architect must obtain a license to practice and renew it annually or biannually. Most states also require that architects complete a minimum number of continuing education credits to maintain their licenses.

To obtain the initial license, a candidate must pass the Architect Registration Examination (ARE) given by the National Council of Architectural Registration Boards (NCARB). An individual state, such as California, may also require the candidate to take and pass a supplemental exam. The state may require that the applicant for licensure hold a degree from a university that is accredited by the National Architectural Accrediting Board (NAAB). This degree is generally a bachelor of architecture or master of architecture degree. Most states also require candidates to complete the Intern Development Program (IDP), during which the candidate serves an internship under the direct supervision of a registered architect and gains diverse experience. (The IDP is discussed in more detail later in this chapter.) Some states allow a candidate to become a licensed architect without a formal degree by completing the requirements of the NCARB's Broadly Experienced Architect (BEA) program; the candidate must also pass the ARE and complete the IDP.

After becoming licensed in one state, an architect can apply for reciprocal licensure in other states by providing documentation of education, experience, and exam status to each state's licensing board; if the architect has current NCARB certification, NCARB will send documentation on request. The architect may need to meet additional state requirements, such as passing the California Supplemental Examination. An architect who is licensed in more than one state must meet each of those states' continuing education requirements.

ETHICAL STANDARDS

An architect must conform to the same federal, state, provincial, and local laws that any other businessperson must follow, as well as any state laws governing the practice of architecture. Beyond this, however, a professional's conduct should be guided by a general sense of what is ethically correct and incorrect. For most professions, ethics are defined by historical practice as well as codified standards developed by a profession's trade organization.

The main source of ethical standards for architects is the American Institute of Architects (AIA). Although the AIA *Code of Ethics & Professional Conduct* applies specifically to AIA members, it provides good guidance for all architects, and all architects and ARE candidates should be familiar with it. The code provides minimum standards of conduct, procedures for enforcement, and sanctions against AIA members who violate the standards.

Any legal or regulatory violation applicable to the *Code of Ethics* must be determined by an appropriate legal authority. If an AIA member is found in violation of the *Code of Ethics*, sanctions may include nonpublic *admonishment*; *censure*, which includes publishing a description of the violation in an AIA periodical; *suspension* of membership; or *termination* of membership.

Over the decades, some of the prohibitions in the original 1909 *Code of Ethics* have been dropped. An architect may

- compete for projects on the basis of fee
- advertise, as long as no misleading or false statements are made
- supplant or replace another architect on a project (though intentionally seeking to interfere with another architect's contractual relationship with a client may be illegal in some cases)
- be involved with construction, as on a design-build project
- offer free design services for the purpose of securing a commission, as long as the prospective client is not deceived or misled (for example, by implying that an informal preliminary sketch is actually a fully thought-out solution to the client's needs)

The AIA *Code of Ethics* is arranged into three tiers of statements, including canons, ethical standards, and rules of conduct. Canons are broad principles of conduct, ethical standards are specific goals toward which members should aspire, and rules of conduct are specific, mandatory statements that members must follow. Violating a rule of conduct is grounds for discipline. Some of the most important guidelines are summarized here; the complete AIA *Code of Ethics*, with commentary, is available on the AIA website.

Canon I, General Obligations

Members should

- maintain and improve their knowledge and skill
- seek to raise architectural standards in aesthetics, education, research, training, and practice
- respect and seek to improve society and the environment
- exercise learned professional judgment
- uphold human rights
- not discriminate on the basis of race, religion, national origin, age, disability, or sexual orientation

Canon II, Obligations to the Public

Members should

- uphold the law
- never try to influence a public official with a payment
- never accept payments intended to influence their judgment
- never help a client with anything fraudulent or illegal
- promote and serve the public interest
- render pro bono services
- be involved in civic activities
- strive to improve public appreciation of architecture

Canon III, Obligations to the Client

Members should

- serve their clients competently and professionally
- exercise unbiased judgment
- not accept projects beyond their professional capacity
- avoid conflicts of interest
- be truthful in professional communications
- keep clients informed about their projects
- maintain client confidentiality

Canon IV, Obligations to the Profession

Members should

- uphold the integrity and dignity of the profession
- practice with honesty and fairness
- not sign and seal documents for which they do not have responsible control
- not knowingly make false statements
- be honest about their qualifications and about the work they claim credit for

Canon V, Obligations to Colleagues

Members should

- respect the rights of their colleagues and acknowledge their professional contributions
- provide associates and employees with suitable working conditions and fair compensation
- nurture fellow professionals through their education, internships, and careers
- give credit to others for their professional work

Canon VI, Obligations to the Environment

Members should

- be environmentally responsible
- promote sustainable design in their professional work
- advocate sustainable buildings and site design
- use sustainable practices within their firms and encourage clients to do the same

HUMAN RESOURCES

Human resource management, or *personnel management* as it is sometimes called, involves the entire range of hiring, compensating, managing, and terminating employees, along with the legal responsibilities of having employees. Although large offices have more complicated human resources operations than small ones, architectural firm with employees must deal with the same issues. Human resource management is vital to the success of a firm because its most valuable assets are the people who provide the services that the business sells.

Hiring

There are many ways to find employees, such as placing advertisements in local newspapers and trade journals, hiring an executive search firm, contacting university placement offices, and posting jobs on the internet and social media sites. Most architectural firms also receive unsolicited resumes, phone calls, and email requesting interviews for employment. Depending on the state of the local economy, these unsolicited requests may be few or many. Word-of-mouth notice that a particular firm is hiring can also be an effective way to find interviewees within the local community.

When interviewing, an architect must be aware of the many legal requirements in regard to speaking with candidates and hiring employees. For example, equal employment opportunity laws make it illegal for an employer to ask a job candidate about age, date of birth, marital status, national origin, race, or maiden name. The Civil Rights Act of 1964, the Equal Employment Opportunity Act of 1972, and the Civil Rights Act of 1991 also make it illegal to discriminate on the basis of sex, race, color, religion, or national origin. The Americans with Disabilities Act (ADA) makes it illegal to discriminate on the basis of disabilities. In most cases, these laws apply only to firms with 15 or more employees. However, all firms should follow these hiring guidelines to minimize the potential for problems. Refer to the section later in this chapter for other legal requirements.

The process of considering someone for employment should include a review of the candidate's past work experience and resume, a portfolio review, and one or more personal interviews. It can also be valuable to speak with the candidate's references.

The firm must be cautious that the freelancer is truly an independent contractor and cannot be classified by the Internal Revenue Service as an employee.

One important legal aspect of human resources is the condition under which employees are hired. In some cases, a firm may have a formal employment contract that both the employee and employer sign. This contract spells out the employee's responsibilities, work duties, and compensation, as well as the firm's benefits, work conditions, termination procedures, and policies on accepting work from outside firms (moonlighting). The contract may include a *noncompete clause*, sometimes called a *restrictive covenant*, which may include limits or prohibitions on such matters as who the employee may work for during a specified amount of time after leaving the firm, setting up a competing business in the same geographical area, working for the firm's clients, and passing on confidential information to others.

If an employment contract is not used, the employee works under the concept of *employment at will*, which means that there is no written contract and the employee can be terminated at any time without explanation. Likewise, the employee can quit at any time without giving a reason. However, the employee is still protected from being terminated because of age, sex, religion, and the other conditions mentioned previously.

If an office does not need a full-time, permanent employee the firm may elect to hire a freelance person, also technically known as an independent contractor, thereby avoiding the need to withhold taxes, pay benefits, or establish any other type of employee-employer relationship. However, the firm must be cautious that the person is truly an independent contractor and cannot be classified by the Internal Revenue Service or other governmental entities as an employee.

The IRS uses three broad areas to determine if a worker is an employee or an independent contractor (freelancer): behavioral control, financial control, and the relationship between the worker and employer. There are many details involved with the determination and all three factors must be considered, but in general the following are the most important. A person is an independent contractor if they are hired for a specific project, they control where and how they perform their work after given their initial assignment, they provide their own supplies and equipment, they receive no benefits from the firm other than payment for services, and they are free to work for other firms at the same time. In addition, the architectural firm should establish the amount of payment as a set fee or on an hourly basis before beginning any work and be sure that the independent contractor is not otherwise financially tied to the firm.

Management and Communication

All staff must have the physical support they need to do their jobs, including a comfortable and well-planned office environment, as well as the most effective electronic tools and programs available. Beyond these basics, good management and a continuous exchange of ideas are the basis for a productive professional team in an architectural firm of any size.

Good management is necessary in all aspects of office operation. This includes development of a sound and workable business plan that outlines a direction for all phases of business operation, policy statements concerning personnel, a stable financial plan, and rigorous project management procedures. All members of the team need clear direction, from understanding how a particular job helps the firm to how the most productive use can be made of a morning's work. Good planning makes this possible. With it, morale will remain high and less time will be wasted.

Management must share the goals and objectives of the organization with all team members. Employees need to see the big picture if they are to understand how their efforts contribute. They should know the prospects for work in both the short and long term, what the firm's marketing strategies are and how staff may help achieve them, and the general business climate.

Employees' complaints and suggestions should be heard. Opening up the lines of communication is one of the best ways to get everyone working together as a professional team rather than struggling with an "us-against-them" relationship between employees and management.

Principals and firm management should continue their own education in the area of personnel management. Architects almost never receive this kind of training in architecture school. Universities and trade groups offer seminars in this area of practice.

Work Organization and Job Descriptions

Every office, regardless of size, should have a defined method of completing projects and an understanding of who is responsible for each task and who reports to whom. For small firms, this may simply be an agreed-upon practice; for large firms, it is often formalized in an organizational chart. In addition an organizational structure, there should be written *job descriptions* for all positions in the firm. Job descriptions define the duties and responsibilities of the person holding a specific job title; they may also include the qualifications and experience required for the position and an explanation of how that position fits into the organizational and reporting structure of the firm.

Individual job titles vary from one firm to another. The AIA publishes standard definitions of various positions, which commonly include principal, project manager, design director, department head, architect, and intern. The AIA defines three architect/designer titles based on the number of years of experience and responsibilities. Other common job titles include receptionist, resource coordinator, librarian, CAD operator, marketing director, and bookkeeper.

All this information can be included in a personnel policy manual. A personnel policy manual should be a positive statement of the firm's commitment to employees, clients, and the public at large. This policy should be viewed as a tool to help maintain clear communication in the firm, not as a book of rules that must be followed on threat of disciplinary action.

A personnel policy manual may also include statements regarding office organization, employment policies, office procedures, salary and benefits, and professional development.Each personnel manual will be different, reflecting the firm's philosophy and method of operating.

Compensation

Compensation is any kind of payment made to employees for their work. For architectural firms, this includes a base salary or wage along with standard benefits. In addition, some firms may offer bonuses, which may be based on the profitability of the firm or employee performance, or be a fixed amount delivered at holidays or other times and based on the employee's base salary. Standard benefits include compensation such as paid vacation and sick leave, health insurance, educational benefits, retirement plans, dental and vision insurance, travel expenses, and life insurance. The benefits offered can vary widely, depending on each firm's size, structure, and financial position. In addition, a firm may offer fringe benefits such as use of a car, gym membership, and use of the company vacation house. Additional benefits are listed below.

Whatever the firm's size or profitability, a significant portion of the budget will be devoted to compensating employees for their efforts. A firm's particular financial plan may allocate more or less to this line item than other firms, but salaries always represent a fixed expense.

A firm should tailor salaries and benefits to fit both its goals and organizational structure as well as the goals of employees. This is especially important if the firm expects to attract and keep the best people. To be competitive in this area, architectural firms need to be creative in their rewards, both monetary and otherwise. Here is a list of benefits that a firm might offer.

- *Flextime.* Being able to set their own hours is a big plus for many workers. Most offices need to be staffed during the standard five-day week, so half or full days off must usually be alternated among employees. A simple option is to allow employees to set their own starting and quitting times while requiring a standard eight-hour day and defining a core time when everyone should be there, such as from 9:30 a.m. to 3:30 p.m. Another variation is to work nine- or ten-hour days to allow for a half or full day off every week or every other week.

- *Flexible benefit packages.* Required statutory benefits are provided, and employees can choose their additional benefits from a menu of options, based on a lump-sum allowance. For example, an unmarried employee may choose extra paid time off while an employee with a large family chooses an increased contribution to a medical insurance plan.
- *Office-sponsored events.* These can include parties, sightseeing "field trips," holiday activities, pizza lunches, wine tastings, skiing trips, educational programs, seminars, and so on. In-house educational programs can benefit both employees and the firm, helping employees stay current with new developments while keep them informed of procedures and topics of special relevance to the office.
- *Floating holidays.* Two or three days per year can be set aside for employee-selected "holidays." This can allow, for example, an employee to take off the Friday after Thanksgiving or extend the Christmas break without taking away from regular vacation time. A variation of this is to provide a certain number of days of "personal leave" for emergencies or "mental health" days.
- *Sabbaticals.* A sabbatical can be given every three to five years to allow a refresher break. This gives an added incentive for someone to stay with the company and furnishes time for travel, special study, or simply a break from the demands of the profession.
- *Flexible days off.* A set number of days can be established for employees to use in any way they want: for sick days, vacation, or to trade in for cash.
- *Compensation alternatives.* Employees can receive compensation in addition to salary. A straight raise or bonus is taxable income for the employee and offers no deduction for the employer. However, such things as educational reimbursements, paying for travel to conventions and seminars, merit awards, day care services (if they are offered to all employees), and group term life insurance may also be given.
- *Annual performance bonuses.* Money is not the only thing that motivates, but recognizing outstanding performance with money is one way of rewarding a good job and encouraging high-quality work.
- *Profit sharing.* Profit sharing is based on individual project performance. If the team produces a job on schedule and is profitable, then each member of the team receives a percentage of that profit in addition to a base salary.
- *Wellness.* Wellness programs can be offered in addition to traditional health insurance. Often, insurance providers assist firms with setting up these programs, which might include health club memberships, weight management programs, or smoking cessation programs. Many see this as a way to reduce the rising costs of health care by preventing problems before they occur. When employees follow a good health care program, they take fewer sick days and have more energy and a better attitude.
- *Company cars.* The economics of providing one or more company cars should be reviewed, especially if extensive traveling is required. Employees will appreciate saving wear and tear on their personal automobiles. In large urban areas, an added benefit is eliminating the hassle of driving to and from work merely to have a car available for trips out of the office.
- *Community involvement.* Employees may be given time off for professional and civic activities. Besides contributing to employees' professional development, the firm can benefit from added exposure among peers and potential clients.
- *Professional dues.* Firms should encourage membership in professional organizations by providing full or partial payment of dues. Likewise, less experienced employees can be encouraged to work for their professional licenses by reimbursing their exam fees.
- *Office amenities.* A stocked snack refrigerator and good coffee can have a significant impact on morale.

- *Continuing education.* Time off can be given for conventions, seminars, and other educational programs. Employees need to keep up with the latest developments in their fields. Not only do most states make it a requirement maintaining one's professional license, but continuing education increases an employee's value to a firm.
- *Family medical leave.*

Any of these ideas can be used if they are consistent with the firm's goals. Some can be implemented inexpensively, others have significant costs. But however much is spent, this is an investment in the most important commodity a firm can offer to clients—the skill and talent of its people.

Evaluations

A *performance evaluation* is a formal review performed by a manager to assess each employee's performance. Evaluations are typically conducted annually for existing employees and may be conducted more frequently for newly hired employees. Generally, evaluations tell employees how they are doing and in what areas they need to improve. More specifically, performance evaluations

- serve as the basis for pay increases, promotions, and terminations
- provide a way to direct improved employee work performance
- help the firm understand the strengths and weaknesses of personnel
- help direct hiring
- help protect the firm from claims by employees

To be useful, the evaluation process must be objective, treat all employees equally, and be based on each employee's job description. To the extent possible, evaluations should be based on objective, measurable criteria or on goals set jointly by the employer and employee.

Personnel evaluations can be one of the most uncomfortable parts of running an architectural practice, but they are also one of the most crucial. Employees want to know how they are doing. Evaluation is necessary for the growth of both the firm and the employee. Individual performance needs to be measured against goals periodically to determine if any corrective action is needed.

To make the best use of evaluations, there are a few fundamentals to keep in mind.

- Each employee should be evaluated in regard to how successfully he or she is performing to reach stated goals; the firm as a whole should be evaluated by the same measure.
- The goal of the evaluation is to improve both the firm and the employee, not simply to criticize past actions.
- Evaluations should be focused on results. It is less important to evaluate specific actions than it is to evaluate how well they achieved their intended effects.
- Personnel assessments should be made as a result of ongoing management and project decisions, rather than on the basis of one or two evaluations per year.

A productive evaluation can be made only if there is something against which performance can be measured. It is crucial that employees clearly understand their expected roles and that these roles be formalized in some way for use during the evaluation. It is likewise necessary that the firm's goals and objectives are clearly communicated to the staff so that the firm can be evaluated.

Objectives should be measurable. It is not enough just to tell an employee that his or her performance has been poor. If an architect has had the specific goal of reducing the average design time of a particular kind of project by two weeks, it is possible to evaluate whether the goal has been achieved, the reasons that it has or has not, and what steps can be taken next toward the employee's improvement and development.

The type of evaluation used, as well as the timing, forms used, procedures, and other aspects of evaluations, will vary depending on the firm's operating philosophy, size, services offered, and commitment to a program. Certain guidelines, however, should be included in almost any evaluation process.

- Employees must know what kind of performance is expected of them. Clear job descriptions or similar statements are important. They also help eliminate personal bias from the review process.
- Evaluations should be performed at least once a year. Holding them twice a year is often helpful so that issues can be addressed expediently. Some firms schedule fixed dates related to bonus time; others schedule evaluations based on the date each staff member started working for the firm. The latter approach has the advantage of spreading out the work load of giving evaluations.
- Standard forms should be used. These will help evaluators maintain consistency from one session to another, keeping attention focused on areas most important to the firm.
- If possible, more than one person should evaluate each employee. This helps prevent a one-sided judgment that might be based on personality differences or something else unrelated to job performance. It is helpful for the reviewers to discuss their evaluations before meeting with the employee and to develop a shared agenda for the discussion, so that the employee does not receive mixed messages.
- Strengths as well as weaknesses should be discussed. Give praise where warranted and be tactful and respectful when discussing shortcomings. Instead of simply pointing out weaknesses, offer suggestions on how to correct them.
- Unusual incidents should not be the primary basis for evaluation. Performance over the entire time period should be considered, not just the highs and lows.
- A thorough evaluation consists of many independent parts. Opinions about one part of an employee's performance should not affect the evaluation of others. A staff member may be doing very well in every area except one; this one area should not be given undue weight or dominate the review.
- The evaluation should conclude with definite steps for the employee to take to improve on weaknesses during the next review period. New objectives or expectations that will be reviewed at the next evaluation should be discussed with the employee.
- It is helpful to give each employee a written summary of his or her evaluation, both to review after the meeting is over and to prepare any questions or comments for later discussion. Written documentation also allows progress to be tracked over the long term, and can be referred to later if disputes arise.
- Salary adjustment reviews should be kept separate from performance reviews. Salary is based on other items in addition to performance, such as length of service, job category, cost-of-living increases, comparison with other professionals in similar positions, general performance and prospects of the firm, and other factors. Financial rewards may be a result of good performance but are not necessarily dependent on it. Similarly, a firm may wish to recognize exemplary performance with a bonus or increase in salary, yet may not be in a financial position to do so.

Architectural Experience Program

Young professionals gain most of their knowledge and experience not from schoolwork and reading but from actually participating in projects and working in a firm. Traditionally, people new to the architecture profession interned in a firm under the guidance of senior members and performed entry-level jobs while they "looked over the shoulders" of more experienced professionals. This approach had mixed results. Some interns were assigned a wide range of responsibilities, representing all that architects do, and benefited from the mentoring and guidance offered by their employers. Others ended up with less than desirable experiences, spending their time on repetitive tasks and never being exposed to the wide range of skills an architect needs to practice independently.

This haphazard approach to intern work has been replaced by NCARB's *Architectural Experience Program* (AXP). Participating in the AXP is one of the prerequisites for taking the ARE. As the term is used today, an *intern* is someone in the process of satisfying a state registration board's experience requirement prior to or while taking the ARE. The AXP provides a formalized way to make the transition from school to the profession.

NCARB has established the *AXP Guidelines*, which state the type and amount of experience an intern must have before becoming eligible for the ARE. These include the number of hours an intern is required to devote to various professional tasks, as well as requirements for documenting and reporting this time to NCARB. Each intern is also required to have a supervisor who is a licensed architect in the intern's firm. The supervisor guides the intern on a daily basis, is responsible for providing opportunities for the intern to gain the experience required for an architecture career, gives feedback on the quality of the intern's work, and certifies the intern's experience reports. An intern may also select a mentor, who may or may not be a part of the intern's firm and who can provide professional guidance from a different perspective than the intern's employer. The intern/mentor relationship tends to be less formal than the intern/supervisor relationship.

Employee Involvement

Nearly all architectural firms can benefit from increased participation by staff in both the short- and long-term success of the office. Most employees want to do more than receive orders, carry them out, and go home. They want to be actively involved in all aspects of the work and want to make an important contribution not just to their own careers but to the overall effort of the firm. This kind of involvement is crucial to the spirit of the firm and, ultimately, its productivity.

The functional organization of the firm and the desires of the owners will help determine exactly how employee participation can be most useful for both the employee and the employer. It may range from the simplest "gripe session" to actual financial ownership. The following three methods are often used.

Most employees want to make an important contribution not just to their own careers but to the overall effort of the firm.

A *quality control circle* is a small group of employees who meet regularly among themselves and with management representatives to identify and resolve issues that affect their area of work. The philosophy is that employees know better than management what their immediate problems are and how to solve them. Quality control circles are not set up in response to an immediate situation, but are ongoing groups that seek to improve the quality of work.

When the group doesn't have specific problems to confront, it can take on special research activities in areas that may improve productivity. A group of administrative staff, for example, could explore ways to speed clerical activities or find out how automation could improve their work flow. Project managers could study methods for streamlining job administration.

Quality control group meetings may take an hour or two per week of company time, but the benefit-to-cost ratio is usually high. The overall results can be great because employee-generated actions produce more enthusiasm than employer-mandated ones, and they can pull company goals and personal goals closer together.

Another way employees can be involved with the firm is through special *study groups* that work on specific projects. Ideas are generated, evaluated, and submitted to the firm principals for study and implementation. Some firms have committees made up of the heads of each department, who meet regularly to coordinate actions and do long-range planning.

A third method of encouraging employee involvement is financial, by giving employees partial ownership in the firm. One of the ways to do this is with an *Employee Stock Ownership Plan* (ESOP). The company sets up a trust, through which it gives employees stock, or possibly cash with which to buy stock. The contributed stock is then allocated to each employee based on one of several allowable formulas. Over a period of time, usually from ten to fifteen years, the employee becomes fully vested. (Usual vesting is 10 percent per year.) Voting rights may or may not be given depending on how the plan is set up, and the amount of stock the trust holds for the employees may range from 1 percent to 100 percent.

In addition to the benefits of ownership and significant participation in the firm, ESOPs offer tax advantages and financing opportunities for the business. There are also several disadvantages to ESOPs. They are generally for larger firms and definitely only for the architectural firm that is on stable financial and management footing to begin with.

ESOPs are complicated and often expensive to set up, requiring legal advice and careful planning. If properly established, however, they can result in greater employee job satisfaction and increased firm profit and productivity.

Termination

Terminating an employee is one of the most difficult tasks a manager or firm principal performs. Reasons for termination generally fall into one of two broad categories: Employees may be terminated because of low business volume (layoffs) or because of some unacceptable behavior. Unacceptable behavior may include incompetence, low productivity, chronic lateness or absences, negligence, dishonesty, sexual harassment, fraud, misappropriation of company property, insubordination, illegal activity, or noncompliance with company policies. Employees cannot be terminated for age, activities outside of work hours (except for moonlighting, if it is against company policy), missing work for required military obligations or jury duty, or reporting company violations of health or safety laws.

Legal Requirements

In addition to the previously mentioned legal requirements for hiring, there are many other federal laws that regulate the employee-employer relationship. Which of these laws apply is often based on the number of employees in the firm.

All Employers Regardless of Number of Employees

The *National Labor Relations Act* (also called the *Wagner Act*) allows private sector employees to organize into trade unions and protects union employees from unfair labor practices by employers.

The *Equal Pay Act* requires equal pay for employees who have the same work duties, responsibilities, and experience.

Employee Eligibility Verification requires employers to verify the employee's right to work in the United States by maintaining an employee's I-9 form for at least three years as well as for one year after termination.

The *Wages and Fair Labor Standards Act* (FLSA) establishes minimum wage, overtime, pay, recordkeeping, and child labor standards in both the private sector and in government employment.

The *Occupational Safety and Health Act* of 1970 (OSHA) requires employers to provide a safe work environment. Although primarily aimed at construction sites, factories, and industrial plants, OSHA can inspect offices and levy fines for failure to provide things such as first aid kits, posted material safety data sheets, and fire extinguishers.

The *Health Insurance Portability and Accountability Act* of 1996 (HIPAA), among other provisions, protects the privacy of individually identifiable health information.

The *Employee Retirement Income Security Act* (ERISA) sets minimum standards for pension plans in the private sector for those employers who have a pension plan program.

Employers with More than 15 Employees

The *Consolidated Omnibus Budget Reconciliation Act* of 1986 (COBRA) requires employers with 20 or more employees to continue group medical coverage if employment is terminated, working hours are reduced, employment is changed, or in the event of death, divorce, and other significant life events.

The *Civil Rights Act* of 1991 prohibits discrimination on the basis of sex, race, color, religion, or national origin.

The *Age Discrimination in Employment Act* of 1967 (ADEA) prohibits age discrimination in employment for persons age 40 or over, including hiring, firing, segregation in the workplace, and reducing wages or salary.

Employers with 50 or More Employees

The *Family and Medical Leave Act* (FMLA) requires that companies give an employee up to 12 weeks of unpaid leave for child, spousal, or parental care, without initiating retribution or jeopardizing the employee's job. This also applies to an employee with a serious health condition.

Firms that do any work for the federal or state government must comply with additional regulations.

BUSINESS DEVELOPMENT

In the competitive marketplace of professional services, it is no longer possible for an architect to sit in the office waiting for a phone call about a new job or for a referral from a previous client. Marketing and public relations have become integral parts of successful firms, and ARE candidates should be familiar with the basic techniques.

Marketing Plan

The first step in successful business development is to create a sound marketing plan. This includes first identifying the type of work the firm wants to do, in what geographical areas the firm wants to work, what the competition is, how much work the firm needs, and a budget for active marketing and public relations. Only then can the firm begin to formulate an approach to meeting its goals.

A number of marketing techniques are used by architectural firms. Some are traditional, while others have developed with the growth of electronic communications. The strategies that should be used depend on the type of market the firm is hoping to capture, the geographical area the firm markets in, the type of work the firm wants to perform, and the budget and personnel available for marketing, among other factors. The following marketing techniques are some of the more common methods.

- *Networking:* Person-to-person contact is one of the primary and often one of the most effective ways to market services. Networking, whether in person or through electronic means, is a way to understand the market, identify the needs of potential clients, develop trust, and maintain contact when a business opportunity arises. Through networking, an architect can identify a *lead*, or a source of information about a potential client who may need the services of an architect now or in the future. A lead can also be a planned building project that requires design services. Networking can be done by staying active in professional architectural organizations, becoming a member of a potential client's trade organization or going to their conventions, getting involved in civic groups, and talking with consultants who work with the firm's market.
- *Corporate identity:* Although a corporate identity is not a specific marketing technique in itself, it is a fundamental requirement for a professional firm and is important to other marketing efforts. A corporate identity is a distinct and consistently applied graphic image that brings the architect's firm to the mind when people see it. may include a specially designed logo or mark that is unique to the firm or a unique treatment of the firm's name. Every firm should have a well-designed corporate identity program that encompasses all the graphic and promotional items the firm produces, such as letterhead, envelopes, brochures, business cards, proposals, newsletters, forms, websites, and social media accounts and pages. A properly designed corporate identity program can visually communicate the firm's philosophy, present a strong, visible identity to support the firm's marketing efforts, organize the firm's internal office procedures and project documentation, and give the firm a visual coherence and consistency.
- *Brochures:* A brochure is a basic marketing tool for all architectural firms. gives a brief description of the firm and its capabilities and service specialties, and includes representative photographs of past projects. Brochures are produced in a wide range of sizes and styles, from simple, pocket-size folders to hardbound books. In most cases, a brochure should be well designed, fairly brief, and laid out to give potential clients an overall impression of the firm and its abilities. should serve as a reminder of

the firm and encourage a potential client to seek more information from the architect. The traditional printed brochure is now often supplemented with or even replaced by a well-designed website that can be updated more frequently and easily than a full-color brochure.

- *Websites:* Most firms have websites that provide an overview of the firm, examples of the types of work the firm does, photographic images, and a listing of staff experience and capabilities. Websites may also contain links to other sites, basic helpful information for potential clients, a method to submit resumes, and online newsletters.
- *Social media:* Social media and networking services such as LinkedIn, Facebook, Instagram, and Twitter allow virtual networking and may be useful in communicating the capabilities of an architectural firm and its professionals.
- *Newsletters:* A newsletter is an effective way to keep an architectural firm's name and work in front of a large audience on a regular basis. Promotional newsletters (as opposed to the in-house types that are intended for staff) are well-designed pieces that are sent to past, present, and potential clients. Newsletters are a relatively inexpensive marketing tool, but to be effective they must be produced on a regular basis, which takes a commitment of time and money. Newsletters can also be produced in electronic format and made available through a firm's website.
- *PowerPoint presentations:* Audiovisual presentations are often used to present more detailed information about a firm and its work or to focus on how a designer might approach a particular client's design problem. These are fairly easy to customize for each type of client and reproduce as needed.
- *Advertising:* Advertising is any paid communication in some type of media, such as on websites or television or in newspapers and magazines. Advertising was once considered professionally unethical, but it is now accepted in architecture and can be used to reach a wide market. Unlike press releases, articles, and other publicity tools, advertising has the advantage of being guaranteed to reach a given audience because firms do not have to depend on the decision of an editor to place their promotions.
- *Past clients:* One of the best sources for new work is through current and past clients. If an architectural firm has done a good job providing service, the client is more likely to hire the firm again. A satisfied client is also a good source of word-of-mouth advertising.

Example 1.3

An architectural firm's practice consists of a wide range of building types from higher education to professional sports facilities to health care clinics. Over the years, the firm has designed football stadiums, basketball and ice hockey arenas, and tennis stadiums. Professional football is expanding the number of teams in three new U.S. markets and one international location to be determined. What are the three most effective ways for this architecture firm to begin the marketing effort to these potential clients? (Choose the three that apply.)

(A) improve the firm's website to showcase sports facilities designed by the firm

(B) post on social media

(C) an electronic brochure sent to new team owners

(D) advertise in a sports magazine

(E) team up with a local architecture firm that has been a past project partner

(F) visit team locations

Solution

Social media and magazine advertising do not target specific clients. Visiting the teams would not ensure contact with the owners, and the international sites are not yet selected. The firm has a long-standing reputation in designing sports facilities. This strength should be communicated through improvements in the website and by sending a firm brochure to each new franchise owner. Teaming up with a local partner would help the firm understand the local politics, timing, and players to be targeted in order to make further marketing efforts in the project.

The answers are (A), (C), and (E).

Public Relations

Public relations (PR) differs from marketing in that it is not tied to a particular potential job or single potential client. Rather, PR establishes and communicates the firm's presence to various groups of people on many different levels. The goal of PR is to create a positive image of the firm in the minds of targeted audiences. Of course, the most important group that an architect tries to communicate with are the people who may need the firm's services or who are able to recommend the firm to others.

A PR program should be a part of any firm's marketing plan. To be effective, a PR effort must identify who the target audience is and what its needs are, because the firm is ultimately trying to communicate how its services mesh with the interests of a particular community of people. To get the firm's message across most effectively, all PR efforts must communicate on the target audience's terms and in the language it understands best.

There are several ways to promote an architectural firm through good PR. One of the most common is through a press release, a short statement concerning some newsworthy event related to the firm that is sent to appropriate publications with the hope that the editors will use it. These may be local newspapers, trade newspapers, regional magazines, or national trade magazines.

Press releases are one of the most economical ways to publicize a firm. Unfortunately, many releases never go to press because they are poorly written or incorrectly presented, do not conform to the requirements of the publication, or do not contain anything really newsworthy. Before sending a press release to a publication, it is important to follow the publication's format and editorial standards and determine to whom the release should be sent.

Another excellent form of publicity is an article about one of the architectural firm's projects in a magazine. Highly publicized projects may offer opportunities for media coverage. Although it is flattering to be featured in a trade magazine, is better to be published in a magazine received by potential clients. For instance, a bank project that is featured in banking magazines will be more likely to reach and impress other bankers looking for architectural services than if the job is shown in an architectural trade journal. Wherever the article appears, however, reprints can be sent to existing and potential clients.

Technical articles written by an architect can also be used to promote a firm and its services. Architects can write and publish articles in local magazines or newspapers, on LinkedIn or their firm's website, or in trade association newsletters. Before releasing project-related information or photographs, however, it is customary to request permission from the client, and to let the client review and approve the material to ensure that the article does not violate any nondisclosure agreements.

Other methods of public relations include organizing seminars or workshops on a topic of interest to the firm's target audiences, volunteering for local service groups or projects, getting involved with local politics, winning design awards, and setting up open houses for the public.

2

FINANCIAL AND RISK MANAGEMENT

FINANCIAL MANAGEMENT

The financial management of an architectural firm includes two broad categories of accounting. The first is basic accounting, which all businesses must do. Keeping track of money flowing into and out of the business is needed for day-to-day operations, banking, taxes, and auditing. Often called *general ledger accounting*, this provides firm-wide statements about the overall financial status of the business so that firm owners can make decisions crucial to the firm's profitability and survival.

The second type of accounting is *project cost accounting*, which tracks revenue, expenses, and profit by individual projects. Project cost accounting is vital for professional service businesses, such as architectural firms, that depend on knowing how the amount of time spent on specific projects affects the financial health of the firm. Firm principals need to be able to differentiate between projects that are making money and those that are losing money, and that goes beyond the scope of general ledger accounting. Information from project cost accounting reports can help managers decide how to allocate resources, manage projects, and develop accurate proposals for new work.

FINANCIAL TERMINOLOGY

Financial management is a complex subject. Some basic terms include

- *accounts payable:* Amounts owed to the suppliers of goods or services (such as consultants, reproduction companies, or the utility company) that have not yet been paid.
- *accounts receivable:* Money that others owe to the business through invoices for services.
- *assets:* Any type of tangible or intangible resource that can be measured in monetary terms, including current assets, fixed assets, and other assets.
- *chart of accounts:* A list of the various accounts a business uses to keep track of money, along with corresponding account numbers used for data processing.
- *current assets:* Resources of a business that are converted into cash within one year.
- *direct labor:* All labor of technical staff, principals, and support staff that is directly chargeable to projects.
- *direct personnel expense:* The expense of employee salaries plus the cost of mandatory and discretionary expenses and benefits such as payroll taxes and health insurance.
- *discretionary distribution:* Voluntary distribution of profits to owners and nonowners, such as performance bonuses, profit sharing, and incentive compensation.[1]
- *fixed assets:* Resources that the firm uses and retains for a long period of time, such as equipment and property.
- *gross revenue:* All the revenue generated by a business during a stated period of time.
- *indirect labor:* All labor not charged to a specific project or revenue-producing account, such as administration, general office time, and marketing.
- *liabilities:* Claims by people outside the business and claims by the owners of the business against the total assets of the business.
- *net operating revenue* (or *net revenue*): The money that remains from billing after deducting fees and expenses, reimbursable expenses, and non-reimbursable project-related expenses.
- *other assets:* Miscellaneous resources such as securities and copyrights.
- *overhead:* Expenses incurred to keep a business operating whether or not any revenue is being generated, such as rent, software leases, and fees for power and telephone service.

---

[1]Some architectural firms view this as an expense that is necessary to attract qualified personnel, while other firms view it as a profit-related item.

Accounting Methods

There are two basic accounting methods: cash accounting and accrual accounting. With *cash accounting,* revenue and expenses are recognized at the time the business receives the cash or pays a bill. With *accrual accounting,* revenue and expenses are recognized at the time they are earned or incurred, whether or not cash changes hands. For example, if a firm sends an invoice to a client for $50,000, that money is listed as revenue even though the client has not yet paid the invoice.

Both methods have their advantages and disadvantages. Cash accounting is better at tracking actual cash flow, while accrual accounting gives a better picture of a business's long-term financial status and provides information that is important for active financial management. Cash accounting is fairly simple and is often used by single-person businesses and small businesses; businesses above a certain size or that maintain inventory are required by the IRS to use accrual accounting.

A slight variation of the accrual method typically used by architectural firms is the *modified accrual basis* method. This method records fee revenue, expenses billed to the client, and invoices to the firm by outside consultants. However, it does *not* include the amounts of fees that have been earned but not yet billed to the client.

In both cash and accrual accounting, revenue and expenses are grouped into individual accounts for the purposes of auditing, review, tax preparation, management, and analysis. For example, there are separate expense accounts for wages, rent, telephone, supplies, and so on. The accrual accounting method uses *double-entry bookkeeping,* in which all transactions are listed chronologically in a *journal.* They are then posted to a *ledger* where transactions are grouped into individual accounts. (Although legacy terms such as journal and ledger are still used in accounting, nearly all but the smallest businesses do their accounting with computer programs, some of which are designed specifically for architectural firms.)

Accounting Statements

From the basic information entered in journals and ledgers, various types of *accounting reports* can be generated. Some of the more common include the following.

A *balance sheet* summarizes all assets and liabilities and shows the financial position of a business. All the assets listed must exactly equal all the liabilities listed. One important part of a balance sheet is the net worth of the business or the owner's equity. The *net worth* of a firm is the total assets less the total liabilities. *Owner's equity* is the money invested in a business by the owners or stockholders. Another way to view this, and the way it normally shows on a balance sheet, is that the total assets must equal the total liabilities plus the net worth or owner's equity.

A *profit and loss statement* (or *income statement*) lists all the income and expenses of a business for a certain period of time. The difference between all the income and all the expenses gives either the profit or the loss for that period.

A *cash flow statement* shows actual inflows and outflows of cash or cash equivalents. Cash is defined as money, checks, or anything else accepted by banks. *Cash equivalents* are short-term investments that can be quickly converted into cash, such as short-term certificates of deposit. Cash flow statements are important because a business's month-to-month financial health depends on being able to meet payroll and pay bills.

In addition to reports that show the overall financial health of a business, the basic information obtained from journals, ledgers, and project data can be used to develop reports for individual projects so that project managers and firm management can track the progress of each job.

Profit Planning and Financial Management

Beyond basic bookkeeping and accounting activities is *financial management.* Financial management includes active planning, monitoring, and controlling of financial information as well as acting on that information.

The most fundamental equation for financial planning in any profit-oriented business is

$$\text{profit} + \text{expenses} = \text{revenue}$$

This equation is often shown in the form

$$\text{revenue} - \text{expenses} = \text{profit}$$

Even though the two equations are mathematically equal, the second equation suggests that profit is whatever may be left over after expenses are subtracted from revenue. The first equation suggests that the business will make its targeted profit, and that the business must then control expenses and generate appropriate revenue to make the equation work.

Controlling expenses generally means reducing overhead cost wherever possible. One of the highest percentages of overhead is for *indirect labor*, personnel who do not directly work on projects. Increasing revenue generally means either increasing how much work the firm does or increasing fees.

An invoice older than 90 days means in effect that the firm is lending money to the client without charging interest.

Financial management software can generate a variety of reports based on information from accounting journals, time sheets, and project financial data. These reports can help firm principals and project managers control the work the firm performs.

In addition to basic accounting reports, one of the most important reports for architectural firms is the *project progress report*, which is a more detailed, computer-generated version of the manually produced charts shown in Fig. 4.4 and Fig. 6.1. The project progress report shows the hours and labor costs for each phase of a project, both for the current reporting period and the total to date, and compares these numbers with the estimated hours and costs. The report also shows direct costs, such as for consultants, overhead allocations, and reimbursable expenses. These reports give the project manager and firm management an accurate look at the status of a project and can be used to take corrective action as necessary.

An *office earnings report* summarizes each of the firm's projects in terms of the amount of revenue it has generated, the expenses it has incurred, unbilled services, percentage of completion, and profit or loss to date. This report can help firm management find any projects that may be hurting overall profitability and need remedial action.

An *aged accounts receivable report* shows the status of all invoices for all projects, whether or not they have been paid, and the "age" of each invoice, which is the time from the invoice date to the payment date, or to the current date if still unpaid. Generally, any unpaid invoice more than 60 days old needs attention from the firm principal or whoever is responsible for collections. In architectural firms, the average collection period for invoices runs between 60 and 75 days. An invoice older than 90 days means in effect that the firm is lending money to the client without charging interest.

A *time analysis report* lists each employee along with the number of hours he or she has spent on direct labor, indirect labor (including marketing and professional development), vacation time, sick leave, and holidays. Every firm has a targeted percentage of time that technical employees should spend on direct labor, and this report is an excellent way of monitoring such time. The most important information this report generates is the chargeable ratio. The *chargeable ratio* (or *utilization rate*) is the percentage of time (sometimes calculated as percentage of dollars) spent on direct labor, divided by the total time (or dollars) spent on direct and indirect labor, vacation, holiday, and sick leave. A chargeable ratio of about 65% for the whole firm is generally thought to be the break-even point, or the minimum that should be allowed. For the professional and technical staff, this ratio should be higher, in the range of 75% to 85%, as most of their time is spent working on projects. The chargeable ratio of principals may be on the low end because much of their time is devoted to non-chargeable work like promotion, marketing, and management.

Financial Ratios

There are many other ratios and values that firm management, accountants, and banks use to measure a business's financial health. These ratios and values can be compared against industry benchmarks to determine whether corrective action is needed.

- *current ratio:* Total current assets divided by total current liabilities. This is a measure of a firm's ability meet current obligations. Generally, the higher the ratio, the better, with 1.5 or more indicating a healthy business and 1.0 being about the minimum acceptable level.
- *net profit before tax:* The percentage of profit based on net revenue—the total annual revenue minus consultants' fees and reimbursable expenses.
- *overhead rate:* Total office overhead (or total indirect expenses) divided by total direct labor. This ratio should be in the range of 1.30 to 1.50. When used to calculate fees, this ratio is multiplied by the estimated cost of direct labor, and the resulting product is added to the direct labor amount.
- *quick ratio:* A refinement of the current ratio including only cash and cash equivalents, plus accounts receivable, plus revenue earned but not billed, divided by total current liabilities. The quick ratio is a more conservative measure than the current ratio because it includes only the most liquid assets. The quick ratio and the current ratio are commonly included on balance sheets.
- *revenue per technical staff:* The amount of net revenue produced per technical staff member, or those staff members most directly involved with charging direct time and producing jobs. This number can be used to estimate the required net operating revenue for future budgets. If a firm's operating revenue is known, revenue per technical staff can be used to estimate staffing levels.
- *revenue per total staff:* The amount of net revenue produced per staff member per year, including principals and part-time employees. This ratio is the annual net operating revenue divided by the total number of employees. It can be used in the same way as revenue per technical staff.

Example 2.1

For accounting purposes, a large plotter is considered

(A) a current asset

(B) a fixed asset

(C) a liability

(D) an overhead expense

Solution

An asset is anything a business owns that can be given a value. A current asset is either cash or an asset that is expected to be converted into cash within one year, such as accounts receivable. An item that is used in the long term, such as a plotter, is considered a fixed asset. A liability is a claim made against the total assets of a business, either by a person outside the business or by an owner of the business. An overhead expense, such as salaries, rent, power, or telephone, is an expense incurred in order to keep a business operating whether or not any revenue is being generated.

The answer is (B).

Setting Fees

One of the most important aspects of making an architectural business profitable is setting suitable fees. The most common method is to charge an hourly rate per staff member working on a project. This hourly rate is known as the *billing rate*, and it may vary with the position and experience of the staff member as well as the type of service provided. (See Chap. 5 for a discussion of the various methods of charging professional fees.) Even if the client asks for a stipulated lump sum fee proposal, that number is most often determined by estimating the number of hours it will take for each staff member to complete his or her work on the project and multiplying each number by that staff member's billing rate.

Billing rates are determined based on the employee's salary, plus the costs for that employee's fringe benefits, plus the cost of office overhead, plus an allowance for profit. Often, calculations are simplified with a *net multiplier* found by dividing the net revenue of the firm (excluding consultants' fees and reimbursables) by the cost of direct labor. The net multiplier accounts for fringe benefits, indirect labor, overhead, and profit. For most architectural firms, this value is from 2.7 to 3.0. For example, at a firm using a net multiplier of 3.0, if an employee is paid $40 per hour, the billing rate to the client for that employee would be $120 per hour.

The *break-even rate* is similar to the net multiplier and is the total cost of operations divided by total money spent on direct labor. This rate accounts for the salary of the employee plus the amount of overhead attributed to the employee. As described above, the recommended overhead rate should be from 1.30 to 1.50, so the break-even rate should be from 2.30 to 2.50. The employee's base salary is multiplied by the break-even rate to determine the minimum hourly fee that must be charged to the client in order for the firm to break even on the employee's salary. This number can then be increased by whatever percentage of profit is wanted to arrive at an hourly fee.

Related to the net multiplier is a multiplier based on *direct personnel expense* (DPE). With DPE, the costs of providing taxes, benefits, and the like are included with the employee's base salary. The multiplier is then calculated to account for indirect labor and profit. Because benefits are already included in the DPE, this multiplier is slightly lower than the net multiplier. This way of calculating fees is not used as frequently as the net multiplier.

Billing rates are based on the employee's salary, plus that employee's benefits, plus office overhead, plus an allowance for profit.

Once hourly rates are established for all employees in the firm, the next step in setting fees is estimating the amount of time it will take to complete a project and deciding which employees (with their respective billing rates) will be doing what work. Hours are then multiplied by billing rates to get the total estimated fee. In addition to hourly fees, the person estimating the total project budget must add costs for estimated non-reimbursable direct expenses, consultants' fees (if not billed separately), and a contingency (if any).

Many firms also use information about past projects to develop benchmark fees based on area, construction costs, project type, or other measures. Comparing the proposed fees for a current project against these benchmarks serves as an additional check.

The approaches to setting fees described in this section are the most common, but there are many others. For example, some firms may base fees on the square footage of the project area or on a percentage of the construction cost.

Managing Accounts Receivable

Getting paid promptly for services rendered is basic to an architect's financial success. Timely payment is critical for cash flow to pay employees and current bills. There are four basic steps to collecting accounts receivable: contract terms, timely billing, complete invoices, and regular procedures for tracking accounts.

Put Terms of Fee Collection in the Contract

Having a clear understanding with the client, before work starts, about the fee and how it will be paid is fundamental to avoiding misunderstandings later. If problems do develop, there is little procedural or legal recourse unless everything is itemized in the agreement with the client. The contract should include the basis for the fee, when invoices will be sent and in what form, when payment is due, and any penalties for late payment, such as interest charges after 45 days or some other reasonable period of time. The contract should also contain provisions for nonpayment, including stopping work on the client's project and making no presentations until the payment has been received. An attorney should be consulted for specifics in this area and for the language to use in the contract.

Submit Invoices Promptly

Invoices should be sent as soon after the payroll period as possible. Every day of delay is one more day until payment is made. If possible, a billing cycle of a month at most should be maintained; some firms bill twice a month to keep cash coming in more regularly. Avoid agreeing to a lump sum payment at the end of phase completion—on a large project this can sometimes delay cash inflow for months. Faster billing also helps the client associate the invoice with the work performed during the billing cycle and may forestall questions.

Make Each Invoice Complete

Every invoice should be easy to read and understand. The name and address of the client, the project name and number, and a reference to a contract must be included. In addition, a detailed breakdown of the work performed and the billing associated with each item should be included. Invoices should also include reimbursable expenses with backup documentation and any past due amount.

The exact format of the invoice will depend on the firm's method of operating and tracking professional time, as well as on the conditions of the contract. Invoices may include a breakdown of the time each team member spent on the job, their billing rates, and the total cost. Alternatively, each phase of work or work task that was outlined in the contract may be itemized. Invoices should have a consistent format so that the client always knows what to expect and where to look for information. Whatever form is chosen, an invoice that includes only the amount due, with no backup information, should not be submitted. That is an open invitation for the client to question the amount and delay payment.

Regular Procedures for Tracking Accounts

The firm should have a policy on how accounts receivable are handled. If payment for an invoice hasn't been received after about two weeks, it is a good idea to follow up with the person the invoice was sent to. This gives the firm an opportunity to verify that the invoice was received and ask whether the client has any questions. Simple problems, such as a lost invoice or an easily answered question, can be taken care of quickly, and this also lets the client know that the account is being closely followed.

Additional actions that can be taken include sending a past-due notice after 30 days, making personal calls and visits after an additional amount of time, and taking legal action if the account becomes too far overdue. Any procedure should be consistent with contract provisions, and these procedures should be known to the client before work begins. If the policy is not fully stated in the contract, the firm may want to consider providing a standard policy statement to every client at the start of a project.

A written record should be kept of all the office's actions regarding collections. If legal problems develop later, this record will be useful. Some additional suggestions for collecting fees are as follows.

- At the beginning of the project, verify the client's billing procedures and be careful to follow them. The client's project representative may not be the right person to send invoices to. The client may require that invoices be sent to a particular office, be in a specific format, and include specific information such as a purchase order number. If the procedures are not followed, payment may be delayed.
- Use the personal approach in collecting fees. A cover letter can be sent with an invoice can be sent with invoices explaining the progress on the job and what efforts the billing represents. The project architect or project manager should sign the invoices to let the client know they have been reviewed. When problems develop, a phone call or personal visit should be made, rather than sending a threatening letter. A face-to-face approach is always more successful than an impersonal one.
- Use project accounting software that develops aged accounts receivable (as discussed in the previous section). The report should show 30-, 60-, 90- and 120-day outstanding accounts. The oldest accounts should be dealt with first since these are the most likely not to be collected unless immediate action is taken.

- Be familiar with the client's payment procedures. Often, an invoice must travel a tortuous route through a large organization with multiple approvals before a check is issued. Understand how long the process should take and who to contact with questions if there is a delay.
- Plan for cash flow. Use project accounting software that develops cash flow reports. When cash flow positions can be viewed a month or two in advance, it becomes very clear how important collecting fees is.
- All invoices should include the name and telephone number of the person to contact if the client has any questions. It is better to encourage the resolution of problems than to create distance between the firm's and client's accounting departments.
- Consider offering a discount of 1% to 2% for payment made within two weeks or some other specified period of time. Encouraging prompt payment in this way may cost less than borrowing in the short term to cover a weak cash position, losing interest on short-term investments, or paying for legal assistance with late collections.
- Require a retainer before work starts. This may be anywhere from 10% to 20% of the fee, or it may be based on an average anticipated monthly billing amount. Most projects require some up-front money, and there is no reason why the architect should not receive some of it. Explain to the client the amount of time and money the office must expend before a normal billing payment is made. If a client has objections to a reasonable retainer, it may be worth investigating further to verify financial solvency.
- If the firm's involvement with the project is expected to last more than a year, include provisions in the contract to allow for the renegotiation of terms, billing rates, and other financial considerations that may change over a long period of time.
- Beware of delaying tricks. A delinquent client may send a letter of dissatisfaction to justify not paying. As long as the firm has fulfilled its contractual obligations, it should not be dissuaded from aggressively seeking payment.
- Be prepared to file a lien against the client's project if necessary. Because lien laws vary from state to state, an attorney should be consulted.

Controlling Overhead

Overhead expenses are necessary for the functioning of an office, but they don't produce revenue as professional fees do. Keeping overhead to a minimum can increase the firm's profits or allow the firm to offer lower fees than the competition. Some ways to minimize overhead include the following.

- The single largest overhead expense is non-billable labor. Every firm's highest priority in reducing overhead should be to minimize this component. The first step is to carefully control time reporting. Often, much of the time legitimately spent on a project ends up listed as "office" time or in some other non-chargeable category. This often happens when staff fills in time cards or time-tracking software at the last minute, trying to remember an entire week or two weeks of work late on a Friday afternoon. Principals are often the worst offenders, listing their efforts as general coordination, marketing, or administration when they were actually working on specific projects. Some firms require time information to be turned in daily; others require that task sheets or project management software logs be completed during the day as jobs are worked. This is especially useful for project managers and others who may be involved in several projects every day. The project coordinator or project manager should check all time spent and verify that all legitimate time is being charged.
- All significant non-labor direct expenses should be reported. Most firms know to include costs for project-related travel, construction document printing, and the like in invoices, but many chargeable expenses are often thought of as general overhead. Firms should keep accurate records of these project-related expenses and charge them to the client. Some non-labor direct expenses include
  - progress prints made during the course of the job
  - all copy machine reproduction

- computer expenses charged by an outside company
- model supplies for a specific project
- postage and delivery
- all local travel expenses
- presentation supplies used for a project

Some of these may seem like small expenditures, but they can add up. Some other strategies for controlling overhead expenses include the following.

- Shop around for the best prices on telephone service, internet access, and other communications services.
- Reevaluate where the firm's offices are located. The firm may be spending extra for a office space in a location that does not really benefit the business. Review how the space is used, too, to make sure the firm is not paying for more space than it needs.
- Team up with other firms to share the costs of continuing education. Instead of three firms each sending a staff member to a trade show or seminar, one firm can send one employee who then shares what he or she learned with the staffs of all three firms. The firm that sends an employee can alternate so that each firm has a chance to be represented at the show or seminar.
- Study the firm's insurance policies to see if there is too much coverage or overlapping coverage. Consider raising the deductible on health care coverage in order to lower premiums. Shop around for insurance to get the lowest possible price. Consider getting low base coverage, and then adding supplemental project insurance as needed. The project insurance may then be billed as a reimbursable expense to the client.

Example 2.2

An architect can determine which clients have not paid by looking at the

(A) aged accounts receivable

(B) balance sheet

(C) cash flow statement

(D) income statement

Solution

Aged accounts receivable are accounts with invoices that are still unpaid after a certain length of time, such as 90 days. A list of aged accounts receivable should be kept and regularly updated, and used to follow up with clients who have outstanding invoices.

The answer is (A).

LEGAL ISSUES

Architects need to be familiar with many legal issues, pertaining not only to contracts but also to the organizational structure of the firm, human relations, financial management, insurance, professional conduct, copyright, expert witness involvement, and obligations to the public. It is helpful to understand the fundamental principles on which contract language is based. Some of the more important ones are briefly described.

Agency

The legal concept of *agency* is that one person, the *agent*, acts on behalf of another, the *principal*, in dealings with another, the *third party*. In architecture and construction, the agent is the architect, the principal is the owner or client, and the third party is the contractor. Legally speaking, when the agent consents to act on behalf of and represent the interests of the principal, the agent is empowered to create a legal relationship between the principal and third parties.

When architects work with and convey information to contractors, the contractors may assume the architects have more authority than they actually do. The contractors may blame the architects for instructions the owners may not be aware of, and the owners may blame the architects for inadequately or incorrectly carrying out their wishes. Architects must be careful to act on the owner's behalf and to keep the owner informed of progress or issues. The standard agreement forms and general conditions of the contract attempt to minimize potential problems by clearly defining the duties and responsibilities of the various parties. This is one reason, for example, why change orders must be signed by owners as well as architects.

Contractors are considered to be *vendors*. A vendor supplies a specific product for a fixed price. Unlike architects/agents, vendors act primarily in their own interest.

Duties

The law defines what one person "owes" another in particular relationships, including contracts, by applying the term *duties* to a set of terms or requirements. Duties are important in the construction industry because of the many formal (contractual) and informal relationships involved. For architects, there are three ways that duty is established.

The first is by the terms of a contract, whether written or oral. The standard forms of agreement established by the American Institute of Architects (AIA) outline the services and responsibilities of the architect and state that these may not be extended without the written consent of the owner.

The second way that duty is established is by legislative enactment, such as by means of building codes and architectural licensing laws.

The third way duty is established is by the architect's conduct. Courts often look to the *implied duties* that depend on how the parties have conducted themselves in the course of performing their work. Situations may arise that are not covered by the contracts or general conditions. In these cases, architects are not free to act unilaterally without consulting clients. Architects may be held liable for the consequences of either action or inaction.

Some examples of implied duties are as follows.

- *cooperating with contractors.* While some actions related to this duty are clearly stated in contracts, others are not.
- *not interfering with the contractor's work.* Such interference includes actions that might cause delay or additional costs, or that cause the contractor to modify standard methods and procedures of construction.
- *giving relevant information to contractors.* This includes anything that may affect the progress of the job, including any problems or errors the architect has observed.
- *assisting the owner in coordinating work.* This includes helping owners coordinate the schedules and requirements of other contractors and vendors who are not under the control of the general contractor.

Liability and Negligence

Liability is the legal responsibility for injury to another person or damage to property. Architects are constantly exposed to liability through their actions and inactions or simply by being named as a responsible third party in other claims. An important way that architects can be liable is through *negligence*, which is the failure to use due care to avoid harming another person or damaging property.

For an architect to be found negligent, three conditions must be met. First, there must be a legal duty established between the parties. Second, it must be shown that the architect breached that duty. Third, it must be shown that the breach of duty was the cause of the damage or injury suffered by the other party.

Architects represent themselves as having special knowledge and skill, and the law holds such professionals liable for their professional actions. However, the prevailing legal concept is that professionals are not expected to be perfect. An architect is expected only to use the same degree of skill, knowledge, and judgment that is normally used by other professionals in similar circumstances and communities. This is the *standard of care* discussed in Chap. 1. Architects are expected to perform to the standards of the professional community, which means that an architect should display the generally accepted knowledge and use the generally accepted practices and procedures of that community.

Defense of Claims

While the design professional should do everything possible to avoid liability and negligence, there are times when a claim will be made against the architect for which there may be a viable defense. Three of these are commonly used.

Betterment

The concept of *betterment* often can apply to claims of omission by the architect. For example, if a client originally approved the use of wood paneling in a room but the architect mistakenly showed a painted finish, a change order would have to be issued to correct the mistake. The client may claim that the architect should bear the full cost of the change. However, to minimize the consequences of having to pay the full amount of the change order, the architect could claim that the owner would have had to pay for the wood paneling anyway (a betterment to the project), so that the architect should have to pay only for any extra charges caused by the change order above what the original cost of labor and materials would have been; for example, to add blocking for the paneling and to call back the workers to redo the room.

Statute of Limitations

A *statute of limitations* sets a time limit within which a claim can be made. After the time limit, the claim is permanently barred. Each state has its own statute of limitations on construction claims against architects, but the time limit is generally between three and ten years. A claim of breach of contract may have a different time limit, even within the same state. In many states, the statute of limitations begins with the date of substantial completion.

Statute of Repose

A *statute of repose*, used in some states, is similar to a statute of limitations, except that the time limit is usually much shorter and does not begin until the problem is first discovered. There is also a second time limit within which any claim can be made. For example, the statue of repose for a claim against an architect may be three years from discovery, with the absolute cutoff date six years from substantial completion. In this case, if a client discovered a problem five years after substantial completion, he or she would have only one year in which to file a claim.

Risk Management

Although architects cannot avoid all liability, they can limit their exposure to liability through good risk management. Some strategies for managing risk are as follows.

- *Know the client.* In some cases, an architect should not even agree to accept a client who is unknowledgeable about construction, expects too much, has a history of poor payment, or has a history of litigation. (See Chap. 3 for a discussion of client selection.)
- *Use well-written contracts and follow them thoroughly.* The standard AIA documents have been written to coordinate with each other and are based on decades of experience. If these cannot be used, employ an attorney to write the contract or to review the client's contract.
- *Make sure the appropriate employees are assigned to each project.* Experienced project managers and design staff should be in charge of the design and production of each project as well as construction administration. Less experienced staff—with correspondingly lower billing rates—can be assigned to tasks appropriate to their skill levels while they experience their on-the-job training.
- *Maintain an active quality control program.* Establish a well-defined program and set of objectives for each project. Use standard checklists of procedures. Use proven construction methods, details, and specifications. Maintain communication among everyone on the architectural and construction team, including the client. Make sure everyone in the firm who works on a project understands the contractual obligations and their responsibilities. (See Chap. 6 for a discussion of project quality control.)
- *Maintain thorough documentation.* Document every decision, meeting, action, and observation throughout the entire life of the project. (See Chap. 4 for more information on documentation.) Documentation is invaluable in establishing a sequence of events, who each decision was made by, and what standard of care the architect took in completing the work.
- *Be very careful about last-minute changes and substitutions.* Many claims and lawsuits are caused by last-minute actions, which result in modifications that the architect does not have time to fully research and consider.
- *Carry liability insurance.* Be sure it's sufficient for the types of work the firm does. (See the following discussion on types of insurance.)

Exposure to Third-Party Claims

Through the concept of *privity*, architects are in theory protected from claims by parties with whom they have no direct contractual relationship. This is clearly stated in the *General Conditions of the Contract for Construction*, AIA Document A201, as an indemnification clause. An *indemnification clause* holds harmless both owners and architects for any damages, claims, or losses resulting from the performance of any work on the project, whether by contractors or others with whom the architects have no contractual relationship.

However, there are cases where courts may not support the enforcement of this clause for a variety of reasons, one of which may be that instructions the architects gave or failed to give were the primary cause of the damage or injury. In addition to making sure an indemnification clause is in the contract and general conditions, architects can minimize third-party claims by these actions.

- Don't include language in the contract that expressly states or implies responsibility to provide management, supervision, coordination, or planning of construction, unless those services are specifically being provided.
- Do not give directions concerning methods of construction. Actions or directions to contractors during construction may imply that the architects' responsibility extends to portions of the work beyond what the contract requires.
- Point out obvious construction safety problems to contractors. Follow up in writing with both the contractors and owners. If the problems are not corrected, suggest to the owners that construction be stopped until they are corrected.

Copyright

Copyright protection for architectural work falls into two categories. The first, and traditional, category includes copyright for the drawings, specifications, and other pictorial or graphic representations of an architect's work. The second category is for the building itself. This latter category of copyright protection was established under The Architectural Works Copyright Protection Act, which applies to buildings erected after December 1, 1990. Under current copyright protection, the rights retained by the copyright holder include the graphical representation of the building as well as the overall form, arrangement, and composition of spaces and elements in its design. This means that a building owner cannot construct buildings based on unauthorized copies of an architect's design. Likewise, derivative works may not be made. Derivative works are buildings designed after the original building that are substantially similar to the original. Making modifications to the original building falls under derivative works.

Generally, the architect owns the copyright unless the architect is an employee of the building owner or specifically assigns the copyright to the owner. This is something that should be clearly stated in the Owner-Architect Agreement. AIA Document B101, *Standard Form of Agreement Between Owner and Architect*, states that the architect is the owner of the instruments of service and retains all common law, statutory, and other reserved rights, including copyrights. In addition, the architect should specifically claim ownership rights of the building copyright. To do this, the owner-architect agreement should state that these rights belong to the architect, and the architect should register the work with the U.S. Copyright Office. Although not technically required, official registration is advisable and allows the architect to bring a lawsuit for infringement, to collect attorneys' fees, and to recover statutory damages. Registration should be made within three months of "publication," which is the completion of the building.

As is discussed in Chap. 5, the architect grants to the owner a license to use the instruments of service solely and exclusively for the purposes of constructing, using, maintaining, altering, and adding to the project. If the owner terminates the owner-architect agreement for the owner's convenience, or if the architect terminates the agreement due to the owner's suspension of the project, the owner cannot continue to make use of the architect's instruments of service without paying a licensing fee to the architect.

The architect can transfer copyright to the owner, if desired, or grant a license to reproduce the building or a derivative work one or more times.

Example 2.3

According to the legal concept of implied duties, which of the following should an architect be diligent about following when conducting construction observation? (Choose the three that apply.)

(A) performing only those actions related to the contractor and site visitation that are explicitly required by the *General Conditions*

(B) notifying the contractor if the architect thinks there is poor quality construction

(C) working with the general contractor to coordinate schedules of the owner's separate contractors

(D) notifying a subcontractor if a dangerous situation is observed with the subcontractor's work

(E) making suggestions to the contractor about the processes by which work should be carried out

(F) giving the contractor information regarding local laws and regulations regarding the project

Solution

Option A is incorrect because the architect has the duty to cooperate with the contractor even if a particular action is not in the *General Conditions* or any other relevant contract. Option D is incorrect because if a safety problem is observed, the architect should notify the contractor, not the subcontractor. Option E is incorrect because the architect should not advise the contractor about methods of construction. Options B, C, and F are reasonable implied duties that any architect should follow.

The answer is (B), (C), and (F).

INSURANCE

There are many types of insurance, some required and some optional, that pertain to doing business and completing an architectural project. In a sense, insurance is a risk management strategy for architects. Each of the three main parties to a project—the architect, the owner, and the contractor—must have certain kinds of insurance to protect against liability, property loss, and personal loss. Because the issue of insurance is so complex, and because architects are not qualified to give insurance advice, it is best that the owner receive insurance recommendations for specific projects from an insurance counselor. Architects and contractors should also have their own insurance advisers recommend needed insurance for their businesses.

Architect's Insurance

AIA Document B101, the owner-architect agreement, requires architects to maintain professional liability, general liability, automobile liability, and workers' compensation insurance. If the owner requires the architect to carry insurance at limits greater than the architect normally does, the owner is responsible for paying the additional cost. The following are some of the common types of insurance architects carry.

- *professional liability insurance:* Sometimes called *malpractice insurance* or *errors and omissions insurance.* This type of insurance protects architects in case one of their actions causes bodily injury, property damage, or other damage. This covers problems resulting from things such as incorrect specifications, mistakes on drawings, and negligence. However, it excludes intentional wrongful acts, claims for cost estimates being exceeded, and claims arising from express warranties.
- *general liability insurance:* This term includes a range of insurance that protects against claims of property damage, liability, and personal injury caused by architects or their employees, consultants, or other people hired by the architects. Sometimes an architect will also buy insurance to protect against the possibility that a contractor or subcontractor does not have the needed, valid insurance coverage.
- *property insurance:* Property insurance protects the architects' building and the building's contents against disasters such as fire, theft, and flood. Even if office space is rented, property insurance protects the contents of the office.
- *personal injury protection:* This insurance protects architects against charges of slander, libel, defamation of character, misrepresentation, and other torts. (A *tort* is a civil wrong, as contrasted with a criminal act, which causes injury to another person.)
- *automobile insurance:* Automobile insurance covers liability and property damage to vehicles owned and used by the business. This insurance can include protection against claims made by employees who use their own cars while on company business.
- *workers' compensation:* This insurance is mandatory in all states and protects employees in the event of injuries caused by work-related activities.

Other types of insurance that architects may carry include health and life insurance for employees, special flood insurance, valuable papers insurance, and business life insurance.

Owner's Insurance

As stated in AIA Document A201, *General Conditions of the Contract for Construction*, the owner is required to carry liability insurance as well as property insurance for the full insurable value of the work. This insures against physical loss or damage caused by fire, theft, vandalism, collapse, earthquake, flood, windstorm, and malicious mischief. It also provides for reasonable compensation for architect and contractor services and expenses that may be needed as a result of insured losses.

The policy must be the "all risk" type rather than the "specified peril" type. All-risk insurance is broader in coverage and includes all hazards except those that are specifically excluded by the policy. If the property insurance requires deductibles, any costs that are not covered because of the deductibles are paid by the owner. All-risk insurance also covers work stored off site and portions of the work in transit.

The owner is also required by the *General Conditions* to carry boiler and machinery insurance.

Contractor's Insurance

The *General Conditions of the Contract for Construction* require that contractors carry insurance that will protect from the following types of claims.

- workers' compensation
- damages because of bodily injury, occupational sickness, or death of employees
- damages of bodily injury or death to people other than employees
- personal injury, which includes slander, libel, false arrest, and similar actions
- damages other than to the work because of destruction of tangible property, including loss of use resulting from such damages
- damages related to use of motor vehicles
- bodily injury or property damage arising when an injury occurs after the job is complete and the contractor has left the site
- contractual liability insurance

Practice Management

3

DELIVERY OF SERVICES

This chapter discusses four important aspects of practice management:

- how to decide whether or not to accept a project
- how to decide on the type of project delivery method to use
- how to implement each of the possible project delivery methods
- how to determine what types of practice methodologies will best meet the needs of the client and the selected project delivery method

ACCEPTING A PROJECT (CLIENT SERVICES REQUESTS)

One of the first decisions an architect must make, and one of the most important, is whether to accept or turn down a project that is offered by a prospective client. Some architects think that almost any project should be accepted for the well-being of the firm, but sometimes it is much better not to accept an offer. In fact, making good decisions about which projects to accept (or to reject) is one of the most important ways that an architect can reduce risk for the firm.

There are many factors involved in this decision, including the firm's current workload, how well the project matches the type of work the firm is qualified to do or wants to do, and how feasible the project is. Two especially important factors are

- whether the client's budget is sufficient to cover construction and professional fees
- the reliability and reputation of the client

Sometimes the client requests work that the architect expects will exceed the construction budget, the budget for professional fees, or both. In such a case, the architect may decide to accept a lower profit margin on the project, possibly because it will give the firm experience in a project type that the architect wants to pursue. Another possibility is to negotiate with the client to reduce the scope of the project, the scope of services, or both. When neither of these is an acceptable option, however, the architect must decline the job.

If the prospective client is unknown to the architect, some investigation is called for. This can include researching on the internet, reviewing trade journal indexes in the client's line of business, doing a credit check, contacting other professionals who have worked with the prospective client, and talking with the client's business associates, vendors, and customers. Specifically, look for information about the client's ability to fund the project, history with building projects, and history working with design professionals. If the prospective client's experience in these areas is questionable or nonexistent, the architect must carefully weigh the potential rewards of accepting the project against the possible risks.

Some other considerations are as follows.

- Does the prospective client want to use a nonstandard contract? If so, it will probably be written to the client's benefit, not the architect's. Ask the client why he or she wants to use a nonstandard contract, and suggest the use of a standard AIA owner-architect agreement. Explain how this contract is coordinated with the AIA owner-contractor agreement and how this integration is beneficial during the construction administration phase of the project.

  If the owner still insists on using a nonstandard contract, the architect should have it thoroughly reviewed by an attorney familiar with construction law.

- Is the prospective client using bidding as a method of selecting design professionals? This indicates the client is very concerned with costs and may be likely to file a claim to save or recover money.

- Does the prospective client have a history of litigation with professionals, consultants, and contractors?
- In initial meetings, has the prospective client made unreasonable requests or shown unreasonably high expectations? These should be "red flag" indications. The client may continue to have unreasonable expectations throughout the project. These expectations most often involve schedule and budget constraints, but can also include strong preconceived ideas about design solutions and products.

If the architect decides accept the job, the architect must first negotiate an agreement with the client that determines the scope of the work, fees required, and other aspects of the contract. (See Chap. 5 for more information on owner-architect agreements.) Part of the negotiations may involve developing a preliminary design and construction schedule to help determine the project's feasibility—and the architect's expected fees—before a complete owner-architect agreement is written. Having such an agreement in writing, even if just in the form of a simple letter or memo, reduces potential risk.

If another architect or design professional has been involved with the project, the architect should determine whether any formal or informal agreement currently exists between the owner and the other design professional. The architect should not accept work from the owner unless the agreement with the other architect or design professional has been dissolved. Under the current versions of the AIA *Code of Ethics & Professional Conduct*, an architect may supplant or replace another architect on a project; however, seeking to interfere with an existing contractual relationship is still often regarded as unethical and in some cases may also be illegal.

SELECTING A PROJECT DELIVERY METHOD

The term *project delivery* describes the entire sequence of events that is needed to provide an owner with a completed building. It includes the selection of people who will design and construct the project, the establishment of contractual relationships, and some method of organizing contractors to perform the work. This section reviews some of the elements of project delivery and discusses the main project delivery methods.

Responsibility for Design and Construction

Traditionally, the owner hires an architect to design the project and a contractor to build it. The architect acts as agent for the owner, looking after the owner's best interests, with no financial stake in the project. The contractor agrees to provide, for a fixed price and within a certain time period, the materials and labor needed to construct the project according to the plans and specifications. In this project delivery model, the owner has separate contracts with the architect and the contractor.

More recent project delivery methods include a single entity being responsible for both designing and building a project, the involvement of a construction manager, and having all those involved in the design and construction process working together on one team.

Factors in Selecting a Method

Although the owner is often the one who selects the project delivery method (especially if the owner has had experience with other construction projects), the architect may be in the best position to evaluate the many variables that affect the choice.[1] These variables include cost, schedule, project scope, building quality, and risk.

Cost

Cost is an important factor is choosing the project delivery method. Traditionally, owners have chosen the design-bid-build method in order to achieve the lowest cost. There is considerable risk, though, that in the end the building will cost more than the lowest bid.

---

[1] The project delivery method should be confirmed before the architect's agreement with the owner is made final, as different delivery methods will demand different levels of design and detailing effort from the architect, and will determine the extent of the architect's involvement in the project beyond the design phase.

Bidding puts the contractor in the role of adversary to the owner and architect. On the one side, the owner and architect want a high-quality project completed at the lowest cost; on the other side, the contractor wants to win the contract and still make a profit on construction. To achieve a low bid, a contractor will often underestimate the requirements of the project or base the bid on low-quality materials and labor, and then try to make up costs with change orders. A contractor may also try to take advantage of discrepancies or ambiguities in the construction documentation to force change orders that could be considered errors or omissions and may be charged to the architect.

Unless the project is well designed and well detailed and the specifications are thoroughly researched and written, the design-bid-build approach is fraught with risks for both the owner and architect. An owner who prefers to avoid the bidding process may choose a different project delivery method and negotiate a contract with a guaranteed maximum price instead.

Schedule

The project schedule is another important factor in selecting the project delivery method. Nearly any owner, whether private and public, will be under pressure to complete a building project as quickly as possible, whether the reason is to minimize the cost of financing, to meet a certain move-in date, or so that the building can begin generating income. Everyone loses when a project is delayed.

This scheduling pressure led to the development of the fast-track method of construction, discussed in the section on construction management. When the fast-track method is used with multiple prime contracts and with a construction manager as constructor, projects can proceed quickly.

Project Scope

Project scope refers to the size and complexity of the project, as well as what is unknown about the project when the construction contract is signed. For large and complex projects, it may be best to have a construction manager who organizes multiple contracts, either with or without a fast-track schedule. When a project has many unknowns, any of the project delivery methods may be employed using a cost-plus-fixed-fee price from the contractor, either with or without a guaranteed maximum price.

Building Quality

Finally, building quality must be considered. The developer of a speculative office building may want a lower-quality building that can be built quickly for a low cost, while the development of a government-owned civic building may call for a structure with durable materials, energy-efficient systems, low maintenance, and low life-cycle costs, all of which will demand a higher initial investment. For a low-cost building, the design-bid-build project delivery method may be right, while a construction-manager-as-constructor method or an integrated project delivery approach may be better for a higher-quality building.

Risk

There are many risks involved in the design and building process. One of the ways the architect can reduce these risks is by helping the owner select the best delivery method for the project. To minimize risks during both design and construction, the architect may want the advice of someone with construction expertise. This may suggest using a design-build team, hiring a construction manager (either as adviser or constructor), or creating an integrated project delivery arrangement. These methods largely remove the adversarial relationship between architect, owner, and contractor in the traditional design-bid-build approach and encourage the team to avoid potential problems early in design as well as during construction.

PROJECT DELIVERY METHODS

There are six main types of project delivery methods.

- design-bid-build (DBB)
- construction manager as adviser (CMa)
- construction manager as constructor (CMc)

- design-build (DB)
- design-assist contracting
- integrated project delivery (IPD)

Each method may include a different method of compensation, such as a stipulated sum or cost plus a fee, either with or without a guaranteed maximum price.

See Chap. 49 for a description of the architect's preconstruction responsibilities under the various types of project delivery methods.

Design-Bid-Build

The design-bid-build approach is the traditional method of project delivery.[2] With this approach, the architect designs the project and prepares the construction drawings and specifications. These documents are used as the basis for pricing the project and awarding a construction contract, either through competitive bidding or through negotiation with one contractor. The contractor then builds the project, while the architect provides contract administration services. The owner has separate contracts with both the architect and contractor.

This method of project delivery is fairly simple because all the roles are well defined and the work proceeds in a linear fashion, from selection of the architect to final build-out. Coordination problems are minimized, contractual relationships are straightforward, and the owner can be quoted a fixed price before proceeding with construction.

The main disadvantage is that the design phase must be completely finished before the construction phase proceeds. This can be a problem if the owner needs the building quickly or if extended design and construction times result in higher financing costs. If the contractor is not selected by negotiation, this method often leads to an adversarial relationship between the architect and contractor or between the owner and contractor.

The roles and responsibilities of the architect, owner, and contractor using standard AIA contracts are described in Chap. 5.

Construction Manager as Adviser (CMa)

A construction manager (CM) can be either the construction contractor or an independent third party who acts as the owner's agent (as does the architect) without any financial interest in the project. The CM is generally hired by the owner, outside of the architect's contract. The CM advises on the constructability of the design as it is developed, provides early cost estimating and value analysis, completes project scheduling, assists with contract negotiations, manages multiple construction contracts and fast-track construction, makes early material purchases, and, in some cases, gives a guaranteed price and completion date.

There are two important disadvantages of using a CM. First, because the CM is hired before the design work is finished, there is no competitive bidding on the cost of building the project, which may mean higher costs for the owner. Second, there is a more complicated management structure due to having one more person on the design and build team. These disadvantages can be reduced considerably, however, if the contractor also acts as CM (see the next section).

If the CM is an independent adviser (CMa), different AIA agreements should be used from those for a design-bid-build project. These include

- AIA Document B132, *Standard Form of Agreement Between Owner and Architect, Construction Manager as Adviser Edition*
- AIA Document A132, *Standard Form of Agreement Between Owner and Contractor, Construction Manager as Adviser Edition*

[2]Design-bid-build is sometimes called design-award-build because one of the contractors bidding on the project is awarded the contract.

- AIA Document A232, *General Conditions of the Contract for Construction, Construction Manager as Adviser Edition*
- AIA Document C132, *Standard Form of Agreement Between Owner and Construction Manager as Adviser*

There are also versions of these agreements for use on a sustainable project.

When the CM acts as an adviser, there are three common methods for establishing the total construction cost of a project. The first is the fixed-price method, also known as the stipulated sum or lump sum method, in which the contractor gives the owner a set price for completing the project. With this method, the owner knows the final cost before construction begins and is not responsible for cost overruns. However, the owner does not share in any savings that the contractor may realize.

The second is the cost-plus-fee method with a guaranteed maximum price (GMP). In this case, the owner pays the actual cost of construction (direct plus indirect costs) plus a fee that is agreed on before construction begins, and the CM guarantees a maximum price. If the project is completed for less than this amount, the client receives the cost savings.

The third method is the cost-plus-fee without a GMP.

Fast-Tracking

When the overall time for design and construction must be compressed, the fast-track method can be used. In this method, the construction process is allowed to begin before the design process is completed. This is possible because the architectural and engineering documents are issued in stages, often called *bid packages*. For example, construction drawings and specifications for foundations can be completed based on design development drawings and sent to bid, even though the architect is still working on interior finish design.

Fast-track construction requires many prime contracts and a great deal of coordination, but it can reduce the time and cost of a project substantially. Although fast-track construction can be used with any project delivery method, including design-bid-build, it is most commonly used when a CM is involved.

Architect's Roles and Responsibilities with a CMa

AIA Document A232 requires the architect and the CM to perform joint construction administration services in regards to visiting the site, certifying applications for payment, rejecting work, reviewing submittals, investigating concealed and unknown conditions, determining dates of substantial completion and final completion, issuing certificates of substantial completion, deciding matters of performance, and reviewing requests for information from the contractor.

The CMa schedules and coordinates the activities of the contractor and other multiple prime contractors, facilitates communication between the owner and contractor, and prepares change orders and construction change directives; the CMa must keep the architect informed about these actions.

The architect's construction administration services are similar to those provided on a design-bid-build project, but the architect must advise and consult with *both* the owner and CM and report to both any known deviations from the contract documents and the most recent construction schedule as well as any observed defects and deficiencies in the work. The architect's decisions on matters relating to aesthetic effect are final if consistent with the intent in the contract documents.

Construction Manager as Constructor (CMc)

Under a CMc method of project delivery, the construction manager is part of the contracting firm, which has a single agreement with the owner covering the construction management services as well as the construction services provided. The owner-CMc agreements divide the CMc's services into two phases: the preconstruction phase and the construction phase, portions of which may proceed concurrently in order to fast-track the process.

As with the CMa method, during the preconstruction phase the CMc provides advice to the owner on constructability of the design, cost estimating, value analysis, scheduling, contract negotiations, and early material purchasing. Unlike the CMa method, however, there are only two ways to price the project—on cost of the work plus fee, either with or without a GMP. There is no stipulated sum option.

In most cases, the CMc bases cost estimates and GMP on partially completed documents, typically after the design development phase is complete. Establishing a GMP before all details, specifications, and drawings are complete puts the CMc at risk, which is why many construction managers prefer the cost-plus-fee method without a GMP. This method is often referred to as Construction Manager at Risk (CM@R) for this reason. This way, the owner and CMc can monitor cost through periodic review of the original estimate as the project proceeds, and the fee to the construction manager can be adjusted accordingly if the scope of work changes. The CMc can also advise the architect on the cost implications of the architect's work as drawings are finalized.

During the construction phase, the roles and responsibilities of the contractor and architect become essentially what they are under the *General Conditions of the Contract for Construction*, AIA Document A201.

If the CM is also the contractor, different AIA agreements should be used from those used for a design-bid-build project or a CMa-managed project. These include

- AIA Document B133, *Standard Form of Agreement Between Owner and Architect, Construction Manager as Constructor Edition*
- AIA Document A133, *Standard Form of Agreement Between Owner and Construction Manager as Constructor where the basis of payment is the Cost of the Work Plus a Fee with a Guaranteed Maximum Price*
- AIA Document A134, *Standard Form of Agreement Between Owner and Construction Manager as Constructor where the basis of payment is the Cost of the Work Plus a Fee without a Guaranteed Maximum Price*

All documents are intended to be used with AIA Document A201, *General Conditions of the Contract for Construction*, which is discussed in Chap. 5. There are also versions of these agreements for use on a sustainable project.

Architec's Roles and Responsibilities with a CMc

In addition to the architect's responsibilities during preconstruction (see Chap. 49), the architect provides construction administration services as described in AIA Document A201. This responsibility begins once one of three things happens: the owner accepts the CMc's GMP, the owner approves the CMc's control estimate, or the owner issues a notice to proceed to the CMc.

The *control estimate* is the sum of the CM's estimate of the cost of the work plus the CM's fee. The control estimate establishes the expected date of substantial completion and includes a list of drawings and specifications as well as other items used by the CMc in the preparation of the control estimate.

During the construction phase services, the architect must also advise and consult with the owner and CM.

Design-Build

With the design-build method of project delivery, the owner contracts with one entity (a person or a firm) to provide both design and construction services; that entity then subcontracts portions of the work to others as needed. The design-build entity could be a construction contractor with in-house design services, a construction contractor collaborating with an architect or other design professional through a joint venture or other project-specific legal entity, a real estate developer subcontracting both design and construction services, or any other person or firm legally permitted to do business as a design-builder in the location where the project is located.

Most often, the design-build entity is led by a construction contractor, and an independent architect and engineer act as consultants. The architect and engineer have agreements with the contractor, not with the owner. A design manager from the contracting firm then works with the contracted architect to coordinate the efforts of the two firms.

Less commonly, the design-build process may be led by an architect, and the construction contractor and engineer are subcontractors to the architect. Another possibility is that the design-build entity is an organization with in-house capabilities for both design and construction.

It is also possible for a design firm and construction firm to establish a joint venture, which is a project-specific legal entity. In a joint venture, the new entity becomes something separate from the firms that have joined to create it and bears responsibility for the project. It is important to research and understand all of the legal, regulatory, and tax implications before agreeing to a joint venture.

In the design-build method of project delivery, the owner provides the design-builder with a set of criteria that establishes the owner's requirements for the project. The design-builder then uses this information to develop a preliminary design and provide a proposed contract sum. If the proposal is accepted, the owner and design-builder execute the agreement.

The design-build method can be used for small or large projects and for private or public works. However, local or state laws and regulations may limit or otherwise control how a public project is completed.

The design-build approach offers the owner several advantages. Because the design and construction firms are under one contract, there is a single source of responsibility, and all the parties work together to give the owner the best value. A skilled constructor gives advice early in the design stages of the project when time- and cost-saving measures can be implemented. The owner receives a fixed price early in the process; this price is generally lower than with other project delivery methods. The total time of design and construction is usually less than it would be with more traditional approaches.

However, the design-build approach also has several disadvantages for the owner. Once the contract is signed, the owner has less control over design and construction than with other project delivery methods. There may be disagreements about what should have been included in the design. The design-build entity has control over the quality of the materials and construction methods used, and may substitute lower-quality or less expensive materials or finishes to stay within the project budget.

With the design-build method, the owner is responsible for developing a set of performance requirements that will act as a program for the designers and constructors. For this reason, design-build contracts are typically used by owners who have experience with building projects and who can define and state their needs clearly and precisely.

Example 3.1

A community college district wants to build a new campus, which will be financed through local and state bonds. The most important considerations are controlling costs and sharing in any savings that the contractor may realize as the project progresses. Transparency of costs is also important, as board members will follow the project carefully. State laws have established minimum quality standards for the project. What is the best method of project delivery under these conditions?

(A) construction manager as constructor (CMc) with a guaranteed maximum price (GMP)

(B) construction manager as adviser (CMa)

(C) design-build

(D) design-bid-build

Solution

Controlling costs and sharing in savings are the most important considerations. In option B, the CMa method, the CM does not act as the contractor and cannot directly control costs. Option D, the design-bid-build method, is competitively bid, but once the contract is signed, the cost is fixed with no opportunity for the owner to share in any savings.

The feature that allows the owner to control costs and also share in savings is a GMP in the contract. Both the design-build and CMc methods lend themselves to the use of a GMP, but in this case state law will not allow the contractor to substitute lower-quality materials to achieve savings in the design-build method.

The answer is (A).

Example 3.2

Which series of AIA contract documents includes a joint venture agreement between two architecture firms?

(A) A-series

(B) B-series

(C) C-series

(D) D-series

Solution

The AIA contract documents are organized into six series according to their end users. Each series is identified with a letter as follows.

A-series	owner-contractor agreements
B-series	owner-architect agreements
C-series	other agreements
D-series	miscellaneous documents
E-series	exhibits
G-series	contract administration and project management forms

An agreement involving an architect but not an owner is part of the C-series. AIA Document C101 is *Joint Venture Agreement for Professional Services.*

The answer is (C).

Requirements for Success

For a design-build project to be successful, the following conditions should be met.

- The owner must be educated in the unique aspects of the design-build method or have experience working with the method.
- The owner's project criteria must be clearly and completely stated. This is what the design-builder will use to develop a proposal, analyze costs, and design the building. The project criteria include the building program and the objectives for cost, time, and design excellence, as well as performance specifications, sustainable criteria, and other project-specific requirements.
- An owner may choose to hire a consultant to analyze project needs and develop a building program and statement of performance requirements. This consultant may also develop and issue a request for proposal (RFP) and assist the owner in evaluating, interviewing, and selecting a design-build entity. (This is discussed in greater detail under "Bridging" later in this section.)

- Although competitive bidding can be used to solicit pricing for many parts of the project, it is best if the key contractors, such as the structural and mechanical engineers, are selected early and are involved in the design process.
- Whatever form of contract is used should allow for adjustments in cost and time as the project proceeds, even when a GMP contract is used based on the owner's original criteria.
- Because a design-build project depends on cooperation among all parties, the contract should provide for a method of dispute resolution to solve problems quickly.
- Forms of communication that allow for close working relationships between the parties should be established, such as building information modeling (BIM) and the location of representatives from all the parties in the same space.
- There must be trust among the parties and willingness to work together to get the best value for the price while meeting the owner's requirements.

The main AIA contract for a design-build approach is AIA Document A141, *Agreement Between Owner and Design-Builder.* There are several other agreements that can be used instead, depending on what type of entity the design-builder is. For example, if the architect is hired as a consultant or subcontractor to the prime contractor, AIA Document B143, *Standard Form of Agreement Between Design-Builder and Architect* may be used. On the other hand, if the architect is already on the staff of the design-builder, then that architect performs the design duties required by the applicable laws, and no separate agreement is needed.

The Design-Build Institute of America (DBIA) also offers a series of standard agreements that can be used for this type of project delivery. The DBIA agreements tend to be more neutral for all parties, while the AIA documents tend to favor the architect.

Owner's Responsibilities

In addition to providing the project criteria, the owner also assumes many of the construction contract administration duties normally performed by the architect, including reviewing and approving submittals, approving changes submitted by the design-builder, visiting the site, and rejecting nonconforming work. When using AIA documents, the owner must also certify substantial completion using AIA Document G744, *Certificate of Substantial Completion for a Design-Build Project.*

The agreement between the owner and the design-builder can be based on a stipulated sum, the cost of the work plus a fee, or the cost of the work plus a fee with a GMP. AIA Document A141 includes the provisions for the unit prices, allowances, and assumptions on which a GMP is based.

Architect's Responsibilities

Under AIA Document B143, the architect's roles and responsibilities during all phases of the project are defined in an exhibit to the agreement. From a list of services, the design-builder, architect, and owner select the specific ones the architect will provide. These design services may (but do not necessarily) include

- normal design administration services, including design scheduling, consultant coordination, design presentations, and assistance with submissions to governmental authorities
- evaluation of the project criteria provided by the owner
- normal design of the project based on the owner's project criteria
- providing construction documents, including specifications

See Chap. 50 for the architect's responsibilities during construction administration.

Example 3.3

The owner of a proposed five-acre office park is planning to develop the property in phases. A consultant is hired to analyze how the property might be best utilized and to develop a master plan showing where the multiple buildings will be located on the property and how the zoning requirements will be met. The master plan also shows how the buildings could be phased depending on the demands and needs of the ultimate users. The owner has signed an agreement with the first tenant, who will occupy the whole of the first building to be constructed. To control costs and expedite the construction of this building, the owner has selected a design-build delivery method using a GMP. The design-build team will consist of an architect and contractor who have worked with the owner on traditional design-bid-build but not design-build projects. Which of the following topics are most likely to become problems or risks for the architect? (Choose the three that apply.)

(A) the type of agreement used between the architect and contractor

(B) the guaranteed maximum price

(C) rejection of nonconforming work

(D) adequate design staff

(E) communication and coordination of documentation with the contractor's staff

(F) certificate of substantial completion

Solution

The GMP is provided by the contractor. Under the design-build-method, the construction administration duties of rejecting work and providing a certificate of substantial completion become the duty of the owner. Since the architect and the contractor have not worked as a design-build team the major issues will be: what type of agreement is used, providing enough design staff to meet the expedited schedule, and coordinating communication and documentation with the contractor's staff.

The answers are (A), (D), and (E).

Bridging

A variation of the design-build approach is *bridging*, which combines the advantages of the traditional design-bid-build process and the design-build approach. Using this method, the owner hires an architect or engineer (AE) to be the project manager. The AE acts as an adviser and works with the owner to develop the project requirements that will be used by the selected design-build firm. This relieves the owner of the responsibility to develop the project criteria. As project manager, the AE (sometimes called the criteria architect) also works with public and private groups to gain the needed approvals for the project, and develops preliminary scope drawings and specifications so that design-build firms interested in bidding for the project can understand the extent of the project and the owner's design intent.

Using the documents developed by the AE, the owner makes the project available for bidding by design-build firms. When a design-build firm is selected, this firm takes over the AE's responsibilities and produces the final, detailed construction documents. The AE reviews the final documents on the owner's behalf, to ensure that the owner's design goals have been achieved, but is not legally responsible for them. The design-build firm then uses the final documents it has prepared to secure the necessary permits, review submittals, and construct the project.

Bridging is based on the idea that the design-build firm is in the best position to work with manufacturers, subcontractors, and other suppliers to determine the best way to construct the project at the lowest possible cost while meeting the requirements of the owner. For the owner, bridging combines an important advantage of design-build—someone to represent the owner's interests throughout the process—with the advantages of competitive bidding, a fixed cost, and single-source responsibility for construction.

Design-Assist Contracting

Design-assist contracting is a project management method in which specialty subcontractors or trades are included early in the design and construction document phases to help with the development of complex or unique portions of the building. This method is based on the assumption that in some cases subcontractors, trades, and product suppliers will be more knowledgeable about their portions of the work than the architect or the general contractor.

For example, a unique and innovative exterior cladding system may be better designed and detailed by the supplier of the system than by the architect. The details and specifications of the system can then be shared with the general contractor and other subcontractors whose work is affected by the system. The shop drawings and specifications of the specialty subcontractor or supplier can then be incorporated into the architect's construction documents.

The design-assist contracting method does take some additional work to make it effective. The owner must develop a clear statement and scope of work, along with a budget and schedule. The architect must help with developing the requirements of the work and then with the selection of the best subcontractor to meet the design, budget, and schedule requirements.

Integrated Project Delivery

In the integrated project delivery (IPD) method, all participants collaborate closely from the project's earliest conceptualization to move-in. The theory behind IPD is that the best design and the most efficient and cost-effective building will be produced when everyone works together throughout the process, without the adversarial positions that sometimes develop in the traditional design-bid-build approach or other project delivery methods.

IPD has many things in common with the design-build approach. A key difference is that in IPD the owner often has multiple agreements with independent design and construction firms, whereas in the design-build method the owner always has only one agreement.

At the beginning of the project, during what is called *conceptualization* (or *pre-design* in traditional terms), the owner, building users, architect, engineers, contractors, subcontractors, suppliers, and others begin to work together. They continue their collaboration as the project design is developed, finalized, and constructed. IPD depends heavily on technology, communication, and an integrated building information model (BIM) that everyone on the team has access to.

A unique and innovative exterior cladding system may be better designed by the supplier of the system than by the architect.

The phases of IPD include *conceptualization* (pre-design), *criteria design* (schematic design), *detailed design* (design development), *implementation documents* (construction documents), *agency review, buyout* (bidding from participants not included in the integrated team), *construction* (construction administration), and *closeout.* Because more participants are involved, the early design phases may take slightly longer than with traditional approaches. The implementation documents, agency review, and buyout phases will take less time, however, and the total project delivery time will be shorter overall. The *MacLeamy curve,* illustrated in Fig. 3.1, shows how IPD places more design effort earlier in project development when there is a greater ability to affect costs and the functional aspects of the building.

The advantages of IPD include a better design, shorter project delivery time, lower project cost, quality construction, and fewer problems during construction. Although there are many considerations unique to this delivery method, such as compensation, legal responsibilities, and technology standards, IPD has the potential to improve how projects are designed and built. The AIA has developed standard documents to address these issues, including AIA Document A295, *General Conditions of the Contract for Integrated Project Delivery.*

Figure 3.1 MacLeamy Curve

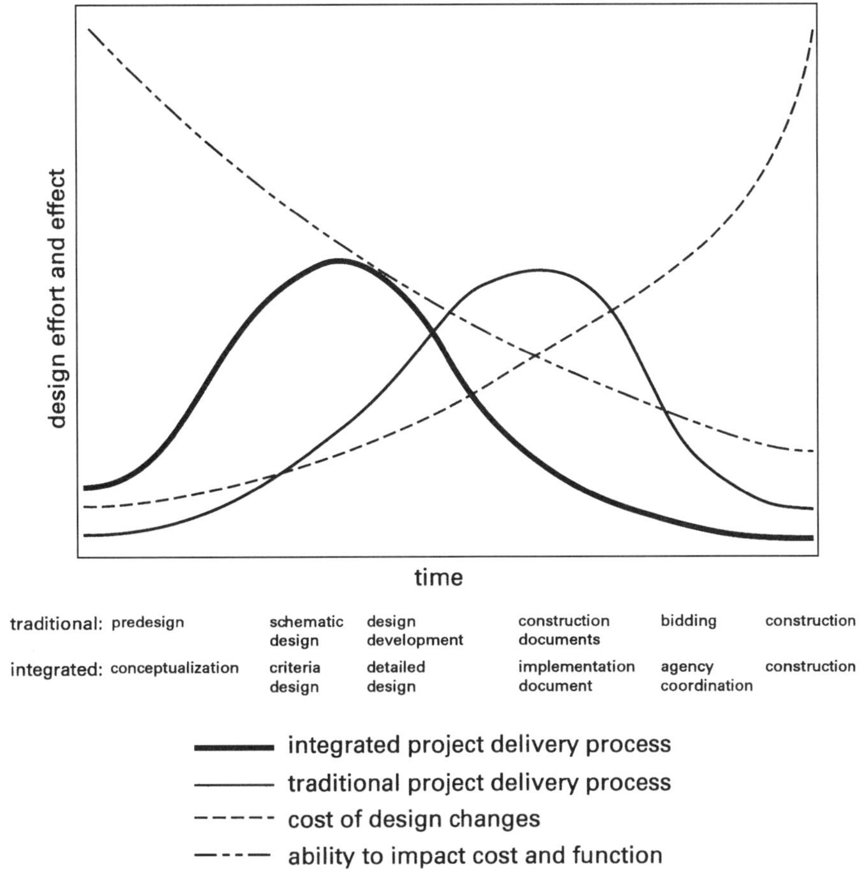

Using standard AIA documents, there are three ways to establish the contractual relationships between the primary participants in IDP.

- with transitional forms
- with a multi-party agreement
- with a single purpose entity

Transitional Forms

Transitional forms are modeled after existing CM agreements and include AIA Document B195, *Standard Form of Agreement Between Owner and Architect for Integrated Project Delivery*; AIA Document A195, *Standard Form of Agreement Between Owner and Contractor for Integrated Project Delivery*; and AIA Document A295, *General Conditions of the Contract for Integrated Project Delivery.*

Multi-party Agreements

A *multi-party agreement* is a single agreement executed by the owner, architect, contractor, and other key project participants for the design, construction, and commissioning of a project. This type of agreement is governed by AIA Document C191, *Standard Form Multi-Party Agreement for Integrated Project Delivery.* As with other IPD documents, the multi-party agreement outlines a collaborative working relationship that encourages the parties to meet the cost and performance goals they jointly established. An IPD project is managed by a project management team; in addition, a project executive team provides a second level of project oversight and conflict resolution. Each team consists of one representative from each major party to the agreement.

Single Purpose Entities

A *single purpose entity* (SPE) is an independent limited liability company newly created for the sole purpose of planning, designing, and constructing a particular project. An SPE provides for a complete sharing of risk and reward in a fully integrated collaborative process. AIA Document C195, *Standard Form Single Purpose Entity Agreement for Integrated Project Delivery*, requires the SPE to contract with an architect—who will become a member of the SPE—for planning, design, construction contract administration, and other services as necessary. An SPE is normally used for large and complex projects.

Once a project reaches the construction phase, the architect's construction contract administration roles and responsibilities are about the same as with AIA Document A201. See Chap. 49 for the architect's roles and responsibilities during preconstruction.

PRACTICE METHODOLOGIES

Practice methodologies are the various approaches that an architectural firm may use to complete various aspects of a project, including design, documentation, and coordination. The methods chosen by a firm often depend on the expertise and size of the staff, the overall philosophy of the firm, how the firm is organized as a business, the techniques used to develop designs, and how the firm produces the drawings and specifications.

This section reviews those aspects of practice management that apply to all phases of the architect's work. The various forms of business and office organizations are discussed in Chap. 1, methods of project management are discussed in Chap. 4, and contracts are discussed in Chap. 5. See Chap. 10 for a review of project budgeting, cost estimating, and scheduling during pre-design. See Chap. 46 for information on the content and coordination of the architectural and consultant drawings. Chapter 49 reviews the architect's role in construction procurement through the bidding or construction contract negotiation process. The duties and responsibilities of the architect during construction administration are covered in Chap. 50.

Design Methodologies

There are several ways an individual architect or an architectural firm can approach the design process.

Some firms are design-based; they concentrate on developing solutions to problems that are unique and easily identifiable with the firm. Such a firm is typically headed by a well-known architect who has a distinctive style; the architect is often sought after by clients who want signature buildings. In a firm of this sort, the initial conceptual design is developed mainly by the principal, and it is left to the project managers and production team to develop and implement the concept. The time and fees required by these design practices can be considerable.

Some firms focus on one particular type of project. Some specialize in complex building types such as hospitals, airports, or laboratories; a firm like this looks for projects that demand expertise in the firm's area of specialization. Other firms specialize in less complicated building types such as residential, retail, or religious buildings. Some of these firms become skilled at delivering one kind of project quickly and inexpensively; efficiencies in design and production can be found, solutions can be repeated, and most of the staff can be less experienced and less costly, though some senior staff are needed to manage projects well. A specialized firm may pursue projects on its own, or it may team with another, more generalist architectural firm that can provide the work force needed for full development of a design concept.

Some firms are generalist in nature and will complete a variety of project types. A firm of this sort needs principals and support staff with a broad range of experience, because taking on a new or complex building type can require more time and effort from a generalist firm than it would from a specialist firm. This can strain the firm's fee budget and resource. A generalist firm is more likely to see wide swings in staff employment due to changes in the marketplace; however, such a firm also tends to be better equipped to move quickly from one market to another, because its staff is more flexible and less locked into a particular building "formula." There is also the option of bringing in a specialist in a certain building type as a consultant, to provide expertise that the firm lacks.

As described in Chap. 1, most firms are organized on either the departmental or the studio model. A firm that specializes in a few building types or that wants to maximize efficiency will often use departmental organization; each project moves through each department in the overall design and production process, and individual specialists apply their expertise at each stage. A design-based firm can also manage projects in this way once the principal has developed the overall design. Generalist firms and some specialist firms often use studio organization, where most of the design and production for each project is responsibility of a single group of employees. Some larger offices have studios that specialize in certain building types, combining the advantages of expertise with the advantages of close communication and group problem solving.

Documentation Methodologies

The methods a firm uses to document a project and generate the needed construction drawings and specifications can affect productivity and profitability. Each firm uses its own preferred set of software and hardware tools.

For the design development phase, there are a variety of computer programs available to help the architect visualize and analyze project design. Once a project has reached the construction document phase, however, there are just a few computer-aided drafting (CAD) programs to choose from: either a two-dimensional (2-D) drafting program or the document production component of a three-dimensional (3-D) *building information modeling* (BIM) program. Some firms employ experienced architects who are also proficient with the office's CAD programs, while other firms use the more traditional model, in which experienced staff design plans and elevations and develop details that are then documented by entry-level staff who are experts at using the CAD or BIM programs. See Chap. 46 for a discussion of BIM.

While most firms use in-house staff to complete drawings, some elect to outsource portions of the work on a project-by-project basis, either locally or to overseas companies. *Outsourcing* is the practice of contracting with another company for the production of a certain part of the architect's work product. Most often, this includes drafting work that would traditionally be done by junior-level employees, such as construction documents, renderings, and 3-D modeling. Outsourcing can be an economical way to produce construction drawings, and it can help a firm manage fluctuating workloads, reduce production time, and take on more work. However, it also requires additional management and coordination by the firm.

For specifications, most firms either hire the services of a specification-writing firm, or they subscribe to a master specification system and use the system's software to produce documents in-house. Some large firms have an in-house specification writer and a master set of specifications. Regardless of how it develops specifications, a firm should follow the guidelines discussed in Chap. 49. The architect always bears the final responsibility for the content of specifications and their coordination with drawings.

Consultant Coordination

Professional consultants who will be involved in a project should be brought in as early as possible. Their advice and expertise is vital to determining the scope of the building project (especially if the project involves the renovation of an existing building), developing broad conceptual approaches to designing the building, and understanding the concerns of the client and other design professionals working on the project.

One of the most important tasks an architect has during pre-design is to assemble and coordinate a team of professional consultants to work on the project. Most project teams will include, at a minimum, structural and building systems engineers (mechanical, electrical, and plumbing). Additional consultants may include geotechnical engineers, civil engineers, fire protection engineers, historic preservation specialists, security consultants, interior designers, and audiovisual consultants. The architect can hire consultants to perform energy analyses, create renderings, build models, and perform dozens of other services. What services are expected from each consultant must be determined with the advice of the consultant and the approval of the client.

The contractual arrangement between the consultant and the architect or owner must also be determined. If the owner contracts directly with the consultant, the owner assumes all responsibility for coordinating the architect's work with the consultant's work. The architect avoids any issues with contract provisions and payment, but may lose some ability to direct the consultant.

If, on the other hand, it is the architect who contracts directly with the consultant, then the architect becomes responsible for coordination between the architectural work and the consultant's work. In this arrangement, the architect holds the primary contract with the owner, receives all payments, and is responsible for paying consultants their shares of the total fee. If payments from the owner are delayed, the architect may encounter problems paying consultants' fees. For this reason, many architects include a "pay when paid" clause in their contracts with consultants. This clause states that the consultant will be paid when payments are received from the owner.

Although being the one to contract with the consultant means more work for the architect, many architects prefer it, as it ensures them of the opportunity to comment on any portions of the consultant's design that affect the aesthetic objectives for the project. On the other hand, some architects object to working with outside consultants because it takes extra time, lessens the architect's control over a project, and reduces the amount of immediate contact among all team members.

One of the most important tasks an architect has during pre-design is to assemble and coordinate a team of professional consultants to work on the project.

As stated in Chap. 5, the architect is responsible for informing consultants about the applicable code requirements and about any design decisions that may have code implications. The architect is also responsible for understanding any design decisions the consultants make that will affect portions of the architect's work.

In addition to the standard types of consultants, such as structural, mechanical, and electrical engineers, a firm may want to use independent consultants to outsource work as described in the previous section. In addition to outsourcing production work the architect can hire consultants for energy analysis, rendering, model building, and dozens of other services.

The usual objections that most architects have are that working with non-engineering consultants is more time consuming and that it lessens the control and immediate contact that management would have if the work were being done in house. With proper working procedures and clearly defined agreements, however, these objections can be easily overcome with good coordination using the following techniques.

- Develop a list of reliable people in the area who can be called on when needed. Include several contacts for each type of work, so that there are alternatives if one's first choice is too busy. Research and interview consultants before an immediate need arises so that there will be time to choose the most appropriate one and develop the necessary agreements. Be sure to include the costs for this work in the initial project budget.
- Check references and past work before hiring a consultant. Only a small percentage of consultants available will be appropriate for the project. Speaking with colleagues in other firms and searching the internet may help narrow the choices.
- Plan and outline the work needed before giving it to the consultant. This may lead the architectural firm to study this aspect of the project in greater detail than it normally would, resulting in better coordination and less risk of omissions.

- Establish a lump-sum contract price for the work that is to be outsourced. This is usually possible for tasks like creating drawings and specifications. This makes it possible to develop a budget for the project. Be explicit in the written agreement about the extent of the work to be done and its quality.
- Set up a strict schedule of progress meetings, methods of communication, and reviews. This is the only way to catch problems before they become serious and to ensure that deadlines will be met.
- Do not assume that all work is being completed as contracted. The architect must still control overall coordination and review all the work the consultant does. This is not extra effort: Even if the work were being done in house, oversight and review would have to be provided by someone in the office.

DIVISION 2: PROJECT MANAGEMENT

PROJECT PLANNING AND MANAGEMENT

Project management is one of the most important jobs in an architectural firm. Someone must be responsible for coordinating all the tasks that must be done from start to finish for each architectural project. The job of project management includes project planning, scheduling, monitoring, coordinating and directing, updating documentation, closing out the job, and following up with clients. Whether a project is small or large, planning and coordination warrant a concentrated management effort in addition to the project's design and production.

Depending on the size of the project and how the firm is organized, the project manager may also be the office principal and project designer. Alternatively, the project manager may be a separate staff member and may manage more than one project at a time. The project manager often sees the project through all the way from the initial proposal through contract administration and follow-up.

While project management is often the responsibility of a single person, another method of managing a project is through *partnering*. In partnering, various stakeholders in a project—such as the architect, owner, contractor, and vendors—all participate in the decision-making process. Partnering can produce closer communication on a project and can result in shared responsibilities; on the other hand, the day-to-day management of a project can be difficult with so many people involved. With either method, the lines of communication and of delegation of responsibility should be established clearly at the beginning of the project.

PROJECT MANAGEMENT RESPONSIBILITIES

The project manager should coordinate the activities of all members of the design and construction teams who are related to the firm. Figure 4.1 shows the ideal position of the project manager in relation to others involved with the project. In this central role the project manager may have some or all of the following responsibilities.

Figure 4.1 Project Management

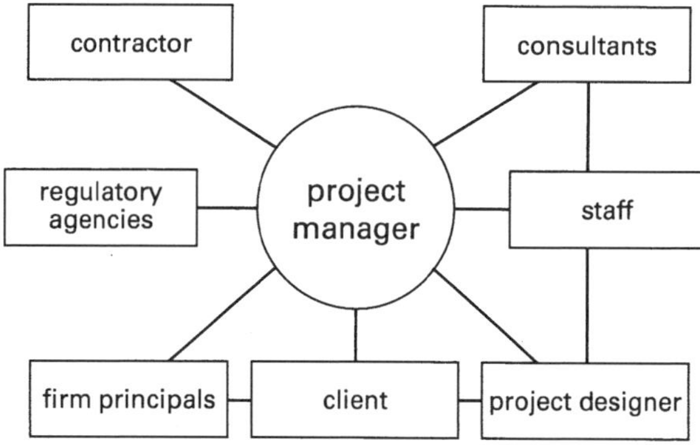

Possible Project Manager Responsibilities

- Take part in team marketing efforts.
- Take part in writing proposals and fee estimates.
- Take part in preparing the agreement between the architect and the owner.
- Assemble the project team.
- Prepare the time estimate for the project.
- Create the project schedule.
- Take part in the hiring and coordination of consultants.
- Organize and coordinate all activities needed to complete the project.
- Keep the project on track to meet the goals laid out by the client and the design team.

- Schedule meetings and coordinate progress among all team members.
- Manage the personnel assigned to the project.
- Take part in resolving conflicts among team members.
- Be the primary link between the principals and the project team.
- Provide status reports to the principals.
- Be the contact person for the project with governmental agencies and other regulatory groups.
- Attend client presentations.
- Obtain client approvals at important project milestones.
- See that all aspects of the project are documented.
- Process all change orders, certificates for payment, work authorizations, and similar documents.
- Make sure that the office meets all its contractual obligations.
- Review all invoices that the firm will send to the client.
- Review all invoices that consultants have sent to the firm, and approve payment as appropriate.
- Keep track of personnel time spent on the job, compare it against initial estimates, and take corrective action when needed.
- Keep track of construction cost estimates as design and production proceed, and compare them against the client's budget.
- Coordinate the production of construction documents.
- Take part in bidding or negotiation procedures.
- Confirm that proper contract administration and construction observation are carried out.
- Help collect overdue billings.
- Help the client with construction-related problems during and after move-in.
- Close out the job.
- Follow up with the client periodically after move-in.
- Work with upper management and other project managers to maintain overall office workload scheduling.

This list contains only a few of the hundreds of responsibilities that a project manager may take on during the course of a project. Giving these responsibilities to one person helps ensure that the client's project is completed on time and within budget, and that the design goals are met in a profitable manner.

The project manager often uses project management software to

- project personnel time and fees
- track actual time and fees in comparison to budgeted figures
- track consultant costs
- schedule work within the office
- generate invoices
- maintain project documentation such as correspondence, transmittals, and meeting notes
- track construction-related documents such as change orders and site visits
- maintain information about individual project design and specification decisions

- keep a project address book with all team contacts
- track employee productivity
- compile information from individual jobs into office-wide financial management reports

Assembling the Project Team

Having the right team is vital to the success of the project, and to the financial and business success of the architectural firm. There are, in fact, two project teams: the overall group of people involved in producing the job (of which the architectural firm is only one part), and the group of people assembled within the architect's office.

The overall team includes, at a minimum, the architect, consultants, and the owner. It may also include a construction manager, contractor, and major subcontractors, depending on what type of project delivery method is used. If the architectural firm associates with another architectural firm, that second firm is also part of the team.

A team is usually formed partly before the project is secured and partly after. If architectural firms are submitting proposals in competition, they are usually required to identify the major players on their teams—the firm principal overseeing the project, the lead designer, the project manager, and the consulting firms that will be used (such as structural, mechanical, and electrical engineers). It may even be necessary to have decided on specialty consultants, commissioning agents, and major suppliers to the job, particularly if the costs associated with their services should be included in the architect's total fee proposal. For design-build projects and projects led by construction management, the construction manager, contractor, and possibly major subcontractors should also be identified. Once the proposal is accepted and the contract signed, the project manager, with the assistance of the firm principal and others, assembles the appropriate staff in the office to complete the design work. At this time, the project manager may also make some additional decisions about specialty consultants.

When selecting consultants to bring into the project, the architectural firm usually considers a number of factors. Past working relationships are often the most important. If the consultants have performed well on previous projects, then the architect and consultant will be comfortable working with each other and already familiar with each other's methods of collaborating. In some cases, the firm may need to retain someone new because a particular kind of expertise is needed. The available staff and the fee proposal may also be considerations, but they are usually not deciding factors.

Sometimes the architect will have two or more consultants of the same discipline to call on, and the project manager will decide which is best suited to the particular job. For smaller, simpler jobs, the choice may not be important and one may be as good as another; for larger, more complex projects, one consultant may have the added expertise or the larger staff needed to handle the job.

Similar considerations apply when the architect selects a construction manager or contractor for a design-build project. Occasionally, the client may suggest (or even insist on) certain consultants.

How the project manager selects the team depends on how the office is organized and how it works. As mentioned in Chap. 1, offices can be organized into departments (horizontal organization), studios (vertical organization), or a combination of both. If the office is organized into studios, the project manager will need to assemble a project team and should consider the following issues.

- *the type and complexity of the project.* Some projects may require experience and expertise that only a few people in the office have.
- *the size of the project,* Small projects can be completed by just a few staff members with nominal experience, but large projects need more staff members with a wider range of experience and knowledge.
- *staff availability.* Some staff members will already be committed to other projects and unavailable to work on the new one.

- *experience levels.* The project manager must determine the tasks that the project team will need to perform over the life of the project, and then match these tasks with the skills and knowledge that available staff members have.
- *billing rates.* The budget for the project may suggest that certain billing rates be kept to a minimum, but this must be balanced with the experience and knowledge needed for the job. For example, the project manager may decide to use several less skilled staff members with lower billing rates, and have them supervised by one experienced professional.
- *personalities.* A project team requires close, long-term cooperation and mutual support, so team members must have compatible personalities and working methods. A good project manager is aware of which working relationships in the office are good and which are problematic.

If the firm associates with another architectural firm, the same considerations apply. In addition, there should be a clear, written understanding of each firm's duties and responsibilities.

Example 4.1

A project manager has been assigned to the construction of a new office building using the design-build project delivery method. The site has been fully designed by a landscape architect except for utilities. The contractor determines that the building systems will use design-build subcontractors. Which team members must the project manager include as consultants and staff to complete the project? (Choose the four that apply.)

(A) specification writer

(B) fire protection engineer

(C) in-house project designer

(D) mechanical, electrical, and plumbing engineers

(E) civil engineer

(F) structural engineer

Solution

Building systems include mechanical, electrical, plumbing, and fire protection engineering, and these will be handled by design-build subcontractors. The project manager will need to hire consultants or assign in-house staff to design the building and write the specifications, as well as consultants to provide structural and civil engineering services.

The answers are (A), (C), (E), and (F).

Scheduling the Project

There are two methods commonly used for scheduling design and construction projects. The simpler and more common of the two is the *bar chart* or *Gantt chart.* (See Fig. 4.2.) All the various *tasks* (also called *activities*) that must be done in order to complete the project are listed in chronological order along the vertical axis of a bar chart; the time period that the entire project will cover is represented by the horizontal axis. For each task, a horizontal bar is drawn from the task's start date to its end date. If one task must be completed before another can start, an arrow is drawn from the end of the earlier task to the beginning of the later one; this relationship is called a *dependency.* A bar chart can show at a glance which tasks should be happening at any given time and which tasks must occur in sequence. Bar charts are easy to create and understand and are suitable for projects of almost any size.

Figure 4.2 Scheduling Using a Bar (Gantt) Chart

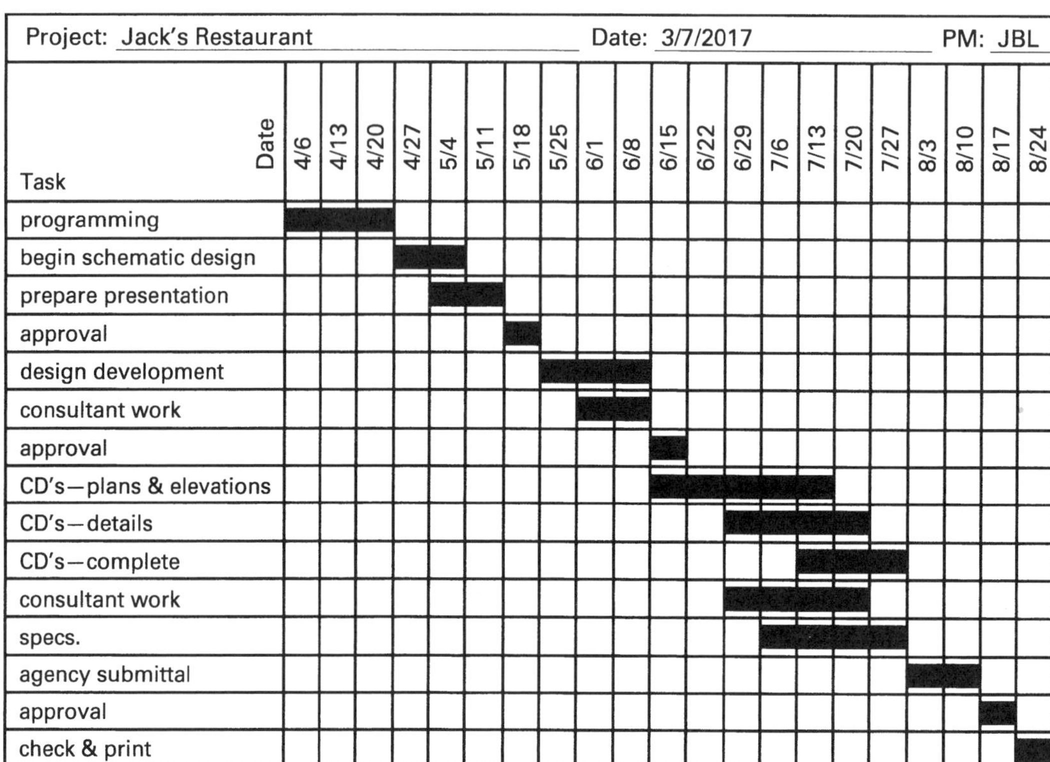

The other common scheduling tool is the *critical path method* (CPM), though this is used more often with construction projects than with design projects. A CPM chart graphically depicts all the tasks needed to complete a project, the sequence in which the tasks must occur, and each task's duration, earliest and latest possible starting times, and earliest and latest possible finishing times.

A CPM chart for a simple design project is shown in Fig. 4.3. Each solid arrow represents a task; each task's beginning and end points are represented by numbered circles. A task cannot begin until all the tasks that lead into its beginning circle have been completed. The number under each arrow is the number of days that the task will take to complete.

Dependencies are represented by dashed arrows, known as *dummies*. Dummies do not represent tasks, so they have no duration. Dummies are used to give each activity a unique beginning and ending number.

The heavier arrows in Fig. 4.3 show the *critical path*, the sequence of those tasks (called *critical tasks*) that must start and finish on time if the project's final deadline is to be met. Delaying the start or increasing the duration of any critical task delays the whole project. A noncritical task, however, may start somewhat later or take somewhat longer without affecting the final completion date. The maximum length of time that a noncritical task can be delayed or extended before it causes a delay in the overall project is called the *float* of that task.

Figure 4.3 Critical Path Method Chart

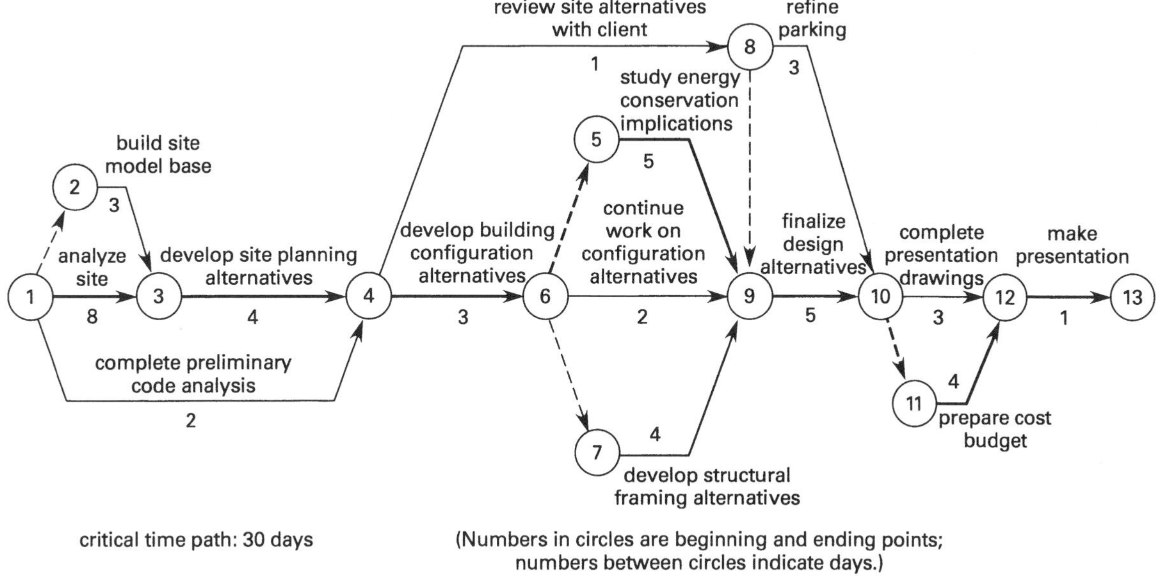

Example 4.2

Using the Gantt chart from Fig. 4.2, determine which of the following project phases will require the longest time to complete.

(A) specifications

(B) design development

(C) construction documents

(D) schematic design

Solution

The schematic design, design development (including approval), and specifications will each require four weeks. The construction document phase (including approval) is scheduled to be completed in ten weeks.

The answer is (C).

Creating the Work Plan

A *work plan* is a detailed project schedule, breaking the project down into its component tasks and assigning staff members and other resources to each task. Creating the work plan is one of the earliest and most important tasks that a project manager must complete.

The work plan also details how the fee that the firm receives—after deductions for profit, overhead, and other expenses—will be used to pay staff members and cover other costs over the course of the project. For this reason, the work plan is also sometimes called a *fee projection*.

A good work plan includes the following items.

- *the scope of services in the agreement.* This is drawn directly from the owner-architect agreement, and states what the architect is legally required to provide. It is important that all members of the project team understand what services are included in and excluded from the contract. If the client requests additional services, the project manager should request additional compensation.
- *a breakdown of the services to be provided into phases and individual tasks.* This is the heart of the work plan. It requires the project manager to think though the entire project in detail and identify exactly what needs to be done to complete the project.
- *dependencies.* The work plan should identify all the cases where one task cannot be started until some other task has been completed.
- *milestones.* The work plan should identify specific points and events in the project's schedule that will act as markers of the progress made toward completion. Typical milestones can include a crucial meeting, the completion of a phase, the completion of a deliverable, the client's approval of a deliverable, or the approval of a governmental agency.
- *the staff needed to do the work.* The project manager assigns specific members of the project team to the individual tasks.
- *allocation of time and fees to phases and individual tasks.* This is crucial for project monitoring.
- *what work will be done by consultants, and what fees and other costs will be associated with their work.* The work plan should also give the major components of the consultants' schedules. See Chap. 10 to learn how to include time for construction as part of the work plan schedule.

The primary element of a work plan is the *schedule*, most often presented in the form of a bar chart. The project manager begins planning the schedule by considering the scope of the project, which includes the project's type, size, and budget, and the services that must be completed. The project manager defines each task, establishing the start and end dates both for design services and any construction that is required. Finally, the project manager assigns staff members for the completion of each task within its allotted time.

The level of detail that a work plan needs depends on the complexity of the project. The plan must be detailed enough that the project manager can assign specific tasks to individual staff members, so that the staff members can understand and perform their assigned tasks, and so that their progress can be tracked. For example, in the design development phase there may be individual tasks such as *develop exterior cladding details*, *finalize toilet room layouts*, and *complete outline specifications.* The tasks are listed in chronological order along the vertical axis of a bar chart so that the first task is at the top of the schedule and the final task is at the bottom, closest to the horizontal axis. The time needed for each task is listed along the horizontal axis. The timeline is usually divided into weeks for easy and accurate planning and monitoring, but may be divided into months for projects with very long durations. Each task is plotted on the chart, with the first task beginning at the top left corner of the schedule and the last task in the lower right corner.

One of the more difficult parts of the work plan process is estimating how much time will be required for various tasks. A project manager must have sufficient experience in all phases of design in order to accurately determine how much time a task will take based on the experience level of the person who will perform the task.

The work plan in Fig. 4.4 shows part of a very simple project. Whether a project is small (with a short duration) or very large (to be completed over a year or more), the basic form of this work plan applies.

Figure 4.4 Work Plan

Project: Mini-mall   Project No.: 9274   Date: 10/14/2017
Completed by: JBL   Project Manager: JBL   Total Fee: $26,400

Phase or Task	Period / Date	1	2	3	4	5	6	7	8	9	% of total fee	fee allocation by phase or task	person-hrs. est.
	Date	11/16–22	11/23	11/30	12/7	12/14	12/21	12/28	1/4	1 /11			
SD-design		1320	1320								10	2640	
SD presentation			1320								5	1320	
DD—arch. work				1980	1980						15	3960	
DD—consultant coord.				530	790						5	1320	
DD—approvals					1320						5	1320	
CD—plans/elevs.						1056	1056	1056	1056	1056	20	5280	
CD—details								2640	2640		20	5280	
CD—consultant coord.						440		440	440		5	1320	
CD specs.									1320	1320	10	2640	
CD—material sel.						660	660				5	1320	
budgeted fees /period		1320	2640	2510	4090	2156	1716	4136	5456	2376	100%	$26,400	
person–weeks or hours		53 / 1.3	106 / 2.6	100 / 2.5	164 / 4	108 / 2.7	86 / 2.2	207 / 5	273 / 6.8	119 / 3			
staff assigned		JLK	JLK AST JBC	JLK AST EMW-(1/2)	JLK AST JBC EMW	JLK AST EMW	JLK AST	JLK AST EMW →	JLK SBS BFD	JLK AST EMW			
actual fees expended													

Assigning Fees

After creating the schedule, the project manager's next step is to assign fees to the various tasks. Estimating fees can be done with a top-down approach or a bottom-up approach. Most often, the project manager estimates the fees both ways and compares the results.

The Top-Down Approach

The project manager begins by estimating the total fee needed to complete the project. This estimate is generally made using a combination of rules of thumb (such as a certain percentage of the construction cost or a certain amount per square foot, the amount varying with the building's size and type) and historical data (data about similar buildings in the past).

A total fee that is estimated using this approach will include fees for both direct and indirect labor, consultants' fees, non-reimbursable expenses, and a contingency. To determine the portion of the total fee that is available for direct labor, the amounts of the other elements must be estimated and subtracted from the total fee. These estimates are typically based on historical data and are often calculated as a percentage of the total fee. For example, a firm might know from experience that, for a particular type of building, consultants' fees will be about 35% of the total fee.

The project manager's next step is to assign fees to the various tasks. This can be done with a top-down approach or a bottom-up approach.

Once the fee for direct labor is determined, the project manager allocates it to the various phases. Rules of thumb can be used to allocate the expected total labor budget among the various phases. For a traditional design-bid-build project, for example, the fees needed for schematic design, design development, construction documentation, bidding, and construction administration will be about 15%, 20%, 40%, 5%, and 20% of the total project budget, respectively. If additional services such as programming and post-construction work are included, the percentages will vary. Percentages will also differ with the project delivery method (discussed in Chap. 3). The project manager will allocate fees quite differently if an integrated delivery method is used, for example, instead of design-bid-build.

Figure 4.4 shows the top-down approach. The *total working fee*—that is, the fee available to pay people to do the job after subtracting fees for profit, consultants, and other expenses—is listed in the upper right corner of the chart. The phases or tasks needed to complete the job are listed in the left column, and the time periods are listed (most commonly in weeks) across the top of the chart.

As shown in this example, the percentage of the total amount of work or fee for each phase is estimated. This estimate is based on the firm's experience and common rules of thumb. The percentages are noted in the third column from the right; a phase's percentage is multiplied by the total working fee to find the allotted fee for that phase, which is given in the second column from the right. This allotted fee is then divided over the number of time periods in this phase, and the result is noted under each time period.

If phases or tasks overlap (as they do in the example in Fig. 4.4), fees in each period are totaled and placed at the bottom of the chart. If this dollar amount is divided by the average billing rate for the people working on the project, the result is the approximate number of hours that the firm can spend on the project each week and still make a profit. If the budgeted number of hours exceeds about 40, of course, more than one person will be needed to do the work, or overtime will be required.

The Bottom-Up Approach

In this approach, the project manager begins by breaking the project down into individual tasks, listing the tasks in order along the left side of the chart, and estimating how much time will be needed (in hours or weeks) to complete each one. Then the project manager charts bars showing the time estimated under the appropriate calendar dates. The total estimated fee can be calculated by assigning a specific staff member with a defined billing rate to each task.

Combining the Two Approaches

The bottom-up approach is more accurate than the top-down method, but usually both are used and then the results are compared. If the fees found using both approaches are about equal, the project manager can feel confident that the estimate is sound. If the work plan is used for diligent monitoring (discussed in greater depth in Chap. 6), there should be enough money to complete the project within the allotted time and generate a profit for the firm.

Monitoring the Project

By monitoring employees' time sheets weekly, the project manager can compare the actual hours (or fees) expended to the budgeted time (or fees) and take corrective action if the actual time exceeds the budgeted time. This can be done using a *project monitoring chart.* A project monitoring chart can also be produced manually, like the one in Fig. 4.5 (which is based on the fee projection chart in Fig. 4.4). For a larger project, the project manager may use project management software to create the work plan and project monitoring chart. Project management software can also often be linked with a firm's financial management system to produce reports like those described in Chap. 2.

A useful technique for involving all members of the design and construction team (including the client) in developing a schedule is to bring the entire team together to complete a *full wall schedule.* This is a low-tech process, but sometimes nothing works as well as having everyone in the same room and able to see the entire project laid out. Vertical lines are drawn five inches apart on an entire wall. The space between each pair of lines represents one week. The project manager develops a preliminary list of project tasks and who may be responsible for completing the tasks. Each task is written on two 3 × 5 index cards with one labeled "start" and one labeled "finish."

Figure 4.5 Project Monitoring Chart

Project: Mini-mall		time												
Phase/People/Departments	fee dollars	1	2	3	4	5	6	7	8	9	10	11	12	total
schematic design	budgeted	1320	2640											
	actual	2000	2900											
design development	budgeted			2510	4090									
	actual			3200										
construction docs.	budgeted					2156	1716	4136	5456	2376				
	actual													
	budgeted													
	actual													
	budgeted													
	actual													
	budgeted													
	actual													
	budgeted													
	actual													
total (cumulative)	budgeted	1320	3960	6470	10,560	12,716	14,432	18,568	24,024	26,400				
	actual	2000	4900	8110										

At beginning of job, plot budgeted total dollars (or hours) on graph. Plot actual expended dollars(or hours) as job progresses. Also plot estimated percentage complete as job progresses.
Budgeted
Actual
% completed
100
80
60
40
20

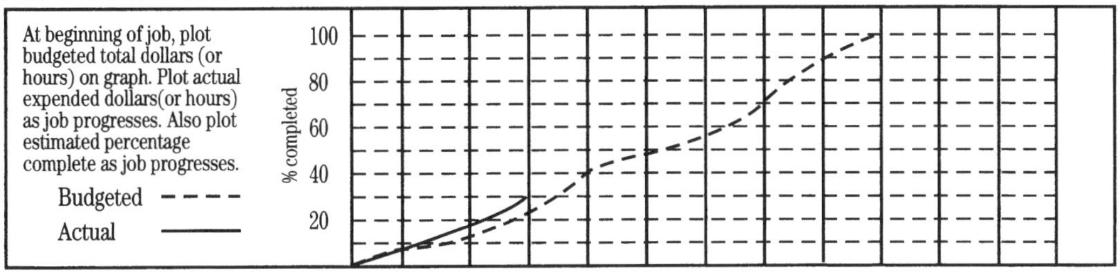

Along the left edge of the chart are placed the names of everyone who is responsible for any of the tasks. Each person is asked to place the start and finish cards where they think the activity should be placed in the total schedule to indicate the time they need allotted for the task. Fixed dates, such as regulatory board meetings or submission deadlines, should be included to ensure that all deadlines are met and the project is not delayed. This large, interactive schedule serves as a starting point for discussion among everyone on the project team. Cards can be moved around easily, and when everyone has agreed to the dates, the schedule can be copied to project management software or some other more convenient format and used by everyone on the team.

COORDINATION

An important part of the project manager's job is coordinating the work of the design office staff, consultants, and the client, while making sure all codes and regulations requirements are met. Some of the tools the project manager can use for coordination include project management software, project websites, checklists, weekly project meetings, consultant drawing exchange, and building information modeling.

Design Office Staff Coordination

Project management is fundamentally people oriented. Its ultimate success depends on the project manager's ability to understand interpersonal relationships within the context of a business environment and use this knowledge to organize and motivate all the people involved in the project.

One of the most important groups of people with which the project manager must interact is the design office project team. The following list highlights some of the actions a project manager can take to add a personal dimension to the everyday direction of team coordination.

- *Communicate.* Communication is one of the most important aspects of project management. There are four basic kinds of communication in a design office: work assignments, instructions, reward and punishment, and social interaction. For the greatest impact, each kind of communication should be handled separately. For example, chatting with a staff member about yesterday's football game and then mentioning that he is doing a good job lessens the emphasis and effect of the praise. It is better to tell him directly that he is valuable to the team, that his efforts are appreciated, and so on, without mixing it with social communication. A message with a single purpose is more likely to be understood.

- *Always clarify the expectations of project team members.* Outline the task, the time allowed, and the results that are expected. Make sure each team member understands exactly what is wanted, when it needs to be completed, and at what level of detail or quality. Employees may interpret instructions differently depending on their levels of experience, familiarity with the project, and roles on the team. For example, telling an engineering consultant to "look into" a problem is too ambiguous, and the results may not be what is needed. Instead, the project manager should define the problem, outline his or her thoughts, tell the engineering consultant what is wanted, specify a time limit, and suggest an approximate maximum fee limit. Use the same approach for in-house staff.
- *Never give responsibility to an employee who does not have enough authority to make decisions and carry out actions.* If a task is assigned to a junior staff member, the project manager should be available to answer questions and review the work frequently.
- *Be sensitive to the manager-subordinate relationship.* Recognize that the different points of view may affect work output. A subordinate may be concerned with moving up in the organization, wanting due credit, protecting position, and wondering what kind of job he or she is doing and whether the manager is a partner or a competitor. A manager may be concerned with advancing in the organization, wondering whether the subordinate wants his or her job, and wondering whether the manager's work is as important to the project and as valued in the organization as the subordinate's. The various points of view will affect communication, work assignments, quality of work, and general enthusiasm for the project. The effective project manager must recognize these feelings and work within the limitations they create or take steps to minimize their negative effects.
- *Stay calm when people get angry.* A good project manager recognizes anger as a symptom of a significant problem, not just a personality trait. It may indicate a problem with the project that would not come to the surface any other way until it was too late. The manager should analyze the anger, find out what is causing it, and work with the person to solve the problem. Don't simply dismiss the anger or get angry in return.
- *Commit to resolving conflicts as they occur.* The natural tendency for most people is to avoid a problem and hope it will go away. It seldom does; it usually just gets worse. Solve the problem as soon as possible.
- *Provide ways for staff members to grow and advance.* Some of these opportunities may be determined by office policy and general personnel practices, but on the project management level, each person can be challenged with work assignments and encouraged to expand their knowledge and skill levels.
- *Give recognition when it is due.* Every person needs to be recognized. Give praise publically, and encourage self-esteem.
- *Evaluate the performance of the staff members on the project team.* People like to know what kind of job they are doing, so this evaluation should be on a continuing basis, not just the formal six-month or one-year company evaluation. If criticism is needed, give it constructively and privately; suggest techniques for improvement and offer help if it is needed.
- *Open up communication among team members.* It is too easy for everyone to get so involved in the pressures of completing a job that the overall view is lost. Encourage general discussions at appropriate times of the broad issues involved in a project, and encourage participation in decision making to the extent possible.
- *Model the behavior you want to see.* Keep everyone informed of job progress, problems, schedules, goals, and general status. Listen to complaints and suggestions for improvements, and take time at in-house seminars, retreats, or social gatherings to review what everyone is doing and why.

- *Don't shut the client out.* Most clients want to be involved with the design of their buildings or spaces. The client will have a deep knowledge of his or her organization and a point of view that the design team does not.
- *Direct the client's interest to areas where his or her contributions will be most valued.* Clients who are more analytical can help with defining the needs of their organizations (programming). Clients who are focused primarily on the broad view can become involved in design reviews and presentations.
- *Establish an environment in which initiative is encouraged.* Design is a creative business, and an atmosphere that stifles fresh thinking and the willingness to explore is unpleasant and counterproductive. When employees feel that their contributions are valued and they are invested in the success of the work, the results will be better morale and a better project.

Consultant Coordination

For most medium to large projects, the project team will need to include consultants. A *consultant* is an expert who is not part of the firm's regular staff but is employed to work on one or more specific projects. Consultants most often engaged by architectural firms include structural engineers, mechanical engineers, and electrical engineers. Other needed consultants may be experts in

- acoustical design
- construction specifications
- building code compliance
- fire protection
- hardware
- commercial food service
- security systems
- audiovisual systems
- telecommunication systems

The project manager is responsible for coordinating the work of all consultants. The project manager must understand the typical scope of each consultant's work. Refer to Chap. 17 for more information on structural, mechanical, and electrical systems.

The project manager should involve the consultants in the project as early as possible.

A structural engineer designs any new structure or structural modifications, including the building foundation, frame, floors, and load-bearing walls. The structural engineer also produces any drawings and specifications for the structural portion of the project.

A mechanical engineer designs and produces the drawings and specifications for the heating, ventilating, and air conditioning (HVAC) systems on a project, as well as any plumbing systems needed. The mechanical engineer often also designs the fire protection systems, including sprinkler systems, but sometimes a separate fire protection consultant is used.

The electrical engineer designs and produces the drawings and specifications for the power system (outlets and equipment) and the lighting system. On most projects the electrical engineer will also design the telephone system, signal systems, and security systems. On larger commercial projects, which have more sophisticated security, computer, and signal systems, specialized consultants may complete these portions of the job instead. Their work must be carefully coordinated by the electrical engineer to ensure that what they do complies with the design intent. A separate lighting designer may also be retained.

The project manager should involve the consultants in the project as early as possible. Consultants are an integral part of the team, and their early input is valuable in developing design concepts and avoiding misdirected design efforts. Their advice and expertise is vital to determining the scope of the project, developing broad conceptual approaches to solving the client's problem, and understanding the concerns of the client and other design professionals working on the project. A few basic assumptions laid out by the mechanical engineer early in the project, for example, could save weeks of design time that might be wasted in exploring an inappropriate scheme.

Once the consultants are retained, the project manager should inform the appropriate consultants about any applicable code requirements. The project manager is also responsible for informing the consultants of any design decisions that may have code implications. Although the project manager and design team are responsible for ensuring that the drawings and specifications conform to the applicable codes, the consultants are responsible for code compliance regarding their areas of work in the same way the architect is responsible to the owner. By signing their drawings, the engineering consultants become responsible for compliance with applicable codes and regulations.

Each consultant is also responsible for the accurate production of his or her own drawings and specifications, and for checking his or her own documents for consistency. The architect, however, is the main consultant and is liable to the owner for the consultant's work.

For information on coordination with the consultant's drawings, see Chap. 48.

Coordination of Code Requirements

Reviewing and applying code requirements should begin during programming and early space planning and should continue throughout the project. Different levels of detail are appropriate depending on the design phase: general principles during early planning, and detailed requirements during the construction document phase. Code checklists are useful for coordinating code requirements. Some important code requirements for programming and early design work are listed in Chap. 8 and Chap. 14.

During design development, all preliminary information used in schematic design should be verified. This is especially important if changes are being made to the space plan, occupancy type, occupant load, or other building configuration. The project manager assigns someone to check the basic exiting requirements, including those pertaining to the number of exits, separation between exits, travel distance, common path of egress travel, exit width, dead-end corridors, and door swings.

It is often acceptable if very detailed code requirements are not verified and applied until later, during the construction document stage. This is not true, however, for design elements that could affect the overall space plan or have significant cost implications. For example, the design decision to use expensive fire-rated glazing instead of gypsum wallboard partitions would have a serious budget impact. It would be better if the project manager, designers, and client verified the fire safety requirements and studied the cost implications of the design during the schematic design phase rather than waiting until later.

TECHNIQUES FOR DAILY PROJECT MANAGEMENT

Project Notebook

A *project notebook* is one of the most useful project management tools. The notebook may be a traditional paper binder or it may be kept on a tablet or laptop computer. With the use of cloud-based data, essentially all project information can be at the project manager's fingertips at any time.

In either form, the project notebook gives the project manager immediate access to information for planning, coordinating, and monitoring the job. It can be used in the office or taken to meetings and the job site. When the notebook is kept in electronic form, it is also easy to share notes with the rest of the project team, including the client.

A project notebook should contain most of the following items. This list can be modified to suit the unique needs of individual offices and project types.

- *general reference:* the index of the notebook, the project directory (names, addresses and telephone numbers of the client, consultants, contractors, regulatory agencies, major vendors and others), and the filing index (names and code numbers of the office filing system for the job)
- *contracts:* the owner-architect agreement, architect-consultant agreements, and work authorizations
- *fees and schedules:* preliminary schedule, detailed schedule, time projections, fee budgets, task assignments, and financial management report summaries
- *programming:* goal statements, program or program summary, code and zoning search, special equipment needs, other special needs, and utility information
- *budget:* overall project budget, construction budget, furnishings budget, other special items, and updates
- *job communication:* major correspondence, meeting minutes, telephone and email logs, transmittal log, design review notes, and written client approvals
- *construction administration:* shop drawing/sample log, minutes or notes from job conferences and site visits, bulletins, change orders, field orders, field reports, test and site observation reports, and applications and certificates for payment
- *close-out and follow-up:* punch list, certificate of substantial completion, summary of construction costs, summary of fee expenditures and other job-related costs, commissioning reports, testing and balancing reports, comments on completed job, consultant evaluations, and notes on follow-up visits

Meeting Tips

Meetings are a necessity of any office, but they can also be large time wasters. Some ways that project managers can make meetings more efficient are as follows.

- Every meeting should have a clearly stated purpose. Prepare an agenda and distribute it in advance to all invitees. The agenda should list things that need to be discussed, decided, or accomplished at the meeting. If it has been a long time between meetings, attach a copy of the minutes and action items from the last meeting.
- Don't schedule a meeting unless it is truly necessary.
- Ensure that the correct team members are invited to the meeting.
- Require that everyone turn off cell phones.
- Send a reminder email to all participants the day before.
- Arrive early and start on time.
- If there is a lot to accomplish and the topics to be discussed are independent, arrange the meeting in shifts. For example, it may be possible to ask the civil engineer to arrive at 9 a.m. to discuss site development issues, the mechanical engineer to arrive at 10 a.m. to discuss the building systems, and the interior designer to arrive at 11 a.m. to go over the furniture plan, while asking only the owner and architect to be present for the entire discussion. This is respectful of your colleagues' time.
- A conference call is often more productive than an in-person meeting, especially if the latter would require participants to travel. If the firm's telephone system doesn't support conferencing, it is easy to set up a telephone conference through any of a number of free online services.
- If the project manager will be leading the meeting, appoint another team member to take notes. If no one is available, it may be advantageous to record the meeting, but as a courtesy, ask permission from participants before doing so.
- If the meeting will include use of audiovisual aids (such as reviewing a plan or a BIM model) and the project manager will be leading the meeting, appoint another team member to manage the computer and projector.

- Establish an ending time—and stick to it. Limit meetings to an hour, if possible; if the meeting must be longer, plan for a short break midway through.
- Organize your notes and prepare the minutes as soon after the meeting as possible.
- Minutes should include decisions, accomplishments, and action items. This information can be expressed either in sentences or can be simplified into a table.
- If a follow-up meeting is needed, set the date and time for it at the end of the meeting, and include this information in the minutes.
- Use stand-up meetings to reduce the tendency of people to stay longer than necessary.
- Schedule meetings just before lunch or at the end of the workday, to encourage participants to keep them short.

Meeting Notes

Documentation of all meetings is vital to a properly managed project. Trying to reconstruct from memory what happened in the past is unreliable and leads only to disagreements. Minutes of every meeting should be taken and promptly distributed to the participants, with the opportunity for participants to submit corrections. These minutes will improve communication, help the team avoid misunderstandings, and provide a written or electronic record should disputes or legal problems arise.

The best technique for taking meeting minutes is to use a template. There should be a place for the project name and number, date, place of the meeting, time, people attending and the subjects covered. If the meeting is held at a construction site, it may be prudent to record the weather conditions and temperature on the day of the visit. It is also advantageous to prepare a blank sign-in sheet in advance, to be completed by meeting participants. The sign-in sheet (which can be on paper or on a laptop or other device) can serve as a record of attendees and will ensure that the email addresses and phone numbers for all participants have been recorded. The meeting minutes may include a column for follow-up, including who is assigned to perform a task and by when.

Taking good notes requires a little practice. The meeting notes must be complete, accurate, unbiased, and to the point. The meeting minutes serve as the formal record of the proceedings and may have legal implications later on. Handwritten notes should be typed and formatted immediately after the meeting, and then promptly distributed to all attendees, the client, and any other project team members who may need to know what happened. At the end of the form include a statement such as, "If there are any additions or corrections to these minutes, please notify this office within five days." This gives everyone a chance to set the record straight while the meeting is fresh in their minds, and it also protects against someone disagreeing later.

Example 4.3

The construction administrator has returned from a visit to the construction site to review the project progress with the contractor's superintendent. While on site, the construction administrator and the superintendent note that metal conduit material stored on site by the electrical subcontractor is located in an unsecured and unsafe area. How should the administrator respond?

(A) Call the electrical subcontractor.

(B) Include this observation in a written memo or report.

(C) Stop the work and call the owner immediately.

(D) Assist the superintendent in moving the conduit to a safe location.

Solution

Since the meeting took place on the construction site, the construction administrator has limited authority to take direct action on the site condition. The administrator is an agent of the owner and does have the authority to record the observation and send this report to the owner and contractor. It is always important, in addition to reporting the date, time, and location, to record the people attending the meeting. The report could become an important document if a dispute were to arise over the metal conduit.

The answer is (B).

Project Perfection Syndrome

In their efforts to complete a job, a project team spends time working toward some established or idealized level of quality. Early in the project, the time they spend results in rapid progress toward this goal. As the job continues to be worked on and refined, however, more and more time is needed to get closer to the "perfect" level of quality. Eventually, the point is reached where marginal progress toward "perfection" can be made only with a great deal of additional time (and therefore additional fees as well). This is illustrated schematically in Fig. 4.6.

Figure 4.6 Time to Reach Perfection

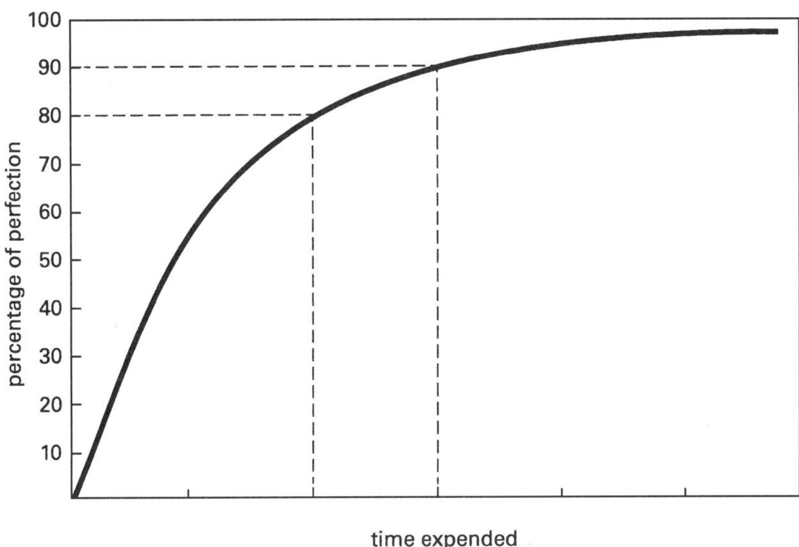

The desire to continue to pursue perfection is called *project perfection syndrome.* In Fig. 4.6, for example, an increase in project perfection from 80% to 90% requires half again as much time as was expended to reach the 80% level.

The project manager must decide whether the additional time and money are justified. If fees are available and the time was allocated originally, it may be a simple decision to proceed. If, on the other hand, fees have already been spent or are close to running out and more work should be done but may not absolutely have to be done, then the choice is more difficult. A joint decision by the project manager, project designer, firm principals, and others has to be made.

The most common situation in which project perfection syndrome can occur is when contractual and office quality standards have been met, but the designers or production staff want to continue refining and improving the design. Although this is a natural tendency, it can mean the difference between a profit and a loss on the job with no real improvement to show for the extra time expended. In order to curb this tendency, the project manager should make sure that everyone on the project team understands how much time is budgeted for each task and which tasks must be completed.

Every office has its unique project perfection curve. Its form depends on the skill and talent of the people involved and how efficiently design and production are managed. For some offices, the curve may not level out so quickly; for others it may not rise so steeply in the initial stages of work. The project manager must know the special characteristics of the office's project perfection curve and be prepared to judge how far to go before stopping work.

5

CONTRACTS

For each project that an architect works on, there is some form of mutual understanding about what the architect will do and what the client will give in return for services rendered. There are similar understandings with the contractor and any consultants and subcontractors who are also working on the project. These understandings are formalized in the *contract documents* for the project.

The American Institute of Architects (AIA) provides standardized forms and contracts that define the relationships and terms involved in design and construction projects. Architects may use these documents, though they are not required to. The AIA contract documents have been developed over many years with the consensus of owners, contractors, attorneys, architects, and others. As a result, these documents are comprehensive and widely recognized as the industry standard. They are also used as the basis for contract-related questions on the Architect Registration Exam.

The AIA contract documents include the

- standard owner-architect agreement
- owner-architect agreement for sustainable projects
- owner-contractor agreement
- owner-contractor agreement for sustainable projects
- general conditions of the contract
- supplementary conditions of the contract
- general conditions of the contract for sustainable projects
- architect-consultant agreement
- architect-consultant agreement for sustainable projects

There are other standard AIA contract documents and forms, but these are the ones typically referred to on the Architect Registration Exam, and the ones that are discussed in this chapter.

The AIA contract documents are organized and coordinated so that the architect's responsibilities to the owner, contractor, and project are clearly and uniformly defined across documents. Although the architect is not a party to the owner-contractor agreement, the documents that make up the owner-contractor agreement (AIA Documents A101 and B201) do assign responsibilities and roles to the architect. If the AIA owner-architect agreement is used in conjunction with the AIA owner-contractor agreement, the role of the architect and the terms for his or her compensation will be clear and delineated.

Other organizations, such as the Design-Build Institute of America, also provide standard contracts. Design-build contracts are typically used by owners who have building experience with multiple facilities and who have clearly defined needs that can be precisely stated in performance requirements. However, the AIA contract documents are the only ones covered on the Architect Registration Exam. The various agreements discussed in this chapter are long and cover a great deal of material, so it is a good idea to become familiar with the primary agreements before taking the exam. Sample documents are available for download from the AIA's website.

OWNER-ARCHITECT AGREEMENT—AIA DOCUMENT B101

The AIA publishes several types of owner-architect agreements. The most common is AIA Document B101, *Standard Form of Agreement Between Owner and Architect.* This document includes both the provisions of the agreement and the architect's scope of services specific to the project. Other AIA standard agreements are available for large and complex projects, small projects of limited scope, jobs where construction management services are performed, jobs that require interior design work, and other specialized services.

In AIA Document B101, two separate articles describe the architect's services: one for basic services and one for additional services. *Basic services* include the five traditional phases of a design-bid-build project: schematic design, design development, construction documents, bidding or negotiation, and construction administration. Other services are considered to be *additional services*; these include programming, building information modeling, LEED or other sustainable building rating system certification, and post-occupancy evaluation. The architect may be entitled to additional compensation for additional services, whether these services are part of the original agreement or the need for additional services arises as the project progresses. If additional services are to be provided, they must be noted in AIA Document B101 and described either in the agreement or in an attachment.

Initial Information

Article 1, "Initial Information," requires the architect and owner to give certain information and assumptions about the project as known at the time of the contract's execution. This information includes the project's objective; site information; the owner's program; the physical, legal, financial, and time parameters; and the key personnel for both the owner and the architect. The architect may choose to use AIA Document G612, *Owner's Instructions to the Architect*, to help gather initial information.

The intent of this article is to encourage communication at the beginning of the project. The article also states, however, that the information may materially change. If it does, the owner and architect are required to adjust the schedule, the architect's services, and the architect's compensation appropriately.

The Architect's Responsibilities

The architect's responsibilities are spelled out in the next three articles of AIA Document B101. Article 2 covers general responsibilities, Article 3 covers basic services, and Article 4 covers additional services.

In Article 2, "Architect's Responsibilities," a *standard of care* paragraph requires the architect to perform his or her services in a manner consistent with the level of professional skill and care that is ordinarily provided by architects practicing in similar locations under similar circumstances. The architect must perform these services as expeditiously as is possible while meeting this standard of professional care and seeing to the orderly progress of the project. (For a more detailed discussion of the principle of standard of care, see Chap. 1.)

The architect must not take part in any activity or accept any employment, interest, or contribution that could reasonably appear to compromise the architect's judgment. (Refer to the discussion of ethical standards in Chap. 1 for more information.)

If the architect becomes aware of anything that is incorrect, incomplete, or inconsistent, he or she must notify the owner promptly and in writing.

Article 2 also requires the architect and owner to agree on and list the types and amounts of insurance that the architect must carry for the project. The article specifically mentions general liability, automobile liability, workers' compensation, and professional liability. The owner must reimburse the architect for the cost of any insurance beyond what the architect normally carries. (For information on types of insurance, see Chap. 2.)

Basic Services

Article 3, "Scope of Architect's Basic Services," covers the structural, mechanical, and electrical engineering services the architect customarily provides. The architect must coordinate his or her services with those provided by the owner and the owner's consultants. The architect is entitled to trust that all information and services provided by the owner and the owner's consultants are correct and complete. But if the architect does become aware of anything that is incorrect, incomplete, or inconsistent, he or she must notify the owner promptly and in writing.

As soon as is practical after the agreement is signed, the architect must prepare a schedule for the performance of his or her services and submit it for the owner's approval. This schedule must include time for the owner's review, the performance of the owner's consultants, and the approval of submissions by authorities having jurisdiction. It must also include the expected dates for the start of construction and substantial completion. Once the owner has approved the schedule, these time limits cannot be exceeded by the architect or owner except for reasonable cause.

One provision in Article 3 requires the architect to consider environmentally responsible design alternatives during the schematic design phase. These alternatives may include choices of materials, building orientation, and other considerations, as long as they are consistent with the owner's program, schedule, and budget.

Other important provisions of Article 3 include the following.

- *project administration services.* The architect must manage the architect's own services and administer the project. This includes consulting with the owner, researching design criteria, attending project meetings, coordinating both the architect's and owner's consultants, and issuing progress reports. A progress report may consist of copies of correspondence, memos detailing the progress of the project, the architect's field reports, minutes of meetings, and any other writings that keep the owner informed of the project's status.

  The architect must prepare a project schedule and keep it updated during the project. This schedule identifies estimated milestone dates for decisions required of the owner, services furnished by the architect, time required for governmental and other approvals, completion of documents provided by the architect, commencement of construction, and substantial completion. The project schedule is not the construction schedule, which is prepared by the contractor and only runs from commencement of construction to the proposed date for substantial completion.

  The architect must also consider alternative materials and building systems, make presentations to the owner, submit design documents to the owner for evaluation and approval, and assist the owner in filing documents required for approval of governmental authorities.

- *evaluation of budget and cost of the work.* The architect must prepare a preliminary estimate of the cost of the work and refine it as design work progresses during the preparation of construction documents. The cost estimate should be routinely compared with the owner's budget. If the estimate exceeds the budget, the architect must make recommendations to the owner to adjust the project's size, quality, or budget. The owner must cooperate with the architect in making the adjustments.

  All cost estimates prepared by the architect represent the best professional judgment. Neither the architect nor the owner, however, can guarantee that bids or negotiated prices will not vary from the owner's budget or from any estimate that the architect has made. Only the contractor can guarantee prices.

- *evaluation and planning services.* The architect must provide a preliminary evaluation of the information furnished by the owner, including information about the site, program, schedule, budget, and proposed method of contracting for construction. In this evaluation the architect should review the balance between quality, cost, and time. The architect should notify the owner of any impact that the budget, schedule, site, or method of contracting may have on the project.

- *design services.* Article 3 covers the bulk of the architect's standard services, including schematic design, design development, and construction document production, and describes generally what is involved in each of these design phases. At the end of each phase the owner's approval is a precondition that must be received before the architect can begin work on the next phase. When schematic designs are presented to the owner, the owner is not obligated to approve the scheme if it fails to match the agreed-upon program, budget, or time frame. However, the owner must act in good faith to work with the architect as revisions are made. During the construction document production phase the architect must assist the owner in the development and preparation of bidding documents and the conditions of the contract for construction. However, the architect should make it clear that he or she is *not* providing legal services to the owner and is *not* a party to the owner-contractor agreement. The owner-contractor agreement must be drafted by the owner's attorney or other authorized representative.

- *construction procurement services.* During this phase the architect must assist the owner in obtaining competitive bids or negotiated proposals and must assist in awarding the contract and preparing contracts for construction; the architect is authorized to act as an agent for the owner in order to perform these tasks. The architect produces the bidding documents, distributes the documents, considers requests for substitutions, holds pre-bid conferences, answers questions, prepares addenda, and participates in the bid opening. Similar requirements are defined if the project is negotiated with a contractor. Refer to Chap. 49 for more information on bidding procedures and documents and the architect's responsibilities during this phase of the work.
- *contract administration services.* The architect must make site visits at intervals appropriate to the stage of construction to generally determine whether, when completed, the project will be in accordance with the contract documents. The architect must keep the owner informed of the progress and endeavor to protect the owner against defects. However, the architect is not required to make exhaustive or continuous on-site inspections.

  The architect is not responsible for the means of construction, building techniques, or safety precautions. These are the sole responsibility of the contractor. The only time this is not true is if the architect has actually specified means and methods of construction. (This provision is in AIA Document A201, *General Conditions of the Contract for Construction*, not in AIA Document B101.) Refer to Chap. 50 for more information on construction administration services and the architect's responsibilities during this phase.

  The owner and contractor are supposed to communicate through the architect. Communications by and with consultants and the contractor's subcontractors are also supposed to be through the architect.

The Owner's Responsibilities

Under AIA Document B101, the owner must provide the architect with certain information such as a program, schedule, and budget. The owner must provide the architect with a program that defines the owner's objectives, schedule, constraints, and design criteria, including space requirements and relationships, special equipment, systems, and site requirements. The owner may request the architect's assistance to develop this program as an additional service with additional compensation. In this case, this service should be listed in the agreement.

The owner must also either furnish the services of consultants or authorize the architect to furnish these services as a change in services. The owner must furnish land surveys to describe the legal limits of the site, grades, locations of utilities, easements, right-of-way, and other aspects of a standard survey. The architect may assist the owner in procuring these services (using AIA Document G601, *Request for Proposal—Land Survey*), but this would be an expansion of the architect's standard services.

The owner must furnish the services of a geotechnical engineer; these services may include test borings, determinations of soil bearing values, percolation tests, evaluation of hazardous materials, and other investigations made necessary by the site and the project. A report with recommendations should be provided. The architect is entitled to rely on the accuracy of these geotechnical services. The architect may assist the owner in procuring these services and coordinating the necessary information (using AIA Document G602, *Request for Proposal—Geotechnical Services*). The owner also has certain responsibilities regarding site information and geotechnical engineering services under the terms of the *General Conditions of the Contract for Construction*, AIA Document A201.

In addition, the owner must furnish all tests, inspections, and reports required by law or by the contract documents. These could include structural, mechanical, and chemical tests, along with tests for pollution or hazardous materials. The owner must also furnish all insurance, legal, and accounting services needed for the project.

Example 5.1

On a large, privately funded project, the lowest bid is 15% higher than the owner's original budget. Under the provisions of AIA Document B101, the owner elects to revise the project scope and quality to reduce the cost. In this case the architect must

(A) proceed to reduce the project scope and quality on a time and materials basis

(B) develop an addendum to the owner-architect agreement for additional services

(C) work with the owner to revise the project with additional compensation

(D) modify the contract documents as necessary, without additional compensation, to comply with the budget

Solution

Section 6.7 of AIA Document B101 requires that the architect shall, without additional compensation, modify the documents for which the architect is responsible as necessary to comply with the budget.

The answer is (D).

Terms and Conditions of the Contract

Other important provisions in AIA Document B101, the owner-architect agreement, include the following.

- *instruments of service.* Drawings, specifications, and other documents, including those in electronic form, are considered instruments of service whose authors and owners are the architect and the architect's consultants. They retain all common law, statutory, and other reserved rights, including copyrights. Under the terms of the agreement, the architect grants the owner a license to use the instruments of service solely and exclusively for constructing, using, maintaining, altering, and adding to the project. This license is terminated if the architect rightfully terminates the agreement for cause as described elsewhere in the agreement.

  Unless the architect terminates the agreement for cause, the owner retains the license to use the instruments of service after completion of the project or the owner's termination of the agreement, for the purposes described in the previous paragraph. If the owner later uses the instruments of service without retaining the architect, the owner agrees to release and indemnify the architect and the architect's consultants for all claims and causes of action arising from such uses.

- *waiver of consequential damages.* Both the architect and owner waive consequential damages. This limits claims to damages resulting directly from a breach of the agreement.

- *hazardous materials.* The architect and architect's consultants have no responsibility for the discovery, presence, handling, removal, or disposal of hazardous materials such as asbestos, PCBs, and other toxic substances, nor for the exposure of persons to these hazardous materials.

- *third-party claims.* Section 10.5 of AIA Document B101 states, "Nothing contained in this Agreement shall create a contractual relationship with or a cause of action in favor of a third party against either the Owner or Architect." This provision is in support of *privity*, the principle that a contract cannot be used as the basis of a legal claim except by those who are parties to it. No one but the owner and the architect can sue to enforce the agreement or to claim damages based on it.

- *causes of action.* Any claim or cause of action taken by either the architect or the owner against the other must be initiated within a time period prescribed by applicable law (generally the law of the state in which the project is constructed), and in any case not more than 10 years after the date of substantial completion of the work. Each state defines the period of time within which a claim must be filed (often called the *statute of limitations* or *statute of repose*). Because it can take time for construction defects to become apparent, in some states the statute of limitations for construction claims is longer than for general claims. This period generally begins at the time the problem or injury is first discovered. For example, if the client discovers a leaky roof two years after substantial completion, and state law has a five-year statute of limitations, then the claim may be filed up to seven years after substantial completion.

- *waiver of rights.* This clause, also known as a *waiver of subrogation,* is a waiver of damages that are covered by property insurance during construction. It means the owner and architect cannot sue each other for damages if they are covered by property insurance, as is required by the owner-contractor agreement. The waiver prevents the insurance company from suing any of the principal participants in the project (architect, contractor, subcontractors, engineers, and consultants) to recover what has been paid for an insured loss.
- *right to photograph.* The architect has the right to photograph the project and include photographs or other artistic representations of the design in the architect's promotional materials unless the owner has specifically notified the architect in writing that some or all of what the architect wants to photograph is confidential or proprietary information. Unless such notice has been given, the owner must give reasonable access to the completed project for photography.
- *termination.* Either party can terminate the agreement with no less than seven days' written notice if the other party fails substantially to perform according to the terms of the agreement. The architect is also allowed to suspend performance of services with seven days' written notice to the owner if the owner fails to make fee payments when due. If the owner suspends work or terminates the agreement, the architect must be compensated for services performed prior to termination or suspension. The owner may terminate the contract, without cause and for the owner's convenience, as long as the owner gives seven days' written notice.

Cost of the Work

The *cost of the work* is the cost of labor and materials furnished by the owner and the cost of items specified or designed by the architect (including costs of management or supervision of construction provided by a separate construction manager or contractor), plus a reasonable allowance for overhead and profit. Costs are figured at current market rates. The cost of the work does not include professional fees, land cost, financing costs, or other costs (such as land surveys) that are the responsibility of the owner; these must be considered as a part of the overall project budget.

The architect does not guarantee that bids or negotiated costs will accord with the owner's budget or any estimate that the architect has prepared; however, the architect must adhere to the owner's budget. If the lowest bid or negotiated proposal is greater than the budget, the owner has five options.

- increase the budget
- authorize rebidding or renegotiation
- terminate the project
- cooperate with the architect to revise the project's scope or quality
- implement some other mutually acceptable alternative

If the owner decides to revise the project, the architect must revise any documents he or she is responsible for without additional compensation. For this reason, the architect should regularly check that the expected costs of the design accord with the available budget. The architect may suggest that the owner hold a portion of the available funds in reserve to cover unforeseen increases in construction prices.

Additional Services

In Article 4, "Additional Services," Sec. 4.1 of AIA Document B101 gives a list of additional services that may be added to the architect's responsibilities. These services include programming, preparing measured drawings of an existing facility, building information modeling, landscape design, interior design, on-site project representation, post-occupancy evaluation, security evaluation and planning, LEED or other sustainable building rating system certification, and historic preservation.

For each item in this list, the parties can indicate whether the service will be the responsibility of the architect, the responsibility of the owner, or not provided by either. The architect is not responsible for any of these services unless it is specifically indicated in this section of the agreement. The architect is entitled to be compensated by the owner for each of these additional services.

Each service that the architect will provide should be described in more detail, either in Sec. 4.2 of AIA Document B101 or in an exhibit attached to the agreement. The B-series of AIA documents includes standard forms to describe many of the services that may be listed.

- AIA Document B202, *Standard Form of Architect's Services: Programming*
- AIA Document B203, *Standard Form of Architect's Services: Site Evaluation and Planning*
- AIA Document B204, *Standard Form of Architect's Services: Value Analysis, for use where the Owner employs a Value Analysis Consultant*
- AIA Document B205, *Standard Form of Architect's Services: Historic Preservation*
- AIA Document B206, *Standard Form of Architect's Services: Security Evaluation and Planning*
- AIA Document B207, *Standard Form of Architect's Services: On-Site Project Representation*
- AIA Document B209, *Standard Form of Architect's Services: Construction Contract Administration, for use where the Owner has retained another Architect for Design Services*
- AIA Document B210, *Standard Form of Architect's Services: Facility Support*
- AIA Document B211, *Standard Form of Architect's Services: Commissioning*
- AIA Document B212, *Standard Form of Architect's Services: Regional or Urban Planning*
- AIA Document B214, *Standard Form of Architect's Services: LEED Certification*
- AIA Document B252, *Standard Form of Architect's Services: Architectural Interior Design*
- AIA Document B253, *Standard Form of Architect's Services: Furniture, Furnishings and Equipment Design*

Additional Services Not in Agreement

Section 4.3 of AIA Document B101 covers two kinds of situations in which the architect must provide services not specifically listed. Unless the services are required due to the fault of the architect, the architect is entitled to additional compensation and an appropriate adjustment in the architect's schedule.

The first case is described in Sec. 4.3.1 of AIA Document B101. When the architect sees that any of the services listed in this section are needed, the architect must notify the owner with reasonable promptness and explain the circumstances. The architect should not proceed, however, until the owner has given authorization in writing. These services include the following.

- making changes to initial information, previous instructions, or approvals given by the owner
- making material changes in the project, such as to the owner's schedule, the budget, the delivery method, or the size, quality, or complexity of the project
- fulfilling the owner's request for extensive environmentally responsible design alternatives, including LEED or other sustainable building program certification
- making changes to instruments of service already prepared because of changes in codes, laws, or regulations
- preparing digital data for transmission to the owner's consultants and contractors
- preparing design and documentation for alternate bid or proposal requests by the owner

- preparing for and attending public presentations, meetings, or hearings
- preparing for and attending dispute resolution proceedings or legal proceedings (unless the architect is a party)
- evaluating the qualifications of bidders or persons providing proposals
- providing consultation about the replacement of work due to fire or other cause during construction
- assisting the initial decision maker[1], if this is someone other than the architect
- any service that has become necessary because the owner failed to make a decision in a timely manner, or due to any other failure of performance by the owner or the owner's consultants

Section 4.3.2 of AIA Document B101 covers times when the architect must provide additional services to avoid a delay in construction. In such cases, the architect may begin the services and notify the owner with reasonable promptness, explaining why the services are needed. The owner may decide that all or part of the services are not needed, in which case the owner must notify the architect of this promptly in writing, and is not obligated to compensate the architect for the unneeded services. Services that fall into this category include the following.

- reviewing a contractor's submittal out of sequence from the original submittal schedule
- responding to the contractor's requests for information, in cases where the requests have not been prepared according to the contract documents or the contractor could have found the information from the contract documents, from other information provided by the owner, or from correspondence and documentation from a prior project
- preparing change orders and construction change directives that require evaluation of the contractor's proposals and supporting data
- evaluating an extensive number of claims
- evaluating substitutions proposed by the owner or contractor and making subsequent revisions to the instruments of service
- providing construction phase services 60 days or more after the expected date of substantial completion given in the initial information (or 60 days or more after the actual date of substantial completion, if this is earlier), when this affects the architect's basic services

Owner-Architect Dispute Resolution

Article 8 of AIA Document B101 describes how disputes are to be handled. When one party begins a claim or cause of action, mediation must be tried first. *Mediation* is a process in which a neutral third party helps the disputing parties negotiate a settlement, using rules established by the American Arbitration Association (AAA).

No dispute resolution proceedings whose outcome would be binding may be held before at least 60 days from the date that the request for mediation was filed, in the hope that a mutually acceptable agreement can be reached within that time period. The parties to the mediation share the costs involved. Parties may not seek other forms of binding dispute resolution unless mediation fails.

When writing the contract, architect and owner must decide what method they will use next if mediation fails, and they must specify it in AIA Document B101 Sec. 8.2.4. This may be arbitration, litigation, or another method. *Arbitration* is a formal, legally binding process for resolving disputes without litigation. One or more arbiters with experience in the construction industry will hear the arguments of both disputing parties and then render a decision, which is binding. The arbitration proceedings are conducted according to rules and guidelines established by the AAA. The demand for arbitration cannot be made

[1]The *initial decision maker* (IDM) is the person named in the agreement to render initial decisions on claims and to certify termination of the agreement. The architect is generally the IDM, but the owner and contractor may hire a third-party IDM for dispute resolution.

before a request for mediation has been filed (although it can be made at the same time as the filing), and it cannot be made beyond the time indicated by the applicable statute of limitations.

Compensation Methods

In Article 11 of AIA Document B101, "Compensation," the parties specify how the architect will be compensated. There are several methods of compensation that the owner and architect can negotiate. The most common methods are these.

- *stipulated sum (fixed fee).* The owner pays the architect a fixed sum for a specific set of services. The money is usually paid out monthly according to the percentage of completion of the five basic phases of services. When agreeing to a stipulated sum, the architect must accurately estimate what it will cost for the office to do the job and still make a profit.

  The architect's fee does not include *reimbursable expenses*, which are expenses paid by the architect that are directly related to the project. The architect is reimbursed for these by the owner, and this reimbursement is in addition to the fee paid for the architect's services. Section 11.8.1 gives a list of reimbursable expenses, which include postage, reproductions, transportation or travel expenses, project-specific communication costs, project websites, project insurance, renderings, and models.

- *cost plus fee.* The architect is compensated for the actual expenses of doing the job plus a reasonable fee for profit. The actual expenses include salaries, employee benefits, direct expenses, and office overhead. Several variations of the cost-plus-fee approach are used.

  With the *multiple of direct personnel expense* approach, the direct salary of employees is determined and multiplied by a factor to account for normal and required personnel expenses such as taxes, sick leave, health care, and so on. Then, the amount is increased by a multiplier that includes provisions for overhead and profit. For example, if a particular employee's direct personnel expense is calculated at $30.00 per hour and the multiplier is 2.5, then the cost to the client for that person is $75.00 per hour.

  The *multiple of direct salary expense* method (sometimes called the *net multiplier method*) is similar, but the multiplier is larger to provide for employee benefits.

  In the *hourly billing rates* method, the multiplier is built into the hourly rate. The client sees only one number for each type of employee working on the project. A variation of this is hourly with a "not to exceed" amount given.

- *percentage of construction cost.* In this method, the professional fee is a fixed percentage of the cost of construction. This was a popular method in the past, but it is less commonly used than the other methods. From the owner's viewpoint, it appears to give the architect an incentive to keep the cost of construction high; from the architect's viewpoint, a low-cost project can require just as much work as an expensive project, sometimes even more.

- *unit cost.* Using the unit cost method, fees are based on a definable unit, such as square footage, for such work as tenant planning in a leased building, or on a per-house basis in a large residential project. This approach can work well for projects with a great deal of repetition.

Several factors should be considered when choosing a compensation method. The method chosen should compensate the architect fairly for the actual work required and the value of that professional service. It should also allow for the rising cost of providing services. (This is especially important when the project will be of long duration.) Finally, the client should be comfortable with the method and should understand where the money is being spent.

OWNER-ARCHITECT AGREEMENT FOR A SUSTAINABLE PROJECT—AIA DOCUMENT B101 SP

When an owner requests a sustainably designed and constructed project the architect should use AIA Document B101 SP, *Standard Form of Agreement Between Owner and Architect, for use on a Sustainable Project.* When this document is used, other related forms should also be used with it, including AIA Document A201 SP, *General Conditions of the Contract for Construction, for use on a Sustainable Project*, and one of the owner-contractor agreements for sustainable projects.

In addition, the architect may use AIA Document C401 SP, *Standard Form of Agreement Between Architect and Consultant, for use on a Sustainable Project*; AIA Document D503, App. F, *Example of a Sustainability Plan*; and AIA Document B214, *Standard Form of Architects Services: LEED Certification.*

The Sustainability Process

Each of the standard agreements previously described defines a standard process for completing a sustainable project. To begin the process, the owner must set a *sustainable objective*, a goal to be achieved by incorporating sustainable measures into the design, construction, maintenance, and operations of the project. For example, the objective may be to achieve certification through LEED or another sustainable building rating system, to reduce the building's impact on the environment, to enhance the health and well-being of building occupants, or to improve energy efficiency.

A sustainable objective may be based on a code or other jurisdictional requirement, such as meeting the requirements of a state energy code, or it may be voluntary, such as wanting the project to achieve a LEED platinum rating. Although the architect may suggest a sustainable objective, it is the owner's responsibility to make the final decision. It is also important that the architect explain the cost implications of the sustainable objective so that the owner can make an informed decision.

Before the end of the schematic design phase, the architect, owner, consultants, and other relevant team members should hold a *sustainability workshop*. This may even be held earlier as part of the programming process. At the sustainability workshop, the team members confirm the sustainable objective, establish the goals and expectations for the project, and discuss possible sustainable measures. A *sustainable measure* is a specific design or construction element, or a post-occupancy use, operation, maintenance or monitoring requirement, that must be completed in order to achieve the sustainable objective. The team also reviews the effect that the sustainability measures will have on the project's feasibility and budget.

Next, the architect prepares a sustainability plan. A *sustainability plan* is a contract document that identifies and describes the

- sustainable objective
- sustainable measures that will be used to achieve the objective
- strategies that will be used to implement the sustainable measures
- associated responsibilities of the owner, architect, and contractor
- details about design reviews
- details about the testing required to verify achievement of the sustainable measures
- details about the sustainability documentation required for the project

From the architect's viewpoint, a low-cost project can require just as much work as an expensive project, sometimes even more.

AIA Document D503 provides a format for completing a sustainability plan.

Sustainability certification is certification of sustainable design, construction, environmental performance, or energy performance. Certification is issued by an agency *certifying authority* such as Green Building Certification Inc., which issues LEED certification. If the objective is certification, the sustainability plan can take the form of a spreadsheet that lists these items.

- the sustainable measures needed to achieve the sustainable objective
- the potential and expected value of each credit from the certifying authority
- the responsible party (owner, architect, contractor, or other) and whether the party is primarily responsible for implementing the measure or just provides support
- detailed description of the implementation strategies selected to achieve the sustainable measures, the details about design reviews or testing, and the sustainability documentation required

The sustainability plan is submitted to the owner for approval. The architect must then incorporate the sustainable measures into the drawings and specifications as appropriate. The sustainability plan may be bound into the project manual with the specifications. The architect must prepare the schematic design, design development, and construction documents that incorporate the sustainable measures identified in the sustainability plan.

Additional Responsibilities of the Architect

If some of the materials and equipment that the architect proposes to use have had limited testing or verification of performance, then the architect must discuss with the owner how the sustainable objective may be affected if the materials and equipment do not perform according to the manufacturer's or supplier's representations. If the owner agrees to use the materials and equipment anyway, the owner must put this decision in writing. As long as this is done, the architect is not responsible for any damages arising from the failure of the materials or equipment.

The architect must implement those sustainable measures that were identified as the architect's responsibility in the sustainability plan and make adjustments as needed as the design work and construction move forward. The architect has a duty to keep the owner informed of how the project is progressing toward achievement of the sustainable measures, as well as of any deficiencies that will affect that achievement. The architect must also notify the owner of proposed changes that will materially affect the achievement of a sustainable measure or the sustainable objective.

If the sustainable objective of the project includes sustainability certification, the architect must register the project, first providing the owner with copies of all the agreements that the certifying authority will require in order to register the project and pursue the sustainability certification. The owner must agree to the certification requirements, and the owner and architect must review them before moving forward with additional sustainability services. The owner must give written notice to the architect to proceed with the registration. The architect performs these services as an agent of the owner. Any fees paid to the certifying authority are reimbursable expenses.

As the project nears completion, the architect must collect the sustainability documentation, submit the documentation to the certifying authority, and prepare and submit the application for certification to the certifying authority. The architect may also be required to prepare and file necessary documentation with the certifying authority to appeal a ruling or other interpretation denying a requirement, prerequisite, credit, or point necessary to achieve the sustainability certification.

See Chap. 50 for the architect's responsibilities under AIA Document B101-SP during the construction administration phase for a sustainable project.

Owner's Responsibilities

The exact nature of the owner's responsibilities depends on what was specifically identified in the sustainability plan (such as applying for certification), but may include some or all of the following.

- providing any information requested by the architect that is relevant for achieving the sustainable objective, such as design drawings, record drawings, operation and maintenance manuals, building operation costs, historical building data, or repair records
- complying with the requirements of the certifying authority as they relate to the ownership, operation, and maintenance of the project during construction and after completion of the project (for example, the owner may be required to submit utility bills)
- preparing, filing, and prosecuting any appeals to the certifying authority in the event that sustainability certification is awarded and then later revoked or reduced
- providing the services of a commissioning agent, unless the architect is specifically contracted to do so as an additional service

OWNER-CONTRACTOR AGREEMENT—AIA DOCUMENT A101

The owner enters into an agreement directly with the contractor for construction of the project. The owner-contractor agreement, however, will assign responsibilities and tasks to the architect during the construction phase. For this reason, the architect should be familiar with the various types of owner-contractor agreements.

AIA Document A101, *Standard Form of Agreement Between Owner and Contractor, where the basis of payment is a Stipulated Sum,* is commonly used. Many of the provisions of AIA Document A101 are also used in other agreement types and in non-AIA owner-contractor agreements.

Variations on the owner-contractor agreement are usually based on the method of compensation for the contractor.

Identification of Contract Documents

Article 1 of AIA Document A101, "The Contract Documents," specifies that the contract documents include the agreement, the general and supplementary conditions of the contract, drawings, specifications, addenda, modifications, and other documents listed elsewhere in the agreement. All the documents are listed in detail in Article 9.

Example 5.2

Which of the following are standard elements of the contract documents? (Choose the four that apply.)

(A) addendum

(B) change order

(C) contractor's bid

(D) program

(E) special supplementary conditions

(F) written amendment signed by owner and contractor

Solution

The contractor's bid form, like other bidding documents, is not part of the contract documents unless specifically stated in the agreement. The amount of the bid, or contract amount, would be incorporated into the agreement, but the bid form itself is not included. The program is used in creating the contract documents, but is not itself part of them.

The answers are (A), (B), (E), and (F).

Basic Provisions

Some basic provisions are common to all owner-contractor contracts. These include a description of the work being contracted, the times of commencement and substantial completion, and the contract sum.

Article 2 of AIA Document A101, "The Work of This Contract," says that the contractor is to execute the work that is described in the contract documents—primarily the drawings and specifications—with the exception of any tasks that are specifically stated in the agreement or other contract documents to be the responsibilities of others.

Article 3 is titled "Date of Commencement and Substantial Completion." The date of commencement is important because it is from this date that the construction completion time, or the *contract time*, is measured. The date can be a specific calendar day or it can be the day when the contractor receives a notice-to-proceed letter from the owner.

Substantial completion is the stage at which the work, or a designated portion of it, is sufficiently complete that the owner can occupy it or use it for its intended purpose, in accordance with the contract documents. The time of substantial completion can be expressed with a specific calendar date or by a number of calendar days from the date of commencement. The completion time may be extended, as provided for in the general conditions, when the delay is due to weather or other circumstances beyond the control of the contractor.

If a particular completion date is important to the owner, a provision for liquidated damages may be included. *Liquidated damages* are fees paid by the contractor to the owner for every day the project is late (except for delays due to uncontrollable circumstances). To be enforceable in court, these must represent reasonable losses that the owner realistically expects to incur if the project is not completed on time. For example, if an owner cannot occupy the project and must pay double rent, the liquidated damages may be the amount of extra rent.

In many cases, a liquidated damages provision is accompanied by a bonus provision, so that the contractor receives a payment for early completion. This is usually based on the amount that the owner realistically expects to save if the project is completed early.

Sometimes an additional penalty is also included on top of the liquidated damages. However, if a penalty clause is included, a bonus provision must also be included or the penalty is likely to be unenforceable.

Article 4, "Contract Sum," covers the compensation the contractor will receive for the work.

The completion time may be extended when the delay is due to weather or other circumstances beyond the control of the contractor.

Progress Payments

Article 5, "Payments," covers how the owner will pay the contractor. Section 5.1, "Progress Payments," describes periodic (usually monthly) payments that the owner makes as the project progresses; these are based on applications for payment that the contractor submits to the architect. Section 5.2, "Final Payment," covers the payment of the unpaid balance of the contract sum to the contractor at the end of the project.

In AIA Document A101, the amount due in any time period is based on the percentage of completed work, plus the amount allocated for any materials and equipment that have been purchased and stored on site for later use on the project. (Materials and equipment stored off site also require payment, but only if approved in advance by the owner in writing.)

The percentage of completed work is based on a schedule of values that the contractor submits to the architect. This schedule of values allocates the total contract sum to various portions of the work, such as mechanical, electrical, foundations, and so forth. The *retainage,* a percentage of each payment (usually 10%), is withheld until final completion of the work.

In order to receive payment, the contractor must submit an application for payment to the architect, listing the completed work and stored materials according to the schedule of values. The architect reviews and verifies the contractor's application, then recommends payment to the owner, who makes payment. If there is work in dispute, the architect may choose not to certify payment of all or a portion of the amount until the problem is resolved.

Example 5.3

The architect has received an Application and Certification for Payment (progress payment) from the contractor. Included in the application within the schedule of values for the electrical work is a request for $10,000 for stored materials. What step should the architect take next?

(A) Certify the payment request as it has been submitted and increase the retainage to 15%.

(B) Reject the payment request.

(C) Require the contractor to submit written proof of quantity, type of material, delivery date and documentation of the location of the stored material. Include this documentation with the payment request.

(D) Delete the stored material from the request and subtract $10,000 minus retainage.

Solution

The architect has the authority to certify, reject or revise the amount of the payment request from the contractor. The architect does not have the authority to revise the retainage without the permission of the owner. The stored material must be located in a secure location that is covered by the contractor's insurance so the owner will not be at risk if lost or damaged.

The answer is (C).

Owner-Contractor Dispute Resolution

As with AIA Document B101, AIA Document A101 gives a specific procedure for resolving disputes. In Article 6, "Dispute Resolution," the architect is indicated as the initial decision maker (IDM), unless the owner and contractor have agreed to appoint another person to be the IDM. Article 6 makes reference to Sec. 15.2 of AIA Document A201, *General Conditions of the Contract for Construction*, where the procedures for resolving claims and disputes are described in more detail.

When disputes arise, they are first referred to the IDM, who reviews the claims and supporting evidence. Within 10 days of receiving the claim, the IDM must take one or more of the following actions.

- request additional supporting information from the claimants
- reject the claim in whole or in part
- approve the claim
- suggest a compromise
- advise the owner and contractor that the IDM is unable to resolve the claim

If the IDM renders a decision, it is binding but subject to mediation. If the parties fail to resolve their dispute through mediation, the dispute is subject to binding dispute resolution. As with the owner-architect agreement, the owner and contractor must specify a method of binding dispute resolution when they write the contract: arbitration, litigation, or some other specified means. Arbitration is not mandatory, but it is an option.

Enumeration of Contract Documents

Article 9, "Enumeration of Contract Documents," lists all the contract documents.

- AIA Document A101, *Standard Form of Agreement Between Owner and Contractor, where the basis of payment is a Stipulated Sum*
- AIA Document A201, *General Conditions of the Contract for Construction*
- any supplementary general conditions
- all specification sections
- all drawings
- addenda, if any
- additional documents, if any, that are made part of the contract

Compensation Methods

There are several ways in which the owner can pay the contractor for the work. One of the most common methods is by a *stipulated sum*, a fixed price that the owner agrees to pay the contractor for the work as shown in the contract documents. This is a simple way to arrange things, and it is attractive to owners because the cost is known as soon as the bids are made or negotiation is completed. Competitive bidding always uses a stipulated-sum method.

Another method is the *guaranteed maximum price* (GMP). In this method, the contractor or construction manager guarantees the owner a fixed, maximum price. If the project is completed for less than this amount, the owner receives the cost savings. If the project costs exceed the GMP, the contractor must pay the excess.

Cost-plus-fee methods compensate the contractor for the actual expenses of labor, materials, and subcontracts and then add a fixed fee. Cost-plus-fee contracts have more flexibility than fixed-fee contracts, and they allow construction to proceed before design is complete. Their main disadvantage is that the cost is not known; however, this can be mitigated with guaranteed maximums, target prices with incentives, or partial cost guarantees. Target prices establish a likely project cost, and the contractor may share in a percentage of savings below the target price or be responsible for a percentage over the price. Partial cost guarantees involve obtaining fixed prices from certain subcontractors or material suppliers.

Construction can sometimes be based on *unit prices.* Entire projects are seldom based this way, but portions of a project may be. Where it is not possible to firmly establish an important quantity at the time of bidding, a unit price can be set. This happens frequently in excavation projects, when a cost per cubic yard of material is established. The final quantity is then multiplied by this unit price to arrive at the total cost. In other cases, when changes or additions are expected, the contractor may be asked to include unit prices in the bid. These can be used to evaluate the possible cost consequences of making a change, and as a check against the final cost of a change order.

GENERAL CONDITIONS OF THE CONTRACT FOR CONSTRUCTION—AIA DOCUMENT A201

AIA Document A201, *General Conditions of the Contract for Construction*, is one of the most important contract documents. It is incorporated by specific reference into AIA Document B101, the owner-architect agreement, as well as into AIA Document A101, the owner-contractor agreement. Obtain a copy of the *General Conditions* and read the entire document before the exam. This section outlines many of the most important provisions. Other portions that pertain to bidding and contract administration are discussed in Chap. 49 and Chap. 50.

General Provisions

Article 1 of AIA Document A201, "General Provisions," contains six sections. Section 1.1, "Basic Definitions," defines a number of terms used in the rest of the document. One of the most important definitions is that of the *contract documents.* These consist of

- the agreement between owner and contractor
- the conditions of the contract (general, supplementary, and special)
- the drawings
- the specifications
- addenda issued before the contract is executed
- other documents listed in the agreement
- modifications issued after the contract is executed

The contract documents do not include other documents such as the bidding documents. Section 1.1.2 specifically states that the contract documents do not create a contractual relationship between the architect and contractor, between the owner and any subcontractor, between the owner and the architect, or between any other persons other than the owner and the contractor.

Two more important definitions are those of work and project, which do not mean the same thing. *Work* consists of the contractor's obligations to provide improvements to the project. The *project*, on the other hand, may also include construction by other contractors or the owner's own forces. The work may be the whole of the project or just a part of it.

Section 1.1 also defines *instruments of service*, which are any representations of the tangible and intangible creative work of the architect and the architect's consultants. These may include studies, surveys, models, sketches, drawings, specifications, and similar materials. Section 1.5 states that the architect and the architect's consultants are the owners of their respective instruments of service.

Section 1.6 states that if the parties intend to transmit information in digital form, they must try to establish necessary protocols for data transmission.

The Owner

Article 2, "Owner," outlines the duties, responsibilities, and rights of the owner. Among these is the responsibility to furnish reasonable evidence, should the contractor request it in writing before work begins, that financial arrangements have been made to fulfill the owner's obligations under the contract—in other words, to show that the contractor can be paid. Once work has begun, the contractor can only request such evidence if

- the owner fails to make payments
- a change in the work materially changes the contract sum
- the contractor identifies in writing a reasonable concern regarding the owner's ability to pay

If the contractor makes a written request, the owner must give the information that the contractor would need to file for a mechanic's lien to be placed on the property. This is usually the legal description of the property and proof of legal title. This information allows the contractor to evaluate, give notice of, or enforce mechanic's lien rights. (Mechanic's liens are discussed in Chap. 50.)

The owner must secure and pay for the approvals and permits that are required to construct permanent structures or make changes in existing structures. These might include zoning permits, easements, assessments, environmental impact studies, and the like, so they will generally be required before the execution of the contract. The owner is not responsible, however, for those approval and permits that the contractor must pay for after the execution of the contract, such as building permits and other governmental fees and permits.

The owner must supply the contractor with one free copy of the contract documents, which the contractor may reproduce for use on the project. The contractor is also entitled to any information the owner has about site conditions. The contractor has the right to rely on the accuracy of the information that the owner has furnished.

If the contractor fails to correct work that does not accord with the contract documents, or if the contractor repeatedly carries out work that does not accord, the owner may order the contractor to stop the work until the reason for the order is eliminated.

The owner also has the *right to carry out the work* if the contractor fails to do so correctly. To exercise this right, the owner must give written notice to the contractor demanding correction of the problem. The contractor has ten days from receiving written notice to begin to correct the problem. If there is no response, the owner can begin work while still retaining the right to arbitration or legal action for breach of contract. The owner may execute a change order or construction change directive that states that the reasonable cost of correcting the work—including both the owner's expenses and the compensation for any additional services that the architect must provide—should be deducted from the contract sum. However, both the owner's actions in regard to carrying out the work and the amount that is to be deducted from the contract sum must first be approved by the architect.

The Contractor

Article 3, "Contractor," details the responsibilities of the contractor. Before starting the work, the contractor must review and study the various drawings, specifications, other contract documents, and information furnished by the owner. The contractor must also observe site conditions and take any field measurements necessary.

The contractor is responsible for supervising and directing the work. Unless the contract documents give specific instructions, the contractor is solely responsible for how the construction is done and for coordinating the work under the contract. If the contract documents do specify the means of construction, however, the contractor is responsible only for job site safety, not for the results of the architect's specifications.

The contractor is not liable to the owner or architect for any damage that results from errors or omissions in the contract documents, unless the contractor recognized such an error and knowingly failed to report it to the architect.

It is not the contractor's responsibility to make sure that the contract documents are in accordance with building codes, ordinances, and other regulations. However, if the contractor does notice a problem, the contractor must notify the architect and owner in writing. If the contractor does not give this notice and knowingly performs work that is in variance with a regulation, the contractor assumes full responsibility for such work.

The contractor's responsibilities include making sure that work already performed is in proper condition to receive subsequent work. They also include controlling the contractor's own work force, coordinating the subcontractors, and being responsible to the owner for the acts and omissions of all the people performing work under the contract.

The constructor's other responsibilities include the following.

- *substitutions.* If the contractor wants to make a substitution, he or she can do so only with the consent of the owner, after evaluation by the architect, and in accordance with a change order.
- *warranty.* Section 3.5 states that the contractor guarantees that the materials and workmanship furnished under the contract are of good quality, free of defects, and conform to the requirements of the contract documents. This warranty is in addition to other warranties from manufacturers or fabricators, and is separate and distinct from the one-year correction period mentioned later in Sec. 12.2.2.
- *permits, fees, and taxes.* The contractor must secure and pay for the building permit and other permits, governmental fees, licenses, and inspections necessary for the execution of the work. These permits are ordinarily obtained after the execution of the contract. The contractor also pays sales, consumer, use, and similar taxes for work provided by the contractor.
- *concealed or unknown conditions.* If the contractor discovers concealed or unknown conditions that are materially different from those indicated on the contract documents, the contractor must notify the owner and architect within 21 days of first noticing them. The architect must investigate the conditions and determine whether they make it necessary to increase the contract sum, the contract time, or both. If changes are justified, the architect will recommend an equitable adjustment.

  During the course of the work, if the contractor encounters human remains or recognizes the existence of burial markers, archaeological sites, or wetlands not indicated in the contract documents, the contractor must immediately suspend work that would affect them and notify the owner and architect. The owner must then take any action needed to obtain governmental authorization to resume operations. The contractor may then request adjustments in the contract time, contract sum, or both.
- *allowances.* When developing the contract sum, the contractor must include all allowances that are listed in the contract documents. An *allowance* is the architect's estimated cost of a particular material or piece of equipment when the actual cost cannot be precisely determined at the time of the bid or negotiated proposal. It is, in effect, a placeholder so that some amount of money can be set aside for the item. Section 3.8, "Allowances," states that each allowance should cover the cost to the contractor of the item, its delivery at the job site, and all required taxes. The allowance, however, is not intended to cover the costs of unloading, handling, and installing the item, nor does it include the contractor's overhead and profit; the contractor must include these in the contract sum. If the actual costs turn out to be different from the allowance, the contract sum is adjusted accordingly by change order.

- *construction schedule.* The contractor is obligated to provide a construction schedule for the owner's and architect's information, to keep it up to date, and to conform to it.
- *record documents.* The contractor must maintain record documents at the job site. *Record documents* are copies of all construction drawings, specifications, and other contract documents, marked to record exactly how the project was built, noting any changes or deviations from the original documents. The record documents are available for the architect's reference during construction. The architect should include the exact requirements for record documents in Division 01 of the specifications.
- *submittals.* The contract documents may require the contractor to submit shop drawings, product data, and samples to show how the contractor proposes to carry out the design concept expressed in the contract documents. These submittals are not contract documents, and they are subject to the architect's review. The contractor must keep one copy of all submittals at the job site. See Chap. 50 for more information on submittals.
- *design services.* The contractor can be required to provide professional design services or certifications if specifically required to do so by the contract documents or if the contractor needs to provide such services in order to carry out the work of the contract. The architect must specify all the performance and design criteria that such services must satisfy.

  This requirement is sometimes called *design delegation.* Legally, however, it is a form of design allocation by the owner because there is no contractual relationship between the architect and the contractor. Design delegation allows the use of performance specifications for products and building assemblies; it can also let the contractor select the best approach to completing the work. For example, specialized temporary shoring may be needed to support cutting and patching operations for a portion of the work. The contractor is responsible for carrying out this work, but may require the services of a registered professional engineer to design the shoring according to the contractor's needs.
- *indemnification.* To the extent provided by law, the contractor will indemnify and hold harmless the owner, architect, architect's consultants, and agents against claims, damages, and expenses arising from performance of the work. To *indemnify* is to secure against loss or damage. This does not relieve the architect of his or her liability for errors in the drawings, specifications, or administration of the contract, but it protects the owner and architect against situations where a person is injured or property (other than the work itself) is damaged due to the negligence of the contractor or the contractor's agents.

The Architect

Article 4 of the *General Conditions,* "Architect," states the architect's roles and responsibilities in contract administration. In general, this article provides for the typical duties the architect performs. These are discussed in more detail in Chap. 50.

The architect visits the site regularly to become familiar with the progress of the work and to determine whether the work is proceeding in general accordance with the contract documents. However, the architect is not required to make exhaustive or continuous on-site inspections.

The architect has the authority to reject work that does not conform to the contract documents. This authority, however, does not create any duty or responsibility of the architect toward the contractor, subcontractors, or others.

The architect does not have control over how the construction is performed, nor over the safety precautions taken, as these are the sole responsibility of the contractor. The architect does not have the right to stop the work if something is wrong or if the architect observes some safety problem. Instead, the architect should notify both the contractor and the owner.

The architect reviews shop drawings and other submittals, but only to see that they conform with the design intent expressed in the contract documents. The contractor remains responsible for the accuracy, completeness, and overall coordination of the work.

The architect prepares change orders and may authorize minor changes in the work, if they are consistent with the intent of the contract documents and do not involve adjusting the contract sum or contract time.

At the owner or contractor's request, the architect interprets and decides on matters about the performance of the contract.

The architect's decisions about aesthetic effect are final, as long as they are consistent with the intent shown in the contract documents.

The architect must review and respond in writing to requests for information about the contract documents. If necessary, the architect must prepare and issue supplemental drawings and specifications related to the request.

Construction by Owner or by Separate Contractors

The owner has the right to perform construction on the project with his or her own forces. If so, the owner is responsible for the coordination of his or her own forces with the work of the contractor, and must act with the same obligations and rights as any contractor would.

The owner also has the right to award separate contracts for different portions of the work. The owner is responsible for the coordination of the activities of the separate contractors.

When requested, the contractor must work with the owner and other contractors in coordinating construction schedules and following any revisions that have been agreed on. The contractor must also give the others reasonable opportunity to store their materials and perform their work.

If the contractor discovers that construction by the owner or other contractors will adversely affect his or her work, the contractor must notify the architect promptly. The owner is responsible for any costs that the contractor incurs due to another contractor's delays, improperly timed activities, or defective construction. However, if the contractor's own delays, improperly timed activities, or defective construction cause another contractor to incur costs that the owner must pay for, the contractor must reimburse the owner.

Changes in the Work

Under the *General Conditions of the Contract*, changes may be made in the work after execution of the contract. These changes are made by a change order, a construction change directive, or an order for a minor change in the work.

A *change order* is written by the architect and signed by the owner, contractor, and architect. The order states the extent of the change and how it affects construction cost and time.

A *construction change directive* requires agreement only between the owner and architect; it may or may not be agreed to by the contractor. It instructs the contractor to proceed with the stated changes in the work, even if the contractor does not agree with the basis for adjustment in contract sum or contract time. When the changes in cost and time are finally determined and submitted by the contractor and reviewed by the architect and owner, a change order is issued. In the meantime, the contractor can include the work completed under the construction change directive in regular applications for payment.

A *minor change in the work* can be ordered by the architect alone, provided that the change is consistent with the intent of the contract documents and does not affect the construction cost or time. The architect must submit the order in writing.

See Chap. 50 for a more detailed procedure for making changes.

Time

The *contract time* is the period from the starting date established in the agreement to the time of substantial completion, including any authorized adjustments. The contractor is expected to proceed expeditiously, with adequate work forces, and to complete the work within the allotted time.

Payments and Completion

The contractor makes monthly applications for payment based on the percentage of work completed, in accordance with a schedule of values allocated to various portions of the work. The architect reviews these applications and either issues the owner a certificate for payment or withholds issuance if there are valid reasons. See Chap. 50 for a more detailed procedure for issuing payment.

Liens

A *mechanic's lien* is a claim by one party against the property of another party for the satisfaction of a debt. This is a common method for an architect, contractor, or material supplier to gain payment. If a property carries a mechanic's lien, it cannot be sold or transferred until the lien is disposed of (or bonded), except through foreclosure. If a contractor does not pay a subcontractor or material supplier, and the unpaid party files a mechanic's lien against the property, the owner becomes responsible for payment. If the lien is not paid, the property can be foreclosed by the lien holder, the lender, or a taxing entity.

Because the owner is not responsible for paying subcontractors or material suppliers, methods for protecting the owner from liens are provided in Sec. 9.10 of the *General Conditions of the Contract.* These include requiring the contractor to submit a release or waiver of liens to the owner before final payment is made or retainages of previous payments are released. The contractor must also furnish to the owner and architect an affidavit of payment of all debts and claims, and an affidavit of release of liens stating that all obligations have been satisfied. The release or waiver of liens is attached to this affidavit.

The exact laws governing liens and the time period during which a lien may be filed vary from state to state, so the architect and owner must be familiar with local regulations.

Protection of Persons and Property

According to Article 10, "Protection of Persons and Property," the contractor is solely responsible for taking on-site precautions against injury or damage to

- the contractor's employees
- other people affected by the work
- the work itself
- other property at the site or adjacent to it

If the work sustains damage due to inadequate protection, the contractor must repair or correct it (unless the damage was caused by the owner or architect's actions).

Section 10.3 contains provisions concerning the discovery of asbestos, PCBs, or other hazardous materials. If such substances are found or suspected by the contractor, the contractor must stop work and notify the owner and architect in writing. The owner must then obtain the services of a licensed laboratory to determine whether the hazardous materials reported by the contractor are present. The owner is responsible for the removal of discovered hazardous materials. Work can then resume upon written agreement of the owner and contractor.

The owner is responsible for the removal of discovered hazardous materials. Work can then resume upon written agreement of the owner and contractor.

When the contract documents require that hazardous materials be brought onto the site, the owner is responsible for those materials, except to the extent that the contractor is negligent in using and handling them.

The contractor must indemnify the owner for any costs incurred for the remediation of a hazardous material that the contractor brings to the site and negligently handles, or because the contractor fails to fulfill his or her obligations in handling hazardous materials.

Insurance and Bonds

For the duration of the project, both the owner and contractor are required to maintain insurance to protect against various types of losses. The provisions for insurance are spelled out in Article 11 of the *General Conditions of the Contract*, "Insurance and Bonds." Additional provisions as required by the unique nature of each project are included in the supplementary conditions.

The architect is not responsible for giving advice to either the owner or the contractor on matters related to insurance and bonds. In fact, an architect's professional liability insurance does not protect against any adverse consequences of giving such advice. Both the owner and contractor should receive advice from their respective legal counsels and insurance advisers as needed.

The contractor must furnish liability insurance to cover the entities for whom the contractor is legally liable. This coverage includes workers' compensation, bodily injury or death, damages to the work, personal injury, motor vehicle insurance, and claims involving contractual liability. The contractor should require that all subcontractors carry similar insurance. The contractor must add the owner, architect, and architect's consultants as additional insured parties for claims caused by the contractor's negligence.

The amount of coverage must be at least the maximum liability specified in the contract or required by law, whichever is greater. Coverage must be maintained without interruption from the beginning of the work until the date of final payment.

At the beginning of the project, the architect should write a letter to remind the owner of his or her responsibilities under the terms of the agreement and to request that the owner determine, with his or her legal and insurance advisers, the type and amount of coverage required. This information, including the owner's requirements on bonds, should be given to the architect so that the architect can help the owner prepare the contract and bidding documents.

The architect should also have certificates of insurance from the contractor on file and should not issue any certificate of payment until this evidence is available, or until the architect has been advised by the owner that such insurance has been obtained.

The owner must also purchase and maintain the liability insurance needed to protect himself or herself against claims and losses arising from operations under the contract. This includes insurance for property damage and loss of use.

The owner's property insurance protects against fire, theft, vandalism, and other hazards. It must be an all-risk policy that insures against all perils that are not specifically excluded. The amount of coverage must be for the full value of the work (usually the contract sum plus any subsequent modifications).

The owner may require the contractor to furnish a surety bond to cover the faithful performance of the contract. A *surety bond*, also called a *contract bond*, is an agreement among at least three parties. The *surety* (the bonding company) agrees to be responsible to the *obligee* (in this case, the owner) for the default or debts of the *principal* (the contractor). A surety bond is a protection for the owner against default by the contractor. Bonds are discussed in more detail in Chap. 49.

Uncovering and Correction of the Work

If the contract documents require that certain portions of the work remain uncovered for the architect's observation, and the contractor covers them, then the contractor must uncover them at no additional charge when architect requests this in writing.

The architect may request that work be uncovered even if he or she did not specifically request to examine a portion of the work before it was covered. If the uncovered work is found not to be in accordance with the contract documents, the cost of uncovering, correcting, and covering the work is the responsibility of the contractor. If the uncovered work is found to be in accordance with the contract documents, the cost is the responsibility of the owner.

Prior to substantial completion, if the architect rejects work because it does not conform to the requirements of the contract documents, the contractor must correct the work. The contractor must also bear the cost of such corrections, including testing, inspections, and compensation for the architect's services connected with the corrections. For a period of up to a year after substantial completion or within the effective dates of warranties, if any work is found not to be in accordance with the contract documents, the contractor must correct the defective work after written notice from the owner. If the contractor does not correct the work within a reasonable time, the owner may exercise his or her right to carry out the work. To do this, the owner gives the contractor another written notice and the contractor then has 10 days to correct the work. If the work is not corrected, the owner can have others correct it.

If the owner chooses, he or she can accept nonconforming work as long as it meets code. Because this entails a change in the contract, it must be done by written change order. If appropriate, the contract sum may be reduced.

Termination or Suspension of the Contract

Either the owner or the contractor may terminate the contract for any of the reasons given in Sec. 14.1 the *General Conditions of the Contract.*

The contractor may terminate the contract if work has stopped for more than 30 days, through no fault of the contractor or anyone working for the contractor, for any of the following causes.

- a court order
- an act of government
- the architect's failure to issue a certificate of payment or give a reason for not doing so
- the owner's failure to make payment on a certificate of payment within the time stated in the contract documents
- the owner's failure to give proper evidence that financial arrangements have been made to fulfill the owner's obligations

The contractor may also terminate the contract if the work has been repeatedly delayed by the owner for a total of 120 days in any 365-day period or for a total number of days equal to the construction time given in the original contract documents. The delays must not be due to the contractor or anyone working for the contractor.

If the architect certifies that sufficient cause exists, the owner can terminate the contract if the contractor fails to supply enough properly skilled workers or proper materials, fails to make payment to subcontractors, disregards laws and ordinances, or is guilty of substantial breach of a provision of the contract documents. The owner may also suspend or terminate the work for convenience, without any cause.

In all these cases, seven days' written notice must be given.

Claims and Disputes

Article 15, "Claims and Disputes," describes the procedures required for dispute resolution, including those for mediation and arbitration.

A *claim* is an assertion, made by one of the parties to the contract, that he or she is owed payment or some other form of relief under the contract's terms. A claim may also include other disputes between the owner and contractor relating to the contract.

A claim must be initiated by giving written notice to both the other party and the initial decision maker (IDM). This notice must be given within 21 days of the event that gives rise to the claim, or within 21 days after the claimant first discovers the condition that gives rise to the claim, whichever is later. While the claim is being resolved, the contractor must continue with the work and the owner must continue to make payments in accordance with the contract.

A claim is first referred to the IDM. If the IDM does not render a decision, or if either party does not agree with this decision, the claim goes to mediation. If mediation is not successful, the claim is resolved by the method of binding resolution that was agreed to by the owner and contractor in their contract. This may be arbitration, litigation, or another method.

Claims can only be made for *direct damages*. These include the cost of repairing defective work or completing unfinished work. The contractor and the owner agree to waive claims for *consequential damages* (or *indirect damages*), which are damages that are not caused directly and immediately by the other party's actions, but from the consequences of those actions. For example, if a contractor does not finish a retail store by the original completion date, the rent the owner must continue to pay on the unopened store and the profits lost from not being able to operate the store are both examples of consequential damages.

Section 15.1.6 specifies that the consequential damages waived by the owner include

- rental expenses
- loss of use, income, profit, financing, business, or reputation
- loss of management or employee productivity

Consequential damages waived by the contractor specifically include

- expenses in running the contractor's principal office, including compensation for staff there
- loss of financing, business, or reputation
- loss of profit other than anticipated profit arising directly from the work

GENERAL CONDITIONS OF THE CONTRACT FOR A SUSTAINABLE PROJECT—AIA DOCUMENT A201 SP

AIA Document A201 SP, *General Conditions of the Contract for Construction, for use on a Sustainable Project*, is similar to the standard *General Conditions*, but it is modified to give the requirements for a sustainable project. AIA Document A201 SP is coordinated with and intended to be used with other sustainability project documents, including AIA Document B101 SP, the owner-architect agreement, AIA Document A101 SP, the owner-contractor agreement, AIA Document C401 SP, the architect-consultant agreement, and AIA Document D503, Appendix F, *Example of a Sustainability Plan.*

Definitions

In addition to the terms defined in AIA Document A201, Sec. 1.1 of AIA Document A201 SP includes definitions of terms pertaining to a sustainable project, such as *sustainable measure* and *certifying authority.*

Owner Responsibilities

In addition to the owner's responsibilities given in AIA Document A201, Article 2 of AIA Document A201 SP states that the owner must

- perform the sustainable measures that are specified in the sustainability plan as being the owner's responsibility
- comply with the requirements of the certifying authority as they relate to the ownership, operation, and maintenance of the project

Responsibilities of the Contractor

Article 3 of AIA Document A201 SP adds these items to the contractor's responsibilities given in AIA Document A201.

- The contractor must perform any sustainable measures specified in the sustainability plan as being the contractor's responsibility.
- If the owner or architect recognizes a condition that will affect the achievement of a sustainable measure, the contractor must meet with the owner and architect to discuss alternatives and remedy the condition.

- The contractor is not required to ascertain that the contract documents are in accordance with the requirements of the certifying authority, but if the contractor becomes aware of such conditions, the contractor must notify the architect.
- If the contractor wants to make a substitution, he or she must include a written description identifying any potential effect the substitution may have on the project's achievement of a sustainable measure or the sustainable objective.
- The contractor must complete any sustainability documentation required by the sustainability plan or other contract documents. This may include documentation that must be submitted after substantial completion.
- For construction waste management, the contractor must recycle, reuse, remove, or dispose of materials as required by the contract document. As part of this requirement, the contractor must prepare and submit to the architect and owner a construction waste management and disposal plan.

SUPPLEMENTARY AND SPECIAL CONDITIONS OF THE CONTRACT

Because each construction project is unique, not every condition can be covered in a standard document such as AIA Document A201, *General Conditions of the Contract for Construction.* Each job must accommodate a different combination of client needs, governmental regulations, and local laws.

In most cases, the conditions unique to the job are handled by modifying AIA Document A201. If desired, however, they may also be given in a separate document referred to as the *supplementary conditions.* Because the AIA contract documents are coordinated with one another and contain numerous cross references, using a separate document is preferable when modifying AIA Document A201 would involve deleting entire sections and renumbering others. There is no AIA standard form for supplementary conditions, but AIA Document A503, *Guide for Supplementary Conditions,* gives guidance and model language that can be used in modifying or supplementing the *General Conditions.*

In two cases, additional conditions should be separate from the contract. Matters pertaining only to the bidding process should be included in the bidding documents. Administrative and procedural requirements should be given only as broad provisions in the *General Conditions* and should be explained in detail in Division 01 ("General Requirements") of the specifications.

It is impossible to give a complete list of the provisions that may be included in the supplementary conditions, but examples include

- permission for the architect to furnish the contractor with instruments of service in electronic form
- additional information and services provided by the owner
- the cost for the architect to review the contractor's requests for substitutions
- provisions for the owner, instead of the contractor, to pay for utilities
- the requirement that the contractor employ a superintendent to coordinate mechanical and electrical work
- provisions for fast-tracked scheduling
- reimbursement by the contractor for extra site visits by the architect that are made necessary by the fault of the contractor
- additional protection for the owner against claims for additional time or for consequential damages
- requirements for more detailed information on costs and overhead
- additional requirements for payment procedures
- requirements for liquidated damages and bonuses
- additional requirements for bonding and insurance

In addition to the supplementary conditions, a project may require *special conditions*, which are provisions that are completely unique to a particular project or project site. Special conditions are always given in a separate document attached to the contract. Although the supplementary conditions document is also written for a particular project, its individual provisions could be used again on different projects for the same client or that are governed by the same regulations or local laws. Each provision of a special conditions document, however, is written only once for unique circumstances.

ARCHITECT-CONSULTANT AGREEMENT—AIA DOCUMENT C401

When consultants are retained for a project, AIA Document C401, *Standard Form of Agreement Between Architect and Consultant* is often used. This document sets forth the roles and responsibilities of the consultant and the architect. It states that the consultant is an independent contractor for his or her portion of the project and must perform services with the same standard of care as other professionals practicing in the same or similar locality under the same or similar circumstances. The agreement states that all communication between the consultant and the owner, contractor, or other consultants must go through the architect. It further states that the consultant is not responsible for the acts or omissions of the architect; the architect's other consultants, contractors, and subcontractors; any of their agents or employees; or other persons performing any of the work.

Consultant's Responsibilities

In addition to the previously listed responsibilities, the architect-consultant agreement requires the consultant to

- recommend to the architect the appropriate surveys, tests, analyses, reports, and services of other consultants that are needed
- coordinate his or her services with the architect and other consultants
- provide copies of drawings, reports, specifications and other necessary information to the architect and other consultants as needed
- provide a schedule for the consultant's work for the architect's approval
- assist the architect in determining whether or not the architect will reject work for the consultant's portion of the project or whether additional inspection or testing is required

Architect's Responsibilities

The architect is required to provide in a timely manner all the relevant project information that pertains to the design and coordination of the consultant's portion of the work. This includes (when appropriate to the consultant's area) detailed layouts that show the location of connections, and tabulations that give size, loads, and other information on equipment designed, specified, or furnished by others.

For example, the electrical consultant must be provided with, among other information, an itemized list of equipment, model numbers, and detailed electrical requirements of any equipment determined in the programming phase of the project.

The architect is entitled to rely on the accuracy and completeness of services and information furnished by the consultant.

Coordination of Code Information

Once the consultants are retained, the architect informs each of them about the code requirements that apply to that portion of the work. The architect is also responsible for informing the consultants of any design decisions that may have code implications. Although the architect is responsible for ensuring that the drawings and specifications conform to the applicable codes, each consultant is responsible for code compliance in his or her area of work, in the same way that the architect is responsible to the owner under AIA Document B101. By signing their drawings, engineering consultants become responsible for compliance with applicable codes and regulations.

Each consultant is responsible for the accurate production of his or her own drawings and specifications. The consultant is also responsible for checking his or her own documents for consistency. The architect, however, is the primary consultant and is liable to the owner for the consultant's work.

ARCHITECT-CONSULTANT AGREEMENT FOR A SUSTAINABLE PROJECT—AIA DOCUMENT C401 SP

Another standard document in the family of AIA documents for sustainable projects is AIA Document C401 SP, *Standard Form of Agreement Between Architect and Consultant, for use on a Sustainable Project.*

Terms in AIA Document C401 SP have the same definitions as in AIA Document A201 SP, *General Conditions for use on a Sustainable Project.* The roles and responsibilities of the consultant are the same as those described in AIA Document C401, but with some added provisions.

- The consultant is responsible for the sustainable consultant services designated under the primary agreement between the owner and architect.
- The consultant must perform the sustainable measures to the extent applicable.
- At the architect's request, the consultant must also attend the sustainability workshop.
- As is true of the architect, the consultant does not warrant or guarantee that the project will achieve the sustainable objective.

The architect must provide the consultant with a copy of the sustainability plan when it is approved by the owner.

CONSENSUSDOCS

In some instances a client may want to use his or her own contracts or use another set of standard construction contract forms. One example is the Design-Build Institute of America's family of documents, which is mentioned earlier in this chapter; another set of standard documents is published by ConsensusDocs.

The ConsensusDocs standard contract documents were developed by a consortium of construction industry organizations including the Associated General Contractors of American, the Associated Builders and Contractors, the Mechanical Contractors Association of America, the Construction Specifications Institute, and nearly 40 other trade groups. These documents were developed with the goal of ending what was perceived as a bias in favor of the architect in the AIA documents. The stated purpose is to take a balanced approach in defining the rights, obligations, and risks of the various parties involved in a construction project and to reduce the number and severity of disputes.

While there are many similarities between the ConsensusDocs and the AIA documents, there are also important differences. If a client insists on using contracts different from the AIA documents, the architect could be put at risk. The architect should have any alternative documents reviewed by the architect's and owner's attorneys and insurance agents and be able to modify any unacceptable clauses.

6 PROJECT EXECUTION AND QUALITY CONTROL

After the professional contracts have been signed and the work of the architectural office is underway, the project manager must make sure that the project proceeds according to the work plan, stays on budget, and meets the client's objectives for the project with the expected level of quality. To do this, the project manager uses a combination of software, people skills, and simple paper-based documentation. Refer to Chap. 4 for a discussion of additional activities and methods of project management.

PROJECT EXECUTION

The most important aspects of project execution include

- monitoring fees and time
- controlling and responding to changes in the scope of work
- monitoring the construction budget
- documenting the design and construction phases
- adhering to the requirements of the authorities having jurisdiction
- maintaining overall quality control of the project

Monitoring Fees and Time

One of the main tasks of project management is ensuring that the job's planned budget, schedule, and tasks are being met in a timely and satisfactory manner. The primary tool for monitoring fees and time is the work plan as described in Chap. 4. The work plan schedule can be developed on paper or with the help of project management or financial planning software. Comparing weekly time sheet data with the original fee projections can show how far over or under budget a project is at a given phase of work. Figure 6.1 shows a simple example of how this can be done. This example uses the same numbers that were used in Fig. 4.4.

In this chart, each budgeted weekly fee is placed in its appropriate time-period column and phase-of-work row. The amount actually expended for each fee is written below the budgeted amount. At the bottom of the chart, a simple graph is plotted that shows the actual money expended against the budgeted fees.

The project manager should estimate the percentage of actual work completed and plot it against the money and time expended so far. If the project is large or complex, the estimate of work completed may be obtained from staff members working on the project. If the actual fees and time expended exceed the estimate, or if the percentage of work completed dips below the estimate, the project manager must identify the problem and correct it.

Depending on the size and complexity of the project, the project manager can monitor fees and work completed every month, every two weeks, or every week. The less time between reviews, the easier it will be to identify problems and take corrective action before it is too late.

Figure 6.1 shows a chart created without the help of a computer, but project management or financial management software is also commonly used. Software can make it easier to track information in more detail, such as by comparing actual time and fees with budgeted amounts for individual staff members. This can make it easier to identify possible problem areas. Such software can also easily track expenses and consultants' fees against budgeted amounts.

In all cases, the main sources of information are the paper-based or electronic timesheets that are filled out by each staff member. Part of the project manager's job is to make sure that these are filled out in a timely manner and that they accurately reflect the time charged to each project. If time spent on one project is mistakenly charged to another job, or time not actually spent working is charged to a job, the tracking system begins to break down.

Figure 6.1 Project Monitoring Chart

Project: Mini-mall		time												
Phase/People/Departments		1	2	3	4	5	6	7	8	9	10	11	12	total
schematic design	budgeted	1320	2640											
	actual	2000	2900											
design development	budgeted			2510	4090									
	actual			3200										
construction docs.	budgeted					2156	1716	4136	5456	2376				
	actual													
	budgeted													
fee dollars	actual													
	budgeted													
	actual													
	budgeted													
	actual													
	budgeted													
	actual													
total (cumulative)	budgeted	1320	3960	6470	10,560	12,716	14,432	18,568	24,024	26,400				
	actual	2000	4900	8110										

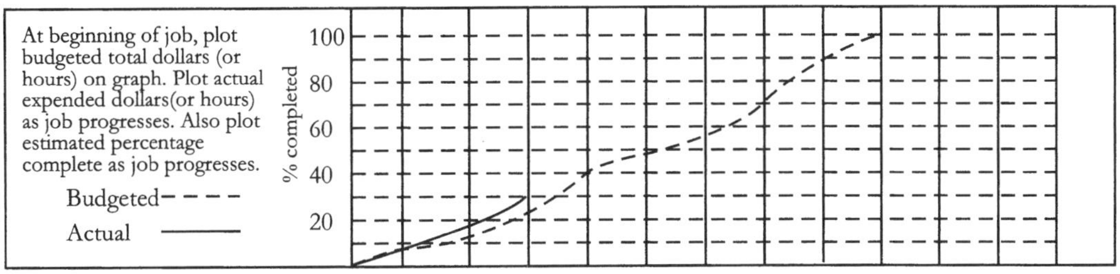

At beginning of job, plot budgeted total dollars (or hours) on graph. Plot actual expended dollars(or hours) as job progresses. Also plot estimated percentage complete as job progresses.

Budgeted - - - -

Actual ———

% completed: 100, 80, 60, 40, 20

Accurate timesheets are important to the success of any architectural office. They provide the basis for billing and give the ongoing data needed for project monitoring. Direct labor expenses derived from timesheets are also used to determine important financial ratios the office uses for financial planning, such as the overhead rate and the net multiplier as described in Chap. 2. Timesheet data also provides important historical information that can be used to accurately estimate fees for new projects.

When the project manager discovers that the project is going over budget or work progress is lagging, corrective action should be taken immediately. The problem may be due to one or more of the following personnel issues.

- *The wrong people are working on the project.* Inexperienced staff need more guidance and cannot work as fast as more experienced people. The project manager may be able to replace inexperienced staff members with more experienced ones. However, this must be balanced with the fact that a more experienced person may have a higher billing rate, so that the substitution will affect the allocation of fees. For this reason, it is important that the project manager assemble the project team best suited for a given project.
- *The people doing the work are not keeping pace.* This may be the result of inexperience, or it may just be slow work. If staff members are not being diligent about their work effort, this becomes a human resources problem and appropriate action should be taken.
- *The people doing the work are spending too much time on the project.* This can be due to the project perfection syndrome described in Chap. 4. However, it also may be due to incomplete or unclear instructions from the project manager to the staff members, and in that case, the project manager must determine how to communicate the project objectives and work plan steps more definitively.
- *Time sheets are not being filled out properly.* Different offices use different methods to encourage accurate time reporting, but at the very least timesheets should be filled out daily; twice daily, once for the morning and once for the afternoon, is even more accurate. Time should be recorded in 15-minute increments for accurate tracking and billing. Staff members can keep informal time logs on their

desks for as-you-go recording and then summarize the time on office time sheets, or online if a computerized system is used.

Example 6.1

Which of the following project management activities would most likely ensure that construction documents are completed on schedule and within budget?

(A) documenting all meetings and correspondence

(B) establishing time and fee projections

(C) monitoring timesheets

(D) setting milestones

Solution

Monitoring the progress of a job is critical to ensuring that the original schedule and fee projects are being met.

Although establishing time and fee projections is a critical component of project management early in the project, continual monitoring is also required. Setting milestones for when certain intermediate work is to be completed is also important, but actual work completion must be compared with the estimated schedule to meet the final deadline.

The answer is (C).

Changes in Scope of Work

When a project is not meeting the fee or time budgets, this may also be a result of changes in the scope of work; that is, more work is being performed than was originally planned. *Scope creep* happens when the client or the architect makes uncontrolled changes to the original list of services set forth in the owner-architect agreement.

Sometimes it can be obvious, such as a client asking for the development of a new floor plan after the first one was already approved. The architect may choose to proceed with the work anyway, rather than risk offending the client by refusing to do the work or asking for more money. At other times, scope creep can occur in more subtle ways, such as by a client asking the architect to review another product. This may not sound like much additional work, but even minor requests, if repeated, can add up quickly.

Scope creep often happens when the architect or other staff members fall into the "project perfection syndrome" described in Chap. 4. A given task may have been completed successfully, but the architect wants to try just one more design scheme or develop just one more refinement to some detail, to see if the project can be made still better. However, the minor improvement that might be found does not justify the disproportionate added time and fee.

Another common cause of scope creep is that employees are not fully aware of the scope of work. For example, staff members may spend time on detailed designs for interior finishes, not realizing that these are not included in the contract.

The solution to this problem is to rigorously and continuously compare the work being done with what was agreed to in the contract. This is why it is so important to develop a detailed work plan before the owner-architect agreement is signed, so that the full extent of the job is known and shared with all project team members. Then, the project manager can monitor the work by project staff against the budget and objectives.

If the scope creep is due to additional work requests by the client, then the project manager, with possible involvement of the firm principal, must ask for an increase in fees from the client, citing the extra work provisions in the agreement. The project team must be aware of the scope so that if the client makes such requests directly, it will know to bring these additional work requests to the project manager for authorization to proceed with those tasks.

Monitoring the Construction Budget

During the various phases of design and document production, the architect must make sure that the design conforms to the original project budget. This can be difficult in the early stages of schematic design if the original cost estimate has been based on the cost per square foot for a similar building type. As the project design is developed and refined, new cost estimates should be developed. These projections are compared against the original budget, and modifications to the design are made as needed. For example, if the assembly or system method is used, as described in Chap. 10, and the exterior cladding proposed for the building causes the overall budget to be exceeded, then the architect can find a less expensive exterior material.

During design development and the early stages of construction document production, the parameter method of budgeting, described in Chap. 30, can be used to adjust decisions about materials, products, and systems in order to meet the owner's budget. One advantage of project delivery with a construction manager, design-build, or integrated project delivery method is that the architect can get accurate cost information throughout the design process and work with the constructor to maintain the project budget.

Any changes in the project scope may increase construction cost, affecting time and fees. If a decision made by the client changes the scope of the project, the architect must immediately inform the client in writing of how the change may affect costs—both construction costs and additional design fees. The client must give written approval for any scope changes.

Refer to Chap. 10 and Chap. 30 for more on budgeting during programming and on methods of refining the construction budget as a project progresses from schematic design through the production of construction documents.

Documentation

All work done on a project must be documented, either electronically or on paper. This documentation lets the designer look back at the project's development, provides a record in case disagreements arise, and serves as a project history that the firm may use for planning future jobs.

Documentation is a vital part of project communication. An email or written memo is more accurate, communicates more clearly, and is more difficult to forget than a phone call or casual conversation. By sending copies of the correspondence or documentation to the members of the project team, all parties involved in the project can stay informed of questions or decisions in a timely manner. Fortunately, digital technology makes this easier than it was when all written communication was on paper.

Most design firms use standard forms or project management software for common documents such as transmittals, job observation reports, and time sheets. Standard forms and software make it easy to record the necessary information. In addition, all meetings should be documented, and meeting notes should be distributed promptly to all participants and others who need to be informed of the proceedings. Phone call logs (listing date, time, participants, and discussion topics), emails, personal daily logs, and formal communications like letters and memos should also be generated and preserved to serve as project documentation.

With proper networking and setup, computers, smart phones, and other electronic devices greatly aid documentation and recordkeeping. Records can be generated, shared, and filed digitally, as well as automatically backed up on servers for future reference. This makes it easy to transmit information to project team members, clients, and subcontractors.

PROJECT QUALITY CONTROL

Quality control (QC) is an organized set of procedures, systems, and tools established by an office that aid in meeting the expectations of the client, maintaining a high level of professional service, and reducing risks and liability. Quality control may also be known as *quality management, quality planning,* and *quality assurance*, but all these terms mean basically the same. An advantage in using the term "quality control" is that control is precisely what an architectural firm can do to achieve it.

There are two aspects to quality: that which is normally expected of an architect (such as designing, detailing, and specifying a roof that doesn't leak), and that which is defined by the client (such as obtaining a functioning building at the lowest possible cost). Quality does not necessarily mean high-cost finishes or an award-winning building, but it does mean determining what the client expects in regard to design, cost, and other aspects of the project and then meeting those expectations.

Sometimes the client and architect have different expectations. The architect may want to design an award-winning, precedent-setting building, but the client may want a time-tested, economical structure in which a business can operate. A building that wins awards will not be a quality product in the eyes of this client if it also exceeds the budget.

Quality does not necessarily mean high-cost finishes or an award-winning building, but it does mean determining what the client expects and then meeting those expectations.

Because meeting the needs and expectations of the client is an integral component of quality control, these needs and expectations must be clearly defined during the programming phase of the project. A successful program will define the client's overall goals. If a program was prepared by another firm and these goals are not delineated in the program document, then the architect must help the client express these goals and get the client's written approval of this statement before design work begins.

There are two methods of achieving quality for both client goals and professional services: process and checking. Both are valid methods, and both are necessary.

Achieving quality through *process* means making sure that tasks are performed correctly the first time so that there is no need to redo them later. Team members' efforts are carefully supervised, and the work of individuals is coordinated. For example, an office may establish step-by-step procedures and checklists for completing floor plans; these are then used by everyone in the office on all projects to make sure that the drawing contains the necessary information and that various key elements are drawn correctly.

Achieving quality through *checking* means making sure a finished product is correct before it is delivered to the end user. In the architectural profession, reviewing, redlining, and correcting the drawings before they are released to the owner for review or to the contractor for bidding or construction is an example of checking.

Example 6.2

What are the basic goals of a quality control program? (Choose the four that apply.)

(A) meeting the community's expectations

(B) meeting the client's expectations

(C) providing the standard of care for professional practice

(D) reducing risk and liability

(E) designing an award-winning project

(F) using the best employees for the project

Solution

Conforming with codes, regulations and requirements is part of the standard of care. Designing to win awards may only be a by-product of a good quality control program. The goals for this program should be to reduce risk and liability, while providing the client with the standard of care required to practice architecture.

The answer is (B), (C), and (D).

Establishing a Quality Control Program

A comprehensive quality control program involves everyone in the firm, each with different responsibilities, each acting at different times and at various levels of detail. In addition, the type of services offered by the company will determine many aspects of the checking and approval processes. An architectural firm will have issues that are quite different from an interior design firm, even though many elements of quality control will be the same. The following guidelines can be used to establish a quality control program.

- Top management must support and encourage the quality control program.
- Give one person or a small committee the responsibility to guide the daily efforts of the quality control program.
- Involve everyone in the office. This is especially important when the quality control program is first being formed. All employees should contribute their thoughts about problem areas and how procedures can be modified to make improvements. A quality control program forced on employees with no room for adjustments or fresh perspectives will not work. Quality circles, described below, are especially useful in motivating and involving employees.
- Review past problem areas. Those that cause the firm the greatest difficulties or that have the most potential to harm the firm should be corrected first.
- Once the firm's particular problem areas are identified, set priorities and a schedule for action. The list of problem areas can be used as a starting point. One office may find that improving standard agreements is the most needed action, while another may find that documentation is what most needs to be improved.
- The quality control program must be maintained and used continually. Over time, eliminate what doesn't work and replace it with new techniques.

An effective quality control program takes time and money to set up and maintain. However, the advantages include fewer errors, reduced exposure to liability, a more efficient practice, and improved service to clients. Although it usually isn't necessary, if an architectural firm wants to implement a very formal quality control program, it can follow the guidelines of ISO 9000 (iso.org/iso/iso_9000).

Quality Control Techniques

The techniques of quality control were first implemented by manufacturing companies in the early part of the twentieth century. Since then, quality control has been elevated to a science and profession. By using some of these basic approaches, an architectural firm can greatly improve the quality of its service.

Programming

Good programming is crucial to successful quality control. The architect must have a written record defining the client's goals, needs, and expectations. This program is the document against which the architect can direct the project and judge whether or not it is achieving the level of quality expected by the client.

Checklists

A *checklist* is a list of things that need to be considered or accomplished in order to complete a particular task. Checklists have a long history in the architectural profession as reminders of what must be done to complete a project.

One of the most common types is the building code checklist. Because a building code has hundreds of requirements that may apply to any given project, a code checklist can remind the architect, project manager, or job captain of what must be reviewed and shown correctly on the construction documents to meet the code.

A checklist can be developed for a specific task such as the completion of a site visit form or for a broad, multifaceted process such as design development. The latter sort of checklist may be long and involved, while the former can be short and easily completed.

Checklists are useful for achieving consistency and quality in tasks that must be done on every project but that are not always done by the same people, especially if some are less experienced staff members. They are also useful in embedding corporate memory into office documentation. For example, if a mistake is made on a project, one or more items can be added to the relevant checklist to avoid the problem on future projects. For offices that specialize in certain building types, checklists can address the unique needs of those buildings. Specific checklists can also be attached to standard details for technical construction reminders. After a project is completed, checklists also serve as a record of work performed.

The staff should include graduates and interns who show promise of developing into good architects and who can bring fresh ideas and new knowledge to the firm.

Checklists can be obtained from various sources, such as practice management books and AIA Document D200, *Project Checklist.* However, most firms develop their own checklists based on their own particular needs and traits, including size of staff and projects, project types, experience of staff, project delivery methods used, and any special problems historically encountered.

Requests for information (RFIs) from contractors on previous projects are a good source of useful items to add to checklists. An RFI usually indicates that there was a problem in the project's drawings or specifications, such as an omission or conflicting information. The method used to resolve the problem can be added to a checklist, a standard detail, a master specification section, or other documentation.

Process-Based Systems

A *process-based system* automates a procedure so that a task can be performed accurately and consistently with little or no human intervention. In architectural practice, quality control has been greatly improved by the growing number of activities that can be performed with computer assistance. For example, project management or financial management software can present in a consistent format the precise information needed to develop a cost estimate or project proposal and to monitor the progress of the work. In design, building information modeling software can accurately detect clashes between structure, building elements, and HVAC systems, a difficult and error-prone job when performed by a human.

Quality Management Meetings

At regular intervals during a project, the project manager, designers, and office principals should hold quality management meetings to review the progress of the project. At these meetings, the group can determine whether the original problems are being solved and whether the job is proceeding according to the client's and design firm's expectations. The work in progress can also be reviewed to see whether it is technically correct, adheres to all codes and regulations, and is being properly documented.

Staffing

The quality of any endeavor depends on the people engaged in it. The primary goal of any architectural firm is to provide a design service that solves difficult problems, so the knowledge, skill, experience, and diligence of the staff is important for quality control. Any number of checklists, meetings, computers, and standard details, no matter how well prepared, will be of little use if the people involved don't apply them correctly.

The best professionals and support staff possible should be recruited and hired. This should include not just experienced architects but also graduates and interns who show promise of developing into good architects and who can bring fresh ideas and new knowledge to the firm. A good in-house mentoring and training program is important to this effort. The firm should provide all employees with training, and continuing education outside the firm should be encouraged. This may include paying for classes and sending staff to workshops, tradeshows, and conventions as part of a human resources benefits package.

Quality Circles

A *quality circle* is a small group of employees who meet regularly to identify, analyze, and solve problems related to their particular sphere of work. Employees are a valuable resource and often know better than management what their immediate problems are and how they might be solved. Additional benefits of quality circles include increased motivation, improved communication, teamwork, more involvement by employees, and higher productivity.

The structure of a quality circle is flexible, based on the company, its needs, the members' schedules, and circumstances, but typically follows some general guidelines. The number of participants ranges from six to ten, but can be slightly smaller or larger. Membership is voluntary. Generally, the quality circle meets once a week for about an hour. Members of a circle should come from the same work group so they can all focus on their particular problems.

In a large office, several quality circles may be organized. For example, in a large architectural firm, one quality circle might be composed of people in the production group while another might be made up of project managers. In a small office, a quality circle can be more informal while still doing the work needed.

In an ideal quality circle program, each circle will be led by a facilitator trained in quality control techniques; if there are multiple quality circles, there will also be a *steering committee* to oversee them and coordinate their efforts. The steering committee includes representatives from major departments in the firm as well as from top management. The committee's purpose is to guide the quality circle program, set goals and objectives, monitor progress, and, in general, to see that the program is consistent with the overall goals of the firm.

Once the quality circle has been set up, it should follow a consistent pattern in dealing with problems and quality control issues. First, problem areas or specific projects should be identified. The ideas may come from anywhere: circle members, management, staff members, or others. Next, the ideas or problems are discussed and defined so that the circle has something definite to work on. Once a problem has been defined, it is analyzed, alternate solutions are discussed, and a solution is developed. The final step in the process is presenting the solution to management and the steering committee, if there is one. At this point, management may decide whether to implement the quality circle's recommendation.

If the firm's resources allow it, training in quality circle techniques can come from management training programs and private management consulting firms, which can provide ongoing support and advice. Some additional guidelines include the following.

- The concept and process must have support from top management, including a commitment to consider seriously suggestions made by the quality circles. In larger firms, middle management must also support the idea.
- The quality circles must be ongoing activities. They cannot run for a few months or a year and then be forgotten.
- Quality circles must not become gripe sessions; they are problem-solving units.
- Quality circles should be kept small. For larger firms or firms with several service areas, more than one circle may be established.
- Although quality circles can work with a firm of any size, they are often more valuable for large firms, where communication between management and staff may be more difficult. A twenty- to

thirty-person firm could probably benefit from a single quality circle, while larger firms might want to institute more.

- Quality circles should be considered a means to help employees develop while generally improving the quality of the work output.

Corporate Knowledge

Corporate knowledge is the documentation of information that an architectural firm has gained through the work it has done and that can be applied to new projects. The term also often refers to the knowledge of experienced people in the firm, but memory can be fleeting, and employees come and go, so the accumulated knowledge should be in a fixed, tangible form so that it can be shared with present and future employees.

Checklists, as previously discussed, are one way to document corporate knowledge. Another common form of documentation is through *standard details*, which not only record information for future project use but can also be used to streamline the production of future construction documents. Although standard details can be used alone, accompanying notes can document what is most important, how details may be modified for certain uses, applicable industry standards, and reference sources, so that less experienced staff can understand the proper use of the detail. Figure 6.2 shows an example of such a detail.

Figure 6.2 Standard Details of a Parapet

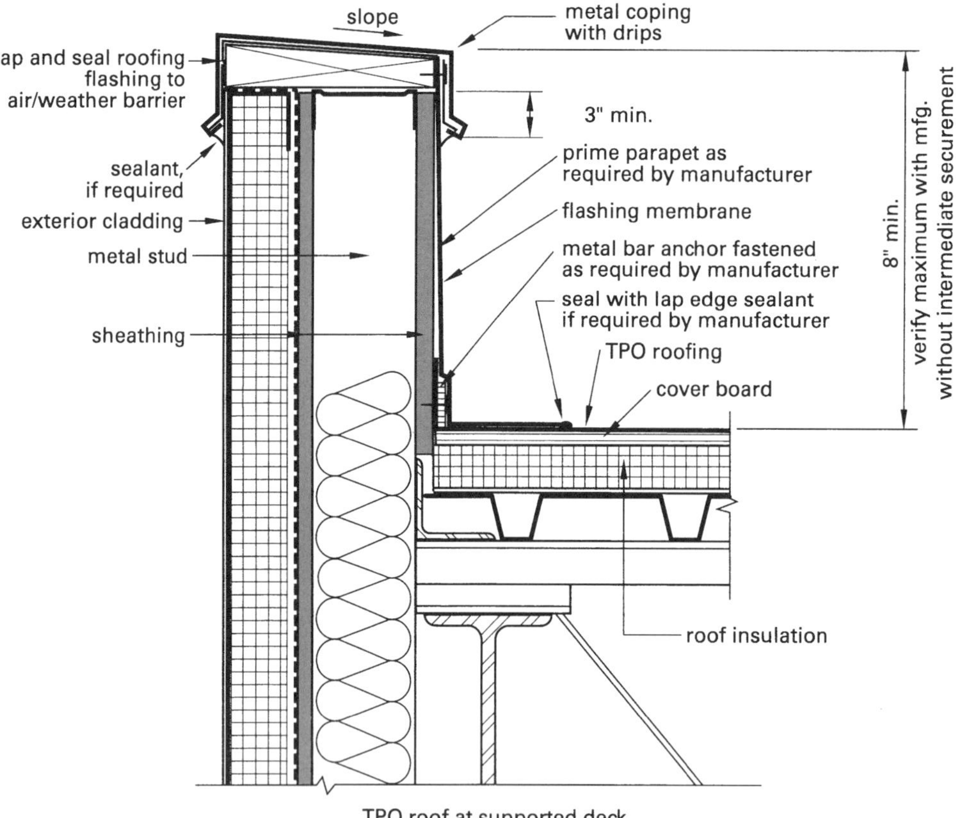

- Provide walkways to mechanical equipment and other roof mounted facilities that require frequent access. These may be an additional layer of membrane or separate pavers or walkways.
- Grease vents may require special treatment to protect against deterioration of the membrane. Exposure to petroleum based products or other chemicals may required special treatment.
- For wind design, follow the recommendations of ANSI/SPRI WD-1, ANSI/SPRI RP-4 and the requirements of the local authority having jurisdiction. In high wind areas, a ballasted system may not be appropriate and a fully adhered or mechanically fastened system may be required.

Figure 6.2 (continued)

- When the roofing is terminated at the top of a parapet as shown, the TPO membrane should be carried over the wood cap under the coping and at least 1 in over the exterior wall, or as required by the manufacturer. Other terminations may be used including counterflashing on the parapet, a termination bar, or reglet.
- Steel decks must be a minimum of 22 gage, 0.0312 in.

metal stud	ASTM C955, if galvanized, ASTM A653, Grade G-90; Sized for maximum deflection, under full wind load of L/240; Installed per ASTM C1007.
sheathing	Fiberglass mat-faced gypsum board (ASTM C1177) or gypsum fiber panels (ASTM C1278); 1/2 in min. fiberglass mat-faced gyp. board is recommended.
cover board	Glass mat gypsum board, ASTM C1177; verify that surface of board is approved by the TPO manufacturer; cover board may not be necessary depending on type of insulation used; composite board may provide suitable surface for TPO.
roof insulation	Polyisocyanurate, extruded polystyrene, expanded polystyrene, or composite board may be used as recommended by the membrane manufacturer. Expanded polystyrene requires a cover board; thickness as required by thermal resistance needed; insulation with rough surfaces should be covered with separation sheet to protect membrane from rough surfaces; insulation must have sufficient strength to span flutes of decking.
TPO roofing	ASTM D6878; TPO membrane and related products by same manufacturer; install per manufacturers' instructions; install according to SPRI Application Guidelines for Self-Adhered Thermoplastic and Thermoset Roofing Systems.

Master specifications can likewise be used to record corporate knowledge in a form that can be used directly in future construction documents. See Fig. 6.3.

Other ways to document corporate knowledge include in-house computer databases, post-occupancy evaluations, project procedure manuals, and even hand-written notes. However, no matter what techniques are used, information must be organized and indexed so that anyone in the office can find what is needed. These documentation methods, along with technology, quality management meetings, staff training, and quality circles, are all ways to make continual improvement, which is a cornerstone of effective quality control.

Project Documentation Quality Control

Documentation is vital to the function and success of an architectural firm. Good documentation is needed for administration of the project, and it also aids in communication, serves as an archive of information that can be used on future jobs, and most importantly provides a record if disputes arise during the project or in arbitration or litigation after the project.

An architectural firm should maintain two categories of project documentation: first, the construction documents (drawings and specifications), and second, everything else related to the project. The construction documents are unique to each project, representing the sum total of the architect's creative and technical work. Most other documentation is accumulated through the course of the project and is based on standard forms such as contracts, change orders, shop drawing logs, and the like. These can be somewhat repetitive from project to project, and there are standard methods for completing, using, and filing them.

The architect needs to make sure that all types of documentation, including electronic forms and project information, are used correctly and consistently and filed properly during the course of the project. At the end of a job, all documentation should be consolidated into a project file and retained for an amount of time required by records retention guidelines.

Figure 6.3 Master Specifications Sample

2.01 Flush, Solid-Core Doors

A. General: Doors shall be of the types, sizes, and configurations as indicated on the drawings and on the door schedule. Flush wood doors shall conform to WDMA I.S. 1-A.

Coordinate with local code requirements. Note: NFPA 252, Fire Tests of Door Assemblies, and UL 10B, are the same as former ASTM E 152, which has been discontinued. Select one of the lock block options.

B. Fire-rated doors: Fire-rated doors shall comply with test requirements of NFPA 252 and shall bear certifying labels of Underwriters Laboratories, Warnock Hersey, or an independent testing agency approved by the building official. Fire-rated doors shall be provided, as required, with hardware reinforcement blocking and top, bottom, and intermediate rail blocking. Lock blocks shall be manufacturer's standard [not less than 5 inches by 18 inches].

Verify local code requirements regarding the applicability of UBC Standard 7-2, including positive pressure fire testing of doors and the "S" label. There are two components, UBC 7-2 Part I (same as UL 10C), which is the positive pressure test, and the "S" rating requirements of air leakage, which is UBC 7-2, Part II (same as UL 1784). If required, include the following language in the paragraph above. Select below as required. Most wood doors require gaskets to meet test requirements.

In addition, fire-rated door assemblies shall conform to the requirements of UBC Standard 7-2, Part I (UL 10C) for positive pressure fire testing. [20-minute smoke and draft control assemblies shall carry the S label as determined by UBC Standard 7-2, Part II (UL 1874).]

Select one of the grades below. Generally, Custom grade is good enough for most work if veneer matching is not critical. Select Premium grade when you want the highest quality veneers, want veneers to match at the transoms, and want vertical edges to be the same species as the veneer. For opaque finishes, Premium grade provides medium density overlay for the best paintable surface. Don't specify Economy grade.

C. Doors shall be Premium [Custom] [Economy] grade in accordance with WDMA I.S. 1-A.

D. Veneer face doors for transparent finish:

1. Core type: Particleboard [Mineral core] [Lumber core] [Particleboard or mineral core as required for fire rating]

Fill in the desired species. Common choices are red oak, white oak, cherry, walnut, maple, Honduras mahogany, birch, ash, or others. Verify availability of veneers.

2. Face veneer species:__________________

Select slicing method below. Generally plain sliced or quarter sliced is used depending on the amount of grain pattern you want to see. Specify rift slice for red or white oak if you don't want flaking. Not all species may be available in some cuts.

3. Veneer cut: [rotary] [plain sliced] [quarter sliced] [rift sliced]

Select one of the following. Book match is the most common and usually looks the best.

4. Matching between individual veneer leaves: Book match [Slip match] [Random match]

Select one of the following. Center match usually looks the best but is the most costly and is available in Premium grade only. Balance match is a lower cost alternative that still looks good. Running match is the least expensive.

Project Files

Project files should be a record of how the entire job progressed, from initial marketing to project closeout and follow-up. The records should document the sequence of events of a project, including the what, who, when, how, and why of all actions. This kind of record keeping is important, both to ensure that the design solution meets the client's objectives and to reduce risks and liability and defend the architectural office against claims and legal action.

The following lists include some of the most important types of project records to maintain for the standard design-bid-build method of project delivery. For other project delivery methods, other types of records may be generated at different times during the project. The firm should establish a standard office protocol for accumulating, preparing, and distributing notes, minutes, and other information, and must keep adequate backup in case the original source is lost.

General Administration of the Project

- marketing information and proposals, including all communications with the prospective client before the contract is signed
- contact information for the client and client's representatives, including billing information
- contracts and agreements
- documents related to fee negotiations and agreements, including scope of services
- documents related to design and construction schedules, including the client's preliminary schedule, approved schedules, and any changes
- documents related to construction budgets, including the client's preliminary budget, approved budget and any changes during the course of the project
- records of communications with the client after the contract is signed
- fee and staffing allocations
- invoices, statements, and backup documents related to client billing
- records of accounts receivable
- records of expenses billed or assigned to the project, including expense invoices and consultant's billing
- other accounting records pertaining to the project
- all communications between the design office and other parties concerning the project, including correspondence, meeting notes, emails, text messages, and telephone logs

Programming

- copy of the program, if done by an outside firm
- complete program requirements, including functional groupings, occupants, individual space requirements, furniture and equipment needs, and growth projections
- statement of the client's goals and objectives
- documentation of existing conditions, if the project is an addition or renovation
- sustainability goals and requirements
- written client approval of the program
- revised project budget, if changed from the agreement
- survey information, including request for survey, communications with the surveyor, and billing information
- soil test information
- building code checklist and other regulatory requirements
- all communications between the design office and other parties concerning the project, including correspondence, meeting notes, emails, text messages, and telephone logs

Schematic Design

- sketches, models, and other drawings and computer files used to develop schematic design
- final schematic design presentation, including budget and schedule
- client's written approval of schematic design and authorization to proceed
- all communications between the design office and other parties concerning the project, including correspondence, meeting notes, emails, text messages, and telephone logs

Design Development

- sketches, models, and other drawings and computer files used to complete design development
- final design development presentation
- approvals of applicable regulatory agencies
- records of all changes, who made them, and why
- final design development presentation, including budget and schedule
- client's written approval of design development and authorization to proceed
- all communications between the design office and other parties concerning the project, including correspondence, meeting notes, emails, text messages, and telephone logs

Construction Documentation

- supporting information for developing the construction drawings and specifications
- records of materials and product investigation and selection
- written approval of the documents by the client
- records related to advertising for bids or proposals
- all communications between the design office and other parties concerning the project, including correspondence, meeting notes, emails, text messages, and telephone logs

Bidding or Negotiation

- records of each prime bidder or negotiating contractor
- record of issuance of contract documents
- addenda records, including requests for information and distribution log
- bidding records, including submitted bids and bid summary log
- pre-bid conference notes
- all communications between the design office and other parties concerning the project, including correspondence, meeting notes, emails, text messages, and telephone logs

Construction Administration

- record of all prime contractors, including record of receipt of bonds, certificates of insurance, dates of approval, and contract signed
- reference copy of the contract between the owner and contractor
- list of subcontractors with contact information
- copy of the contractor's approved schedule
- copy of payment schedules, schedule of values, and other cost-related documents
- records of issuance of all permits

- shop drawings and shop drawing log
- samples and sample submittal log
- copies of test reports
- field reports
- photographs and videos
- change orders, including pricing requests, approved copies, and change order log
- application and certificates for payment
- all communications between the design office and other parties concerning the project, including correspondence, meeting notes, emails, text messages, and telephone logs

Project Closeout and Follow-up

- punch list and follow-ups
- certificate of substantial completion
- final certificate for payment
- testing and balancing reports (if not part of commissioning)
- commissioning reports
- copies of release of liens or dates of release of liens
- copies of guarantees, bonds, and operating instructions
- copies of record drawings
- project closeout form
- construction cost summary
- all communications between the design office and other parties concerning the project, including correspondence, meeting notes, emails, text messages, and telephone logs

The list of project records for each phase includes a record of "all communications between the design office and other parties concerning the project, including correspondence, meeting notes, emails, text messages, and telephone logs." This is because most problems with documentation—or more commonly, with the lack of documentation—come from the actions of the project participants in the day-to-day progress of the job. Often, in the hectic pace of work, the project manager and other team members have face-to-face conversations, take telephone calls, or send text messages without properly recording them. A pivotal decision made or an instruction given through these forms of communication will too often become a point of contention in a courtroom years later. Over time, participants may come to have different recollections of these communications. Without proper documentation, the architect may be in a difficult position.

Contemporaneous documentation is the recording of communications, decisions, and other actions that are not normally relegated to a standard form or whose occurrence cannot be predicted to take place at a given time or circumstance, such as within a regularly scheduled project meeting. This type of documentation should record spoken communication (in-person conversations and telephone calls), as well as electronic correspondence (emails and text messages). These decisions and discussions may be tracked through use of a daily journal or notebook entries. As previously mentioned, if electronic messages and documents are used, there should be an office protocol for using the associated devices and safely archiving the records. A project website is one way of doing this, and it has the added advantages of allowing communication among all members of the project team and of storing the data safely. It is important that a secure platform is used for sharing and archiving this information, and that access is limited to those involved with the project. Social media is not appropriate for communicating project information or for project records.

Regardless of whether the documentation is paper-based or electronic, keep these additional guidelines in mind.

- Be sure to communicate potential problems to the appropriate members of the team.
- Avoid assigning blame for a problem, whether to others or to oneself. Just give the facts and indicate that the problem must be further investigated.
- Include the date of each communication, and make a note of the parties who are privy to it.
- If using paper journals or notebooks, use a spiral-bound type. This will help establish that the notes were sequential and contemporaneous, and that no new pages were added at a later time.
- If paper-based documentation is used, write in ink.
- When keeping the client informed of progress, as required by the contract, be consistent in how the information is communicated, the length and style of the message, and the amount of information given. Deciding how much information to give is a matter of judgment, but if one communication stands out from the others as being unusually long, is trying to assign blame for a problem, or is giving the appearance of having been written by someone else, a court may look with suspicion on that one document.

From a legal standpoint, it is important that contemporaneous documents follow certain guidelines to avoid the possibility of being considered as hearsay in a court proceeding. *Hearsay* is a written or oral statement that was made outside of the court, usually by another person than the witness. Hearsay is normally not allowed as evidence in court. Project records can be considered hearsay evidence, unless they are found to come under an exception allowed by the law, known as the *business entry rule* or the *business records exception to the hearsay rule*. To qualify under this exception, a project record must have been made during the normal course of business, it must have been made at or shortly after the act, event, or transaction being recorded, and it must be the regular course of business for such a record to be made.

Construction documents are one of the main sources of claims of negligence.

For example, if the firm has made it standard practice to send each client a weekly letter reporting on progress and pointing out existing or potential problems, then any such letter will be more likely to be accepted in court than if there were no weekly correspondence; in the latter case, a letter to the client, being an unusual action, may even give the appearance of having been sent specifically as an attempt to absolve the architect of liability for something. If the firm must communicate to the client in between regular communications (such as to report an urgent safety problem on the job site), the communication should make clear that the contract requires the firm to notify the client in a timely manner.

Construction Documents

Construction documents are one of the main sources of claims of negligence. They are the most complex part of the project delivery process, and preparing them requires a great deal of coordination among many people. Also, they are typically completed when time and fees are running out, and less experienced staff members are often assigned to complete them. For these reasons, it is important that the project manager be able to budget and monitor the progress of the work so that there is not a rush to complete the project under less-than-ideal conditions.

No set of drawings and specifications has ever been perfect, and none ever will be. However, it is the architect's duty to produce a set of documents in accordance with the standard of care of the profession and to exercise reasonable skill and knowledge in their preparation. The following guidelines can be used as the foundation for proper document production.

A Single Source of Control

One person should be in control of construction document production and coordination among the various members of the team: client, consultants, firm management, governmental agencies, and so forth. Ideally, this person should be a competent project manager who maintains continuity throughout the entire project delivery process, from initial proposal to project follow-up. On large jobs, the project manager does not necessarily have to handle daily production issues (these can be handled by a job captain), but the project manager should know and understand the complexities of construction documents and how they are produced.

Industry Standards

Be aware of accepted standards of practice and trade customs in the construction industry. Stay current with standards of quality in the industry, and establish a policy regarding the use of industry standards and under what circumstances it is appropriate to deviate from these standards. If the firm wants a higher standard of workmanship than usual on a project, this needs to be clearly expressed in the drawings and specifications.

Professional Standards

A design professional is expected to exercise the degree of skill, knowledge, and judgment that is normally exercised by other professionals in similar circumstances in similar communities. This is one of the basic legal concepts concerning liability and negligence. If conduct falls below this standard of practice, the professional may be held liable for damages.

One way to achieve this level of performance is to follow generally accepted methods and procedures of practice. This includes using drawing standards and specification standards as discussed in Chap. 46 and Chap. 47. The architect can also use accepted details of trade associations.

Communication and Coordination

Lack of communication is the source of many problems. If a last-minute design change is not conveyed to the draftsperson, or a mechanical engineer does not tell the architect about the change in duct size that will affect light fixture clearances, needless time and effort will be spent later correcting the problems that result. A firm should set policies that encourage and facilitate communication among all members of the project team. These policies can include procedures for meetings and written communications, regular exchange of progress drawings, use of design checklists, and, most importantly, assigning to one person the responsibility for implementing these policies. In most cases, this person should be a project manager. Using a shared building information model (BIM) can also facilitate this coordination.

Work Procedures

All staff should use quality control checklists. Using them maintains consistent quality from job to job and minimizes the possibility of omissions. Standard details should also be used, as they not only save time and money in producing jobs, but are also an excellent way to record the knowledge that the firm develops concerning how to build well. These methods need not stifle creativity; they simply let designers spend more of their time concentrating on design rather than production.

Research

Every firm should make an ongoing commitment to research in all aspects of the practice. This should include research into products, ways to improve specifications, design techniques, and other applicable topics. Because research is not a billable item for most firms, many firms neglect it. But in an increasing number of cases, design professionals have been held liable for incorrect product use, design solutions, and the like. Good research reduces the firm's risk of liability.

Evaluation and Feedback

Every firm should learn from its successes and mistakes. Once a project is completed and the last invoice has been sent out, it can seem difficult to justify taking the time to look back and consider all that was done. But a regular process of evaluation and feedback is integral to quality control and necessary for continuing improvement. This is the way to develop and strengthen corporate memory, one of the most valuable sources of information a design office has.

Construction Documents Checklist

Before the construction documents phase can begin, there are two basic requirements. First, the owner must approve the design development submission in writing as required by the agreement. Second, the architect should settle all design decisions and select the materials needed, so that the drawings and specifications can be completed. Leaving design decisions until the construction documents phase is a sure way to make mistakes and go over budget.

General Quality Control Issues

Before starting construction documents the following tasks should be completed.

- *Verify that the design solution meets all program requirements.* To make this verification, use the checklists developed during programming, correspondence with the client, the final programming report, and other documentation as needed.
- *Verify that the design solution meets all regulatory requirements that apply.* This includes applicable zoning and building code requirements. This should be checked during the design phases, too, but last-minute changes often affect compliance. Be alert to such changes, and reexamine the drawings with this in mind. If preliminary approval from governing agencies is required, verify that this approval has been obtained in writing.
- *Obtain from the client all the information needed for inclusion in the project manual.* This includes the type of contract the client wants to use, insurance and bonding requirements, modifications to the general and supplementary conditions of the contract, approved alternatives, items to be supplied by the owner, and similar concerns.

Issues During Production of Construction Documents

- *Prepare an outline of the scope of construction documents required.* This includes working drawing sheet mock-ups, detail lists, the numbering system for the drawings, a list of required technical sections of the project manual, and other required documents of the project manual. A great deal of time, money, and confusion can be saved if this simple step is completed.
- *Check whether the client has special requirements for the drawings or the project manual.* For example, the client's organization may require a specific sheet size that is not typically used by the architect.
- *Check drawings at 50% completion.* Submit these drawings to the client for review and approval. Make it clear to the client that this review is for checking the drawings against the original program requirements and the design development approval; it is not a time for making changes. Changes made at this time are extra services and could require a time extension.
- *Review completed construction and bidding documents with the client.* Obtain the client's written approval to proceed to the bidding or negotiation phase.

Cost Issues

- *Update the design development budget to reflect any changes or development of details (including mechanical/electrical).* If there is significant variance from previous cost budgets, advise the client immediately. Review with the client and obtain approval before proceeding with construction documents.

Scheduling Issues

- *Determine what staffing is needed to complete the construction documents according to schedule.* To complete the work on time, it may be necessary to bring in staff from other departments or to use a subcontractor to provide drafting services. This phase often requires more detailed scheduling than other phases, so it may be necessary to expand the original schedule.
- *Allow enough time at the end of document production to check for errors and correct them, as well as for reproduction.* When time runs short, checking for mistakes is often done in haste or not done at all. This should be avoided at all costs.

Coordination

- Review with the consultants any changes made during design development.
- Supply consultants with the information they need on desired specification items. This can include information about plumbing fixtures, light fixtures, air diffusers, sprinkler heads, switches, and so on. It can also include performance requirements such as color and appearance.
- Supply consultants with a template for the desired specification format. Include the numbering system, page layout, and the like. To avoid confusion, ask consultants to follow the architect's specifications.
- Hold regular meetings with consultants. Exchange progress drawings weekly or biweekly as needed.
- Verify that the working drawings comply with building code requirements. This includes details, specified materials, measurements, and other elements. Provide to each person working on the construction documents a copy of the code checklist that was completed during the programming or design phases.

Records Management Issues

- Document all decisions and changes made by the firm and client during the construction documentation phase.
- Obtain written approval of the documents from the client.

When the construction documents are complete, they should be thoroughly checked. Ideally, this should be done by someone outside the firm, such as a code consultant. Allow sufficient time for this external review. Alternatively, documents can be checked by someone within the firm who has the knowledge needed but who has not worked on the project. This includes reviewing the consultants' drawings and specification sections to ensure proper coordination.

Refer to Chap. 46 and Chap. 47 for a more detailed discussion of construction documentation and coordination with the consultant's documents.

Coordination with Regulatory Agencies

If the building project requires approval from planning agencies or other governmental bodies before detailed design can begin, the project manager is responsible for guiding the owner's project through the approval process. The work required to gain approval may include developing preliminary site plans and land-use proposals, sketching preliminary building designs, and meeting with governmental agencies and neighborhood groups or presenting before regulatory boards.

Generally, there is an approved procedure and a set of application forms that must be used. The project manager should confirm that the application is complete and all information requested has been provided. This work requires additional fees beyond the normal fee for building design, so the architect must estimate the time and costs needed for the work and obtain the client's approval before proceeding.

If the building presents unusual design challenges, it may require zoning variances or unusual building techniques or materials. In this case, the architect will have to work with building officials or zoning regulators early in the pre-design phase to obtain their advice and approval for any deviation from zoning requirements; alternatively, the architect must find other means and methods of construction as allowed by building codes. In some circumstances, a code consultant may be needed to guide the project through the code approval process.

It is the project manager's responsibility to ensure that as the design develops, it is continually checked against the requirements of the building code and any state and local regulations. The project manager may do this personally, but more often building code checks are done by someone in the firm who is especially knowledgeable in this area. If the project is very large or complex, code consultants can be retained to provide this service.

The project manager should also make sure that the construction documents contain all information required by the local authority having jurisdiction. A list of information commonly required on drawings is given in Chap. 47.

Example 6.3

During which phase of a project should the project team review the code requirements or interact with officials having jurisdiction over the project? (Choose the four that apply.)

(A) at the end of the construction document phase

(B) at the beginning of the schematic design phase

(C) at the beginning of the programming phase

(D) during a scope change in the project

(E) before the end of the predesign phase

(F) midway through construction

Solution

During the programming phase, a site has not been chosen yet. A predesign study should include a list of applicable local, state and federal codes, requirements and regulations. As the site design is developed in the schematic design phase, the local zoning, environmental and historic (if any) requirements should be incorporated into the project. Scope changes should trigger a code check for relevant impact to the original code assumptions. At the completion of the construction documents the project is sent to the code officials for building permit review.

The answers are (A), (B), (D), and (E).

Design Process Reviews

The main goal of a quality control program is to manage the project in such a way that the original design objectives of the client are achieved. To accomplish this, the project manager and the design team must keep in mind the original assumptions about the project design, which are typically formalized in the program. These include the size and relationships of spaces; the overall functionality of the building; the requirements pertaining to building systems, materials, and finishes; sustainability issues; and the general level of quality the owner desires. Design review can be accomplished with checklists, regular comparison with the program, and, most importantly, with regular client reviews and written approvals.

DIVISION 3: PROGRAMMING & ANALYSIS

7

Programming & Analysis

BUILDING CONTEXT

Every proposed building exists within a larger context. The project will be located within a certain physical environment, whether this is urban or rural. It is likely that some form of community already exists in the region, and possibly many communities. The client's needs, local building regulations, climate, site features, and cost limitations will all have their influence on the project, sometimes imposing constraints and, at other times, offering opportunities.

Before starting design work, an architect must understand all these factors and how they affect planning. This chapter reviews some of the larger ways in which context influences the development of a building site, including

- urban development and how it affects social behavior
- community influences
- psychological and social influences
- transportation and utility influences
- basic climatic influences
- some general concepts of sustainable design

Chapter 8 covers building regulations, Chap. 9 covers site analysis, and Chap. 10 covers building analysis, including programming.

URBAN DEVELOPMENT

Modern ideas about city and community planning have their antecedents in the historical development of the city and in the theories developed by designers and planners over the centuries about how rational development of the land and cities can improve people's lives. Many development concepts and city forms have been tried; some have failed, but portions of others have been successfully employed in urban planning.

Knowing the history and theory of city planning helps an architect understand how a building project is related to the community and city in which it is located. First, the larger environment affects how the site is developed and the building is designed, and then the building in turn affects the community of which it is a part.

Historical Influences

The earliest humans led nomadic lives. With the development of agriculture, groups of humans created settlements for the first time. Later, as surplus food became available and as ceremony, religion, and leadership began to develop within these groups, the embryonic form of the city appeared.

In the earliest settlements, life was centered around the granary, where food was stored, and the temple, which had multiple functions. The temple was where the administration of the village was conducted and where ceremonial rites, social interaction, and commerce took place. These central buildings were surrounded by living quarters.

As villages grew, their administration became more complex; this function was taken from the temple and the first palaces appeared. Palaces were modest buildings at first, but as power became increasingly centralized, they became larger and more lavish. For security, villages were often walled in or otherwise protected from other village populations or nomadic tribes seeking to take the food they could not produce. Such settlements developed in many areas throughout the world.

All these basic components of the city were present in ancient Greek cities, but in a more evolved form. The activities of the temple increased to a point where they could not be contained in a single facility. Temples remained as centers for religious activity, while the agora became the marketplace. The agora was not just a place for trading goods but also for meeting people, exchanging news, and conducting other business. The Greek cities were also encased by walls for security and had special facilities, such as theaters and stadiums, for other activities.

The medieval city had a form similar to that of earlier villages; it was born at the crossroads of two main streets and grew outward in an irregular layout. Medieval cities were organized around the church and the market because these represented the two most important aspects of life. These structures were located near the center of the city and were surrounded by an informal ring of streets loosely connected by intersecting streets that ran from the church to the gates of the city wall. See Fig. 7.1.

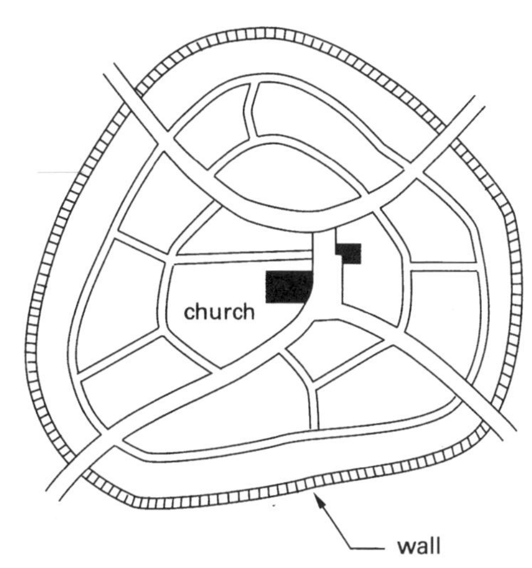

Figure 7.1 Medieval City Form

With the invention of gunpowder, the usual medieval fortification of the high wall was no longer enough to protect the city. The star-shaped city developed, with regularly spaced bastions at points around the wall so that the entire enclosure and all approaches to the city could be defended before the enemy could get close enough for their cannons to be effective. Streets radiated out from the center, thus allowing the defense to be controlled from one point and making it possible to easily move troops and materials. See Fig. 7.2.

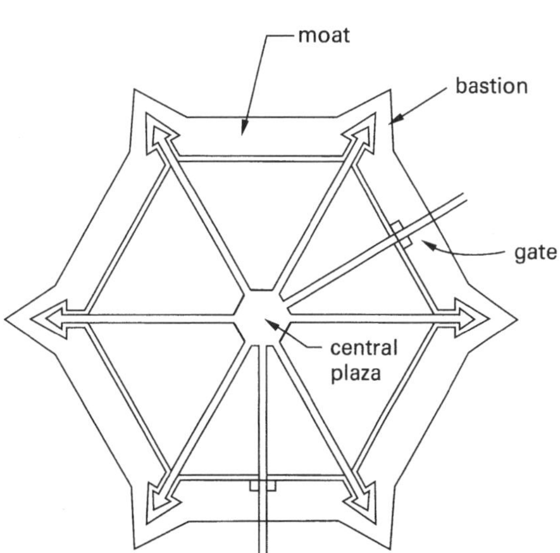

Figure 7.2 Star-Shaped City Form

During the Renaissance, city planning took on greater importance. Although military and defense considerations were still important, planners paid more attention to the aesthetics of urban design. City plans combined symmetrical order with radial layout of streets that focused on points of interest. The primary organization of the radial boulevards was overlaid on a grid of secondary streets or over an existing road system.

Christopher Wren's plan for the rebuilding of London after the great fire of 1666 and Georges-Eugène Haussmann's plan for Paris reflect the Renaissance and Baroque approaches. In the unrealized London plan, Wren proposed main avenues linking major religious and commercial facilities. These were to be superimposed on a gridiron plan for other streets.

In Paris, Haussmann advocated straight, arterial boulevards connecting principal historic buildings, monuments, and open squares. These were designed to create vistas and work in conjunction with the major buildings that were part of the plan. During the period from 1853 to 1869, a large part of Paris was demolished to implement Haussmann's plan. The plan was intended to minimize riots, facilitate defense of the city, and clear out slums, but also succeeded in improving transportation and beautifying the city.

In contrast to the use of straight boulevards promoted by Haussmann, Austrian architect and town planner Camillo Sitte advocated just the opposite. In his book *City Planning According to Artistic Principles*, published in 1889, Sitte proposed that cities be laid out on the principles of medieval towns, with curving and irregular streets. He felt this street configuration would provide a variety of views and be much more interesting than the standard grid and radial city layouts of the time. Sitte proposed using T-intersections to reduce the number of intersection traffic conflicts. He also suggested creating civic spaces around a pinwheel arrangement of streets, which became known as a *turbine square*.

The Industrial Revolution of the eighteenth and nineteenth centuries in England brought about a fundamental change in the design of cities. The factory system required that the work force be close to the factory—the source of power—and to transportation and distribution outlets. As production expanded, so did the populations of the factory towns. The emphasis was on turning out goods, not on social or aesthetic concerns, and the cities soon became overcrowded, filthy, and devoid of open space and recreational activities. These principles spread rapidly from England to northwestern Europe and the northeastern United States, carrying with it the resulting ills.

The living conditions brought about by the Industrial Revolution spawned a reform movement. Many of the first reformers were concerned most with alleviating the deplorable housing conditions that existed, reducing crowding, and improving the water supply and sewage systems. Later reformers and planners, however, realized the need for open space and recreation. All these concerns sparked interest in the planning of cities where factories, housing, and other features of urban life could coexist.

One of the best-known results of the reform movement is the *garden city* concept, first put forth in 1898 by Ebenezer Howard. Howard attempted to combine the best of city and country living in his town-country idea. He proposed that a 6000-acre tract of land be privately owned by the residents. At the center of his idealized city, there would be civic buildings in a park. These would include a town hall, a concert hall, a theater, a library, and other municipal buildings. (See Fig. 7.3.) Surrounding this core would be housing and shops, with industrial facilities in the outermost ring. The urban part of the town would support 30,000 people on 1000 acres of land. The remaining 5000 acres were reserved for a greenbelt and agricultural use and housed 2000 people.

Figure 7.3
Diagram of Ebenezer Howard's Garden City Concept

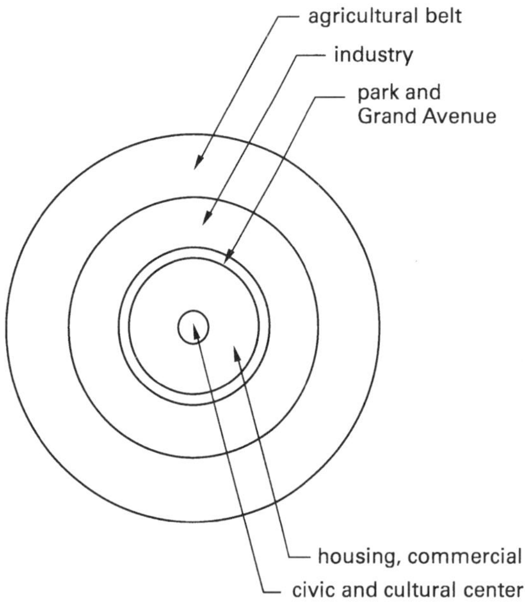

Two cities were built in England using Howard's ideas: Letchworth in 1903 and Welwyn Garden City in 1920. Although they followed the garden city concept, they did not become independent cities but instead became *satellite towns*, smaller towns dependent on larger towns nearby for business.

The *cité industrielle*, proposed by Tony Garnier in 1917, was another reaction to the conditions of the Industrial Revolution. This city plan included separate zones for residential, public, industrial, and agricultural uses, linked by separated circulation paths for vehicles and pedestrians. The buildings were placed on long, narrow lots with ample open space between them. Garnier's plan was one of the first to emphasize the idea of zoning, an idea that would later become vital for city planning.

In the United States, early attempts at city planning reflected the diversity of ideas and styles brought from the Old World. Towns laid out in the colonies were a reaction against the Renaissance ideals and reflected the agrarian lifestyles of the settlers. The towns were planned around a central commons, which was the focus of community life. Houses were free-standing structures set back from the front street, and the lots included backyards as well. This was one of the influences that helped set a precedent for single-family detached housing, which gained prevalence throughout the 20th century.

Philadelphia was typical of many of the early towns. Established in 1682, the city was based on a *gridiron street system* with regularly planned public open spaces and uniform spacing and setback of buildings. Its use of the grid system became the model for later planning in colonial America and for the new towns established as the West was settled.

Savannah, Georgia, was similarly designed in 1733 by its founder, James Edward Oglethorpe. The basic unit of the Oglethorpe Plan was the *ward*, a plot of land about 600 feet square. Each ward contained four residential blocks (containing a total of 40 residential lots) and four civic blocks intended for public buildings, which were arranged around an open central square, two sides of which were reserved for public use. Wards were bounded by major streets arranged in a regular grid.

As the United States expanded into the West, the grid system was encouraged by the Land Ordinance of 1785, which established a rectangular survey system for areas west of the Pennsylvania-Ohio border. This system divided the country into a grid of squares, each 24 miles on a side. Each square was subdivided into 16 *townships*, each six miles on a side. Each township was further subdivided into 36 *sections*, each one mile square. One lot in each township was designated as the location for a school, and others were reserved for government or public facilities.

One early American city that broke with the grid system was Washington, DC. Its layout represented a significant step in city planning, both because of the scale of the project and because it was America's capital city. Pierre Charles L'Enfant was the designer. Unlike the simple grid systems of Philadelphia and Savannah, L'Enfant's design was based on the Renaissance and Baroque planning concepts of diagonal and radial streets superimposed on a rectangular grid.

L'Enfant's plan for Washington centered on the sites for the Capitol, the White House, and a broad pedestrian boulevard that today is known as the Mall. Most streets were north-south or east-west, and key buildings and monuments were located in open circles and plazas at major intersections; these were connected with broad avenues running diagonally across the grid. This created a coherent transportation system based on vistas that terminated in either a building or monument. Modifications were made to the original L'Enfant plan over the years, but the basic layout of the city remains true to L'Enfant's vision.

One early American city that broke with the gird system was Washington, DC.

Frederick Law Olmsted was a leader in landscape and park design. In the 1850s, with architect Calvert Vaux, Olmsted designed New York's Central Park, which inspired similar designs for metropolitan parks across the country and in Canada. Later, Olmsted designed Prospect Park in Brooklyn, Riverside Park in New York, Audubon Park in New Orleans, the Metropolitan Parks System in Boston, and the grounds of the U.S. Capitol in Washington, DC. Olmsted was one of the first landscape architects to preserve the natural features of an area while adding naturalistic elements.

One of the most profound changes in American urban design began with the *Columbian Exposition* in Chicago in 1893. Designed by Olmsted and the architects Daniel Burnham and John Root, the Exposition grouped classical buildings symmetrically around formal courts of honor, reflecting pools, and large promenades. The Exposition started the City Beautiful movement in the United States and revived interest in urban planning. The influence of the Exposition was seen around the country, as civic centers were organized around formal parks, a proliferation of classical public buildings was constructed, and broad, tree-lined parkways and streets were established.

In the 1920s and 1930s, architects such as Frank Lloyd Wright and Le Corbusier envisioned cities with vast open spaces. Wright proposed in his plan for Broadacre City that every home should be situated on at least an acre of land. Many of Wright's ideas of city planning came from his general notion of organic architecture and the idealized notion that all people should have abundant space and be free of the tyranny of centralization. Le Corbusier envisioned a city consisting of office and housing towers surrounded by large green spaces. Corbusier's ideas of city planning were influenced in large measure by Garnier's city planning. Both designers were continuing the reaction against the dense, unsanitary, and haphazard development of city brought about by the Industrial Revolution. Most city planners agree, however, that both schemes would have resulted in very dull cities and a type of urban sprawl probably worse than what exists.

In the twentieth century the suburb became a dominant city form. As with many of the previous planning efforts in the previous two centuries, suburbs developed as a way to escape crowding and other negative aspects of the center city. Modern suburbs first appeared in England and other European countries as those who could afford it built country houses, which could be reached relatively easily from some larger city by means of a network of railroads.

In the United States in the first half of the twentieth century, large suburban developments centered around small towns that had been made more accessible by commuter railroads and an expanding road network. When the population increased after World War II, the suburbs boomed as more and more people wanted the advantages of space, fresh air, light, and a desirable place to raise a family.

As greater numbers of people wanted to move to the suburbs, however, individual plot sizes became smaller and developments sprang up farther from the city. The suburban house surrounded by a small yard became a miniature version of the idealized country estate. As the suburbs grew, so did the need for an even larger network of highways to serve them, as well as for shopping centers to provide necessary services. What became known as *urban sprawl* soon followed.

A fairly recent notion in town planning is the *new town* concept. This is an extension of the idea that entirely new communities can be built away from the crowding and ugliness of existing cities. The idea started in Great Britain in the 1940s and soon spread to the United States and elsewhere. New towns were intended as autonomous centers that included housing, shopping, and business opportunities, surrounded by a greenbelt. Originally, the population was to be limited to about 30,000, but this was later increased to 70,000 and then to 250,000 people.

Several new towns were built in England, but they never became truly independent cities because they lacked significant employment centers and still depended on nearby cities for jobs. In the United States, both Columbia, Maryland, and Reston, Virginia, began as new towns, but suffered from the same problems as their British counterparts. They never became truly separate cities; instead, they depended on the jobs of nearby Washington, DC, and other areas.

New urbanism promotes the connection of neighborhoods and towns to regional patterns of pedestrian, bicycle, and public transit systems while reducing dependence on the automobile.

These new towns and previous visions of utopia have all suffered from the same problems: they are usually static in their conception, and they lack the vitality and interest of a city that has evolved over time.

New urbanism is a more recent planning philosophy that attempts to counter the many undesirable aspects of city development, including suburban sprawl, reliance on the automobile, environmental deterioration, housing segregation, loss of farmland, and single-use development. The movement was begun in the late 1980s with the construction of Seaside, Florida, by Andrès Duany and Elizabeth Plater-Zyberk. Other planners and architects who developed the principles of new urbanism include Peter Calthorpe and Peter Katz.

New urbanism planning concepts are intended to work at the building, neighborhood, district, and regional levels, in new developments as well as urban and suburban infill projects. One of the primary urban design features is the development of neighborhoods intended for mixed use: housing located within walking distance of shops, offices, and other services, and a variety of residential types, from apartments above shops to single-family houses. At the regional level, new urbanism promotes the connection of neighborhoods and towns to regional patterns of pedestrian, bicycle, and public transit systems while reducing dependence on the automobile and establishing connections to open space and natural systems. At the street and building level, new urbanism encourages individual buildings to be integrated with their surroundings, to support the street as a place for pedestrians, and to provide users with a clear sense of location and time. The preservation or reuse of historic structures is also supported.

There are many other precepts of the new urbanism movement, including an emphasis on comprehensive regional planning, a mix of residential types (including affordable housing), safe streets, sustainable design principles, and the integration of civic, institutional, and educational facilities into neighborhoods. Some of the small-scale design features that may be found in new urbanism designs include village squares, backyard garages, front porches, and picket fences.

Development Patterns

The development of a city can be viewed on two scales: the larger scale of the city or metropolitan region and the smaller scale of an individual community and neighborhood.

In the twentieth and twenty-first centuries, the pattern of development at the city scale has been determined primarily by geographic features and the layout of transportation, most notably the highway. In some cases where effective city and regional planning has been undertaken, land use plans have also determined the form of development to a certain degree.

A city established near a major geographic feature, such as by the junction of two rivers or a large body of water, tends to develop along the water first and then expand away from it. When a city begins in less confining circumstances, it tends to grow more or less equally in all directions, usually in a uniform grid pattern.

Since the proliferation of the automobile, cities have tended to expand in a number of typical patterns. These are shown diagrammatically in Fig. 7.4. Each of these patterns has an effect on the planning of smaller-scale communities and neighborhoods, and ultimately on the design of individual building projects.

Figure 7.4 Patterns of Urban Development

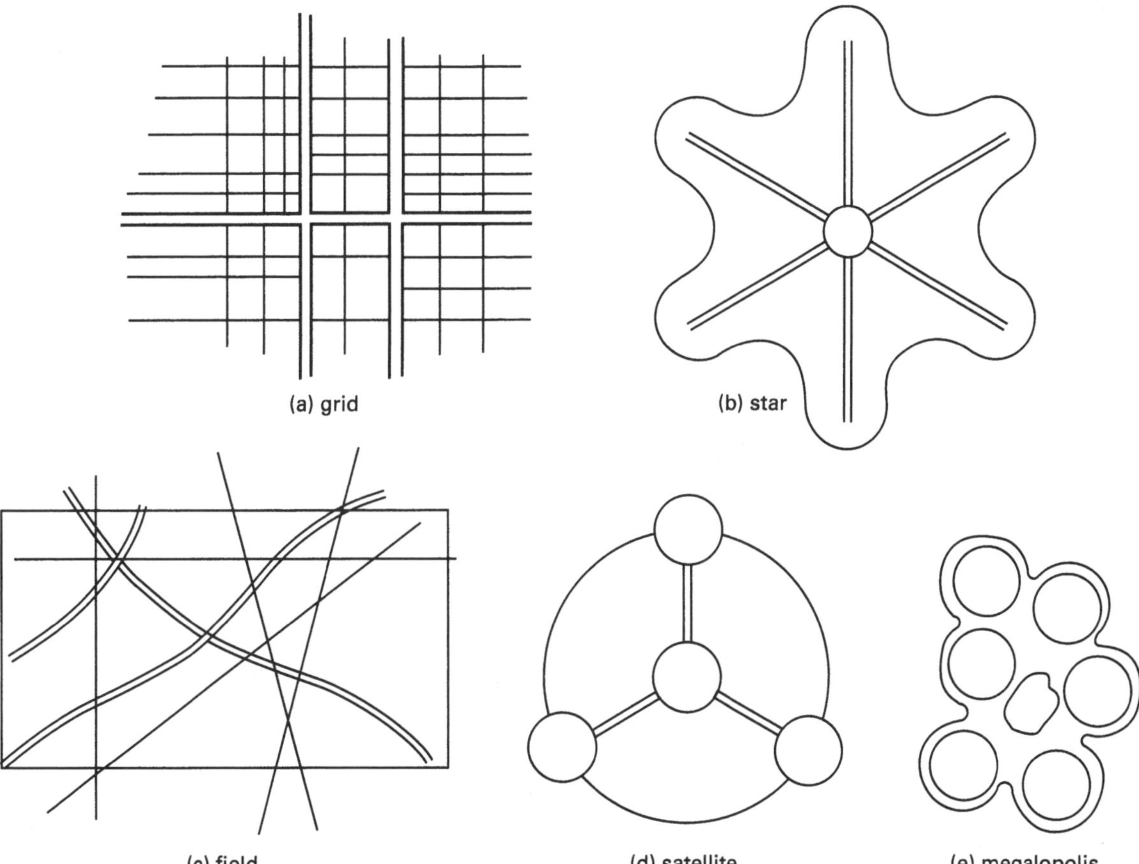

The simplest pattern is the *expanding grid.* In this pattern, the city begins at the junction of two major roads and is methodically laid out in a grid. This pattern is exemplified in the initial plan of Philadelphia. Further growth simply follows the grid pattern until it is stopped by a natural feature, some limit to population, or economics. A strict grid pattern is usually characteristic of smaller cities; larger metropolitan areas in the United States follow other patterns but are almost always filled in with some type of grid. The Commissioners' Plan of 1811 for Manhattan is an example of a grid being superimposed on earlier, organic development, in this case dating from the older city of New Amsterdam on the tip of Manhattan.

The *star pattern* grows out of a dense urban core, with development following the radiating spokes of main highways and mass transit routes out of the center. Higher density development tends to form along the spokes; lower density development tends to fill in the regions between them. The star pattern is similar to the star-shaped city discussed earlier, but developed for reasons other than defense. Chicago is an example of a star-shaped city that developed from railroad and highways radiating from the core (though it takes the shape of only half a star, due to Lake Michigan).

In the *satellite pattern*, a large, dense urban core is surrounded by other major urban areas. The satellite areas are linked to the city in the center by major highways. Often the satellite areas are themselves connected by a circular road system called a *beltway*, making it possible to travel between them without going through the city in the center. The outer urban areas often begin as major shopping areas, peripheral business centers, or transportation centers. Houston is an example of this type of pattern. Often, a satellite pattern starts out as a star pattern.

The *field pattern* has no central focus or apparent overall organization scheme. Development takes place as an amorphous network of highways and natural features. Los Angeles is a typical example of this type of pattern.

The ultimate form of urban development is the *megalopolis*, in which two or more major urban centers near each other grow together as the space between is developed. Many sections of the northeastern United States and Southern California, such as Los Angeles, can be considered megalopolises.

While large-scale urban development can affect the way people view the city and how individual parcels of land are developed, it is within the smaller community and neighborhood scale that architects must plan sites and design buildings. The concept of imageability, first proposed by Kevin Lynch, is useful in linking the urban scale with the community scale.

Imageability is the quality of a physical environment that evokes a strong image in the mind of a given observer. This can be a natural feature or a prominent building or structure. For example, the hills of San Francisco are part of the image of that city in the minds of most people who visit it or live there. These features provoke a mental image of the environment and are vital to orientation, navigating the city, and general well-being.

In his 1960 book *The Image of the City*, Lynch identified five basic elements of the urban image: paths, edges, districts, nodes, and landmarks. These elements are created by buildings, natural features, roads, and other components of the city. New site planning and building design proposals should respond to existing image elements and enhance them if possible.

A *path* is a way of circulation along which people customarily, occasionally, or potentially move. A path may be a street, pedestrian walkway, railroad, transit line, or river. Since circulation is an important part of any physical environment, paths are usually at the center of the image of a city.

An *edge* is a linear element that forms a boundary between two districts or that breaks continuity. An edge could be a shoreline, a line of buildings against a park, a wall, or a similar feature. Sometimes an element can be both a path (if used for circulation) and an edge (if seen from afar). For example, a highway can be perceived as an edge when one is looking at it from within the neighborhood it bounds, and a path when one is traveling on it. Edges may be either solid or penetrable. The line of building development along Central Park in Manhattan is another example of an edge.

A *district* is a two-dimensional area perceived as having some identifying character that distinguishes it from the surrounding city. A district can be perceived from the inside, or can be identified as an element of the city from the outside. Back Bay in Boston and Georgetown in Washington, DC, are two examples of districts.

A *node* is a focal point or center of interest that people can enter. A node could be an intersection of paths, a place where the mode of transportation changes, a plaza or public square, or the center of a district.

A *landmark* is similar to a node in that it is a reference point, but a landmark is viewed from the exterior and may or may not be entered. A tower, monument, building, or natural feature can be a landmark.

Many of the large-scale elements of imageability are interwoven with the smaller community and neighborhood. However, there are additional patterns of development that are also intimately related to an individual site. One is the street pattern. Initially, community and neighborhood development followed the layout of the streets. Blocks between streets were subdivided into lots, and each lot was developed as a separate entity, privately owned, independent, and developed with little regard for its surroundings. Although this development method persists, other approaches have emerged.

One of these approaches is the *superblock*, which is an outgrowth of the new town concept. This is shown in Fig. 7.5. One of the first trials of this development scheme took place in the new town of Radburn, New Jersey, planned by Henry Wright. There, the attempt was made to plan a large piece of land with limited intrusion of the automobile. The superblock is surrounded by a continuous street, and vehicular access is provided with cul-de-sacs.

The superblock concept minimizes the impact of the car on housing and allows the development of pedestrian circulation and park space within the block. This concept was used in the planning of Chandigarh, India, by Le Corbusier, and of Brasilia by Lucio Costa and Oscar Niemeyer. In theory, the separation of the automobile on the side of the house that faces the street from the pedestrian and living area on the other side seems to be an admirable goal. However, because much of contemporary life revolves around the automobile, this separation can be counterproductive to neighborhood social interaction. As a result, the driveways and parking spaces in superblocks are often used more than the quiet park spaces.

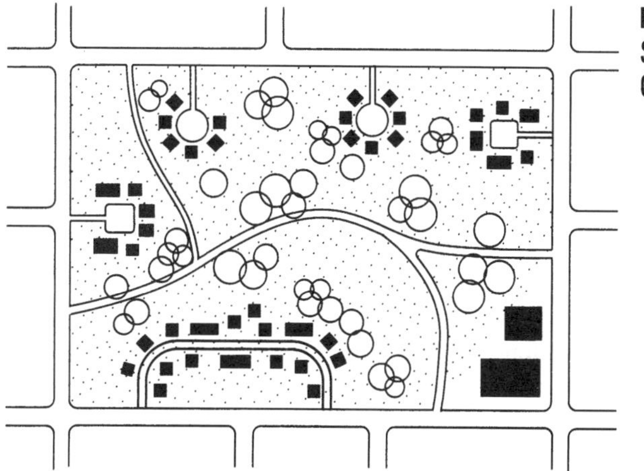

Figure 7.5
Superblock Concept

A variation and extension of the superblock idea is the *planned unit development*, or PUD. With this approach, each large parcel of land is designed to have a mix of uses—residential, commercial, recreational, and open space—and is designed with a variety of lot sizes and densities. Industrial developments can also be planned as PUDs. PUDs must conform to certain standards as communicated by the local planning agency and must be approved by the planning agency, but within the restrictions the planner has wide latitude in determining how the site is developed.

The standards for PUDs include the permitted uses, total floor area ratio (ratio of developed floor space to land area), amount of open space required, number and configuration of parking spaces required, living space ratio (open space less parking space), maximum building heights, and required setbacks at the perimeter of the PUD and proximity of the structures within.

PUDs offer many advantages. They make more efficient use of land by grouping compatible uses without the setback regulations of zoning ordinances. This grouping allows the extra land to be allocated for open space or common use areas. PUDs also provide a variety of housing options, from single-family detached to row houses to high-rise apartments and condominiums, and recapture some of the diversity and variety of urban living that many people find desirable.

Transit-oriented development is becoming more popular as cities work to connect areas of urban sprawl with each other and with downtown areas through construction of light-rail, subways, and other mass transit. Transit-oriented development is construction that takes place in areas surrounding transit stops; it usually includes a relatively high density of living units, commercial development, and other support services. The idea is that residents can live, work, eat, and take care of day-to-day needs without an automobile, and use the transit facility to travel to other parts of the city.

The Effects of Development Patterns on Social Behavior

Physical environment affects human behavior. This is true at any scale, from the plan of a city to the arrangement of furniture in a room. A great deal of research has been conducted in the field of environmental psychology. The results of this research have not always been conclusive, but some theories have been shown to provide a reliable basis for making design decisions.

Density is a characteristic of human settlements, the number of people per unit of area. A city neighborhood with multi-story apartment buildings might have a density of 50 people per acre, while a suburban neighborhood may have only two or three families per acre, each in its own single-family home. Rural or agricultural communities may have an average density of less than one person per acre, with most of the land being undeveloped woodland or devoted to crops.

Density is a ratio, so it doesn't give the total number of people or how they are distributed throughout the area. A density of 50 people per acre could mean 50 people evenly distributed over one acre or 500 people housed in a few high-rise buildings in one corner of an otherwise uninhabited 10-acre land parcel.

For a long time, high population density has been equated with undesirable living conditions. However, research has shown that there is much more involved when talking about density. The first consideration is that density should not be confused with crowding. Four people sharing a bedroom is crowding, but if each of the same four people had adequate personal space while sharing the same overall living space, they probably would not feel crowded, even though the density would be unchanged.

The perception of crowding also depends on cultural influences and circumstances. People from some cultures tend to find living in close proximity normal and desirable, whereas people from other cultures tend to find the same density crowded. Similarly, being in a densely packed restaurant for a few hours would not seem like crowding to most people, but trying to relax on a park bench at the same density would be uncomfortable.

Regardless of the interpretation of density, there are limits to the density under which people can comfortably live, work, and play, depending on cultural context. Studies have shown that excessive density can cause poor physical and mental health and can spawn a variety of antisocial behaviors.

Different cultures and socioeconomic groups respond to and use physical environments differently. The entire range of a particular group's pattern of living, working, playing, and socializing may flourish under one kind of environment and suffer under another. Taking cultural and social differences into account when designing housing and other facilities is critical to the success of a project.

Regardless of the specific culture of a group, all people need and want social interaction with family, friends, neighbors, and other groups to which they belong. A building, neighborhood, or city can promote or hinder such interaction. By providing spaces to gather, to watch other people, to cross paths, and to meet informally, the architect can encourage this vital part of human life.

Spaces, buildings, rooms, and even furniture can be considered sociopetal if they tend to bring people together. A group of chairs facing each other, circular gathering spaces, and radial street plans are examples of sociopetal environments. Sociofugal conditions are those that do the opposite, tending to discourage interaction or social contact.

In addition to interaction, people need a place they can call their own, whether it is a house, a seat at a conference table, or one end of a park bench. Territoriality is a fundamental part of animal behavior, humans included. When a desk at the office is personalized with family pictures, plants, individual coffee mugs, and the like, the person who sits there stakes a claim to a personal territory, small and temporary as it may be. In a more permanent living environment, such as a house or apartment, territorial boundaries are provided by walls, fences, and property lines. Boundaries are often more subtle. A street, a row of trees, or something very small such as a change in level may serve to define a person's or group's territory.

Closely related to territoriality is the concept of *personal space* that surrounds each individual. Anthropologist Edward T. Hall was the first to propose that there are four basic distances that can be used to study human behavior and serve as a guide for designing environments. The actual dimensions of the four distances vary with the circumstances and with cultural and social differences, but they always exist.

The closest is intimate distance. This ranges from physical contact to a distance of about 6 in to 18 in. People only allow others to come within this distance under special conditions. If forced this close together, such as on a crowded bus, people employ defense mechanisms, such as avoiding eye contact, to minimize the effect of the physical contact.

The next distance is personal distance, ranging from about $1\frac{1}{2}$ ft; personal distance extends to about $2\frac{1}{2}$ ft for some cultures, more for others. If given the choice, people will maintain this distance between themselves and other people.

Social distance is the next zone, ranging from about 4 ft to 12 ft. This is the distance used for business communication, interactions with strangers or new acquaintances, and other more formal or impersonal situations.

Public distance is the farthest zone, ranging from about 12 ft outward. This distance is used for lectures, ceremonies, theater, and other occasions involving large audiences or a high degree of formality. This distance also allows people to leave easily if they sense danger or unpleasantness.

The architect should be aware of personal distance needs and design accordingly. Forcing people closer than the situation suggests can affect them negatively.

Closely related to territoriality is the concept of personal space that surrounds each individual.

Another principle concerning the effects of development patterns on social behavior is *diversity*. People need diverse and stimulating environments. In a monotonous urban setting, community, or building, people tend to suffer some type of negative influence, such as becoming depressed or irritated. Over a long period of time, living in a dull, unstimulating environment can even affect personality development.

Environment can also affect criminal behavior and its prevention. In his 1972 book, *Defensible Space*, Oscar Newman described a range of design elements that used the basic concepts of surveillance, territoriality, and real and symbolic barriers to reduce crime. For example, instead of having the entry to an apartment building open directly to the public area of a street, a low wall outside the front entrance indicates a separation of public and semipublic space. A large window placed next to the front door allows residents and passersby to observe activity both inside and outside the door.

Newman further developed these ideas in a later, expanded volume called *Creating Defensible Space*. More recently, the concepts of defensible space have inspired the newer term *crime prevention through environmental design* (CPTED). Newman's research showed that relatively simple changes in design could reduce criminal behavior. CPTED takes the idea further and adds other methods such as electronic surveillance, alarms, and human resources. See Chap. 12 for a discussion of site security.

Example 7.1

An accounting firm occupies a building in a suburban office park. To accommodate the growth planned for the next two years, the firm needs at least twice the space it now occupies. The owner is considering four options.

- A medium-size undeveloped lot on the border of a residential zone and a commercial zone. There is enough space for a new building, a small photovoltaic array to supplement electricity, and plenty of parking. The remaining open space can be left undeveloped.
- An abandoned, single-story warehouse that has been condemned. It was previously used to store books and clothing. There is no evidence of chemical contamination. It is surrounded by other industrial buildings and is within walking distance of an active downtown district with public transportation.

Programming & Analysis

- A vacancy in a three-story office building adjacent to the firm's current location. The building is about 25 years old and has been fairly well maintained. The space would need to be remodeled to meet the needs of the firm.
- Using a space behind the existing location to build an addition that would double the current area. The business would be able to stay open during construction.

Sustainability is an important factor, and the owner is willing to spend more money in order to minimize environmental impact. Which of the four options is most suitable?

(A) the undeveloped site

(B) the abandoned warehouse

(C) the adjacent office building

(D) the addition

Solution

Developing an existing site would have the largest environmental impact. Building an addition to an existing building or developing an existing site such as the abandoned warehouse would have less environmental impact than a brand new building, but these options would still have a larger impact than using an existing building. Moving into the existing adjacent office building has the smallest environmental impact.

The answer is (C).

COMMUNITY INFLUENCES ON DESIGN

Catchment Areas

Nearly all land development is dependent on or affected by some surrounding base of population. The geographical region this population resides within is the *catchment area.* For example, the developer of a grocery store may base a decision about whether to build at a proposed location on how many people live within a certain distance of the site. The population within this catchment area is the primary market for the services of the store. In a similar way, a school district may be the catchment area for a particular school building.

The boundaries of a catchment area may be determined by physical features such as highways and rivers, by artificial political boundaries such as city lines and school district limits, or by more nebulous demarcations such as the division between two ethnic neighborhoods. Often when a site location study is being made the developer knows that a certain number of people must reside within a specified distance from the proposed site to make the project economically feasible. By using population information from census data or other types of surveys, it can be determined whether the catchment area will support the commercial development.

The boundaries of a catchment area and the number of people within it can depend on several factors. Boundaries are often determined by the availability of transportation. A convenience store that depends on neighborhood customers who walk to the store will have a catchment area with closer boundaries than will a shopping center accessible by major highways. A residential catchment area may increase in population as the population of the overall region increases, either because of an expansion in the borders of the catchment area (such as a new residential development on previously undeveloped land) or with the construction of new housing (such as a new high-rise replacing lower-density housing or a vacant lot). Conversely, the expansion of an employment center may create more demand for workers, increasing both the geographical size and the population of the center's catchment area.

In many cases, knowing just the gross population within a catchment area is not enough to make development decisions; the composition of the catchment area must also be known. For example, the developer of a high-end retail store needs to know how many people or families whose average income is over a particular amount reside within a certain distance from the store site. A school district needs to know how many children within a particular age group reside within an area. This kind of information is usually available from census data and local planning agencies.

Accessibility to Transportation

Transportation of all types is critical to the selection and development of a building site. This is true on all scales, from accessibility by major freeways to the individual road system, public transit, and pedestrian paths around a small site. Something as simple as a one-way street that makes the site more difficult to enter from one direction may be enough to render the property undesirable for some uses.

A number of considerations should be examined when analyzing a site for development.

- Is the highway system adequate to bring the catchment area population to the site?
- Are there adequate traffic counts for businesses that depend on drive-by trade?
- Would enough additional traffic be created to overload the existing road system? Would new roads need to be built? Would existing roads need to be expanded?
- Is there adequate access for trucks servicing the site?
- Does the surrounding transportation network create an undesirable environment for the development? For example, a small site bounded by two freeways may be too noisy for an apartment building.
- Is there safe and convenient pedestrian access to the site? Is it needed?
- Is there public transportation nearby? How will people get from the mass transit stops to the site? This is especially important for transit-oriented development.
- If this is an industrial project, are rail lines available?

Neighborhoods

Any development project becomes an intimate part of the area in which it is located. Architects must be sensitive to the existing fabric of a neighborhood and how existing conditions may influence how a project is designed, as well as to the impact the project may have on the surroundings. A *neighborhood* is a relatively small area in which a number of people live and share similar needs and desires in housing, social activities, and other aspects of day-to-day living.

The concept of the neighborhood as a part of city planning was first developed by Clarence Perry in 1929. Although his ideas had physical design implications, they were proposed mainly as a way of bringing people together to discuss common problems and become involved in the planning process. His ideal way of accomplishing this was to plan the neighborhood unit as an area within walking distance of an elementary school, which would serve as the community center for neighborhood activity. Perry also proposed that major streets should be at the boundaries of neighborhoods rather than running through them, so that neighborhood children could walk to and from school without having to cross a major street.

The neighborhood has become the basic planning unit for contemporary American urban design. This is in part due to the need for a manageable size on which to base city planning, as well as to the increased importance placed on citizen participation in the planning process, as suggested by Perry. The neighborhood is the level of scale that most people can readily identify with and understand, the part of a city that people come in contact with daily and that most influences their lives.

Site development must be sensitive to the existing neighborhood. This can include respecting pedestrian paths, maintaining the size and scale of the surrounding buildings, using similar or compatible materials, not creating uses that conflict with the surroundings, respecting views and access to important structures in the area, and trying to fit within the general context of the district.

Public Facilities

Public facilities include such places as schools, shops, fire stations, places of worship, post offices, and recreational centers. Their availability, location, and relative importance in a neighborhood can affect how a site is developed. For example, if a church is the center of social activity in a neighborhood, the designer should maintain easy access to it. Surrounding development should be subordinate to or compatible with it, and the designer should give consideration to maintaining views or enhancing the church's prominence in the community. In another community, the path from a school to a recreation center may have special importance. The neighborhood may want the link maintained and improved by any new construction planned along the way.

Example 7.2

A multistory residential building is proposed for an undeveloped property. The following observations are made during a site visit.

- The property is located in an upper midwestern state that regularly sees snow in the winter months.
- The northeastern edge of the property is considered a wetland.
- There is a small detention area on the adjacent property to the west that drains through the north side of the owner's property to the wetland area.
- The site is accessible from an existing cul-de-sac on the south-west border of the property.

Taking energy conservation into account, which of the following design options would be the best for building orientation and parking location?

(A) Orient the building on the east side of the property with a north-south axis and the parking to the west.

(B) Orient the building on the north side of the property with an east-west axis and the parking to the south.

(C) Orient the building on the west side of the property with a north-south axis and the parking to the east.

(D) Orient the building on the south side of the property with an east-west axis and the parking to the north.

Solution

Location on the property is less important than the axis of the building. Maintaining an east-west axis will allow the building to take advantage of solar heat and light, potentially reducing heating and electric costs. Locating the building to the north provides better access for parking to the south and, potentially, a better view to the north.

The answer is (B).

PSYCHOLOGICAL AND SOCIAL INFLUENCES

Developing physical environments that respond to people's psychological needs is one of the most difficult tasks in programming. Although there has been a great deal of research in the field of environmental psychology, predicting human behavior and designing spaces and buildings that enhance people's lives is an inexact process. Still, the architect must create a realistic approximation of the people who will be using the proposed environment and understand the nature of their activities. This model can then serve as the foundation on which many design decisions involving both site planning and building design are based.

During programming, the architect should make a clear distinction between the client and the actual users. They are not always the same. For example, a public housing agency may be the client for a subsidized housing complex, but the actual users will be the people who live there, who may have entirely different values and lifestyles from those developing the program.

Environmental psychology is a complex subject, but a good starting point is to get familiar with the following concepts.

Proxemics

Proxemics is a term coined by Edward T. Hall to mean "the interrelated observations and theories of man's use of space as a specialized elaboration of culture." Proxemics deals with issues of spacing between people, territoriality, organization of space, and positioning of people in the space, as related to the culture of which they are a part. Some of these issues are discussed in the following sections.

Behavior Settings

A *behavior setting* can be thought of as a place with defined boundaries in which a standing pattern of behavior occurs at a particular time; the place may also contain objects that support the behavior. For example, the weekly meeting of a board of directors in a particular conference room can be considered a behavior setting. The activity of the meeting follows certain procedures (call to order, reading of minutes, discussions, and so forth), it occurs in the same place (the conference room), and the contents of the room are arranged to assist the activity (chairs are arranged around a table, audiovisual facilities are present, lighting is adequate).

Behavior settings are useful for studying and understanding the effects of the environment on human activity. The concept is useful for the architect because it connects the behavioral aspects of human activity with the effects of the physical environment on people. Although a behavior setting is a complex system of activities, human goals, administrative requirements, physical objects, and cultural needs, it provides the architect with a definable unit of design. By knowing the people involved and the activities taking place, the architect can develop programmatic concepts that support the setting.

Territoriality

As mentioned previously, *territoriality* is a fundamental aspect of human behavior. It refers to the need to lay claim to the spaces we occupy and the things we own. Although partially based on the innate need for protection, territoriality in humans is more related to the desire to express self-identity and freedom of choice. In addition to claiming objects and larger spaces in the environment, people also protect their own personal space, the bubble of comfortable distance from others that varies with different circumstances.

Territoriality applies to groups as well as to individuals. A study club, school class, or street gang can claim a physical territory as their own, which helps give both the group and each individual in the group an identity. Environments should allow people to claim territory and make choices about where to be and what activities to engage in.

Personalization

One of the ways territoriality manifests is through the *personalization* of space. Whether in the home, at the office desk, or in a waiting lounge, people need to arrange the environment to reflect their presence and uniqueness. The most successful designs allow this to take place without major adverse effects on other people or on the environment as a whole. At home, people decorate the space the way they want. At the office, people bring in personal objects, family photographs, and other items to make the space their own. In an airport lounge, people place coats and suitcases around them, not only to stake out a temporary territory but also to make the waiting time more personal and a little more comfortable.

Another way space is personalized is by modifying the environment. If a given space does not meet the needs of the person using it, behavior can be modified to adapt to the environment, the relationship to the environment can be changed (by leaving), or minor adjustments can be made to the environment. The simple act of moving a chair to make viewing a screen easier is an example of modifying and personalizing a space. If the chair is fixed, the design is not as adaptable to the varying needs of its users.

Group Interaction

To a certain extent, the physical environment can either facilitate or hinder human interaction. In most behavior settings, groups are predisposed to act in a particular way. If the setting is not conducive to these activities, the environment or behavior is modified to make the activity work. In extreme cases, if the setting is totally at odds with the activity taking place there, stress, anger, and other adverse reactions can occur.

Seating arrangement is one of the most common ways of facilitating group interaction. Studies have shown that people will seat themselves at a table according to the nature of their relationships with others around them. For intimate conversation, two people will sit across the corner of a table from one another or next to each other on a sofa. For more formal situations or when people are competing, they will sit across from one another. Where social contact is not desired, two people will take chairs at opposite corners of a table.

Round tables tend to foster more cooperation and equality among those seated. Rectangular tables tend to make cooperation more difficult and establish the person sitting at the end in a superior position. Strangers do not like to share the same sofa or park bench. Knowing the people and activities expected in a place can help the architect make decisions. For example, individual study carrels in a library will be more efficient than large tables because the tables will seldom be fully occupied by strangers.

Studies have shown that when people interact in informal groups, more than 97% of the groups they form will contain two to four people. Designing to accommodate groups of this size makes more sense than anticipating groups of more people; a flexible plan that can accommodate very large groups when needed as well as meet the needs of small groups is the best combination. In most cases, providing a variety of spaces for interaction is the best approach.

Status

The physical environment can communicate status symbolically. To some people, importance is conveyed by the design of a colonial house or a classically designed bank with a large lobby. In the United States, a corner office is perceived as giving its occupant a higher status than an office with only one exterior wall; in many cultures the size of an office is also equated with status. A house in an affluent neighborhood confers higher status on its owner than one in a less affluent neighborhood.

Status can also operate at the scale of an entire building or complex. A client may want a new building to symbolize some quality of the organization and give him or her physical and psychological status in the community.

The architectural programmer should investigate the needs and implications of status. Some clients will state their status-related goals clearly; with others, the programmer must raise the issue, explore it with the client, and document the response as a programmatic concept.

Example 7.3

While considering development of a site, the owner suspects that part of the land may include a 100-year floodplain. Which of these agencies can confirm the location of this plain?

(A) U.S. Forestry Service (USFS)

(B) U.S. Army Corps of Engineers (USACE)

(C) State Department of Natural Resources (DNR)

(D) U.S. Geological Survey (USGS)

Solution

The USGS keeps topographical information on all parts of the United States, including the location of floodplains.

The answer is (D).

TRANSPORTATION AND UTILITY INFLUENCES

This section reviews some general guidelines for analyzing the transportation and utilities servicing a site. Review Chap. 12 for more detailed design criteria.

Roads

Roads provide a primary means of access to a site. Their availability and capacity may be prime determinants in whether and how a parcel of land can be developed. There are four basic categories of roads: local, collector, arterial, and expressway.

Local streets have the lowest capacity and provide direct access to building sites. They may be in the form of a continuous grid or curvilinear system, or they may be cul-de-sacs or loops. Parking is often available on the street or in nearby parking lots or garages, and the local street connects to the pedestrian circulation system.

Collector streets connect local streets with large arterial streets. Collector streets have a higher capacity than local streets, but are usually not intended for through traffic. Intersections of collector and local roads may be controlled by stop signs, whereas intersections of collector streets and arterial streets will be controlled with stop lights.

Arterial streets are major, continuous circulation routes that carry large amounts of traffic on two or three lanes. They usually connect collector streets to expressways. Parking is typically not allowed on an arterial street, and direct access from arterial streets to building sites should be avoided.

Expressways are limited access roads designed to move large volumes of traffic between, through, and around population centers. Intersections are made by various types of ramp systems, and pedestrian access is not allowed. Expressways have a major influence on the land due to the space they require and their noise and visual impact.

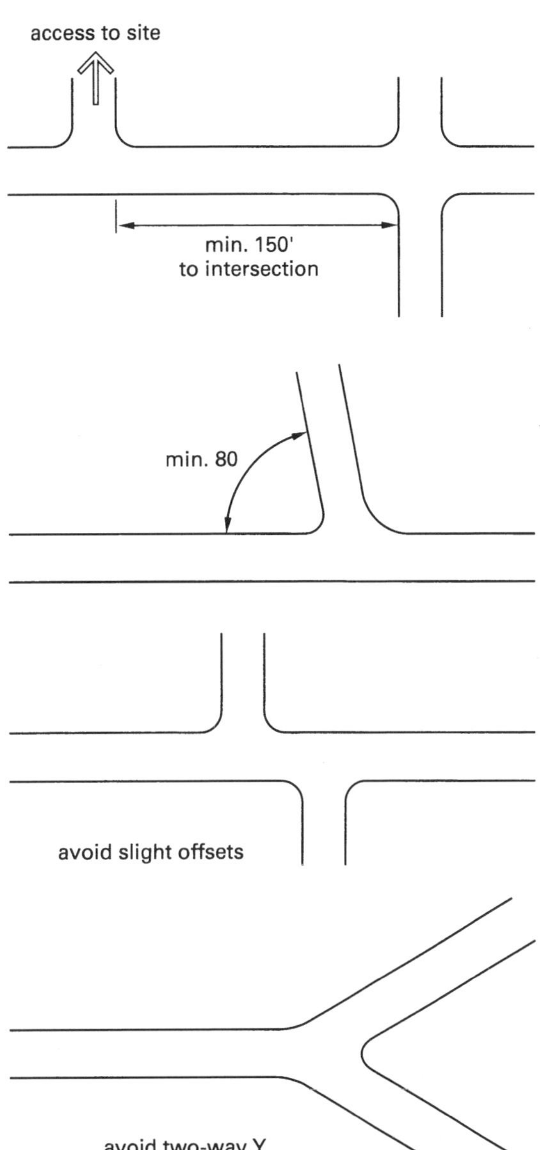

Figure 7.6 Guidelines for Road Layout at Intersections

Site analysis must take into account the existing configuration of the street system and fit new site access points into the hierarchy of roads. Entrances and exits from the site must be planned to minimize congestion and dangerous intersections. Figure 7.6 illustrates some general guidelines for road layout.

A road must be laid out both horizontally and vertically; that is, its *horizontal alignment* and *vertical alignment* must both be designed. A straight section of a road is called a *tangent.* A curved section should form the arc of a circle, and the curve must have a large enough radius to let a vehicle be steered easily and safely. Simple curves of uniform radius between tangents are preferred; a curve of changing radius should be avoided.

There should generally be at least 100 ft between curves in opposite directions and 200 ft between curves in the same direction, but the dimensions of the roadway are influenced by a number of factors, such as the requirements of the state's transportation department, the speed at which vehicles are expected to be traveling, and existing site topography and features.

Vertical alignment must be designed to provide smooth transitions when the grade of the road changes and to avoid overly steep grades. For most streets, the maximum grade ranges from 3% to 10%, depending on terrain, design speed, and the function of the street.

Public Transit

The availability and location of public transit lines can influence site design. This is especially true of transit-oriented development. A site analysis should include determining the types of public access available (whether bus, subway, light- or heavy-rail line, or taxi stop) and its location relative to the site. Building entrances and major site features should be conveniently located near public transit. In large cities, site development may have to include provisions for public access to subway and rail lines.

Service Access

Service access to a site may include provisions for truck loading, moving vans, and daily delivery services. Ideally, service access should be separate from automobile and pedestrian access. Loading dock berths and enough space for large trucks to turn in may need to be provided. Local zoning ordinances usually specify the number and size of loading berths, but generally they should be 10 ft to 12 ft wide, at least 40 ft long, and have a 14 ft vertical clearance. A minimum turning radius of 60 ft should be provided unless some other maneuvering method is possible.

Utilities

Site analysis includes determining the availability, location, and capacity of existing utilities. The development potential of a site depends on the availability of water, sanitary sewers, storm sewers, communication service, gas service, electric service, and other necessary public utilities. Having to extend utility lines from a distance can add greatly to the cost of development.

Generally, utility lines follow the street layout and right-of-way. Sanitary sewers, storm sewers, and water mains are generally located under the road, whereas electric and communication lines are adjacent to the roads, either underground or on poles. Gas lines may either be under the road or next to it within the right-of-way. Utilities can also be located in *easements*, portions of privately owned land that public utility companies are permitted to use for the installation and maintenance of their lines.

When new services must be installed, the location of sanitary and storm sewer lines takes precedence over other types of utility lines because sewers must use the flow of gravity and therefore depend on the natural slope of the land. Collection systems drain to municipal disposal systems or to private, on-site treatment facilities.

Municipal Services

Depending on the location of the site, municipal services may include police protection, fire protection, trash removal, and street cleaning. The development site plan must provide access for these services, which may require large areas of land. For example, local fire protection officials may require an unobstructed strip of land around buildings to allow for fire fighting, in addition to suitable access roads from the street to the building. In some climates, adequate provisions must be made for snow removal or snow stacking.

CLIMATIC INFLUENCES

Climatic analysis must consider both the macroclimate and the microclimate. The macroclimate is the overall climate of the region and is reflected in the weather data available from the National Weather Service. From this information a region can be classified as cool, temperate, hot-arid, or hot-humid. More detailed climate zones have been defined as discussed in Chap. 9 and shown in Fig. 9.2.

The *microclimate* is the site-specific modification of the *macroclimate* by such features as land slope, trees and other vegetation, bodies of water, and buildings.

The microclimate of a site can have a significant influence on its development; undesirable climatic effects can be minimized by careful planning, and desirable effects can be used to enhance the comfort of the inhabitants.

Wind Patterns

Both prevailing wind patterns and microclimate wind effects must be studied during site analysis. Buildings can then be located to take advantage of breezes or to avoid cold winds. Wind speed on the top of a hill, for example, can be about 20% higher than wind speed on flat ground. The leeward side of a hill (the side away from the wind direction) experiences less wind than the windward side. Near large bodies of water, warm air rises over the warmer land during the day and causes a breeze from the water. At night the pattern may be reversed; cold air flows down a hill and settles in low-lying regions, causing pockets that remain colder than higher elevations during the early part of the day. On a large scale, this can result in an inversion, a weather pattern in which colder air near the ground is held in place by the warmer air above it, trapping dust and pollution.

Wind patterns can be modified by buildings and trees. Trees planted in a group 50 ft to 150 ft deep can reduce wind velocity from 30% to 60%, depending on the density of the trees, at a distance of 10 times the tree height. The wind velocity is reduced to about half that at a distance of 20 times the tree height. Buildings can similarly modify wind effects and patterns (see Chap. 44).

In temperate climates, the best microclimates when considering just the wind are generally found on south- or southeast-facing slopes, in the middle or toward the top, rather than at the very top or bottom of the slope.

Solar Orientation

How much solar radiation reaches any given spot on the ground depends on the angle of the sun's rays to the ground. In general, when the sun is high in the sky, more light is reaching the ground at each point than when the sun is low. This is both because the light has traveled a shorter distance through the atmosphere (which reflects and absorbs portions of the energy) and because the light that does reach the ground is concentrated in a smaller area (compare a flashlight beam hitting a wall perpendicularly against the same beam hitting a wall at an angle).

At the macroclimate scale, the two main reasons that summer is warmer than winter are that the sun is higher in the sky and that days are longer. The steeper angle of the sun also accounts for the fact that latitudes nearer to the equator are warmer than latitudes nearer to the poles.

At the microclimate scale, in the Northern Hemisphere south-facing slopes tend to be warmer, especially in the winter, than other slope orientations or flat surfaces. Ski runs in northern latitudes, for example, are usually located on north-facing mountains to avoid the direct radiation of the sun.

Natural materials such as grass and vegetation have low albedos; snow and pavement have high albedos.

The amount of radiation absorbed or reflected from a surface is affected by the surface material. The fraction of the radiant energy received on a surface that is reflected is called the *albedo* or *solar reflectance* (SR) and is expressed as a number from zero to 1.0. A flat black surface that absorbs all the energy striking it and reflects none has an albedo of zero; a mirror that reflects all the energy striking it and absorbs none has an albedo of 1.0. Natural materials such as grass and vegetation have low albedos; snow and pavement have high albedos.

A material's albedo is closely related to its *reflectivity*. In the LEED rating system, reflectivity is used to measure the solar heat rejection of non-roof materials such as vegetation, shading devices, and other less reflective components. Like albedo, reflectivity has a value from zero to 1.0.

Inversely related to albedo is *emissivity*, which is the ability of a surface to emit stored energy. Like albedo, emissivity values can range from zero to 1.0. For an opaque surface, emissivity and albedo add up to 1.0. *Thermal emittance*, sometimes called just *emittance*, is a similar measure of thermal radiation.

The *solar reflectance index* (SRI) is a measure of a roof's ability to reject solar heat, defined so that a standard black surface (with reflectivity of 0.05 and emittance of 0.90) has an SRI of zero, and a standard white surface (with reflectivity of 0.80 and emittance of 0.90) has an SRI of 100. A perfectly reflective surface would have an SRI of about 122.

The LEED rating system combines the SRI value of the roof and the SR values of non-roof surfaces to set minimum requirements for achieving points for the heat island reduction credit. Materials with the highest SRI and SR are the coolest and the most appropriate choices for mitigating the *heat island effect*, the unnatural buildup of heat around buildings, especially in urban areas. The use of cool roofs to reduce the heat island effect is discussed in Chap. 12 and Chap. 27.

Other ways of mitigating the heat island effect and keeping temperatures cooler around a building include planting trees for shade and specifying open-grid paving. Where practical, use of vegetation is preferred to high-albedo materials such as light-colored concrete, because vegetation retains less heat, is more comfortable underfoot, and minimizes stormwater runoff.

SUSTAINABLE DESIGN

Sustainable building design (also known as *green building*) is an increasingly important part of architectural design. Sustainable design includes a wide range of concerns including the environmental impact of a building, the wise use of materials, energy conservation, use of alternative energy sources, adaptive reuse of existing buildings and facilities, indoor air quality, recycling, reuse of building materials, and other strategies to achieve a balance between the consumption of environmental resources and the renewal of those resources.

Sustainable design considers the full life cycle of a building and the materials it comprises. This includes considering the impact of raw material extraction through its fabrication, installation, operation, maintenance, and disposal.

This section discusses sustainable design as it affects preliminary site evaluation, site selection, and the development of project concepts. Refer to Chap. 9 for more detailed information on alternative energy systems and how sustainability principles can be applied to site planning and building design. Refer to Chap. 13 for information on new material technologies, hazardous material mitigation, indoor air quality, energy conservation, and adaptive reuse.

General Ecological Considerations

Ecology is the study of the relation of living organisms to their environments. Although a building is not a living being, designers must understand how the construction of new buildings, modification of the landscape, and use of resources will affect the surrounding natural environment.

This concern has been codified with the requirement that federal agencies file environmental impact statements (EISs). An environmental impact statement is used to analyze and predict how development will affect the environment, including the air, water, land, and wildlife. This requirement was instituted as a provision of the National Environmental Policy Act of 1969 and is enforced by the Environmental Protection Agency (EPA). Many states have similar laws that require EISs for state-sponsored development. Even if a privately developed project is not required to file an EIS, the designer should be cognizant of the impact of smaller-scale building on the surroundings, whether the environment is rural or in the heart of the city.

One concern that should be investigated during site analysis for semirural or rural development is the potential impact on natural landforms, water runoff, wildlife, and existing vegetation. The development should disturb the natural contours of the land as little as possible. Existing drainage patterns must be left intact, and additional runoff caused by impervious roofs and paving should not exceed the capacity of the existing drainage facilities. The development should also avoid significantly disturbing existing ecological systems of plants and wildlife.

Urban sites require a slightly different approach. The relationship of the building and its users to the surrounding environment remains a factor, but the impact of this relationship is more on artificial systems than on natural ecosystems. The proposed development should minimize the production of noise, pollution, or other detrimental emissions. Buildings should be placed so as to avoid creating undesirable wind conditions, either on the site itself or around nearby buildings.

The effects of blocking sunlight to adjacent buildings and outdoor spaces should be studied and minimized when possible. Similarly, the development should avoid any possible annoying reflection or glare on neighboring buildings. Finally, the impact of development on the utility and transportation systems that serve the building must be thoroughly understood. Specific guidelines for achieving these goals are given in the following sections and in Chap. 13.

Wetlands

A *wetland* is defined by the Environmental Protection Agency as an area whose soil is inundated or saturated by surface water or groundwater frequently enough that it can support plants that are adapted to living in saturated soil. Wetlands are sometimes also referred to as *jurisdictional wetlands* when they are administered by the U.S. Army Corps of Engineers. In the United States, wetlands are protected by the federal government through the Clean Water Act of 1972 (CWA). States and local governmental jurisdictions may also have regulations related to wetlands.

Wetlands regulations are aimed at protecting wetlands and areas interrelated with them from damage due to nearby development, discharge of dredged or fill material, and outright destruction. Discharge into wetlands may be allowed, but Sec. 404 of the CWA requires a permit from the U.S. Army Corps of Engineers, except for certain farming and forestry activities.

Site Analysis

Other sustainability issues that should also be considered when analyzing a site include the following.

- Determine what sites or portions of a site are not suitable for development. These include wetlands, sites within 100 ft of wetlands, elevations lower than 5 ft above a 100-year floodplain, habitats for endangered species, potential historic sites (e.g., burial grounds), and prime farmland.
- Determine the historical and cultural qualities of the surrounding area. If these are significant, it may suggest that new development should reflect the massing, architectural style, and landscape design of surrounding development to integrate with the community and preserve the area's cultural heritage.
- Analyze what types of development might surround the site in the future. Such development could affect the location of the building, connection with transportation or other infrastructure, solar access, local microclimate, view corridors, and shared facilities such as parking and service access.
- Analyze existing air quality. This should be done by a qualified laboratory or service and should include an assessment of the existing air quality as well as an estimation of the effects of the proposed development on air quality in the area.
- Have the soil and groundwater tested for contamination. Contaminated soil or water can make the proposed project infeasible or affect building location and mitigation methods.
- Determine the presence of endangered species. These may include plants, insects, and animals.

SUSTAINABLE SITE AND BUILDING CONCEPTS

The early stages of project planning and site analysis offer many ways to help create a sustainable project. The following sustainability guidelines may affect project concepts.

Building Location

- Give preference to urban sites or other sites with existing infrastructure, to minimize disruption of undeveloped land and maximize efficient use of transportation and utility services.
- Encourage mixed-use development of residential, commercial, retail, and entertainment facilities, to give people the option of living near the buildings where they work and do much of their shopping and recreation.
- Locate buildings near public transportation and bicycle or pedestrian routes.
- Locate buildings in such a way as to minimize tree and vegetation clearing, take advantage of solar access, and minimize the detrimental effects of wind.
- Minimize solar shadows on adjacent properties with setbacks or low building heights.
- Locate buildings in such a way as to maximize desirable airflow patterns.
- Locate buildings in such a way as to use gravity sewer systems.

Building Size, Shap, and Design

- Minimize the building footprint by using multiple floors when possible.
- Establish building dimensions that optimize material use and reduce waste.
- Consider using garden roofs or highly reflective roof coverings to reduce the heat island effect.
- Plan buildings to include bicycle storage and shower/changing facilities to encourage use of alternative means of transportation.

Site Disturbance

- Locate buildings and parking on previously disturbed areas.
- Position buildings and roads along landscape contours and shallow slopes, to minimize earthwork and site clearing.
- Plan utility corridors along new road or walk construction or along previously disturbed areas on the site.
- Limit site disturbance to 40 ft beyond the building perimeter, 5 ft beyond primary roadway curbs and walks, and 25 ft beyond constructed areas with permeable surfaces.

Site Development

- Minimize the site development area by providing all or some parking under the building.
- Develop a site plan to minimize road length, parking, and service areas. Consolidate pedestrian, automobile, and service paths whenever possible. Double-load parking lots to share access lanes and minimize paving.
- Do not develop more than the minimum parking required by the local zoning ordinance.
- Reduce heat islands by providing shade or using high-albedo materials with a minimum reflectance of 0.3.
- Use open-grid paving or other pervious paving to reduce stormwater runoff.
- Design pedestrian surfaces using permeable materials, such as loose aggregate, permeable concrete, wooden decks, and spaced paving stones.
- Use mechanical or natural treatment systems for stormwater, such as constructed wetlands, vegetated filter strips, infiltration basins, and bioswales. A *bioswale* is a shallow grass-lined ditch or channel designed to detain storm runoff and remove sediments and other contaminants while allowing the water to seep into the ground through a process known as *phytoremediation*.

- Design vegetative buffer areas around parking lots to mitigate runoff of water containing pollutants such as oil and sediments.
- Minimize site lighting. Prevent light from spilling onto adjacent properties or into the sky.
- Consider using collected rainwater for supplemental irrigation. This may be a possibility if permitted by local and state regulations, if annual rainfall is sufficient, and if air quality at the site yields water suitable for its intended purpose. If this approach is employed, roofing materials must be carefully selected, and the costs of collection, storage, and filtration must be evaluated. Refer to Chap. 13 for more information on rainwater collection.

  If rainwater cannot be collected, an infiltration basin may be used to detain the runoff. An *infiltration basin* is a closed depression in the earth from which water can escape only into the soil. (Do not confuse this with a *catch basin*, which is an area that temporarily contains excessive runoff until it can flow at a controlled rate into the storm sewer system.)
- Use native plant materials, and minimize the use of high-maintenance lawns. Good landscaping practices can improve the aesthetics of a site, reduce water runoff, and minimize erosion while minimizing the need for irrigation and providing habitats for animal and insect species.

8

CODES AND REGULATIONS DURING PROGRAMMING

A vital part of the architect's work during programming and analysis is identifying the legal restrictions that apply to a project. Two of the most common legal restrictions are building codes and zoning ordinances, but there are many others. These may include special rules and regulations of the local fire department, fire zones set by the local municipality, and rules of government agencies such as the Federal Housing Authority (FHA) and the Environmental Protection Agency (EPA). Local health departments may have requirements that apply to restaurants and hospitals; local and state energy conservation regulations may also be in force.

In most cases, the agency that will be enforcing the codes is the local authority having jurisdiction (AHJ), but there are exceptions. For example, a project designed for the federal government, such as a military installation, a post office, or a government office, is exempt from local regulations (but must conform to local zoning codes). In such a case, however, the federal agency with jurisdiction will typically require that local regulations be followed anyway.

Some of the most important subject areas tested in the ARE include building codes and regulations. In all divisions of the exam the candidate must apply knowledge of various regulations and codes to specific areas of practice such as pre-design, building design, structures, mechanical and electrical systems, and material selection.

Although there are many model codes used in the United States, most local and state jurisdictions have adopted the *International Building Code* (IBC) for commercial construction. The IBC is a part of the family of codes published by the International Code Council (ICC). In addition to the IBC, the ICC has developed complementary codes that regulate residential construction, existing buildings, energy conservation, fire protection, green construction, plumbing systems, mechanical systems, and swimming pools and spas. Most of this chapter and Chap. 14 are based on the IBC.

A state may adopt the entire IBC or just some chapters, it may adopt the current version of the code or an earlier one, and it may adopt all, some, or none of the complementary codes. The state may also include additional requirements or modify sections. The IBC also incorporates other documents by reference, such as *Accessible and Usable Buildings and Facilities* (ANSI A117.1), which governs accessibility requirements. It is important that the architect confirm which requirements apply to the specific project. Refer to the section on model building codes later in this chapter for a listing of other common building codes.

This chapter discusses the various types of regulations that affect building design, including building codes, testing and material standards, zoning regulations, land use restrictions, and other local and site-specific requirements. Refer to Chap. 14 for more information on how specific code requirements are applied to a project during design development. Refer to Chap. 48 for a discussion of how to verify conformance to regulatory requirements at the detail level.

Although most basic design decisions related to building codes are deferred until schematic design, it is sometimes necessary to determine some aspects of a building during programming so that a budget can be developed. For example, it may be impossible to estimate a cost accurately until the construction type is determined. Likewise, seismic loading codes will affect the cost of a structural system, and this must be known as part of budgeting. Refer to Chap. 14 for more information on these aspects of codes and regulations.

BUILDING REGULATIONS

Building codes are only one of several types of regulations that affect the design and construction of buildings. Legal and administrative regulations at the federal, state, and local levels may also apply. For example, a state may enforce environmental protection rules, while the building codes used in that state may regulate environmental impact very little. As part of the pre-design phase of a project, the architect must verify which local, state, and federal regulations apply. Refer to Chap. 14 for more information on environmental regulations.

Because applicable regulations vary widely depending on the project type and the geographical location, every office should develop its own set of building regulation checklists. The following is a partial list of regulatory agencies and code provisions that may apply to a project.

- local or state building code (IBC or other, verify edition and any modifications and supplemental documents that may be adopted)
- local zoning ordinance
- fire department
- NFPA 1: *Fire Code*, developed by the National Fire Protection Association (NFPA)
- NFPA 101: *National Life Safety Code*
- NFPA 70: *National Electrical Code*
- energy code adopted by local jurisdiction
- housing codes
- ADA/ABA accessibility guidelines
- local utility company
- drainage/waste water agency
- city engineer or public works department regulations
- local department of health codes and standards
- local department of hospitals
- local ordinances such as height restrictions and view easements
- historic preservation regulations
- waterway and shoreline management agencies
- insurance company requirements
- financial lender requirements
- deed restrictions
- restrictive covenants
- planning or architectural review board rules

Federal Regulations

At the national level, several federal agencies may regulate a construction project, ranging from military construction to the building of federal prisons. Certain federal agencies may also regulate or issue rules covering a specific aspect of construction, such as the safety-glazing requirement issued by the Consumer Product Safety Commission (CPSC).

For architects, one of the most notable federal-level laws is the Americans with Disabilities Act (ADA), which regulates, among other things, removal of barriers to the physically disabled. The ADA requirements are based on the American National Standard Institutes (ANSI) ICC/ANSI Standard A117.1, *Accessible and Usable Buildings and Facilities.* Additional provisions are provided in the ADA regulations. Although very similar to ICC/ANSI Standard A117.1, the ADA is not a code or standard, but civil rights legislation. Still, architects must adhere to the ADA's provisions when designing the facilities covered by it. Chapter 15 addresses requirements for barrier-free design.

State Regulations

Most states have agencies that regulate building in some way. In addition to a state building code (which is usually the IBC or some variation of it), a state government may enforce energy codes, elevator construction requirements, environmental regulations, fabric flammability standards, and specific rules relating to state government buildings, institutions, and other facilities. The requirements of state agencies may also govern design of hospitals, nursing homes, restaurants, schools, and similar institutions.

Local Regulations

Local codes may include amendments to the model building code in use. These amendments usually pertain to specific concerns or needs of a geographical region or are provisions designed to alleviate local problems that are not addressed in the model codes. For example, a local amendment in a mountainous area might require a higher snow-load factor for roof design based on the local climate. Zoning ordinances, described in a later section, are a type of local regulation, as are requirements of fire departments.

Example 8.1

The International Code Council updates the *International Building Code* every three years. After each update is issued, how much time does a U.S. state have to adopt it?

(A) three months

(B) one year

(C) two years

(D) no time limit

Solution

It is up to each state to decide when to adopt each update of the *International Building Code* (IBC)—or even whether to use the IBC at all. A state may use the IBC as it is, amend the IBC for use in that state, or create its own model building code instead of using the IBC. Some cities also have their own local amendments.

The answer is (D).

HISTORY OF BUILDING CODES

The history of building codes dates to as early as 2000 BC. The Babylonian Code of Hammurabi issued a death sentence for the builder of a house that later collapsed and killed the owner. The Greeks and Romans had various types of laws governing construction and the supervision of building. The Laws of the Twelve Tables that governed life in Rome even included setback requirements to allow for repairs and prevent the spread of fire.

In 1189 England's first building code was published as the "Assize of Buildings," written by London Mayor Henry Fitz-Elwyne. It forbade thatched roofs and specified the construction of party walls. After the Great Fire of 1666 in London, an act of Parliament set forth requirements for the rebuilding of the city. This act set up different classes of buildings, described the types of materials that should be used, and established fees to cover the cost of inspection. Nearly 200 years later, Parliament revised the law and established the Metropolitan Buildings Act of 1844, which extended building laws to set building areas and heights, types of buildings, and occupancies, and even established the idea of a building official.

The development of building regulations in the United States was prompted by fires and the spread of diseases as urban areas grew rapidly. The first recorded code in the United States was written in 1625 for the settlement of New Amsterdam (later New York). It regulated the types of roof coverings permitted, to protect buildings from chimney sparks.

As cities were expanding during the latter half of the nineteenth century, tenements in New York City and elsewhere were overcrowded, poorly ventilated, combustible, and lacked basic sanitary facilities. Insurance companies recognized that better fire protection was necessary, especially after the Chicago fire of 1871. In 1905, the National Board of Fire Underwriters wrote a model building code to decrease fire risk, called the *National Building Code*, which was the beginning of the development of the three model building codes. In 1915, the Building Officials Conference of America (BOCA) wrote the *BOCA National Building Code*. The *Uniform Building Code* followed in 1927, and the *Standard Building Code* appeared in 1945. These three groups worked together in the 1990s to develop a single code, the *International Building Code*, in 2000.

One tragedy in particular provided the impetus for improved building codes. In March of 1911, a fire started in one of the sewing rooms of the Triangle Shirtwaist factory in New York City. The factory occupied several upper floors in a building without sprinklers, and the workroom was overcrowded and dangerously loaded with cloth sewing remnants. The building had two internal stairways and an exterior fire escape, but one of the stairways was locked to prevent employee theft, and the fire escape collapsed under the weight of the people trying to exit. The second stairway had doors that opened inward, and it quickly filled with smoke and flames. Ultimately, 145 people, most of them teenage girls, were killed from smoke inhalation, fire, or falling to their deaths.

In the aftermath of the fire, the state's labor laws were revised to better protect workers, and laws were set in place that required better exit facilities, fireproofing, fire extinguishers, and the installation of alarms and automatic sprinkler systems. The safety provisions enacted provided a model for other fire prevention codes and laws throughout the country.

Example 8.2

Which of the following requirements is NOT addressed in the *International Building Code* (IBC)?

(A) number of barrier-free parking spaces

(B) width of an exit stair

(C) maximum number of stories in a building

(D) maximum occupancy of a floor

Solution

Exit stairs, number of stories, and occupancy rate, are all addressed by the IBC. The number and size of barrier-free spaces are addressed in local zoning requirements and by the Americans with Disabilities Act (ADA).

The answer is (A).

BUILDING CODES

Legal Basis of Condes

The authority for adopting and enforcing building codes is one of the police powers given to state governments by the Tenth Amendment to the United States Constitution. Each state, in turn, may retain those powers or delegate some of them to lower levels of government, such as counties or cities. Because of this division of power, the authority for adopting and enforcing building codes varies among the states.

Most often, building codes are adopted and enforced by local governments, either by a municipality or, in the case of sparsely populated areas, a county or district. A few states write their own codes or adopt a model code statewide.

In Canada, the regulation of building is handled by the provincial and territorial governments under the terms of the Constitution Act. The *National Building Code of Canada* (NBC) is a model code that is widely adopted by municipal bylaws or as the basis for a provincial building code. The *National Fire Code of*

Canada and other complementary codes (such as the *National Plumbing Code of Canada*) may also be adopted by local governments.

Codes are enacted as laws, just as any other local regulation would be. Before construction, a building code is enforced through the permit process, which requires that builders submit plans and specifications to the *authority having jurisdiction* (AHJ) for checking and approval before a building permit is issued. During construction, the AHJ conducts inspections to verify that building is proceeding according to the approved plans.

Even though code enforcement is the responsibility of the local building department or the AHJ (unless exempt because it is a government project as mentioned previously), the architect is responsible for designing a building in conformance with all applicable codes and regulations. This is because an architect is required by registration laws to practice lawfully in order to protect the health, safety, and welfare of the public.

Model Building Codes

Local and state jurisdictions may write their own building codes, but in most cases a model code is adopted into law by reference. A model code is one that has been written by a group of experts knowledgeable in the field, without reference to any particular geographical area. Adopting a model code allows a city, county, or district to have a complete, workable building code without the difficulty and expense of writing its own. If certain provisions need to be added or changed to suit the particular requirements of a municipality, the model code is enacted with modification. Even when a city or state writes its own code, that code is usually based on a model code. Exceptions include some large cities, such as New York and Chicago, and a few states that have adopted the *Life Safety Code.*

Adopting a model code allows a city, county, or district to have a complete, workable building code without the difficulty and expense of writing its own.

The primary model code is the *International Building Code* (IBC), published by the International Code Council (ICC). The IBC is an amalgam of the work of the three code-writing groups that previously published three different model codes in the United States. The IBC combines provisions of all three of the previous model codes and is organized in the same format that the three code-writing groups used in the most recent editions of their codes. At the time of this writing, jurisdictions in all states have adopted one or more of the family of international codes and some states have adopted the IBC on a statewide level or have used it as a basis for writing their own codes. The *Life Safety Code*, published by the National Fire Protection Association, is also used by some jurisdictions.

The use of one model code throughout the United States (even state codes that are largely based on the IBC) brings consistency and makes it easier for designers and architects to work across the country. However, to complicate matters, the National Fire Protection Association (NFPA) has written its own code, the NFPA 5000, *Building Construction and Safety Code*, which was published in 2002. It has not, however, seen widespread use, and very few jurisdictions in the United States have adopted it.

The material in this chapter and in this book is based on the IBC, which is the most commonly used model code in the United States, though building design and construction must conform to whatever code is in force in the locale where the structure is erected. Questions on the ARE test knowledge of universal code concepts of model codes, such as the IBC, rather than specifically addressing any one local or state code.

Most of the IBC is prescriptive rather than performance based. This means that most of the code describes specific materials and methods of design and construction for building components and systems, rather than describing how the components and systems are supposed to function. In most cases, the codes refer to nationally recognized standards of materials and testing; if a building component meets the test standard, it can be used. The code does allow for advancement and innovation; new or untested materials and construction methods can be used if they can pass performance-based testing requirements, or if they can otherwise be shown to meet the requirements of the code.

Building codes are written to protect the health, safety, and welfare of the public. As such, model codes are written based on the idea of the *least acceptable risk*, which is the minimum level needed for building and occupant safety. Meeting this minimum level, however, is not always the best construction for a given circumstance.

Administrative Requirements of Building Codes

Every building code includes a chapter dealing with the administration of the code itself. The administrative chapter includes information on what codes apply, the duties and powers of the building official, the permit process, what information is required on construction documents, fees for inspection services, how inspections are handled, and what kinds of inspections are required. Also included are requirements for issuing a certificate of occupancy, instructions on how violations are to be handled, and provisions for appealing the decisions of the building official as to applying and interpreting the code.

The architect may need to coordinate with the local building official during several stages of the project from pre-design to completion of construction if there are questions about how code requirements apply to the project or if the project is unusual in its design. Refer to Chap. 46 for a discussion of the architect's responsibilities for providing required building code information on the construction documents.

Adjuncts to Building Codes

In addition to building codes, there are companion codes that govern other aspects of construction. For example, the ICC also publishes the *International Residential Code*, the *International Fire Code*, the *International Mechanical Code*, the *International Plumbing Code*, and the *International Zoning Code*, among others.

The electrical code used by all jurisdictions is the *National Electrical Code* (NEC), published by the National Fire Protection Association (NFPA). In order to maintain greater uniformity in building regulations, the ICC does not publish an electrical code, but relies on the NEC.

Model codes also make extensive use of industry standards that are developed by trade associations, such as the Gypsum Association, government agencies, standards-writing organizations such as ASTM International and the NFPA, and standards-approving groups such as the American National Standards Institute (ANSI). Standards are adopted into a building code by reference name, number, and date of latest revision. For example, most codes adopt by reference the American National Standard ICC/ANSI A117.1, *Accessible and Usable Buildings and Facilities.* This standard was developed by the ICC based on previous ANSI accessibility standards and is approved by ANSI.

Example 8.3

Zoning requirements typically regulate which three aspects of a site? (Choose the three that apply.)

(A) separation of use groups

(B) setbacks from property lines

(C) minimum green spaces

(D) stormwater from roof drains

(E) loading spaces and parking

(F) accessible paths of travel

Solution

Stormwater is addressed in the *International Plumbing Code.* Separation of use groups and accessible paths of travel are addressed in the *International Building Code.* Zoning typically addresses setbacks to maintain distances between buildings, maximum coverage of development on a site (or, conversely, minimum green spaces that cannot be developed), and loading spaces along with parking.

The answer is (B), (C), and (E).

TESTING AND MATERIAL STANDARDS

All approved materials and construction assemblies referred to in building codes are required to be manufactured according to accepted methods or tested by approved agencies according to standardized testing procedures, or both. There are hundreds of standardized tests and product standards for building materials and constructions. Some of the more common ones are listed in this section.

As previously stated, standards are developed by trade associations, standards-writing organizations, and government agencies. By themselves, standards have no legal standing. When they are referred to in a building code, and that code is adopted by a governmental jurisdiction, then the standards become enforceable.

Standards-Writing Organizations

ASTM International publishes thousands of standards and test procedures that prescribe in detail such requirements as how a test apparatus must be set up, how materials must be prepared, and how long the test must last. Manufacturers will indicate in their product literature what tests each of their materials has passed. Standards are developed by committees of experts in a particular field. ASTM International does not actually perform tests, but its procedures and standards are used by testing agencies.

The National Fire Protection Association (NFPA) is another private, voluntary organization that develops standards related to the causes and prevention of destructive fires. NFPA publishes hundreds of codes and standards in a multivolume set that covers the entire scope of fire prevention, including sprinkler systems, fire extinguishers, hazardous materials, fire fighting, and much more. As mentioned earlier in this chapter, NFPA has published its own building code, NFPA 5000.

Other standards-writing organizations are typically industry trade groups that have an interest in a particular material, product, or field of expertise. There are hundreds of these construction trade organizations, including

- American Society of Heating, Refrigerating and Air-Conditioning Engineers (ASHRAE)
- Illuminating Engineering Society (IES)
- Gypsum Association (GA)
- American Concrete Institute (ACI)
- American Iron and Steel Institute (AISI)
- American Institute of Steel Construction (AISC)
- American Institute of Timber Construction (AITC)

The American National Standards Institute (ANSI) is a well-known organization in the field, but unlike the other standards groups ANSI does not develop or write standards. Instead, it approves standards developed by other organizations and works to avoid duplications between different standards. The ANSI approval process ensures industry consensus for a standard and avoids duplication of standards. For example, ANSI 108, *Specifications for Installation of Ceramic Tile*, was developed by the Tile Council of North America and reviewed by a large committee of widely varying industry representatives. ANSI approval does not always represent unanimity among committee members, but it requires much more than a simple majority. The approval process requires that all views and objections be considered and that a concerted effort be made toward their resolution.

Testing Laboratories

When a standard describes a test procedure or requires one or more tests in its description of a material or product, a testing laboratory must perform the test. A standards-writing organization may also provide testing, but in most cases a Nationally Recognized Testing Laboratory (NRTL) must perform the test. An NRTL is an independent laboratory recognized by the Occupational Safety and Health Administration (OSHA) to test products to the specifications of applicable product safety standards.

One of the best-known NTRLs is Underwriters Laboratories (UL). Among other activities, UL develops standards and tests products for safety. When a product successfully passes the prescribed test, it is given a UL label. There are several types of UL labels, and each means something different.

When a complete product is successfully tested, it is listed. This signifies that the product has passed the safety test and is manufactured under the UL follow-up services program. Such a product receives a *listed label.*

Another type of label is the *classified label.* This means that samples of the product were tested for certain types of uses only. In addition to the classified label, the product must also carry a statement specifying the conditions that were tested for. This allows field inspectors and others to determine if the product is being used correctly.

One of the most common uses of UL procedures is in testing doors and other kinds of protection for openings. For example, fire doors are required to be tested in accordance with UL l0B, *Standard for Fire Tests of Door Assemblies,* and to carry a UL label. Test results and listed products are published in UL's *Online Certifications Directory.*

Types of Tests and Standards

There are hundreds of types of tests and standards for building materials and assemblies that examine a wide range of properties from fire resistance to structural integrity to durability to stain resistance. Building codes indicate what tests or standards a particular type of material must satisfy in order to be considered acceptable for use. For example, gypsum wallboard must meet the standards of ASTM C1396, *Standard Specification for Gypsum Board.*

Fire Safety Tests

The most important tests for building components are concerned with fire safety: those that rate how well a construction assembly can keep fire and smoke from passing from one space to another, and those that rate the flammability of a finish material. The three tests most commonly used to rate the fire resistance of construction assemblies are ASTM E119, NFPA 252 and NFPA 257.

ASTM E119

For wall assemblies and floor/ceiling assemblies, the most commonly used test is ASTM E119, *Standard Test Methods for Fire Tests of Building Construction and Materials.* This test involves building a sample of the assembly in the laboratory and applying a fire to one side of it. The temperature of the fire is controlled and gradually increased, through the use of gas burners, to simulate the temperatures reached by a typical building fire. Monitoring devices measure temperature and other aspects of the assembly as the test proceeds.

The E119 test has two parts. In the first part, heat transfer through the assembly is measured. The goal is to discover how long the fire must be applied to one side of the assembly before the surface of the other side of the assembly, or other materials adjacent to the other side, will combust.

The second part is the "hose stream" test. A duplicate of the assembly is exposed to fire for one-half the time determined by the first part of the test. (In some cases the same assembly is used rather than preparing a duplicate.) Then a stream of water at a standardized high pressure is directed at the assembly. This tests the assembly's ability to maintain its integrity during a fire and to withstand impacts, such as from fire hoses and falling debris, and the cooling and eroding effects of water. Overall, the test evaluates an assembly's ability to prevent the passage of fire, heat, and hot gases for a given amount of time. A similar test for doors is NFPA 252.

A construction assembly tested according to ASTM E119 is given a time rating; in general terms, this rating indicates the amount of time the assembly can resist a standard test fire without failing. The assembly may be given a 1-hour, 2-hour, 3-hour, or 4-hour rating. There are also ratings for 0.5 hours, and 1.5 hours but these are not common. Doors and other opening assemblies can also be given 20-minute, 30-minute, and 45-minute ratings. Refer to Table 14.2 and Table 14.3 for a summary of requirements.

NFPA 252

NFPA 252, *Standard Methods of Fire Tests of Door Assemblies*, is similar to ASTM E119; it evaluates how well a door or other opening assembly resists the passage of flame, heat, and gases. The first part of the test establishes a fire endurance rating; the hose stream test then determines whether the door will stay within its frame when subjected to a standard blast from a fire hose after exposure to fire. Similar tests include UL10B, *Standard for Fire Tests of Door Assemblies*, and UL10C, *Standard for Positive Pressure Fire Tests of Door Assemblies.*

NFPA 257

NFPA 257, *Standard on Fire Test for Window and Glass Block Assemblies*, gives specific fire and hose stream test procedures to use to establish the degree of fire protection, given in units of time, for window openings in fire-resistive walls. This standard determines the degree of protection that the glazing assembly provides from the spread of fire, including flame, heat, and hot gases.

Finish Material Flammability Tests

The three tests most often used for testing the flammability of finish materials in building construction are ASTM E84, NFPA 265, and NFPA 286. (Flammability standards for carpet are described in Chap. 29.) A particular building code will not necessarily include all three. Two more tests, NFPA 289 and NFPA 701, are used to test the flammability of specific kinds of items.

Flammability tests for building and finish materials determine

- whether a material is flammable, and if so, whether it simply burns with applied heat or supports combustion (adds fuel to the fire)
- the material's degree of flammability (how fast fire spreads across the material)
- how much smoke and toxic gas the material produces when ignited

ASTM E84

ASTM E84, *Standard Test Method for Surface Burning Characteristics of Building Materials*, is one of the most common fire testing standards. This method, also known as the *Steiner tunnel test*, rates the surface burning characteristics of interior finishes and other building materials.

The test is performed by placing a sample piece of the material in a narrow test chamber with a controlled flame at one end. The material is given a *flame spread index* (FSI) from 0 to 100. The scale is arbitrary; glass-reinforced cement board is assigned an FSI of 0, and red oak flooring is assigned an FSI of 100.

Table 8.1
Flame Spread Index Ratings

class	flame spread index
A (I)	0–25
B (II)	26–75
C (III)	76–200

With this test, materials are classified into three groups based on their flame-spread characteristics. These groups and their flame spread indexes are given in Table 8.1.

Class A is the most fire resistant, and Class C is the least. Product literature generally indicates the flame spread of the material, either by class (letter or Roman numeral) or by numerical value. Building codes then specify the minimum flame-spread requirements for various occupancies in specific areas of the building. These are discussed in Chap. 14 under Finishes.

ASTM E84 can also be used to generate a *smoke-developed index* (SDI), a measure of the concentration of smoke emitted by a material as it burns.

NFPA 265

NFPA 256, *Standard Methods of Fire Tests for Evaluating Room Fire Growth Contribution of Textile or Expanded Vinyl Wall Coverings on Full Height Panels and Walls*, is also sometimes referred to as the *room corner test.*

This was developed as an alternate to the ASTM E84 test; for textile interior finishes, it is sometimes required in addition to or instead of the ASTM E84 test.

The room corner test measures the contribution of interior textile wall coverings to room fire growth. Real-world conditions are simulated by testing the material in the corner of a full-sized test room. For the test, the textile wall covering is applied to three sides of a room measuring 8 ft by 12 ft by 8 ft high. An ignition source in the room provides a heat output of 40 kW for five minutes and then 150 kW for ten minutes. The textile receives a pass rating if both of the following conditions are met.

- During the 40 kW exposure, flame does not spread to the ceiling.
- During the 150 kW exposure, there is no flashover and no spread of flame to the outer extremities of the 8 ft by 12 ft wall.

If either condition is not met, the textile receives a fail rating.

NFPA 286

NFPA 286, *Standard Methods of Fire Tests for Evaluating Contribution of Wall and Ceiling Interior Finish to Room Fire Growth*, is used to evaluate materials other than textiles. This standard was developed to address concerns about interior finishes that do not remain in place during the Steiner tunnel test (ASTM E84).

This test method—which, like NFPA 265, is also commonly known as the *room corner test*—measures factors such as heat and smoke released, combustion products released, and the potential for fire spread beyond the room, in order to evaluate how much a finish contributes to the growth of fire in a room. NFPA 286 is similar to NFPA 265 in that materials are mounted on the walls inside a room. In the NFPA 286 method, however, a greater area of the wall surface is covered, and the method may be used to test finishes for ceilings as well as for walls.

Refer to Chap. 14 for an explanation of the terms used in building codes.

NFPA 289

NFPA 289 is the *Standard Method of Fire Test for Individual Fuel Packages.* This test determines the fire response of individual fuel packages in a room when exposed to various ignition sources. Three types of fuel packages are covered in the test: single decorative objects, exhibit booths, and theater and motion picture stage sets.

NFPA 701

NFPA 701 is the *Standard Methods of Fire Tests for Flame Propagation of Textiles and Films.* This test establishes two procedures for testing the flammability of draperies, curtains, and other window treatments. Test 1 is used with fabrics lighter than 21 oz/yd^2 used individually or in multilayer composites as curtains, draperies, and other window treatments. Test 2 is for fabrics weighing more than 21 oz/yd^2, such as fabric blackout linings, awnings, and similar architectural fabric structures and banners. NFPA 701 is appropriate for testing materials that are exposed to air on both sides.

ZONING

The most common form of legal constraint on land development is zoning. *Zoning* is the division of a city or other area into districts in order to regulate the use of land and the location and size of buildings within those districts.

For centuries, human settlements have been separated informally into areas intended for different uses, but it was not until the early twentieth century that zoning regulations took on legal status. The legal basis for zoning is founded largely on the right of the state to protect the health, safety, and welfare of the public. State governments, which enact enabling legislation, delegate zoning power to municipalities.

The first zoning ordinance was passed in 1916 in New York City. Zoning was originally an attempt to improve the problems faced by rapidly expanding cities: crowding, factories being built too close to housing, and tall buildings blocking light and air. Although zoning began as a way of regulating land use, it has grown into one means of implementing planning policy.

Zoning primarily regulates

- what a parcel of land may be used for
- how much of the land may be covered with buildings
- how large the structures may be
- how far the buildings must be set back from property lines
- how much parking and loading space must be provided

Other requirements may also be included, such as regulating signs or allowing more building area on sites that will also provide plazas and open space. Although zoning is used primarily in cities, special types of zoning are sometimes used in suburban or rural areas. These types may separate agricultural uses from forestry or recreational use, floodplain zoning, airport zoning, and historic area zoning.

Zoning districts are based on residential, commercial, and industrial occupancies, and each of these may be divided further. Residential zones, for example, may include single-family, low-density multifamily, and high-density multifamily dwellings. For each kind of zoning district, a list of permissible uses is specified, with single-family zones being the most restrictive. Each zone may be used for the purposes listed for that zone, as well as for any use listed in a more restrictive zone. For instance, zoning regulations would not prevent building a single-family house in a dense business zone (though economic and aesthetic considerations probably would).

See Chap. 14 for the application of zoning requirements to site planning.

SITE-SPECIFIC REGULATIONS

Easements

An *easement* is the right to use another's land for a specific purpose, or to prevent the land's owner from using it for a particular purpose. It is a legal instrument and is normally recorded.

One of the most common kinds of easement is a *utility easement*. This allows a utility company to enter the property to install and maintain utility lines above or below the ground within the boundaries of the easement. Although the land belongs to the property owner, no permanent structures can be erected within the easement without the utility company's consent. The utility company also has the right to maintain its equipment within the easement, which may restrict the height of trees or other potential obstructions within the easement.

Another type of easement is the *access easement*. If a parcel of land is not served by a public road, an access easement may be granted that gives the landowner and the public the right to cross an adjacent property.

Other types of easements include *support easements* for the construction of common party walls between properties, *joint use easements* that allow two or more property owners to share a common feature such as a driveway, *scenic easements* that protect views and development in scenic areas, and *conservation easements* that limit land use in large areas. Scenic and conservation easements are often used by public agencies to control land use without the need to purchase large tracts of property.

Rights-of-Way

A *right-of-way* is the legal right of one party or the public to traverse land belonging to another. In its most common form, a right-of-way refers to the public land used for streets and sidewalks. The boundary of a right-of-way usually corresponds to the property line of adjacent property owners. In most cases, the street occupies only a portion of the right-of-way and the remainder is used for sidewalks, landscaping, and utilities. An access easement, as previously described, creates a private or public right-of-way.

Deed Restrictions

Deeds to property can contain provisions that restrict the use of the property by the buyer. These are called *restrictive covenants* and are legal and enforceable if they are reasonable and in the public interest. It is common for the developer of a large tract of land that is being subdivided to include restrictive covenants in the deeds. They may include such limitations as setbacks, minimum square footage of houses, the types of materials that can and cannot be used on exteriors, and the like.

Two other types of deed restrictions are affirmative covenants and conditional covenants. An *affirmative covenant* requires a buyer to perform a specific duty in the future. For example, the purchaser of property may be required to construct and maintain a fence as a condition of purchase. A *conditional covenant* permits the title to the property to revert to the original owner if the restrictions prescribed in the deed are not followed.

Because the covenants are included in the deed, they are known to the potential buyer before purchase, and the buyer can decide not to purchase if the covenants are not acceptable. Restrictive covenants are often used in residential subdivisions to maintain a desired uniformity of appearance, site development, and quality of construction. Most deed restrictions are established for specific periods of time, such as 10 years, 15 years, 20 years, or 30 years.

9

SITE ANALYSIS

Programming & Analysis

Nomenclature

d	vertical distance between contours	ft	L	horizontal distance between points of a slope	ft
G	slope of land	%			

Many factors can influence the placement and design of a building, including the climate, topography, and boundaries of the site on which it is planned. This chapter discusses these considerations, which are typically analyzed during programming and schematic design, and builds on some of the concepts covered in Chap. 7. As a project progresses to design development, more detailed site planning is undertaken; these topics are covered in Chap. 12.

CLIMATIC INFLUENCES AND DESIGN RESPONSES

Some climatic influences that are part of the context of a building were discussed in Chap. 7. As a project moves into the schematic design phase, an architect should analyze

- solar orientation
- design strategies for climatic regions
- alternative energy systems

Solar Orientation

Solar orientation influences three aspects of site planning.

- the orientation of the building to control solar heat gain and heat loss
- the location of outdoor spaces and activities
- the location of building entries

Before design begins, consider the path of the sun and its angle at various times of day in different seasons. In the Northern Hemisphere, the sun's angle is lowest on the winter solstice (around December 21) and highest on the summer solstice (around June 21). At more northern latitudes, the sun's angle is lower all year long than it is at latitudes nearer the equator.

During the winter, the sun rises and sets south of an east-west line through the site, and, depending on the site location, during the summer it may rise and set north of the same line. On the vernal equinox (around March 21) and the autumnal equinox (around September 21), it rises and sets directly above the equator. Some representative values for *solar altitude* (the angle above the horizon) and *azimuth* (the angle north or south from an east-west line) are shown in Table 9.1 for various latitudes and cities. Refer to Chap. 12 for more information on solar design.

Table 9.1 Solar Angles for Representative Latitudes and Cities (all angles are approximate to the nearest degree)

		solar altitudes/noon (degrees)			azimuth at
latitude	nearest city	Dec. 21	Mar./Sept. 21	June 21	sunrise/sunset*
30	Houston	37	60	84	27
34	Los Angeles/Atlanta	32	56	79	28
40	Denver	26	50	73	30
42	Chicago/Boston	24	48	71	32
48	Seattle	18	42	66	34

*Azimuth in this table are degrees from an east-west line. They are the same for sunrise and sunset. For sunrise on December 21, the azimuth is south of east, and for sunset it is the same angle but south of west.

The orientation of a building (the direction its length faces) has a profound effect on energy gains and losses and on the comfort of its users. For example, at 40° latitude, in the winter a southern exposure receives about three times the solar energy as the east or west side does, while in the summer the east and west sides combined receive about twice as much energy as the north and south sides combined.

For most locations in the northern hemisphere, the best overall orientation for a building is with its principal facade facing south or slightly east or west of south. An orientation from 5° to 25° east of south, depending on the climatic region, is considered an ideal balance between maximizing heat gains in winter and minimizing heat gains on the east and west facades in summer. See Fig. 12.16.

Window overhangs can be used to shade windows in summer while letting the sun strike windows in winter for passive solar heating. See Fig 9.1. On east and west facades, however, vertical sun baffles are more effective than overhangs, because the summer sun is lower in the morning and afternoon, when it strikes the windows on these sides.

Louvers can be used to shield a building and its interior from the sun. Both exterior and interior louvers and shades are effective, but exterior louvers are more efficient because they block the sunlight before it enters. Deciduous trees can also shield low buildings from the sun in the summer, while allowing sunlight to enter the building in the winter.

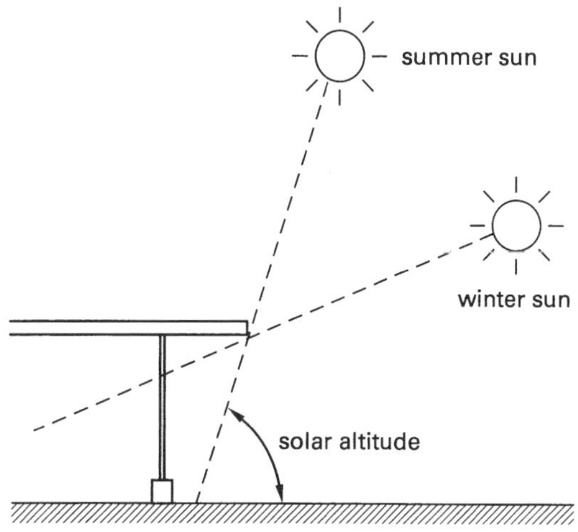

Figure 9.1
South Wall Sun Control

Solar orientation can influence outdoor activities. In hot, humid climates, it is better to locate patios, outdoor restaurants, and the like where they receive shade from the building or trees. In more temperate climates, the same spaces are best located where they receive warmth from the sun in winter, spring, and fall.

In some cases, solar orientation can also affect the placement of building entries. In cold climates, entries are best placed on the south side, where direct sun can melt ice and snow in the winter.

The orientation of the building in regard to winds is a closely related issue. Chapter 7 and Chap. 12 review the effects of wind on building location and how landscaping can be used to mitigate them. The orientation of a building and the locations of windows, plazas, and other elements can either take advantage of cooling breezes in hot, humid climates during the summer or shield the building and occupants from cold winds in the winter. In most temperate climates, prevailing wind patterns change with the seasons, so a wind analysis is needed to determine the direction of summer and winter winds. Shielding a building as much as possible from winter winds can reduce the heat loss through the walls, and providing for natural ventilation can help cool the building during the summer. Windbreaks can be formed with vegetation, buildings, or other manufactured site elements such as screens and fences.

Design Strategies for Climatic Regions

There are four broad climatic regions in the United States.

- The *cool* region includes all of Canada, the northern part of the middle United States, and the mountainous regions of Wyoming and Colorado.
- The *temperate* region includes most of the middle latitudes of the United States, including the northwest and northeast areas of the country.
- The *hot-humid* region includes the southeastern parts of the country.
- The *hot-arid* region stretches from Southern California across the desert southwest to portions of southern Texas.

Traditionally, architects have based their climate-specific design strategies on these four regions. Knowing the characteristics of these regions is usually enough to suggest general approaches to design during site analysis.

Figure 9.2 Climatic Zones of the United States

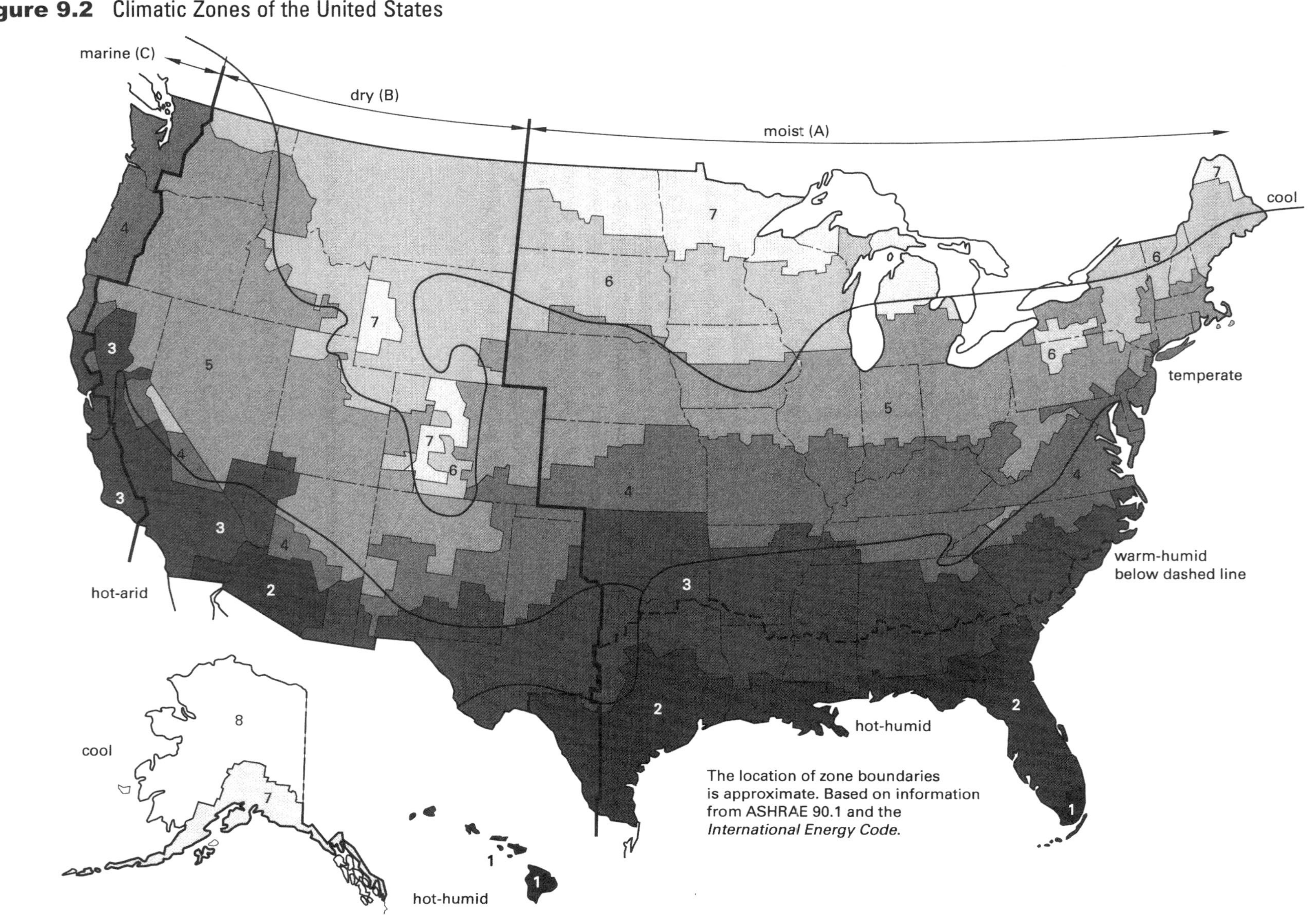

However, an architect needs more specific climatic information to respond adequately to energy conservation requirements, such as the amount of insulation and the type and position of air and water barriers in the exterior envelope. For this reason, most building codes and standards divide the United States into more detailed climate zones that are based on climate data specific to a county. The map of climate zones used for this purpose was developed for the U.S. Department of Energy (DOE) by Pacific Northwest National Laboratory and Oak Ridge National Laboratory. The map has been adopted by the *International Energy Conservation Code* (IECC), the *International Green Construction Code* (IGCC), the *International Residential Code* (IRC), and ANSI/ASHRAE/IESNA 90.1, *Energy Standard for Buildings Except Low-Rise Residential Buildings*, as well as by many states as part of their energy conservation regulations. An appendix in ANSI/ASHRAE/IESNA 90.1 gives a county-by-county listing of each zone in the United States as well as details about the climate zones of other countries.

Eight climate zones are identified by this map, including four subzones of moist, dry, marine, and warm-humid. The eight zones are numbered in Fig. 9.2 and listed by name in Table 9.2. The curved lines overlaid on this figure (which are not part of the DOE map) indicate the approximate boundaries of the four climate regions used by many architects and promoted by Victor Olgyay in his 1963 book *Design with Climate: Bioclimatic Approach to Architectural Regionalism.*

Table 9.2 Climate Zone Descriptions

zone number	description
1A, 2A, and 3A south of the warm-humid line	warm, humid
2B	warm, dry
3A north of the humid line, 4A	mixed, humid
3B, 3C, 4B	mixed, dry
4C	cool, marine
5A, 6A	cool, humid
5B, 6B	cold, humid
7	very cold
8	subarctic

Although the architect should determine what climatic zone is applicable and follow code-regulated guidelines, the four general climatic regions are useful as a basis for preliminary design. Design strategies for each region include the following.

Cold Climates

In cold climates, building designs should ideally minimize the exposed surface area to reduce heat loss. This suggests buildings with cubical shapes and those built partially underground. Northern exposure should be minimized, as should door and window openings on the north side of a building. Entries should have air locks, and landscaping and building design should block winter winds. Because of extremes of temperature and little direct sunlight in the winter, passive solar heating is usually not appropriate. Mechanical heating and active solar heating are needed.

Other strategies include the following.

- Use compact forms with the smallest surface area possible relative to the volume.
- Use large windows facing south, small windows facing east and west, and minimal or no windows facing north.
- Use interior materials that have high thermal mass.
- Include summer shading for glazed areas.
- Use dark or medium-dark colors for the building exterior.

Temperate Climates

In temperate climate zones, heat loss in the winter can be significant, so northern exposure should be minimized and winter winds should be blocked to reduce heat loss. However, solar heat gain is desirable in the winter, so buildings should be oriented to maximize southern exposure. The same south-facing sides of buildings should be shaded with deciduous trees and mechanical devices like awnings to protect from unwanted heat gain in summer. To mitigate the effects of daytime heating, it is best to provide nighttime ventilation for the exhaust of hot air. Solar heating, both active and passive, often works well in locations without excessive cloud cover.

Other strategies include the following.

- Plan rectangular buildings with the long direction oriented generally along the east-west axis and facing slightly to the east. See Fig. 12.16 for suggested building orientations for various climatic regions.
- Provide shade in the summer, and allow the sun to fall on glazing and the building in the winter.
- Use south-facing openings to capture winter sunlight.
- Plan for the cooling effects of wind in the summer; block the wind in the winter.
- Use medium colors for the building exterior.

Hot-Humid Climates

Hot-humid climates are the most difficult to design for without mechanical cooling. Buildings should be planned to maximize the amount of natural ventilation by using narrow floor plans with cross ventilation, large, open windows, porches, and breezeways. Shading is needed, either with vegetation (without blocking ventilation) or with double roofs. Building materials should minimize thermal mass, so that the building does not store up heat during the day and release it at night.

Other strategies include the following.

- Provide shade for all openings.
- Maximize natural ventilation with large openings, high ceilings, and cross ventilation.
- Use light colors for the building exterior.

Hot-Arid Climates

In hot-arid climates, shading from direct sunlight is needed. To take advantage of the wide variations between day and night temperatures, use materials with high thermal mass; the heat stored during the day will be released at night. The same thermal mass then cools at night for daytime comfort. Night ventilation is very useful for removing heat built up during the day.

If enough water is available, pools can reduce local air temperature through evaporation. Roof ponds for one- or two-story buildings provide both evaporative cooling and high thermal mass. Evaporative coolers work well in arid climates because an increase in humidity with a decrease in air temperature is desirable.

Other strategies include the following.

- Use compact forms with the smallest surface area possible relative to the volume.
- Minimize opening sizes.
- Provide shade for openings.
- Use light colors for the building exterior.

Alternative Energy Systems

During the early stages of design, the proposed integration of alternative energy systems and methods can affect the overall project concept. Such systems can affect the choice of location, massing, shape, orientation, and primary material for the building, as well as the configuration of other site elements like parking and landscaping. Refer to Chap. 12 and Chap. 13 for more information on both passive and active energy conservation techniques as well as sustainability principles.

The following are brief summaries of the design strategies that can affect a project concept and overall building configuration during programming and schematic design.

Passive Solar Heating

- If passive solar heating is to be used, orient the long axis of the building in the east-west direction so that southern collection surfaces face within approximately 15° of true south. Passive solar heating methods should be integrated with daylighting design. Both of these design strategies will result in a building that is long and relatively narrow.
- If thermal mass is used, it may be featured as a design element.
- Plant deciduous trees to let sunlight fall on windows in winter and shade windows in summer. Either deciduous or evergreen trees can be used on the east and west facades to block the low angle of morning and afternoon sun. Even bare deciduous trees, however, can block about 20% of winter solar heat gain.

Natural Cooling

- Be aware of and evaluate the possibility of integrating the following natural cooling methods. *Passive solar cooling* utilizes the concepts of shading, natural ventilation, radiative cooling, evaporative cooling, and ground coupling. *Radiative cooling* uses thermal mass to store heat during the day and release heat to the outside at night. *Ground coupling* uses the stable coolness of the earth to cool a building, typically by using a ground-source heat pump.
- Use trees and other landscaping to shade windows and other surfaces, unless direct solar radiation is needed for daylighting or passive or active solar heating. If a site has existing landscaping, locate the building to take advantage of shade.
- To avoid excessive heat gain, use fixed shading devices. These are typically horizontal elements when used on the south side of a building, and vertical elements when used on the east and west sides.
- A building can be made self-shading by designing it to be wider at the upper stories than at ground level.
- Minimize glazed areas on the east and west facades.
- Use water elements and wind for evaporative cooling.
- Use light-colored or reflective materials to minimize radiant heat gains.
- Avoid heat buildup around the structure by limiting the use of paving. Use a pervious paving material that supports vehicles but allows grass or other vegetation to grow through. If extensive paving must be used, select a color with a high reflectance. Provide trees to shade the paving during hot summer months.
- Locate the building on the site so as to take advantage of prevailing winds and natural ventilation strategies. The overall form of the building should be either narrow or spread out so that breezes can filter through the building. Courtyards may also be used.

Active Solar

- Be aware that active solar collectors on a building can make a significant adverse visual statement unless they are placed on sloped roofs or are concealed with parapets.
- Position solar collectors so that they are not shaded by adjacent buildings and trees. If the collectors are to be mounted on the building, this may dictate the building's location. If the collectors are mounted away from the building, an additional area on the site must be designated for the accompanying site disturbance.
- Position solar collectors so that they do not reflect sunlight onto other buildings or occupied areas nearby.

Photovoltaics

- If photovoltaics (PV) are feasible for a building project, large surfaces may be needed for mounting. Using large, flat roofs or sloped surfaces will optimize the PV panel's exposure to the sun.
- Photovoltaics can be integrated with other building materials such as glass and roofing shingles. This technology is known as *facade-integrated photovoltaics* or *building-integrated photovoltaics*. Refer to Chap. 12 for more information on photovoltaics.

Example 9.1

A site analysis is performed to find the best location and orientation for a home to be built on a two-acre lot. Which of these factors would NOT typically be included in the site analysis?

(A) climate and seasonal wind directions

(B) pollution and noise sources

(C) sun angles and views

(D) threatened and endangered species

Solution

Even though threatened and endangered species would be a consideration for selection of a site, the site analysis would not typically include this information.

The answer is (D).

PROPERTY DESCRIPTIONS

The boundaries of a site can be described in one of several ways. One of the most common is based on the U.S. Public Land Survey System (PLSS), which began in 1785. Most of the United States was laid out under this system, with the exception of lands surveyed before the establishment of the system or based on some other system or land grant.

The PLSS starts with a set of east-west lines called *parallels* that follow the lines of latitude of the earth, and with a set of north-south lines called *meridians.* There are several meridians and parallels that serve as the basis for the grid layout. These are called the *principal meridians* and *base lines*, respectively. Other meridians are called *guide meridians*, and other parallels are called *standard parallels.* They are referred to as being east or west of the principal meridians or north or south of the base lines. See Fig. 9.3.

The parallels and meridians are 24 mi apart, and the squares they form are called *checks.* Since the meridian lines converge because of the shape of the earth, the south line of the first and each successive guide meridian is adjusted to be 24 mi from the principal meridian and adjacent guide meridians.

Each 24 mi square is divided into 16 townships, each 6 mi on a side. The townships are referred to by a number referenced to a principal meridian and base line. The row of townships running east and west is referred to as a *township* (the same term but a different meaning), and the row of townships running north and south is referred to as a *range.*

The townships are numbered sequentially beginning at a base line. Those north of the base line are *north townships* and those south are *south townships.* Ranges are also numbered sequentially beginning at a principal meridian, either east or west. A typical designation of a township (the 6 mi^2 parcel of land) might be "township 13 north, range 7 east of the 6th principal meridian." This would typically be abbreviated to T.13N, R.7E, 6th PM.

Each township is then further divided into 36 sections, each section being a one-mile square. These are numbered from 1 to 36 as shown in Fig. 9.3, starting in the northeast section and moving east to west, dropping down to the next row south and moving west to east, and so on.

Sections are commonly further divided into quarter sections, and each of those quarter sections into four more parcels. A complete description of such a portion of a section might read: "The SE 1/4 of the NW 1/4, Section 12, T.13N, R.7E of the 6th PM, located in the County of Merrick, State of Nebraska."

Figure 9.3 U.S. Survey System

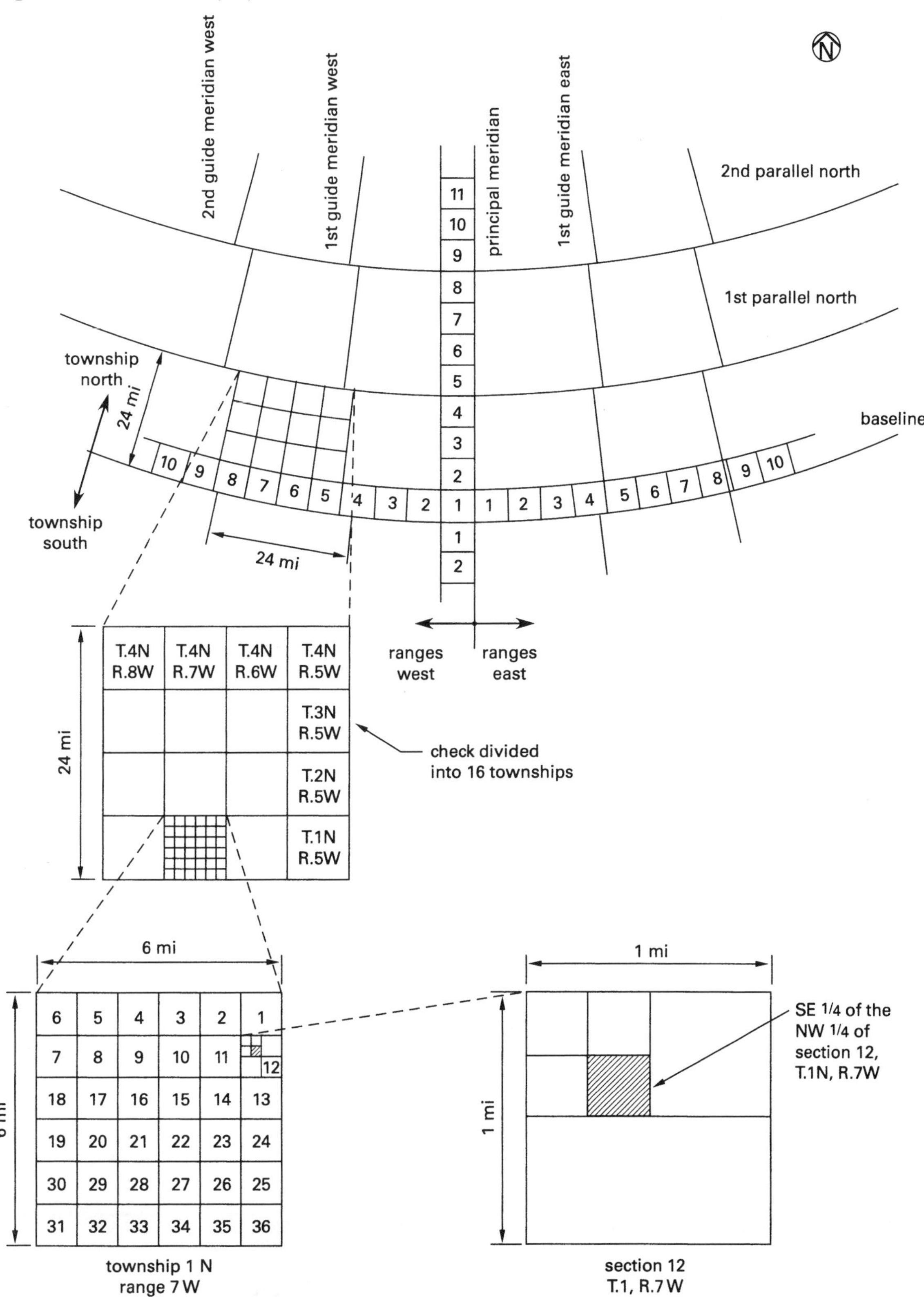

Because so much urbanization has occurred in the past 100 years and subdivision of land has become common, property is often described by its particular lot number within a subdivision, the subdivision having been carefully surveyed and recorded with the city or county in which it is located. Figure 9.4 shows one such property.

In addition to the lot and subdivisions reference, a typical property description will include the bearings of the property lines and their lengths, along with any permanent corner markers set by the original subdivision surveyor. The property line bearings are referred to by the number of degrees, minutes, and seconds the line is located either east or west of a north-south line.

Figure 9.4 Typical Boundary Survey Description

BOUNDARY SURVEY

LOT 18, BLOCK 8, SCANLOCH SUBDIVISION
GRAND COUNTY, COLORADO

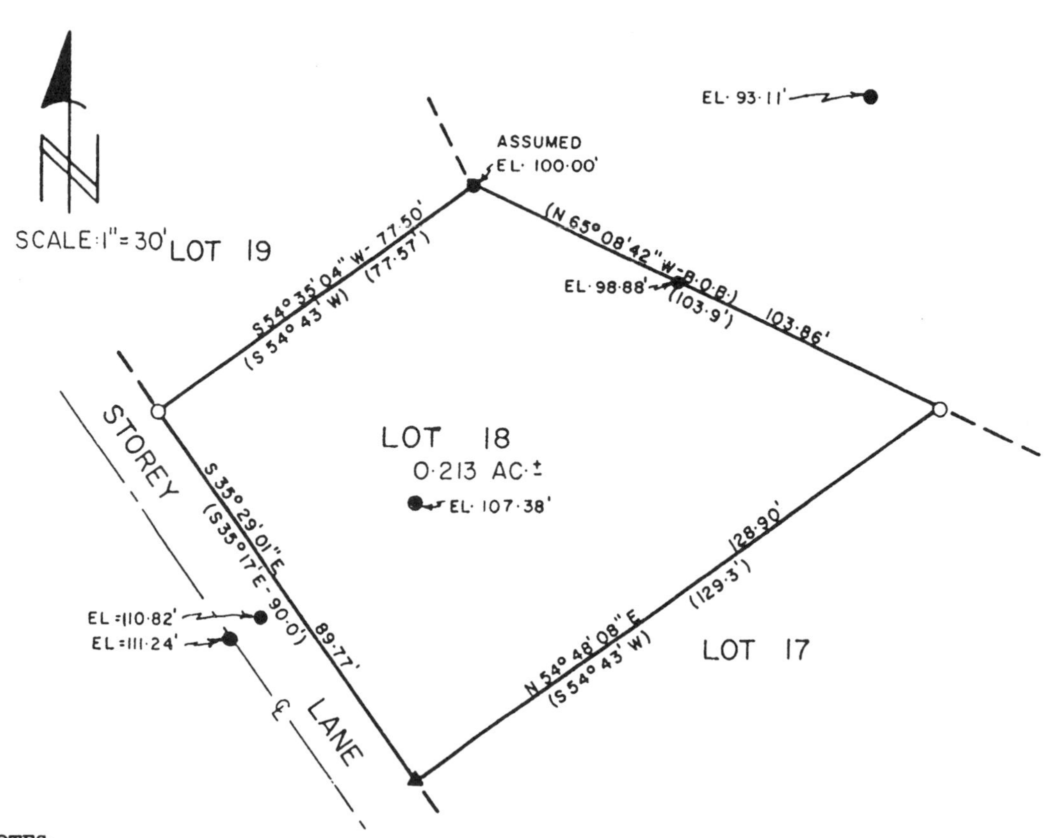

NOTES:

■	FOUND STANDARD BLM BRASS CAP MARKED AP—81 DATED 1950.
○	SET No. 4 REBAR WITH ALUMINUM CAP L. S. No. 11415.
▲	FOUND 1¼" IRON PIPE IN CONCRETE.
●	CALCULATION POINT ONLY, NOTHING FOUND OR SET.
( )	BEARINGS AND DISTANCES AS PER RECORD PLAT RECEPTION No. 759621, GRAND COUNTY RECORDS, COLORADO. ALL OTHER BEARINGS AND DISTANCES ARE ACTUAL FIELD MEASUREMENTS.
B.O.B.	THE BASIS OF BEARING FOR THIS SURVEY IS THE NORTHWESTERLY BOUNDARY LINE OF LOTS 17 & 18. SAID BEARING IS N65°08'42"W.

ELEVATIONS ARE ASSUMED FROM BRASS CAP NORTHEAST CORNER OF LOT 18 AP. 81—1950, ELEVATION = 100.00'.

Another method that is commonly used is the *metes and bounds description.* With this approach, the long description starts at one point of the property and gives the length and direction of each line around the property's boundary, returning to the starting point at the end.

With all types of property descriptions, the area of the parcel is also included, usually in acres (hectares), one acre containing 43,560 ft^2. A section contains 640 ac, and one quarter of a quarter section contains 40 ac. A *hectare* (ha) is 10,000 m^2.

Example 9.2

An architect is hired to create a single-tenant retail building in an outer corner of an existing indoor mall parking lot. The corporate owners of the tenant franchise require minimal levels of sustainable design features to be incorporated as part of the project. The features do not need to be included on the project build site, but would be considered if located within the greater mall property as long as the tenant benefits from the features. Four features desired by the owners are in the following list. At this time, none of these items are available on the greater mall property. Which one of these desired features will be the most problematic to incorporate?

(A) on-site generated power

(B) stormwater runoff treatment

(C) accessibility to public transportation

(D) maximizing green spaces

Solution

On-site generated power can feasibly be satisfied by adding a photovoltaic array to the new building. Stormwater runoff treatment can be satisfied by providing bioswales and natural detention areas within the new building site. Adding a bus stop at the mall through an agreement with a local public bus service would satisfy accessibility to public transportation without any additional cost to the owner.

Maximizing green spaces could be problematic and costly because it would require the removal of some existing parking spaces. Because this is a retail site, a reduction in parking is not advisable.

The answer is (D).

LAND ANALYSIS

Topography

Topography describes the surface features of land. Commonly used in land planning and architectural site development, a *topographic map* shows the slope and contour of the land as well as other natural and artificial features.

Topography affects decisions on where to place major site features such as buildings, parking areas, and drives, as well as how much soil has to be moved to maintain desired slopes and drainage patterns. The study of a site's topography is an important part of environmental analysis because existing land conditions affect how development can take place, what modifications need to be made, and what costs might be involved.

The topography of a site includes the contour lines on a topographic map, as shown in Fig. 9.5. This figure also shows some common contour conditions that are represented by particular patterns of lines. The examinee should be able to immediately recognize these and translate the spacing of the contour lines and the contour interval into a percentage of slope, as described.

Figure 9.5
Common Contour Conditions

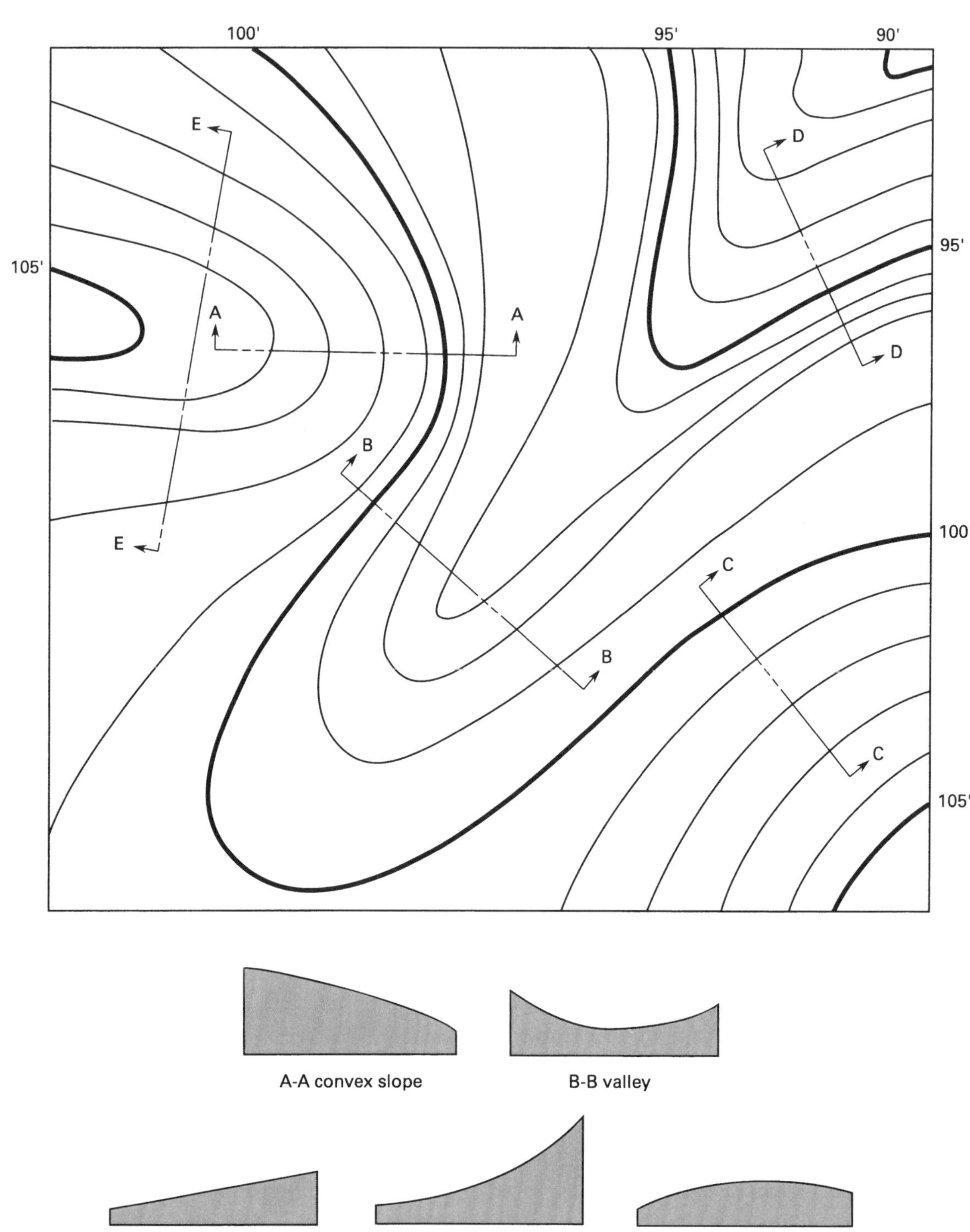

When contour lines represent a ridge, they "point" in the direction of the downslope, and when they represent a valley or swale, they "point" in the direction of the upslope. Equally spaced contour lines represent a uniform slope. As shown in Fig. 9.5, concave slopes have more closely spaced contour lines near the top of the slope, whereas convex slopes have more closely spaced contour lines at the bottom of the slope.

Any site requires some modification of the land, but the changes should be kept to a minimum. There are several reasons for this.

- Moving, removing, or hauling in earth or soil costs money.
- Excavating and building on steep slopes is more expensive than on gentle slopes.
- Excessive modification of the land affects drainage patterns that must be resolved with contour changes, drainage ditches, culverts, or other site work. Runoff that originates on the site must be managed on the site and not allowed to flow onto adjacent sites.
- Large changes in elevations can require retaining walls, which add cost to the project.
- Large amounts of cutting may damage existing tree roots.

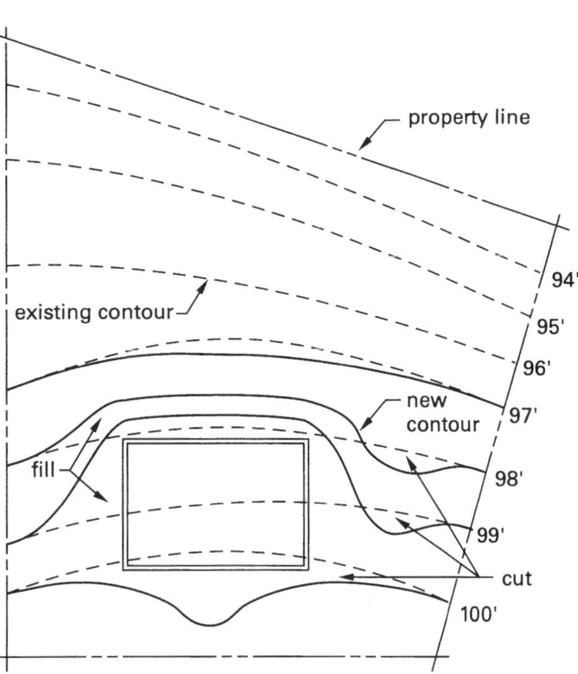

Figure 9.6
New and Existing Contour Lines

When modifications are made to the contours as part of site design, the amount of material cut away should balance the amount of soil needed for fill, to avoid the expense and problems related to removing or hauling in soil. Generally, it is better to orient a building with its length parallel to the direction of the contours, rather than perpendicular to them, to minimize excavation and fill costs.

Both existing contour lines and new contour lines are shown on the same plan; the existing lines are shown dashed and the new ones solid. See Fig. 9.6. New contour lines must match up with existing contours at the property lines, or else retaining walls are needed. Avoid modifying contour lines within the drip line of trees.

A topographic map is developed from a topographic survey by a land surveyor. In addition to information on the contours of a site, a survey will include such data as property boundaries, easements, existing buildings, utility poles, roads and other manufactured features, and trees and other natural features such as rock outcroppings and heavy vegetation. Figure 9.7 shows a simplified example of a topographic map.

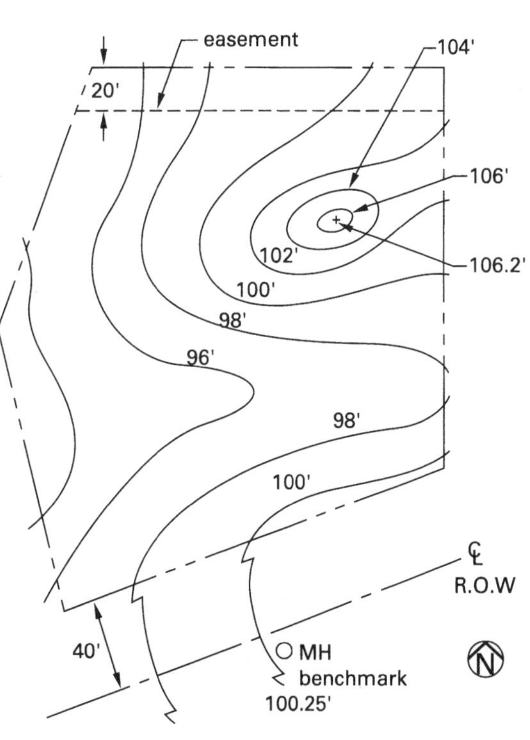

Figure 9.7
Topographic Map

Figure 9.8
Representation of Land Slope with Contour Lines

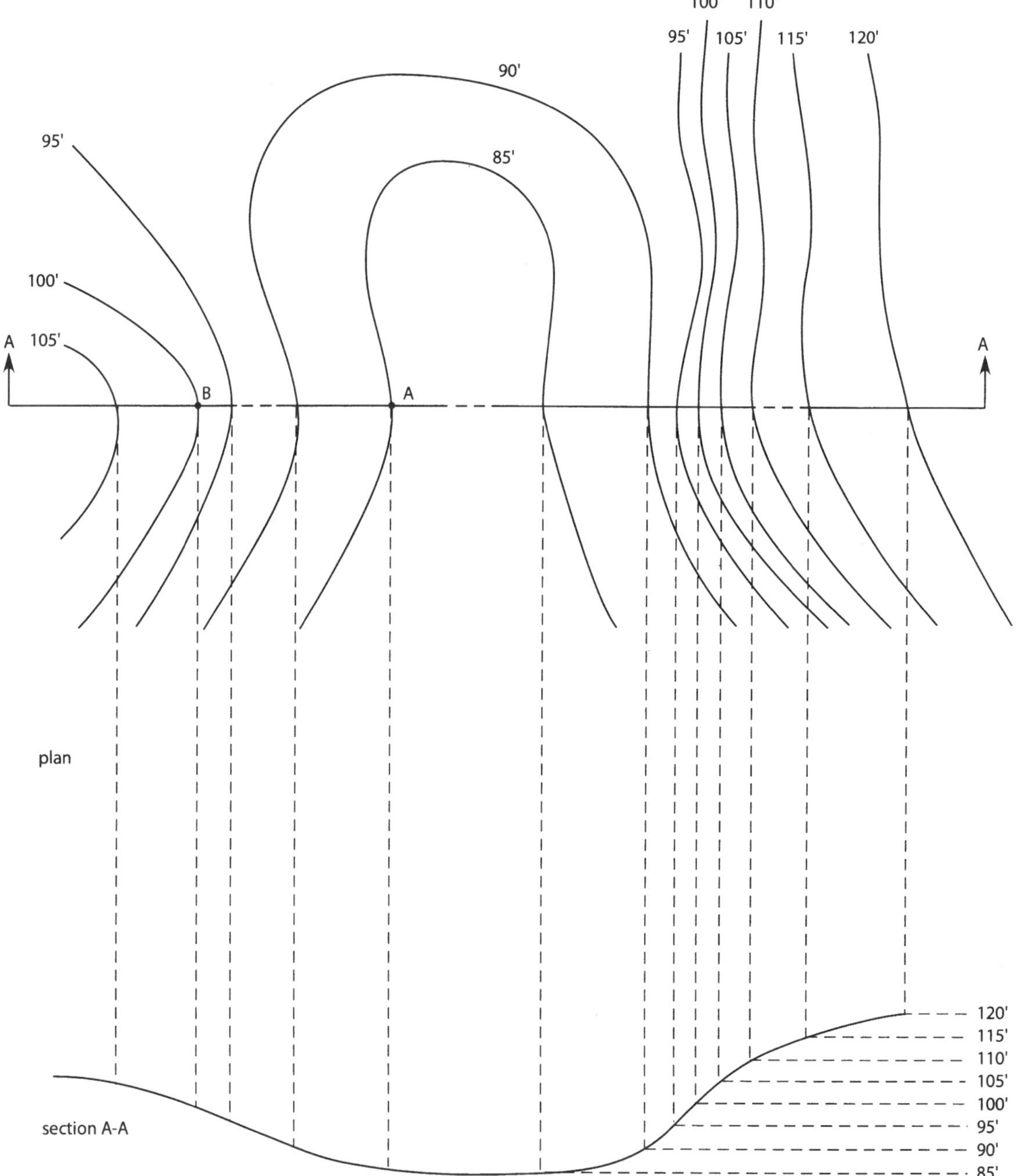

The *contour lines* on a map show the elevations of the land in a plan view and are used to make a slope analysis to determine the suitability of the land for various uses. Each contour line represents a continuous line of equal elevation above some reference benchmark.

The *contour interval* is the difference in elevation between adjacent contour lines. The contour interval on a map will vary depending on the steepness of the slope, the scale of the map, and the amount of detail required. Many large-scale maps of individual building sites use contour intervals of 1 ft, 2 ft, or 5 ft, and small-scale maps of large regions or mountainous areas may use contour intervals of 20 ft or 40 ft.

The relationships between a contour map and a section through the contours is shown in Fig. 9.8.

Knowing the contour interval and the horizontal distance between any two contour lines, the slope of the land at that point can be determined. The slope is represented as a percentage, each 1% being 1 ft of vertical rise for every 100 ft of horizontal distance. Thus, a slope of 6.5% would rise or drop 6.5 ft within 100 ft.

The slope is found using the formula

$$G = \frac{d}{L} \times 100\%$$

Existing contours can be divided into general categories according to their potential for various uses. Slopes from 0% to 4% are usable for all types of intense activity and are easy to build on. Slopes from 4% to 10% are suitable for informal movement and outdoor activity and can also be built on without much difficulty. Slopes over 10% are difficult to climb or use for outdoor activity and are more difficult and expensive to build on. Depending on the condition of the soil, very steep slopes, over 25%, are subject to erosion and become more expensive to build on. Table 9.3 gives some recommended minimum and maximum slopes for various uses.

Table 9.3
Recommended Grade Slopes for Various Uses

	slopes (%)		
	min.	preferred	max.
ground areas for drainage	2.0	4.0	
grass areas for recreation	2.0		3.0
paved parking areas	1.5	2.5	5.0
roads	0.5		10.0
sanitary sewers (depends on size)	0.5–1.5		
approach walks to building	1.0		5.0
landscaped slopes	2.0		50.0
ramps	5.0		8.33

Respecting the natural contours and slope of the land is important not only from an ecological and aesthetic standpoint but also from an economic standpoint. Moving large quantities of earth costs money, and importing or exporting soil to or from a site is not desirable. Ideally, the amount of earth cut away in grading operations should equal the amount required to fill in other portions of the site.

Example 9.3

The horizontal distance between point A and point B in Fig. 9.8 is 80 ft. Most nearly, the slope between point A and point B is

(A) 5.3%

(B) 6.6%

(C) 15%

(D) 19%

Solution

The contour interval is 5 ft, and there are contour intervals between the points, so the vertical distance between point A and point B is 15 ft. The slope is

$$G = \frac{d}{L} \times 100\% = \frac{15 \text{ ft}}{80 \text{ ft}} = 18.75\% \quad (19\%)$$

The answer is (D).

Natural Features

Every site has natural features that may be either desirable or undesirable. A complete site analysis will include a study of these features.

A view analysis may be required to determine the most desirable ways to orient buildings, outdoor areas, and approaches to the buildings. Undesirable views can be minimized or blocked with landscaping or other manufactured features.

Significant natural features such as rock outcroppings, cliffs, caves, and bogs should be identified to determine whether they must be avoided or can be used as positive features in the site design.

Subsurface conditions of groundwater and rock must be known. Sites with high water tables (about 6 ft to 8 ft below grade) can cause problems with excavations, foundations, utility placement, and landscaping. The *water table* is the underground level below which the soil is saturated with water. Generally, the water table follows the slope of the grade above, but it may vary slightly. Boring logs will reveal whether groundwater is present and how deep it is.

Sites with a preponderance of rocks near the surface can be very expensive and difficult—sometimes impossible—to develop. Blasting is usually needed, which can increase the site development costs significantly, and may not be allowed by city code restrictions.

Drainage

Every site has some type of natural drainage pattern that must be taken into account during design. In some cases the drainage may be relatively minor, consisting only of the runoff from the site itself and a small amount from adjacent sites. This type of drainage can easily be diverted around roads, parking lots, and buildings through the use of curbs, culverts, and minor changes in the contours of the land.

In other cases, a major drainage path such as a gully, dry gulch, or river may traverse the site. This will have a significant influence on potential site development, because in most cases such drainage paths must be maintained. Buildings need to be built away from them or must bridge them so that water flow is not restricted and potential damage is avoided. If modification to the contours is needed, the changes must be done in such a way that the contours of the adjacent properties are not disturbed.

Significant natural features such as rock outcroppings, cliffs, caves, and bogs should be identified to determine whether they must be avoided or can be used as positive features in the site design.

Extensive site development may create excessive runoff due to roof areas, roads, and parking lots. All of these increase the *runoff coefficient*, the fraction of total precipitation that is not absorbed into the ground. If the runoff is greater than the capacity of the natural or artificial drainage from the site, holding ponds must be constructed to temporarily collect site runoff and release it at a controlled rate.

During construction, runoff drainage must be controlled to prevent sediment from draining into waterways and stormwater drainage systems. Sediment-laden runoff has been shown to degrade stream habitats for fish and other aquatic species, make it more difficult to filter drinking water, and decrease the capacity of drinking water storage. Construction runoff is controlled by constructing a silt fence before any earth moving or other soil disturbance begins. A *silt fence* is a temporary fence designed to allow water to pass through while filtering out sediment and allowing the sediment to settle. The silt fence is placed along the perimeter of a construction site at places where drainage would normally occur. Although the exact construction requirements vary by jurisdiction, most silt fences are a few feet high and are constructed of a geotextile or other filter fabric stretched between support stakes with the bottom edge of the fabric trenched into the soil. The fence is generally placed perpendicularly to the slope of the land (that is, along a horizontal contour level) with the ends turned uphill so that the fence causes the stormwater to gather and seep through, rather than merely changing the direction of its flow.

Soil

Soil is the pulverized upper layer of the earth, formed by the erosion of rocks and plant remains and modified by living plants and organisms. If the land is undisturbed, the visible upper layer is topsoil, a mixture of mineral and organic material. The thickness of topsoil may range from just a few inches to a foot or more. Below this is a layer of mostly mineral material, which is above a layer of the fractured and weathered parent material of the soil above. Below all of these layers is solid bedrock.

Soil is classified according to grain size and as either organic or inorganic. The grain size classification is

- *gravel:* particles over 2 mm in diameter
- *sand:* particles from 0.05 mm to 2 mm in diameter; the finest grains just visible to the eye
- *silt:* particles from 0.002 mm to 0.05 mm in diameter; the grains are invisible but can be felt as smooth
- *clay:* particles under 0.002 mm in diameter; smooth and floury when dry, plastic and sticky when wet

All soils are a combination of the preceding types, and any site analysis must include a subsurface investigation to determine the types of soil present as well as the water content. Some soils are unsuitable for certain uses, and layers of different soil types may create planes of potential slippage or slides and make the land useless for development.

Gravels and sands are excellent for construction loads, drainage, and sewage drain fields, but they are unsuitable for landscaping.

Silt is stable when dry or damp but unstable when wet. It swells and heaves when frozen and compresses under load. Generally, building foundations and road bases must extend below it or must be elastic enough to avoid damage. Some nonplastic silts are usable for lighter loads.

Clay expands when wet and is subject to slippage. It is poor for foundations unless it can be kept dry. It is also poor for landscaping and unsuitable for sewage drain fields or other types of drainage because it retains water and drains slowly.

Peat and other organic materials are excellent for landscaping but unsuitable for building foundations and road bases. Usually, these soils must be removed from the site and replaced with sands and gravels for foundations and roads. Refer to Chap. 21 for more information on soil.

10

BUILDING ANALYSIS

Building analysis and architectural programming are processes for analyzing, defining, and solving an architectural problem in a way that meets both the client's needs and any applicable code requirements.

As building problems have become more complex and construction costs have risen, determining the client's precise needs has become more important than ever before. Analysis and programming help the client understand the real problem and provide a sound basis for making design decisions. Programming is considered an additional service under the standard AIA documents. Although programming may be done by anyone, the architect is usually the best individual to program, because most of the process relates directly to function, space, budget, and time, all aspects of a client's project that the architect knows best.

Programming is a process of *analysis*, whereas design is a process of *synthesis* once the problem is clearly defined. Analysis may include evaluating existing or historic structures and determining budgets, scheduling, and methods of finance. The process can apply to an individual space or room, a building, or an entire complex of structures.

Thorough programming includes a wide range of information. In addition to stating the goals and objectives of the client, a program report contains a site analysis, aesthetic considerations, space needs, adjacency requirements, organizing concepts, outdoor space needs, codes, budgeting demands, and scheduling limitations. If existing buildings are part of the project a program report may also include an evaluation of those structures for renovation or reuse. The building analysis will generally include the development of concepts for structural systems as well. This chapter covers all these topics except for developing alternatives for the building structure, which is discussed in Chap. 11.

The activities involved in building analysis and programming could include

- evaluating existing structures
- evaluating historic structures
- determining functional requirements
- creating a program
- creating a budget
- creating a schedule

EVALUATING EXISTING STRUCTURES

In many cases, a project is focused on the renovation or reuse of an existing structure, rather than the construction of a new building on a vacant site. In these situations, the architect must evaluate the existing structure to determine whether it is appropriate for the intended use. The evaluation process involves surveying the existing buildings, documenting the building surveys, researching applicable regulations, and evaluating the information.

The evaluation process also includes a preliminary comparison of the building's characteristics and infrastructure with the project program to determine whether the existing space can accommodate the programmatic requirements. If the existing buildings have historic value that the client wants to preserve, the architect will have additional work to do.

How much work, detail, and documentation go into the evaluation process depends on what is needed to test the project's feasibility. A quick survey of the structure's size and condition may be enough to confirm that the project is not feasible within the budget and that no further survey work should be done. If an initial survey indicates that the project might work, a more extensive survey and evaluation may be undertaken. If the preliminary evaluation shows that the structure is workable for the proposed use, another more detailed survey may be scheduled, and documentation may be created to provide the basis for detailed design work and construction documents.

Surveying Existing Buildings

A survey of an existing building must include several components. In most cases, the survey requires laborious field measurements and site-survey techniques, unless accurate as-built drawings are available. An existing building survey should document the following.

- *site features.* Including parking, service access, pedestrian access, adjacent properties, microclimate, and amenities like views and water features.
- *configuration of the building.* Including the building's overall size, shape, and height, as well as the locations of columns, bearing walls, beams, and other major structural components. The locations of partitions, toilets, mechanical rooms, and other service areas should also be noted.
- *structure of the building.* Including the type, load capacity, and condition. The condition of the foundation and primary structural frame is most important, because these support everything else and correcting or reinforcing them is expensive. A structural engineering consultant is usually needed for this portion of the survey.
- *roof.* Including the type, condition, and expected remaining life. This evaluation may include core drilling the existing roof to determine the composition and condition of the assembly, or infrared testing to find weakened areas. Are there any signs of water damage or leaking?
- *exterior envelope.* Including the type and condition. What type of existing insulation does it have and what R-value does the insulation provide? Are the windows in good condition? Infrared testing can also be helpful for envelope analysis.
- *mechanical systems.* Including the type of heating and cooling, the capacity of the central plant, and the condition of the distribution system. A mechanical engineering consultant is usually needed for this portion of the survey.
- *plumbing.* Including the capacity of service to the building, sewer capacity, condition of pipes and fixtures, and number of fixtures. A mechanical engineering consultant is usually needed for this portion of the survey.
- *electrical system.* Including the capacity of service to the building, condition of primary and secondary service, condition of wiring and devices, and condition of lighting and other electrical components. An electrical engineering consultant is usually needed for this portion of the survey.
- *fire protection system.* Including the condition of the system, pipe sizing, and spacing of heads. A fire protection or mechanical engineering consultant may be needed for this portion of the survey.
- *major equipment.* Depending on the building type, this component may not be applicable, or it may include such items as refrigeration equipment, commercial food service equipment, and laboratory equipment.
- *finishes.* Including the condition and expected life of major surface finishes.
- *compliance with accessibility requirements.* The condition of the egress system and fire-rated elements should also be evaluated.

If the building is a designated historic structure or has historic value, additional issues need to be investigated. These are discussed in the next section of this chapter.

The condition of the foundation and primary structural frame is most important.

The architect must ask the client about cost and time constraints. Although this is not a part of the actual building survey, it is a vital part of the evaluation process. In some cases, the client may not have a budget and may want the architect to develop an estimate of the costs involved in adapting an existing building to a new use.

Documenting Building Surveys

A building survey is documented by several means, including hand-drafted drawings and sketches prepared on site, CAD drawings, notes, formal reports, photographs, and videos. If architectural drawings and specifications of the structure exist, the architect should obtain these and verify them against the actual structure. The architect should also obtain any existing site surveys, soils investigations, and other documentation.

Drawings should include the building structure and exterior walls, as well as the locations of interior partitions, doors, equipment, woodwork, plumbing fixtures, and other pertinent items. The measurement accuracy of a survey and its drawings will depend on the structure's size and complexity, the time and equipment available to devote to field measurements, and the requirements of the building's new use. In most cases, accuracy to within $^1/_4$ in is better than adequate, and even $^1/_2$ in accuracy may be sufficient.

The building documentation should include other major features such as elevations of floors above a reference plane. Drawings of some elevations may also be needed. Mechanical and electrical equipment that will remain should be noted on the drawings, and elements that are to be removed should be highlighted.

Finally, the project should be documented with photographs, videos, or both.

Methods of Field Measuring and Recording

Traditionally, collecting information on the size and configuration of an existing building has required the architect to visit the site and take measurements, using a tape measure and traditional surveying equipment. The architect then produces drawings from these measurements. This method is labor intensive and susceptible to human error as well as to errors due to faulty measurement tools. However, hand measuring can be a useful, low-cost method when measuring buildings of moderate size and complexity. Hand measuring is also well suited for recording small details that cannot be seen using instruments with other techniques.

The use of simple tape measures has been augmented by more precise instruments. Low-cost, line-of-sight sonic devices can be used by one person and give reasonable accuracy for many uses. They can measure distance, area and volume and some models include additional measurement modes. However, their range can be limited and they cannot precisely differentiate between closely spaced elements.

Electromagnetic Distance Measurement

Electromagnetic distance measurement (EDM) uses a laser-based instrument with an onboard computer to measure the distance, horizontal angle, and vertical angle of a laser beam to a reflective prism target. These instruments are accurate to $\pm^1/_{64}$ in at 1600 ft. As with hand measuring, this method requires a knowledgeable operator to select the points to be measured. Two people are usually needed to operate this instrument.

A similar technique is *reflectorless electromagnetic distance measurement* (REDM). The device used in this process does not require the use of a prism reflector, but instead relies on the return signal bounced from the object being measured. The accuracy is less precise: $\pm^1/_8$ in at 100 ft. The accuracy of REDM is affected by the obliqueness of the laser beam on the targeted point, the distance from the instrument to the targeted point, and the reflective quality and texture of the targeted point.

Several image-based techniques other than standard photography are available to assist in the accurate surveying of existing structures. These include rectified photography, orthophotography, photogrammetry, and laser scanning.

Rectified Photography

Rectified photography uses digital cameras to photograph facades. The camera's focal plane is set parallel to the facade and gives a flat image with no perspective distortion. Measured points are used to remove distortion and scale the image. Dimensions can then be scaled off of the image, but to improve accuracy the building plane should be relatively flat. Rectified photography makes it possible to scale building elements not readily accessible to hand measuring; in addition, the photograph provides an accurate image of the building, as any photograph would.

Orthophotography

Orthophotography is similar to rectified photography, but uses digital photography and computer software to correct for optical distortion.

Photogrammetry

Photogrammetry is the surveying of objects or spaces through the use of photography and associated software. Common techniques for the application of this method are stereophotogrammetry and convergent photogrammetry.

Stereophotogrammetry uses two overlapping photographs in a computer program to produce a digital stereo image. The stereo image can be used to make an accurate three-dimensional drawing. In addition, this technique produces a photographic record. It requires specialized equipment and computer software, as well as trained technicians to do the work.

Convergent photogrammetry uses multiple photographic images of an object taken at different angles. Measurements and three-dimensional models are derived with the use of software that traces the overlapping photographs. Reference points must be established by standard surveying techniques or by measuring distances between the reference points to establish a correctly scaled coordinate system that the software can use. Although relatively inexpensive, convergent photogrammetry is slower than laser scanning. It has an accuracy of about ±0.05%.

Laser Scanning

Laser scanning uses medium-range pulsing laser beams that systematically sweep over an object or space to obtain three-dimensional coordinates of points on the surface being scanned. The resulting image is a "point cloud" that forms a three-dimensional image. From this image, computer software can develop plans, elevations, sections, and three-dimensional models.

The laser may scan from one or more points, depending on the exact system being used. For multiple room interiors, the images can be stitched together to give an overall image of an entire building. Unlike photogrammetry, no surveyed reference points are needed; all the information can be gathered from a single point rather than from multiple photographs. Laser scanning has an accuracy ranging from ±0.05% to ±0.01% or better.

Researching Applicable Regulations

Just as with a new construction project, with a renovation project the architect must obtain all the applicable codes and regulations. In addition to the relevant building codes, these can include zoning restrictions, easements, deed restrictions, covenants, historic preservation rules, energy conservation codes, and local agency regulations. The architect should consult existing drawings or the local building official to determine the building's construction type and its designated occupancy.

Analyzing Existing Structures

Evaluating whether an existing structure is adequate for a new use involves answering these basic questions.

- Do the location and features of the structure's site work for the new use? If not, can the site be adapted for the new use within the available time and budget?
- Do the structure's size and configuration work for the new use? If not, can the structure be adapted for the new use within the available time and budget?
- Are the appearance and character of the structure consistent with the client's design goals and desired image?

- How much work will be needed to repair, renovate, modify, and add to the structure for the new use, and how much will it cost? Will seismic renovation be required? The analysis should first include the foundation and primary structural elements, as these are the most expensive to modify and are always required for any other work. Additions and modifications to the secondary structural elements are less costly and are easier to accomplish.
- How much work is needed to repair, renovate, modify, and add to the mechanical, plumbing, electrical, and life safety systems to make the building work for the new use, and how much will it cost? If the building is not fully sprinklered, can the cost of adding sprinklers be justified by code requirement trade-offs and lower insurance rates?
- Does the new occupancy work with the existing building's construction type and area? If the maximum allowable area for the new occupancy is exceeded, firewalls may need to be built to separate the building into compartments. This may prove to be economically unfeasible. See Chap. 14 for a discussion of maximum allowable area and height based on occupancy and building type.
- What additional work is needed to bring the structure into compliance with current applicable codes and regulations? How much of the structure must be modified? Can this be done within the available time and budget?
- If a budget and schedule have not yet been established, what is the minimum amount of renovation needed, and how much will it cost? What is the desired amount of renovation needed, and how much will it cost? In both cases, how long might the project take to complete?

If extensive work and cost are needed, a detailed cost analysis should be performed to see if the project is economically feasible. Even an expensive and extensive remodeling project may be less costly than new construction, or the cost may be justified if the return on investment meets the client's needs. During this cost analysis, it is especially important to separate the client's genuine needs from those features that are merely desired.

EVALUATING HISTORIC STRUCTURES

Planning for the reuse of a historic structure presents unique opportunities and challenges. Depending on its age, a historic building may incorporate structural systems and construction materials that are difficult to evaluate based on modern needs and building codes. The Historic Preservation Service of the National Park Service has developed a wealth of information and regulations pertaining to national historic landmarks as well as historic preservation in general. Much of this information can be found on the National Park Service website (nps.gov).

Defining the Scope of the Problem

The first determination the architect must make is whether the structure is actually a designated historic landmark or simply an old building that the client would like to reuse while maintaining its historic character. If the structure is a national historic landmark or has similar landmark status on the state or local level, specific requirements will limit the type and extent of rehabilitation work allowed. In addition, if the owner wants to receive federal tax credits, the rehabilitation must qualify as a certified rehabilitation. In this case, the Secretary of the Interior's Standards for Rehabilitation (described in the next section) must be met. Requirements for national historic landmarks can be found by contacting the National Park Service. If the property is designated as a state or local historic landmark, the state historic preservation officer should be contacted.

A historic building may incorporate systems and materials that are difficult to evaluate based on modern needs and building codes.

Regardless of whether the project falls under the scope of federal, state, or local regulations, the architect, with the client, should determine which of four treatment approaches will be undertaken. If the building is a designated landmark, the state historic preservation officer and National Park Service should also be consulted.

The four treatment approaches (ranked from most historically accurate to least) are preservation, rehabilitation, restoration, and reconstruction.

Preservation attempts to retain all historic fabric through conservation, maintenance, and repair. It reflects the building's continuum over time and the respectful changes and alterations that have been made throughout the building's lifespan.

Rehabilitation emphasizes the retention and repair of historic materials, but gives more latitude to replacement, typically because the property is more deteriorated before work begins.

Both preservation and rehabilitation focus attention on the preservation of those materials, features, finishes, spaces, and spatial relationships that give a property its historic character. Rehabilitation, however, allows for incorporation of newer materials and technologies, as well as modifications to improve the usefulness or efficiency of the building. Most adaptive reuse projects, where a historic property is renovated to allow for a new use (for example, a factory converted into an apartment complex) fall into the category of rehabilitation projects.

Restoration focuses on the retention of materials from the most significant time in a property's history, while permitting the removal of materials from other periods.

Reconstruction is the least historically accurate approach. It allows the opportunity to re-create a non-surviving site, landscape, building, structure, or object in new materials.

Specific standards and detailed guidelines for each of these four treatments are available from the Historic Preservation Service office or at the National Park Service website (nps.gov).

Defining Regulatory Requirements

As codified in 36 CFR 67 for use in the Federal Historic Preservation Tax Incentives program, the Historic Preservation Service of the National Park Service has established ten general standards to guide historic preservation. These are often referred to as the Secretary of the Interior's Standards for Rehabilitation. They are to be applied to specific rehabilitation projects in a reasonable manner, taking into consideration economic and technical feasibility. When federal investment tax credits are involved, these standards take precedence over local historic preservation requirements.

The Standards for Rehabilitation are

1. A property shall be used for its historic purpose or be placed in a new use that requires minimal change to the defining characteristics of the building and its site and environment.
2. The historic character of a property shall be retained and preserved. The removal of historic materials or alteration of features and spaces that characterize a property shall be avoided.
3. Each property shall be recognized as a physical record of its time, place, and use. Changes that create a false sense of historical development, such as adding conjectural features or architectural elements from other buildings, shall not be undertaken.
4. Most properties change over time; those changes that have acquired historic significance in their own right shall be retained and preserved.
5. Distinctive features, finishes, and construction techniques or examples of craftsmanship that characterize a historic property shall be preserved.
6. Deteriorated historic features shall be repaired rather than replaced. Where the severity of deterioration requires replacement of a distinctive feature, the new feature shall match the old in design, color, texture, and other visual qualities and, where possible, materials. Replacement of missing features shall be substantiated by documentary, physical, or pictorial evidence.
7. Chemical or physical treatments, such as sandblasting, that cause damage to historic materials shall not be used. The surface cleaning of structures, if appropriate, shall be undertaken using the gentlest means possible.

8. Significant archeological resources affected by a project shall be protected and preserved. If such resources must be disturbed, mitigation measures shall be undertaken.
9. New additions, exterior alterations, or related new construction shall not destroy historic materials that characterize the property. The new work shall be differentiated from the old and shall be compatible with the massing, size, scale, and architectural features to protect the historic integrity of the property and its environment.

New additions and adjacent or related new construction shall be undertaken in such a manner that if removed in the future, the essential form and integrity of the historic property and its environment would be unimpaired.

The National Park Service has established similar guidelines for preservation, for restoration, and for reconstruction. The ten general standards to guide restoration projects are

1. A property will be used as it was historically or be given a new use which reflects the property's restoration period.
2. Materials and features from the restoration period will be retained and preserved. The removal of materials or alteration of features, spaces, and spatial relationships that characterize the period will not be undertaken.
3. Each property will be recognized as a physical record of its time, place, and use. Work needed to stabilize, consolidate, and conserve materials and features from the restoration period will be physically and visually compatible, identifiable upon close inspection, and properly documented for future research.
4. Materials, features, spaces, and finishes that characterize other historical periods will be documented prior to their alteration or removal.
5. Distinctive materials, features, finishes, and construction techniques or examples of craftsmanship that characterize the restoration period will be preserved.
6. Deteriorated features from the restoration period will be repaired rather than replaced. Where the severity of deterioration requires replacement of a distinctive feature, the new feature will match the old in design, color, texture, and, where possible, materials.
7. Replacement of missing features from the restoration period will be substantiated by documentary and physical evidence. A false sense of history will not be created by adding conjectural features, features from other properties, or by combining features that never existed together historically.
8. Chemical or physical treatments, if appropriate, will be undertaken using the gentlest means possible. Treatments that cause damage to historic materials will not be used.
9. Archeological resources affected by a project will be protected and preserved in place. If such resources must be disturbed, mitigation measures will be undertaken.
10. Designs that were never executed historically will not be constructed.

These guidelines are widely used at the federal level as well as by states, historic district commissions, and planning commissions. However, the architect must research any other specific regulations that may apply.

Surveying the Historic Structure

When surveying a historic building, the components listed in Surveying Existing Buildings apply. In addition, the structural survey of a historic building must include assessments of settlement, deflection of beams, and structural members damaged in previous renovations or for mechanical and electrical services. The physical survey should determine whether original or historic elements have been removed or altered, and if so, what their original appearance was.

The architect should identify the aspects of the building that define its historic character and put them in a list of priorities. These characteristics may include the overall form of the building, its materials, spaces, and workmanship, and other notable features that distinguish it from other buildings. A physical survey of the original appearance of the structure and its current condition may call for the services of a restoration specialist to perform tests and conduct other investigations.

Masonry in Historic Buildings

Many historic buildings were constructed of masonry, so the evaluation, repair, and restoration of masonry are particularly important. The Historic Preservation Service of the National Park Service provides recommendations for the treatment of historic masonry in several categories. The following are often covered in the ARE exam.

Identify, Retain, and Preserve

Unique masonry features from the restoration period should be identified and should not be altered or covered.

Protect and Maintain

To protect masonry, proper drainage should be provided so that water does not accumulate in joints or on horizontal surfaces.

Masonry surfaces should be cleaned only when this is needed to halt deterioration or remove heavy soiling. Tests should be conducted before cleaning in order to study which methods are best and what the long-term effects will be. The gentlest method possible should be used, such as cleaning with low-pressure water, detergents, and natural bristle brushes.

Sandblasting and chemical products that can damage masonry should not be used.

Paint should be removed only if it is damaged or deteriorated, and then, only to the next sound layer using the gentlest method possible. Repainting should be done with colors that are documented to the restoration period of the building, either through historical precedent or microscopic analysis.

Repair

Masonry and mortar may be repaired or replaced if there are signs of deterioration, looseness, or other damage. Mortar should be repointed by hand-raking the joints and duplicating the mortar in strength, composition, color, texture, and joint profile. Electric saws and hammers should not be used to remove mortar from joints. Mortar with high portland cement content should not be used for repointing.

Damaged masonry units should be repaired by patching, piecing in, or otherwise reinforcing the masonry using recognized methods of preservation. To a limited extent, extensively deteriorated or missing parts of masonry features may be replaced with similar pieces of the same material or a compatible substitute.

Replace

If a feature is too deteriorated to repair, it may be replaced with a reproduction. In reproducing the feature, existing physical evidence should be used as a model. If the same kind of material is not technically or economically feasible, then a compatible substitute material may be considered.

Remove Existing Features from Other Historic Periods

When the structure is composed of both original construction and construction from later historic periods, the objects and materials from other periods should be removed and, if possible, stored to facilitate future research.

Recreate Missing Features

If a masonry feature from the restoration period is entirely missing, a new feature may be recreated based on physical or documentary evidence. This should be considered only when none of the previous recommendations are feasible.

PROGRAMMING

Programming is the stage of defining the problem and establishing all the guidelines and needs on which the design process can be based. It is a time for analyzing all aspects of the problem and distilling its complexities into a few clear statements.

One popular programming method is a five-step process that focuses on four major considerations. It is described in *Problem Seeking: An Architectural Programming Primer* by William M. Peña and Steven A. Parshall (Wiley, 2012). The process involves establishing goals, collecting and analyzing facts, uncovering and testing concepts, determining needs, and stating the problem. Each of these steps must include consideration of function, form, economy, and time.

Establishing Goals

Goals are the client's objectives and the reasons behind them. It is not enough to simply list the types of spaces the client needs; the client is trying to achieve some goal with those spaces. For example, a goal for a school administration might be to increase the daily informal interaction between students and teachers.

It is important to identify the goals because, through the process of programming, they ultimately suggest the physical means by which they will be achieved.

Collecting Facts

Facts are the existing conditions and requirements for meeting the client's goals. Facts commonly collected in programming include the number of people to be accommodated, site conditions, space adjacency needs, user characteristics, equipment to be housed, expected growth rate, money available for construction, building code requirements, and climate information.

Because each project relies on so many facts, the programmer must not only to collect facts but also organize them so that they are useful.

Uncovering Concepts

The programming process should develop *programmatic concepts*, abstract solutions for the client's problems that do not define the specific, physical means that will be used to achieve these solutions. These programmatic concepts become the basis for later design concepts.

To continue the example, given the goal of increasing daily interaction between students and teachers, one programmatic concept toward this goal could be to provide common spaces for mixed flow in circulation patterns. A design concept in response to this could be to plan a central court through which all circulation paths pass. Programmatic concepts are discussed in more detail later in this section.

Determining Needs

In this step of the programming process, the architect balances the desires of the client against the available budget, or establishes a budget based on the defined goals and needs. During this step, wants are separated from needs. Most clients want more than they can afford, so a clear statement of true needs at this early stage of the process can help avoid problems later, and can help the client to understand where concessions may be necessary to fit within the budget. At this stage, one or more of the four elements of cost (quantity, quality, budget, and time) may have to be adjusted to balance needs against available resources.

Stating the Problem

Establishing goals, collecting facts, uncovering concepts, and determining needs are all just preludes to the ultimate goal of programming: summarizing the essence of the problem in a few succinct statements. These *problem statements* are the bridge between programming and the design process. In these statements, the client and architect agree on what are the most important aspects of the problem; these statements will then serve as the basis for design as well as the criteria by which the solution can be evaluated. There should be a minimum of four problem statements, one for each of the major considerations of form, function, economy, and time.

Four Major Considerations During Programming

The four major considerations of any design problem are function, form, economy, and time.

- *Function* relates to the people and activities within the space or building and their relationships.
- *Form* relates to the site, the physical and psychological environment of the building, and the quality of construction.
- *Economy* concerns money: the initial costs, operating costs, and life-cycle costs.
- *Time* concerns the past, present, and future as they affect the other three considerations. For example, the required schedule for construction is often a time consideration, as is the need for expansibility in the future.

Programmatic Concepts

Before the architect can develop a physical, three-dimensional design, he or she needs to develop *programmatic concepts*, which are general, abstract solutions to the client's problems. For example, *expansibility* could be a programmatic concept when working with a client whose needs may change significantly in the near future.

Later, in the design process, the architect uses these programmatic concepts as the basis for design concepts, which are specific physical solutions to the client's problems. Working from a programmatic concept of expansibility, for example, the architect's design concept might be to build a structure larger than is currently needed, to allow for expansion; another possible design concept could be to orient the building on the site so as to leave space for a future addition.

In *Problem Seeking*, Peña and Parshall identified 24 programmatic concepts that tend to recur in all types of buildings (though they generally do not all occur in the same building). These include the following.

- *Priority* establishes an order of importance among things such as the size of spaces, the position of spaces relative to one another, and the social or cultural values expressed through architecture. For example, if a client has the goal of enhancing the company's image, the building's entrance and reception area may have higher priority than individual offices.
- *Relationships* include the affinities of people and activities. This is one of the most common programmatic concepts established in any design problem because it most directly affects the organization of spaces and rooms.
- *Hierarchy* relates to the exercise or expression of authority through physical symbols. For example, to reflect the hierarchy of a traditional law firm, senior members may be given larger offices than junior members.
- *Character* is a response to the image that the client wants to project. It is a combination of the look and aesthetic feel of the environment. This is often reflected in design concepts that involve the building's size, shape, materials, organization, and other physical aspects.
- *Density*—typically rated low, medium, or high—describes how a parcel of land or an individual building or space is used. This is often in response to such goals as efficient use of land, compact use of office space, and the desired amount of interaction in a school.

- *Service groupings* include building services, such as mechanical, electrical, communications, and plumbing systems, as well as other functions that support the use of the building. Storage rooms, an information desk and waiting room, vending areas, and loading docks for delivery of supplies, are examples of service groupings. For example, a goal of decentralizing access to information could be accomplished by the physical design concept of using satellite libraries throughout a facility, or by developing an electronic database accessible to all workers through computer terminals.
- *Activity grouping* is a determination of whether activities should be integrated and grouped together or separated and compartmentalized. For example, if a goal is to create an intimate dining atmosphere in a restaurant, compartmentalizing a number of small, private dining areas could be the response.
- *People grouping* is concerned with how people are placed together based on their physical, social, and emotional characteristics. For example, the goal of establishing work teams in a factory might lead to a people grouping concept of keeping small groups together in the same physical space.
- *Home base* is related to the concept of territoriality and is a place where a person can maintain his or her individuality. A home base can be an apartment or an office or just a table in a coffee shop.
- *Communications* promotes the effective exchange of information or ideas by examining who communicates with whom and how exchanges are conducted.
- *Neighbors* refers to how the project will promote or prevent sociality and how the building or facility will relate to surrounding facilities. For example, two buildings may share a common entry court to foster interaction and community among users of both buildings.
- *Accessibility* is concerned with entry into a building and with making the facility accessible to all, regardless of familiarity with the facility or with physical capabilities. It examines the questions of how people find the entrance and make their way into and through the building and whether there should be multiple entrances.
- *Separated flow* relates to segregating the flow of people, automobiles, service access, and other activities of a building. For example, people may need to be separated from automobile traffic, or public visitors to a courthouse may need to be separated from prisoners.
- *Mixed flow* is the opposite of separated flow and is intended to promote interaction among people. Mixed flow may not be a desired programmatic concept in controlled facilities.
- *Sequential flow* is often needed for both people and objects where a specific series of events or processes is needed. For example, a show at an art museum may be designed so as to direct people from a starting point to an ending point. A factory is typically designed so that material progresses from one station to another in a definite sequence.
- *Orientation* is concerned with keeping people from feeling lost within a larger context, typically by providing a point of reference within a building or group of buildings. This could lead to physical design concepts such as a tower among a group of lower buildings, or a central atrium or lobby within a large building.
- *Flexibility* includes three different components. *Expansibility* refers to how a building can accommodate growth through expansion. *Convertibility* refers to how a building can allow for changes in function through the conversion of spaces. *Versatility* provides for several different activities with multifunctional spaces.
- *Tolerance* allows some extra space for an activity that is likely to change in the future, rather than fitting the space precisely. For example, an indoor swimming pool area could be sized to accommodate just the pool and circulation around it; designing for tolerance could give extra room to accommodate future bleachers or extra seating areas.
- *Safety* is focused on how to minimize the risk of injury or death. Building codes and other safety precautions are closely tied to this concept.
- *Security controls* are ways that both people and property can be protected, with the degree of security based on the value of the potential loss.

- *Energy conservation* can be achieved in several ways, such as by keeping the heated or cooled area to a minimum, by keeping heat flow to a minimum, by using materials produced using low amounts of energy, by using recycled materials, or by using recyclable materials.
- *Environmental controls* are controls designed to meet human comfort needs. These needs include levels of air temperature, light, sound, and humidity. This concept encompasses both mechanical systems and natural means of climate control.
- *Phasing* is concerned with completing the project in stages to meet time and cost schedules. It is also concerned with whether the project can use linear scheduling or must use concurrent scheduling to meet urgent occupancy requirements.
- *Cost control* is concerned with establishing a realistic preview of costs and a balanced budget to meet the client's available funds.

EVALUATING FUNCTIONAL REQUIREMENTS

Two important factors in determining the size and configuration of a building are the amount of space needed for activities in the building and the relationships that are needed among spaces.

Determining Space Needs

The main function of a building is to house a specific use. In addition, support spaces—mechanical rooms, toilet rooms, storage, circulation space, and so on—are always needed, and these will add to the overall size of the building.

Often, when programming begins, the client will tell the architect what areas—and in some cases heights—are needed for spaces in the new facility. These may be based on the client's experience or on corporate standards, or they may simply be a list of what currently exists. For example, the space standards of a corporation may dictate that a senior manager should have a 225 ft^2 office while a junior manager should be allotted 150 ft^2. These requirements from the client may be a sound basis for developing space needs, or the architect may need to review them during programming.

Where areas are not defined by one of these methods, the space needed for a particular use is determined in one of three ways.

- by the number of people who must be accommodated
- by an object or piece of equipment that will be within the space (including any clearances needed for using it)
- by an activity that has clearly specified space needs

Space needs are most commonly defined by the number of people who will be engaged in a particular activity. For example, each student sitting in a classroom needs about 15 ft^2 to 20 ft^2; this includes space for sitting in a chair as well as the additional space needed for walking within the classroom, the teacher's desk, shelving, and so on. Each office worker needs from 100 ft^2 to 250 ft^2, depending on whether employees are in private offices or in an open office plan; this includes space needed for walking within the office and may include space for visitors' chairs, personal files, and so on.

Sometimes space needs are based on some other factor that is nevertheless directly or indirectly related to the number of people. For example, preliminary planning of a hospital may be based on the number of beds, while library space may be determined based on the number of books.

In some cases, space needs are determined by fixed seating. Theaters, churches, and sports facilities, for example, call for this type of space planning. Where seating is fixed, the space per person is usually determined by the width of the seats, their row-to-row spacing, and how much additional space per seat must be allocated for aisles. Building codes give minimum requirements for seat spacing and aisle widths based on the occupant load and the arrangement of the seating. In *continental seating*, rows of seats are continuous and accessed only by the two side aisles. In *multiple aisle seating*, rows of seats are not continuous and there are intermediate aisles as well as side aisles. While continental seating requires fewer aisles, the row-to-row spacing must be greater to accommodate the larger number of people exiting each row.

Through experience and detailed analysis, general guidelines have been developed and put into common use for space needs for various types of uses. A representative sample of these is given in Table 10.1.

Table 10.1
Some Common Space Planning Guidelines

space type	area (ft^2)	criteria
offices	100–250	net area per person
restaurant dining	15–18	net area per seat
restaurant kitchens	3.6–5	net area per seat
hotel (1.5 persons/room)	550–600	gross area per room
library reading room	20–35	net area per person
book stacks	0.08	net area per bound volume
theaters with fixed seats	7.5	net area per person
assembly areas; moveable seats	15	net area per person
theater lobbies	30%	of seating area
classrooms	15–20	net area per student
stores	30–50	net area per person

In programming, *benchmarking* is the establishment of common standards for rooms, spaces, and activities based on the measurement of similar facilities. An architectural office may set benchmarks for the types of buildings it designs and use these benchmarks in programming.

However planning is done, the architect must determine the number of people (or seats, beds, etc.) who must be accommodated and then multiply this number by the area needed for each. This will include only the space needed for the specific activity, however, not the space needed to connect several rooms or spaces or for support areas such as mechanical rooms; these must be added to the basic space needs.

The second way space needs are determined is by the size of an object or piece of equipment and the space needed around it for operation. For example, the size of a printing press is part of what determines the area of a press room. Automobile sizes determine the space needs for parking garages.

The third way space needs are determined is through the rules or customs related to the activity itself. The playing area of a sports facility is an example of a space whose needs are determined in this way. The playing area of a basketball court must be a certain size regardless of the number of spectators present, which is then added to the space needed for the desired seating. A courtroom is an example of a space in which the procedures and customs of a process (the trial) dictate an arrangement of human activity and the spacing of individual areas that depend only in part on the number of people using the space.

Determining Total Buiding Area

Taken together, the individual areas determined by these methods make up the *net area* of a facility. The net area does not include space for general circulation between rooms, mechanical rooms, stairways, elevator and mechanical shafts, electrical and telephone equipment rooms, wall and structural thicknesses, and other spaces that do not directly house the primary activities of the building. Sometimes the net area is referred to as the *net assignable area* and these secondary spaces are referred to as the *nonassignable areas* (also called *unassigned* or *unassignable areas*).

Adding the net area to the unassigned areas gives the *gross building area*. The ratio of the net area to the gross area is the *efficiency* of the building, also called the *efficiency ratio* or *net-to-gross ratio*. The efficiency depends on the type of occupancy and how well the building is planned. A hospital, which contains many small rooms and many large corridors, will have a much lower efficiency than a factory, where most of the space is devoted to open production areas and very little space is used for corridors and other secondary spaces.

Building efficiencies most often range from 60% to 80%, though some uses may result in efficiencies outside this range. Some common efficiencies for building types are given in Table 10.2.

In some cases, the client may dictate the efficiency that must be met by the architect's design. This is usually the case when the efficiency is related to the amount of floor space that can be leased, such as in a retail mall or a speculative office building. Increasing the efficiency of a building is usually done by careful layout of the building's circulation plan. A corridor that serves rooms on both sides, for example, is much more efficient than one that serves rooms only on one side.

Once the net assignable area is determined and the appropriate efficiency is established (or estimated), the gross area of the building can be calculated by dividing the net assignable area by the efficiency.

Problems on the ARE may require the examinee to be familiar with various unassignable spaces. The areas may be given in an exhibit to a question, or the examinee may be expected to know how to make a reasonable allowance for mechanical rooms, toilet rooms, elevators, and so on, when their areas are not explicitly given. Table 10.3 lists some typical space requirements for nonassignable areas.

Table 10.2 Some Common Efficiency Ratios

space type	efficiency ratio
offices	0.75–0.85
retail offices	0.75–0.90
restaurants	0.65–0.70
public libraries	0.75–0.80
museums	0.83–0.90
theaters	0.60–0.75
hospitals	0.50–0.65

Programming & Analysis

Table 10.3 Space Requirements for Estimating Non-assignable Areas

space type	required area
mechanical rooms, total	5–9% of gross building area
heating, boiling rooms	3–5% of gross building area
heating, forced air	4–8% of gross building area
fan rooms	3–7% of gross building area
vertical dust space	3–4 ft^2 per 1000 ft^2 of floor space available
toilets	50 ft^2 per water closet
water closets	1 per 15 people up to 55; 1 per 40 people over 55
urinals	Substitute one for each water closet, but total water closets cannot be reduced less than $^2/_3$ of the number required
lavatories	1 per 15 people for offices and public buildings up to 60 people
	1 per 100 people for public assembly use
hydraulic elevator, 2000 lbm (1000 kg)	7 ft 4 in wide by 6 ft 0 in deep
elevator lobby space	6 ft 0 in deep
main corridors	5–7 ft
exit corridors	4 ft 0 in; 44 in minimum by code
monumental stairs	5–8 ft
exit stairs	4 ft 0 in, 44 in minimum by code

Example 10.1

The net assignable area of a small office building has been programmed as 65,000 ft^2. The desired efficiency ratio is 0.73. What should be the gross area of the building?

(A) 80,000 ft^2

(B) 89,000 ft^2

(C) 99,000 ft^2

(D) 110,000 ft^2

Solution

Divide the net assignable area by the efficiency ratio to find the gross area.

$$\begin{aligned} A_{\text{gross}} &= \frac{A_{\text{net}}}{\eta} \\ &= \frac{65{,}000 \text{ ft}^2}{0.73} \\ &= 89{,}041 \text{ ft}^2 \quad (89{,}000 \text{ ft}^2) \end{aligned}$$

The answer is (B).

DETERMINING RENTABLE AREA

When a client plans to lease space in an existing facility rather than construct a new building, the architect needs to determine the *rentable area* needed to accommodate the client's needs. As with the gross and net areas of a building, the needed rentable area is greater than the basic programmed usable area because it includes circulation and service spaces.

In a leased office, retail, residential, or industrial building, the building owner bases rents on the sum of two areas.

- the tenant's *occupant area*, which is the area used exclusively by the tenant's own business or function
- a prorated share of those areas of the building used by all tenants, such as common corridors, restrooms, elevator lobbies, and mechanical rooms, as well as building amenity areas such as building conference rooms, food service facilities, vending areas, and day care centers

Once the architect has determined the occupant area needed by the client (or at least has developed a good estimate), then the architect can determine the rentable area needed. The rentable area is found by multiplying the needed occupant area by a *load factor* to account for the shared portions of the building.

If the available rentable area is known, the architect can work backward to determine the available net area, and then compare this to the net area determined by programming. If the two values vary significantly, the client will have to either rent a larger space or reduce the amount of net space needed.

It is left entirely to the building owner to decide how the shared areas are measured and how each tenant is assigned a prorated portion. However, the Building Owners and Managers Association International (BOMA International) produces standards that give common methods of measuring space for retail, industrial, multi-unit residential, and mixed use buildings. These standards are widely used in the United States, Canada, and many other countries. For office buildings, the BOMA International standard is *Office Buildings: Standard Methods of Measurement* (ANSI/BOMA Z65.1).

The International Facility Management Association (IFMA) also produces standards used for measuring, including *Standard Practice for Building Floor Area Measurements for Facility Management* (ASTM E1836). The building owner could also be using a factor based on competitive market conditions rather than a published standard. In order to determine the rentable area needed by the client, the architect must know not only the occupant area needed but what method the building owner is using to calculate rentable area.

When a tenant occupies an entire floor, the occupant area includes all the space taken by the base building circulation as well as the elevator lobby. The *base building circulation* is the minimum path on a multi-occupant floor necessary for access to and egress from occupant areas, elevators, stairs, restrooms, janitorial closets, and similar areas.

When a leased office space occupies only part of a floor, ANSI/BOMA Z65.1 measures the occupant area to the inside, finished surfaces of multi-occupant corridor partitions and to the centerlines of *demising partitions* (partitions that separate adjacent tenant spaces). Where the measurement is taken to an external wall, then

- if 50% or more of the area of the external wall is glass, the occupant area is measured to the inside surface of the glass
- otherwise, the occupant area is measured to the inside surface of the exterior wall

Columns, recessed entries, and structural projections are ignored. See Fig. 10.1.

ANSI/BOMA Z65.1 uses two methods to determine the rentable area for a tenant: Method A (the *legacy method*) and Method B (the *single load factor method*). Both methods arrive at the rentable area by multiplying the occupant area by a load factor.

- Method A may result in different load factors for different floors of a building, and it uses a separate *R/U ratio* (rentable area divided by usable area) for each floor.
- Method B results in the same load factor for all floors of a building, and it uses the *R/O ratio* (preliminary or net floor area divided by usable area) instead of the *R/U* ratio.

The details for measuring the various areas of a building and calculating load factors are complex and beyond the scope of this book. The building owner is responsible for calculating the load factor, and the architect uses the load factor to help the client determine how much rentable space is needed.

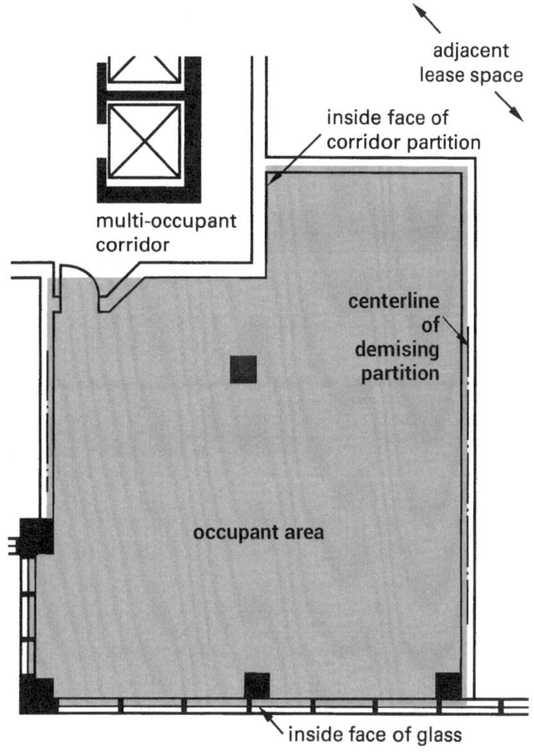

Figure 10.1 Method of Measuring Occupant Area

Example 10.2

A small insurance company is planning to move to a new leased office space. After programming, the architect determines that the client needs approximately 4500 ft^2 of net assignable space. Efficiency for the office building is 0.75. The leasing manager for the building tells the client that the building load factor is 1.20. Approximately how much space does the client need to lease?

(A) 5400 ft^2

(B) 6000 ft^2

(C) 7200 ft^2

(D) 8800 ft^2

Solution

First, calculate the gross area needed by dividing the net assignable area by the efficiency ratio.

$$A_{\text{gross}} = \frac{A_{\text{net}}}{\eta} = \frac{4500\ \text{ft}^2}{0.75} = 6000\ \text{ft}^2$$

Next, calculate the rentable area by multiplying the gross area by the load factor.

$$A_{\text{rentable}} = A_{\text{gross}}\text{LF} = (6000\ \text{ft}^2)(1.2) = 7200\ \text{ft}^2$$

The answer is (C).

DETERMINING SPACE RELATIONS

Not only must spaces be the right sizes for the activities they support, but they must also be located near the other spaces they share functional relationships with. The architect identifies these relationships during programming and assigns a hierarchy of importance to them. The relationships are usually recorded as an *adjacency matrix* or more graphically as an *adjacency diagram*, sometimes called a *bubble diagram*. See Fig. 10.2.

Figure 10.2 Methods of Recording Space Relationships

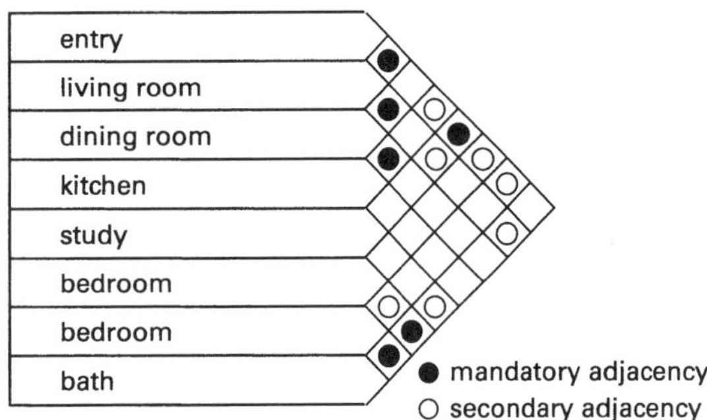

(a) adjacency matrix

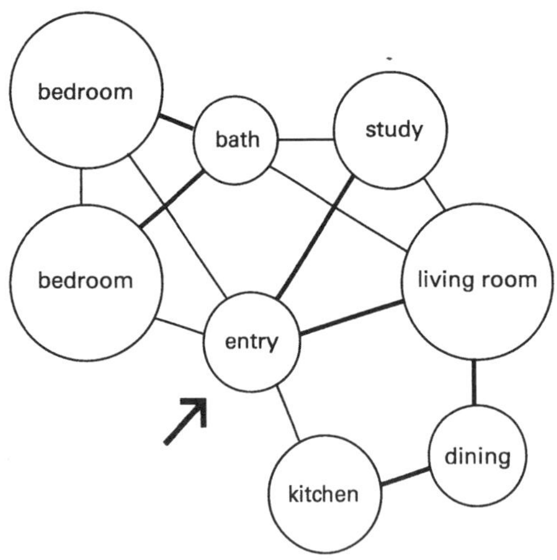

(b) adjacency diagram

There are three basic types of adjacency needs: people, products, and information. How the architect designs the physical space in response to these needs will differ with each type.

Two or more spaces may need to be physically adjacent or located very close to one another when people need face-to-face contact or when people move from one area to another as part of the building's use. For example, the entry to a theater, the lobby, and the theater space have a particular functional requirement for being arranged the way they are. Because of the normal flow of people, these three spaces must be adjacent. In some cases, two or more spaces may need to be accessible to each other but don't need to be directly adjacent; this can be accomplished with a corridor or through another intervening space.

Products, equipment, and other objects may move between spaces and need another type of adjacency. The spaces themselves may not have to be close to one another, but the movement of objects must be facilitated. Dumbwaiters, pneumatic tubes, assembly lines, and other conveying systems can connect spaces of this type.

It may be necessary that people in two or more spaces be able to exchange information but do not need to be physically near each other. The adjacency may then be entirely electronic or be established through a paper-moving system. Though this is a common situation, allowing for informal personal interactions may be advantageous for other reasons.

The programmer analyzes the various types of adjacency requirements and verifies them with the client. Since it is seldom possible to accommodate every desirable relationship, the ones that are mandatory need to be identified separately from the ones that are highly desirable or simply useful.

BUDGETING DURING PROGRAMMING

Establishing a budget is one of the most important parts of programming. The budget influences many design decisions and can determine the feasibility of a project. During later stages of design, an initial budget is refined as more information becomes available. (See Chap. 30 for more information on how a budget and cost estimates are refined during project planning and design.)

There are several common methods for setting a budget.

For a speculative or for-profit project, the owner or developer works out a *pro forma* statement listing the expected income that the project will generate and the expected costs to build the project. An estimated selling price of the developed project or rent per square foot is calculated and balanced against the project costs (e.g., construction price). In order to make the project economically feasible, a limit is set on the building costs. This becomes the budget within which the architect must work.

Budgets for public projects such as government facilities and educational institutions are often established through public funding or legislation. In these cases, the construction budget is often fixed without the architect's involvement, and the project must be designed and built for the fixed amount. Unfortunately, when public officials estimate the cost to build a project, they sometimes neglect to include all aspects of development, such as professional fees, furnishings, and other line items.

At the request of the owner, the architect may set a budget based on the scope of the proposed project. This is the most realistic and accurate way to establish a preliminary budget, because it is based on a specific building type of a defined size on a specific site.

Four basic variables must be considered when developing any construction budget: quantity, quality, available funds, and time. These four are always interrelated; one cannot be changed without changing one or more of the others. For instance, if an owner needs a specific amount of square footage built (quantity), needs the project built by a specific date, and has a fixed amount of money to spend, then the quality of the construction will have to be adjusted to meet the other constraints. If time, quality, and the total budget are fixed, then the amount of space constructed must be adjusted.

In some cases, *value engineering* can be performed. Value engineering involves reviewing individual systems and materials to see if the same function can be accomplished in a less expensive way. Value engineering is typically done during schematic design or design development, but it may be performed during any phase of a project. Value engineering is discussed in more detail in Chap. 30.

Project Cost Items

Many variables affect project cost. Construction cost is only one part of the total project development budget; other parts include site acquisition, site development, fees, and financing. Table 10.4 lists most of the items commonly found in a project budget and a typical range of values based on construction cost. Not all of these are part of every development budget, but they illustrate the types of factors that must be considered.

Table 10.4 Project Budget Line Items

A	site acquisition		$1,100,000
B	building cost	ft^2 times cost per ft^2	(assume) $6,800,000
C	site development	10% to 20% of B	(15%) $1,002,000
D	total construction cost	B + C	$7,820,000
E	moveable equipment	5% to 10% of B	(5%) $340,000
F	furnishings		$200,000
G	total construction and furnishings	D + E +F	$8,360,000
H	professional services	5% to 10% of D	(7%) $547,400
I	inspection and testing		$15,000
J	escalation estimate	2% to 10% of G per year	(10%) $836,000
K	contingency	2% to 10% of G	(8%) $668,800
L	financing costs		$250,000
M	moving expenses		(assume) $90,000
N	total project budget	A + G +H through M	$11,867,200

Building cost is the money needed to construct the building, including structure, exterior cladding, finishes, and electrical and mechanical systems, as well as the contractor's overhead and profit.

Site development costs, such as parking, drives, fences, landscaping, exterior lighting, and irrigation systems, are usually separate from the building cost. If the development is large and affects the surrounding area, a developer may be required to upgrade roads, extend utility lines, and do other major off-site work as a condition of getting approval from public agencies.

Furniture, fixtures, and equipment (FF&E) include movable equipment; furnishings such as furniture, accessories, and window coverings; and major equipment needed to put the facility into operation. These are often listed as separate line items because the funding for them may come out of a separate budget and because they may be supplied under separate contracts.

Professional services include architectural and engineering fees as well as costs for services such as as topographic surveys, soil tests, special consultants, appraisals, and legal consultation. Inspection and testing costs include those for special on-site, full-time inspection (when required), as well as the costs of testing concrete, steel, window assemblies, roofing, and other building materials as needed.

Because construction takes a great deal of time, inflation should be accounted for. Generally, the value of the budget at present rates is multiplied by an inflation factor to get its expected value at the midpoint of construction. The architect can make an educated guess at future inflation by looking at past cost indexes and inflation rates and applying an estimate to the expected condition of the construction.

The budget should include a contingency to account for unforeseen changes by the client, errors in the contractor's pricing or construction, an unanticipated rise in the cost of a key building material, default of a subcontractor, and other possible conditions that would add to the cost. This is generally calculated as a percentage of the total budget. A budget made early in the project should use a higher percentage for this contingency than one made later in the project, because there are more unknowns. A contingency of 5% to 10% is common.

Financing includes the long-term interest paid on permanent financing as well as the immediate costs of loan origination fees, construction loan interest, and other administrative costs. The cost of financing a long-term loan can easily exceed all the original building and development costs. In many cases, long-term interest, called *debt service*, is not included in the project budget because it is an ongoing cost to the owner, similar to maintenance costs.

Many clients include moving costs in the development budget. For large companies especially, the cost of moving can be substantial.

Example 10.3

Which of the following need NOT be accounted for in a project development budget?

(A) professional services

(B) debt service

(C) site development

(D) a contingency

Solution

Debt service is the cost to pay off the construction loan for a project and is generally considered an ongoing cost over many years, not part of the original cost of the project.

The answer is (B).

Methods of Budgeting

The costs shown in Table 10.4 represent a budget that is prepared during programming, or even before programming, to test the feasibility of a project. The numbers are preliminary, often based on incomplete or estimated information. For example, the building cost may be based simply on an estimated cost per square foot multiplied by the estimated gross area needed. The estimated cost per square foot may be derived from historical information on similar buildings in the area, from experience, or from commercially available cost books.

Budgeting, however, is an ongoing activity for the architect. At each stage of the design process, the architect should revise the budget to reflect decisions made up to that point. The AIA owner-architect agreement states that if the cost of the project exceeds the budget, the architect may be required to redesign the project to bring it within the budget, with no additional compensation. To avoid this, the architect should make frequent checks of the expected cost of the work against the budget.

There are three basic methods of preparing budgets and estimating costs during the programming or schematic phase of a project. The method that is most appropriate for a particular project depends on how much accuracy is needed and what stage of development the project is in. Methods of refining the construction budget are discussed in Chap. 30.

In the *project comparison method*, the cost of the new project is estimated using the costs of past projects of similar scope and function. This method is often used when setting a budget or determining a project's feasibility. Most pre-design budgets are based on area, but a different basis can be used. Some companies develop rules of thumb for estimating cost per hospital bed, student, hotel room, or some other functional unit.

The project comparison method is typically accurate within 15% to 25%. It requires information on projects of similar types, scope, and quality. When this estimating method is used, three budgets are often developed: low, midrange, and high.

Another way of estimating costs is the *area method*, also called the *square-foot method* or, when based on volume rather than area, the *volume method*. This type of estimate is usually prepared when preliminary design is completed and the architect has a fairly good idea of the size of the project, its functional components, and the general level of quality or complexity. With this method of estimation, an average cost per unit of area or volume may be used, but the actual area or volume is more precisely known than in the project comparison method. At this stage, the type and extent of site development needed are also known.

The project may be considered as separate parts with different costs per unit of area or volume. For example, a school may include classroom space, laboratory space, shop space, office space, and gymnasium space, each with a different cost per square foot. The area method typically has an accuracy within 5% to 15%.

A third way of estimating costs is the *assembly method*, also called the *system method*. During schematic design, when more is known about the space requirements and general configuration of the building and site, budgeting can be based on major subsystems. Historical cost information on each type of subsystem can be applied to the design. At this point, it is easier to see where the money is being used in the building.

Design decisions can then be based on studies of alternative systems. A typical subsystem budget is shown in Table 10.5.

Table 10.5
Subsystem Cost Budget of Office Buildings

	average cost	
subsystem	($/ft^2)	(% of total)
foundations	3.96	5.2
floors on grade	3.08	4.0
superstructure	16.51	21.7
roofing	0.18	0.2
exterior walls	9.63	12.6
partitions	5.19	6.8
wall finishes	3.70	4.8
floor finishes	3.78	5.0
ceiling finishes	2.79	3.7
conveying systems	6.45	8.5
specialties	0.70	0.9
fixed equipment	2.74	3.6
HVAC	9.21	12.1
plumbing	3.61	4.6
electrical	4.68	6.1
	76.21	100.0

Values for low-, average-, and high-quality construction for different building types can be obtained from cost databases and published estimating manuals and applied to the structure being budgeted. The dollar amounts included in system cost budgets usually include markup for contractor's overhead and profit and other construction administrative costs. The assembly method has an accuracy within about 10%.

Land Values

When making a decision about site selection, whether for potential development or the adaptive reuse of an existing building, the costs associated with the property itself are vital information. In addition to the cost of acquiring the land, the costs of site improvements, building construction, appraisal, financing, professional fees, permits, and maintenance of the completed structure must all be considered. If all these expenses cannot be paid off in a reasonable amount of time and yield a profit to the owner or developer, the site is probably a poor economic choice.

Land values are generally most influenced by three factors: location, local market conditions (which include demand for the land), and the potential for generating profit. Location considerations include the catchment area (the potential surrounding market area), the population density in the region, special features of the site (such as being on a waterfront), and proximity to transportation and utilities, which is especially important to residential and industrial development.

Land appraisal is based on the idea of "highest and best use," which means that the value assumes that the property will be used and developed in such a way as to yield the highest return on investment. Property that is not used to this capacity is said to be *underdeveloped*.

There are three basic ways land value is calculated.

- *market approach*. The surrounding neighborhood or region is investigated to find similar properties that have recently sold or are on the market. The property is assumed to have the same value as the similar properties, possibly with adjustments to reflect the unique nature of the property. For example, if three nearby house lots in a subdivision recently sold for around $400,000 each, and they were all about the same size, then a fourth lot of similar size would also be valued at about $400,000. Land value is often based on value per square foot, acre, or another unit quantity that can be conveniently applied to properties that are not exactly the same.
- *income approach*. The value of the land is calculated based on the potential the property has to yield a profit (i.e., net income). The potential gross income is estimated (allowing for vacancies and credit losses), then various expenses (e.g., taxes, insurance, and maintenance) are deducted. Because potential net income is usually figured on a yearly basis, this amount must be capitalized to estimate the current total value of the property.
- *cost approach*. The value of the land is estimated at its highest and best use. Then, the cost to replace the building or add improvements is calculated. The estimated accrued depreciation is figured and subtracted from the replacement cost or the cost of the improvements. This adjusted amount is then added to the land value to give the total value of the property.

Tax Structure

The taxes to which a developer is subject can influence whether a project is undertaken and how the site is developed. Property taxes are an ongoing operating cost of a development, and can be estimated fairly easily if one knows the tax rate in the municipality and the assessed value of the property on which tax is based.

Property taxes are often expressed as a *mill levy*, which is the number of mills, or thousandths of a dollar, that are charged per $1000 of assessed value. The assessed property value is a percentage of the actual value of the property, and the percentage is set by the taxing authority.

Taxing authorities may offer various tax incentives to developers as a way of implementing public policy. For example, to encourage historic preservation, tax credits may be given for renovating historic structures, or new businesses may be encouraged to move to a particular city by reducing or eliminating taxes for a certain period. Tax incentives may turn an otherwise uneconomical project into a viable one.

Example 10.4

The assessed valuation of developed property is based on 19% of actual value, and the mill levy is 49.31 mills. A developed piece of property is estimated to have an actual value of $150,000. Approximately what is the yearly tax?

(A) $1400

(B) $3000

(C) $3900

(D) $5800

Solution

To find the assessed value, multiply the actual value by the percentage set by the taxing authority.

$$\begin{aligned}\text{assessed value} &= (\$150{,}000)(0.19) \\ &= \$28{,}500\end{aligned}$$

To find the yearly tax, multiply the assessed value by the mill levy (which is in dollars per $1000) and divide by $1000.

$$\begin{aligned}\text{yearly tax} &= \frac{(\$28{,}500)(49.31)}{\$1000} \\ &= \$1405 \quad (\$1400)\end{aligned}$$

The answer is (A).

PUBLIC WORKS FINANCING

There are several methods by which government agencies can finance public works projects. These include general sales and property taxes, special sales taxes, general obligation bonds, revenue bonds (or rate-supported bonds), public enterprise revenue bonds, tax-increment financing, development impact fees, subdivision exactions, and special district assessments. These methods have different requirements and are used for different purposes.

General Sales Taxes and Property Taxes

A *general tax* is any tax imposed for general governmental purposes. Property taxes are an *ad valorem* tax, which is a tax based on the value of the property being taxed. The money collected by a municipality or other jurisdiction is placed in a general fund, and that jurisdiction may use the money as needed.

Although general taxes may be used to fund public works, they are more typically used to pay for ongoing operation and maintenance of existing facilities and normal capital improvements, such as replacing curbs or remodeling schools. Major projects are more often funded with other methods.

Depending on the local or state jurisdiction, an increase to general taxes may be limited or may require a vote of the general population. An increase in property taxes, however, usually occurs when the value of property is increased by the local jurisdiction's tax assessment office, even if the rate of taxation is unchanged.

Special Sales Taxes

A *special sales tax* is any tax that is imposed for a specific purpose or by a single-purpose authority. For example, a special sales tax might be assessed to fund a major transportation project. Special sales taxes require a majority vote of the people in the district.

General Obligation Bonds

General obligation bonds are issued by a city or state and backed by general tax revenue and the issuer's credit. These bonds are typically used to finance the acquisition or construction of specific public capital facilities, such as schools, museums, and libraries, and to purchase real property. The jurisdiction issuing the bond is authorized to levy a property tax at the rate needed to repay the principal and interest of the bonds, usually over a period of 10 to 30 years.

Each general obligation bond measure requires approval of the voters. Because all taxpayers in the jurisdiction issuing the bonds must pay a property tax to pay off the bonds, a voter majority is needed.

Revenue Bonds

Revenue bonds (often called *rate-supported bonds*) are similar to general obligation bonds in that they are issued by a local government to pay for a facility or improvement. However, revenue bonds are backed by the revenue that will come from customers who use the services that the bonds funded. In most cases, rates are increased to pay for retirement of the bonds. Construction, renovation, and expansion of city water and sewer facilities are often funded with revenue bonds.

Public Enterprise Revenue Bonds

Public enterprise revenue bonds are bonds issued by cities or counties to finance facilities for revenue-producing public enterprises. The bonds are paid off from revenues generated by the facilities through the charges they impose. Airports, parking garages, and hospitals are examples of facilities that may use this method of financing.

Tax-Increment Financing

A city can use *tax-increment financing* to pay for improvements that will encourage private development in an area and generate increased taxes due to increased property values. To do this, a city creates a special district and makes public improvements within that district. The assessed values of properties within the district are determined, and taxes based on those values are frozen for a defined period of time set forth in the development plan. Bonds are issued at the beginning of the redevelopment. The revenue from the bond issue is used to ensure that each taxing jurisdiction continues to receive its share of the taxes based on the original assessed valuation. At the end of the development period, the assessed property values increase due to the new development, and the increase in tax revenue (the tax increment) goes into a special fund created to retire the bonds.

Tax-increment financing does not require a vote by the people in the district.

Devolopment Impact Fees

Development impact fees are imposed on developers in order to pay for the improvements to off-site infrastructure (such as roads, utilities, and fire and police departments) that the new development makes necessary. Through these fees, a municipality can make these costs the responsibility of developers rather than existing residents.

Impact fees may be charged in addition to other *exactions*, such as hookup fees for utility service, and can be used for projects such as street improvements or construction of wastewater treatment plants. Impact fees are often controversial because of debate over how the fee is calculated and who really benefits from the new public facilities.

Subdivison Exactions

Subdivision exactions are similar to development fees in that they put a burden on the developer, but subdivision exactions are not used to fund construction. Rather, they are requirements that developers either dedicate some land for public use or contribute cash for the purchase of land and facilities by local governments.

Special District Assessments

There are several variations of *special district assessments*, often called *business improvement districts* (BIDs) or *benefit assessments*. These fees are used to fund public space improvements, such as parks and streetscapes, in order to enhance an area's appeal and, indirectly, increase its property values. A special tax district is established that encompasses the properties that will benefit from the proposed improvements. If a majority of property owners in the area agree to the arrangement, then all owners within its boundaries are required to contribute. Taxes are assessed on all property owners in the district. This type of funding is usually, but not always, used to improve or maintain existing facilities. It is not intended to encourage private development.

Project Financing

Building projects are financed in many ways. The following are some of the most common.

- A *mortgage loan* is used to purchase property. In exchange for the loan, the borrower grants the lender a lien on the property until the loan is repaid. This is the most common method by which individuals purchase homes.
- A *blanket loan* (sometimes called a *blanket mortgage*) is often used to fund the purchase of a large piece of real estate that the borrower intends to subdivide and resell as smaller parcels. If this type of purchase were financed with a traditional mortgage, then each time a parcel was sold the borrower would have to repay the entire loan and secure a new mortgage on the unsold parcels. With a blanket mortgage, each time a parcel is sold a portion of the mortgage is paid back and retired, but the remainder of the mortgage is still in force.
- A *bond* is a type of debt security issued by a government entity (such as a school board, city council, or state or national government) to raise money for a construction project. The issuer of the bond receives money from the buyer, and in exchange the issuer promises to repay the principal with interest on a later date. Bonds are typically sold to individual investors and investment companies.
- A *bridge loan* is a short-term loan used to purchase property or finance a project quickly, before long-term financing can be arranged.
- A *construction loan* is used to finance the building of a project and is in effect only for the duration of construction. Once construction is complete, the loan must be converted into a long-term, permanent loan whereby the lender is repaid monthly.
- A *hard money loan* is a relatively short-term loan used when there is a distressed financial situation such as foreclosure, bankruptcy, or nonpayment of a previous loan. The loan is based on the quick-sale value (which is usually significantly less than the market value) of an asset such as a parcel of property or other real estate. High interest rates are usual.
- A *mezzanine loan* is secured by collateral in the stock of the development company rather than in the developed property. In the event of default, the lender can seize the assets of the borrower more quickly than with a standard mortgage loan. This type of loan is often used by developers for large projects.

  As part of project financing, a developer will create a pro forma statement, which includes a plan for project financing. A *pro forma statement* is a statement or model of all the expected expenses (both initial and long term) of developing a project, compared to the expected income and increase in value of the project. (*Pro forma* is Latin for *as a matter of form.*) A pro forma statement is developed in order to determine whether the project is likely to be financially successful.

SCHEDULING

There are two major parts of a project schedule: *design time* and *construction time*. The architect has control over the design time, including the production of contract documents, but practically no control over the construction time.

However, a design professional must be able to estimate the entire project schedule so that the best course of action can be taken toward meeting the client's goals. For example, if the client must move into the building by a certain date, and normal design and construction schedules would make this impossible, the architect may recommend a fast-track schedule or other alternative approach in order to meet the deadline.

Design-Bid-Build

The traditional *design-bid-build* delivery process consists of several clearly defined phases. Each phase must be substantially finished and approved by the client before the next can begin. The AIA owner-architect agreement references the commonly accepted phases of design-bid-build. See Chap. 3 for a discussion of other project delivery methods that can shorten the total design and construction time.

After programming, the phases of the design-bid-build process are

1. *schematic design.* The general layout of the project is developed and preliminary alternative studies are conducted for materials and building systems. The direction of the project documented in schematic design drawings is reviewed and approved by the client.
2. *design development.* The decisions made during schematic design are refined and developed in more detail. Preliminary or outline specifications are written, and a more detailed cost analysis is developed.
3. *construction document production.* Construction documents include the final working drawings, the full project manual, and any necessary bidding and contract documents.
4. *bidding* (or *negotiation*). Bids are obtained from several contractors and the project is awarded to one of the bidders. (Alternatively, a contract is negotiated with a selected contractor.)
5. *construction administration.* The architect acts as the owner's agent and representative in overseeing and approving construction.

The time needed for these phases can vary greatly and depends on the following factors.

- *the size and complexity of the project.* A 500,000 ft^2 hospital will take much longer to design than a 30,000 ft^2 office building.
- *the number of people working on the project.* Although adding more people to the design or construction team can shorten the schedule, there is a point of diminishing returns. Having too many people creates a management and coordination problem, and for some phases only a few people are needed, even for very large jobs.
- *the abilities and design methodology of the project team.* Younger, less experienced designers typically need more time than more experienced designers to do the same amount of work.
- *the type of client and the client's decision-making and approval processes.* Large corporations and public agencies are likely to have a multilayered decision-making and approval process. Getting necessary information or approval for one phase from a large client may take weeks or even months. However, a small, single-authority client might make the same decision in a matter of days.

The final construction schedule is typically established by the contractor or construction manager after the project is awarded. However, the architect must often create a projected construction schedule while still in the programming phase, to give the client some idea of the total time from project conception to move-in. The architect must make it clear to the client that any such projected schedule is only an estimate and that the architect can in no way guarantee any estimate of the construction schedule.

Many factors can affect construction time. Most can be controlled to some degree, but some (such as the weather) cannot. In addition to the size and complexity of the project, some of the more common variables are

- the contractor's ability to manage both his or her own forces and those of the subcontractors
- material delivery times

- the quality and completeness of the architect's drawings and specifications
- the weather
- labor availability and labor disputes
- new construction or remodeling (remodeling generally takes more time and coordination than new construction)
- site conditions (construction on sites with subsurface problems usually takes more time)
- the architect's construction administration process and skill (e.g., some professionals are more diligent than others in performing their duties during construction)
- lender approvals
- agency and governmental approvals

See Chap. 4 and Chap. 6 for more information on developing and monitoring schedules and setting design fees based on the anticipated schedule.

Example 10.5

Which of the following project management activities would most likely ensure that construction documents are completed on schedule and within budget?

(A) documenting all meetings and correspondence

(B) establishing time and fee projections

(C) monitoring time sheets

(D) setting milestones

Solution

Monitoring the progress of a job is critical to ensuring that the original schedule and fee projects are being met.

Although establishing time and fee projections is a critical component of project management early in the project, continual monitoring is also required. Setting milestones for when certain intermediate work is to be completed is also important, but actual work completion must be compared with the estimated schedule to meet the final deadline.

The answer is (C).

DEFINITIONS

abatement: A reduction in the price of a property due to the discovery of some problem that tends to decrease the property's value.

accessory building: A building whose function is secondary to that of the main structure.

amenities: Desirable features of a building or near a building that have the effect of increasing the property's value.

amortization: The payment of a loan using equal payments at equal intervals over the life of the loan. Each payment provides for a portion to be applied to the principal and the remainder to be applied to the interest.

anchor tenant: A major tenant in a shopping mall, such as a department store, that in theory serves to attract shoppers to the mall to the benefit of other, smaller stores. Compare with *satellite tenant.*

appraisal: An estimation of a property's value made by a qualified appraiser.

aquifer: A natural, underground reservoir from which wells draw water.

assessed value: The value given to a piece of property by a local jurisdiction, to be used in assessing taxes on the property. The assessed value is a percentage of the actual value, which is the value that the property would command on the open market.

bedroom community: A region or small town that contains mainly housing and offers few employment opportunities.

blighted area: An area of a city in which many buildings are in a state of decay and in need of improvement. Some state laws include more specific definitions.

boilerplate: A standard portion (generally a paragraph or longer) of a written document, such as a contract or architectural specification, that appears in all similar documents.

buffer zone: A piece of land used to separate two incompatible uses.

capital expenditure: An amount of money used to make physical improvements to a property to enhance the property's value over an extended period of time.

cash flow: The amount of money that is net income from a property after expenses are paid.

CC&Rs: Abbreviation for "covenants, conditions, and restrictions," which are all the rules that apply to a property owner in a subdivision, condominium, or cooperative housing facility.

cluster housing: A particular type of housing development in which the houses or apartments are placed close to each other and have access to nearby common open spaces.

common area: A portion of a building or development that is available for the use of all tenants or unit owners. Typically, common areas are owned either by the property owners in the development or by a homeowners' association, and property owners pay the maintenance fees.

conditional use permit (CUP): A permit given by a city or other zoning jurisdiction for a proposed use that would otherwise not be allowed in a particular zoning district. The conditional use permit gives the zoning jurisdiction a means of imposing special conditions on the proposed development, to ensure that the development will not adversely affect the surrounding neighborhood or the public safety and welfare.

condominium: A development in which residents own their own living units but share common areas, which are maintained by the condominium corporation.

conveyance: The act of transferring an interest in a property to another person, or the document written to formalize such a transfer.

cooperative (or *co-op*): A type of land ownership where the residents of individual units own an interest in the corporation that owns the entire property. Unlike the residents of a condominium, the residents of a cooperative do not own their own units directly.

cul-de-sac: A dead-end street that has only one way in and often features a large circular turnaround space at the end.

dedication: The donation of a parcel of land by a developer for public use, such as for a park or school.

demising wall: See *party wall.*

despoil: To remove items of value (from a site).

development rights: The legal right of a developer to develop a parcel of land.

discount rate: The rate of interest that reflects the time value of money and that is used to discount future values to present values or to calculate the future value of money invested at the discount rate.

downzoning: A change in zoning resulting in a decrease of allowable density.

easement: The right to use a portion of land owned by another for a specific purpose, such as the right to use a private road through another's property to reach a property otherwise inaccessible from public roads.

eminent domain: The right of a governmental jurisdiction to take ownership of private property for the public good while paying fair market value compensation to the owner.

encroachment: An intrusion onto one property by the improvement of an adjoining property.

equity: The amount of money an owner of a property keeps after selling the property and paying off any mortgages; that is, the difference between the fair market value of a property and the amount of debt on the property.

escalation rate: The rate of change in the price for a particular good or service.

fair market value (or *market value*): The value of a piece of property that a buyer would pay a seller in a free transaction for the property.

fixture: An item that is attached to a building and is typically included in the sale of the building.

ground lease: A long-term lease of a property that allows the tenant to use and improve the land, but that reverts to the owner at the end of the lease.

height zoning: Restrictions on the heights of buildings and structures established by local laws.

improvement ratio: The ratio of the value of improvements on a property to the value of the property alone.

inverse condemnation: A remedy by a court for a private land owner whose land has been taken away by a governmental body. See also *eminent domain.*

landlocked: Descriptive of a parcel of land that does not border any public road.

land sale leaseback: A legal arrangement in which the owner of a property sells the property to someone else but then immediately leases it from the purchaser.

lien: See *mechanic's and materialman's lien.*

lien waiver: A document that gives up a person's right to claim a lien against property.

market value: See *fair market value.*

mechanic's and materialman's lien: A claim placed against a property's deed by someone who has provided work or materials to improve the property but has not been paid for the work. Typically called simply a lien.

minimum property standards: Minimum standards for residential building required by the Federal Housing Administration for construction or for underwriting a mortgage.

modified uniform present worth factor: A discount factor that is used to convert an annual amount that is changing from year to year at a given escalation rate to a time-equivalent present value.

net leasable area: The area of a building that is available for rent, which does not include common areas, structure, stairs, and the like.

occupancy permit: A document, issued by a city's building department, giving permission for a building to be occupied. More commonly called the *certificate of occupancy.* The occupancy permit is part of the building permit process, and its cost is included in the building permit fee paid by the contractor.

pad site: A separate location for development of retail space near (but not in) a shopping center.

party wall: A shared wall between two leased spaces or between two residential units. Often called a *demising wall.*

pro forma: A financial projection for a development project that is meant to determine whether the project is feasible, given estimates on potential income and the cost of developing the project.

restriction: A limit on how the owner of a property or building can use or improve the property. Often called a *restrictive covenant.* It is usually contained in the deed to the property.

riparian: Pertaining to land adjacent to a river or other body of water.

riparian rights: The rights of a landowner to use or control all or a portion of the water in a body of water bordering his or her property.

satellite tenant: A minor or smaller tenant in a shopping center. Compare with *anchor tenant.*

special use permit: An exemption from zoning regulations given to a jurisdiction.

spot zoning: The application of specific zoning regulations to specific properties when nearby land is under different zoning.

underimproved land: Property that is not producing the maximum income it is capable of producing given its size, zoning, and so on.

uniform capital recovery: A method of converting the future value of money to a present worth using the discount rate.

uniform present worth factor: The discount factor that is used to convert a uniform annual value (often an annual cost) to a time-equivalent present value.

uniform sinking fund: The amount of money that has to be invested at today's value at a given interest rate (the discount rate) to become a specified amount of money in the future.

usury: The illegal practice of charging exorbitant interest rates on a loan.

variance: Permission granted by a local jurisdiction to deviate from the literal provisions of a zoning ordinance where strict adherence would cause undue hardship because of conditions or circumstances unique to an individual property.

wetlands: Land that has development restrictions placed on it because it is commonly flooded and may be environmentally sensitive.

zero lot line: Part of a zoning regulation's setback requirements that allows a building to be constructed up to the property line with no setback.

zoning bylaw: The set of zoning regulations established by a local jurisdiction that regulates certain building practices within the jurisdiction.

SELECTION OF STRUCTURAL SYSTEMS

This chapter provides a broad overview of many of the common structural systems and materials used in contemporary construction. Its purpose is to present some of the primary characteristics of structural systems and to review some of the most important criteria for their selection. For more detailed information on specific structural materials and calculation methods, refer to later chapters in this manual.

STANDARD STRUCTURAL SYSTEMS

Wood

Wood is one of the oldest and most common structural materials. It is plentiful, inexpensive, relatively strong in both compression and tension, and easy to work with and fasten. Wood is used primarily in *one-way structural systems*, where the load is transmitted through structural members in one direction at a time.

Joists are light, closely spaced members that span between beams or bearing walls and support floors or ceilings. Typical sizes are 2 × 6, 2 × 8, 2 × 10, and 2 × 12. Typical spacings are 12 in, 16 in, and 24 in on center. The typical maximum normal span is about 20 ft, but spans up to 25 ft are often used.

The space between joists is usually spanned with plywood, particleboard, or oriented strand board subflooring on which underlayment is placed in preparation for finish flooring. Sometimes, a single sheet of $^3/_4$ in subfloor/underlayment is used, although it is not as desirable. See Fig. 11.1(a). Because joists are slender, they must be laterally supported to avoid twisting or lateral displacement. The top edge is held in place by sheathing, but bridging must be used to support the bottom edge. Maximum intervals of no more than 8 ft are recommended. Either solid or cross bridging may be used.

Solid wood beams are still used to a limited degree, but their standard sizes have changed. The availability of solid beams with large cross-sectional areas in suitable lengths is limited, especially in grades that provide the desired strength. Solid wood beams for longer spans have generally been replaced with glued-laminated construction.

The most common use of solid wood beams is with *plank-and-beam framing* in which members of a 4 in or 6 in nominal width span between girders or bearing walls at spacings of 4, 6, or 8 ft. Wood decking, either solid or laminated, is used to span between the beams, with the underside of the decking being the finished ceiling. The normal maximum span for the beams in this system is about 10 ft to 20 ft. See Fig. 11.1(b).

Glued-laminated construction (glulam) is a popular method of wood construction. These structural members are made up of individual pieces of lumber $^3/_4$ in or $1^1/_2$ in thick, glued together in the factory. Standard widths are $3^1/_8$, $5^1/_8$, $6^3/_4$, and $8^3/_4$ in. Larger widths are available. Typical spans for glulam construction range from 15 ft to 60 ft.

One of the advantages of glulam construction is appearance. Structural members are commonly left exposed as part of the architectural expression of the structure on the interior. In addition, glulam members can be manufactured in tapered beams, tapered and curved beams, and various types of arches.

In an effort to employ the many structural advantages of wood and increase utilization of forest products while minimizing the problems of defects and limited strength in solid wood members, several manufactured products have been developed.

One is a *lightweight I-shaped joist* consisting of a top and bottom chord of solid or laminated construction separated by a plywood or oriented strand board web. See Fig. 11.1(c). This type of joist is used in residential and light commercial construction and allows longer spans than are possible with a joist system. It has a very efficient structural shape, like a steel wide flange, and because it is manufactured in a factory, problems such as warping, splits, checks, and other common wood defects are eliminated. This type of product is stronger and stiffer than a standard wood joist.

Another manufactured product is a wood member manufactured with individual layers of thin veneer glued together. See Fig. 11.1(d). It is used primarily for headers over large openings, and singly or built-up for beams. It has a higher modulus of elasticity than a standard wood joist, and its allowable stress in bending is about twice that of a Douglas-fir joist.

A third type of manufactured product is a *truss* made up of standard sized wood members connected with metal plates. See Fig. 11.1(e). Typical spans range from about 24 ft to 40 ft, and typical depths are from 12 in to 36 in. A common spacing is 24 in on center. These types of trusses are useful for residential and light commercial construction and allow easy passage of mechanical ductwork through the truss.

Two other types of wood structural members are possible, but their use is infrequent because of other product availability and the difficulty in constructing them properly since they are usually site-fabricated. One is the *box beam,* fabricated with plywood panels glued and nailed to solid wood members, usually 2 × 4 framing. See Fig. 11.1(f). Box beams are often used in locations where the depth of the member is not critical and where other types of manufactured beams cannot be brought to the building site. *Stressed skin panels* (see Fig. 11.1(g)) are the other type of built-up wood product. Like box beams, they are constructed of plywood glued and nailed to solid 2 in nominal thickness lumber and are used for floor, roof, or wall construction.

Steel

Steel is one of the most commonly used structural materials because of its high strength, availability, and ability to adapt to a wide variety of structural conditions. It is also a ductile material, which simply means that it can tolerate some deformation and return to its original shape and that it will bend before it breaks, giving warning before total collapse. Steel is particularly suited for multifloor construction because of its strength and structural continuity.

Two of the most common steel structural systems are the *beam-and-girder system* and the *open-web steel joist system.* See Fig. 11.2(a) and Fig. 11.2(b). In the beam-and-girder system, large members span between vertical supports, and smaller beams are framed into them.

Figure 11.1 Wood Structural Members

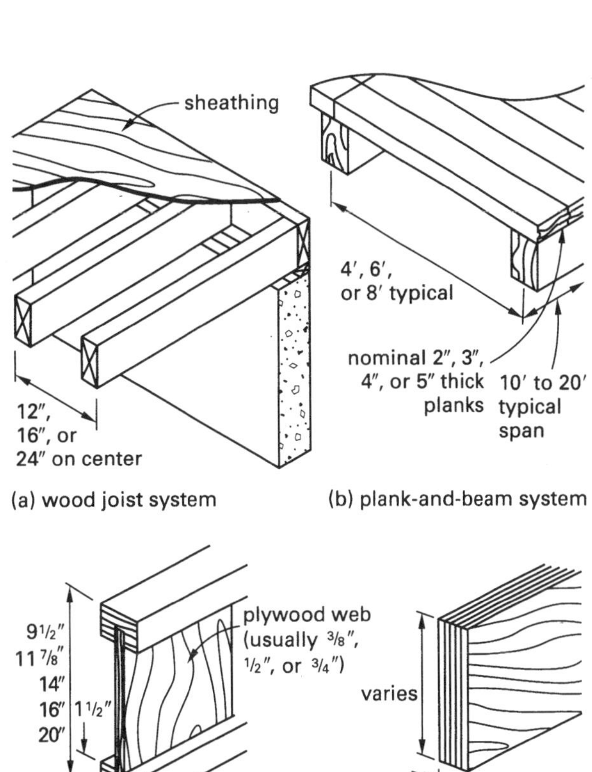

(a) wood joist system

(b) plank-and-beam system

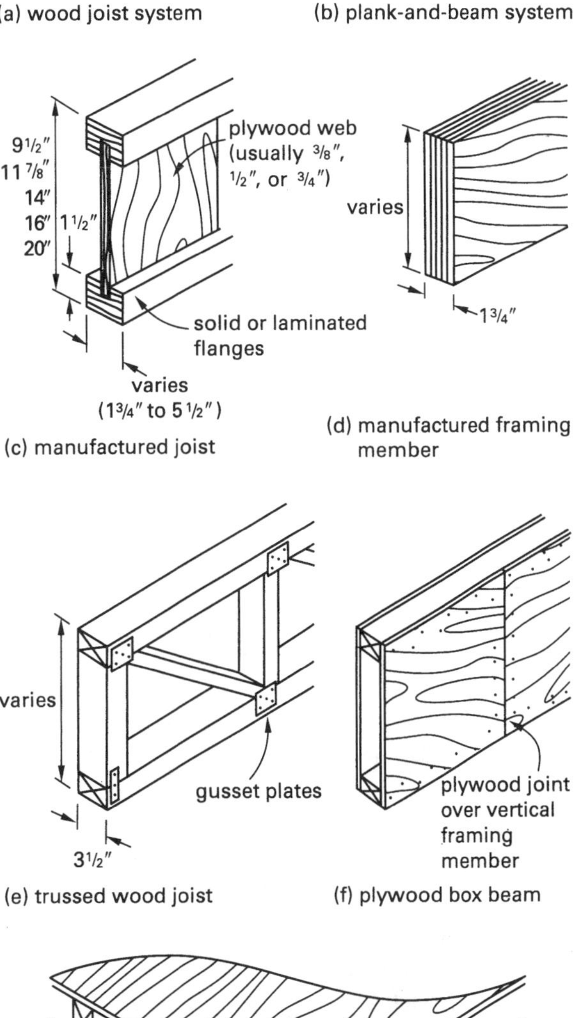

(c) manufactured joist

(d) manufactured framing member

(e) trussed wood joist

(f) plywood box beam

(g) stressed skin panel

Figure 11.2
Common Steel Structural Systems

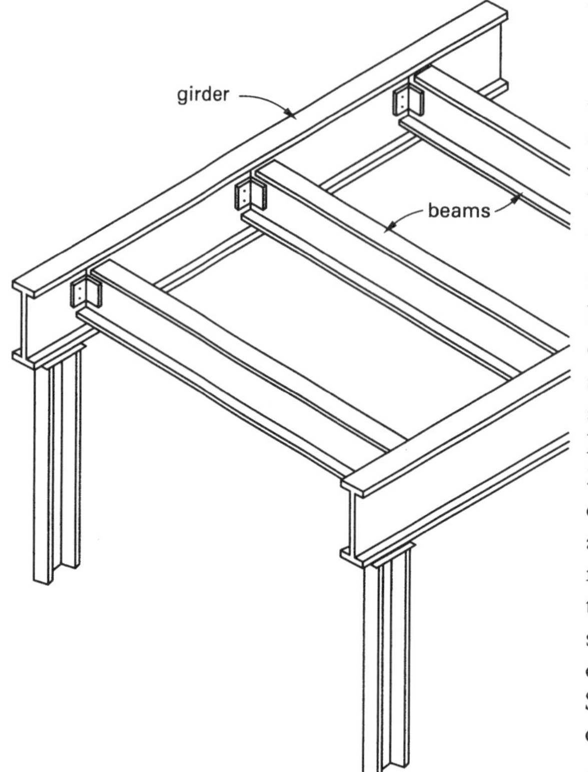

(a) beam-and-girder system

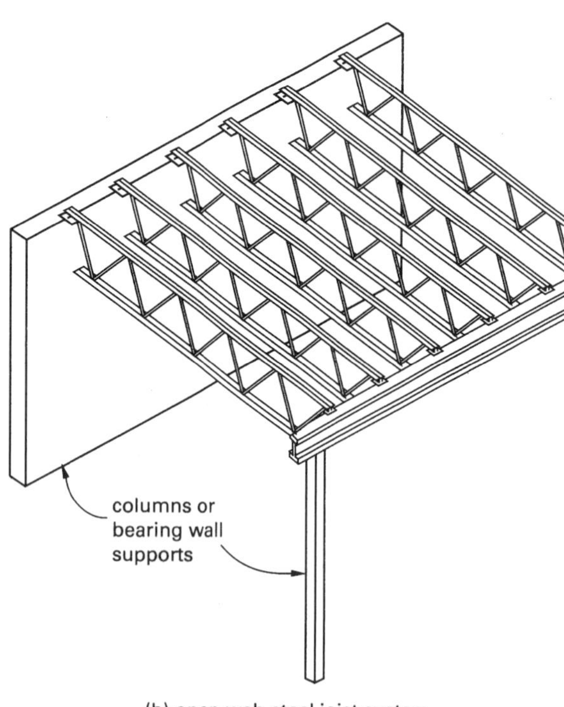

(b) open-web steel joist system

The girders span the shorter distances while the beams span the longer distances. Typical spans for this system are from 25 ft to 40 ft with the beams being spaced about 8 ft to 10 ft on center. The steel framing is usually covered with steel decking that spans between the beams. A concrete topping is then poured over the decking to complete the floor slab.

Open-web steel joists span between beams or bearing walls as shown in Fig. 11.2(b). Standard open-web joists can span up to 60 ft. Long-span joists can span up to 96 ft, and deep long-span joists are capable of spanning up to 144 ft. Depths of standard joists range from 8 in to 30 in, in increments of 2 in. Long-span joist depths range from 18 in to 72 in. Floor joists are typically placed 2 ft to 4 ft on center, while roof joists are usually placed 4 ft to 6 ft on center. Open-web steel joists used in floor construction are usually spanned with steel decking over which a concrete topping is poured. Sometimes wood decking is used, but with closer joist spacings.

Open-web steel joists are efficient structural members and are well-suited for low-rise construction where overall depth of the floor/ceiling system is not critical. They can span long distances and have a combustible construction. Because the webs are open, mechanical and electrical service pipes and ducts can easily be run between the web members.

Concrete

There are many variations of concrete structural systems, but the two primary types are *cast-in-place* and *precast*. Cast-in-place structures require formwork and generally take longer to build than precast buildings, but they can conform to an almost unlimited variety of shapes, sizes, design intentions, and structural requirements. Precast components are usually formed in a plant under strictly controlled conditions so quality control is better and erection proceeds quickly, especially if the structure is composed of numerous repetitive members.

The majority of cast-in-place concrete systems utilize only mild steel reinforcing, but in some instances post-tensioning steel is used. Precast concrete systems, on the other hand, are usually prestressed, although sometimes only mild reinforcing steel is used.

Sometimes concrete is precast on the site, but this is usually limited to wall panels (normally referred to as *tilt-up panels*) of moderate size. Lift-slab construction is still used as well. In this procedure, floor slabs of a multistory building are cast one on top of the next on the ground around the columns and then jacked into place and attached to the columns.

Cast-in-place concrete structural systems can be classified into two general types, depending on how the floors are analyzed: *one-way systems* and *two-way systems*. In one-way systems the slabs and beams are designed to transfer loads in one direction only. For example, a slab will transfer floor loads to an intermediate beam, which then transmits the load to a larger girder supported by columns.

One of the common types of one-way systems is the *beam-and-girder system*. See Fig. 11.3(a). This functions in a manner similar to a steel system in which the slab is supported by intermediate beams that are carried by larger girders. Typical spans are in the range of 15 ft to 30 ft. This system is economical for most applications, relatively easy to form, and allows penetrations and openings to be made in the slab.

A *concrete joist system*, Fig. 11.3(b), is comprised of concrete members usually spaced 24 in or 36 in apart, running in one direction, that frame into larger beams. Most spans range from 20 ft to 30 ft with joist depths ranging from 12 in to 24 in. A concrete joist system is easy to form since prefabricated metal pan forms are used. This system is good for light or medium loads where moderate distances must be spanned.

There are three principal two-way concrete systems: the flat plate, flat slab, and waffle slab. In most cases, all of these are designed for use in rectangular bays, where the distance between columns is the same, or close to the same, in both directions.

The *flat plate* is the simplest. See Fig. 11.3(c). The slab is designed and reinforced to span in both directions directly into the columns. Because loads increase near the columns and there is no provision to increase the thickness of the concrete or the reinforcing at the columns, this system is limited to light loads and short spans, up to about 25 ft with slabs ranging from 6 in to 12 in. It is very useful in

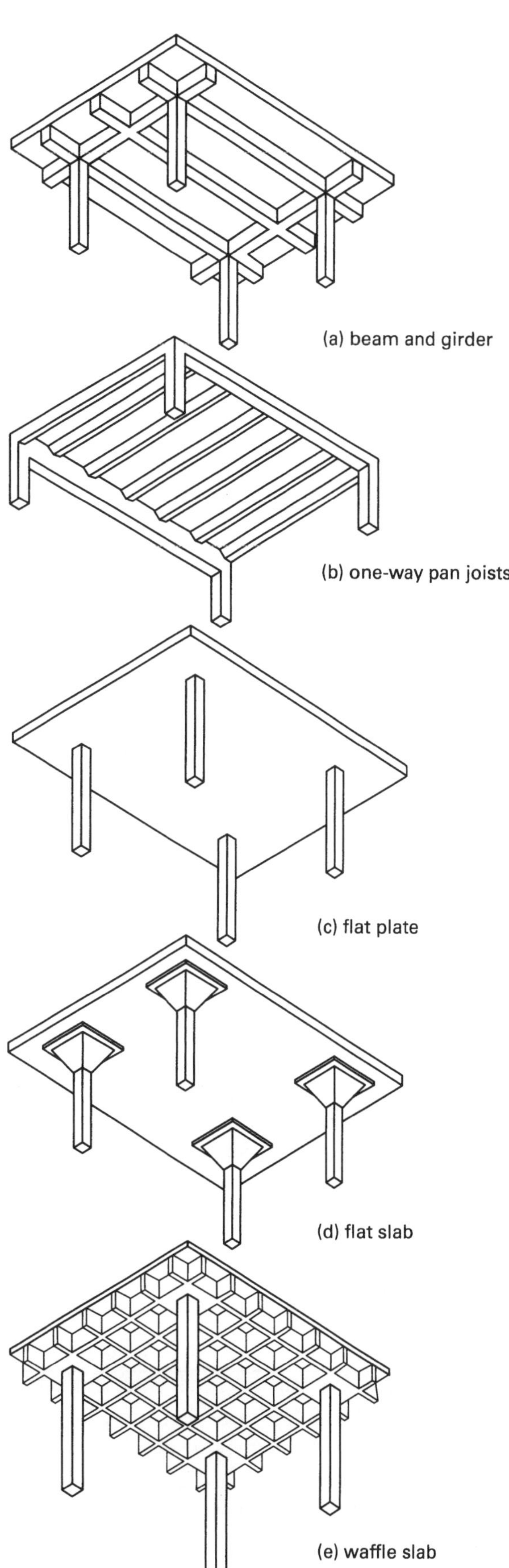

Figure 11.3 Concrete Structural Systems

Programming & Analysis

situations where the floor-to-floor height must be kept to a minimum or an uncluttered underfloor appearance is desired.

When the span of flat plates is large or the live loads are heavier, flat plates require drop panels (increased slab thickness around the columns) to provide greater resistance against punching shear failures. Column capitals (truncated pyramids or cones) are sometimes also used to handle punching shear as well as large bending moments in the slab in the vicinity of the columns. This type of flat plate is usually referred to as a *flat slab*. See Fig. 11.3(d). This system can accommodate fairly heavy loads with economical spans up to 30 ft.

The *waffle slab* system, Fig. 11.3(e), can provide support for heavier loads at slightly longer spans than the flat slab system. Spans up to 40 ft can be accomplished economically. Like the one-way joist system, waffle slabs are formed of prefabricated, reusable metal or fiberglass forms that allow construction to proceed faster than with custom wood forms. Waffle slabs are often left exposed with lighting integrated into the coffers.

Precast structural members come in a variety of forms for different uses. Figure 11.4 illustrates some of the more common ones. They can either be used for structural members such as beams and columns, or for enclosing elements such as wall panels. Concrete for wall panels can be cast in an almost infinite variety of forms to provide the required size, shape, architectural finish, and opening configuration needed for the job. Precast concrete members are connected in the field using welding plates that are cast into the member at the plant.

Figure 11.4
Typical Precast Concrete Shapes

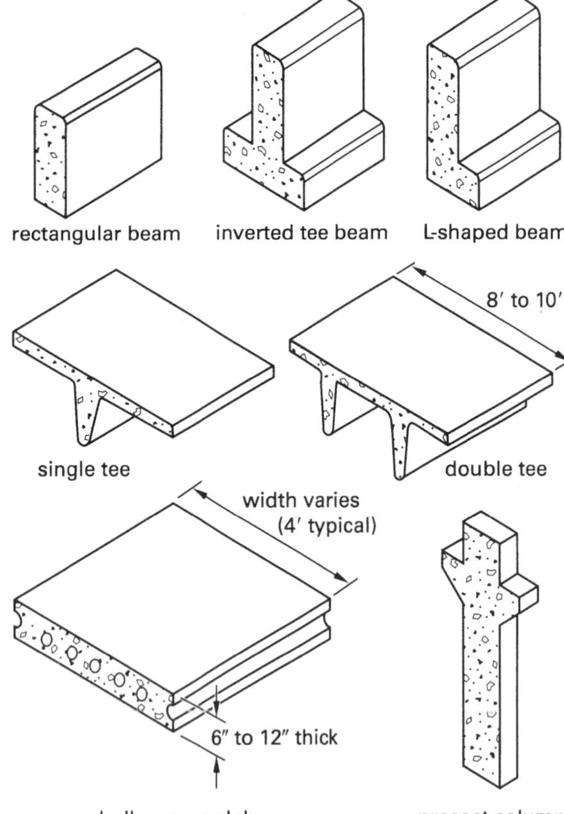

When used for structure, precast concrete is typically prestressed; that is, high-strength steel cables are stretched in the precasting forms before the concrete is poured. After the concrete attains a certain minimum strength, the cables are released, and they transfer compressive stresses to the concrete. When cured, the concrete member has a built-in compressive stress that resists the tension forces caused by the member's own weight plus the live loads acting on the member.

Single tee and *double tee* beams are popular forms of precast concrete construction because they can simultaneously serve as structural supports as well as floor or roof decking, and they are easy and fast to erect. A topping of concrete (usually about 2 in thick) is placed over the tees to provide a uniform, smooth floor surface, and also to provide increased strength when the tees are designed to act as composite beams.

Because of the compressive stress in the concrete caused by the prestressing forces, unloaded beams from the prestressing plant have a camber built into them. This is the upward curvature of the structural member. The stressing in the cables is calculated to provide the correct camber and strength for the anticipated loading so that when the member is in place and live and dead loads are placed on it, the camber disappears or is greatly reduced.

Post-tensioned concrete is yet another structural system that takes advantage of the qualities of concrete and steel. In this system, the post-tensioning steel (sometimes called *tendons*) is stressed after the concrete has been poured and cured. Post-tensioning tendons can be small high-strength wires, seven-wire strands, or solid bars. They are stressed with hydraulic jacks pulling on one or both ends of the tendon with pressures of about 100 psi to 250 psi of concrete area for slabs and 200 psi to 500 psi for beams.

Post-tensioned structural systems are useful where high strength is required and where it may be too difficult to transport precast members to the job site.

Masonry

As a structural system in contemporary construction, masonry is generally limited to bearing walls. It has a high compressive strength, but its unitized nature makes it inherently weak in tension and bending. There are three basic types of masonry bearing wall construction: *single wythe*, *double wythe*, and *cavity* (see Fig. 11.5). Both of the layers in double-wythe construction may be of the same material or different materials. Cavity walls and double-wythe walls may be either grouted and reinforced or ungrouted. Single-wythe walls have no requirements for reinforcing or grouting.

Figure 11.5
Types of Masonry Construction

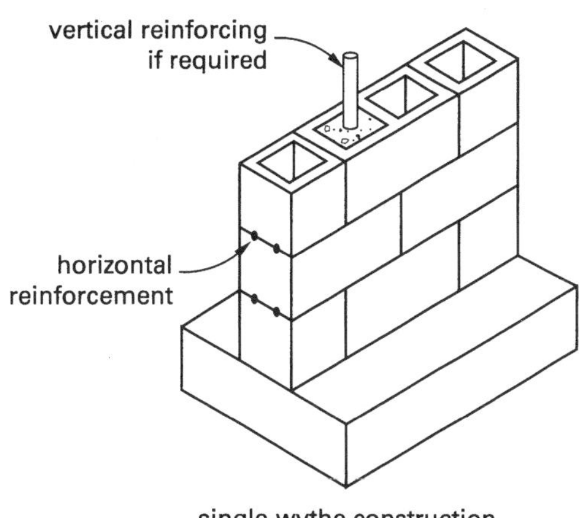

single-wythe construction

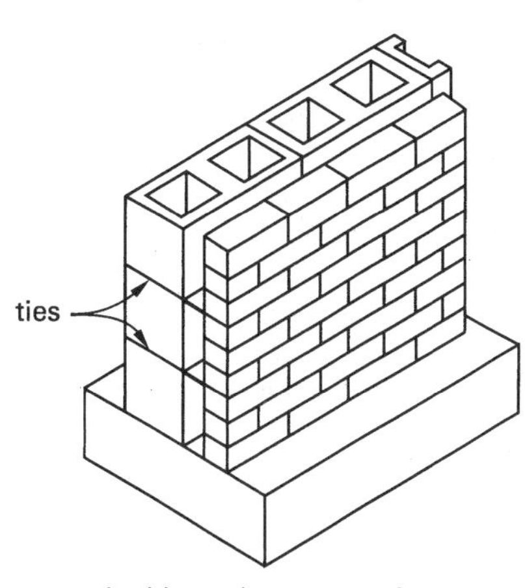

double-wythe construction

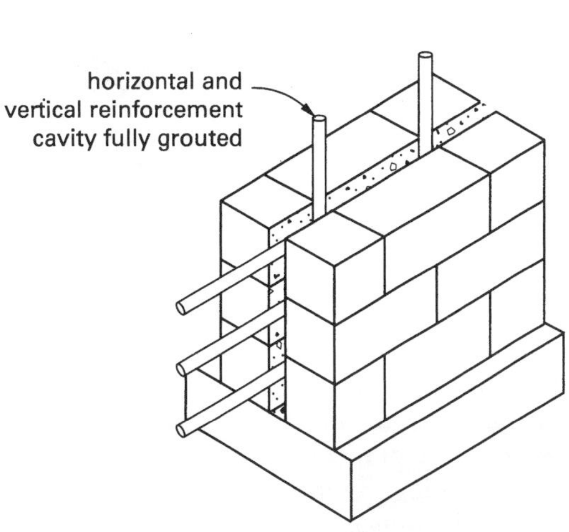

Unit masonry bearing walls offer the advantages of strength, design flexibility, attractive appearance, resistance to weathering, fire resistance, and sound insulation. In addition, their mass makes them ideal for many passive solar energy applications.

The joints of masonry units must be reinforced horizontally at regular intervals. This not only strengthens the wall but also controls shrinkage cracks, ties multi-wythe walls together, and provides a way to anchor veneer facing to a structural backup wall. Horizontal joint reinforcement comes in a variety of forms and is generally placed 16 in on center.

Vertical reinforcement is accomplished with standard reinforcing bars sized and spaced in accordance with the structural requirements of the wall. Typically, horizontal bars are also used and are tied to the vertical bars, with the entire assembly being set in a grouted cavity space. In a single-wythe concrete block wall, only vertical reinforcing is used with fully grouted wall cavities.

One important consideration in utilizing masonry walls is the thickness of the wall, which determines three important properties: the slenderness ratio, the flexural strength, and the fire-resistance rating. The *slenderness ratio* is the ratio of the wall's unsupported height to its thickness and is an indication of the ability of the wall to resist buckling when a compressive load is applied from above. The *flexural strength* is important when the wall is subjected to lateral forces such as from wind. Finally, the *fire-resistance rating* depends on both the wall's material and its thickness. These topics are discussed in more detail in Chap. 14 and Chap. 24.

Composite Construction

Composite construction is any structural system consisting of two or more materials designed to act together to resist loads. Composite construction is employed to utilize the best characteristics of each of the individual materials.

Reinforced concrete construction is the most typical composite construction, but others include composite steel deck and concrete, concrete slab and steel beam systems, and open-web steel joists with wood chords. See Fig. 11.6.

Figure 11.6
Typical Composite Construction

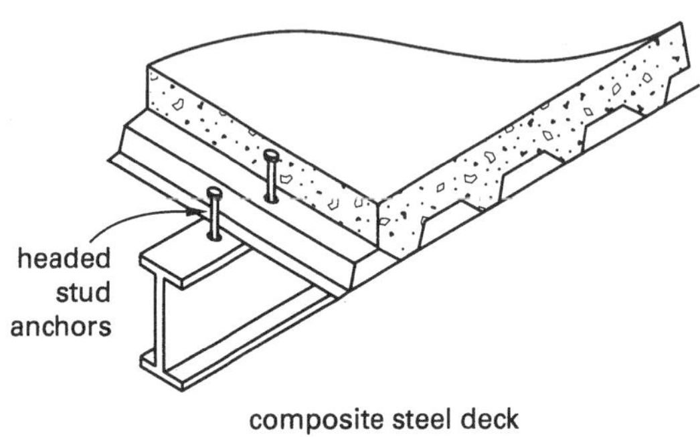

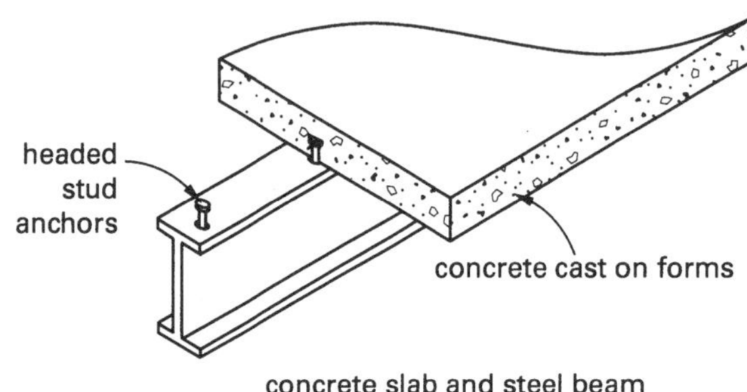

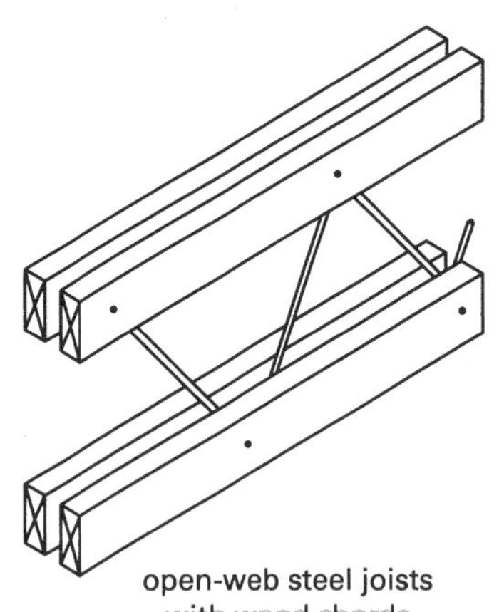

In composite construction with concrete and steel beams, headed stud anchors are used to transfer load between the concrete and steel, making the two materials act as one unit. Composite steel deck is designed with deformations or wires welded to the deck to serve the same purpose. Composite open-web joists are used to provide a nailable surface for the floor and ceiling while using the high strength-to-weight ratio of steel for the web members.

There are many other types of composite constructions that are less frequently used. These include trusses with wood for compression members and steel rods for tension members, concrete-filled steel tube sections, and composite steel joists.

Walls and the Building Envelope

Nonbearing walls are generally not considered part of the structural system of a building, but there are two important structural considerations when deciding how to attach the exterior, nonstructural envelope to the structural frame. The first is how the weight of the envelope itself will be supported. The second is how exterior loads, primarily wind, will be transferred to the structural frame without damaging the facing.

How an exterior facing is attached depends, of course, on the specific material and the type of structural frame. Panel and curtain wall systems are attached with clips on the mullions at the structural frame. The size and spacing of the clips is determined by the structural capabilities of the curtain wall or panel system.

Stone and masonry facings are attached with clip angles, continuous angles, or special fastenings to the structural frame at the floor lines. If additional attachment is required, a grid of secondary steel framing is attached to the primary structure to serve as a framework for the facing. Lightweight facings such as wood siding, shingles, and stucco need to be applied over continuous sheathing firmly secured to the structural wall framing.

One of the most important considerations in attaching exterior facing to the structural frame is to allow for expansion and contraction due to temperature changes and slight movement of the structural frame. Materials with a high coefficient of thermal expansion, such as aluminum, require space for movement within each panel, at the connection with the structural frame, and sometimes at the perimeter of large sections of the facing. Movement can be provided for by using clip angles with slotted holes, slip joints, and flexible sealants.

Materials with a low coefficient of expansion, such as masonry, still require expansion joints at regular intervals and at changes in the plane of the wall. If these are not provided, the joints or masonry may crack or the facing itself may break away during extreme temperature changes.

Usually, steel-framed buildings do not present many problems with movement of the structural frame, but concrete and wood structures will move enough to present problems. Concrete structures are especially subject to creep, a slight deformation of the concrete over time under continuous dead load. This condition must be accounted for when designing and detailing connections. Wood structures also deform over time due to shrinkage of the wood and long-term deflection. Since most wood buildings are relatively small, this is not always a problem, but it should be considered when attaching exterior facings.

Example 11.1

A small business plans to build an addition to its office building to use for manufacturing. This new space needs to be as open as possible with few or no obstructions and a minimum clear height of 12 ft. The floor will be concrete. Which type of structural system will be the most time and cost effective?

(A) post-tensioned concrete slab roof on concrete columns

(B) pre-engineered rigid steel frame

(C) open-web trusses on steel columns

(D) steel beams on concrete masonry walls

Solution

A pre-engineered rigid steel frame is the best options for several reasons. This type of structural system is designed to span the width of a building without the need for internal supporting columns and, as a result, is usually less expensive due to reduced material and labor costs. The erection time for pre-engineered rigid steel frame is also usually less than other systems.

The answer is (B).

COMPLEX STRUCTURAL SYSTEMS

Trusses

Trusses are structures comprised of straight members forming a number of triangles with the connections arranged so that the stresses in the members are either in tension or compression. Trusses can be used horizontally, vertically, or diagonally to support various types of loads when it would be impossible to fabricate a single structural member to span a large distance.

Although trusses are primarily tension/compression structural systems, some amount of bending is present in many of the members. This is due to loads applied between the connections and secondary bending and shear stresses at the connections themselves caused by minor eccentric loading.

Trusses can be field-fabricated or assembled in the factory as is the case with open-web steel joists and wood-trussed rafters. The primary limiting factor is the ability to transport them from the factory to the job site.

Trusses are discussed in more detail in Chap. 36.

Arches

Arches may have hinged or fixed supports. A hinged arch is a structural shape that is primarily subjected to compressive forces. For a given set of loads, the shape of an arch to resist the loads only in compression is its *funicular shape*. This shape can be found by suspending the anticipated loads from a flexible cable and then turning the shape upside down, as Antonio Gaudi did in many of his structural studies. For a hinged arch supporting a uniform load across its span, this shape is a parabola. No arch, however, is subjected to just one set of loads, so there is always a combination of compression and some bending stresses.

At the supports of a hinged arch there are two reactions: the *vertical reactions* and the *horizontal reactions*, or *thrust*, as shown in Fig. 11.7. Since the loads on the arch tend to force it to spread out, the thrust must be resisted either with tie rods that hold the two lower portions of the arch together or with foundations that prevent the spread. For a given span, the thrust is inversely proportional to the rise, or height, of the arch; if the rise is reduced by one-half, the thrust doubles.

Figure 11.7
Reactions of a Hinged Arch

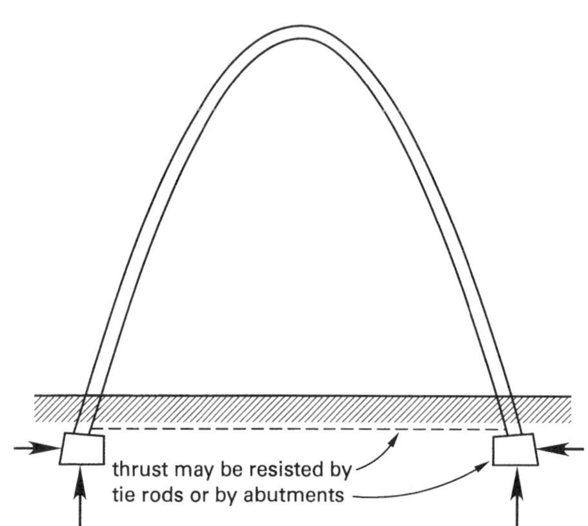
thrust may be resisted by
tie rods or by abutments

Arches can be constructed of any material: steel, concrete, wood, or stone, although each has its inherent limitations. Arches can also take a variety of shapes, from the classic half-round arch of the Romans, to the pointed Gothic arch, to the more decorative Arabic arches, to functional parabolic shapes. Since the shape of a building arch is often selected for its aesthetic appeal, it is not always the ideal shape and must be designed for the variety of loads it must carry in addition to simple compression. Arches typically span from 50 ft to 240 ft for wood, 20 ft to 320 ft for concrete, or 50 ft to 500 ft for steel.

Although arches may have fixed supports, they are usually hinged. This allows the arch to remain flexible and avoids developing high bending stresses under live loading and loading due to temperature changes and foundation settlement. Occasionally, an arch will have an additional hinge connection at the apex and is called a *three-hinged arch*. The addition of the third hinge makes the structure statically determinate, whereas two-hinged or fixed arches are statically indeterminate.

Rigid Frames

In contrast to a simple *post-and-beam system*, a *rigid frame* is constructed so that the vertical and horizontal members work as a single structural unit, as shown in Fig. 11.8.

This makes for a more efficient structure because all three members resist vertical and lateral loads together rather than singly. The beam portion is partially restrained by the columns and becomes more rigid to vertical bending forces, and both columns can resist lateral forces because they are tied together by the beam.

Because the three members are rigidly attached, there are forces and reactions in a rigid frame unlike those in a simple post-and-beam system. This is shown in Fig. 11.8(b) and Fig. 11.8(c) and results in the columns being subjected to both compressive and bending forces and a thrust, or outward force, induced by the action of the vertical loads on the beam transferred to the columns. As with an arch, this thrust must be resisted with tie rods or with appropriate foundations.

The attachment of the columns to the foundations may be rigid or hinged. This results in slightly different loads on the columns. The fixed frame as shown in Fig. 11.8(c) is stiffer than the hinged frame, and the thrust in the fixed frame is also greater.

When a horizontal beam is not required, such as in a single-story structure, a rigid frame often takes on the appearance of a *gabled frame* as shown in Fig. 11.9. This shape decreases the bending stresses in the two inclined members and increases the compression, making the configuration a more efficient structure. Because rigid frames develop a high moment at the connections between horizontal and vertical members, the amount of material is often increased near these points as shown in the tapered columns and roof members in Fig. 11.9.

Figure 11.8 Post-and-Beam and Rigid Frames

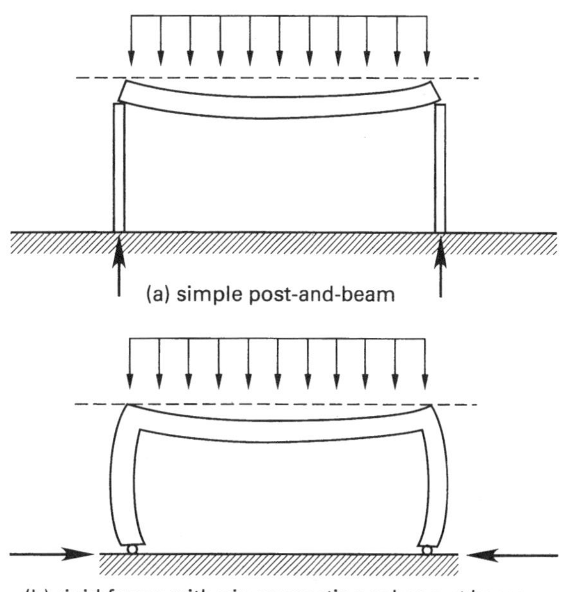

(a) simple post-and-beam

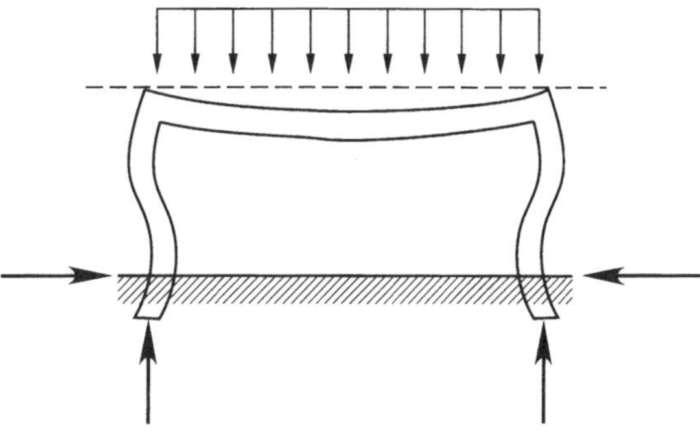

(b) rigid frame with pin connecting column at bases

(c) rigid frame with fixed connection column at bases

Space Frames

In simplest terms, a *space frame* is a structural system consisting of trusses in two directions rigidly connected at their intersections. With this definition it is possible to have a rectangular space frame where the top and bottom chords of the trusses are directly above and below one another. The bays created by the intersection of the two sets of trusses then form squares or rectangles. The more common type of space frame is a *triangulated space frame* where the bottom chord is offset from the top chord by half a bay, and each is connected with inclined web members. See Fig. 11.10.

Space frames are very efficient structures for enclosing large rectangular areas because of the two-way action of the components acting as a single unit. This results in a very stiff structure that may span up to 350 ft.

Span-to-depth ratios of space frames may be from 20:1 to 30:1. Other advantages include light weight and the repetitive nature of connectors and struts so that fabrication and erection time is minimized.

Figure 11.9 Gabled Rigid Frame

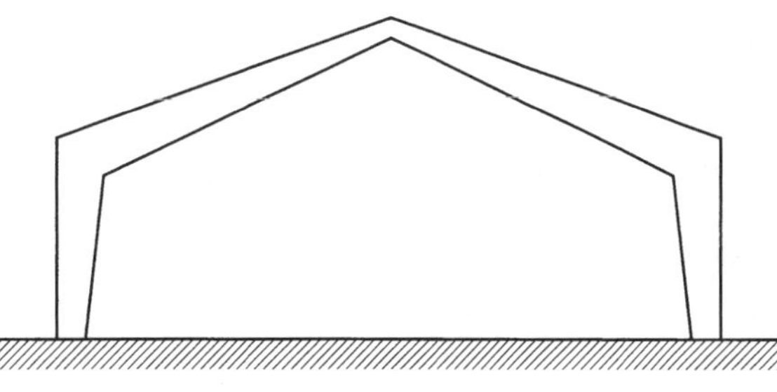

The structural design of space frames is complex because they are statically indeterminate structures with numerous intersections. A computer is needed for analysis and design.

Figure 11.10
Typical Space Frame

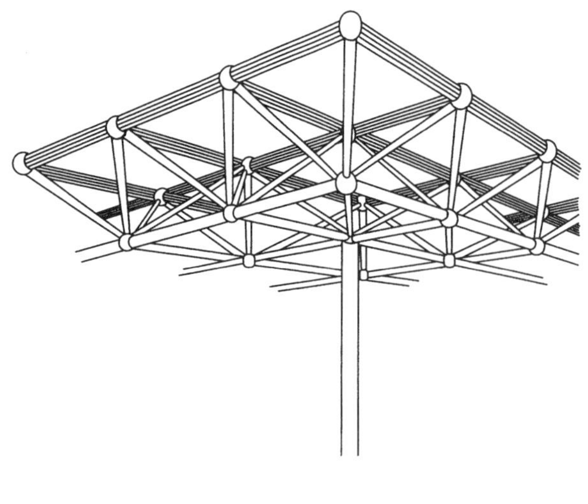

Folded Plates

A *folded plate* structure is one in which the loads are carried in two different directions: first in the transverse direction through each plate supported by adjacent plates, and second in the longitudinal direction with each plate acting as a girder spanning between vertical supports. See Fig. 11.11. Since the plates act as beams between supports, there are compressive stresses above the neutral axis and tensile stresses below.

Folded plates are usually constructed of reinforced concrete from 3 in to 6 in thick, although structures made of wood or steel are possible. Typical longitudinal spans are 30 ft to 100 ft with longer spans possible using reinforced concrete.

Figure 11.11
Folded Plate Construction

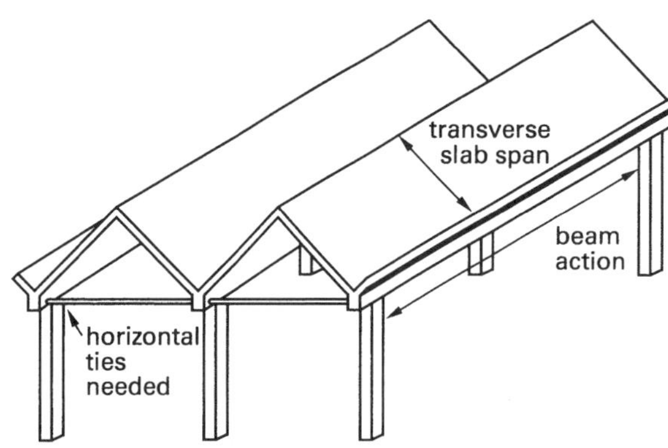

Thin-Shell Structures

A *thin-shell structure* is one with a curved surface that resists loads through tension, compression, and shear in the plane of the shell only. Theoretically, there are no bending or moment stresses in a thin-shell structure. These structures derive part of their name (thin) because of the method of resisting loads; a thick structure is not necessary since there are no bending stresses.

Since thin shells are composed of curved surfaces, the material is practically always reinforced concrete from about 3 in to 6 in thick. The forms can be domes, parabolas, or barrel vaults or can take on the more complex form of a saddle-shaped hyperbolic paraboloid. Thin-shell domes can span from 40 ft to over 200 ft, while hyperbolic paraboloids may span from 30 ft to 160 ft.

Stressed-Skin Structures

Stressed-skin structures comprise panels made of a sheathing material attached on one or both sides of intermediate web members in such a way that the panel acts as a series of I-beams, with the sheathing being the flange and the intermediate members being the webs. Since the panel is constructed of two or more pieces, the connection between the skin and the interior web members must transfer all the horizontal stress developed. Stressed-skin panels are typically made of wood, as shown in Fig. 11.1(g), but are also fabricated of steel and other composite materials. Although long-span steel stressed-skin panels do exist, most panels of this type span intermediate distances from 12 ft to 35 ft.

Suspension Structures

Suspension structures are most commonly seen in suspension bridges, but their use is increasing in buildings, most notably in large stadiums with suspended roofs. The suspension system was boldly used in the Federal Reserve Bank in Minneapolis, where two sets of cables were draped from towers at the ends of the building. These, in turn, support the floors and walls, leaving the space on the grade level free of columns.

Cable suspension structures are similar to arches in that the loads they support must be resisted by both vertical reactions and horizontal thrust reactions. The difference is that the vertical reactions are up and the horizontal thrust reactions are outward, since the sag tends to pull the ends together. As shown in

Fig. 11.12(a), the horizontal reaction is dependent on the amount of sag in the cable. Shallow sags result in high horizontal reactions, while deep sags result in lower horizontal reactions.

Since suspension structures can only resist loads with tension, the shape of the cable used changes as the load changes. No bending stresses are possible. With a single concentrated load, the cable assumes the shape of two straight lines (not counting the intermediate sag due to the weight of the cable). With two concentrated loads, the shape is three straight lines, and so on.

If the cable is uniformly loaded horizontally, the shape of the curve is a parabola. If the cable is loaded along its length uniformly (such as when it is supporting its own weight), the shape will be a catenary curve. See Fig. 11.12(b) and Fig. 11.12(c).

The fact that a suspension structure can only resist loads in tension creates a disadvantage: instability due to wind and other types of loading. Suspension structures must be stabilized or stiffened with a heavy infill material, with cables attached to the ground or with a secondary grid of cables either above or below the primary set.

Figure 11.12 Cable-Supported Structures

(a) horizontal reaction depends on sag

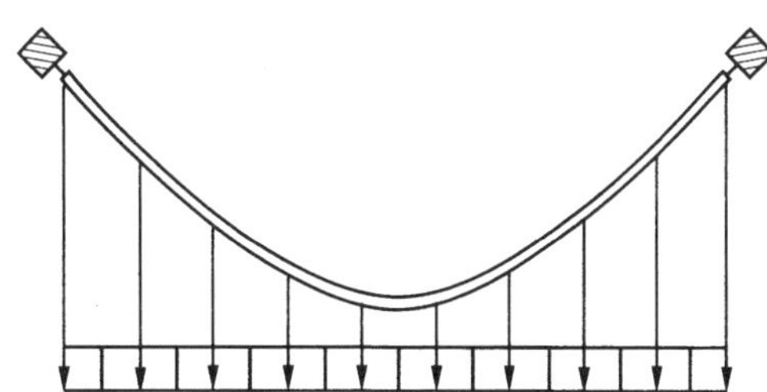

(b) uniform horizontal load results in parabolic curve

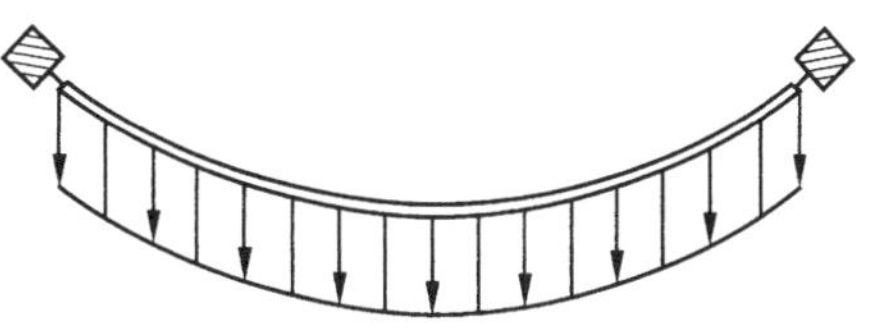

(c) uniform load on cable results in catenary curve

Inflatable Structures

Inflatable structures are similar to suspension structures in that they can only resist loads in tension. They are held in place with constant air pressure that is greater than the outside air pressure. The simplest inflatable structure is the single membrane anchored continuously at ground level and inflated.

A variation of this is the *double-skin inflatable structure* in which the structure is created by inflation of a series of voids, much like an air mattress. With this system, the need for an air lock for entry and exit is eliminated. Another variation is a double-skin structure, with only one large air pocket supported on the bottom by a cable suspension system and with the top supported by air pressure.

Like cable suspension buildings, inflatable structures are inherently unstable in the wind and cannot support concentrated loads. They are often stabilized with a network of cables over the top of the membrane. Inflatable structures are used for temporary enclosures and for large, single-space buildings such as sports arenas.

Example 11.2

A long-span, high-hazard warehouse does not have an automatic sprinkler system installed. Which of the following would be LEAST likely to fail after several hours of exposure to fire?

(A) steel-reinforced concrete posts and beams

(B) heavy wood timber

(C) structural steel

(D) concrete masonry walls with open-web roof joists

Solution

Heavy timber is large enough to burn and char, forming a protective "crust" on the outside of the wood. This leaves the interior fibers of the wood protected from the fire and able to remain intact. The other options would more likely fail in the continued high heat of a building fire.

The answer is (B).

STRUCTURAL SYSTEM SELECTION CRITERIA

The selection of an optimum structural system for a building can be a complex task. In addition to the wide variety of structural systems available and their many variations and combinations, there are dozens of other considerations that must be factored into making the final selection. The architect's job is to determine the full scope of the problem and find the best balance among often conflicting requirements. This section briefly outlines some of the major selection criteria to be familiar with when analyzing possible systems.

Resistance to Loads

Of course, the primary consideration is the ability of the structural system to resist the anticipated and unanticipated loads that will be placed on it. These include the weight of the structure itself (*dead load*); loads caused by external factors such as wind, snow, and earthquakes; loads caused by building use, such as people, furniture, and equipment (*live loads*), as well as others.

The anticipated loads can be calculated directly from known weights of materials and equipment and from requirements of building codes that set down what is statistically probable in a given situation—the load caused by people in a church, for example. Unanticipated loads are difficult to plan for but include such things as changes in the use of a building, overloading caused by extra people or equipment, unusual snow loads, ponding of water on a roof, and degradation of the structure itself.

When deciding on what material or system to use, there is always the consideration of what is reasonable for the particular circumstance. For example, wood can be made to support very heavy loads with long spans, but only at a very high cost with complex systems. A wood system does not make sense if other materials and systems, such as steel and concrete, are available.

Often, very unusual loads will be the primary determinant of the structural system and its effect on the appearance of the building. Extremely tall high-rise buildings like the Sears Tower or the John Hancock Building in Chicago, with its exterior diagonal framing, are examples of load-driven structural solutions.

Building Use and Function

The type of occupancy is one of the primary determinants of a structural system. A parking garage needs spans long enough to allow the easy movement and storage of automobiles. An office building works well with spans in the 30 ft to 40 ft range.

Sports arenas need quite large open areas. Some buildings have a fixed use over their lifespan and may work with fixed bearing walls, while others must remain flexible and require small, widely spaced columns.

These are all examples of somewhat obvious determinates of building systems. There are, however, many other needs that are not so apparent. For example, in a location where building height is limited, a client may want to squeeze as many floors into a multistory building as possible. This may require the use of concrete flat-plate construction with closely spaced columns even though another system would be more economical.

In another instance, a laboratory building may need large spaces between usable floors in which to run mechanical services. This may suggest the use of deep-span, open-web trusses. If the same laboratory were to house delicate, motion-sensitive equipment, then the use of a rigid, massive concrete structure might be warranted.

Integration with Other Building Systems

Although a building's structure is an important element, it does not exist alone. The building must have exterior cladding attached to it. Ductwork and pipes run around and through it, electrical wires run among it, and interior finishes cover it. Some materials and structural systems make it easy for other services to be integrated. For instance, a steel column-and-beam system with open-web steel joists and concrete floors over metal decking yields a fairly penetrable structure for pipes, ducts, and wiring while still allowing solid attachment of ceilings, walls, and exterior cladding.

On the other hand, reinforced prestressed concrete buildings may require more consideration as to how mechanical services will be run so there is not an excess of dropped ceilings, furred-out columns, and structure-weakening penetrations. Exposed structural systems, such as glued-laminated beams and wood decking or architectural concrete, present particularly difficult integration problems.

Cost Influences

As with most contemporary construction, financial concerns drive many decisions. Structure is no exception. It is one portion of a building that is most susceptible to cost cutting because it quite often cannot be seen and the client sees no reason to spend more on it than absolutely necessary.

Programming & Analysis

Changing the direction of the beams and girders may result in a savings in the weight of steel and therefore a savings in money.

There are two primary elements of selecting a structural system based on cost. The first is selecting materials and systems that are most appropriate for the anticipated loads, spans required, style desired, integration needed, fire resistance called for, and all the other factors that must be considered. This generally leads to major decisions such as whether to use a concrete flat-slab construction instead of steel, or to use a steel arch system instead of glued-laminated beams.

The second part is refining the selected system so that the most economical arrangement and use of materials is selected regardless of the system used. In a typical situation, for example, a steel system is selected, but various framing options must be compared and evaluated. Changing the direction of the beams and girders or slightly altering the spacing of beams may result in a savings in the weight of steel and therefore a savings in money. Or, a concrete frame may be needed, but the one with the simplest forming will generally cost less.

Fire Resistance

Building codes dictate the fire resistance of structural systems as well as other parts of a building. These range from 1 hour to 4 hours; the time is an indication of how long the member can withstand a standard fire test before becoming dangerously weakened. The structure is, of course, the most important part of a building because it holds everything else up. As a consequence, required fire resistances are generally greater for structural members than for other components in the same occupancy type and building type.

There are two considerations in the fire resistance of a structural member. One is the combustibility of the framing itself, and the other is the loss of strength a member may experience when subjected to intense heat. Steel, for instance, will not burn but will bend and collapse when subjected to high temperatures. It must, therefore, be protected with other noncombustible materials. Heavy timber, on the other hand, will burn slightly and char, but will maintain much of its strength in a fire before it burns completely.

Some materials, such as concrete and masonry, are inherently fire resistant and are not substantially weakened when subjected to fire (assuming any steel reinforcing is adequately protected). Other materials, such as wood and steel, must be protected for the time period required by the building codes.

Since it costs money to protect structural members from fire, cost must be factored into the decision to use one material instead of another. Even though steel may be a less expensive structural material to use than concrete, it may be more expensive to fireproof and, in the long run, cost more than a concrete-framed building.

Construction Limitations

The realities of construction often are a decisive factor in choosing a structural system. Some of these include construction time, material and labor availability, and equipment availability.

Construction time is almost always a factor due to high labor costs typical in the United States. However, other things influence the need to shorten the construction period as much as possible. The cost of financing requires that the terms of construction loans be as short as feasible. This may dictate the use of large, prefabricated structural elements instead of slow, labor-intensive systems such as unit masonry. Another factor can be climate and weather. In locations with short construction seasons, buildings need to be erected as quickly as possible.

Material and labor are the two primary variables in all construction cost. Sometimes both are expensive, but usually one dominates the other. In the United States, labor costs are high in relation to materials; in many developing countries labor is extremely cheap while most modern materials are expensive or even unattainable. Even within the United States, labor and material costs for the same material or structural system in different states may vary enough to influence the structural system decision.

Related to labor costs are the skills of the workforce. A sophisticated structural system may require a technically skilled workforce that is not available in a remote region. The cost to transport and house the needed workers could very well make such a system infeasible.

Finally, equipment needed to assemble a structural system may be unavailable or prohibitively expensive. The lack of heavy cranes near the job location, for example, could suggest that large, prefabricated components not be used.

Style

Some structural systems are more appropriate as an expression of a particular style than others. One of the most obvious examples is the International Style, which could only be achieved with a steel post-and-beam system. Even when fireproofing requirements might have implied a concrete structure, steel was used.

The architect and client usually determine what style the building will be and then require that any structural solution adapt to that need. In some instances, the structural engineer may devise a structural solution that becomes the style itself. Once again, there should be a balance between what style may be desired and what is practical and reasonable from a structural point of view.

Social and Cultural Influences

Related to the style of a building are the social and cultural influences on the architecture of a geographical location and particular time period. The architect must be sensitive to these influences. For example, in a historic area where most buildings are constructed of brick, a masonry bearing wall structural system certainly should be considered. In a newly developing industrial park, more contemporary and daring structural systems might be appropriate.

Example 11.3

While running a sprinkler line across the ceiling of the middle floor in a multistory building, a contractor discovers a joist that spans the back of the suspended ceiling tile and the underside of the floor deck above. A 3 in hole must be drilled through the beam. A structural engineer is consulted, approves the proposed hole, and indicates specifically where the hole must be located. What location did the engineer most likely indicate?

(A) the middle of the web and close to one of the bearing ends

(B) close to the bottom of the web, anywhere except the middle third of the beam span

(C) close to the top of the web, anywhere in the middle third of the beam span

(D) the middle of the web and as close to the midspan as possible

Solution

The strength of a beam comes from the compression and tension of the top and bottom fibers of the material, so holes near the top and bottom webs or flanges should be avoided. The shear of the beam is greatest at the bearing ends, so holes near the ends should also be avoided. Typically, the best location for a hole is in the middle of the web and midspan of the beam length.

The answer is (D).

M. BATH
MASTER BEDROOM
KIT
DINING ROOM
SOIL GAS VENT
RETURN
SLOPED WALL
2x4 POST FASTENED TO SIDING TO WHICH PORCH RAIL SHOULD BE FASTENED
2x4 POST FASTENED TO SIDING TO WHICH PORCH RAIL SHOULD BE FASTENED
NOTE:
CONFIRM R.O. SIZES WITH WINDOW MANUFACTURER AND ADJUST WALL FRAMING ACCORDINGLY.

DIVISION 4: PROJECT PLANNING & DESIGN

Project Planning

Chapter

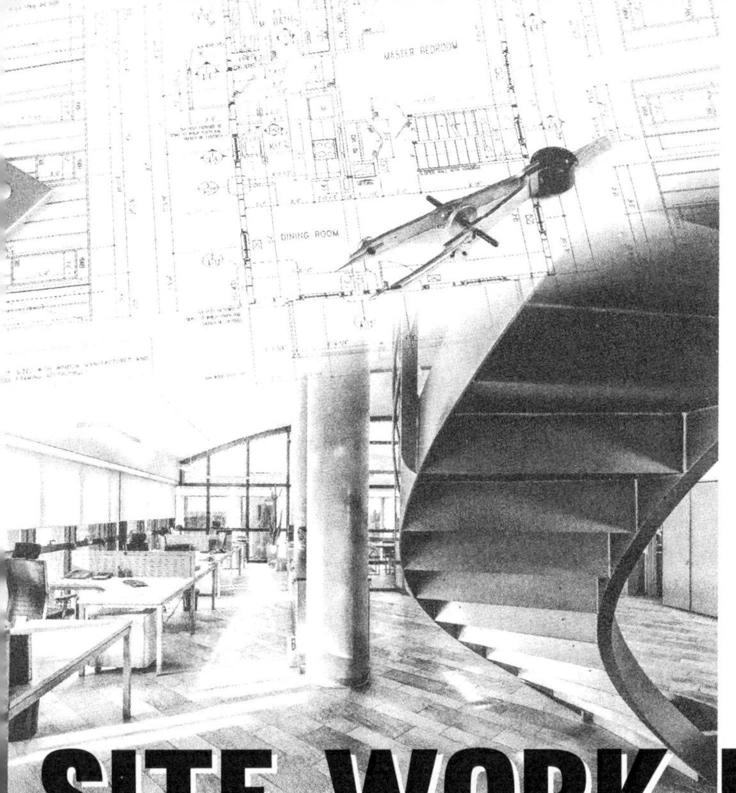

12

SITE WORK DESIGN DEVELOPMENT

Project Planning

Nomenclature

A	distance from noise source to top of sound barrier	ft	f	sound frequency	Hz
B	distance from noise source to bottom of sound barrier	ft	H	effective height	ft
D	line-of-sight distance from sound source to receiver	ft	N	noise level	dB
			ε	emissivity	–

Among the first tasks an architect performs after completing programming and analysis are to determine how best to locate the building on the site, what site improvements should be made, what additional sustainability principles can be applied, and how the neighborhood context will influence the design. This chapter discusses these activities as part of the overall design development of a project.

Some preliminary sustainability concepts are discussed in Chap. 7, and more detailed principles of sustainable design are discussed in Chap. 13.

Later in the design process, the basic building configuration is determined, and structure, building systems, and cost considerations are integrated into the building as discussed in Chap. 30.

BUILDING LOCATION AND SITE IMPROVEMENTS

Some of the influences that help determine the location of a building on a site are discussed in Chap. 7 as part of the schematic design process. As a project moves into design development and more detailed decisions are made additional issues need to be addressed.

Drainage

Any development of a site interrupts the existing drainage pattern and creates additional water flow. This is because some of the naturally porous ground is replaced with impervious areas of roof and paving.

The architect must provide for any existing drainage patterns through the site, and accommodate any expected increase in *runoff*, which is stormwater that accumulates on the site in excess of what can be absorbed by the ground. The site design must also create positive drainage away from the buildings, parking areas, and walks to avoid flooding, erosion, and standing water.

Drainage systems fall into two types: aboveground and underground. *Aboveground drainage systems* use pervious paving, sheet flow, gutters built into roadways and parking areas, ground swales as part of the landscaping, and channels to manage runoff and direct it appropriately. Pervious paving is discussed in Chap. 21. *Underground drainage systems* use perforated drains and enclosed storm sewers to carry the runoff from the site, either to a municipal storm sewer system or to a natural drainage outlet such as a river. Several methods of drainage may be combined in a single project.

Sheet flow is water that drains across a sloping surface, whether that surface is paved, grassy, or otherwise landscaped. In most cases, sheet flow is directed to gutters or channels, which empty into a natural watercourse or storm sewer. Gutters are often used because they can be built along with the roadway or parking area and naturally follow the same slope as the paved surface. They can easily drain into sewers, which also typically follow the paths of roads.

When the stormwater management strategy includes surface drainage, minimum *slopes* are needed to provide positive drainage. Some minimum slope values are listed in Table 9.3. Although the table indicates that a slope as little as 0.5% may be sufficient for some drainage, this is true only for very smooth, carefully constructed surfaces. For most paved surfaces, a slope of at least 1.5% is needed to account for paving roughness and variations in installation tolerances.

Underground systems use piping with a minimum slope of 0.3%. *Storm drains* collect water from roof *downspouts*, drain inlets, catch basins, and drain tiles surrounding the building foundation. A *drain inlet* is an opening in the ground that allows stormwater to run directly into the storm sewer; the opening is usually covered with a metal grate for safety and to keep out debris. A *catch basin* is an underground reservoir that has a sump built into it; debris settles into the sump instead of flowing down the sewer and potentially clogging the pipes.

Periodically, the sump must be cleaned out. Large *storm sewer* systems must have manholes for service access; these are located wherever the sewer changes direction, or a maximum of 500 ft apart. Storm sewers are always completely separate from *sanitary sewer* systems.

The required capacity of a drainage system is based on the size of the area to be drained, the *runoff coefficient* (that fraction of water not absorbed), and the amount of water to be drained during the most severe storm anticipated by the design.

This storm is referred to as an *n-year storm*, where the value of n is based on the probability that a storm of this magnitude or greater will occur at this location in any given year. For example, a *100-year storm* for a given location is a storm of such magnitude that there is only a 1% probability that a storm at least as large will occur in any given year. A *25-year storm* has a 4% probability, and a *10-year storm* has a 10% probability.

It is common to design drainage systems for 25-year storms; systems designed for 10-year storms are also common.

If the site development creates a volume of runoff in excess of the capacity of the existing municipal storm sewer or natural drainage course, a *holding pond* may be constructed on the site. The holding pond collects the site runoff and releases it into the sewer system at a controlled rate; it also prevents excess water from flooding other areas. Refer to Chap. 13 for more information on drainage as it relates to sustainability.

1/8 in/ft
house sewer
invert 92.0 ft
1/8 in/ft
80 ft
main line slope 1-1/2%
100 ft
invert
90.0 ft
invert
91.5 ft
theoretical shortest distance from building to sewer line
Actual required house sewer needs to intercept main sewer downline where main sewer has dropped sufficiently to allow house sewer to drain into it.
Shortest line dropping at 1/8 in/ft for 80 ft length (10 in) would intercept main line at 91.16 ft—too low to drain into line.
At 1/8 in/ft for approximately 130 ft, the house sewer invert, where it intersects the main line, is about 90.7 ft.

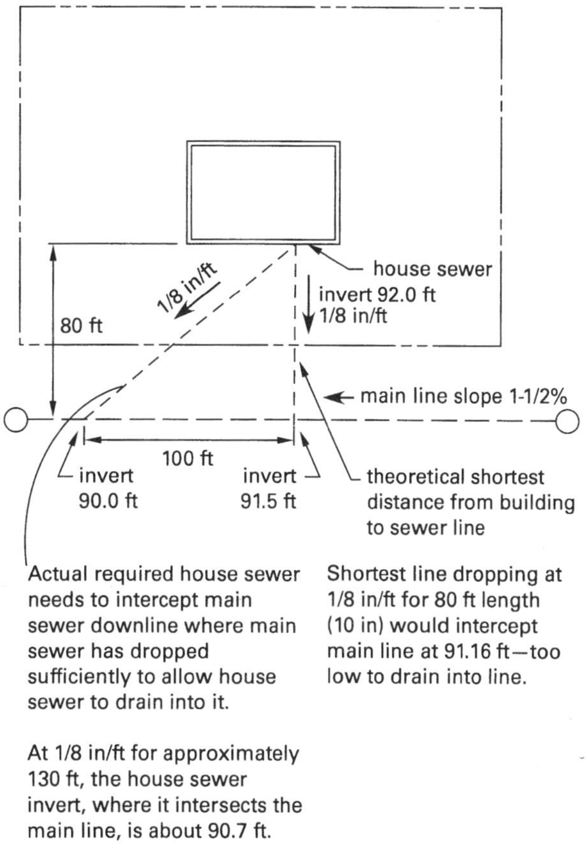

Figure 12.1 Sewer Layout Based on Slope Required

Utilities

The architect should determine the locations of existing utilities before beginning design, and should contact the utility companies early in the design process to confirm their requirements for providing service to the proposed building. These utilities may include sanitary sewers, storm sewers, water lines, natural gas, electricity, steam, telephone, internet, cable television, and others.

If possible, the building should be located so as to minimize the length of utility lines between the structure and the main line. If the existing utility mains are not convenient to the site, it will be necessary to coordinate with the utility companies to determine how the utilities will reach the structure, and to establish the associated costs so that these expenses can be included in the project budget.

Sanitary sewers and storm sewers usually take precedence in planning because they depend on gravity flow. The invert, or lowest, elevations of the existing public sewer line should be established, because the effluent must flow from the lowest point where the sewer line leaves the building to the main sewer. (See Fig. 12.1.) The size and slope of the sewer piping will depend on the capacity needed to service the building. This portion of the horizontal piping of the sanitary sewer system outside the building is known as the building sewer. The actual connection of the building sewer to the main line must be at an elevation above the invert of the main line at any given point in order not to interfere with the free flow through the main line.

The minimum slope of the building sewer is 0.5% to 2.0% depending on the size of the pipe. A greater slope is required for smaller pipes. A pipe with a diameter of $2\frac{1}{2}$ in or less must be placed at a slope of

$^1/_4$ in/ft, a pipe with a diameter of 3 in to 6 in must be placed at a slope of $^1/_8$ in/ft, and a pipe with a diameter of 8 in or more must be placed at a slope of $^1/_{16}$ in/ft. In some cases, the run of the building sewer will have to be longer than the shortest distance between the building and the main line simply to intercept the main line at a point low enough to allow for proper slope, and the point where the sewer line enters the building will have to be adjusted to allow a greater distance. (See Fig. 12.1.)

Other utilities, such as water and electricity, do not depend on gravity, so there is more flexibility in locating the building relative to these services. However, the total distance should still be minimized. In the case of electrical service, the location of the main electric lines may dictate the location of transformers and service entry to the building.

Automobile Circulation

Fig. 12.2 gives some design guidelines for on-site *road design*. Roads should be of sufficient width to make driving easy and at least wide enough to allow two vehicles to pass. Curves should be gradual and should follow the natural topography, and there should be no blind curves.

Figure 12.2 Design Guidelines for On-Site Roads

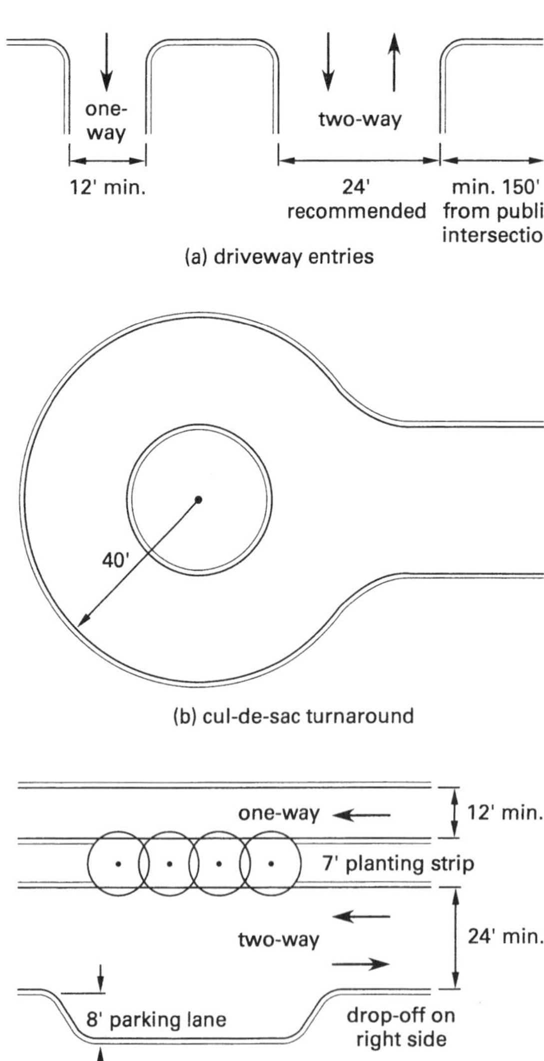

Planning for *automobile circulation* includes locating the entry drives to the site and providing on-site roads to reach the parking areas and the building drop-off point. The entire automobile circulation system should provide direct, easy access to the parking areas and building without excessive drives, turnarounds, dead ends, or conflicts with service areas and pedestrian circulation.

The size of the site, its relationship to existing public roads, and the expected volume and type of traffic will help the designer determine whether to use a one-way loop system with two entry drives or a two-way system with one entry drive. In either case, roads should be laid out so a driver can go directly to the parking area, to a drop-off point, or to the loading area without intersecting the roads to the other areas. Forcing traffic through the parking area to reach the loading area or a drop-off point should be avoided.

A road should not be laid out perpendicular to a slope unless the slope is very gentle. The road should slightly cross the slope, however, to minimize the grade. A road should be limited to a maximum slope of 15% for short distances, although 10% or less is preferable. If a road does slope more than 10%, there should be transition slopes of one-half of the maximum slope between the road and level areas. *Ramps* crossing sidewalks must have a level area between the ramp and the sidewalk (see Fig. 12.3(a)).

A road should have a gradual cross slope for drainage from the center of the roadway, called the *crown*, to the sides. This slope should be a minimum of $^1/_4$ in/ft. If the road has a gutter, the edge of the gutter should be 6 in high.

Figure 12.3 Design Guidelines for Road Grades

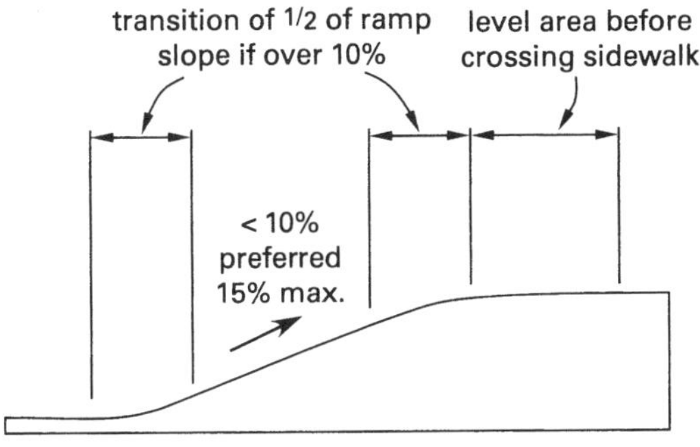

(a) automobile ramps

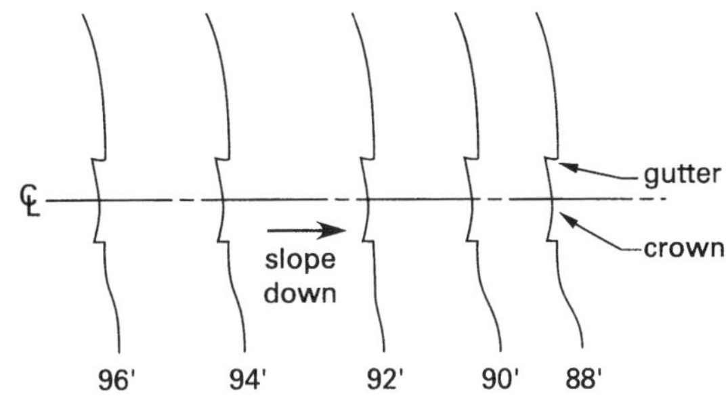

(b) representation of road with gutters on contour map

Sometimes the representation of roads and gutters on a topographic map or site plan can be confusing. Figure 12.3(b) shows a simple road sloping down, with a uniform pitch from the crown, and with gutters on either side. As shown in Fig. 9.5, the curving contours of the road point toward the direction of the slope, and the pointed contours representing the gutters point in the direction of the "valley" (in this case, the low point of the gutter).

Entry drives to the site should usually be as far away as possible from street intersections and other intersecting roads in order to avoid conflicts with vehicles waiting to turn and to avoid confusion about where to turn. In the case of a shopping center or other development that receives a high volume of vehicular traffic, however, the primary entrance may be located at an intersection so that access to the site can be controlled by traffic light.

Pedestrian Circulation

Pedestrian circulation routes should provide convenient, direct access from the various points on the site, including parking areas, to the building entrances. If connections with adjacent buildings, public sidewalks, public transportation stops, and other off-site points are needed, the circulation system must take these into account as well. *Sidewalks* should provide for the most direct paths from one point to another, since people generally opt to take the shortest route possible. If possible, pedestrian circulation paths should not cross roads, parking lots, or other areas of potential conflict.

Collector walks should be located next to parking areas so people can travel from their cars directly to a separate walk.

When these walks are next to parking where car bumpers might overhang the walk, the path should be a minimum of 6 ft wide. Required amenities such as seating, trash containers, and lighting should be provided along the walk, but placed so that they will not reduce the usable width. A walk should have a slope of $^1/_4$ in/ft perpendicular to the walking surface of the paving for drainage, unless the walk is an accessible route, in which case the cross slope can be no more than $^1/_4$ in/ft. Figure 12.4 summarizes some of the design guidelines for exterior walks.

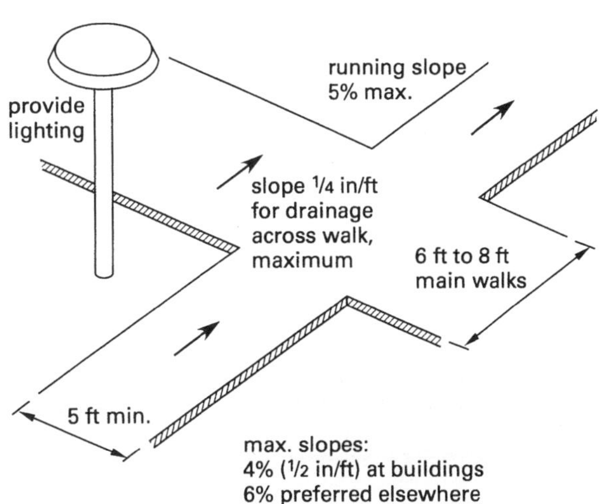

Figure 12.4 Design Guidelines for Exterior Walks

Changes in elevation are accomplished with *ramps* and *stairs*. There must be provisions for making the site accessible to the physically disabled, and all elements of accessible routes from handicapped parking areas to the building entrances must comply with the required slopes and widths prescribed by accessibility guidelines. Requirements

Figure 12.5 Access Requirements for the Physically Disabled

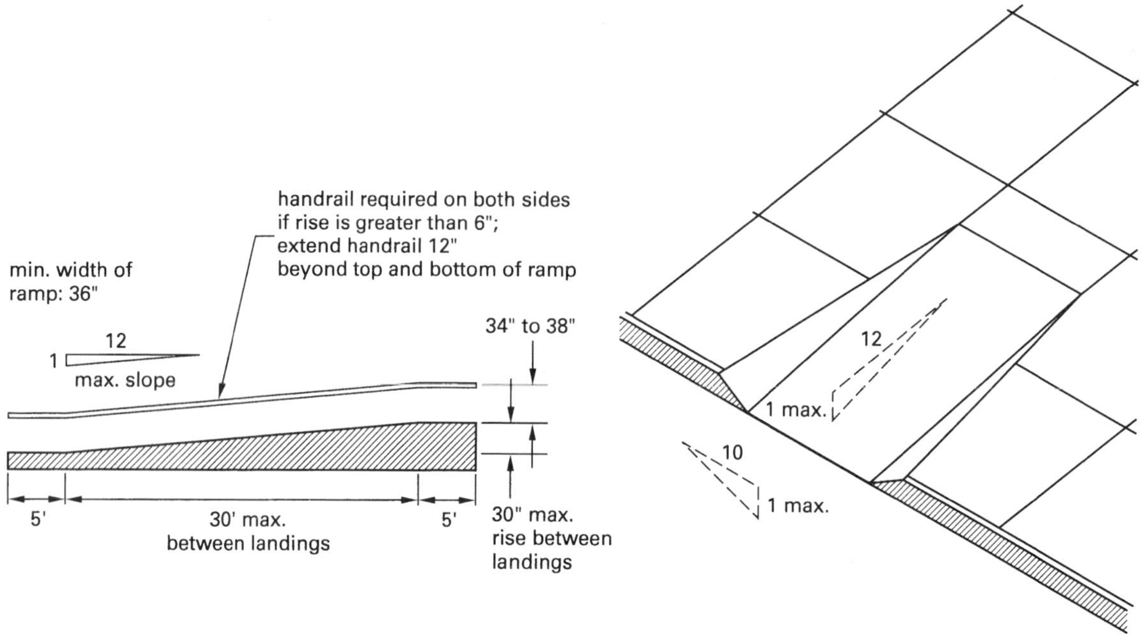

handrail required on both sides
if rise is greater than 6";
extend handrail 12"
beyond top and bottom of ramp
min. width of
ramp: 36"
12
1
max. slope
34" to 38"
5'
30' max.
between landings
5'
30" max.
rise between
landings
12
1 max.
10
1 max.

(a) ramps

(b) curb cuts

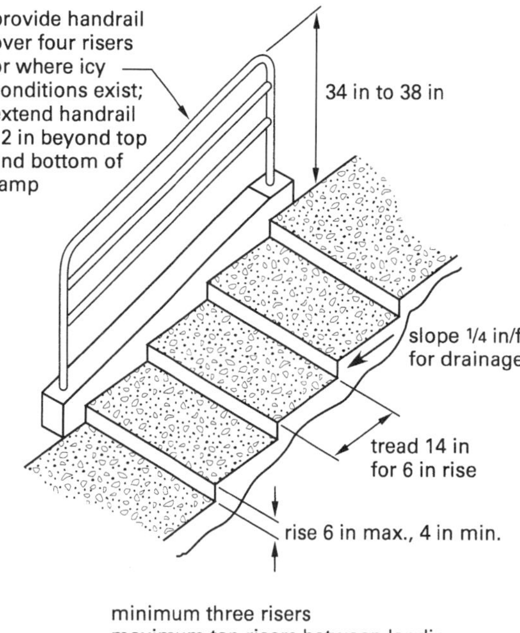

Figure 12.6 Design Guidelines for Exterior Stairs

provide handrail
over four risers
or where icy
conditions exist;
extend handrail
12 in beyond top
and bottom of
ramp
34 in to 38 in
slope 1/4 in/ft
for drainage
tread 14 in
for 6 in rise
rise 6 in max., 4 in min.
minimum three risers
maximum ten risers between landings

for *curb cutouts* and ramps are shown in Fig. 12.5, and general guidelines for exterior stairs are shown in Fig. 12.6. When a ramp and an adjacent stairway serve the same areas, both the bottoms and the tops of the ramp and the stairway should be adjacent if possible. As with walks, stairways and ramps should be illuminated.

Service Access

Service access and automobile circulation should be kept separate whenever possible. Service access is typically related to some space in the building program, such as a loading dock, receiving area, or storage area; although service trucks and automobiles may use the same entry and drives if necessary, this service area should be kept apart from automobile circulation. Enough space should be provided to allow service vehicles to turn around or back up. If the service area is enclosed, enough clearance should be provided around the vehicle for loading and unloading goods from side doors. Figure 12.7 shows some common guidelines for service drives for moderate-size trucks.

Parking

Parking should be planned so that it is efficient, convenient to the building, and separate from *pedestrian circulation.* Placement of the parking area is usually based on the size of the site, topography, location of entry drives to the property, and relationship to the service drive and building drop-off area. The parking capacity is determined by the requirements of the zoning ordinance or by the building program.

The basic planning unit for parking is the *parking space* (also called a *parking bay*, *parking stall*, or *car stall*). The standard size of a parking space is 9 ft 0 in wide and 19 ft 0 in long for standard-size cars, and 7 ft 6 in wide and 15 ft 0 in long for compact cars. However, individual zoning ordinances may have slightly different requirements and should be verified before planning. Most zoning ordinances allow a certain percentage of required parking spaces to be sized for compact cars.

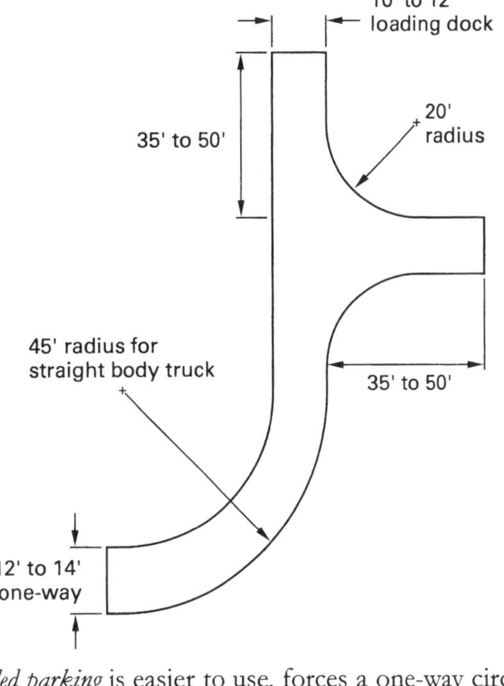

Figure 12.7 Design Guidelines for Service Drives

Parking spaces are arranged along *aisles* (often called *drive aisles* or *access aisles*, but the latter term also has a separate use in regard to accessible parking spaces). A *single-loaded aisle* has spaces on only one side; a *double-loaded aisle* has spaces on both sides.

Layouts for two types of parking arrangements are shown in Fig. 12.8. 90° *parking*, in which parking spaces are perpendicular to the aisle, is the most efficient in terms of land use. However, *angled parking* is easier to use, forces a one-way circulation pattern, and requires less total width for either a *single-loaded* or *double-loaded* layout.

Most parking lots should allow for continuous through circulation. Back-up space is needed in dead-end parking areas, and such areas are appropriate for parking only a few cars. The most efficient layouts are those with double-loaded aisles or that use a drive as the back-up space.

To estimate the area required for parking a value of 400 ft^2 per car can be used. This allows for parking, aisles, drives, and minimal parking lot landscaping. Of course, the final area depends on a more precise layout but a value of 400 ft^2 per car is a good place to start.

The area needed per car depends on several factors, including the parking spaces, aisles, drives, landscaping, and layout. However, an approximate value of 400 ft^2 per car is often used for preliminary estimation.

Accessible Parking

The number of parking spaces required for the physically disabled is set by the *2010 ADA Standards for Accessible Design* and by local codes, based on the total number of parking spaces in a parking facility. Design guidelines for accessible spaces are shown in Fig. 12.9. These spaces should be located close to the building entrance and should be identified with the international symbol for accessibility.

Figure 12.8 Parking Layouts

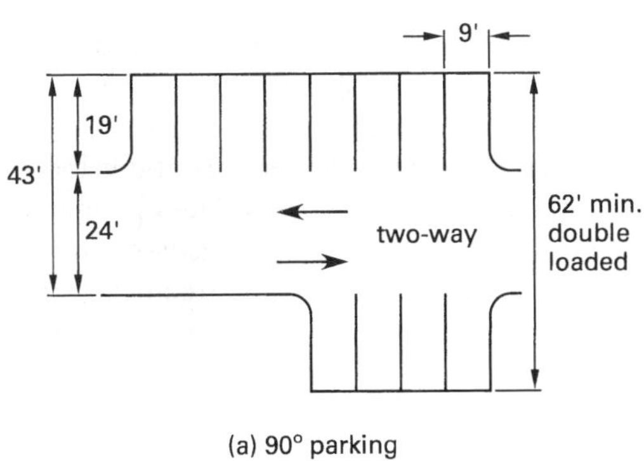

(a) 90° parking

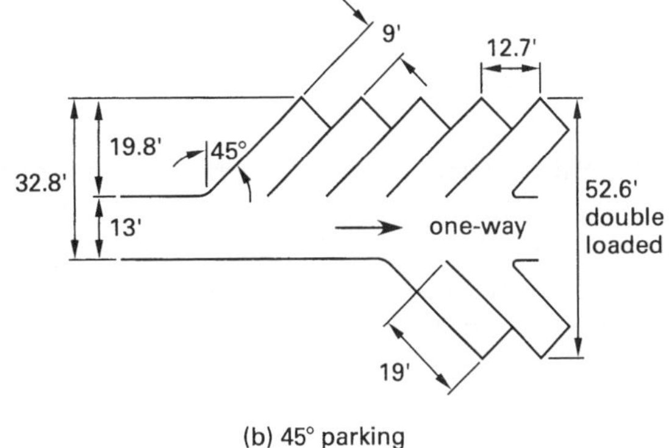

(b) 45° parking

Project Planning

Each accessible parking space should be adjacent to a *parking access aisle* (or just *access aisle*) that is part of an accessible route between the parking space and the building.

Figure 12.9
Parking for the Physically Disabled

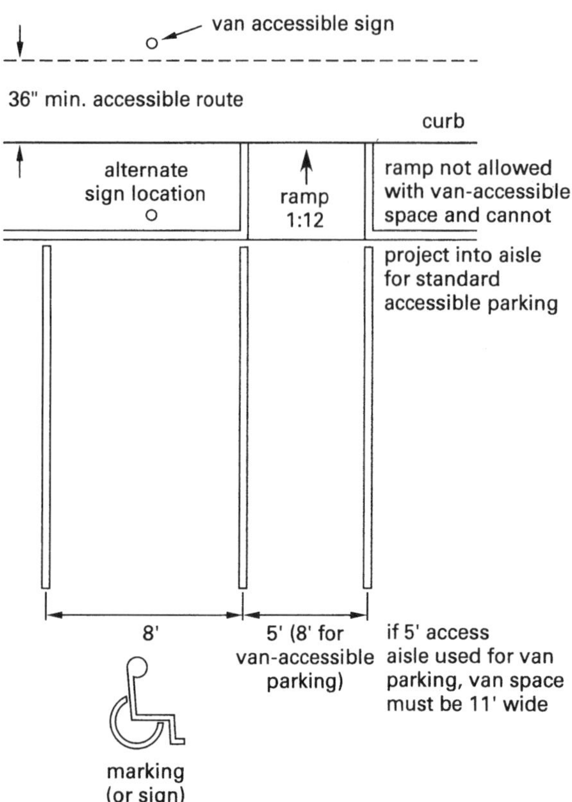

A percentage of the accessible spaces may be required to be van accessible; for a van-accessible space, the adjacent access aisle must be 96 in wide and level with the accessible route. A maximum slope of 2% must be maintained.

Drainage

Drainage in parking areas should be established as part of the site design. The slope should be between 1.5% and 5%, but for convenience in calculating, 2% or 3% can be used when figuring the slope of parking lots. Water should drain toward the edges of the parking area where it can run off into the landscaping or be collected and diverted to storm sewers, holding ponds, or other natural or engineered water courses. If curbs are used, there must be some way for the water to drain out, either through curb cutouts or through drains connected to the storm sewer. Figure 12.10 shows three basic drainage patterns for different relationships between the length of the lot and the contour lines.

One useful way to check new contour lines quickly during design is to use an estimate of the change in elevation from one side of a double-loaded parking area to the other (62 ft). For a minimum slope of 1.5%, this change in elevation is about 1 ft. With a maximum slope of 5%, the maximum change in elevation across the same 62 ft parking row is about 3 ft.

Landscaping

Landscaping is a vital part of site development. In addition to its purely aesthetic qualities, landscaping can improve energy conservation, moderate noise, frame desirable views, block undesirable views, create privacy, fashion outdoor spaces, provide shade, retard erosion, and visually connect a building to its site. Some communities prescribe guidelines for landscape installation in their zoning ordinances.

Deciduous trees can be placed to block sunlight from a building in the summer while letting the light through in the winter. Trees can moderate the wind and thereby reduce heat loss from wall surfaces. Slowing the normal wind patterns can also make outdoor spaces more pleasant to use. Protecting a house or other external-load dominated building from the effects of a cold wind can reduce the heating load substantially.

How effectively trees shield against wind varies depending on the types of trees chosen, the width of the row or rows, how densely the trees are planted, and tree height. As mentioned in Chap. 7, a very deep row of trees can reduce wind velocity substantially. However, most site designs allow space for only a single or double row of trees. In general, a row of trees of a certain height will decrease the velocity of the wind between 30% and 40% at a distance about five times the height of the trees. Trees planted next to a building may reduce wind velocity between 20% and 60%, depending on the density of the trees. The effect of trees on reducing wind velocity decreases greatly at about 10 times the tree height and is negligible beyond 20 times the tree height. If trees are employed as a windbreak, evergreens should be used so that they will remain effective in the winter. The use of landscaping to moderate the microclimate is discussed in greater detail in Chap. 7.

Like any other design material, plants have form, size, color, texture, and other qualities that can serve the purposes of the designer and create the kind of image desired. Unlike other materials, however, plants grow. The mature size and height of a tree or shrub must be known so that adequate spacing can be provided between plants and between plants and buildings. Generally, *planting strips* with trees in parking areas and between other paved areas should be at least 7 ft wide. Landscaping strips for grass or groundcovers between paved areas should be at least 4 ft wide.

Most trees and shrubs take years to grow, so existing healthy landscaping, especially large trees, should be saved whenever possible. The contours of the land cannot be changed within the *drip line* of an existing tree (i.e., within the edge of its canopy), so careful planning is needed to preserve established trees. Trees and other landscaping also need protection during construction.

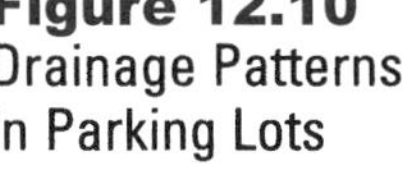
Figure 12.10
Drainage Patterns in Parking Lots

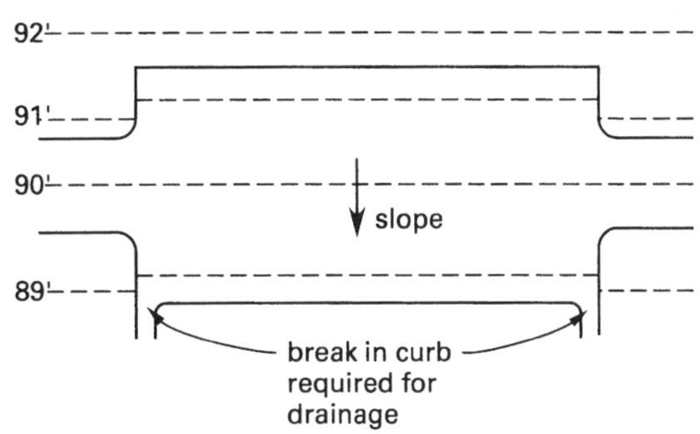

(a) drainage perpendicular to length of lot

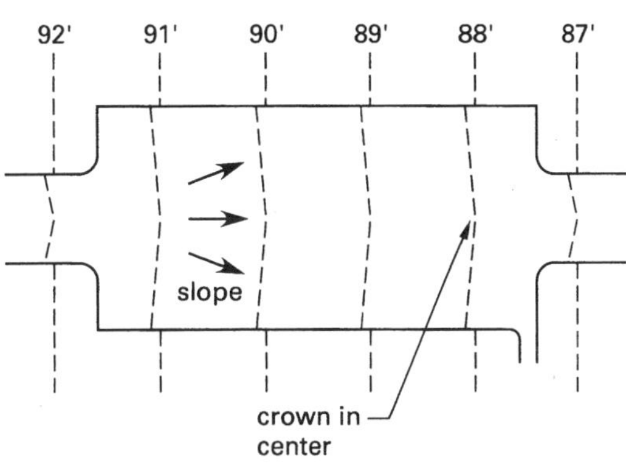

(b) drainage parallel to length

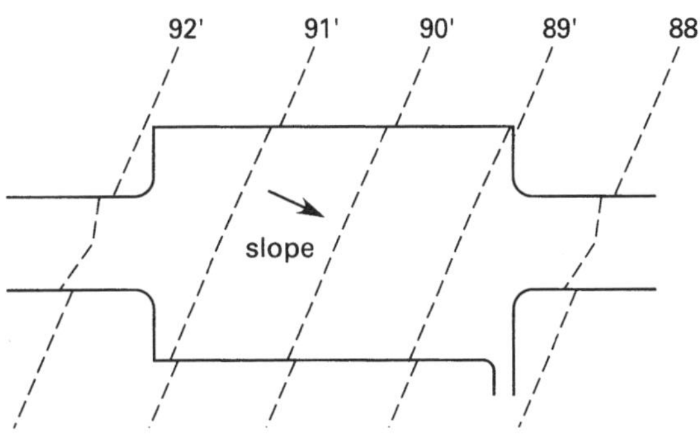

(c) drainage across lot

ALTERNATIVE ENERGY SOURCES

Using *alternative sources* to meet the building's energy needs is one of the best ways to improve a building's sustainability while decreasing the building's life-cycle costs. Although most buildings designed to use alternative energy sources have a higher initial cost, they have relatively short payback periods.

Other aspects of sustainable design, as well as the Leadership in Energy and Environmental Design (LEED) program and other sustainable building programs, are described in greater detail in Chap. 13.

Solar Design

Good *solar design* can have a tremendous impact on *energy conservation* because of the vast amount of solar energy that is striking the earth at every moment. This energy can be harnessed to provide energy for heating and cooling buildings and for heating water. The sun's light can be used for daylighting and for electrical generation by means of photovoltaic cells.

Solar Design Basics

Like most natural phenomena, *daylighting* is highly variable, and using it for building design requires an understanding of how daylight varies during different times of the day and year and in different geographical locations.

The *sun's position* varies by season because of the relationship between the sun and the earth. The seasons are a result of the change in angle between the earth and sun. The north-south axis of the earth is tilted at an angle of 23.4° relative to the north-south axis of the sun. This is called the *declination angle* (or *declination*) of the earth and remains constant as the earth revolves around the sun during a one-year period.

As shown in Fig. 12.11, when the northern pole of the earth's axis is tilted toward the sun, it is summer in the Northern Hemisphere. This is the season in which the rays of the sun are closest to being perpendicular to the surface of much of the northern part of the earth; in the summer the sun is highest in the sky, and the Northern Hemisphere receives the most solar radiation.

Figure 12.11 Seasonal Variation of Sun Angle

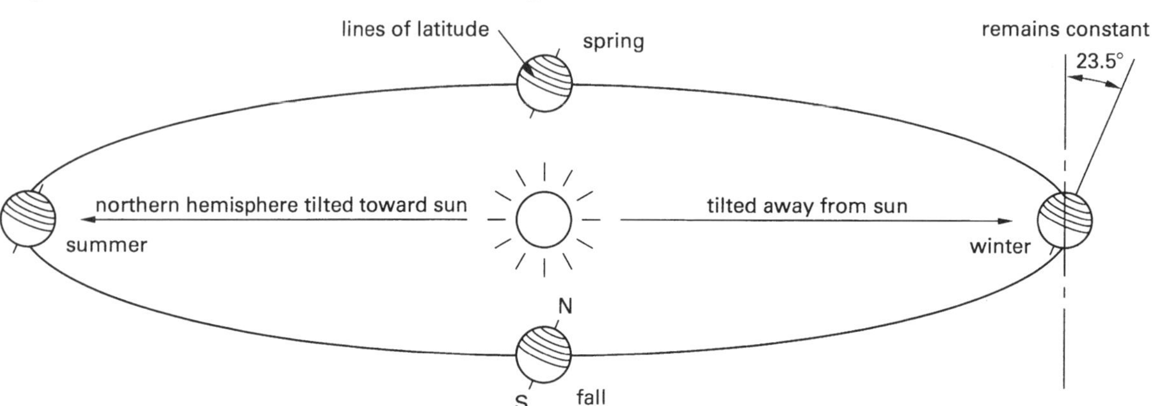

During the winter months, the earth's northern pole is tilted away from the sun, decreasing the sun's angle relative to the horizon and reducing the amount of solar energy striking the earth. The times of maximum tilt in relation to the sun are approximately December 21 for the *winter solstice* and June 21 for the *summer solstice*. On about March 21 and September 21, the earth is tilted sideways in relation to the sun, and day and night are of equal length; these are the *spring equinox* and *fall equinox*, respectively.

How high above the horizon the sun is at any given time during the day depends on two factors. One is the variation of the seasons, and the other is the latitude of the observer on the earth. At the equator, or 0° latitude, the surface of the earth is closer to being perpendicular to the sun's rays than it is at 90° latitude, the north pole.

The position of the sun as viewed from the earth can be described by two angles, the azimuth and the altitude. (See Fig. 12.12.) The *azimuth* is the compass orientation of the sun. For solar design purposes, this is usually the number of degrees either east or west of due south. For example, if the sun is halfway between south and west, the azimuth is 45° west of south. Sometimes, the azimuth is measured in a 360° circle with due north at 0°, due east at 90°, south at 180°, and west at 270°.

Figure 12.12 Sun Angles

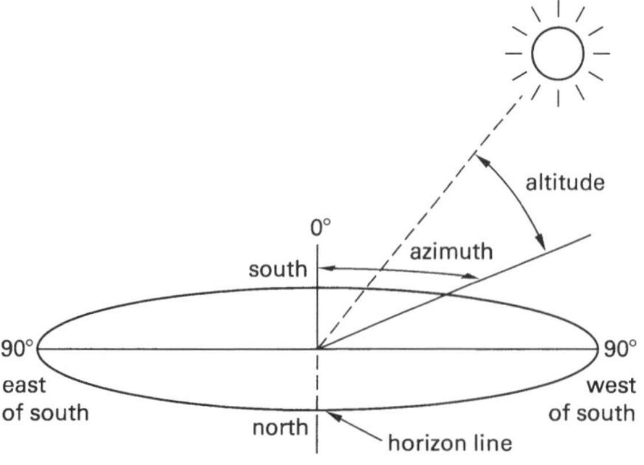

The *altitude* is the apparent height of the sun measured as an angle from the horizon. The horizon is at 0°; directly overhead is 90°.

Because the earth follows a similar path around the sun every year, the relative position of the sun at any location on earth on any given day and at any given time can be calculated with various formulas.

Sun charts (or *sunpath projections*) plot the altitude and azimuth at different times during a day. Alternatively, various web sites and tablet applications are available that can provide exact values of azimuth, altitude, sunrise, and sunset for any position on earth for any time and date of the year. Although exact figures for a specific site will be required for detailed design, for preliminary design, any of the traditional sun charts and solar plots can be used. These graphic representations of the values are often quicker and easier to use for a given latitude on earth than a more complex computer-based version, particularly in the early stages of design. One such solar plot for a particular latitude is shown in Fig. 12.13.

The sun chart shown in Fig. 12.13 is known as a *rectilinear projection.* In this kind of chart, the solar azimuth is plotted along the horizontal axis, and the solar altitude is found along the vertical axis. Several lines represent the sun at yearly time intervals (usually the 21st day of each month).

Solar altitude varies with latitude; a different sun chart could be plotted for every fraction of a degree of latitude. In practice, sun charts are usually plotted for every 2°, 5°, or 10° of latitude, depending on what level of accuracy is needed. Data for dates and latitudes between the plotted lines can be interpolated.

Three other types of sun charts are the equidistant horizontal projection, the gnomonic projection, and the stereographic projection (also known as the *fish-eye projection*).

The *equidistant horizontal projection* (also known as the *horizontal polar projection*) plots the path of the sun at various times of the year on a circular chart. Fig. 12.14(a) shows a simplified version of this type of chart. The spokes of the chart represent the solar azimuth. The curved lines overlaid on the chart show the path of the sun on different dates based on the latitude. Intersecting lines represent the time of day.

At low angles of the sun, the lines extend to infinity, as shown in Fig. 12.14(b). A *gnomonic projection* (also called a *sunpeg chart*) is derived from a sundial projection. This is less useful as a solar chart than the other types, but it is useful for shadow studies. As with the other charts, a separate projection is needed for each latitude. A gnomonic projection is used by placing the chart next to the building model to be studied, then placing a small peg perpendicular to the chart in the location shown. The model and chart are tilted in sunlight until the tip of the shadow cast by the peg intersects the selected date and time. The shadows on the model are then the same as they would be in the actual building at that time and date.

Figure 12.13 Typical Sun Chart

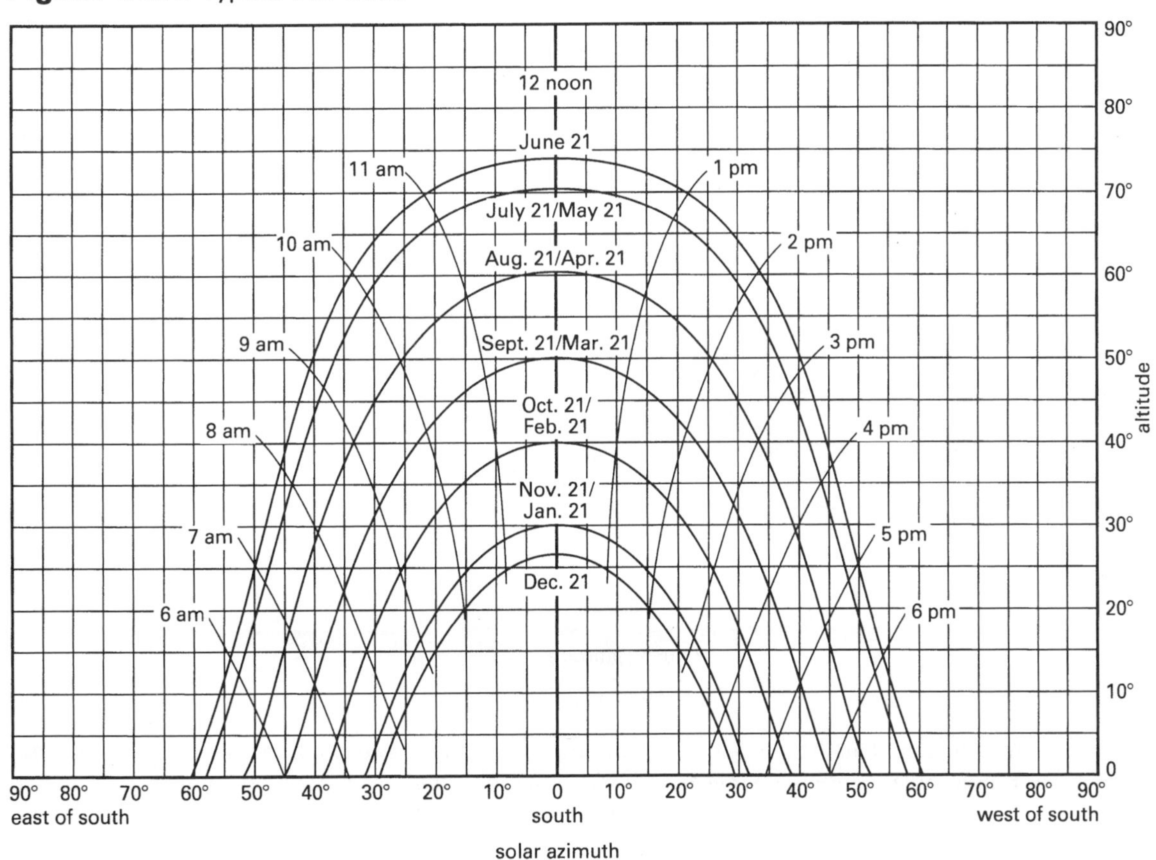

Figure 12.14 Sun Path Projections

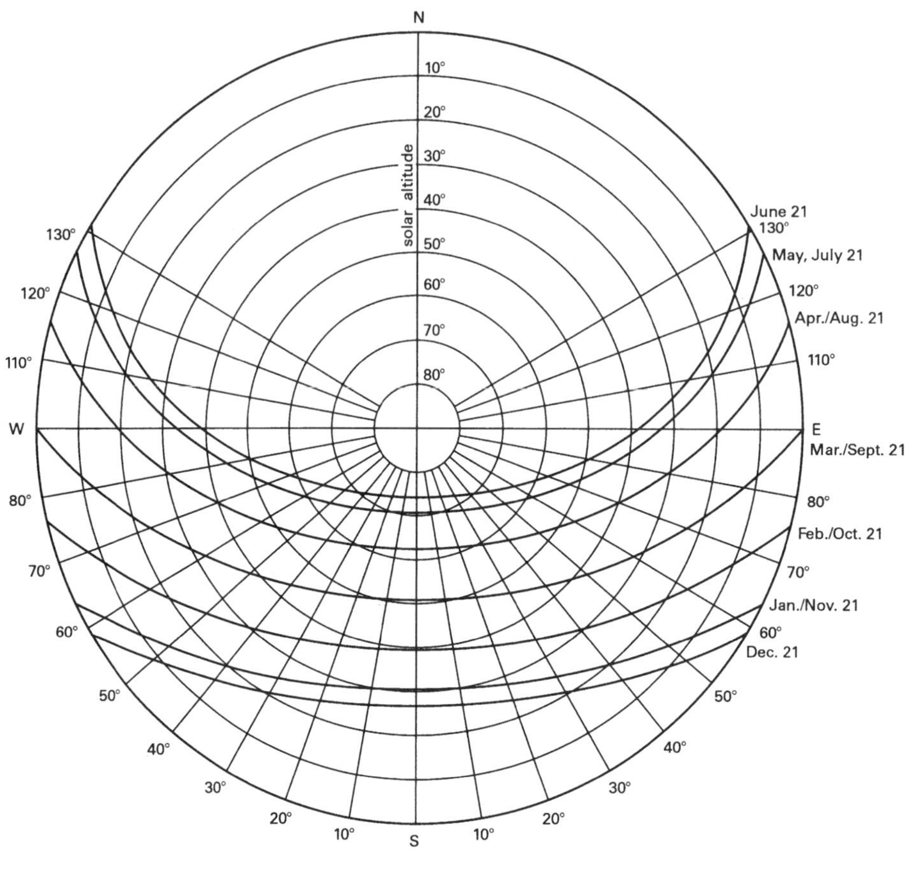

40° N. latitude

(a) equidistant horizontal projection

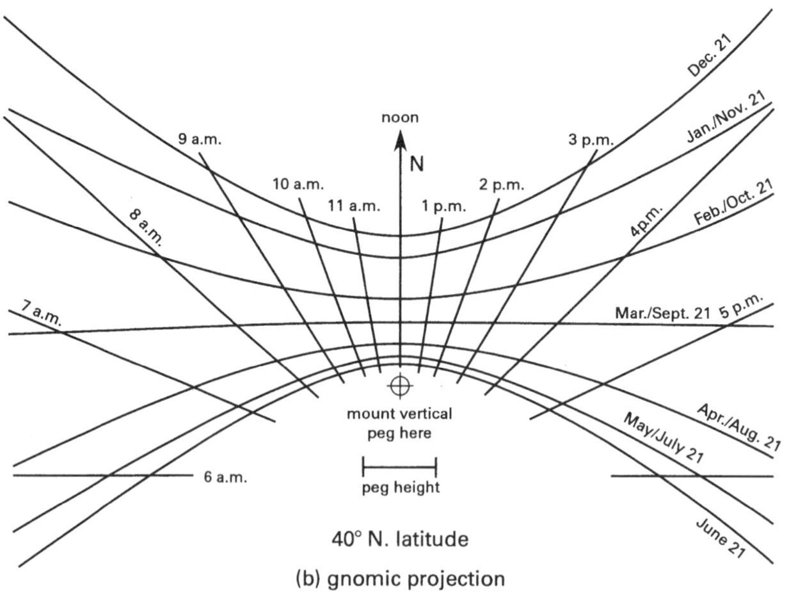

40° N. latitude

(b) gnomic projection

Use of any type of sun chart begins with knowing the direction of *solar south*, the direction of the geographic south pole. Solar south is not necessarily the same as *magnetic south*, which is south as determined by a compass. The earth's magnetic field is irregular and is not aligned with its geographic north and south poles. In most places on earth, a compass does not point toward the true north pole, and due to regional irregularities in the magnetic field, a compass may not even point directly toward the north magnetic pole. Magnetic north may be easterly or westerly from true north, and this difference varies with the compass's location on the earth.

To determine the direction of true north from a compass reading, the *magnetic declination*—the angle of difference between magnetic north and true north—must be known for that location. The compass reading is adjusted by the magnetic declination to give the direction of true north. True south, or solar south, is then the opposite direction.

Sun charts can be used to determine the best design for overhangs and other shading devices and to plot the shading effects of surrounding structures and vegetation on a building using solar heating or daylighting. Such a plot is called a *shadow mask*. Although hard copy sun charts and shadow masks are useful for preliminary design and quick studies, there are computer programs that can quickly give exact data based on a project's location. Many three-dimensional design programs can calculate sun position and show accurate shadows on a model.

Charts and tables are also available in printed form or on various web sites that give the amount of solar radiation in British thermal units per foot per day for different geographical locations. This data can be used to design passive and active solar energy systems.

Figure 12.15 Passive Solar Heating Types

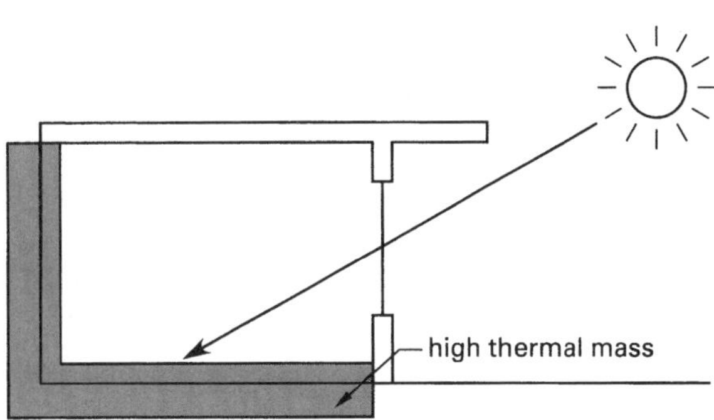

(a) direct gain space

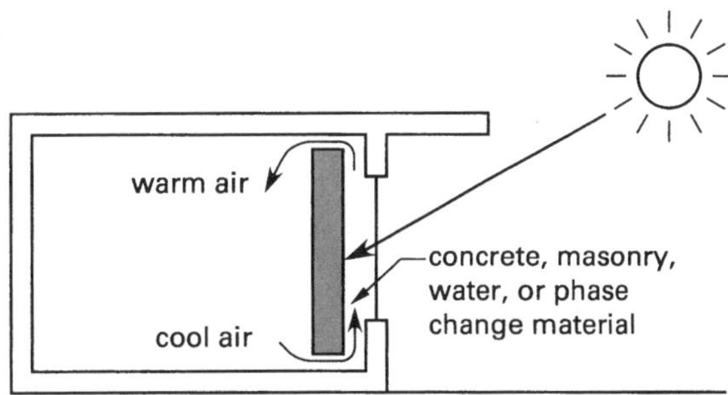

(b) thermal storage wall (Trombe wall)

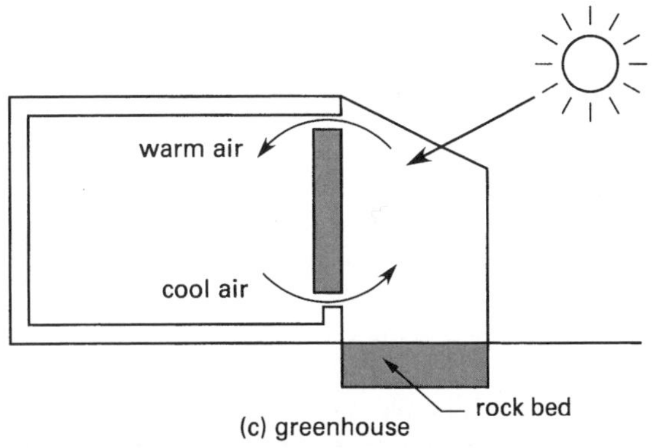

(c) greenhouse

Passive Solar Design

A *passive solar energy system* collects, stores, and distributes solar energy without the use of mechanical equipment. The most commonly used passive solar design techniques, shown in Fig. 12.15, fall into the following general categories.

- *Direct gain systems* collect heat through south-facing glass and then store this heat in high-mass materials such as concrete floors, masonry walls, tile, stone, and terrazzo. See Fig. 12.15(a). During nighttime hours, the high-mass materials slowly release the heat they captured during the day. To make this system effective, the glass area must be well insulated at night or the glazing must be *low-emissivity glass* (also called *low-ε*) glass. Glazing used for passive solar heating should have a *U*-factor of less than 0.35 Btu/ft^2-hr-°F. Because movable nighttime insulation is not very efficient and requires human intervention, newer glazing materials such as triple-pane glass units, low emissivity glass, and *spectrally selective glazing* can be used instead. The mass areas should be dark colored and free of rugs, wall hangings, and other materials that would interfere with the storage and release of heat.

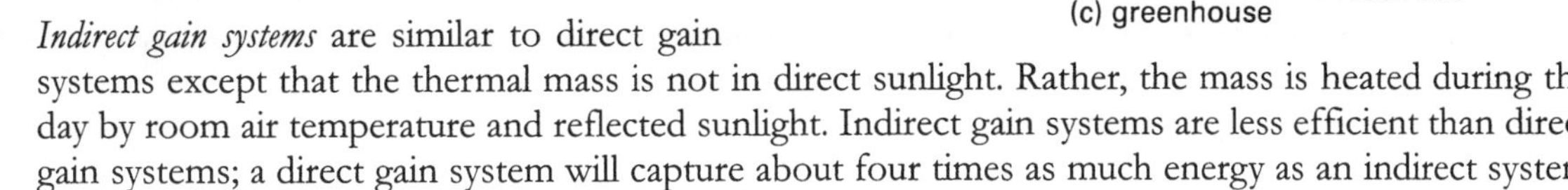

- *Indirect gain systems* are similar to direct gain systems except that the thermal mass is not in direct sunlight. Rather, the mass is heated during the day by room air temperature and reflected sunlight. Indirect gain systems are less efficient than direct gain systems; a direct gain system will capture about four times as much energy as an indirect system with the same mass. However, an indirect gain system can be used in conjunction with a direct gain system to even out temperature variations in different parts of a building.

- A *thermal storage wall* is a high-mass wall placed directly behind a south-facing glass wall. The high-mass wall collects solar energy during the day for release at night, as a form of direct gain system. Most thermal storage walls are vented, which allows cool air to circulate in the space between the glass and wall, become heated, and travel by convection up and over the wall and back into the space.
- A common form of thermal storage wall, as shown in Fig. 12.15(b), is the *Trombe wall*, which is constructed of masonry with vents at the top and bottom to allow heated air to circulate out to the rest of the building. Thermal storage walls can also be constructed of water containers, phase change materials, or any material that is able to store heat. Water is more effective than concrete or masonry because it has a higher specific heat and can store more energy.
- *Phase change materials* are used to avoid the overheating and wide swings in temperatures that can occur with concrete, masonry, and water. Eutectic salts that change from a solid to a liquid at a fairly low temperature, around 70°F, are commonly used phase change materials. They store large amounts of heat because they also store latent heat as they undergo the phase change from solid to liquid. At night, the heat is released as they again change state, from liquid back to solid.
- A *greenhouse design* features a large glazed area on the south side of the building, with a heavy thermal mass wall separating the greenhouse from the rest of the structure. A rock bed or high thermal mass floor is built in the greenhouse. While the greenhouse often overheats and is subject to heat loss at night, the stored heat circulates into the rest of the building at night. See Fig. 12.15(c).
- A *roof pond* stores heat in large water-filled bags on the roof of a building. In winter during the day, the bags heat up. At night, insulation is moved over the roof pond, and the bags release heat downward into the building.
- The same system can be reversed in the summer to cool the building by radiation. During the day, the bags are covered with insulation so that they absorb heat only from the building. At night, the insulation is removed and the absorbed heat is transferred upward and away from the building.
- *Convective loop systems*, or *thermosiphons*, place the solar collector below the inhabited space. The air within the space is circulated by natural convection as the warm air rises and cool air falls back to the collector. The cycle continues indefinitely. Convective loop systems can be used to circulate either air or water.

Active Solar Design

Active solar energy systems use pumps, fans, ducts, pipes, and other mechanical equipment to collect, store, and distribute solar energy. In order of most common use, active solar systems are used for domestic and process water heating, space heating, space cooling, and electricity generation. Practical generation of electricity is still limited due to the expense of photovoltaic (PV) cells, but this is slowly changing as more efficient and economical PV cells are developed.

One of the most common types of active systems consists of an otherwise passive system used with ductwork and fans to distribute the heated air without relying solely on natural convection. This can be thought of as a "passive system with active assist."

A typical active solar system requires three components: a collector, a storage device, and a distribution system.

The *collector* may be either a flat-plate collector or a focusing collector. *Flat-plate collectors* consist of a network of pipes located on an absorptive black surface with low emissivity, placed below a covering of glass or plastic. The pipes carry the heat transfer medium, which is usually water with antifreeze but can also be another liquid or air. *Focusing collectors* are parabolic reflectors that focus the incoming radiation to a single pipe that carries the heat-transfer medium. Because the reflectors direct the sun's energy to a specific point, focusing collectors operate at a much higher temperature than flat-plate collectors.

However, they must be continuously aimed at the sun for maximum benefit, so they are usually attached to mechanisms that automatically track the sun's path.

Common *storage devices* are water for water systems and rock beds for air systems. *Phase change materials* can also be used, but they are more expensive.

Distribution components are the same as for standard HVAC systems: ducts for air, pipes for water, and associated fans, pumps, registers, and control devices. When solar energy is used for water heating, the system may be either open loop or closed loop. In an *open-loop system*, the water is heated directly in the solar collector. In a *closed-loop system*, antifreeze or some other transfer medium is heated in the collector and circulated to a heat exchanger, where the domestic water is heated by the transfer medium. This allows use of a nontoxic chemical that facilitates the heat transfer but guarantees that it will be kept separate from the domestic water supply. See Chap. 17 for more information on solar water heating.

A typical active solar system requires three components: a collector, a storage device, and a distribution system.

When solar energy is used for space heating, either air or water can be used as the transfer medium. If air is used, the heated air is circulated to a rock bed, normally located under the building, where the heat is stored in the mass of the rocks. At night, fans circulate cool air over the rock bed, where the air warms and is distributed to the building. If water is used as the transfer medium, it is stored in a large tank and then, when needed, it is pumped to baseboard heaters, radiant panels, or a heat exchanger in a forced air furnace.

Solar energy can be used for cooling if high enough temperatures are reached in the transfer medium. The heated water is used as the energy source for absorptive cooling, as shown in Fig. 17.2.

The *International Building Code* requires photovoltaic elements to comply with the general code requirements for roofing materials and rooftop structures. This includes requirements for fire resistance, wind resistance, material standards, and installation according to manufacturers' instructions. These systems must also comply with the applicable provisions of the *International Fire Code.*

Wind

Wind power offers an extremely sustainable method of generating electricity from a renewable and free source. There are many commercial wind farms across the United States and Canada that help reduce the need for fossil-fuel-burning power plants.

However, the specific conditions needed for generating wind power tend to make on-site generation impractical for individual building use. The equipment is costly, and most jurisdictions will not allow its use on urban or suburban sites. It is also unlikely that the project site will satisfy the wind speed and direction needs for wind power.

Even where a wind-driven generating system can be installed, in most cases the electricity must be used as it is generated. Using wind energy to charge batteries has limited use for most building sites. However, some power companies will purchase excess electricity that is generated on private sites, when the electricity is transferred to the utility power grid.

Geothermal

Geothermal energy draws on heat sources within the earth. The earth absorbs and holds solar radiation within its great mass, keeping the temperature underground relatively constant year round. In the winter, when the air temperature is colder than the underground temperature, a geothermal system uses the heat in the ground to warm an embedded piping system, transferring the heat to the heating system. In the summer, the underground piping system releases excess heat from the air into the cooler ground. The water is cooled and is used to cool the air in the building.

Geothermal energy uses *ground-source heat pumps* (*GSHPs*). GSHPs are electrically powered systems that work like air-source heat pumps by either extracting heat from the ground in winter or giving off excess heat to the ground in summer. Within a GSHP, the heat from the ground is increased through a vapor-compressor refrigeration cycle.

The main feature of a GSHP is the assemblage of durable plastic pipes buried in the ground. The pipes can be arranged either vertically or horizontally depending on the space available and the geology of the site. About 400 ft of pipe is required for every 12,000 Btu/hr of heating or cooling capacity needed. For heating, water is pumped through the plastic tubing in the earth to the heat pump, where the water's heat is increased. The GSHP can then be used to preheat water or exchange heat in a water-water or water-air heat exchanger. The cycle is reversed for cooling. GSHPs can be used for space heating and cooling and for preheating water for domestic hot water. They can reduce energy consumption of space heating and cooling by 20% to 50% and use up to 50% less energy for water heating.

Although the initial cost of a geothermal system is higher than that of conventional equipment, long-term costs are lower, and the system reduces the need for fossil fuel-based energy supplies. Geothermal systems can be used for either residential and commercial buildings; they are most beneficial in buildings that require significant space and water heating and cooling over extended hours of operation (e.g., single-family homes, multifamily residential buildings, and schools).

Photovoltaics

Photovoltaics is the direct conversion of sunlight into electricity. Photovoltaic (PV) cells are made from various types of semiconductor materials, deposited or arranged on a variety of substrate materials to form flat panels. There are also concentrator systems that focus sunlight on the PV cells to increase energy production, but these are generally limited to use in large-scale power generation. The PV cells convert the sunlight into direct current electricity, which is then converted into alternating current electricity. The electricity can be used immediately, stored in batteries, or sold back to the power utility if the system is connected to the power grid.

The use of PV technology has many advantages. It reduces demand on nonrenewable energy sources, such as coal- and gas-fired power plants. It can reduce energy costs because the power is generated on site and the excess can, in many states, be sold back to the utility. It produces electricity with no pollution, and the energy captured comes from a free resource.

PV technology reduces demand on nonrenewable energy sources, can reduce energy costs, and the excess can be sold back.

Disadvantages include high initial cost, the need for collectors to be placed in a location that receives adequate sunlight, low winter production, and the lack of electricity production during night hours. The use of storage batteries introduces its own challenges, such as high initial and maintenance costs, and potentially high physical space requirements depending on the storage capacity needed. In addition, some local jurisdictions, especially homeowners' associations, may limit the use of photovoltaics.

The development of PV technology is ongoing, and the efficiency is increasing while the cost is decreasing. Manufacturers now provide 20-year warranties for PV cells. PV use continues to grow, with some states offering tax rebates or other financial incentives to make PV use more feasible.

There are many types of PV cells, including some that are still in experimental stages. However, the three most common types of PV cells in use are crystalline, polycrystalline, and thin-film cells. *Crystalline cells* are the most widely used. *Polycrystalline cells* are less expensive than crystalline cells, but produce less power. *Thin-film cells* can be deposited onto other materials such as glass, metal, and plastic, and are ideal when the cells need to be fused to other building materials as part of building-integrated PV systems. However, thin-film cells produce as little as one-third the power of crystalline PV cells.

PV cells can be placed on a building in one of two ways.

Individual PV cells can be assembled into multicell *arrays*, which can be constructed in frames and attached to the roof, walls, or elsewhere as a distinct visual element. When a PV array is used on a roof, its ideal angle and location is determined by the latitude of the building site. For maximum year-round energy generation, the tilt angle should be the same as the latitude of the building site. For maximum energy generation in the winter, the tilt angle should be 10° to 15° greater than the latitude.

Alternatively, thin-film cells can be built into other building materials, such as shingles, metal roofing, membrane roofing, and glass. When the PV cells are incorporated into more traditional materials, their aesthetic impact is minimized and their use may be permitted in more locations.

SUSTAINABLILITY PRINCIPLES

This section covers passive design methods for energy efficiency, including those the architect may consider during development of the site design concept. The careful use of these strategies can greatly reduce reliance on mechanical systems, reduce operating costs, improve human comfort, and reduce the use of fossil fuels.

Additional sustainable design issues and building techniques are discussed in Chap. 13.

Sustainable design techniques that can be employed during the pre-design and schematic design phases are discussed in Chap. 7. Energy conservation techniques that incorporate features into HVAC systems to make them more efficient and energy efficiency in electrical systems are discussed in Chap. 17.

Building Orientation

By orienting a building carefully, an architect can maximize solar heat gain in the winter (if desired), reduce solar heat gain in the summer, encourage cooling with prevailing winds, minimize exposure to cold winter winds, and optimize daily use of the prevailing climate. Preliminary siting decisions based on climatic influences are discussed in Chap. 7.

Selecting the optimum building orientation for energy efficiency is often difficult because of interrelated and sometimes conflicting considerations such as heat gain, protection from overheating, daylighting, use of PV and solar heating panels, use of beneficial cooling breezes, protection from cold winds, and the practical aspects of site topography and the building program. However, building orientation for energy conservation is a natural way to help balance overheated and underheated periods during the year and react to daily temperature fluctuations.

Many studies have been performed to determine optimum building orientation. All recommend that a rectangular building should be oriented with its longer dimension approximately east-west, in order to minimize the more intense solar radiation from east and west while taking advantage of the heating potential of south-facing surfaces in the winter. In summer, on the other hand, the sun is higher in the sky and its rays strike a south-facing wall from a higher angle, so there is less solar radiation striking the wall than in winter, and what there is can be shaded more easily.

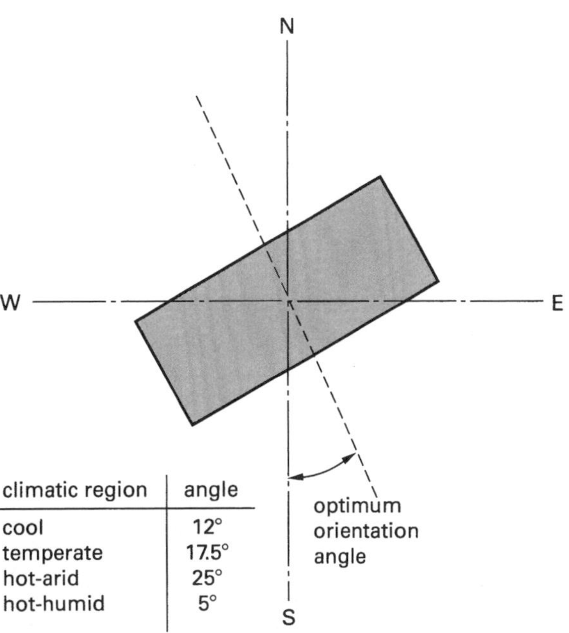

climatic region	angle
cool	12°
temperate	17.5°
hot-arid	25°
hot-humid	5°

Figure 12.16
Optimum Building Orientation

However, the precise angle at which the building should be placed in relation to the east-west datum depends on the climatic region and location of the site. Considering the slightly lower morning temperatures, a rectangular building is generally best oriented slightly east of south as shown in Fig. 12.16. The ideal angle of the south face varies slightly depending on the climatic region but is approximately 15° east of south. In hot-arid and hot humid climates, the building may have to be rotated slightly from this angle to pick up the cooling breezes of the local climate.

In cold climates, a building's entrances are best located on the leeward side of the building to avoid winter winds. In temperate climates, entrances should be located on the south side to make them more inviting and to capitalize on the natural snow-melting effects of the sun. In hot climates, the long side of a building can be oriented to catch cooling breezes.

Building orientation for energy conservation is a natural way to help balance overheated and underheated periods during the year and react to daily temperature fluctuations.

Building Shape

As with building orientation, the shape of a building is the result of many interrelated and sometimes conflicting requirements and programmatic needs. In regard solely to energy conservation, however, some general guidelines for building shape can be established.

Building shape can affect energy use in a number of ways. Because both heating and cooling loads depend on the thermal conductance of the walls and roof and the respective areas of those surfaces, a building with a smaller total surface area will generally use less energy. A sphere would be the ideal shape because it has the least possible surface area for a given volume, but spheres are not practical for buildings. Among the practical shapes, a cube has the least *surface area* for a given volume. (See Fig. 12.17.) For example, a two-story building, being closer in shape to a cube, will generally use less energy than a one-story building of the same floor area.

However, the goal of minimal surface area must be balanced with the gains provided by other building shapes that are better suited to solar heating, natural ventilation, and similar techniques. Minimizing surface area usually works best in cold climates; in a different climate, reducing heat loss through the exterior envelope may be less important than other factors. As already mentioned, a long, thin building can be oriented with a long surface facing toward the south to maximize solar heating and minimize heat gain. Long, thin buildings also make it easier to use daylighting strategies and to capture prevailing winds for natural ventilation. Larger buildings may need courtyards and rambling shapes for daylighting and ventilation. See Fig. 12.17(b).

Figure 12.17 Building Shape Affects Energy Use

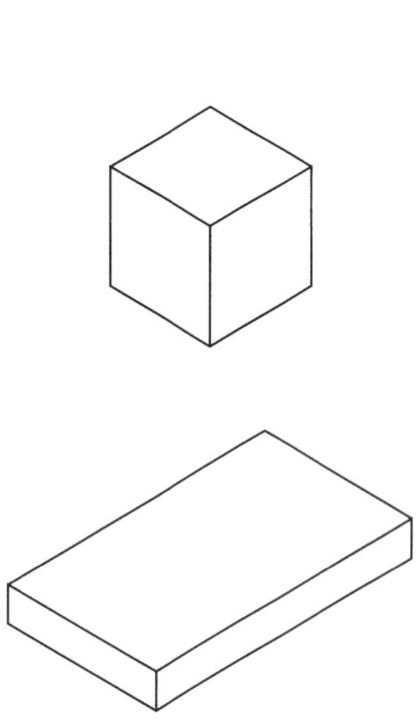

(a) For same floor area, cubic buildings have less surface area.

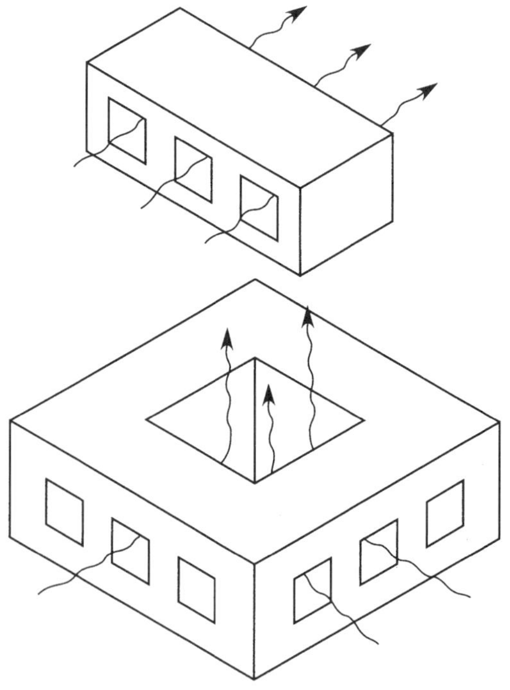

(b) Thin sections are best for natural ventilation and daylighting.

For energy efficiency, the ideal shape of a building depends on its climatic region and whether it is an external-load dominated building or an internal-load dominated building.

An *external-load dominated building* (also called a *skin-load dominated building*) is one whose energy use is determined mainly by the amount of heat loss or gain through its exterior envelope. Buildings of this type generally have few occupants per unit area and a small amount of heat gain from lighting, equipment, and people. Examples are houses, apartments, condominiums, and warehouses.

An *internal-load dominated building* is one whose energy use is driven by high heat gain from occupants, lighting, and equipment. Buildings of this type include office buildings, hospitals, retail stores, schools, and laboratories.

In most cases, the shape of an internal-load dominated building has less of an effect on energy efficiency than it does for an external-load dominated building, unless the building shape is designed to allow extensive use of daylighting or other passive or active energy conservation techniques. Figure 12.18 shows the optimal building shape for each type of load in each of the four climatic regions of the United States. (See Fig. 9.2 for a map of the climatic zones in the United States.)

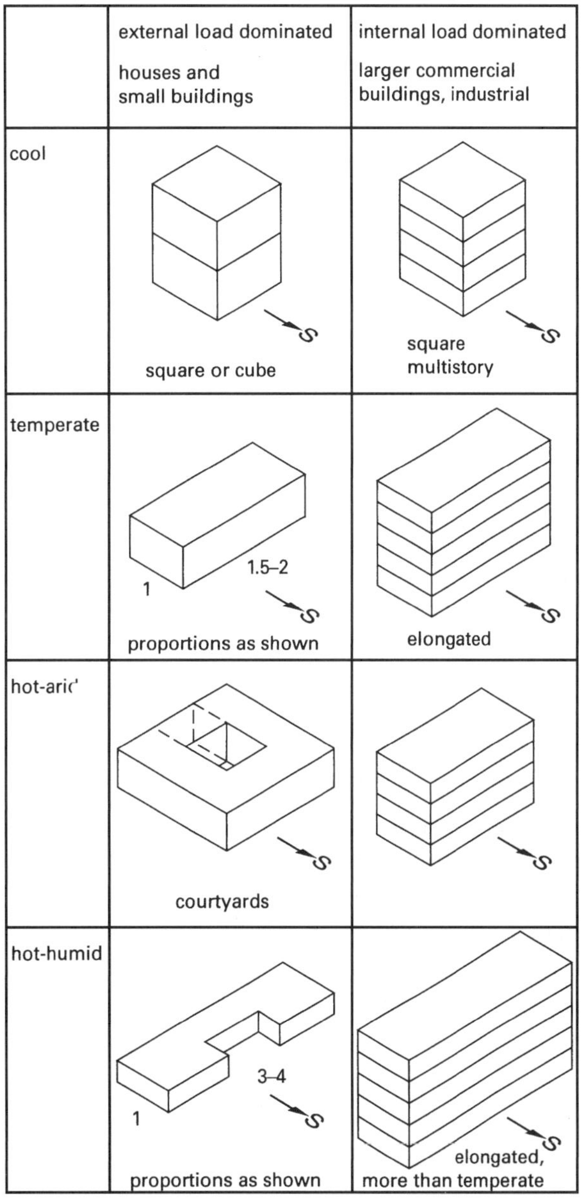

For cool and cold regions, a cubic shape generally works best because the extremes of winter temperature suggest that the surface area should be minimized in both types of load dominated buildings. For the same floor area, a two-story house is better than a one-story house.

For temperate climates, *building shape* has less of an effect. However, a building elongated in the east-west direction still offers some advantages for winter solar heat gain, daylighting, and minimizing heat gain in the summer.

For hot-arid regions, squarer shapes are better. For external-load dominated buildings, the plan should include open courtyards; for internal-load dominated buildings, a solid, multistory arrangement works best.

For hot-humid regions, shapes elongated in the east-west direction are preferable to allow breezes, provide natural cooling, and minimize severe heat gain from the east and west directions. Courtyards and broad overhangs are also useful.

Figure 12.18 Building Shapes Based on Climate Type and Type of Load

	external load dominated houses and small buildings	internal load dominated larger commercial buildings, industrial
cool	S square or cube	S square multistory
temperate	1 1.5–2 S proportions as shown	S elongated
hot-arid	S courtyards	S
hot-humid	1 3–4 S proportions as shown	S elongated, more than temperate

Building Shading

Building shading should be used selectively to minimize solar heat gain in the summer and maximize it in the winter. This can be done naturally with deciduous trees, or with horizontal or vertical shading devices attached to the building. The shading devices can be either fixed or movable. If daylighting strategies have been employed, horizontal blinds can both shade the glass and provide reflective surfaces to direct sunlight into a building, depending on needs.

Figure 12.19 Building Shading

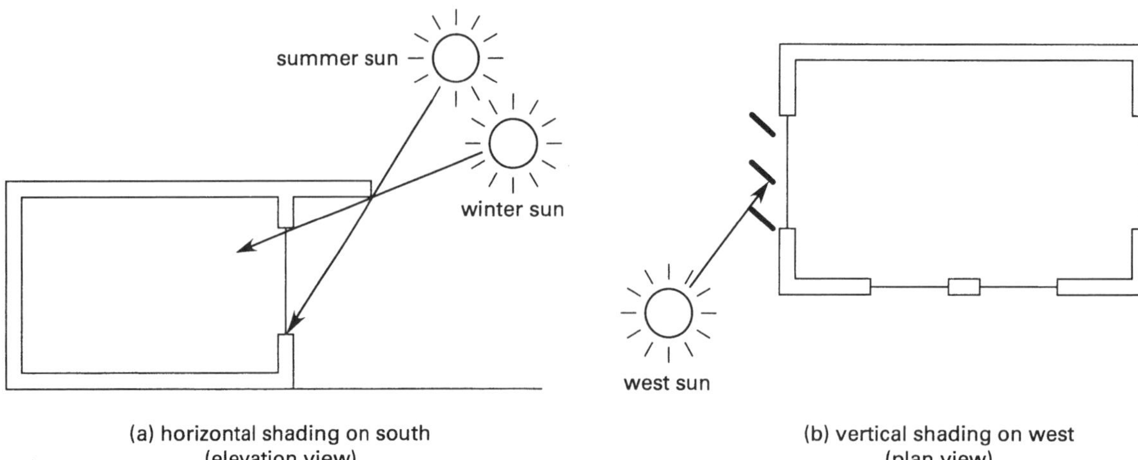

(a) horizontal shading on south (elevation view)

(b) vertical shading on west (plan view)

The orientation of a building's facade determines the most effective type of shading device. South-facing facades need moderate overhangs or horizontal louvers, while east- and west-facing facades should be protected with vertical *louvers* (see Fig. 12.19). Southeast- and southwest-facing facades may need either very wide overhangs or vertical louvers, or both. Fixed exterior shading devices are usually supplemented with interior *window coverings.*

Insulation and Weather Sealing

One of the most basic passive energy conservation strategies is to adequately insulate and seal a building against air infiltration. How much insulation to use, in terms of cost-benefit analysis, depends on the climate, but in most buildings the money spent on insulation, weather-stripping, and caulking is recovered within a few years. In addition to reducing heat flow, adequate insulation also keeps wall and ceiling surfaces warmer, raises the mean radiant temperature so the comfort level is increased, and improves acoustic qualities.

Insulation

Insulation is made from a variety of materials, such as fiberglass, mineral wool, polystyrene, polyisocyanurate, polyurethane, and cellulose. Newer, less common insulation materials include cementitious foam, autoclaved aerated concrete, straw panels, straw-bale construction, and plastic fiber.

Insulation is available in several forms, such as loose fill, batts, rigid foam boards, spray-on foam, and as part of other construction assemblies such as structural insulated panels.

Before the type and form of insulation can be selected, the required *R*-value must be determined. The local or state building codes will either prescribe *R*-values or reference the requirements from a model energy code such as the *International Energy Conservation Code* or a standard such as ANSI/ASHRAE/IES Standard 90.1, *Energy Standard for Buildings Except Low-Rise Residential Buildings.*

For example, the *International Residential Code* provides a prescriptive table that lists thermal component criteria for each element of the building envelope, including ceilings, walls, floors, basement walls, perimeter slabs, and crawl space walls, based on the climatic zone (see Fig. 9.2) and the number of heating degree days (see Chap. 17). Commercial buildings may be subject to energy budgets.

However, for increased energy savings, a life-cycle analysis can be performed, comparing the initial cost of installing more insulation of various types (and costs) with the expected long-term energy savings, calculated based on local fuel costs and other factors. Most insulation types must be installed with a vapor barrier to be effective.

Insulation that uses *hydrochlorofluorocarbons* (HCFCs) in the production process should not be used; these chemicals have been identified as ozone-depleting compounds and will be phased out by 2030. (*Chlorofluorocarbons* (CFCs), which also deplete the ozone, were similarly used at one time; their use ended in

1996.) Closed-cell polyurethane foam insulation is produced with a non-CFC gas as the blowing agent. When possible, use foamed-in-place insulations that use carbon dioxide (rather than pentane or HCFCs) in the manufacturing process.

Chapter 13 contains more information on insulation and sustainability, and Chap. 27 describes specific insulation types and weather barrier concepts.

Superinsulation

Superinsulation is the technique of providing higher levels of insulation than normally used, tightly sealing all joints and cracks, and preventing any thermal bridges between the outside and inside, such as through studs. All portions of the building are carefully detailed so that every piece is insulated. Gaps, such as electrical outlets on exterior walls, are avoided or placed inside the insulation. In many cases, exterior walls have to be made thicker than would otherwise be needed to accommodate the added insulation. For homes, this includes using 2 × 6 studs instead of 2 × 4 studs.

Transparent Insulation

Transparent insulation consists of a relatively thick layer of polycarbonate honeycomb material, acrylic foam, or fiberglass sandwiched between layers of glazing. It is used to admit light while providing a high degree of insulation. It can also be used over another thermal mass material to trap solar heat and then slow the loss of the stored heat back into the atmosphere. Although good for diffusing light, transparent insulation cannot be used where a view is desired.

Movable Insulation

Movable insulation is typically used on windows that provide passive solar heating. The insulation is removed during sunlight hours and replaced at night or during cloudy weather to prevent heat loss. This type of insulation can be manually operated, power operated, or automated. Common types of movable insulation include roll-down shutters, insulated shades or curtains, swinging panels of insulation, and expanded polystyrene beads blown between panes of glass.

Air Barriers

Much energy is lost from *infiltration* and *exfiltration* (also called *air leakage*), the movement of air into and out of a building by natural means rather than through mechanical ventilation. Infiltration and exfiltration are caused by differences in pressure between the indoor and outdoor air. These differences can be caused by a combination of wind, the stack effect, the mechanical system in the building, and other factors.

The *stack effect* (or *chimney effect*) is a difference in pressure between the top and bottom of a building due to a temperature differential. The effect is most pronounced in high-rise buildings. In a cold climate, air will be warmer in the upper part of the building and cooler in the lower part, which causes exfiltration at the top and consequently infiltration near the ground to replace the lost air.

Infiltration and exfiltration are usually unwanted for several reasons.

- Air that enters through infiltration rather than through the ventilation system must still be conditioned to meet indoor requirements, which adds to the building's heating or cooling load. Typically, 25% to 40% of the heating and cooling energy used by a building is lost due to infiltration.
- Similarly, conditioned air from within the building can be lost to exfiltration.
- Infiltration carries dust and pollutants into the building.
- Infiltration carries water vapor into the building, which can condense and contribute to mold growth and the degradation of building materials.

The solution to air leakage is to provide a continuous barrier around the conditioned spaces in the building. An *air barrier* is the part of a building envelope system that controls infiltration and exfiltration. It consists of materials, components, and assemblies on all vertical and horizontal surfaces exposed to the exterior. An effective air barrier can reduce energy consumption and help keep out pollutants and excess moisture.

Some air barriers are made from vapor-impermeable material. A *vapor-impermeable barrier* acts as both an air barrier and a vapor retarder in the same material. Vapor transmission can be caused by diffusion through materials, as discussed in Chap. 27. However, vapor transmission by air movement is a larger problem. It is estimated that the amount of water vapor carried by air infiltration is 10 to 200 times greater than that carried by diffusion through materials.

Other air barriers are vapor permeable. Common *vapor-permeable barriers* include relatively thin sheets of spunbonded polyolefin (*house wrap*), polyethylene, elastomeric coatings, liquid applied spray-on or trowel-on materials, self-adhesive membranes, various types of sheathing sealed with tape, silicon-based materials, fluid-applied products, and combinations of these materials.

Permeance is a measure of how readily a material or membrane allows water vapor to pass through it. The unit of permeance is the *perm*, which is one grain of moisture per hour per square foot per inch of mercury difference in vapor pressure (1 perm = 1 g/hr-ft^2-in Hg). If an air barrier is vapor permeable, it should have a permeance rating of 5 perms or greater.

The maximum permeance of an air barrier material should be 0.004 cfm/ft^2 at a pressure difference of 1.57 lbf/ft^2 when tested according to ASTM E2178. (The pressure difference of 1.57 lbf/ft^2 is equal to 0.3 in wg at 68°F.) This value is approximately equal to the permeance of a sheet of $^1/_2$ in unpainted gypsum wallboard.

ANSI/ASHRAE/IESNA Standard 90.1, *Energy Standard for Buildings, Except Low-Rise Residential Buildings*, requires that one of the following three options be used for many commercial buildings.

- Individual air barrier material cannot exceed 0.004 cfm/ft^2 at 0.30 in wg.
- Air barrier assemblies cannot exceed 0.04 cfm/ft^2 at 0.30 in wg when tested according to ASTM EI677.
- Whole-building air barriers cannot exceed 0.4 cfm/ft^2 at 0.30 in wg when tested according to ASTM E779.

For individual projects, the requirements of the local building code regarding air and vapor barriers must be determined.

In order for an air barrier system to function properly, the following conditions must be met.

- The air barrier, assemblies, and whole building must meet the minimum permeance ratings listed above or as prescribed by the local building code.
- The air barrier must be continuous around the conditioned spaces, including walls, roof, foundation walls, and slabs on grade.
- All joints between materials, components, and assemblies must be sealed.
- The air barrier must be securely and tightly joined at other building components such as windows, doors, the roof air barrier component, and foundations.
- All penetrations for pipes, ducts, and similar elements must be sealed.
- The barrier must be securely attached to the structure to prevent billowing, tearing, or breaking away from attachments and other building components. It must resist the loads on it caused by wind, stack effect, and HVAC systems, both as positive and negative air pressure.
- The air barrier at movement joints must be capable of moving with the joint without breaking or tearing.
- The air barrier must be durable and last the life of the building, or maintaining it must be possible.

- If both a vapor retarder and an air barrier are used and they are separate membranes, the air barrier should be 10 to 20 times more permeable to water vapor diffusion than the vapor retarder, to prevent trapping moisture between the two layers.

An air barrier controls infiltration and exfiltration, can reduce energy consumption, and can help keep out pollutants and excess moisture.

The location of the air barrier within a wall or roof assembly is not important for its effectiveness. However, for ease of construction and durability, the air barrier generally should be located behind the exterior cladding and outside the sheathing. This makes it easier to install, seal, join to other building components, and properly support. If the same material performs the functions of both air barrier and vapor retarder, it is usually placed outside the structure and sheathing but behind the cladding. If the air barrier and vapor retarder are different materials, their locations within the building envelope depend on the climatic region, interior environmental conditions, and the specific construction of the envelope.

Earth Sheltering

Earth sheltering, or burying a portion of a building underground, has several advantages. A few feet below the surface, the temperature of the earth is fairly stable. Since earth's temperature is cooler in the summer and warmer in the winter than the air aboveground, unwanted heat gain and loss are reduced, and the effect of extreme outdoor air temperatures is minimized. Earth sheltering also protects a structure from cold winter winds. Additional advantages include natural soundproofing, less outside maintenance, and better protection from natural threats such as hail and tornados.

There are three types of earth-sheltered design. The first design type is built above grade, and fill earth is bermed against the walls on one or more sides. The second design type is similar to the first, but the building is built into the excavated side of a hill. Ideally, for buildings in the Northern Hemisphere, the north side of the building built into the hill and the south side is exposed for solar heating, views, and daylight. The east and west sides may be partially or completely buried. In either of these types of designs, the roof may also be covered with earth. The third type of earth-sheltered design is completely buried below grade with a courtyard in the middle to allow for access, daylight, an outdoor living area, and ventilation.

Usually, earth sheltering is only used on a portion of a building, so that the south side of the building can remain exposed. This approach combines the advantages of earth sheltering with the need to permit desirable heat gain and admit light.

There are a number of practical considerations in regard to earth-sheltered designs.

- Ideally, there should be a natural slope to the land so that earthmoving can be minimized.
- The soil should be granular. Gravel, sand, and sandy loam are all appropriate soils. Clay soils are not appropriate for earth-sheltered designs because they do not drain well and can expand with moisture.
- The site should be tested for radon concentrations.
- The groundwater level must be below the building, and positive drainage away from the building should be maintained.
- Extra care must be taken to waterproof the underground portions adequately.

Even though earth-sheltered designs do not require much insulation, the insulation must be correctly designed to keep the indoor temperature comfortable and to prevent condensation from forming on cool inside walls, especially in a humid environment.

With fewer windows on all sides, the building will need adequate ventilation to control humidity and maintain good air quality.

Figure 12.20 Green Roof Construction

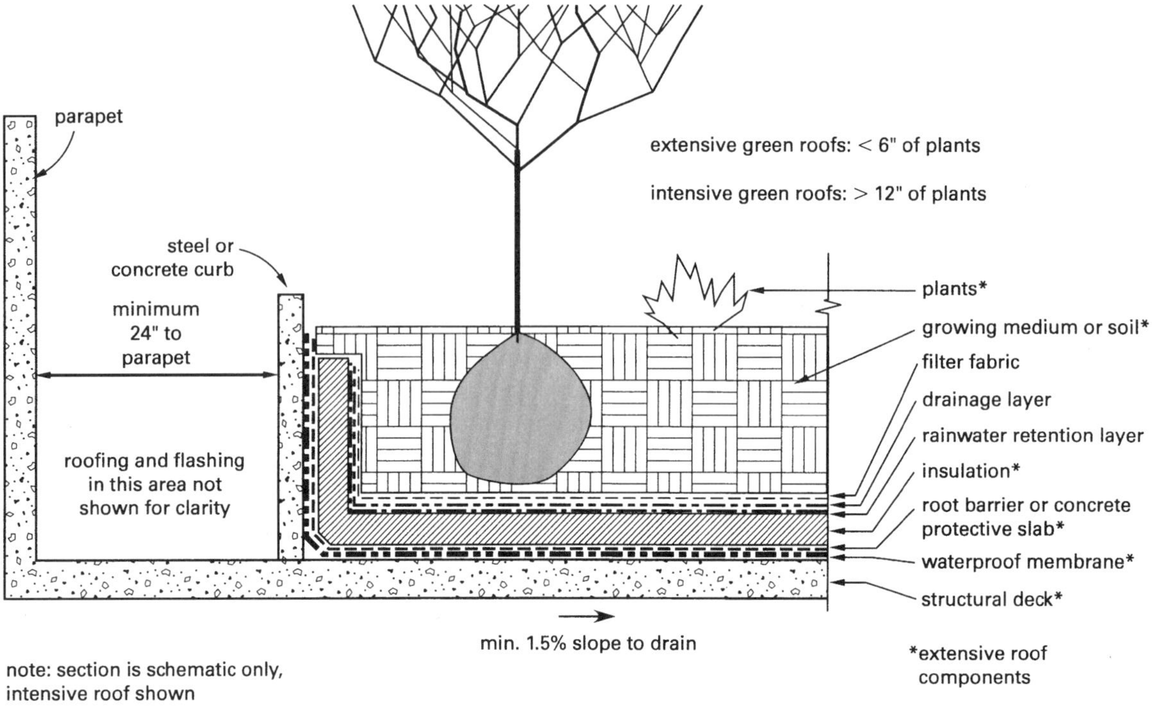

parapet
steel or concrete curb
minimum 24" to parapet
roofing and flashing in this area not shown for clarity
extensive green roofs: < 6" of plants
intensive green roofs: > 12" of plants
plants*
growing medium or soil*
filter fabric
drainage layer
rainwater retention layer
insulation*
root barrier or concrete protective slab*
waterproof membrane*
structural deck*
min. 1.5% slope to drain
*extensive roof components

note: section is schematic only, intensive roof shown

Green Roofs

A *green roof*, also called a *vegetated roof*, *garden roof*, or *eco-roof*, is a system consisting of planting containers filled with soil and a layer of vegetation, that is installed on top of a roof that has been designed for this purpose. Some advantages of a green roof include

- conserving energy by reducing cooling and heating loads
- reducing storm runoff
- absorbing carbon dioxide
- reducing ambient air temperatures
- filtering the air and binding dust particles
- reducing the heat island effect normally caused by exposed roofing membranes
- protecting roofing membranes from ultraviolet light degradation, temperature extremes, wind, and hail
- adding acoustical insulation
- adding aesthetic appeal to the roof

There are two types of green roofs: extensive and intensive. *Extensive green roofs* use soil less than 6 in deep, which is capable of supporting meadow grasses, sedums, herbs, and perennials.

Intensive green roofs use deeper soil (usually 12 in or more) and support complex landscapes, including shrubs and small trees. Intensive green roofs may feature landscape elements such as ponds and fountains, and building inhabitants may be invited to use the roof as they would use a garden at grade.

In either case, a subsurface irrigation system is generally recommended to help the plants become established. The system usually remains in place and is used for supplemental watering as needed.

Most green roofs include a continuous layer of *growth medium*, a material with the proper nutritive and drainage characteristics for the proposed plants. Alternatively, the plants can be placed in modular plastic containers. In most cases, the modular systems weigh less, are more flexible, and can be easily removed to replace plants or make roof repairs.

A green roof must be constructed over a structural deck strong enough to hold the wet weight of the assembly. Depending on the type of system used, a green roof may weigh from 12 psf to 300 psf. This means that in most cases an intensive green roof should be used only in new buildings where the structure can be designed correctly from the beginning. However, in some cases it may be possible to place a lighter-weight green roof system over an existing structure without additional support. Although there are many variations in design and detailing, a typical intensive roof over a concrete deck is constructed as shown in Fig. 12.20.

The steps involved in constructing a green roof over a concrete deck are as follows.

1. A waterproof membrane is placed over the structural deck. Common membrane materials include polyvinyl chloride (PVC), ethylene propylene diene monomer (EPDM), thermoplastic polyolefin (TPO), and a polymer modified bituminous membrane.
2. If necessary, a root barrier is placed over the waterproofing. Some materials, such as PVC, EPDM, and TPO, are inherently root resistant.
3. Rigid insulation is placed over the root barrier. In addition to providing thermal insulation, this helps prevent water stored in the growth media from extracting heat from the building's interior during the winter. Some systems use a retention layer over the insulation to provide a long-term water supply.
4. A drainage layer is installed over the insulation to allow water that is not absorbed by the plants and growing media to flow to drains or scuppers. A green roof should be constructed on a deck with a slope of at least 1.5%. The maximum recommended slope is 30%, but stabilization panels, battens, or other devices are needed on steep slopes to prevent the growing medium from shifting.
5. A filter fabric above the drainage layer prevents the fine particles of the soil or growing medium from entering and clogging the drainage layer. Common filter fabric materials include polypropylene mats, polyethylene mats, and water-resistant polyester fiber mats.
6. Finally, the growth medium is placed in thicknesses from 2 in to 12 in or more. The growth medium is an engineered mixture of soil and organic and mineral additives such as peat, sand, lava, and expanded clay. The growth medium is designed for the particular types of plants that will be used.

Constructing a green roof over a metal deck is slightly different.

1. A thermal barrier is placed over the metal deck to protect the insulation from heat transfer. This is required by the IBC and most local codes, and can consist of $\frac{1}{2}$ in of gypsum sheathing or other approved material.
2. Rigid insulation is placed over the thermal barrier in a thickness appropriate for the climate and as required by the local code. *Extruded polystyrene* (XPS) is typically used because it is resistant to moisture and has a high compressive strength. *Polyisocyanurate insulation* can also be used and, if allowed by local code, may not need a thermal barrier. However, it has a lower compressive strength than XPS and needs to be covered with a protection board to protect it from damage during subsequent construction operations.
3. A waterproofing membrane is placed over the insulation. If necessary for the type of membrane selected, a separation layer is placed between the waterproofing membrane and the insulation. As with membranes over concrete decks, the membrane may be PVC, TPO, or EPDM.

4. If necessary for the type of waterproofing membrane selected, a root barrier is placed over the membrane.
5. A drainage layer is placed over the membrane (or root barrier, if used). Drainage layers can be made from entangled filaments, thermoformed dimpled cups, or geonets.

Finally, the growth medium is placed on top of the drainage layer, and the plants are installed.

Because the waterproofing layer is such a critical part of any green roof system, quality control measures must be taken to ensure a watertight system. There are several ways to do this.

A *flood test* is a common way to verify watertightness. The area is flooded with 2 in of water for 48 hours, and the interior of the building is inspected for leaks.

An independent inspection company can also be hired to evaluate the installation of the waterproofing membrane and other components, either visually, with infrared testing that can be used to identify leaks, or with *electric field vector mapping* (EFVM) techniques. For EFVM, the growing medium is wetted to provide an electrically conductive layer, and the deck is grounded. A leak will cause electric flow from the growing medium to the deck below. Using probes connected to a potentiometer, a technician can walk the roof and detect the precise location of any electric current.

The best plant material for a given project varies depending on whether the green roof is extensive or intensive, the local climate, maintenance availability, and the aesthetic needs of the project. A drip irrigation system is usually recommended instead of a spray system because it is more water efficient, delivering the moisture directly to the roots of the plants rather than allowing some of the water to evaporate.

Use of a green roof can contribute to a LEED credit for the building if the roof satisfies certain area requirements relative to total site paving area. However, a green roof must be used in conjunction with non-roof measures to fulfill the requirements of this credit. Refer to the LEED rating systems for exact requirements.

Cool Roofs

One alternative to a green roof is *reflective roofing*, commonly known as a *cool roof*. A cool roof is a roof covered with a light-colored material that reflects more of the sun's heat than it absorbs. Generally, a roof must have a minimum reflectivity of 0.65 when new and a three-year aged value of at least 0.50 to be considered a cool roof according to the EPA's Energy Star cool roofing requirement. Buildings with cool roofs have been shown to have lower cooling needs, thus reducing energy use, as well as to help reduce the heat island effect in urban areas.

Cool roofs are most appropriately used in climates where cooling degree days exceed heating degree days (see Chap. 17), although internal-load dominated buildings in cool climates may also benefit from a cool roof. In addition to considering the sustainability benefits of a cool roof during early project planning, the architect may also need to evaluate possible problems with glare into adjacent buildings and the aesthetic aspects of very light-colored roofs.

As with a green roof, use of a cool roof can help a building earn LEED credit for heat island reduction if the roof satisfies certain area requirements relative to the total paving area. However, the cool roof must be used in conjunction with non-roof measures. Refer to the LEED rating systems for exact requirements.

See Chap. 7 for more information on the related concepts of albedo, reflectivity, solar reflectance, and solar reflectance index. Materials for cool roofs are discussed in Chap. 27.

Air Locks

A *vestibule entry system* (or *air lock system*) is desirable in cold and temperate climates and can be beneficial in hot climates where a building is mechanically cooled. In addition to preventing cold drafts from entering when an exterior door is opened, air locks minimize heat loss when people enter and leave a building. In lieu of a vestibule, revolving doors can be used.

Glazing

Glass can be a major source of heat loss and heat gain in a building. Heat can move through glass both by convection and by radiation, and standard float glass has little resistance to either. In the winter, the low insulation value of float glass results in large heat losses; in summer, the same glass can be a significant source of heat gain by radiation unless it is shaded. A single pane of glass has a *U*-value of about 1.11 Btu/ft^2-hr-°F.

Two common ways of expressing how well a window or a kind of glass reduces solar radiation are its solar heat gain coefficient and its shading coefficient. The *solar heat gain coefficient* (SHGC) is the amount of solar radiation that is transmitted through the entire window assembly, expressed as a fraction of the total amount that strikes it. The SHGC is a decimal fraction between zero and one; a value of one would indicate a window assembly that lets all solar radiation pass through, and a value of zero would indicate a window assembly that lets none pass through.

Glazing can help balance the conflicting requirements that glass must offer views, admit daylight, provide for solar heating, and insulate against extremes of temperature.

While the SHGC includes the effects of the frame, glass spacer, and other parts of the window assembly, the *shading coefficient* (SC) applies to just the glass itself. The SC is the ratio of the amount of solar radiation that passes through a piece of glass to the amount that would pass through a similar piece of unshaded, clear, double-strength glass $^1/_8$ in thick under the same conditions. Like the SHGC, the SC is a decimal fraction between zero and one. In the United States, use of the SC has largely been superseded by the SHGC.

Glazing has long been a weak point in constructing energy-efficient buildings. For a long time, designers looking for a more energy-saving alternative to float glass were limited to double-paned glass, tinted glass, reflective glass, and a few other types. No longer—there are numerous glazing products that can help the designer balance the often conflicting requirements that glass must offer views, admit daylight, provide for solar heating, and insulate against extremes of temperature. The proper type of glass for a project is the one that will provide the desired characteristics; for example, glass that will admit more than 70% of visible light while blocking nearly 95% of the infrared spectrum is available for daylighting use. Refer to Chap. 28 for more information on glazing types.

Insulating glass (also called *double glazing* or *double-pane glass*, or *triple glazing* or *triple-pane glass* when three panes are used) is used to control heat loss. This is a glazing assembly in which two or three panes of glass are separated by sealed air spaces or partially evacuated spaces that act as insulators. *U*-values for insulated glazing decrease to about 0.57 Btu/ft^2-hr-°F, assuming two panes separated by a $^1/_4$ in air space. However, air currents within the air space still allow heat loss by convection. In addition, some of the desired solar heat gain admitted through the glass is lost by radiation, as objects in the building get warm and begin to emit infrared radiation that passes back outside.

Some insulating glass is manufactured so that panes of glass are separated by partial vacuums rather than air. However, using an inert gas fill instead of a vacuum makes the double or triple glazing more efficient at stopping heat transfer by convection. Argon gas is commonly used because it offers good thermal performance at a low cost. Krypton gas can also be used, but it costs about 200 times as much. Krypton is more efficient than argon when the space between glass panes is small (up to $^3/_8$ in). A double-glazed unit with argon gas in a $^1/_4$ in space has a *U*-value of about 0.52 Btu/ft^2-hr-°F. However, the gas can leak out over time at a rate of approximately 0.5% to 1% per year, so long-term energy calculations should consider the decrease in performance that may occur over time.

Tinted glass, *reflective glass*, and *heat-absorbing glass* have long been used to reduce *solar heat gain*. However, because about half the incident solar radiation on glass is in the visible spectrum and about half is in the infrared spectrum, tinted glass and reflective glass also reduce the visible light transmittance. This reduces or eliminates the potential for using daylighting to conserve energy; it also generally makes both views out and interiors seem darker, especially on cloudy days. These glass types also eliminate the possibility of making use of solar heat gain when it is desirable.

The following glazing types have been developed more recently for better control of heat gain.

Low-ε glass, also known as *low-emissivity glass* or *low-e glass*, is double glazing that includes a thin film or coating placed somewhere in the glazing cavity. The film or coating allows both visible and near-infrared radiation to be transmitted through the glass. However, as objects in the room are heated and emit long-wave radiation, the film or coating prevents the loss of this heat; instead, the heat is reflected back into the room. When used with an argon gas fill to reduce convection, low-ε window units are very efficient at preventing heat loss. For example, a double-glazed unit with argon gas in a $^1/_4$ in space with a low-ε coating ($\varepsilon = 0.15$) has a U-value of about 0.36 Btu/ft^2-hr-°F. With a $^1/_2$ in space, the U-value drops to approximately 0.28 Btu/ft^2-hr-°F.

Spectrally selective glazing transmits a high proportion of the visible solar spectrum while blocking up to 80% of the heat from the infrared portion of the spectrum. Used with a low-ε coating, a double-glazed window can achieve an SHGC of approximately 0.25. Spectrally selective glazing materials are especially good for buildings that have a long cooling season and that need high interior light levels.

Super windows are glazing units that combine two low-ε coatings with gas-filled cavities between three layers of glass. With a U-value of 0.15 Btu/ft^2-hr-°F or less, these units can gain more thermal energy than they lose over a 24-hour period in winter.

More recent technologies allow the glazing to serve the multiple functions of daylighting, view, maximizing heat gain when wanted, and minimizing heat loss in winter.

Switchable glazings are *chromogenic window* products that change their characteristics based on particular environmental conditions or through human intervention. They include the following types of products.

- *Electrochromic glazing* consists of a multilayered thin film, applied to glass, that can change between opaque and clear or change colors when a burst of low-voltage electrical current is applied. Once the change has been made, the current does not need to be maintained. This type of glazing allows variable transmittance in the visible portion of the spectrum while reflecting in the infrared spectrum, thereby reducing solar heat gain. The voltage can be controlled manually or automatically. Refer to Chap. 28 for more information on this type of glazing.
- *Photochromic glazing* darkens under the direct action of sunlight, in the same way that some sunglasses do. As the light intensity increases, the window becomes darker. Although offering the advantage of automatic action, this type of glazing does not offer the control of electrochromic glazing. For example, there could be times when clear glazing is desirable, such as on a cold, sunny day.
- *Thermochromic glazing* changes darkness in response to temperature; it becomes translucent when it reaches a certain temperature. Like photochromic glazing, the change is an inherent property of the material, so this technique offers less control than electrochromic glazing does.
- *Transition-metal hydride electrochromics* make it possible to have a glazing material that changes from transparent to reflective. These products are based on coatings of nickel-magnesium instead of the oxides used in other electrochromic materials.

Double Envelope

In a *double envelope system*, the outer skin of a building consists of two glazed layers that are typically separated by about 2 ft to 3 ft. Some type of sun control (louvers, blinds, or shades) and either a passive or active ventilation system is incorporated within this space. The system may include devices to redirect sunlight so as to enhance daylighting of the interior spaces.

The outer shell moderates the effects of the environment. The cavity between the outer layer and the inner shell may be passively heated, depending on the climate and needs of the overall building design. Air flowing between the layers can exhaust excessive heat buildup directly to the outside in hot weather, or it can be redirected to a heat exchanger to warm incoming air in cold weather.

Although the cost is significantly higher than that of a single envelope structure, the advantages of a double envelope system include reduced cooling loads, enhanced sun control, reduced operating costs, optimized daylighting, and enhanced air quality when natural ventilation is used.

When a new outer layer of glazing is built around an existing building, the system is referred to as a *dynamic buffer zone system*. This type of system prevents and controls condensation that may result from remodeling and upgrading the existing building's ventilation, heating, and cooling systems to higher humidity levels. In a dynamic buffer zone system, the space between the existing building and the new facade is ventilated with dry, preheated air during winter months.

Daylighting

Electric lighting and the cooling needed to offset the heat gains from the fixtures typically account for 30% to 40% of a commercial building's total energy use and can sometimes be as high as 50%. *Daylighting* is the placement of windows, reflective surfaces, and other design elements so that natural light can give effective internal lighting during the day. In addition to providing energy savings and a sustainable design, daylighting can increase occupant satisfaction and productivity. Well-daylighted spaces can make it easier to lease space and reduce tenant turnover.

In order to make daylighting feasible and cost effective, several conditions must be met. First, there must be enough view of the sky. Daylighting may not be practical for buildings on dense urban sites or for houses or small buildings nestled among tall trees. Second, the glazing must transmit sufficient light. This is rarely a problem in new building design, but it may be problematic in remodeling or historic building renovations where glazing cannot be changed. Finally, the daylighting design must be coordinated with artificial lighting control and mechanical systems design.

The daylighting design must be coordinated with artificial lighting control and mechanical systems design.

The *daylight factor* (DF) is often used in daylighting calculations. The DF is the ratio of the illuminance at a point on a horizontal surface indoors to the illuminance at a point on a horizontal surface outdoors and fully open to the sky, measured at the same time under overcast skies; direct sunlight is excluded. The DF is expressed as a percentage, but the percent sign is sometimes omitted (for example, a DF of 2% is sometimes expressed as a DF of 2).

Various DFs are recommended for different tasks, ranging from about 1.5% for ordinary visual tasks to about 4% for difficult visual tasks such as drafting. At a DF of about 5% or more, glare and excessive heat gain and heat loss can become issues.

Daylighting Variables

Some of the variables that must be accounted for when developing a daylighting strategy include the compass orientations of the facades utilizing daylight, the brightness of the sky (which is affected by solar altitude, cloud conditions, and time of day), the area of the glass, the height of the head of the glass, the transmittance of the glass, the reflectances of interior room surfaces and nearby outdoor surfaces, and obstructions such as overhangs and trees. Figure 12.21 illustrates some of these variables.

The advantages of daylighting must be weighed against the potential disadvantages. Large areas of glazing can lead to glare and unwanted heat gain and heat loss; imbalanced lighting can be a problem if side lighting is too strong. Control must also be addressed, because daylighting will not conserve energy if electric lights are used even when natural light is sufficient. Automatic switching is often used to overcome this problem. (See Chap. 17.)

Building Design

The preliminary design of a building can have a significant impact on daylighting. To optimize daylighting, the building or building portion should be long and narrow, with the long dimension running east-west. A building with a deep facade can provide a space for shading devices and light shelves. If the building is one or two stories, the glazed areas should be located away from tall trees or other obstructions. Surfaces on the exterior of the building should be light in color to reflect more daylight. The building should have ceilings as high as the budget allows; high ceilings increase the penetration of daylight into the interior and make it easier to incorporate light shelves into the design.

Figure 12.21 Daylighting Variables

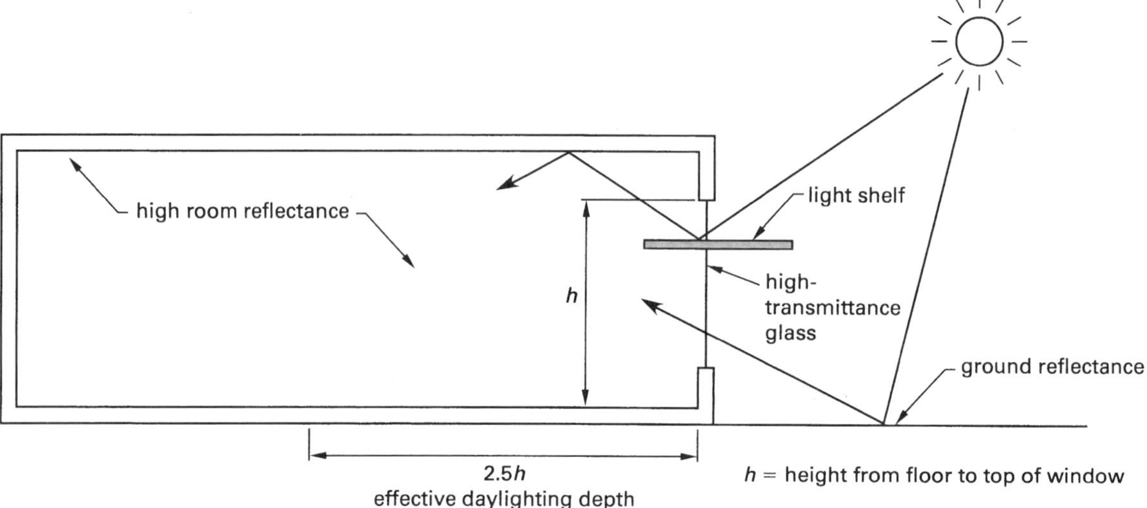

Window Design

Two important variables to consider when designing windows for daylighting are the height of the window head above the floor and the effective aperture. The head of the window should be as high above the floor line as possible. With a standard window that has no overhang protection or light shelf, the effective *daylighted zone* extends about 1.5 times the window head height into the room. When a *light shelf* is used, the effective daylighted zone is from 2.0 to 2.5 times the window head height.

The *effective aperture* (EA) is the product of two variables: visible light transmittance and window-to-wall ratio. The *visible light transmittance* (VLT) is the percentage of visible light that passes through a glazing material. The *window-to-wall ratio* (WWR) is the net glazing area in a room or space divided by the gross exterior wall area. It does not include window frames or mullions.

Small, punched windows have low WWRs, while large, continuous windows have high WWRs. Generally, an EA of between 0.20 and 0.30 provides good daylighting. Thus, if the glazing has a low VLT, the size of the window should be increased.

For best uniform light distribution, use continuous windows instead of punched windows.

Light Shelves

One problem with using large, high windows for daylighting on the south side of a building is the resultant glare and heat gain of direct sun. One of the most effective ways to solve this problem is by using a light shelf. A *light shelf* is a horizontal surface placed above eye level that reflects direct daylight onto the ceiling while shading the lower portions of the window and the interior of the room. A light shelf also has the desirable effect of distributing the light more evenly from the window to the back of the room, as shown in Fig. 12.22.

However it is designed, a light shelf should have a diffuse and highly reflective surface. A light shelf can provide a practical dividing point for different types of glass in a glazing assembly; glass with a higher VLT can be used above the shelf, while tinted glass may be specified below for glare control.

Glazing Selection

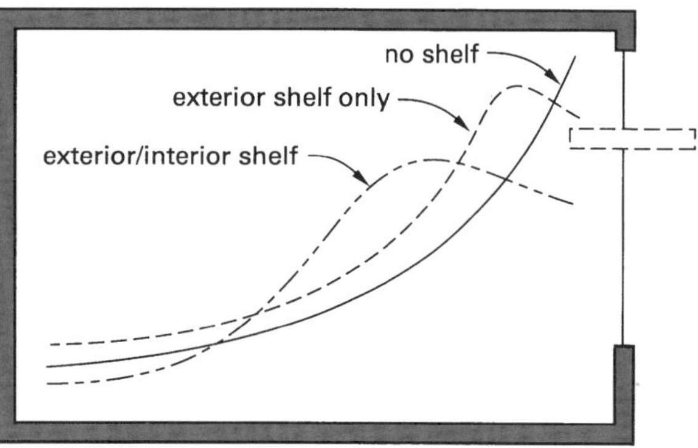

Figure 12.22
Effect of Light Shelf

An important issue with daylighting is balancing the need for a high VLT against the need for control of glare and unwanted heat gain and loss. To control heat loss through convection, a glass with a low *U*-value is desirable. To control heat gain from the sun's radiation, a low SHGC is desirable. Various types of *tinted glass* have been used to achieve these goals. *Spectrally selective glazing* can also be used, which provides a fairly high VLT with a low SHGC.

A good choice for *glare control* is a glass with a VLT from 50% to 70% combined with the lowest possible SHGC. If glare control is critical and if the size of the glazing area can be increased to achieve an EA between 0.20 and 0.30, a glass with a lower VLT can be selected.

Shading

Some type of shading is needed on every window, regardless of which direction the window faces. Exterior shading is generally more effective than interior shading at blocking solar heat gain, although some type of interior window covering is usually needed for occupant control and for times when glare is excessive or the inside space needs to be darkened.

For daylighting applications, horizontal shading above the window on the south side of a building provides effective control. If a sufficient projection cannot be provided, a series of horizontal shades can be provided along the height of the glazing, but this is often expensive and blocks views. If light shelves are used, they should be partially inside and partially outside the building.

Room Design

There are several factors in *room design* that should be considered for effective daylighting. The reflectance of interior surfaces should be as high as possible; minimum reflectance should be 80% for ceilings, 50% to 70% for walls, and 20% to 40% for floors. The wall facing the window should always be as light as possible to improve light distribution.

The placement of furniture and equipment should be coordinated to make optimum use of the daylight. Low furniture should be used to ensure that light is not blocked from reaching the center of the space and the areas farthest from the windows. Tasks that require higher light levels should be located closer to the windows. Computer monitors should be positioned so that they avoid reflected glare; that is, they should face away from windows, with the screens oriented approximately perpendicular to and tilted slightly away from the window. Partial partitions can also be used to darken the area immediately around computer screens.

Top Lighting

Top lighting with daylight involves the use of light pipes, skylights, roof monitors, saw-toothed roofs, or sloped glazing. An additional, overhead source of daylight helps distribute the light evenly and provide daylight to a larger portion of the building. Top lighting works only in one-story buildings, low-rise stepped-back buildings, on the top floor of multistory buildings, and in buildings with one or more large, skylit atriums.

An insulated glazing panel or transparent insulation can be used to provide light without direct sunlight, as described earlier in this section. This diffuses the light and reduces heat loss.

Light Pipes

Light pipes are round or square tubes with highly reflective interior coatings. They extend from the roof to the space to be lighted. Sunlight is captured through a clear plastic dome and directed down to a translucent diffusing plate at the bottom. Light pipes are available in diameters from 10 in to 16 in. These devices are a relatively inexpensive way to bring natural light to the interior of a building, but they only work in spaces near the roof.

SITE ACOUSTICS

Controlling site noise makes outdoor activities more pleasant and reduces the noise that reaches the building interior. Several design strategies are available for improving site acoustics. Some are more effective than others, but in general, mitigating unwanted noise is usually more successful than enhancing wanted sounds.

The most effective method of controlling site noise is the use of solid *sound barriers.* These can be thin-wall barriers constructed of wood or concrete blocks, or earth berms. A barrier does not completely stop sound transmission; sound will travel over and around it through *diffraction*, which is the bending of sound waves (or other kinds of waves) around the edge of a barrier or through a small opening.

The effectiveness of a solid barrier depends on its height and position, the distance between the source and the receiver, and the frequency of the noise that the barrier is designed to block, as shown in Fig. 12.23. When the values of these valuables are known, the reduction in noise in decibels (NR_{db}) from a point source can be calculated with the *Maekawa equation.*

$$NR_{dB} - 20\log\frac{\sqrt{2\pi N}}{\tanh\sqrt{2\pi N}} + 5 \qquad 12.1$$

In Eq. 12.1,

$$N = \left(\frac{f}{565}\right)(A + B - d) \qquad 12.2$$

f is the frequency of the sound (in hertz), d is the distance (in feet) of the acoustical line of sight from the source of the sound to the receiver, and $A + B$ is the length (in feet) of the shortest path around the barrier, as shown in Fig. 12.23. The Maekawa equation is empirically derived, and units are not consistent.

As Eq. 12.1, Eq. 12.2, and Fig. 12.23(a) indicate, the critical factor is not the actual height of the barrier but the *effective height*, which is the distance from the top of the barrier to the point where the acoustical line of sight intersects the barrier. This difference is usually not significant on level ground, but when the source and receiver are at substantially different heights, the effective height can decrease. Figure 12.23(b) shows how the effective height changes when a barrier of the same overall height is located in two different positions.

The Maekawa equation is for point sources; for a linear source such as a highway, the noise reduction is about 20% to 25% less than that calculated by the equation.

The following are some basic principles for designing outdoor sound barriers.

- Solid barriers are generally better at blocking high-frequency sounds than they are at blocking low-frequency sounds. For high frequencies, the acoustic shadow shown in Fig. 12.23 is larger.
- The barrier is best placed as close as possible to either the source of the noise or the receiver.
- If the barrier is placed close to the noise source, it should be at least four times as high as the distance from the source to the barrier.
- The greater the effective height, the greater the attenuation. (See Fig. 12.23.)

Figure 12.23 Outdoor Sound Barriers

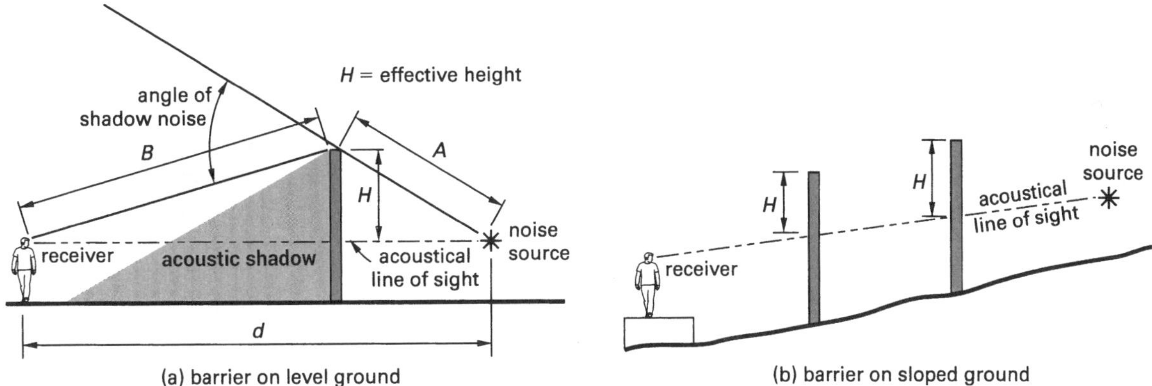

(a) barrier on level ground

(b) barrier on sloped ground

- For blocking noise from a point source, a short barrier should be at least four times as long as the distance from the barrier to the source, or the distance from the barrier the receiver, whichever is shorter.
- A barrier should have a density of at least 5 lbm/ft^2 and be solid. However, densities greater than this do not improve sound attenuation significantly.

Some other methods of controlling site noise are as follows.

- *Maximize the distance between the source of the noise and the receiver.* In free space, sound from a point source decreases by about 6 dB each time the distance doubles. This is enough of a decrease to be noticeable, but not significant; a decrease of 10 dB is needed for the noise to be perceived as half as loud. When the noise comes from a linear source, such as a highway, it will only decrease by about 3 dB for each doubling of the distance. Locating a building as far as possible from a source of loud noise, such as a busy street, can mitigate the noise that reaches the building. However, on most urban and suburban sites, it will be difficult or impossible to make a significant difference.
- *Avoid hard surfaces near the source of noise.* Hard surfaces reflect sound and help it travel.
- *Avoid parallel hard surfaces.* They can intensify the noise. Where possible, orient buildings, walls, and other hard surfaces at angles from one another.
- *Plant evergreen trees and shrubs densely between the noise source and the receiver.* Plants have limited usefulness as sound barriers unless they are planted in large, deep groupings. To be effective (a sound attenuation of around 10 dB or more), the depth of the grouping must be 100 ft or greater. Planting is more useful when coupled with solid barriers or earth berms.
- *Control sources of noise that are in or near the building.* Locate mechanical equipment, service entrances, loading docks, and other noise sources away from usable outdoor spaces, building entrances, and any other areas where noise should be minimized.
- *Make use of masking sounds.* For example, the sound of a fountain or other source of running water in a usable outdoor space can mitigate noises at lower levels.
- *Design building features to block noise.* The overall shape of a building can be used to create isolated courtyards or block a source of noise. A solid balcony can block the path of a noise from outside before it strikes the glazing near the balcony. For glazing in critical areas, laminated glass can reduce how much noise penetrates the building.

Refer to Chap. 19 for more information on the basics of sound and controlling noise in buildings.

SITE SECURITY

Site security involves protecting a building or group of buildings from threats, which can range from common vandalism to intruders to vehicle-borne attacks.

Security systems for building interiors are discussed in Chap. 32. While some interior security systems, such as microwave detectors and locking devices, can also be used to protect the building exteriors, site security presents unique problems and design responses.

The first step in designing for site security is to define the risk and the level of protection needed. This must be done in consultation with the client, security experts, and—in the case of governmental clients—other governmental departments at the local, state, or federal level, as appropriate. As a part of building programming or preliminary design, this step determines the overall goals and objectives for site design and sets the direction of the design process with design concepts and defined constraints. The design solution must balance the desired level of protection with provisions included for accessibility, sustainability, and usability. The visual impact of the security measures should be minimized so that the facility is sensitive to its neighborhood and does not take on the appearance of a fortress.

Design for site security can be accomplished by viewing the site at four different levels.

- perimeter protection
- access and parking
- on-site security
- building envelope protection

Perimeter Protection

Perimeter protection is the first line of defense on a site. It is a physical barrier that discourages or prevents unauthorized people or vehicles, or both, from entering the site or getting close to the building. For low-security sites, this may be as simple as a fence; for high-security buildings, it may include holding all unapproved vehicles at a required standoff distance from the building.

Fences are used more often to prevent individual intruders from entering than to keep vehicles out. They may be placed on the property line or, if enough land is available, they may be set back to lessen their visual impact. Fences are available in a variety of materials and designs and can provide a high level of security, especially if combined with camera surveillance, motion detectors, and other electronic devices. If solid fences are used, they should be planned carefully to maintain a clear field of view and avoid areas of concealment.

When unauthorized vehicles must be kept off the site or at a *standoff distance* from the building, various physical elements can be used including walls, changes of elevation, bollards, dry moats, water features, landscaping, and hardened street furniture. These elements can be used in combination to lessen their visual impact, and they can be combined with fences if individuals must be prevented from entering the site as well. When a standoff distance is needed due to the threat of explosions, a competent expert should perform a blast analysis to determine the safe minimum distances from the building, building protection, and other aspects of the final building and site design.

Access and Parking

Authorized personnel, visitors, and vehicles must be allowed onto the site and into parking areas or drop-off areas. For low-security facilities, access may be secured by limiting the number of access points and by using card-controlled gates or guard stations, as well as by incorporating visual or camera surveillance of critical areas. When more protection is needed, these methods can be combined with guard booths, retractable bollards or other retractable devices, heavy-duty gates, or sally ports. A *sally port* is an entrance consisting of two secure gates or doors with a small area between them. The outer door or gate is opened to admit a person or vehicle into the sally port and is then closed and secured while authorization is checked. If the person or vehicle is cleared for entrance, the inner door or gate is opened to allow entrance to the facility. This arrangement makes it difficult for unauthorized people to gain entrance through force or by following closely behind someone who is authorized to enter.

Parking lots, parking garages, loading docks, building entrances, and circulation routes on the site should be adequately illuminated, with clear signage to direct people to the proper areas, and monitored with personnel, cameras, or other electronic means as appropriate for the level of security needed.

On-Site Security

At some facilities, the outdoor area between the building (or buildings) and the site perimeter is used for purposes other than just access and parking, such as gathering, eating lunch, recreation, public events, and landscaping. At these sites, amenities such as water fountains, pools, planters, low walls, kiosks, benches, and lighting poles can be hardened to provide protection from vehicle access without calling attention to their security purposes. Other site features like signage, landscaping, bicycle racks, and trash containers can add to the usefulness of a site while minimizing the visual impact of security measures. For sites that hold vehicles away but allow public pedestrian access up to the building, this aspect of security is especially important.

Site design may also include provisions at the building entrance for queuing when entrance inspection is used.

Building Envelope Protection

The final layer of site security involves protecting the building and its occupants. If needed, *building envelope materials* may be used that are designed to prevent forced entry as well as damage by explosions. However, the need for such protection must be balanced with the need to avoid giving the building a forbidding, fortress-like look, especially if the owner wants the facility to appear open and inviting.

Exterior walls can be designed to withstand explosions and forced entry while disguising this function. Solid walls can be designed with textured surfaces, murals, water features, step-backs, or decorative stone. Alternatively, the secure wall can be built as an inner wall set back from the perimeter of the building, with the visible exterior wall constructed of glass and with the space between them used for displays, waiting areas, or public use. When glass and doors are used, they can be designed, specified, and constructed to withstand forced entry and blasts.

The need for protection must be balanced with the need to avoid giving the building a forbidding, fortress-like look.

Building entrances and egresses should be easy to use and accessible for building personnel as well as visitors. In some cases, entrances for authorized persons should be separated from visitor entrances. Egress for emergency evacuation must be adequately designed and clear space must be provided on the outside of the building for the dispersal of occupants.

Lighting and camera surveillance must be planned at the building line to provide the needed coverage while being protected from weather and vandalism. Lighting is needed for surveillance and for the general safety of the building occupants. However, site lighting levels should not contribute to night sky light pollution, and fixtures should be shielded to direct the light down and to appropriate locations.

Depending on the level of threat, air intakes and HVAC equipment may need to be separated from access to the building or otherwise protected to prevent the introduction of chemical or biological materials.

NEIGHBORHOOD CONTEXT

The *context* of the surrounding development is an important factor in designing the location, orientation, configuration, and other features of a building. The design of a building should be sensitive to the scale, massing, and fenestration patterns of nearby buildings. The design should also consider any functional adjacency requirements relative to other structures or outdoor activities. For example, the entry to a student union building should be located near major campus circulation routes.

Views are also an important consideration. Pleasant, desirable views can be used to advantage, whether they are seen from important spaces within the building or from outdoor spaces. Service spaces or less important spaces can be planned to face undesirable views. Off-site sources of noise can be similarly avoided by minimizing windows near the noise source.

Frequently, a building is located so as to stand on an important axis in relation to surrounding structures or to complete the enclosure of a major outdoor space. The site planning process should not overlook these kinds of symbolic criteria.

DEFINITIONS

analemma: The figure-eight curve that represents the angular offset of the sun from its mean position as viewed from the earth. At any given point on the earth, if the position of the sun is noted at the same time every day for a year, the figure of the analemma is produced.

balance-point temperature: The outdoor temperature at which a building makes a transition from a heating need to a cooling need.

daylight autonomy (DA): Also referred to as *spatial daylight autonomy* (sDA). The percentage of an area that meets a minimum daylight illuminance level for a specified fraction of the operating hours per year (e.g., 300 lux for 50% of the time). It is one of the options for receiving LEED credit in the Daylight category.

daylight factor (DF): The ratio, expressed as a percentage, of the indoor illuminance at a point on a horizontal surface to the unobstructed exterior horizontal illuminance. Direct sunlight is excluded.

effective aperture (EA): The product of visible transmittance and the window-to-wall ratio.

equation of time: The factor used to account for the difference between solar time and clock time. Solar time is based on the position of the sun. Its basic unit is the *solar day*, the time the earth takes to make one complete rotation on its axis. A solar day may be slightly more than or less than 24 hours by clock time; its exact length changes from day to day due to the earth's elliptical orbit around the sun and the tilt of the earth's axis. Depending on the time of year, solar days may pass more quickly or more slowly than days on the clock. As the small differences accumulate, solar time can be ahead or behind clock time by as much as about $16\frac{1}{2}$ minutes. The equation of time is also expressed in the analemma. The difference between solar time and clock time is also affected by one's position east or west within a time zone; this is a separate factor from the equation of time.

glazing factor: A LEED-based number calculated by taking into account window area, floor area, a window geometry factor, light transmission, and a window height factor.

ground light: Visible light from the sun and sky, reflected by exterior surfaces below the plane of the horizon.

light shelf: A horizontal element positioned above eye level and designed to reflect daylight on the ceiling for improved daylighting effectiveness

net metering: The requirement that a utility pay and charge equal rates regardless of which way electricity flows as part of the utility grid. Thus, excess electricity generated with photovoltaics or wind systems can be sold back to the utility.

radiation spectrum: The entire range of electromagnetic radiation extending from 0 Hz to about 1023 Hz. This includes visible light as well as infrared radiation, radio waves, and gamma rays, among others.

radiative cooling: Also known as *nocturnal cooling* or *night-cooled mass.* A passive or active design strategy that uses thermal mass to collect and store heat during the day for release at night. This works best in climates where there is a significant difference between daytime and nighttime temperatures, such as the southwest and temperate climates.

shading coefficient (SC): The ratio of the solar heat gain through a glazing product to the solar heat gain through an unshaded $\frac{1}{8}$ in thick, clear, double-strength glass under the same set of conditions. This is a value for the glass only and does not include the frame. The SC is a decimal value between zero and one. Because this rating includes only the glass, the solar heat gain coefficient is usually considered a more accurate rating.

solar constant: The amount of solar energy that falls in a unit time on a unit area that is 93,000,000 miles from the sun and oriented on a plane perpendicular to the sun's rays. The mean value of the solar constant is 433 Btu/hr-ft^2. Some of this energy is lost as the energy travels through the earth's atmosphere.

solar heat gain coefficient (SHGC): The ratio of the solar heat gain through a fenestration to the total solar radiation incident on the glazing. Solar heat gain includes directly transmitted solar heat and absorbed solar radiation, which is then re-radiated, conducted, or convected into the space. This rating includes the effects of the frame and glass spacer. The SHGC is a decimal value between zero and one.

solar savings fraction: The fraction of the total energy used by a system that is provided by a solar technology. The solar savings fraction, represented by the variable f, is a decimal fraction from zero (where no solar energy is used) to one (where all energy used by a system is solar energy).

solar time: The time as defined by the sun and its position relative to the earth. Because the length of the solar day varies, most references use the mean solar day as a basis for timekeeping. This is the average length of a solar day.

visible light transmittance (VLT): The fraction of visible light that passes through a glazing material.

window-to-wall ratio (WWR): The ratio of the net glazing area in a room or space (glass only, not including frame or mullions) to the gross exterior wall area.

workplane: The assumed height at which work is performed, usually considered to be at desk height, 30 in above the floor.

13

SUSTAINABLE DESIGN

Sustainability, in its broadest sense, is the practice of meeting the needs and wants of the present generation through judicious use of resources, without harming or compromising the ability of future generations to meet their needs. Sustainability encompasses a wide range of concepts and strategies, and the specifics will vary depending on the context.

As it applies to architecture, *sustainable design* (also called *green building*, *environmental design*, and *ecological design*, among other terms) involves the use of many planning, design, operational, and reuse concepts to create functional, healthy, nonpolluting, and environmentally friendly buildings without compromising practical requirements or human comfort. In addition, the long-term costs are no greater, and are often less, than those of comparable buildings designed without sustainability in mind.

There are many *green building rating programs* that can be used to assess a building's environmental footprint. Leadership in Energy and Environmental Design (LEED) is a program of the U.S. Green Building Council designed to encourage the implementation of sustainable building practices. A building receives credits for using various sustainable design practices; if the building receives enough credits, it is awarded a LEED certificate. LEED has established itself as the premier comprehensive building rating program, but there are alternatives, including the Green Building Initiative's Green Globes program. Some other programs, such as the Energy Star Buildings initiative, evaluate a building's performance in terms of energy management only.

Some elements of sustainable design are an inherent part of other aspects of the design process. See Chap. 5 for contract provisions when AIA documents related to sustainable design are used. See Chap. 4 for more information on how sustainability practices affect site design and project concepts. See Chap. 12 for more information on how topography, utilities, climate, and alternative energy systems, and new material technologies affect project concepts. See Chap. 17 for information on energy efficiency in mechanical systems and alternative energy sources.

SITE DEVELOPMENT

The first step in planning a sustainable building project is to develop a site strategy that will disturb the natural site as little as possible, by minimizing the building footprint, parking, and other development. The natural topography should be respected, and climatic conditions should be considered. All these will affect the final building form.

Building sites should be located in areas where occupants can make the best use of community services, such as public transportation, utilities, and pedestrian paths. Buildings should not be developed on sites designated as prime farmland, in floodplains, on or within 100 ft of wetlands, on land designated as habitat for threatened species, or on land that was previously public park land. A project can receive LEED credit for meeting these requirements.

WATER USE

Sustainable water use involves controlling and directing stormwater runoff, preventing erosion and contamination of runoff, using rainwater or graywater for site irrigation, and practicing general water conservation (for example, using low-flow plumbing fixtures).

Each type of water should be kept separate from the others; at minimum, potable water must always be kept separated from the other types.

In architectural design, water can be classified in four ways: potable water, rainwater, graywater, and blackwater. *Potable water* is water that has been treated to make it suitable for drinking. *Rainwater* is natural precipitation that falls on a site. *Graywater* is wastewater that is not from toilets and urinals, such as wastewater from sinks, showers, bathtubs, and clothes washing machines. *Blackwater* is water containing toilet or urinal waste; in some jurisdictions, wastewater from kitchen sinks and laundry facilities is also classified as blackwater because of the detergents and other contaminants it may contain.

Ideally, each type of water should be kept separate from the others; at minimum, potable water must always be kept separated from the other types. In some cases, and where local regulations permit it, it is possible to reuse water of other types so as to reduce the use of potable water; this can also reduce the load on sewage systems. For example, rainwater and graywater can be collected and filtered or otherwise treated for use in an underground irrigation system, for flushing toilets, or as the circulating fluid in a heat exchanger that preheats cold water before its final heating in a water heater. Blackwater can also be used for these purposes, but it requires more extensive treatment, and some jurisdictions do not permit it. Because of high initial costs and strict local and state health regulations, it is seldom feasible to make extensive use of graywater and blackwater, especially in an urban or suburban setting.

Storm Runoff and Erosion Control

The first consideration in managing water use should be to protect existing watersheds on a site and within the surrounding areas and waterways. Improper water control during and after construction can create a number of problems.

- increased load on local storm sewer systems
- increased potential for flooding
- pollution of waterways with sediment, road salts, petroleum products, fertilizers, heavy metals, and pathogenic bacteria
- erosion of sites and waterways
- erosion of stream banks
- accelerated soil creep or landslides
- stream warming
- loss of aquatic biodiversity

All development sites should have a stormwater management plan. *Stormwater management* is the use of structural or nonstructural practices designed to reduce stormwater runoff pollutant loads, discharge volumes, and peak flow discharge rates.

During construction, erosion must be controlled while natural surfaces are stripped and subjected to building conditions. Most states and local municipalities have regulations to control erosion and sediment. Silt fences, sediment traps or basins, vegetated buffer strips, hay bales, and other methods are used to control water flow and pollutants onto adjacent property, and ultimately, into natural waterways.

The final constructed site should minimize areas of impervious coverage, utilize the natural filtration and cleansing actions of soils and plants, and capture and control excessive runoff. Some common ways to accomplish this are to use pervious paving, develop constructed wetlands, and build grass-lined swales. *Pervious paving* is a material that can withstand vehicular or pedestrian traffic, depending on its application, but that will allow water to pass through and seep into the ground below. Pervious paving products include manufactured grids of concrete, plastic, or other materials that allow grass or other ground covers to grow through, or it can be porous asphalt or concrete.

Additional guidelines for sustainable site design are given in Chap. 7.

Rainwater Collection

If local regulations allow, rainwater can be collected and used for irrigation and, in some cases, for other nonpotable uses such as flushing toilets. The use of rainwater also reduces the amount of site runoff, lightening the burden on storm sewer systems. However, the collection of rainwater is appropriate only in locations that receive adequate rainfall and where the quality of the rainwater is not compromised by, for example, air pollution. Local regulations should be checked.

Devices can be used to divert the first flush of water during a rainfall, to prevent it from entering the cistern. This water is the most likely to contain contaminants.

A *rainwater collection system* is composed of a water collection system, a storage cistern, and a water distribution system. The water collection system is commonly a series of gutters and downspouts at the perimeter of the roof area of the building. If a roof is used as the catchment surface, the roofing materials should be selected to minimize contamination of the water and the addition of sediment. Good materials include epoxy-coated metal, clay or slate tiles, and new concrete tiles. Avoid using asphalt shingles, treated wood shakes, old concrete tiles (which may contain asbestos), or lead-containing materials such as flashing. Steep roofs work better than low-sloped roofs because they shed water more quickly, and they are scoured by winds and collect less dust and debris.

The area of the roof or other catchment surface is referred to as the catchment area. The catchment area is measured in terms of its "footprint" as projected onto a horizontal plane; the slope of the roof does not affect the size of the catchment area.

To calculate the amount of rainwater available, multiply the catchment area by the average annual rainfall for the region and by a factor, typically 75% or 0.75, to account for evaporation and other losses. One inch of rain yields about 0.6 gal of rainwater per square foot of catchment area.[1]

After the rainwater is collected it is stored in a cistern. This is a large tank, placed underground or at a convenient location on the site or on the building. Cisterns can be made from fiberglass, steel, or concrete. They must be watertight and covered to prevent contamination, and opaque to prevent algae growth. They also must be accessible for cleaning. If cisterns can be located above the area of use, water can flow by gravity; otherwise, small pumps are used to distribute the water.

In order to size a cistern with sufficient capacity, the amount of water to be drawn over a period of time must be calculated and subtracted from the available rainwater.

If the collected water will be used for irrigation, the runoff can be filtered first with screens on the gutters and then passed through a series of with graded screens, paper filters, or sand filters. Additional treatment may be needed if the water is to be used flushing toilets and similar nonpotable applications.

Example 13.1

A small commercial building with a roof area of 10,000 ft^2 is located in an area that receives an annual rainfall of 20 in. 25% of the water is lost in evaporation, run-off, absorption, and impoundment. The amount of rainwater that can be collected in a year is

(A) 9000 gal

(B) 15,000 gal

(C) 90,000 gal

(D) 150,000 gal

Solution

The total annual rainfall is equal to the catchment area times the average annual rainfall.

$$\text{total rainfall} = \left(20\ \frac{\text{in}}{\text{yr}}\right)(1\ \text{year})\left(10{,}000\ \text{ft}^2\right) = 200{,}000\ \text{in-ft}^2$$

Multiply the total annual rainfall by 0.75 to account for losses, and convert to gallons.

$$\text{available rainwater} = (1 - 0.25)(200{,}000\ \text{in-ft}^2)\left(0.6\ \frac{\text{gal}}{\text{in-ft}^2}\right) = 90{,}000\ \text{gal}$$

The answer is (C).

[1]More precicely, 0.623 gallons per in-ft^2.

Graywater and Blackwater Systems

Graywater recycling is the collection, treatment, storage, and distribution of wastewater from sources that do not contain human waste, such as showers and sinks. Depending on the treatment methods employed and local health regulations, graywater may be used for irrigation, toilet flushing, vehicle washing, janitorial cleaning, cooling, and similar uses.

Even if graywater is used only for irrigation, health regulations may require that it be filtered and be applied subsurface so that the water is not released into the air.

Graywater systems are generally only cost effective in new construction where separate piping can be installed easily and where the ratio of the demand for nonpotable to potable water is relatively high, such as for laundries and car washes. Graywater is not "clean" water—it may contain detergents, chemicals, and debris. If a graywater recycling system is in use, building occupants must not use it to dispose of detergents, cleaning products, or other substances that are toxic or inappropriate for the ways in which the graywater will be reused. For example, if graywater will be used for irrigation, chemicals that are harmful to plants must be kept out of the graywater system. Water from kitchen sinks and dishwashers is sometimes excluded from graywater systems as it is more likely to contain harsh chemicals, oils, bits of food, and so on. All graywater systems should have interceptors to prevent the flow of grease and hair into the system.

Graywater cannot be stored for long periods of time without treatment. Other cost considerations include the net reduction in water consumption, the price of potable water, and economies of scale.

Even if graywater is used only for irrigation, health regulations may require that it be filtered and be applied subsurface, using drip irrigation pipes or other methods than sprinklers, so that the water is not released into the air.

If graywater is not reused directly for irrigation or flushing toilets, it can be run through a heat exchanger so that the heat it carries can be used to preheat potable water flowing to a water heater. This can reduce energy demand, increase the availability of hot water, allow downsizing of heated water storage, and lower energy costs. Heat recovery systems are best for buildings that have large domestic hot water needs, such as restaurants, laundries, apartments, and arenas. The heat exchanger can be either a direct system, recycling in which the graywater flows past a coil of cold water, or a tank system, recycling where the graywater is held around coils of incoming cold water. Tank systems can extract more heat from the graywater but require periodic maintenance. Both kinds of systems must protect against contamination of the potable water supply, such as by using a double-walled heat exchanger. Building officials and health departments must be consulted to determine the local requirements for these types of systems.

Blackwater recycling is the collection, treatment, storage, and distribution of wastewater from nearly any source, including from toilets and urinals. Because of the contamination, blackwater needs more extensive treatment before use. Generally, blackwater recycling is not cost effective except on a large scale, although commercial systems are available for single-building use.

Plumbing Fixtures

The simplest way to conserve water is to use less of it. The Energy Policy Act of 2005, issued by the Environmental Protection Agency, governs how much water various types of plumbing fixtures may use. Low-flow toilets, showerheads, and faucets are widely available in response to these guidelines. In the United States, toilets may not use more than 1.6 gal per flush, and toilets that use even less water are available.

The WaterSense label indicates fixtures that meet even stricter guidelines. By using air pressure tanks or vacuum systems, some toilets use as little as 1.5 qt (0.375 gal) of water per flush. Low-consumption appliances are also available that reduce water use without compromising function. For example, a front-loading washing machine uses less water than does a top-loading model.

ALTERNATIVE ENERGY SOURCES AND ENERGY EFFICIENCY

Alternative energy sources are those that are renewable, such as solar and wind power. While it is seldom possible satisfy all of a building's energy needs with alternative energy sources alone, alternative energy can substantially reduce reliance on depletable energy sources such as fossil fuels, and can reduce pollution.

Energy efficiency is the reduction of the energy that must be consumed in providing various services and functions, particularly as compared to standard baselines.

Both of these topics are discussed in Chap. 7. Energy efficiency using conventional fuels and mechanical systems is discussed in Chap. 17.

MATERIALS

The total sustainability of a building project is affected significantly by the selection and use of materials. As with energy consumption and other sustainability issues, material selection must be made with consideration of the entire life cycle of the building. However, sustainability issues must be balanced with the traditional concerns of function, cost, appearance, and performance.

Life-Cycle Assessment

A life-cycle assessment (LCA) is a method of evaluating the environmental impact of using a particular material or product in a building. LCAs are an important part of the Materials and Resources category of the LEED rating system. There are usually four phases to an LCA.

1. *Define the goals and scope of the study.* Limits must be established for the study and for the units for study, so that alternatives can be compared and the framework for data acquisition can be developed.

2. *Perform an inventory analysis.* The *inventory analysis* is often the most difficult part of the assessment, because it involves determining and quantifying all the inputs and outputs of the product under study. These might include the energy needed to obtain the raw materials and to process or manufacture them, the energy used for transportation, the need for ancillary materials, and the pollution or waste disposal methods involved in the manufacturing, use, and disposal processes. The recyclability of the material is also considered. Some of the criteria used for evaluating building materials are listed in the next section.

3. *Perform an impact assessment.* The *impact assessment* examines the processes identified in the inventory analysis and evaluates how they will affect the environment. The analysis may include such things as resource depletion, the generation of pollution, and effects on health and social welfare. For example, the energy that is needed to produce a product may make it necessary to increase the electrical generating capacity at the manufacturing plant, which in turn may produce both waterborne and airborne pollution.

4. *Perform an improvement analysisand report the results of the study.* The improvement analysis, or interpretation, suggests ways to reduce the environmental impact of the raw materials, energy, and processing used to create the product or construction activity.

There are four main stages in a product's life cycle: raw material acquisition, manufacturing, use in the building, and disposal or reuse. The potential individual elements of each stage are as follows.

Raw Material Acquisition

- acquisition of raw materials through mining, drilling, or other activities and evaluation of the energy consumption associated with these processes
- processing of raw materials
- transportation of raw materials to processing points

Manufacturing

- conversion of processed raw materials into useful products
- manufacturing or fabrication of materials necessary to generate the final product
- packaging of the product
- transportation of the finished product to the job site or distribution channel

Use and Maintenance

- installation or construction of the product into the building
- long-term use of the product throughout its life or the life of the building
- maintenance and repair of the product throughout its life

Disposal

- demolition or removal of the product from the building
- conversion of the waste into other useful products
- waste disposal of the product
- reuse or recycling of the product if not disposed or converted

At any point in the life cycle of a building material or product—but most commonly during inventory analysis—consideration must be given to all the inputs and outputs needed to produce the material or product under study. These include the energy and other resources needed to acquire, process, or use the product, as well as the materials released to the air, water, and land as a result of its use. A model for analyzing these effects is shown in Fig. 13.1.

Figure 13.1 is helpful in directing the collection of data. Inputs for energy are typically in British thermal units or megajoules, inputs for raw materials are in pounds or kilograms, and water is in gallons or liters. Output is typically given by weight, in pounds or kilograms.

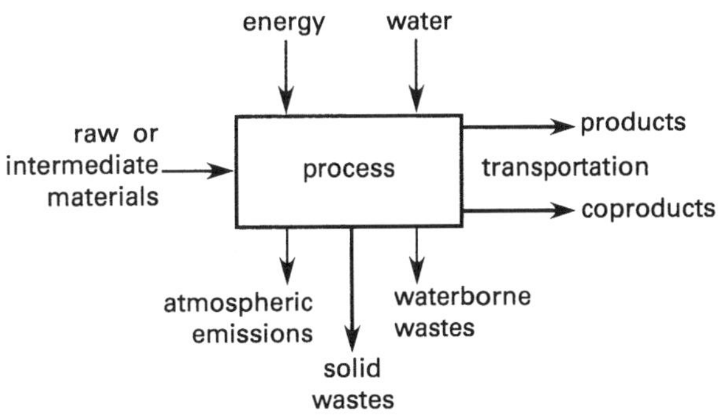

Figure 13.1
Life-Cycle Inventory Model

Whole-Building Life-Cycle Assessments

To perform a *whole-building life-cycle assessment*, a building is modeled both as a base case and a design case. The base case, or reference model, reflects the typical construction practices for buildings of that type, size, and location. The design case reflects the building's actual construction. The models are limited to the structure and enclosure of the building and do not include interior finishes or site work.

A whole-building LCA is a credit option in the LEED program. To receive LEED credit, the modeling must demonstrate that the design case outperforms the base case in at least three of six categories: global warming, ozone layer depletion, acidification, eutrophication, formation of ground-level ozone, and depletion of non-renewable energy resources.

Acidification is the generation of waste materials that can lower the pH of surrounding waterways or soil. (A material with a pH of less than 7 is an acid, a material with a pH of 7 is neutral, and a material with a pH greater than 7 is a base.)

Eutrophication is the formation of excessive nutrients in a body of water that promotes increased algae growth. The algae block the penetration of sunlight into the water, resulting in less oxygen production and the loss of aquatic life.

To earn LEED credit, the design must be at least 10% better than the reference case in the global warming category and two others of choice, and it cannot be more than 5% worse than the reference case in any of the categories.

Environmental Product Declarations

An LCA is a useful tool for understanding the amount of energy, water, and materials consumed in the production and use of a product, as well as what emissions are produced in its manufacture or use. However, an LCA cannot give a complete view of a product, nor does it allow consumers to compare multiple products within a particular category.

An *environmental product declaration* (EPD) is a standardized report of a product's environmental impact throughout its life cycle. An EPD is based on information gathered from an LCA, but it gives additional information and is verified by a third party in accordance with guidelines established by the International EPD System. These guidelines reference the International Standard Organization's ISO 14025, *Environmental Labels and Declarations—Type III Environmental Declarations—Principles and Procedures.*

There are two types of EPDs: industry-wide and product-specific. An *industry-wide EPD* covers a generic type of product that several manufacturers make, such as building products like cement, acoustic ceilings or carpet yarn. A *product-specific EPD* is specific to a single manufacturer's product and usually contributes more to sustainable credits.

One thing that makes an EPD useful for comparing similar products, and differentiates it from an LCA, is the use of *product category rules* (PCR). A product category rule is a set of guidelines for a particular type of product that establishes what data should be collected in the LCA, how LCA results are reported, and what other information must be reported in the EPD. *Product categories* are general types of items, such as flooring, insulation, wood products, and doors. Each type of product has a different environmental impact based on the raw materials used, the energy used in manufacture and transportation, and the emissions created during manufacture, use, and disposal. The use of uniform PCRs makes it possible to compare one product to another more accurately and determine the complete environmental effects of using a particular manufacturer's product.

EPDs are developed by manufacturers following standards defined in ISO 14025. The process must be administered by a *program operator,* which is an organization that coordinates the involvement of stakeholders, takes responsibility for completing or overseeing the LCA and PCR process, writes the EPD itself, and generally makes sure that the process follows ISO standards. Examples of program operators include ASTM International and the UL Environment and Scientific Certification Systems (SCS).

Developing an EPD is a five-step process.

1. An applicable PCR is found or developed in accordance with ISO 14025.
2. The manufacturer conducts and independently verifies an LCA.
3. The EPD is prepared.
4. The EPD is submitted to an independent third party for review and verification.
5. If approved, the EPD is registered and published.

EPDs can be used along with other product certification systems, such as GREENGUARD for flooring materials or the Forest Stewardship Council for wood products, to help an architect select an environmentally preferable product for a particular use, and for owners to understand the impact of their facility throughout its life cycle.

For more information consult the following sources.

- American Center for Life Cycle Assessment (ACLCA), lcacenter.org
- Global Environmental Declarations Network (GEDnet), gednet.org
- Institute for Environmental Research and Education (IERE), iere.org

- The International EPD System, environdec.com
- SCS Global Services, scsglobalservices.com
- UL Environment, industries.ul.com/environment
- U.S. Life Cycle Inventory Database published by the National Renewable Energy Laboratory, nrel.gov/lci

Criteria for Evaluating Building Materials

These are some of the criteria used for evaluating the sustainability of a product or construction process. Not every criterion will apply to every product.

- *embodied energy.* The material or product should require as little energy as possible for its extraction as a raw material, initial processing, and subsequent manufacture or fabrication into a finished building product. This includes the energy needed to transport materials and products during their life cycle. Production of the material should also generate as little waste or pollution as possible. Table 13.1 lists the approximate embodied energy of some common building materials.
- *renewable materials.* A material is renewable if it comes from sources that can renew themselves within a fairly short time through new growth. LEED credits are given for using rapidly renewable building materials and products for at least 5% of the total value of all building materials and products used in the project. These include products typically made from plants that are harvested within a cycle of 10 years or shorter. Products that meet this criterion include wool carpets, bamboo flooring and paneling, straw board, cotton batt insulation, linoleum flooring, poplar oriented strand board (OSB), sunflower seed board, and wheatgrass cabinetry.
- *recycled content.* The more recycled content a material contains, the less energy and raw materials are required to process the raw materials into a final product. Each of the three types of recycled content should be considered: post-consumer materials, post-industrial materials, and recovered materials.
- *energy efficiency.* Materials, products, and assemblies should reduce the energy consumption in a building.
- *use of local materials.* Using locally produced materials supports the region's economy, reduces transportation costs, and can add to the regional character of a design. Integration of regional materials can be used to earn LEED credits.
- *durability.* Durable materials will last longer and generally require less maintenance over the life of a product or building. Even though initial costs may be higher, the life cycle costs may be lower.
- *low volatile organic compounds* (VOC) *content.* VOCs in paint, carpet, composite wood products, and so on, can be released into the indoor air and create health risks.
- *low toxicity.* Materials should be selected that emit little or no harmful gases, such as chlorofluorocarbons (CFCs), formaldehyde, and others listed on the EPA's list of hazardous substances.
- *moisture problems.* If possible, materials should be selected that prevent or resist the growth of biological contaminants.
- *water conservation.* Products should reduce water consumption in a building and in landscaping.
- *maintainability.* It should be possible to clean and maintain materials and products using only nontoxic or low-VOC substances.
- *potential* for reuse and recycling. Some materials and products are more readily recycled than others. For example, steel can usually be separated from other materials and melted down to make new steel products. On the other hand, plastics used in construction are difficult to remove and separate.
- *reusability.* A product should be reusable after it has served its purpose in the original building. This type of product becomes a salvaged material in the life cycle of another building.

Table 13.1 Embodied Energy in Common Building Materials

material	embodied energy Btu/lbm	MJ/kg
limestone	129	0.3
stone (local)	340	0.79
terrazzo tile	603	1.4
marble	862	2.0
clay brick	1080	2.5
lumber	1080	2.5
cork	1724	4.0
gypsum wallboard	2630	6.1
stone (imported)	2930	6.8
particleboard	3450	8.0
aluminum (recycled)	3490	8.1
steel (recycled)	3830	8.9
plywood	4480	10.4
MDF	5130	11.9
glass	6850	15.9
ceramic tile	8390	19.5
mineral wool insulation	9223	21.4
tempered glass	11,290	26.2
fiberglass insulation	12,067	28.0
steel (virgin)	13,790	32.0
zinc	21,980	51.0
brass	26,720	62.0
PVC	30,170	70.0
copper	30,430	70.6
vinyl flooring	34,090	79.1
expanded polystyrene	38,183	88.6
paint	40,210	93.3
GFRP	43,096	100.0
wool carpet	45,690	106.0
linoleum	49,990	116.0
nylon carpet	63,790	148.0
aluminum (virgin)	82,320	191.0

All information should be viewed as approximate due to different sources, different methods of calculating values, varying assumptions, and what factors may have been used in the calculations. It is best to view the information in terms of relative differences in magnitude and what other sustainable factors may be involved in the decision to use a particular material. For example, a material with a high embodied energy may otherwise be desirable because it has a long life span, can be recycled, is very durable, and reduces energy consumption in the building during occupancy.

Sources: *Environmental Resource Guide*, American Institute of Architects; *The Energy Embodied in Building Materials—Updated New Zealand Coefficients and Their Significance*, George Baird; *Environmental Building News*, July 1, 2001; United States Gypsum; University of Bath, UK, 2010.

Use of Salvaged Materials

Salvaged materials should be used as much as possible, if the building owner permits them and they satisfy other design requirements. These materials may include doors, window units, cabinetry, furnishings, equipment, and other items. There may be additional costs associated with preparing salvaged materials for reuse, but they can be offset by the savings from not buying new, more expensive materials and from reducing the costs associated with disposing of old items and producing new ones.

Reusing certain materials, such as brick or timber from old buildings, can add to the aesthetic appeal of a new building. Materials can also be used in new ways in the new facility. For example, if a stained glass window salvaged from a demolished building is not well insulated enough to become part of the new building's exterior envelope, it can be used as an interior partition.

Concrete

Concrete is often not considered a sustainable material, because the manufacture and production of portland cement consumes substantial energy and raw material consumption and produces environmental emissions. However, when properly constructed, concrete has many environmental advantages, including long life, heat storage capability, no appreciable emissions after curing (although some admixtures can produce odors and emissions when the concrete is in the plastic state), and a lower embodied energy than steel. Concrete can also be recycled as crushed aggregate for highway base, fill, or subsequent concrete manufacture. The reinforcing steel used within the concrete can be recycled indefinitely. Except for the cement, concrete is composed of abundant and readily available natural materials such as sand or gravel aggregate; these materials are typically sourced close to where they are used, reducing transportation costs.

When properly constructed, concrete has many environmental advantages, including long life, heat storage capability, no appreciable emissons after curing, and a lower embodied energy than steel.

The environmental impact of concrete can be reduced by incorporating fly ash admixtures, using recycled aggregates when possible, and using low-waste formwork. Fly ash is a waste material obtained from coal-fired power plants. It can be used to increase concrete strength, decrease permeability, reduce temperature rise during placement, increase sulfate resistance, and improve the workability of concrete. It may also reduce the total amount of cement needed. In high-volume fly ash concrete mixes, between 15% and 35% of the portland cement can be replaced by fly ash with no adverse impact, though if high proportions of fly ash are used, the concrete may take longer to set. If use of fly ash is encouraged, the optimum amount should be determined and specified as part of the mix design.

Using lightweight aggregates such as pumice and perlite can reduce the need for standard aggregates, reduce the structural load, and improve insulation values.

Using forms made from reusable steel or permanent rigid plastic foam can reduce the waste associated with standard wood forms. Rigid plastic foam forms that remain in place after the concrete is poured have the additional advantage of improving the thermal resistance of foundation walls.

Autoclaved aerated concrete (AAC) is a lightweight, precast concrete made with aluminum powder as an extra ingredient. This type of concrete is hardened in molds and cured in an autoclave, which is a steam-filled pressure chamber. The concrete is formed into blocks, typically 10 in by 25 in, in thicknesses of 4 in, 8 in, and 10 in. AAC can easily be cut and shaped with normal woodworking tools. ACC is used for non-load-bearing residential and light commercial walls. It provides excellent insulation value, low air infiltration, and good acoustic qualities. ACC also needs less cement than standard concrete.

Masonry

As with concrete, masonry and mortar require large amounts of energy and raw materials to produce, regardless of whether they are concrete or clay based. However, brick and *concrete masonry units* (CMUs) are generally manufactured close to the place of use and formed from locally quarried natural materials, reducing transportation costs. Masonry is also a durable material with a long life. Like concrete, masonry produces no pollution or emissions once in place and provides excellent thermal mass. It can be recycled, and it produces no toxic substances when placed in landfills. Environmental impacts can be minimized by using fly ash, recycled aggregates (such as ground granulated blast furnace slag) and lightweight aggregates.

Metals

Although metals require large amounts of energy for their production, they have a high potential for recycling. Steel is the most common metal used in buildings and is often recycled as scrap to produce more steel. Steel with a recycled content up to 30% or more is readily available. Aluminum is also widely used and is available with a recycled content of 20% or more. Copper has great value as a recycled material, and brass, bronze, and stainless steel can also be recycled if separated.

Problems can arise with some metals that are plated or coated with chemicals. Electroplating processes produce high levels of pollution and by-products. Alternatives to these processes include powder coatings and plastic polymer coatings. A finish should be selected that is easily removable to facilitate recycling.

Wood and Plastic

Lumber and wood products are used in both residential and commercial construction for myriad purposes, from rough framing to furniture. This includes both softwoods and hardwoods, harvested from domestic and foreign sources. Deforestation and the processing and manufacture of wood products are large ecological problems, but architects can reduce these effects by applying three sustainable strategies:

- using reclaimed wood
- specifying sustainable or alternate materials
- using certified wood products

Reclaimed wood is timber salvaged from demolished buildings and other structures that has been prepared for a new use. Preparation may include removing nails and other fasteners, drying, and cutting or planing. In addition to being ecologically sound, reclaimed wood has a unique visual character that many architects and clients find desirable, and it is possible in this way to obtain kinds of wood that are no longer available, such as American chestnut. Reclaimed wood is generally old-growth material, which is harder than lumber from trees that are planted and harvested in a short period of time. Because it has had many years to acclimate and dry, it is less likely to warp or split than materials with a higher moisture content.

Sustainable materials (or *alternative materials*) include a wide range of products. Standard solid-wood framing products can be replaced with engineered wood products such as wood I-joists, laminated veneer lumber, and structural insulated panels (SIPs). These products are discussed in Chap. 25. Panel products that use waste material from other processes, such as particleboard and medium-density fiberboard (MDF), are good sustainable products as long as they do not contain adhesives and resins that outgas formaldehyde or other pollutants such as urea formaldehyde. Formaldehyde-free MDF and low-emission panels are available that use phenol-formaldehyde or urethane adhesives. These materials have a formaldehyde level of 0.04 ppm or less, which is below the commonly accepted level of 0.05 ppm. Another alternative to urea formaldehyde is methylene diphenyl diisocyanate (MDI). This resin does not emit toxic gases during use and requires less dryer energy and lower press temperatures than traditional binders.

Other innovative products can be used in some instances to replace rough lumber. Straw particleboard, for example, is made from wheat straw, a waste product from farming. The straw is milled into fine particles and hot pressed together with formaldehyde-free resins. It can be used for both construction and furniture making. Other useful agricultural by-products are rice straw and bagasse, the residue from the processing of sugar cane. Some products also use postconsumer recycled waste paper in building panels.

A building can receive LEED credit for using low-emitting materials such as wood and agrifiber products that contain no added urea-formaldehyde resins.

For finish carpentry and architectural woodwork, many alternative products exist. Molding can be made from medium-density fiberboard or molded high-density polyurethane foam. Composite wood veneers are manufactured from readily available and fast-growing trees by slicing veneers, dying them, and gluing them back into an artificial "log." The manufactured log is then sliced. By varying the dye colors and how the artificial log is cut, a wide variety of veneers is possible, from those that look like standard wood to highly figured and colored products.

Certified wood products are obtained through sustainable forest management practices. While there are many forest certification groups in North America, the most well known is the Forest Stewardship Council (FSC). The FSC is an international body that oversees the development of national and regional standards based on basic forest management principles and criteria. It accredits certifying organizations that comply with its principles. There are many U.S. and international certifying groups, including Rainforest Alliance, the FSC Chain of Custody Program of SCS Global Services, and Sustainable Northwest.

The FSC has established 10 basic principles and 56 individual criteria that it uses to evaluate organizations for accreditation. It also uses additional regional criteria for different parts of the United States. The 10 principles can be summarized as follows.

- Forest management must respect all applicable laws of the country in which it occurs and must comply with FSC *Principles and Criteria.*
- Long-term tenure and use rights to the land and forests must be defined, documented, and legally established.
- The rights of indigenous peoples to own, use, and manage their land must be recognized and respected.
- Forest management practices and operations must maintain or enhance the long-term social and economic well-being of workers and local communities.
- Forest management must encourage the efficient use of the forest's multiple products to ensure economic viability and environmental and social benefits.
- Forest management must conserve biological diversity, water resources, soils, ecosystems, and landscapes to maintain the ecological functions of the forest.
- A management plan must be written, implemented, and maintained.
- Monitoring must be conducted to assess the condition of the forest, yields, chain of custody, and management activities and their social and environmental impacts.
- Management activities in forests with high conservation value must maintain or enhance the attributes that define such forests.
- Plantations must follow the first nine principles as well as the criteria that apply to plantations. Plantations should reduce pressures on natural forests, complement their management, and promote their restoration and conservation.

A building can receive LEED credit for using products that comply with approved leadership extraction practices for at least 25%, by cost, of the total value of permanently installed building products. This includes wood products certified by FSC or a USGBC-approved equivalent, as well as reused and recycled materials. When calculating the percentage of products that meet this criterion, products sourced within 100 miles of the site are valued at 200% of their cost.

Plastic building materials and consumer products identified as recyclable should be reused and recycled. Recycled plastics have many uses. Polyethylene terephthalate (PET) from soft drink containers, for example, can be used to manufacture carpet with properties similar to polyesters.

Compostable plastics are also available, although they are primarily used for disposable containers and trash bags rather than for building materials. These should be identified, separated, and delivered to appropriate processing facilities. Compostable plastics either take a long time to break down or will not decompose in a household compost bin; they require treatment in commercial facilities that grind materials and compost at very high temperatures.

Plastic lumber is used for decking, fencing, and other outdoor applications. This material may be either all plastic (a mixture of recycled plastic and pure high-density polyethylene (HDPE)), or a wood-plastic composite that is a mixture of recycled plastic resin (usually polyethylene) combined with wood fiber, which can be also be recycled material. In addition to providing a use for post-consumer and post-industrial waste materials, plastic lumber is also an alternative to using pressure-treated wood containing the preservative chromated copper arsenate (CCA), which can pose an environmental risk during disposal. All-plastic lumber is durable, and it will not rot, absorb water, or crack; it can be worked with standard woodworking saws and carbide blades. However, it is not suitable for load-bearing applications. Some wood-plastic composite lumber, on the other hand, has been graded for structural use.

Two recent developments may improve the sustainability of plastic. The first is *bioplastics*, specifically *polylactide* (PLA). PLA is a biodegradable plastic derived from harvested corn. It is currently used in the manufacture of carpet fibers. The second advance is the development of *metallocene catalysis polymerization*, a process that makes it possible to manufacture polyolefins with specific properties. This may lead to the development of materials that can replace PVC and other plastics while doing less harm to the environment, and which could be used in the manufacture of window frames, membrane roofing, siding, and wire sheathing.

Thermal Insulation and Moisture Protection

Materials that provide insulation and moisture protection are some of the most important for energy efficiency and the control of mold and other water-related problems. Very efficient plastic-based insulations with high thermal resistance are available, but their manufacture requires the use of petroleum products, which cause pollution; also, the products are subject to outgassing and the disposal of used and waste materials is difficult.

There are several types of insulation that are resource efficient and pose little danger to indoor air quality. The conductivity of each is given in Table 27.2.

- *Cellulose insulation* is available in loose-fill form and is made from 80% to 100% postconsumer recycled paper combined with a fire-retardant additive. This material has a low embodied energy.
- *Compressed straw* can be used as infill in structural insulated panels.
- *Cotton insulation* is made from pre-consumer recycled cotton denim scrap material with a small amount of polyester for binding and stability. It also has a low embodied energy.
- *Glass fiber insulation* containing at least 30% postconsumer recycled glass is available in rigid boards, batts, and loose-fill form.
- *Mineral-fiber insulation*, which is made from steel mill slag or basalt rock, is available in rigid boards, batts, and loose-fill form. Most manufacturers use from 50% to 95% recycled material, with 75% postindustrial content being about average.
- *Spray-on cellulose* is manufactured as loose-fill insulation with about the same recycled content as mineral-fiber insulation. The EPA recommends that spray-on cellulose insulation contain at least 75% post-consumer recovered paper.
- *Perlite* is made from volcanic rock expanded by heat. It is used as a lightweight aggregate for plaster and concrete and as loose-fill insulation.
- *Vermiculite* is made from mica expanded by heat. It can be used for loose-fill insulation applications. It is also a component of some spray-applied fireproofing products.

Doors and Windows

Window design is one of the best tools for sustainable design. When properly tuned, windows can be used for daylighting, solar heat gain, and ventilation while maintaining good insulation qualities. Modern glazing products offer a variety of options to suit the individual needs of each building. In addition to controlling solar heat gain, insulated glazing assemblies can have very high *R*-values.

Special consideration should be given to the framing supporting the glazing. If aluminum or steel is used for the frame, there should be a thermal break between the inside and outside surfaces. Wood and plastic (vinyl or PVC) are much better insulators than metal, and frames constructed of these materials do not require a thermal break. The type of glazing specified, the spacing between panes, and the gases used to infill the cavities significantly affect the product's energy efficiency. The energy efficiency of windows, doors, and skylights should be certified by an independent laboratory according to the standards of the National Fenestration Rating Council (NFRC) for *U*-factor (*U*-value), solar heat gain coefficient (SHGC), and visible light transmittance (VLT) coefficients. Windows may be certified with the Green Seal label if they meet the criteria given in Green Seal's Standard GS-13.

See Chap. 28 for more information on windows and glazing products.

Finishes

Selecting interior finish materials with recycled content and low VOCs is an effective way to improve a building's sustainability. By virtue of their location within the building envelope, interior finish products are one of the main sources of potential indoor air pollution. These materials are typically replaced several times over the life of a building. Finish types are grouped into the following categories.

Adhesives

With many types of finishes, it is the adhesives or coatings used during installation that affect indoor air quality, not the finish material itself. Most adhesives emit gases because they contain plastic resins and other materials that can outgas. Three types of low-emission and zero-VOC adhesives can be used for installing carpet, resilient flooring, plastic laminates, sheet metal, wood veneers, and some types of wall coverings: *dry adhesives* that contain resins stored in capsules released by pressure, *water-based adhesives* containing latex or polyvinyl acetate, and *natural adhesives* containing plant resins in a water dispersion system. A building can receive LEED credits for using adhesives and sealants with a VOC content at least as low as that defined in the California South Coast Air Quality Management District (SCAQMD) Rule 1168, which is among the lowest VOC content standards in the country.

Flooring

When specifying carpet, there are three major considerations for sustainability: raw material use, raw material disposal, and impact on indoor air quality. Good raw materials include polyester and nylon-blended carpet made from recycled soft drink containers (PET) and wool. Although wool has a higher initial cost, it is a renewable resource, wears well, and may have a lower life-cycle cost than less expensive carpet, which typically needs to be replaced more frequently. Carpet cushions made from recycled materials, such as tire rubber and synthetic and natural fiber from textile mill waste, should also be selected.

Disposal of carpet is a problem because of the total quantity that is placed in landfills, the fact that it does not decompose easily, the difficulty of separating the various components for recycling, and the costs of recycling compared to the cost of landfill disposal. While some carpet materials, such as nylon 6, can be recycled easily, the amount of carpet that is recycled is just a fraction of the total amount of carpet disposed. Generally, carpet tiles are more sustainable than broadloom carpet. This is because only a small number of tiles need to be replaced when they are damaged or worn, the adhesives used to apply them tend to offgas less than broadloom adhesives, and several manufacturers have programs to recycle the tiles.

Carpet can affect indoor air quality because of its construction and the adhesives used in direct-glue applications. Most carpet is made by bonding the face fiber to a backing with a synthetic latex resin. The latex can be replaced with fusion bonding, in which the face fiber is heat-welded to a sponge plastic backing. Carpets made with a needle punching process also avoid the use of latex bonding. The Carpet and Rug Institute (CRI) has a voluntary testing program under which manufacturers have their carpet products tested by an independent agency for four types of emissions: total volatile organic compounds, styrene, formaldehyde, and 4-phenylcyclohexene (4-PC). Carpet that passes the test criteria is allowed to carry the CRI IAQ carpet testing program label, also known as the "Green Label." The CRI also recommends that the building ventilation system be operated at maximum capacity during installation and for 48 to 72 hours afterward to evacuate gases. A building can receive LEED credit for using carpet systems that meet or exceed the requirements of the CRI IAQ program. To qualify, carpet must meet the requirements of the Green Label Plus program, cushion must meet the requirements of the Green Label program, and carpet adhesives must have a VOC limit of 50 g/L.

Vinyl flooring provides many benefits in both commercial and residential applications, including durability, easy cleaning, a wide choice of patterns and colors, and relatively low cost. However, its manufacture uses highly refined petrochemicals, and it contains a large percentage of PVC that can cause environmental problems during manufacture and disposal. Because of the high concentration of chlorine in the tile, hazardous substances can be given off if vinyl flooring is incinerated. Some vinyl tile is manufactured from recycled PVC, and at least one brand is made without chlorine. As with carpet, low-VOC adhesives should be specified for laying vinyl flooring.

Rubber flooring made from recycled tires is available as both tile and sheet goods. This flooring is durable, slip-resistant, and resilient. However, because of the methods of manufacture and the binders that are used, recycled rubber flooring may emit indoor pollutants. This type of flooring should only be used where there is adequate ventilation, such as in outdoor sports areas, locker rooms, and other utility spaces.

Linoleum is available in tile and sheet form and can also be used for baseboards. Linoleum is made from natural, renewable products, including linseed oil, rosin, cork powder, and pigments. It is a durable floor material and is biodegradable, waterproof, fire resistant, naturally antibacterial, and does not generate static electricity. When used with low-VOC adhesives, it emits low levels of contaminants, less than those of vinyl flooring.

Cork flooring is made from a renewable resource, the bark of cork oak trees, which regenerates every nine to ten years. Cork forests are well managed and protected by the countries in which they are located. Cork flooring is an excellent absorber of sound, has a rich, warm texture, and provides a cushioned walking surface. However, its softness and porosity makes it prone to scratching and indentation.

Prefinished flooring eliminates the need for finishing on the job site, which could create indoor air quality problems.

Cork should be installed with a water-based, low-VOC latex adhesive. It can be finished with water-based urethanes with very low VOCs that provide durability along with water and chemical resistance.

The only disadvantage to using cork as a natural material is that it must be imported from Mediterranean countries, increasing the transportation energy used. Although cork requires binders to hold the individual pieces together, modern cork products are usually bound with phenol formaldehyde, polyurethane, or all-natural protein products. Cork flooring bound with urea-formaldehyde should not be used.

Wood flooring offers many advantages for use in a sustainable design project. First, wood originating from well-managed forests can be selected; both domestic and tropical hardwoods are available from sustainable, FSC-certified sources. Second, veneered and laminated products using a plywood or MDF core can be used. Finally, salvaged solid-wood flooring is available. Whenever possible, prefinished flooring should be used to eliminate the need for sanding and finishing on the job site, which could create indoor air quality problems. If adhesives are required, they should be low-VOC types. On-site finishing processes should only use water-dispersed urethanes; varnishes, acid-cured varnishes, and hardening oils should be avoided.

Bamboo or *palm wood* can be used as an alternative to standard wood floors. Bamboo is a fast-growing grass that reaches maturity in three to four years. It is almost as hard, and is twice as stable, as red oak and maple. Bamboo is sold in tongue-and-groove strips prefinished with a durable polyurethane coating. Palm wood is harvested as a byproduct of commercial coconut plantations.

Ceramic tile is generally considered a sustainable material in spite of the high embodied energy required to produce it and the transportation costs to get it from the factory to the job site. It uses readily available natural materials, is very durable, produces practically no harmful emissions, and requires very little maintenance. Some tile is made from post-consumer or post-industrial waste products and may contain up to 100% recycled material. Cement mortars and grouts are also environmentally friendly and produce very few emissions. Avoid epoxy-modified grout, plastic adhesives with solvents, and sealers that contain VOCs.

Wall Finishes

Gypsum wallboard is manufactured with 100% recycled content for its paper faces and with some recycled content in the core. Some manufacturers mix recycled newspaper with gypsum as the core material.

About 7% of the industry's total use of gypsum is synthetic gypsum. Synthetic gypsum is chemically identical to natural, mined gypsum but is a by-product of various manufacturing, industrial, and chemical processes. The main source of synthetic gypsum in North America is flue-gas desulfurization, a process used by power plants (and similar plants) to remove polluting gases from their stacks and thus reduce harmful emissions. Synthetic gypsum is an efficient application for refuse material.

By itself, gypsum wallboard does not contribute in any significant way to indoor air pollution. However, adhesives, paints, and caulking used for installing and finishing gypsum board can be pollution sources and should be specified carefully.

Disposal of gypsum wallboard is problematic because wallboard taken out of an old building cannot be reused. Some gypsum wallboard plants have developed ways to pulverize old wallboard and turn it into a soil additive. However, the wallboard must be separated from other materials and be free of screws, nails, and lead paint, and the cost of collecting and transporting the old wallboard is a disincentive for recycling.

Sisal is a natural material used for wall and floor coverings. It is made from the fibers of the sisal plant (or the closely related henequen plant). Both are agaves with fibrous leaves, grown in Central and South America and similar climates. The branches are harvested and the fiber is extracted, dyed, and spun into yarn. Although fairly rough and not suitable for wet areas, sisal wall and floor coverings are durable, low maintenance, and reduce sound reflection and transmission. Sisal wall covering should be applied with a zero-VOC adhesive and detailed to allow slight expansion and contraction with absorption and release of humidity.

Paints and other coatings should be selected and used with care. Although federal, state, and local regulations have eliminated coatings containing dangerous components such as lead and cadmium, and have limited the use of volatile organic compounds, some commercial coatings may still contain them. Generally, new paint must conform to VOC limits set by the EPA per the Clean Air Act. The limits are defined in the National Volatile Organic Compound Emission Standards for Architectural Coatings, 40 CFR Part 59. Many types of coatings are listed in the standard. For example, the VOC content of flat interior paint cannot exceed 250 g/L, while non-flat interior paint cannot exceed 380 g/L. (Enforcement of the rule is based on SI units.) California has stricter standards, limiting paint to 50 g/L for flat paint and 100 g/L for non-flat coatings. A building can receive LEED credit for using interior paints and coatings that comply with the VOC and chemical component limits of the California Air Resources Board or the South Coast Air Quality Management District Rule 1113.

Ceiling Finishes

Acoustical ceiling tile that uses recycled content of old tiles, newsprint, or perlite is available. Other materials, such as clay and wood fibers, may also be incorporated into the products. Fiberglass ceiling panels are also available with recycled content; the quantity varies but can be up to 95%, depending on the manufacturer and the product type. Old tile can be repainted if the correct type of paint and procedures are used, which can help to extend the tile's life span. At least one manufacturer offers a recycling program that allows customers to ship old tile to their plant if the manufacturer's own tile will be used as a replacement; in this case, the cost to recycle the tile is typically less than the cost of sending the material to a landfill. The grid itself can be recycled as scrap steel.

Ceiling tile may shed fiber if it is damaged or as it ages. This fiber can be collected by the HVAC system if the plenum is used as a return air space. This problem can be partially alleviated by using separate ducts for return air or by regularly cleaning the plenum with vacuums.

Furnishings

In addition to other sustainability issues, furnishings can be a significant source of formaldehyde in residential and commercial settings because of the particleboard, MDF, and coatings used in their construction. The following strategies can be used to improve sustainability through the selection and specification of furnishings.

- Use refurbished or reused office furniture.
- Consider using furniture made from steel, solid wood, and glass, which can readily be recycled.
- Specify that furnishings be fabricated with wood certified under standards established by the FSC, or with reclaimed wood.
- Specify that furnishings be fabricated with formaldehyde-free MDF or strawboard.

- Use furniture with cushions, workstation panels, and fabrics made with recycled PET from soda bottles.
- Specify fabrics with biodegradable and nontoxic dyes.
- Use upholstery made of chemical-free organic cotton, wool, ramie, blends, or other natural materials.
- Use low-VOC finishes.
- Specify powder coatings for finishes instead of standard paint.
- Specify that cushions be foamed with CO2-injected foam or other environmentally friendly materials.

INDOOR AIR QUALITY

Maintaining health is an important aspect of sustainable design, and one of the basic requirements of health is good *indoor air quality* (IAQ). In addition to the impact on basic health, the quality of indoor air affects a person's sense of well-being and can affect absenteeism, productivity, creativity, and motivation. IAQ is a complex subject because there are hundreds of different contaminants, dozens of causes of poor IAQ, many possible symptoms building occupants may experience, and a wide variety of potential strategies for maintaining good IAQ. Because IAQ has become such an important topic in building design, there is no shortage of laws and standards devoted to regulating indoor air quality. Some of the more significant ones are given at the end of this section.

Indoor Air Contaminants

Indoor air contaminants can be classified into two groups: chemical contaminants and biological contaminants. *Chemical contaminants* include substances such as volatile organic compounds, inorganic chemicals, tobacco smoke, while *biological contaminants* include mold, pollen, bacteria, and viruses.

Volatile organic compounds (VOCs) are chemicals that contain carbon and hydrogen and that vaporize at room temperature and pressure. They are found in many indoor sources, including building materials and common household products. Building materials likely to contain VOCs include paint, stains, adhesives, sealants, water repellents and sealers, particleboard, furniture, upholstery, and carpeting. Other sources include copy machines, cleaning agents, and pesticides.

The EPA has established regulations for VOCs in coatings. The 1998 regulation on VOCs in architectural, industrial, and maintenance coatings lists the maximum content of VOCs permitted in various types of coatings. However, state laws also regulate VOCs, and each state may permit a different level. For example, the California South Coast Air Quality Management District has very strict limits on the volatile organic content of paints.

Formaldehyde is a colorless gas with a pungent odor. It is used in the preparation of resins and adhesives most commonly found in particleboard, wall paneling, furniture, carpet adhesives, and other glues used in the construction and furniture industries. Formaldehyde is designated as a probable human carcinogen and causes irritation of the eyes and respiratory tract.

The maximum suggested or allowable exposure rates vary depending on the agency publishing the guidelines. ASHRAE recommends a maximum continuous indoor air concentration of 0.081 ppm. OSHA specifies concentrations not to exceed 0.75 ppm in an eight-hour time period, but allows a 2 ppm short-term exposure, not to exceed 15 minutes. In order to be GREENGUARD certified, a product cannot produce more than 0.0073 ppm.

The problems associated with formaldehyde can most easily be solved by minimizing the source, using two or three coats of sealants to prevent the outgassing, or airing out the building before occupancy.

There are hundreds of organic and inorganic chemicals that may potentially be harmful to humans. The California Office of Environmental Health Hazard Assessment lists chemicals that the state regulates, along with the chronic inhalation reference exposure level (REL) for each, in micrograms per cubic meter ($\mu g/m^3$). This list was developed as a result of California's Proposition 65, which was passed in

1986. Proposition 65 requires businesses to provide a clear and reasonable warning before knowingly and intentionally exposing anyone to a listed chemical. The Proposition 65 list includes hundreds of chemicals known to cause cancer or reproductive toxicity.

The GREENGUARD Environmental Institute also produces a list of products, chemicals in those products, and allowable maximum emission levels. Some of the common chemicals include VOCs, formaldehyde, aldehydes, 4-phenylcyclohexene, and styrene, as well as particulates and biological contaminates. In order to be certified by GREENGUARD, a product must meet these standards after being tested according to ASTM D5116 and D6670, the State of Washington's protocol for interior furnishings and construction materials, and the EPA's testing protocol for furniture.

Tobacco Smoke

Secondhand smoke, also called environmental tobacco smoke (ETS), is a mixture of the smoke given off by the burning end of a cigarette, pipe, or cigar and the smoke exhaled from the lungs of smokers. Secondhand smoke has been found to contain over 4000 substances, more than 40 of which are known to cause cancer in humans, and many of which are strong irritants. The EPA and the California EPA have found that exposure to secondhand smoke increases the risk of cancer and other serious health effects. To improve indoor air quality, either smoking should be banned completely from buildings and near entrances, or isolated smoking rooms should be constructed that have a separate ventilation system that exhausts directly to the outside.

Biological Contaminants

Potential biological contaminants in a building include the common problem of mold and mildew in addition to bacteria, viruses, mites, pollen, animal dander, dust, and insects. Even protein in urine from rats and mice is an allergen.

Molds and mildew are microscopic fungi that produce enzymes to digest organic matter. Their reproductive spores are present nearly everywhere. When exposed to spores, people sensitive to molds and mildew may experience eye irritation, skin rashes, running noses, nausea, headaches, and similar symptoms.

Mold spores require three conditions to grow: moisture, a nutrient, and a temperature range from 40°F to 100°F. Nutrients are any organic materials (e.g., wood, carpet, the paper coating of gypsum wallboard, paint, wallpaper, insulation, and ceiling tile) that serve as a nourishing food source for organisms. Because nutrients and a suitable temperature are always present in buildings, the only way to prevent and control mold is to prevent and control moisture in places where mold growth should be prevented.

Causes of Poor Indoor Air Quality

There are four main causes of poor indoor air quality.

- chemical contaminants from indoor sources
- chemical contaminants from outdoor sources
- biological contaminants
- poor ventilation

Any of these factors may be present alone or in combination with one or more of the others.

One of the most common sources of poor indoor air quality is chemical contaminants from indoor sources. Some common sources of chemical contaminants include VOCs, environmental tobacco smoke, respirable particles, and outdoor contaminants carried in through improperly located vents, doors, and windows. Lists of harmful chemicals can be obtained from the following sources.

- *Hazardous Chemicals Desk Reference*, Richard J. Lewis, Sr. New York: John Wiley & Sons.
- National Toxicology Program (NTP), a part of the National Institutes of Health. The NTP lists chemicals known to be carcinogenic. (ntp.niehs.nih.gov)

- International Agency for Research on Cancer (IARC), a part of the World Health Organization. IARC classifies chemicals that are known to be carcinogenic. (www.iarc.fr)
- Chronic Reference Exposure Levels. California Office of Environmental Health Hazard Assessment. This list identifies hazardous chemicals recognized by this office, with links to more information about each chemical. (oehha.ca.gov/air/general-info/oehhc-acute-8–hour-and-chronic-reference-exposure-level-rel-summary)
- California Health and Welfare Agency, Safe Drinking Water and Toxic Enforcement Act of 1986 (Proposition 65) identifies chemicals known to cause cancer and reproductive toxicity. (oehha.ca.gov/proposition–65)
- California Air Toxics. California Environmental Protection Agency, Air Resources Board (ARB). The ARB maintains a list of toxic air contaminants (arb.ca.gov/toxics/toxics.htm)

Chemical contaminants from outdoor sources can be introduced to a building when air intake vents, windows, or doors from parking garages are improperly located, allowing pollutants from the outside to be drawn into the building. Indoor pollutants from exhausts and plumbing vents can also be sucked back into the building through improperly located air intakes.

Biological contaminants such as mold, bacteria, and viruses may develop from moisture infiltration, standing water, stagnant water in mechanical equipment, and even from insects or bird droppings that find their way into the building.

Poor ventilation allows indoor pollutants to accumulate to unpleasant or unhealthy levels and affects the general sense of well-being of building occupants. One of the most difficult aspects of providing proper ventilation is balancing the need for proper ventilation with energy conservation. However, this problem can be solved by using heat exchangers and other conservation methods. (See Chap. 17.) Guidelines for minimum levels of ventilation are given later in this section.

Symptoms of Poor Indoor Air Quality

Poor indoor air quality causes many symptoms, from temporary, minor irritations to serious, life-threatening illnesses. These are grouped into three classifications.

Sick building syndrome (SBS) is a condition in which building occupants experience a variety of health-related symptoms that cannot be directly linked to any particular cause. Generally, symptoms disappear after the occupants leave the building. Symptoms may include irritation of the eyes, nose, and throat; dry mucous membranes and skin; redness of the skin; mental fatigue and headache; respiratory infections and cough; hoarseness of voice and wheezing; hypersensitivity reactions; and nausea and dizziness.

Building-related illness (BRI) describes a condition in which the health-related symptom or symptoms of a building's occupants are identified and can be directly attributed to specific building contaminants. The symptoms do not immediately improve when the occupant leaves the building. Legionnaires' Disease, a type of severe pneumonia, is an example of BRI.

Multiple chemical sensitivity (MCS) is a condition induced by exposure to VOCs or other chemicals. People with MCS may develop acute, long-term sensitivity and show symptoms each time they are exposed to the chemicals. These sensitivities can remain with some people for the rest of their lives. In many cases, only a slight exposure to the chemical can be enough to produce symptoms.

Strategies for Maintaining Good Indoor Air Quality

Methods of maintaining good indoor air quality that the architect can use or suggest to the building owner can be classified into five broad categories: eliminate or reduce the sources of pollution, control ventilation rates in the building, establish good maintenance procedures, control occupant activity as it affects IAQ, and provide appropriate filtration.

Eliminate or Reduce Sources of Pollution

- Establish the owner's criteria for indoor air quality early in the project. This may be part of the programming process. It should include the budget available.
- Select and specify building materials and furnishings with low emissions and VOCs. The standards listed in the next section provide guidance on choosing materials. Because it is not always possible to eliminate all sources of pollutants, set priorities by identifying materials that are the most volatile and that represent large quantities.
- Specify materials that are resistant to the growth of mold and mildew, especially in areas that may become wet or damp.
- Request emissions test data from manufacturers. This can be the safety data sheets (SDSs) or other data provided by the manufacturer. OSHA regulations require all manufacturers to develop and supply SDSs for their products if they contain harmful chemicals.
- Design the building envelope to properly control moisture.

Prior to occupancy, the HVAC system in a new building or occupied space should be operated at full capacity for two weeks to reduce the emissions due to outgassing chemicals and moisture and new filtration media should be installed.

Control Ventilation

- During the programming phase, determine the owner's and occupants' needs for ventilation. Also determine applicable energy conservation code requirements.
- Provide minimum outdoor air ventilation levels as recommended by ASHRAE for the specific activity of the building or individual space. These minimums, as defined in ANSI/ASHRAE 62.1, range from 5 cfm/person to 20 cfm/person. The minimum recommendation of 5 cfm/person is for office spaces; the high range of 20 cfm/person is for smoking lounges.
- Locate fresh air intakes away from loading docks, bus stops, and parking garages where carbon monoxide, carbon dioxide, nitrous oxide, and odors can be drawn into the building.
- Avoid placing fresh air vents near landscaped areas where irrigation moisture could be drawn into the building.
- Provide separate rooms and ventilation systems for equipment that emits high concentrations of pollutants. In an office, a high-volume copier might require a separate room. Health clubs, laboratories, and kitchens also commonly have high-emittance equipment.
- When thermal insulation is needed, place it on the outside of ductwork. Use acoustical insulation that is encapsulated for the inside of ducts.
- Design the HVAC system with local controls so building maintenance personnel can correct heating, cooling, and ventilating problems as they arise.
- Specify independent building commissioning and testing, adjusting, and balancing (TAB) of the HVAC system at the completion of construction and any future renovation projects.

Establish Cood Maintenance Procedures

Once a building is completed, it must be properly maintained. The architect has little control over this aspect of indoor air quality, but through the proper selection of materials, development of maintenance manuals, and establishment of operating guidelines, the architect, mechanical engineer, interior designer, and other design professionals can provide the building owner with the basis for proper maintenance.

- Select and specify building materials and finishes that are easy to clean and maintain.
- Include requirements for warranties and maintenance contracts in the specifications.

- Suggest that the building owner conduct post-occupancy evaluations at regular intervals to review procedures for maintaining good IAQ.
- In the specifications, require that the contractor assemble an operation and maintenance manual with information provided by the various suppliers of HVAC and electrical equipment giving performance criteria, operation requirements, cleaning instructions, and maintenance procedures. This should be reviewed by the architect and mechanical engineer and then delivered to the owner for future reference.
- In the maintenance manual, include materials and procedures for regular cleaning of specified products, including furnishings. These techniques should use only low-emission cleaning agents recommended by the manufacturer of each product or finish. This manual should be reviewed by the architect and delivered to the owner for future reference.

Control Occupant Activity

As with maintenance procedures, the architect has little control over occupant activity once the building is completed. However, the architect can make suggestions to the building owner regarding methods of controlling occupant activity as it affects IAQ. The architect can also add long-term occupancy IAQ suggestions to the operation and maintenance manual. For example, the architect could do the following

- Suggest a no smoking policy for the building.
- Suggest that the building owner or manager monitor individual space use to determine when major changes to occupant load, activities, or equipment occur. When changes are made, the building HVAC system may need to be adjusted accordingly.
- Install sensors for CO, CO_2, VOCs, and other gases; these sensors should be connected to the building management system.

Provide Appropriate Filtration

Filtration is an effective way to keep indoor air free of particle air pollutants. The selection of filtering methods should be based on the needs of the type of occupancy. There are three basic types of filters that can be incorporated into an HVAC system.

- *Particulate filters* remove large particles such as dust and lint from the air and trap them in the filter. Particulate filters must be cleaned or replaced frequently. *Panel filters* trap only the largest particles, while *media filters* use finer filter paper. The most efficient filter is the *high-efficiency particulate arrestance filter* (or HEPA filter). Particulate filters other than HEPA filters are commonly located in front of the HVAC equipment to clean the air before it enters the unit. HEPA filters are located downstream from the cooling coils to ensure any microbiological contaminants from wet surfaces are removed.
- *Adsorption filters* remove unwanted gases from the air with activated carbon, which is produced from coal or from coconut shells. The structure and properties of the activated carbon remove vapors that are too small to be captured in HEPA filters, such as benzene and naphthalene (which was used in the past to make mothballs); these are found in small quantities in interior finish materials. As with particulate filters, adsorption filters must be replaced or regenerated to remain effective. Adsorption filters are typically located downstream from the HVAC unit to trap microbiological contaminants.
- *Electronic filters* trap particles by creating different electrostatic charges between the particles and the filter.

Indoor Air Quality Standards

Many laws, regulations, and standards have been enacted at the federal, state, and local levels that attempt to control and IAQ. OSHA has also proposed rules for IAQ. Some of the more important laws and regulations with which architects should be familiar include:

- Clean Air Act (CAA) of 1970. This law regulates air emissions from area, stationary, and mobile sources. This law requires the EPA to establish the National Ambient Air Quality Standards (40 CFR Part 50) to protect public health and the environment. These standards establish acceptable levels for six principal pollutants; carbon monoxide, lead, nitrogen dioxide, ozone, particle pollution, and sulfur dioxide. The CAA has been amended several times since 1970, most recently in 1990, to extend deadlines for compliance and add other provisions.

- ANSI/ASHRAE Standard 62.1, *Ventilation for Acceptable Indoor Air Quality.* This is an industry standard and, as such, compliance with it is voluntary unless the building code has incorporated all or a part of this standard by reference, thereby giving it the force of law. In addition to setting minimum outdoor air requirements for ventilation, the standard includes provisions for managing sources of contamination, controlling indoor humidity, and filtering building air, as well as requirements for HVAC system construction and startup, and operation and maintenance of systems.

- ANSI/ASHRAE Standard 62.2, *Ventilation and Acceptable Indoor Air Quality in Low-Rise Residential Buildings.* This is also a voluntary industry standard which may be incorporated into a building code by reference. The standard applies to single-family houses and multifamily buildings of three stories or less, including manufactured and modular homes. It defines the roles of and minimum requirements for mechanical and natural ventilation systems as well as requirements for the building envelope.

- National Volative Organic Compound (VOC) Emission Standards for Architectural Coatings (40 CFR Part 59). This rule implements part of the CAA and sets limits on the amount of volatile organic compounds that manufacturers and importers of architectural coatings can put into their products.

- South Coast Air Quality Management District (SCAQMD) Rule 1113, *Architectural Coatings.* This rule limits the VOC content of architectural coatings used in the South Coast Air Quality Management District in California. The limits it sets are more restrictive than the national VOC.

- Emission standards published by the EPA. Rule 1168 limits the VOC content of adhesives and sealants.

- California Safe Drinking Water and Toxic Enforcement Act of 1986 (Proposition 65). This law prohibits businesses from discharging chemicals that cause cancer or reproductive toxicity into sources of drinking water and requires that warning be given to individuals exposed to such chemicals. The California Environmental Protection Agency's Office of Environmental Health Hazard Assessment (OEHHA) is the lead agency for the implementation of Proposition 65.

- GREENGUARD Certification. To achieve GREENGUARD Certification, products are tested in accordance with ASTM Standards D5116 and D6670, the EPA's testing protocol for furniture, and the State of Washington's protocol for interior furnishings and construction materials. GREENGUARD lists emission levels that products must meet before they are certified by the organization.

- Documentation of the Threshold Limit Values and Biological Exposure Indices, American Conference of Governmental Industrial Hygienists (ACGIH). This document defines exposure limits—called *threshold limit values* (TLVs) for chemicals in the workplace.

- ASTM D5116, *Standard Guide for Small-Scale Environmental Chamber Determinations of Organic Emissions from Indoor Materials/Products.* This guide describes the equipment and techniques suitable for determining organic emissions from small samples of indoor materials. It cannot be used for testing complete assemblages or coatings. Another standard, ASTM D6803, is used for testing levels of volatile organic compounds in paint using small environmental chambers.

- ASTM D6670, *Standard Practice for Full-Scale Chamber Determination of Volatile Organic Emissions from Indoor Materials/Products.* This practice details the method to be used to determine the VOC emissions from building materials, furniture, consumer products, and equipment under environmental and product usage conditions that are typical of those found in office and residential buildings. It is referenced by other standards or laws as a way to determine the level of VOC emissions.

- ASTM E1333, *Standard Test Method for Determining Formaldehyde Concentrations in Air and Emission Rates from Wood Products Using a Large Chamber.* This test method measures the formaldehyde concentration in air and the emission rate from wood products in a large chamber under conditions designed to simulate product use.

  For a listing of additional regulations and industry standards related to sustainability, refer to the section later in this chapter.

RECYCLING AND REUSE

Recycling and reuse of materials and products is an important part of the total life cycle of a building. When a building is demolished or elements are removed, as many materials as possible should be recycled into other products or reused for their original purpose. In turn, new buildings should incorporate as many recycled and reused materials as possible to provide a market for those products. Ideally, all materials specified for a building project should be durable, biodegradable, or recyclable.

Adaptive Reuse

Adaptive reuse encourages reusing as much of the existing building stock as possible instead of constructing new buildings. Buildings can be either updated to return to their original use or adapted to a new use. Turning an old warehouse into residences is a common example of adaptive reuse. A project can receive LEED credit for reusing or renovating historic buildings or renovating abandoned or blighted buildings.

On a smaller scale, individual products can be reused in new buildings. These include building elements such as plumbing fixtures, doors, timber, and bricks. For example, heavy timber can be reused by re-sawing and planing. In most cases, using these old materials adds to the architectural character of the new building.

Reuse of existing materials conserves natural resources, reduces the amount of energy required to construct new buildings or products, lessens air and water pollution due to burning or dumping, and keeps materials from entering the waste stream.

Recycled Materials

Recyclability is the capacity of a previously used material for reuse as a resource in the manufacture of a new product. Melting down old steel to manufacture new steel is an example of recyclability.

Recycling materials is often difficult because the construction process requires the joining and integration of materials; when the products are removed from the building, it is difficult to separate different substances so that they can be individually marketed. Most of this separating must be done by hand, and in some cases (e.g., gypsum wallboard), the cost of separating all the component parts may be more than the cost of sending the material to a landfill.

Before selecting and specifying materials, the architect should research the recycled content of each product. A project can receive LEED*Adaptive reuse* encourages reusing as much of the existing building stock as possible instead of constructing new buildings. Buildings can be either updated to return to their original use or adapted to a new use. Turning an old warehouse into residences is a common example of adaptive reuse. A project can receive LEED credit for reusing or renovating historic buildings or renovating abandoned or blighted buildings. credit by using products that optimize the extraction process, which may include using reused materials or using recycled content.

Recycling of consumer products can be encouraged by providing bins, sorting and storage rooms for recycling, and other provisions as part of the building design. In some areas, local codes require that a portion of the trash area be reserved for recycling bins.

Building Disposal

If discarded products and materials cannot be reused or recycled, they must be incinerated or placed in a landfill for disposal. If a biodegradable material is placed in a landfill, it can break down quickly and return to the earth. Some materials, such as aluminum, most plastics, and steel, can take tens or even hundreds of years to decompose naturally. A project can receive LEED credits by diverting materials from the waste stream through reuse and recycling, or by minimizing the amount of construction waste generated.

Biobased products, or products made primarily from plant or animal materials, may be used to minimize disposal problems while conserving depletable raw materials. Using biobased products, such as adhesives, composite panels, gypsum wallboard substitutes, ceiling tiles, and carpet backing, also helps maintain good IAQ and provides a market for products of the rural economy. Biobased products may also be used to earn LEED credits.

HAZARDOUS MATERIAL MITIGATION

Hazardous materials are biological substances and other chemicals that pose a threat to the environment or to human health if released or misused.

In many cases, building sites or existing buildings may be contaminated with harmful chemicals, mold, mildew, and other hazardous materials. These contaminants can be building products, or components of products, that were installed before the hazards of the materials were fully understood, or they can be contaminants such as mold that were introduced through flooding or poor moisture management. These contaminants need to be identified and removed in accordance with best practices and in compliance with federal, state, and local regulations.

There are thousands of products and substances that can be defined as hazardous. A few of the more common ones found in buildings are described in the following sections.

Asbestos

Asbestos is a naturally occurring fibrous mineral found in certain types of rock formations. After mining and processing, asbestos consists of very fine fibers. Asbestos is known to cause lung cancer, asbestosis (a scarring of the lungs), and mesothelioma (a cancer of the lining of the chest or abdominal cavity). Oral exposure may be associated with cancer of the esophagus, stomach, and intestines. In buildings, exposure generally comes from airborne particles of asbestos that has become friable (easily crumbled) or that has been disturbed accidentally or by construction activities. Although generally not a problem in new construction, asbestos can be found in many types of building materials in older construction, such as pipe and blown-in insulation, asphalt flooring, vinyl sheet and tile flooring, construction mastics, ceiling tiles, textured paints, roofing shingles, cement siding, caulking, and vinyl wall coverings.

Asbestos is regulated under two federal laws and one federal agency restriction: the Clean Air Act (CAA) of 1970, the Toxic Substances Control Act (TSCA) of 1976, and the U.S. Consumer Product Safety Commission (CPSC). Under authority of the TSCA, in 1989 the EPA issued a ban on asbestos.

However, much of the original rule was vacated by the U.S. Fifth Circuit Court of Appeals in 1991. Products still banned include flooring felt, corrugated or specialty paper, commercial paper, and wallboard. The ban also prevents the use of asbestos in products that have not historically contained asbestos. Under the authority of the CAA, the National Emission Standards for Hazardous Air Pollutants (NESHAP) rules for asbestos ban the use of sprayed-on or wet-applied asbestos-containing materials (ACMs) for fireproofing and insulation. These rules took effect in 1973. NESHAP also bans the use of ACMs for decorative purposes. This took effect in 1978. The CPSC bans the use of asbestos in certain consumer products, such as textured paint and wall-patching compounds.

Testing for asbestos and mitigation efforts must be done by an accredited company following strict procedures. In many cases, if the asbestos has not been disturbed, it can be left in place because the EPA and NIOSH (National Institute for Occupational Safety and Health) have determined that intact and undisturbed asbestos materials do not pose a health risk. The asbestos may be encapsulated to protect it from becoming friable or from accidental damage. During building demolition or renovation, however, the EPA does require asbestos removal. This must be done by a licensed contractor certified for this type of work.

Vermiculite

Vermiculite is a hydrated laminar magnesium-aluminum-iron silicate that resembles mica. It is separated from mineral ore, which may include asbestos. When heated during processing, vermiculite expands into wormlike pieces. In construction, it is used for pour-in insulation, acoustic finishes, fire protection, and sound-deadening compounds. Vermiculite obtained from a mine in Montana is known to contain some amount of asbestos; the mine was closed in 1990. Vermiculite is still mined at other locations, but those have low levels of contamination and can be safely used.

Althought generally not a problem in new construction, asbestos can be found in many types of buiding materials in older construction.

The EPA recommends that attic insulation that may contain asbestos-contaminated vermiculite not be disturbed, and that any cracks in the ceiling be sealed. If the insulation must be removed, only a trained and certified professional contractor should perform the work.

Lead

Lead is a highly toxic metal that was once used in a variety of consumer and industrial products.

Exposure to lead can cause serious health problems, especially in children, including damage to the brain and nervous system, slowed growth, behavior problems, seizures, and even death. In adults, it can cause digestive and reproductive problems, nerve disorders, muscle and joint pain, and difficulties during pregnancy. Most exposure to lead comes from paint in homes built before 1978, and from soil and household dust that contains material from deteriorating lead-based paint. The federal government banned lead-based paint from housing in 1978.

Federal law requires that lead-based paint be removed by a certified professional and that lead-based paint be removed from some types of residential occupancies and child-occupied facilities by a certified company using approved methods for removal and disposal. Lead-based paint should not be removed by sanding, using a propane torch or heat gun, or dry scraping. Depending on the building type, covering the wall with a new layer of gypsum wallboard or simply repainting instead of removing the lead paint may be an acceptable alternative.

Lead-coated copper was also used in flashing, sheet metal panels, gutters, and downspouts before its health effects were understood. This material is no longer used due to the potential for soil contamination.

Radon

Radon is a colorless, odorless, tasteless, naturally occurring radioactive gas found in soils, rock, and water throughout the world. Radon causes lung cancer; most of the risk comes from breathing air contaminated with radon and its decay products.

Radon accumulates in spaces within a building that are in direct contact with the soil, such as basements. Most radon exposure occurs in places where people spend a lot of time in these lower-level spaces, such as homes, schools, and office buildings that were constructed before radon testing and installation of mitigation equipment was common, so most remedial work is done in existing buildings.

Testing for radon is easy and can be done by a trained contractor or by homeowners with kits available in hardware stores or through the mail. The EPA recommends that remedial action be taken if a radon level over 4 pCi/L is detected.

Remedial work should follow the radon mitigation standards of the EPA and ASTM E2121 and can include any or a combination of the following actions.

- sealing cracks in floors, walls, and foundations
- venting the soil outside the foundation wall
- depressurizing the voids within a block wall foundation (block wall depressurization)

- ventilating the crawl space with a fan (crawl space depressurization)
- using a vent pipe without a fan to draw air from under a slab to the outside (passive sub-slab depressurization)
- using a fan-powered vent to draw air from below the slab (active sub-slab depressurization)
- using a fan-powered vent to draw air from below a membrane laid on the crawl space floor (sub-membrane depressurization)

Polychlorinated Biphenyls (PCBs)

Polychlorinated biphenyls (PCBs) are mixtures of synthetic organic chemicals, with physical properties ranging from oily liquids to waxy solids. PCBs were used in many commercial and industrial applications, including building transformers, fluorescent light transformers, paints, coatings, and plastic and rubber products. PCBs are known to cause cancer and other adverse health effects afflicting the immune system, reproductive system, nervous system, and endocrine system. Because of concerns regarding the toxicity and persistence of PCBs in the environment, their manufacture and importation was banned in 1977 in the United States under the Toxic Substances Control Act (TSCA). The TSCA strictly regulates the use and disposal of PCBs.

If PCBs are discovered in building components or on site, they must be handled by a certified contractor and disposed of by incineration, dechlorination, or placement in an approved chemical waste landfill.

LIFE-CYCLE COST ANALYSIS

Life-cycle cost analysis (LCCA) is a method for determining the total cost of a building, building component, or system over a period of time. LCCA takes into account the initial cost as well as the costs of financing, operation, maintenance, and eventual disposal.

These costs are estimated over a length of time called the study period; the duration of the study period varies according to the needs of the client and the anticipated useful life of the item. For example, investors in a building may be interested in comparing various alternative materials over the expected investment time frame, while a city government may be interested in a longer time frame representing the expected life of the building. All future costs are discounted back to a common time, usually the base date, to account for the time value of money. The discount rate is used to convert future costs to their equivalent present values.

Using life-cycle cost analysis allows two or more alternatives to be evaluated and their total costs to be compared. This is especially useful when evaluating energy conservation measures where one design alternative may have a higher initial cost than another, but a lower overall cost because of energy savings. Some of the specific costs that factor into the life cycle cost of a building element include:

- initial costs, which include the cost of acquiring and installing the building, component, or system
- operational costs for electricity, water, and other utilities
- maintenance costs for the element over the length of the study period, including any anticipated repair costs
- replacement costs, if any, during the length of the study period
- finance costs required during the length of the study period
- taxes, if any, for initial costs and operating costs

The *residual value* is the remaining value of the element at the end of the study period based on resale value, salvage value, value in place, or scrap value. All the costs listed are estimated, discounted to their present value, and added together. Any residual value is discounted to its present value and then subtracted from the total to determine the final life-cycle cost of the element.

A life-cycle cost analysis is not the same as an LCA. An LCA analyzes the environmental impact of a product or building system over the entire life of the product or system.

SUSTAINABLE BUILDING PROGRAMS, RATING SYSTEMS, AND STANDARDS

Throughout the United States, Canada, and Great Britain, several organizations have emerged that provide industry-recognized ratings and standards for environmental design. These organizations develop objective criteria that designers must follow in order for a building or interior build-out to adhere to a particular standard or receive a particular rating. Although conforming to the criteria that these organizations establish is not mandatory by any building code, some governmental entities and large corporations may require that their designers follow an organization's guidelines. The following are the major programs, rating systems, and standards used in the United States, Canada, and Great Britain.

Building Research Establishment Environmental Assessment Method (BREEAM)

The *BRE Environmental Assessment Method* (BREEAM) is a certified environmental assessment method offered by the Building Research Establishment (BRE), a British organization that provides research-based consultancy, testing, and certification services covering all aspects of the built environment and associated industries.

BREEAM measures the environmental performance of building materials and products by evaluating buildings—including offices, industrial buildings, retail buildings, and homes—in the areas of management, energy use, health and well-being, pollution, transportation, land use, waste management, ecology, materials, and water use. Credits are awarded in each area and are added to produce a total score. The building is then given a rating of pass, good, very good, excellent, or outstanding, and awarded a certificate. A rating from one to five stars is also provided. For more information, visit the BREEAM website at breeam.com.

Collaborative for High Performance Schools (CHPS)

The Collaborative for High Performance Schools is a membership-based organization composed of public, private, and nonprofit organizations. Its goal is to increase the energy efficiency of schools in California and improve the quality of education offered within. CHPS publishes several manuals on best practices, holds training seminars, and maintains a list of low-emitting materials meeting the criteria of California's *Special Environmental Requirements, Specifications Section 01350* governing IAQ in buildings.

CHPS provides resources including assessment tools and criteria for recognition that are used by over 50 schools and districts in California and other states. For new construction and major modernizations, CHPS provides two different recognition programs: CHPS Designed is self-monitored, while CHPS Verified involves an independent review. Depending on the state in which it is located, a project may be eligible for either program or just one. For more information, go to the CHPS website at chps.net.

Section 01350

The state of California developed its *Special Environmental Requirements, Specifications Section 01350* in 2003 for construction of an addition to the state capitol complex. *Section 01350* was so successful in defining sustainability goals for that project that it was released for general use. The section has since been revised to comply with current CSI format and is known as "Section 01 35 00, General Requirements—Special Project Procedures" or simply as Section 01350.

Section 01350 covers key environmental performance issues related to the selection and handling of building materials. It gives specifications for testing emissions from interior finish materials and other elements that affect indoor air quality, screening building materials for hazardous content, and avoiding mold and mildew from construction. For more information, search for "Section 01350" at the website of California's Department of Resources Recycling and Recovery, calrecycle.ca.gov.

ENERGY STAR Buildings & Plants

ENERGY STAR Buildings & Plants is part of the EPA's ENERGY STAR program, which began in 1992. To earn an ENERGY STAR label, buildings and energy generation plants record a year's worth of energy performance, which is then compared to other, similar facilities and given a rating from 1 to 100. Facilities scoring 75 or higher are eligible for the ENERGY STAR label. The program also offers an online tool called Portfolio Manager that can be used to track the building's energy and water consumption over time. For more information, visit the ENERGY STAR website at energystar.gov.

Green Globes

Green Globes is a green building guidance and assessment program available in Canada and the United States. The program was developed by the Green Building Initiative (GBI), a nonprofit organization promoting practical green building approaches for residential and commercial construction.

Green Globes offers certification for commercial buildings in the categories of new construction, existing buildings, and sustainable interiors. Each building is assessed in areas such as energy use, indoor environment, site strategies, water use, use of resources, emissions, and project management. Assessment is on a 100-point scale for new construction and existing buildings and on a 1000-point scale for interiors. After the initial assessment, third-party assessors review the building and documentation; they may grant certification and award a rating of one to four globes. For more information, visit the GBI website at thegbi.org.

Project Planning

Leadership in Energy and Environmental Design (LEED)

The *Leadership in Energy and Environmental Design (LEED) Green Building Rating System* is a consensus-based building rating system designed to accelerate the development and implementation of green building practices in the United States. It was introduced in 2000 by the U.S. Green Building Council (USGBC), which is a national coalition of leaders from all aspects of the building industry working to promote buildings that are environmentally responsible and profitable and that provide healthy places to live and work. Since that time, it has been frequently updated to require improved building performance and address new technologies and best practices. The current version of the rating system, LEED v4, was opened in 2013.

There are several LEED rating systems that can be used for different building types, including new construction, existing buildings, operations and maintenance, commercial interiors, core and shell, schools, retail, health care, data centers, hospitality, warehouses and distribution, homes, and neighborhood development. To be LEED certified, a building must meet certain prerequisites as well as the requirements for additional credits in a variety of categories such as water efficiency, environmental quality, and materials and resources. Each LEED credit is worth one or more points. Depending on the total number of points earned, the building can be certified as one of five levels: effort, certified, silver, gold, and platinum. Table 13.2 shows the categories for one of the LEED rating systems.

For more information about LEED, visit the USGBC website at usgbc.org.

Leadership in Energy and Environmental Design Canada (LEED Canada)

The Canada Green Building Council (CaGBC) has adapted the LEED program for use in Canada. The requirements are largely the same, but some requirements can be met in alternative ways, and credits are included that address regional priorities. In addition, SI units are used and reference is made to Canadian standards and regulations. For more information, visit the CaGBC website at cagbc.org.

Table 13.2 LEED for New Construction (v4) Point Categories

category	possible points	percent of total
integrative process	1	1%
location and transportation	16	15%
materials and resources	13	12%
water efficiency	11	10%
energy and atmosphere	33	30%
sustainable sites	10	9%
indoor environmental quality	16	15%
innovation	6	5%
regional priority credits	4	3%

National Green Building Standard

The National Association of Home Builders (NAHB) and the International Code Council (ICC) developed ICC/ASHRAE 700, *National Green Building Standard*, along with companion publications, to provide guidance for builders engaged in or interested in green building products and practices for residential design, development, construction, and remodeling.

The standard covers seven areas.

- site design and development
- lot design, preparation, and development
- resource efficiency
- energy efficiency
- water efficiency
- indoor environmental quality
- operation, maintenance, and building owner education

After a home is constructed, the builder can request a third-party inspection and review. A successful project can be awarded a bronze, silver, gold, or emerald rating (emerald is the highest).

As a joint project of NAHB and ICC, this document is referenced by or references other ICC publications such as the *International Green Construction Code* (IgCC) and the *International Energy Conservation Code* (IECC). For more information, visit the NAHB website at nahbgreen.org.

WELL Building Standard

The *WELL Building Standard*, administered by the International WELL Building Institute (IWBI), is a standard that combines the best practices in design and construction with evidence-based health and wellness interventions. It measures the attributes of buildings by looking at seven factors.

- air
- water
- nourishment
- light
- fitness
- comfort
- mind

The *WELL Building Standard* is composed of 102 features that are applied to each building project. The standard is optimized for commercial and institutional buildings and can be applied to three project types: new construction and major renovations, tenant improvements, and core and shell developments. Future refinements are anticipated to address the unique requirements of multifamily residences, retail buildings, restaurants, sports facilities, convention centers, schools, and healthcare facilities. For more information, visit the WELL Building Standard website at wellcertified.com.

PRODUCT CERTIFICATION

A number of organizations and programs evaluate and certify building products as environmentally sound. The following are some of the most notable.

BIFMA

The Business and Institutional Furniture Manufacturer's Association (BIFMA) maintains two ANSI-approved standards for limiting volatile organic compound emissions from office furniture. These are ANSI/BIFMA M7.1, *Test Method for Determining VOC Emissions*, and ANSI/BIFMA X7.1, *Standard for Formaldehyde & TVOC Emissions.*

BIFMA has also developed ANSI/BIFMA e3, *Furniture Sustainability Standard.* This standard establishes minimum criteria in the four areas of materials, energy and atmosphere, human and ecosystem health, and social responsibility. A product that goes through the certification process conducted by one of two accredited third-party certifiers—NSF International or Scientific Certification Systems—can earn a rating of silver, gold, or platinum. For more information, visit the BIFMA website at bifma.org.

Cradle to Cradle

The Cradle to Cradle (C2C) Certified Product Standard program of McDonough Braungart Design Chemistry (MBDC) certifies products that use environmentally safe materials, are designed so that their materials that can be recovered and reused, use water and energy efficiently in their manufacturing, and are manufactured by socially responsible organizations. Acceptable materials are classified as *technical nutrients*, which are synthetic materials that can be reused without a loss in quality, or as *biological nutrients*, which are organic materials that will safely decompose into the natural environment after use. Products are assessed in five categories.

- material health
- material reutilization
- renewable energy and carbon management
- water stewardship
- social fairness

Levels of certification are basic, bronze, silver, gold, and platinum. For more information, visit the MBDC website at mbdc.com.

Eco-Certified Composite Sustainability Standard

The *Eco-Certified Composite (ECC) Sustainability Standard* is a voluntary standard developed by the Composite Panel Association (CPA) for manufacturers of products made with particleboard, MDF, hardboard, engineered wood siding, and engineered wood trim. The standard establishes requirements for the manufacture of unfinished composite panels and for finished products, including components and laminated panels.

Products are evaluated based on their carbon footprint, as determined through use of the CPA Carbon Calculator, use of local and renewable resources, use of recycled or recovered materials, sustainability, and wood sourcing. Unfinished panels must comply with the California Air Resources Board formaldehyde emission regulation before being considered for other ECC criteria. The ECC sustainability standard replaces the Composite Panel Association's Environmentally Preferable Product (EPP) specification and voluntary certification program. For more information, visit the Composite Panel Association's website at compositepanel.org.

ENERGY STAR

In addition to its building rating system, ENERGY STAR also offers a voluntary labeling program designed to identify energy-efficient products such as consumer appliances, office equipment, residential furnaces and air conditioning equipment, lighting, and consumer electronics. Products that qualify may place the ENERGY STAR label on their products, with their energy-saving features noted. For more information, visit the program's website at energystar.gov.

FloorScore

The FloorScore program of the Resilient Floor Covering Institute (RFCI) tests and certifies hard-surface flooring products and adhesives that comply with strict indoor air quality requirements in California's *Section 01350* specification and qualify for use in high-performance schools and office buildings in California. Products bearing the FloorScore seal have been certified by Scientific Certification Systems as meeting the requirements. For more information, visit the RFCI website at rfci.com.

Forest Stewardship Council (FSC)

The Forest Stewardship Council (FSC) is an international organization that oversees the development of national and regional standards for responsible forest management based on its FSC Principles and Criteria for Forest Stewardship. It accredits certifying organizations that comply with these principles.

The FSC logo on a wood product ensures that materials have come from environmentally conscious management and have followed the other FSC principles. For more information on the FSC, visit the FSC website at fsc.org.

Green Label Plus

The Green Label Plus program of the Carpet and Rug Institute (CRI) is a voluntary testing program for carpet, cushion, and adhesive that conforms to CHPS. Products carrying the Green Label Plus mark are certified as being low-emitting and meet the CHPS requirements as defined in California's *Section 01350* specification. For more information, visit the CRI website at carpet-rug.org.

Green Seal

Green Seal is an independent, nonprofit organization that strives to achieve a more sustainable world by promoting environmentally responsible production, purchasing, and products. Among other programs, Green Seal develops environmental standards for products in specific categories and certifies products that meet these standards. The organization meets the criteria of the International Organization for Standardization's ISO 14020 and ISO 14024 for eco-labeling. Green Seal's product evaluations are conducted by third-party organizations using a life-cycle approach that considers energy, resource use, and emissions to air, water, and land, as well as other effects on health and the environment. The Green Seal is awarded to products that meet the high standards of the program. For more information, visit the Green Seal website at greenseal.org.

GreenFormat

GreenFormat is a web-based database developed by the Construction Specifications Institute (CSI) to allow manufacturers to self-report sustainability properties of their products using a standard questionnaire format. The information is reported in six categories:

- general information
- product details
- product lifecycle
- manufacturer sustainability policies
- manufacturer support documentation
- manufacturer certification

Designers, contractors, and others can search the database according to these criteria. Although the information is self-reported, sustainability claims are verified by relating questions on the questionnaire to standards and certifications. For more information, visit the GreenFormat website at csinet.org.

GREENGUARD Certification

The GREENGUARD Certification Program, part of UL Environment, helps manufacturers to create, and buyers to identify, interior products and materials that have low chemical emissions. This program tests indoor products for emissions to ensure that they meet guidelines and standards for pollutants affecting indoor air quality. Products are tested for emissions of total VOCs, formaldehyde, total aldehydes, respirable particles, carbon monoxide, nitrogen oxide, and carbon dioxide.

If a product meets the standards of GREENGUARD, it is given GREENGUARD Certification or GREENGUARD Gold Certification. The Gold classification indicates that the product meets stricter criteria and is acceptable for use in environments such as schools and healthcare facilities. Certified products may carry a certification mark and are on placed on a searchable online database. For more information, visit the program's website at greenguard.org.

Health Product Declaration (HPD)

The Health Product Declaration, created and administered by the Health Product Declaration Collaborative, is an open standard format used by manufacturers for the reporting of contents and potential health hazards of materials. It is intended to provide transparency, openness, and innovation in the building industry's product supply chain. A HPD uses hazard information from governmental agencies and toxicology experts around the world and uses them in their GreenScreen List Translator screening tool and full GreenScreen analysis. The List Translator tool categorizes chemicals based on two types of lists. The first are authoritative lists that are maintained by government bodies. The second are screen lists, that include chemical that government bodies think need further evaluation, as well as chemical lists not recognized by any government body. During screening a chemical is then categorized into a particular hazard level. A full GreenScreen analysis looks at the full life cycle of a material or product, including the chemicals it's made from and the chemicals it's likely to break down into.

The HPD is an option for achieving credit in LEED version 4, in the Materials and Resources credit category, Building Product Disclosure and Optimization—Material Ingredient Reporting.

For more information, visit the HPDC website at www.hpd-collaborative.org.

International Organization for Standardization (ISO)

The International Organization for Standardization is a nongovernmental organization comprising national standards bodies from over 120 countries. ISO 14000 is a collection of standards and guidelines covering issues such as performance, product standards, labeling, environmental management, and life-cycle assessment as these relate to the environment. Several of the individual standards and guidelines are applicable to building products.

ISO 14020 describes a set of principles that should be followed by any practitioner of environmental labeling. ISO 14024 covers labeling programs and specifies the procedures and principles that third-party certifiers, or *ecolabelers*, should follow. For example, an organization should not have any financial interest in the products it certifies, it should conduct scientific evaluations using internationally accepted methods, and it should use a life-cycle approach when evaluating products. The ISO 14040 series of standards covers requirements for life-cycle assessments. For more information, visit the ISO website at iso.org.

Pharos Project

The Pharos Project, created by the Healthy Building Network, is a subscription-based online database that can be used for identifying health hazards associated with building products. The Pharos Project encourages manufacturers to disclose all ingredients in their products and helps architects and buildings owners avoid using products that contain harmful chemicals. For more information, visit the Pharos website at pharosproject.net.

SCS Global Services (SCS)

SCS Global Services (formerly Scientific Certification Systems) is a private organization that performs third-party environmental, sustainability, and food quality certification, auditing, testing, and standards development. SCS certifies other product rating programs and *environmentally preferable products*, which are products that have a reduced environmental impact when compared to similar products performing the same function. SCS's work is based on scientifically defensible, field-verifiable, performance measurement systems. Building products that are certified include carpet, nonwoven flooring, composite panel products, adhesives and sealants, furniture, paints, casework, ceiling tiles, and other wall coverings. SCS also certifies qualifying forests under their Forest Certification Program. For more information, visit the SCS's website at scsglobalservices.com.

SMaRT

The Sustainable Materials Rating Technology (SMaRT) program, overseen by the Institute for Market Transformation to Sustainability (MTS), identifies sustainable products by awarding points in several categories:

- safety for public health and environment
- renewable energy and energy reduction
- biobased or recycled materials
- facility or company based requirements
- reclamation, sustainable reuse and end of life management
- innovation in manufacturing

Products are certified at one of four levels: sustainable, sustainable silver, sustainable gold, and sustainable platinum. For more information, visit the MTS website at mts.sustainableproducts.com.

Sustainable Forestry Initiative (SFI)

The Sustainable Forestry Initiative is an independent, nonprofit organization dedicated to promoting sustainable forest management. The SFI's programs include forest certification, chain-of-custody certification, establishment of fiber sourcing requirements, and awarding of SFI labels. It has developed a *sustainable forestry initiative standard* (SFIS) that includes 13 principles and 15 objectives in the areas of land management, procurement, forestry research, training and education, legal and regulatory compliance, public and landowner involvement, and management review and continual improvement. An FSI label on a product indicates that the product has come from a certified forest.

The SFI program gives different types of product labels to participating companies that meet the SFI requirements based on both environmental and market demands. For more information, visit the SFI website at sfiprogram.org.

UL Environment

UL Environment is a program of Underwriters Laboratories that helps support the growth and development of sustainable products, services, and organizations in the global marketplace. It provides independent green claims validation, product certification, training, and advisory services and standards development. Among the claims UL Environment can validate are recycled content, rapidly renewable materials, regional materials, volatile organic compound emissions, volatile organic compound content, energy efficiency, water efficiency, hazardous or toxic substances, reclamation programs, mold resistance, manufacturing energy audits, degradability, and compostability.

UL Environment maintains the Sustainable Product Guide, a web-based database of products it has certified, which can streamline the verification process and paperwork required for compliance with LEED and other sustainable building programs. UL Environment also runs the GREENGUARD Certification Program. For more information, visit the UL Environment website at industries.ul.com/environment.

WaterSense

WaterSense is a program of the U.S. Environmental Protection Agency (EPA) that helps consumers identify water-efficient programs and products by the WaterSense label. Products are certified by independent, third-party licensed certifying bodies following testing and certification protocols specific to each product category. Certification is based on EPA criteria for water efficiency and performance. For more information, visit the WaterSense website at epa.gov/watersense.

REGULATIONS AND INDUSTRY STANDARDS RELATED TO SUSTAINABILITY

- ANSI/ASHRAE/IES Standard 90.1, *Energy Standard for Buildings Except Low-Rise Residential Buildings.* This is a voluntary industry standard that gives information on minimum standards for energy efficiency, building envelope requirements, zone isolation, insulation for floors, ceilings, and roofs, and power allowance calculation. Standard 90.1 is written in mandatory enforceable language suitable for code adoption and is referenced by the International Energy Conservation Code.
- ANSI/ASHRAE/USGBC/IES Standard 189.1, *Standard for the Design of High-Performance Green Buildings Except Low-Rise Residential Buildings.* This is a voluntary standard developed by the American Society of Heating, Refrigerating and Air-Conditioning Engineers (ASHRAE), in conjunction with the American National Standards Institute (ANSI), the Illuminating Engineering Society (IES), and the U.S. Green Building Council (USGBC). Although voluntary, it is written in such a way that it can be adopted by building code organizations or local jurisdictions. It covers a wide range of requirements including site sustainability, water efficiency, energy efficiency, indoor environmental quality, and the building's impact on the atmosphere, materials, and resources.
- ASTM Standard E2114, *Standard Terminology for Sustainability Relative to the Performance of Buildings*
- ASTM Standard E2129, *Standard Practice for Data Collection for Sustainability Assessment of Building Products*
- GS-11, *Green Seal Standard for Paints, Coatings, Stains, and Sealers*, product standard for paints and coatings applied on-site
- GS-13, *Green Seal Standard for Windows*, product standard for residential fenestration products
- *International Energy Conservation Code* (IECC). This model code was developed by the International Code Council (ICC) to regulate minimum energy conservation requirements for new buildings. It addresses requirements for all aspects of energy uses in both commercial and residential construction, including heating and ventilating, lighting, water heating, and power usage for appliances and building systems. The code is designed to work with the other ICC codes and incorporates ANSI/ASHRAE/IES Standard 90.1 as an alternative path to compliance.
- *International Green Construction Code* (IgCC). This model code was also developed by the ICC and provides a way to include sustainability measures for the entire construction project and its site. It provides a regulatory framework for new and existing buildings for commercial construction, as well as applies to all residential buildings over three stories. The code is designed to work with the other ICC codes and incorporates ANSI/ASHRAE/USGBC/IES Standard 189.1 as an alternative path to compliance.
- ICC/ASHRAE 700, *National Green Building Standard.* This was developed by the National Association of Home Builders and the ICC to provide a sustainable standard for residential building. ICC/ASHRAE 700 uses the IECC as a basis and applies to single-family houses, low- and high-rise multifamily buildings, home remodeling, hotels and motels, and the site work associated with these projects.
- *Toxic Substances Control Act (TSCA) of 1976.* This law was enacted to give the Environmental Protection Agency (EPA) the authority to track and regulate over 75,000 industrial chemicals produced or imported into the United States. It allows the EPA to ban the manufacture and import of those chemicals that pose an unreasonable risk.

DEFINITIONS

coproduct: A marketable by-product from a process. Materials traditionally considered to be waste but that can be repurposed as raw materials in a different manufacturing process are considered coproducts.

demand control ventilation: A system designed to adjust the amount of ventilation air provided to a space based on the extent of occupancy. The system normally uses carbon dioxide sensors but may also use occupancy sensors or air quality sensors.

detention: The temporary storage of storm runoff in a detention facility to control peak discharge rates and to provide gravity settling of pollutants. The detention facility is designed to provide for a gradual release of stored water at a controlled rate.

drainage easement: The legal right granted by a landowner to a grantee, commonly a governmental entity, allowing the use of private land for stormwater management.

embodied energy: The total energy required to extract, produce, fabricate, and deliver a material to a job site, including the collection of raw materials, the energy used to extract and process the raw materials, transportation from the original site to the processing plant or factory, the energy required to turn the raw materials into a finished product, and the energy required to transport the material to the job site.

fee in lieu: Payment of money by a developer in place of meeting all or part of stormwater performance standards.

hydrologic soil group (HSG): Soils, classification for runoff potential A classification of soils based on their potential for runoff when thoroughly wet. As defined by the National Resources Conservation Service (NRCS), there are four groups ranging from Group A, which contains soils high in gravel and sand that have high permeability and low runoff potential, to Group D, which contains clayey soils that have low permeability and high runoff potential.

infiltration: The process of percolating stormwater into the subsoil.

post-consumer: Referring to a material or product that has served its intended use and has been diverted or recovered from waste destined for disposal, having completed its life as a consumer item.

post-industrial: Referring to materials generated in manufacturing processes, such as trimmings or scrap, that have been recovered or diverted from solid waste. Also called *pre-consumer.*

pre-consumer: see *post-industrial.*

recovered materials: Waste or by-products that have been recovered or diverted from solid waste disposal. This term does not apply to materials that are generated from or reused within an original manufacturing process.

renewable product: A product that can be grown or naturally replenished or cleansed at a rate that exceeds human depletion of the resource.

sustainability: The condition of being able to meet the needs of the present generation without compromising the needs of future generations.

watercourse: Any body of water, such as a lake, pond, river, or stream.

waterway: A channel that directs surface runoff to a watercourse or to a public storm drain.

14

CODES AND REGULATIONS DURING DESIGN DEVELOPMENT

Nomenclature

A	area	ft^2
A_a	allowable area	ft^2
A_t	tabular allowable area, from Table 14.10	ft^2
F	length of portion of building that fronts a public way or open space ($\geq$ 20 ft)	ft
I_f	area factor increase based on frontage	–
L	length of portion of building perimeter	ft
NS	tabular allowable area factor for non-sprinklered buildings	ft^2
P	building perimeter	ft
S_a	number of building stories above grade plane	–
w	width of public way along a particular portion of a building's perimeter	ft
W	width of public way or open space (fixed value or weighted average)	ft

During the entire design process, from programming to the development of construction documents, the architect must be mindful of what building codes and zoning regulations apply and what they require.

Most of the effort of researching and complying with codes and regulations, however, is made during the design development stage. This is when the myriad code requirements must be applied to the project design as the basic shape of the building takes form. These requirements will affect the egress system, fire protection, materials selection, energy conservation, accessibility, structural needs, mechanical and electrical systems, and other aspects of the design.

This chapter reviews many of the code and zoning requirements that must be applied during design development. It expands on the preliminary considerations that are discussed in Chap. 8. See Chap. 15 for requirements for barrier-free design and Chap. 48 for requirements for detailed building code reviews.

FIRE-RESISTANCE STANDARDS

Building codes recognize that there is no such thing as a fireproof building; there are only degrees of fire resistance. Because of this, the codes specify requirements for two broad classifications of fire resistance: the resistance of construction materials and assemblies, and the surface burning characteristics of finish materials.

Construction Materials and Assemblies

The *fire-resistance rating* of a construction material or assembly is typically the length of time that the item can withstand a standardized fire resistance test. For example, ASTM Standard E119, *Standard Test Methods for Fire Tests of Building Construction and Materials* defines standard test methods for walls, ceiling/floor assemblies, columns, beam enclosures, and other building elements. NFPA 252, *Standard Methods of Fire Tests of Door Assemblies*, and NFPA 257, *Standard on Fire Test for Window and Glass Block Assemblies*, define standard test methods for doors and glazing, respectively. See Chap. 8 for a discussion of these standards.

Building codes typically specify the minimum fire-resistance ratings that building elements must have in various circumstances. For example, exit-access corridors are often required to have at least a 1-hour rating, and the door assemblies in such a corridor may be required to have a 20-minute rating.

Various building elements must be protected with the types of construction specified in Table 601 in the *International Building Code* (IBC) (see Table 14.1) and elsewhere in the code. When a fire-resistive barrier is required, any penetrations in the barrier must also be fire rated. This includes doors, windows, and ducts.

Other sources of information for acceptable construction assemblies include the *Online Certifications Directory* by Underwriters Laboratories (UL), UL's online *Product SPEC* search engine, and manufacturers' proprietary product literature.

Duct penetrations are protected with fire dampers placed in line with the wall. A *fire damper* is a listed device installed in ducts and air transfer openings that is designed to close automatically on detection of heat, to resist the passage of flame. If a fire occurs, a fusible link in the damper closes a louver that maintains the rating of the wall.

Table 14.1
Fire-Resistance Rating Requirements for Building Elements (hours)

building element	type I		type II		type III		type IV (heavy timber, HT)	type V	
	A	B	A	B	A	B	HT	A	B
primary structural frame[f]	3[a]	2[a]	1	0	1	0	HT	1	0
bearing walls									
exterior[e,f]	3	2	1	0	2	2	2	1	0
interior	3[a]	2[a]	1	0	1	0	1/HT	1	0
nonbearing walls and partitions exterior	See IBC Table 602.								
nonbearing walls and partitions interior[d]	0	0	0	0	0	0	See IBC Sec. 602.4.6.	0	0
floor construction and associated secondary members (see IBC Sec. 202)	2	2	1	0	1	0	HT	1	0
roof construction and associated secondary members (see IBC Sec. 202)	$1\frac{1}{2}$[b]	1[b,c]	1[b,c]	0[c]	1[b,c]	0	HT	1[b,]	0

[a]Roof supports: Fire-resistance ratings of primary structural frame and bearing walls are permitted to be reduced by 1 hour where supporting a roof only.
[b]Except in Group F-1, H, M, and S-1 occupancies, fire protection of structural members shall not be required, including protection of roof framing and decking where every part of the roof construction is 20 ft or more above any floor immediately below. Fire-retardant-treated wood members shall be allowed to be used for such unprotected members.
[c]In all occupancies, heavy timber shall be allowed where a 1-hour or less fire-resistance rating is required.
[d]Not less than the fire-resistance rating required by other sections of this code.
[e]Not less than the fire-resistance rating based on fire separation distance (see IBC Table 602).
[f]Not less than the fire-resistance rating as referenced in IBC Sec. 704.10.

2015 International Building Code, International Code Council, Inc., Washington, D.C. Reproduced with permission. www.iccsafe.org

Smoke dampers may also be required in certain locations. A *smoke damper* is a listed device installed in ducts and air transfer openings that is designed to resist the passage of smoke. Smoke dampers may be controlled by a smoke detection system to operate automatically, or may be operable, where required, from a fire command center. There are also combination fire/smoke dampers. Section 717.5 in the IBC details the required locations of fire and smoke dampers and lists many exceptions to the requirements.

Determining the fire resistance ratings of existing building components is important in determining the construction type of the building.

Individual materials by themselves do not create a fire-rated barrier. It is the construction assembly of which they are a part that is fire resistant. A 1-hour rated suspended ceiling, for example, must use rated ceiling tile, but it is the entire assembly—including the tile, the suspension system, and the structural floor above—that carries the 1-hour rating. In a similar way, a 1-hour rated partition may consist of a layer of $\frac{5}{8}$ in Type X gypsum board attached to both sides of a wood or metal stud according to certain conditions. A single piece of gypsum board does not have a fire-resistance rating by itself, except under special circumstances defined by the IBC.

Types of Fire-Resistance-Rated Walls and Partitions

One of the most common types of construction assemblies is the partition. The IBC makes important distinctions between various types of fire-resistance-rated walls and partitions. These include fire partitions, fire barriers, fire walls, and smoke barriers. Fire partitions are one of the most common fire-resistance-rated partitions used.

A *fire partition* is a wall assembly with a 1-hour fire-resistance rating. Fire partitions must be used in the following designated locations.

- walls separating dwelling units such as rooms in apartments, dormitories, and assisted living facilities
- walls separating guestrooms in Group R-1 occupancies, such as hotels, as well as Group R-2 and Group I-1 occupancies
- walls separating tenant spaces in covered and open mall buildings
- corridor walls
- elevator lobby separation for Groups I-2, I-3, and high-rise buildings and elsewhere where required by the code

Figure 14.1
Options for Fire Partition Construction

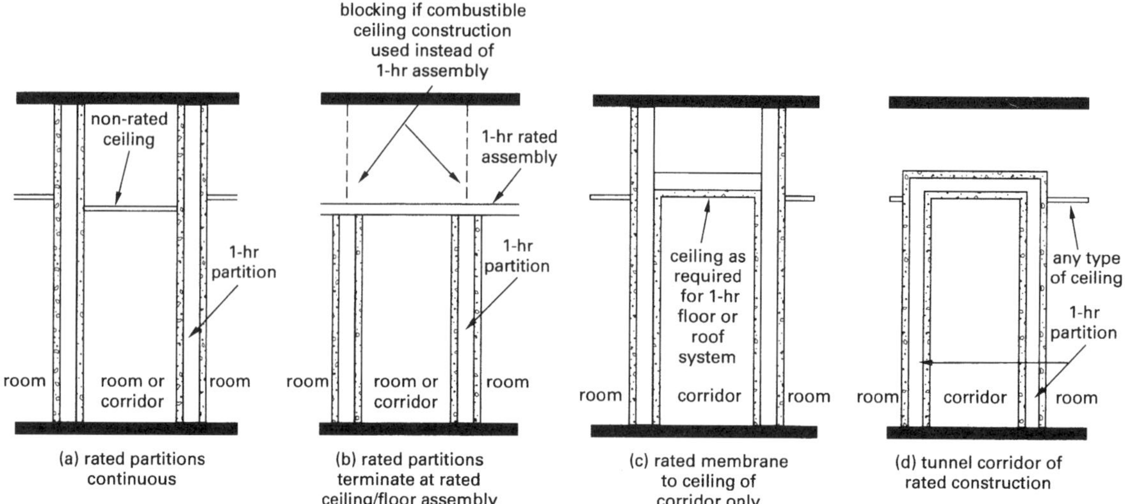

There are some exceptions, including corridor walls permitted to be nonrated by the IBC (see Table 14.14) and dwelling and guestroom separations in Types IIB, IIIB, and VB buildings equipped with automatic sprinkler systems. In these construction types, separation walls may be $^{1}/_{2}$-hour rated. Fire partitions are also not required for corridors in a dwelling unit or sleeping unit in Groups I-1 and R occupancies, for corridors in Group B occupancies where only a single means of egress is required, or for corridors in Group E occupancies where each classroom has at least one door that opens directly to the exterior at ground level.

In most cases, fire partitions must provide a continuous barrier. This means that they must extend from the floor to the underside of the floor or roof slab above, or to the ceiling of a fire-resistance-rated floor/ceiling or roof/ceiling assembly. They must be securely attached top and bottom and extend continuously through concealed spaces, except where permitted to terminate below a fire-resistance-rated floor/ceiling or roof/ceiling assembly. There are several exceptions. Some of the more commonly used fire partitions are shown in Fig. 14.1. See Sec. 708 of the IBC for complete information.

Openings in fire partitions must have a minimum rating of $^{3}/_{4}$ hour, except for corridors, which must be protected by 20-minute fire-protection assemblies.

Although two options are available for separating rooms with fire partitions (as shown in Fig. 14.1(a) and Fig. 14.1(b)) and four options are available for corridor separation, continuous slab-to-slab partitions are usually the best option for commercial construction. These partitions provide the best passive control of smoke and fire without relying on the integrity of a ceiling assembly, and are often the easiest and least costly for contractors to construct, although there could be instances where other methods may be preferred.

A *fire barrier* is a vertical or horizontal assembly that is fire-resistance rated and that is designed to restrict the spread of fire, confine it to limited areas, and/or afford safe passage for protected egress. In general terms, a fire barrier offers more protection than a fire partition. Fire barriers are used to

- enclose vertical exit enclosures (stairways), exit passageways, horizontal exits, and incidental use areas
- separate different occupancies in a mixed occupancy situation
- separate single occupancies into different fire areas
- otherwise provide a fire barrier where specifically required by a code provision in the IBC as well as the other international codes

Unlike fire partitions, fire barriers must always be continuous from the floor slab to the underside of the floor or roof slab above. There are only a few exceptions. Fire barriers may also be required to have a fire-resistance rating greater than 1 hour.

The degree of protection that an opening in fire barrier must have can vary from 45 minutes to 3 hours, depending on the rating of the fire barrier itself. Requirements for typical interior partitions and exterior walls and high-rated interior partitions are summarized in Table 14.2 and Table 14.3; see IBC Table 716.5 for complete information. This includes requirements and limitations for window and sidelight glazing, as well as for doors and glazing in doors.

These tables are organized according to partition type and location within a building, but in all cases, openings are limited to a maximum aggregate width of 25% of the length of the wall. Any single opening cannot exceed 156 ft^2 in area.

Some exceptions to these requirements are

- Openings can be greater than 156 ft^2 if adjoining fire areas are equipped throughout with an automatic sprinkler system.
- Fire doors serving an exit enclosure can exceed the previous limitation.

Openings are not limited to 156 ft^2 or 25% of the length of the wall if the opening protective assembly has been tested according to ASTM E119 and has a fire-resistance rating equal to or greater than that of the wall. This allows special fire-rated glazing to be used.

Each glazing assembly must be marked with an abbreviation to indicate the fire test standard that it meets. A number following the abbreviation gives the time, in minutes, of the fire resistance or fire protection rating.

- W: meets the wall assembly criteria of ASTM E119
- OH: meets the fire window assembly criteria, including the hose stream test, of NFPA 257
- D: meets the fire door assembly criteria of NFPA 252, UL 10B, or UL 10C
- H: meets the fire door assembly hose stream test of NFPA 252, UL 10B, or UL 10C
- T: meets for 30 minutes the 450°F temperature rise criteria of NFPA 252, UL 10B, or UL 10C

Not just openings, but also penetrations (as for pipes and conduit), joints (between the partition and other construction), ducts, and air transfer openings must be protected as specified in the code.

A *fire wall* is a fire-resistance-rated wall that is used to separate a single structure into separate construction types or to provide for allowable area increases by creating what amounts to separate buildings even though they are attached. Fire walls are unique in that, in addition to having 2- to 4-hour fire-resistance ratings, they must extend continuously from the foundation to or through the roof, and they must be designed and constructed in such a way that, under fire conditions, the structure on one side can collapse without affecting the structural stability of the adjacent building.

A *smoke barrier* is a continuous vertical or horizontal membrane with a minimum fire- resistance rating of 1 hour that is designed and constructed to restrict the movement of smoke. It is a passive form of smoke control. Openings in smoke barriers must have at least a 20-minute rating.

When a single fire assembly is designed to serve multiple purposes, such as to be both a fire barrier and a fire wall, the assembly must meet the applicable requirements of both.

Finishes

Single layers of finish material are rated according to ASTM E84, and their use is restricted to certain areas of buildings based on their rating, the occupancy group, and whether or not the building is sprinklered. See Table 14.4. This type of regulation is intended to control the flame-spread rate along the surface of a material and to limit the amount of combustible material in a building.

The finishes that are tested and rated according to surface burning characteristics include wainscoting, paneling, heavy wall covering, and other finishes applied structurally or for decoration, acoustical correction, surface insulation, or similar purposes. In most cases, the restrictions do not apply to trim, such as chair rails, baseboards, and handrails; to doors, windows, or their frames; or to materials that are less than 0.036 in (about $^1/_{28}$ in) thick and are cemented to the surface of noncombustible walls or ceilings.

Project Planning

Table 14.2 Opening Protective Requirements for Interior Partitions

partitions				doors		sidelight/transom glazing			
						fire-protection-rated glazing		fire-resistance-rated glazing	
use of partition	type[a]	fire rating	fire rating (hr)	max. glass area (in^2)	glazing marking[b]	glazing fire rating and marking	max. glass area	glazing fire rating and marking IBC Table 716.5	max. glass area[c]
corridor wall, nonsprinklered A, B, E, F, M, S, U (occupant load > 30)	FP	1	1/3	MST	D-20	3/4D-H-OH-45	MST	3/4D-H-OH-45	MST
corridor wall, sprinklered A, B, E, F, M, S, U, occupant load > 30; I-2[d], I-4, all occupant loads	FP	0	0	NL	not required	NL	NL	not required	NL
corridor wall, sprinklered, occupant load > 10, R	FP	0.5	1/3	MST	D-20	1/3D-H-OH-20	MST	1/3D-H-OH-20	MST
walls separating dwelling units	FP	1	3/4	MST	D-H-45	3/4D-H-45	MST	3/4D-H-45	MST
same, types IIB, IIIB, VB[e]	FP	0.5	1/3	MST	D-H-20	1/3D-H-20	MST	1/3D-H-20	MST
walls separating guestrooms, Groups R-1, R-2, I-1	FP	1	3/4	MST	D-H-45	3/4D-H-45	MST	3/4D-H-45	MST
same, types IIB, IIIB, VB[e]	FP	0.5	1/3	MST	D-H-20	1/3D-H-20	MST	1/3D-H-20	MST
party walls in covered malls	FP	1	3/4	MST	D-H-45	3/4D-H-45	MST	3/4D-H-45	MST
elevator lobby separation, where required, see 3006	FPSB	1	3/4	MST	FP: D-H-45SB: D-20	3/4D-H-OH-45	MST	3/4D-H-OH-45	MST
stairway walls, < 4 stories; exit passageways, 1 hour	FB	1	1	100	≤100 in^2 D-H-60; >100 in^2 D-H-T-60 or D-H-T-W-60	NP	NP	1W-60	MST
stairway walls, ≥ 4 stories; exit passageways, 2 hour	FB	2	1 1/2	100	≤100 in^2 D-H-90; >100 in^2 D-H-T-90 or D-H-T-W-90	NP	NP	2W-120	MST
1 hour occupancy separation; separate incidental uses	FB	1[h]	3/4[b]	MST	D-H-NT-45	3/4D-H-NT-45	see 707.6	3/4D-H-NT-45	MST
occupancy separation	FB	2[I]	1 1/2	100	≤100 in^2 D-H-90; >100 in^2 or D-H-W-90	NP	NP	2W-120	MST
smoke barriers	SB	1	1/3	MST	D-20	3/4D-H-OH-45	see 716.6	3/4D-H-OH-45	MST

[a]Assembly types: FB = fire barrier; FW = fire wall; SB = smoke barrier; NL = no limit; NP = not permitted; MST = maximum size tested. See the IBC for definitions of assembly types.
[b]See IBC Sec. 716.3.
[c]See manufacturer's data for size limitations for fire-resistance-rated glazing.
[d]I-2 occupancies also require smoke barrier.
[e]Must be sprinklered in these construction types.
[f]Smoke barrier allowed if building is sprinklered.
[g]See the IBC for four instances where 2-hour separation may be required. In most, but not all, cases sprinkler system may substitute for 1-hour rating.
[h]1-hour occupancy separation requires 3/4-hour door and is most common for most interior design situations.
[I]See the IBC for required hourly ratings, sprinkler use, and other exceptions.

Table 14.3 Opening Protective Requirements for Exterior Walls, High-rated Fire Walls and Fire Barriers

walls and partitions			doors			window/sidelite/transom glazing			
						fire-protection-rated glazing		fire-resistance-rated glazing	
use of wall or partition	type[a]	fire rating	fire rating (hr)	max. glass area[b] (in^2)	glazing marking[b]	glazing fire rating and marking	max. glass area	glazing fire rating and marking IBC Table 716.5	max. glass area[c]
3-hour exterior wall	FW	3	$1\frac{1}{2}$	100[a]	≤100 in^2 D-H-90; >100 in^2 D-H-W-90	NP	NP	3W-180	MST
2-hour exterior wall	FW	2	$1\frac{1}{2}$	100[a]	≤100 in^2 D-H-90; >100 in^2 D-H-W-90	NP	NP	2W-120	MST
1-hour exterior wall	FW	1	$\frac{3}{4}$	MST	D-H-45	$\frac{3}{4}$D-H-45	MST	$\frac{3}{4}$D-H-45	MST
fire wall; H-1, H-2	FW	4	3	NP	NP	NP	NP	4W-240	MST
fire wall; F-1, H-3, H-5, M, S-1	FW	3	3[d]	NP	NP	NP	NP	3W-180	MST
fire wall; A, B, E, H-4, I, R-1, R-2, U	FW	3	3[d]	NP	NP	NP	NP	3W-180	MST
fire wall; A, B, E, H-4, I, R-1, R-2, U for Type II or V construction	FW	2	$1\frac{1}{2}$	100[b]	≤100 in^2 D-H-90; >100 in^2 D-H-W-90	NP	NP	2W-120	MST
fire wall; F-2, S-2, R-3, R-4	FW	2	$1\frac{1}{2}$	100[b]	≤100 in^2 D-H-90; >100 in^2 D-H-W-90	NP	NP	2W-120	MST
horizontal exit	FW	2	$1\frac{1}{2}$	100[b]	≤100 in^2 D-H-90; >100 in^2 D-H-W-90	NP	see IBC Sec. 706.8	2W-120	MST
fire area separation; H-1, H-2	FB	4	3	NP	NP	NP	NP	4W-240	MST
fire area separation; F-1, H-3, S-1	FB	3	3[d]	NP	NP	NP	NP	3W-180	MST
fire area separation; A, B, E, F-2, H-4, H-5, I, M, R, S-2	FB	2	$1\frac{1}{2}$	100[b]	≤100 in^2 D-H-90; >100 in^2 D-H-W-90	NP	NP	2W-120	MST
fire area separation; U	FB	1	$\frac{3}{4}$	MST	D-H-NT-45	$\frac{3}{4}$D-H-NT-45	see IBC Sec. 707.6	$\frac{3}{4}$D-H-NT-45	MST
3-hour occupancy separation	FB	3	3[d]	NP	NP	NP	NP	3W-180	MST
4-hour occupancy separation	FB	4	3[d]	NP	NP	NP	NP	4W-240	MST

[a]Assembly types: FB = fire barrier; FW = fire wall; NP = not permitted; MST = maximum size tested. See the IBC for definitions of assembly types.
[b]Fire-resistive-rated glazing may be the maximum size tested if tested according to ASTM E119.
[c]See manufacturer's data for size limitations for fire-resistance-rated glazing.
[d]Two doors, each with a rating of $1\frac{1}{2}$ hour, installed on opposite sides of the same opening is deemed equivalent to one 3-hour door.
[e]In Type II or V construction, walls are permitted to have a 2-hour fire-resistive rating.

2015 International Building Code, International Code Council, Inc., Washington, D.C. Reproduced with permission. www.iccsafe.org

Project Planning

Table 14.4
Interior Wall and Ceiling Finish Requirements by Occupancy[k]

	sprinklered[l]			nonsprinklered		
group	interior exit stairways and ramps and exit passageways[a, b]	corridors and enclosure for exit access stairways and ramps	rooms and enclosed spaces[c]	interior exit stairways and ramps and exits passageways[a, b]	corridors and enclosure for exit access stairways and ramps	rooms and enclosed spaces[c]
A-1 & A-2	B	B	C	A	A[d]	B[e]
A-3[f], A-4, A-5	B	B	C	A	A[d]	C
B, E, M, R-1	B	C	C	A	B	C
R-4	B	C	C	A	B	B
F	C	C	C	B	C	C
H	B	B	C[g]	A	A	B
I-1	B	C	C	A	B	B
I-2	B	B	B[h, i]	A	A	B
I-3	A	A[j]	C	A	A	B
I-4	B	B	B[h, i]	A	A	B
R-2	C	C	C	B	B	C
R-3	C	C	C	C	C	C
S	C	C	C	B	B	C
U		no restrictions			no restrictions	

[a]Class C interior finish materials shall be permitted for wainscotting or paneling of not more than 1000 ft^2 of applied surface area in the grade lobby where applied directly to a noncombustible base or over furring strips applied to a noncombustible base and fireblocked as required by IBC Sec. 803.13.1.
[b]In other than Group I-3 occupancies in buildings less than three stories above grade plan, Class B interior finish for nonsprinklered buildings and Class C interior finish for sprinklered buildings shall be permitted in interior exit stairways and ramps.
[c]Requirements for rooms and enclosed spaces shall be based upon spaces enclosed by partitions. Where a fire-resistance rating is required for structural elements, the enclosing partitions shall extend from the floor to the ceiling. Partitions that do not comply with this shall be considered enclosing spaces and the rooms or spaces on both sides shall be considered one. In determining the applicable requirements for rooms and enclosed spaces, the specific occupancy thereof shall be the governing factor regardless of the group classification of the building or structure.
[d]Lobby areas in Group A-1, A-2, and A-3 occupancies shall not be less than Class B materials.
[e]Class C interior finish materials shall be permitted in places of assembly with an occupants load of 300 persons or less.
[f]For places of religious worship, wood used for ornamental purposes, trusses, paneling, or chancel furnishing shall be permitted.
[g]Class B material is required where the building exceeds two stories.
[h]Class C interior finish materials shall be permitted in administrative spaces.
[i]Class C interior finish materials shall be permitted in rooms with a capacity of four persons or less.
[j]Class B materials shall be permitted as wainscotting extending not more than 48 in above the finished floor in corridors and exit access stairways and ramps.
[k]Finish materials as provided for in other sections of the IBC.
[l]Applies when protected by an automatic sprinkler system installed in accordance with IBC Sec. 903.3.1.1 or Sec. 903.3.1.2.

2015 International Building Code, International Code Council, Inc., Washington, D.C. Reproduced with permission. www.iccsafe.org

The test defined in ASTM E84 is the most common for interior finishes, but as an alternative, the IBC also allows the use of finish materials other than textiles if they meet certain requirements when tested in accordance with NFPA 286, *Standard Methods of Fire Tests for Evaluating Contribution of Wall and Ceiling Interior Finish to Room Fire Growth* and when a Class A finish would otherwise be required. The NFPA 286 test is described in Chap. 8.

Textile wall coverings must comply with one of three conditions.

- be rated as Class A according to ASTM E84 and be protected by an automatic sprinkler system
- meet the requirements the Method B test protocol of NFPA 265
- meet the requirements of NFPA 286

Textile finishes for ceilings must meet the requirements of either ASTM E84 with sprinklers or NFPA 286.

The *International Building Code* (IBC) regulates the ratings of some floor coverings, including textile coverings or those composed of fibers (i.e., carpet). It specifically excludes traditional flooring types such as wood, vinyl, linoleum, and terrazzo.

The IBC requires textile or fiber floor coverings to belong to one of two classes as defined by the flooring radiant panel test described in NFPA 253, *Standard Method of Test for Critical Radiant Flux of Floor Covering Systems Using a Radiant Heat Energy Source.* In this test, the amount of radiant energy needed to sustain flame is measured and defined as the critical radiant flux. Class I materials have a critical radiant flux of not less than 0.45 W per square centimeter, and Class II materials have a critical radiant flux of not less than 0.22 W per square centimeter. Class I materials are more resistant to flame spread than Class II materials. Class I finishes are typically required in vertical exits, exit passageways, and exit access corridors in Group I-I, I-2, and I-3 occupancies (hospitals, nursing homes, and detention facilities). Class II flooring is typically required in the same areas of Groups A, B, E, H, I-4, M, R-1, R-2, and S occupancies. In other areas, carpet must conform to DOC FF-1 (CPSC 16 CFR, Part 1630), the pill test, or to ASTM D2859. See Chap. 29 for more information on the pill test.

Exceptions apply if the building is equipped with an automatic sprinkler system; Class II materials are permitted in any area where Class I materials would otherwise be required. In addition, materials complying with DOC FF-1 may be used in other areas.

See Chap. 29 for a discussion of carpet flammability and tests specifically related to carpet.

Decorations and Trim

Curtains, draperies, hangings, and other decorative materials suspended from walls or ceilings in other than Group I-3 occupancies must be flame resistant and meet the flame propagation performance criteria of Test 1 or 2, as appropriate, of NFPA 701, or exhibit a maximum heat release rate of 100 kW when tested in accordance with NFPA 289 using a 10 kW ignition source. See Chap. 8 for a description of the NFPA 701 and 289 tests. Decorative materials are defined as materials applied over the building interior finish for decorative, acoustical, or other effect and do not include wall coverings, ceiling coverings, ordinary window shades, interior finish, and materials less than 1.25 in thick applied directly to and adhering tightly to a substrate.

The amount of noncombustible decorative materials is not limited, but the amount of combustible materials is limited to 10% of the specific wall or ceiling area to which the material is attached, except in A occupancies, where up to 75% is allowed if the building is fully sprinklered, and in Group R-2 dormitories and dwelling units where up to 50% is allowed if the building is fully sprinklered. In Group B and M occupancies, the amount of combustible fabric partitions suspended from the ceiling is not limited.

Materials used as interior trim must have a minimum Class C flame spread index and smoke-developed index. Combustible trim (such as wood trim), excluding handrails and guardrails, cannot exceed 10% of the specific wall or ceiling area to which it is attached.

REQUIREMENT BASES ON OCCUPANCY

The *occupancy* of a building or interior space is its use, such as an office, a restaurant, a private residence, or a school. Uses are grouped into occupancy classes based on similar life-safety characteristics, fire hazards, and combustible contents.

The idea behind occupancy classification is that some uses are inherently more hazardous than others. For example, a building where flammable liquids are used is more dangerous than a single-family residence. It also considers the mobility of the occupants and their ability to exit the space. For example, residents of a nursing home will have more trouble exiting than will young schoolchildren who have participated in fire drills. In order to achieve equivalent safety in building design, each occupancy group has different fire protection requirements, area and height limitations, restrictions on type of construction, and means of egress requirements.

There are additional requirements for special occupancy types such as covered mall buildings, high-rise buildings, atriums, underground buildings, occupancies involving motor vehicles, hazardous occupancies, and institutional occupancies.

Occupancy Groups

Every building or portion of a building is classified according to its use and is assigned to an occupancy group. The IBC classifies occupancies into 10 major groups.

- assembly
- business
- educational
- factory and industrial
- hazardous
- institutional
- mercantile
- residential
- storage
- utility

Six of these groups are further divided into categories to distinguish subgroups that define the relative hazard of the occupancy. For example, in the assembly group, an A-1 occupancy includes assembly places, usually with fixed seats, used to view performing arts or motion pictures, while an A-2 occupancy includes places designed for food and/or drink consumption. Table 14.5 briefly summarizes the occupancy groups and subgroups and gives some examples of each. This table is not complete; consult the IBC for specific requirements.

If a particular project does not seem to fit any of the categories, the architect should consult with the local building official for a determination of the occupancy classification of that project.

Knowing the occupancy classification is important in determining other building requirements such as the maximum area, the number of floors allowed, and how the building must be separated from other structures. The occupancy classification also affects

- calculation of the occupant load
- egress design
- interior finish requirements
- the use of fire partitions and fire barriers
- fire detection and suppression systems
- ventilation and sanitation requirements
- other special restrictions particular to any given classification

Mixed Occupancy and Occupancy Separation

When a building or area of a building contains two or more occupancies, it is considered to be of *mixed occupancy*. For instance, the design of a large office space can include office workspaces (B occupancy) adjacent to an auditorium used for training, which would be an assembly occupancy (A occupancy) if it has an occupant load over 49. Each occupancy must be separated from the other occupancies by a fire barrier, so as to increase the level of fire protection between occupancies as the relative hazard increases; the minimum fire-resistance rating of the barrier is defined by the building code that applies.

Table 14.5
Occupancy Groups Summary

occupancy	description	examples
A-1	assembly with fixed seats for viewing of movie theaters, live performance	performances or movie theaters
A-2	assembly for food and drink consumption	bars, restaurants, clubs
A-3	assembly for worship, recreation, etc. not classified elsewhere	libraries, art museums, conference rooms > 50
A-4	assembly for viewing of indoor sports	arenas
A-5	assembly for outdoor sports	stadiums
B	business for office or service transactions	offices, banks, educational above the 12th grade, post office
E	educational by > 5 people through 12th grade	grade schools, high schools, day care if > 5 children and > 2.5 years old
F-1	factory moderate hazard	see IBC
F-2	factory low hazard	see IBC
	hazardous—see IBC	see IBC
I-1	> 16 ambulatory people on 24-hour basis	assisted living, group home, convalescent facilities
I-2	medical care on 24-hour basis	hospitals, skilled care nursing
I-3	> 5 people restrained	jails, prisons, reformatories
I-4	daycare for > 5 adults or infants (< 2.5 yr)	daycare for infants
M	mercantile	department stores, markets, retail stores, drug stores, sales rooms
R-1	residential for transient lodging	hotels and motels
R-2	residential with 3 or more units	apartments, dormitories, condominiums, convents
R-3	1 or 2 dwelling units with attached uses or child care < 6, less than 24-hour care	bed and breakfast, small child care
R-4	residential assisted living where number of occupants > 5 but < 16	small assisted living
dwellings	must use *International Residential Code*	
S	storage—see IBC	see IBC
U	utility—see IBC	see IBC

This is just a brief summary of the groups and examples of occupancy groups in the IBC. Refer to the IBC for a complete list or check with local building officials when a use is not clearly stated or described in the code.

The required rating determines the specific design and detailing of the partition that separates the two spaces. IBC Table 508.4 shows required occupancy separations ranging from 1 to 4 hours. When a building is equipped with an automated sprinkler system, the required ratings are generally reduced by 1 hour; this can mean that a fire-rated partition is not required between some occupancies when the building is fully sprinklered.

One exception related to mixed occupancies concerns small storage rooms. If a room or space used for storage is less than 100 ft^2 and is accessory to another occupancy, it is classified as part of that occupancy. For example, a 75 ft^2 storage room in a business office would be a B occupancy, not an S occupancy. Storage rooms greater than 100 ft^2 are generally classified as S occupancies, but the local building official may classify them as the same occupancy in which they are located. Unseparated mixed occupancies are allowed in many cases; where there is no separation between occupancies, the maximum allowable area and height of a building or a portion of a building is based on the most restrictive allowance for the occupancy groups under consideration.

In the IBC, there are two variations of the concept of mixed occupancies: accessory occupancies and incidental uses. Each of these has its own particular, but related, requirements.

Accessory Occupancies

An *accessory occupancy* is a space or room that is ancillary to a main occupancy but that does not exceed 10% of the floor area of the story in which it is located. An accessory occupancy does not need to be separated from the main occupancy with a fire barrier. For example, a small gift shop in a hospital would be considered an accessory occupancy, and it would not require the 2-hour occupancy separation that would ordinarily be required between an M occupancy and an I-2 occupancy.

There are three exceptions to this. First, as long as a live/work unit complies with all other IBC requirements, portions with different uses are not considered separate occupancies. Second, most kinds of Group H (hazardous) occupancies must be separated from other occupancies. Third, dwelling units and sleeping units in Group I-1, R-1, R-2, and R-3 occupancies must be separated from other units and from accessory occupancies with a fire partition.

Incidental Uses

An *incidental use* is ancillary to a main occupancy and has the same classification as the nearest main occupancy, but poses a greater level of risk than that occupancy. The incidental use must be separated from the main occupancy by a fire barrier, be equipped with an automatic sprinkler system, or both. An incidental use area cannot exceed 10% of the area of the story on which it is located.

Table 14.6 lists types of incidental accessory occupancies along with the separations or sprinkler systems required for each. For example, a small incinerator room in an apartment building would pose a greater risk than the apartments' occupancy; the room would have to be separated from the rest of the apartment building with a 2-hour rated partition and have a sprinkler system installed.

This requirement does not apply to incidental uses within and serving a dwelling unit.

Where Table 14.6 allows a sprinkler system to substitute for a fire barrier, the incidental use area must be separated from the main occupancy by a smoke barrier, and the sprinklers are required only in the incidental use area. Doors must be self closing or automatic closing.

CLASSIFICATION BASED ON CONSTRUCTION TYPE

In the IBC, each building is classified as belonging to one of five major types of construction. Type I buildings are the most fire resistive, while Type V buildings are the least fire resistive. Type I and II buildings are noncombustible, while Type III, IV, and V buildings are considered combustible.

This classification is based on the fire-resistance rating of its major construction components, including the structural frame, bearing walls, exterior and interior nonbearing walls, floor construction, and roof construction. The construction type categories and fire-resistance rating requirements for each building element are shown in Table 14.1. The fire-resistance requirements for exterior, nonbearing walls are based on the distance from the building to the property line, the type of construction, and the occupancy group as shown in Table 14.7.

These classifications are used to protect the structural elements of a building from fire and collapse, and to divide the building into compartments so that a fire in one area will be contained long enough to allow people to evacuate the building and firefighters to arrive. Detailed requirements for the various construction types are contained in Chap. 6 of the IBC. It is advisable to read through IBC Chap. 6 and become familiar with the IBC provisions.

In combination with occupancy groups, construction type limits the area and height of buildings. For example, Type I buildings of any occupancy (except certain hazardous occupancies) can be of unlimited area and height, while Type V buildings are limited to only a few thousand square feet in area and one to three stories in height, depending on their occupancy. Limiting height and area based on construction type and occupancy recognizes that it becomes more difficult to fight fires, provide time for egress, and rescue people as buildings get larger and higher. It also recognizes that the safety of a building is affected by the type and amount of combustibles present due to the building's use. Allowable height and area are discussed in later in the chapter.

Fire zones are another consideration often encountered in urban areas. A municipality may, by action of the local government, divide a city into fire zones representing the degree of fire hazard. The *fire hazard* is usually based on factors such as density, access for fire fighting equipment, existing building heights, and so forth. The dense, central business district of a city is typically classed as fire zone 1. The local code may then restrict the types of construction that are allowed in the various fire zones.

Table 14.6 Incidental Uses

room or area	separation and/or protection
furnace room where any piece of equipment is over 400,000 Btu per hour input	1 hour or provide automatic sprinkler system
rooms with boilers where the largest piece of equipment is over 15 psi and 10 horsepower	1 hour or provide automatic sprinkler system
refrigerant machinery room	1 hour or provide automatic sprinkler system
hydrogen fuel gas rooms, not classified as Group H	1 hour in Group B, F, M, S, and U occupancies; 2 hours in Group A, E, I, and R occupancies
incinerator rooms	2 hours and provide automatic sprinkler system
paint shops, not classified as Group H, located in occupancies other than Group F	2 hours or 1 hour and provide automatic sprinkler system
in Group E occupancies, laboratories and vocational shops not classified as Group H	1 hour or provide automatic sprinkler system
in Group I-2 occupancies, laboratories not classified as Group H	1 hour and provide automatic sprinkler system
in ambulatory care facilities, laboratories not classified Group H	1 hour or provide automatic sprinkler system
laundry rooms over 100 ft^2	1 hour or provide automatic sprinkler system
in Group I-2, laundry rooms over 100 ft^2	1 hour
Group I-3 cells and Group I-2 patient rooms equipped with padded surfaces	1 hour
in Group I-2, physical plant maintenance shops	1 hour
in ambulatory care facilities or Group I-2 occupancies, waste and linen collection rooms with containers that have an aggregate volume of 10 ft^3 or greater	1 hour
in other than ambulatory care facilities and Group I-2 occupancies, waste and linen collection rooms over 100 ft^2	1 hour or provide automatic sprinkler system
in ambulatory care facilities and Group I-2 occupancies, storage rooms greater than 100 ft^2	1 hour
stationary storage battery systems having a liquid electrolyte capacity of more than 50 gallons for flooded lead-acid, nickel cadmium or VRLA, or more than 1000 lbf for lithium-ion and lithium metal polymer used for facility standby power, emergency power, or uninterruptable power supplies	1 hour in Group B, F, M, S, and U occupancies; 2 hours in Group A, E, I, and R occupancies

Table 14.7 Fire-Resistance Rating Requirements for Exterior Walls Based on Fire Separation Distance[a, b, c]

fire separation distance, x (ft)	type of construction	occupancy group H[d]	occupancy group F-1, M, S-1[e]	occupancy group A, B, E, F-2, I, R, S-2, H[f]
$x < 5$[g]	all	3	2	1
$5 \leq x < 10$	IA	3	2	1
	others	2	1	1
$10 \leq x < 30$	IA, IB	2	1	1[h]
	IIB, VB	1	0	0
	others	1	0	1[h]
$x \geq 30$	all	0	0	0

[a]Load-bearing exterior walls shall also comply with the fire-resistance rating requirements of IBC Table 601.
[b]The fire-resistance rating of an exterior wall is determined based upon the fire separation distance of the exterior wall and the story in which the wall is located.
[c]Where IBC Table 705.8 permits nonbearing exterior walls within the unlimited area of unprotected openings, the required fire-resistance rating for the exterior walls is 0 hours.
[d]For special requirements for Group H occupancies, see IBC Sec. 415.6.
[e]For special requirements for Group S aircraft hangars, see IBC Sec. 412.4.1.
[f]For a building containing only a Group U occupancy in private garage or carport, the exterior wall shall not be required to have a fire-resistance rating where the fire separation distance is 5 ft or greater.
[g]See IBC Sec. 706.1.1 for party walls.
[h]Open parking garages complying with IBC Sec. 406 shall not be required to have a fire-resistance rating.

Project Planning

For renovation or remodeling work, knowing the construction type is important if major changes are proposed. For example, if the occupancy of a building or portion of a building is being changed from a B (business) occupancy to an A (assembly) occupancy, the architect must know the construction type to verify that the maximum area is not exceeded. If it is, a fire wall may need to be constructed or sprinklers may need to be added. In addition, construction type can affect the required fire ratings of coverings of structural elements, floor/ceiling assemblies, and openings in rated walls. For example, a protected beam may be damaged or changed during remodeling to accommodate new construction, degrading its required fire rating. The architect would have to detail or specify repairs or new construction as required to return the assembly to its original rating.

ALLOWABLE HEIGHT AND FLOOR AREAS OF BUILDINGS

Allowable Height

Chapter 5 of the IBC sets forth the requirements for determining the maximum height (in stories as well as in feet) and area of a building based on its construction type, its occupancy, and whether there is an automatic sprinkler system installed throughout the building. It also gives the conditions under which the height and area may be increased. The concept behind these limits is that the more hazardous a building is, the smaller it should be, to make it easier in the event of an emergency for occupants to exit and for a fire department to fight the fire.

Table 14.8 (IBC Table 504.3) gives the allowable building height in feet above the grade plane. To use the table, find the building construction type column across the top of the table and the occupancy row along the left side of the table. Each occupancy row is divided into a sprinklered and non-sprinklered row. These three variables determine the maximum allowable height. Some occupancies, such as H, must always be sprinklered, so the table gives only one row of values.

Table 14.9 (IBC Table 504.4) is similar, but gives the allowable building height in number of stories above the grade plane.

Table 14.8
Allowable Height in Feet Above Grade Plane[a]

		type of construction								
		type I		type II		type III		type IV	type V	
occupancy classification	see footnotes	A	B	A	B	A	B	HT	A	B
A, B, E, F, M, S, U	NS[b]	UL	160	65	55	65	55	65	50	40
	S	UL	180	85	75	85	75	85	70	60
H-1, H-2, H-3, H-5	NS[c, d]	UL	160	65	55	65	55	65	50	40
	S	UL	160	65	55	65	55	65	50	40
H-4	NS[c, d]	UL	160	65	55	65	55	65	50	40
	S	UL	180	85	75	85	75	85	70	60
I-1 Condition 1, I-3	NS[c, d]	UL	160	65	55	65	55	65	50	40
	S	UL	180	85	75	85	75	85	70	60
I-1 Condition 2, I-2	NS[d, e, f]	UL	160	65	55	65	55	65	50	40
	S	UL	180	85	55	65	55	65	50	40
I-4	NS[d, g]	UL	160	65	55	65	55	65	50	40
	S	UL	180	85	75	85	75	85	70	60
R	NS[d, h]	UL	160	65	55	65	55	65	50	40
	S13R	60	60	60	60	60	60	60	60	60
	S	UL	180	85	75	85	75	85	70	60

[a]See IBC Chap. 4 and Chap. 5 for specific exceptions.
[b]See IBC Sec. 903.2 for the minimum thresholds for protection by an automatic sprinkler system for specific occupancies.
[c]New Group H occupancies are required to be protected by an automatic sprinkler system in accordance with IBC Sec. 903.2.5.
[d]The NS value is only for use in evaluation of existing building height in accordance with the *International Existing Building Code.*
[e]New Group I-1 and I-3 occupancies are required to be protected by an automatic sprinkler system in accordance with IBC Sec. 903.2.6. For new Group I-1 occupancies Condition 1, see Exception 1 of IBC Sec. 903.2.6.
[f]New and existing Group I-2 occupancies are required to be protected by an automatic sprinkler system in accordance with Sec. 903.2.6 and Sec. 1103.5 of the *International Fire Code.*
[g]For new Group I-4 occupancies, see Exceptions 2 and 3 of IBC Sec. 903.2.6.
[h]New Group R occupancies are required to be protected by an automatic sprinkler system in accordance with IBC Sec. 903.2.8.

Allowable Floor Areas

The allowable area of a building is based on construction type, occupancy, whether or not there is an automatic sprinkler system installed throughout the building, and the amount of building frontage on a public way or open space. The IBC gives requirements for single-occupancy buildings and for mixed-occupancy buildings. For ease of use, the IBC combines the variables of construction type, occupancy, and sprinklers into one table; then any allowable area increase for building frontage is added.

The basic allowable areas for a single-story building are given in IBC Table 506.2. A portion of this table is reproduced in Table 14.10. The allowable area of a single-occupancy, one-story building is determined using Eq. 14.1.

$$A_a = A_t + (\text{NS})I_f \qquad 14.1$$

A_t is the allowable area factor from Table 14.10; use the NS, S1, SM, or S13R value as appropriate.

The term $(\text{NS})I_f$ is the increase in allowable area due to building frontage. NS is the allowable area factor from Table 14.10 for non-sprinklered buildings (the NS factor is used in calculating this term whether or not the building is sprinklered). I_f is the area factor increase, which is explained later in this chapter.

The area of a single-occupancy, multistory building is determined using Eq. 14.2.

$$A_a = \left(A_t + (\text{NS})I_f\right)S_a \qquad 14.2$$

S_a is the actual number of building stories above grade plane. If the building is sprinklered throughout, S_a may be no greater than four; otherwise, S_a may be no greater than three.

No individual story can exceed the allowable area, A_a that results from using the value S_a=1.

Area Factor Increase Based on Frontage

If at least 25% of the building's perimeter is located on a public way or open space, the basic allowable area may be increased. Such open areas must be either on the same lot or dedicated for public use, and they must be accessible from a street or approved fire lane.

To qualify, the public way or open space must be at least 20 ft wide, measured at right angles from the building face to any of the following.

- the closest interior lot line
- the entire width of a street, alley or public way
- the exterior face of an adjacent building on the same property

The amount of increase allowed is represented by the term $(\text{NS})I_f$ in Eq. 14.1 and Eq. 14.2. The factor I_f is calculated with Eq. 14.3.

$$I_f = \frac{\left(\frac{F}{P} - 0.25\right)W}{30} \qquad 14.3$$

P is the total building perimeter, and F is the length of the portion of the building perimeter that fronts on a public way or open space. W is the width of the public way or open space, which must be at least 20 ft; also, W may not be taken as greater than 30 ft, even if the actual width is greater.

If the width of the public way or open space varies along the building perimeter, the IBC includes instructions for calculating a weighted average.

The maximum value of I_f, which is for a free-standing building with 30 ft or more of open space on all sides, is 0.75. Thus, 75% of the value of NS is Table 14.10 is the maximum that can be added to the basic allowable area, as indicated in Eq. 14.1 and Eq. 14.2.

Table 14.9 Allowable Number of Stories Above Grade Plane[a,b]

occupancy classification	see footnotes	type I A	type I B	type II A	type II B	type III A	type III B	type IV HT	type V A	type V B
A-1	NS	UL	5	3	2	3	2	3	2	1
	S	UL	6	4	3	4	3	4	3	2
A-2	NS	UL	11	3	2	3	2	3	2	1
	S	UL	12	4	3	4	3	4	3	2
A-3	NS	UL	11	3	2	3	2	3	2	1
	S	UL	12	4	3	4	3	4	3	2
A-4	NS	UL	11	3	2	3	2	3	2	1
	S	UL	12	4	3	4	3	4	3	2
A-5	NS	UL	UL	UL	UL	UL	UL	UL	UL	UL
	S	UL	UL	UL	UL	UL	UL	UL	UL	UL
B	NS	UL	11	5	3	5	3	5	3	2
	S	UL	12	6	4	6	4	6	4	3
E	NS	UL	5	3	2	3	2	3	1	1
	S	UL	6	4	3	4	3	4	2	2
F-1	NS	UL	11	4	2	3	2	4	2	1
	S	UL	12	5	3	4	3	5	3	2
F-2	NS	UL	11	5	3	4	3	5	3	2
	S	UL	12	6	4	5	4	6	4	3
H-1	NS[c,d]	1	1	1	1	1	1	1	1	NP
	S									
H-2	NS[c,d]	UL	3	2	1	2	1	2	1	1
	S									
H-3	NS[c,d]	UL	6	4	2	4	2	4	2	1
	S									
H-4	NS[c,d]	UL	7	5	3	5	3	5	3	2
	S	UL	8	6	4	6	4	6	4	3
H-5	NS[c,d]	4	4	3	3	3	3	3	3	2
	S									
I-1 Condition 1	NS[d,e]	UL	9	4	3	4	3	4	3	2
	S	UL	10	5	4	5	4	5	4	3
I-1 Condition 1	NS[d,e]	UL	9	4	3	4	3	4	3	2
	S	UL	10	5						
I-2	NS[d,f]	UL	4	2	1	1	NP	1	1	NP
	S	UL	5	3						
I-3	NS[d,e]	UL	4	2	1	2	1	2	2	1
	S	UL	5	3	2	3	2	3	3	2
I-4	NS[d,g]	UL	5	3	2	3	2	3	1	1
	S	UL	6	4	3	4	3	4	2	2
M	NS	UL	11	4	2	4	2	4	3	1
	S	UL	12	5	3	5	3	5	4	2
R-1	NS[d,h]	UL	11	4	4	4	4	4	3	2
	S13R	4	4						4	3
	S	UL	12	5	5	5	5	5	4	3
R-2	NS[d,h]	UL	11	4	4	4	4	4	3	2
	S13R	4	4						4	3
	S	UL	12	5	5	5	5	5	4	3
R-3	NS[d,h]	UL	11	4	4	4	4	4	3	2
	S13R	4	4						4	3
	S	UL	12	5	5	5	5	5	4	3
R-4	NS[d,h]	UL	11	4	4	4	4	4	3	2
	S13R	4	4						4	3
	S	UL	12	5	5	5	5	5	4	3
S-1	NS	UL	11	4	2	3	2	4	3	1
	S	UL	12	5	3	4	3	5	4	2
S-2	NS	UL	11	5	3	4	3	4	4	2
	S	UL	12	6	4	5	4	5	5	3
U	NS	UL	5	4	2	3	2	4	2	1
	S	UL	6	5	3	4	3	5	3	2

Note: UL =Unlimited; NS = Buildings not equipped throughout with an automatic sprinkler system; S = Buildings equipped throughout with an automatic sprinkler system installed in accordance with IBC Sec. 903.3.1.1; S13R = Buildings equipped throughout with an automatic sprinkler system installed in accordance with IBC Sec. 903.3.1.2.

[a]See IBC Chaps. 4 and 5 for specific exceptions to the allowable height in this chapter.
[b]See IBC Sec. 903.2 for the minimum thresholds for protection by an automatic sprinkler system for specific occupancies.
[c]New Group H occupancies are required to be protected by an automatic sprinkler system in accordance with IBC Sec. 903.2.5.
[d]The NS value is only for use in evaluation of existing building height in accordance with the *International Existing Building Code.*
[e]New Group I-1 and I-3 occupancies are required to be protected by an automatic sprinkler system in accordance with IBC Sec. 903.2.6. For new Group I-1 occupancies Condition 1, see Exception 1 of IBC Sec. 903.2.6.
[f]New and existing Group I-2 occupancies are required to be protected by an automatic sprinkler system in accordance with Sec. 903.2.6 and Sec. 1103.5 of the *International Fire Code.*
[g]For new Group I-4 occupancies, see Exceptions 2 and 3 of IBC Sec. 903.2.6.
[h]New Group R occupancies are required to be protected by an automatic sprinkler system in accordance with IBC Sec. 903.2.8.

Project Planning

Table 14.10 Allowable Area Factor (A_t = NS, S1, S13R, or SM, as applicable) in Square Feet[a,b]

		type of construction								
		type I		type II		type III		type IV	type V	
occupancy classification	see footnotes	A	B	A	B	A	B	HT	A	B
A-1	NS	UL	UL	15,500	8500	14,000	8500	15,000	11,500	5500
	S1	UL	UL	62,000	34,000	56,000	34,000	60,000	46,000	22,000
	SM	UL	UL	46,500	25,500	42,000	25,500	45,000	34,500	16,500
A-2	NS	UL	UL	15,500	9500	14,000	9500	15,000	11,500	6000
	S1	UL	UL	62,000	38,000	56,000	38,000	60,000	46,000	24,000
	SM	UL	UL	46,500	28,500	42,000	28,500	45,000	34,500	18,000
A-3	NS	UL	UL	15,500	9500	14,000	9500	15,000	11,500	6000
	S1	UL	UL	62,000	38,000	56,000	38,000	60,000	46,000	24,000
	SM	UL	UL	46,500	28,500	42,000	28,500	45,000	34,500	18,000
A-4	NS	UL	UL	15,500	9500	14,000	9500	15,000	11,500	6000
	S1	UL	UL	62,000	38,000	56,000	38,000	60,000	46,000	24,000
	SM	UL	UL	46,500	28,500	42,000	28,500	45,000	34,500	18,000
A-5	NS	UL	UL	UL	UL	UL	UL	UL	UL	UL
	S1	UL	UL	UL	UL	UL	UL	UL	UL	UL
	SM	UL	UL	UL	UL	UL	UL	UL	UL	UL
B	NS	UL	UL	37,500	23,000	28,500	19,000	36,000	18,000	9000
	S1	UL	UL	150,000	92,000	114,000	76,000	144,000	72,000	36,000
	SM	UL	UL	112,500	69,000	85,500	57,000	108,000	54,000	27,000
E	NS	UL	UL	26,500	14,500	23,500	14,500	25,500	18,500	9500
	S1	UL	UL	106,000	58,000	94,000	58,000	102,000	74,000	38,000
	SM	UL	UL	79,500	43,500	70,500	43,500	76,500	55,500	28,500
F-1	NS	UL	UL	25,000	15,500	19,000	12,000	33,500	14,000	8500
	S1	UL	UL	100,000	62,000	76,000	48,000	134,000	56,000	34,000
	SM	UL	UL	75,000	46,500	57,000	36,000	100,500	42,000	25,500
F-2	NS	UL	UL	37,500	23,000	28,500	18,000	50,500	21,000	13,000
	S1	UL	UL	150,000	92,000	114,000	72,000	202,000	84,000	52,000
	SM	UL	UL	112,500	69,000	85,500	54,000	151,500	63,000	39,000
H-1	NS[c]	21,000	16,500	11,000	7000	9500	7000	10,500	7500	NP
	S1	21,000	16,500	11,000	7000	9500	7000	10,500	7500	NP
H-2	NS[c]	21,000	16,500	11,000	7000	9500	7000	10,500	7500	3000
	S1	21,000	16,500	11,000	7000	9500	7000	10,500	7500	3000
	SM	21,000	16,500	11,000	7000	9500	7000	10,500	7500	3000
H-3	NS[c]	UL	60,000	26,500	14,000	17,500	13,000	25,500	10,000	5000
	S1	UL	60,000	26,500	14,000	17,500	13,000	25,500	10,000	5000
	SM	UL	60,000	26,500	14,000	17,500	13,000	25,500	10,000	5000
H-4	NS[c,d]	UL	UL	37,500	17,500	28,500	17,500	36,000	18,000	6500
	S1	UL	UL	150,000	70,000	114,000	70,000	144,000	72,000	26,000
	SM	UL	UL	112,500	52,500	85,500	52,500	108,000	54,000	19,500
H-5	NS[c,d]	UL	UL	37,500	23,000	28,500	19,000	36,000	18,000	9000
	S1	UL	UL	150,000	92,000	114,000	76,000	144,000	72,000	36,000
	SM	UL	UL	112,500	69,000	85,500	57,000	108,000	54,000	27,000

UL = Unlimited; NP = Not permitted; NS = Buildings not equipped throughout with an automatic sprinkler system; S1 = Buildings a maximum of one story above grade plane equipped throughout with an automatic sprinkler system installed in accordance with IBC Sec. 903.3.1.1; SM = Buildings two or more stories above grade plane equipped throughout with an automatic sprinkler system installed in accordance with IBC Sec. 903.3.1.1.

[a]See IBC Chaps. 4 and 5 for specific exceptions to the allowable height in this chapter.
[b]See IBC Sec. 903.2 for the minimum thresholds for protection by an automatic sprinkler system for specific occupancies.
[c]New Group H occupancies are required to be protected by an automatic sprinkler system in accordance with IBC Sec. 903.2.5.
[d]The NS value is only for use in evaluation of existing building area in accordance with the *International Existing Building Code*.

Example 14.1

An office building is being built with Type IIB construction and a sprinkler system. Each floor will have the same area. The allowable area factor increase has been determined to be 25%. What is the maximum allowable area for the building?

(A) 300,000 ft^2

(B) 370,000 ft^2

(C) 460,000 ft^2

(D) 550,000 ft^2

Solution

From the problem statement, the allowable area factor increase is $I_f = 0.25$. From Table 14.9, for occupancy classification B, Type IIB construction, and a sprinkler system, the maximum number of stories above grade plane is $S_a = 4$. From Table 14.10, the tabular allowable area is A_t = is 69,000 ft^2, and the tabular allowable area factor, NS, is 23,000 ft^2. Calculate the allowable area, A_a.

$$A_a = (A_t + (\text{NS})I_f)S_a = (69{,}000\ \text{ft}^2 + (23{,}000\ \text{ft}^2)(0.25))(4) = 299{,}000\ \text{ft}^2$$

Check the allowable area for an individual floor by using a value of $S_a = 1$.

$$\begin{aligned} A_a &= (A_t + (\text{NS})I_f)S_a = (69{,}000\ \text{ft}^2 + (23{,}000\ \text{ft}^2)(0.25))(1) \\ &= 74{,}750\ \text{ft}^2 \end{aligned}$$

If each floor has the same area (299,000 ft^2/4 = 74,750 ft^2), each is well under the maximum allowable for an individual floor.

Project Planning

Example 14.2

A building has a 240 ft perimeter. 180 ft of the perimeter fronts an open space 24 ft wide. (The building could be a square 60 ft on a side.) Most nearly, the value of the factor I_f is

(A) 0.1

(B) 0.2

(C) 0.3

(D) 0.4

Solution

Use Eq. 14.3 to calculate the value of I_f.

$$\begin{aligned} I_f &= \frac{\left(\frac{F}{P} - 0.25\right)W}{30} \\ &= \frac{\left(\frac{180\ \text{ft}}{240\ \text{ft}} - 0.25\right)(20\ \text{ft})}{30} \\ &= 0.33 \end{aligned}$$

The answer is (C).

Table 14.11 Maximum Floor Area Allowances per Occupant

function of space	occupant load factor (floor area in ft^2/ occupant)
accessory storage areas, mechanical equipment room	300 gross
agricultural building	300 gross
aircraft hangars	500 gross
airport terminal	
baggage claim	20 gross
baggage handling	300 gross
concourse	100 gross
waiting area	15 gross
assembly	
gaming floors (keno, slots, etc.)	11 gross
exhibit galley and museum	30 net
assembly with fixed seats	see IBC Sec. 1004.4
assembly without fixed seats	
concentrated (chairs only—not fixed)	7 net
standing space	5 net
unconcentrated (tables and chairs)	15 net
bowling centers (allow 5 persons for each lane including 15 ft of runway, and for additional areas)	7 net
business areas	100 gross
courtrooms—other than fixed seating areas	40 net
day care	35 net
dormitories	50 gross
educational	
classroom area	20 net
shops and other vocational room areas	50 net
exercise rooms	50 gross
Group H-5 fabrication and manufacturing areas	200 gross
industrial areas	100 gross
institutional areas	
inpatient treatment areas	240 gross
outpatient areas	100 gross
sleeping areas	120 gross
kitchens, commercial	200 gross
library	
reading rooms	50 net
stack area	100 gross
locker rooms	50 gross
mall buildings—covered and open	see IBC Sec. 402.8.2
mercantile	60 gross
storage, stock, shipping areas	300 gross
parking garages	200 gross
residential	200 gross
skating rinks, swimming pools	
rink and pool	50 gross
decks	15 gross
stages and platforms	15 net
warehouses	500 gross

2015 International Building Code, International Code Council, Inc., Washington, D.C. Reproduced with permission. www.iccsafe.org

Project Planning

Mixed-Occupancy Buildings

There are several requirements for the maximum area and height of mixed-occupancy buildings.

- The allowable area and height must be based on the most restrictive allowances for the occupancy groups under consideration for the type of construction of the building.
- When the area of each separated occupancy is expressed as the ratio of its actual building area to its allowable building area, the sum of the ratios in each story must not be greater than one. For example, if a story contains two separated occupancies, and the actual building area of occupancy 1 is 0.35 of its allowable building area, then the actual building area of occupancy 2 may not be more than 0.65 of its allowable building area.
- Each separated occupancy must comply with the building height limitations based on the type of construction.
- Hazardous occupancies (H), dwelling units, accessory occupancies, and nonseparated occupancies are subject to additional requirements and exceptions.

For multistory buildings of mixed occupancy, each story must individually comply with the sum of ratios as above. In addition, for non-sprinklered buildings more than three stories above grade plane, when the area of each story is expressed as the ratio of its actual area to its allowable area (as determined from Eq. 14.1), the sum of the ratios for all stories must not exceed three. For sprinklered buildings, this sum cannot exceed four.

There are two ways to use the tables for basic allowable height and building area (see Table 14.9 and Table 14.10, as well as IBC Table 504.4 for the maximum number of stories).

If the occupancy, construction type, and sprinkler conditions are known, simply find the intersection of the rows designating occupancy and sprinkler conditions and the column designating construction type, read the permitted area or height, and then increase the areas according to the percentages allowed for perimeter open space.

More often, however, the occupancy and required floor area are known from the building program, and the architect must determine the construction type that will allow a building that meets the client's size needs. The architect may also need to decide at this time whether to install sprinklers; often, however, the decision to use sprinklers will already have been made in the pre-design phase because of the advantages the IBC gives to fully sprinklered buildings.

Example 14.3

A one-story building with a total area of 10,000 ft^2 is divided into a 7000 ft^2 restaurant (A2 occupancy) and a 3000 ft^2 office (B occupancy). The building is of type V-B construction and does not have a sprinkler system. The open space around the building gives it a 25% allowance for area increase. Does this building comply with IBC maximum area requirements?

Solution

First, determine the maximum allowable area factors for each occupancy. From Table 14.10, NS_{A2} = 6000 ft^2 and NS_{B} = 9000 ft^2.

Next, determine the allowable area for both the A2 occupancy, $A_{a,\text{A2}}$, and the B occupancy, $A_{a,\text{B}}$.

$$\begin{aligned} A_{a,\text{A2}} &= A_{t,\text{A2}} + (\text{NS}_{\text{A2}})I_{f,\text{A2}} \\ &= 6000\ \text{ft}^2 + (6000\ \text{ft}^2)(0.25) \\ &= 7500\ \text{ft}^2 \end{aligned}$$

$$\begin{aligned} A_{a,\text{B}} &= A_{t,\text{B}} + (\text{NS}_{\text{B}})I_{f,\text{B}} \\ &= 9000\ \text{ft}^2 + (9000\ \text{ft}^2)(0.25) \\ &= 11{,}250\ \text{ft}^2 \end{aligned}$$

Check the sum of the ratios of the actual building areas to the allowable building areas.

$$\begin{aligned}\text{sum} &= \frac{A_{\text{actual,A2}}}{A_{a,\text{A2}}} + \frac{A_{\text{actual,B}}}{A_{a,\text{B}}} \\ &= \frac{7000 \text{ ft}^2}{7500 \text{ ft}^2} + \frac{3000 \text{ ft}^2}{11{,}250 \text{ ft}^2} \\ &= 1.20 \quad [\text{must be} \le 1]\end{aligned}$$

The sum of the ratios is greater than 1, so the building as configured is not permitted. Either the building needs to be sprinklered, or a higher construction type (e.g., V-A) must be used.

Changes in Occupancy

Occasionally, an architect may be asked to remodel a building for a use other than that originally intended. If the existing building is not large enough to accommodate the new occupancy, other significant steps may need to be taken to make the project feasible (for example, adding a sprinkler system or adding a fire wall to separate the space into two fire areas).

For example, consider a one-story, 12,000 ft^2, type V-B building formerly used as a low-hazard factory (F-2 occupancy). The client wants to remodel it for use as a nightclub (A-2 occupancy). According to the IBC, the basic maximum allowable floor area for the F-2 occupancy as 13,000 ft^2, but the basic maximum allowable floor area for the A-2 occupancy is only 6000 ft^2 (see Table 14.10). While the entire floor area of the building could be used when the building was as a factory, only 6000 ft^2 of the building can be used as a nightclub. If the client wants to use more than that, other steps must be taken.

A common approach in this sort of situation is to use a *fire wall* (or *area separation wall*) to divide the single structure into two portions, called *fire areas*, that may be as treated separate buildings. This approach works as long as all requirements for fire walls are met.

In the IBC, the minimum fire-resistance rating that a fire wall must have depends mainly on the occupancy. A 4-hour fire-resistive wall is required in H-1 and H-2 occupancies. A 2-hour fire wall is required in F-2, S-2, R-3, and R-4 occupancies. A 3-hour fire wall is required in other occupancies, except that in a Type II or V constructions the fire wall may have a 2-hour fire-resistance rating. Other codes may base the required ratings of fire walls on other factors such as construction type.

Location on Property

IBC Sec. 602 lists requirements for the siting of buildings relative to adjacent property lines based on occupancy group and construction type. The siting requirements are determined by specifying the fire resistance of exterior walls based on distance from property lines or adjacent buildings. The purpose is to prevent the spread of fire from one building to another. If the exterior wall has openings such as windows, provisions in IBC Chap. 7 regulate the maximum allowable area of openings based on distance from the property lines.

As with maximum allowable area, requirements for the location of a building on a site can be approached two ways during pre-design and site planning. If the building must be placed a certain distance from the property line, then the code specifies the minimum fire-protection rating and limitations on openings. On the other hand, if the architect wants to minimize the required fire ratings, increase the allowable opening area, or both, then the minimum allowable setback can be determined from the tables in the IBC.

MEANS OF EGRESS

The Egress System

Means of egress is one of the most important provisions of any building code and one with which the architect must be intimately familiar. Several parts of the exam will contain questions related to egress.

The IBC defines *means of egress* as a continuous and unobstructed path of vertical and horizontal egress travel from any point in a building or structure to a public way. The means of egress consists of three parts.

- the exit access
- the exit
- the exit discharge

These must lead to a *public way*, which is any street, alley, or similar parcel of land essentially unobstructed from the ground to the sky that is permanently appropriated to the public for public use and has a clear width of not less than 10 ft. See Fig. 14.2.

The *exit access* is the portion of the means of egress that leads to an exit. Exit access areas may or may not be protected depending on the specific requirements of the code, based on occupancy and construction type. Exit access areas may include components such as rooms, spaces, aisles, intervening rooms, hallways, corridors, ramps, and doorways. The exit access does not provide a protected path of travel. In the IBC, even fire-protection-rated corridors are considered exit access. The exit access is the portion of the building where travel distance is measured and regulated. (Maximum travel distance is discussed later in this section.)

The *exit* is the portion of the egress system that provides a protected path of egress between the exit access and the exit discharge. Exits are fully enclosed and protected from all other interior spaces by fire-resistance-rated construction with protected openings (such as doors, glass, and so on). An exit may be as simple as an exterior exit door at ground level, or it may include exit enclosures for stairs, exit passageways, and horizontal exits. In the IBC, exits may also include exterior exit stairways and ramps. Depending on building height, construction type, and passageway length, exits must have either a 1- or 2-hour rating. Travel distance is not an issue once the exit has been reached.

The *exit discharge* is the portion of the egress system between the termination of an exit and a public way. Exit discharge areas typically include portions outside the exterior walls such as exterior exit balconies, exterior exit stairways, and exit courts. Exit discharge may also include building lobbies of multistory buildings, if one of the exit stairways opens onto the lobby and certain conditions are met. These conditions require that the exit door in the lobby is clearly visible, that the level of discharge is sprinklered, and that the entire area of the area of discharge is separated from areas below by the same fire-resistance rating as the exit enclosure that opens onto it. In the IBC, exterior exit stairways and ramps are considered exits (see Fig. 14.2).

Occupant Load

The *occupant load* is the number of people that a building code assumes will occupy a given building or portion of a building. It is based on the occupancy classification. Occupant load is based on the assumption that some types of spaces will be more densely populated than others, and that exiting provisions should respond accordingly. For example, an auditorium needs more exit capacity to allow safe evacuation than does an office space with the same floor area.

The IBC requires that the occupant load be established by taking the largest number determined by one of three methods: by actual number, by table, or by combination.

Occupant Load by Actual Mumber

In the first method, the actual number of people the building or space is designed to accommodate is used to determine the occupant load. For example, the occupant load of an auditorium with fixed seating can be calculated by counting the number of seats. This method is typically used only where there are fixed seats, because otherwise it is easy for a space to be used for multiple purposes and for its uses to change over time.

Occupant Load by Table

In the second method, the occupant load is determined by calculating the area in square feet assigned to a particular function, and dividing by an occupant load factor as given in the code. In the IBC the occupant load factor is given in IBC Table 1004.1.2, reproduced here as Table 14.11. This is the most common method of calculating occupant load. Other model codes have similar tables and use the same technique to calculate occupant load.

The *occupant load factor* is the amount of floor area presumed to be occupied by one person. It is based on the generic functions of building spaces and is not the same as the occupancy groups. Over time, occupant load factors have been found to consistently represent the densities found in various uses. Table 14.11 also shows whether the occupant load is to be calculated based on net or gross area. *Gross floor area* includes stairs, corridors, toilet rooms, mechanical rooms, closets, and interior partition thickness. *Net floor area* includes only the space actually used by the occupant. Most common uses are included in the table, but the IBC gives the local building official the power to establish occupant load factors in cases where a use is not specifically listed.

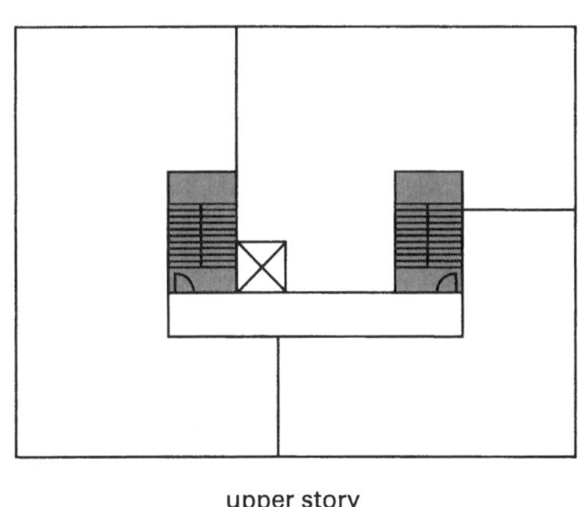

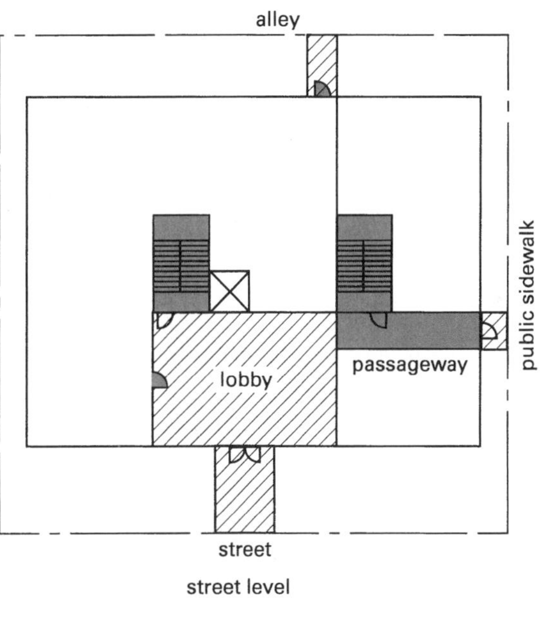

Figure 14.2 The Egress System

Occupant Load by Combination

In the third method, when an occupant load from an intervening space or accessory area exits through a primary space, the egress facilities from the primary space occupant load must include the occupant load of the primary space plus the occupant load of the intervening or accessory space.

This provision simply requires that occupant loads are cumulative as occupants exit through intervening spaces to an ultimate exit access or exit. However, this only applies to determining the capacity (width) of the egress, not the number of means of egress.

In determining the occupant load, all portions of the building are presumed to be occupied at the same time. However, the local building official may reduce the calculated occupant load if the official determines that some areas of a building would not normally be occupied at the same time.

If there are mixed occupancies or uses in a building, each area is calculated with its respective occupant load factor, and then all loads are added together.

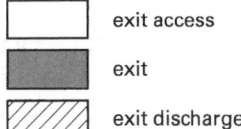

Example 14.4

What is the occupant load for a restaurant dining room that is 2500 ft^2 in area?

(A) 167 occupants

(B) 184 occupants

(C) 202 occupants

(D) 222 occupants

Solution

Table 14.11 includes dining rooms under the use "Assembly without fixed seats, unconcentrated," with an occupant load factor of 15 ft^2 per occupant.

$$\begin{aligned}\text{occupant load} &= \frac{A}{\text{occupant load factor}} = \frac{2500\ \text{ft}^2}{15\ \frac{\text{ft}^2}{\text{occupant}}}\\ &= 166.67\ \text{occupants} \quad (167\ \text{occupants})\end{aligned}$$

The answer is (A).

Example 14.5

A building includes an office with a gross area of 3700 ft and two training classrooms of 1200 ft each. What is the occupant load for the entire building?

(A) 92 occupants

(B) 120 occupants

(C) 157 occupants

(D) 206 occupants

Solution

As a business occupancy, the office has an occupant load factor of 100 ft^2/occupant gross.

$$\begin{aligned}\text{occupant load}_{\text{office}} &= \frac{A}{\text{occupant load factor}}\\ &= \frac{3700\ \text{ft}^2}{100\ \frac{\text{ft}^2}{\text{occupant}}}\\ &= 37\ \text{occupants}\end{aligned}$$

Classrooms have an occupant load factor of 20 ft^2/occupant, so

$$\begin{aligned}\text{occupant load}_{\text{classroom}} &= \frac{A}{\text{occupant load factor}}\\ &= \frac{(2)(1200\ \text{ft}^2)}{20\ \frac{\text{ft}^2}{\text{occupant}}}\\ &= 120\ \text{occupants}\end{aligned}$$

The total occupant load of all the spaces is

$$\begin{aligned}\text{total occupant load} &= 37 \text{ occupants} + 120 \text{ occupants} \\ &= 157 \text{ occupants}\end{aligned}$$

The answer is (C).

Required Number of Exits

The number of exits or exit access doorways required from a space, a group of spaces, or an entire building is determined based on several factors, including the occupant load and occupancy of the space, the limitations on the length of the common path of egress travel, whether or not the building is sprinklered, and specific requirements for large occupant loads.

All buildings or portions of a building must have at least one exit. The IBC requires two exits or exit access doorways when the occupant load of a space or the common path of egress travel exceeds the numbers given in Table 1006.2.1, reproduced as Table 14.12.

Table 14.12 Spaces with One Exit or Exit Access Doorway

		maximum common path of egress travel distance (ft)		
		without sprinkler system (ft)		
occupancy	maximum occupant load of space	occupant load ≤ 30	occupant load > 30	with sprinkler system (ft)
A[c], E, M	49	75	75	75[a]
B	49	10	75	100[a]
F	49	75	75	100[a]
H-1, H-2, H-3	3	NP	NP	25[b]
H-4, H-5	10	NP	NP	75[b]
I-1, I-2[d], I-4	10	NP	NP	75[a]
I-3	10	NP	NP	100[a]
R-1	10	NP	NP	75[a]
R-2	10	NP	NP	125[a]
R-3[e]	10	NP	NP	125[a]
R-4[e]	10	75	75	125[a]
S[f]	29	100	75	100[a]
U	49	100	75	75[a]

NP = Not permitted

[a]Buildings equipped throughout with an automatic sprinkler system in accordance in IBC Sec. 903.3.1.1 or Sec. 903.3.1.2. See IBC Sec. 903 for occupancies where automatic sprinkler systems are permitted in accordance in IBC Sec. 903.3.1.2.
[b]Group H occupancies equipped throughout with an automatic sprinkler system in accordance in IBC Sec. 903.2.5.
[c]For a room or space used for assembly purposes having fix seating, see IBC Sec. 1029.8.
[d]For the travel distance limitations in Group I-2, see IBC Sec. 407.4.
[e]The length of common path of egress travel distance in a Group R-3 occupancy located in a mixed occupancy building or within a Group R-3 or R-4 congregate living facility.
[f]The length of the common path of egress travel distance in a Group S-2 open parking garage shall not be more than 100 ft.

2015 International Building Code, International Code Council, Inc., Washington, D.C. Reproduced with permission. www.iccsafe.org

There are several exceptions where the danger to life safety has been determined to be small enough that having only one exit or exit access doorway is acceptable. One such exception is an individual dwelling unit of R-2 or R-3 occupancy with a maximum occupant load of 20, where the dwelling is equipped with a sprinkler system. Another exception is for care suites in Group I-2 occupancies (where medical care is provided on a 24-hour basis for more than five persons who are incapable of self-preservation) that meet the special egress requirements for that occupancy.

The conditions under which an occupancy requires only one exit are given in IBC Table 1006.3.2(2), reproduced here as Table 14.13. These conditions apply only to one- and two-story buildings. For basements and the first three stories above grade, R-2 occupancies with a maximum number of four dwelling units and a maximum common path of egress travel of 125 ft are allowed to have just one exit. Three exits are required when the occupant load is between 501 and 1000, and at least four exits are required when the occupant load exceeds 1000.

Table 14.13
Stories with One Exit or Access to One Exit for Other Occupancies

story	occupancy	maximum occupant load per story	maximum common path of egress travel distance (ft)
first story above or below grade plane	A, B[a], E, F[b], M, U	49	75
	H-2, H-3	3	25
	H-4, H-5, I, R-1, R-2[b,c], R-4	10	75
	S[a,d]	29	75
second story above grade plane	B, F, M, S[d]	29	75
third story above grade plane and higher	NP	NA	NA

NP = not permitted

NA = not applicable

[a]Group B, F, and S occupancies in buildings equipped throughout with an automatic sprinkler system in accordance with IBC Sec. 903.3.1.1 shall have a maximum exit access travel distance of 100 ft.
[b]Buildings classified as Group R-2 equipped throughout with an automatic sprinkler system in accordance with IBC Sec. 903.3.1.1 or IBC Sec. 903.3.1.2 and provided with emergency escape and rescue openings in accordance with IBC Sec. 1030.
[c]This table is used for R-2 occupancies of sleeping units. For R-2 occupancies consisting of dwelling units, use IBC Table 1006.3.2(1).
[d]The length of exit access travel distance in a Group S-2 open parking garage shall not be more than 100 ft.

Common Path of Egress Travel

The *common path of egress travel* is the portion of the exit access travel distance measured from the most remote point within a story to the point where the occupants have separate access to two exits or exit access doorways and can make a choice about which direction to go (see Fig. 14.3).

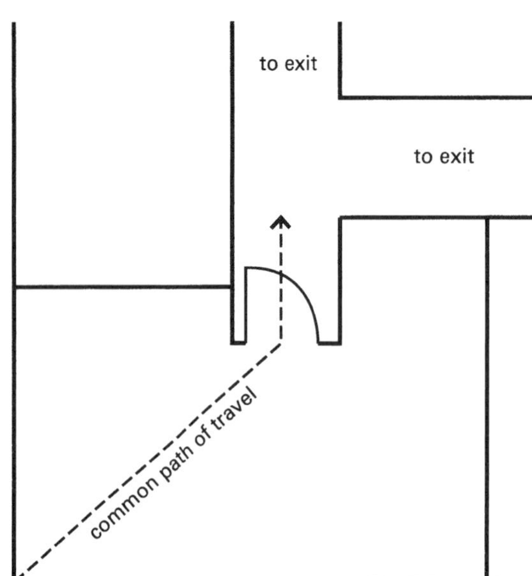

Figure 14.3
Common Path of Egress Travel

Even if the occupant load of a building space is less than that shown in Table 14.12, two exits are still required if the common path of egress travel exceeds the limits given in the same table. As indicated in the footnotes to the table, there are some exceptions and specific requirements for certain occupancies.

Exit Access Travel Distance

Exits are protected, but exit access areas are not. For this reason, the code limits how far someone in an exit access area should need to travel in order to get to an exit. Once a person is safely in an exit, travel distance is no longer an issue.

Exit access travel distance is the distance that an occupant would have to travel to get from the most remote point in the occupied portion of the exit access area, along the natural and unobstructed path of horizontal and vertical travel, to the entrance to the nearest exit.

Maximum travel distances are based on the occupancy of the building and whether or not the building is sprinklered. The exit access travel distance encompasses common paths of egress travel but extends to an exit, such as an exit stairway or an exit door leading outside the building.

There are special requirements in the IBC that decrease the allowable travel distances in some occupancies and situations such as malls, atriums, hazardous locations, educational uses, and assembly seating.

The maximum exit access travel distances are given in Table 1017.2 of the IBC (see Table 14.14). The footnotes of this table refer to other sections of the code for specific occupancy requirements.

Table 14.14
Exit Access Travel Distance[a]

occupancy	without sprinkler system (ft)	with sprinkler system (ft)
A, E, F-1, M, R, S-1	200	250[b]
I-1	not permitted	250[b]
B	200	300[c]
F-2, S-2, U	300	400[c]
H-1	not permitted	75[d]
H-2	not permitted	100[d]
H-3	not permitted	150[d]
H-4	not permitted	175[d]
H-5	not permitted	200[c]
I-2, I-3, I-4	not permitted	200[c]

[a]See the following sections for modifications to exit access travel distance requirements:
IBC Sec. 402.8: for the distance limitation in malls
IBC Sec. 404.9: for the distance limitation though an atrium space
IBC Sec. 407.4: for the distance limitation in Group I-2
IBC Sec. 408.6.1 and Sec. 408.8.1: for the distance limitations in Group I-3
IBC Sec. 411.4: for the distance limitation in special amusement buildings
IBC Sec. 412.7: for the distance limitation in aircraft manufacturing facilities
IBC Sec. 1006.2.2.2: for the distance limitation in refrigeration machinery rooms
IBC Sec. 1006.2.2.3: for the distance limitation in refrigerated rooms and spaces
IBC Sec. 1003.2: for buildings with one exit
IBC Sec. 1017.2.2: for increased distance limitation in Group F-1 and S-1
IBC Sec. 1029.7: for increased limitation in assembly seating
IBC Sec. 3013.4: for temporary structures.
IBC Sec. 3014.9: for pedestrian walkways
[b]Buildings equipped throughout with an automatic sprinkler system in accordance with IBC Sec. 903.3.1.1 or Sec. 903.3.1.2. See IBC Sec. 903 for occupancies where automatic sprinkler systems are permitted in accordance with IBC Sec. 903.3.1.2.
[c]Buildings equipped throughout with an automatic sprinkler system in accordance with IBC Sec. 903.3.1.1.
[d]Group H occupancies equipped throughout with an automatic sprinkler system in accordance with IBC Sec. 903.2.5.1.

2015 International Building Code, International Code Council, Inc., Washington, D.C. Reproduced with permission. www.iccsafe.org

Separation of Exits

Once the required number of exits or exit access doorways for each room, space, group of rooms, or story is known, the arrangement of those exits can be determined.

When two exits are required in a non-sprinklered building, they must be separated by a distance not less than one-half the length of the maximum overall diagonal dimension of the building or area to be served. For the purposes of the IBC requirement this distance is measured in a straight line between the exits or exit access doorways, from and to any point along the width of the doorways. See Fig. 14.4(a) and Fig. 14.4(b).

When interior exit stairways are interconnected with a 1-hour rated corridor, the required exit separation distance is measured along the shortest direct line of travel in the corridor. This requirement is intended to prevent a fire or other emergency from blocking both exits because they have been positioned too close together.

If the building is fully sprinklered, the minimum separation distance is reduced to one-third the maximum diagonal dimension of the room or area to be served.

If three or more exits are required, two of them must comply with the one-half (or one-third) diagonal distance rule, and the third (and any additional) exits must be arranged a reasonable distance apart so that if one becomes blocked, the others will still be available.

Exits and exit access doorways must be located so that their locations are obvious.

Project Planning

Figure 14.4
Arrangement of Exits

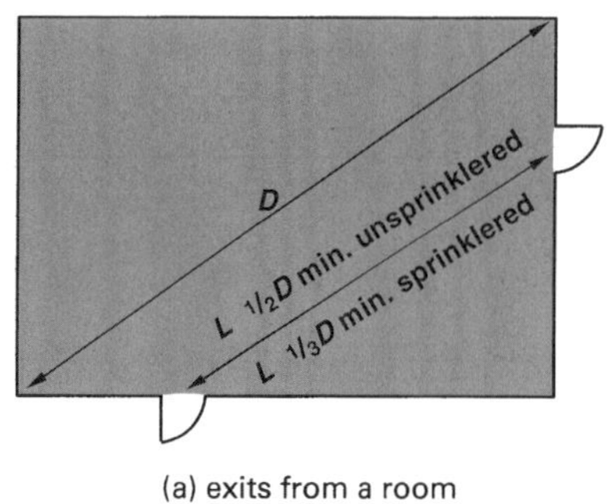

(a) exits from a room

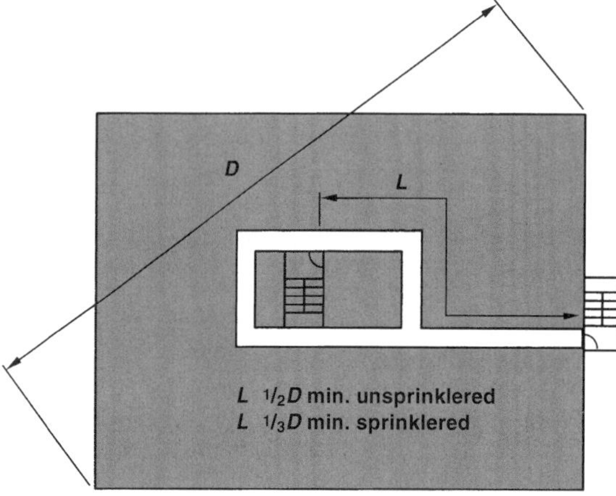

(b) exits from a building or group of rooms

Width of Exits

In general, the required minimum width of exits is determined by multiplying the occupant load by a factor of 0.3 in for stairways or 0.2 in for egress components other than stairways. Where stairways serve more than one story, only the occupant load of each story considered individually is used in calculating the required width of the stairways serving that story. For occupancies other than H and I-2, if the building is equipped throughout with both an automatic sprinkler system and an emergency voice/alarm communication system, the multiplying factors may be reduced to 0.2 in for stairways and 0.15 in for egress components other than stairways.

However, if the calculated width is less than the minimum width required elsewhere in the IBC (minimum corridor width, for example), the larger width must be used.

For example, consider the calculated office occupant load of 157 determined in Ex. 14.5. In this office, the minimum width of a corridor that is part of a means of egress system is

$$\begin{aligned}\text{minimum corridor width} &= (\text{occupancy load})(\text{width factor}) = (157 \text{ persons})\left(0.2\ \frac{\text{in}}{\text{person}}\right) \\ &= 31.4 \text{ in}\end{aligned}$$

However, IBC Table 1020.2 also specifies a minimum width of 44 in for a corridor that serves an occupant load greater than 50. The larger value must be used, so the minimum width is 44 in.

If two or more exits are required, the total width must be divided such that the loss of any one means of egress would not reduce the available capacity to less than 50% of the required capacity.

The IBC also requires that if doors are part of the required egress width, their clear width must be used, not the width of the door. For example, a 36 in door actually provides about 33 in of clear width when the thickness of the door in the 90° open position and the width of the stop are subtracted from the full width.

Exiting Through Intervening Spaces

In most cases, the means of egress from a room or space must lead directly to a corridor, exit enclosure, exterior door, or some other type of egress element. However, the IBC allows that egress can pass through an adjoining or intervening room or space, provided that three conditions are all met.

- One of the two rooms or spaces is an accessory to the other.
- Neither room or space is a Group H (high hazard) occupancy.
- There is a discernible path of egress travel to an exit.

For example, the door to a private office could lead into a larger general office area, which then leads into a corridor.

The IBC also states that egress cannot pass through kitchens, storerooms, closets, or spaces used for similar purposes, nor through any room that can be locked to prevent egress.

CORRIDORS

A *corridor* is a fully enclosed portion of an exit access that defines and provides a path of egress travel to an exit. The purpose of a corridor is to provide a space where occupants have limited choices regarding paths or directions of travel. When two exits are required, corridors must be laid out so that it is possible to travel in either direction to an exit. If one path is blocked, occupants always have an alternate way out.

As part of the exit access portion of the egress system, corridors may or may not be required to be constructed of fire-resistive construction depending on the occupancy, the occupant load, and whether or not the building is fully sprinklered. This is discussed in greater detail later in the chapter.

As mentioned earlier in this section, the size of a corridor must be determined by multiplying the occupant load by the appropriate factor. Also, the width of an exit must not be less than 44 in, with the exceptions given in Table 14.15.

Table 14.15
Exceptions to Minimum Corridor Width of 44 in

minimum exit width (in)	type of corridor
24	access to electrical, mechanical, and plumbing
36	all occupancies, where occupant load is less than 50
36	within a dwelling unit
72	Group E occupancies serving an occupant load of 100 or more
72	Group I occupancy corridors serving stretcher traffic in ambulatory care facilities
96	Group 1-2 occupancies where bed movement is required

The minimum width of a corridor as required by a building code, however, should be checked against the minimum width required by the *2010 ADA Standards* or other accessibility guidelines, as discussed in Chap. 15.

The width of a corridor cannot be encroached upon, with the following exceptions. See Fig. 14.5. Projecting objects cannot reduce the minimum clear width of an accessible route.

- Doors opening into the path of egress travel may reduce the required width up to one-half during the course of the swing, but when fully open the door must not project more than 7 in into the required width.
- Handrails may not reduce the required means of egress width more than 4.5 in on each side.
- Nonstructural horizontal projections such as trim and similar decorative features may project horizontally from either side up to a maximum of 1.5 in.
- Structural elements such as light fixtures or furnishings must not project more than 4 in between the heights of 27 in and 80 in above the walking surface.

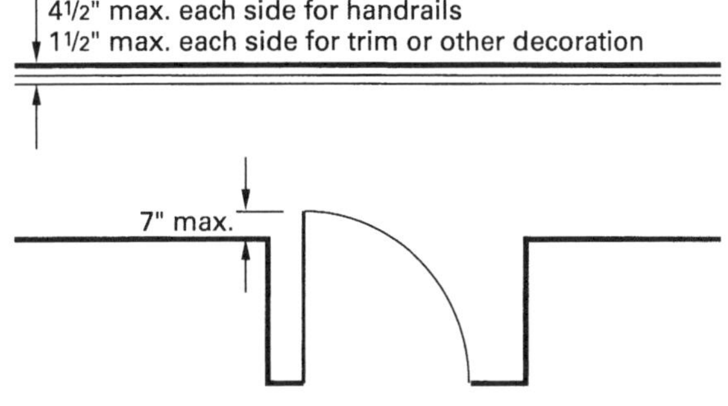

Figure 14.5
Allowable Projections into Exit Corridors

Corridor Construction

Corridors must be fire-resistance-rated in accordance with IBC Table 1020.1, shown as Table 14.16, and they must be constructed as fire partitions, as described in IBC Sec. 708. This means that the corridor walls must extend from the floor to the underside of the structural slab above, or to the underside of a fire-resistance-rated ceiling. Some of the options are shown in Fig. 14.1.

There are four exceptions when corridors do not have to be fire-resistance-rated.

- Group E occupancies where classrooms and assembly rooms have half their required egress leading directly to the exterior at ground level
- corridors in a dwelling unit or a guest room in a Group R occupancy or sleeping units in Group I-1 and Group R occupancies

- corridors in open parking garages
- Group B occupancies that require only one exit by other provisions in the code

Table 14.16
Corridor Fire-Resistance Rating

		required fire-resistance rating (hours)	
occupancy	occupant load served by corridor	without sprinkler system	with sprinkler system[c]
H-1, H-2, H-3	all	not permitted	1
H-4, H-5	greater than 30	not permitted	1
A, B, E, F, M, S, U	greater than 30	1	0
R	greater than 10	not permitted	0.5
I-2[a], I-4	all	not permitted	0
I-1, I-3	all	not permitted	1[b]

[a]For requirements for occupancies in Group I-2, see IBC Sec. 407.2 and Sec. 407.3.
[b]For a reduction in the fire-resistance rating for occupancies in Group I-3, see IBC Sec. 408.8.
[c]Buildings equipped throughout with an automatic sprinkler system in accordance with IBC Sec. 903.3.1.1 or Sec. 903.3.1.2 where allowed.

2015 International Building Code, International Code Council, Inc., Washington, D.C. Reproduced with permission.

Openings in Corridors

A door placed in a 1-hour corridor must have a fire rating of at least 20 minutes and must have approved smoke- and draft-control seals around it. The door also must either be self-closing (with a door closer) or close automatically on actuation of a smoke detector. Both the door and the frame must bear the label of an approved testing agency such as Underwriters Laboratories (UL).

Glazing may be used in a 1-hour rated corridor wall only if the glass is listed and labeled as having a $^3/_4$-hour fire-protection rating. The glass must make up no more than 25% of the area of a common wall with any room, unless the glass used is fire resistance rated (tested according to ASTM E119); in that case, there is no limitation on the percentage of glass.

When a duct penetrates a rated corridor, it must be provided with a fire damper. The damper must have a fire rating of at least 20 minutes.

Glazing and other opening protective requirements in fire partitions and fire walls are shown in Table 14.2 and Table 14.3 and discussed in more detail in Chap. 28. Doors are discussed later in the chapter.

Corridors Continuity

Once an occupant has reached a certain level of safety in the egress path, that level of safety should persist until the occupant has exited. From this principle it follows that, when a corridor is required to be fire resistance rated, that corridor must continue to an exit. The egress path from that corridor must not pass through intervening rooms.

There are a few exceptions. First, the egress path may pass through foyers, lobbies, and reception rooms as long as these spaces are constructed as required for the corridors. In essence, these spaces become enlarged portions of the corridor.

Second, corridors in fully sprinklered Group B buildings may pass through enclosed elevator lobbies if all areas of the building have access to at least one required exit without passing through the lobby.

Dead Ends

A *dead end* exists when a person in any part of the building required to have two means of egress has only one choice of direction that leads to an exit access doorway or an exit. When a corridor is required to lead to two or more exits, a person in that corridor should always have at least two choices of direction.

The IBC limits the length of a dead-end corridor to 20 ft. There are three exceptions based on occupancy and sprinklering.

- Group B, E, F, I-1, M, R-l, R-2, R-4, S, and U occupancies may have 50 ft dead-end corridors if the entire building is equipped with an automatic sprinkler system.

- Dead-end corridors may be 50 ft long in Group I-3 occupancies of Conditions 2, 3, or 4. These condition numbers refer to specific security arrangements in detention facilities.
- A dead-end corridor may be longer than 20 ft if its length is less than 2.5 times its width at the narrowest part.

DOORS

Doors are potential obstructions to egress throughout the egress system, so they are highly regulated by the IBC and other model codes. Means of egress doors must meet the following design criteria.

- They must be readily distinguishable from the adjacent construction.
- They must be readily recognizable as means of egress doors.
- They cannot be covered with mirrors or other reflective materials.
- They cannot be concealed with curtains, drapes, decorations, or similar materials.

If the design provides more than the minimum required number of doors, the additional doors must meet the same criteria as the required doors.

Size of Doors

The minimum width of egress door openings must be sufficient for the occupant load served, and the clear width must always be at least 32 in. The clear opening width must be measured between the face of the door and the doorstop when the door is open 90°. In practical terms, this means that 36 in doors must be used as exit doors. The maximum width of swinging egress doors is 48 in. The minimum height of egress doors is 80 in.

There are several exceptions to the size requirements, including doors in residential occupancies and sleeping rooms in I-3 occupancies. Refer to IBC Sec. 1010.1.1 for details on these exceptions.

Project Planning

Door Swing

Egress doors must be pivoted or side-hinged, so that its operation is easy and familiar to the user. There are some exceptions to the requirement for side-swinging doors, including private garages; office areas; factory and storage areas with an occupant load of 10 or less; individual dwelling units of R-2, R-3, and R-4 occupancies; power-operated doors; and a few others. Refer to IBC Sec. 1010.1.2 for a complete list of exceptions.

In most cases, special doors (such as revolving, sliding, and overhead doors) cannot be used in required exits. Power-operated doors and revolving doors are sometimes allowed if they meet certain requirements. A revolving door, for example, must have leaves that collapse under opposing pressure and must have a diameter such that at least 36 in of exit width is provided when the leaves are collapsed; there must also be at least one conforming egress door in close proximity. The IBC does allow the use of manually operated horizontal sliding doors as a means of egress element in occupancies other than Group H, provided that the occupant load is 10 or less. For additional requirements for special doors, refer to IBC Sec. 1010.1.4.

Egress doors must swing in the direction of travel when the area served has an occupant load of 50 or more, or if the area is a Group H occupancy. This is to prevent a door from being blocked when people are trying to get out in a panic. Exam candidates frequently make the mistake of not showing required doors—all building exit doors, stairway doors, and doors from spaces with a high occupant load—swinging in the direction of travel. See Fig. 14.6(a).

Doors must not swing into a required travel path such as a corridor. In many instances, exit doors must be recessed as shown in Fig. 14.6(b) to meet this requirement. Recessed doors must be compensated for by providing at least 18 in, and preferably 24 in, on the pull side of the door next to the latch jamb for accessibility. See Chap. 15 for other maneuvering clearance requirements.

Interior swinging egress doors without closers must have a maximum opening force of 5 lbf. Other doors must have a maximum opening force of 15 lbf. The maximum allowable force needed to set the door in motion is 30 lbf. The door must swing to a full-open position when subjected to 15 lbf. All these required maximum forces are measured on the latch side of the door.

Figure 14.6 Exit Door Swing

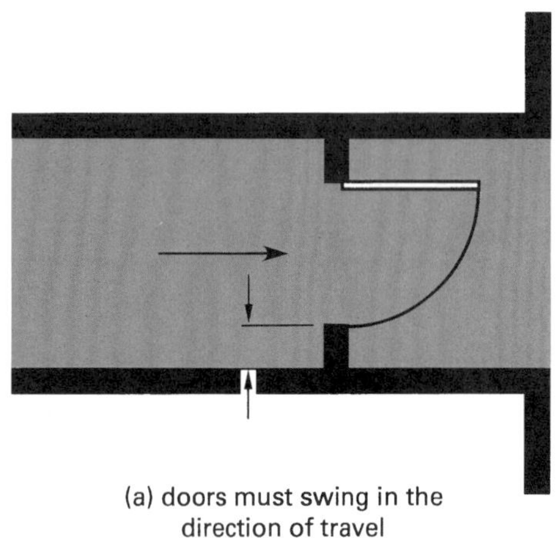

(a) doors must swing in the direction of travel

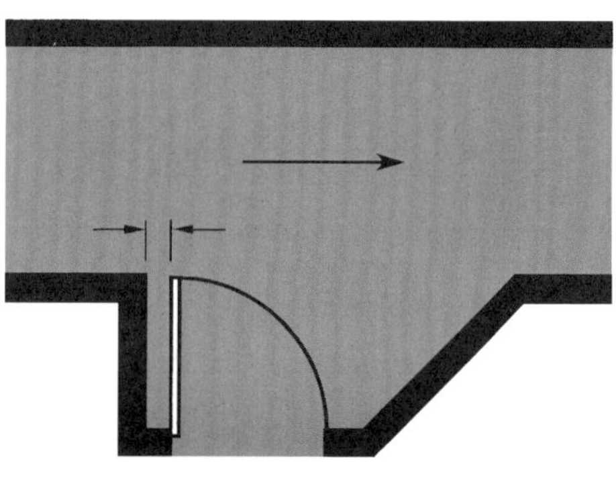

(b) doors must not swing into the required exit path more than 7 in

Fire-Resistance Rating Requirements

An egress door in a fire-resistance-rated partition is required to have a fire rating. The specific fire rating varies depending on the rating of the partition. These ratings are shown in Table 14.2 and Table 14.3. For most applications, only a few door assembly ratings are commonly encountered. These are summarized in Table 14.17. If a building is fully sprinklered, corridors in A, B, E, F, M, S, and U occupancies (and in some other situations) do not need to have a fire rating, so in these cases fire-protection-rated doors are not required under the IBC.

Table 14.17 Required Ratings of Doors Based on Partition Type

use of partition	rating of partition	required door assembly rating
corridors, smoke barriers	1 hour or less	20 minutes
fire partitions	1 hour	$\frac{3}{4}$ hour
exit passageways	1 hour	1 hour
exit stairs	1 hour	1 hour
occupancy separations	1 hour	$\frac{3}{4}$ hour
exit stairs	2 hours	$1\frac{1}{2}$ hour
fire separations	2 hours	$1\frac{1}{2}$ hour

2015 International Building Code, International Code Council, Inc., Washington, D.C. Reproduced with permission. www.iccsafe.org

In addition to having a 20-minute fire rating, doors in corridors and smoke barriers must meet the requirements for positive-pressure fire testing (NFPA 252 or UL 10C, excluding the hose stream test) as discussed in Chap. 8. These doors must also meet the requirements for smoke and draft control, tested in accordance with UL 1784, *Standard for Safety for Air Leakage Tests for Door Assemblies*, with an automatic bottom seal installed across the full width of the bottom of the door during the test. These may need to carry "S" (smoke) labels if required by the local authority having jurisdiction. Smoke barriers are commonly used to split health care and detention facilities into separate zones. Smoke barriers are also required in vertical shafts, vestibules to stairways, and areas of refuge.

Additional requirements for power-operated doors, horizontal sliding doors, and revolving and access-control doors, as well as for delayed-egress locks, gates, thresholds, floor elevation, and door arrangement, are given in IBC Sec. 1010.1.4 and Sec. 1010.1.5.

See Chap. 28 for more information on building code requirements for doors, hardware, and glazing in fire-rated doors.

STAIRWAYS

A *stair* is defined by the IBC as a change in elevation accomplished by one or more risers. A *stairway* consists of one or more flights of stairs with the necessary landings and platforms connecting them to form a continuous passage from one level to another. An *interior exit stairway* is an exit component that meets one or more means of egress requirements. An *exit access stairway* is an interior stairway (for example, a monumental stair serving two floors of a retail store) that is not a required interior exit stairway.

Exit Stairways

Because vertical shafts provide the most readily available path for fire and smoke spreading upward from floor to floor, interior exit stairways must be completely enclosed. In buildings four or more stories in height, they must be enclosed with 2-hour rated walls; in buildings less than four stories, 1-hour rated construction is required. The stories include basements but exclude mezzanines. 2-hour stairways must have $1\frac{1}{8}$-hour rated doors, and 1-hour stairways must have 1-hour rated doors.

Generally, the floor openings between stories created by exit access stairways must be enclosed. However, the IBC provides eight exceptions to this requirement, three of which are commonly encountered.

- An exit access stairway that serves only two stories is not required to be enclosed unless it is in a Group I-2 or Group I-3 occupancy.
- An exit access stairway with a single residential dwelling unit or sleeping unit in a Group R-1, Group R-2, or Group R-3 occupancy does not have to be enclosed.
- In any occupancy other than B and M, an exit access stairway may be open if all the following conditions are met.
  - The floor opening does not connect more than four stories.
  - The building has an automatic sprinkler system.
  - The area of the floor opening between stories is not greater than twice the horizontal projected area of the stairway.
  - The opening is protected by a draft curtain and closely spaced sprinklers in accordance with NFPA 13.

Refer to IBC Sec. 1019 for other exceptions.

Requirements for All Stairways

As with corridors, stairways serving an occupant load of 50 or more must be at least 44 in wide or as wide as determined by multiplying the occupant load by 0.3 in or 0.2 in, whichever is greater. Stairways serving an occupant load of less than 50 must not be less than 36 in wide. Handrails may project into the required width $4\frac{1}{8}$ in. If the stairway is also the accessible means of egress, the minimum clear width is 48 in between handrails.

Stair risers cannot measure less than 4 in or more than 7 in, and the tread must not be less than 11 in. Risers for barrier-free stairs cannot exceed 7 in; treads must have an acceptable nosing design as shown in Fig. 14.7. For residential occupancies and private stairways in R-2 occupancies, the maximum riser may be 7.75 in and the minimum tread may be 10 in.

There are other requirements for circular stairways, winders, spiral stairways, and stairs serving as aisles in assembly seating areas. Winding, circular, and spiral stairways may be used as exits in R-3 occupancies and in private stairways of R-l occupancies only if they meet the requirements shown in Fig. 20.6.

Project Planning

Figure 14.7 Acceptable Nosing Shapes for Safety and Accessibility

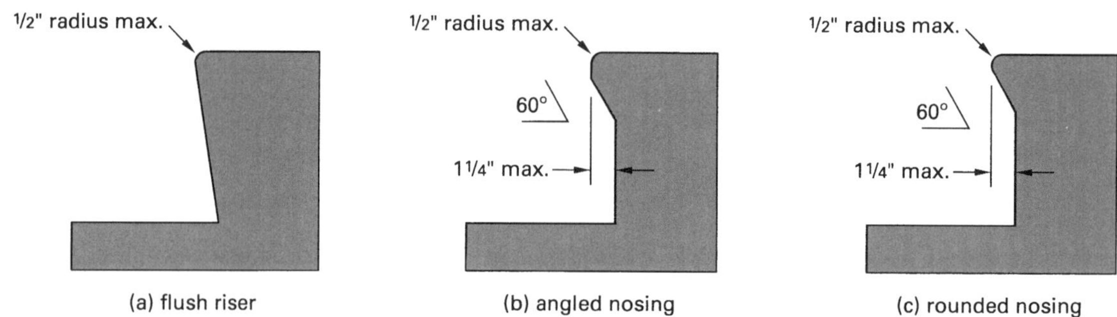

Figure 14.8 Code Requirements for Stairways

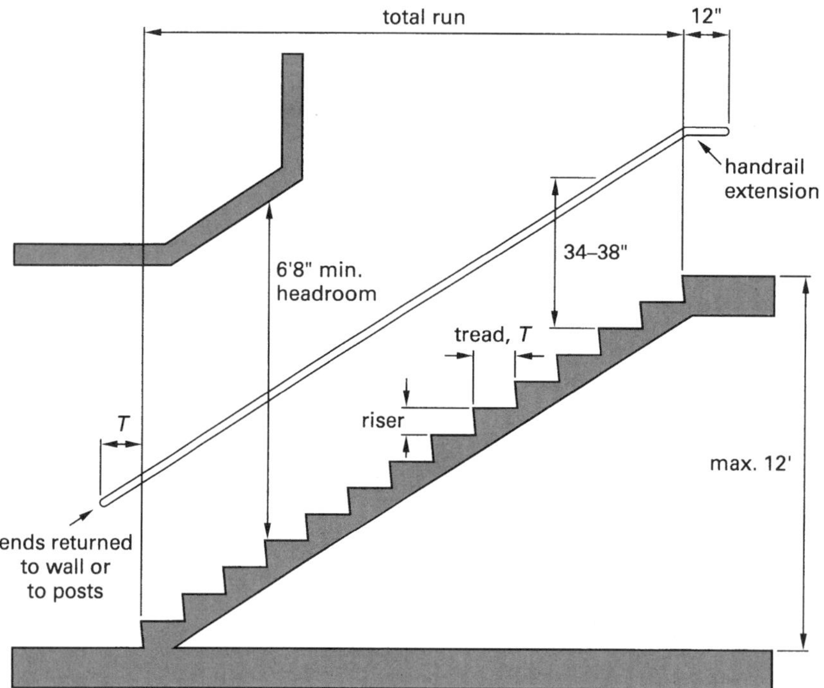

Landings must be provided at the top and bottom of every stairway, and the minimum dimension of the landing in the direction of travel must not be less than the width of the stair, but need not be more than 48 in if the stairway is a straight run (that is, if it does not change direction). The maximum distance permitted between landings is 12 ft, measured vertically.

Handrails must be provided on both sides of stairs, even if there is only one riser. However, stairways in dwelling units, spiral stairways, and aisle stairs that only serve seating on one side require a handrail on only one side. Stairways wider than 5 ft must have intermediate handrails.

Handrails are not required in the following locations.

- decks, patios, and walkways that have a single change in elevation, where the landing depth on each side is greater than that is required for landings
- single risers in Group R-3 occupancies at an entrance or egress door
- changes in room elevations of three or fewer risers within dwelling units and sleeping units in Group R-2 and Group R-3 occupancies

Refer to IBC Sec. 1029 for specific requirements for handrails in assembly occupancies.

As shown in Fig. 14.8, the top of the handrail must be between 34 in and 38 in above the nosing of the treads. The handrail must extend not less than 12 in horizontally beyond the top riser, and not less than the depth of one tread beyond the bottom riser. Each end must be returned to the wall or floor or terminate in a newel post. The gripping portion cannot be less than 1.25 in or more than 2 in in cross-sectional dimension. There must be a space at least 1.5 in wide between the wall and the handrail.

When handrails are used, they must be easily graspable and mounted far enough away from the wall to allow gripping. The IBC and *2010 ADA Standards* limit the size and shape of handrails, as shown in Fig. 14.9. A standard Type I handrail must have a perimeter of at least 4 in and no more than 6.25 in. A handrail may have a perimeter greater than 6.25 in if it is of Type II, with a graspable finger recess on both sides. Type II handrails are allowed in Group R-3 (residential) occupancies, within dwelling units in Group R-2 occupancies (apartments, condominiums), and in Group U occupancies that are accessory to a Group R-3 occupancy or accessory to individual dwellings in Group R-2 occupancies.

Figure 14.9 Handrail Configurations

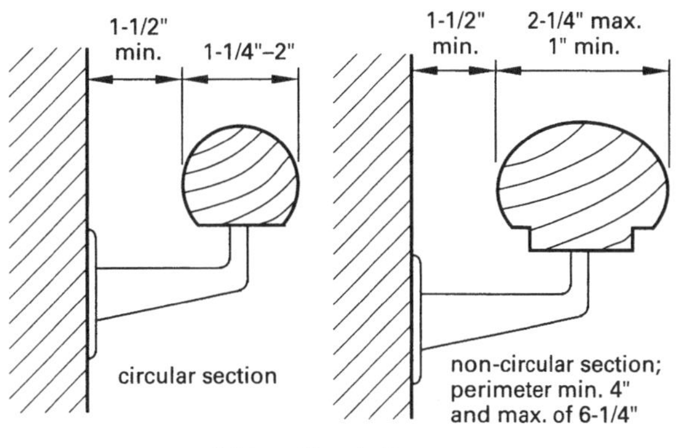

(a) type I handrails

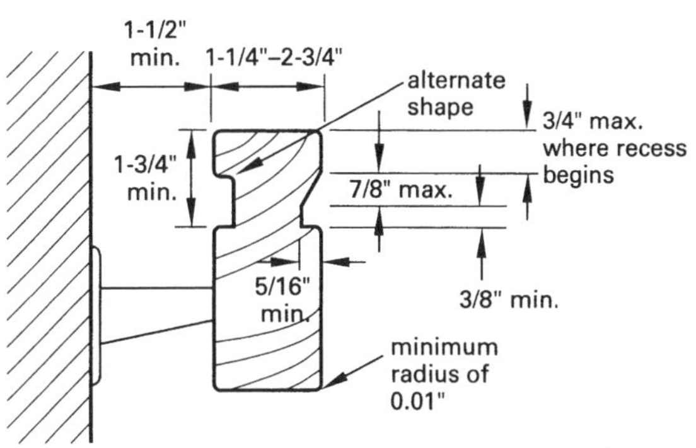

(b) type II handrail

See Chap. 20 for additional diagrams and more information regarding building code requirements for stairway layout. See Chap. 15 for accessibility requirements.

OTHER CODE REQUIREMENTS

High-Rise Buildings

High-rise buildings pose a unique problem for fire and life safety. The IBC defines a *high-rise building* as one with occupied floors more than 75 ft above the lowest level of fire department vehicle access. Buildings this high are often office buildings, hotels, and apartment buildings. Fire department apparatus may not be able to reach above 75 ft, so special precautions must be taken.

IBC Chap. 4 gives specific requirements for these buildings. High-rise buildings must be provided with an automatic sprinkler system, smoke detectors and alarms, communication systems, a central control station for fire department use, smoke control for exit stair enclosures, and standby power systems, among other special requirements.

Glazing

Building codes regulate the use of glass in exterior windows (limiting the area and type based on wind loading, energy conservation, and other factors), fire-rated assemblies, hazardous locations subject to human impact, and sloped glazing and skylights. See Chap. 28 for more information on code requirements for glazing.

Guards

A *guard* (or *guardrail*) is a component whose function is to prevent falls from an elevated area. For example, a second-floor opening that overlooks the first floor must be protected with a guard. Guards are required along open-sided walking surfaces, mezzanines, industrial equipment platforms, stairs, ramps, and landings that are more than 30 in above the floor or grade below, measured vertically at any point within 36 in horizontally to the edge of the open side. There are several exceptions, including stages and raised platforms.

Guards must be a minimum of 42 in high and designed such that a 4 in diameter sphere cannot pass through any opening up to a height of 36 in; above 36 in, the maximum opening may be $4\frac{3}{8}$ in. Guards must be designed to resist a load of 50 lbf/ft applied in any direction at the top of the guard. Additional design requirements and exceptions are detailed in IBC Sec. 1015.

One exception allows the use of a 36 in minimum height guard in Group R-3 occupancies (one- and two-family dwellings, small congregate living facilities), which are not more than three stories above grade, and within individual dwelling units in R-2 occupancies (apartments, dormitories) not more than three stories above grade with a separate means of egress.

In addition, guards are required at operable windows in Group R-2 and and Group R-3 occupancies, and in one-, two-, and multiple-family dwellings. When the sill of an operable window is more than 72 in above the exterior surface below, then the lowest part of the clear opening of the window cannot be less than 36 in above the finished floor surface of the room in which the window is located. Operable windows below 36 in cannot allow passage of a 4 in diameter sphere. There are other exceptions for windows with fall prevention devices.

Fire Detection and Suppression

Fire detection, alarm, and suppression systems are important parts of a building's overall life safety and fire protection strategies. Almost every new building is required to have some type of detection device, even if it is a single smoke detector in a residence. Other occupancies, such as high-rise buildings and hotels, must have elaborate detection and alarm systems, including communication devices on each floor to allow firefighters to talk with each other and with occupants in the event of an emergency. Both audio and visual alarms are required for people with hearing or visual impairments. See Chap. 32 for more information on fire suppression systems and detection and alarm systems.

Mechanical Systems

The companion volumes for the IBC are the *International Mechanical Code* (IMC), *International Fuel Gas Code* (IFGC), *International Energy Conservation Code* (IECC), and the *International Green Construction Code* (IgCC). (See Chap. 13 for more information about the IECC and the IgCC.)

The IMC regulates the design, installation, maintenance, alteration, and inspection of HVAC systems, as well as components, equipment, and listed appliances, except for fuel gas-fired equipment and residential structures.

Detached one- and two-family dwellings and multiple one-family dwellings (that is, townhouses) not more than three stories high with separate means of egress must comply with the *International Residential Code* (IRC).

The IFGC regulates the installation of fuel gas distribution piping and equipment, fuel gas-fired appliances, and fuel gas-fired appliance venting systems. Together, the IMC and the IFGC cover all currently used fuels.

Separate chapters in the IMC include requirements for ventilation; exhaust systems; duct systems; combustion air; chimneys and vents; specific appliances, fireplaces, and solid fuel-burning equipment; boilers, water heaters, and pressure vessels; refrigeration; hydronic piping; fuel oil piping and storage; and solar systems.

The IECC regulates the design and installation of HVAC systems for efficient energy use. Additionally, the IMC refers to the *International Plumbing Code* when mechanical equipment is connected to plumbing systems, and to NFPA 70 for electrical wiring, controls, and connections to equipment and appliances. See Chap. 17 and Chap. 31 for information on mechanical systems.

Ventilation

The IECC requires that attics, crawl spaces, and similar spaces be ventilated in order to prevent the accumulation of detrimental moisture, such as the condensation of moist air on cold surfaces. Accumulated moisture can cause dry rot on wood surfaces and rust on ferrous metals, and it can lessen the effectiveness of insulation.

In an attic, the net free ventilating area provided must be at least $^1/_{150}$ of the area of the space ventilated. The required ventilating area may be reduced to $^1/_{300}$ of the area if both of two conditions are met.

- If 40% to 50% of the required ventilating area is provided by ventilators located in the upper portion of the space (at least 3 ft below the ridge or highest point of the space, with the balance provided by eave or cornice vents), then the $^1/_{300}$ value may be used.
- In climate zones 6, 7, and 8, if a Class I or II vapor barrier is installed on the warm-in-winter side of the ceiling below the attic (at least 1 in of space must be maintained between the insulation and the underside of the roof sheathing), then the $^1/_{300}$ value may be used.

In a crawl space without a vapor retarder, the net free ventilation area must be at least $^1/_{150}$ of the crawl space area. If the ground surface is covered with a Class I vapor retarder, the total area may be reduced to $^1/_{1500}$ of the underfloor area. A Class I vapor retarder has a permeance of 0.1 perm or less. In all cases, the ventilating openings must be arranged to provide cross ventilation of the space.

Crawl spaces, attics, and other uninhabited spaces may also be mechanically ventilated. When this is done, the IMC requires a minimum exhaust rate of 0.02 cfm (cubic feet per minute) per square foot of horizontal area. The ventilation must be automatically controlled to operate whenever the relative humidity in the space exceeds 60%. In the IBC, this rate is expressed as 1.0 cfm for each 50 ft^2 of crawl space floor area. A mechanically ventilated crawl space also requires a Class I vapor retarder.

Chimneys and Vents

According to the IMC, a *chimney* is a primarily vertical structure containing one or more flues to carry gaseous products of combustion and air from a fuel-burning appliance to the outdoors. A chimney is capable of venting flue gases at higher temperatures than vents can. Chimneys may be either masonry or factory-made.

A *vent* is a pipe or factory-made component that contains a passageway for carrying combustion products and air to the atmosphere. Vents must be listed and labeled for use with specific types or classes of appliances.

The ventilation requirements for chimneys and vents are distinct from those discussed earlier in this section and from the requirements for exhaust systems discussed in Chap. 17. The IMC defines requirements for chimneys and vents, including size, location, construction, and installation. Requirements for factory-made fireplace chimneys are given in the IMC, while requirements for masonry fireplaces are detailed in the IBC.

Plumbing Systems

The *International Plumbing Code* (IPC) is the companion volume to the IBC that regulates plumbing design and construction. The IPC gives the minimum number of toilets, lavatories, drinking fountains, and other sanitary fixtures required in a building. The number required is based on occupancy and the number of people served, as described in IBC Table 2902.1. The numbers given in the IBC are minimum numbers, not optimum numbers.

The IPC also outlines detailed requirements for plumbing system design, individual materials, and methods of installation. Candidates should be able to use the IPC table to determine the required number of fixtures based on occupancy. See Chap. 17 for more information on plumbing systems.

Figure 14.10 Fireplace Hearth and Trim Dimensions

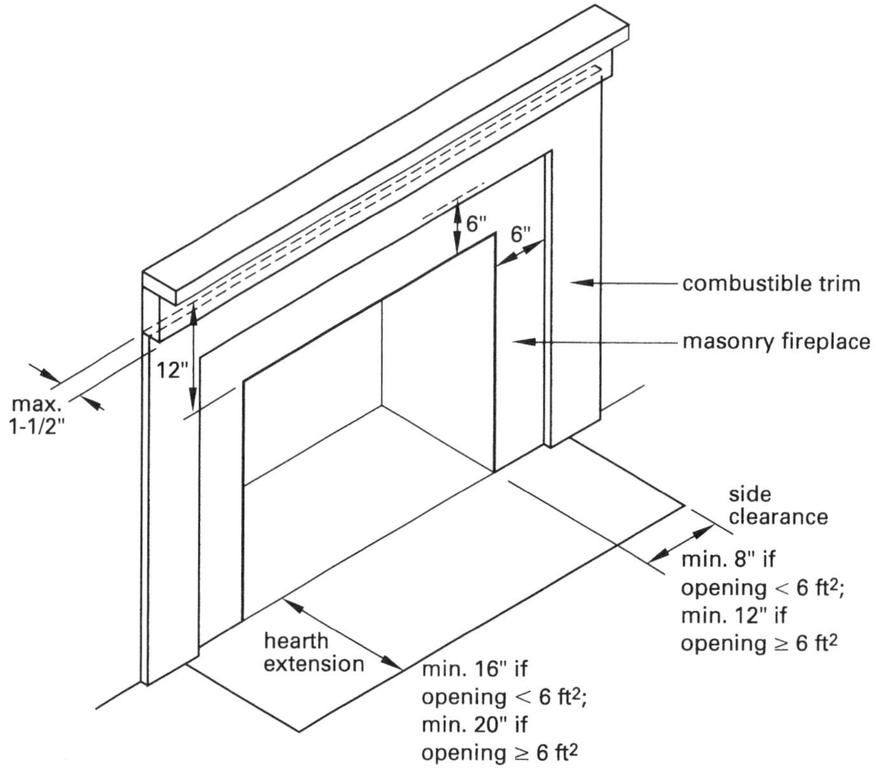

Project Planning

Electrical Systems

The IBC references the *National Electrical Code* (NEC), published by the National Fire Protection Association. The NEC details the requirements for materials and the design of the power supply and lighting systems of buildings. See Chap. 17 for more information on electrical systems.

Sound Ratings

The IBC requires that wall and floor/ceiling assemblies in residential occupancies that separate dwelling units or guestrooms from each other and from public spaces be designed and constructed to provide for control of sound transmission. The IBC specifies a minimum sound-transmission class (STC) of 50, or 45 if field tested, for walls. This provision does not apply to dwelling unit entrance doors, but these doors must fit tight to the frame and sill. The minimum impact insulation class (IIC) for floors must be 50, or 45 if field tested. Construction details that satisfy these requirements must be selected. For example, penetrations in a sound wall must be sealed or otherwise treated to maintain the required rating. See Chap. 19 and Chap. 32 for more information on acoustics.

Fireplaces

There are two basic types of fireplaces: *factory-built*, or *prefabricated fireplaces*, and traditional masonry fireplaces. A factory-built fireplace must be installed in accordance with the IMC and the manufacturer's directions, including requirements for minimum clearances between the fireplace and any combustible construction or trim nearby.

The IBC gives detailed requirements for construction of a masonry fireplace, including the foundation dimensions and materials, wall thickness, firebox configuration, and chimney construction. Seismic reinforcement is required in all seismic design categories except A and B. No part of a masonry fireplace located in a building may be closer than 2 in to combustible materials along the front and sides of the fireplace, nor closer than 4 in along its back face. The airspace created must be kept clear except for any fire blocking required at floor and ceiling penetrations.

For the interior, exposed parts of a fireplace opening, the main requirements defined in the code are those governing the materials and the dimensions of the hearth extensions, the trim around the opening, and the mantel. A hearth extension must be made of concrete or masonry, supported by noncombustible materials, and reinforced to carry its own weight as well as all imposed loads. The hearth extension must be a minimum of 2 in thick while the hearth itself must be a minimum of 4 in thick. Figure 14.10 shows some of the required dimensions for masonry hearths and trim.

No combustible trim is allowed within 6 in of the fireplace opening. Any combustible trim between 6 in and 12 in from the opening may only project $^1/_8$ in from the masonry surface of the fireplace for every 1 in of space between the trim and the opening. For example, at a point 6 in from the opening, any combustible trim may project only 6 times $^1/_8$ in, or $^3/_4$ in, out from the face of the fireplace. At 12 in from the opening, trim may project only 12 times $^1/_8$ in, or 1.5 in, out from the face. Beyond 12 in, combustible trim or a mantel can project any amount. Combustible materials located along the sides of the fireplace opening that project more than 1.5 in from the face of the fireplace must have an additional clearance equal to the projection.

ZONING REQUIREMENTS

This section describes how some important zoning requirements are applied to site and building design. Some of the history and basic concepts of zoning are reviewed in Chap. 8.

Floor Area Ratios

The amount of land on a site that can be covered by a building is determined by the interrelationship of two zoning restrictions: floor area ratio and setbacks. *Floor area ratio* (FAR) is the ratio of the gross floor area within a structure to the area of the lot on which the structure is situated. For example, if the floor area ratio is 1.0, and a lot is 75,000 ft^2 in area, the maximum permissible gross floor space is 75,000 ft^2. Within the constraints of setbacks and bulk planes, this 75,000 ft^2 of floor space may be configured in any number of ways.

Figure 14.11
Examples of Floor Area Ratios

FAR = 1.0

(a) 50% site coverage

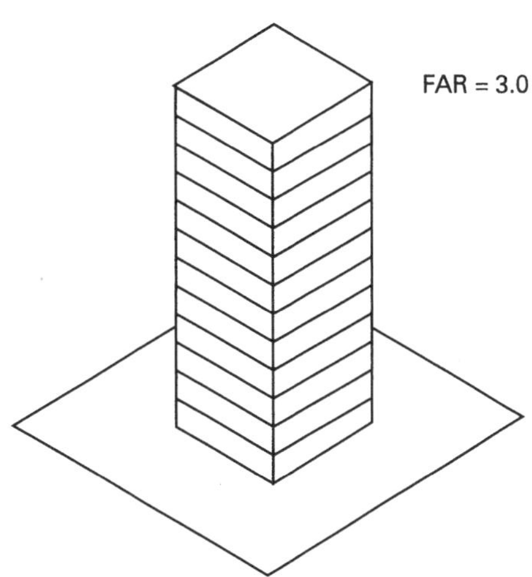

(b) 25% site coverage 12 stories

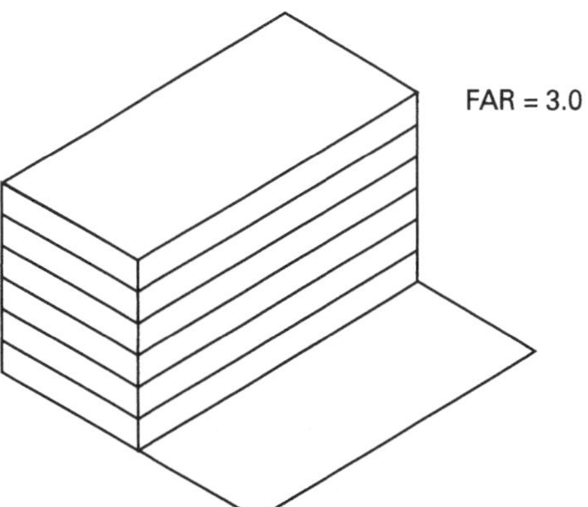

(c) 50% site coverage 6 stories

Figure 14.11(a) shows a structure occupying only 50% of the ground area. If the FAR is 1.0, then a two-story building can be constructed.

Figure 14.11(b) and Fig. 14.11(c) illustrate two instances where the same floor area ratio can result in two different building forms. In Fig. 14.11(b), the building occupies only 25% ground area. If the FAR is 3.0, then a 12-story building can be erected. In Fig. 14.11(c), the building occupies 50% of the land, so only six stories can be built. In both cases, the building area is three times the land area. The maximum height of a building may also be limited by construction type and occupancy.

Floor area ratios must always be developed with regard to setbacks. A *setback* is the minimum distance a building must be placed from a property line. Setback distances usually vary depending on which property line is involved. The distance from the property line facing the street or the primary front of the property is known as the *front setback*; this is usually the greatest setback distance. The distance from the back of the lot is the *rear setback*, and the distance from the side property line is known as the *side setback*. In the example of Fig. 14.11(a), for instance, setbacks might preclude covering 50% of the site, so to reach the maximum allowable floor area ratio, the building would have to be more than two stories. Setbacks also regulate the bulk of a building and how much space results between structures.

Bulk Plane Restrictions

A *bulk plane restriction* is a zoning technique that establishes an imaginary inclined plane beginning at the lot line or the center of the street at a given elevation and slopes at a prescribed angle toward and over the lot. The building cannot extend beyond this plane. This restriction ensures adequate light, air, and solar access for neighboring properties and for the open space and streets around the land.

Sometimes, zoning ordinances will also place maximum limits on a building's number of stories or height in feet above grade level.

Variances in Zoning

There are many instances when zoning restrictions create an undue hardship on a property owner, or a zoning ordinance does not completely cover unusual conditions. In these cases, the property owner can apply for a *variance*, or permission to deviate from the zoning regulations. Municipalities or other local jurisdictions establish a procedure by which owners can describe their situation and apply for a variance. Typically, a public hearing is held to allow nearby property owners and other interested parties the opportunity to object.

If a new zoning ordinance is applied to existing development, there may be properties with nonconforming uses. These are allowed to remain unless the owner stops using the property in its original fashion or the property is demolished or destroyed by fire. Then, any new use and new construction must conform to the zoning requirements.

A zoning board or planning commission may also grant a *conditional use permit*, which allows a nonconforming use or other use in the zoning ordinance if the property owner meets certain conditions. A conditional use permit is often granted if the exception is in the public interest. For example, a zoning board may allow a temporary street fair in a location where it would normally be prohibited, or it might allow a church to violate a setback provision to build a new, accessible entrance, with the condition that other open space be provided for the community.

ENVIRONMENTAL REGULATIONS

There are many environmental regulations with which an architect should be familiar. These are established at the federal, state, and local levels, and are in addition to voluntary building rating systems, such as LEED, as well as more general building codes and zoning ordinances.

At the federal level, regulations include requirements under the jurisdiction of the Environmental Protection Agency, including environmental impact statements, wetlands, and laws under the Clean Water Act. There are also federal laws related to hazardous materials and consumer products (see Chap. 8).

At the state and local levels, there are varying requirements for state environmental impact statements, erosion and sediment control, solar access, indoor air quality, and energy conservation. Many of these are discussed in Chap. 13.

DEFINITIONS

The following terms are frequently used by building codes to precisely communicate meaning. Additional terms are defined in the main text of this chapter. Although the differences between terms are sometimes subtle, it is advisable to become familiar with them.

area of refuge: An area where people unable to use stairways can remain temporarily while waiting for assistance.

automatic closing door: A door that is normally held in the open position but is released to close on activation by a smoke detector or other type of fire alarm system. An automatic closing door must be self-closing.

combustible material: Material that will ignite and burn, either as a flame or glow, and that undergoes this process in air at pressures and temperatures that might occur during a fire in a building.

common path of egress travel: The portion of exit access travel distance measured from the most remote point within a story to the point where the occupants have separate access to two exits or exit access doorways.

corridor: An enclosed exit access component that defines and provides a path of egress travel to an exit. A corridor may or may not be protected depending on the particular requirements of the code.

exit access doorway: A door or access point along the path of egress travel from an occupied room, area, or space where the path of egress enters an intervening room, corridor, unenclosed exit access stair, or unenclosed exit access ramp.

exit court: A court or yard (considered part of an exit discharge) that provides access to a public way for one or more required exits. The IBC refers to this as an *egress court.*

exit enclosure: A fully enclosed portion of an exit that is only used as a means of egress and that provides for a protected path of egress either in a vertical or horizontal direction. Depending on construction type, height, and building occupancy, an exit enclosure must have either a 1- or 2-hour rating, and all openings must be protected. An exit enclosure must lead to an exit discharge or the public way.

exit passageway: A horizontal, fully enclosed portion of an exit that is only used as a means of egress. An exit passageway leads from an exit doorway to an exit discharge or a public way. A common example of an exit passageway is an exit from the door at the ground level of an interior stairway that leads through the building to an outside door.

fire area: The area enclosed and bounded by fire walls, fire barriers, exterior walls, or horizontal assemblies of a building.

fire assembly: An assembly of a fire door, fire window, or fire damper, including all required anchorage, frames, sills, and hardware.

fire barrier: A fire-resistance-rated vertical or horizontal assembly of materials designed to restrict the spread of fire, in which openings are protected.

fire door assembly: Any combination of a fire door, frame, hardware, and other accessories that provides a specific degree of fire protection to an opening.

fire exit hardware: Panic hardware that is listed for use on fire-door assemblies.

fire partition: A fire-resistive component used to separate dwelling units in R-2 construction, to separate guest rooms in Group R-l construction, to separate tenant spaces in covered mall buildings, or as a corridor wall. Fire partitions are generally required to have a minimum 1-hour rated construction except in certain circumstances. They are similar to fire barriers, but the requirements for support are not as strict.

fire-protection rating: The period of time for which an opening assembly, such as a door or window, maintains the ability to confine a fire, or maintains its integrity, or both, when tested in accordance with NFPA 252, UL 10B, UL 10C (for doors), or NFPA 257 (for windows). An assembly that is required to have a fire-protection rating must withstand fire exposure and thermal shock (the same as for a fire-resistance rating), but is not required to withstand heat transmission (unlike for a fire-resistance rating).

fire-rated: See *fire-protection rating.*

fire-rated glazing: Glazing with either a fire-protection rating or a fire-resistance rating.

fire resistance: The property of a material or assembly to withstand or resist the spread of fire or give protection from it.

fire-resistance rating: The period of time a building component such as a wall, floor, roof, beam, or column is able to confine a fire or maintain its structural integrity, or both, when tested in accordance with ASTM E119, *Standard Methods for Fire Tests of Building Construction and Materials.* This is different from the fire-protection rating, which involves protected opening assemblies.

fire-resistive construction: See *fire resistance.*

flame resistance: The ability to withstand or give protection from flame impingement. This applies to individual materials as well as combinations of components when tested in accordance with NFPA 701, *Standard Methods of Fire Tests for Flame-Resistant Textiles and Films.*

flame spread: The propagation of flame over a surface.

flame spread index: The numerical value assigned to a material tested in accordance with ASTM E84, *Standard Test Method for Surface Burning Characteristics of Building Materials.*

flammable: Capable of burning with a flame and subject to easy ignition and rapid flaming combustion.

horizontal exit: An exit component consisting of fire-resistance rated construction and opening protectives intended to compartmentalize portions of a building thereby creating refuge areas that afford safety from fire and smoke from the area of fire origin. The fire-resistance rated construction is typically 2-hour rated.

noncombustible material: Material that will not ignite and burn when subjected to a fire. The IBC qualifies a material as noncombustible only if it is tested in accordance with ASTM E136, *Noncombustible Material—Tests*, or if it has a structural base of noncombustible material with a surfacing not more than $\frac{1}{8}$ in thick that has a flame-spread index no greater than 50.

occupant load: The number of people for which the means of egress of a building or part of a building is designed.

panic hardware: A door-latching assembly that includes a device that releases the latch when a force is applied in the direction of egress travel.

self-closing door: A door equipped with a device (most commonly a door closer) that will ensure closing after the door has been opened.

stair: A change in elevation, consisting of one or more risers.

stairway: One or more flights of stairs, either exterior or interior, with the necessary landings and platforms connecting them to form a continuous and uninterrupted passage from one level to another.

travel distance: The distance between the most remote occupied point of an area or room to the entrance of the nearest exit that serves it. Travel distance is part of the exit access and is measured along the natural and unobstructed path of egress travel.

trim: Picture molds, chair rails, baseboards, handrails, door and window frames, and similar decorative or protective materials used in fixed applications.

15

BARRIER-FREE DESIGN

Project Planning

Barrier-free design, or *universal design*, is an important part of the ARE, especially since the *Americans with Disabilities Act* (ADA) became law in 1990. Although building codes and many federal and state agencies contain accessibility requirements, the overriding regulation is the ADA. This federal law requires, among other things, that all commercial and public accommodations be accessible to people with disabilities. Although the ADA is not a national building code and does not depend on inspection for its enforcement, building owners must comply with its requirements or be liable for civil suits. Architects are likewise responsible for designing buildings that conform to the ADA requirements as well as local building code regulations.

The ADA is a complex, four-title civil rights law. Title III, Public Accommodations and Commercial Facilities, is the part that most affects designers.

The design requirements for construction are found mainly in the *2010 ADA Standards for Accessible Design*. The *ADA Standards* apply to facilities covered by the ADA, including places of public accommodation, commercial facilities, and state and local government facilities. With some minor changes, these standards are closely based on the earlier *Americans with Disabilities Act* and *Architectural Barriers Act Accessibility Guidelines* published in 2004. The original *ADA Accessibility Guidelines* appeared as Appendix A to 28 CFR 36, the *Code of Federal Regulations* rule that implemented Title III.

In some cases, the *ADA Standards* reference provisions of the *International Building Code* (IBC) and other industry standards. This coordination of standards is meant to make compliance simpler and more straightforward. When architects and others refer to the ADA, they are usually referring to the design criteria contained in the *ADA Standards*.

Other local and federal laws and regulations also govern accessibility. For example, multifamily housing is regulated mainly by the federal Fair Housing Act and by some state laws. For some federal buildings, the *Uniform Federal Accessibility Standards* govern. Although there are differences among these regulations, they all follow most of the standards set forth in ICC/ANSI Standard A117.1, *Accessible and Usable Buildings and Facilities*.

The main differences among the standards are in scoping provisions, which set how many accessible elements must be provided. For example, scoping provisions tell the designer how many seats in a restaurant must allow for wheelchair access or how many housing units in a complex must be accessible. The *ADA Standards* also include design and scoping requirements for

- social service center establishments
- housing at places of education
- assembly areas
- medical care facilities
- residential dwelling units constructed by state and local governments
- detention and correction facilities
- places of lodging
- play areas
- swimming pools
- amusement rides

The standards discussed in this chapter include some of the basic requirements for accessibility inside a building as defined in the ADA and with ICC/ANSI Standard A117.1 with which the candidate should be familiar. Additional accessibility provisions for site work are discussed in Chap. 12.

ACCESSIBLE ROUTES

An *accessible route* is a continuous, unobstructed path that connects all accessible elements and spaces in a building or facility. It includes corridors, doorways, floors, ramps, elevators, lifts, and clear floor space at fixtures. The standards for accessible routes are designed to accommodate a person with a severe disability who uses a wheelchair, and they are also intended to provide ease of use for people with other disabilities.

Each *site arrival point* must be connected by an accessible route to the accessible building entrance or entrances served. Site arrival points include such elements as parking, passenger loading zones, sidewalks, public transportation stops, and connections with other buildings or sites.

The accessible routes connecting site arrival points must coincide with or be located in the same general area as the general circulation paths. There is one exception to this: An accessible route is not required between accessible buildings, accessible facilities, accessible elements, and accessible spaces if the only means of access between them is a vehicular way not providing pedestrian access.

Accessible routes and other clearances are based on basic dimensional requirements of wheelchairs. The minimum clear floor space required to accommodate one stationary wheelchair is 30 in by 48 in. For maneuverability, a minimum 60 in diameter circle is required for a wheelchair to make a 180° turn. In place of this, a T-shaped space may be provided as shown in Fig. 15.1.

The minimum clear width for an accessible route is 36 in continuously and 32 in clear at a passage point such as a doorway. The passage point cannot be more than 24 in long. The minimum passage width for two wheelchairs is 60 in. If an accessible route is less than 60 in wide, passing spaces at least 60 in by 60 in must be provided at intervals not to exceed 200 ft. These requirements are shown in Fig. 15.2.

In toilet rooms , the turning space may overlap with the required clear floor space at fixtures and controls and with the accessible route. If turns in corridors or around obstructions must be made, the minimum dimensions are as shown in Fig. 15.3.

An accessible route may have a slope up to 1:20 (a 1 in rise for every 20 in of distance) or 5%. Any slope greater than this is classified as a ramp and must meet the requirements given in Ramps and Stairs section.

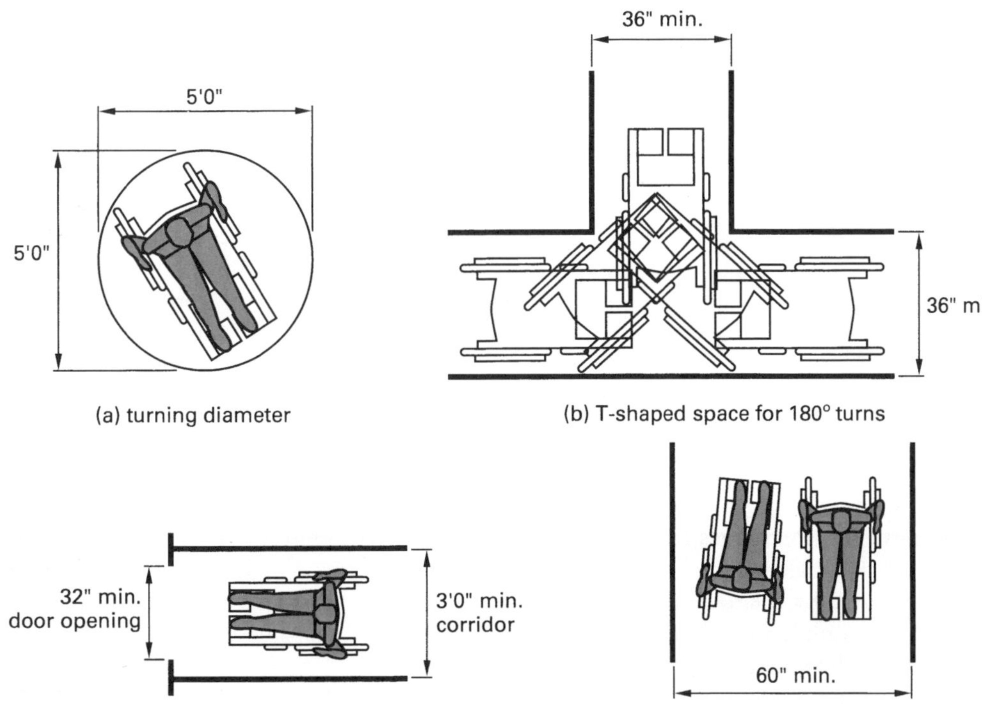

Figure 15.1 Maneuvering Clearances

(a) turning diameter

(b) T-shaped space for 180° turns

Figure 15.2 Wheelchair Clearances

(a) corridor and door clearances

(b) minimum clear width for two wheelchairs

Project Planning

Figure 15.3
Turn in Corridors or Around Obstructions

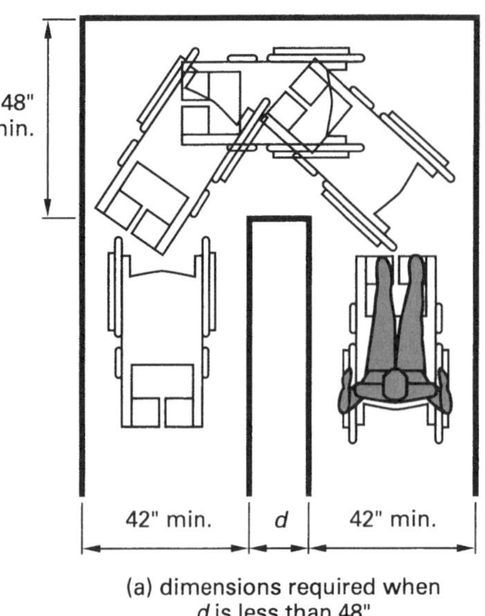

(a) dimensions required when *d* is less than 48"

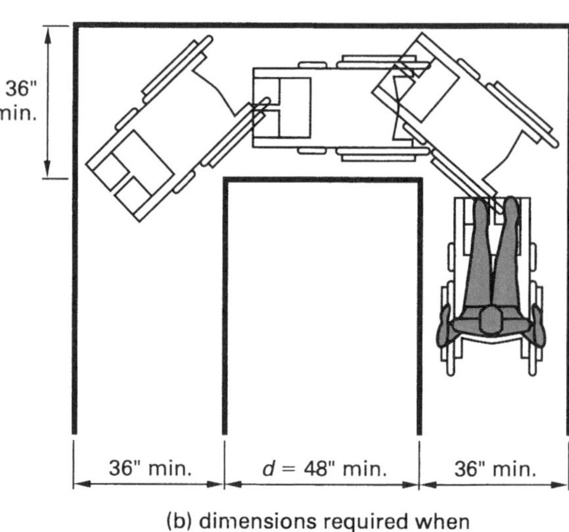

(b) dimensions required when *d* is 48" or greater

REACH RANGES

When a forward reach is unobstructed, the high forward reach is 48 in and the low reach is 15 in minimum above the floor. For example, outlets must be located no less than 15 in above the floor. When the forward reach is over an obstruction, like a countertop, the high forward reach for obstructions over 20 in up to 25 in is a maximum of 44 in. When a clear floor space allows a parallel approach to an element the side reach is a maximum of 48 in. When there an obstruction and a parallel approach is possible the side reach is still 48 in if the obstruction has a maximum depth of 10 in and a maximum height of 34 in. Refer to the *ADA Standards* for reach ranges for children and other exceptions.

DOORWAYS

Width and Arrangement

Doors must have a minimum clear opening width of 32 in when the door is opened at 90°. The maximum depth of a doorway 32 in wide is 24 in. If the area is deeper than this, the width must be increased to 36 in. See Fig. 15.4.

Figure 15.4
Doorway Clearances

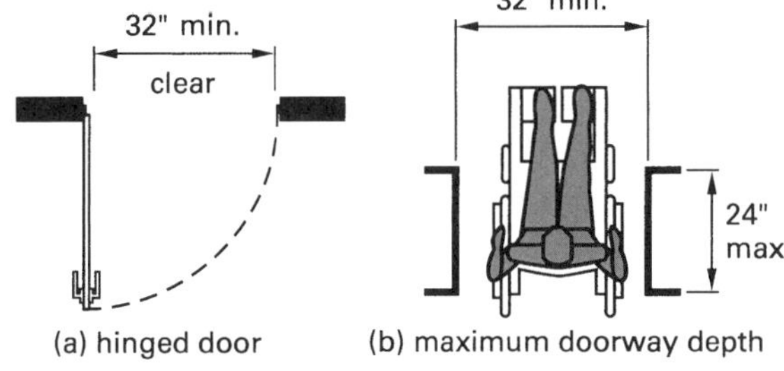

(a) hinged door (b) maximum doorway depth

Maneuvering clearances are required at standard swinging doors to allow easy operation of the latch and provide for a clear swing. For single doors the clearances are shown in Fig. 15.5. For two doors in a series the minimum space is shown in Fig. 15.6. Note the 48 in space requirement. If sufficient clearance is not provided, the doors must have power-assisted mechanisms or be automatic opening.

Opening Force

The maximum opening force (torque) required to push or pull open interior hinged doors cannot be more than 5 lbf-ft. This force does not include the force required to retract the latch bolts or disengage other devices that may hold the door closed. Maximum opening forces may be greater if the door is a fire door and regulated by the local code jurisdiction. Automatic doors and power- assisted doors may also be used if they comply with ANSI/BHMA Standard A156.10 (automatic doors) or ANSI/BHMA Standard 156.19 (low-powered, automatic doors).

When closers are used, the sweep period of the door must be adjusted so that from an open position of 70°, the door will take at least 3 sec to move to a point 3 in from the latch as measured to the leading edge of the door.

Figure 15.5 Maneuvering Clearances at Single Doors

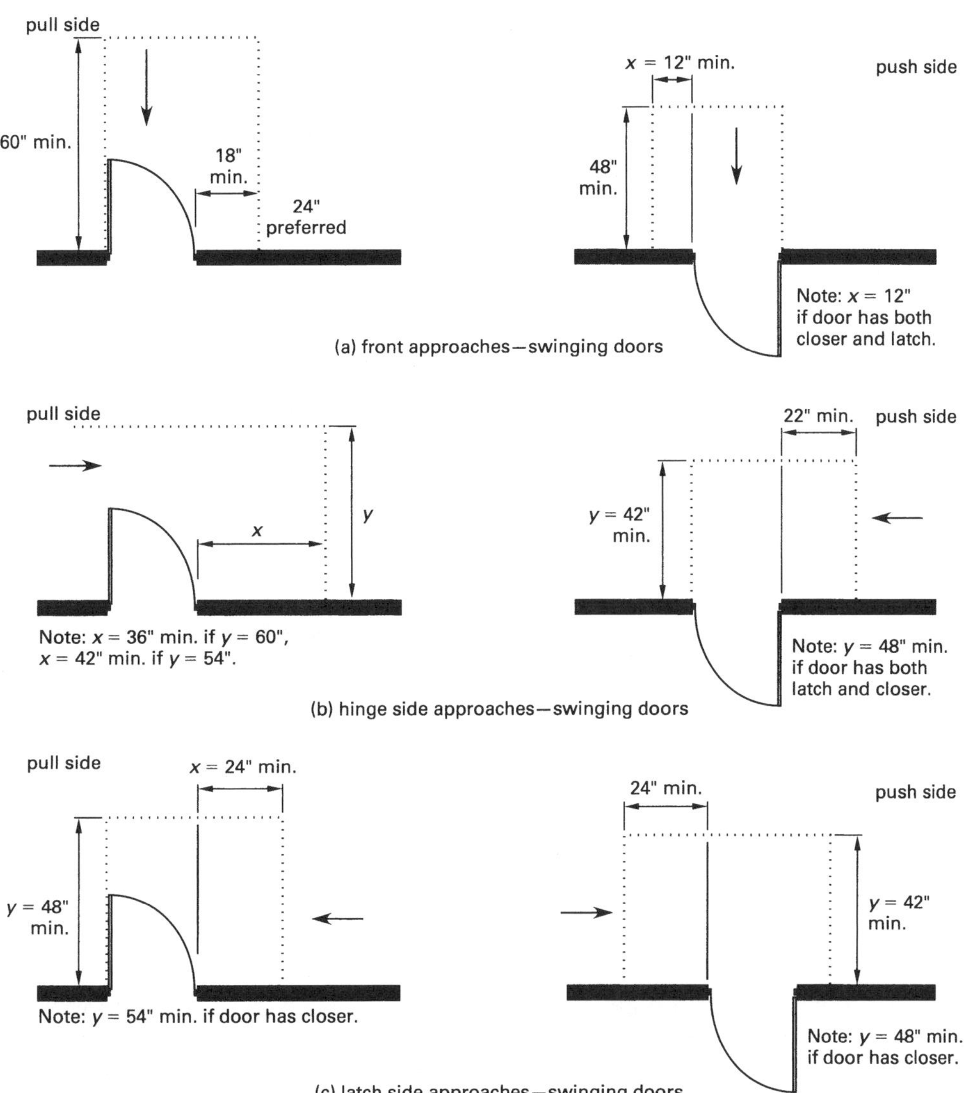

Figure 15.6 Maneuvering Clearances at Double Doors

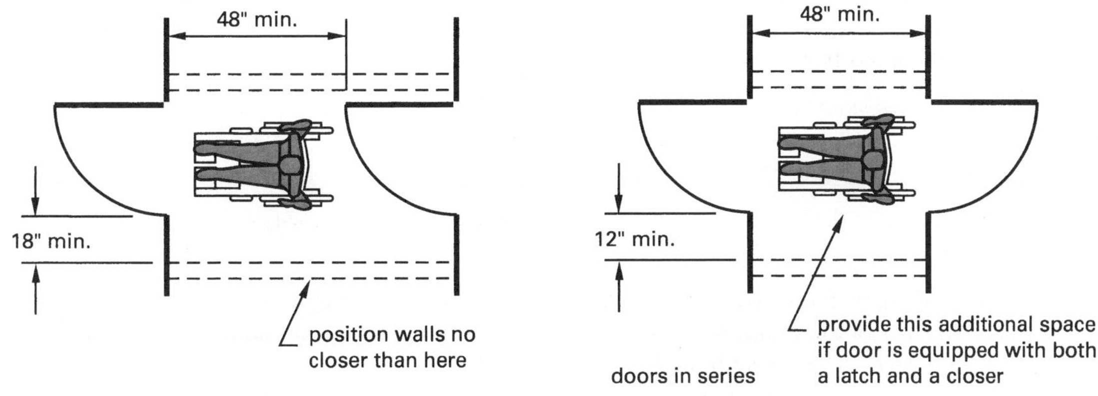

Figure 15.7 Toilet Stall Dimensions

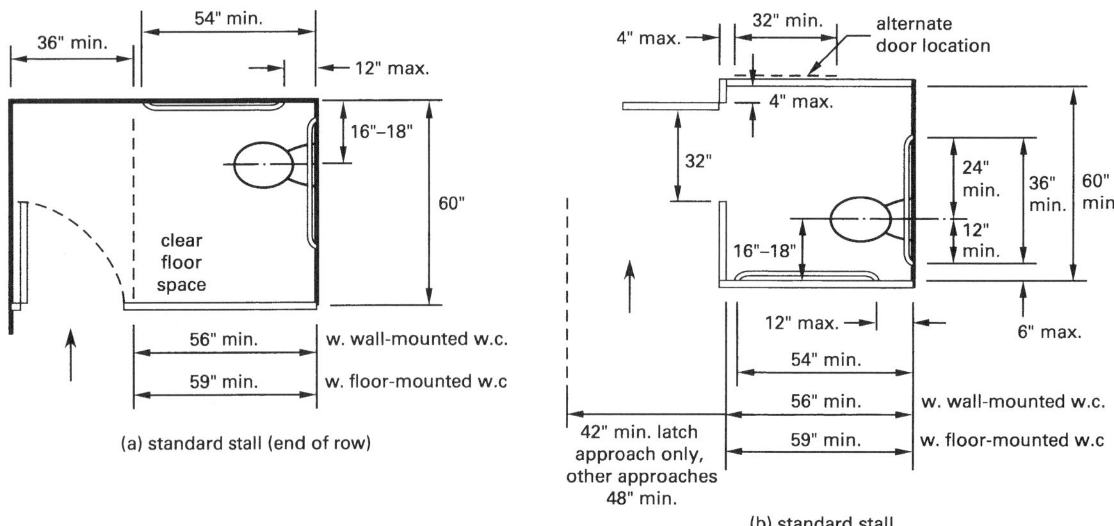

Hardware

A threshold at a doorway cannot exceed a $^1/_4$ in vertical change. A change in elevation between $^1/_4$ in and $^1/_2$ in in height must be beveled so that no part of the threshold slopes more than 1 vertical unit for each 2 horizontal units. In other words, each $^1/_4$ in vertical change in elevation, after the first $^1/_4$ in, must be made over a horizontal distance of at least $^1/_2$ in.

Operating devices must have a shape that is easy to grasp. This includes lever handles, push-type mechanisms, and U-shaped handles. Round doorknobs are not allowed. If door closers are provided, they must be adjusted to slow the closing time. Hardware for accessible doors may not be mounted more than 48 in above the finished floor.

PLUMBING FIXTURES AND TOILET ROOMS

ICC/ANSI Standard A117.1 and the ADA govern the design of the components of toilet rooms as well as individual elements such as drinking fountains, bathtubs, and showers. Toilet rooms must have a minimum clear turning space of a 5 ft diameter circle in addition to the minimum access areas required at each type of fixture. The 5 ft circle can overlap with required access at controls and fixtures and with the accessible route.

Toilet Stalls

There are several acceptable layouts for toilet stalls. Minimum clearances for two standard stall layouts are shown in Fig. 15.7. The clearance depth in both cases varies depending on whether a wall-hung or floor-mounted water closet is used. In most cases, the door must provide a minimum clear opening of 32 in and must swing out, away from the stall enclosure. Grab bars must also be provided as shown in the illustrations, mounted from 33 in to 36 in above the floor.

In addition to the dimensional requirements shown in Fig. 15.7, the *ADA Standards* require that at least one ambulatory toilet stall be provided where there are six or more toilet stalls or where the combination of urinals and water closets totals six or more fixtures. An ambulatory toilet stall is shown in Fig. 15.8.

In all cases, the clearance depth varies depending on whether a wall-hung or floor-mounted water closet is used in the stall.

All toilet stalls must have toe clearance below the front partition and below at least one side partition. This clearance must be a minimum of 9 in above the floor and extend a minimum of 6 in beyond the compartment-side face of the partition. Refer to the full text of the *ADA Standards* for additional requirements for children's toilets and toilet stalls.

In residential units, the edge of a lavatory may be located a minimum of 18 in from the centerline of the toilet. In all other cases, there must be a clear floor space as shown in Fig. 15.9.

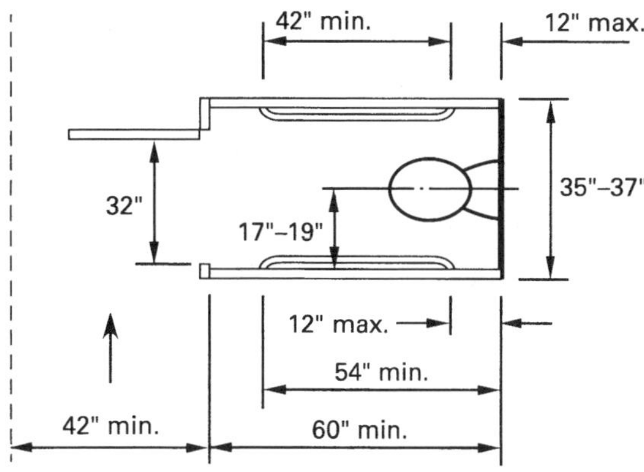

Figure 15.8
Ambulatory Toilet Stall Dimensions

If toilet stalls are not used, the centerline of the toilet must still be 16 in to 18 in from a wall with grab bars at both the back and side of the water closet. A clear space in front of and beside open water closets should be provided as shown in Fig. 15.9. Toilet paper dispensers must be 7 in minimum and 9 in maximum in front of the water closet measured to the centerline. The outlet of the dispenser must be between 15 in and 48 in above the floor. It may be mounted either above or below the grab bar. If mounted above the grab bar, there must be a minimum of 12 in between the top of the bar and the outlet. If mounted below the grab bar, there must be a minimum clearance of $1\frac{1}{2}$ in between the bottom of the bar and the top of the dispenser.

Dispensers must not be of a type that controls delivery or that does not allow continuous paper flow.

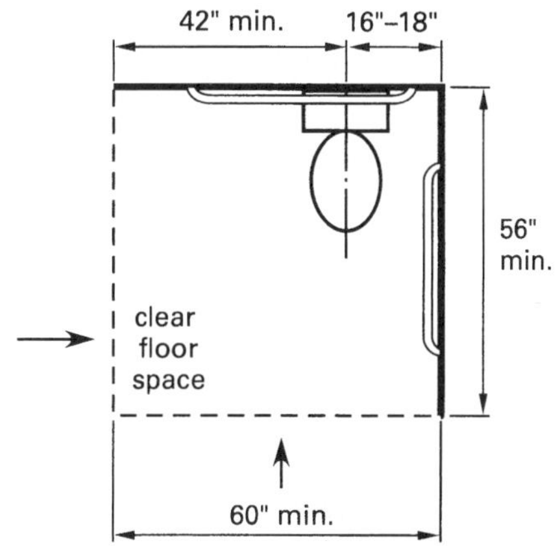

Figure 15.9
Clear Floor Space at Water Closets

Urinals

Urinals must be stall-type or wall-hung with an elongated rim at a maximum height of 17 in above the floor and a minimum depth of $13\frac{1}{2}$ in from the wall to the face of the rim. A clear floor space of 30 in by 48 in must be provided in front of the urinal, which may adjoin or overlap an accessible route. Urinal shields that do not extend beyond the front edge of the rim may be provided with 30 in clearance between them.

Lavatories and Sinks

Lavatories must allow someone in a wheelchair to move under the sink and easily use the basin and water controls. The required dimensions are shown in Fig. 15.10. Because of these clearances, wall-hung lavatories are the best type to use when accessibility is a concern. If pipes are exposed below the lavatory, they must be insulated or otherwise protected, and there must not be any sharp or abrasive surfaces under lavatories or sinks. Faucets must be operable with one hand and cannot require tight grasping, pinching, or twisting of the wrist. Lever-operated, push-type, and automatically controlled mechanisms are acceptable types.

Mirrors must be mounted with the bottom edge of the reflecting surface no higher than 40 in from the floor.

Requirements for sinks are the same as those for lavatories. The maximum depth of the sink bowl is $6\frac{1}{2}$ in. The clear floor space requirement is the same as it is for lavatories.

Drinking Fountains

Requirements for drinking fountains with a front approach are shown in Fig. 15.11. A drinking fountain that is freestanding or built-in without clear space below must have a clear floor space in front of it at least 30 in by 48 in wide with the long dimension parallel to the fountain, which allows a person in a wheelchair to make a parallel approach. The spout must be a maximum of 5 in from the front edge of the unit, for users making a forward approach.

The IBC requires that two drinking fountains be provided, one for wheelchair users and one for persons who are standing. A combination unit that accommodates both may be provided instead.

Figure 15.10 Clear Floor Space at Lavatories

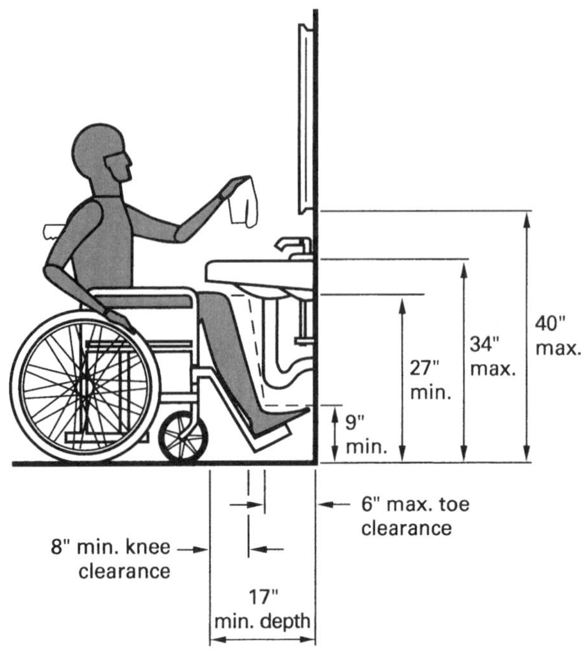

(a) lavatory clearances

17" min.
clear
floor
space
30"
min.
19" max.
48" min.

(b) clear floor space at lavatories

Figure 15.11 Water Fountain Access

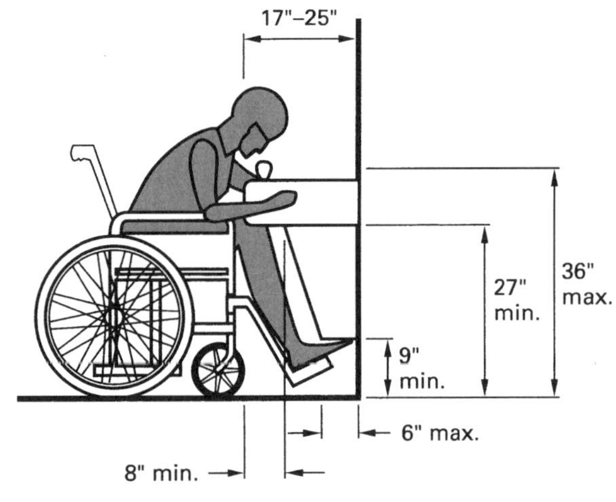

(a) spout height and knee clearance

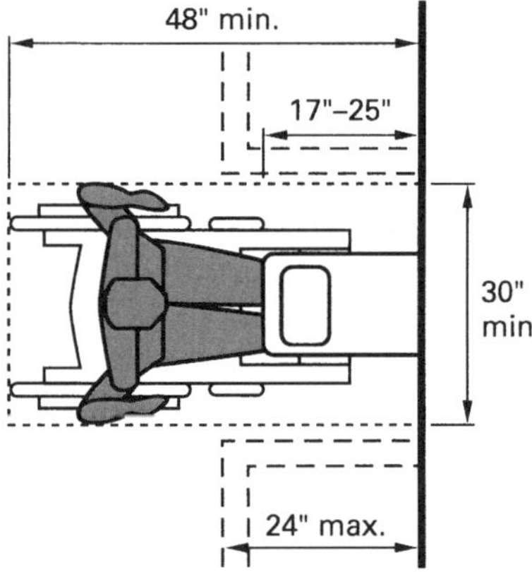

(b) clear floor space

Bathtubs

Bathtubs must be configured as shown in Fig. 15.12. An in-tub seat or a seat at the head of the tub must be provided as shown in the drawing. Grab bars must be provided as illustrated in Fig. 15.13. If an enclosure is provided, it cannot obstruct the controls or transfer from wheelchairs onto seats or into the tub. Enclosure tracks cannot be mounted on the rim of the tub.

Showers

Shower stalls may be one of two basic types as shown in Fig. 15.14. When facilities with accessible sleeping rooms or suites are provided, a minimum number of rooms having roll-in showers must be provided, as specified in the ADA or the Federal Fair Housing Act. A seat is required in the smaller shower stall configuration, while a folding seat is required in the larger configuration if a permanent seat is provided. Grab bars must be provided and mounted 33 in to 36 in above the floor.

Figure 15.12 Clear Floor Space at Bathtubs

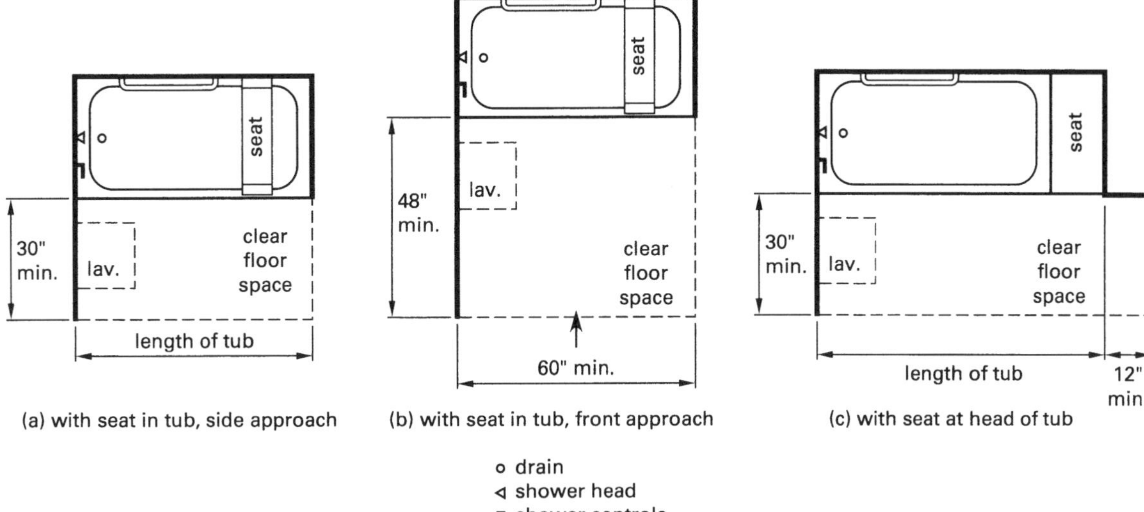

Figure 15.13 Grab Bars

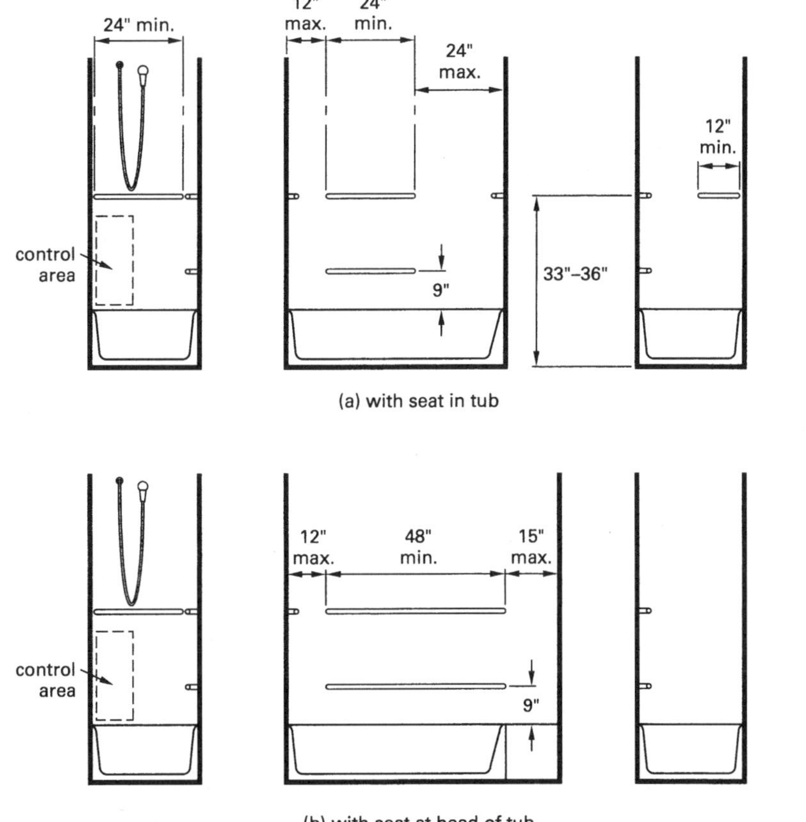

FLOOR SURFACES

Floor surfaces must be stable, firm, and slip resistant. If there is a change in level, the transition must meet the following requirements. If the change is less than $^1/_4$ in, it may be vertical and without edge treatment. If the change is between $^1/_4$ in and $^1/_2$ in, it must be beveled with a slope no greater than 1:2 ($^1/_2$ in of rise requires 1 in of length, for example). Changes greater than $^1/_2$ in must be accomplished with a ramp meeting the requirements in the next section.

Figure 15.14 Accessible Shower Stalls

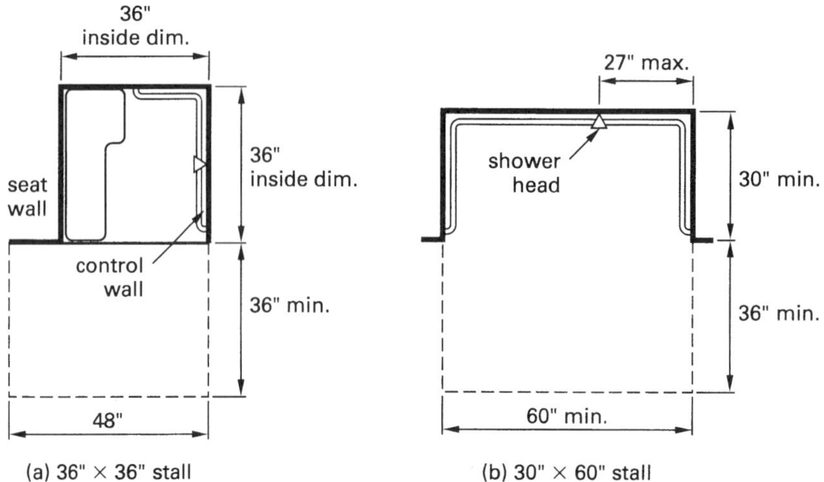

(a) 36" × 36" stall (b) 30" × 60" stall

If carpet is used, it must have a firm cushion or backing, or it must have no cushion and a level loop, textured loop, level cut pile, or level cut/uncut pile texture with a maximum pile height of $^1/_2$ in. It must be securely attached to the floor and have trim along all lengths of exposed edges.

RAMPS AND STAIRS

Ramps must be provided for smooth transitions between changes in elevation for wheelchair-bound persons and those whose mobility is otherwise restricted. In general, the least possible slope should be used, but in no case can a ramp have a slope greater than 1:12 (1 in rise for every 12 in of run). The maximum rise for any ramp is limited to 30 in. Changes in elevation greater than this require a level landing before the next run of ramp is encountered. In some cases where existing conditions prevent the 1:12 slope, a 1:10 slope is permitted if the maximum rise does not exceed 6 in, and a 1:8 slope is permitted if the maximum rise does not exceed 3 in.

The minimum clear width of a ramp is 36 in with landings at least as wide as the widest ramp leading to them. Landing lengths must be a minimum of 60 in. If ramps change direction at a landing, the landing must be at least 60 in square.

Ramps with rises greater than 6 in or lengths greater than 72 in must have handrails on both sides, with the top of each handrail from 34 in to 38 in above the ramp surface. They must extend at least 12 in beyond the top and bottom of the ramp segment and have a diameter or width of gripping surface from $1^1/_4$ in to $1^1/_2$ in. Handrails are not required for ramps adjacent to seating in assembly areas.

Stairs that are required as a means of egress and stairs between floors not connected by an elevator must be designed according to certain standards specifying the configuration of treads, risers, nosings, and handrails. The maximum riser height is 7 in, and the treads must be a minimum of 11 in as measured from riser to riser as shown in Fig. 15.8. Open risers are not permitted. The undersides of the nosings must not be abrupt and must conform to one of the styles shown in Fig. 15.7. There should be contrasting strips at the top and bottom tread nosings.

Stairway handrails must be continuous on both sides of the stairs. The inside handrail on switchback or dogleg stairs must always be continuous as it changes direction. Other handrails must extend beyond the top and bottom risers as shown in Fig. 15.8. The top of the gripping surface must be between 34 in and 38 in above stair nosings. The handrail must have a diameter or width of gripping surface from $1^1/_4$ in to 2 in. There must be a clear space between the handrail and the wall of at least $1^1/_2$ in.

When an exit stairway is part of an *accessible route* in a non-sprinklered building (not including houses), there must be a clear width of 48 in between handrails.

In most cases, there must be an area of refuge within an enlarged floor-level landing for a stairway to be considered part of an accessible means of egress. An *area of refuge* is an area where people unable to use stairways can remain temporarily while waiting for assistance. Each area of refuge must accommodate a wheelchair space of 30 in by 48 in for each 200 occupants or portion thereof. An area of refuge is not required if a building is equipped with an automatic sprinkler system.

PROTRUDING OBJECTS

Because objects and building elements that project into corridors and other walkways present a hazard for visually impaired people, there are restrictions on their size and configuration. These are shown in Fig. 15.15 and are based on the use of a cane by people with severe vision impairments. Protruding objects with their lower edge less than 27 in above the floor can be detected so they may project any amount (as long as the minimum passage width is maintained).

Regardless of the situation, protruding objects cannot reduce the clear width required for an accessible route or maneuvering space. In addition, if vertical clearance of an area adjacent to an accessible route is reduced to less than 80 in, a guardrail or other barrier must be provided. For example, if there is clear floor space below a stairway extending to the floor, some type of barrier must be provided at the point where the underside of the stair is less than 80 in.

Figure 15.15 Requirements for Protruding Objects

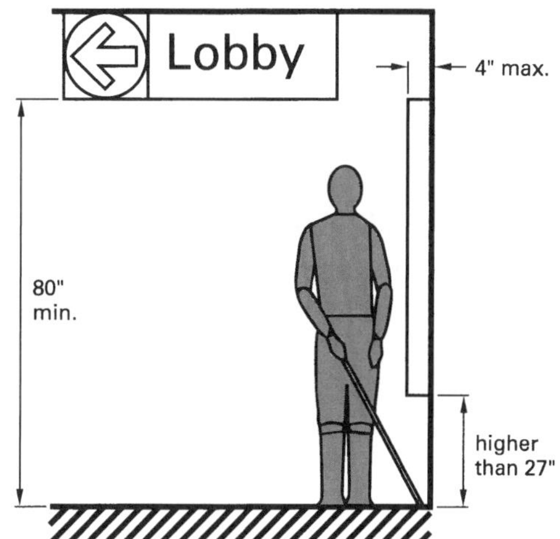

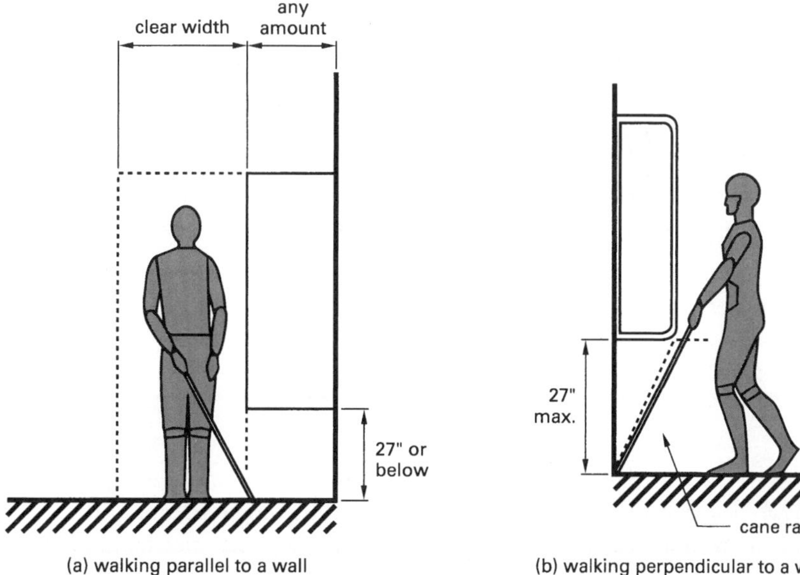

(a) walking parallel to a wall

(b) walking perpendicular to a wall

DETECTABLE WARNINGS

A *detectable warning* is a surface feature built in or applied to a walking surface or other element to warn of hazards on a circulation path. Detectable warning surfaces consist of truncated domes 0.2 in in height spaced between 1.6 in and 2.4 in on center in a square grid pattern.

Continuous detectable warning surfaces 24 in wide are generally required at passenger transit platform edges where there is no guard or other protection. Other locations where detectable warning surfaces are required depend on the locally adopted regulation. Both the ADA and the IBC require detectable warning surfaces at platform boarding edges, but the IBC does not require them at bus stops. ICC/ANSI Standard A117.1 makes reference to detectable warning surfaces in both exterior and interior locations but provides no scoping provisions stating precisely where they are required. Local codes should be verified to determine which rules might apply to a particular design project.

SIGNAGE AND ALARMS

Signage that gives emergency information and general circulation directions for visually impaired people must be provided. Signage is also required for elevators.

Emergency warning systems that provide both a visual and an audible alarm are required. Audible alarms must produce a sound that exceeds the prevailing sound level in the room or space by at least 15 dB. Visual alarms must be flashing lights that have a flashing frequency of about 1 Hz (1 cycle per second).

The ADA requires that certain accessible rooms and features be clearly identified with the symbol for accessibility and that identification, directional, and information signs meet certain specifications.

Permanent rooms and spaces must be identified with signs having lettering from $^5/_8$ in to 2 in high, raised $^1/_{32}$ in above the surface of the sign. Lettering must be all uppercase, in sans serif or simple serif type accompanied with Grade 2 Braille. If pictograms are used, they must be at least 6 in high and must be accompanied with the equivalent verbal description placed directly below the pictogram. Signs must be eggshell matte or use some other nonglare finish with characters and symbols contrasting with their background. Permanent identification signs must be mounted on the wall adjacent to the latch side of the door such that there is a minimum clear floor space of 18 in by 18 in centered on the tactile characters and beyond the arc of the door swing. The mounting height to the baseline of the lowest tactile character must be 48 in minimum and 60 in maximum to the baseline of the highest tactile character. When there is no wall space to the latch side of the door, including for double-leaf doors, the sign must be placed to the right of the right-hand door.

The ADA requires that certain accessible rooms and features be clearly identified with the symbol for accessibility and that identification, directional, and information signs meet certain specifications.

Directional and informational signs must have lettering from $^5/_8$ in to 3 in high, depending on the viewing distance, which is detailed in a table in the *ADA Standards*. Contrast and finish requirements are the same as those for permanent room identification. Lettering can be uppercase or lowercase.

The international symbol for accessibility is required on parking spaces, passenger loading zones, accessible entrances, and toilet and bathing facilities when not all are accessible. Building directories and temporary signs do not have to comply. Refer to the *ADA Standards* for the detailed requirements for signage.

TELEPHONES

If public telephones are provided, there must be at least one telephone per floor conforming to the requirements as shown in Fig. 15.16 and as specified in the ADA requirements. If there are two or more banks of telephones, there must be at least one conforming telephone per bank. When four or more public pay telephones are provided, then at least one interior public text telephone is required.

Accessible telephones may be designed for either front or side access. The dimensions required for both of these types are shown in Fig. 15.16. In either case, a clear floor space of at least 30 in by 48 in must be provided. The telephones should have pushbutton controls and telephone directories within reach of a person in a wheelchair.

The international TDD (*telecommunication device for the deaf*, also called a *text telephone*)) is required to identify the location of those phones, and volume control telephones must have a sign depicting a telephone handset with radiating sound waves. In assembly areas, permanently installed assistive listening systems must display the international symbol of access for hearing loss. See Fig. 15.17.

Refer to the *ADA Standards* and local codes for detailed rules on telephone types and installation requirements.

Figure 15.16 Telephone Access

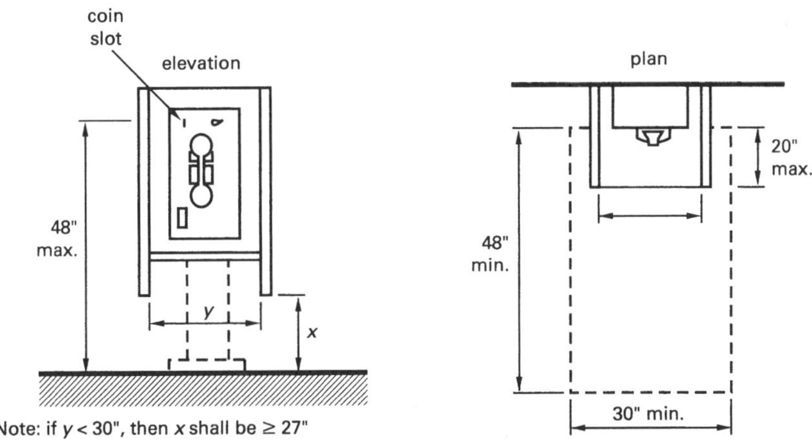

(a) forward reach possible

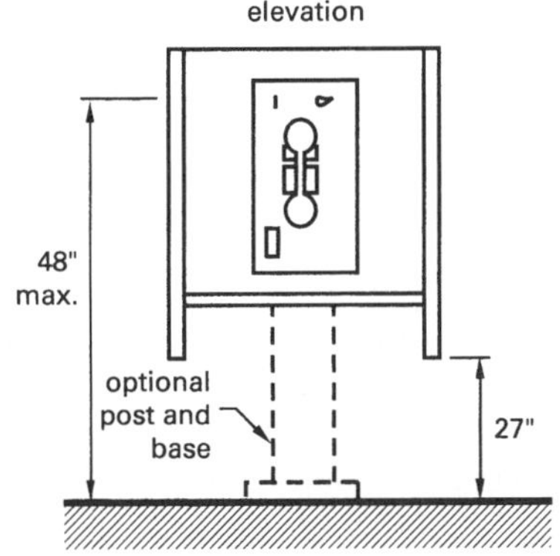

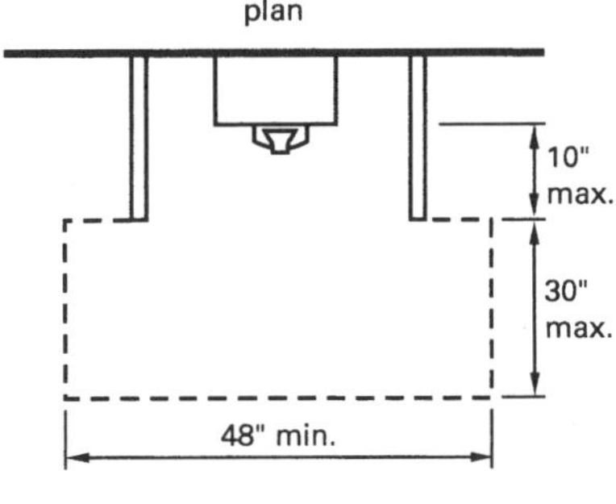

(b) side reach possible

Figure 15.17 International TDD and Hearing Loss Symbols

(a) TDD symbol

(b) access for hearing loss symbol

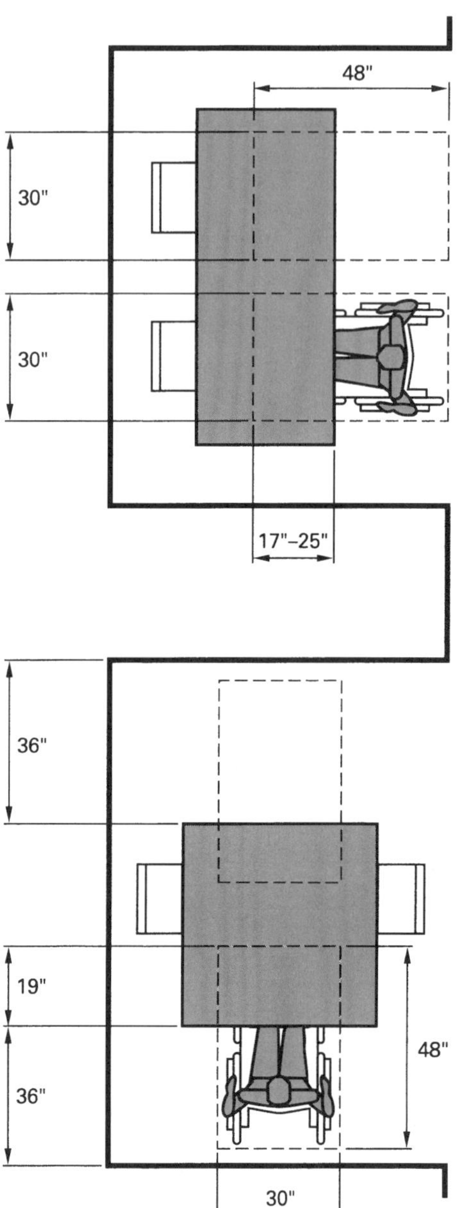

Figure 15.18
Minimum Clearances for Seating and Tables

SEATING

If fixed or built-in seating or tables are provided in accessible public or common-use areas, then at least 5%, and no fewer than one, of the seating areas must be accessible. This includes facilities such as restaurants, nightclubs, churches, and similar spaces. In new construction and when possible in remodeling, the accessible tables should be dispersed throughout the facility. If smoking and nonsmoking areas are provided, the required seating spaces must be proportioned between the smoking and nonsmoking areas. The area for this type of seating must comply with the dimensions shown in Fig. 15.18.

In places of assembly with fixed seating, the minimum number of wheelchair locations is given in Table 15.1. At least 5% of the total number of aisle seats provided must be located closest to accessible routes and must have removable or folding armrests on the aisle side. Each designated aisle seat must be identified by a sign or marker. The wheelchair areas must be an integral part of the overall seating plan and must be provided so people have a choice of admission prices and lines of sight comparable to those available for members of the general public. At least one companion seat must be provided next to each wheelchair area. Each wheelchair area must adjoin an accessible route that also serves as a means of emergency egress. Lines of sight must be designed so that a person in a wheelchair can see over the heads of people standing in the row immediately in front of them.

When assembly areas are part of a remodeling and it is not feasible to disperse the seating areas throughout, the accessible seating areas may be clustered. These clustered areas must have provisions for companion seating and must be located on an accessible route that also serves as a means of emergency egress.

Refer to the *ADA Standards* for details of assembly seating, requirements for audio-amplification systems and assisted listening devices, and signage required for assembly areas.

ELEVATORS

The ADA requires that elevator signals be located as shown in Fig. 15.19. The call buttons, hall lantern, and floor designators must all be located within easy reach and visual access. The call button must indicate when each call is registered and answered. The hall lantern must give a visual and audible signal. For audible signals, the lantern can sound once for up and twice for down, or it may be equipped with a verbal annunciator that sounds out "up" and "down."

Inside the car, floor buttons can be no higher than 48 in above the floor. However, when a side approach is possible and the elevator panel serves more than 16 openings, floor buttons may be a maximum of 54 in above the floor. Emergency controls must be grouped at the bottom of the panel with the centerline of the group no less than 35 in above the floor. Refer to the *ADA Standards* for other requirements, including the minimum size of cars, door and signal timing, and safety reopening devices.

Table 15.1 Minimum Number of Wheelchair Spaces for Assembly Areas

capacity of seating in assembly area	number of required wheelchair spaces and companion seats
4 to 25	1
26 to 50	2
51 to 150	4
151 to 300	5
301 to 500	6
501 to 5000	6, plus 1 for each 150, or fraction thereof, between 501 through 5000
5001 and over	36, plus 1 for each 200, or fraction thereof, over 5000

Source: 2010 *ADA Standards for Accessible Design*

Figure 15.19 Elevator Entrances

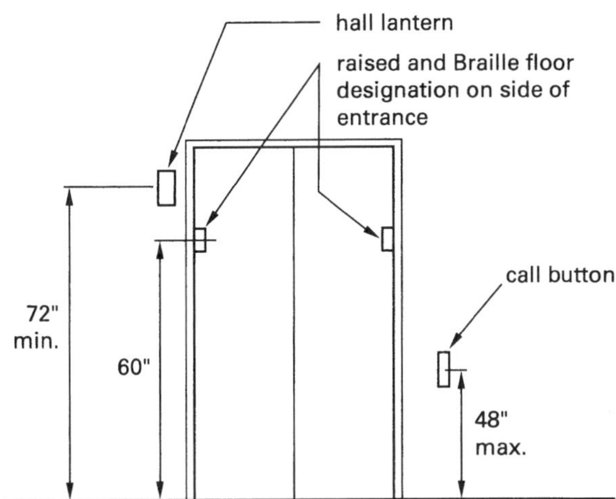

16 HUMAN COMFORT AND MECHANICAL SYSTEM FUNDAMENTALS

Nomenclature

A	area of a building assembly	ft^2	R	resistance	$hr\text{-}ft^2\text{-}°F/Btu$
C	conductance	$Btu/hr\text{-}ft^2\text{-}°F$	ΔT	temperature difference	°F
e	emittance	$hr\text{-}ft^2\text{-}°F/Btu$	T_e	sol-air temperature	°F
E_t	total solar radiation	$Btu/hr\text{-}ft^2$	T_o	outdoor dry-bulb temperature	°F
h_o	coefficient of heat transfer	$Btu/hr\text{-}ft^2\text{-}°F$	U	coefficient of heat transmission	$Btu/hr\text{-}ft^2\text{-}°F$
k	thermal conductivity (for 1 in thickness)	$Btu/hr\text{-}ft^2\text{-}°F$	V	volumetric airflow rate	ft^3/min
q	rate of heat loss	Btu/hr	a	absorbance	–
q_v	rate of sensible heat loss or gain due to infiltration or ventilation	Btu/hr	ε	thermal emissivity	–

HUMAN COMFORT

Human comfort is based primarily on the quality of the following environmental factors.

- temperature
- humidity
- air movement
- temperature radiation to and from surrounding surfaces
- air quality
- sound
- vibration
- light

For each of these factors, there are certain ranges within which people are comfortable and can function most efficiently. Acoustics and lighting are reviewed in later chapters. This section discusses human comfort relative to the thermal environment. Chapter 16 deals with the mechanical systems used to modify internal environments to maintain human comfort.

Human Metabolism

The human body is a heat-producing machine. It takes in food and water and, through the metabolic process, converts these to mechanical energy and the other bodily processes necessary to maintain life. Because the body is not very efficient in this conversion, it must give off excess heat in order to maintain a stable body temperature.

The body's heat production is measured in metabolic units, or mets. A *met* is the energy produced per unit of surface area per hour by a seated person at rest. One met is 18.4 $Btu/hr\text{-}ft^2$. Given the average surface area of an adult, this means that at rest, the human body gives off from 360 Btu/hr to 400 Btu/hr. This increases to around 700 Btu/hr to 800 Btu/hr for moderate activities like walking and work, and up to 2000 Btu/hr for strenuous exercise.

The body loses heat in three primary ways: convection, evaporation, and radiation. It can also lose heat by conduction, but this accounts for a very small portion of total body heat loss.

Convection is the transfer of heat through the movement of a gas or liquid. This occurs when the air temperature surrounding a person is less than the body's skin temperature, around 85°F. The body heats the surrounding air; the heated air rises and is replaced with cooler air.

Heat loss through *evaporation* occurs when moisture changes to a vapor as a person perspires or breathes.

Radiation is the transfer of heat energy through electromagnetic waves from one surface to a colder surface. The body can lose heat to a cooler atmosphere or to a cooler surface.

Conduction is the transfer of heat through direct contact between two objects of different temperatures.

The body loses heat (or is prevented from losing heat) through these four processes in various proportions depending on the environmental conditions. If the body cannot lose heat one way, it must lose it in another. For example, when the air temperature is above the body temperature of 98.6°F, there can be no convection transfer because heat always flows from a higher level to a lower level. (This is the second law of thermodynamics.) The body must then lose its heat by evaporation (i.e., perspiration). Figure 16.1 illustrates how the total amount of heat generated by a person at rest is transferred depending on the surrounding temperature.

The body maintains its proper temperature by regulating physiological processes, mainly the control of blood flow to the various parts of the body. This is done by the hypothalamus in the brain. When the body is too hot, the hypothalamus signals the sweat glands to increase secretion and sends more blood to the skin surface, a process called *vasodilation.* This carries body heat to the skin, where the heat energy is lost to the atmosphere through evaporation, or sweating. When the body is too cold, the hypothalamus signals the body to decrease blood flow to the skin surface and to the extremities, a process called *vasoconstriction.*

The sensation of *thermal comfort* depends on the interrelationship of many factors, including

- air temperature
- humidity
- air movement
- surface temperature
- clothing
- ventilation

Other factors that are more difficult to quantify objectively include personal metabolic rate, age, and psychological variables such as light, color, and aroma.

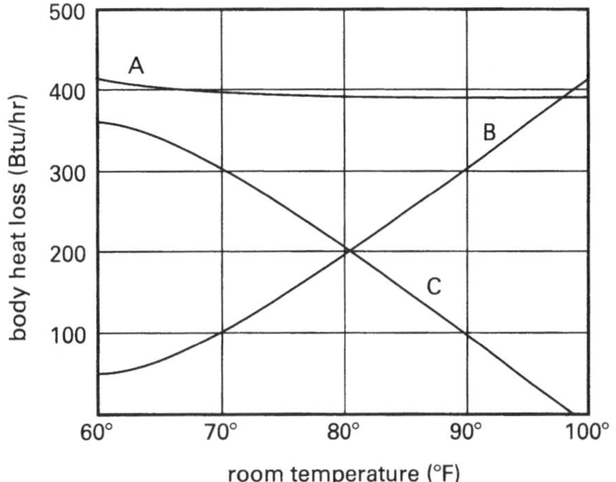

Figure 16.1 Body Heat Generated and Lost at Rest

Air Temperature

Temperature is the primary determinant of comfort. It is difficult to precisely state a normal range of comfortable temperature limits because the range depends on many factors, including the humidity levels, radiant temperatures, air movement, clothing, cultural factors, age, and sex.

However, a general comfortable range is between 69°F and 80°F, with a tolerable range from 60°F to 85°F, depending on relative humidity. *The International Mechanical Code* (IMC) and the *International Building Code* (IBC) both require that any space intended for human occupancy be provided with an active or passive space-heating system capable of maintaining a minimum indoor temperature of 68°F at a point 3 ft above the floor on the design heating day.

The *effective temperature* (ET) is a derived value that combines the effects of air temperature, humidity, and air movement.

Dry-bulb temperature is measured with a standard thermometer. Wet-bulb temperature is measured with a *sling psychrometer*, a device that consists of a thermometer with a moist cloth around the bulb. The thermometer is swung rapidly in the air, causing the moisture in the cloth to evaporate. In dry air, the moisture evaporates rapidly and acquires latent heat, which produces a low wet-bulb temperature. A large difference between the wet-bulb temperature and the dry-bulb temperature indicates low relative humidity. In moist air, less moisture evaporates from the cloth, so the wet-bulb temperature is higher.

In recent years, electronic *hygrometer sensors* that can accurately measure relative humidity have been taking the place of sling *psychrometers.*

Humidity

Relative humidity is the ratio of the percentage of moisture in the air to the maximum amount of moisture that the air can hold at a given temperature without condensing. Comfortable relative humidity ranges are between 30% and 65%, with tolerable ranges between 20% and 70%.

Relative humidity is particularly important in the summer months because as the air temperature rises, the body can lose less heat through convection and must rely mostly on evaporation. However, as the humidity rises, it is more difficult for perspiration to evaporate, so a person may feel much hotter than the air temperature would indicate.

Air Movement

Air movement tends to increase evaporation and heat loss through convection. This is why a person will feel more comfortable in high temperatures and high humidity conditions when there is a breeze. This is also the cause of the *windchill effect*, when a tolerable cold air temperature becomes unbearable in a wind. Wind speeds from 50 ft/min to about 200 ft/min are generally acceptable for cooling without causing annoying drafts.

Surface Temperature

Because the body gains and loses heat through radiation, the temperature of the surrounding surfaces is an important factor in determining human comfort. If the *surface temperatures* of the surroundings are colder than the surface temperature of the skin, which is about 85°F, the body loses heat through radiation; if the surrounding surfaces are warmer than the skin, the body gains heat. The rate at which radiation occurs depends on the surface temperatures of the body and the nearby object, the viewed angle, and the emissivity.

The *viewed angle* is the solid angle formed between the measuring position and the outer edges of the object. For example, when sitting close to a fireplace, a person experiences relatively high radiant heat because the fireplace occupies a large angle of view relative to the body. When the person sits across the room, the same fireplace occupies a much smaller angle of view, so it will not feel as warm.

Because the body gains and loses heat through radiation, the temperature of the surrounding surfaces is an important factor in determining human comfort.

The *emissivity*, ε, of an object is a measure of its ability to absorb and then radiate heat. The *emittance* of an object is the ratio of the radiation emitted by a given object or material to that emitted by a black body at the same temperature. Shiny objects or materials have very low emissivity, so they do not absorb or radiate heat as well as black objects. The shiny foil on many insulation materials is an example of the use of the emissivity properties of a material to reduce heat transfer.

To determine the effects of surface temperatures on human comfort, all room surfaces and their temperatures and positions must be taken into account. The value used to calculate these factors is the *mean radiant temperature* (MRT). The MRT is a weighted average of the various surface temperatures in a room and the angle of exposure of the occupant to these surfaces, as well as of any sunlight present.

The MRT is an important comfort factor in cold rooms or in the winter, because as the air temperature decreases, the body loses more heat through radiation than by evaporation, as shown in Fig. 16.1. Even a room with an adequate temperature will feel cool if the surfaces are cold. Warming these surfaces and providing radiant heating panels are two ways to counteract this effect.

Another way to factor in the effects of surface temperatures on human comfort is with operative temperature. *Operative temperature* is an average of the air temperature of a space and the MRT of the space. It can be measured with a *globe thermometer* (sometimes called a *black-globe thermometer*), which is a thermometer inside a black globe. This type of thermometer can account for both the air temperature and radiant effects from surrounding surfaces.

Clothing

Nearly all measurements and standards for human comfort are based on wearing clothing. To quantify the effects of clothing, the unit of the *clo* was developed. One clo is about equal to the thermal insulation given by the typical business suit, or about 0.15 clo per pound of clothing.

Ventilation

There are two basic types of *ventilation* requirements: one for unoccupied spaces such as attics and crawl spaces, and one for occupied spaces. See Chap. 14 for ventilation requirements for attics and crawl spaces.

Ventilation is needed in occupied spaces for many reasons: to provide oxygen and remove carbon dioxide, to remove odors, to carry away contaminants, and to remove unwanted moisture. The IMC requires that every occupied space be provided with either natural or mechanical ventilation. In addition, certain spaces and uses, such as toilet rooms, clothes dryers, cooking appliances, refuse conveyor systems, and laboratories, are required to have a separate exhaust system to remove contaminants, odors, and moisture.

Where *natural ventilation* is used, the IMC and the IBC both require that the area that can be opened to the outdoors be equal to at least 4% of the floor area being ventilated. When a room or space without outside openings is ventilated through an adjoining room, the opening to the adjoining room must have an unobstructed area of at least 8% of the floor area of the interior room or space, and not less than 25 ft^2. In this case, the minimum area that can be opened to the outdoors is calculated based on the total floor area being ventilated.

Where *mechanical ventilation* is used, the rate of supply air brought into the room or space must be approximately equal to the rate of return air, or exhaust air, carried out of it. However, the development of positive or negative pressure is allowed when it is needed for the use of the space. For example, in a hospital room there may be a need for positive pressure to prevent the entry of outside, germ-laden air. Likewise, in stair towers positive pressure can prevent the entry of smoke during a fire. The amount of outdoor ventilation air that must be brought in depends on the type of use and the occupant load. A table in the IMC gives the minimum ventilation rates in both cubic feet per minute per person (cfm/person) and cubic feet per minute per square foot of area (cfm/ft^2), based on the occupancy classification. The table also gives the occupant density, in number of people per square foot, that must be used when calculating the occupant load.

The *occupancy classifications* and the occupant density used in these calculations are not the same as those used in the IBC for calculation of egress requirements. The IMC table assumes that smoking is not present. If smoking is expected in a space other than a smoking lounge, the ventilation system must be designed to provide more ventilation than what is required by the table. Smoking lounges have a separate ventilation and exhaust requirement in the table. Once the ventilation rates are known from the IMC table, a series of complex calculations is required to design a specific mechanical system to meet the requirements.

This same table also gives required *exhaust airflow rates*, in cubic feet per minute per square foot of area, for spaces that require a separate exhaust system. See Chap. 17 for more information on exhaust systems.

MEASUREMENT SYSTEMS

Because the relationships between temperature, humidity, radiation, and other factors are complex, various methods have been developed to show these relationships and to assist in designing mechanical systems. Two of the more common methods are comfort charts and psychrometric charts.

Comfort Charts

Comfort charts show the relationships among temperature, humidity, and other comfort factors. A simplified version is shown in Fig. 16.2. It shows the comfort zones for both winter and summer for temperature zones in the United States (about 40° latitude) for elevations less than 1000 ft above sea level, and for people normally engaged in sedentary or light work.

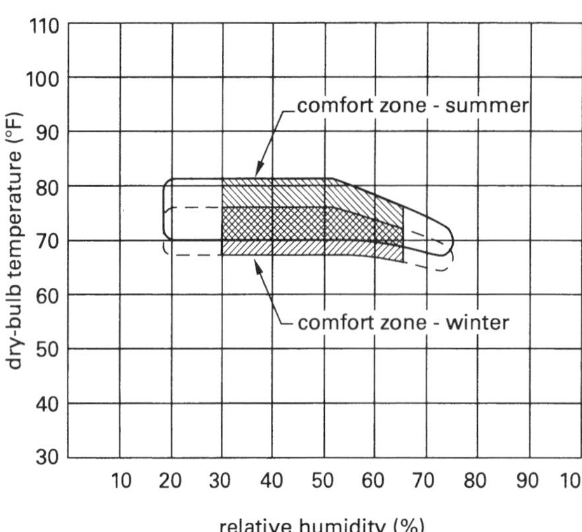

Figure 16.2
Comfort Chart for Temperate Zones

The tolerable humidity limits of about 20% and 75% are shown, but limits between 30% and 65% are preferred. The chart shows that as humidity increases, the air temperature must also decrease to provide the same amount of comfort as is felt at lower humidity levels.

If the temperature drops below the recommended levels, radiation in the form of sunshine or mechanical radiation is needed to maintain comfort. The lower the temperature, the more radiation is required. As the humidity and temperature increase, air movement is required to maintain comfort levels.

Psychrometric Chart

The *psychrometric chart* is a graphical representation of the complex interactions between heat, air, and moisture. (See Fig. 16.3.) The study of the water vapor content of air is known as *psychrometry.*

Because warm air can hold more moisture than cold air can, and because the amount of moisture in the air (humidity) affects human comfort, especially at high temperatures, a way is needed to calculate how much heat and moisture needs to be added or removed by an HVAC system for comfort. The psychrometric chart is the tool used to make these calculations.

Figure 16.3 shows a simplified version of the psychrometric chart. For illustrative purposes, this figure does not show all the graph lines that are present on the full chart. The vertical lines show dry-bulb temperatures, while the lines sloping from upper left to lower right show wet-bulb temperatures. The curved lines represent relative humidity from 0% to 100%. The 100% line is also known as the *saturation line* or *dew-point line.* This indicates when water vapor will form when saturated air comes in contact with any surface at or below the air's *dew-point temperature.* At 100% relative humidity, the wet-bulb and dry-bulb temperatures are the same.

Along the upper-left side of the chart is a scale representing *enthalpy,* or the total amount of both sensible and latent heat in the air-moisture mixture. Its lines run approximately parallel to the wet-bulb temperature lines and are in units of Btu/lbm of dry air. The *enthalpy line* is used to determine the total amount of heat that must be either removed (through cooling) or added (through heating) from conditioned air. This is more than just the heat represented by air temperature (sensible heat), because the latent heat contained in the moisture in the air must also be removed or added.

The amount of moisture that must be removed or added can also be read along a horizontal scale at the right side of the full chart. These lines are not shown in the simplified Fig. 16.3, but they represent the *humidity ratio,* or the amount of moisture by weight within a given weight of air.

The psychrometric chart illustrates why evaporative coolers work only in hot, dry climates. An *evaporative cooler* (also called a *swamp cooler*) reduces the temperature of the air but does not reduce the enthalpy (total heat). For example, by selecting the wet-bulb temperature line of 70°F (which is nearly parallel to the enthalpy lines) where it crosses the vertical dry-bulb temperature line of 90°F and following it up and to the left until it crosses the vertical 80°F dry-bulb temperature line, the psychrometric chart shows that without changing the enthalpy and dropping the air temperature 10°F, the humidity has increased from about 40% to more than 60%.

In addition to providing a wide range of information for HVAC design, the psychrometric chart can also be used to plot the comfort zone based on combinations of temperature and humidity. This also is shown in Fig. 16.3.

Figure 16.3 Psychrometric Chart

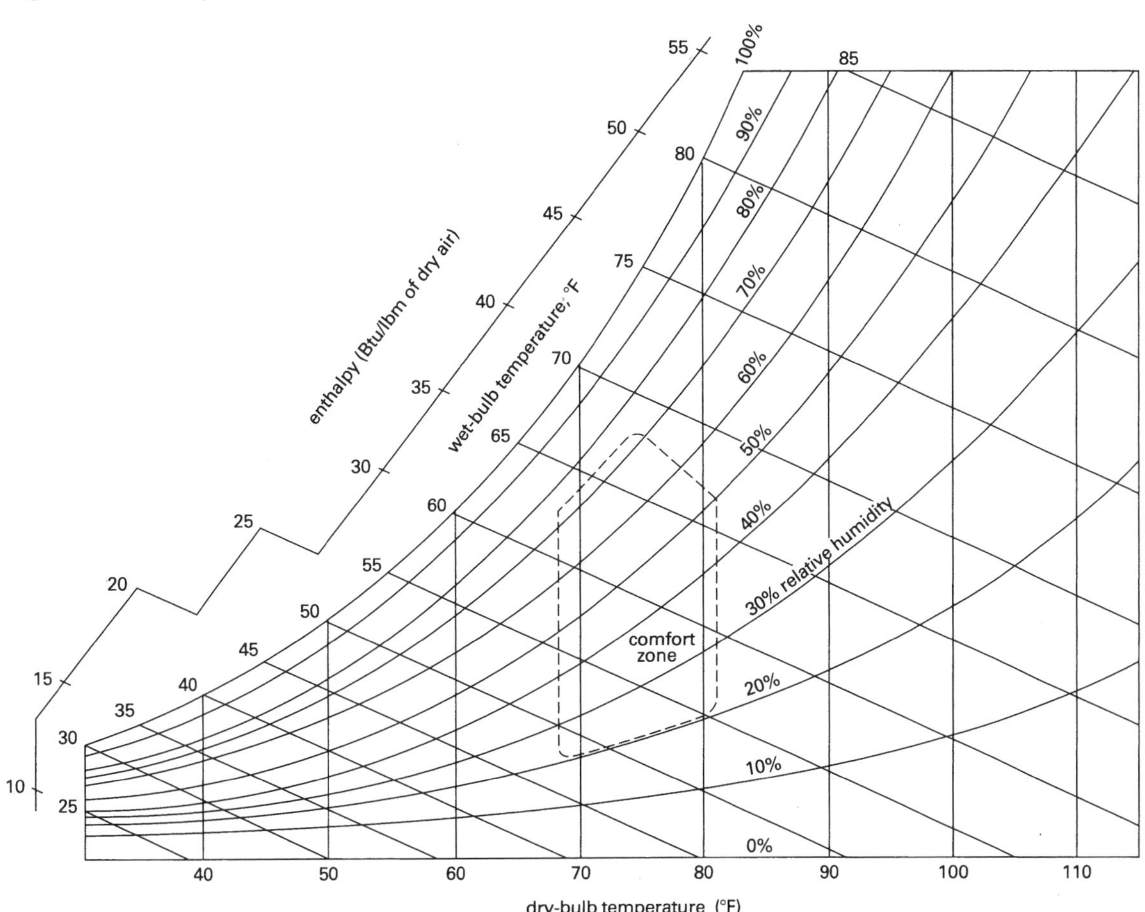

EXTERNAL AND INTERNAL LOADS

To maintain *human comfort*, a building must resist either the loss of heat to the outside during cold weather or the gain of heat during hot weather. Any excess heat gain or loss must be compensated for with passive energy conservation measures or with mechanical heating and cooling systems.

External factors that cause heat loss include air temperature and wind. External factors that cause heat gain include air temperature and sunlight. Internal factors that produce heat loads include people, lights, and equipment.

Heat is transferred between the outside and inside of a building through conduction, convection, and radiation. *Conduction* is the transfer of heat through direct contact between molecules. *Convection* is the transfer of heat through the movement of air. *Radiation* is the transfer of heat energy through electromagnetic waves from one surface to a colder surface.

Heat Loss Calculations

In order to determine the size of a heating system for a building, the total amount of heat lost per hour must be calculated. Heat is lost in two basic ways: through the building envelope and through air infiltration. The *building envelope* consists of the building's walls, roof, doors, windows, and foundation. Each material that is part of the building envelope resists the transfer of heat that occurs through the processes of conduction, convection, and radiation.

A material's *thermal conductivity, k*, is the rate at which heat passes through 1 ft^2 of a 1 in thickness of the material when the temperature differential is 1°F. *Conductance, C*, is the same property when the material is a thickness other than 1 in. The *resistance*, R, of a material, is the number of hours needed for 1 Btu to pass through a material of a given thickness when the temperature differential is 1°F. Total conductance and total resistance are related by Eq. 16.1.

$$R = \frac{1}{C} \tag{16.1}$$

Values for k, C, and R for various materials are given in standard reference texts as well as in the American Society of Heating, Refrigerating and Air-Conditioning Engineers (ASHRAE) *Handbook of Fundamentals*. If any heat loss calculations are required on the exam, the necessary tables will be included with the on-screen reference materials.

When a building assembly consists of more than one material, the value used to calculate heat loss is the *overall coefficient of heat transmission*, U. However, the value of U is not simply the sum of all the conductances of the individual materials. Instead, the coefficient of heat loss must be calculated according to Eq. 16.2.

$$U = \frac{1}{\sum R} \tag{16.2}$$

The amount of heat loss through one unit of area of building material or assembly is dependent on the coefficient of heat transmission of the material or assembly and the temperature differential between the inside and outside. For an entire area made of one type of material, this value is multiplied by the total area to get the total heat loss, q, as shown in Eq. 16.3.

$$q = UA\Delta T \tag{16.3}$$

In order to calculate the heat loss for an entire room or building, the heat losses of all the different types of assemblies—walls, windows, roofs, and so forth—must be determined and then added together.

Example 16.1

Find the coefficient of heat transmission for the wall assembly shown.

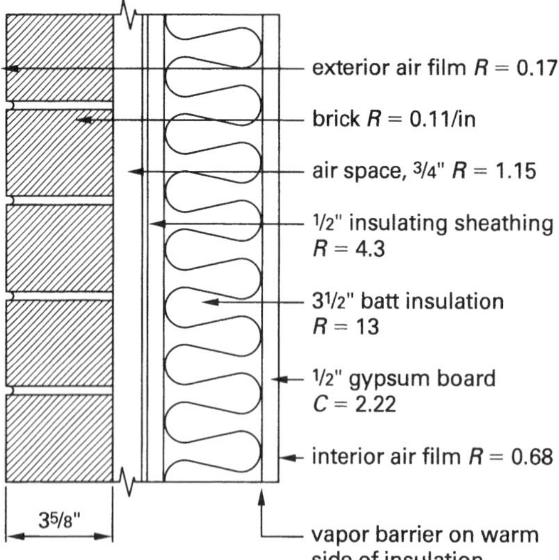

Solution

The R- and C-values for the various components are given in the table. However, they must all be converted to conductances for the thicknesses used. Air spaces and the thin layer of air on the exteriors and

Project Planning

interiors of buildings have some thermal resistance. The brick has an *R*-value of 0.11 hr-ft^2-°F/Btu per inch and is 3⅝ in thick, so its total *R*-value is 0.40 hr-ft^2-°F/Btu.

The conductance, *C*, of the gypsum board is 2.22 hr-ft^2-°F/Btu, so its resistance, *R*, is

$$R = \frac{1}{C} = \frac{1}{2.22\ \frac{\text{hr-ft}^2\text{-°F}}{\text{Btu}}}$$
$$= 0.45\ \text{hr-ft}^2\text{-°F/Btu}$$

The sum of the total *R*-values of the assembly is

material	*R*-value (hr-ft^2-°F/Btu)
exterior air film	0.17
brick	0.40
airspace	1.15
sheathing	4.30
insulation	13.00
gypsum board	0.45
interior air film	0.68
$\sum R$	20.15

The overall coefficient of transmission, *U*, is

$$U = \frac{1}{\sum R} = \frac{1}{20.15\ \frac{\text{hr-ft}^2\text{-°F}}{\text{Btu}}}$$
$$= 0.0496\ \text{Btu/hr-ft}^2\text{-°F}$$

The value for ΔT is determined by subtracting the outdoor design temperature from the desired indoor temperature in the winter, usually 70°F. Outdoor design temperatures vary with geographical region and are found in the *ASHRAE Handbook* or are set by local building codes.

Heat loss calculations and the *psychrometric chart* are used to avoid condensation on interior surfaces and especially inside building construction by determining the dew point of the moisture in the air. For example, air at 70°F and 35% relative humidity has a dew point of 41°F. Moisture will condense on surfaces at or below this temperature.

Heat is lost in two basic ways: throught the building envelope and through air infiltration.

In Ex. 16.1, if the outdoor temperature is 0°F and the indoor temperature is 70°F, somewhere inside the wall assembly the temperature is 41°F or less. Water vapor from inside the building permeating the construction would condense on this surface, damaging the wood construction and possibly negating the effectiveness of the insulation. To avoid this problem, a *vapor barrier* must be placed on the warm side of the insulation, as shown in Ex. 16.1. Vapor barriers can be thin plastic films, or they can be a part of sheathing or insulation batts.

In most cases, it is obvious which side of the insulation is the warm side. However, if the location of dew-point temperature must be determined, a thermal gradient can be calculated through a section of the construction assembly. A *thermal gradient* shows variance in temperature through a cross section of a construction assembly. Figure 16.4 shows an example using the same wall assembly from Ex. 16.1.

Figure 16.4 Example Wall Assembly

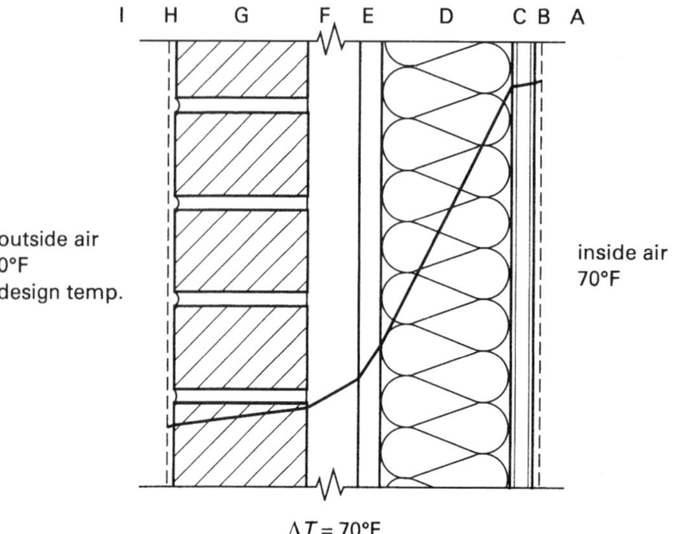

ref. point	thermal component	component resistance, R	cumulative resistance, R_c	$\Delta T_d = \left(\frac{R_c}{R_t}\right)\Delta T$ temp. difference to ref. point, T_d	temp. at ref. point, °F
A	inside air	–x	–x	–x	70
B	interior air film	0.68	0.68	2.36	67.6
C	gypsum board	0.45	1.13	3.93	66.1
D	insulation	13.00	14.13	49.09	20.9
E	sheathing	4.30	18.43	64.02	6.0
F	airspace	1.15	19.58	68.02	2.0
G	brick	0.40	19.98	69.41	0.6
H	exterior air film	0.17	20.15	70.00	0.0
I	outside air	–x	–x	–x	0.0
		R_t = 20.15			

Note: R of vapor barrier is zero.

Heat Loss Through Infiltration

Infiltration is the transfer of air into and out of a building through open doors, cracks around windows and other openings, flues and vents, and other gaps in the exterior construction. Unless a building is well sealed, infiltration can account for more heat loss than transmission through the walls and roof. However, no building is perfectly sealed; there is always some infiltration.

Heat loss through infiltration is calculated by Eq. 16.4.

$$q_v = V(1.08)\Delta T \qquad 16.4$$

The factor of 1.08 Btu-min/ft^3-°F-hr accounts for the specific heat of air; that is, the amount of heat that air at a certain density can hold. The volumetric flow rate, V, of air infiltration can be calculated from the volume of air lost through cracks, doors, and other openings, or it can be estimated using tables that give air changes per hour based on certain criteria.

Because infiltration can greatly affect energy use in a building, current codes and energy conservation standards require the use of air barriers and other construction methods to minimize the unwanted transfer of air into and out of a structure. See Chap. 27 for more information on air barriers.

Heat Gain Calculations

There are several sources of *heat gain* in buildings. There is heat gain produced when the outside temperature is high and heat is transferred by conduction, convection, and radiation, just as there is heat loss when the outside temperature is low. Heat gain through infiltration is also a factor when the outside temperature is high. In addition, heat is produced by the radiation of the sun on glazing, and by interior elements such as the building's occupants, lighting, and equipment such as motors.

The percentage of heat generated by each of these factors varies with the occupancy of the building. For example, a residence is dominated by gains from the building envelope and through glazing. Heat gain from occupants and lighting is negligible. A large office building, however, has a great many occupants, each of whom produces a minimum of 400 Btu/hr at rest. Office buildings also have a large number of light fixtures and a significant amount of equipment. The ratio of room area to wall surface may be quite low for an office building as compared to a residence. Because of conditions like these, for many occupancies it is not unusual to need air conditioning even in the winter months.

Heat gain through the building envelope is calculated in a manner similar to heat loss, using the overall coefficient of heat transmission and the area of the building assembly (as shown in Eq. 16.3), but the temperature differential is not used directly. Instead, a derived value known as the *design equivalent temperature difference* (DETD) must be used. The DETD takes into account the air temperature differences, effects of the sun, thermal mass storage effects of materials, colors of finishes exposed to the sun, and daily temperature range. DETD values are published in tables produced by ASHRAE.

An alternative to the DETD is the *sol-air temperature*, a value for outdoor temperature that combines the effects of temperature difference with solar radiation. This value can be used as the ΔT value in heat gain calculations. The sol-air temperature is

$$T_e = T_o + \frac{aE_t}{h_o} - 7°\text{F} \qquad 16.5$$

In Eq. 16.5, T_e is the sol-air temperature, T_o is the outdoor dry-bulb temperature, and a is the surface's absorbance for solar radiation. Light-colored surfaces are usually assumed to be 0.45; dark surfaces are assumed to be 0.90. Detailed values are given in the *ASHRAE Handbook*. E_t is the total solar radiation incident on the surface, given in units of Btu/hr-ft^2; solar heat gain factors are given in the *ASHRAE Handbook*. h_o is the film coefficient of heat transfer by long-wave radiation and convection at the surface; this is usually assumed to be 3.0 Btu/hr-ft^2-°F.

As Eq. 16.4 illustrates, heat flow through construction assemblies is strongly affected both by the amount of solar radiation and by the color of the surface, with dark surfaces resulting in much greater heat flow than light surfaces.

Heat gain through glazing can be a very significant factor. It is calculated by multiplying the area of the glazing by the *design cooling load factor* (DCLF). Like the DETD, the DCLF takes into account several variables that affect how solar heat gain occurs, including the type of glazing, the type of interior shading, and the outdoor design temperature. Design cooling load factors are also published by ASHRAE.

The occupants of abuilding produce two kinds of heat: sensible heat and latent heat in the form of moisture from breathing and perspiration.

The occupants of a building produce two kinds of heat: *sensible heat* and *latent heat* in the form of moisture from breathing and perspiration. Sensible heat gain from occupants can be assumed to be about 225 Btu/hr, although this varies slightly with occupancy type. Total sensible heat is estimated by multiplying the number of occupants by 225 Btu/hr.

Project Planning

Because 1 W = 3.41 Btu/hr, heat gains from lighting can be calculated by multiplying the total wattage load of the building's lighting by 3.41. For fluorescent and other discharge lights, the energy used by the ballast must also be included. A general rule is to multiply the Btu/hr generated by these types of fixtures by 1.25.

Heat generated by equipment such as motors, elevators, appliances, water heaters, computer servers, and cooking equipment can be a significant factor in commercial buildings. The methods of calculating such heat are complex and depend in part on horsepower ratings and efficiencies of motors, load factors, and any latent heat produced.

Latent heat must be accounted for in calculating heat gains because, for cooling purposes, moisture in the air must be removed to maintain a comfortable relative humidity level while the sensible heat level is being reduced. In heat gain calculations, latent heat gain is either calculated separately or estimated as a percentage of the total sensible heat; the percentage is based on experience and the type of occupancy. Latent heat gain in residential and many other occupancies is about 30% of the sensible heat gain.

Using building materials with high mass is an effective passive method of mitigating the effects of heat gain from solar radiation and air temperature. Materials such as masonry, concrete, and tile slow the transmission of heat into a building. During the day, these materials absorb the heat energy and store it. During the night, when the air temperature is cooler than the surface of the mass, much of this energy is lost to the atmosphere instead of being transmitted into the building.

Heat Gain Through Infiltration

The method for calculating sensible heat gain through infiltration is similar to the method for calculating heat loss. The total heat gain is found by multiplying the total area by an infiltration factor. However, if a building is mechanically ventilated, the volume of air being introduced into the building is multiplied by the amount of heat that must be extracted both to cool the air and to remove excess humidity (i.e., latent heat). In humid climates, the energy needed to do this can be substantial.

DEFINITIONS

British thermal unit (Btu): The amount of heat required to raise the temperature of 1 lbm water by 1°F.

coefficient of heat transmission (*U*): The overall rate of heat flow through any combination of materials, including air spaces and air layers on the interior and exterior of a building assembly. It is the reciprocal of the sum of all the resistances in the building assembly.

conductance (*C*): The number of British thermal units per hour that pass through 1 ft^2 of homogeneous material of a given thickness when the temperature differential is 1°F.

conductivity (*k*): The number of British thermal units per hour that pass through 1 ft^2 of homogeneous material 1 in thick when the temperature differential is 1°F.

dew point: The temperature at which water vapor in the air becomes saturated and begins to condense into drops of water.

dry-bulb temperature: The temperature of the air-water mixture as measured with a standard dry-bulb thermometer.

enthalpy: The total heat in a substance, including latent heat and sensible heat.

latent heat: Heat that causes a change of state of a substance, such as the heat required to change water into steam. The amount of heat required to change the state of a substance is much greater than the heat required to raise the temperature of the substance (sensible heat). The average value of latent heat per pound of moisture is 1061 Btu.

resistance: The number of hours needed for 1 Btu to pass through 1 ft^2 of material or assembly of a given thickness when the temperature differential is 1°F. It is the reciprocal of conductance.

sensible heat: Heat that causes a change in temperature of a substance but not a change of state. For example, the sensible heat needed to raise the temperature of 1 lbm of water from 50°F to 100°F is 50 Btu. In contrast, the latent heat needed to change liquid water at 212°F to steam at 212°F is 1061 Btu.

specific heat: The number of Btus required to raise the temperature of a specific material by 1°F. Specific heat is a measure of a material's capacity to store heat as compared with the storage capacity of water.

wet-bulb temperature: The temperature of the air as measured with a *sling psychrometer.* The wet-bulb temperature is a more critical measure of heat in high humidity because it is an indicator of physical stress caused when the human body is near the upper limits of temperature regulation by perspiration.

17

MECHANICAL, ELECTRICAL, AND PLUMBING SYSTEMS

Nomenclature

E	energy	W-hr	R	resistance	Ω
I	electrical current	A	t	time	hr
P	electrical power	W	V	voltage	V
pf	power factor	–	Z	impedance	Ω

During project planning and the design development phase of a project, the architect must make some fundamental decisions regarding the selection of mechanical, electrical, and plumbing systems. This chapter reviews the basics of energy sources, types of HVAC systems, energy conservation strategies in mechanical systems, water supply, electrical system fundamentals, and power supply in buildings. The fundamentals of human comfort and mechanical systems are discussed in Chap. 16.

ENERGY SOURCES

Regardless of what energy conservation measures are adopted for a building, either the primary or backup energy source will likely be one of the conventional fuels. Only in a few instances will the building be a *net zero structure*; that is, one that consumes only as much energy as it produces on site through renewable means.

The selection of fuel type will depend on the fuel's availability in the region and the dependability of supply; the fuel's cost, cleanliness and convenience of storage; and the needs of the building's equipment. For example, in an urban area, steam may be readily available as a by-product of a local utility company, whereas in a suburban area, oil may have to be the energy source. Electricity is inexpensive and readily available in some locations, while in others, its use for heating is cost prohibitive.

Natural Gas

Of all the fossil fuels, *natural gas* is the most efficient. It is clean burning and relatively low in cost. Depending on the location of the site and local market conditions, however, natural gas service may not always be available, or the price may fluctuate significantly. In rural or remote locations, it may not be available at all. Natural gas has a heating value of about 1050 Btu/ft^3.

Propane is a type of gas that can be used in areas where natural gas is not available. It is delivered and stored in pressurized tanks and has a heating value of about 21,560 Btu/lbm, or 2500 Btu/ft^3.

Oil

Oil is widely used in some regions, but because it is a petroleum product, its cost and availability depend on world and local market conditions. It must be stored in or near the building where it is used, and the equipment needed for burning it often requires more maintenance than gas-fired boilers.

Oil for residential and commercial heating use is produced in six grades: no. 1, no. 2, no. 4, no. 5 light, no. 5 heavy, and no. 6. (The designation for no. 3 was merged into that for no. 2 in the mid-twentieth century.) Grades with lower numbers are more refined and thus more expensive. No. 2 fuel oil is the grade most commonly used in residential and light commercial boilers, while no. 4 and no. 5 grades are used in larger commercial applications. The heat value for no. 2 oil is from 137,000 Btu/gal to 141,000 Btu/gal, while no. 5 has a heat value from 146,800 Btu/gal to 152,000 Btu/gal.

Electricity

Electricity has many advantages as an energy source. It is easy and relatively inexpensive to install, simple to operate, easy to control, and flexible in zoning. It does not require storage facilities, exhaust flues, or supply air.

The primary disadvantage of electricity is its cost as compared to other fuels. Most electric utilities charge more for *peak use*, electricity consumed during periods in which public consumption is expected to be high. For this reason, heating with electricity during a cold period can be very expensive. However, on-site *photovoltaics* can reduce the reliance on utility-supplied electricity.

Electricity is ideal for *radiant heating*, whether it is installed in a ceiling or in individual panels. It can be used in baseboard units as well as to operate electric furnaces for forced air systems. Electricity can be used directly to produce heat in radiant panels or to heat water that is circulated in a *hydronic system*. Supplemental space heating is one of the most common uses of electric heating. Electricity has an equivalent heating value of 3413 Btu/kW.

Steam

Steam is not considered a basic fuel like gas and oil, but in many urban locations and large campuses, it is available from a central plant and is distributed as a by-product of the generation of electricity. Steam is not generally used directly for heating. Typically, steam is piped into a building and used to heat water for water or air heating systems and to drive absorption-type water chillers for air conditioning.

Heat Pumps

Heat spontaneously travels from warmer locations to cooler ones. A *heat pump* is a device that can reverse this, absorbing heat from a cooler location and transferring it to a warmer one, using the principles of refrigeration.

A heat pump's heating efficiency decreases as the outdoor air temperature decreases. It is more effective in mild climates where winter temperatures are usually moderate.

A heat pump can provide heat in the winter and cooling in the summer. During the summer, the heat pump acts as a standard air conditioner. A refrigerant circulates inside the heat pump through a cycle that includes an evaporator and a condenser. In the evaporator, the refrigerant absorbs heat from the inside air. This warmed refrigerant then flows to the condenser, where it releases heat, which is sent to the outside air. The cooled refrigerant then flows back to the evaporator to absorb more heat, and the cycle continues.

In the winter, the refrigerant flow is reversed so that the heat pump absorbs heat from the outside air and releases it to the inside.

A heat pump's heating efficiency decreases as the outdoor air temperature decreases. At exterior temperatures below about 40°F, a heat pump is not economically competitive with oil or gas as a heating source. Heat pumps are more effective in mild climates where winter temperatures are usually moderate. To provide supplemental heating, electrical resistance coils are often placed in supply ductwork.

To increase its efficiency, a heat pump can be connected to a solar energy system. With this approach, solar energy provides heat when the outdoor temperature is between 47°F and 65°F. Below this range, a heat pump automatically turns on and provides heat until the temperature becomes too cold for the pump's efficient use. At that point, both systems are used; the heat pump preheats the air, and the solar energy system heats the warmed air further so that its temperature is high enough for space heating.

Electrical resistance heating may also supplement on very cold or cloudy days. Ground source heat pumps, described in Chap. 12, can use the temperature of the earth to both heat and cool.

Natural Energy Sources

Energy from natural sources includes solar (either passive or active), photovoltaic (PV), geothermal, wind, and tidal energy. These are described in Chap. 12. Solar energy has been developed to the point where it is readily available and efficient for residential and some commercial uses.

PV panels are available, but the cost per kilowatt hour is high, and their general use is limited. This is changing as more research is conducted and more efficient panels are manufactured. See Chap. 12 for more information on photovoltaics.

Use of other natural energy sources is still largely in the research and development stage; their use is limited to large-scale generation rather than use for individual buildings.

Selecting Fuel Sources

The regional prices of different kinds of fuel are not the only factor to consider when selecting fuel sources. The amount of fuel that will be needed and the various efficiencies of the available fuels are two other important factors that should be taken into account.

The fuel needed for heating can be estimated with the help of degree days, which are a rough measure of how much heating is needed for human comfort in a particular location over the course of a year.

The fuel needed for heating can be estimated with the help of *degree days*, which are a rough measure of how much heating is needed for human comfort in a particular location over the course of a year. The number of degree days for a given location on a given day of the year is found by taking the difference between a baseline indoor temperature of 65°F and the average outside temperature for the day. 65°F is used as a baseline as it is adequate for human comfort, given that internal gains raise the temperature a few more degrees.

For example, if the 24-hour average for April 8 in Pennsylvania is 36°F, then the number of degree days for that day at that location is 65 − 36 − 29. If the average outside temperature is 65°F or above, there are no degree days for that day.

The daily values for the year are added to get the total number of degree days for the year. Degree days are used to estimate yearly fuel consumption, to size some passive solar energy systems, and to factor into other heating computations.

Sometimes degree days are called *heating degree days* to distinguish them from *cooling degree days*, a similar but opposite measurement. Cooling degree days measure how much the average daily temperature exceeds 65°F; they can be used to estimate energy needs for cooling.

Table 17.1 Approximate Efficiencies of Fuels

fuel	efficiency (%)
natural gas	70–80
propane	70–90
no. 2 oil	65–85
anthracite coal	65–75
electricity	95–100

Because different fuel types convert energy into heat with varying levels of efficiency, efficiency is an important consideration in the selection of fuel, assuming all fuels are available. Table 17.1 shows the typical efficiency ranges of several fuels.

ENERGY CONVERSION

Any type of fuel selected for heating or cooling must be converted into a useful form, such as heated or chilled air, for distribution throughout a building. Distribution usually requires an additional energy source, such as electricity, to operate fans, motors, and other components of the system.

Heat Generation Equipment

Two of the most common devices for converting fuel to heat are the furnace and the boiler.

A *furnace* burns fuel inside a combustion chamber. Air is circulated around the chamber by a fan. As the cool air from return air ducts passes over the combustion chamber, it is heated for distribution to the building. The hot exhaust gases pass through a flue that is vented to the outside. Replaceable filters are used on the return air side of the furnace to trap dust and dirt that enters the system.

Forced air furnaces come in three types: upflow, downflow, and horizontal. In an *upflow furnace*, the return air is supplied at the bottom of the unit and the heated air is delivered to the bonnet above the furnace where it is distributed through ductwork. A *downflow furnace* operates in exactly the opposite way and is typically used in cases where ductwork is located in a basement or crawl space and the furnace is located on the first floor. A *horizontal furnace* is designed to be used in areas where headroom is limited, such as in crawl spaces.

A *boiler* uses fuel to create hot water or steam. The fuel source can be gas, oil, electricity, or steam. In a typical boiler, tubes containing the water to be heated are situated within the combustion chamber, where the heat exchange takes place. As with furnaces, the gases and other products of combustion are carried away through breeching into the flue or chimney. If the primary fuel source is electricity or steam, there is no need for an exhaust flue.

Principles of Refrigeration

There are two types of refrigeration processes that can produce chilled air or water.

- compressive refrigeration
- absorption

A third type, evaporative cooling, can be used in some climates to produce cool air.

Compressive Refrigeration

Compressive refrigeration is based on the transfer of heat during the liquefaction and evaporation of a refrigerant. As a refrigerant in a gaseous form is compressed, it liquefies and releases latent heat as it changes state. As the same liquid expands and vaporizes back to a gas, it absorbs latent heat from the surroundings into the gas. These principles are used in the basic refrigeration cycle shown in Fig. 17.1.

In the past, refrigerants such as Freon were used in compressive refrigeration. However, these compounds contain chlorofluorocarbons (CFCs) that contribute to the depletion of the earth's ozone layer when leaked into the atmosphere; as a result, their use is prohibited. Newer refrigerants such as hydrofluorocarbons (HFCs) have replaced CFCs. However, although HFCs do not harm the ozone layer, they pose a threat to the atmosphere because of their global warming potential, which is much higher than that of carbon dioxide, and because of their increased use. Other common refrigerants such as ammonia, sulfur dioxide, and propane are friendlier to the environment if accidentally released, but raise concerns of their own about toxicity and flammability.

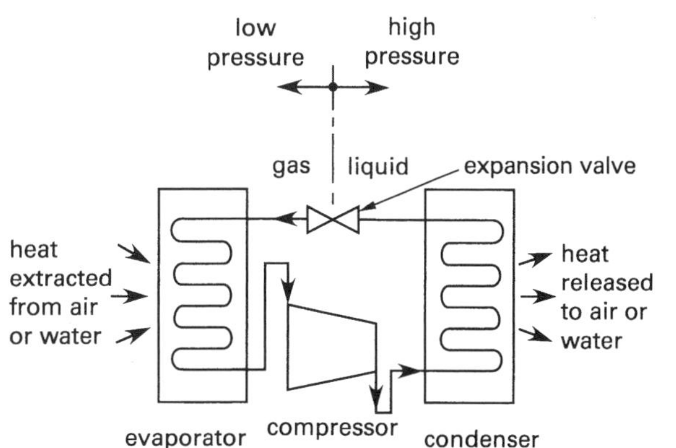

Figure 17.1
Compressive Refrigeration

There are three fundamental components of a compressive refrigeration system: the *compressor*, the *condenser*, and the *evaporator*. The compressor receives the refrigerant as a gas and compresses it, turning it into a liquid. The liquid refrigerant leaves the compressor and flows into the condenser, where its latent heat is released. The condenser is usually located on the outside of the building, and the heat is released to the outside air or to water. The refrigerant then leaves the condenser and enters the evaporator, where it draws heat from its surroundings (either air or water) and expands, becoming a gas again. The gaseous refrigerant leaves the condenser and enters the compressor, and the process repeats.

For many small cooling units, air is forced over the evaporator coils by a fan, and it is this cooled air that is then circulated through the room or space. However, water is a much more efficient medium than air for carrying heat. In larger units designed for large buildings, water is pumped over the evaporator coils, and this chilled water is then pumped to remote cooling units where air is circulated over the chilled water pipes. On the condenser side, water draws the heat from the condenser pipes and then flows to remote cooling towers where it releases the heat to the air.

Absorption

Refrigeration by *absorption* also produces chilled water through the loss of heat when water evaporates, as shown in Fig. 17.2. This evaporation is produced in a closed system; a salt solution draws water vapor from the evaporator.

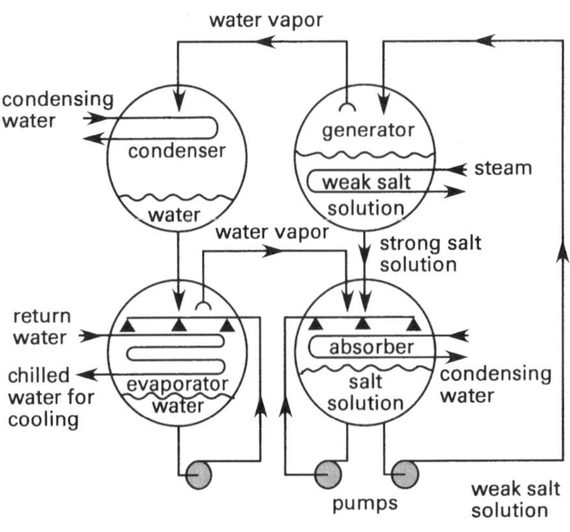

Figure 17.2 Absorption Cooling

As the salt solution absorbs water, it is diluted and must be regenerated by boiling off the water and returning the strong salt solution to the absorber. This is most often done with steam, but it can also be done with high-temperature water produced by solar collectors. The water that is boiled off in the generator is returned to a liquid state in the condenser and then returned to the evaporator. Both the condenser and the absorber receive the condensing water, which removes the waste heat and carries it to cooling towers.

Absorption systems are less efficient than compressive systems. They are most often used when waste heat is available for energy input to the generator part of the system.

Evaporative Cooling

A third type of conditioning is *evaporative cooling.* Water is dropped over pads or fin tubes through which outdoor air or water is circulated. As the free water evaporates (becomes vapor), heat is drawn from the air or from the water circulating. This cooled air is then distributed to the indoor spaces. Evaporative cooling only works in hot-arid climates where the outdoor air has a low enough humidity level to allow the moistened air to evaporate. It can be more economical than refrigeration cooling because it uses only one motor instead of three. An evaporative cooler is also simpler in construction and operation because it needs no refrigerant line and uses fewer parts.

A *ton of refrigeration* (or *ton of cooling*) is a unit used to describe the capacity of a refrigeration system. A ton of cooling is the cooling effect obtained when 1 ton of 32°F ice melts to water in 24 hours. This is equivalent to 12,000 Btu/hr. In general, the needed capacity of a refrigeration machine in tons can be calculated by dividing the calculated total heat gain in Btu/hr by 12,000.

HVAC SYSTEMS

Heating, ventilating, and air conditioning (HVAC) *systems* can be categorized by the medium that is used to heat or cool a building. The two media most often used to transport heat are air and water. Electricity can also be used directly for heating. Some systems use a combination of media. This section outlines some of the more common systems with which an examinee should be familiar.

Direct Expansion Systems

The simplest type of HVAC system is the *direct expansion* (DX) *system*, also known as an *incremental unit.* A DX system is a self-contained unit that passes non-ducted air over an evaporator, which cools the air. The air is then discharged into the room. Ventilation comes directly from the outside, which can help improve ventilation rates and indoor air quality (IAQ). Direct expansion units can be through-wall types, roof mounted, or packaged.

Smaller units with $^1/_3$ ton to 2 ton capacities are adequate for individual rooms, while a larger unit with a capacity over 2 tons can serve several rooms in a single zone. With the addition of a heating coil, a DX system can provide both heating and cooling functions.

All-Air Systems

An all-air system cools or heats a space using conditioned air alone. Heat is transported to and from the space through supply and return air ducts. The most basic type of all-air system is the constant-volume single-duct system. Single-duct systems are most often used in residential and small commercial applications. Air is heated (or cooled) in a central furnace (or air conditioner) and is distributed throughout the

Project Planning

building in ductwork at a constant volume. One centrally located thermostat controls the operation of the furnace. Return air ducts collect cooler air and return it to the furnace for reheating.

This type of system is simple and easy to operate, but it cannot be zoned so that different rooms or areas of the building receive varying amounts of heat (or cooling). The only way to control the system is by adjusting dampers on each supply air register to adjust the amount of heated (or cooled) air coming into a room. The need for individual zone or room control is one reason that many homes use hydronic, or all-water systems (discussed later in this section).

For larger buildings there are four main types of all-air systems.

- *variable air volume* (VAV) *system:* Air is heated or cooled as needed in a central plant and distributed to the building at a constant temperature through a single duct. At each zone, a thermostat controls a damper that varies the volume of conditioned air that enters the space to respond to the user's needs. Dampers on the return air side of the system allow variable amounts of fresh air (up to 100%) to be introduced into the building for ventilation and for cooling when outdoor conditions make it unnecessary to mechanically condition the air. A VAV system is somewhat limited in its ability to compensate for extremes in simultaneous heating and cooling demands in a building, but it offers a very efficient means of air conditioning large internal load dominated buildings. (See Fig. 17.3(a).)

- *high-velocity dual-duct system:* Two parallel ducts run to each space; one carries hot air, and one carries cool air. These two streams of air are joined in a mixing box in proportions to suit the temperature requirements of the conditioned space. A thermostat controls pneumatic valves in the mixing box to create the proper mixture. Figure 17.3(b) shows a simplified diagram of this type of system.

  Because both hot and cool air are available at each location in a building, a dual-duct system can respond to varying requirements throughout the building. For example, on a cold day, heating may be needed on the north side of a structure with a high percentage of glazing, but on the south side of the same building, the combination of solar heat gain, lighting, and occupancy may create a need for cooling. Because the air travels at a high velocity (about 3000 ft/min), the ducts can be smaller, which saves space in high-rise buildings.

  However, a dual-duct system is inherently inefficient because both hot and cool air have to be supplied at all times, so previously cooled air may need to be heated or previously heated air may need to be cooled. In addition, moving air at high velocity takes larger, more powerful fans, which need more energy. Air moving at high velocity can cause noise problems in the ductwork. Finally, the initial cost of a dual-duct system is high because of the quantity of ductwork needed.

- *reheat (constant volume) system:* Return air and fresh outdoor air are mixed. The system cools and dehumidifies the mixture, which is then distributed in a constant volume at low temperature throughout the building. At or near the spaces to be conditioned, the air is reheated as needed based on the cooling load of each space. See Fig. 17.3(c).

  Reheating of the air is usually accomplished with heated water, but it can also be done with electricity. If the reheating equipment is located near the conditioned space, the unit is called a terminal reheat system. If the reheating coils are located in the ductwork that serves an entire zone, the unit is called a zone reheat system. Thermostats are used to control valves in the water supply line and regulate the temperature.

  In many cases, an economizer cycle is used. This cycle allows outdoor air to be used for cooling when temperatures are low enough. The economizer works by adjusting dampers on the return air ducts and fresh air intakes.

  The advantages of the reheat system are that humidity and temperature can be carefully controlled, and that the low supply temperature equates to smaller duct sizes and lower fan horsepower. However, a reheat system uses more energy than other types of systems, because the primary air volume must be cooled most of the time and then reheated.

Figure 17.3
Types of All-Air Systems

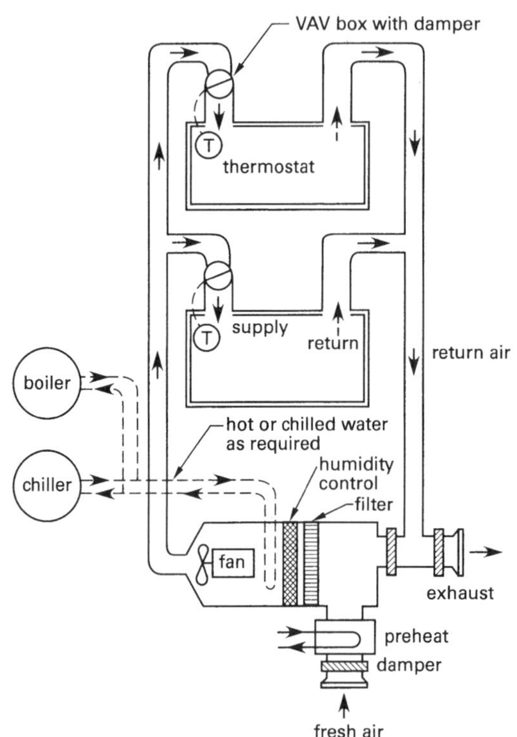

(a) variable air volume system

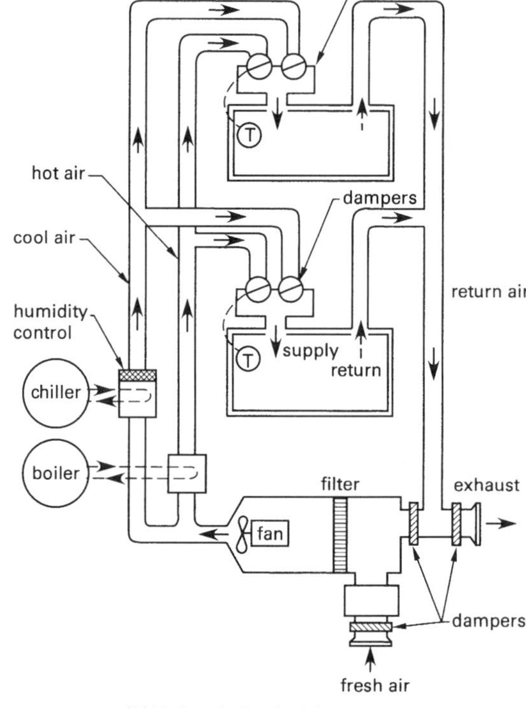

(b) high-velocity dual-duct system

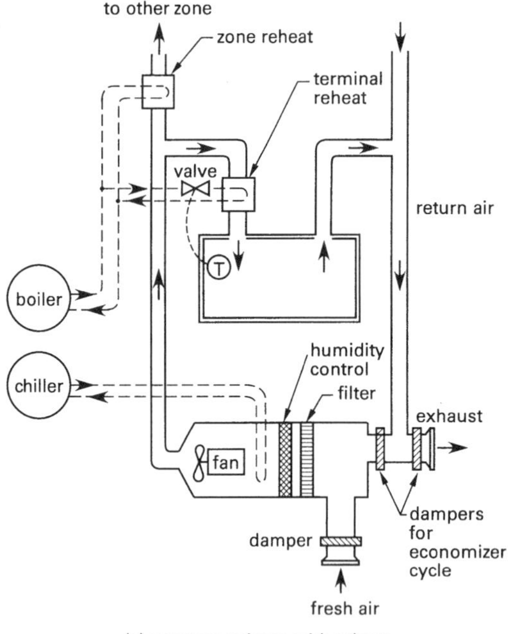

(c) constant volume with reheat

T
zone 2
dampers
return air
boiler
T
zone 1
chiller
filter
exhaust
fan
dampers
preheat
damper
fresh air

(d) multizone system

- *multizone system:* A multizone system (see Fig. 17.3(d)) supplies air to a central mixing unit where separate heating and cooling coils produce separate hot and cold airstreams. These are mixed with dampers controlled by zone thermostats, and the resulting tempered air is delivered to the zones. Multizone systems offer the same advantage as dual-duct systems in that simultaneous cooling and heating of different zones can be accommodated.

  The main disadvantage is that the amount of duct space increases rapidly as more zones are added. This type of system is usually only used for medium-size buildings, or where a central mixing unit can be located on each floor.

All-Water Systems

An *all-water system* uses a fan coil unit in each conditioned space. The fan coils are connected to one or two water circuits. Ventilation is provided with openings through the wall at the location of the fan coil unit, from interior zone air heating, or by simple infiltration.

In a two-pipe system, either hot or chilled water is pumped through one pipe and returned in another. In a four-pipe system, as shown in Fig. 17.4, one circuit is provided for chilled water and one for hot water. There are two supply pipes and two return pipes. A three-pipe system uses a single return pipe for both hot and cold water.

An all-water system is an efficient way to transfer heat. It is easily controlled, as the thermostat in each room regulates how much water flows through the coils. However, humidity control is not possible at the central unit.

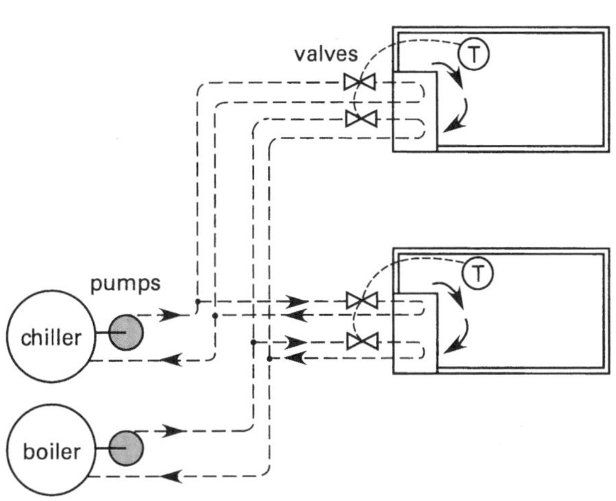

Figure 17.4
Four-Pipe All-Water System

Air-Water Systems

An air-water system relies on a central air system to provide humidity control and ventilation air to conditioned spaces. However, the majority of the heating and cooling is provided by fan coil units located in each space. Air-water systems are often used where return air cannot be recirculated because of the potential for contamination, such as in hospitals and laboratories. In these cases, 100% outside air is supplied, and return air is completely exhausted to the exterior.

With an *induction system*, shown in Fig. 17.5(a), air is supplied throughout the building under high pressure and velocity to each induction unit, where the velocity and noise are attenuated before the air passes over the coils and is heated or cooled as needed. The water supply system delivers heated or chilled water to the coils through either a two- or four-pipe system. Thermostatic control is provided to each unit or group of units by regulating the amount and temperature of water flowing through the coils.

Another type of air-water system uses a fan-coiled unit for primary heating and cooling but has a separate air supply to provide humidity control and ventilation. See Fig. 17.5(b).

Electric Systems

The most common method of electric heating uses a grid of wires in the ceiling of a room to provide radiant heating. Electric baseboard radiators are also available. An electric system provides a uniform, clean, inconspicuous form of heating that can be controlled with a separate thermostat in each room. No space is needed for piping or ductwork.

The biggest disadvantage is that electric heat is generally not economical except in areas where electricity is inexpensive. Most often, electric heat is used for supplemental heating in localized radiant panels, or where water or air systems may need a boost in temperature.

Figure 17.5
Air-Water Systems

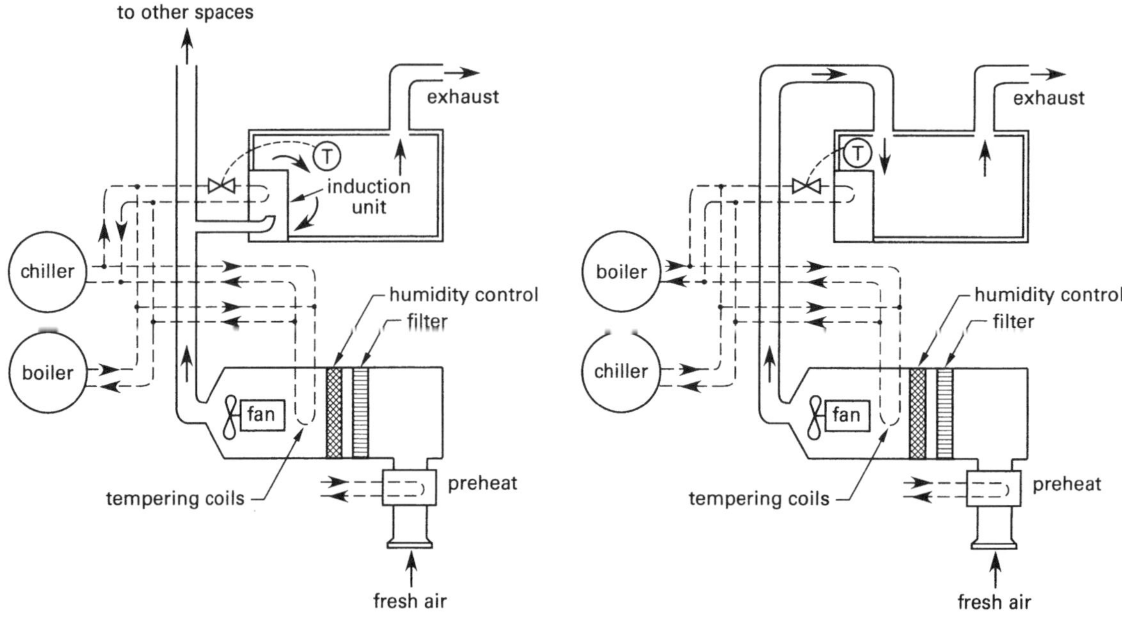

Project Planning

Selection of Systems

Buildings have different HVAC needs because of differences in size, zoning, economics, need for individual control, need for humidity control, and so on. An apartment building, for example, needs a system that will allow each tenant to adjust heating and cooling levels individually. Some common types of HVAC systems and the kinds of buildings in which they are often used are summarized in Table 17.2.

Table 17.2
HVAC Systems for Building Types

	direct expansion	constant volume single duct	variable air volume	dual duct, high velocity	constant volume, terminal reheat	multizone	all-water system	all-water induction	closed loop heat pumps	fan coil	electric
apartments									•	•	
auditoriums/theaters		•	•			•					
churches		•	•			•					
commercial—small			•			•	•				•
hospitals		•		•	•	•		•		•	
hotels/motels		•							•	•	
laboratories		•	•	•	•						
libraries			•			•					
office buildings			•			•		•		•	
residential—single family	•	•					•				•
schools										•	
shopping centers		•	•								

Selecting the most appropriate HVAC system for a building depends on several interrelated variables.

- *use profile of the building:* Some occupancies, such as office buildings and retail stores, need a flexible system to account for changes during the life of the building and for the different requirements of multiple tenants. Variable air volume systems and induction systems satisfy this requirement. A building with multiple uses or a building subject to simultaneous variations in heating or cooling loads may need a dual-duct system or a multizone system.
- Occupancies such as hospitals and laboratories need induction systems or fan coil systems with supplementary air, so that all air supply is 100% outdoor air with complete exhaust to the outside.
- *building scale:* The size of the building helps determine whether to use a central system or individual units. If the air conditioning load is less than about 25 tons, direct expansion units or heat pumps

can usually be used; they can be either rooftop mounted or the through-wall variety. For larger cooling needs, a central station is more economical and provides the needed flexibility.

- *control needs:* Hotels, motels, apartments, and some office buildings need thermostatic control over individual rooms or areas. Other buildings such as theaters need less individual control.
- *fuels available:* Although chillers, boilers, and furnaces that operate with a variety of fuels may be used, the designer will likely select an HVAC system according to which system is most readily and economically available. If steam pipes are adjacent to the building site, for example, absorption-type chillers may be more appropriate than refrigeration equipment.
- *climatic zone:* If the proposed building is in a hot-arid climate, the requirement for dehumidification will not be as great, so an all-water system may be appropriate. Locations that experience a wide swing in temperatures during the day may need a dual-duct system or four-pipe system to provide flexibility and quick response as outdoor conditions change.
- *flexibility:* Flexibility is important for buildings that will change internally (for example, an office building with leased tenant spaces) or be added onto in the future. An all-water system or air-water system can be sized to accommodate the ultimate capacity of the building. Expansion is then a simple matter of extending the piping runs from the central heating and cooling plant.
- *integration with building systems:* The structural system used for the building may suggest using one type of system over another. For example, for a cast-in-place concrete structure with a low floor-to-floor height, it may be easier to use an all-water system with its smaller piping than an all-air system that requires large ductwork. There may also be extensive plumbing, exhaust, and other systems that need to be coordinated with the primary HVAC system.
- *economics:* The initial costs of an HVAC system, its long-term maintenance, and the cost of operating the system must be considered. Speculative developers may want a low initial-cost system, whereas owners and occupants of a structure will be more concerned with the long-term energy efficiency of the system, including the expected costs of fuel and maintenance over the life of the system. Usually, a life-cycle cost analysis of several alternatives is required in order to make an informed decision.

Exhaust

Exhaust systems include systems designed to handle hazardous and nonhazardous exhaust, as well as systems needed for specific equipment operations and those intended to exhaust away from sources of contamination.

In the *International Mechanical Code* (IMC), requirements for exhaust systems are distinct from the requirements for ventilation, which are discussed in Chap. 14, and the requirements for the exhaust components of standard HVAC systems, which are illustrated in Fig. 17.3.

The following systems and equipment may need dedicated exhaust systems.

- equipment and processes that produce or throw off dust or particles sufficiently light to float in the air
- equipment and processes that emit heat, odors, fumes, spray, gas, or smoke in such quantities so as to be irritating or injurious to health or safety
- hazardous materials used in production
- garages and motor vehicle repair facilities
- clothes dryers
- domestic kitchen exhaust
- commercial kitchen hoods and grease ducts
- laboratories
- dust, stock, and refuse conveying systems

- sub-slab soil exhaust systems
- smoke control systems (see Chap. 32)
- energy recovery ventilation systems

Exhaust air must be discharged outdoors at a place where it will not cause a nuisance, and where it cannot be drawn back into the building by an intake for the ventilating system. A *nuisance* in this case is a legal term meaning that which is dangerous to human life or detrimental to health. The IMC does not specify exact distances from general HVAC exhaust outlets and air intakes, leaving that determination to the local code official. Exhaust air cannot be discharged into an attic or crawl space; it must be vented to the building exterior. The IMC also details the minimum distances required between the termination points of exhaust air and other building elements. These are given in Table 17.3.

Table 17.3
Location of Exhaust Outlets

	distance in ft from					
exhaust type	property lines	operable openings	exterior walls and roofs	combustible walls and operable openings in the direction of exhaust discharge	above adjoining grade	mechanical air intakes
ducts conveying explosive or flammable vapors, fumes, or dusts	30	3	6	30	10	
other product-conveying outlets	10	3	3		10	
environmental air exhaust (domestic kitchen, bath, and clothes dryer)	3	3	3			10
clothes dryer, ktichen hoods, dust stock systems, subslab soil exhaust systems, smoke control, refrigerant discharge, machinery room discharge	requirements specified in individual sections of the IMC					

ENERGY CONSERVATION

In many cases, mechanical techniques can be used to reduce reliance on HVAC. These techniques involve mechanical system components, heat transfer methods, building automation systems, and building commissioning.

Mechanical System Components

The amount of energy used by HVAC systems is usually between 40% and 60% of the overall energy consumption of the building, depending on the building type, climate, design, and other variables. Because some type of mechanical system is always required in large buildings and most small buildings, it is reasonable to include energy-efficient mechanical systems in an overall strategy for energy conservation and sustainability.

In order to make standard HVAC equipment more efficient, the National Appliance Energy Conservation Act of 1987 established minimum efficiency standards for both small and large heating and cooling equipment. The performance of this equipment is rated based on several factors, including annual fuel utilization efficiency, the coefficient of performance, the energy efficiency ratio, the integrated part load value (IPLV), and the seasonal energy efficiency ratio (SEER).

In addition to specifying more efficient equipment, a designer can minimize reliance on standard HVAC systems by applying various mechanical techniques and devices to conserve energy. The following sections describe some of the most commonly used methods.

Economizer Cycle

An *economizer cycle* uses outdoor air when it is cool enough to mix with recirculated indoor air. This reduces the energy needed for refrigeration and can be useful when the outdoor air temperature is about 60°F. As the temperature drops, less outdoor air is introduced because it would need to be heated.

An economizer cycle is essentially a mechanical substitute for an open window, providing fresh air into the building to improve indoor air quality, with the advantages of filtering the air and facilitating more even distribution. The control system balances the need for fresh air intake with the outdoor temperature and other variables of the heating system. For a large commercial building where internal loads and heat gain make cooling necessary even in winter months, an economizer cycle can save a significant amount of energy.

Dual-Condenser Cooling

In *dual-condenser cooling*, refrigeration equipment uses two condensers instead of one. When heat is needed in the building, the heat recovery condenser is used, which sends the waste heat to fan coil units or other devices. When the heat is not needed, the heat rejection condenser sends heat to the cooling towers. The building automation system controls which condenser is active, based on the outdoor temperature and the heating and cooling needs of the building.

A similar option is to use multiple chillers with units of varying sizes instead of one large chiller. The system can operate more efficiently by using the chiller with the best size for the load.

Gas-Fired Absorption Cooling

Unlike conventional air conditioning chillers, *absorption chillers* do not rely on electricity and ozone-depleting refrigerants. They are usually powered by natural gas, which is generally a more economical fuel than electricity. If steam or high-temperature water from an industrial process is available, that can also be their energy source.

Absorption chillers are not as efficient as electrically driven chillers, they have a higher initial cost, and they reject more heat to cooling towers. However, they may be more energy efficient for large buildings, especially in areas where electricity costs are high and where low-cost heat sources from steam or industrial processes are available. As an added benefit, equipment can be selected that will also provide hot water for heating.

Solar-Powered Absorption Cooling

Absorption chillers can be made more efficient and sustainable if they are powered by hot water from solar collectors. Standard flat-plate solar collectors can supply water from 175°F to 195°F.

Using such a system may be less expensive than running compressive chillers with electricity, even though the efficiency of the solar collectors is low. Efficiency can be increased by using parabolic concentrating solar collectors to provide water at a higher temperature.

Solar-Powered Desiccant Cooling

Another type of solar-powered cooling system uses desiccants to dehumidify and cool air by means of evaporative cooling. A *desiccant* is a material, either liquid or solid, that absorbs water.

Designs vary, but a typical system passes incoming air over a desiccant, which is usually mounted on a wheel rotating in the airstream. As the air passes over the desiccant, it is cooled and dehumidified. Thermal energy from solar collectors is used to dry out the desiccant so it can be used again in the cycle. Desiccants commonly used in these systems include silica gel, zeolite, lithium bromide, and monoethylene glycol.

Direct Contact Water Heaters

A *direct contact water heater* passes hot gases directly through water to heat it. Natural gas is burned to provide flue gases that transfer heat to the water. To further improve efficiency, a heat exchanger on the combustion chamber reclaims any heat lost from the chamber. Although the gases are in direct contact with the water, the water is considered safe for human consumption.

Direct contact water heaters can be up to 99% efficient when the inlet water temperature is below 59°F. They also produce lower emissions of carbon monoxide and nitrous oxides than other heating systems. Because direct contact water heaters are a high-cost alternative, they are best used where there is a continuous demand for hot water, such as for food processing, laundries, and industrial purposes.

Recuperative Gas Boilers

Flue gases are exhausted at very high temperatures. A *recuperative gas boiler* (also called a *fuel economizer* or *boiler economizer*) recovers the heat in the flue gases that would normally be discharged to the atmosphere. A recuperative gas boiler is designed to cool the flue gas enough to achieve condensation, so that both sensible heat and latent heat are recovered. The reclaimed heat is used to preheat the cold water entering the boiler or to preheat combustion air. Standard gas boilers tend to have a maximum efficiency of around 83%, but a recuperative gas boiler can increase efficiency to about 95%. Some systems also reduce emissions of carbon monoxide and nitrous oxides.

The flue gases are cool when finally emitted, so plastic vent pipe can be used, making installation easier. This also permits the use of a smaller flue, with more turns in the piping if needed.

Displacement Ventilation

Displacement ventilation is an air distribution system in which supply air is dispensed at floor level and rises to return air grilles in the ceiling as it warms, as shown in Fig. 17.6. Because the supply air is delivered at floor level, close to users, it does not have to be cooled as much, resulting in energy savings. Displacement ventilation is a good system for removing heat generated by ceiling-level lights and for improving indoor air quality, because this kind of system typically uses a high percentage of outdoor air. It can also be used with personal temperature control and flexible underfloor wiring.

Figure 17.6 Displacement Ventilation

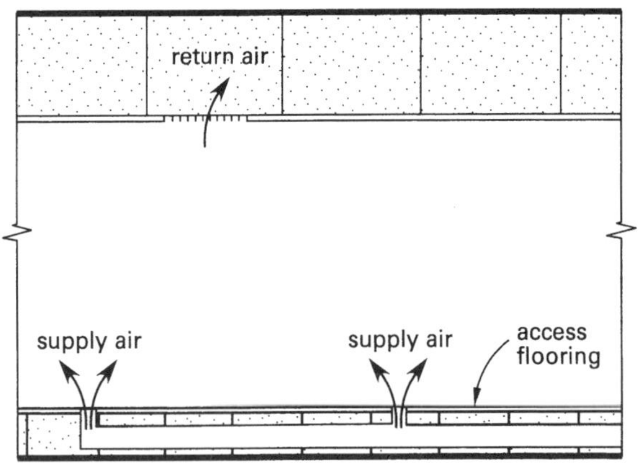

Most displacement ventilation systems need an access flooring system to provide space for underfloor ducting and to allow rearrangement of supply air outlets as the space layout changes. This makes displacement ventilation appropriate only for new construction, where the additional floor-to-floor height can be set to accommodate the 12 in or more needed for ductwork, and where the elevations of stairway landings and elevator stops can be coordinated to match the elevation of the access floor.

A variation of this system uses supply air outlets located low on exterior walls, but this system only works for spaces next to the exterior wall to a depth of about 16 ft.

Water-Loop Heat Pumps

A *water-loop heat pump system* uses a series of heat pumps for different zones of a building. These heat pumps are all connected to the same piping system of circulating water, as shown in Fig. 17.7. The water loop is maintained at a temperature between 60°F and 90°F. When some zones are in cooling mode and are dumping heat into the loop, other zones are in heating mode and are extracting heat from the loop; therefore, no additional energy has to be added or removed when the heating and cooling modes are balanced. Only when most of the units are in the same mode does the water in the loop have to be cooled or heated with a cooling tower or boiler. Automatic valves at the cooling tower and boiler direct the water as needed.

This type of system is very efficient where there is a simultaneous need for heating and cooling in different parts of the building. It also reduces piping costs in comparison to two- or four-pipe water heating systems. It is not appropriate for buildings where cooling loads are small.

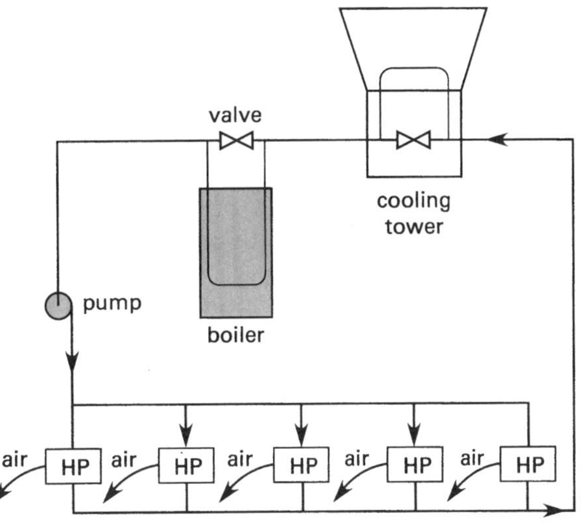

Figure 17.7
Water-Loop Heat Pump System

Thermal Energy Storage

Thermal energy storage uses water, ice, or rock beds to store excess heat or coolness for use at a later time. Thermal storage makes it possible to manage a building's energy needs over climatic temperature swings throughout the day or week, and it allows the use of less expensive, off-peak energy costs to cool.

For example, in the summer, chillers can cool water at night, when utility rates are typically lower and the cooling needs of the building are not as great as they are during the day. During the next day, the stored coolness can be used to minimize the energy needed for cooling.

Heat and coolness can be stored in water, rocks, or other appropriate thermal masses. Coolness can also be stored in ice. Ice can absorb and give off more heat than the other storage media, both as sensible heat and as the latent heat used in melting and freezing. For any given amount of heat capacity, ice will occupy about one-eighth as much space as water.

HEAT TRANSFER

The desire for energy conservation is not always compatible with indoor air quality (IAQ) needs and requirements. Historically, the first efforts at energy conservation resulted in tightly sealed buildings in which both the infiltration of fresh air and the reuse of conditioned air were reduced. This led to problems with human comfort, sick building syndrome, and other building-related illnesses.

One way to alleviate some IAQ problems in tightly sealed buildings is to introduce more outdoor air through the ventilation system while exhausting more of the used, conditioned air. However, heating or cooling the incoming air uses energy. Balancing these incompatible needs for energy conservation and IAQ involves careful evaluation and selection of heat transfer methods. The following methods are all based on the concept of heat exchange, in which heat is moved from a place it is not wanted to a place where it is desirable.

Energy Recovery Ventilators

Energy recovery ventilators, also called *air-to-air heat exchangers,* reclaim waste energy from the exhaust airstream and use it to condition incoming fresh air. The use of energy recovery ventilators can reduce the energy needed to condition incoming air by 60% to 70%.

Energy recovery ventilators are especially efficient in very cold, hot, or humid climates, where the temperature differential between indoor and outdoor air is high. They are most efficient in buildings with continuous occupancy, such as hotels and hospitals. Their use is generally not justified in temperate climates or in buildings that are not occupied at all times.

Three conditions should be met when using energy recovery ventilators.

- The fresh air intake must be kept as far away from the exhaust outlet as possible, to avoid sucking the exhaust air back into the building.
- Exhaust air that contains excessive moisture, grease, or other contaminants should be separated from the heat exchanger air.
- In cold winter conditions, a defroster in the device may be needed to prevent the condensate in the exhaust air from freezing.

Energy recovery ventilators do not completely eliminate leakage between the exhaust and supply airstreams. Although the *International Mechanical Code* (IMC) generally prohibits recirculation of outdoor air introduced into a mechanical system, it does allow the use of up to 10% of recirculated air so as to allow the use of energy recovery ventilators. However, energy recovery ventilators are prohibited in hazardous exhaust systems; in dust, stock, and refuse systems that convey explosive or flammable vapors; in smoke control systems; in commercial kitchen exhaust systems; and in clothes dryer exhaust systems.

Three common devices are used to facilitate air-to-air heat exchange: flat-plate heat recovery units, energy transfer wheels, and heat pipes.

Flat-plate heat recovery units have two separate ducts of various designs—one for incoming air and one for exhaust air—separated by a thin wall that facilitates the heat transfer. These units can only exchange sensible heat, and they offer no humidity control.

Energy transfer wheels, also called *enthalpy heat exchangers*, transfer heat between two airstreams through the use of a heat exchanger wheel. Air passes through small openings in the wheel; these openings are impregnated with lithium chloride or another substance that absorbs moisture and transfers it to the other airstream.

Energy transfer wheels are typically used in commercial buildings. Their advantage over other types of heat exchangers is that they can transfer latent heat as well as sensible heat. In winter, heat from the warm, humidified exhaust air is transferred to the cool, dry incoming air. In summer, the cool exhaust air removes some of the heat and excess humidity from the hot incoming air, as shown in Fig. 17.8.

Energy transfer wheels conserve energy, reduce the cooling load, and minimize the need to humidify indoor air during the winter. Some units have a transfer efficiency up to 80%.

Figure 17.8
Energy Transfer Wheel

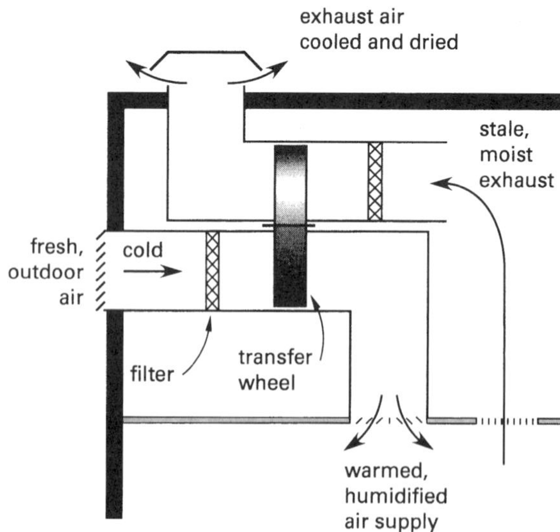

A *heat pipe* is a self-contained device that transfers sensible heat energy from hot exhaust air to cool outdoor air. As the hot exhaust air passes over the heat pipe, it vaporizes a refrigerant inside the pipe, which then moves to a section of the pipe that is exposed to cool incoming air. As the refrigerant condenses, it releases heat to the incoming air, warming it. A wick material inside the pipe then carries the refrigerant back to the hot side through capillary action. For heat pipes to work, the incoming and outgoing airstreams must be adjacent.

Water-to-Water Heat Exchangers

Water-to-water heat exchangers, sometimes called *runaround coils*, use water or some other liquid transfer medium to exchange heat. The main advantage of this type of system is that the incoming and exhaust airstreams do not have to be adjacent. In winter operations, hot exhaust air passes over coils that contain a heat transfer fluid; this fluid is pumped into coils that cool incoming air passes over. In summer, the cooled indoor air being exhausted is used to reduce the temperature of the hot incoming air.

Water-to-water heat exchangers are commonly used in large buildings. They eliminate the possibility that incoming air could be contaminated with exhaust air. The efficiency of water-to-water heat exchangers ranges from 50% to 70%.

Extract-Air Windows

An *extract-air window* uses a double-paned insulated glass unit over which another pane of glass is placed on the inside of the building. Air is drawn up between the interior pane and the main window unit and is extracted into the return air system. This warms the glass in winter and cools it in summer to maintain a comfortable radiant temperature and eliminate the need for a separate perimeter heating system.

Ground-Coupled Heat Exchangers

Ground-coupled heat exchangers heat or cool outside air by circulating it through pipes buried in the ground. In the summer, the air can be used directly if the outdoor air temperature is higher than the ground temperature. In the winter, the system can preheat air for an energy recovery ventilator (to prevent frosting) or for a standard fan-coil heating unit.

Ground-coupled heat exchangers are typically suitable only for low-rise buildings. Their disadvantage is that long runs of pipes are needed for efficient operation. Because the air is forced through the pipes, the energy saved by using such a system must outweigh the energy needed to run the fans. An alternative to this type of system that takes advantage of geothermal energy is the ground-source heat pump.

Chilled Beams

A *chilled beam* is a ceiling-mounted unit that uses water to provide cooling and heating. There are two types of chilled beams: passive and active.

A *passive chilled beam system* relies on natural convection and can provide only cooling. The unit is usually installed above a suspended ceiling. Cool water is circulated through piping attached to aluminum fins. These units are similar to fin tube radiators used for domestic heating. Warm room air, rising by natural convection, enters the unit and comes into contact with the fin tubes. The air is cooled by this contact, and the cool air sinks naturally back into the room. Because no ventilation air is used, separate ventilation ducts are required. However, because heating and cooling are separate from the ventilation system, air ducts and fans can be smaller, reducing energy consumption.

For a passive chilled beam system to function, the temperature of the water must be a little higher than the room's dew point to avoid condensation. Because this water temperature is higher than the standard temperature of chilled water supplied to HVAC units, the building's central chillers can be smaller than usual, saving additional energy. However, the humidity of the ventilation air must be controlled through separate equipment.

An *active chilled beam system* is integrated with a ventilation system and can provide both heating and cooling. Fresh air is drawn into the unit, where it is either cooled or warmed by water; the air is then forced out of the unit and into the room. In this way, an active chilled beam system can handle temperature control and ventilation at the same time.

A *multiservice chilled beam system* combines an active chilled beam system with other building services such as lighting, sprinklers, data cabling, and building management system sensors.

Although chilled beams have a high initial cost, they offer significant energy savings over traditional all-air and air-water HVAC systems. Because they have fewer parts, they also offer lower maintenance, more compact design, and quieter operation.

Variable Refrigerant Flow Systems

A *variable refrigerant flow* (VRF) system uses a single compressor and condenser unit located outdoors, connected to multiple evaporators located in different zones of the building. Refrigerant is supplied to each zone instead of the chilled and heated water used in more traditional all-water systems. Each evaporator is individually controlled, and the amount of refrigerant supplied to each zone varies based on the needs of the zone.

Because both the compressor and all the evaporators operate at varying speeds to precisely meet the load in each zone, power consumption is reduced. VRF systems can also be designed to use heat pump technology or heat recovery to allow simultaneous cooling and heating in different zones, further reducing life-cycle energy costs. If ventilation is needed, individual units in each zone can accept ductwork to mix fresh air with return air.

VRF systems are ideal for office buildings, hotels, schools, multifamily residential, and any building with varying loads and different zones. They are also ideal for renovation work because of the small size of piping and the smaller size of compressors and evaporators compared with conventional systems. They are not appropriate for buildings with large, open volumes like theaters, gyms, and arenas.

In addition to saving energy and providing zoning flexibility, VRF systems also provide the advantages of quicker installation than other systems, quiet operation, flexibility in location of equipment, reduced piping, central control, and the ability to continuously monitor energy use as part of a building management system.

Building Automation Systems

A *building automation system* (BAS) is a computer-based integrated system used to monitor and control building systems. The systems controlled by the BAS will vary depending on the complexity of the building and the needs of the owner, but they typically include HVAC, energy management, lighting, life safety, and security. Other systems that may be part of a BAS include vertical transportation, communications, material handling, and landscape irrigation.

A BAS reduces energy costs through better systems management; allows for monitoring of large, complex buildings; reduces the number of personnel needed to supervise a large building; improves occupant comfort; and provides detailed documentation of the performance of the building's subsystems. If problems arise, the BAS notifies the building systems manager and, if necessary, outside authorities.

The energy conservation component of a BAS is the *energy management system* (EMS), which detects environmental conditions both inside and outside the building, monitors the status of all equipment (including temperature, humidity, and flow rates), and optimizes the control of the equipment (including start and stop times and operational adjustments).

See Chap. 51 for a discussion of building commissioning.

ELECTRICAL FUNDAMENTALS

Definitions

ampere: Also called *amp.* Abbreviated A. The unit flow of electrons in a conductor, equal to 6.251 × 1018 electrons passing a given section in 1 sec.

energy: The product of power and time, also called *work.*

impedance: The resistance in an alternating current (AC) circuit, measured in ohms.

ohm: Abbreviated Ω. The unit of resistance in an electrical circuit.

power factor: The phase difference between voltage and current in an alternating current circuit.

reactance: Part of the electrical resistance in an alternating current circuit, caused by inductance and capacitance.

volt: Abbreviated V. Unit of electromotive force or potential difference. 1 V is the amount of force or potential difference that will cause a current of 1 A to flow through a conductor whose resistance is 1 Ω.

watt: Abbreviated W. Unit of electrical power.

Basic Relationships

Electricity is the energy generated by the flow of electrons. A basic electric circuit consists of a *conductor*, the actual flow of electrons (i.e., *current*), an electric potential difference to cause the electrons to move (i.e., *voltage*), and some type of *resistance* to the flow of electrons. The circuit can be interrupted with a *switch*. These basic components are shown in Fig. 17.9.

Ohm's law for DC circuits, Eq. 17.1, states that the current in a circuit is directly proportional to the voltage and inversely proportional to the resistance.

$$I = \frac{V}{R} \qquad 17.1$$

Power is the rate at which work is done or the rate at which energy is used. In electric circuits, power is expressed in units of *watts*. In DC circuits, wattage is the product of voltage and current, as shown in Eq. 17.2. A watt is the amount of power in a circuit when V is one volt and I is one amp.

$$P = VI \qquad 17.2$$

A useful mnemonic is the word PIE: *power* (P) equals *current* (I) times *electromotive force* (E). Electromotive force is another term for voltage. (Strictly speaking, electromotive force and voltage are closely related concepts but not exactly the same; however, they are often used loosely as synonyms.)

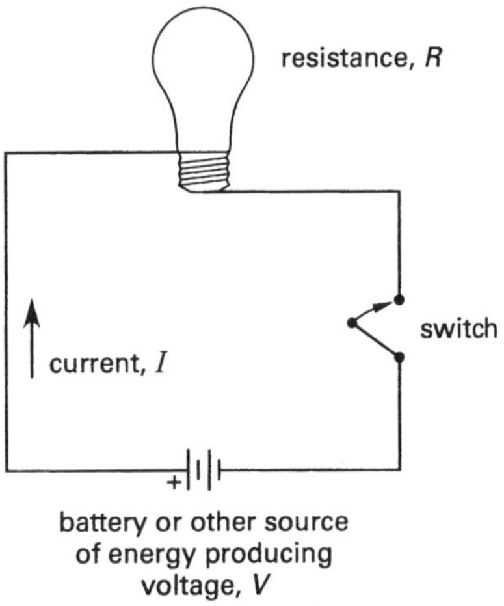

resistance, R

switch

current, I

battery or other source of energy producing voltage, V

Figure 17.9
Basic Electric Current

Electrical circuits for *alternating current* (AC) are slightly different because of the way that AC is generated. AC circuits operate according to the principle of electromagnetic induction, discovered by Michael Faraday in 1831. When a conductor is moved in a magnetic field, a voltage is induced. The direction of the movement determines the polarity of the voltage, either positive or negative. When a coil of a conductor (typically wire) is rotated within a magnetic field, or when the magnetic field is rotated around a fixed coil, a voltage of alternating polarity is produced.

AC voltage is represented graphically with a *sine wave*, as shown in Fig. 17.10. The *amplitude* of the wave represents the voltage, and the distance between peaks represents one *cycle*. The *frequency* is measured in units of *hertz* (Hz), or cycles per second. In the United States, AC is produced at a frequency of 60 Hz. In Europe and other countries, the frequency is 50 Hz.

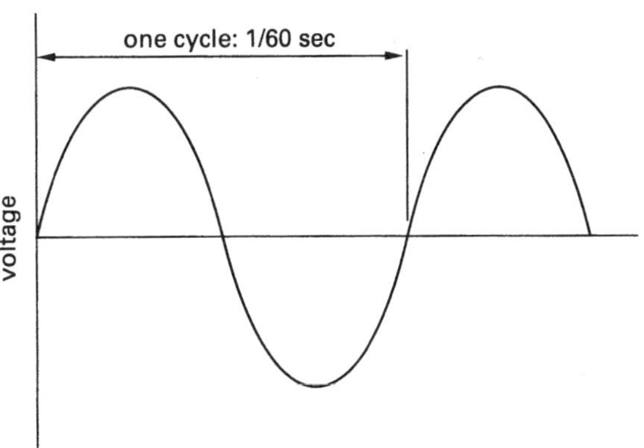

Figure 17.10
Sine Wave of Alternating Current

In AC circuits, resistance is known as *impedance*, which comprises both resistance and reactance and causes a phase change difference between voltage and current. The difference is represented by the *power factor* (pf) and can be a significant factor in calculating power in an AC circuit. For circuits with only resistive loads, such as incandescent lights or electric heating elements, the power factor is 1.0. Sometimes capacitors are used to improve the power factor.

Ohm's law for AC circuits, Eq. 17.3, is similar to Eq. 17.1.

$$I = \frac{V}{Z} \qquad 17.3$$

The calculation for power in AC circuits, , is similar to Eq. 17.2, but with the power factor included.

$$P = VI(\text{pf}) \qquad 17.4$$

Figure 17.11
Basic Circuit Types

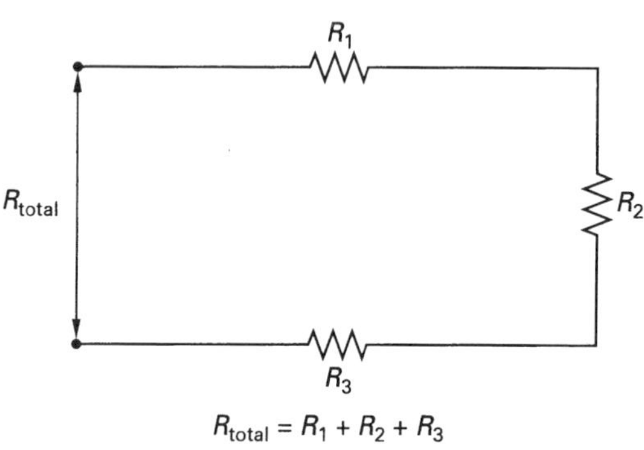

(a) series circuit

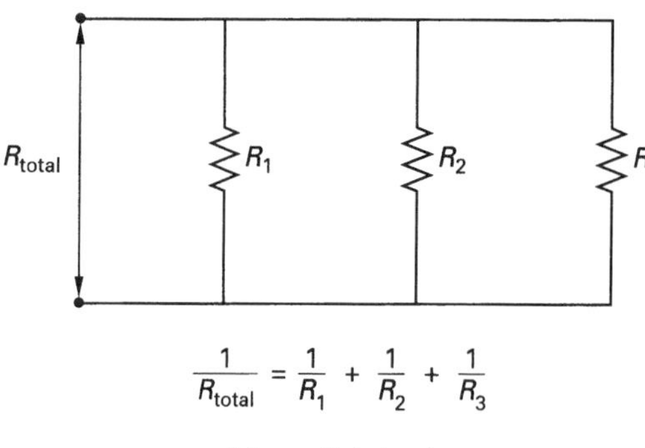

(b) parallel circuit

Energy can be measured in watt-hours (W-hr), but is more commonly measured in thousands of watt-hours, or kilowatt-hours (kW-hr). To calculate the energy used in a system, multiply power by time, as shown in Eq. 17.5.

$$E = Pt \qquad 17.5$$

There are two basic types of electric circuits: series and parallel. These are shown in Fig. 17.11. In a *series circuit*, the loads (represented in the diagrams by zigzag lines) are placed in the circuit one after another. The current, I, remains constant throughout the circuit, but the voltage potential changes, or drops, across each load.

In a *parallel circuit*, the loads are placed between the same two points. The voltage remains the same, but the current is different across each load. However, adding up the individual currents results in a total current that is applied to the circuit as a whole.

If one load is removed in a series circuit (e.g., a light bulb burns out in a string of lights), the entire circuit is opened. For this reason, and because of the voltage drops across individual loads, series circuits are not used in building construction.

Example 17.1

What is the approximate current in a 120 V circuit serving nine 150 W downlights?

(A) 11 A

(B) 15 A

(C) 20 A

(D) 26 A

Solution

The power in the circuit is $9 \times 150 \text{ W} = 1350 \text{ W}$. Rearrange Eq. 17.4 to solve for current, I. Because the circuit has only resistive loads (incandescent lights), use a power factor of 1.0.

$$P = VI(\text{pf})$$

$$I = \frac{P}{V(\text{pf})} = \frac{1350 \text{ W}}{(120 \text{ V})(1.0)} = 11.25 \text{ A} \quad (11 \text{ A})$$

The answer is (A).

Materials

The *conductor* is the basic material of an electrical system. Conductor sizes are based on *American Wire Gauge* (AWG) and *thousand circular mil* (MCM) designations. AWG sizes range from 16 gage to 0000 (4/0) gage. The actual size of the conductor increases as the number designation decreases, so 16 gage is the smallest size (0.0508 in diameter), and 4/0 is the largest (0.460 in diameter). A single insulated conductor, no. 6 AWG or larger, or several conductors assembled into a single unit, is referred to as *cable*. Conductors no. 8 AWG and smaller are called *wire*.

Cable larger than 4/0 gage is designated with the MCM nomenclature. A *circular mil* is a derived area measurement representing the square of the cable diameter in thousandths of an inch (mils). The MCM cable sizes are 250, 300, 400, and 500. The current-carrying capacity (or *ampacity*) of a conductor depends on its size, the type of insulation around it, and the surrounding temperature. There are many different types of conductors and insulating materials. The two most common conductors are copper and aluminum. Aluminum conductors must be larger than copper conductors to carry the same amperage, but they are lighter and generally have a lower installation cost in larger sizes. Copper is more cost effective in small and medium-size wire and cable. Aluminum conductors require special care in installation because joints can loosen and oxides can form, causing resistance and overheating. As a result, the use of aluminum is limited to primary circuits that are installed by skilled workers.

The following are some common cables, based on the type of insulation they use.

Nonmetallic sheathed cable, also known by the trade name *Romex*, consists of two or more plastic-insulated conductors and a ground wire surrounded by a moisture-resistant plastic jacket. This type of cable can be used in wood-frame residential buildings not exceeding three stories, as long as it is used with wood studs and is protected from damage by being concealed behind walls and ceilings. Because it does not require conduit, it is inexpensive to install.

Flexible metal-clad cable, also known by the trade name *BX*, consists of two or more plastic-insulated conductors encased in a continuous spiral-wound strip of steel tape. It is often used in remodeling work because it can be pulled through existing spaces within a building. It does not require conduit.

The most common type of wire and cable is a single conductor covered with thermoplastic or rubber insulation. Several different types are available for different voltages and service conditions. This cable must be placed in metal conduit or other approved types of carriers.

When high currents are involved, the use of very large cables becomes expensive and awkward to tap into when connecting to transformers and branch circuits. Instead, rectangular bars of copper, called *busbars*, are used. When several busbars are assembled in a special metal housing, it is called a *busduct* or *busway*.

For commercial construction and large residential construction, individual conductors must be placed in metal conduit or other approved carriers. Conduit supports and protects the wiring, serves as a system ground, and protects surrounding construction from fire if the wire overheats or shorts.

There are three types of metal conduit: rigid steel conduit, intermediate metal conduit, and electric metallic tubing.

- *Rigid steel conduit* is the heaviest type of metal conduit and is connected to junction boxes and other devices with threaded fittings.
- *Intermediate metal conduit* (IMC) has thinner walls but the same outside diameter as rigid steel conduit. It is also installed with threaded fittings.
- *Electric metallic tubing* (EMT) is the lightest of the three and is installed with special pressure fittings because it is too thin to thread. It is easier and faster to install, but it cannot be used in hazardous areas. In certain situations, flexible metal conduit can also be used to minimize vibration transmission from equipment to the structure and for areas where installation of rigid conduit is not possible. It is commonly referred to as *flex*.

The number of conductors that can be placed in a single conduit is limited to prevent damage from trying to pull too many conductors through a small space and to control the heat buildup inside the conduit. The limit depends on the conductor type, the conductor size, and the size of the conduit. The *National Electrical Code* (NEC) sets limits on the length, number, and radius of bends permitted in conduit between pull boxes, to prevent damage to the conductors and to make pulling the conductors easier. In most cases, there can be no more than four 90° bends between pull boxes.

Underfloor raceways and undercarpet cable are two more types of power distribution often used in office buildings and wherever the locations of receptacles must be changed frequently.

There are two varieties of ***underfloor raceways:*** underfloor ducts and cellular metal floors.

- *Underfloor ducts* are proprietary steel raceways cast into a concrete floor at regular spacing, usually about 4 ft, 5 ft, or 6 ft. Feeder ducts run perpendicular to the distribution ducts and carry power and signal wiring from the main electrical closet to each distribution duct. Preset inserts are placed along the distribution ducts at close intervals and are tapped wherever an outlet or telephone connection is needed.
- *Cellular metal floors* use the same basic concept but are actually a part of the structural floor. This is essentially metal decking designed for use as cable raceways. Cellular floors differ from underfloor ducts in that the cells are closer together. Alternating cells can be used for power, telephone, and signal cabling. Cellular floors also have preset locations that can be easily tapped to install electrical outlets, telephone jacks, and computer outlets.

Undercarpet cable (also called ***undercarpet wiring***) is thin, flat, protected wire that can be laid under carpet without protruding or telegraphing through the carpet. Cable for both 120 V circuits and telephone and signal lines is available. However, this wiring must be used with carpet tiles so that it is readily accessible. Undercarpet cable connects pedestals in the middle of the room, which contain electrical outlets and telephone connections, to junction boxes in nearby walls where the wiring is connected to standard conduit-enclosed cable.

POWER SUPPLY

The most common form of electrical energy used in buildings is *alternating current* (AC). *Direct current* (DC) is used for some types of elevator motors and for low-voltage applications such as signal systems, controls, and similar equipment. Electricity is supplied by the local power company and is distributed as described in the following sections. For emergency power, generators and batteries are used.

Primary Service

Electrical service is provided by the utility company to the property line. It is the owner's responsibility to install and pay for wiring, metering, transformers, and distribution beyond that point, although most utility companies will, for a charge, extend the power supply from the property line to the building's service entrance.

Service may be either overhead or underground. *Underground service* is more expensive but avoids the clutter of overhead wires and protects the lines from snow, wind, and other potentially damaging conditions. When *overhead service* is provided to smaller projects, the service cable is connected to a weatherhead mounted at least 12 ft above the ground. This is the part of the conduit that leads to the meter and distribution panel.

Power is supplied to buildings in several different voltages. The voltage or voltages provided depend on what is available from the utility company at the property, the expected electrical loads of the building, and what types of transformers the owner is willing to provide. In some cases, it is less expensive for the owner of a large commercial building to buy power from the utility company at higher voltages and supply the transformer to step it down for use within the building, than to pay a higher charge for lower voltages.

The most common for residences and very small buildings is a 120/240 V, single-phase, three-wire system, as shown in Fig. 17.12(a). It consists of two hot wires, each carrying 120 V, and one neutral wire. This is used where the actual load does not exceed 80 A, although minimum service is considered 100 A. Appliances that need 240 V (e.g., electric ranges and dryers) use the two hot wires, while 120 V service is obtained by tapping one hot wire and the neutral wire.

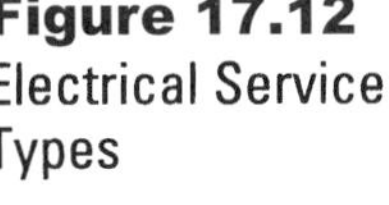

Figure 17.12
Electrical Service Types

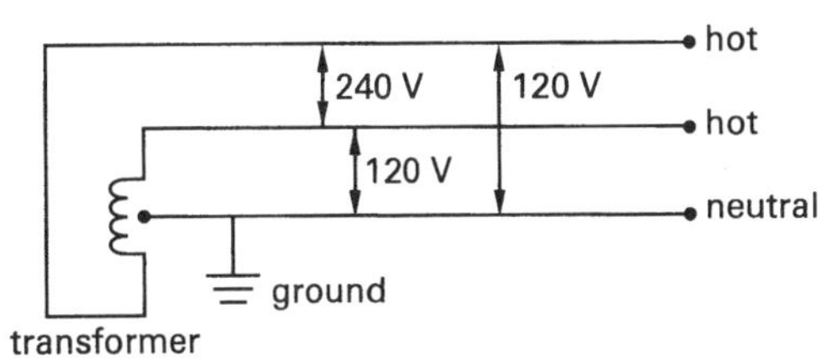

(a) 120/240 V, single-phase, 3-wire system

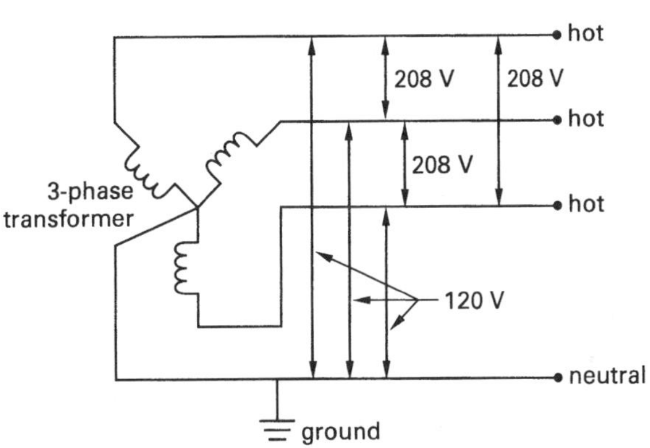

(b) 120/208 V, 3-phase, 4-wire system

A system often used for larger buildings is the 120/208 V, three-phase, four-wire system, as shown in Fig. 17.12(b). It is frequently used because it allows use of a variety of electrical loads.

For larger buildings, a 277/480 V, three-phase, four-wire system is used. It is the same as the 120/208 V system except the voltage is higher. Since higher voltages are used, and thus the equipment has to carry smaller currents, this type of system can use smaller feeders, smaller conduit, and smaller switchgear. Buildings with this type of system have predominantly 277 V fluorescent lighting, which can use smaller wiring. Small step-down transformers are used where 120 V service is needed for receptacles and other equipment.

For very large commercial buildings and factories with a great deal of machinery, 2400/4160 V, three-phase, four-wire systems are available.

Transformers

Transformers are used to change alternating current voltages either up or down. In most cases, power is supplied to buildings at high voltages because the transmission lines can be smaller and because at higher voltages there is less voltage drop. The building owner must supply the transformer to convert the power as it is delivered from the utility to one of the types of service described in the Power Supply section. For residences and very small buildings, the utility company usually supplies step-down transformers to serve a small group of houses with 120/240 V service.

Transformers are rated on their capacity in units of kilovolt-amperes (kVa) and are described by their type, phase, voltage, method of cooling, insulation, and noise level. For cooling, transformers are either dry, oil-filled, or silicone-filled. When there is a possibility of fire, as with oil-filled transformers, the equipment must be placed in a fire-resistive transformer vault room. Because transformers generate a great deal of heat, the vault must be at an exterior wall and vented to the outside. Locating a transformer vault near the exterior wall also makes it easier to move the large, heavy device into place and replace it when necessary.

Metering and Load Control

Metering must be provided at a building's service entrance to allow the utility company to charge for energy used. For residences and other single-use buildings, one meter is typically used. For multiple-occupancy buildings such as shopping centers and apartments, banks of meters are installed so that each unit can be metered independently because in most cases every tenant must pay for the energy used. This also encourages energy conservation.

The most common meter is the *watt-hour meter.* This registers the use of power over time in kilowatt-hours. The meter is placed on the incoming power line in front of any master service switch so that it can operate continuously.

In order to encourage the conservation of energy and pay for the cost of providing power to customers, many energy companies levy energy charges based not only on the total amount of energy used but also on *peak demand.* If a customer uses a nominal amount of energy over a billing period but uses a great deal of energy only at times of high demand, the utility company must still provide facilities to supply this peak demand. The actual amount of energy used during those peak times may be relatively low, but the utility company must be ready to supply the occasional maximum amount.

To compensate for this, most utility companies make charges based on the *maximum interval demand,* which is the average amount of energy used in a certain time period, such as 15 min or 30 min. The ratio of the average power used to the maximum power demand is called the *load factor.* A low load factor implies an inefficient use of energy and a high demand charge.

From the user's standpoint, a building's electrical system should be designed to avoid peak electricity use. There are several methods of doing this, which are called *load control.* Other terms used include *load shedding, peak demand control,* and *peak load regulation.*

Manual and automatic devices are available to accomplish load control. With automatic load shedding, for example, a device automatically monitors the use of energy, and when a certain point is reached the device shuts off nonessential electrical loads. Such loads can include nonessential lighting, water heating, and space heating. Load scheduling can also be used if the energy consumption characteristics of the building are known. With this method, different electrical loads are automatically scheduled to operate at different times to control the peak demand.

Primary Distribution

Large buildings need a *switchgear,* or central electrical distribution center. The switchgear consists of an assembly of switches, circuit breakers, and cables or bus ducts that distribute power to other parts of the building. A transformer and metering are also often included with the switchgear. The equipment is usually housed in a separate room, depending on the type of transformer used and the security needed. This equipment room may be required to have fire-rated walls and doors, with panic hardware installed at the exits.

Power coming through the meter and transformer is split into separate circuits, each with a master switch and circuit breaker to protect the circuit from overload or short circuits. From the switchgear, power is distributed to substations for further transforming and distribution, to motor control centers, to elevator controls, and to individual panel boxes as part of the secondary distribution system.

Power Quality

The power supplied by an electric utility is not always provided at a steady, regulated voltage. There can be power surges and voltage variations from various causes. Building use and equipment such as electronic devices, lighting dimmers, and motor controls can cause these and other problems, including radio frequency (RF) interference and overheating. Individual problems can be corrected with specific pieces of equipment such as voltage regulators, surge suppressors, and filters. For example, an individual computer can be protected with a plug-in surge suppressor. For larger installations such as computer rooms and other sensitive electronic equipment, one-piece units called *power conditioning units* can be used.

Harmonic currents are a problem for many buildings containing computers and other electronic equipment. A *harmonic current* is a voltage or current at a frequency that is a multiple of the fundamental frequency. For U.S. power supply at 60 Hz, harmonic currents could occur at 120 Hz, 180 Hz, and so on. Harmonic currents are produced by electrical loads that are nonlinear, which includes almost any load other than simple resistive loads such as incandescent lights, heaters, and motors. In large buildings with many nonlinear loads such as computers, copiers, electronic ballasts, variable-speed motors, and other solid-state equipment, harmonic currents can create significant problems. These problems can include overheating of the neutral conductor wiring, nuisance tripping of circuit breakers, overheated transformers, and telephone interference.

In some cases, the problem can be solved by oversizing the neutral conductor and adding passive harmonic filters to the distribution system. More commonly, *active line conditioning* is used; this introduces a variable power conditioning unit controlled by computer that continuously analyzes the harmonics of the line voltage and adds an equal but out-of-phase voltage to cancel the harmonics.

Secondary Distribution and Branch Circuits

Power from the main switchgear is distributed to individual panelboards where it is further split into individual branch circuits used for power, lighting, motors, and other electrical needs of the building. Secondary distribution involves the typical lower voltages of 120 V, 240 V, and 277 V Secondary distribution is made with wires in conduit, various types of underfloor raceways, or flexible cabling systems.

Each circuit is protected with circuit breakers in the panelboard. These are rated for the amperage the circuit is expected to carry, ranging from 15 A and 20 A circuits for general lighting and power circuits to 100 A or more for main disconnect switches or large loads.

There are three important kinds of protection for electric circuits: grounding, ground-fault protection, and arc-fault protection.

Grounding provides a path for a fault. The ground wire and the neutral wire are both grounded at the building service entrance to either a grounding electrode buried in the earth or in the foundation or to a buried cold water pipe. This helps to prevent a dangerous shock if someone simultaneously touches an appliance with a short circuit and touches a ground path such as a water pipe. All new construction is grounded with a separate wire in addition to the hot and neutral wiring of each circuit.

A *ground fault*, however, can create other problems, because the current required to trip a circuit breaker is high and small current leaks can continue unnoticed until someone receives a dangerous shock or a fire develops.

There are three important kinds of protection for electric circuits: grounding, ground-fault protection, and arc-fault protection.

Ground fault circuit interrupters (GFCIs), often also called *ground fault interrupters* (GFIs), are devices that can detect small current leaks. If a leak is detected, the device immediately disconnects the power to the circuit or appliance. A GFCI can be a part of a circuit breaker or installed as an outlet. In dwelling units, GFCIs are required in bathrooms, garages, accessory buildings at or below grade, crawl spaces, unfinished basements, countertop receptacles in kitchens, laundry and utility rooms, and boathouses, as well as outdoors and within 6 ft of the outside edge of a wet bar. They are also required for receptacles in bathrooms in commercial (nondwelling) occupancies, and in other locations specified in the NEC.

An *arc-fault circuit interrupter* (AFCI) helps protect against the effects of arc faults by recognizing characteristics that are unique to arcing and by de-energizing the circuit when an arc fault is detected. In some jurisdictions, AFCIs are required in bedroom branch circuits that serve both receptacles and lighting, as well as in other locations. The bedroom branch circuits must be run separately from all other circuits in the dwelling. The NEC also requires AFCIs on 15 A and 20 A branch circuits that supply outlets in family rooms, dining rooms, living rooms, libraries, dens, sunrooms, recreation rooms, closets, hallways, and similar rooms.

Wiring Devices

Wiring devices are receptacles, switches, pilot lights, and other such devices normally installed in outlet boxes. The most common receptacle for normal power distribution is the *duplex receptacle*, or *duplex outlet*. It is also called a *convenience outlet* because it is designed for normal use by building occupants for portable lamps, clocks, electronic devices, appliances, and similar devices that operate at 120 V. Special receptacles are used for appliances and equipment that require higher voltages, such as electric ranges, dryers, and large copy machines. Electrical devices that are connected to the building circuits in junction boxes rather than being plugged in are said to be *hardwired*.

A convenience outlet has two holes to receive the prongs of the plug supplying power and a third hole for the grounding prong. The grounding pole is connected to a green wire that is part of the wiring in the conduit. Alternately, the grounding pole of the outlet may be connected to the metal conduit that acts as the system ground. A *split-wired receptacle* can be installed so that one outlet is always energized but the other is controlled from a wall switch. This allows floor lamps and other devices that normally plug in to be controlled with a switch.

Outlets are normally mounted vertically from 12 in to 18 in above the floor, although a minimum 15 in mounting height is required for forward and side reach accessibility for persons in wheelchairs. In residential construction, outlets must be located no more than 12 ft apart, or such that no point is more than 6 ft from an outlet. If a wall space is shorter than 6 ft long but longer than 2 ft and is unbroken by doorways, fireplaces, and similar openings, it must also have an outlet.

Most residential convenience outlet circuits are 15 A, but at least two 20 A appliance circuits must be provided for the kitchen, pantry, breakfast room, and dining room. The outlets serving the kitchen countertop area must be supplied from at least two different circuits, with no more than four outlets per 20 A circuit. The outlets in the kitchen must be located so that no point on a wall above a countertop is more than 24 in from an outlet. There must also be at least one outlet between appliances and the sink so that no cord has to be draped across an appliance or the sink. Outlets must be of the GFCI type.

Switching

Switches are used to control power to lights, receptacles, and other electric devices. The most common is the *toggle type*, which simply switches on or off with a *toggle*, or lever. Other types that perform the same function include the rocker switch, push switch, and key switch. Some specialized switches provide additional functions, such as dimmer switches, automatic timer switches, and programmable switches.

Traditionally, individual switching and dimming controls have been used for most lighting situations. However, energy conservation often requires the use of more sophisticated lighting controls and switching methods than can reduce a building's total energy use.

When one switch controls a light or other device, it is called a *two-way switch* because the switch needs two conductors (not including the ground) in order to function. Similarly, a *three-way switch* requires three conductors to make it possible to control a light from two different switches. A *four-way switch* is used to control the same device from three or more locations.

Low-voltage switching is also available. With this system, individual switches are operated on a 24 V circuit and control relays that provide the 120 V switching. Although more costly to install, low-voltage switching has several advantages over line-voltage switching. First, the same light or device can be controlled from several positions that are remote from each other. Second, a central control station can be set up to monitor the entire system and override local control. For example, pilot lights at the central station in a house can show which lights are on and which are off and allow switching from that station. Third, control devices such as timers and energy management systems can be wired to override local control. Finally, for large installations that require flexibility of control, low-voltage wiring and switches are a less expensive alternative to installing the same scope of line-voltage wiring and devices.

Another approach to remotely controlling line-voltage lighting and outlets is the use of a *power line carrier* (PLC) *system*. A PLC system uses the power lines to carry control signals, which are low-voltage, high-frequency coded signals. Each control device, such as a light switch, can respond to its unique code. These systems have the advantage that no additional wiring is needed.

Traditionally, individual switching and dimming controls have been used for most lighting situations. However, current energy conservation codes and building rating systems, such as the LEED rating systems, often require the use of more sophisticated lighting controls and switching methods that can reduce a building's total energy use.

The most basic approach is to provide individual switches for each use area, instead of one switch to control several areas. When an area is not in use, the lighting can be turned off. Individual area switching is required by model codes and energy conservation codes.

Alternatively, one luminaire can be controlled with two switches. For example, two switches can control a four-lamp fluorescent luminaire, providing two levels of illumination.

Other methods can be used to provide more than two levels of illuminance. *Multilevel lighting control* is a variation of this idea that allows lighting power to be reduced in steps, while maintaining a reasonably uniform level of illuminance through the area controlled.

Dimmers make it possible to reduce light levels when the maximum light output of the luminaires is not needed. However, neither individual switching nor dimmers will reduce energy usage unless they are consciously used to do so, and studies have shown that this is not an effective approach. To conserve energy, automatic lighting controls are needed.

The most common type of automatic control is a programmable *time-of-day controller*. This device turns off the power at designated times. A single device can be mounted in an individual switch box, or many devices can be integrated into a complex building management system. They can be programmed to turn off lights in response to the normal time schedules of the users, while still providing egress lighting or dimmed lighting for after-hours building maintenance. The ability to override a controller can be incorporated into the system for use when an occupant needs to work overtime.

An *occupant sensor* can turn lights on and off in response to the presence of people in a room or area. This kind of sensor can be passive infrared, ultrasonic, or a mix of both. Manually operated switches can override the sensor function.

A *daylight compensation control* uses photocells to dim lights or turn lights on and off automatically as the level of daylight changes. Well-designed daylighting compensation controls can reduce energy use along the inside perimeter of a building by up to 60%, depending on the climate, effectiveness of the daylighting design, hours of building use, and other variables. Refer to Chap. 12 for more information on daylighting design. How effectively and economically daylighting can be used varies with the latitude, climate, surrounding buildings and landscaping, direction of window exposure, and type, size, and configuration of glazing. In most cases, daylight compensation controls can be used in a perimeter zone to the depth at which the zone receives at least one-half of its illuminance from daylight for several hours a day. Daylighting studies can be done manually or with available computer programs to determine if daylight compensation controls are economically feasible.

Although the specific requirements for switching and other lighting control may vary by jurisdiction and by what version of a particular code that jurisdiction is using, most requirements are very similar, if not identical, to ANSI/ASHRAE/IES Standard 90.1, *Energy Standard for Buildings Except Low-Rise Residential Buildings*. This standard requires that automatic lighting shutoff be used in most buildings larger than 5000 ft^2. There are three approved methods for accomplishing this.

- Time-of-day controllers may be used that are programmed to shut off lighting at specific times. Each controller may govern an area of up to 25,000 ft^2 and no more than one floor.

- Occupant sensors may be used that turn off lighting within 30 minutes of an area becoming unoccupied.
- A separate control or alarm system, such as a building security system, may be set up to send a signal to a lighting control device when an area is unoccupied.

There are exceptions for 24-hour operations, spaces where patient care is rendered, and spaces where automatic shutoff would endanger the safety or security of the room or building occupants.

ASHRAE/IESNA Standard 90.1 also requires that every space enclosed by ceiling-height partitions must have at least one device that controls the general lighting in that space. This device must automatically turn lighting off within 30 minutes of the space becoming unoccupied. In classrooms, conference/meeting rooms, and employee lunch/break rooms, a manual switch is not required. In all other spaces, the control device must also have an easily accessible manual switch that can override any time-of-day scheduled shutoff, but not for more than four hours. Depending on the size of the space, two or more devices may be required. The area that each device controls may not be more than 2500 ft^2 if the enclosed space is 10,000 ft^2 or less, or more than 10,000 ft^2 if the enclosed space is greater than 10,000 ft^2.

Control devices are also required for exterior lighting, with exceptions for safety and security needs. Outdoor control devices must operate by photosensors or by a programmable time switch with astronomic correction.

Additional controls are required for the following uses.

- Display and accent lighting must have separate control devices.
- Hotel and motel guest rooms must have a master control device at the main room entry that controls all permanently installed luminaires and switched receptacles.
- Supplemental task lighting, including undercabinet lighting, must have a control device integral to the luminaires or be controlled by a wall-mounted device.
- Nonvisual lighting, such as for food warming, must have a separate control device.
- Lighting equipment that is for sale or used in demonstrations must have a separate control device.

The type of control can affect how lights must be circuited. When many lights are connected to a single dimmer switch, they must be on their own circuit. Both incandescent and fluorescent lights can be dimmed, but fluorescent dimmers are more expensive, and special fixtures are needed to minimize flicker when they are dimmed.

Generally, a single circuit should not include both incandescent and fluorescent lights. In many large commercial installations, 277 V circuits are used for fluorescent lights for greater efficiency, while incandescent lights are on 120 V circuits, so the two kinds of lights must be on separate circuits in any case.

Emergency Power Supply

Emergency power is required for electrical systems that relate to the safety of occupants or community needs. This includes systems for exit lighting, alarms, elevators, telephones, and fire pumps, as well as equipment that could have life-threatening implications if power were lost, such as some medical equipment. *Standby power*, on the other hand, provides electricity for functions that the building owner needs to avoid an interruption in business. This often includes computer operations or industrial processes.

Emergency power is supplied by generators or batteries. Generators provide the capacity for large electrical loads for long periods of time, limited only by the available emergency fuel supply. They are expensive to install and must be maintained and checked periodically for proper operation.

Batteries are used for smaller loads for shorter time periods. Emergency lighting often consists of separate lighting packs with their own batteries, placed in strategic locations such as corridors and stairways.

Large installations have racks of batteries in separate rooms connected to lights and other equipment with wiring.

WATER SUPPLY

Depending on geographic location, water is available from a variety of sources. It comes from rivers, lakes, wells, surface runoff, oceans, and even recycled wastewater. In some cases, water may be pure enough in its natural state for immediate human use. In most instances, however, it must be treated to remove impurities. Water suitable for human drinking is called *potable water*. If it is not suitable for drinking, it is called *nonpotable*, but this type of water may still be used for other purposes like irrigation and flushing toilets.

Two of the most common sources of large water supplies for cities are surface water and groundwater. *Surface water* comes from rain and snow that runs off into rivers and lakes. *Groundwater* seeps into the ground until it hits an impervious layer of rock or soil. It then forms a water table that is tapped by drilling. Large regions of subsurface water are called *aquifers*.

Generally, the best sources for water are those that require little or no treatment, including water from deep wells, relatively clean rivers, and surface runoff. This type of water can be easily treated in most cases and can be made available in large quantities. However, with increasing pollution and the scarcity of water in some locations, greater use of treated seawater and recycled wastewater will be necessary. The processing is more expensive for these types of water than it is for water from cleaner sources.

Water Treatment

Many factors determine the proper treatment and use of water from different sources.

The *pH level* is a measure of the relative acidity or alkalinity of water. It is based on a scale of 0 to 14, with a pH of 7 being neutral. Anything below 7 is considered *acidic* and can be corrosive; anything above 7 is considered *alkaline*. Knowing the pH of water is useful in determining the water treatment needed for corrosion, chemicals, and disinfection. For example, acidic water, along with entrained oxygen, can cause iron and steel pipes to rust. The problem can be corrected by adding a neutralizer to raise the water's alkaline content. *Rainwater* is slightly acidic in its natural state, but in many industrialized areas, the acid level is greater due to sulfur and nitrogen compounds in the atmosphere. The compounds combine to form sulfuric or nitric acid and fall as "acid rain."

Hardness of water is caused by calcium and magnesium salts in water. If untreated, hard water can cause clogged pipes and corrosion of boilers. It also makes laundry and other types of washing difficult because it inhibits the cleaning action of soaps and detergents. Treatment methods for hardness are discussed later in this section.

Turbidity is caused by suspended material in the water, such as silt, clay, and organic material. Although it is not hazardous, turbidity is unpleasant and can be treated by filtration.

Color problems and *odor problems* are caused by organic matter, inorganic salts, or dissolved gases. Odor problems can be corrected with filtration through activated carbon. Color problems can be corrected with fine filtration or chlorination.

Biological contamination in water can be caused by bacteria, viruses, and protozoa, all of which can be dangerous to health. Bacteria in the coliform group are some of the most common kinds found in water supplies, especially well water. *Escherichia coli* (commonly *E. coli*) is the most well known of this group. Water tests commonly check for *E. coli*. Another bacterium of concern to building designers is *Legionella pneumophila*, which causes Legionnaires' disease. Although these types of bacteria are usually not a problem in drinking water, they grow in warm water such as that found in cooling towers, air conditioning systems, large plumbing systems, and hot tubs.

Two types of protozoa that can cause diarrheal illness are *Giardia* and *Cryptosporidium*. These protozoa exist in the form of microscopic cysts and are most commonly transmitted through improperly treated drinking water. Slow sand filters can remove nearly all *Giardia* cysts.

There are hundreds of hazardous materials that can cause chemical contamination, including chemicals from industrial processes, mining, and pesticides. Some chemicals affect only the color and taste of water, but others can be deadly. Treatment can be expensive and complex.

Water Treatment Methods

Several methods are used to treat water, depending on both the problem and the intended use of the water. Multiple methods are often used in combination to filter and disinfect the various types of contaminants found in natural water sources.

Water treatment methods can be categorized into four general groups.

- pretreatment
- filtration
- demineralization
- disinfection

Pretreatment

Pretreatment is often necessary before other treatment methods can be used. This step of water management is designed to remove suspended matter and large particles from the water.

- *Sedimentation* uses gravity and still water, allowing heavy particles to sink to the bottom of a holding basin or tank. The clear water is then piped out into a secondary filtration system or treatment facility. Sedimentation can take place with or without coagulation and flocculation.
- *Coagulation* is the process of getting particles in the water to stick together by adding alum or other chemicals.
- *Flocculation* is the next step after coagulation. The mix of water and alum is sent to still water, where the particles and alum form a loosely aggregated mass called floc, and are heavy enough for sedimentation to take place.

Filtration

- *Slow sand filtration* allows water to seep through a bed of fine sand about 3 ft to 4 ft deep. As a biological slime forms on the sand filter, it traps small particles and degrades organic matter. Sand filters do not require coagulation or flocculation. Slow sand filters are excellent at filtering out *Giardia* and particulates, but they are not good for water with high turbidity.
- *Direct filtration* passes water under pressure through a filter medium. This process always includes coagulation and filtration, and may require a flocculation tank. Direct filtration is good for eliminating nearly all *Giardia* and most viruses.
- *Packaged filtration* is the same as direct filtration except that all the elements used are placed in a single unit for direct hookup to a water supply.
- *Diatomaceous earth filtration* uses a thin layer of diatomaceous earth from $^1/_8$ in to $^1/_5$ in thick placed on a septum or filter element. Diatomaceous earth is a light-colored, soft sedimentary rock formed mainly of the siliceous shells of diatoms (phytoplankton). This filtration method is good for removing cysts, algae, and asbestos, but not as good at removing bacteria and turbidity.
- *Membrane filtration* forces water at high pressure through a thin membrane that removes particles 0.2 μm and larger, as well as *Giardia*, other bacteria, some viruses, and other microorganisms.
- *Cartridge filtration* uses self-contained units placed along the water supply line to filter out particles 0.2 μm and larger. The cartridges must be replaced as they get fouled, but are useful for individual faucets as well as on small supply systems.

Demineralization

Demineralization removes dissolved solids and the chemicals that cause hard water.

- *Ion exchange* is used in water softeners to treat hard water and to remove cadmium, chromium silver, radium, and other chemicals. Hard water is piped into the softener, which contains zeolite. The calcium or magnesium ions are exchanged for the sodium ions in the zeolite. The water softener must be recharged periodically by passing a brine solution through the zeolite; this is done automatically by the water softening equipment. Water run through an ion exchange unit must be pretreated to reduce suspended solids.
- *Reverse osmosis* (RO) removes contaminants by using a semipermeable membrane that allows only water to pass through and not dissolved ions. RO is useful for removing inorganic chemicals, bacteria, and suspended particles. The unit is cleaned by forcing clear water through the membrane, which leaves the contaminants behind in a brine that must be carefully disposed of.

Electrodialysis places charged membranes at the inflow stream of water to attract counterions. Electrodialysis can remove barium, cadmium, selenium, fluoride, and nitrates. Electrodialysis systems are expensive to buy and operate, and they require high water pressure and a source of direct current power.

Disinfection

Disinfection destroys microorganisms that can cause disease in humans. There are several methods used to disinfect water. The EPA Surface Water Treatment Rule (SWTR) requires disinfection of water supply systems that get their water either from surface water or from groundwater under the direct influence of surface water.

- *Chlorination*, the most common form of treatment, kills organisms by introducing chlorine into the water stream. The chlorine may be in the form of a gas, liquid, or solid, depending on the type of system used.
- *Chloramine* is used in a way similar to chlorination, but it is a weaker disinfectant than chlorine. Chloramine is produced by adding ammonia to water that contains chlorine, or by chlorinating water that contains ammonia. Chloramine is generally used as a secondary disinfectant to prevent bacterial regrowth in a distribution system.
- *Ozonation* disinfects water through the use of ozone, a powerful oxidizing and disinfecting agent. Ozonation is used mainly as a primary disinfectant, and typically requires a secondary disinfectant for water supplies. It is typically used for treating cooling tower water to prevent *Legionella pneumophila*, scale, and algae.
- *Ultraviolet* (UV) *light* destroys a cell's ability to reproduce and is effective against bacteria and viruses. UV light is not effective against *Giardia* or *Cryptosporidium* and is not useful for water that contains high levels of turbidity, suspended solids, or soluble organic matter. UV light must be used with a secondary disinfectant to prevent regrowth of microorganisms.
- *Nanofiltration* uses filter membranes that are capable of trapping particles as small as one nanometer (one billionth of a meter, or 10^{-9} m) in size. At this scale the filter can remove bacteria, viruses, pesticides, and organic material. Because the filter is small, the water must be forced through at high pressure.

Distillation and Aeration

Additional methods of water treatment include distillation and aeration.

In *distillation*, water is treated by boiling it and then condensing the vapors. This results in very clean water with all solids, bacteria, salts, and other materials removed. Distillation is often used to treat seawater.

Aeration (or *oxidation*) is used to improve the taste and color of water. It also aids in the removal of iron and manganese by oxidizing them so that they can be more easily removed by filtration. Aeration is a simple process through which as much of the water as possible is exposed to air through the use of sprays, fountains, or waterfalls. For drinking water treatment, the water should be aerated in an enclosed space or in a tank.

Private Water Supply

Private water supplies include wells, springs, and collected rainwater. Wells are the most common type, and they are used for residences and small buildings where a municipal supply is not available. Wells are most commonly drilled or bored. A well is usually drilled using a rotary bit, which is the only method that will through rock; a *bored well* uses a rotary auger to make the hole.

Two of the most important considerations in drilling a well are depth and yield. The *depth* of a well may range from less than 25 ft, known as a *shallow well*, to several hundred feet. Of course, the depth affects the cost of the well, and there is no sure way of knowing prior to drilling how deep the well may have to be. Before drilling, the architect should talk to neighbors, local well drillers, and geologists in the area to see what their experience has been.

The *yield* of a well is the number of gallons per minute (gpm) it provides. A yield from 5 gpm to 10 gpm is about the minimum required for a private residence. If a yield is too low for the project, the system may need to include a large storage tank that can be filled during periods of low use, such as during the night, so enough water is available during peak periods.

As a well is drilled or bored, a pipe casing is lowered into the hole to prevent the hole from caving in and to prevent seepage of surface contamination into the well. The casing is a steel pipe from 4 in to 6 in in diameter. Lower in the well, perforated casings are used to allow the water to seep into the well from which it is pumped out.

Pumps

Several kinds of pumps are used in wells, including suction, deep-well jet, turbine, and submersible. Most pump systems have three fundamental components: a well, a pump, and a storage tank.

Suction pumps are only suitable for water tables less than 25 ft, while deep-well jet pumps can operate at depths from 25 ft to over 100 ft. Turbine pumps are used for high-capacity systems with deep wells. One of the most common types for moderate to deep wells serving private residences or small buildings is the submersible pump. This type has a waterproof motor and pump that are placed below the water line and pump water to a pressure tank.

Jet pumps (also known as *Venturi pumps*) have the pump and motor aboveground and lift water using the *Venturi effect*. Water is forced through a pipe in the well where a jet stream of small diameter is created in another pipe. The low pressure sucks up the well water and drives it to the surface. Water is pumped to a pressure tank where air pressure circulates the water and operates fixtures.

Pressure tanks are used to maintain a constant water pressure for use in the building and to compensate for brief peak use demand that exceeds the capacity of the pump. Pressure tanks also reduce the amount of time the pump must be run because small quantities of water can be used from the tank without the need for the pump to operate. As the pressure tank is emptied, a pressure gage senses the loss and activates the pump. In a jet pump system, an air volume control senses the depletion of the tank. When the yield of a well is too low to meet the demand, a larger storage tank may be used to provide water for normal use. During nighttime or periods of low use the pump slowly fills the tank.

Municipal Water Supply

Most cities get their water from rivers, lakes, or snow melt. Water treatment typically involves first settling out heavy materials and coagulation (or flocculation) with a chemical such as alum. Suspended particles combine with the alum and settle out. The water is then filtered and treated with chlorine or some other chemical to kill organic materials. The water may also be aerated to improve its taste, and fluoride may be added to help prevent tooth decay. Other treatments can adjust the pH level.

Once the water is treated, it is piped through water mains at a pressure of about 50 psi, although this can vary from 40 psi to 80 psi depending on location and other factors. If the pressure is too high, a pressure-reducing valve must be used between the water main and the building meter.

One of the first tasks in a building project is to determine the location of the public water main, its size, its pressure, and the cost for tapping it. This information is available from the local water company. If a main is not adjacent to the property, the property owner is often required to extend the line to the site at his or her own cost. If the water main is a substantial distance from the proposed building, the cost impact can be significant. The designer needs to know the pressure in the line to determine what kind of supply system can be used, as described in Chap. 31.

SOLAR WATER HEATING

Solar energy is commonly used to heat water for domestic use, industrial use, and swimming pools. Nearly all solar heating systems have certain components in common: some type of solar collector, a storage tank, associated piping to move the fluids, and a backup heater. If it is an *active system*, it will use pumps and associated controls and sensors. The collectors are usually flat plate, but they can also be focusing collectors, or in the case of batch systems, they can be as simple as black tanks behind glass or plastic.

Many types of solar water heating systems exist, but they can be broadly classified by how the heat transfer occurs, how the heating fluid is circulated, and their means of protection from freezing.

Solar heat is transferred either directly or indirectly. In a *direct system*, or *open-loop system*, the water used in the building is the same water that is heated in the solar collectors. An *indirect system*, or *closed-loop system*, uses a separate fluid for collecting heat, which is then transferred to the domestic hot water. Direct systems are simple and highly efficient, but they are subject to freezing. Indirect systems are easier to protect from freezing because the heat-collecting fluid can contain antifreeze. These systems can also operate at a lower pressure than that required for the domestic hot water. However, an indirect system needs a heat exchanger, which reduces efficiency.

The heating fluid is circulated either passively or actively. *Passive circulation systems* rely on gravity and the thermosiphoning action of heated water. They are simple and low-cost systems, but their storage tanks must be placed above the solar collectors, and the points of use must be close to the storage tanks. *Active circulation systems* use pumps to circulate the heat-collecting fluid. These systems are much more flexible and reliable but add costs for equipment and operation.

Protection from freezing is provided either by using a nonfreezing medium (antifreeze solution or phase change material) or by draining the fluid at night and during cloudy weather. Direct systems must use some type of drainage system.

Some of the common types of solar heating systems with which examinees should be familiar include

- *batch system:* Heats water directly in a black-painted tank inside a glazed box. This passive system is simple, but it is subject to freezing and nighttime heat loss.
- *thermosiphon system:* Relies on the natural movement of heated water to circulate the water in a passive, open-loop system. This system is also simple, but the storage tanks must be located above the collectors, and the piping must be kept simple to minimize pipe friction. To address the problem of freezing, a variation of this method uses a closed-loop system with antifreeze fluid.
- *closed-loop active system:* One of the most common types of systems for both residential and commercial applications. A separate, nonfreezing fluid is circulated by pumps through the solar collectors and into a heat exchanger where the domestic hot water is heated. A differential controller senses when the temperature of the collector is lower than that of the stored water and turns the pumps off. This system is flexible and provides control but suffers from some loss in efficiency because of the need for a heat exchanger.
- *drain-down system:* A direct, active system that solves the problem of freezing by automatically draining the water from the collectors when the outside temperature is near freezing. Because water is wasted

whenever the system is drained, this method is best for climates with mild winters where the draining process would not occur frequently.

- *drain-back system:* An indirect, active system that uses water as the heat-collector fluid. The heated water is pumped to a heat exchanger where a coil of domestic hot water is heated. When the controller senses the temperature is too low, it turns off the pump, and the collector water drains back into the solar storage tank.
- *phase change system:* Hot water systems can also take advantage of phase change materials as the collector fluid. As discussed in Chap. 51, phase change materials store large amounts of latent heat as well as sensible heat.

DEFINITIONS

actuator: A device in a building control system that receives commands from a controller and activates a piece of equipment.

annual fuel utilization efficiency (AFUE): The ratio of annual fuel output energy to annual input energy. This includes nonseasonal pilot light input losses.

coefficient of performance (COP): A unitless number that is a rating of the efficiency of heating or cooling equipment. It is derived by dividing the steady-state rate of energy output (or the rate of heat removal, in the case of cooling equipment) of the equipment by the steady-state rate of energy input to the equipment. The output and input values must be in equivalent units, such as watts out to watts in.

controller: A device that measures, analyzes, and initiates actions in a building control system.

deadband: In a building control system, the range of temperatures within which neither heating nor cooling is needed.

energy efficiency ratio (EER): The ratio of net cooling capacity in Btu/hr to the total rate of electrical input in watts under designated operating conditions.

energy management system (EMS): A computer-based system used to monitor and control facility energy use. An EMS is typically part of a building automation system.

ground-coupled cooling: A method of cooling a building by direct contact with the earth or by circulating air through underground tunnels to cool it.

heating seasonal performance factor (HSPF): A measure of the performance of a heat pump operating in the heating cycle. See also *seasonal energy efficiency ratio.*

home energy rating system (HERS): A standardized system for rating the energy efficiency of residential buildings using the HERS Council Guidelines and the Mortgage Industry HERS Accreditation Procedures. A HERS score is a numeric value between 0 and 100 indicating the relative energy efficiency of a given home as compared with the HERS Energy-Efficient Reference Home.

integrated part load value (IPLV): The single-number figure of merit based on part-load EER or COP expressing part-load efficiency for air conditioning and heat pump equipment on the basis of weighted operation at various load capacities for the equipment, as determined using the applicable test method in the Appliance Efficiency Regulations.

relative solar heat gain (RSHG): The ratio of solar heat gain through a window, corrected for external shading, to the incident solar radiation. This heat gain includes directly transmitted solar heat and absorbed solar radiation, which are conducted or convected into the space.

seasonal energy efficiency ratio (SEER): The total cooling output of a central air conditioning system or heat pump in the cooling mode, measured in Btus per hour, during its normal usage period for cooling divided by the total electrical input in watt-hours, as determined by specific test procedures. The higher the SEER, the more efficient the equipment performance. The minimum SEER permitted for residential air conditioning equipment in the United States is 13.

18

STRUCTURAL SYSTEMS

LONG SPAN STRUCTURES—ONE-WAY SYSTEMS

A *long span* is generally considered to be one over 60 ft in length. The study of long spans as distinct structural entities is important because of the unique design problems that arise when structures cover long distances. These problems include such things as temperature expansion and contraction, shipping, and deflection, among others. These will be discussed in detail in later sections.

One of the most important characteristics of long span structures is their lack of redundancy. In structures with many separate, small bays, the collapse of one beam would be damaging, but the majority of the building would remain standing supported by other parts of the framing system. With a long span structure, failure of one portion affects a much greater area and can even cause collapse of the entire building. The potential for catastrophic loss of life and property is much greater.

Long span structures can be categorized into two broad divisions: one-way and two-way systems. *One-way systems* are characterized by linear members that span in one direction and resist loads primarily by beam action, or bending. A one-way long span generally consists of primary members that bridge the long distance, and a series of secondary members that span between the primary one, also with simple beam action, and support the floor or roof system. *Two-way systems* distribute loads to supports in both directions and involve complex, three-dimensional methods of resisting loads. Two-way systems will be covered later in this chapter.

Types of One-Way Systems

The following sections outline some of the more typical long span, one-way systems. Most of these use steel or concrete as their primary material because of the high strength-to-weight ratio of steel and concrete. Wood is used for long span construction in trusses and glued-laminated beams.

Many variables determine the exact size and configurations of a member that is to span a particular distance, such as loading and the allowable stress of the material. Table 18.1 summarizes several of the one-way systems along with typical span ranges, depths, and depth-to-span ratios.

Table 18.1
One-Way Long Span Systems

system	typical spans (ft)	typical depths (ft)	typical depth-to-span ratios
steel girders	10–72	$^2/_3$–3	1/20
steel rigid frames	30–150	2–5	1/20–1/30
glued laminated rigid frames	30–120	$1^1/_2$–4	1/20–1/30
flat wood trusses	40–120	4–12	1/10
pitched wood trusses	40–100	7–17	1/6
flat steel trusses	40–300	4–30	1/10–1/12
pitched steel trusses	40–150	5–20	1/6–1/8
long span joists	25–96	$1^1/_2$–4	1/20–1/24
deep, long span joists	90–144	$1^1/_3$–6	1/20–1/24
joist girders	20–100	2–10	1/10–1/12
glued laminated beams	10–60	1–4	1/24
prestressed single tee concrete	20–120	1–4	1/20–1/30
prestressed double tee concrete	20–60	1–$2^1/_2$	1/20–1/30
prestressed concrete girders	40–120	3–6	1/15–1/20
steel arches	50–500	1–5	1/100
concrete arches	40–320	1–7	1/50
wood arches	50–240	$1^1/_2$–6	1/40

Steel Girders

Rolled steel members are sometimes used for long spans if the loads are not excessive. The largest rolled section available is 44 in deep, and its practical span length is about 72 ft. If additional moment-carrying capacity is required, cover plates can be welded to the top or bottom flanges as shown in Fig. 18.1(a).

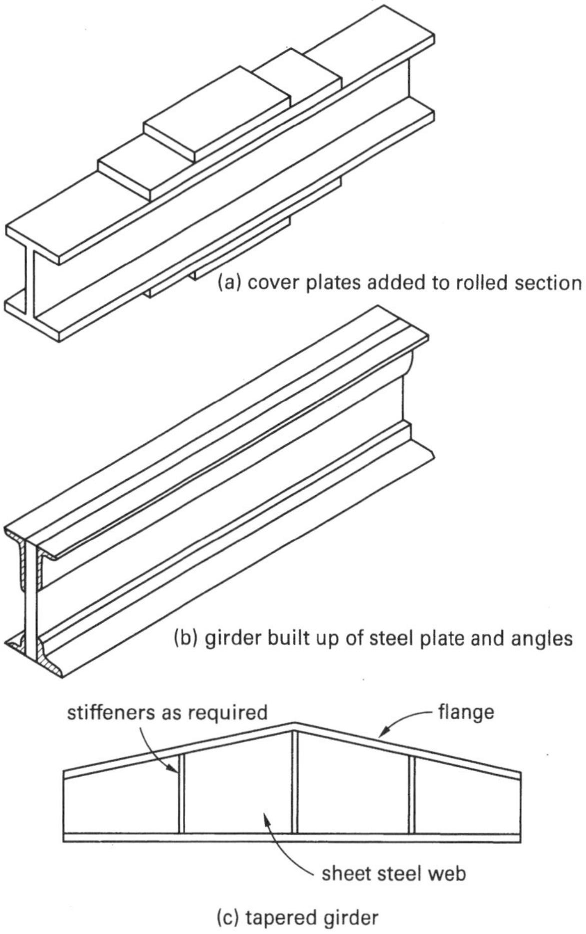

Figure 18.1
Built-Up Steel Sections

(a) cover plates added to rolled section

(b) girder built up of steel plate and angles

stiffeners as required

flange

sheet steel web

(c) tapered girder

If longer spans are required for steel sections, they must be fabricated from individual components. The most common type of section is the plate girder, which is composed of sheet steel for the web and either steel bars or angles for the flanges. Figure 18.1(b) shows a plate girder built up of angles. Plate girders are efficient long span members because most of the material is in the flanges separated by a large distance, which results in a high moment of inertia.

In order to minimize the amount of steel required (and, therefore, the weight and cost), plate girders used as roof beams can be tapered toward the middle of the span where the moment is the greatest. See Fig. 18.1(c).

Plate girders are often 8 ft deep or more. They are sometimes used to transfer the load of a column to two wider spaced columns to create a clear span below as shown in Fig. 18.2. This is often required in buildings such as hotels, where the lobby requires a more open space than the rooms above. In most cases, because the web is relatively thin compared with its length, intermediate stiffeners are required to prevent buckling of the web. These are usually angles welded perpendicular to the length of the web.

Rigid Frames

A *rigid frame* is a structural system in which the vertical and horizontal members and joints resist loads primarily by flexure, and in which moments are transferred from beams to columns. When discussing long span structures, a rigid frame has a sloped roof with a rigid, moment-resisting connection between the columns and the roof structure, or the column/roof structure is one continuous member. See Fig. 18.3. A rigid frame may have fixed connections between the columns and foundation and between the two halves, or it may have pinned connections at these points. With pinned connections, the structure is determinate and does not develop secondary stresses caused by temperature differences. If the entire frame is rigidly connected, it is an indeterminate structure.

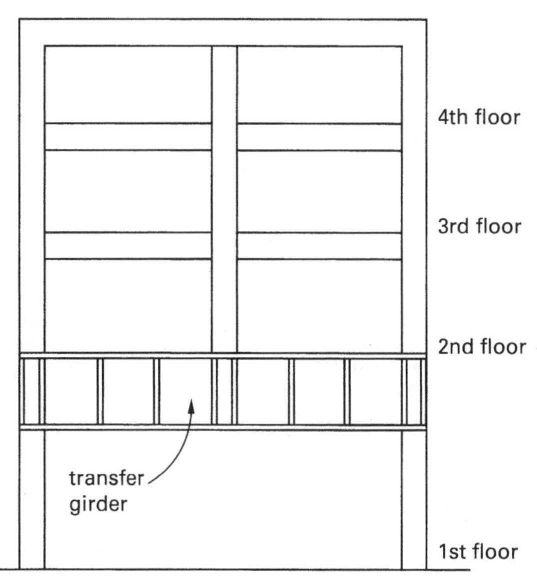

Figure 18.2
Transfer Girder

Figure 18.3
Rigid Frame

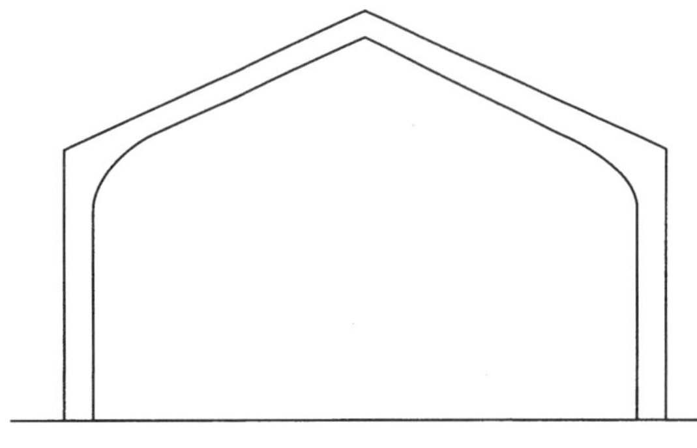

Part of the spanning capability of a rigid frame comes from the arch action of the sloping beams, through which vertical loads are transferred to the columns through compression as well as bending. In addition, since the two columns are tied together, lateral loads are transferred to both columns, resulting in a more efficient structure. As shown in the illustration, the column and beam are often tapered toward the foundation and ridge. This reflects the fact that the moment is greatest at the junction where more material is needed to resist the forces in the structure.

Rigid frames are used for industrial facilities, warehouses, manufacturing plants, and other instances where a simple, rectangular open space is required. They are primarily constructed of steel, but are also made of glued laminated lumber because each half can be easily fabricated as a single, continuous unit.

Trusses

A *truss* is a structure composed of straight members that form a number of triangles, with the connections arranged so that the stresses in the members are either in compression or tension. Trusses are very efficient structures to span long distances because of their primary reliance on compression and tension to resist forces, rather than bending, and their high strength-to-weight ratios. Trusses are usually constructed of steel or wood and sometimes a combination of materials.

Figure 18.4
Truss Configurations

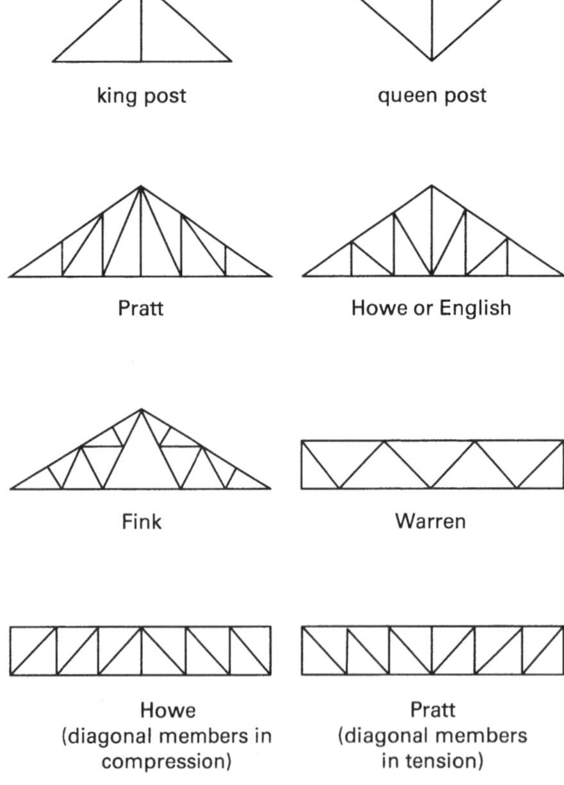

Trusses offer many advantages in bridging large spaces. They are relatively lightweight, the space between the members can be used for mechanical services, they can be partially prefabricated for fast erection, they make efficient use of material, and they can theoretically be made as deep and large as needed to span most any distance, although there are practical limits to the span. One disadvantage of a truss, however, is the number of connections, which can increase fabrication or erection time.

Trusses are usually spaced from 10 ft to 40 ft on center with intermediate purlins spanning between them and bearing on the *panel points*, those points where the web members intersect the top chord. Roof or floor decking then spans between the purlins.

The typical spans and depths of the various types of trusses are shown in Table 18.1. Some of the more common truss configurations are shown in Fig. 18.4. Refer to Chap. 36 for more information on truss analysis.

Open-Web Steel Joists and Joist Girders

Open-web joists are prefabricated truss members using hot-rolled or cold-formed steel members. These joists have been standardized into three major groups: K-series, LH-series, and DLH-series. The K-series spans up to 60 ft, so the

Project Planning

LH- and DLH-series are considered long span. The LH-series is suitable for the direct support of floors and roof decks, and the DLH-series is suitable for direct support of roof decks.

parallel chords, underslung

parallel chords, square ends

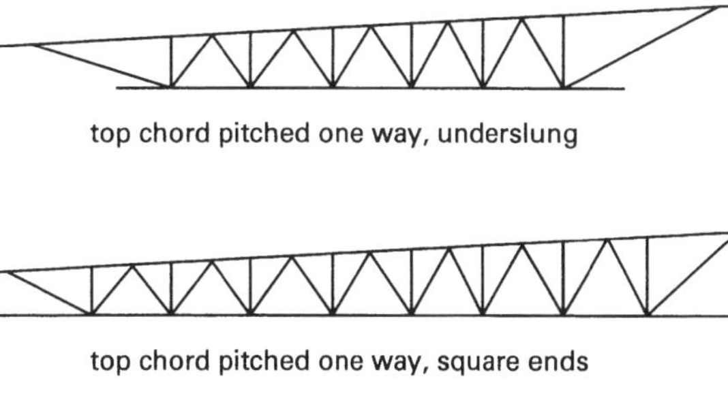

top chord pitched one way, underslung
top chord pitched one way, square ends

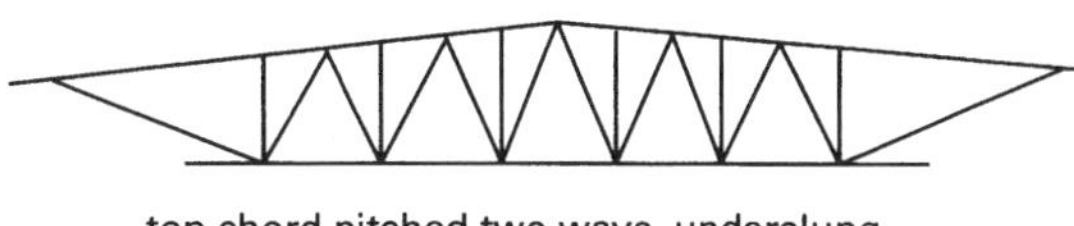

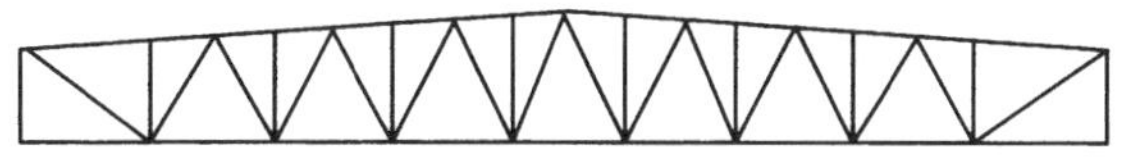

Figure 18.5 Open-Web Steel Joist Configurations

Even though each manufacturer has its own chord and web profiles, the sizes and specifications for the manufacturing have been standardized by the Steel Joist Institute. Long span joists, the LH-series, come in depths from 18 in to 48 in and span up to 96 ft. The deep, long span joists, the DLH-series, come in depths from 52 in to 72 in and span up to 144 ft. The depths increase in 2 in or 4 in increments.

Open-web joists typically bear on the top chord and have underslung ends. However, square end trusses can be purchased that bear on the bottom chord. The depth of the bearing portion is standardized at 5 in for the LH-series and for chord sizes through 17 in the DLH-series. For chord sizes of 18 and 19 in the DLH-series, the standard bearing depth is $7\frac{1}{2}$ in.

There are a number of standard chord configurations. These are illustrated in Fig. 18.5. Of course, parallel chord trusses are required for floor systems, but the pitched top chord configuration is useful for roof structures to provide for positive drainage. In addition, there are a number of accessories such as bottom chord ceiling extensions, extended ends for the top chord, and various types of anchoring devices.

Both LH-series and DLH-series joists are manufactured with camber, the amount depending on the length of the top chord. *Camber* is the rise in a beam to compensate for deflection. The cambers range from $\frac{1}{4}$ in for a 20 ft length to $8\frac{1}{2}$ in for the longest, 144 ft span.

Open-web joists are very flexible. By varying the spacing, depth, and chord size, a wide variety of floor and roof loads and spans can be accommodated. They can bear on steel beams, masonry walls, concrete walls, and joist girders. The top chord can likewise support a variety of flooring and roofing systems. Because they are lightweight and prefabricated, erection is quick and simple. For more information, including design methods, refer to the section on open-web joists in Chap. 24.

Joist girders are designed to serve as primary structural members that support evenly spaced open-web joists. Joist girders are available in depths of 20 in to 120 in and can span up to 100 ft. They are manufactured with steel angle sections. Although each manufacturer may have its own particular configuration, there is a standard way of designating a joist girder. For example, in the designation 48G8N8.8K, the 48G indicates the depth in inches, the 8N indicates the number of joist spaces, and the 8.8K indicates the required design load in kips at each panel point.

Vierendeel Trusses

A *Vierendeel truss* is a structure composed of a series of rigid rectangular frames. However, it is not a true truss because there are no triangles and the members must resist bending as well as tension and compression. See Fig. 18.6. A Vierendeel truss is used when diagonal members

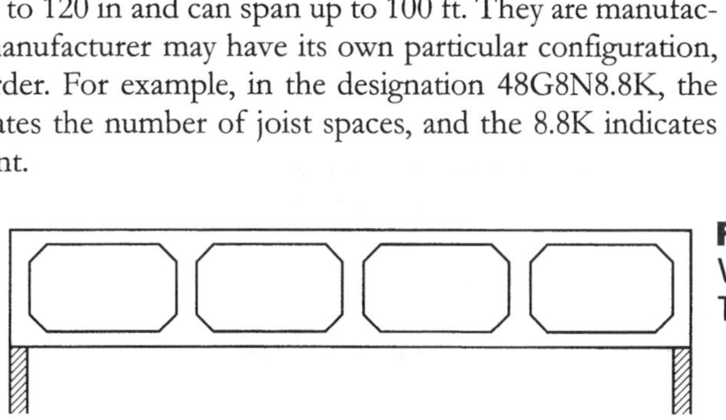

Figure 18.6 Vierendeel Truss

Project Planning

are undesirable, and in many instances will occupy an entire story height when used to transfer loads from closely spaced columns above to column-free spaces below.

The top and bottom chords of a Vierendeel truss are in compression and tension, respectively, just as with any beam or true truss. However, there is bending moment in the chords as well as in the vertical members. As a result, all portions of a Vierendeel truss must be designed with larger members than would be necessary with a regular truss, and the joints must be capable of resisting moments as well. This is why these trusses often have triangular brackets or short knee braces as shown in Fig. 18.6.

Glued-Laminated Beams

Although glued-laminated construction seldom exceeds the 60 ft distance arbitrarily considered long span, it is included here because it is used for spans and loads that regular sawn timber is incapable of supporting, and because many of the special considerations of long spans apply to this type of construction. Long distances are spanned by glued-laminated members in two primary ways: with straight, rectangular beams and with rigid frame arches.

Glued-laminated members consist of a number of individual pieces of lumber, either $^3/_4$ in or $1^1/_2$ in thick, glued together and finished in a factory (see also Chap. 25). See Fig. 18.3. Because the individual pieces can be hand-selected free from major defects and the entire member can be properly seasoned, glulams, as they are called, have higher stress ratings than standard sawn lumber sections. In addition, much larger sizes are possible, so the span and load-carrying capabilities are much greater for glulam construction than for standard wood frame buildings.

Glulam beams are designed with the same formulas used for other wood construction, except a few additional formulas are required to account for modifications in stress ratings when curved members are used. As with sawn members, there are load tables that make selection easier by giving the allowable load per foot based on span and size of beam.

Prestressed Concrete

When concrete is used for one-way systems to span long distances, it is nearly always prestressed or post-tensioned. Prestressed concrete consists of a member that has had an internal stress applied before it is subjected to service loads. This stress is applied by stressing high-strength steel strands in a form into which concrete is poured. When the concrete cures, the external stress is removed and it is transferred to the concrete. This process effectively counteracts the tension that concrete is not capable of carrying. The prestressing process also reduces cracking and deflection, and permits concrete to span longer distances with smaller sections than is possible with reinforced, cast-in-place construction.

There are several types of precast sections suitable for long span concrete sections. The three most common ones are shown in Fig. 18.7 and include the single tee, the double tee, and the AASHTO (American Associations of State Highway and Transportation Officials) girder.

Single tees are typically 4, 6, or 8 ft wide with an 8 in to 12 in thick web. Depths range from 1 ft to 4 ft with span capabilities up to about 120 ft.

Double tees are usually 8 ft or 10 ft wide with a 2 in flange thickness and depths ranging from 8 in to 32 in. Span distances are less than with single tees; the maximum span is 60 ft to 80 ft. Double tees typically have a 2 in thick concrete topping that covers the joints, smooths out any irregularities between adjacent panels, and strengthens the floor or roof assembly.

Double tees are used frequently because of their many advantages. They function both as a structure and a decking, are relatively inexpensive to produce, can be erected quickly, and can be used either as horizontal or vertical members. In addition, the space between the webs can be used for mechanical and electrical service runs.

The use of AASHTO girders is generally limited to highway bridges. However, similar rectangular beams can be precast to span long distances, with lengths up to 120 ft possible.

Other precast shapes include box girders and channel slabs, but these are not used for building as frequently as the sections shown in Fig. 18.7.

Post-tensioned Concrete

With post-tensioned concrete construction, the concrete member is cast with hollow sleeves embedded in it. High-strength steel cables, called *tendons*, are placed in the hollow sleeves, and after the concrete has cured, tension is applied to the tendons by hydraulic jacks. When the design stress is reached, the cables are anchored to the ends of the concrete member with steel plates or by grouting the space between the tendon and the sleeve. The post-tensioning equipment is removed, and the resulting member functions in a way similar to prestressed concrete.

Post-tensioning can be used in beams, floor slabs, or other sections to increase the load-carrying capacity of the member and to allow for longer spans.

Figure 18.7 Typical Prestressed Concrete Shapes

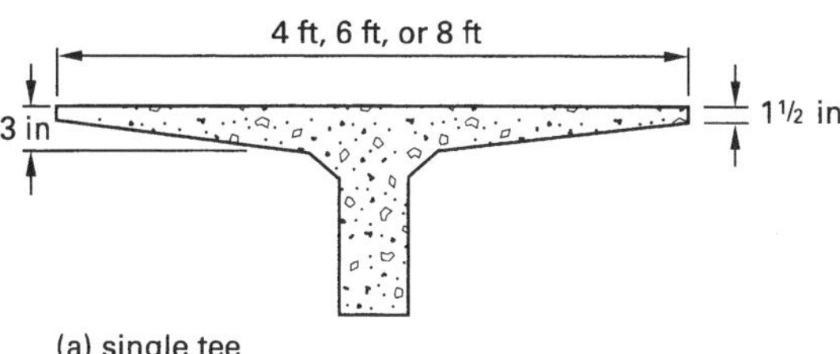

(a) single tee

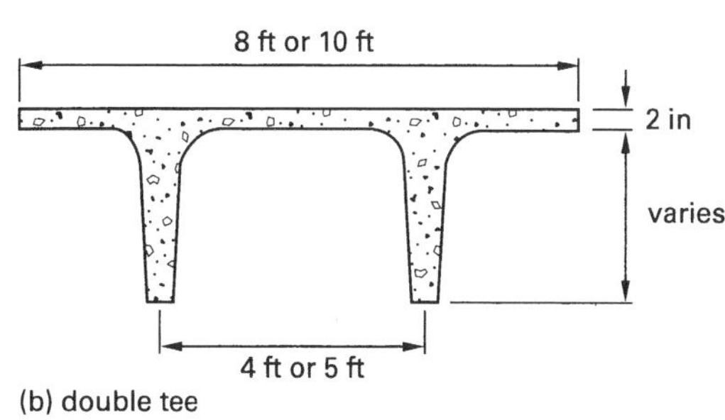

(b) double tee

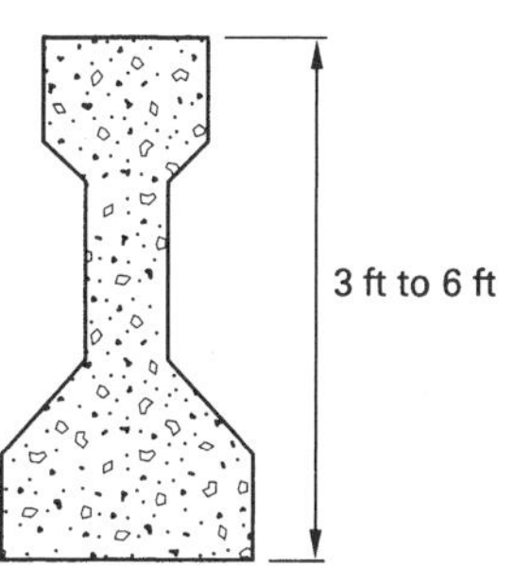

(c) AASHTO girder

Arches

Arches are one of the oldest long span structural systems. This is because an arch depends primarily on compression to resist loads, and ancient materials like stone were very strong in compression. In a true arch, all of the load is carried in compression. For a given set of loads, the shape of an arch that acts in this way is its funicular shape. For an arch supporting a uniform load across its span, this shape is a parabola.

However, in practical terms, there are no true arches, because there are always combinations of loads that place both compressive and bending stresses in an arch. A good working definition for an *arch* is a structure that resists imposed loads primarily by compression with some bending stresses involved.

There are several arch shapes. Some of the more common ones are shown in Fig. 18.8. The A-frame and gabled frame are not immediately apparent as arches, but they represent the concept of arch action, in which there is some compression in the spanning member as well as bending. As the slope of the arch approaches vertical, there is more compression and less bending.

Internal loads tend to cause an arch to spread out unless it is restrained with foundations or a tie rod. For a given span, this tendency to spread, or the *thrust* of the arch, is inversely proportional to the rise, or height, of the arch. As the rise increases, the thrust decreases.

Arches can be constructed with wood, concrete, and steel, and some spans have reached over 1000 ft. For most purposes, however, the typical spans for arches range from 50 ft to 240 ft for wood; 40 ft to 320 ft for concrete; and 50 ft to 500 ft for steel. Typical depth-to-span ratios are about 1:40 for wood arches and up to 1:100 for steel arches.

Arches can be either fixed or hinged. If the arch is hinged at the supports, it can move slightly under loads caused by temperature, soil settlement, and wind without developing high bending stresses.

When used in one-way structural systems, arches are the primary structural member, and the space between is spanned with secondary members that in turn support the roofing system.

Figure 18.8
Types of Arches

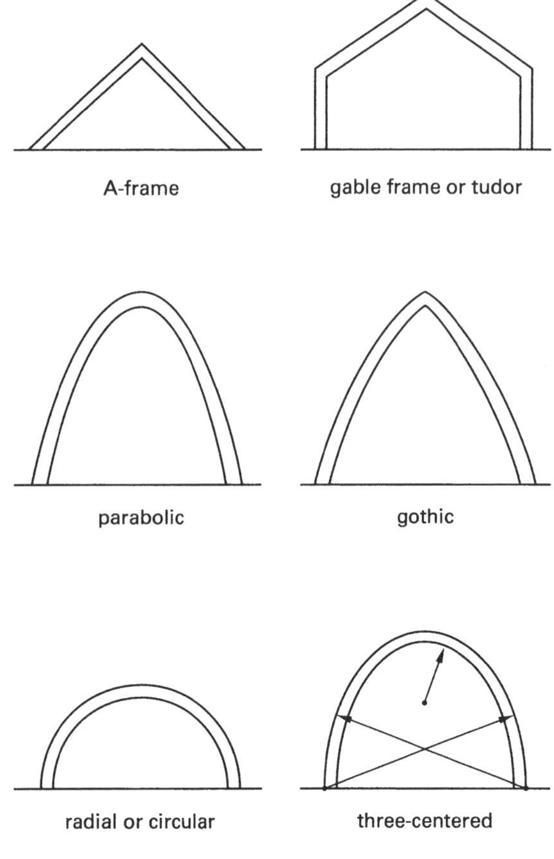

Design and Selection Considerations

The selection of the most appropriate long span system for a particular project involves finding a balance between many different factors. This section and the next will outline some of the more important factors for both one-way and two-way systems.

Function

All structural systems must meet the functional needs of the building being designed. An auditorium may need a clear span of 150 ft, a sports arena may require an open area large enough for hockey and thousands of spectators, or a manufacturing plant may simply need narrow, but very long, unobstructed bays. A system appropriate for one use may not be the best choice for another use. For example, it would not make sense to use a steel arch capable of spanning 400 ft if long span open-web joists clearing 60 ft would do just as well.

Cost and Economy

Selecting and designing an economical long span structural system for a particular project requires that the architect and engineer balance many interrelated factors.

There are six general considerations that affect the cost of any structure.

- structural system
- material
- labor
- equipment
- construction time
- integration with other building systems

Regardless of the relative efficiency of a long span structural system, bridging great lengths always comes at a cost. The first determinant, therefore, is the structural system itself. Generally speaking, it is less costly to build more columns to decrease spans as much as possible than it is to provide deeper and heavier beams or complex two- or three-dimensional systems. All other things being equal, the most economical structure is the one that spans just the required distance and no farther without stretching the limits of the system.

Since most materials are more efficiently used in compression and tension than in bending, a system that reflects this fact will often cost less than one that relies on flexure. X-braced buildings, for example, may use less steel than moment-resisting frames, or trusses may require less weight than comparable solid beams. However, material use may be offset by higher fabricating costs or labor required for assembly.

Finally, deeper bending members are more efficient and require less material than shallow ones. A deep steel beam will weigh less (and cost less) than a shallow one that supports the same load. If other considerations allow it, the architect should provide as much space as possible for structural members.

Material is the second consideration affecting cost. In addition to the size and amount required by the system selected, cost can be affected by the availability of material. For instance, in some parts of the country, steel may be more readily available and at a lower cost than concrete, or a job site may be quite remote from a precasting plant, which would rule out prestressed concrete.

The choice of material may also have repercussions for other materials. Steel will require fireproofing while concrete will not, or masonry walls in cold climates may require more complex insulating systems than simple steel stud cavity walls.

It is less costly to build more columns to decrease spans as much as possible than it is to provide deeper and heavier beams or complex two-or three-dimensional systems.

One of the major determinates of cost is labor. This is especially true in the United States. Generally, any structural system that minimizes the amount of labor, especially on-site labor, has an economic advantage. This is why precast concrete is often preferred over cast-in-place concrete.

The other aspect of labor cost is the availability of skilled labor to perform certain building tasks. A brick structure needs skilled masons, and a welded steel frame requires competent welders, for example. In metropolitan areas, this may not be a problem. In more remote areas, the best structural system may be one that is prefabricated and requires simple site assembly.

Equipment required for the erection of long span structures is usually large and expensive. Here, there is a balance between the cost of equipment, and speed and ease of construction. Larger cranes may cost more to rent than smaller ones, but may allow the use of larger, prefabricated members and therefore reduce construction time and the number of connections required.

Construction time is very important in many building situations due to the high cost of financing. Anything that reduces the building period saves money. Readily available material, prefabrication, simple long span systems, and easy on-site labor can significantly affect the economy of a building.

Finally, any long span structure must be selected so that it integrates with other building systems and components. There must be room for mechanical ductwork without excessive floor-to-floor heights, the exterior configuration must work with the fenestration system, and there must be provisions for easy installation of partitions and finishes.

Shipping

Because of their very nature, most long span structures, especially one-way systems, require large components to be shipped to the job site. There are many advantages to prefabricating structural members in sizes as large as possible, but these must be weighed against the practical limits of the transportation system serving the site. For instance, with precast concrete, the largest size possible should be shipped in order to reduce the number of field connections required and to speed erection. However, this goal must be balanced with the practical limits of weight and truck size.

In most cases, the maximum length is 60 ft for truck shipment and 80 ft for railroad shipment. Maximum height for truck shipment is 14 ft. In some special situations, these dimensions are exceeded, but only at greater cost and with unusual provisions for transportation.

Access to the site must also be considered. In constricted urban locations, it may be impossible to maneuver a large truck into proper position for unloading.

Acoustics

Acoustics can be a factor in the selection of a long span structural system if the system's shape concentrates sound reflections. Barrel vaults, domes, and some polygonal shapes can increase the noise level or produce undesirable echoes. This can be a critical concern in sports arenas, manufacturing plants, and other buildings where the normal noise level is usually high. Adding a false ceiling or making other provisions for acoustical control can add to the cost of the structure.

Assembly and Erection

There are several things to consider about the assembly and erection of long span structures. The first is the speed and ease of construction, both of which can affect the cost of the building. In addition, the equipment required for erection must be taken into account, as previously mentioned. More important are the structural and safety requirements of long span construction. Because long span members are usually large, correspondingly large erection stresses can be developed. Sometimes these stresses are greater than those the member will encounter in use, and the piece must be designed and sized accordingly.

Due to the lack of redundant members to support the structure, materials, and workers during erection, it is critical that correct procedures and sequences of construction be followed to avoid instability or overstressing until the entire building is complete and all bracing components are in place.

Due to the lack of redundant members to support the structure, materials, and workers during erection, it is critical that correct procedures and sequences of construction be followed to avoid instability or overstressing until the entire building is complete and all bracing components are in place.

For example, when open-web steel joists are erected, several procedures must be followed. The hoisting cables must not be removed until bolted diagonal bridging near the midspan is installed. The number of bridging lines that must be installed before the hoisting cables are released depends on the span. If the joist is bottom bearing, the ends must be restrained and bridging must be installed before the hoisting cables are released. Further, all bridging and bridging anchors must be completely installed before construction loads are placed on the joists.

During erection of joist girders, it is recommended that a loose connection of the lower chord be made to the column, or that some other support is provided to stabilize the lower chord laterally and help brace the joist girder against possible overturning. For both open-web joists and joist girders, concentrated construction loads must not be placed so as to exceed the load-carrying capacity of any member.

Precast concrete presents special problems with erection because of its weight. While it is desirable to fabricate large members to speed construction and minimize joints and field connections, the practical limits of crane capacities must be considered, as well as the space available around the building site to maneuver trucks, cranes, and large precast sections. Additionally, each individual member must be properly braced until the complete system is assembled.

Fire Protection

As mentioned previously, the requirement for fire protection of structural members may influence the selection of a particular system. In some instances, the cost and difficulty of installing fire-resistant covering may offset the initial economy of an otherwise efficient material. Steel, of course, is especially vulnerable to weakening when exposed to high temperatures.

The *International Building Code* (IBC) allows an exception to the fire protection of structural steel in some instances. In Group A (assembly) and E (educational) occupancies, if the structural framework of the roof is more than 25 ft above the floor, fire protection may be omitted. This is why there is no fire protection in many sports stadiums, exhibition halls, and concert halls.

Technical Considerations

Long span structures pose special problems that are not present, or at least not significant, with standard structural systems. For example, a 30 ft long steel beam will expand so slightly with an increase in temperature that it is of little consequence. The expanson of a 120 ft truss, however, can be significant. Because of the nonredundant nature of long span structures and the potential for catastrophic failure, the following considerations are especially important.

Connections

Many of the failures of long span structures (as well as standard structures) occur not with the primary spanning members but with the connections. As with other aspects of long span structures, there is less redundancy with connections. If one fails, it can lead to a progressive failure of others when they are overstressed.

In addition to building code requirements, it is often wise to build in extra connections. Shop drawings should also be carefully reviewed to make sure changes were not made by the fabricator, and this should be followed up by meticulous field observation to verify that the connections are properly installed and in the proper sequence for the type of material and system being used.

For example, if a rigid connection is made between a joist girder and a column, it must be made only after the application of the dead loads. In such a case, the girder must be investigated for continuous frame action because the girder is no longer a simply supported beam.

Envelope Attachment

The connection of roofing and exterior wall materials to long span structures requires special attention. This is due to the larger movements experienced by both the structural system and the building envelope. Expansion and contraction of the primary frame caused by temperature differentials can exert unusual stresses on cladding, so expansion joints must be designed to accommodate this type of movement.

Deflection of a long span floor or roof is also significant in terms of weatherproof attachment of the roofing material and flooring and ceiling finish.

For simple, one-way structural systems, the end rotation of a beam or girder can be significant for a long span member where it is of little consequence in normal span construction. There must be enough room at the end of the beam to allow for this type of movement without stressing or dislodging the exterior envelope.

Ponding

Ponding is one of the most dangerous conditions with long span roofs. It occurs when a roof deflects enough to prevent normal water runoff. Instead, water collects in the middle of the span. With the added weight, the roof deflects a little more, which allows additional water to collect, which in turn causes the roof to deflect more. The cycle continues until structural damage or collapse occurs.

The IBC specifically requires that all roofs be designed with sufficient slope or camber to ensure adequate drainage after long-term deflection, or that roofs be designed to support maximum roof loads, including possible ponding.

For glued-laminated construction, the IBC requires that the roof slope provide a positive slope not less than $^1/_4$ in/ft between the level of the drain and the highest point of the roof. This slope must be in addition to the camber provided by the beams, which must be $1^1/_2$ times the calculated dead load deflection.

The best design approach is to plan roofs so that there is more than enough slope to provide positive drainage while allowing for the usual construction variances. Instead of $^1/_4$ in/ft, provide at least $^1/_2$ in/ft. In addition, pay particular attention to situations that can create ponding. If a roof area depends on drains, some kind of provision must be made for drainage if the primary drain is clogged.

Temperature Movement and Stresses

The greater length of long span structures over standard length members means that any movement caused by temperature differentials will be increased in proportion to the length of the member. Where an expansion of $^1/_{10}$ inch in the length of a short steel beam may not pose any particular problem, an increase of $^3/_{10}$ inch may overstress a connection or crack an attached brick wall.

Particular attention must be paid to detailing long span structures to account for these kinds of movement. The situation is more critical if the structure is exposed to the weather; temperature differentials and movement will be greater than for interior structural members. Temperature stresses can be avoided by using flexible joints, providing clearance for the anticipated movement, providing slip joints, and so on.

Tolerances

Just as with temperature-induced movement, fabrication and erection tolerances are greater for long span structures. Details and connections must be designed to accommodate a member whose length or depth may vary by an inch or more from what is designed and shown on the drawings. Hinged connections, slotted bolt holes, shims, and similar devices are often used to allow for tolerance variations.

Stability

Many long span structures depend on secondary framing and horizontal or vertical diaphragms for complete rigidity. During erection, the primary elements, such as arches and rigid frames, must be braced temporarily until enough of the remainder of the structure can be built to make the entire assembly self-supporting. Although the contractor is responsible for construction methods, the drawings and specifications must be clear in their instructions. In all cases, industry standards and the recommendations of the manufacturer or fabricator should be followed.

Figure 18.9 One-Way and Two-Way Systems

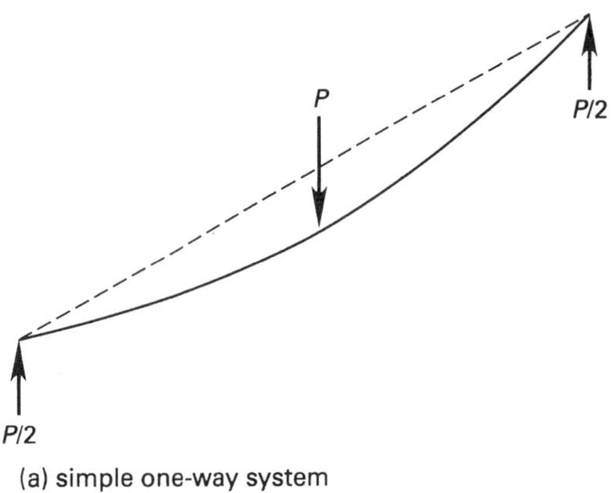

(a) simple one-way system

P/4
P
P/4
P/4
P/4

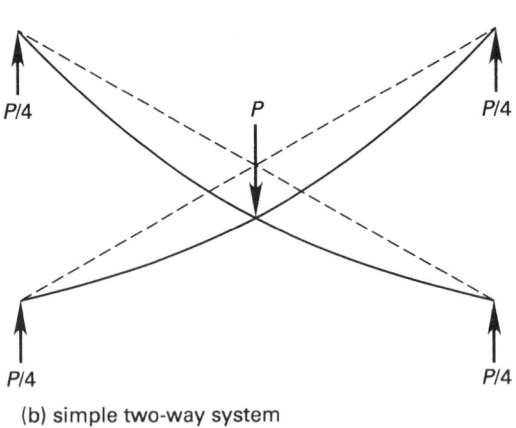

(b) simple two-way system

Shop Drawing Review

Minor changes in the preparation of shop drawings are a fact of life in the design and construction industry. However, where a slight change from the original details or specifications may be acceptable in a normal structure, such a change can have disastrous consequences in long span construction. Architect should fulfill their role in the shop drawing review process and verify that the structural engineer, contractor, and erection subcontractor have thoroughly reviewed the shop drawings, and that any deviation from the original design is completely studied and approved by all parties.

Construction Observation

The final step in the correct design and construction of a long span structure is the thorough observation of the erection sequence. Both the architect and structural engineer must be involved in this process to verify that construction is in accordance with the plans and specifications.

LONG SPAN STRUCTURES—TWO-WAY SYSTEMS

Two-way structural systems distribute loads in two or more directions and consist of members that are all considered to be primary. Because the load is shared by many members in the system and generally distributed to more supports, two-way systems are structurally more efficient than one-way systems. This can be seen by comparing a simple one-way system with a two-way system. See Fig. 18.9.

Fig. 18.9(a) shows a single concentrated load on a flexure member. The beam carries the entire load with one-half of the load carried by each support. With a two-way system, as shown in Fig. 18.9(b), the same load is distributed to two flexure members with each support only having to carry one-fourth of the load.

With this type of two-way system, the structure is most efficient if the shape is square so the loads are equally distributed. If the shape becomes rectangular, more and more of the load is carried in the short dimension and less in the long dimension. When the proportion becomes 2:1, nearly all the load is carried in the short dimension. This is why systems such as a waffle slab and flat plate construction are most efficient when the bays are square.

Some two-way systems also offer the advantage of redundancy, which is lacking in most of the one-way systems. For example, the failure of one joint or member of a space frame will not cause the entire structure to collapse.

Two-way systems are more efficient in their use of material and can span farther and carry heavier loads than comparable one-way systems. However, one disadvantage is that they are more complicated to design and build. The design work is a minor problem because of computer programs that can calculate highly indeterminate structures. The problem of complex construction still remains, however. Most two-way systems require a large number of pieces and connections, which require a great deal of fabrication time.

An additional limitation of long span, two-way systems is that nearly all of them can only be used for roof structures due to their basic shape. Space frames are the one exception, but even these are almost always used only for roofs and occasionally wall systems. Note that this limitation applies only to long span structures. Other two-way systems, like flat slabs and stressed skin floor panels, do utilize the efficiency of two-way action.

Types of Two-Way Long Span Systems

As with one-way systems, there are many types and variations of two-way, long span structural systems. This section discusses the major ones with some of the most used variations. Table 18.2 summarizes the typical two-way systems, giving typical span ranges, thicknesses, and height-to-span ratios. With the exception of space frames, the height-to-span ratio is not the same as the depth-to-span ratio used with one-way structures. Since all of the systems listed are three-dimensional, they all have an optimum total height that is different from the size or thickness of individual members.

Table 18.2 Two-Way Long Span Systems

system	typical spans (ft)	typical thickness (in)	typical height-to-span ratios
space frames	80–220	–	1/15–1/25
geodesic domes	50–400	–	1/3–1/5
thin shell domes	40–240	3–6	1/5–1/8
hyperbolic paraboloids	30–160	3–6	1/6–1/10
barrel vaults	30–180	3–5	1/10–1/15
lamella arches	40–150	–	1/4–1/6
folded plates	50–100	3–6	1/6–1/10
suspended cable structures	50–450	–	1/8–1/15

Space Frames

A space frame is a three-dimensional structural system that transfers loads through a network of members attached to each other at nodal connection points. Space frames are very efficient structures because of the large number of members and because they resist loads primarily in compression or tension.

One of the unique features of a space frame that is uncharacteristic of many other long span structures is redundancy. Buckling of one member under a concentrated load does not lead to the collapse of the whole structure. This is because the system distributes concentrated loads evenly throughout the entire frame.

There are many configurations for space frames. They all have a top chord grid and a bottom chord grid connected with diagonal bracing. The two grids can be identical and run in the same direction, or run in different directions while still forming a regular pattern. Grids can be square or triangular, although the square grid is more common.

The simplest type of space frame is a two-way truss system. With this, trusses spanning two directions are interconnected and form a grid of square openings. The diagonal members are vertical and in the plane of each truss, just as with a one-way truss system. See Fig. 18.10.

Figure 18.10 Two-Way Truss Space Frame

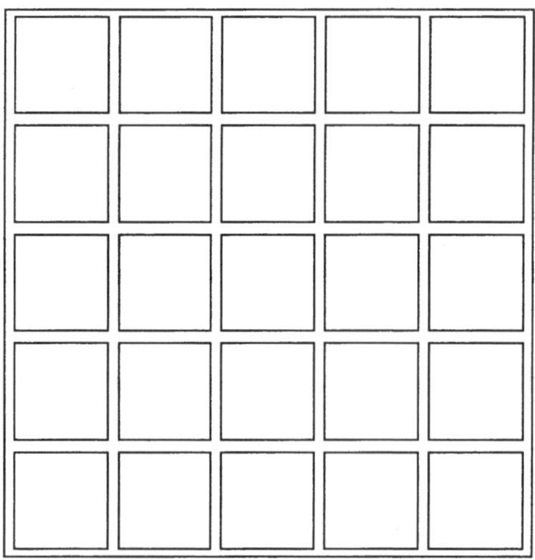

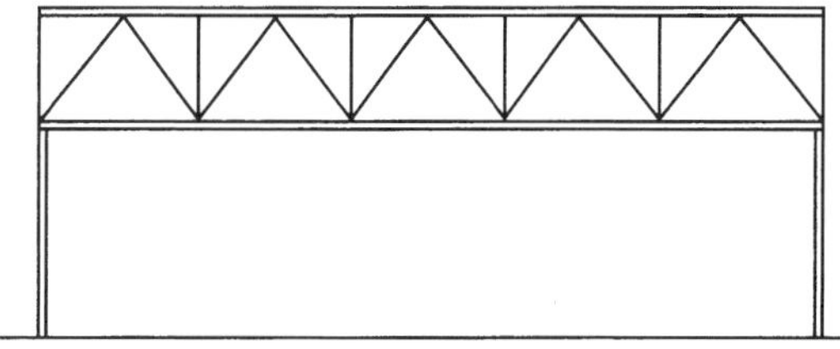

Figure 18.11 Offset Grid Space Frame

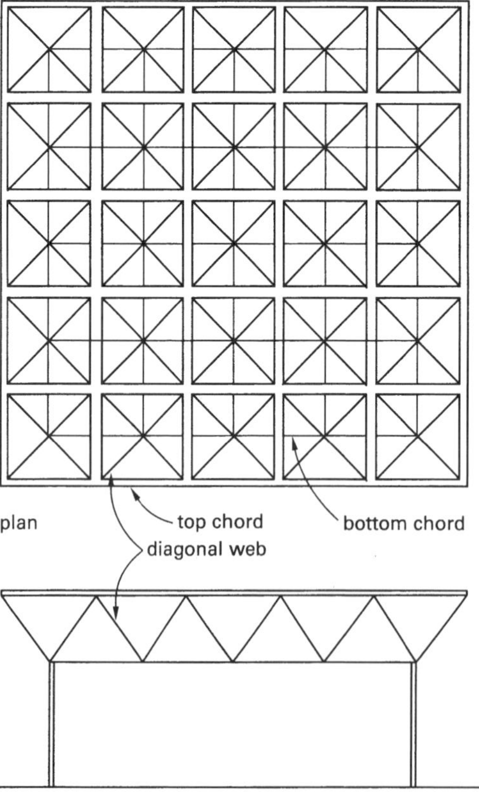

A more common type of space frame is the offset grid illustrated in Fig. 18.11. The top and bottom grids consist of identical squares, but the bottom one is offset from the top by one half grid. The two grids are connected with skewed diagonal members.

The module size of a space frame can be varied to suit the functional needs of the building and the structural limitations of the grid members. The depth of the grid can also be varied as necessary, but the most economical depth-to-module ratio is about 0.707. Of course, the larger the module size, the fewer the number of connections, which saves fabrication and erection time and money.

There are many types of connections. They may be formed of hollow or solid sections with tapped holes for screw attachment of the members. They may be bent plates to which the members are bolted or welded, or prefabricated units that are slipped over the spanning members. Whatever type is used, the connection must provide for attaching the supporting structure and for attaching the roofing and sidewall system to the primary frame. Some of the typical methods of support are shown in Fig. 18.12.

The supports for a space frame can be located at any node, but for greatest efficiency they are usually spaced symmetrically. Cantilevers of 15% to 30% of the span are possible and even desirable since less chord material is required.

Domes

Domes are one of the most efficient structural systems. This is because the shape of the structure itself helps resist loads placed on it primarily through compression and tension, and in the case of thin-shell structures, shear. There are three basic variations of domes: the *frame dome*, the *geodesic dome*, and the *thin-shell dome*.

The forces in all domes can be visualized by viewing a simple circular frame dome (see Fig. 18.13(a)). The meridian lines act as individual arches, transferring loads to the ground through compression. The meridians are supported laterally by the hoops, those lines running parallel to the horizontal.

For very shallow, or low-rise domes, the entire structure can be placed in compression, without any tensile stresses at all. The vertical load at the bottom of the dome must then be resisted by the ground or a foundation.

For high-rise domes (the most typical situation) when the dome is under a uniform load, such as from its own weight or from a snow load, each meridian tends to compress in the upper part of the dome and expand in the lower part. See Fig. 18.13(b). This deflection is held in check, however, by the hoops. But because of the deflection, the hoops in the upper part of the dome compress, and the hoops in the lower part are placed in tension. If there is sufficient hoop material at the base of the dome that can resist the tensile forces, the dome is self-supporting without the need for a foundation to carry the thrust. The foundation only needs to carry the vertical component of dead and live loads.

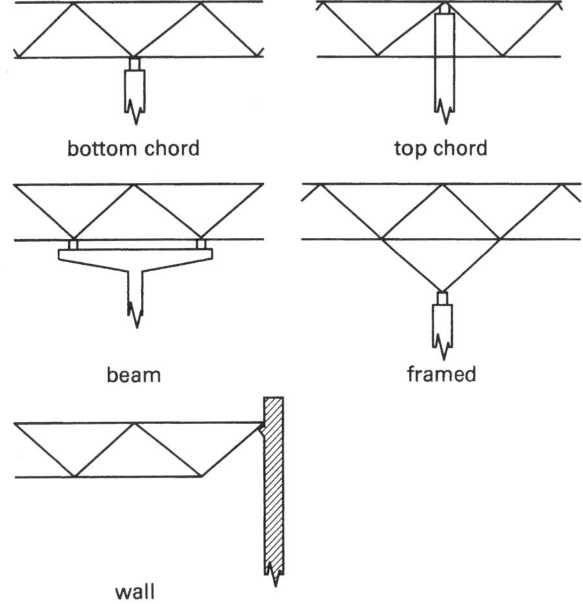

Figure 18.12 Methods of Space Frame Support

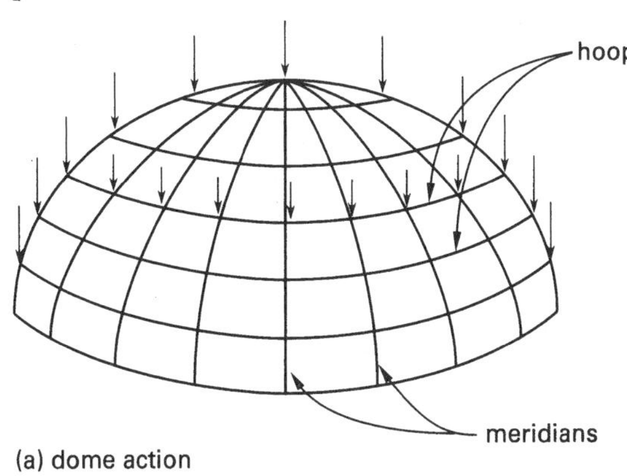

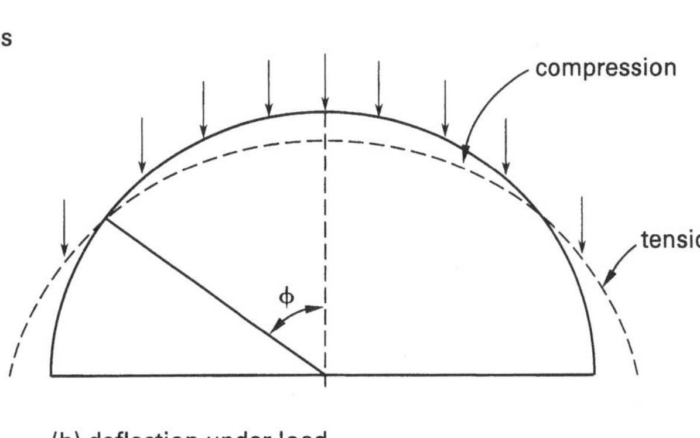

Figure 18.13 Dome Structural Behavior

The point at which the stresses change from compression to tension varies with the load. Under dead load the angle ϕ, as shown in Fig. 18.13(b), is about 52°; under snow load the angle is 45°.

As a consequence of all the stresses being in compression or tension, the strains are relatively small. This is why a dome is a very stiff structure with very little deflection.

There are several variations of the framed dome. All are approximations of a true dome because only straight members are used. One of the common types of framed domes is the *Schwedler dome* as shown in Fig. 18.14. The areas between the meridians and the hoops are braced with single or double diagonals and spanned with purlins or directly with the roofing.

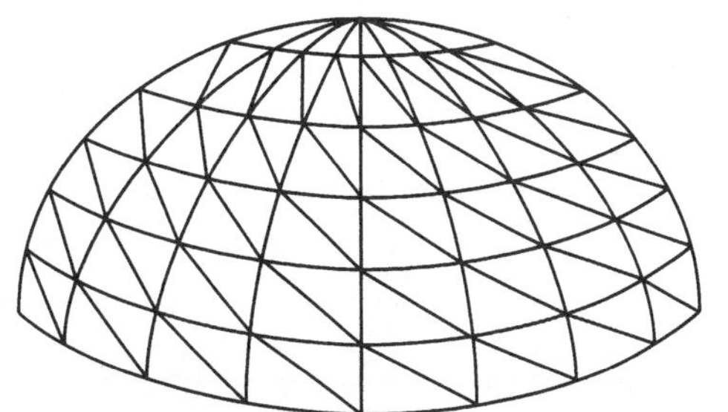

Figure 18.14 Schwedler Dome

Geodesic Domes

Geodesic domes, invented by Buckminster Fuller, are like space frames formed in the shape of a sphere. The grid of a geodesic dome is based on great circle arcs and is composed of spherical polyhedrons, usually formed of equilateral triangles. A geodesic dome can be constructed with a single or double layer of struts.

Geodesic domes are extremely strong, stiff, and lightweight, and they enclose the greatest volume with the least surface area. They can easily span 400 ft or more.

Figure 18.15
Thin-Shell Barrel Vault

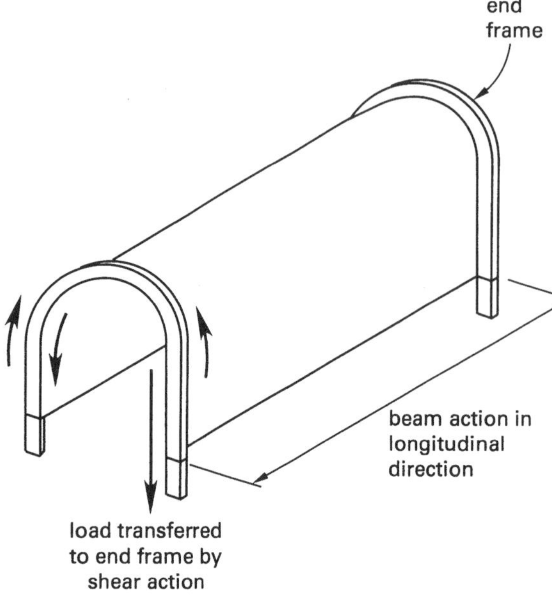

Thin-Shell Structures

Thin-shell structures are a class of form-resistant structures whose strength is a result of their ability to support loads through compression, tension, and shear in the plane of the shell because of their basic shape. The other broad category of form-resistant structure is the membrane, which can only support loads through tension. Membranes will be discussed in the next section.

Shells are classified as either singly curved or doubly curved. The most common example of a singly curved thin shell structure is the *barrel vault* as shown in Fig. 18.15. Barrel vaults with end frames act as curved beams, with the upper portion in compression and the lower portion in tension. Beam action carries the loads to the two ends where it is transferred by shear action to the end frames.

Figure 18.16
Types of Thin-Shell Surfaces

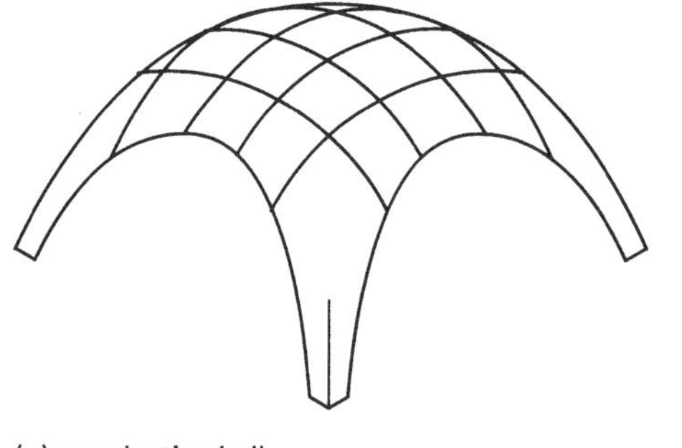

(a) synclastic shell

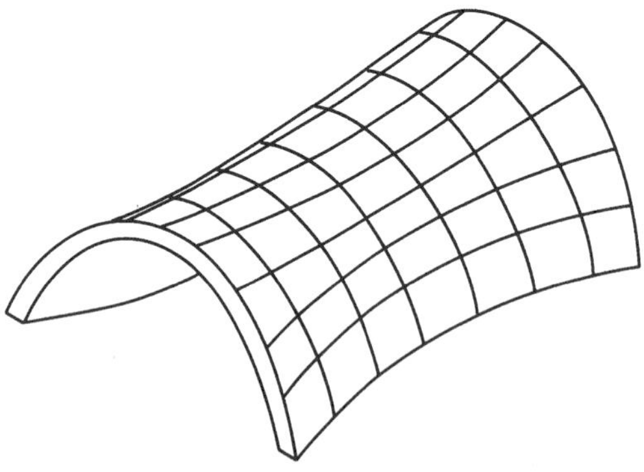

(b) anticlastic shell (hyperbolic paraboloid)

This structural condition is true only for a long barrel; that is, a barrel whose length is larger than its radius. It is also only true for a barrel supported by end frames and end supports. With such a barrel, there is a tendency for the longitudinal edges of the barrel to deform inward. This is usually counteracted by an adjacent vault or with longitudinal stiffeners. If a barrel vault is only supported by its longitudinal edges, arch action develops along with the corresponding thrust common to arches. If the shape of the barrel is not the funicular shape for the loads, some bending stresses will also be present. Such a barrel vault will have to be thicker than an end-supported vault to account for these additional loads.

A barrel vault shape with rounded hip ends can also be created with a *lamella roof*. This is a structure formed by two intersecting grids of parallel skewed arches covering a rectangular area. Lamella arches are very efficient because of the interaction between the beams of the two grids and because the short lengths of the beams near the corners have small spans, thus reducing the length of the span of the beams framed into them.

The second class of thin-shell structures is the doubly curved shell. There are two types of doubly curved shells. *Synclastic shells* are those with curves on the same side of the surface. *Anticlastic shells* are those with the main curves on opposite sides of the surface. See Fig. 18.16. A dome is an example of a synclastic shell, and a hyperbolic paraboloid is an anticlastic shell.

Thin-shell domes are very rigid and efficient structures. They are stable for either symmetric or asymmetric loads. In theory, they behave like the frame domes discussed in a previous section, but because they consist of one continuous surface, each infinitesimal portion is resisting compression, tension, and shear. See Fig. 18.17. Compression is acting in the lines of the meridian, and either tension or compression is acting in the hoop direction. Shear is therefore developed in any section to keep the structure in equilibrium.

Another common thin shell is the *hyperbolic paraboloid.* This anticlastic shell is formed by moving a vertical parabola with downward curvature along an upward curving parabola that is perpendicular to it. The resulting form is that shown in Fig. 18.16(b). The shape that a horizontal plane makes with the curve is a hyperbola.

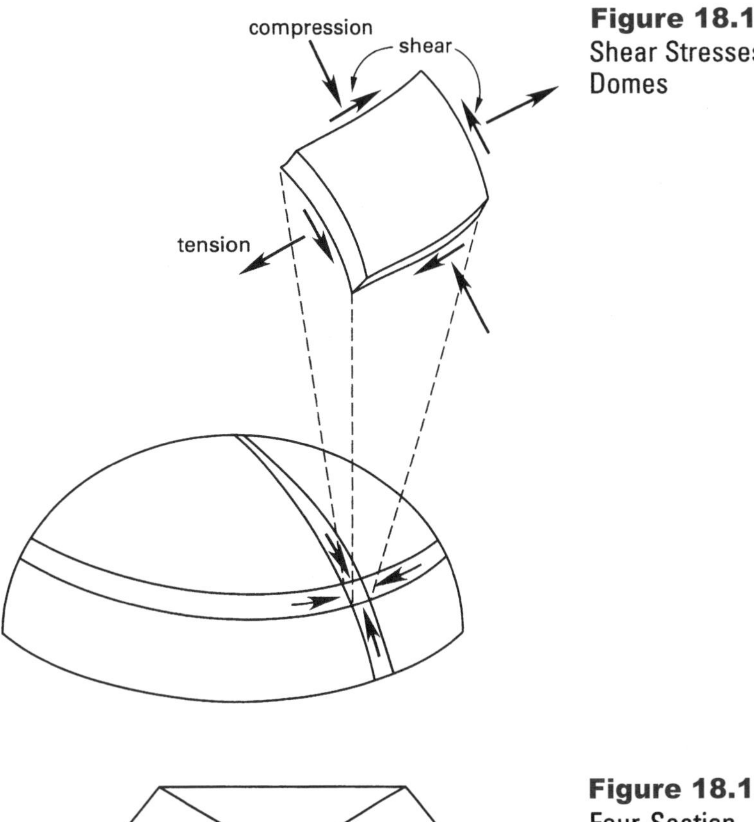

Figure 18.17
Shear Stresses in Domes

Hyperbolic paraboloids can also be formed by straight lines moving along two nonparallel lines. There are many variations of this method of generating these thin-shell forms, but one of the most common is shown in Fig. 18.18. This form is actually four separate hyperbolic paraboloids arranged to cover a square. In this form, the loads are resisted in the plane of the shell and transferred to the boundaries of the hyperbolic paraboloids, where they become compression forces in the edge stiffeners and are transmitted to the foundations. There is an outward thrust caused by this arch action that must be resisted by the tie rods or suitable foundations.

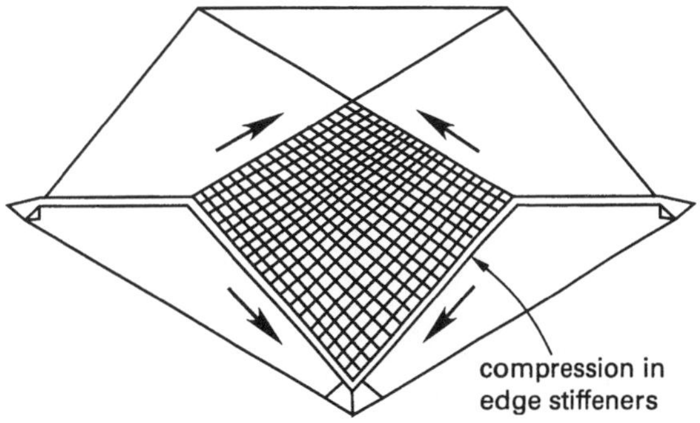

In most cases, thin shells can be made only a few inches thick and still be structurally stable, but the minimum thickness is usually determined by the space required for reinforcing steel, minimum cover distances over the steel, and a sufficient thickness to allow for placing the concrete by machine. Building codes also limit the minimum thickness in order to provide for possible bending moments that may be induced in the structure from concentrated loads.

compression in edge stiffeners

Figure 18.18
Four-Section Hyperbolic Paraboloid Roof

Although thin shells are very efficient in their minimal use of material and have great strength and stiffness, they are often not the structural system of choice in the United States because they are labor-intensive structures to construct. It is typically less expensive to pay for more, less-efficient structural material if it can be erected quickly with as little on-site labor as possible.

Membrane Structures

Membranes are the second class of form-resistant structures. Unlike shells, membranes can only resist loads in tension. As such, the membrane must be anchored between elements that can be placed in compression like the poles of a tent. Although membranes are very efficient in the amount of material they require, their biggest disadvantage is that they move and change shape in response to varying loads. They also flutter in the wind.

Figure 18.19
Membrane Structures

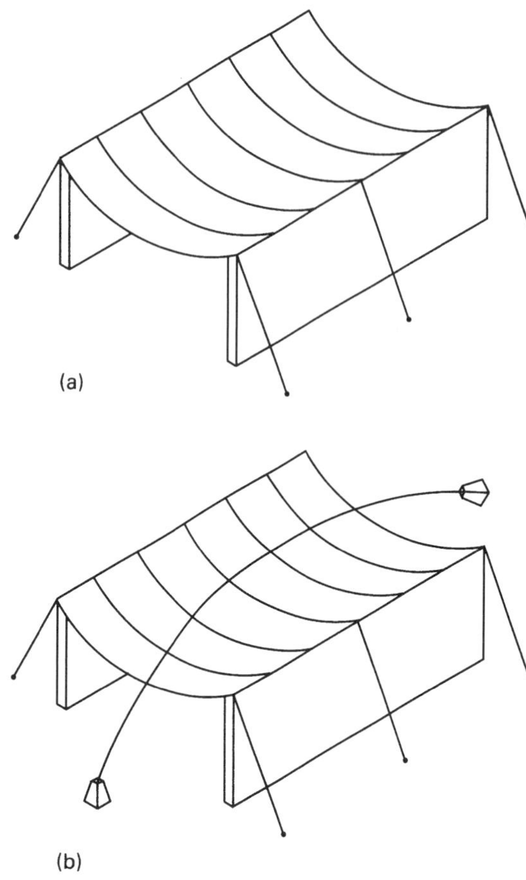

These problems can be counteracted to a great degree by prestressing the membrane with anticlastic shapes. Figure 18.19(a) shows a simple membrane draped between two horizontal supports. Fig. 18.19(b) shows the same configuration except that a cable perpendicular to the transverse drape has been pulled tightly over the membrane, resulting in a doubly curved surface. The resulting shape is much more stable.

Air-Supported Structures

Another form of the membrane structure is the air-supported or pneumatic roof. The membrane can still only support loads through tension but the membrane is held in place by air pressure rather than by cables and compression members. The simplest type of air-supported structure is the single membrane inflated like a balloon. Very little air pressure above the atmospheric air pressure is needed to keep a pneumatic structure inflated, but the interior does have to be kept closed to the outside.

Air-supported structures suffer from the same problems as other types of membrane roofs. Specifically, they are unstable under concentrated and varying loads and flutter in the wind. To minimize these problems, they must be stabilized. One way of doing this is to run cables over the top of the structure so that it is stiffened both from within by the pressure and on the outside by tension in the cables.

Other methods of stabilization include using a double skin structure inflated like a large pillow or with a large number of individual air pockets like an air mattress. These kinds of pneumatic structures also eliminate the need for air lock doors and the continuous pumping of air into the building to maintain the required pressure.

Figure 18.20
Folded Plate Structure

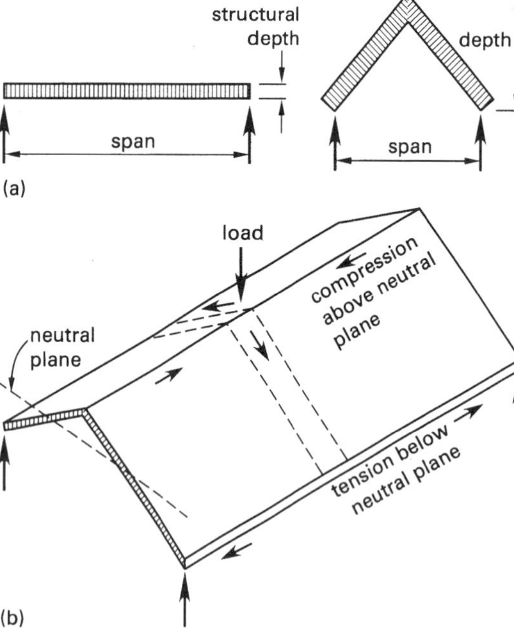

Folded Plates

A folded plate structure consists of thin slabs bent to increase the load-carrying capacity. A typical folded plate roof is illustrated in Fig. 11.11. Folded plate structures are stronger than simple horizontal flat plates because instead of having a structural depth just the thickness of the slab, the structural depth is as deep as the fold of the plate. Additionally, the span is much less, only the distance from one edge of the slab to the other. See Fig. 18.20(a).

Folded plates resist loads with a combination of slab action in the transverse direction and beam action in the longitudinal direction. However, as shown in Fig. 18.20(a), the slab only has to support loads within the distance from one fold to the next, and the load at the apex of each fold is divided into two components, half transferred to one plate and half to the other. In the longitudinal direction, the entire plate assembly acts as a beam with compressive stresses above the neutral plane and tensile stress below. See Fig. 18.20(b).

Folded plate structures can span up to about 100 ft in the longitudinal direction and about 25 ft to 35 ft between outer folds of each plate assembly. They are most commonly built of concrete but can be constructed of plywood, steel, or aluminum as well. One of their primary advantages is that the shapes are simple flat pieces so they can be prefabricated, or if cast in place, the formwork is easy to build.

Since the exterior slabs of any flat slab construction are more highly stressed than interior slabs, a short stiffening slab is usually placed at both edge boundaries to compensate for the additional stress.

Suspension Structures

Suspension structures are similar to membranes in that they can only resist loads by tension. However, this is also one of their great advantages since any given cross section of cable is uniformly stressed because no variable bending stresses can be developed. This results in the material being utilized to its fullest unit stress capability.

Because a cable structure is not inherently rigid, it assumes its funicular shape for any given set of loads. A simple cable supporting one load in midspan will assume a symmetrical triangular shape. If the load is shifted to one side, the shape of the cable changes.

In cable structures, the amount of tensile force is inversely related to the sag of the cable: the greater the sag, the less the tension in the cable. This can be visualized by examining two cables with different sags supporting the same amount of weight in the middle of the cable. See Fig. 18.21(a). If the load is weight P, each of the vertical components of the reaction must be one-half of the weight as dictated by the laws of equilibrium. However, the resultant of the vertical and horizontal forces acts in the direction opposite from the direction of the cable so a simple force polygon as discussed in Chap. 36 can be constructed.

For a cable with a small sag, the resultant (tension) and corresponding horizontal component are large. For a large sag, the resultant and horizontal component are small. In the extreme case of maximum sag, the cable would hang vertically and there would be no horizontal component.

Of course, as the sag increases, the tensile force and hence the amount of cable cross-sectional area required decreases, but the length of the cable increases. If the efficiency and cost of the structure is dependent on the amount of cable material, then there must be some optimum sag that balances cable length with cable cross section. For a cable supporting a single load in the middle, the ideal proportion is that the sag is one-half the span so that the cable is at a 45° angle.

Figure 18.21 Cable Structures

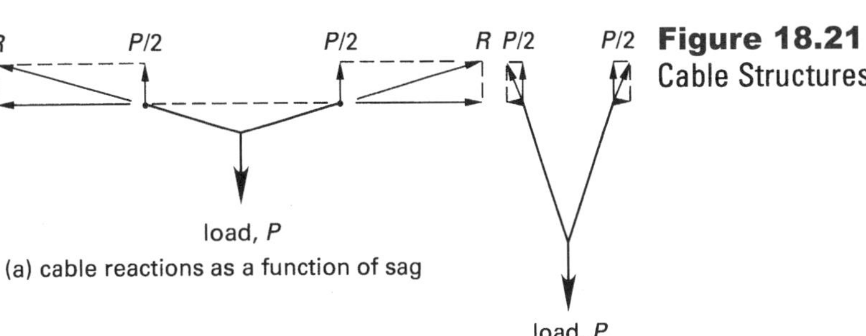

(a) cable reactions as a function of sag

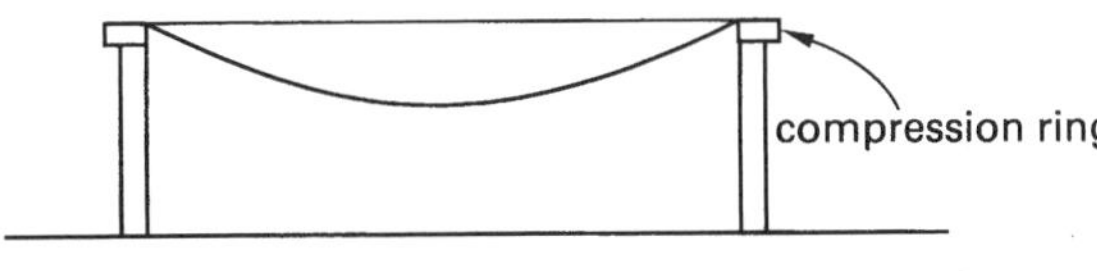

(b) circular cable suspension structure

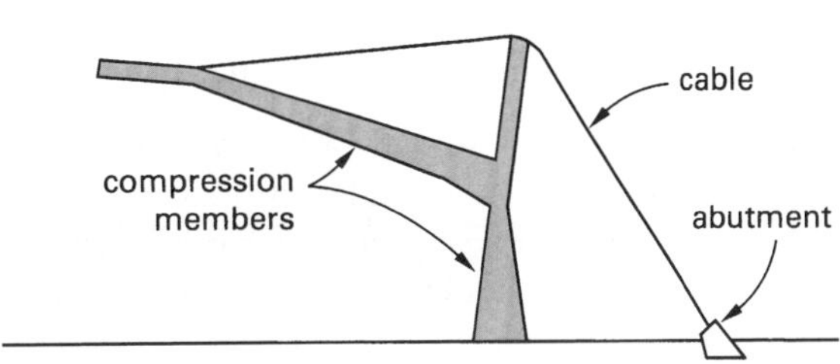

(c) one-way cable structure

In building situations, however, single concentrated loads are the exception. A cable structure supports uniform loads. There are two typical uniform loading conditions for cable structures: (1) where the load is uniformly applied on the horizontal projection of the cable and (2) the load is uniformly applied along the length of the cable. See Fig. 18.21(b) and (c). A uniform horizontal load results in the cable assuming the shape of a parabola, and a uniform load along the length of the cable (such as supporting its own weight) results in a catenary curve.

For these loading conditions, the optimum sag for a parabolic cable is three-tenths of the span, and for a catenary curve the optimum sag is one-third of the span. In practice, however, these sags are not achieved because the low sags would interfere with the function of the building.

For cable-supported structures, there must always be some way of balancing the tensile forces in the cable. This is done with compression members or by extending the cable across a support to a foundation that holds the cable in place, or with some combination of both.

For circular buildings, the tensile forces can be balanced with a continuous compression ring at the perimeter of the roof as shown in Fig. 18.21(b). If the building is not circular, the cable can be draped over a compression member and anchored to a massive foundation. See Fig. 18.21(c). Circular buildings with cable roofs pose a particular problem, however, because the lowest point of the roof for drainage is in the middle of the span.

Cable-suspended structures have the same problem as membrane structures. Because they can only resist loads in tension, they are inherently unstable in the wind and with concentrated loads or other types of changing loads. Sometimes the flexibility of the cable structure can be stabilized simply with the weight of the roof or other structure. More often, additional cables and a stiffening structure must be included.

Design and Selection Considerations

Many of the design considerations concerning one-way long span systems apply to two-way systems as well. There are, however, a few additional factors that must be taken into account.

Function

Most two-way systems are used exclusively for roofs because of their three-dimensional configuration. Two-way, long span systems are also used primarily for enclosing large, open, single-use spaces such as sports arenas and auditoriums. Therefore, the size and use of the building is the first consideration in deciding on the type of two-way system to use.

Additional functional considerations include provisions for drainage, insulation, and waterproofing. Of course, some shapes, such as domes, some thin-shell structures, and air-supported roofs, are well suited for positive drainage. Others, such as cable-suspended roofs with their low point in the center, membrane structures that drain toward the interior, and some folded plates that trap water in their folds, present definite problems.

Insulating a long span, two-way structure can be a problem since such structures are often selected because of their appearance and architectural drama, in addition to their ability to bridge large distances. Adding insulation to the interior may be difficult or impossible, or may mar the internal appearance. Placing insulation on the exterior may be equally difficult, especially if the shape is complex.

Waterproofing presents similar problems for some types of systems. Structures such as space frames, frame domes, and cable-suspended structures have many parts and facets, resulting in a large number of joints that are always difficult to waterproof easily. Other forms, such as domes and folded plates, can easily be covered with liquid-applied waterproofing membranes.

Cost and Economy

Most two-way structures are very efficient in their use of material and can easily span long distances. However, other factors mitigate these advantages. The most notable disadvantage with many two-way systems is the increased labor cost required for either their fabrication or erection, or both. A space frame is an example of one such framing type with a great number of connections. The problem can be minimized somewhat by using large module sizes, which reduces the number of connections. This means a lower labor cost and lower material costs for the nodes, which are usually the most expensive material part of a space frame.

Likewise, thin-shell structures are very efficient in material use, but are often prohibitively expensive to form because of all the complex curves and careful placement of concrete required.

Occasionally, some prefabrication of shells, folded plates, and space frames is possible to save money. Shot concrete can also be used to speed up concrete placement on thin shells.

For some two-way systems, the attachment of roofing and glazing to the structure may be uneconomical. For example, a geodesic dome must have provisions for attaching the nonstructural, somewhat flexible skin to the rigid framing members. Then, each joint between the panels must be sealed against the weather. For a large dome, this process can be very expensive.

Shipping

Shipping is less of a problem with two-way systems than it is with one-way systems, because most of the assembly is done on site. Components such as connectors and members of a geodesic dome, or the cable for a cable-suspended structure, can easily be shipped to the site.

Acoustics

Some shell configurations and membrane structures can focus sounds. If the use of the building requires a good acoustical environment, the choice of a two-way system should be carefully evaluated since adding acoustical control can be difficult and expensive to achieve.

Assembly and Erection

Since most of the construction of a two-way system is done on site, either by casting concrete or assembling small pieces, shipping large members to a job site or building in remote areas is usually not a problem. However, this advantage is often offset by the higher erection costs due to more labor components.

Technical Considerations

The technical considerations pertaining to one-way systems apply to two-way systems as well.

Preliminary Structural Systems

It is important to do a preliminary sizing of the structural system in the early design stage. This will make it much easier to integrate all systems effectively during the schematic design and design development stages.

The most common method of preliminary sizing is to calculate the depth-to-span ratio, because this can be done even if only the structural layout and the basic use of the system are known. and use this approach.

Many other variables can also affect the sizing of the structural system and should be considered as a part of the analysis. For instance, if the system will be supporting construction that is likely to be damaged by the normal deflections of some members, then the depths of these members should be increased to develop greater stiffness and reduce deflection. A simple approach for this condition would be to double the stiffness of those members. For a bending member, this would result in the following formula.

$$d = \sqrt[3]{2d_T^3} \tag{18.1}$$

In Eq. 18.1, d_T is the depth of the member as taken from a standard selection table, and d is the depth needed to double that member's bending stiffness. A member with depth d will exhibit one-half the deflection of the member with the tabulated depth d_T.

Table 18.3
Wood Structural Systems

system	depth-to-span ratio
sawn wood decking	1/36
sawn wood joists	1/16
sawn wood beams	1/14
sawn wood girders	1/12
glued laminated lumber	1/20
trussed wood joists	1/18
laminated veneer lumber	1/24

Table 18.4
Steel Structural Systems

system	depth-to-span ratio
formed steel/concrete deck	1/12
steel joists	1/20
steel joist girders	1/12
steel beams	1/20
steel girders	1/16
composite steel/concrete deck	1/18
composite steel beams	1/24
composite steel girders	1/20

Table 18.5
Concrete Structural Systems

system	depth-to-span ratio
reinforced concrete slabs	1/24
reinforced concrete joists*	1/20
reinforced concrete beams*	1/18
reinforced concrete girders*	1/16
reinforced concrete flat plates*	1/33
reinforced concrete flat slabs*	1/36
reinforced concrete waffle slabs*	1/24
prestressed concrete slabs*	1/33
prestressed concrete beams	1/25
prestressed concrete girders	1/20

*Members are part of a continuous system

Table 18.3, Table 18.4, and Table 18.5 summarize typical depth-to-span ratios for members used in several standard structural systems. These are typical, average values based on a variety of references; some references give single values, while others give a range. These three tables are organized by material—wood, steel, and concrete, respectively—and in some cases are further classified by use. These ratios are for floor systems, and they may be reduced by 15% when calculating the structural systems for roofs.

The depths given in these tables are for normal conditions and should be increased when necessary. They can also be decreased when conditions such as lighter loading exist.

19

FUNDAMENTALS OF LIGHTING AND ACOUSTICS

Nomenclature

a	coefficient of absorption	–
A	total acoustic absorption	sabins
c	velocity of sound	ft/sec
f	frequency	Hz
H	height	ft
I	sound intensity	W/cm^2
I_o	minimum sound intensity audible to human ear, 10^{-16}	W/cm^2
IL	sound intensity level	dB
L	length	ft
n	number of sources	–
r	radius, or distance from point source	ft
S	surface area	ft^2
t	coefficient of transmission	–
T	reverberation time	sec
TL	transmission loss	dB
V	room volume	ft^3
w	wavelength	ft

In addition to mecha ical, electrical, and plumbing systems, two additional specialty systems are critical in the design development phase of a project. These are lighting and acoustic systems. This chapter reviews the fundamentals of these topics, while Chap. 32 describes how to integrate these systems into a building design. Chapter 20 discusses conveying systems.

LIGHTING FUNDAMENTALS

Light and Vision

Light is defined as visually evaluated radiant energy. *Visible light* is a form of electromagnetic radiation with wavelengths that range from about 400 nm (10^{-9} m for violet light to about 700 nm for red light), a range known as the *visible spectrum.* White light is produced when a source emits approximately equal quantities of energy over the entire visible spectrum.

When light strikes a surface, it can be transmitted, reflected, or absorbed. If a material is transparent, such as window glass, most of the light is transmitted. The ratio of the total transmitted light to the total incident light is the *transmittance*, also called the *coefficient of transmission*, expressed as a percentage.

Clear glass has a transmittance of about 85%, while frosted glass has a transmittance of between 70% and 85%. The rest of the light is either reflected or absorbed. A material that allows the transmittance of light but not of a clear image is said to be *translucent.* In clear materials, light is *refracted,* or bent slightly, as it passes through the material. Refraction is the principle used to design lenses; light passing through a lens is bent toward the thicker part of the lens.

An opaque material allows no light to pass through, and all incident light is either reflected or absorbed. For example, a flat, black material absorbs most of the incident light. A white material reflects most of the incident light. The ratio of the total reflected light to the total incident light is the *reflectance* or *reflectance coefficient*; like transmittance, this is expressed as a percentage.

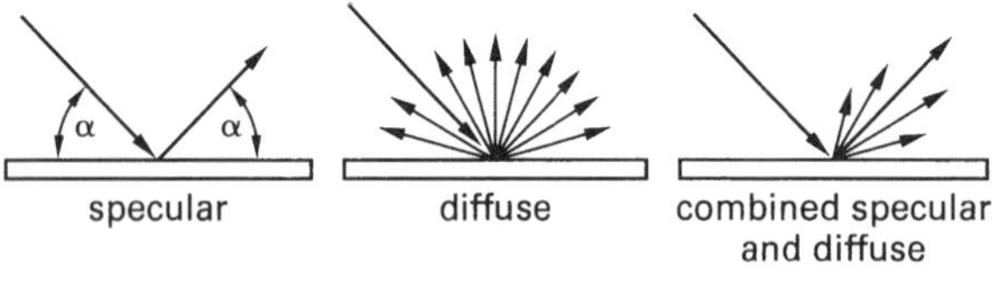

Figure 19.1 Light Reflections

How light is reflected depends on the finish of the material it is striking. As shown in Fig. 19.1, reflection can be specular, diffuse, or combined specular and diffuse. *Specular reflection* results from a smooth, polished surface such as a mirror. The angle of incidence equals the angle of reflection. *Diffuse reflection* results from a uniformly rough surface. The reflection appears uniformly bright, and the image of the source cannot be seen. *Combined specular and diffuse reflection* makes surfaces appear to be brighter at the point where the source is shining than in the surrounding areas.

Light is received through the eye and processed by the brain. In the process of seeing, light enters the eye through the pupil, as shown in Fig. 19.2. The amount of light entering the eye is controlled by the iris. The lens focuses the image (upside down) on the *retina*, where the light stimulates cells that send messages to the brain for interpretation.

The retina contains two types of cells: cones and rods. *Cones* are cone-shaped cells located near the fovea, or central portion of the retina. They are extremely sensitive to detail and color. However, they are only located within a 2° cone of vision around the line of sight.

The remainder of the retina is populated by rod-shaped cells. These *rods* are extremely sensitive to light and motion. However, rods are not as good as cones at discriminating color or detail. That is why, in dim light, people lose their sense of color vision; rods are responsible for night vision, and objects perceived by the rods appear in shades of gray.

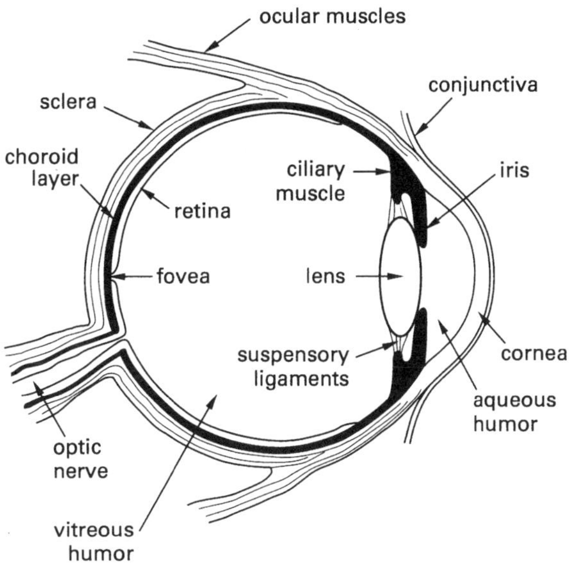

Figure 19.2 Human Eye

Measuring Light

Examinees should be familiar with the relationships between several illumination definitions. Figure 19.3 shows these units of light.

candlepower: The unit of luminous intensity approximately equal to the horizontal light output from an ordinary wax candle. In the SI system of measurement, this unit is the *candela.*

illuminance: The density of luminous flux incident on a surface, expressed in lumens per unit area. One lumen uniformly incident on 1 ft^2 of area produces an illuminance of 1 foot-candle (fc).

lumen: Abbreviated *lm.* The unit of luminous flux equal to the flux in a unit solid angle of 1 steradian from a uniform point source of 1 candlepower. On a unit sphere (1 ft radius), an area of 1 ft^2 will subtend an angle of 1 steradian. Because the area of a unit sphere is 4π, a source of 1 candlepower produces 12.57 lm.

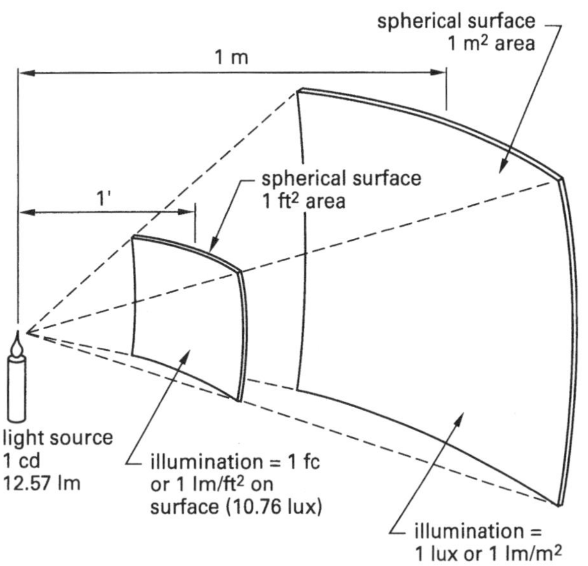

Figure 19.3 Relationship of Light Source and Illumination

luminance: The luminous flux per unit of projected (apparent) area and unit solid angle leaving a surface, either reflected or transmitted. The SI unit is the candela per square meter (cd/m^2), also called the *nit.* In the customary U.S. system, the unit is the *footlambert* (fL), where 1 fL is $1/\pi$ candlepower per square foot. Luminance takes into account the reflectance and transmittance properties of materials and the directions in which they are viewed. Thus, 100 lux striking a 1 m^2 surface with 50% reflectance would result in a luminance of 50 candelas per square meter. In U.S. units, 100 fc striking a surface with 50% reflectance would result in a luminance of 50 fL. Luminance is sometimes called *brightness,* although brightness includes the physiological sensation of the adaptation of the eye, whereas luminance is the measurable state of object luminosity.

Luminous intensity: The solid angular flux density in a given direction measured in candlepower or candelas.

Light Levels

Different visual tasks performed under different conditions need different levels of illumination. Proper illumination is determined by the nature of the task itself, the age of the person performing the task, the reflectances of the surfaces in the room, and the demand for speed and accuracy in performing the task.

The Illuminating Engineering Society of North America (IESNA) has established a method for determining a range of illumination levels appropriate to particular design conditions and for different age ranges. Various areas and activities are each assigned an illuminance category, and these categories are used along with other factors to establish the recommended task and background illuminances.

The basic illuminance targets are based on the assumption that the observers are between the ages of 25 and 65. If it is known that more than 50% of the population using the proposed lighting system is older than 65, the recommended illuminance is doubled. If it is known that more than 50% of the population is younger than 25, then the recommended illuminance is halved.

The illumination level needed for an individual task, room, or area must be balanced with energy conservation needs. ASHRAE/IESNA Standard 90.1 and other energy conservation codes and standards set a maximum limit on the total power that may be used for lighting a building or space. This limit is given in units of watts per square foot and is based on the type of building or individual space. It takes careful design and the use of high-efficacy lamps and luminaires to light the building or space effectively while staying under the limit. Refer to Chap. 32 for a discussion of lighting power densities.

Design Considerations

Good lighting design involves providing not just the proper quantity of light needed to perform a task, but the proper quality of light as well. Important considerations are glare, contrast, uniformity, and color.

Glare

There are two types of *glare:* direct and reflected. *Direct glare* results when a light source in the field of vision causes discomfort and interference with the visual task. Not all visible light sources cause direct glare problems. The extent of the problem depends on the brightness of the source, its position, the background illumination, and the adaptation of the eye to the environment.

The *visual comfort probability* (VCP) is a metric used in evaluating the problem of direct glare. The VCP is the percentage of normal observers who may be expected to experience visual comfort in a particular environment with a particular lighting situation. Many manufacturers publish VCP ratings for their light fixtures when the fixture is used under defined conditions.

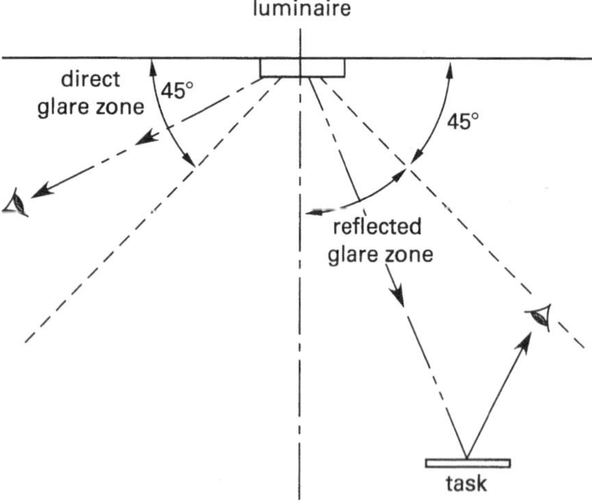

Figure 19.4
Glare Zones

For most situations, the critical zone for direct glare is in the area above a 45° angle from the light source. See Fig. 19.4. This is because the field of vision (when looking straight ahead) includes an area approximately 45° above a horizontal line. Many direct glare problems can be solved by using a luminaire with a 45° cutoff angle or by moving the offending luminaire out of the field of view.

Reflected glare occurs when a light source is reflected from a viewed surface into the eye. If it interferes with the viewing task, it is also called *veiling reflection.* The effect of reflected glare is to decrease the contrast between the task and its background. For example, a strong light on paper with pencil writing can bounce off the relatively reflective graphite, making it almost as bright as the paper and effectively obscuring the writing.

A veiling reflection is a complex interaction of light source and brightness, position of the task, reflectivity of the task, and position of the eye. One of the simplest ways to correct a veiling reflection is to adjust the position of the task or the light source. Because the angle of incidence is equal to the angle of reflection, this can be calculated if the exact use of a room and its furniture arrangement are known. Another approach is to provide general background illumination and specific task lighting, the position of which can be controlled by the user.

Contrast

Contrast is the difference in illumination level between a given point and nearby points. Because contrast is the means by which people see, it is vital to the quality of an environment. A printed word on a page is only visible because the ink contrasts with the brightness of the surrounding paper. However, too much contrast can be detrimental. The eye adapts by opening and closing the iris, which causes eye strain and fatigue. For example, it is difficult to see fine detail on a small, dark object when the object is viewed against a bright background because the eye has adapted to the brighter background (i.e., the iris of the eye is smaller) and cannot admit enough light to see the darker object.

In most situations, brightness ratios should be limited to 3:1 between the task and adjacent surroundings, to 5:1 between the task and more remote darker surfaces, and to 1:10 between the task and more remote lighter surfaces.

Uniformity

Uniformity of lighting affects a person's perception of a space as being comfortable and pleasant. Complete uniformity of lighting is usually not desirable, except for certain detail-oriented tasks such as drafting or machine shop work. Because people see by contrast, some amount of shade and shadow provides highlight and interest to a space.

Color

Color in lighting is an interaction between the color of the light source (lamp or daylighting) and the colors of the objects that reflect the light. Color in lighting is a complex subject, but color has a tremendous effect on people's comfort and impressions of an environment. For example, most people think of reds and yellows as "warm" colors and greens and blues as "cool" colors. Light also can be characterized as "warm" or "cool."

Colors of light sources and the use of color in lighting design are discussed in Chap. 32. See Chap. 29 for a discussion of color systems.

LIGHT SOURCES

In addition to daylight, there are four primary types of light sources.

- incandescent lamps
- fluorescent lamps
- high-intensity discharge (HID) lamps
- light-emitting diodes (LED)

The best type of light source for a given space can depend on the color rendition characteristics, initial cost, operating cost, efficacy, size, operating life, and ability to control output from a luminaire.

Efficacy is the ratio of luminous flux emitted to the total power input to the source and is measured in lumens per watt. It is an important measure of the energy efficiency of a light source. The amount of heat generated by a light source is also an important selection consideration, because waste heat from lighting systems usually needs to be removed or compensated for with the air conditioning system, which can add to the total energy load of a building.

Some characteristics of common light sources are given in Table 19.1.

Table 19.1 Characteristics of Common Light Sources

lamp description	efficacy (lm/W)	color temperature (K)	CRI	approx. lamp life (h)
incandescent	5–20	2700–2800	100	750–4000
tungsten-halogen	18–22	300–3100	100	1000–4000
fluorescent (T12 and T8)	65–105	2700–7500	55–98	6000–24,000
fluorescent (T5)	95–105	3000–4100	75–95	6000–16,000
compact fluorescent	25–48	2700–4100	82	10,000
mercury-vapor	20–60	5500–5900	15–52	14,000–25,000
metal-halide	35–95	3200–4300	65–85	5000–20,000
ceramic metal-halide	80–100	3000–4100	80–90	15,000
high-pressure sodium	80–140	1800–2800	22–70	10,000–24,000
GU-24	40–70	varies	84	10,000–30,000
LED	80–150+*	varies	varies	10,000–50,000

Note: The values listed in the table are approximate and representative only. Individual manufacturers and lamps may provide different values.

*Values for the efficacy of LEDs are difficult to compare with other sources because as yet there are no industry standard test procedures for rating the luminous flux of LED devices and arrays. Values are also expected to increase rapidly as improvements in LEDs take place.

Figure 19.5 Incandescent Lamp Shapes

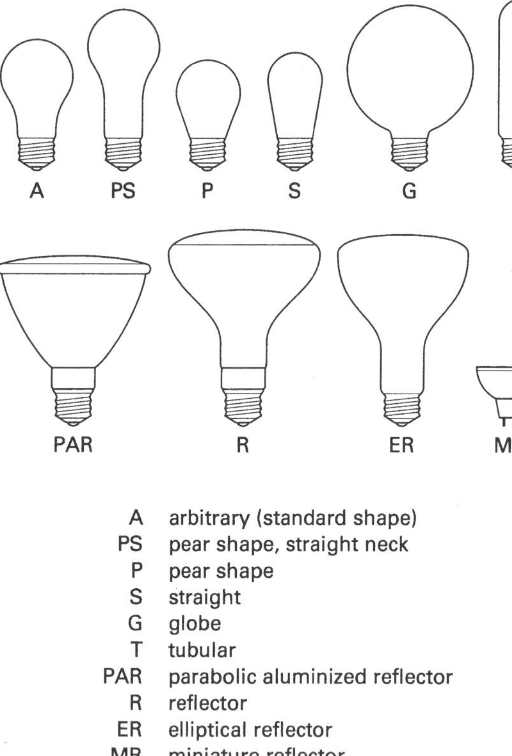

A arbitrary (standard shape)
PS pear shape, straight neck
P pear shape
S straight
G globe
T tubular
PAR parabolic aluminized reflector
R reflector
ER elliptical reflector
MR miniature reflector

The Energy Policy Act (EPAct) of 1992 set minimum energy efficiency standards for incandescent and fluorescent light sources. As a result, some types of incandescent and fluorescent lamps that have traditionally been used in architectural applications are no longer manufactured in or imported into the United States; the rest must satisfy EPAct requirements for minimum lumens per watt.

Incandescent Lamps

An *incandescent lamp* consists of a tungsten filament placed within a sealed glass bulb containing an inert gas. When electricity passes through the lamp, the filament glows, producing light. Incandescent lamps are produced in a wide variety of shapes, sizes, and wattages for different applications. Some of the more common shapes are shown in Fig. 19.5.

A typical designation of an incandescent lamp is a letter followed by a number; the letter indicates the shape or type, and the number indicates the size of the bulb at its widest point, in eighths of an inch. For example, an A-21 bulb has the standard arbitrary shape and the diameter of the bulb at its widest point is $^{21}/_8$ in ($2^5/_8$ in).

Incandescent lamps are inexpensive, compact, easy to dim, can be repeatedly started without a decrease in lamp life, and have a warm color rendition. In addition, their light output can be easily controlled with reflectors and lenses. Their disadvantages include low efficacy, short lamp life, and high heat output. The combination of low efficacy and heat production makes incandescent lamps undesirable for large, energy-efficient installations. For example, a standard 150 W lamp produces less than 20 lumens per watt, whereas a 40 W cool white fluorescent lamp has an efficacy of about 80 lm/W with much less heat output.

Another type of incandescent lamp is the *tungsten halogen lamp*. Light is produced by the incandescence of the filament, but there is a small amount of a halogen, such as iodine or bromine, in the bulb with the inert gas. Through a recurring cycle, part of the tungsten filament is burned off as the lamp operates, but it mixes with the halogen and is redeposited on the filament instead of on the wall of the bulb as in standard incandescent lamps. This results in longer bulb life, low lumen depreciation over the life of the bulb, and a more uniform light color. Because the filament burns under higher pressure and temperature, the bulb is made from quartz and is much smaller than a standard incandescent lamp. Halogen lamps are often referred to as *quartz-halogen lamps.* Both standard-voltage (120 V) and low-voltage tungsten-halogen lamps are available.

Tungsten-halogen lamps are compact and have a greater efficacy than standard incandescent lamps. Their higher operating temperature produces more light in the blue end of the spectrum, resulting in a light that looks whiter.

However, because these lamps operate at high temperatures and pressures, a failure results in explosive shattering of the lamp. For this reason, halogen lamps are usually enclosed in another bulb or are covered with a piece of glass or a screen.

Reflector lamps (*R lamps*) and *parabolic aluminized reflector lamps* (*PAR lamps*) contain a reflective coating built into the lamp. This increases the efficiency of the lamp and allows more precise beam control. Both are available in *flood* (wide) and *narrow* (spot) beam dispersal patterns. PAR lamps are made with heavier glass and are also suitable for outdoor use.

Elliptical reflector lamps (*ER lamps*) are an improved version of R lamps. They provide a more efficient throw of light from a fixture by focusing the light beam at a point slightly in front of the lamp before it spreads out. The spread of an ER lamp is slightly smaller than that of an R lamp. This design is used for downlights with deep baffles or with small openings, so that less of the light's output is trapped in the fixture.

Low-voltage miniature reflector lamps (*MR lamps*) are small tungsten-halogen lamps that are available in a variety of wattages (20 W to 75 W) and beam spreads. The regenerative halogen cycle provides consistently high output and a lamp life of 2000 to 3000 hours. Typical color temperatures range from 2000K to 3400K, which makes many of them whiter than standard incandescent lights. MR lamps are available as MR-11 and MR-16. MR-16 lamps are also available for use in 120 V circuits where they can be screwed directly into a socket without the need for a transformer.

Effective October 31, 1995, EPAct prohibits the manufacture or importation of several types of incandescent lamps that do not meet minimum energy standards. These include all medium-base PAR and R lamps of 40 W and higher. Production of 100 W bulbs ended in 2012, followed by production of 75 W bulbs. Production of 40 W and 60 W bulbs ended in 2014. In place of these, some types of ER lamps and lower-wattage lamps can be used. Low-voltage and tungsten-halogen lamps can also be used in place of the old lamps. Incandescent bulbs are still available for purchase until stock runs out, but most homeowners will need to switch to more energy efficient lamp types.

Fluorescent Lamps

Fluorescent lamps contain a mixture of an inert gas and low-pressure mercury vapor. When a fluorescent lamp is energized, a mercury arc is formed that creates ultraviolet light. This invisible light, in turn, strikes the phosphor-coated bulb, causing the bulb to fluoresce and produce visible light.

Fluorescent lamps have a high efficacy (about 80 lm/W), relatively low initial cost, and long life. They are available in many color temperatures, ranging from a "cool" FL/D (daylight) lamp of 6500K color temperature to a WWD (warm white deluxe) with a color temperature of 2800K, which has a large percentage of red in its spectral output. They can also be dimmed, although fluorescent lamp dimmers are more expensive than their incandescent counterparts. Because fluorescent lamps are larger than incandescent lamps, it is more difficult to control them precisely, so they are usually more suitable for general illumination. However, with the development of the smaller and brighter *compact fluorescent lamp* (CFL), several manufacturers produce downlights with reflector designs for compact fluorescent lamps that can replace traditional incandescent downlights.

There are three types of fluorescent lamps.

- *Preheat lamps* do not carry a current unless in operation and will not begin luminescing until the cathode has reached operating temperature. Preheat lamps have been supplanted by rapid-start types.
- *Rapid-start lamps* maintain a constant low current in the cathode that allows them to start within about 2 seconds.
- *Instant-start lamps* maintain a constant voltage high enough to start the arc in the tube directly without preheating the cathode.

Every gaseous discharge lamp, including a fluorescent lamp, has a *ballast.* This is a device that supplies the proper starting and operating voltages to the lamp and limits the current once the lamp has started. There are several types of ballasts.

- *Magnetic ballasts* are constructed from laminated steel plates wrapped with copper windings. They operate at 60 Hz. Magnetic ballasts are considered obsolete, but they may still be found in older luminaires.
- *Electronic ballasts* are solid-state electronics that operate at much higher frequencies (from 25 kHz to 60 kHz) and use much less power than the older magnetic ballasts. In addition, electronic ballasts operate without noise or flicker, generate less heat, and can allow dimming over a continuous range of levels from 1% to 100%.
- *Multilevel ballasts*, either two-level or three-level, are used to change lighting levels evenly to conserve energy.
- *Energy-saving ballasts* reduce the total wattage of the lamp-ballast combination by using a lower current, by efficient design of the ballast, and by disconnecting the lamp filaments after the lamp starts.

Other types of ballasts include *low-current* and *high-current* ballasts designed to be matched with specific lamp types.

All ballasts are rated for efficiency according to one or more factors.

- *ballast factor* (BF): The ratio of the light output of a lamp when operated on a tested ballast to the light output when the lamp is operated by a standard reference (or "perfect") ballast according to a standard testing procedure. Although the ballast factor is not a measure of energy efficiency, matching a ballast factor with a particular lamp for a particular application can reduce energy usage.
- *ballast efficacy factor* (BEF): The ratio of the ballast factor multiplied by 100 (for example, a 0.75 ballast factor would be 75 as used in the ratio) to the power in watts. The BEF gives a way to compare the efficacy of different ballasts when used with the same kind and number of lamps, even when the wattages used by the different lamp-ballast combinations are different. The BEF does not give a valid comparison, however, when comparing different kinds or different numbers of lamps.
- *power factor:* How effectively the ballast converts supplied power into usable power (watts) for the lamps. In most cases, ballasts with higher power factors cost more but are more energy efficient. A power factor of 0.90 or above is considered to be high. A power factor corrected ballast has a power factor from 0.80 to 0.90.

Some electronic ballasts and all magnetic ballasts produce noise. Ballasts are rated for noise using letters from A to F. An A-rated (or Class A) ballast is the quietest and is appropriate for spaces with the lowest ambient noise levels. Most electronic ballasts are Class A. A Class F ballast is suitable only for noisy environments.

Fluorescent lamps are produced in tubular shapes. They are normally straight, but U-shaped and circular lamps are also produced. They are designated according to their type, wattage, diameter, color, and method of starting. Like incandescent lamps, size is designated in eighths of an inch. For example,

F40T12WW/RS describes a fluorescent lamp (F), 40 W (40), tubular (T), $^{12}/_{8}$ in in diameter (12), warm white color (WW), with a rapid start (RS) circuit.

Fluorescent lamps come in several lengths; 4 ft is the most common, but 2 ft, 3 ft, and 8 ft lengths are also available, as well as special U-shaped sizes. Compact fluorescent lamps have either a T-4 or T-5 glass envelope bent into a U-shape, double U-shape, or in a spiral form and mounted on a special base that houses the ballast and allows the lamp to be screwed into existing incandescent luminaires. Other CFLs require luminaires specifically designed for them.

The *ENERGY STAR Program Requirements for Residential Light Fixtures* require that residential lighting fixtures seeking the ENERGY STAR label do not use the standard Edison screw base. A GU-24 lamp is a high-efficacy compact fluorescent with a two-pin base that makes it impossible to use any other type of lamp in a GU-24 luminaire. The GU-24 socket and base system is designed to replace the standard Edison screw base, and it is becoming the most common type of energy-efficient lamp. It is available in a spiral CFL shape and a spiral squat version and is intended for use in 120 V or 277 V circuits. Several color temperatures are available with a CRI of 80 or higher. GU-24 lamps have efficacies from 40 lm/W to 70 lm/W, depending on wattage and the specific manufacturer. Rated lamp life ranges from 10,000 hours to 30,000 hours.

The EPAct prohibits the manufacture or importation of several types of fluorescent lamps that do not meet minimum energy standards. These include the standard F40T12 lamp, U-shaped lamps, and other full-wattage lamps. The F40T12 lamp has been replaced with the F32T8, which has a higher efficacy and better color rendering than the F40T12. However, it requires an electronic ballast, so retrofitted T-12 fixtures must include the ballast along with replacement lamps. T-8 fixtures also include triphosphor coatings, which give the lamps improved color rendering.

High-Intensity Discharge Lamps

High-intensity discharge lamps (*HID lamps*) include mercury vapor, metal halide, and high- and low-pressure sodium. In a *mercury vapor lamp*, an electric arc is passed through high-pressure mercury vapor, which produces both ultraviolet light and visible light, primarily in the blue-green band. For improved color rendition, various phosphors can be applied to the inside of the lamp to produce more light in the yellow and red bands. Mercury lamps have a moderately high efficacy, in the range of 30 lm/W to 50 lm/W, depending on the voltage and type of color correction used.

A *metal halide lamp* is similar to a mercury lamp except that a combination of metal halides has been added to the arc tube. This increases the efficacy and improves the color rendition, but also shortens the life of the lamp. Among the HID lamps, metal halide lamps provide the best combination of features for many purposes. They have color rendering indexes between 60 and 90, high efficacy, and relatively long life. The main disadvantage of a metal halide lamp is that its apparent color temperature shifts significantly over its life. (See Chap. 32 for a discussion of color temperature.)

Like all HID lamps, a metal halide lamp has an outer bulb to protect the arc tube and to protect people from dangerous ultraviolet light. There are three types of outer bulbs.

- *Clear bulbs* are used when optical control is required.
- *Phosphor-coated bulbs* are used for better color rendition.
- *Diffuse bulbs* are specified in recessed downlight fixtures installed in low ceilings.

A newer type of metal halide lamp is the *ceramic metal halide lamp* (*CMH lamp*). A CMH lamp uses a ceramic arc tube rather than a quartz tube, which allows the lamp to burn at a higher temperature, improving color rendition and light control. The efficacy of CMH lamps is better than the older metal halide lamps, and there is better color consistency over the lamp's lifetime. Disadvantages of CMH lamps include higher initial costs, difficulty in dimming, and the need for a ballast. They are useful in spaces with high ceilings where long life and high efficacy are desirable, and in retail uses where point source control and excellent color rendition are needed.

A *high-pressure sodium lamp* (*HPS lamp*) produces light by passing an electric arc through hot sodium vapor. The arc tube must be made of a special ceramic material to resist attack by the hot sodium. HPS lamps have efficacies from 80 lm/W to 140 lm/W, making them among the most efficient lamps available. They also have extremely long lives, about 10,000 hours for the improved-color lamps and up to 24,000 hours for other types. Unfortunately, standard HPS lamps produce very yellow light. However, HPS lamps are also available with color correction, and their color rendition is acceptable for some interior applications. It is possible to get HPS lamps with color rendering indexes of up to 70.

Low-pressure sodium lamps (*LPS lamps*) have even higher efficacies, about 150 lm/W, but they produce monochromatic light of a deep yellow color. Therefore, they are suitable only when color rendition is not important, such as for street lighting.

All HID lamps need time to restart after being shut off or in case of a power failure. The lamp must cool first and then warm up again. Mercury-vapor lamps need about 3 min to 10 min to relight, metal halide lamps need about 10 min to 20 min, and HPS lamps need about 1 min.

Light-Emitting Diodes (LEDs)

A *light-emitting diode* (LED) is a semiconductor device that uses solid-state electronics to create light. The basic unit of an LED is the *LED package*, which is combined with other packages into a lamp and then into an entire LED luminaire. LEDs are a class of solid-state lighting that also includes *organic light-emitting diodes* (OLEDs) and *polymer light-emitting diodes* (PLEDs).

LEDs have been used for many years as indicator panel lights and in other small electronic devices. More recently, it has become common to use LEDs in traffic signal lights, signage lights, outdoor decorative lighting, railroad and automotive applications, and general building lighting as well as outdoor applications.

The advantages of LED lamps include brightness, long life, a lack of heat production, and low power consumption. Lamp life ranges from 50,000 hours to 100,000 hours. LEDs can be directly controlled by a digital interface. They can be manufactured to produce a number of colors or white light. Their main disadvantages have been their low efficacy (lumens per watt) and high cost. However, as the technology improves, LEDs are being used in an increasing number of architectural and interior design applications. LED lighting is commonly used for decorative purposes, exit lights, emergency lighting, and anywhere a life-cycle cost analysis shows that their low power consumption and long life justifies the higher initial cost.

Recent developments in the technology have produced luminaires with efficacies averaging 80 lm/W to 100 lm/W, with some as high as 120 lm/W. The U.S. Department of Energy has established a target efficacy of LED luminaires exceeding 150 lm/W, which may be reached by 2020. LED luminaires are available in a variety of configurations, including reflector lamps, downlights, outdoor lights, undercounter lights, 2 ft × 2 ft and 2 ft × 4 ft luminaires designed to replace standard fluorescent recessed troffers. As their efficacy improves and their cost decreases, LEDs are rapidly replacing CFLs and many types of incandescent lamps.

Other Light Sources

In addition to the four common types of lamps, there are neon lamps, cold-cathode lamps, and fiber optic luminaires.

Neon lamps are glass tubes filled with gas that can be formed into an unlimited number of shapes. These can be used for signs and specialty accent lighting. By varying the gases within the tube, a variety of colors can be produced.

Cold-cathode lamps are similar to neon in that they can be produced in long runs of thin tubing and bent to shape, but they have a higher efficacy, are slightly larger (with about a 1 in diameter), and can produce several shades of white as well as many colors.

A *fiber optic luminaire* carries light from a remote light source to the area or object to be illuminated. Bundled optical fibers deliver light to the ends of the fibers with little or no loss. A *fiber optic system* is often used where ultraviolet radiation and heat must be kept away from the illuminated object, such as in a museum display of delicate objects. Other uses include lighting swimming pools, spas, storage areas for highly flammable materials, other areas where electrical wiring could be a hazard, and bringing light to hard-to-reach areas while locating the light source where it can be easily accessed for maintenance.

FUNDAMENTALS OF ACOUSTICS

Definitions

amplification: The increased intensity of sound by mechanical or electrical means.

articulation index: A measure of speech intelligibility calculated from the number of words read from a selected list that are understood by an audience. A low articulation index (less than 0.15) is desirable for speech privacy, whereas a high articulation index (above 0.6) is desirable for good communication.

attenuation: The reduction of sound.

decibel: 10 times the common logarithm of the ratio of a quantity to a reference quantity of the same kind, such as power, intensity, or energy density. It is most often used as the unit of sound intensity.

dBA: Unit of sound intensity that is weighted to account for the response of the human ear to various frequencies.

frequency: The number of pressure fluctuations or cycles occurring in 1 sec, expressed in hertz.

hertz (Hz): A unit of frequency equal to one cycle per second. Equipment manufactured before the 1960s may list specifications in cycles per second (cps) or just "cycles" rather than in hertz.

impact insulation class (IIC): A single-number rating of a floor-ceiling assembly's impact sound transmission performance at various frequencies.

intensity: The amount of sound energy per second across a unit area.

intensity level: 10 times the common logarithm of the ratio of a sound intensity to a reference intensity. See *decibel.*

noise: Any unwanted sound.

noise criteria (NC): A set of single-number ratings of acceptable background noise corresponding to a set of curves specifying sound pressure levels across octave bands. Noise criteria curves can be used to specify continuous background noise, achieve sound isolation, and evaluate existing noise situations.

noise isolation class (NIC): A single-number rating of noise reduction.

noise reduction (NR): The arithmetic difference, in decibels, between the intensity levels in two rooms separated by a barrier of a given transmission loss. Noise reduction is dependent on the transmission loss of the barrier, the area of the barrier, and the absorption of the surfaces of the receiving room.

noise reduction coefficient (NRC): The average sound absorption coefficient to the nearest 0.05, measured at the four one-third octave band center frequencies of 250 Hz, 500 Hz, 1000 Hz, and 2000 Hz.

octave band: A range of frequencies in which the upper frequency is twice that of the lower frequency.

phon: A unit of loudness level of a sound equal to the sound pressure level of a 1000 Hz tone judged to be equally loud.

reverberation: The persistence of a sound in a room after the source has stopped producing the sound.

reverberation time: The time it takes the sound level to decrease 60 dB after the source has stopped producing the sound.

sabin: The unit of absorption. Theoretically, 1 ft^2 of surface has an absorption coefficient of 1.0.

sabin formula: The formula that relates reverberation time to a room's volume and total acoustical absorption.

Project Planning

sound: A small compressional disturbance of equilibrium in an elastic medium, which causes the sensation of hearing.

sound absorption coefficient: The ratio of the sound intensity absorbed by a material to the total intensity reaching the material. Theoretically, 1.00 is the maximum possible value of the sound absorption coefficient.

sound power: The total sound energy radiated by a source per second, in watts.

sound transmission class (STC): An average of a barrier's ability to reduce sound over several frequency bands. The higher the STC rating, the better the barrier's ability to control sound transmission.

transmission loss (TL): The difference, in decibels, between the sound power incident on a barrier in a source room and the sound power radiated into a receiving room on the opposite side of the barrier. The transmission loss varies with the frequency being tested.

FUNDAMENTALS OF SOUND AND HUMAN HEARING

Qualities of Sound

Sound has three basic qualities: velocity, frequency, and power.

The *velocity of sound* depends on the medium in which it is traveling and the temperature of the medium. For acoustical purposes in buildings, however, the temperature effect on velocity is not significant. In air at sea level, the velocity of sound is approximately 1130 ft/sec.

Frequency is the number of cycles completed per second, measured in hertz (Hz). One hertz equals one cycle per second.

Frequency, f, velocity of sound, c, and wavelength, w, are related by Eq. 19.1.

$$f = \frac{c}{w} \tag{19.1}$$

Power, P, is the quantity of acoustical energy as measured in watts. In free space, a point source emits waves in all directions equally, so the sound intensity, I, at a given point at a distance of r from the source is equal to the power divided by the area of a sphere of radius r, as shown by Eq. 19.2.

$$I = \frac{P}{4\pi r^2} \tag{19.2}$$

To use Eq. 19.2 to find the sound intensity in watts per square centimeter, the radius must be in centimeters. If the radius is in feet and the sound intensity is wanted in watts per square centimeter, Eq. 19.3 can be used.

$$I = \frac{P}{\left(930\ \frac{\text{cm}^2}{\text{ft}^2}\right)4\pi r^2} \tag{19.3}$$

Inverse Square Law

The *inverse square law*, , states that the intensity of a force or energy (such as a sound wave) at a given point is inversely proportional to the square of the distance from the source of that energy. It is derived from Eq. 19.2.

$$\frac{I_1}{I_2} = \frac{r_2^2}{r_1^2} \tag{19.4}$$

Sound Intensity

The sensitivity of the human ear covers a vast range, from 10^{-16} W/cm^2 to 10^{-3} W/cm^2, and hearing is proportional to the logarithm of the source intensity. The sound *intensity level*, which is measured in decibels (dB), relates the sound intensity to the way humans experience sound. By definition, 0 dB is the threshold of human hearing and 130 dB is the threshold of pain.

In mathematical terms, this relationship is expressed by Eq. 19.5.

$$\text{IL} = 10\log\frac{I}{I_o} \qquad 19.5$$

Some common sound intensity levels and their subjective evaluations are shown in Table 19.2.

Table 19.2 Common Sound Intensity Levels

IL (dB)	example	subjective evaluation	intensity (W/cm^2)
140	jet plane takeoff	painful and dangerous	
130	gunfire	threshold of pain	10^{-3}
120	hard rock band, siren at 100 ft	deafening	10^{-4}
110	accelerating motorcycle	sound can be felt	10^{-5}
100	auto horn at 10 ft	conversation difficult to hear	10^{-6}
90	loud street noise, kitchen blender	very loud	10^{-7}
80	noisy office, average factory	difficult to use phone	10^{-8}
70	average street noise, quiet typewriter, average radio	loud	10^{-9}
60	average office, noisy home	usual background	10^{-10}
50	average conversation, quiet radio	moderate	10^{-11}
40	quiet home, private office	noticeably quiet	10^{-12}
30	quiet conversation	faint	10^{-13}
20	whisper	very faint	10^{-14}
10	rustling leaves, soundproof room	very faint	10^{-15}
0	threshold of hearing	hardly audible	10^{-16}

Loudness

The sensation of loudness is subjective, but some common guidelines are given in Table 19.3. These guidelines are useful in evaluating the effects of increased or decreased decibel levels in architectural situations. For example, spending money to modify a partition to increase its sound transmission class by 3 dB probably would not be worth the expense because it would hardly be noticeable.

Table 19.3 Subjective Change in Loudness Based on Decibel Level Change

change in intensity level (dB)	change in apparent loudness
1	almost imperceptible
3	just perceptible
5	clearly noticeable
6	change when distance to source in a free field is doubled or halved
10	twice or half as loud
18	very much louder or quieter
20	four times or one-fourth as loud

Addition of Decibels of Uncorrelated Sounds

Because decibels are logarithmic, they cannot be added directly. While exact results can be calculated, a more convenient guideline gives results accurate to within 1%. Given two decibel values, use the values in Table 19.4 to add decibels. For three or more sources, add the first two, then add the result to the third number, and so on.

Table 19.4 Addition of Decibels

where difference between the two values is	add this value to the higher value
0 or 1 dB	3 dB
2 or 3 dB	2 dB
4 to 8 dB	1 dB
9 or more dB	0 dB

For the addition of an arbitrary number, *n*, of sources of identical value, use Eq. 19.6.

$$\text{IL}_{\text{total}} = \text{IL}_{\text{source}} + 10\log n \qquad 19.6$$

Example 19.1

One office machine produces 70 dB of sound, and a second machine generates 76 dB. What is the combined sound intensity level of the two office machines?

(A) 77 dB

(B) 95 dB

(C) 118 dB

(D) 146 dB

Solution

Use Table 19.4. The difference between 76 and 70 is 6; therefore, add 1 dB to 76, which gives 77 dB.

The answer is (A).

Example 19.2

A room in an office contains eight machines, each of which produces 73 dB of sound. What is the overall sound level?

(A) 78 dB

(B) 82 dB

(C) 87 dB

(D) 92 dB

Solution

Use Eq. 19.6.

$$\begin{aligned} IL_{total} &= IL_{source} + 10 \log n \\ &= 73 \text{ dB} + 10 \log 8 \\ &= 82 \text{ dB} \end{aligned}$$

The answer is (B).

Human Sensitivity to Sound

Although human response to sound is subjective and varies with age, physical condition of the ear, background, and other factors, some common guidelines are useful to remember.

The normal human ear of a healthy young person can hear sounds in the range of 20 Hz to 20,000 Hz and is most sensitive to frequencies in the 3000 Hz to 4000 Hz range. Speech is composed of sounds primarily in the range of 125 Hz to 8000 Hz, with most energy in the range of 100 Hz to 600 Hz.

Among sounds of equal energy, the human ear is less sensitive to low frequencies (less than 500 Hz) than to middle frequencies (500 Hz to 2000 Hz) and high frequencies (greater than 2000 Hz).

Most common sound sources contain energy over a wide range of frequencies. Because frequency is an important variable in how a sound is transmitted or absorbed, it must be taken into account in building acoustics. For convenience in measurement and analysis, the frequency range is often divided into a scale of eight octave bands. A band is one octave wide when its highest frequency is twice its lowest frequency. These bands are identified by their center frequencies, which are 63 Hz, 125 Hz, 250 Hz, 500 Hz, 1000 Hz, 2000 Hz, 4000 Hz, and 8000 Hz. For more detailed purposes, narrower bands can also be used.

Because the human ear is less sensitive to low frequencies, a modified decibel scale, called the *dBA scale*, is used to predict human response to sounds and for acoustical design when low frequencies are part of the sound.

SOUND TRANSMISSION

Transmission Loss and Noise Reduction

One of the primary objectives of architectural acoustics is to reduce the transmission of sound from one space to another. Transmission of sound is primarily retarded by the mass of the barrier. The stiffness of the barrier is also important. Given two barriers of the same weight per unit area, the one that is less stiff will perform better than the other.

There are two important concepts in noise reduction: transmission loss and actual noise reduction. *Transmission loss* is the difference (in decibels) between the sound power incident on a barrier in a source room and the sound power radiated into a receiving room on the opposite side of the barrier. This measurement is typically derived in a testing laboratory.

Noise reduction (NR) is the arithmetic difference (in decibels) between the intensity levels in two rooms separated by a barrier of a given transmission loss. Noise reduction is dependent on the transmission loss of the barrier, the area of the barrier, and the absorption of the surfaces in the receiving room.

Noise reduction is calculated using Eq. 19.7.

$$\text{NR} = \text{TL} + 10\log\frac{A}{S} \qquad 19.7$$

In SI units, A is in metric sabins and S is in m^2. One metric sabin equals 10.76 English sabins.

Equation 19.7 shows that noise reduction can be increased by increasing the transmission loss of the barrier, by increasing the absorption in the receiving room, by decreasing the area of the barrier separating the two rooms, or by some combination of the three. The second term of Eq. 19.8 can be a negative number, resulting in a noise reduction less than the transmission loss of the wall.

The actual transmission loss of a barrier varies with the frequencies of the sounds being tested. Test reports, often published with manufacturers' literature, include the transmission loss over six or more octave bands. A commonly used single-number rating is the *sound transmission class* (STC). The higher the STC rating, the better the barrier (theoretically) is at stopping sound.

STC ratings represent the ideal loss under laboratory conditions, but walls, partitions, and floors built in the field are seldom constructed as well as those in the laboratory. Also, breaks in the barrier such as cracks, seams, electrical outlets, doors, and the like will significantly reduce the overall noise reduction.

In critical situations, transmission loss and selection of barriers should be calculated using the values for specific frequencies rather than the single STC average value. Some materials may allow an acoustical "hole," stopping most frequencies but allowing transmission of a certain range of frequencies. This often happens with very low or very high frequencies. However, for preliminary design purposes in typical situations the STC value is adequate.

There are many times when a partition will include two or more types of construction; for example, a door in a wall, or a glass panel in a wall. The combined transmission loss can be found using Eq. 19.8.

$$\text{TL}_{\text{composite}} = 10\log\frac{A_{\text{total}}}{\sum tS} \qquad 19.8$$

Equation 19.9 can be used to find the value of t if the value of the transmission loss of the individual materials is known.

$$t = 10^{-(\text{TL}/10)} \qquad 19.9$$

Project Planning

Example 19.3

A conference room and an office are separated by a common wall that is 13 ft long and 9 ft high, with an STC rating of 54. The total absorption of the office has been calculated to be 220 sabins. What is the total noise reduction from the conference room to the office?

(A) 46 dB

(B) 57 dB

(C) 64 dB

(D) 72 dB

Solution

Use Eq. 19.7.

$$\begin{aligned} \text{NR} &= \text{TL} + 10\log\frac{A}{S} \\ &= 54\ \text{dB} + 10\log\frac{220\ \text{sabins}}{(9\ \text{ft})(13\ \text{ft})} \\ &= 57\ \text{dB} \end{aligned}$$

The answer is (B).

Example 19.4

A wall is 9 ft high and 15 ft long and contains a 7 ft by 3 ft door. The transmission loss of the wall alone is 54 dB. The transmission loss of the door with full perimeter seals is 29 dB. What is the combined transmission loss of the wall and door?

(A) 25 dB

(B) 37 dB

(C) 56 dB

(D) 83 dB

Solution

The total area of the wall and door combined is

$$A_{\text{total}} = H_{\text{total}}L_{\text{total}} = (9\ \text{ft})(15\ \text{ft}) = 135\ \text{ft}^2$$

The area of the door is

$$S_{\text{door}} = H_{\text{door}}L_{\text{door}} = (7\ \text{ft})(3\ \text{ft}) = 21\ \text{ft}^2$$

The area of the wall alone is

$$S_{\text{wall}} = S_{\text{total}} - S_{\text{door}} = 135\ \text{ft}^2 - 21\ \text{ft}^2 = 114\ \text{ft}^2$$

From the problem statement, the transmission loss for the wall alone is 54 dB. From Eq. 19.9, the coefficient of transmission for the wall alone is

$$t = 10^{-(\text{TL}/10)} = 10^{-(54/10)} = 10^{-5.4}$$

Similarly, the coefficient of transmission for the door is

$$t = 10^{-(\text{TL}/10)} = 10^{-(29/10)} = 10^{-2.9}$$

From Eq. 19.8, the transmission loss for the wall and door together is

$$\begin{aligned}\mathrm{TL}_{\mathrm{composite}} &= 10\log\frac{A_{\mathrm{total}}}{\sum tS} = 10\log\frac{135\ \mathrm{ft}^2}{(10^{-5.4})(114\ \mathrm{ft}^2)+(10^{-2.9})(21\ \mathrm{ft}^2)}\\ &= 37\ \mathrm{dB}\end{aligned}$$

The answer is (B).

Noise Criteria Curves

All normally occupied spaces have some amount of background noise. This is desirable because some noise is needed to avoid the feeling of a "dead" space and to help mask other sounds. However, the acceptable amount of background noise varies with the type of space and the frequency of sound. For example, people are generally less tolerant of background noise in bedrooms than they are in public lobbies, and they can generally tolerate higher levels of low-frequency sound than of high-frequency sound.

These variables have been consolidated into a set of *noise criteria curves* (*NC curves*) relating frequency in eight octave bands to noise level, as shown in Fig. 19.6. Accompanying these curves are noise criteria ratings for various types of space and listening requirements. A representative sampling is shown in Table 19.5. Noise criteria curves can be used to specify the maximum amount of continuous background noise allowable in a space, to establish a minimum amount of noise desired to help mask sounds, and to evaluate an existing condition.

For example, if the noise spectrum of an air conditioning system was plotted on the NC chart, as shown in Fig. 19.6, the noise criteria rating would be defined by that curve that was not exceeded by the air conditioning spectrum curve at any frequency.

When background noise conforms to an NC curve, it usually still contains too many low-frequency and high-frequency sounds for comfort. A modification of the NC curves, called the *preferred noise criteria* (PNC), has been established that has sound-pressure levels lower than the NC curves on the low- and high-frequency ends of the chart.

Table 19.5 Some Representative Noise Criteria

type of space	preferred NC (db)
concert halls, opera houses, recording studios	15–20
bedrooms, apartments, hospitals	20–30
private offices, small conference rooms	30–35
large offices, retail stores, restaurants	35–40
lobbies, drafting rooms, laboratory work spaces	40–45
kitchens, computer rooms, light maintenance shops	45–55

Guidelines for Transmission Loss

In addition to using calculations for acoustical design, many guidelines can be used for preliminary estimating and for noncritical situations.

- In general, transmission loss through a barrier tends to increase with the frequency of sound.
- A wall with 0.1% open area (from cracks, holes, undercut doors, etc.) will have a maximum transmission loss of about 30 dB. A wall with 1% open area will have a maximum transmission loss of about 20 dB.
- A hairline crack will decrease a partition's transmission loss by about 6 dB. A 1 in^2 opening in a 100 ft^2 gypsum board partition can transmit almost as much sound as if the entire partition did not exist.
- Although placing fibrous insulation in a wall cavity increases its STC rating, the density of the insulation is not a significant variable.
- In determining the required STC rating of a barrier, the guidelines in Table 19.6 may be used.

Table 19.6
Effect of Barrier STC on Hearing

STC	effect on hearing
25	normal speech can clearly be heard through barrier
30	loud speech can be heard and understood fairly well; normal speech can be heard but barely understood
35	loud speech is not intelligible but can be heard
42–45	loud speech can only be faintly heard; normal speech cannot be heard
45–50	loud speech is not audible; loud sounds other than speech can only be heard faintly, if at all

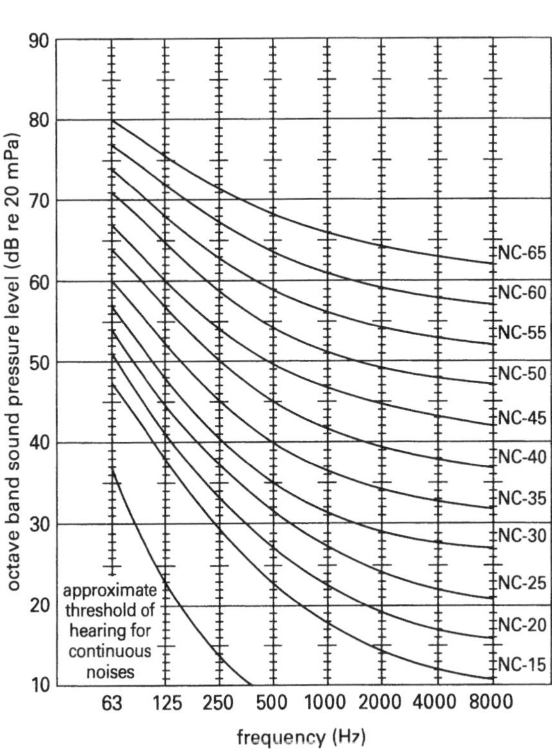

Figure 19.6
NC (Noise Criteria) Curves

SOUND ABSORPTION

Fundamentals

Controlling sound transmission is only one part of good acoustical design; proper sound absorption must also be included. Although the sound intensity level decreases about 6 dB for each doubling of distance from the sound source in free space, this is not the case in a room or semi-enclosed outdoor area. In a room, sound level decreases very near the source as it does in free space, but then it begins to reflect, and it levels out at a particular intensity.

In addition to reducing the intensity level of sound within a space, *sound absorption* is used to control unwanted sound reflections, improve speech privacy, and decrease or enhance reverberation.

The absorption of a material is defined by the coefficient of absorption, a, which is the ratio of the sound intensity absorbed by the material to the total intensity reaching the material. The maximum absorption possible is 1.0, the absorption of free space. Generally, a material with a coefficient of absorption below 0.2 is considered reflective, and one with a coefficient above 0.2 is considered sound absorbing.

The coefficient of absorption varies with the frequency of the sound, and some materials are better at absorbing some frequencies than others. All frequencies should be checked for critical applications, but for convenience, the single-number *noise reduction coefficient* (NRC) is used. The NRC is the average of a material's absorption coefficients at 250 Hz, 500 Hz, 1000 Hz, and 2000 Hz, rounded to the nearest multiple of 0.05.

Although most product literature still lists NRC ratings, the NRC has been superseded by the *sound absorption average* (SAA). The two are similar, and each provides a single number rating. The SAA is the average of the absorption coefficients for the 12 one-third-octave bands from 200 Hz to 2500 Hz when tested in accordance with ASTM C423.

The total absorption of a material is dependent on the area of the material and the material's coefficient of absorption, as shown in Eq. 19.10.

$$A = Sa \qquad 19.10$$

Because most rooms contain several materials with different areas, the total absorption in a room is the sum of the various individual material absorptions.

Noise Reduction Within a Space

Increasing sound absorption within a space will result in noise reduction according to Eq. 19.11, where A_1 is the original total room absorption in sabins and A_2 is the total room absorption after the increase.

$$\mathrm{NR} = 10\log\frac{A_2}{A_1} \qquad 19.11$$

The overall reverberant noise level in a room does not apply to noise level very near the source. (See Eq. 19.12.)

Example 19.5

A room 15 ft by 20 ft with a 9 ft ceiling has a carpeted floor with a 44 oz carpet on pad ($a = 0.40$), gypsum board walls, and a gypsum board ceiling ($a = 0.05$). What will be the noise reduction achieved by directly attaching acoustical tile with an NRC of 0.70 to the ceiling?

(A) 1.5 dB

(B) 3.4 dB

(C) 5.1 dB

(D) 11 dB

Solution

Use Eq. 19.10 to find the total absorption of the original room.

$$\begin{aligned} A_1 &= A_{\text{floor}} + A_{\text{ceiling}} + A_{\text{wall 1}} + A_{\text{wall 2}} + A_{\text{wall 3}} + A_{\text{wall 4}} \\ &= (15\ \text{ft})(20\ \text{ft})(0.40) + (15\ \text{ft})(20\ \text{ft})(0.05) \\ &\quad +(15\ \text{ft})(9\ \text{ft})(0.05) + (20\ \text{ft})(9\ \text{ft})(0.05) \\ &\quad +(15\ \text{ft})(9\ \text{ft})(0.05) + (20\ \text{ft})(9\ \text{ft})(0.05) \\ &= 120\ \text{sabins} + 15\ \text{sabins} + 7\ \text{sabins} + 9\ \text{sabins} \\ &\quad +7\ \text{sabins} + 9\ \text{sabins} \\ &= 167\ \text{sabins} \end{aligned}$$

After the tiles are installed, the absorption of the ceiling is

$$A_{\text{ceiling+tile}} = (15\ \text{ft})(20\ \text{ft})(0.70) = 210\ \text{sabins}$$

The total absorption of the room after the increase, A_2, is

$$\begin{aligned} A_2 &= A_{\text{floor}} + A_{\text{ceiling+tile}} + A_{\text{wall 1}} + A_{\text{wall 2}} + A_{\text{wall 3}} + A_{\text{wall 4}} \\ &= 120\ \text{sabins} + 210\ \text{sabins} + 7\ \text{sabins} + 9\ \text{sabins} \\ &\quad +7\ \text{sabins} + 9\ \text{sabins} \\ &= 362\ \text{sabins} \end{aligned}$$

Use Eq. 19.11 to find the noise reduction, NR, achieved by installing the tiles.

$$\mathrm{NR} = 10\log\frac{A_2}{A_1} = 10\log\frac{362\ \text{sabins}}{167\ \text{sabins}} = 3.4\ \text{dB}$$

Increasing the absorption by this amount helps a little, but the difference is barely perceptible (see Table 19.3). However, tripling the absorption would be clearly noticeable.

The answer is (B).

Guidelines for Sound Absorption

There are several guidelines related to sound absorption that are useful to remember.

- The average absorption coefficient of a room should be at least 0.20. Indoor-outdoor carpet has an absorption coefficient of about 0.20, while heavy carpet on a concrete floor has an absorption coefficient of about 0.30. An average absorption coefficient above 0.50 is usually not desirable, nor is it economically justified. Materials with lower values are suitable for large rooms, while materials with higher values are suitable for small or noisy rooms.
- Each doubling of the amount of absorption in a room results in a noise reduction of only 3 dB.
- If additional absorptive material is being added to a room, the total absorption should be increased at least three times (amounting to a change of about 5 dB, which is clearly noticeable). The increase may need to be more or less than three times to bring absorption to between 0.20 and 0.50.
- When adding extra absorption, an increase of 10 times (a reverberant noise reduction of 10 dB) is the approximate practical limit. Beyond this, more absorption results in a decreasing amount of noise reduction as the practical limit of 0.50 total average absorption coefficient is approached.
- Each doubling of the absorption in a room reduces reverberation time by one-half.
- Although absorptive materials can be placed anywhere, ceiling treatment for sound absorption is more effective in large rooms, whereas wall treatment is more effective in small rooms.
- Generally, absorption increases with an increase in thickness of a porous absorber. However, excessive low-frequency noise may require special design treatment.
- The amount of absorption of a porous type of sound absorber such as fiberglass or mineral wool is dependent on (1) the material's thickness, (2) the material's density, (3) the material's porosity, and (4) the orientation of the fibers in the material. A porous sound absorber should be composed of open, interconnected voids.

Project Planning

Reverberation

Reverberation is an important quality of the acoustical environment of a space. It affects both the intelligibility of speech and the quality of conditions for music of all types. *Reverberation time* is the time it takes the sound level to decrease 60 dB after the source has stopped producing the sound. The reverberation time in seconds, T, is calculated using Eq. 19.12.

$$T = 0.05\left(\frac{V}{A}\right) = 0.05\left(\frac{V}{aS}\right) \qquad 19.12$$

V is the volume of the room in cubic feet. (If cubic meters are used, the factor is 0.16 instead of 0.05.)

Each type of use has its own preferred range of reverberation time, shorter times being best for smaller spaces and longer times working best for larger spaces. (See Table 19.7.)

Table 19.7 Recommended Reverberation Times

space	reverberation time (sec)
auditoriums (speech and music)	1.5–1.8
broadcast studios (speech only)	0.4–0.6
churches	1.4–3.4
elementary classrooms	0.6–0.8
lecture/conference rooms	0.9–101
movie theaters	0.8–1.2
offices, small rooms for speech	0.3–0.6
opera halls	1.5–1.8
symphony concert halls	1.6–2.1
theaters (small dramatic)	0.9–1.4

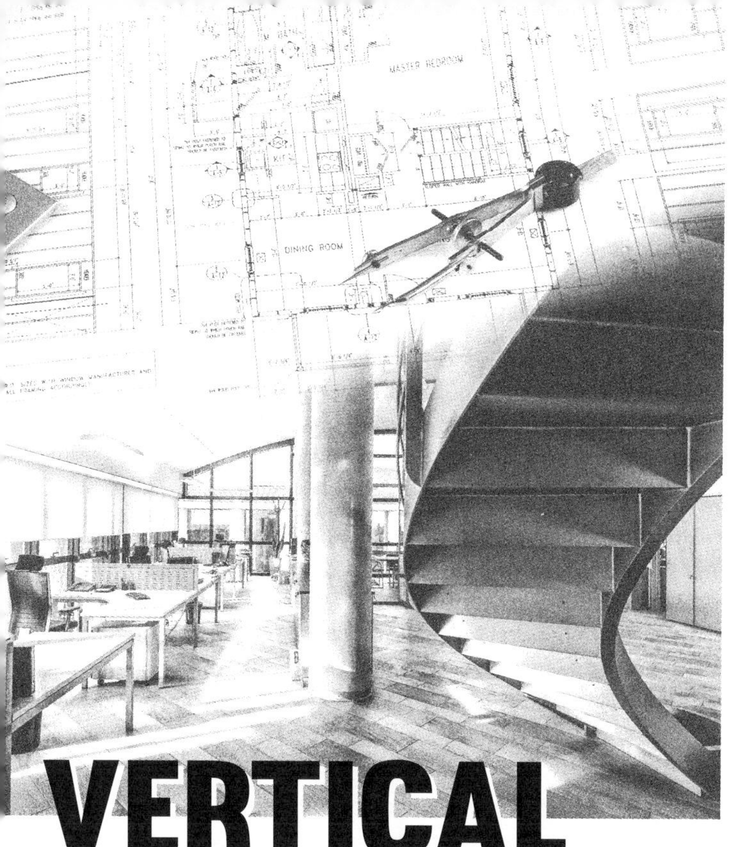

20

VERTICAL TRANSPORTATION

Vertical transportation is a term that describes all the methods used to move people and materials vertically. This includes passenger and freight elevators, escalators, dumbwaiters, vertical conveyors, moving ramps, wheelchair lifts, and platform lifts, as well as stairs, ramps, and ladders.

HYDRAULIC ELEVATORS

Hydraulic elevators are one of the two major elevator types used for the movement of people and freight; the other is electric elevators. Hydraulic elevators are lifted by a plunger, or *ram*, set in the ground directly under the car and operated with oil as the pressure fluid. As a consequence, the cylinder for the ram must be extended into the ground to a depth the same as the elevator's full height.

Because the ram must be set in the ground and speed is limited, hydraulic elevators are only used for passenger and freight loads in buildings from two to six stories high, or about 50 ft. They have speeds much lower than those of electric elevators, traveling from 25 ft/min to 150 ft/min and are, therefore, not appropriate for moving large numbers of people quickly. Single-ram elevators have weight capacities from 2000 lbm to 20,000 lbm, and multiple-ram units can lift from 20,000 lbm to 100,000 lbm.

A few variations of the standard hydraulic elevator are available. The holeless hydraulic uses a telescoping plunger set in the shaft next to the cab. Lift is provided by applying force to the upper members of the car frame. Another type uses a roller chain mounted over a wheel mounted on top of the hydraulic plunger. With this type, the plunger is mounted above the ground in the side of the shaft.

ELECTRIC ELEVATORS

Electric elevators are the most common elevator type used for passenger service. They are capable of much higher lifts and greater speeds than hydraulic types and can be precisely controlled for accelerating and decelerating. The system employs a cab suspended by cables (known as *ropes*) that are draped over a sheave and attached to a counterweight. A motor drives the sheave, which transmits lifting power to the ropes by the friction of the ropes in grooves of the sheave. For this reason, electric elevators are also referred to as *traction elevators*. The common components of a traction elevator are shown in Fig. 20.1.

Electric passenger elevators travel from 250 ft/min to 1800 ft/min and have capacities from 2000 lbm to 5000 lbm. Higher capacities are available for electric freight elevators.

Types

The two types of electric elevators are the gearless traction and the geared traction. *Gearless traction elevators* use a direct current (dc) motor directly connected to the sheave. The brake is also mounted on the same shaft. Gearless machines that are dependable and easy to maintain are used on high-speed elevators.

The *geared traction elevator* is used for slow speeds from 25 ft/min to 450 ft/min. A high-speed DC or AC motor drives a worm gear reduction assembly to provide a slow sheave speed with high torque. With the many possible variations in gear reduction ratios, sheave diameters, motor speeds, and roping arrangements, geared traction machines provide a great deal of flexibility for slow-speed, high-capacity elevators.

Roping

Roping refers to the arrangement of cables supporting the elevator. The simplest type is the *single wrap*, in which the rope passes over the sheave only once and is then connected to the counterweight. For high-speed elevators, additional traction is usually required so that the rope is wound over the sheave twice. This is known as a *double-wrap* arrangement. The disadvantage to double wrapping is that there are more bends in the cable and consequently a shorter rope life.

When the rope is directly connected to the counterweight, the cable travels just as far as the car, only in the opposite direction. This is known as *1:1 roping*. When the rope is wrapped around a sheave on the counterweight and connected to the top of the shaft, the rope moves twice as far as the elevator cab. This is known as *2:1 roping* and requires that less weight be lifted. Therefore, a smaller, higher-speed motor can be used, which is desirable for speeds up to 700 ft/min.

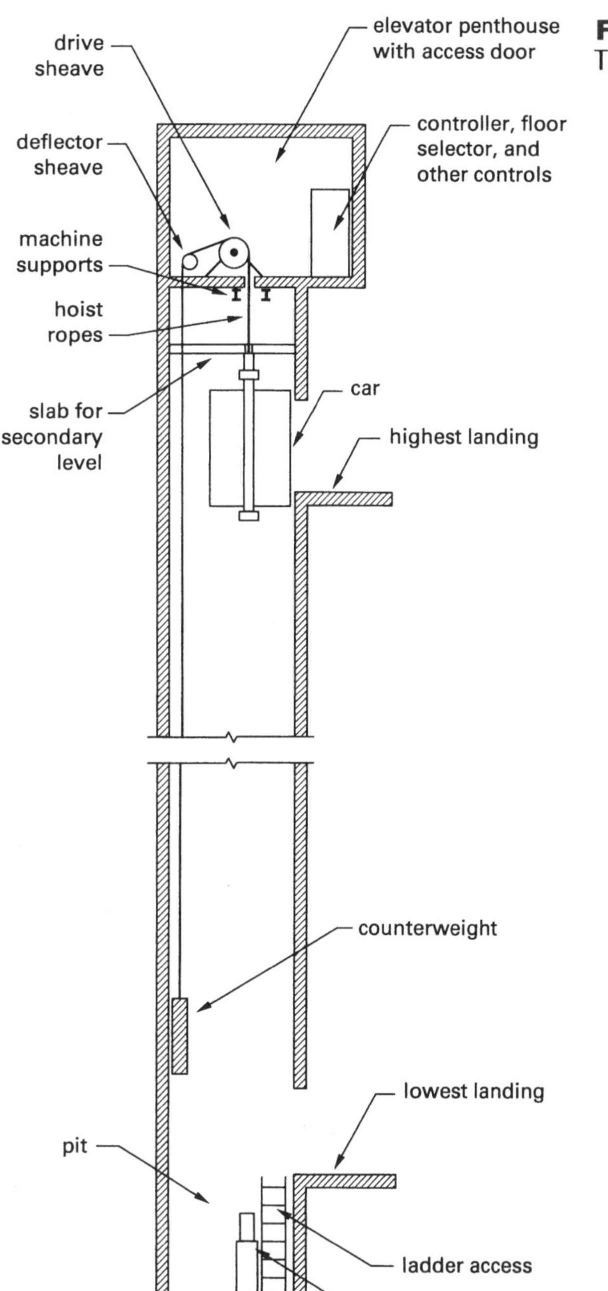

Figure 20.1 Traction Elevator

Operation and Control

Operation is the term used to describe the way the electrical systems for an elevator or group of elevators answer calls for service. *Control* describes the method of coordinating and operating all the aspects of elevator service, such as travel speed, accelerating and decelerating, door opening speed and delay, leveling, and hall lantern signals.

Many types of operating methods are available. The purpose of an operating system is to coordinate elevator response to signal calls on each floor so that waiting time is minimized and the elevators operate in the most efficient manner possible.

The simplest type of system is the *single automatic*. This was the first type of automated system for elevators without attendants and consists of a single call button on each floor and a single button for each floor inside the car. The elevator can only be called if no one is using it, and once inside, the passenger has exclusive use of the car until the trip is complete. This type of system has limited use, and is therefore best for small buildings with little traffic where exclusive use is desired.

The most common type of system for many buildings is the *selective collective operation*. With this system, the elevator remembers and answers all calls in one direction and then reverses and answers all calls in the opposite direction. When the trip is complete, the elevator can be programmed to return to a home landing, usually the lobby.

The selective collective system works well for light to moderate service requirements, but for large buildings with many elevators, *group automatic operation* is employed. This is simply the control of all elevators with programmable microprocessors to respond to calls in the most efficient manner possible, taking into account all the variables involved. In addition, such things as the time of day or day of the week can be included in the programming. This provides precise response to any building's needs.

A newer method of elevator system control is the *destination floor guidance system*. This kind of system uses computer control with artificial intelligence to put riders into the same car who are going to the same floor or to floors near each other. With this system, each rider selects a destination floor in the lobby, either on a wall panel or on a kiosk, and the control system assigns a particular car based on what other riders have selected. Once in the car, the riders do not press any destination buttons; the car stops at the floors that were chosen in the lobby. The system reduces total travel time to the destination floor and results in fewer stops for each car.

Drive Control

An elevator installation contains a *drive control* that controls the speed of the motor that drives the traction machine. There are three basic types of drive controls.

The *unit multivoltage* (UMV) control system, also called the Ward-Leonard control system, uses an alternating current (AC) motor to operate a direct current (DC) generator. The DC current from the generator is then varied to run a DC traction motor. Before the advent of electronic motor control in the 1980s, this was the only way to obtain the precise motor speeds needed for smooth elevator operation. However, the system is noisy, requires three machines, and is subject to high thermal losses and low overall efficiency. Many UMV control systems are still in use, but other systems have become more common in new elevators.

The *silicon-controlled rectifier* (SCR) control system (also called a *thyristor* control system) provides variable DC voltage to a DC traction motor. This system provides good drive and leveling control, but it also has a low power factor and high thermal losses. The older AC system had many disadvantages, and the DC system is generally used.

The *variable-voltage, variable-frequency* (VVVF) AC control system uses a rectifier and an inverter to convert AC power to DC power and then to variable-voltage, variable-frequency, three-phase AC current. This current controls a standard AC motor, which operates at the speed corresponding to the frequency of the input. The result is very accurate and efficient speed control. The VVVF control system does not have the disadvantages of the thyristor system and is energy efficient. It is useful for elevators of all speeds and travel distances, and maintenance is minimized due to its solid-state design.

Safety Devices

Modern elevators use many safety devices. The main brake on the sheave or motor shaft is normally operated by the control mechanism. If a power failure occurs, the brake is automatically applied. A governor also senses the speed of the car, and if the limit is exceeded, the brake is applied. There is also a safety rail clamp that grips the side rails if there is an emergency. In the pit of the elevator below the lowest landing, car buffers stop a car's motion if it over-travels the lowest stop; however, they are not designed to stop a free-falling elevator cab.

Elevators must be accessible to the physically disabled. In lobbies this usually means visual signals that can be easily seen as well as audible signals.

Hoistway door interlocks prevent the elevator from operating unless the hoistway door is closed and locked. In addition, various devices prevent the doors from closing on someone in their path. *Safety edges* are movable strips on the leading edge of the door that activate a switch to reopen the door if something contacts it. Photoelectric devices serve the same purpose. There are also proximity detectors that sense the presence of a person near the door and can stop the closing motion.

To prevent overloading of a car, sensors under the floor detect when the maximum weight is reached by deflection of the floor. This then makes a warning noise with additional loading and prevents the elevator from picking up any more people. Additional safety devices include multiple ropes, escape hatches in the top of the cab, alarm buttons on the car control panel, and telephones for direct communication in an emergency.

In the case of a power failure all cars will stop where they are, but most codes require that emergency power be available to operate at least one car at a time. This allows the unloading of occupied cars. Building codes require that if a fire alarm is activated, all cars return to the lobby without stopping and switch control to manual mode. The cars can then only be operated by fire fighting personnel using a manual key.

Elevators must also be accessible to the physically disabled. In lobbies this usually means visual signals that can be easily seen as well as audible signals indicating car approach, car landing, and directions of approach. Call buttons and raised and braille floor designations must be placed within certain height limitations. There is also a formula for calculating the minimum time between notification that a car has answered a call and the moment the doors of that car start to close, with a minimum time of 5 sec.

Elevator cars themselves must be sized to allow a person in a wheelchair to enter, maneuver within reach of the controls, and exit the car. Minimum clear door opening width is 36 in. All car controls must be no higher than 54 in for side approaches and 48 in for front approaches. The car controls must be designated by braille and by raised standard alphabet characters. Main entry floor, door open, door closed, emergency alarm, and emergency stop buttons must also be designated by standard raised character symbols.

Example 20.1

What type of elevator should be specified for a 40-story office building?

(A) hydraulic

(B) gearless traction

(C) geared traction

(D) electric

Solution

A gearless traction elevator will be an appropriate choice for the office building. Gearless traction elevators can travel at the highest speeds of the types listed, and to accommodate the rush of people entering and exiting the building in the morning, at lunch time, and in the evening, the quick cycles will be a necessity.

Gearless traction and geared traction are two different types of electric elevators. Both operate on DC current. The geared traction elevator travels at slower speeds but offers many options for adjusting the speed to suit the building conditions.

Hydraulic elevators are lifted by a ram, which must be sunk into the ground the same distance as the height of the elevator's path of travel. Therefore, they are used only in low-rise buildings (generally less than six stories). They travel much more slowly than electric elevators and are better used for freight or for low-occupancy passenger elevators where speed is not an issue.

The answer is (B).

ELEVATOR DESIGN

In simplest terms, elevator design involves selecting the capacity, speed, and number of elevators to adequately serve a particular building's population and then arranging the location of each elevator bank and the arrangement of the lobby. In addition, the roping method, machine room layout, control system, and cab decoration must be determined.

Capacity and Speed

Determining the number, capacity, and arrangement of elevators to serve a building is a complex process because there is an optimal interrelationship between the number of people to be served in a given time period, the maximum waiting time desired, cost, and particular requirements of the building. For example, a hospital elevator moves large numbers of people but also must have provisions for stretchers and large quantities of supplies. The elevator in a corporate headquarters building may handle a great deal of interfloor traffic, whereas one in an apartment building will primarily move people from the lobby up to their floors and back down again.

For most buildings the *handling capacity*, or number of people to be served, is usually based on a five-minute peak period. For office buildings, this is usually the time in the morning when everyone is coming to work. The number of people an elevator car can carry is a function of its capacity, which is measured in weight. Some general guidelines have been established for recommended capacities based on building types and rough building areas. These are shown in Table 20.1.

Table 20.1 Recommended Elevator Capacities (in lbm)

building type	building size			service elevator
	small	medium	large	
offices	2500/3000	3000/3500	3500/4000	4000–6500
garages	2500	3000	3500	–
retail	3500	3500	4000	4000–8000
hotels	3000	3500	3500	4000
apartments	2000/2500	2500	2500	4000
dormitories	3000	3000	3000	–
senior citizens	2500	2500	2500	4000

The maximum number of passengers in an elevator car is directly related to the capacity in weight. Table 20.2 gives the elevator car passenger capacity based on weight capacity.

Table 20.2 Car Passenger Capacity

elevator capacity (lbm)	maximum passenger capacity
2000	12
2500	17
3000	20
3500	23
4000	28

General recommended elevator speeds are also available based on the number of floors served and the general size of the building. The higher speed translates to shorter intervals, or waiting time, but there are some limits due to overall travel distance (number of floors). Higher-speed elevators also generally cost more. Recommended elevator speeds are shown in Table 20.3.

Table 20.3 Recommended Elevator Speeds (in ft/min)

number of floors	elevator speed (ft/min)			
	small	medium	large	service
offices				
2–5	250	300/400	400	200
5–10	400	400	500	300
10–15	400	400/500	500/700	400
15–25	500	500/700	700	500
25–35	–	800/1000	1000	500
35–45	–	1000/1200	1200	700
45–60	–	1200/1400	1400/1600	800
over 60	–	–	1800	800
garages				
2–5	200			
5–10	200–400			
10–15	300–500			
hotels				
2–6	100–300			200
6–12	200–500			300
12–20	400–500			400
20–25	500/700			500
25–30	700/800			500
30–40	700–1000			700
40–50	1000–1200			800
apartments/dormitories, senior citizen housing				
2–6	100			200
6–12	200			200
12–20	300–500			200
20–25	400/500			300
25–30	500			300

Number of Elevators Required

Based on the car capacity and speed, along with such particular characteristics of the elevator functioning as door opening and closing time, delays at stops, and so forth, the average round trip time can be calculated, and then the handling capacity of one car in a given five-minute period can be determined. The exact procedure for doing this is complicated and involves probability of number of stops, highest floor reached, and other variables.

The number of elevators required is then found by taking the total number of people to be accommodated in a five-minute peak period and dividing by the handling capacity of one car. The *interval*, or average waiting time for an elevator to arrive, can then be checked to see if it is acceptable. Recommended intervals vary with the type of building. For diversified offices the time is between 30 and 35 sec. For hotels and apartments it is from 40 to 70 sec or more.

Location and Lobby Design

Elevators should be grouped near the center of a building whenever possible. At the lobby level, they should be easily accessible from the entrance and plainly visible from all points of access. In all but the smallest installations, there should be a minimum of two elevators so that one is available if the other is being serviced. Consideration should also be given to obvious traffic generators such as subway entrances, parking garage doors, and the like. Service elevators may be remotely located from passenger elevators as required by the building function.

Elevator lobbies should be designed so that it is easy to see all hall lanterns from one point and to minimize walking distance from any one point to the car that happens to arrive. This is especially important for barrier-free design. Adequate space must also be available so that people can wait without interfering with other circulation. There should never be more than eight cars in a group or more than four cars in a line. Figure 20.2 shows the recommended lobby layouts for various numbers of cars and the minimum lobby widths based on the depth of the car.

As buildings get taller and larger, the number of elevators required to adequately serve all floors increases, and the proportion of elevator shaft area to total floor area increases beyond economic levels. In addition, it becomes impossible for a single elevator to serve more than about 12 to 15 floors without exceeding acceptable waiting and total travel times. To solve these problems, several methods of elevatoring have been developed.

The first method simply divides the total number of elevators into banks that serve separate zones of the building. For example, the first bank may serve floors 1 through 14 while the second bank serves the lobby floor and floors 14 through 28. Additional banks can be added for taller buildings. Although this method keeps waiting and total travel times at acceptable levels, the elevator shafts still take up considerable floor space, especially on the lower floors.

Figure 20.2 Elevator Lobby Space Requirements

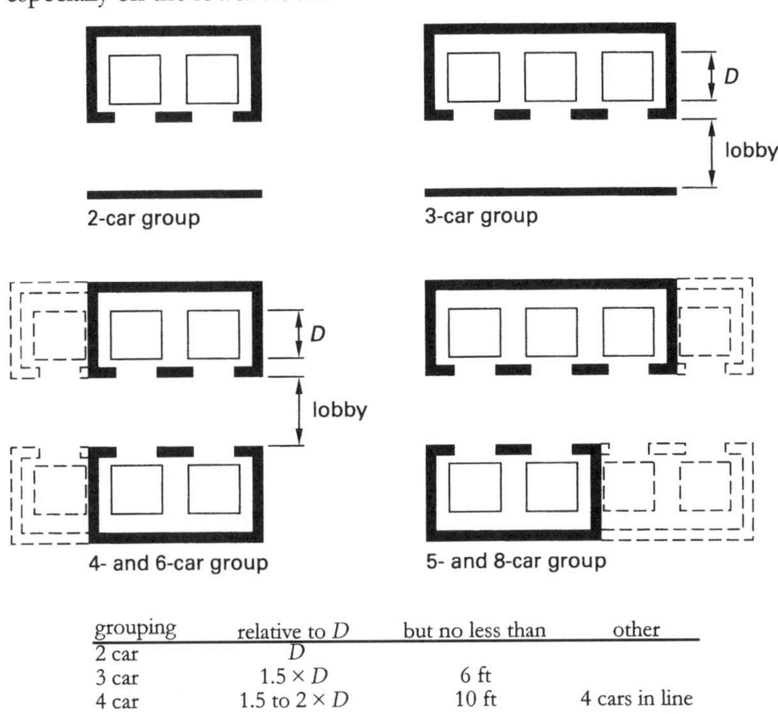

grouping	relative to *D*	but no less than	other
2 car	*D*		
3 car	1.5 × *D*	6 ft	
4 car	1.5 to 2 × *D*	10 ft	4 cars in line 1.5 × *D*, min. 8 ft
5 car	1.5 to 2 × *D*	10 ft	
6 car	1.75 to 2 × *D*	10 ft	
8 car	2 × *D*	max. 14 ft	lobby open both ends

The second method is the sky lobby concept. One or more intermediate lobbies are placed in very tall buildings and large-capacity, high-speed elevators take people from the first floor lobby to the sky lobby where they transfer to elevators serving the upper floors. This method reduces the amount of space occupied by elevators, because the shafts do not extend the full height of the building. It also works well for multi-occupancy buildings such as those with apartments, offices, and parking.

The third method uses stacked, or double-deck, elevator cabs. At the main terminal level, traffic going to even-numbered floors is directed to one floor, and traffic going to odd-numbered floors is directed to an adjacent floor. This method effectively doubles shaft capacity, reducing the area required for elevators while decreasing the number of local stops.

Elevator Shaft and Pit Design

The *hoistway*, or elevator shaft, provides a dedicated, fire-resistive space through which the elevator travels. The hoistway provides space for the guide rails on which the elevator cars travel, the cables that support the cars, the counterweights, and various electrical and control devices.

Each hoistway must be provided with not less than 1 fc of illumination for its entire length. This lighting must activate when an emergency operation by firefighters is active.

As with stairways and other vertical shafts, hoistways must be fire rated in accordance with the IBC. A hoistway must be contained within a fire-rated enclosure, and doors and other openings through the enclosure must also be fire rated. If the enclosure connects no more than three floors, then both the enclosure and any openings through it must have at least a 1-hour fire rating. If the enclosure connects four or more stories, then it must have at least a 2-hour fire rating, and doors and other openings must have at least a 1 $^1/_2$-hour fire rating.

A maximum of four elevator cars may be located in a single hoistway enclosure. Moreover, if four or more elevator cars serve the same floor, they must be in at least two separate hoistway enclosures. For example, if six elevator cars serve a floor, they must be located in at least two separate hoistway enclosures; if there are two enclosures, the cars must be divided either 3-3 or 2-4.

The *elevator pit* at the bottom of the hoistway provides space for the car buffer, the compensating cables (if any), and other elevator equipment. It also gives room for maintenance of the cars from underneath. The *car buffer* is a device to bring an elevator car to a cushioned stop if the car travels beyond the lowest stop. The elevator pit must be provided either with an access ladder from the lowest stop or with a separate access door. The pit must also be provided with permanent lighting and either a drain or a sump to remove any water that accumulates.

Doors

Doors are an important part of elevator design because of their effect on passenger convenience and round-trip time. If a car makes 10 stops on a trip, a difference in opening and closing time of only $^1/_2$ sec can add 10 sec to the interval time and make an otherwise satisfactory design unacceptable. Doors can be either center opening or side opening and single speed or two speed. Single-speed, center-opening doors are common and allow faster passenger loading and unloading than do side-opening doors.

Two-speed, side-opening doors have two leaves, one of which telescopes past the other as they move. Two-speed, center-opening doors have four leaves. The minimum opening width is 3 ft 6 in, but 4 ft 0 in is better because it allows two people to easily and quickly enter or leave at the same time.

Machine Rooms

Machine rooms are best located directly above the hoist-way and must provide adequate space for the motor, sheave, brake, controller board, speed governor, floor selector mechanism, and motor generator. All of these require minimum clearances for servicing and access. The exact size varies with manufacturer and type of elevator, but in general the machine room must be about as wide as the hoistway and from 12 ft to 16 ft deeper than the hoistway.

Minimum ceiling height ranges from 7 ft 6 in to over 10 ft 0 in. In addition to this dimension, the distance from the floor of the top landing to the underside of the machine room floor can be substantial, from about 15 ft to 30 ft depending on the type, speed, and capacity of the elevator.

Machine rooms are no longer necessary for some hydraulic elevators or for gearless elevators in low- and mid-rise buildings. A *machine-roomless elevator* (MRL) has the motor and controller within the hoistway rather than in a dedicated machine room. MRLs also use coated steel belts with a smaller bending radius than traditional wire rope, which make it possible to use smaller and more efficient drive sheaves that can be placed in the hoistway.

By eliminating the need for machine rooms, MRLs free up more space for other uses and reduce the costs and electrical and mechanical services usually associated with machine rooms. MRLs can also reduce energy consumption through the use of more efficient motors, LED lighting, sleep mode, and the ability to use regenerative drives. In sleep mode, the car lights and fans are shut down when not in use. *Regenerative drives* generate electricity when a heavily loaded car travels in the down direction (outweighing the counterweight) or when a lightly loaded car travels in the up direction (when the counterweight outweighs the car).

Other advantages of MRLs include

- reduced noise and vibration due to the coated steel belts
- elimination of the lubrication needed for traditional wire ropes
- the ability to place call buttons in the elevator door jambs, simplifying coordination with other trades
- shorter ordering lead times
- faster installation

FREIGHT ELEVATORS

Freight elevators are designed and intended to transport only equipment and materials and those passengers needed to handle the freight. Elevator codes classify these elevators into five groups: A, B, C1, C2, and C3. Class A is for general freight, and no item can exceed one-fourth of the rated capacity of the elevator. The rating cannot be less than 50 lbm/ft^2 of platform area. Class B elevators are those used for motor vehicle loading and are rated at no less than 30 lbm/ft^2. Class C elevators are for industrial truck loading based on 50 lbm/ft^2. Class C1 includes the truck; Class C2 does not include the truck; and Class C3 is for concentrated loading with the truck not carried and with increments greater than 25% rated capacity.

Freight elevators are commonly available in capacities from 2500 lbm to 8000 lbm, with some multiple-ram hydraulic elevators capable of lifting up to 100,000 lbm. Speeds range from 50 ft/min to 200 ft/min, with speeds up to 800 ft/min available for very tall buildings. With freight elevators, interval time is not as important as capacity, so the speeds are much less than those of passenger elevators.

ESCALATORS

Escalators are very efficient devices for transporting large numbers of people from one level to another. They are also useful for directing the flow of traffic.

Escalators are rated by speed and size. The industry standard speed is 100 ft/min. A second speed of 120 ft/min is available for transportation and sports facilities but is not used often in other applications. Three sizes are available: 32, 40, and 48 in. The actual tread widths of these sizes are 24, 32, and 40 in, respectively. Because the 40 in size does not increase the capacity of a 32 in escalator in actual use, the two most common sizes are 32 in and 48 in.

The actual observed capacity of people using escalators is somewhat less than the theoretical maximum capacity. This is because under crowded conditions, people tend to space themselves on every other step on 32 in models and on an average of every step on 48 in models. Observed capacity ranges from 2300 people per hour for a 32 in escalator to 4500 people per hour for a 48 in model.

Escalators are housed in a trussed assembly set at a 30° angle. The motors, drives, and other mechanisms extend below the treads and floor at both the top and bottom of the assembly, so this must be taken into account when calculating head height clearance and floor-to-floor heights. See Fig. 20.3.

Figure 20.3
Escalator
Configuration

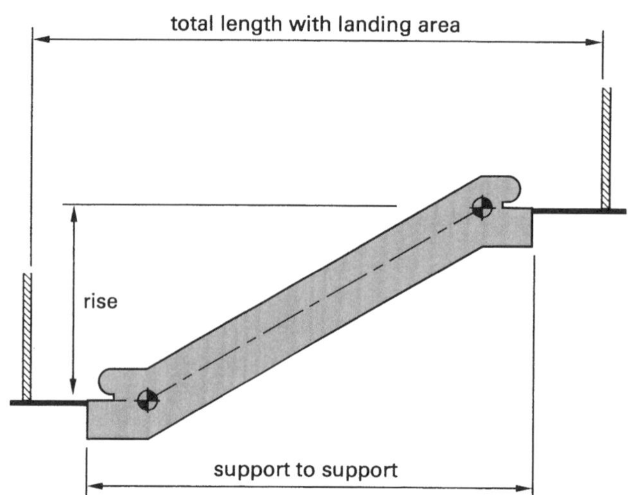

When more than two floors are to be served by escalators, how to arrange the units can become a more complicated decision for the designer. The various possible arrangements have different advantages and disadvantages.

There are two basic arrangements. In a *crisscross arrangement* the up and down escalators between each pair of floors form an X when viewed in elevation. This separates the entrances to the up and down escalators from a floor, which sometimes leads to confusion for riders. In a *parallel arrangement*, the up and down escalators between each pair of floors are parallel to each other, and the entrances to the up and down escalators from a floor are side by side. Each of these arrangements has two variations.

The *crisscross spiral arrangement* is the most common. After exiting at one floor, the rider makes a simple U-turn to enter the escalator that continues to the next floor. This reduces travel time for trips of two or more floors.

The *crisscross walkaround arrangement* places all the up escalators above each other and all the down escalators above each other. After exiting at one floor, the rider must walk around to the other side of the escalator area to enter the escalator that continues to the next floor. This lengthens any trip of two or more floors, but is sometimes used in retail stores so that riders will pass more displays of merchandise as they travel.

Both types of crisscross arrangement take up a total width on each floor equal to the width of two escalators.

In the *parallel spiral arrangement* the rider can reach the escalator that continues to the next floor with a simple U-turn. This arrangement is the only one that has both advantages of reducing travel time for longer trips and placing entrances to up and down escalators near each other. But as the entrances and exits of four escalators must therefore be side by side, this arrangement requires a total width of four escalators.

The *stacked parallel arrangement* also forces the rider to walk around to the other side of the escalator area to continue to the next floor, but this arrangement takes up the width of only two escalators instead of four.

Example 20.2

Which of the following is NOT a standard nominal width for an escalator?

(A) 32 in

(B) 40 in

(C) 48 in

(D) 54 in

Solution

54 in is not a standard nominal width for an escalator.

Most manufacturers make escalators in nominal widths of 32 in, 40 in, and 48 in with corresponding actual widths of 24 in, 32 in, and 40 in.

The answer is (D).

STAIRS AND RAMPS

Stairs are one of the most basic types of vertical circulation—as old as buildings themselves. Because they affect the safety of all buildings in which they are used, they must be designed correctly.

Stairways may be classified into two broad categories: those used for strictly utilitarian purposes, such as exit stairs, and monumental stairs designed to be a prominent design feature as well as provide vertical access. Whichever type is used, there are common design features that must be incorporated. This section elaborates on some of the basic building code requirements given in Chap. 39.

A stair's design and detailing begins with deciding on its basic configuration and shape, the approximate amount of space it requires, and the geometry of its layout. Some of the most common configurations are shown in Fig. 20.4. Each of these types has many variations. For example, a simple straight-run stair may be enclosed or partially open, it may be interrupted with several landings, or the landings may project from the face of the open side of the stair. L-shaped stairs can have equal or unequal legs.

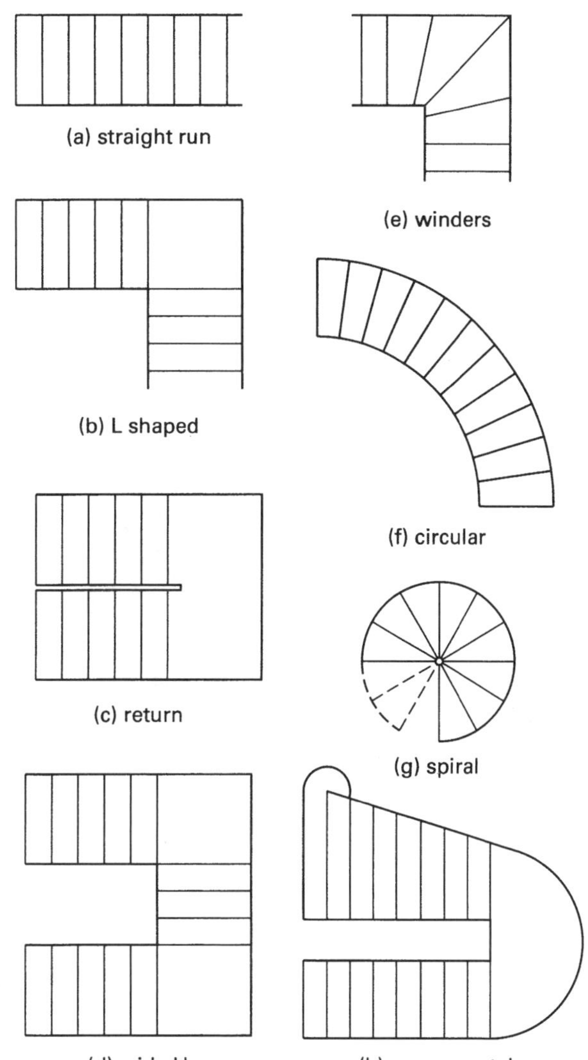

Figure 20.4 Basic Stair Configurations

Once the basic configuration of a stairway has been determined, the width, total run, and landing depths and widths determine how much space is required. Figure 20.5 shows the minimum dimensions for laying out a stairway in plan view, including a landing. The total run depends on the depth of the treads and the number of risers and landings that will be used.

The minimum width of any stair is 36 in, or 44 in when the occupant load exceeds 50. Handrails may project a maximum of $4^1/_2$ in on both sides of a stairway.

In addition to the requirements shown in Fig. 20.5, building codes limit the use of special types of stairs. These include winding, circular, and spiral stairways. They are only allowed as private stairways in homes, apartments, condominiums, and the like.

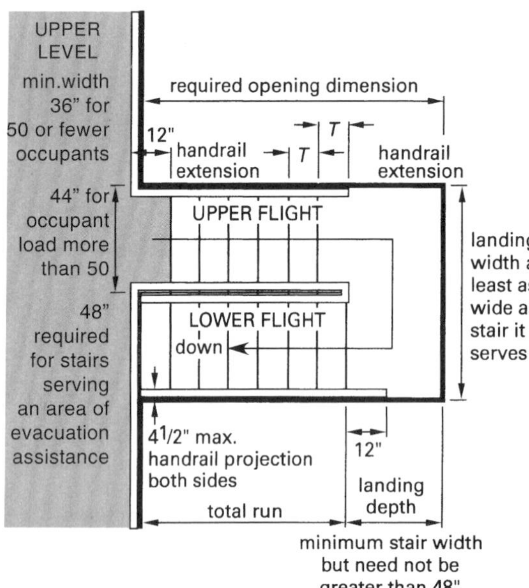

Figure 20.5
Stair Planning Guidelines

Winding stairways have tapered treads that are wider at one end than at the other. See Fig. 20.6(a). When circular stairways have a smaller radius than is required by code, they are classed as winding stairways. When winders are used they should all be the same shape and size.

Circular stairways have sides shaped as a circular arc. The inside, smaller arc cannot be less than twice the width of the stair. See Fig. 20.6(b). If it is, the stairway is considered a winding stairway.

Spiral stairs use wedge-shaped treads that radiate from a center support column, as shown in Fig. 20.6(c). The allowable riser height is greater than for other stairs; it must be enough to provide a minimum headroom height of 6 ft 6 in but cannot be greater than $9\frac{1}{2}$ in.

Figure 20.6
Building Code Requirements for Nonstraight Stairs

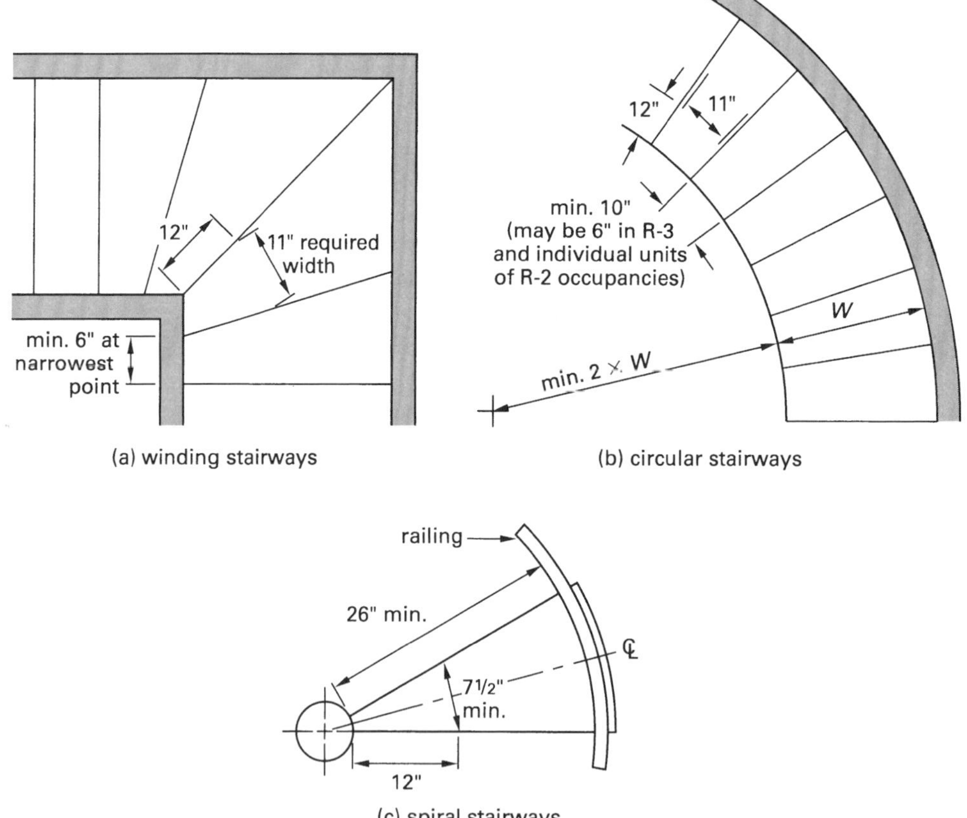

Project Planning

For enclosed exit stairways with doors adjacent to landings, the codes require that the door not intrude into the required exit path more than a certain distance, either as the door is opening or when the door is fully opened. IBC requirements are shown in Fig. 20.7. Although the dimensions in Fig. 20.7 do not include any allowance for evacuation assistance space, if it is required, these areas are normally provided in the building exit stairways.

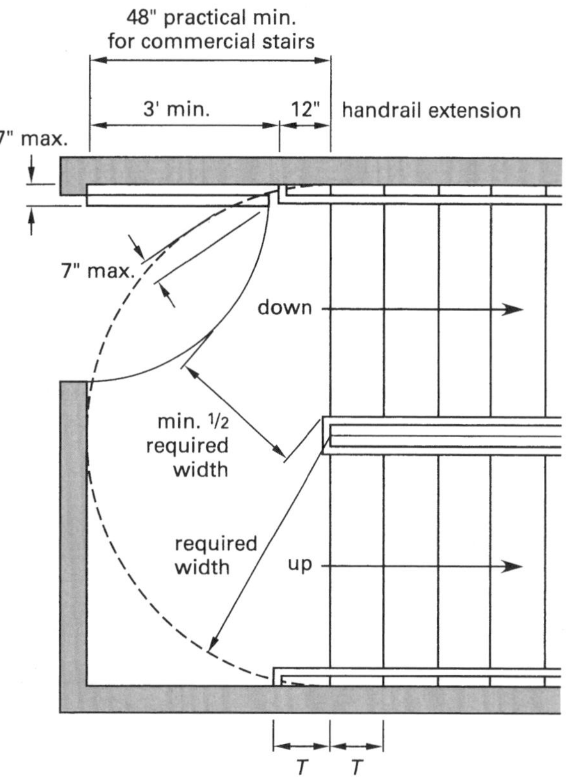

Figure 20.7 IBC Requirements for Enclosed Exit Stairs

The basic design and code requirements for vertical dimensions of stairs are shown in Fig. 14.8 along with the related discussion in that chapter.

Extensive research has determined the best dimensions for the rise and treads of stairs and the safest and most comfortable proportion between the two. The maximum rise and minimum tread dimensions of 7 in and 11 in, respectively, represent some of the most current research, including considerations for the physically disabled. Some researchers recommend that treads be even wider, from 12 in to 14 in. The tread of a stair is considered the horizontal projection of the distance from the edge of one nosing to the next. It does not include any part of the tread under the nosing.

Because stair dimensions are based on the normal stride of a person while ascending and descending a stair, various formulas have been used to determine one dimension based on the other. For example, a formula can be used to determine the total number of stairs when the total rise is known and the number of risers must be a whole number without exceeding 7 in or 8 in on private stairways. Some of these formulas include the following (where R equals riser height and T equals tread depth, both in inches).

$$2R + T = 25 \qquad 20.1$$

$$RT = 75 \qquad 20.2$$

$$R + T = 17 \qquad 20.3$$

$$T = 20 - \frac{4R}{3} \qquad 20.4$$

Some of these formulas are rather old and represent proportions that were comfortable for people who, on average, were slightly smaller than the average size of people today. Equation 20.1, for example, was developed in the seventeenth century and originally stipulated that twice the riser plus the tread be between 24 and 25. The minimum should be 25 and may be increased to 26. Of the four formulas, Eq. 20.1 gives the widest tread based on a given riser height if the value of 25 is used, and can be used in most designs. A wider tread is generally the safest, especially when descending.

The total run of a stair is calculated by taking the total rise in inches and dividing by an estimated riser height, usually 7 in. If the result is not a whole number, the required number of risers is the next highest whole number. This number is then divided into the total rise to obtain the actual required riser height. The number of treads for a straight-run stair is one less than the number of risers, and this number is multiplied by the tread dimension to obtain the total required run.

The maximum distance between landings is 12 ft; however, some research suggests that 9 ft is a better dimension, especially for the physically disabled. The top and bottom treads should have contrasting strips at nosings for visually impaired people.

Tread design is an especially important part of stair design. The important parts of treads include their depth, material, and nosing design. The depth of treads must be enough to provide safe footing for both ascending and descending as discussed previously. The material should be a nonslip surface, but not so rough that people get their feet caught on the nosing when descending. Any nonslip material designed into the nosing should be level with the rest of the tread.

Safe and accessible design requires that nosings not be abrupt and that they have a maximum rounded edge of $^1/_2$ in.

Ramps are another type of vertical transportation used for minor transitions between floor levels. The requirements for ramps are covered in Chap. 15.

21

SITE WORK

Project Planning

Site work includes demolition and clearing of land, earthwork, installation of piles and caissons, paving and other types of surfacing, drainage, site improvements, and landscaping. Included in this chapter are those aspects of site work encountered on almost any architectural project.

SOIL

Because all aspects of site work depend on the nature of the soil, the architect must have a basic understanding of this element. *Soil* is the general term used to describe the material that supports a building. It is generally classified into four groups: sands and gravels, silts, clays, and organics.

Sands and gravels are granular materials that are low in plasticity. *Sand* consists of particles from about 0.002 in to $^1/_4$ in in size. *Gravel* consists of rock particles from $^3/_4$ in to $3^1/_2$ in in size. Both sands and gravels are very good bases for building foundations. In addition, they provide good drainage because of the voids between the individual particles.

Silt is fine-grained sedimentary soil composed of material smaller than sand but larger than clay. Silts behave as granular materials, but they are sometimes slightly plastic in their behavior.

Clays are composed of smaller particles than silts. Clays have some cohesion, or tensile strength, and are plastic in their behavior when wet. Clay is very unpredictable because it swells when it absorbs water and shrinks when it dries. In some cases silts and clays can provide an adequate base for foundations if soil investigations show they are stable. Generally, they make better foundations if they are mixed with other types of soil.

Organics are materials of vegetable or other organic matter and make poor bases for foundations.

In addition to these general types there are other commonly used terms for various types of soil. *Hardpan* refers to an unbroken mixture of clay, sand, and gravel. It is a good base for building foundations. *Shale* and *slate* are soft rocks with a fine texture. *Boulders* describe rocks that have broken off of bedrock. Finally, *bedrock* is the solid rock that forms the earth's crust. Bedrock has the highest bearing capacity of all soil types. Shale and slate make up the group with the second highest bearing capacity.

Soil Tests

Prior to design and construction, the exact nature of the soil must be determined. This is done with one of a variety of soil tests used to determine such things as the bearing capacity, water table level, and porosity. Porosity must be known if the land is to be used for private sewage disposal systems. Two of the most common soil tests for bearing capacity are borings and test pits.

With typical core borings, undisturbed samples of the soil are removed at regular intervals and the type of material recovered is recorded in a *boring log*. This log shows the material, the depth at which it was encountered, its standard designation, and other information, such as moisture content, density, and the results of any borehole tests that might have been conducted at the bore site. A typical boring log is shown in Fig. 21.1.

One of the most common borehole tests is the *standard penetration test* (SPT), which is a measure of the density of granular soils and the consistency of some clays. In this test, a 2 in diameter sampler is driven into the bottom of the borehole by a 140 lbm hammer falling 30 in. The number of blows, N, required to drive the cylinder 12 in is recorded.

The recovered bore samples can be tested in the laboratory. Some of the tests include strength tests of bearing capacity, resistance to lateral pressure, and slope stability. In addition, compressibility, grain size, specific gravity, and density tests are sometimes performed. Because laboratory tests are expensive and not always necessary, they are not performed for every building project.

The number of borings taken at a building site is determined by many factors, such as the size of the building, suspected subsurface geological conditions, and requirements by local codes. Usually, a minimum of four borings is taken, one near each corner of the proposed building. If wide variations are found in the initial boring logs, additional tests may be warranted.

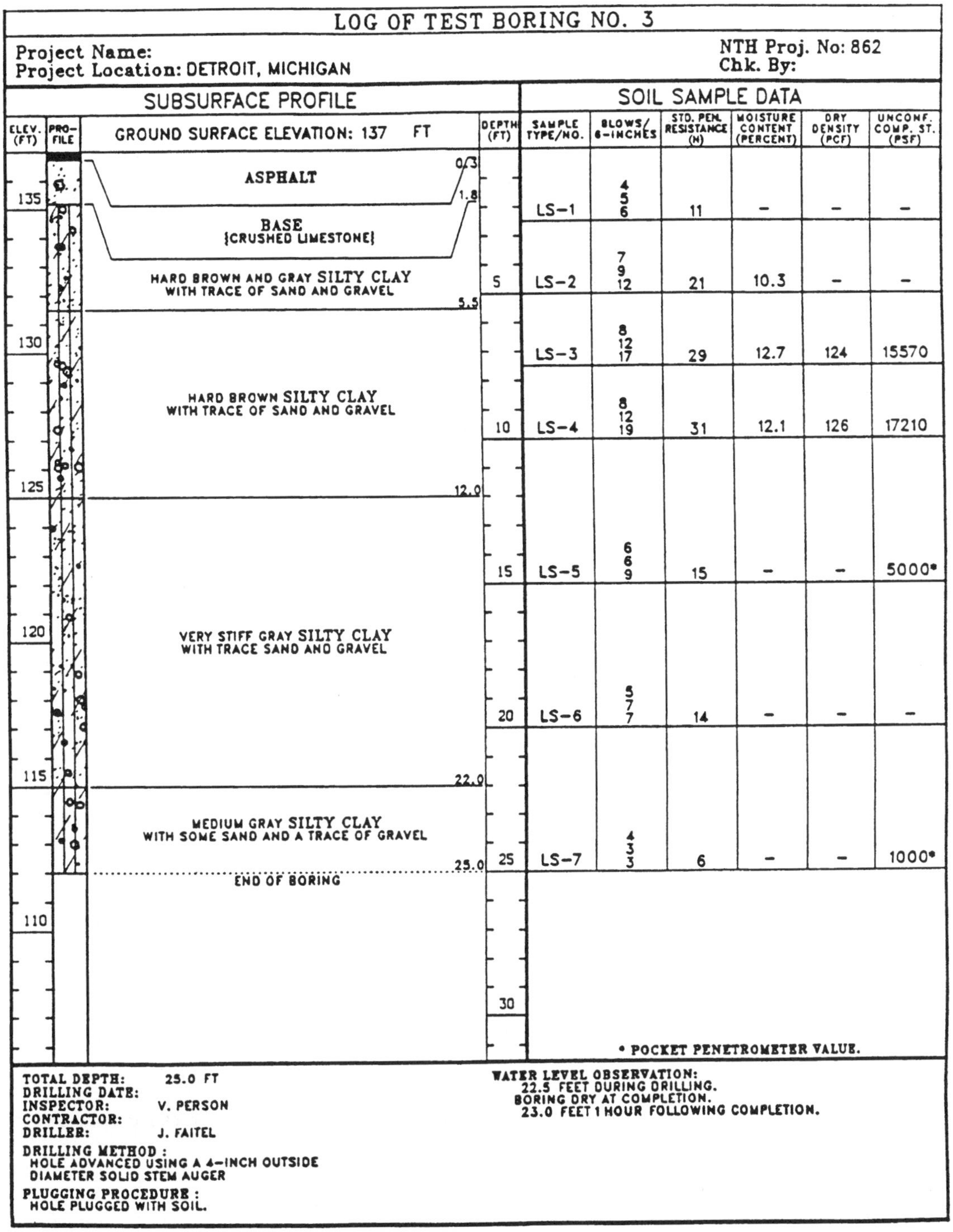

Figure 21.1
Typical Boring Log

LOG OF TEST BORING NO. 3

Project Name:
Project Location: DETROIT, MICHIGAN

NTH Proj. No: 862
Chk. By:

SUBSURFACE PROFILE — GROUND SURFACE ELEVATION: 137 FT

ELEV. (FT)	DESCRIPTION	DEPTH (FT)	SAMPLE TYPE/NO.	BLOWS/ 6-INCHES	STD. PEN. RESISTANCE (N)	MOISTURE CONTENT (PERCENT)	DRY DENSITY (PCF)	UNCONF. COMP. ST. (PSF)
	ASPHALT	0.3						
135	BASE (CRUSHED LIMESTONE)	1.8	LS-1	4 5 6	11	-	-	-
	HARD BROWN AND GRAY SILTY CLAY WITH TRACE OF SAND AND GRAVEL	5.5	LS-2	7 9 12	21	10.3	-	-
130	HARD BROWN SILTY CLAY WITH TRACE OF SAND AND GRAVEL		LS-3	8 12 17	29	12.7	124	15570
125		12.0	LS-4	8 12 19	31	12.1	126	17210
120	VERY STIFF GRAY SILTY CLAY WITH TRACE SAND AND GRAVEL		LS-5	6 6 9	15	-	-	5000*
115		22.0	LS-6	5 7 7	14	-	-	-
	MEDIUM GRAY SILTY CLAY WITH SOME SAND AND A TRACE OF GRAVEL	25.0	LS-7	4 3 3	6	-	-	1000*
110	END OF BORING							

* POCKET PENETROMETER VALUE.

TOTAL DEPTH: 25.0 FT
DRILLING DATE:
INSPECTOR: V. PERSON
CONTRACTOR:
DRILLER: J. FAITEL

DRILLING METHOD:
HOLE ADVANCED USING A 4-INCH OUTSIDE DIAMETER SOLID STEM AUGER

PLUGGING PROCEDURE:
HOLE PLUGGED WITH SOIL.

WATER LEVEL OBSERVATION:
22.5 FEET DURING DRILLING.
BORING DRY AT COMPLETION.
23.0 FEET 1 HOUR FOLLOWING COMPLETION.

Test pits are the second common type of subsurface exploration. These are trenches dug at the job site that allow visual inspection of the soil strata and direct collection of undisturbed samples. Because they are open pits, the practical limit on depth is about 10 ft, so the soil below that depth cannot be directly examined.

The location of each test boring or test pit is shown on the plot plan and given a number corresponding to the boring log in the soil test report. Soil tests are usually requested by the architect but paid for by the owner. They are typically referred to in the specifications for information only. However, soil tests are not part of the contract documents.

Other types of tests include auger borings, wash borings, dry sample borings, and soil load tests. *Auger borings* raise samples of the soil by using a standard auger bit. The test is best used in sand or clay for shallow or intermediate depths because the auger cannot penetrate hard obstructions such as bedrock or hardpan soil.

Wash borings are made with a 2 in to 4 in diameter pipe through which a water jet is maintained to force up the soil material. The resulting samples are so thoroughly mixed that analysis is difficult, but the test is useful for soils too hard for an auger test. Wash borings can extend down about 100 ft or more.

Dry sample borings extract material by driving a pipe with a split sampling pipe on the leading edge about 5 in into the soil. The pipe is lifted out, and the samples are removed for analysis. Subsequent samples are taken in approximately 5 in increments.

Soil load tests involve building a platform on the site, placing incremental loads on it, and observing the amount of settlement during given time periods until settlement becomes regular after repeated loading. The design load is usually half the test load.

The soil tests performed by the geotechnical engineer should reveal any unusual problems with the site, including soil that has been contaminated by previous building operations on the site, by mining activity, or by runoff and seepage from adjacent sites. Any of these would be cause to classify the site as a brownfield.

A *brownfield*, as defined by the EPA, is property whose redevelopment or reuse may be complicated by the presence or potential presence of a hazardous substance, pollutant, or contaminant. A brownfield requires remediation, which may include removing the contaminated soil and replacing it with new soil.

Geological tests and site review should also indicate if the land is in a karst region or subject to sinkholes from other causes. *Karst* is landscape in which soluble rocks such as limestone, dolomite, and gypsum have dissolved, forming caves and other voids below the surface. These voids can cause sinkholes on the surface.

After the field sampling is done, the soil is tested in a laboratory and the soils engineer issues a report stating the results of the testing. From this the soils engineer gives the allowable soil bearing pressure and recommends a foundation type to use. Some of the properties that can be tested include the following.

- *grain size and shape.* These determine (for granular soil) the shear strength of the soil, its permeability, the likely result of frost action, and compaction ability.
- *liquid and plastic limits.* These values give the compaction and compressibility values for cohesive soil.
- *specific gravity.* This is used to determine void ratio, which determines compressibility of the soil.
- *unconfined compression.* The shear strength for cohesive soil is measured from this value.
- *water content.* This number is used to get the compressibility and compaction values for cohesive soil.

Soil Types

Soils are classified according to the *Unified Soil Classification System* (USCS). This system divides soils into major divisions and subdivisions based on grain size and laboratory tests of physical characteristics and provides standardized names and symbols. A summary chart of the USCS is shown in Fig. 21.2.

Bearing capacities are generally specified by the building code based on the soil type. Other bearing capacities may be used if acceptable tests are conducted that show higher values are appropriate.

Water in Soil

The presence of water in soil can cause several problems for foundations as well as other parts of the site. Water can reduce the load-carrying capacity of the soil in general, so larger or more expensive foundation systems may be necessary. If more moisture is present under one area of the building than another, differential settlement may occur, causing cracking and weakening of structural and nonstructural components. In the worst case, structural failure may occur. Improperly prepared soil can also cause heaving or settling of paving, fences, and other parts of the site.

Foundations below the groundwater line, often called the *water table*, are also subjected to hydrostatic pressure. This pressure from the force of water-saturated soil can occur against vertical foundation walls as well as under the floor slabs. Hydrostatic pressure creates two difficulties: it puts additional loads on the structural elements, and it makes waterproofing more difficult because the pressure tends to force water into any crack or imperfection in the structure. See Fig. 27.1 for a typical method of waterproofing a foundation.

Even if hydrostatic pressure is not present, moisture in the soil can leak into the below-grade structure if not properly dampproofed and can cause general deterioration of materials.

Figure 21.2 Unified Soil Classification System (USCS)

<table>
<tr><td rowspan="8">coarse-grained soils
more than 50% of material is larger that no. 200 sieve</td><td rowspan="4">gravels
more than 50% of coarse fraction retained on No. 4 sieve</td><td rowspan="2">clean gravels
less than 5% fines</td><td>GW</td><td>well-graded gravel</td></tr>
<tr><td>GP</td><td>poorly graded gravel</td></tr>
<tr><td rowspan="2">gravels with fines
more than 12% fines</td><td>GM</td><td>silty gravel</td></tr>
<tr><td>GC</td><td>clayey gravel</td></tr>
<tr><td rowspan="4">sands
50% or more of coarse fraction passes No. 4 sieve</td><td rowspan="2">clean sands
less than 5% fines</td><td>SW</td><td>well-graded sand</td></tr>
<tr><td>SP</td><td>poorly graded sand</td></tr>
<tr><td rowspan="2">sands with fines
more than 12% fines</td><td>SM</td><td>silty sand</td></tr>
<tr><td>SC</td><td>clayey sand</td></tr>
<tr><td rowspan="6">fine-grained soils
50% or more passes the no. 200 sieve</td><td rowspan="3">silts and clays
liquid limit less than 50</td><td rowspan="2">inorganic</td><td>CL</td><td>lean clay</td></tr>
<tr><td>ML</td><td>silt</td></tr>
<tr><td>organic</td><td>OL</td><td>organic silt</td></tr>
<tr><td rowspan="3">silts and clays
liquid limit 50 or more</td><td rowspan="2">inorganic</td><td>CH</td><td>fat clay</td></tr>
<tr><td>MH</td><td>elastic silt</td></tr>
<tr><td>organic</td><td>OH</td><td>organic clay</td></tr>
<tr><td>highly organic soils</td><td colspan="2">primary organic matter, dark in color, and organic odor</td><td>PT</td><td>peat</td></tr>
</table>

Soil Treatment

In order to increase bearing capacity, decrease settlement, or do both, several methods of soil treatment are used.

- *drainage.* As mentioned in the previous section, proper drainage can solve several types of problems. It can increase the strength of the soil and prevent hydrostatic pressure.
- *fill.* If existing soil is unsuitable for building, the undesirable material is removed and new engineered fill is brought in. This may be soil, sand, gravel, or other material as appropriate. In nearly all situations, the engineered fill must be compacted before building commences. Controlled compaction requires moisture to lubricate the particles. With all types of fill, there is an optimum relationship between the fill's density and its optimum moisture content. The method for determining this is the Proctor test, in which fill samples are tested in the laboratory to determine a standard for compaction. Specifications are then written that call for fill to be compacted between 90% and 100% of the optimum Proctor density; higher values are necessary for heavily loaded structures, and lower values are appropriate for other loadings. Moisture contents within 2% to 4% of the optimum moisture content at the time of compaction must also be specified. Fill is usually placed in lifts of 8 in to 12 in with each lift compacted before placement of the next.
- *compaction.* Sometimes existing soil can simply be compacted to provide the required base for construction. The same requirements for compaction of fill material apply to compaction of existing soil. One device used to compact large areas is the *sheepsfoot roller.*
- *densification.* This is a type of on-site compaction of existing material using one of several techniques involving vibration, dropping of heavy weights, or pounding piles into the ground and filling the voids with sand. The specific technique used depends on the grain size of the soil.
- *surcharging.* Surcharging is the preloading of the ground with fill material to cause consolidation and settlement of the underlying soil before building. Once the required settlement has taken place, the fill is removed and construction begins. Although suitable for large areas, the time and cost required for sufficient settlement often preclude this method of soil improvement.
- *mixing.* In lieu of complete replacement of the soil, a layer of sand or gravel can be placed on less stable soil and mixed in, thus improving the soil's bearing capacity. By varying the type of added material, a soil with required properties can be created.
- *geotextiles.* Geotextiles are permeable, flexible fabrics and mattings, typically synthetic. Geotextiles are used in a wide variety of building applications, including silt fences, drainage planes against foundations, and landscaped roofs. For site work, geotextiles are used to stabilize engineered fill below footings, to stabilize marginal soils under paving, and as erosion control on steep slopes.

Other Considerations

Frost. Because most soils expand and heave when they freeze, footings and foundations must be placed below the frost line to prevent the structure from lifting up. The depth of the frost line varies, of course, with location and local climatic conditions. It is usually specified by the local building code or building official.

Expansive soil. Many clays, such as bentonite, expand when they get wet and shrink when they dry. If such soils are below a proposed building, the foundations must be isolated from them. One method of doing this is to use pile or caisson foundation piers that bear on material below the expansive soil. Concrete grade beams span between the piers with voids below the beams so any expansion does not cause stress on the foundation. The building walls are then built on the grade beams. The remainder of the ground level slab is usually built over select fill material, although in some instances it is suspended from beams and piers.

Concrete grade beams span between the piers with voids below the beams so any soil expansion does not cause stress on the foundation.

Repose. When sands, gravels, and other types of soils are piled up, they come to rest with a characteristic slope. The angle of the slope depends on the granular size of the material and the material's moisture content. The slope is known as the *angle of natural repose* and is the maximum practical angle for changing grades without using retaining walls or other stabilization techniques. However, even though a slope may conform to the angle of repose of a material, it may still be unsuitable to prevent erosion or allow for the desired type of landscaping.

Example 21.1

A soil investigation for a building site reveals that the soil type is sandy clay and that bentonite is present. Which of the following foundation types would be most appropriate?

(A) spread footings

(B) mat foundation

(C) belled piers

(D) grade beam on piers

Solution

Grade beams on piers are used where expansive soil such as bentonite is present. The beams transfer the building weight to the piers, which are commonly placed on bedrock. Voids under the beams allow the soil to expand without heaving the foundation.

Each soil type has a certain bearing capacity, which is the load (measured in pounds per square foot or kilopascals) from a building foundation that the soil can resist. Of the various soil types, bedrock and sedimentary rock have the highest bearing capacities.

The answer is (D).

EARTHWORK

Earthwork includes excavating soil for the construction of a building foundation, water and sewer lines, and other buried items as well as modifying the site's land contours.

Excavation

Excavation is the removal of soil to allow construction of foundations and other permanent features below the finished level of the grade. It is usually done with machinery, although small areas may be excavated by hand. When a relatively narrow, long excavation is done for piping or for narrow footings and foundation walls, it is called *trenching.*

Because excavations can pose a hazard to workers, unshored sides of soil should be no steeper than their natural angle of repose or not greater than a slope of $1\frac{1}{2}$ horizontal to 1 vertical. Where this is not possible, the earth must be temporarily shored as discussed in the next section.

For large excavations, excess soil has to be removed from the site. However, to minimize cost, it is best to use the soil elsewhere on the site for backfill or in contour modification.

Grading

Grading is the modification of the contours of the site according to the grading plan. Rough grading involves the moving of soil prior to construction to approximate levels of the final grades. It also includes adding or removing soil after construction to the approximate final grades. In both of these operations, the grade is usually within about 6 in to 1 ft of the desired level. Often, excavating is part of the rough grading as soil removed from the building is placed in low spots where the grade must be built up.

Finish grading is the final moving of soil prior to landscaping or paving, where the level of the earth is brought to within 1 in of the desired grades. This operation is done with machines and by hand and often includes the placement of topsoil.

SHORING AND BRACING

Figure 21.3 Excavation Shoring

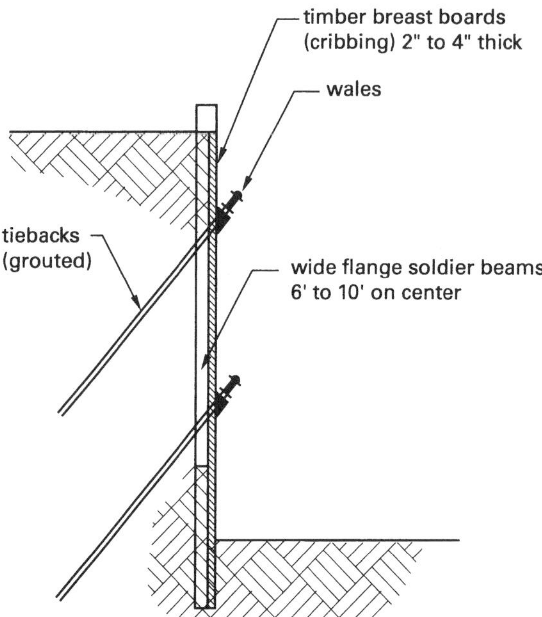

(a) soldier beams and breast boards

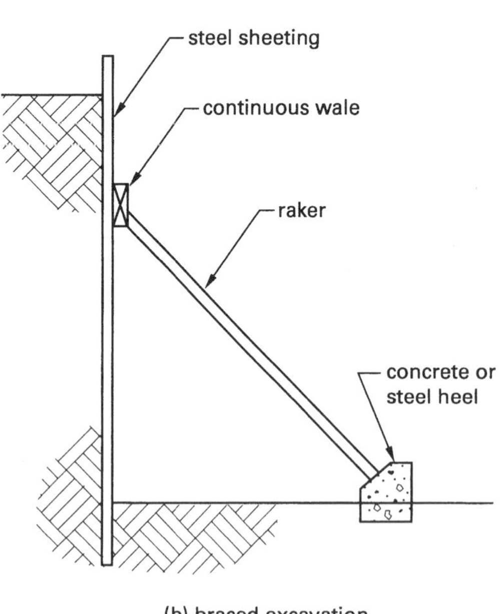

(b) braced excavation

For shallow excavations in open areas, the sides of the excavation can be sloped without the need for some supporting structure. However, if the depth increases or the excavation walls need to be vertical in confined locations, temporary support is required. There are two common methods of doing this.

The first method employs a system of vertical beams and horizontal timbers. See Fig. 21.3(a). Prior to excavation, steel wide-flange soldier beams are driven at 6 ft to 10 ft intervals to a length slightly deeper than the anticipated excavation. As soil is removed, horizontal timbers 2 in to 4 in thick, called *breast boards* or *cribbing*, are placed between the soldier beams so they bear against the inside face of the flange.

When the excavation reaches a certain point, holes are drilled diagonally into the earth or deeper rock. Rods or tendons are inserted into the holes and grouted into place. These tiebacks are connected to horizontal wales that hold the soldier beams back against the pressure of the excavation. As the excavation proceeds, more breast boards and tiebacks are added. The advantage of this method of shoring is that the excavation is free from bracing and allows drilling of piers, forming of foundation walls, and other construction to proceed unimpeded.

The second method uses vertical sheeting, either wood or steel, supported by diagonal braces, as shown in Fig. 21.3(b). Steel sheeting is composed of interlocking Z-shaped sections supported by continuous horizontal members called *wales*. The wales, in turn, are supported by diagonal rakers that are anchored to the bottom of the excavation with steel or concrete heels. For very small excavations, the diagonal rakers can be replaced with horizontal braces connecting opposite sides of the excavation.

Shoring and bracing are used to temporarily support adjacent buildings and other construction with posts, timbers, and beams when excavation is proceeding and to temporarily support the sides of an excavation.

being extended to a lower level. Needle beams supported by the adjacent grade and hydraulic jacks are used to temporarily support the building while the new foundation is constructed.

SITE DRAINAGE

Water must be properly drained from a site to carry off excess rain and other surface water, to avoid leakage into the building, and to make other parts of the site, such as walks, parking areas, and outdoor activity areas, usable. There are two primary types of drainage to consider: subsurface and surface.

Subsurface Drainage

Water below ground can reduce the load-carrying capacity of the soil, cause differential settlement, and leak into a building. For these reasons, the site for a building must be examined and tested for potential water problems, and steps must be taken to drain excess water.

A small amount of moisture in the soil normally does not pose significant problems. However, if there is a high percentage of water in the soil or if the water table is high, these problems must be dealt with. The *water table* is the level below which the soil is saturated with groundwater. If any part of a structure is below this level, it is subject to hydrostatic pressure, putting additional loads on the structural elements of the foundation and making waterproofing more difficult.

In order to minimize subsurface water, the land around the building must be sloped to drain surface water before it soaks into the ground near the structure. A minimum slope of $^1/_4$ in/ft is recommended. All water from roofs and decks should also be drained away from the building with gutters and drain pipes.

Below ground, perforated drain tile should be laid around the footings at least 6 in below the floor slab to collect water and carry it away to a storm sewer system, drywell, or some natural drainage area. The drain tile is set in a gravel setting bed, and more gravel is placed above the drain. This is commonly known as a "French drain" or sub-drain.

If hydrostatic pressure against the wall is a problem, a layer of gravel can be placed next to the wall. Open-web matting (geotextile material) can also be used. With either of these methods, when water is forced against gravel or matting, it loses its pressure and drips through the gravel or matting into the drain tile.

To relieve pressure against floor slabs, a layer of large gravel is placed below the slab. If the presence of water is a significant problem, the gravel layer is used in conjunction with a waterproofing membrane, and drain tiles are placed below the slab. See also Chap. 27.

Surface Water Drainage

Surface water should be drained away from a building by sloping the land and otherwise modifying the finish contours to divert water into natural drainage patterns or artificial drains. Gutters can be built into curbing to collect water from paved areas. In some cases, large paved or landscaped areas need to be sloped to drain inlets or catch basins that connect with storm sewers.

A drain inlet allows stormwater to run directly into the storm sewer. A catch basin has a sump built into it so that debris will settle instead of flowing down the sewer. The sump can be cleaned out periodically. Large storm sewer systems require manholes for service access, located wherever the sewer changes direction, or a maximum of 500 ft apart.

Refer to Chap. 9 and Chap. 13 for more information on sustainable design during the site analysis and design phases.

SITE IMPROVEMENTS

Site improvements include items not connected to the building, such as parking areas, walks, paving, landscaping, sprinkler systems, outdoor lighting, fences, retaining walls, and various types of outdoor furnishings.

Paving

Paving is used for parking areas, driveways, and large, hard-surfaced activity areas. Paving is normally constructed of concrete, asphaltic concrete, or unit pavers.

Concrete paving is placed on compacted soil or a gravel bed and is normally reinforced with welded wire fabric to resist temperature stresses. If heavy loading is anticipated, the concrete is often reinforced with standard reinforcing bars. Concrete paving should be a minimum of 5 in thick, but the actual thickness required depends on the anticipated loading. Concrete paving is poured in sections, with joints between the sections. Expansion joints should be located every 20 ft separated with a $^1/_2$ in premolded joint filler. Construction joints or control joints are placed where separate sections of concrete are poured, and they are intended to control the locations of the inevitable minor cracking that occurs in concrete.

Asphaltic concrete paving is a general term that includes several types of bituminous paving. The most common type of asphaltic concrete consists of asphalt cement and graded aggregates. This is laid on the base and rolled and compacted while still hot. Cold-laid asphalt is the same except that cold liquid asphalt is used. Before the asphalt is applied, a subbase of coarse gravel is overlaid with finer aggregate and compacted and rolled to the desired grade. The asphalt is laid over this base to a depth of 2 in or 3 in.

Unit pavers can be any of a number of types of materials, including concrete, brick, granite, and flagstone. Unit pavers should be laid on a level, compacted base of sand over crushed gravel. For greater stability they may also be laid on a bituminous setting bed over a poured concrete slab. Figure 21.4 shows a typical unit paver section, and Fig. 21.5 shows common paving patterns.

Figure 21.4
Unit Paving

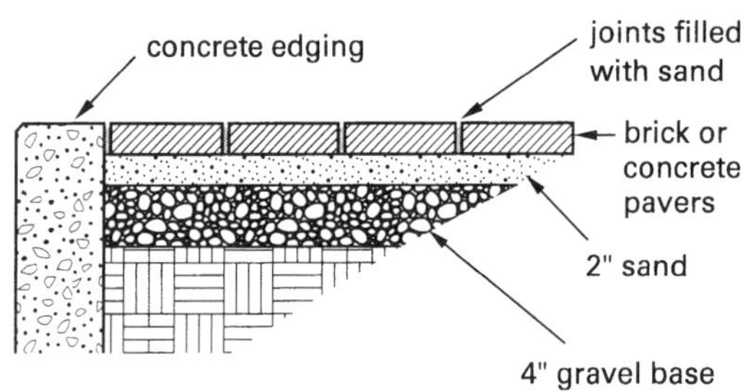

For better sustainability, pervious paving can be used. *Pervious paving* is a hard-surfaced paving material designed to let stormwater infiltrate through voids in the surface into the soil below, rather than directing the water into storm drains or waterways. Once in the ground, the water is naturally filtered and pollutants are removed.

Gravel is a naturally pervious material. If a harder surface is needed for parking or pedestrian walks, pervious paving can be made from concrete, asphalt, stone, or brick. There are many proprietary products designed to be laid like standard unit pavers, but with wider openings that can be filled with sand, small stones, grass, or other appropriate vegetation. For heavy-duty applications such as parking lots, pervious paving may be laid on a base of stone and engineered to support the expected loads. For soil with a low infiltration rate, an underdrain may be needed to carry off excess water.

Light-colored pervious paving materials may be used to earn LEED credits both for reducing the heat island effect and for rainwater management. The amount of impervious paving on a site can be reduced further, meeting further LEED requirements, by using covered parking instead of open parking lots.

Walks

Walks are common site improvements. Like paving, walks can be constructed of a number of materials, such as asphalt or brick, but the most common is concrete because of its strength and durability. Concrete walks should be laid over a gravel subbase with control joints every 5 ft and expansion joints every 20 ft. Walks are usually 4 in thick. Additionally, expansion joints should be located where walks abut buildings, curbs, paving, and other permanent structures.

Low Retaining Walls

The *International Building Code* (IBC) requires that retaining walls be designed for lateral loads, overturning, sliding, and water uplift. Some of the types of retaining walls and how they are designed are discussed in Chap. 37. In some cases, such as residential or small commercial site work, a low retaining wall with no surcharge may be constructed of interlocking concrete or stone blocks designed for that use, large treated timbers, or similar materials, without engineering analysis. These walls are usually limited to approximately three or four feet high depending on the requirements of the local authority having jurisdiction. When timbers or large blocks are used, the retaining wall may be anchored back to the earth with a deadman. A *deadman* is a timber, plate, or similar object placed perpendicular to the face of the retaining wall and that serves to anchor the wall by means of earth friction or pressure. Deadmen may also be used in larger, engineered walls, such as those discussed in Chap. 37.

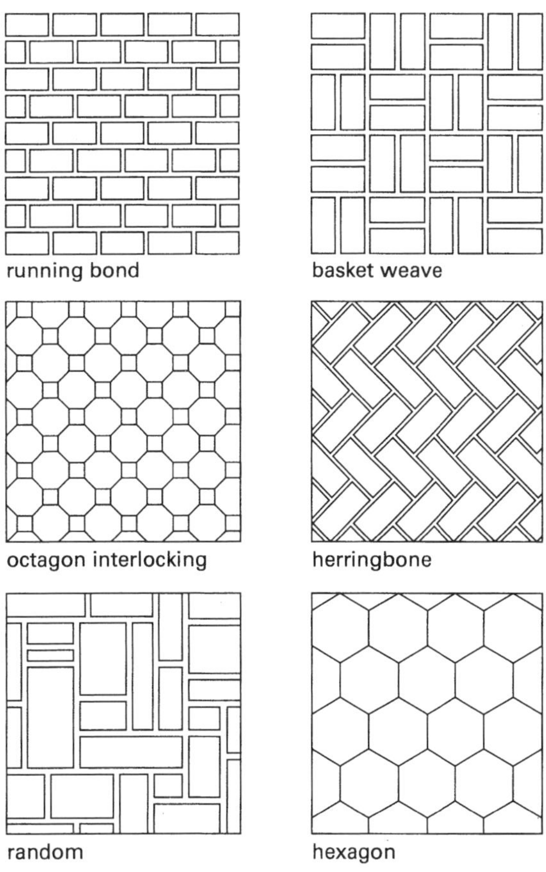

Figure 21.5 Unit Paving Patterns

Project Planning

Example 21.2

Which of the following statements is INCORRECT?

(A) A $1\frac{1}{2}\%$ slope is suitable for rough paving.

(B) Landscaped areas near buildings should have at least a 2% slope away from the structure.

(C) A safe sidewalk slopes no more than $2\frac{1}{2}\%$.

(D) Roads in northern climates can safely have up to a 12% grade.

Solution

Most roads should be kept at a grade of less than 10%; very short roads and parking garage ramps are exceptions. In northern climates, where snow and ice are a problem, it is even more important to maintain gentle slopes. A 12% grade would not be safe and could make driving difficult.

The answer is (D).

22

CONCRETE

Project Planning

Concrete is one of the most versatile of basic building materials. It is durable, strong, weather resistant, and sustainable, and it can be formed into a wide variety of shapes and finished in a number of ways. It can be used in both structural and nonstructural applications. Although concrete has many advantages, its use requires knowledge of many variables and construction steps. These include formwork, reinforcing, placing, curing, testing, and finishing.

Refer to Chap. 11 and Chap. 18 for discussions of selecting structural systems, including concrete and to Chap. 43 for a more detailed discussion of concrete structural design. Refer to Chap. 13 for sustainability issues.

HISTORY OF CONCRETE

Concrete was first developed by the Romans. As early as the third century B.C., Roman builders used a mortar made of lime and sand. Later they discovered that if they mixed pozzolana, a volcanic ash, with lime and water, the mixture would set underwater. They mixed their new cement with stone and brick rubble to form walls, and they cast it in wooden forms to create vaults, arches, and domes.

Concrete fell out of popular use until the late eighteenth century, when John Smeaton found that quicklime containing clay would harden underwater. He used a primitive form of this mortar for a stone lighthouse. In 1824, Joseph Aspdin developed portland cement, the first manufactured hydraulic binder—that is, a binder that could set underwater. Reinforced concrete, or ferroconcrete as it was first known, was developed in the latter part of the century when both wire and bars were used to strengthen the construction.

Although there was some experimentation with concrete during the nineteenth century (the Paris Exhibition of 1867 used concrete in portions of the main building), it was not until the first two decades of the twentieth century that engineers and architects began to fully exploit the possibilities of the material.

The Swiss engineer Robert Maillart used concrete extensively in his bridges and industrial buildings. One of his best known works was Cement Hall, completed in 1939 in Zurich. It was a thin-shell parabolic vault that fully exploited the possibilities of reinforced concrete.

Auguste Perret was another innovator with concrete. However, he used the material for structural frames in simple rectangular constructions. The area between the concrete frames was frequently filled in with other materials. A contemporary of Perret, Tony Garnier, envisioned using ferroconcrete as the basis for the buildings in his proposed town plan, the *cité industrielle*, designed between 1901 and 1904.

Engineer Pier Luigi Nervi used reinforced concrete for many of his most innovative structures. His stadiums in Florence, bridges, and airplane hangars use exposed concrete in daring and innovative forms. His most famous works include the Exhibition Building in Turin (1948) and the sports palace in Rome (1957). Nervi also experimented with and used precast reinforced concrete units in many of his buildings.

Le Corbusier used concrete extensively in many of his later buildings. The apartment block at Marseilles, France (1946-1952), the chapel of Notre Dame du Haut in Ronchamp, France (1950-1954), and the Palace of Justice in Chandigarh, India (1953), are examples of a master architect exploiting the plastic possibilities of the material. Frank Lloyd Wright used reinforced concrete in many of his later buildings such as Fallingwater (1938), the Johnson Wax Headquarters (1936), and the Guggenheim Museum (1959). Wright also experimented with concrete masonry units in his "textile block" houses built in California in the 1920s.

FORMWORK

Formwork refers to the system of boards, ties, and bracing used to construct the mold in which wet concrete is placed. Formwork must be strong enough to withstand the weight and pressure created by the wet concrete and must be easy to erect and remove.

Types of Forms

Forms are constructed of a variety of materials. Unless the concrete is finished in some way, the shape and texture of the surfaces of the formwork will affect the appearance of the final product. Wood grain, knotholes, joints, and other imperfections in the form will leave a negative image in the concrete when the form is removed.

Plywood is the most common forming material. It is usually $^3/_4$ in thick and is coated on one side with oil, a water-resistant glue, or plastic, which prevents water from penetrating the wood and increases the reusability of the form. Oil on forms also keeps the concrete from adhering, so that the forms are easier to remove. The plywood is supported with solid wood framing, which is braced or shored as necessary.

Figure 22.1 shows two typical wood-framed forms.

Figure 22.1 Concrete Formwork

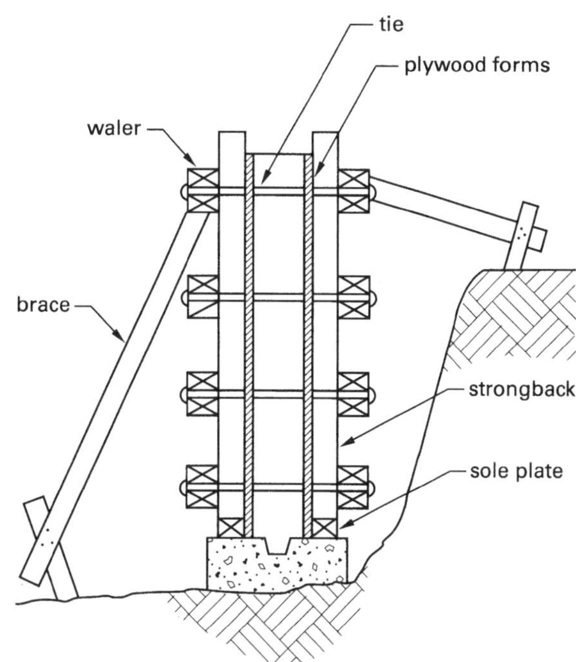

(a) wall formwork

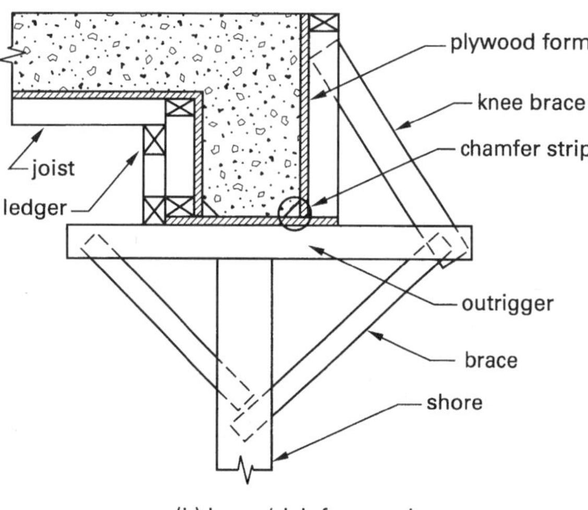

(b) beam/slab formwork

Prefabricated steel forms are often used because of their strength and reusability. They can form one-way joist systems, waffle slabs, round columns, and other special shapes. Forms can also be made of glass-fiber-reinforced plastic, hardboard, and various kinds of proprietary systems. Plastic forms are manufactured with a variety of patterns embedded within. These patterns are transferred to the concrete and influence the texture of the final surface. Special form liners can also be used to impart a deeply embossed pattern.

For exposed architectural surfaces, the method of construction and design of the formwork must receive careful consideration because the pattern of joints and form ties will be visible. Joints are often emphasized with *rustication strips,* continuous pieces of neoprene, wood, or other material that, when removed, will show a deep reveal in the concrete.

Form ties are metal wires or rods used to hold opposite sides of the form together and prevent their collapse. When the forms are removed, the wire remains in the concrete, and the excess is twisted or cut off. Some form ties are threaded rods that can be unscrewed and reused.

Tie holes are made with cone-shaped heads placed against the concrete form. When these are removed, a deep, round hole is left, allowing the tie to be cut off below the surface of the concrete. These holes can remain exposed as a design feature or be patched with grout.

Special Forms

Most formwork is designed and constructed to remain in place until the concrete cures sufficiently to stand on its own. However, one method called *slip forming* moves as the concrete cures. Slip forming is used to form continuous surfaces such as tunnels and high-rise building cores. The entire form is constructed with working platforms and supports for the jacking assembly. Various types of jacking systems are used to support the form as it moves upward. The form moves continuously upward at about 6 in to 12 in per hour while concrete is poured. By the time the form moves up enough that the concrete is exposed, it is sufficiently cured to support the jacks that keep the form moving upward.

Flying forms are large fabricated sections of framework that are removed once the concrete has cured and reused in forming an identical section above. They are often used in buildings with highly repetitive units, such as hotels and apartments. After forming a floor for a hotel, for example, the form assembly is slid outside the edge of the building where it is lifted by crane to the story above. After that floor is poured, the process is repeated.

Insulating Concrete Forms

Insulating concrete forms (ICFs) are polystyrene foam forms that provide the formwork for poured concrete and remain in place after the concrete cures. Finish materials are applied directly to plastic or metal ties that are integral to the forms. ICFs speed construction and provide insulation in one operation. When used for above-grade walls, they produce a strong exterior wall with significant sound attenuation and less air infiltration.

There are three basic varieties of ICF systems: block, plank, and panel. *Block systems* use foam blocks about the size of concrete blocks. These blocks have interlocking edges and integral ties and can be stacked like simple building blocks. The ties that hold the two sides of the block together are attached to the plastic or metal strips that are used for the attachment of finishes. *Panel systems* use flat foam panels up to 4 ft × 12 ft. *Plank systems* use flat forms up to 12 in high and from 4 ft to 8 ft long. In all systems, reinforcement is placed in the forms as called for by the structural requirements of the project.

ICFs are used most often for single- and two-family houses and small commercial construction. They can be used for the basement portion of the building only, or for both the basement and one or two stories above grade.

Insulating concrete forms speed construction and provide insulation in one operation.

Depending on the wall height and the type of system used, ICFs can reduce the amount of bracing needed. For block forms, the concrete is usually placed in lifts (or layers) to prevent blowout of the forms. In all cases, codes require that both sides of the wall be protected from fire and exposure to sunlight and weather. This can be accomplished by installing a layer of gypsum wallboard of a minimum $\frac{1}{2}$ in thickness directly to the interior for finish and fire protection, or furring may be attached for application of other materials. Below grade, the exterior of the wall must be protected from moisture with dampproofing or waterproofing as required by the soil conditions.

Economy in Formwork

One of the biggest expenses for cast-in-place concrete is the formwork. The architect can reduce the overall cost by following some basic guidelines. Forms should be as reusable as possible, meaning that uniform bay sizes, beam depths, column widths, opening sizes, and other major elements should be repeated throughout the building. Slab thicknesses and walls should be kept constant, without offsets. Structural requirements will necessitate variations in many elements, but it is often less expensive to use a little more concrete to maintain a uniform dimension than to form offsets.

Tolerances

Because of the nature of the material and the forming methods, concrete construction cannot be perfect. Certain tolerances are accepted as industry standards. Construction attached to concrete must be capable of accommodating these tolerances. For columns, piers, and walls, the maximum variation in plumb will be $\pm\frac{1}{4}$ in in any 10 ft length. The same tolerance applies for horizontal elements, such as ceilings, beam soffits, and slab soffits.

The maximum variation out of plumb for the total height of the structure is 1 in for interior columns and $^1/_2$ in for corner columns for buildings up to 100 ft tall, while the maximum variation for the total length of the building is $\pm$1 in. Elevation control points for slabs on grade can vary up to $^1/_2$ in in any 10 ft bay and $\pm^3/_4$ in for the total length of the structure.

For elevated, formed slabs the tolerance is $\pm^3/_4$ in. Finished concrete floors can be specified anywhere from $\pm^1/_8$ in in 10 ft for very flat slabs, to $\pm^1/_2$ in for bull-floated slabs. When a slab is bull floated, a 10 ft straightedge is laid on the floor and any high or low spots are identified and measured.

Another way to specify and measure the flatness and levelness tolerance of a concrete floor is with the *F-number system* (*Face floor profile numbers*). With this system, an electronic instrument is used to take multiple readings over 12-inch intervals and develop a statistical evaluation of the flatness and levelness of a floor, which is reflected in a single number value for each ranging from 10 to 150. Although there is no direct equivalence between F-numbers and the older straightedge method of measuring flatness, a $^1/_4$ in gap is about the same as an F-number of 25. A $^1/_8$ in gap is about the same as an F-number of 50. As F-numbers increase, the flatness and levelness of the slab improves. F-numbers are only used for on-grade slabs, due to the initial and developed deflection of elevated slabs with an airspace below them.

MOISTURE MIGRATION AND VAPOR BARRIERS

In all construction, water and moisture can cause a variety of problems. For concrete construction the potential problem of water migration through slabs on grade is one of the most significant. Moisture is not as much of a threat for suspended slabs.

Moisture Migration Through Slabs on Grade

Moisture can migrate through slabs by capillary action or by movement of water vapor. Capillary action causes water to be drawn up through the slab through the forces of adhesion, surface tension, and cohesion. Water vapor moves from areas of high vapor pressure to areas of lower vapor pressure by the process of diffusion, which can occur in concrete and soil when water changes from a liquid to a vapor as it evaporates.

For slabs on grade, a vapor barrier must be provided under the slab to prevent the migration of moisture through the slab, onto the surface of the slab, or into the space above the slab. Moisture can cause damage to water-sensitive floor finishes, such as vinyl tile, and can create problems in indoor air quality by supplying one of the necessary components of mold and mildew growth.

Water problems inside the building can be reduced by specifying a low *water-cementitious materials ratio* (abbreviated as *w/cm ratio* or just *w/cm*) in the concrete mix. (This ratio was more commonly known in the past as the *water-cement ratio* or *w/c ratio*, but cementitious materials other than portland cement have become more common.) If possible, construction should be scheduled so that slabs have as much time as possible to cure and dry before any sealants or floor finishes are applied. This will help provide a vapor barrier.

Because it takes so long for the free water (the water not used in the curing process) to evaporate out of the slab, it is recommended that the maximum w/cm ratio be set at 0.45 to 0.50. Ideally, concrete slabs should be allowed to cure and dry for a minimum of six weeks before resilient flooring is installed.

Vapor Barriers

The best way to stop the migration of moisture is with a vapor barrier placed directly below the concrete slab and on top of any sand cushion layer or subbase. This recommendation is contrary to the traditional method of placing the vapor barrier under the sand cushion. However, the traditional method is no longer recommended, because the sand acts as a sponge to hold any water present during construction.

A *vapor barrier* is a thin sheet material, generally plastic, designed to prevent water vapor from passing through it. A *vapor retarder*, on the other hand, only slows the rate of water vapor transmission. A vapor barrier should have a permeance not exceeding 0.04 perm and be at least 10 mils thick.

Permeance is a measure of a material's resistance to water-vapor transmission, expressed in perms. As discussed in Chap. 12, a *perm* is the passage of one grain of water vapor per hour through one square foot of material at a pressure differential of one inch of mercury between the two sides of the material.

REINFORCEMENT

Concrete is strong in compression but weak in tension. As a result, a reinforcing material that is strong in tension is needed to resist the tensile stresses in beams, slabs, and columns, and to reduce the size of columns. There are two types of reinforcing steel for cast-in-place concrete: deformed bars and welded wire fabric for reinforcement of slabs.

Reinforcing Bars

Reinforcing bars, often called *rebar*, are available in diameters from $^3/_8$ in to $2^1/_4$ in, with $^1/_8$ in increments up to $1^3/_8$ in. There are also two special large sizes of $1^3/_4$ in and $2^1/_4$ in. Bars are designated by numbers that represent the number of $^1/_8$ in increments in the nominal diameter of the bar. Thus, a no. 6 bar has a diameter of $^6/_8$ in, or $^3/_4$ in. See Table 42.1 for the cross-sectional areas and other dimensional properties of standard sizes of rebar.

Reinforcing steel and concrete must be bonded together to provide maximum strength. For this reason, rebar is deformed to mechanically interlock the two materials. Additional bonding is provided by the chemical adhesion of the concrete to the steel and by the normal roughness of the steel. There are several types of deformation patterns depending on the mill that manufactures the bar, but they all serve the same purpose. In order to clearly identify bars on the job site, standard designations have been developed for marking bars at the mill. These are shown in Fig. 22.2.

Project Planning

Figure 22.2 Reinforcing Bar Identification

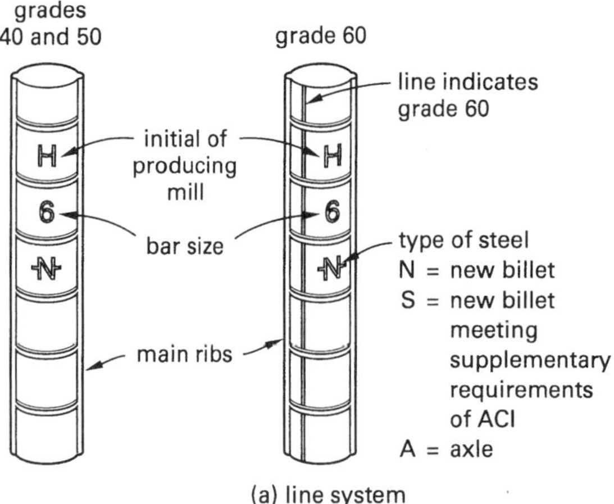

(a) line system

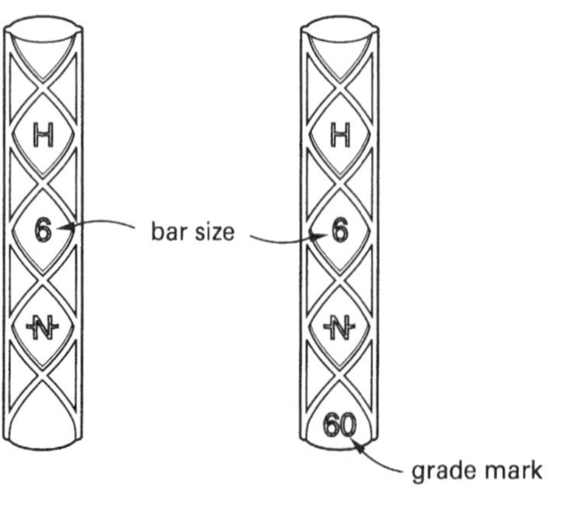

(b) number system

Rebar comes in two common grades: grade 40 and grade 60. Grades 50 and 75 are also available. These numbers refer to the yield strength of the steel in kips per square inch. Grade 60 is the type most commonly used in building construction. Wire for prestressing (discussed later in this chapter) has a much higher tensile strength, up to 270 $kips/in^2$. Rebar is classified as axle, rail, and billet, the last of which is the most commonly used.

In order to protect the reinforcing, certain minimum clearances between the steel and the exposed face of the concrete must be maintained according to project conditions. These distances, listed in Table 22.1, can be maintained by using metal or plastic rebar supports that keep the reinforcing steel in place, as discussed later in this section. There are also minimum allowable clearances between rebar to allow the coarse aggregate to pass through as the concrete is poured.

Alternative Types of Reinforcing Members

There are several types of reinforcing bars that can be used instead of plain steel, including galvanized steel, stainless steel, epoxy-coated steel, and glass-fiber-reinforced polymer. These are used in special applications, such as corrosive environments, where the concrete will be exposed to chlorides in seawater or deicing salts.

Galvanized steel rebar provides the same type of protection as most galvanized product as long as the coating remains intact. Special care must be taken in the bending process so that the coating is not cracked.

Where extreme corrosion resistance or non-magnetic characteristics are needed, *stainless steel bars* can be used. Although this is more expensive than ordinary rebar, the additional cost of stainless steel is justified where the highest level of durability and extended service life are needed, or where the cost of repairing or replacing corroded bars would be high, such as in a large highway bridge or nuclear facility.

Table 22.1 Minimum Concrete Protection for Reinforcement (distances from edge of rebar to face of concrete)

location	distance (in)
surfaces not exposed directly to the weather or ground:	
slabs and walls	3/4
beams and columns	1 1/2
surfaces exposed to the weather or in contact with the ground:	
no. 5 bars and smaller	1 1/2
larger than no. 5 bars	2
concrete poured directly on the ground	3

Like stainless steel, *epoxy-coated rebar* is used where corrosion presents a problem, such as road pavement, bridges, parking structures, and marine structures. Epoxy-coated steel is less expensive than and almost as durable as stainless steel and has a proven record of performance.

Glass-fiber-reinforced polymer rebar (*GFRP rebar*) is used where corrosion is present or where nonferrous reinforcement is needed due to electromagnetic considerations, such as MRI facilities or high-voltage transformer vaults. Because its physical properties are different from those of steel, GFRP rebar cannot be used in primary structural members, like columns and beams, in moment frames, in seismic zones, or for prestressing tendons.

Welded Wire Fabric

Welded wire fabric is used for temperature reinforcement in slabs. It consists of cold-drawn steel wires set at right angles to each other and welded at their intersections. The wires are usually in a square pattern with spacings of 4 in or 6 in.

The system used to designate welded wire fabric gives the size first and then the gage. The size is stated in inches and the gage is given in cross-sectional area in hundredths of a square inch. For example, "6 × 6—W1.4 × 1.4" means that the grid is 6 in by 6 in, and the size of the wire is 1.4 hundredths of a square inch, or 0.014 in^2. The letter preceding the gage is either W for smooth wire or D for deformed wire. See Carbon Fiber Concrete section for information on carbon fiber mesh, which can also be used for reinforcement of slabs.

Accessories

Before concrete is poured into the forms, various types of embedded items must be placed in addition to the reinforcing. These include

- welding plates for attachment of steel and other structural members
- electrical boxes and conduit
- sleeves for pipes to pass through the concrete
- other types of anchoring devices for suspended components and finish walls

Embedded items must be accurately placed and are temporarily held in position with nails, by wiring the object to the reinforcing, or with other proprietary devices until secured by the concrete.

Other accessories also hold reinforcing bars in their proper locations. Intersecting reinforcing bars are wired together and held in place with spacers in walls and with chairs in slabs. *Chairs* are metal wire or plastic devices placed on the form to hold the rebars above the bottom of the form at the proper distance.

CONCRETE MATERIALS

Basic Components

Concrete is a combination of cement, fine and coarse aggregates, and water. These components are mixed in the proper proportions and allowed to cure to form a hard, durable material. *Admixtures* can be added to impart particular qualities to the mix. Because the strength of concrete depends on the materials and their proportions, it is important to understand the relationship between the constituent parts.

The binding agent in concrete is *portland cement*, which is made from lime, silica, iron oxide, and alumina (also called aluminum oxide) under strictly controlled conditions. Portland cement interacts chemically with water to form a paste that binds the other aggregate particles together in a solid mass. Cement is supplied in bulk or in 94 lbm bags containing one cubicfoot of cement mix.

Too much water can decrease concrete's strength. Excess water remains in the paste and forms pores that cannot resist compressive forces.

There are five different types of cement, all used for specific purposes. Type I is called *standard cement*, or *normal cement*, and it is used for most general construction where the special properties of other types are not needed. Type II is called *modified cement*, and it is used in places where a modest amount of sulfate resistance is needed and the heat of hydration needs to be controlled, such as in dams or other massive structures. Type III is *high-early-strength cement* and is used where a quick set is needed; type III also has a higher heat of hydration, so it is suitable for cold-weather concreting. Type IV, used in massive structures to minimize cracking, is called *low-heat cement*, and it is very slow setting; this is no longer commonly used. Type V is *sulfate-resisting cement* and is used for structures that will be exposed to water or soil with a high alkaline content.

Although water is needed for *hydration* (the chemical hardening of concrete) and makes it possible to mix and place the concrete into forms, too much water can decrease the concrete's strength. Excess water not used in the chemical process remains in the paste and forms pores that cannot resist compressive forces. For complete hydration to occur, an amount of water equal to 25% of the weight of the cement is needed. An extra 10% to 15% or more is needed to make a workable mix. The water itself must be potable to ensure that it is free of any foreign matter that could interfere with adhesion of the aggregates to the cement paste.

For most concrete mixes, the minimum water-cementitious materials (w/cm) ratio is about 0.35 to 0.40 by weight. Based on the weight of water, this works out to about 4 gal to 4.5 gal of water per 94 lbm sack of cement.

Because of the way water and cement interact, the w/cm ratio is the most important factor in determining the strength of concrete. For a given mix, there should be just enough water to produce a workable mix without being too watery. If too much water is added, *laitance* may develop. This is a chalky surface deposit of low-strength concrete. If additional concrete will be poured on top of an existing pour, the laitance must be removed in order for the new concrete to bond. A w/cm ratio of 0.25 is used where high strength is required, such as for high-rise buildings, but a super plasticizer must be used to make this type of mix workable. Common residential walks and driveways, on the other hand, can have a w/cm ratio of 0.55 and still be serviceable.

Aggregates are available in coarse and fine varieties. Fine aggregates are those that pass through a no. 4 sieve (one with four openings per linear inch). Coarse aggregates specified for most concrete mixes are typically $^3/_4$ in or 1 in. Because cement is the most expensive component of concrete, the best mix is one that uses a combination of aggregate sizes that fill most of the volume, so that the minimum amount of cement is used to achieve the desired strength. Aggregates typically occupy about 65% to 70% of the total volume of the concrete.

Generally, concrete aggregates are materials such as sand and gravel, but other materials may be used. Materials such as expanded clays, slags, and shales are used for lightweight structural concrete. Pumice or cinders are used for insulating concretes. Whereas standard concrete weighs about 150 lbm/ft^3, lightweight mixes can range from 50 lbm/ft^3 for insulating concretes to 120 lbm/ft^3 for lightweight structural concrete.

The size of coarse aggregates is determined by the size of the forms and the spacing between the reinforcing. In most instances, the size of the largest aggregate should not be more than three-fourths the smallest distance between reinforcing bars, one-fifth the smallest dimension of forms, or one-third the depth of slabs, whichever is smallest.

Proportioning

The proportions of materials in a concrete mix determine its properties of strength, workability, durability, economy, and sustainability. Achieving the highest level of all these properties at once is usually not possible because they are often in conflict. For example, lowering the w/cm ratio will improve strength but decrease workability. The goal is to determine the best balance of these properties to meet the particular requirements of the project.

When the mix design has been developed, several methods are used to specify the proportions of the concrete mix. One is to define the ratio of cement to sand to gravel by weight using three numbers such as 1:2:4, which means one part cement, two parts sand, and four parts gravel. In addition, the amount of water must also be specified. Another method is to specify the weight of materials, including water, per 94 lbm bag of cement. A useful method for large batch quantities is to define the weight of the materials needed to make up one cubic yard of concrete; this includes the cement, the aggregates, admixtures, and other cementitious materials.

The strength of the final mix is specified by the compressive strength of the concrete after it has cured and hardened for 28 days. This is known as the *design strength* of concrete. Typical specified design strengths, indicated by the variable f_c', are 2000 psi, 3000 psi (one of the most common), and 4000 psi. Higher strengths, up to 12,000 psi, are available for special applications, but they are more expensive than the standard mixes.

Admixtures

Admixtures are chemicals or other materials added to concrete to impart certain qualities. They are used to speed hydration, slow hardening, improve workability, add color, improve durability, and serve a variety of other purposes. Some of the more common admixtures are the following.

- An *air-entraining agent* forms tiny, dispersed bubbles in the concrete. This increases the workability and durability of the concrete and improves its resistance to freezing and thawing cycles. The agent also helps reduce separation of the components as the mix is poured into forms.
- An *accelerator* speeds up the hydration of the cement so that the concrete achieves strength faster. This allows faster construction and reduces the length of time needed for protection in cold weather.
- A *plasticizer* reduces the amount of water needed while maintaining the needed consistency for correct placement and compaction. Reducing the water makes it possible to mix higher-strength concrete.
- A *retarder* slows down the setting time to help reduce the heat of hydration.
- A *waterproofing agent* decreases the permeability of the concrete.

There are also admixtures for corrosion resistance, underwater use, alkali-silica resistance, shrinkage reducers, and super retarders.

Supplementary Cementitious Materials

Supplementary cementitious materials (SCMs) are added to concrete as part of the total cementitious system and also impart other desirable qualities to a concrete mix. Unlike admixtures, SCMs have cementing properties similar to portland cement and are often used as a partial replacement for portland cement.

- *Fly ash* is a waste material obtained from coal-fired power plants. In concrete, fly ash improves workability, reduces temperature rise, minimizes bleeding, reduces permeability, inhibits alkali-silica reaction (ASR), and enhances sulfate resistance. Like other SCMs, fly ash can also be used to decrease the total amount of cement needed. See later in this chapter for more information on ASR. Refer to Chap. 13 for more information on how fly ash is used to make concrete a more sustainable material.
- *Ground-granulated blast-furnace slag* (GGBFS) is produced from the material formed from molten slag that is a by-product of iron and steel manufacturing. The material is dried and ground to a fine powder to produce a hydraulic cementing material that is substituted for portland cement in different ratios; a 25% to 50% substitution is common. Slag improves workability, decreases the need for water, and increases setting time in concrete, all of which can be a benefit in large pours and during hot weather. It also reduces bleeding, improves resistance to sulfate and chloride attack, and can prevent damage from ASR. Concrete that contains slag develops strength more slowly than standard concrete, particularly in the first seven days, but it continues to gain strength beyond 28 days and has a higher ultimate strength than standard portland cement concrete.
- *Silica fume* is collected by filtering the smoke created during the production of silicon and ferrosilicon metals. It consists mostly of particles of silicon dioxide about $1/100$ the size of cement grains. Silica fume is also available in liquid form. It is added to concrete in a proportion of 7% to 10% by weight of the cement. Silica fume decreases permeability, increases compressive strength, improves abrasion resistance, and reduces bleeding.
- A *pozzolan* is a siliceous or aluminosiliceous material that, in finely divided form and in the presence of moisture, reacts chemically with the calcium hydroxide released by the hydration of portland cement to form various cementitious compounds. Pozzolans are used as a partial replacement for portland cement and to decrease permeability, increase strength, and improve resistance to ASR and sulfate attack. Natural pozzolans, which are formed from clay, shale, and other materials with cementitious properties, include calcined shale, calcined clay, and metakaolin. The Romans used volcanic ash, another natural pozzolan, to mix the earliest form of concrete.

Other Concrete Products

Concrete is improved through the use of new materials, admixtures, equipment, and construction techniques. The following are some innovations that have become common in mainstream construction practices.

- autoclaved aerated concrete
- self-consolidating concrete
- carbon fiber concrete
- ultra high performance concrete
- poured gypsum decks

Autoclaved Aerated Concrete

Autoclaved aerated concrete (AAC) is a precast concrete product manufactured by adding aluminum powder to concrete, hardening it in molds, and then curing the molds in a pressurized steam chamber (autoclave). The resultant blocks have approximately one-fifth the density of conventional concrete. They are typically manufactured in blocks 10 in high by 25 in long and in thicknesses of 4 in, 8 in, and 10 in. The blocks are laid with a thinset mortar and can be cut and shaped with woodworking tools. Unreinforced and reinforced panels of ACC are also produced for use as floor, roof, and wall panels.

AAC requires less material and results in less construction site waste than building with standard concrete block, making it a sustainable alternative to standard concrete in some applications. It provides sound control and thermal retention and has greater air tightness than wood stud walls. It is resistant to insects, rodents, and mold. However, it does not have the strength of standard concrete, so construction is limited to nonloadbearing walls and low-rise structures. It must also be protected from the exterior environment with plaster, masonry, or some other exterior finish.

Self-Consolidating Concrete

Self-consolidating concrete (SCC) is a concrete mixture that can be placed by means of its own weight without the use of vibration. SCC is made possible with the use of a superplasticizer admixture called a polycarboxylate polymer. Because no vibration is needed, SCC placement finishes faster, requires less labor, and increases productivity. This type of concrete flows easily around dense reinforcement and provides a smoother, more uniform surface than standard concrete, so less time is required to make minor cosmetic repairs. Because SCC develops strength faster than conventional concrete, forms can be stripped sooner.

Carbon Fiber Concrete

Carbon fiber concrete uses epoxy-coated carbon fiber mesh in place of standard steel mesh for secondary steel reinforcement. It is used to make precast panels thinner and lighter. Because carbon fiber is noncorrosive, less concrete cover is required. The resulting panels require smaller foundations and support structures, reduce transportation costs, and speed the erection process.

The carbon fiber is manufactured by extruding industrial-grade carbon into ultrathin fibers. The fibers are bundled together to form pieces resembling yarn, called *tows*. The tows are laid perpendicular to each other in a grid, with the intersecting tows bound together by a heat-cured epoxy resin. The resulting grid, or fabric, is about 0.04 in thick. The various components of the grid can be modified to meet different strength requirements, with a typical grid having nearly seven times the tensile strength of standard steel mesh.

Ultra High Performance Concrete

Ultra high performance concrete (UNPC) is a type of concrete characterized by high strength, low water absorption, and high resistance to waterborne and airborne chemical degradation. Compressive strength can range from 17,000 psi to 25,000 psi with flexural strength from 3600 psi to 6000 psi. UHPC is comprised of cement, sand, water, silica fume, and plasticizers along with a small percentage of alkali resistant glass fibers or steel fibers. The unique properties of UHPC are achieved by using extremely small particle sizes and unique particle chemistry mixed, vibrated, and cured in the factory under controlled conditions. Because of the unique characteristics of the material it is typically delivered precast and not mixed on the job site.

Although it is used for structural members it is often used in architectural applications for exterior cladding, curtain walls, shading devices, and landscape elements. For exterior cladding, precast elements can be as thin as $^5/_8$ in. For textured panels, a $^3/_4$ in or $^1/_{18}$ in thickness is used. This compares with 4 in to 6 in thicknesses for standard concrete precast panels and $1^1/_2$ in to 2 in for glass fiber reinforced concrete panels.

Because of the exacting mixing and production processes involved in UHPC, there are few manufacturers producing the product.

Poured Gypsum Decks

A poured gypsum deck is used for roofs and is similar to concrete in that a liquid mixture is poured on reinforcing material. In typical gypsum deck construction, purlins support fiber plank or rigid insulation. Wire mesh reinforcing is placed over the insulation and gypsum is poured on the assembly to a minimum depth of $2^1/_2$ in. Gypsum provides a highly fire-resistant roof deck.

Precast gypsum planks with tongue-and-groove edges are also available in 2 in and 4 in thicknesses. These planks are reinforced with wire fabric and can span up to 10 ft.

Curing and Testing

Curing Concrete

Because concrete hardens and gains strength by curing—through chemical reaction between the water and the cement—rather than by drying, it is essential that the proper moisture and temperature conditions be maintained for at least seven days and up to two weeks for critical work, such as a cantilevered stadium seating area. If concrete dries too fast, it can lose strength, up to 30% or more in some instances. With high-early-strength cements, the time can be reduced. This is because concrete gains about 70% of its strength during the first week of curing, and the final 28-day design strength depends on the initial curing conditions.

There are many techniques for maintaining proper moisture levels, including covering with plastic, using sealing compounds, or continually sprinkling the surfaces with water.

Concrete must also be kept from freezing while curing or it will lose strength, sometimes as much as half. Because concrete produces heat while it cures (known as *heat of hydration*) it is often sufficient to cover the fresh material with insulated plastic sheets for a few days. In very cold conditions, Type III cement may be used and external heat supplied. Alternatively, the water and aggregate may be heated prior to mixing.

Testing Concrete

Because there are so many variables in concrete construction, the material must be continually tested at various stages to maintain quality. There are several tests with which the architect must be familiar, including the following.

- slump test
- cylinder test
- core cylinder test
- Kelly ball test
- impact hammer test
- K-slump test

Usually performed at the job site, the *slump test* measures the consistency of the concrete. In this test, concrete is placed in a 12 in high truncated cone, 8 in at the base and 4 in at the top. It is compacted in the cone by hand with a rod, and then the mold is removed from the concrete and placed next to it. The distance the concrete slumps from the original 12 in height is then measured in inches. The amount of slump desired depends on how the concrete is going to be used, but it is typically specified to be in the range of 2 in to 6 in. Too much slump indicates excessive water in the mix, and a very small slump indicates that the mixture will be difficult to place properly.

The *cylinder test* measures compressive strength. As the concrete is placed, samples are put in cylinder molds that are 6 in in diameter and 12 in high, and are moist-cured and tested in the laboratory according to standardized procedures. Plastic cylinders are sometimes used for this test and are 4 in in diameter and 8 in high. The compressive strength in pounds per square inch is calculated and compared with the value used in the design of the structure. Cylinders are tested at a specified number of days, normally 7 and 28 days. Seven-day test results are usually about 60% to 70% of the 28-day strength.

The *core cylinder test* is used when a portion of the structure is in place and cured but needs to be tested. A cylinder is drilled out of the concrete and tested in the laboratory to determine its compressive strength.

In the *Kelly ball test*, also known as the *ball penetration test*, a hemispheric mass of steel with a calibrated stem is dropped onto a slab of freshly laid concrete. The amount of penetration of the ball into the concrete is measured and compared to one-half the values of the slump test.

The *impact hammer test* is a nondestructive way to test concrete strength after it has hardened. A spring-loaded plunger snaps against a concrete surface, and the amount of rebound is measured. The amount of rebound gives an approximate reading of the concrete strength. If this test is not accurate enough, the cylinder cores can be cut from hardened concrete and tested in the laboratory.

The *K-slump test* uses a $^3/_4$ in tube that contains a floating scale. The tube is placed on the wet concrete, and the scale is pushed into the mixture and released. The distance the scale floats out directly measures the consistency of the concrete, comparable to the slump measure by the traditional slump test.

Testing Concrete for Moisture Content and Alkalinity

Because unwanted moisture in a slab on grade can create many problems, the moisture level of the concrete should be tested prior to the application of any important finishes such as vinyl, rubber, linoleum, urethane, or wood. The flooring industry recommends that these types of flooring not be installed until the moisture emission from the concrete has reached a certain level. This maximum limit for moisture emission is 3.0 lbm per 1000 ft^2 per 24 hr when exposed to 73°F temperature and 50% relative humidity. There are several tests by which moisture level can be determined.

- calcium chloride test
- hygrometer test
- polyethylene sheet test
- mat test
- electrical impedance test

The *calcium chloride test* (sometimes called the *moisture dome test*) is one of the most common tests for moisture in concrete because it is inexpensive and easy to complete. It gives results in the same form that many flooring manufacturers use to determine if their products can be successfully installed. This test is conducted by placing a standard mass of calcium chloride below a plastic cover and sealing the cover to the concrete floor. After 60 to 72 hours, the calcium chloride is weighed and compare with its pretest weight. Through a mathematical formula, the amount of moisture the calcium chloride absorbed is converted to the standard measure of pounds per 1000 ft^2 per 24-hour period. One test should be conducted for every 500 ft^2 to 1000 ft^2 of slab area.

The *hygrometer test* (sometimes called the *relative humidity test*) determines the moisture emission by measuring the relative humidity (RH) of the atmosphere confined adjacent to the concrete floor. In this test, a pocket of air is trapped below a vapor-impermeable box, and a probe in the device measures the RH. Test standards recommend that moisture-sensitive flooring not be installed unless the RH is 75% or less.

The *polyethylene sheet test* is a qualitative test conducted by sealing an 18 in × 18 in sheet of plastic to the floor to trap excessive moisture. After a minimum of 16 hours, a visual inspection is made of the floor and the sheet. The presence of visible water indicates the concrete is insufficiently dry for the application of finishes.

Similar to the sheet test is the *mat test*. This is also a qualitative method that uses a 24 in × 24 in sample of a vapor-retardant floor finish. The sample is applied with adhesive, and the edges are sealed with tape. After 72 hours a visual inspection is made. If the mat is firmly bonded or if removal of the mat is difficult, the level of moisture present is considered to be sufficiently low for installation of the flooring material.

The *electrical impedance test* uses proprietary meters to determine the moisture content of the concrete by measuring conductance and capacitance. Probes of the meter are placed on the concrete, and the percentage of moisture content in the slab is read out directly.

In addition to testing for moisture, the slab should be tested for pH level and alkalinity. *pH level* is a measure of the acidity or alkalinity of a material rated on a scale from 0 to 14 with 7 being neutral. Materials with a pH lower than 7 are considered acidic while those above 7 are considered alkaline. The scale is logarithmic, so a material with a pH of 12 is actually ten times more alkaline than one with a pH of 11. Concrete normally has a pH of about 12.0 to 13.3.

Although pH level is an indication of the presence of alkalinity, pH level and alkalinity are not synonymous. Alkalinity cannot exist without moisture because the moisture causes the soluble alkalis in the concrete to enter into the solution.

In addition to the alkalis within the concrete slab itself, excess alkalinity can be carried from the soil below the slab through the migration of water vapor. This is another reason why vapor barriers are important. Although pH level is an indication of the presence of alkalinity, pH level and alkalinity are not synonymous. Two slabs can have the same pH level, but one can have a much higher alkalinity. Alkalinity cannot exist without moisture because the moisture causes the soluble alkalis in the concrete to enter into the solution. This is why it is important to control moisture in slabs.

Alkalinity in concrete can cause problems in two ways. High alkalinity on the surface of a slab can damage a tile installation by causing the adhesive to re-emulsify, or revert to its original liquid state. It can also negatively affect other coatings. At a pH level of about 9 or 10, most tile adhesives begin to experience problems, although professional-grade adhesives can sometimes be used on a slab that has a pH of 11. Surface alkalinity can be controlled with various proprietary coatings.

Alkalinity is also responsible for the phenomenon known as *alkali-silica reaction* (ASR). In this process, strongly alkaline cement begins to dissolve the sand and rock within the concrete. The chemical reaction produces a gel-like material that creates tremendous pressures in the pores of the concrete surface. These pressures can buckle or blister floor finishes. The risk for ASR can be reduced by specifying aggregates that are not susceptible to ASR, by using low-lime cement, by proper curing, or by not finishing the concrete with a hard trowel surface. Resistance to ASR can also be improved by using SCMs as discussed in the previous section.

A *pH test* is used to test the surface of concrete that will come in contact with flooring adhesives or other floor coatings. This simple test uses a coated paper strip or a small pH meter. If the paper test strip is used, it will turn a color that corresponds to the color on a key, indicating the pH level. A pH meter is a device measures the voltage between electrodes when the electrodes are in contact with the material being tested. Once the pH level is known, it can be compared with the maximum pH recommended by the flooring manufacturer. A pH of 8.5 is considered ideal for flooring installation; this is about the minimum pH that concrete can have, with values up to 9.0 being acceptable.

In addition to the pH test, a *titration test* can be used to determine the level of alkalinity in concrete. This involves grinding portions of the concrete, mixing the resulting powder with demineralized water, and performing laboratory chemical analysis. A testing laboratory must perform this test.

Placing and Finishing

Concrete Placement

Placing concrete involves several steps, from transporting the material from the truck or mixer to using the forms. First, the concrete must be mixed according to the proportions specified in the mix design, which is developed based on the desired properties of the product. The concrete can be mixed in small amounts on site, but larger quantities are blended at a plant and delivered to the project site in an agitating truck.

If the concrete will be transported from the plant to the site, the mix design of the concrete can be adjusted to allow for the length of the trip; usually the allowable time is less than two hours. When it arrives on site, preliminary performance tests may be performed to verify that the mix is as specified. If the concrete fails the preliminary tests, it may be rejected. If it passes the tests, it is conveyed to the formwork to be placed. The concrete is moved and placed with bottom-dump buckets, by pumping, or in small buggies or wheelbarrows. The method used depends on the available equipment, the quantity of concrete, and the physical size and layout of the job. Concrete can even be placed underwater with a long, cylindrical steel chute called a *tremie.*

Once at the formwork, the concrete must be placed to avoid *segregation*, which is the separation of the aggregates, water, and sand from each other. Dropping concrete long distances from the conveying device to the forms is one of the typical causes of segregation. Typically, 5 ft is the maximum distance that concrete should be dropped. Excessive lateral movement of the concrete in forms or slab work should also be minimized.

After placement, the concrete must be consolidated to ensure the following.

- The wet material has flowed into all the forms and around all the rebar.
- It has made complete contact with the steel.
- There has been no *honeycombing*, the formation of air pockets within the concrete and next to the forms.

Consolidating also removes air voids trapped in the concrete and decreases permeability. For small jobs, hand compaction can be used. More typically, it is done with vibrators.

As-Cast Finishes

Concrete can be finished in a variety of ways. A *rough form finish*, the simple method of leaving the concrete as is when the forms are removed, shows the pattern of the formwork and joints between forms. Defects and tie holes may be left unfinished or finished. This roughest finish, it is usually used for concrete that will not be visible.

A *smooth form finish* is similar in that the profile of the interior of the form will be embossed in the face of the concrete. However, smooth forms of wood, metal, or hardboard are used, and the locations of joints and tie holes are planned so that they are symmetrical. Any fins left from concrete seeping into joints between forms are removed.

Architectural Finishes

Architectural finishes are used where concrete will be exposed and appearance is a consideration. There are several varieties of these finishes.

- *form liner:* The concrete form is constructed and liners of plastic, wood, or metal are attached to the inside of the formwork. Parallel rib liners are a common type. Joints and form tie holes are treated as desired—either left exposed or patched. Custom form liners can be used to give the finished concrete almost any pattern that the architect designs, or the designer can choose from standard patterns offered by the liner manufacturer. Some form liners are designed to allow thin brick to be installed in the formwork before the concrete is poured; the thin brick becomes the exterior finish with the concrete acting as the "mortar" between the masonry units.
- *scrubbed:* The surface of the concrete is wetted and scrubbed with a wire or fiber brush to remove some of the surface mortar and expose the coarse aggregate.
- *acid wash:* The surface of the concrete is wetted with muriatic acid to expose and bring out the full color of the aggregate.
- *water jet:* A high-pressure water jet mixed with air is used to remove some of the mortar and expose the aggregate.

Tooled and Sandblasted Finishes

Tooled finishes are produced by mechanically modifying the concrete surface.

- *bush hammering:* A bush-hammered finish gives a rugged, heavy texture by removing a portion of the surface with a manual or electric hammer with a head that has rows of small pyramids, similar to a meat tenderizer.
- *grinding:* This finishing technique uses a grinder to smooth out the surface of the concrete, giving it a similar appearance to terrazzo.
- *applied:* Applied finishes include the application of other materials, such as stucco, to the concrete.
- *sandblasted finishes:* Sandblasted finishes are produced by removing surface material from the concrete. This exposes the fine and coarse aggregate to varying degrees, depending on whether the sandblasted finish is specified as light, medium, or heavy.

Rubbed Finishes

Rubbing gives concrete a smooth, uniform, durable finish. However, creating the finish can be labor intensive.

- *smooth:* The surface of the concrete is wetted and rubbed with a carborundum abrasive brick to produce a smooth, uniform color and texture.
- *grout cleaned:* Grout is applied over the concrete and smoothed out. This results in a uniform surface with defects concealed.

Concrete Slab Finishes

After a concrete slab is poured, the first finishing operation is to *strike off* the concrete by drawing a straightedge (metal or wood) across the forms to yield a roughly level surface. If a smooth surface is required, the slab is then floated. *Floating* brings cement paste to the surface, where it is consolidated and smoothed over the coarse aggregate; floating can be done with a wood or magnesium float or a bull float. A *float* is a handheld wood or magnesium trowel. A *bull float* is wider than a standard float and is attached to a long handle that allows finishers to smooth large concrete surfaces while standing away from the fresh concrete.

At this point in the finishing operation the following finishes are available.

- If no further work is done after floating, the finish is called a *float finish*. It gives a sandpaper-like texture and is appropriate for exterior surfaces or where smooth surfaces are not needed for other finish materials. A wood float gives a rougher finish texture than a magnesium float does.
- A *light steel-troweled finish* is achieved by using a steel trowel several hours after floating. This further consolidates the concrete. Either hand trowels or large, mechanically driven rotary trowels may beused.
- A *hard steel-troweled finish* continues the consolidation of the concrete and greatly densifies the top $^1/_8$ in of the concrete, making a very smooth surface.
- After floating, a *broom finish* is created by running an industrial broom with medium bristles over the surface of the concrete. This process dislodges fine aggregate and products a rough-textured surface useful for slip-resistance on outdoor slabs.

- A *superflat floor finish* typically has a hard steel troweled finish, but the term refers to the smoothness and levelness of a concrete slab. A superflat floor is commonly used in industrial warehouses where automated or special forklift vehicles are used to rapidly locate and retrieve materials from high-rack storage. Because of the small distances between the storage racks, the vehicles, and the high reach of the lifts, the vehicle must travel on a very smooth, level floor.
- A *stamped finish* gives the slab an embossed surface and may be used in locations where the concrete is to become a decorative element, such as a patio. A plastic stamp is pressed into the wet concrete to create the desired pattern. The concrete can be colored after it is placed, but the installation tends to look and weather better if the color is incorporated into the mix.

Joints and Accessories

Purposes and Types of Concrete Joints

There are four main types of concrete joints: control, construction, expansion, and isolation. Each serves a different function and is constructed differently. See Fig. 22.3.

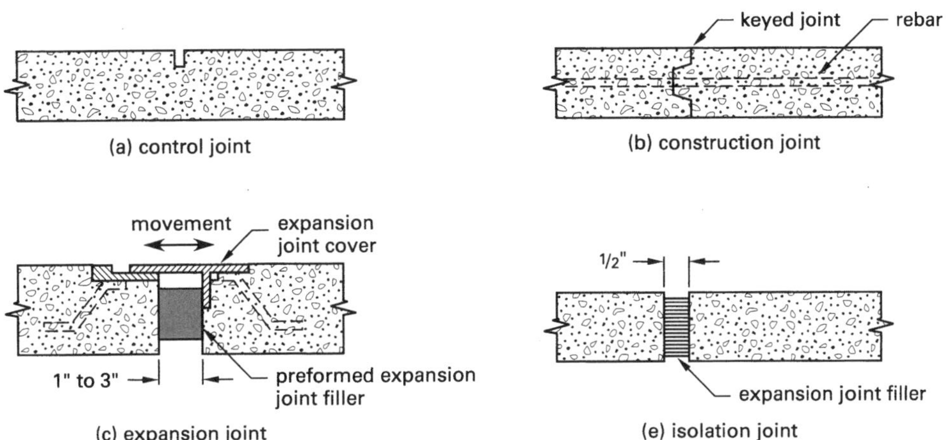

Figure 22.3
Concrete Joints

A *control joint* is a weak section intentionally created in the slab so that normal temperature and stress cracking will occur along the joint instead of at random locations. Control joints are normally formed by tooling when the concrete is still wet, by sawcutting or using premolded sections in the formwork. The joints are cut to a depth of one-fourth the slab thickness.

A *construction joint* occurs wherever there are two successive pours; the joint is created and a new pour is made against a section of concrete already cured. Because a construction joint creates a plane of weakness, it should be located at a point of minimum shear. Normally, reinforcing extends from one pour to another to tie the two sections together. A construction joint is also a point where water leakage can occur. To prevent this, prefabricated waterstops that extend from the first pour into the second can be inserted in the first pour, as shown in Fig. 22.3.

An *expansion joint* allows entire sections of a concrete structure to move independently of one another. This movement could be caused by shrinkage of the concrete or by temperature changes. Because the movement can be cyclical, the expansion joint must be capable of moving in two directions. Expansion joints are complex fabrications, portions of which are embedded in the concrete and other portions of which are exposed. In most instances, the expansion joint extends through the entire structure—walls, floors, roof, and so on—so there is no rigid connection between any two components of adjacent building sections.

An *isolation joint* also allows two adjacent sections to move independently of one another, but this kind of joint is not as complex as an expansion joint. An isolation joint typically consists of two separate pours of concrete separated with a premolded joint material. Isolation joints are often used to separate columns from slabs and slabs from foundations and other types of walls.

Inserts

Concrete inserts include a wide range of anchoring devices used to attach other materials and components to concrete construction. For example, *weld plates* are steel plates cast flush with the surface of concrete, to which steel members are welded. The weld plate is attached to a steel anchor that extends into the concrete for positive anchorage. In some cases, the anchors are welded to the reinforcing bars.

Concrete Sealers

A *concrete sealer* is a proprietary product applied to concrete to protect against weather and water penetration, provide resistance to chemicals, prevent dusting of the surface, or harden the surface. Some products help cure the concrete while sealing it. Other coatings are applied for decorative purposes.

There are two general types of concrete sealers: coating types and penetrating types. Coating types dry as a surface film and are made from a variety of materials including acrylics, urethanes, and epoxies. Penetrating types seep into the pores of the concrete and include proprietary products made with silicones, silanes, and siloxanes. Because of the way they work, penetrating sealers do not wear off as some surface sealers do. Some proprietary formulations can be used to stop moisture and alkaline migration through an existing concrete slab.

Figure 22.4
Typical Precast Concrete Shapes

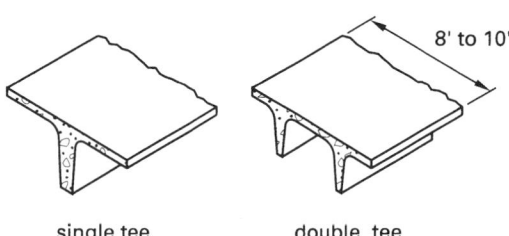

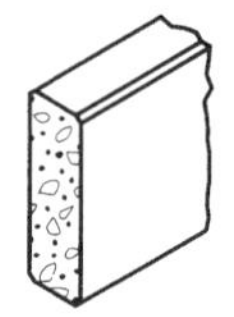

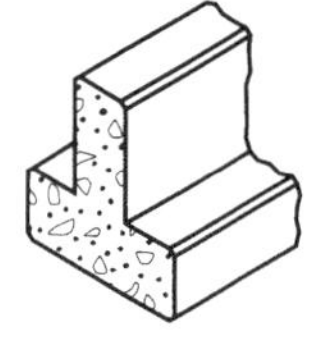

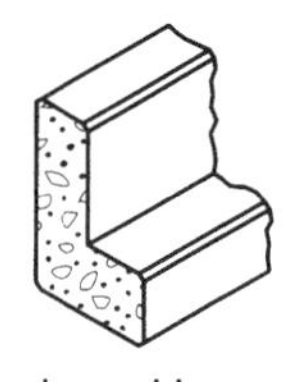

8' to 10'

single tee

double tee

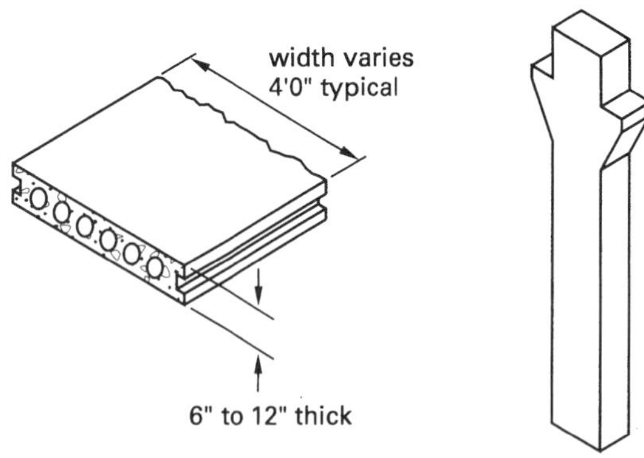

Precast Concrete

Precast concrete consists of components cast in separate forms in a place other than their final position. Precast concrete can be cast on site or in fabricating plants where conditions are more carefully controlled and where work can proceed regardless of the weather.

Beams and Columns

Precast concrete beams for buildings are usually rectangular, T-shaped, or L-shaped, as shown in Fig. 22.4. T-shaped and L-shaped beams allow the floor structure to be flush with the top of the beam and minimize the total depth needed for the structure. Single-T and double-T sections are efficient and widely used. These combine a deep section for efficient beam action and a wide flange for the floor structure. When T-sections are used, a topping slab is poured to cover the joints and provide a level floor. T-sections are often used with T-shaped and L-shaped beams in precast buildings.

Precast concrete columns are usually rectangular in shape and cast with welding plates at the top and bottom. The casting also often includes haunches that support beams, as shown in Fig. 22.4.

Floor and Roof Panels

As with precast T-sections, simple reinforced concrete slabs may serve as a floor and roof structures. For light loads and short spans, the slabs may be solid; for heavier loads and longer spans, hollow core slabs are used. These allow the depth of the slab to be increased for more efficient load-carrying capability while minimizing weight. Cored slabs are 6 in to 12 in thick and normally 4 ft wide. They can span up to 36 ft.

Lift-slab construction is a technique for multistory construction in which entire floor sections are cast on the ground, one on top of another around pre-erected columns. The slabs are poured with a bond breaker between successive pours. Once cured, the slabs are lifted into place with jacks attached to the columns. The slabs are connected to the columns with weld plates. This type of construction minimizes the amount of formwork required and generally reduces total construction time.

Wall Panels

Wall panels can be cast in a variety of sizes and shapes. For greatest economy, the number of types of panels and openings should be minimized Wall panels are generally 5 in to 8 in thick (although they can be thicker) and long enough to span columns or beams. If the panels span beams in a multistory building, casting exterior wall panels to span two floors can increase cost savings.

Wall panels can be precast at a plant or cast on site. A typical method of building is with *tilt-up construction.* With this procedure the panels are cast in a horizontal position near their final location and are lifted into place when sufficiently cured. In many cases, the panels are cast directly on the building's floor slab with temporary boards forming the edges. A bond breaker is used to prevent the wall panel from sticking to the casting surface. A bond breaker may be a liquid solution or a sheet of plastic, but liquids result in a better finish.

Precast, Prestressed Concrete

Prestressed concrete consists of members that have internal stresses applied to them before they are subjected to service loads. The prestressing consists of compressive forces applied where the member experiences tension in use. This greatly reduces or eliminates tensile forces that the member is not capable of carrying. In addition to making a more efficient and economical structural section, prestressing reduces cracking and deflection, increases shear strength, and allows longer spans and greater loads. Prestressing is accomplished in one of two ways: pretensioning and post-tensioning.

Pretensioning

With this system, concrete members are produced in a precasting plant. High-strength pretensioning stranded cable or wire is draped in forms according to the required stress pattern, and a tensile force is applied. The concrete is then poured and allowed to cure. Once the concrete cures, the cables are cut and the resulting compressive force is transferred to the concrete through the bond between cable and concrete.

Post-tensioning

In post-tensioned construction, hollow sleeves or conduits are included with the installation of the forms on the site, and concrete is poured around them. Within the sleeves are high-strength steel tendons, which are stressed with hydraulic jacks after the concrete has cured. Once the desired stress has been applied, the ends of the cables are secured to the concrete and the jacks are removed. If the tendons are to be unbonded, no further action is taken. In bonded construction, the sleeves are removed and grout is forced into the space between the tendons and the concrete.

Typically, unbonded systems use monostrand tendons, which are composed of seven wire strands wound together and coated with corrosion-inhibiting grease. Monostrand, unbonded post-tensioning is commonly used in slabs and beams for buildings, in parking structures, and in slabs on grade. Bonded systems use multistrand tendons, which are composed of two or more tendons stressed with a large, multistrand jack and anchored in a common anchorage device. Multistrand systems are used in bridges and in heavily loaded beams in buildings.

23

MASONRY

Project Planning

Masonry construction is one of the oldest building techniques known, having survived through the centuries because of its many advantages. Masonry is durable and strong, it can be formed into a variety of building shapes, and the raw materials are available in most parts of the world. Combined with modern materials, such as improved mortars, reinforcing, and flashing, brick and stone remain timeless materials.

In simplest terms, masonry consists of an assembly of relatively small units of stone, burned clay, or other manufactured material, held in place with mortar. Traditionally, masonry has been used to support loads in compression because stone, brick, and mortar have negligible resistance to tensile or bending forces. Horizontal spanning with masonry is traditionally accomplished with some form of arch.

However, with the introduction of steel reinforcing, high-strength mortars, steel lintels, and the like, brick and unit masonry can be used in an even wider variety of situations, both horizontally and vertically. Philosophically, however, many architects still feel that, since masonry is compressive by nature, it should be used in the traditional way and that the design should express the properties of the material.

MORTAR

Mortar is the cementitious material used to hold masonry units together. It must be compatible with the masonry units being used, provide the needed strength, and be resistant to the environmental conditions at the site. Three aspects of mortar that must be considered in its use are

- components of mortar
- types of mortar
- grout

Components of Mortar

Mortar is a mixture of cement, lime, sand, and water. Usually, portland cement is used. Lime is added to plasticize the cement so that it is more workable, to add resilience, and to increase the water retention of the mortar. Resilience is important for the mortar's ability to accommodate movement caused by temperature change and brick swell. Water retention is important to improve the hydration of the cement as it sets.

Masonry cement is a prepared mixture of portland cement and pulverized limestone. It is not as strong or expensive as portland cement, but it has greater plasticity. It is suitable for low-rise building veneers and for interior, non-load-bearing applications.

Various other types of cements are available for special applications. One of the most common is non-staining cement, which should be used for marble, limestone, terracotta, cut stone, and glazed brick.

Types of Mortar

There are four basic types of mortar, called N, S, M, and O. Each has a different compressive strength and a different proportion of cement, lime, and aggregate. A job should never use a mortar that is stronger in compression than required. In addition, because lime helps retain water in the mortar for hydration, a mortar with a high lime content is appropriate for bricks with a high initial rate of absorption or for summer construction where evaporation is a factor.

Type N mortar is one of the most commonly used types for exterior, above-grade walls exposed to severe weather; it is also used for laying soft stone masonry. Type S is suitable for at- or below-grade applications due to its higher compressive strength. Type M has the highest compressive strength and is recommended for harder stone and walls bearing heavy loads. Type O mortar is generally limited to interior non-load-bearing walls, tuckpointing, and historic structures. For older historic structures, a lime putty mortar without any portland cement can be used that is compatible with mortar used prior to the 1870s and that allows water to wick out.

Table 23.1 summarizes some guidelines for mortar selection.

Table 23.1 Selection of Mortar

location	building component	mortar type first choice	mortar type alternative
exterior, above grade	load-bearing walls	N or S	M
	non-load-bearing walls	N	
	parapet walls	N	S
exterior, at or below grade	foundation walls, retaining walls	M	S
	driveways	M	
interior	load-bearing walls	N	S
	non-load-bearing walls	N	O

Note: compressive strengths: type M: 2500 psi; type S: 1800 psi; type N: 750 psi

Grout

Similar to mortar, *grout* is mixed to a pouring consistency and is used to fill wall cavities or cores of hollow masonry units and to bond masonry to reinforcement. Grout may be categorized as either fine or coarse. Coarse grout includes no. 4 aggregate (pea gravel). Fine grout is used when the dimensions of the space in which the grout is placed are less than 2 in.

BRICK

Types of Brick

A *brick* is a relatively small masonry unit made from burned clay, shale, or a mixture of these materials that is not less than 75% solid. The two basic types of brick are facing brick and building brick (also called *common brick*). As the name implies, *facing brick* is used for exposed locations where appearance and uniformity of size are important. *Building brick* is made without regard for color or special finish.

Building brick is graded according to its resistance to exposure.

- severe weathering (SW)
- moderate weathering (MW)
- negligible weathering (NW)

Among other things, these grades reflect the ability of brick to resist freeze-thaw cycles. Facing brick is available in SW and MW grades and is further classified into three types: FBS, FBX, and FBA. FBS is for general use where a wide range of color and variation in size are acceptable or required. FBX is used when a high degree of mechanical perfection, narrow color range, and minimal variation in size are required. FBA is nonuniform in color, size, and texture.

Hollow brick is also available in SW and MW grades. Like facing brick, hollow brick is further classified according to its appearance. HBS is for general use where a range of size and color variation is acceptable or desired. HBX is used when a high degree of mechanical perfection, narrow color range, and minimum variation in size are required. HBA is nonuniform in color, size, and texture.

Although brick comes in many sizes, not all sizes are available from all manufacturers. Some typical sizes are shown in Fig. 23.1, along with the common terms used to describe the various surfaces. The most common size is manufactured to an actual dimension of $3^5/_8$ in thick, $2^1/_4$ in high, and $7^5/_8$ in long. With a mortar joint of $^3/_8$ in, this gives a modular size of 4 in thick and 8 in long. Three courses equal 8 in, the same as a standard concrete block course.

Brick manufacturers offer a variety of specialty shapes, such as angled brick, brick with rounded edges or ends, or sloped brick for window sills. Custom shapes and sizes can also be manufactured.

Figure 23.1
Sizes and Faces of Brick

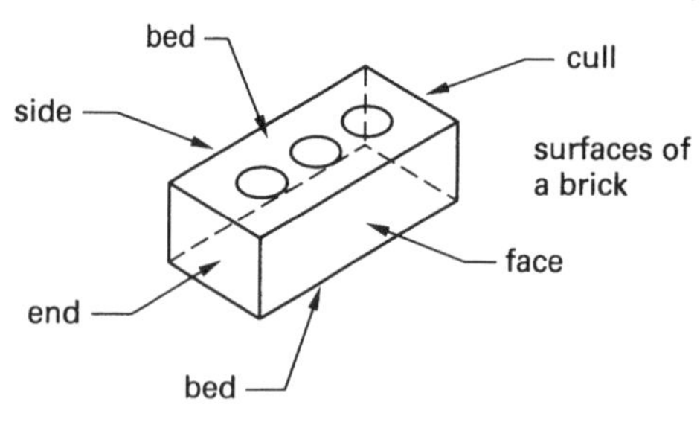

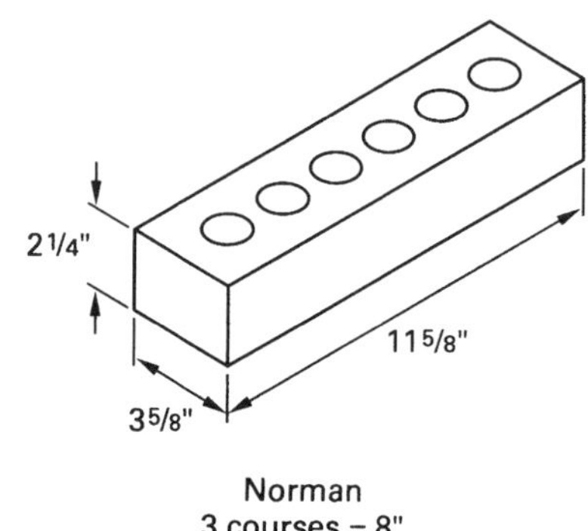

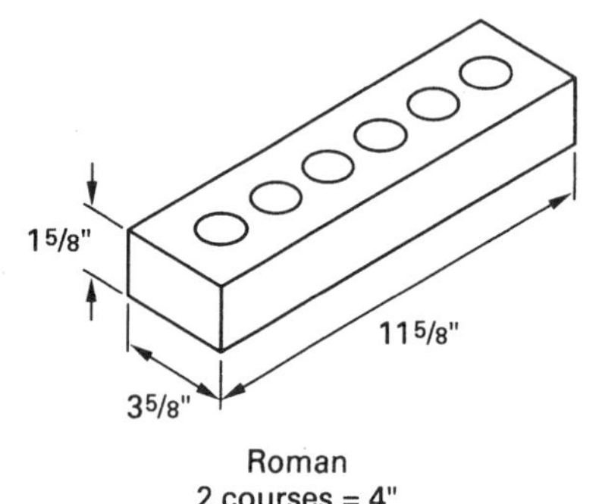

Figure 23.2
Brick Courses

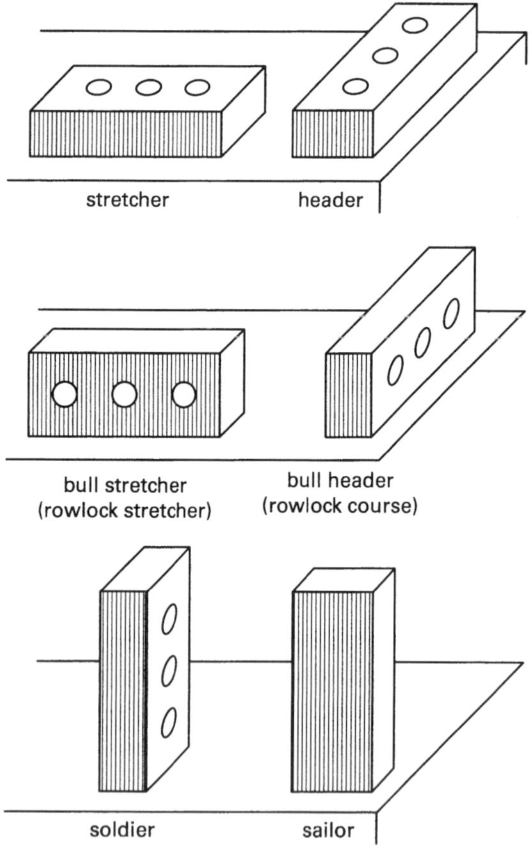

Brick Coursing

Brick can be laid in a variety of patterns depending on which surface of the brick is oriented to the outside and what position it is in. A *course* is one continuous horizontal layer of masonry. Figure 23.2 illustrates the methods of laying brick courses and the terms used to describe them.

The method of laying several courses in a wall is called the *bond pattern* (or *bonding pattern*). Some common bond patterns are shown in Fig. 23.3. A brick wall is stronger if the joints do not align and the bricks overlap. Before steel joint reinforcing was used, bond patterns were a way to accomplish this and to tie several wythes of brick together. A *wythe* is a continuous vertical section of a wall one masonry unit in thickness. For example, a header course was designed to hold a two-wythe wall together, since the length of the brick was the same as the thickness of the double wall.

With modern joint reinforcement and metal brick ties, bond patterns are less important structurally than they once were, and brick coursing is most commonly used for decorative purposes. Different coursing patterns can be used to differentiate among different parts of a building or to highlight wall openings and other features. Belt courses are often used to create a strong horizontal line in a masonry building. A *belt course*, sometimes called a *string course*, is a continuous band of masonry across the facade of a building or entirely around it; it is differentiated from other masonry by projecting from the face of the main surface, by being a different color or style, or by being made of a different type or thickness of masonry. If the belt course is located at the level of the window sills, it is called a *sill course*.

Brick Joints

Joints are an important part of any masonry wall. The mortar in the joints not only holds the entire wall together, it also prevents infiltration of water and air. Bricks should be set in full beds of mortar, on both the bed joints (horizontal) and head (vertical) joints.

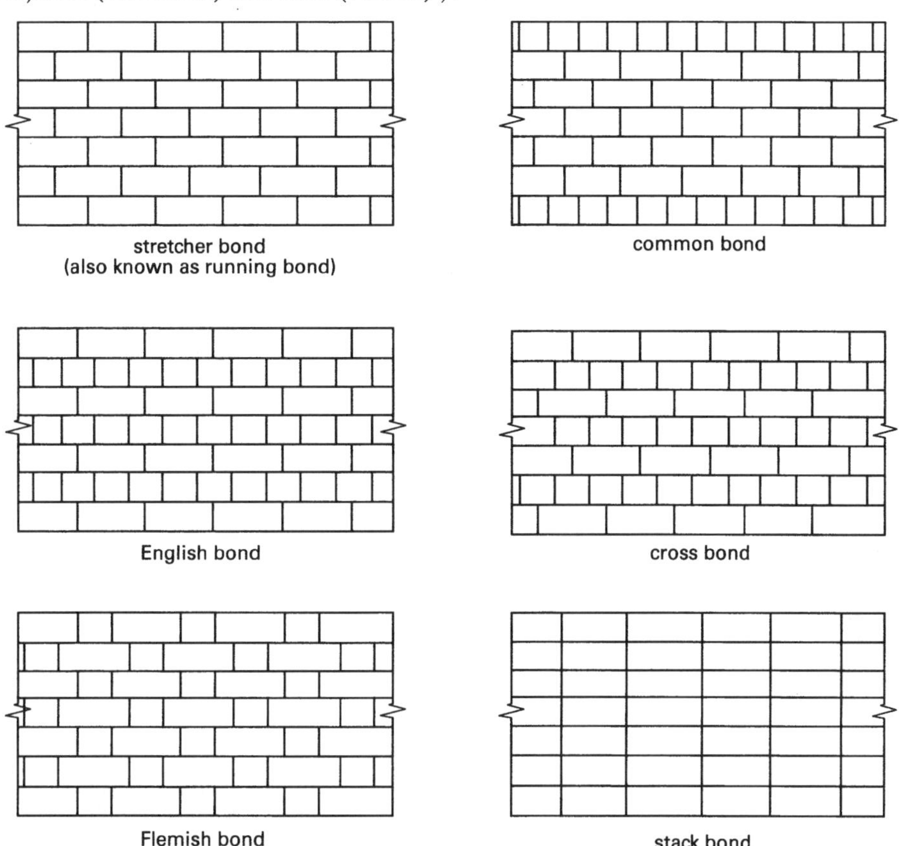

Figure 23.3 Brick Bond Patterns

After the brick is laid, the joints must be tooled. *Tooling* imparts a decorative effect to the wall, but more importantly, it makes the joint more watertight by compressing the mortar near the exposed surface. There are various types of mortar joints, as shown in Fig. 23.4, but only a few are recommended for exterior use because they shed water more effectively. These are the concave, flush, and vee joints.

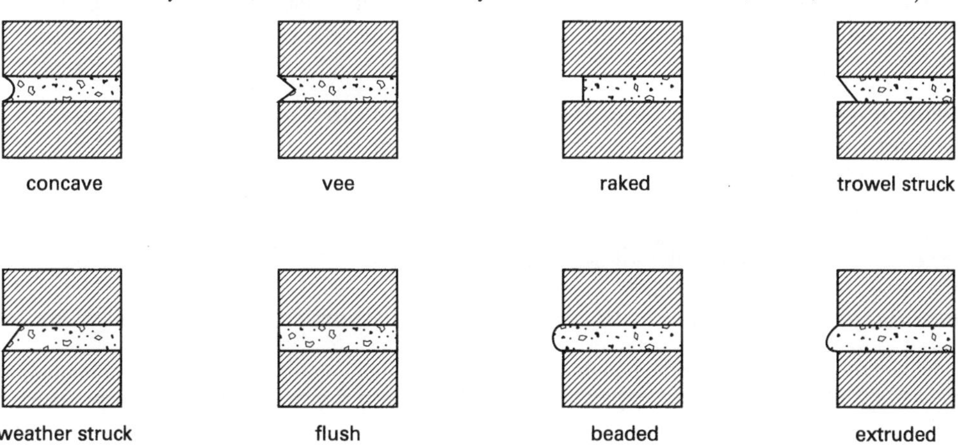

Figure 23.4 Brick Joint Tooling

Project Planning

Figure 23.5 Masonry on Shelf Angle

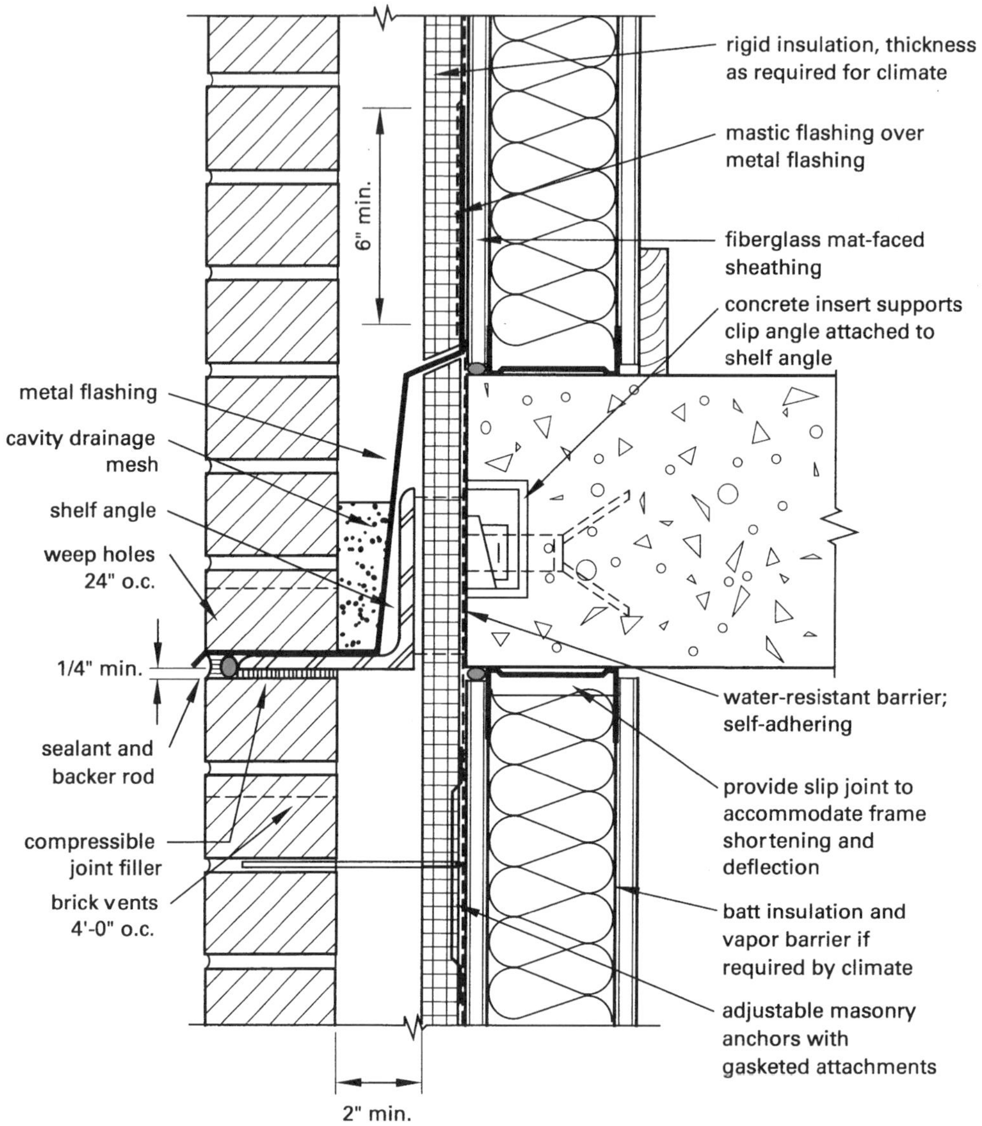

A weather-struck joint is sometimes acceptable for exterior use, but water running down the brick above the joint may not drip off and may instead run horizontally under the brick. If the joint is not tight, or if its shape allows water to accumulate on a horizontal surface, the water can be drawn through the joint by capillary action or by a pressure differential between the outside and inside of the wall.

In addition to the joints between individual masonry units, horizontal and vertical joints must accommodate building movement caused by temperature changes and differential movement between materials. If joints do not provide for such movement, cracking can occur in the joints or the bricks themselves, resulting in water and air leakage and an unsightly appearance. In the worst case, stresses can be great enough that the brick can crack and spall off.

There are several types of joints, including the following.

- A *construction joint*, also known as a *cold joint*, isolates the masonry from through-wall elements, such as doors and windows.
- An *expansion joint* accommodates expansion and contraction due to changes in temperature, temperature differentials, and moisture absorption of the brick, as well as allowing for any tolerances of the brick and its installation. A designer can size a joint using a formula that combines these variables

and the movement capabilities of the sealant. For a 100°F temperature differential and a sealant with 50% movement capability, for example, the joints range in size from $^3/_8$ in for a 10 ft joint spacing to $^5/_8$ in for a 25 ft spacing. Joints are constructed by separating two sections of masonry to create a space, then filling the space with a backing covered with a sealant. In many cases, a neoprene gasket is placed within the wall between the two sections of masonry.

- A *through-building expansion joint* is much larger and is used to completely separate two sections of a building.

Major through-building expansion joints are usually spaced every 100 ft to 150 ft in large buildings. Expansion and control joints are spaced about every 15 to 25 ft and at places where the wall changes direction, height, or thickness. When several windows align in a multi-story building, vertical expansion joints are often aligned with the brick window jambs.

Horizontal expansion joints should be placed below beams and slabs above brick and below shelf angles that support intermediate sections of brick. One such detail is shown in Fig. 23.5. These types of joints prevent excessive stress from being placed on the brick due to deflection of the angle or beam above.

Brick Construction

Although brick is a simple construction material, it must be designed, detailed, and installed correctly in order to function properly. There are many types of brick and masonry walls. The more common ones are shown in Fig. 23.6. The illustrations only show the basic configuration without insulation, water-resistant barriers, air barriers, or interior finish.

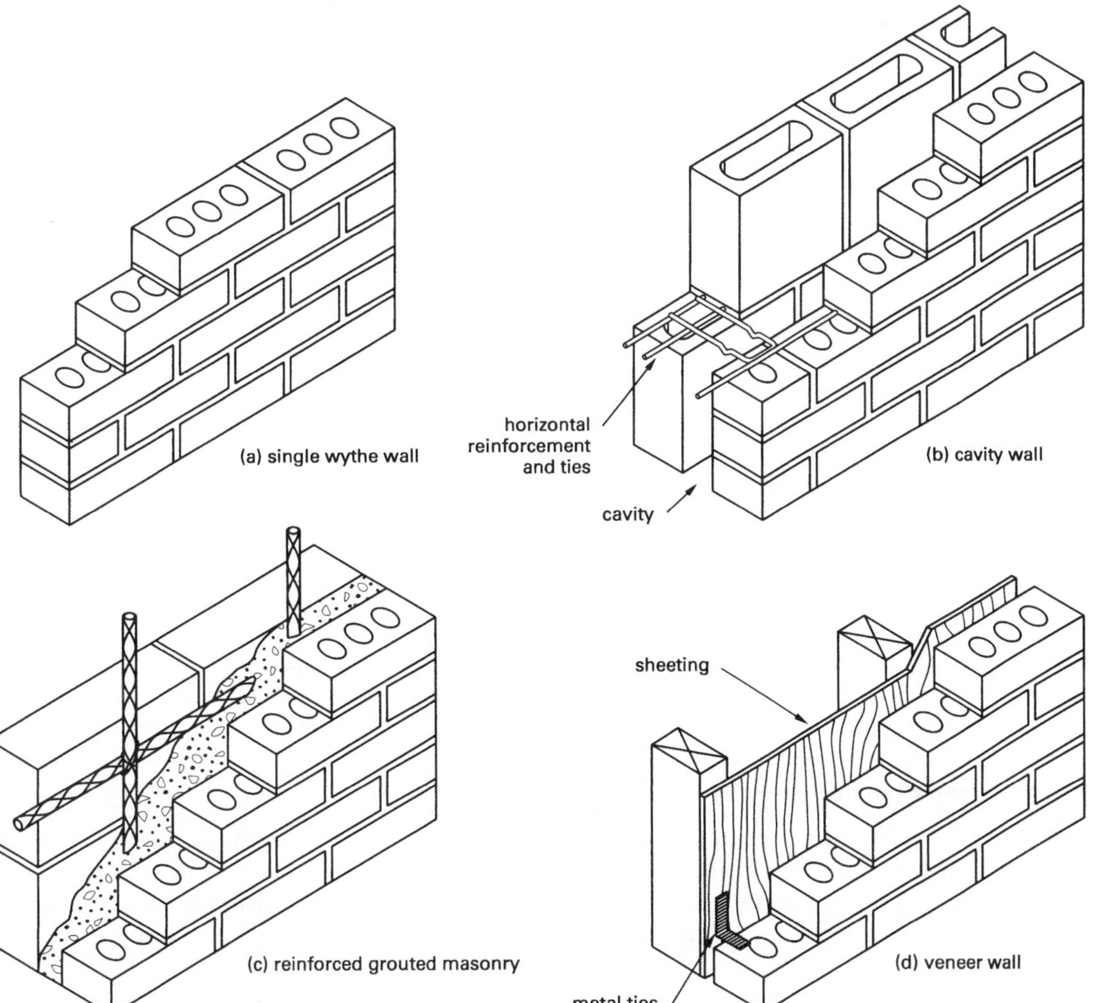

Figure 23.6 Types of Brick Walls

A *single-wythe wall* consists of one layer of brick that acts as either a load-bearing or non-load-bearing wall. Because it is non-reinforced, the maximum ratio of unsupported height or length to thickness cannot exceed 20:1 for a solid wall or 18:1 for a hollow masonry wall.

A *cavity wall* consists of two wythes of brick separated by an air space. The two sections must be tied together with galvanized metal wall ties or continuous horizontal reinforcement placed 16 in on center vertically. When two wythes of masonry are used, the inside wythe is often built with concrete unit masonry (CMU) to save cost and speed construction. In this type of construction, both wythes require vertical expansion joints as shown in Fig. 23.7.

Figure 23.7 Masonry Composite Wall Expansion Joints

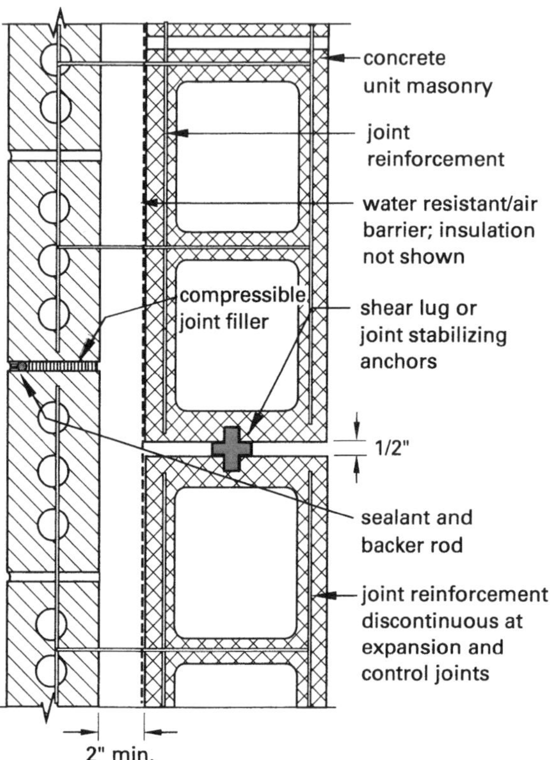

A *reinforced grouted wall* also consists of two wythes of brick, but the cavity contains vertical and horizontal reinforcing bars and is completely filled with grout. Compared with cavity walls, grouted walls can carry heavier loads, have higher unsupported heights, and are better able to resist lateral loading.

A *veneer wall* is a single wythe of brick attached to some other type of construction, usually a wood-frame wall in residential construction, as shown in Fig. 23.6(d), or a steel stud backup wall for commercial construction. In a veneer wall, the masonry is for decorative and weather-resisting purposes rather than for structural support.

One of the most important considerations in designing a brick wall is watertightness. In order to achieve this, the proper brick and mortar must first be selected for the climate conditions and loading, as discussed earlier in this section. The brick joints must be tooled correctly to shed water and prevent expansion, and control joints must be located correctly to allow the wall to move without opening up cracks. The tops of walls and parapets should be flashed and capped with coping, which should extend beyond the face of the wall and include drips to allow water to drain off instead of run down the wall. The slope of the coping is called the *wash*.

Next, the wall must be flashed and finished to prevent water from entering and to allow water that does enter to flow out. Base flashing should be installed at the bottom of the exterior wythe, extend up 8 in to 10 in; it should also be set in a reglet or masonry joint in the interior wythe, as shown in Fig. 23.8. A *reglet* is a preformed metal shape that is cast into a concrete wall and set flush with the wall to allow the insertion of the edge of flashing and a sealant. Weep holes should be located 24 in on center horizontally in the lowest course of brick to allow any water that penetrates the wall to drip out; these are usually small prefabricated plastic tubes or vents that are embedded in the joint space. Louvers or screen may be a part of the design to keep out insects. This type of detail should also be used over windows and at shelf angles, similar to that shown in Fig. 23.5.

Brick is often used to form chimneys, both for fireplaces and for the venting of furnaces and other appliances. The top of a chimney must be at least 2 ft higher than any point of the structure within a radius of 10 ft. The tops of adjacent flue liners must be offset in height from 4 in to 12 in. If clay chimney flue liners are used in brick chimneys, they must extend a minimum of 2 in above the top of the chimney cap.

Figure 23.8 Masonry Cavity Wall at Grade

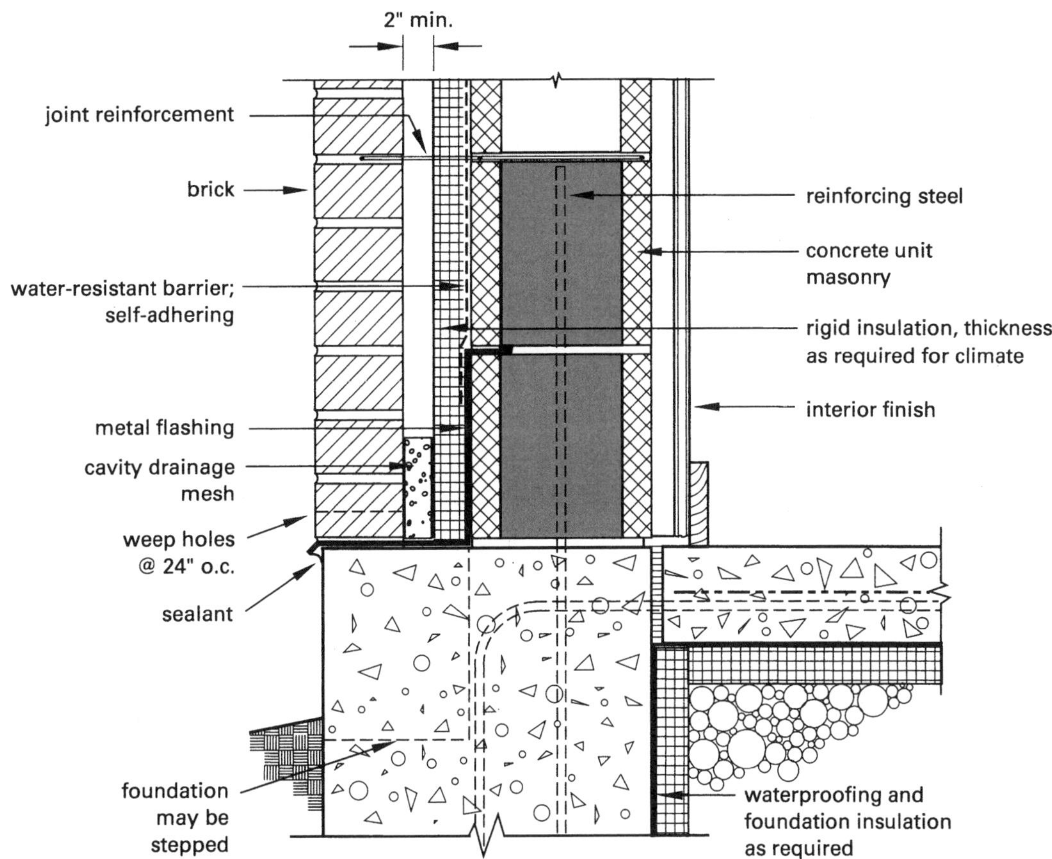

Openings

Most openings in masonry construction are spanned with steel lintels. Steel lintels are inexpensive and simple to install, and their size and thickness can be varied to suit the span of the opening. Lintels should bear on each end of the supporting masonry in such a way that the bearing capacity is not exceeded, but in no case should the bearing length be less than 6 in. Several alternatives to steel lintels are shown in Fig. 23.9.

An *arch* is the traditional method of spanning a masonry opening, because this shape makes full use of the compressive capabilities of the material. Alternatively, a reinforced concrete beam (see Fig. 23.9(c)) or a fully grouted and reinforced concrete unit masonry bond beam (see Fig. 23.9(d)) can be used.

Whatever type of lintel is used, there is always arch action over the opening. This is shown diagrammatically in Fig. 23.10. Unless a concentrated load or a floor load is near the top of the opening, the lintel carries only the weight of the wall above the opening in a triangular area defined by a 60° angle from each side of the opening.

Efflorescence

Efflorescence is a white, crystalline deposit of water-soluble salts on the surface of brick masonry. When water seeps into the masonry, it can dissolve soluble salts present in the masonry, backup wall, mortar, or anything in contact with the wall. The dissolved salts are brought to the surface of the brick and appear when the water evaporates. Although unsightly, efflorescence is usually not harmful to the brick.

Figure 23.9
Masonry Lintels

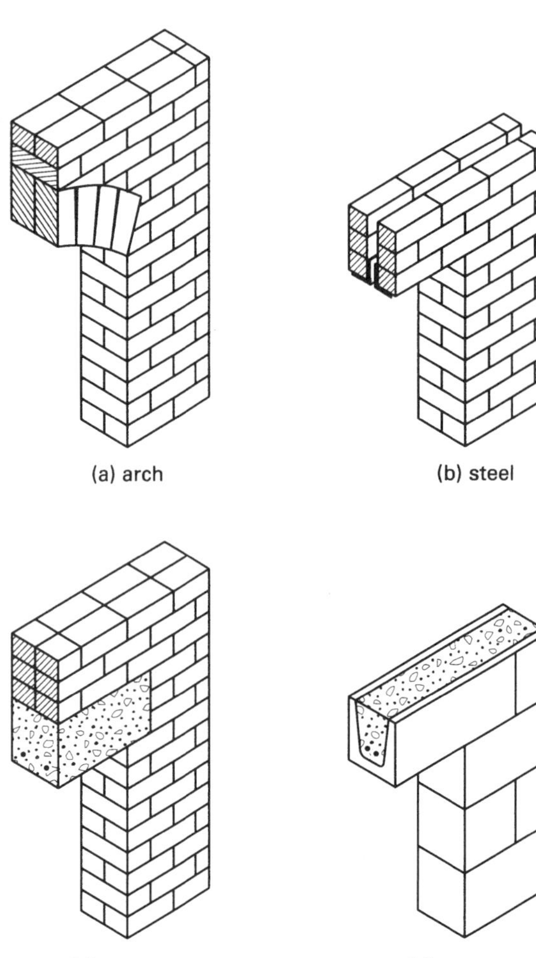

Efflorescence can be prevented or minimized by using materials with few or no soluble salts, by forming tight joints, and by detailing the wall to avoid water penetration. Both brick and mortar can be specified to contain no or limited soluble salts. If efflorescence does occur, it can be removed by dry brushing or by washing with a 5% solution of muriatic acid. A simple water wash can also be used, but this should be done in warm, dry weather to avoid additional moisture.

Cleaning and Restoration

At the completion of a job, brick should be cleaned with a mild 5% to 10% solution of muriatic acid in water and then washed off with clean water. A stiff brush can be used to remove loose mortar pieces, stains, and efflorescence.

Restoration of brick is more difficult. Over time, brick can be physically damaged, mortar joints can deteriorate, and the entire surface can become dirty and stained. Damaged units must be carefully removed and replaced with new brick that matches the existing surface as closely as possible. If mortar has fallen out, it must be replaced though a process known as *tuckpointing* or *repointing*. In this process, the mortar in the areas to be redone is removed to about $2^1/_2$ times the depth of the joint. The joint is then cleaned and wetted with water. New mortar is pressed into the joint with a special tuck-pointing tool. High-lime mortar is best and it should be applied in layers; each layer is applied after the previous one becomes thumbprint hard.

There are several ways to clean brick. The method chosen should be selected for the following attributes.

- compatibility with the nature of the soiling
- amount of cleaning desired
- surrounding environment in which the cleaning must take place
- type of brick involved

High-pressure water washing is often effective, but can wash away mortar and create swirl marks across the surface of the wall. Scrubbing the wall by hand with a brush and water may be required for soft brick. Acid solutions and other types of chemicals may be used to remove stubborn dirt and stains, but this is not appropriate for some brick and can damage surrounding surfaces. Abrasive cleaning using sand, sodium bicarbonate, glass beads, or walnut shells can be used in certain circumstances, but this can erode both brick and mortar. Refer to Chap. 10 for more information on cleaning historic structures.

OTHER UNIT MASONRY

Unit masonry is a term used to describe various types of building products assembled with mortar, of which brick is one kind. Other types of unit masonry include

- concrete block
- clay tiles
- ceramic veneer
- stone
- terracotta
- gypsum block
- glass block

Figure 23.10 Arch Action in a Masonry Wall over an Opening

Concrete Block

Concrete block is the common term for concrete unit masonry, also known as *concrete masonry units* (CMUs). This building product is manufactured with cement, water, and various types of aggregate, including gravel, expanded shale or slate, expanded slag or pumice, and limestone cinders.

Concrete block is classified in the following categories.

- hollow, load-bearing
- solid, load-bearing
- hollow, non-load-bearing
- solid, non-load-bearing

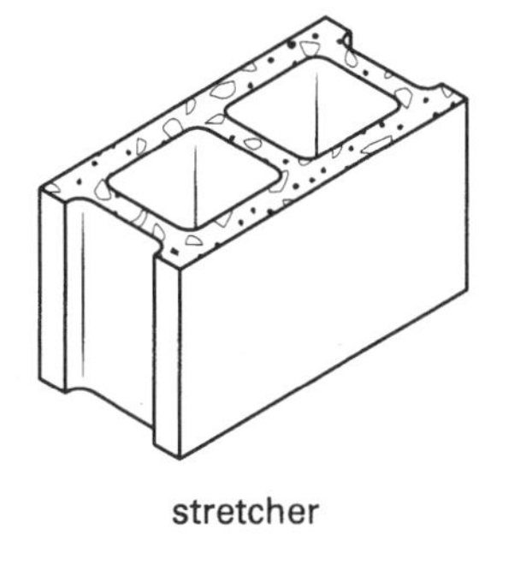
stretcher

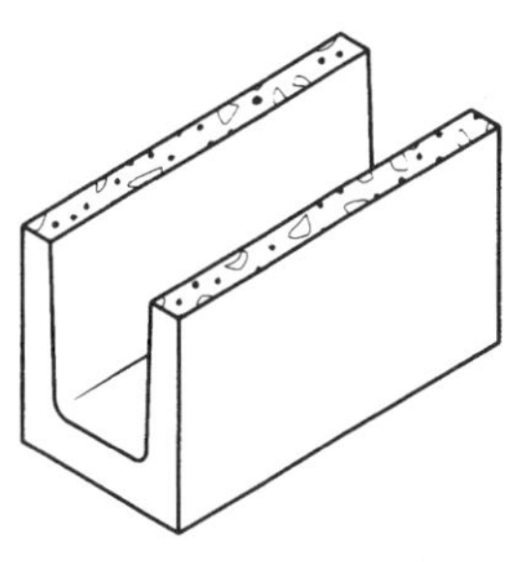
bond beam

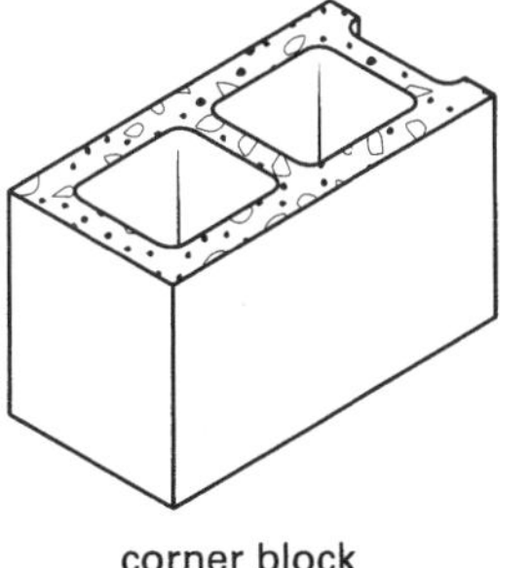
corner block

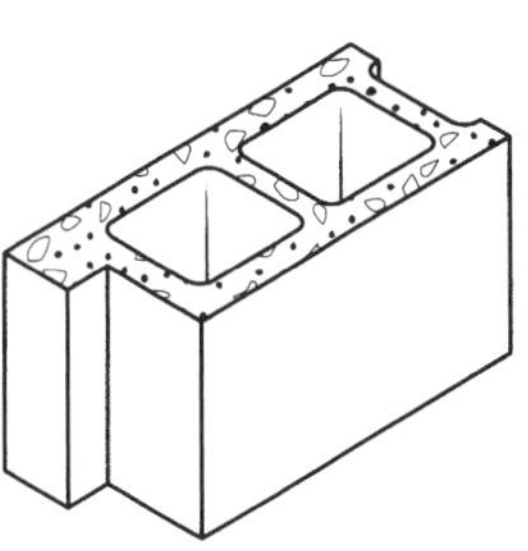
jamb block

Figure 23.11 Typical Concrete Block Shapes

Solid units are those that are 75% or more solid material in any general cross section. Hollow units are those that are less than 75% solid material.

The dimensions of a CMU are given with width first, then height, and finally length. CMU dimensions are based on a nominal 4 in module. The most common thicknesses are 4 in, 6 in, 8 in, 10 in, and 12 in, and the most common lengths are 8 in, 12 in, and 16 in. The actual dimensions of the CMU are $^3/_8$ in less than the nominal dimensions to allow for mortar joints. One of the most common sizes is nominally 8 in × 8 in × 16 in; this is actually $7^5/_8$ in × $7^5/_8$ in × $15^5/_8$ in long.

Concrete block is manufactured in a wide variety of shapes to suit particular applications. A few of the most common shapes are shown in Fig. 23.11.

Concrete block walls can be either single or double wythe, but they are more often single wythe for economy and speed of construction. The cores of the blocks allow walls to be reinforced and grouted if additional strength is required for vertical or lateral load bearing. As with brick walls, horizontal reinforcing is required every 16 in on center. Walls can also be grouted if additional fire resistance or sound resistance is required. Figure 23.12 shows a typical reinforced, grouted concrete masonry wall. It also shows the use of a bond beam at the top of the wall that can serve as a lintel over openings, to provide bearing for the floor and roof structure, and to resist lateral loads from floor and roof diaphragms.

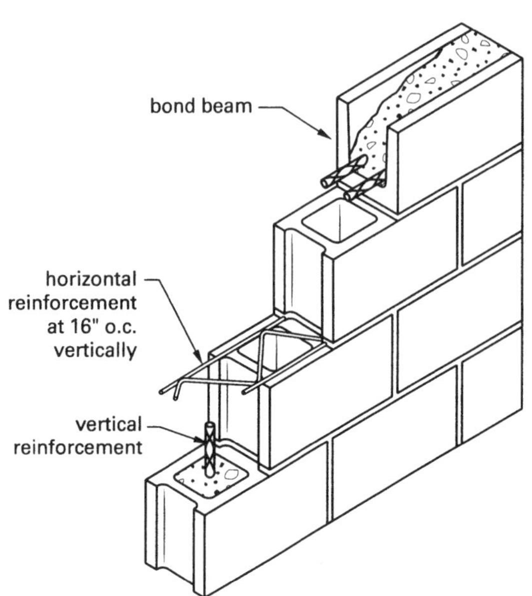

Figure 23.12 Reinforced, Grouted Concrete Masonry Wall

Because most concrete block walls consist of hollow units, it is important to understand equivalent thickness. *Equivalent thickness* is the solid thickness that would result if the concrete contained in a hollow unit were recast without core holes. The value is calculated from the actual thickness of the block and the percentage of solid materials.

The fire rating for a masonry wall is based on this value and the type of material used in the manufacture of the block. Building codes give the required equivalent thicknesses for various hourly fire ratings. The architect must determine whether the thickness and type of concrete block being used meet the required fire rating.

Detailing for concrete block and brick walls is especially important for the prevention of cracking, leaking, and structural instability. Adequate expansion and control joints should be provided, and recommended horizontal joint reinforcing should be installed, as stated previously. In addition, the connection of other materials to the masonry must be well detailed to maintain weathertightness and prevent other problems from developing.

One example of masonry detailing is shown in Fig. 23.13. This illustration shows a typical concrete block wall with brick veneer and a parapet. The concrete block acts as a bearing wall for an open-web steel joist roof system. The concrete masonry is fully grouted and reinforced to provide the required bearing capacity, and a continuous bond beam with steel bearing plate is provided for the attachment of the bar joist. Generally, the height of the parapet should not exceed three times its nominal thickness unless additional lateral support is provided. In this example, the vertical reinforcing is continued into the brick parapet to anchor it to the rest of the wall and provide additional lateral support. Brick is used on the back side of the parapet to minimize differential movement caused by weather and temperature acting on dissimilar materials; alternatively, a single wythe of concrete block could be used as the parapet backing.

In this example, a stone coping is used to keep water out of the wall. The coping is sloped toward the roof to minimize the amount of water dripping on the side of the building. Drips keep water from running under the coping; a metal or precast concrete coping could be used instead. If a metal coping is selected, it can be built up over the top of the parapet to provide space for insulation, thus minimizing the thermal bridge through the brick backup. To prevent leakage from moisture on the roof or from snow piled next to the parapet, the roofing is carried up the wall and terminated in a reglet set in the masonry joint or continued over the top of the wall and protected by the coping. Additional flashing is used on the outside of the roof slab and joists.

Example 23.1

What is the equivalent thickness of a concrete block with a nominal thickness of 8 in that is 60% solids?

(A) 4.58 in

(B) 5.50 in

(C) 6.60 in

(D) 7.91 in

Project Planning

Solution

The actual thickness of the block is $7\frac{5}{8}$ in. The equivalent thickness is

$$(7.625 \text{ in})(0.60) = 4.58 \text{ in}$$

The answer is (A).

Figure 23.13 Masonry Cavity Wall at Parapet

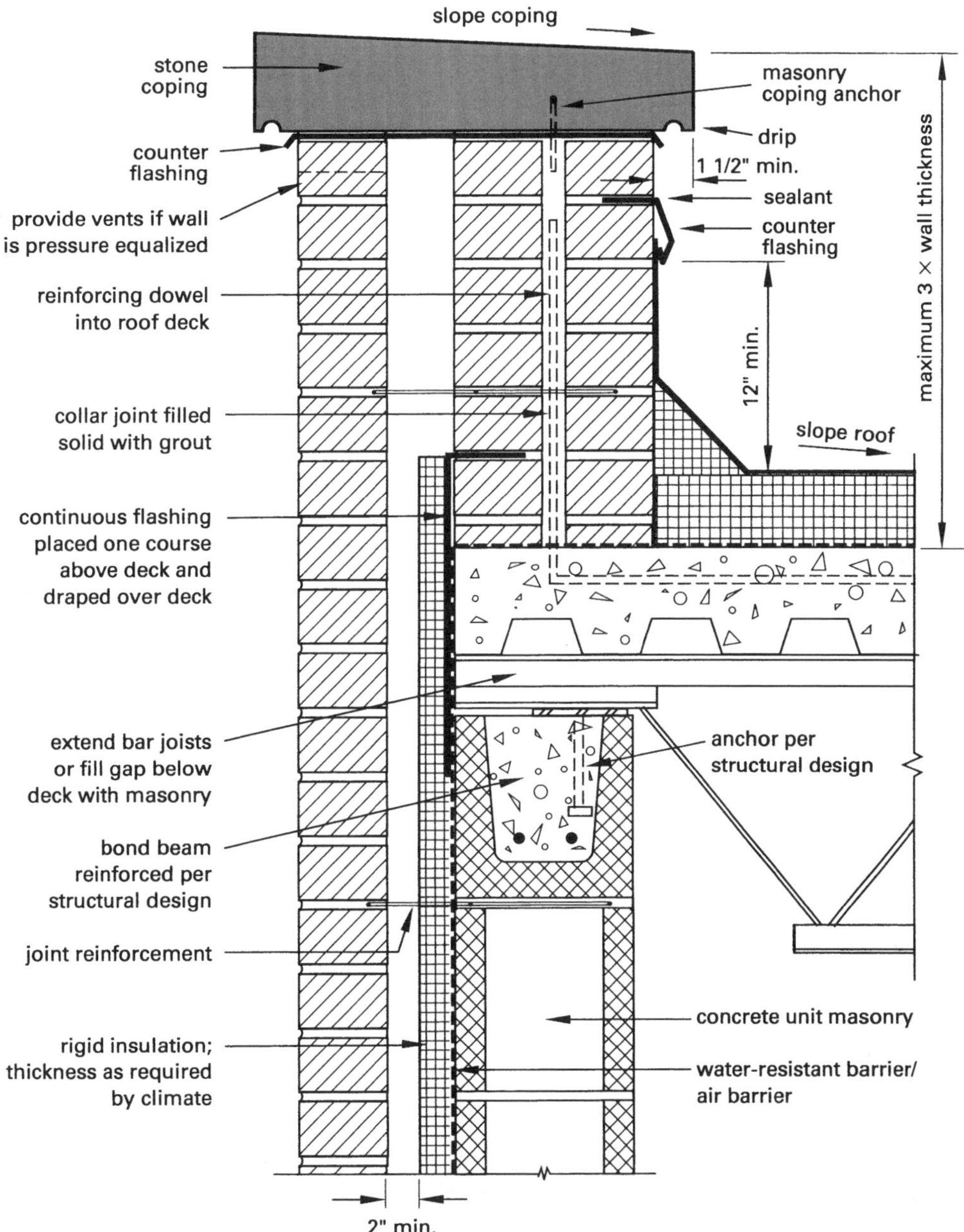

Structural Clay Tile

Structural clay tile is made from burned clay formed into hollow units with parallel cells. Clay tile is available in load-bearing and non-load-bearing types and with glazed surfaces appropriate for finished exterior or interior walls.

Two types of structural clay tile are produced: side construction and end construction as shown in Fig. 23.14. Side construction tile is designed to receive its principal stress at right angles to the axis of the cells, and end construction tile is designed to receive principal stress parallel to the axis of the cells. Various sizes are produced in nominal 3 in, 4 in, 6 in, and 8 in widths and 6 in, 8 in, 12 in, and 16 in heights and lengths.

Figure 23.14
Structural Clay Tile

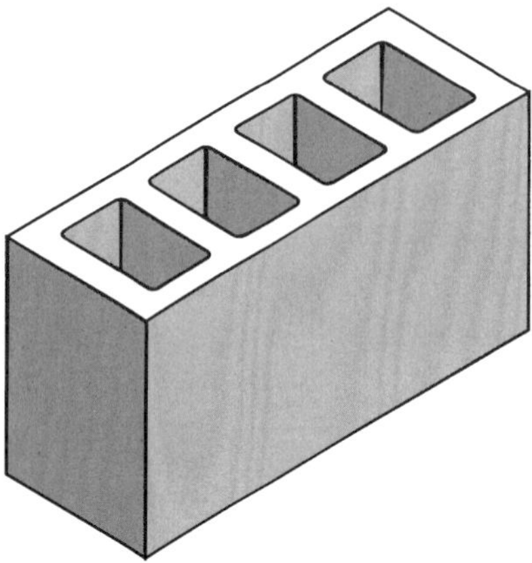

(a) load-bearing and non-loadbearing

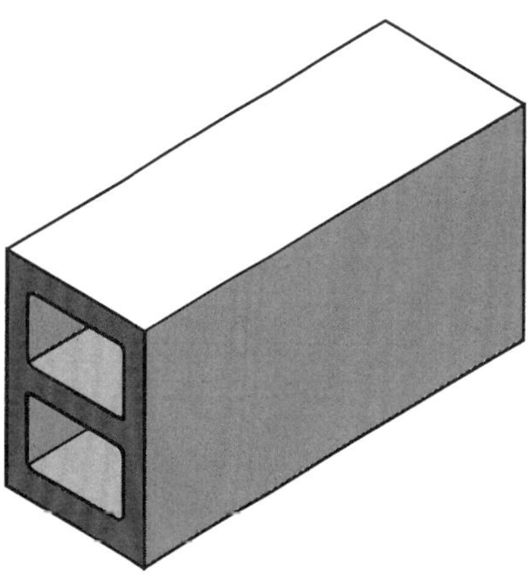

(b) side construction for structural clay facing tile

Structural clay tile is used as backup for exterior walls, as non-load-bearing interior partitions, and for load-bearing masonry walls that will be finished with other materials. For interior partitions, glazed structural clay tile provides a wall with a hard, durable, decorative finish in one unit.

Glazed structural clay facing tile is a load-bearing clay tile with a finish consisting of ceramic glaze fused to the body at above 1500°F. There are two grades of glazed structural tile: S grade (select) is for use with relatively narrow mortar joints, and SS grade (select sized) is for use where the variation of face dimensions must be very small.

Terra Cotta

Terra cotta (also spelled *terracotta* and *terra-cotta*) is a high-fired clay unit used for cladding and decorative purposes in building construction. Also known as *ceramic veneer*, terra cotta is made from enriched clay materials and fired at a high temperature that gives it a hardness and density that are not possible with other clay units. The base unit without the glaze is called the bisque. In most cases, to the glazing makes it weather resistant and provides a limitless range of colors.

Terra cotta is often manufactured to provide replacement pieces for building restoration. However, it has also gained popularity in new construction because it can be produced in a variety of custom shapes and sizes. Terra cotta can also be formed to look like stone, but with about one-tenth the weight of stone.

Terra cotta is manufactured by machine extrusion, molding, or hand carving for ornate work. The finished pieces are attached to a suitable substrate either by the adhesion method or the anchored method. For adhesion application, the back of the terra cotta is cast with dovetail slots and applied on a mortar bond. As with other veneer stone, building codes limit the maximum size of any one piece and the total weight to 15 lbm/ft^2. Adhered units cannot exceed $1^1/_4$ in in thickness.

Anchored terra cotta is attached with stainless steel or galvanized metal anchors (usually 8-gage wire) and a full grout backing. The anchors must be at least $1^1/_4$ in thick.

Because moisture can potentially deteriorate the glaze and base unit, terra cotta must be carefully detailed, flashed, and caulked to prevent water penetration. If moisture seeps between the bisque and the glaze, alternate freezing and thawing cycles can delaminate the glaze from the bisque. Water seeping into the clay body can also cause the clay to deteriorate.

Gypsum Block

Gypsum block or *tile* is solid or cored units cast of gypsum plaster. Historically, these were used for non-load-bearing partitions and for fire protection of structural elements. They available in thicknesses from $1^1/_2$ in to 6 in with a standard face size of 12 in high and 30 in long. Gypsum block may be encountered when remodeling older buildings.

Glass Block

Glass block is manufactured as either a hollow or a solid unit with a clear, textured, or patterned face. The area inside the block is under a partial vacuum that improves the thermal insulating properties of the material. This property, along with the light-transmitting value and availability of obscuring patterns, makes glass block useful in both interior and exterior applications where a combination of light transmission, privacy, and insulation is needed. Solid block can also be used for flooring if it is correctly supported.

Generally, glass block does not provide rated fire resistance, but some assemblies are available that qualify as 30-minute and 45-minute fire-rated enclosures in 1-hour walls. Underwriters Laboratories has classified some manufacturer's blocks for 60- or 90-minute ratings in openings up to 100 ft^2 if no dimension is greater than 10 ft.

Glass block is manufactured in the United States in nominal thicknesses of 3 in and 4 in and in face sizes of 6 in × 6 in, 8 in × 8 in, 12 in × 12 in, and 4 in × 8 in. The two standard thicknesses are $3^1/_8$ in and $3^7/_8$ in, and other sizes are available from foreign manufacturers. The thinner block is commonly used for interior partitions. Glass block is available in clear, textured, or patterned faces, and special blocks made by most manufacturers can be used to form 90° angles, end caps, and curves.

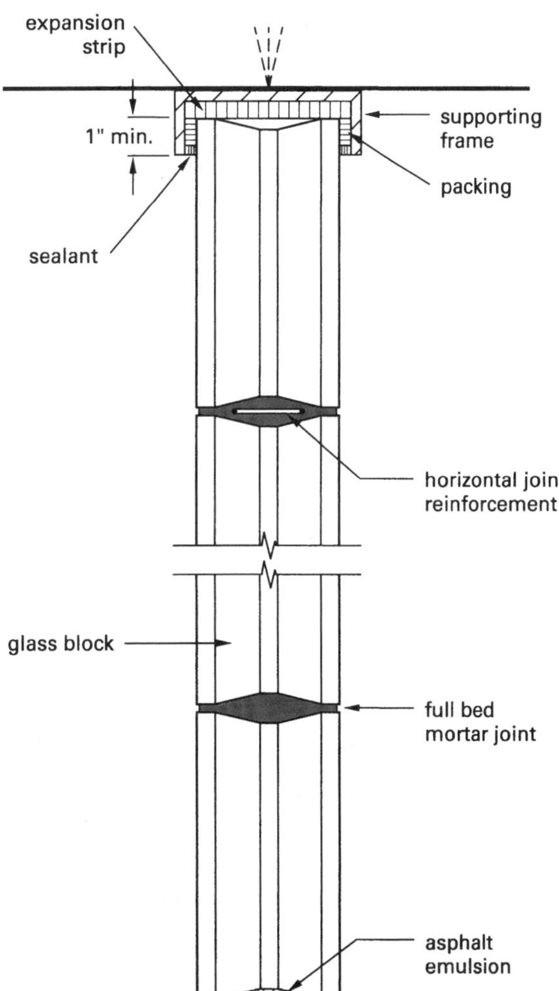

Figure 23.15 Glass Block Partition at Sill and Head

Glass block walls are laid in stack bond (with joints aligned rather than staggered) with Type S or Type N mortar and horizontal and vertical reinforcement in the joints. Because of the coefficient of expansion of glass, the possible deflection of the floor structure, or some other building movement, it is recommended to provide expansion strips at the tops and sides of glass block partitions. Figure 23.15 shows typical detailing for the sill and head of an interior glass block wall.

Because glass block cannot be load-bearing, individual exterior panels are limited to certain maximum sizes based on the design wind pressure. Historically, there was a limit of 144 in^2 total area. This was based on an assumed wind loading of 20 lbm/ft^2 and a safety factor of 2.7. More recent codes allow an area up to about 250 ft^2 when the design wind pressure is about 16 lbm/ft^2. Interior panels are limited by code to 250 ft^2 for standard units and 150 ft^2 for thin unit panels. For both exterior and interior panes, intermediate structural supports between panels are required at a maximum dimension of 25 ft horizontally and 20 ft vertically.

Cast Stone

Cast stone is a precast concrete building product made of portland cement, sand, and light aggregates used to simulate natural stone. It is often used as a substitute for limestone and other smooth-faced stones for facing panels, trim, ornaments, columns, moldings, and copings, among other architectural elements. Normally it is used in non-load-bearing applications.

Table 23.2
Stones Used in Construction

types	uses
granite	exterior wall panels
	interior finish panels
	flooring
	base
	trim
	water courses
	countertops
	thresholds
	lintels
	windowsills
	stair treads
	hearths
	sculpture
	chips for terrazzo
marble	exterior wall panels
	interior finish panels
	flooring
	base
	trim
	toilet partitions
	thresholds
	tabletops
	stair treads
	hearths
	windowsills
	sculpture
	chips for terrazzo
limestone	exterior wall panels
	coping
	lintels
	sculptured trim
slate	flooring
	stair treads
	roofing
	blackboards
	countertops
sandstone	flooring
	exterior paving

STONE

Stone is a construction material made from various types of naturally occurring rock. *Rock* is a geologic term meaning solid and unconsolidated material in the earth's crust, whereas small, quarried pieces of rock are called *stone.*

There are three classifications of rock.

- *Igneous rocks* are formed from the solidification of molten rock. Granite is a type of igneous rock.
- *Sedimentary rocks* consist of consolidated products of rock disintegration, sea shells, and various clays and silts. Sandstone and limestone are examples of common sedimentary rocks.
- *Metamorphic rocks* are formed of either igneous or sedimentary rocks that have been altered by pressure or intrusion of molten rock or other liquids over a long period of time. Marble and slate are metamorphic rocks.

Types of Construction Stone

Stone is one of civilization's oldest building materials. In the past, stone was used as both a structural material and a finish material; however, with the increased cost of stone and the labor to place it, solid stone is seldom used for structural purposes. In new construction stone is used in thin slabs for exterior and interior finish, as flooring, countertops, stair treads, and various types of trim pieces in masonry construction. Stone chips are widely used with cement to form terrazzo.

Five of the most common stones used in construction include granite, marble, limestone, slate, and sandstone. Table 23.2 lists the most common uses of the various types of stone.

Stone Finishes

A wide variety of finishes are available for the different types of stone used in construction. Each type of stone has its own nomenclature, which is summarized in Table 23.3.

Stone finishes should be selected for the conditions in which they will be used. For example, highly polished surfaces are not appropriate for flooring or stairs, where a small amount of water will make them slippery and dangerous. Rough finishes may not be appropriate for exterior walls in an environment where dirt and pollution may collect and be difficult to clean off.

Table 23.3 Types of Stone Finishes

marble finishes	
polished	a glossy surface that brings out the full color and character of the marble (not recommended for floor finishes)
honed	a satin-smooth surface with little or no gloss (recommended for commercial floors)
sandblasted	a matte-textured surface with no gloss (recommended for exterior use)
abrasive	a flat, nonreflective surface suitable for exterior use, stair treads, and other nonslip surfaces
wet-sand	a smooth surface suitable for stair treads and other nonslip surfaces
granite finishes	
polished	mirror gloss with sharp reflections
honed	dull sheen without reflections
fine-rubbed	smooth and free from scratched; no sheen
rubbed	plane surface with occasional slight "trails" or scratched
shot-ground	plane surface with pronounced circular markings or trails having no regular pattern
thermal (flame)	plane surface with flame finished applied by mechanically controlled means to ensure uniformity; surface coarseness varies, depending on grain structure of granite
sandblasted, fine stipple	place surface, slightly pebbled, with occasional slight trails or scratches
sandblasted, coarse stipple	coarse plane surface produced by blasting with an abrasive; coarseness varies with type of preparatory finished and grain structure of granite
8-cut	fine bush-hammered; interrupted parallel markings not over $^3/_{32}$ in apart; a corrugated finish
6-cut	medium bush-hammered; markings not more than $^1/_8$ in apart
4-cut	coarse bush-hammered; markings not more than $^7/_{32}$ in apart
sawn	relatively plane surface, with texture ranging from wire sawn (a close approximation of rubbed finish) to shot sawn, with scorings $^7/_{32}$ in in depth; gang saws produce parallel scorings; rotary or circular saws make circular scorings; shot-sawn surfaces are sandblasted to remove all rust stains and iron particles
limestone finishes	
smooth finish	machine finish producing a uniform honed finish; uses only select grade or standard grade
plucked	rough texture produced by rough planing the surface of the stone
machine tooled	finish made up by cutting parallel, concave grooves in the stone with 4, 6, or 8 grooves to the inch; depth of the grooves range from $^1/_{32}$ in to $^1/_{16}$ in
chit-sawed	coarse, pebbled surface that closely resembles the appearance of sandblasting; sometimes contains shallow saw marks or parallel scores; direction of score or saw marks will be vertical and/or horizontal in the wall unless the direction is specified
shot-sawed	coarse, uneven finish ranging from a pebbled surface to one rippled with irregular, roughly parallel grooves; steel shot used during gang-sawing rusts during process, adding permanent brown tones to the natural color variations
split face	rough, uneven, concave-convex finish produced by splitting action; limits stone sized to 1 ft 4 in high by 4 ft 0 in long; available in ashlar or similar stone veneer only
rock face	similar to split face except that the face of the stone has been dressed by machine or by hand to produce bold convex projection along the face of the stone

Stone Coursing

Stone is classified by the way it is shaped and prepared prior to installation. Stone used with little or no shaping is called *rubble*, stone with slightly shaped edges resulting in vertical joints is called *squared stone*, and highly shaped stone is called *ashlar*. Ashlar is also referred to as *cut stone* and consists of thick pieces of stone.

Methods of arranging stones in a wall are categorized into range, broken range, and random. *Range masonry* arranges stones in uniform courses for the entire length of the wall. In *broken range masonry*, stones are coursed for short distances. *Random masonry* is devoid of coursing or any attempt to align vertical joints. Figure 23.16 shows some common stone wall patterns.

Figure 23.16 Stone Patterns

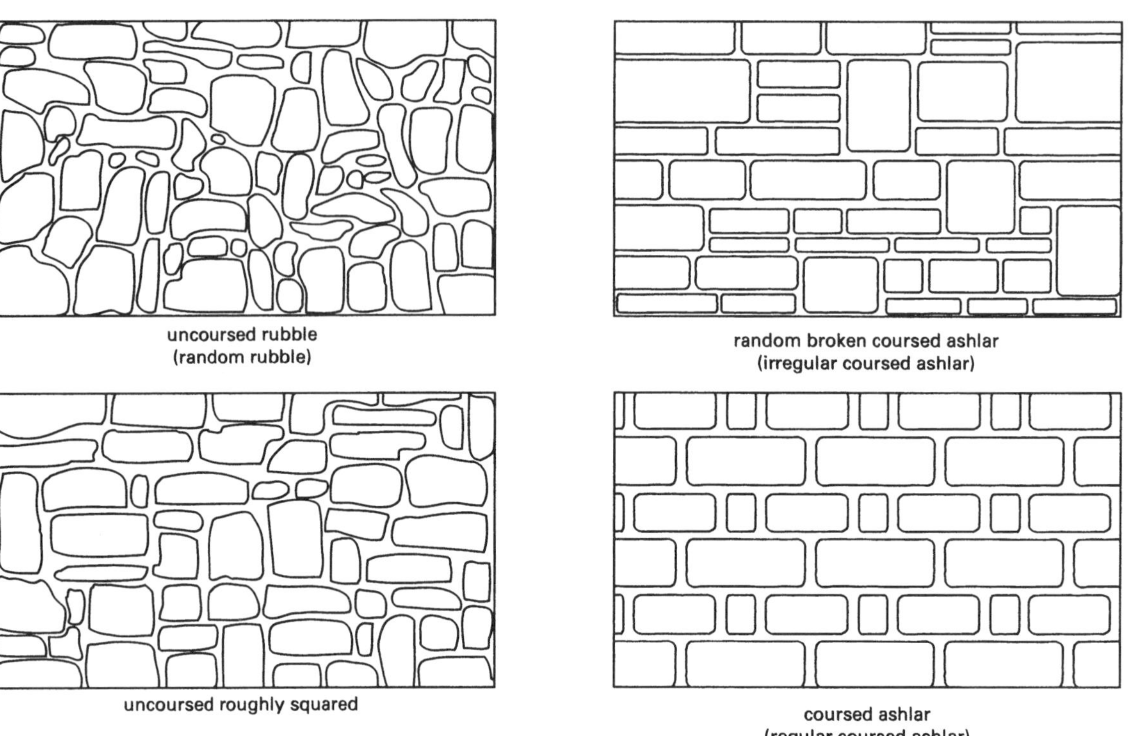

Another commonly used classification of stone is ***veneer stone***, so called because $^3/_4$ in to $1^1/_4$ in thick sheets are applied over a structural support system. With improved cutting methods, it is possible to cut very thin slabs, about $^3/_8$ in thick, which can be applied with mastic to a suitable backup wall. These tiles are commonly manufactured in small shapes, normally 12 in × 12 in or similar sizes. Thin stone veneer in larger sizes can also be applied with adhesive to honeycomb or other types of lightweight backing and then installed on framing applied to the building structure.

Figure 23.17 Veneer Stone Corner Joints

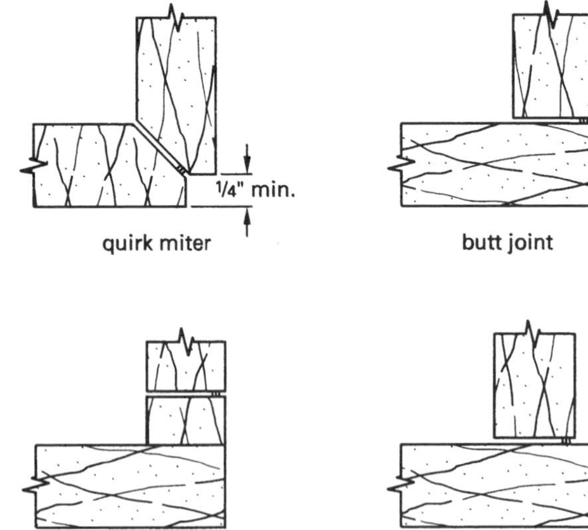

Stone Construction

Some types of stone work, such as steps, trim, coping, and belt courses, still employ cut stone, often called ***dimension stone***. However, because the majority of stone wall finishes use veneer, it is important to know how such work is applied and anchored to structural backup walls. Many types of metal clamps and anchors are available for attaching cut stone and veneer stone to concrete, masonry, and steel construction. A few of the common methods of anchoring and forming corner joints are shown in Fig. 23.17 and Fig. 23.18. In many cases, the space around the anchoring device, between the back of the stone and the structural wall, is filled with plaster of paris to plumb the stone and hold it away from the wall. The joints of stone should be filled with non-staining portland cement mortar.

Figure 23.18 Veneer Stone Anchoring Details

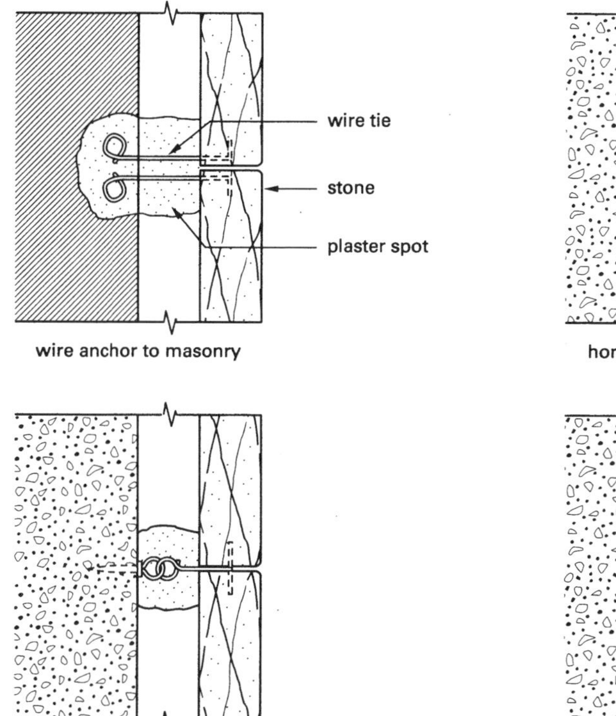

wire anchor to masonry

power actuated anchor

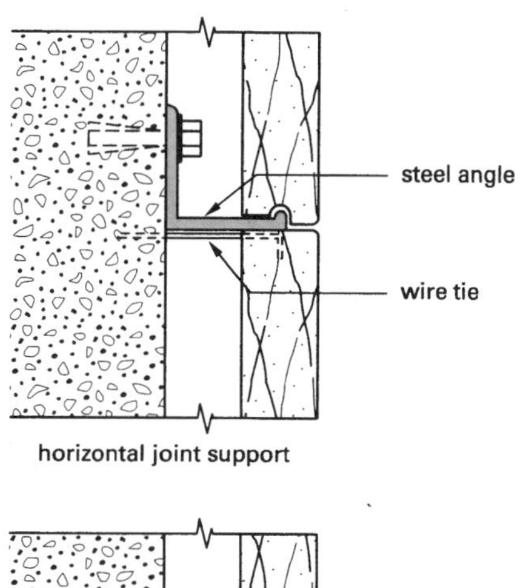

horizontal joint support

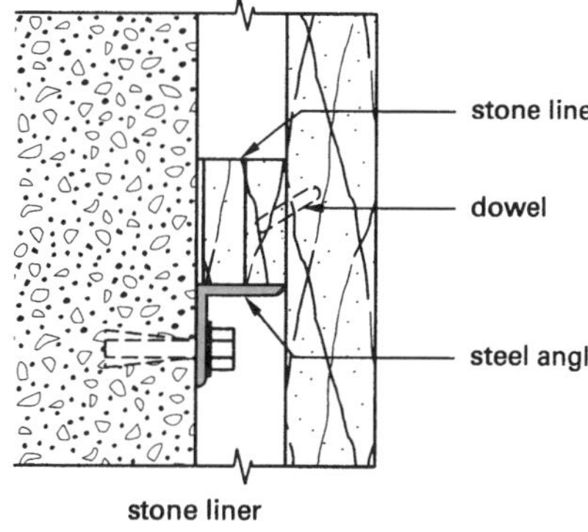

stone liner

24

METALS

Metals are the most versatile of all construction materials. Although they begin as natural elements, the process of refining, manufacturing, forming, and finishing metals allows an almost unlimited variety of forms and uses. Metals have been used in construction in a limited way for centuries, from the lead pipes of the Romans to the decorative grilles and doors of the English Medieval period. However, it has only been in the last 200 years that metals have seen widespread use in both structural and decorative applications.

HISTORY OF METALS

The first use of metals began over 3000 years before Christ when copper was produced by melting ores. Later, humans discovered that the copper could be strengthened by adding small amounts of tin to produce bronze. The Bronze Age continued until about 1200 B.C. when iron smelting was discovered and iron replaced bronze as the basic material for weapons, tools, and other utensils.

By the fourteenth century, cast iron was generally available in Europe, but its use in construction was largely restricted to door fittings, decorative grilles, and other small building parts. Structurally, iron chains were used by Brunelleschi to prevent the dome of Florence Cathedral from spreading (1463) and by Michelangelo for the same purpose on the dome of St. Peter's Cathedral (1585). Cast iron pipes were used to supply water to the gardens at Versailles around 1664.

The invention that started the widespread use of iron in construction (and that helped fuel the Industrial Revolution) occurred when Abraham Darby introduced the use of coke for smelting the metal in 1709. Substituting coke for charcoal eliminated the impurities caused by charcoal and resulted in stronger, higher quality iron. By 1876 iron was being used for roof structures in France.

In 1779, Abraham Darby III made the first major use of cast iron structural elements in a bridge over the river Severn at Coalbrookdale, England. Other cast iron bridges followed this, and at about the same time cast iron columns replaced wood columns in some English cotton mills.

The invention that started the widespread use of iron in construction occurred when Abraham Darby introduced the use of coke for smelting the metal in 1709. Substituting coke for charcoal eliminated the impurities caused by charcoal and resulted in stronger, higher quality iron.

As the nineteenth century began, cast iron columns were commonly used for interior columns in the English mills. In other construction, the new material was being employed for railway station roofs, exhibition halls, and greenhouses. The first use of cast iron for both columns and I-beams for the entire framework of a building was in a cotton mill at Salford, Manchester. It was built by Matthew Boulton and James Watt. Although this building still used exterior masonry bearing walls, it is considered the precursor to the steel-framed buildings in Chicago during the latter part of the century.

Notable buildings during the first half of the century included the Royal Pavilion at Brighton by John Nash (1818), the Greenhouse of the Botanical Gardens in Paris by Rouhault (1833), and the Library of Saint Geneviève in Paris by Henri Labrouste (1843). At midcentury (1851), the Crystal Palace in London became the symbol of the age when Joseph Paxton designed the huge building using prefabricated parts and plate glass, which allowed the structure to be completed in only nine months. The Crystal Palace was followed by the Eiffel Tower, built for the Paris exhibition of 1889, and by the Halle des Machines, which used a 375 ft arch formed of cast iron.

A major technical improvement in iron construction happened in 1856 when Henry Bessemer developed the Bessemer process for making steel inexpensively. Although the process was first used to make railroad rails, it produced better-quality steel (lower carbon content) and provided the raw materials for buildings that followed. In 1868 the open-hearth process improved on this further by shortening the time required for production and allowing scrap iron to be used in larger quantities.

In the United States in 1848, James Bogardus constructed a five-story factory in New York. This building was significant because it used cast iron columns instead of masonry for the outside walls. Ten years later Bogardus designed a similar building for Harper and Brothers where he used an iron framework with large expanses of glass as infill.

The period from 1850 to the late 1880s was called the *Cast Iron Age* in the United States because of the widespread use of the material in New York, Chicago, Saint Louis, and elsewhere across the country.

In 1885 William Le Baron Jenney designed what is considered the first skyscraper, the ten-story Home Insurance Building in Chicago. The building utilized cast iron columns for both the interior and exterior columns and employed the new Bessemer steel girders. In addition, the building was fireproofed.

Jenney also designed the Leiter Building in Chicago. This eight-story structure was one of the first where the architecture and engineering construction were integrated into one expression. The skeleton frame determined the form even though the exterior columns were protected by masonry. Other architects were quick to adopt the new iron and steel materials. Because most of the early and innovative work occurred in Chicago, the use of the iron skeleton came to be called "Chicago Construction."

As a strictly structural device, the steel skeleton was quickly adopted. Most architects during the latter half of the nineteenth and first half of the twentieth century still cloaked the steel in masonry and other materials. It was Mies van der Rohe who was one of the first architects to make the material and its structural purpose part of the form of the building. From his early studies for glass skyscrapers in 1919 to his later work, the steel frame was always elegantly detailed and shown, even if a false grid of steel had to be applied over the fireproofed structural frame. His most notable buildings include structures for the Illinois Institute of Technology in Chicago (from 1939 on) and the 860 Lake Shore Drive apartments (1951), also in Chicago.

BASIC MATERIALS AND PROCESSES

In their natural form, metals exist in combination with other elements and substances in metallic ores. *Smelting* is the process of refining the ores to extract the pure metal. Once the basic metal is obtained, it usually undergoes further treatment to eliminate any impurities that might affect its use.

Metals for construction are seldom used in their pure form but are combined with other elements to form alloys. The addition of other substances to the base metal imparts desirable characteristics. For example, adding chromium and nickel to steel makes the steel corrosion resistant, or stainless. It is the ability to form alloys that makes metals so versatile.

Fabricating Metals

Fabrication is the process of forming and shaping refined metal into the desired condition. The most basic fabrication method is *casting*, which has been used for centuries. In this process, molten metal is poured into a form where it is allowed to cool and harden into the desired shape. The iron columns used in the nineteenth century were cast shapes. The casting process is still used for decorative shapes, pipe valves, and some hardware.

Rolling is the process of passing metal through rollers to produce the needed shape. Rolling can be done while the metal is hot or cold. Hot rolling tends to eliminate flaws in the metal, whereas cold rolling increases the metal's strength and elastic limit but decreases its ductility. Most of the structural steel shapes such as wide-flange beams and channel sections are hot rolled. Many smaller, relatively thin steel shapes are cold rolled for increased strength. All metals except iron can be formed by this method.

Extruding pushes metal through a die to form a shape. Many aluminum sections are formed this way, especially decorative sections and those used for door and window frames. One advantage to the extruding process is that if a sufficiently large quantity is required, special dies can be made and custom shapes extruded for a particular job.

Drawing is similar to extruding, but the metal is pulled through a die instead of being pushed through. The drawing process usually reduces the size of the piece or changes its shape and also improves the strength and surface qualities of the metal. Drawing is applicable for all metals except iron.

There are also many ways metal can be fabricated with mechanical forming. *Bending* changes the shape of tubes and extruded shapes by passing them through various kinds of rolling machines and presses. *Brake forming* takes plates and sheets of metal and makes successive one-directional bends to fabricate the shape. *Spinning* forms round shapes on a lathe. *Embossing* makes patterns on flat sheets of metal by passing them through a machine with the embossing pattern on rollers.

Part of the fabrication process of many metals includes some type of heat treatment. Thermal treatments are used to change the strength or workability of the material. Although any metal can be heat treated, the process is most often used with steel for various structural purposes.

Annealing is a process in which the metal is reheated and slowly cooled to obtain a more ductile metal, which will have improved its machinability and cold-forming characteristics.

Quenching involves heating the metal (most often steel) to a certain temperature and then rapidly cooling it by complete submersion in water or some other liquid. This strengthens the steel.

Tempering is similar to quenching but does not involve rapid cooling. It is also used to improve the strength and workability of steel.

Case hardening produces a hard-surface steel over a relatively softer core.

Finishing Metals

There are three general types of metal finishes. Not all of these finishes are used on all metals, but the classification helps in understanding the processes involved. Each metal type has its particular finishing systems and its own terminology, which will be discussed in the individual sections concerning each metal.

Mechanical finishes alter the surface of the metal in some way. This alteration may be as simple as the way the metal comes from the final forming process or may result from more refined finishing methods, such as grinding or buffing.

Chemical finishes are produced by altering the surface of the metal with some type of chemical process. They may simply clean and prepare the surface for other types of finishes or they may protect or color the metal. Anodizing of aluminum is one type of chemical finish in which the metal is immersed in an electrolytic bath and a current is applied to the metal. In the process, the finish, which can include various colors, becomes an integral part of the aluminum structure, producing a very durable surface.

Coatings are finishes that consist of applied materials that may be for protection of the metal or purely decorative. Coatings may be clear or opaque.

In deciding on the type of finish, several considerations should be reviewed. These include appearance, the amount of protection required, initial cost, long-term or life-cycle cost, and required maintenance.

Joining Metals

There are several methods of joining metals. The selection depends on the type of metal being joined, the working space available for the operation, and the final appearance desired.

All metals can be mechanically joined using accessories such as screws, bolts, and clips. It is common to use high-strength bolts in fastening structural steel. Bolts can also be used to fasten lighter metals such as aluminum and bronze. Bolts are useful when it is necessary to join two dissimilar metals. If potentially damaging galvanic action (electrolysis) might take place between the two metals, a plastic or rubber washer is used to separate them.

Screws can be used to join light-gage metal. Self-tapping screws are typically used to fasten metal or other materials to steel studs or other light framing. Screws are also appropriate for securing light-gage metals to other substrates, such as wood. However, heavier metals must be tapped with threads before screws can be used.

Welding is the joining of two metals by heating them above their melting point. When they cool, the metals physically form one piece of metal. Welding is commonly used for joining structural steel. Welding is not appropriate for thin metals or situations where appearance is important unless the weld can be ground smooth and finished to match the adjacent metal.

Brazing is the joining of two metals at an intermediate temperature using a nonferrous filler metal with a melting point that is above 800°F but lower than welding. Brazing is usually used for brass, bronze, and some aluminums. It results in a clean joint, although some buffing may be required if a completely smooth joint is desired.

Soldering is the joining of two metals using lead-based or tin-based alloy solder filler metal that melts below 500°F.

Metals can also be fastened with adhesives. This method is usually reserved for small trim pieces and sheet stock where the strength of the bond is not critical. Normally, adhesives are used when fastening metals to other substrates such as plywood and particle board.

Properties of Metals

In selecting, detailing, and specifying metals, the architect must have a rudimentary knowledge of several of the unique properties of the various metals. These include gage sizing, galvanic action, and coefficients of expansion.

The thickness of large steel members is usually expressed in fractions or decimals of an inch. However, sheet steel and nonferrous metals of tubing, strips, and sheets are expressed with a gage number. Gage sizing to indicate the thickness of metal started in the early days of the metal industries and was based on the weight of a square foot of a metal. Obviously, the weight would depend on the density of the metal and whether there were any coatings, such as galvanized steel. To confuse matters, different companies had their own gages and different standards have been adopted over the years. As a result, gage is only a rough approximation of a metal's thickness. Even within the same company, the actual thickness may vary even though the gage is the same. Because of the variations, it is preferable to call out the actual thickness desired in decimals of an inch or in millimeters.

Galvanic action is the corrosion resulting when dissimilar metals come in contact with each other in the presence of an electrolyte such as moisture. In the process, called *electrolysis*, a mild electric current is set up between the two metals, gradually corroding one while the other remains intact.

The thickness of large steel member is usually expressed in fractions or decimals of an inch. However, sheet steel and nonferrous metal of tubing, strips, and sheets are expressed with a gage number. Gage is only a rough approximation of a metal's thickness.

The following list represents the galvanic series in the presence of seawater, which is a powerful electrolyte; the metals are listed in the order of their susceptibility to corrosion. The farther apart the metals are from each other on the list, the greater the possibility for corrosion when they are in contact.

In many cases, the electromotive scale of adjacent metals in this list is so close together that few problems would be encountered. For example, the electromotive difference between brass and tin is only 0.01 V while that between zinc and aluminum is 0.24 V.

- zinc
- aluminum
- steel or iron
- 304 stainless steel (active)
- copper
- bronze

- brass
- tin
- lead
- 316 stainless steel (active)
- titanium
- 304 stainless steel (passive)
- gold

Table 24.1 Coefficients of Thermal Expansion by Materials (temperature range 68–212°F)

material	coefficient of expansion $\times 10^{-6}$ in/°F
structural steel	6.5
copper, alloy 110	9.3
stainless steel, 302	9.9
commercial bronze, alloy 220	10.2
red brass, alloy 230	10.2
aluminum	12.8
lead	15.9
other materials	
wood	2.7
glass	5.1
concrete	5.5

To avoid galvanic action, use identical metals when they must be in contact, or separate the metals with nonconducting materials such as neoprene, plastic, or rubber. If these precautions are not possible, use metals as close to each other on the galvanic series as possible. Electrolysis is most severe in humid, marine environments where there is an abundance of seawater; it is less severe in dry climates.

Metals expand and contract with changes in temperature more than many other materials, so it is important to allow for changes in size when designing and detailing metal building components. Table 24.1 lists some of the coefficients of thermal expansion for various metals, along with a few other materials for comparison. Most often, slip joints or expansion joints are provided to accommodate such movement when the building assembly is primarily composed of metal. When metal is used within other materials, such as an aluminum frame within a concrete opening, allowances must be made for the differential movement.

Example 24.1

Galvanic action can be avoided by

(A) using neoprene spacers

(B) increasing the thickness of the materials

(C) reducing contact with dripping water

(D) all of the above

Solution

Dissimilar metals should be physically separated by nonconducting materials such as neoprene in order to prevent galvanic action.

Increasing the thickness of the materials may postpone their complete deterioration but will not prevent it, so option B is incorrect. Direct contact with water will speed up galvanic action, but even moisture in the air is sufficient to cause it, so option C is incorrect.

The answer is (A).

FERROUS METALS

There are two major classifications of metals: ferrous and nonferrous. *Ferrous metals* are those that contain a substantial amount of iron; *nonferrous metals* are those that do not. The primary types of ferrous metals used in the construction industry include iron, steel, stainless steel, and other special steel alloys.

Wrought and Cast Iron

All ferrous metals contain a majority of iron, some carbon, and other elements in the form of impurities or components mixed with the iron to form an alloy. The amount of carbon and other elements determines the strength, ductility, and other properties of the ferrous metal.

Wrought iron is iron with a very low carbon content (less than about 0.30%) and a substantial amount of slag. It is similar in chemical composition to low-carbon steel, but most of the impurities are in the slag, which is mechanically mixed with the iron. Because of its low carbon content, wrought iron is soft, ductile, and resistant to corrosion. Its use in construction is limited to ornamental iron work such as gates, grilles, and fences.

Cast iron is iron with a carbon content above 2%. With this high percentage of carbon, it is very hard, but brittle. Cast iron was used extensively in the nineteenth century for columns and beams in such structures as the Crystal Palace, mill buildings in New England, and some of the early commercial buildings in New York City.

Cast iron with a low silicon content is called white cast iron and has little use in construction unless it is processed in such a way as to produce malleable iron. Cast iron with a high silicon content is called *grey cast iron* and is used for various types of castings such as plumbing valves, pipes, and hardware.

Steel

Steel is one of the most widely used metals because of its many advantages, which include high strength, ductility, uniformity of manufacture, variety of shapes and sizes, and ease and speed of erection. *Ductility* is a property that allows steel to withstand excessive deformations due to high tensile stresses without failure. This property makes steel useful for earthquake-resistant structures. Steel is used in a variety of structural and nonstructural applications including columns, beams, concrete reinforcement, fasteners of all types, curtain wall panels, interior finish panels and trim, pipes, flashing, and electrical conduit.

Because steel is manufactured under carefully controlled conditions, its composition, size, and strength can be uniformly predicted. Therefore, steel structures do not have to be overdesigned to compensate for manufacturing or erection variables as do concrete or timber structures.

Because steel is manufactured under carefully controlled conditions, its composition, size, and strength can be uniformly predicted.

In spite of the advantages, however, steel does have properties that must be accounted for. Most notable are its reduction in strength when subjected to fire and its tendency to corrode in the presence of moisture. Steel itself does not burn, but it deforms when exposed to high temperatures. As a result, steel must be protected with fire-resistant materials, such as sprayed-on cementitious material, gypsum board, or concrete. This adds to the overall cost but is usually justified when the many advantages are considered.

As with any ferrous material, steel will rust and otherwise corrode if not protected. This can be prevented by including other elements in the steel to resist corrosion (stainless steel is an example of a material that uses this method) or by covering the steel with paint or some other type of protective coating.

Steel can also be bonderized. To *bonderize* steel (or any metal) is to coat it with an anticorrosive phosphate solution in preparation for the application of paint, enamel, or lacquer.

Steel is composed primarily of iron with small amounts of carbon and other elements that are part of the alloy, either as impurities left over from manufacturing or deliberately added to impart certain desired qualities to the alloy. In medium-carbon steel used in construction, these other elements include manganese (from 0.5% to 1.0%), silicon (from 0.25% to 0.75%), phosphorus, and sulfur. Phosphorus and sulfur in excessive amounts are harmful because they affect weldability and make steel brittle.

The percentage of carbon present affects the strength and ductility of steel. As carbon is added, the strength increases but the ductility decreases. *Low-carbon steel* contains from 0.06% to 0.30% carbon, *medium-carbon steel* has from 0.30% to 0.50% carbon, and *high-carbon steel* contains from 0.50% to 0.80% carbon. *Standard structural steel* has from 0.20% to 0.50% carbon.

The most common type of steel for structural use is ASTM A992, which means that the steel is manufactured according to ASTM International specification number A992. The yield point for this steel is 36 ksi. Other high-strength steels include A242, A440, and A441 steel, which have yield points of 46 ksi or 50 ksi.

Steel and other metals can be heat treated in a number of ways. There are many types of heat treatment used to alter the physical properties of the metal. Some of the more common for architectural metals are quenching and tempering, annealing, and case hardening. *Quenching and tempering* involves heating the steel to a certain temperature, to alter its crystalline structure, and then cooling it quickly. At this point the steel is too brittle, so it is tempered by heating it again at a lower temperature and cooling it slowly. *Annealing* is a process of heating the metal and then slowly cooling it. This relieves stresses in the metal caused by cold working, and can alter ductility, strength, and other mechanical properties. *Case hardening* is a process for heating a metal and diffusing a gas or liquid, commonly carbon or nitrogen, into its surface, creating a thin layer of a harder alloy. The metal is then given an appropriate heat treatment.

Stainless Steel

Stainless steel is a steel alloy containing a minimum of 11% chromium. In addition, nickel is often added to increase the corrosion resistance and improve cold workability. Additional trace elements such as manganese, molybdenum, and aluminum are added to impart certain characteristics.

Stainless steel is highly corrosion resistant and stronger than other architectural metals. Its resistance to corrosion results from the formation of a chromium-oxide film on the surface of the metal. If the film is scratched or otherwise damaged it will re-form as the metal is exposed to oxygen in the air. This chromium-oxide film layer gives the stainless steel *passivity*, which means that a layer of nonreactive molecules does not allow metal ions at the surface to migrate into solution. Most stainless steel remains passive, but when this layer is lost by abrasion or chemical etching that introduces free iron or chlorides, the surface can become active. The stainless steel can also become active when exposed to certain chemical agents. This affects not only resistance to corrosion but also to the position of the stainless steel in the galvanic series.

Of the nearly 40 types of stainless steel produced, only eight are used for building purposes, six for products, and two for fasteners. They are labeled by number designation of the American Iron and Steel Institute (AISI) and include the following, which are the most commonly used in construction.

- *Type 302*. This contains 18% chromium and 8% nickel and has traditionally been one of the most widely used stainless steel types. It is highly resistant to corrosion, very strong and hard, and can be easily fabricated by all standard techniques.
- *Type 304*. Type 304 has largely replaced type 302 for architectural uses because of its improved weldability. Its other properties are identical to 302.
- *Type 301*. This alloy is similar to type 302, but with slightly smaller amounts of chromium and nickel. It is still very corrosion resistant. Its advantage is its improved work-hardening properties, which can result in very high tensile strengths.
- *Type 316*. For extreme corrosive environments such as industrial plants and marine locations, this type is often used. It has a higher percentage of nickel than the other alloys and includes molybdenum.
- *Type 430*. This type does not contain any nickel, so it is less corrosion resistant than the other types. Its use is generally limited to interior applications.

Stainless steel is available in a variety of forms including sheets, wire, bars, and plates. Structural shapes of H sections, channels, tees, and angles are also available, as are custom extrusions. Stainless steel can be finished in a variety of ways, including mechanical and coatings.

The most common polished finishes for architectural work include the following.

- *No. 3 finish:* an intermediate, dull finish, coarser than no. 4.
- *No. 4 finish:* a general-purpose polished finish that is dull and prevents mirror reflection. It is one of the most frequently used architectural finishes.
- *No. 6 finish:* a dull satin finish.
- *No. 7 finish:* a highly reflective polished surface.
- *No. 8 finish:* the most reflective finish, used for mirrors and reflectors. It is seldom used for general architectural applications; a no. 7 finish is usually used instead.

There are also patterned finishes available that are produced by passing a sheet between patterned rollers. Color coatings are also available. Organic coatings consist of acrylic or other plastic-based enamels, which are fairly elastic, that can be applied to the metal prior to forming. Inorganic coatings such as porcelain enamel are less elastic but add color to the metal.

Other Alloy Steels

Various elements can be added to steel to impart certain qualities. In addition to stainless steel as described, many types of alloy structural steel are produced, which are designated by specification numbers of the American Society of Testing and Materials (ASTM).

ASTM A36 is the most common type of structural steel. It has a minimum yield point of 36,000 lbf/in^2 and a carbon content from 0.25% to 0.29%. ASTM A440 is a high-strength structural steel used for bolted or riveted structures. ASTM A441 is a high-strength, low-alloy manganese vanadium steel intended for welded construction.

Weathering steel is an alloy that contains a small amount of copper. When exposed to moisture in the air or from rain, it develops a protective oxide coating with a distinctive sepia-colored finish. It is used in structures where it is difficult to maintain the steel, or it is used simply for its appearance. However, because small amounts of oxide are carried off by rain, structures using weathering steel should be detailed so the runoff does not stain other materials.

NONFERROUS METALS

Nonferrous metals are those that do not contain iron. The types most often used in construction include aluminum, copper, and copper alloys such as bronze and brass. Other nonferrous metals such as zinc, lead, and gold are of limited use in their pure state or are used in conjunction with other metals and materials.

Aluminum

Aluminum is an abundant element. The primary source of aluminum is bauxite, which is hydrated oxide of aluminum and iron with small amounts of silicon. Aluminum by itself is soft and weak; however, alloying it with manganese, zinc, magnesium, and copper improves its strength and hardness.

Aluminum is used in a wide variety of applications including structure, wall panels, curtain walls, window and door frames, and other decorative uses. In most uses, its high strength-to-weight ratio makes aluminum a desirable building material. It can be formed by casting, drawing, and rolling, although it is most often formed by extruding.

Aluminum can be finished mechanically, chemically, and with coatings. Mechanical finishes include the following.

- *buffed finishes:* smooth specular and specular.
- *directional textured finishes* (satin sheen with tiny, parallel scratches): fine satin, medium satin, coarse satin, hand rubbed, and brushed.

- *nondirectional textured finishes* (formed by abrasion methods, not applicable to thicknesses under $^{1}/_{4}$ in): extra-fine matte, fine matte, medium matte, coarse matte, fine shot blast, medium shot blast, and coarse shot blast.
- *patterned finishes:* formed by rollers and other methods.

Chemical finishing for aluminum is usually an intermediate process for some other final finishing such as cleaning, etching, or preparing for some other coating.

Coating finishes for aluminum include the most familiar *anodizing process*, which is an electrochemical process that deposits an integral coating on the metal. It is called an anodic coating and can include the familiar silvery color of aluminum or a number of colors in the black and brown ranges. The problem with this finish is that it can be scratched.

Other finishes include impregnated color coatings such as baked enamel, vitreous coatings, powder coatings, and laminated coatings.

Aluminum can be joined by screwing, bolting, welding, brazing, soldering, adhesive bonding, and with concealed fasteners. Welding, brazing, and soldering should only be used when the joint is concealed or prior to final finishing. Adhesive bonding should be limited to thin material in situations where high strength is not required.

One of the primary disadvantages of aluminum is the amount of energy required for its refining and manufacture. Although the material is recyclable, the amount of embodied energy to install a finished product into a building is considerable.

Copper and Copper Alloys

Copper is widely used in construction because of its resistance to corrosion, its workability, and its high electrical conductivity. The two primary alloys of copper are bronze and brass. Bronze, by definition, is an alloy of copper and tin, whereas brass is an alloy of copper and zinc. However, traditional nomenclature calls many true brasses by the name bronze. The confusion is clarified by referring to the alloys by their standard designation numbers developed by the Copper Development Association (CDA) or by the Unified Numbering System (UNS). Table 24.2 lists some of the alloys used in construction, including their number designations and common names as well as their nominal compositions.

Copper and copper alloys are used in a variety of applications. Of course, copper is used for electrical wiring because of its high electrical conductivity. The copper alloys are also used for hardware, curtain walls, piping, gutters, roofing, window and door frames, wall panels, railings, and many other ornamental purposes.

- Copper and copper alloys can be formed by casting, rolling, bending, brake forming, extrusion, spinning, and several other methods. They are joined by mechanical fasteners, brazing, and adhesive bonding.
- As with aluminum, copper alloys can be finished several ways using the three methods of mechanical finishes, chemical finishes, and coatings.
- Mechanical finishes include buffed, directional textured (in a variety of grain sizes), nondirectional textured, and patterned.
- Chemical processing is usually used as an intermediate step in a total finishing process, but it can also be used to color the copper alloy.

Coatings can involve clear organic coatings, metallics, and oils and waxes. Although one of the advantages of copper, brass, and bronze is their ability to resist corrosion, if left unprotected many of the alloys develop a patina that is very different in color from the original finish of the metal. The distinctive green color of aged copper is the most notable example. In some cases, this is undesirable, especially in interior applications. To prevent this, various types of thin, clear organic coatings can be applied to the metal. In other situations, a coat of oil or wax can bring out the rich luster of the metal, although continued maintenance is required.

One special alloy, used primarily for roofing, is *Monel metal* (a trade name), which is a combination of copper and nickel with small amounts of other elements. It is also highly resistant to corrosion and is easily worked.

Table 24.2 Composition and Description of Copper Alloys

alloy	UNS no.	name	nominal composition
110	C11000	copper	99.9% copper
220	C22000	commercial bronze	90% copper 10% zinc
230	C23000	red brass	85% copper 15% zinc
260	C26000	cartridge brass	70% copper 30% zinc
280	C28000	Muntz metal	60% copper 40% zinc
385	C38500	architectural bronze	57% copper 40% zinc 3% lead
655	C65500	silicon bronze	97% copper 3% silicon
745	C74500	nickel silver	65% copper 25% zinc 10% nickel

Miscellaneous Nonferrous Metals

Zinc is resistant to corrosion and is sometimes used for sheet roofing and flashing. Zinc fasteners are also made. The metal is more commonly used for coating steel to produce galvanized steel.

Lead is also resistant to corrosion and is occasionally used to cover complex roofing shapes because it is very easy to form around irregularities. However, its density makes it ideal for acoustical insulation, vibration control, and radiation shielding. An alloy of 75% lead and 25% tin can be used to plate steel for roofing. This is known as *terneplate.*

STRUCTURAL METALS

Sleel Shapes

The two metals used in structural applications are steel and aluminum, although steel is by far the most common. The structural use of aluminum is limited to small structures or minor portions of structures. Steel is used for beams, columns, and plates; in light-gage framing such as steel studs; for floor and roof decking; as prefabricated truss joists; and for many types of fasteners.

Structural steel comes in a variety of shapes, sizes, and weights, giving the designer a great deal of flexibility in selecting an economical member that is geometrically correct for any given situation. Figure 24.1 shows the most common shapes of structural steel.

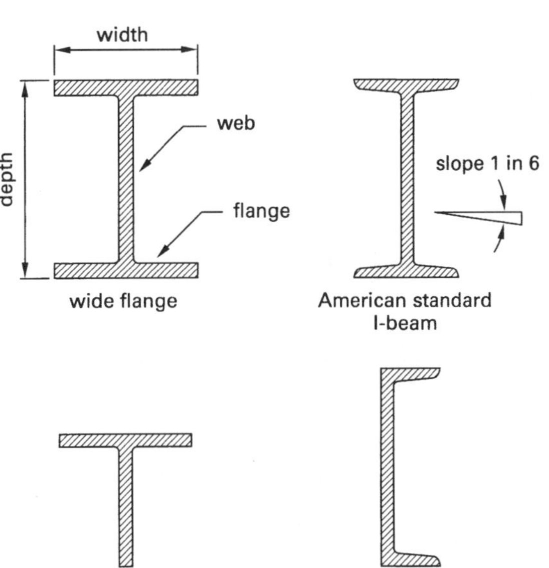

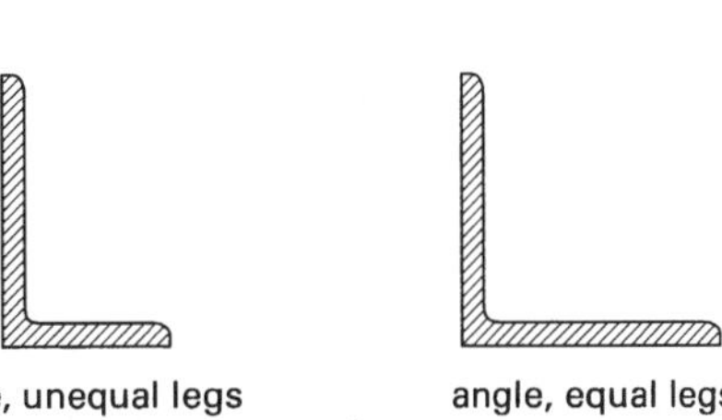

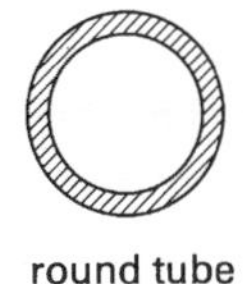

Figure 24.1 Structural Steel Shapes

Wide-flange members are H-shaped sections used for both beams and columns. They are called wide flange because the width of the flange is greater than that of standard I-beams. Many of the wide-flange shapes are particularly suited for columns because the width of the flange is very nearly equal to the depth of the section, so they have about the same rigidity in both axes.

Wide-flange sections are designated with the letter W followed by the nominal depth in inches (millimeters) and the weight in lbm/ft. For example, a W18 × 85 is a wide flange nominally

18 in deep and weighing 85 lbm/ft. Because of the way these sections are rolled in the mill, the actual depth varies slightly from the nominal depth.

American standard I-beams have a relatively narrow flange width in relation to their depth, and the inside faces of the flanges have a slope of one in six. Unlike the wide flanges, the actual depth of an I-beam in any size group is also the nominal depth. The designation of depth and weight per foot for these sections is preceded with the letter S. These sections are usually used for beams only.

American standard channel sections have a flange on one side of the web only and are designated with the letter C followed by the depth and weight per foot. Like that of the American standard I-beams, the depth is constant for any size group; extra weight is added by increasing the thickness of the web and the inside face of the flanges. Channel sections are typically used to frame openings, to form stair stringers, or in other applications where a flush side is required. They are seldom used by themselves for beams or columns because they tend to buckle due to their asymmetrical shape.

Structural tees are made by cutting either a wide-flange section or I-beam in half. If cut from a wide-flange section, a tee is given the prefix designation WT and, if cut from an American standard I-beam, it is given the designation ST. A WT9 × 57, for example, is cut from a W18 × 114. Because they are symmetrical about one axis and have an open flange, tees are often used for chords of steel trusses.

Steel angles are available with either equal or unequal legs. They are designated by the letter L followed by the lengths of the angles and then followed by the thicknesses of the legs. Angles are used in pairs as members for steel trusses or singly as lintels in a variety of applications. They are also used for miscellaneous bracing of other structural members.

Square and rectangular tube sections and round pipe are also available. These are often used for light columns and as members of large trusses or space frames. *Structural tubing* of various sizes is available in several different wall thicknesses, while *structural pipe* is available in standard weight, extra strong, and double-extra strong. Each of the three weights has a standard wall thickness depending on the size. Pipe is designated by its nominal diameter, although the actual outside dimension is slightly larger, while the size designation for square or rectangular tubing refers to its actual outside dimensions. Standard designations for structural steel shapes are summarized in Table 24.3.

Table 24.3 Standard Designations for Structural Shapes

structural shape	example of standard designation
wide-flange shapes	W12 × 22
American standard I-beams	S12 × 35
miscellaneous shapes	M12 × 11.8
American standard channels	C15 × 40
miscellaneous channels	MC12 × 37
angles, equal legs	L3 × 3 × $\frac{3}{8}$
angles, unequal legs	L3 × 4 × $\frac{1}{2}$ LLV*
structural tees—cut from wide flange shapes	WT7 × 15
structural tees—cut from American standard I-beams	ST9 × 35
plate	PL$\frac{1}{2}$ × 10
structural tubing	TS8 × 8 × 0.03750
pipe	pipe 4 std.

*LLV and LLH are used on drawings to indicate the orientation of the long leg of the angle: long leg vertical and long leg horizontal, respectively.

Finally, steel is available in bars and plates. *Bars* are considered any rectangular section 6 in or less in width with a thickness of 0.203 in and greater or sections 6 in to 8 in wide with a thickness of 0.230 in and greater.

Plates are considered any section over 8 in wide with a thickness of 0.230 in and over, or sections over 48 in wide with a thickness of 0.180 in and over.

Open-Web Steel Joists

Open-web steel joists are standardized, shop-fabricated trusses with webs composed of linear members and chords of back-to-back steel angles. The chords are typically parallel, but some types have top chords that are pitched for roof drainage. See Fig. 24.2.

There are three standard series of open-web joists: the K-series, the LH-series, and the DLH-series. The typical spans and depths of each are summarized in Table 24.4. The depths in the K-series increase in 2 in increments, and the depths in the LH- and DLH-series increase in 4 in increments. The standard designation for an open-web joist consists of the depth, the series designation, and the particular type of chord used. For example, a 36LH13 joist is 36 in deep and of the LH-series, with a number 13 chord type. Within any size group, the chord type number increases as the load-carrying capacity of that depth of joist increases.

Open-web steel joists have many advantages for spanning medium to long distances. They are lightweight and efficient structural members, they are easy and quick to erect, and the open webbing allows for ductwork and other building services to be run through the joists rather than under them. In addition, a variety of floor decking types can be used, from wood systems to steel and concrete decks. They can easily be supported by steel beams, by masonry or concrete bearing walls, or by heavier open-web joist girders.

There are also various types of composite joists that use wood top and bottom chords with steel webs. These are ideal for wood-frame buildings where wood decking is used and where spans exceed the limits of standard wood joists.

Metal Decking

Metal decking is available in steel or aluminum, although steel is the more common form. Steel decking consists of formed panels that are laid over steel beams or open-web steel joists to serve as formwork for poured concrete slabs. Before the concrete is poured, the decking also provides a convenient working deck during construction.

Steel decking is available in a wide variety of types, shapes, depths, and gages to satisfy nearly any span and loading condition. A few of the more common shapes are illustrated in Fig. 24.3. Decking is available that simply serves as a form for concrete or that is deformed to bond with the concrete and act as a composite structural material. Cellular decking provides structural support as well as raceways for power and communication cabling.

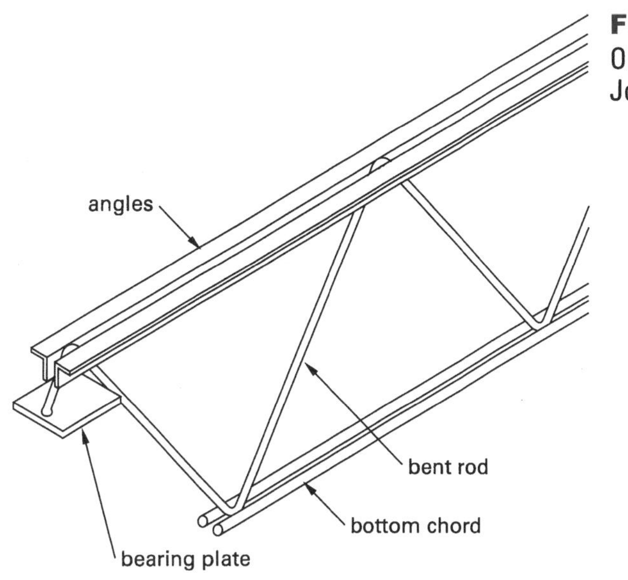

Figure 24.2 Open-Web Steel Joist

Light-Gage Metal Framing

Light-gage metal framing consists of steel members with thicknesses from 10 gage to 25 gage. It is used for interior partitions, exterior bearing and nonbearing walls, joists, rafters, and similar framing. Unlike structural steel, light-gage framing comes in shapes more suitable for lighter loads and easier handling. Light-gage framing is noncombustible, is easily cut and assembled, and does not shrink or otherwise decay.

Manufacturers supply a variety of shapes, sizes, and gages for various uses. Most commonly, light-gage framing is used for interior partitions in noncombustible buildings. However, joists and deeper studs are used for floor and roof framing, as well as for some bearing wall applications. Some of the common shapes of light-gage framing are shown in Fig. 24.4.

Table 24.4 Open-Web Steel Joists—Spans and Depths

series	name	span limits (ft)	depths in series (in)
K	standard	8–60	8–30
LH	long span	25–96	18–48
DLH	deep long span	89–144	52–96

Framing used for interior partitions ranges from 20 gage to 25 gage. Studs are available in depths of $1^{5}/_{8}$, $2^{1}/_{2}$, $3^{5}/_{8}$, 4, and 6 in. For higher walls, bearing walls, and exterior walls, heavier gages and depths are available. Joists are available in depths from 6 in to 14 in and in thicknesses from 10 gage to 20 gage. Light-gage joists and rafters are capable of spanning up to 40 ft.

Light-gage framing is erected with screws, bolts, or welds depending on the thickness of the member and its application.

METAL FABRICATIONS

In addition to structural metals, there are individual building components fabricated partially or entirely of steel, aluminum, or other metals that belong in the category of "metals." These include items such as spiral stairs, expansion joints, gratings, and ladders.

Figure 24.3 Steel Decking

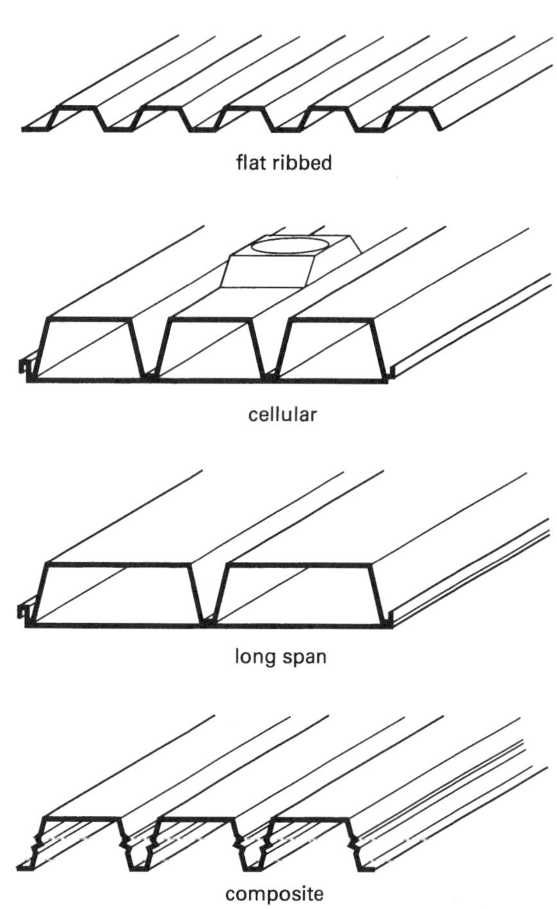

Spiral Stairs

Spiral stairs have a closed circular form with wedge-shaped treads supported from a central, minimum-diameter column (usually 4 in). Standard prefabricated spiral stairs are commonly made from steel. Treads can be exposed steel, hardwood over a steel support, recessed steel pans for infill with concrete or stone, or particleboard over a steel support that can be finished with carpet or resilient flooring. Handrails can be specified as steel pipe, wood, or other ornamental metal. Custom spiral stairs can be fabricated of nearly any combination of steel, wood, and other ornamental metal. Spiral stairs are available in standard diameters from 3 ft 6 in to 7 ft 0 in, in 6 in increments.

Spiral stairs can be fabricated with 22.5°, 27°, and 30° treads, with 30° treads being the most common. This means that there are twelve treads in a full 360° turn or three treads for each quarter circle of the stair. The riser height is set between $7^1/_2$ in and $9^1/_2$ in to make up the total floor-to-floor height so each riser is the same and headroom is adequate. At the top of the stair, a square landing is used to make the transition between the stair and the rest of the floor when a square opening is used. Depending on the floor-to-floor dimension, a spiral stair must be planned so the first riser at the bottom and the last riser at the top are situated so people enter and exit the stair traveling in the right direction.

Expansion Joints

Expansion joint cover assemblies are fabrications designed to allow for major movement between independent structural units of the building. They are different from control joints or isolation joints in that the movements between adjacent portions of a building are significant—on the order of $^1/_2$ in to several inches.

Expansion joints separate two sections of a building completely and continuously, from the foundation through floors, walls, and the roof. Two examples of expansion joint cover assemblies are shown in Fig. 24.5. The first, Fig. 24.5(a), illustrates an expansion joint between two floor slabs; Fig. 24.5(b) shows the separation between a floor and wall. Expansion joints that provide for lateral movement only or for both lateral and vertical movement are available. Seismic expansion joints are also available, but they require special engineering study to determine what type and amount of movement must be accommodated.

Other Miscellaneous Metal Fabrications

Other common miscellaneous metal fabrications include gratings, steel ladders for service areas, stair treads, pipe handrails and guardrails, sheet metal enclosures, prefabricated utility stairs, and protective steel bollards, bumpers, and corner guards.

Example 24.2

The stringers of prefabricated steel utility stairs are normally constructed of

(A) angle iron

(B) channel sections

(C) steel plate

(D) tube sections

Solution

Although any of the listed forms can be used, the stringers are *normally* constructed of steel channel sections with the flanges turned away from the stair. The steel treads and risers are welded to the webs of the sections.

The answer is (B).

Project Planning

ORNAMENTAL METALS

Ornamental metals include a wide variety of both functional and decorative products, such as handrails, guardrails, and elevator interiors. Metal may also be used for custom doors and door facings, partition and architectural woodwork facing, building directories and kiosks, signs, custom light fixtures, ceilings, or as part of nearly any construction assembly. The decorative options available to the architect are almost limitless. The most commonly used ornamental metals include stainless steel, the copper alloys of bronze and brass, and aluminum. Carbon steel, copper, iron, and porcelain enamel are used less frequently.

Stainless steel and copper alloys are available in several stock forms that fabricators use to construct custom assemblies. Some of the common shapes for brass and bronze are shown in Fig. 24.6. Sheet and bar stock are also available in a number of thicknesses.

Detaling Stainless Steel

Custom details for stainless steel are developed in the same way as for plain carbon steel or any other metal. Combinations of bar, plate, tubing, sheet stock, and other shapes are detailed to nearly any configuration and in any combination. Stainless steel can be joined by welding, mechanical fasteners, and in some cases, with adhesives. For the smoothest joint, welding is preferred. However, the finish specified must make it possible to smooth and work the weld to match the adjacent finish. Some rolled and proprietary finishes cannot be matched after shop welding. When mechanical fasteners such as screws, bolts, and rivets are used, they should also be stainless steel to prevent galvanic action and rust stains caused by carbon steel fasteners. Adhesives are typically used to laminate sheet stock to other materials. In order to simplify fabrication and minimize cost, the smallest sizes and gages that satisfy the application should be used.

Detailing with Brass and Bronze

As with stainless steel, basic shapes are used to fabricate custom assemblies by various forming and fastening methods. Brass can also be extruded and cast. Extrusion is common for door and window frames, railings, and trim, whereas casting is used to manufacture hardware and plumbing fixtures.

Brass can be fabricated to any size required, but it is more economical to design and detail ornamental brass using standard shapes (see Fig. 24.6) and sizes whenever possible. Hexagonal and octagonal tubing is also available on special order as well as some T-shapes, Z-shapes, and proprietary shapes. Note that square and rectangular tubing, channels, and angles of brass have sharp corners as contrasted with the rounded corners of stainless steel and regular steel tubing, channels, and angles. Although there are some standard shapes and sizes, several manufacturers use brass to fabricate proprietary shapes and products. For example, several manufacturers produce lines of brass railings for bars, guardrails, and handrails, including brackets and other accessories for a complete installation.

Figure 24.4
Light-Gage Metal Framing

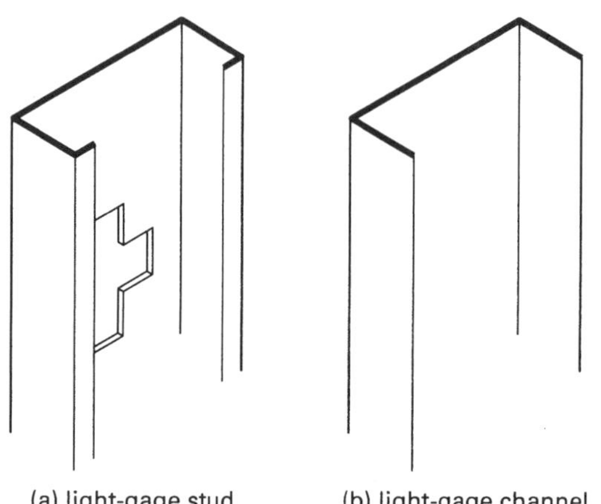

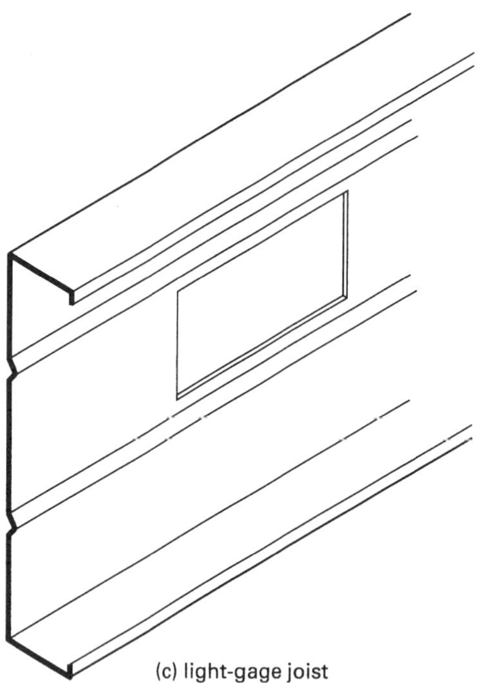

Brass and bronze can be formed into an unlimited number of shapes and sizes, and different pieces can be fastened to fabricate nearly any type of detail. Brass and bronze can also be combined with other materials such as wood, plastic, and stone to construct specialty items. However, standard shapes, sizes, and metal alloys should be used to minimize cost and fabrication difficulty. Following are some general guidelines for designing and detailing with these metals.

For details with large expanses of smooth, flat sheet stock, the gage of metal must be thick enough to avoid oil canning or showing other surface imperfections. A minimum of 10-gage brass (0.1019 in) is used when large areas are unsupported or unbacked. If the sheet has an embossed pattern, thinner material is used because the patterning imparts stiffness to the sheet. When brass is laminated to particleboard or other backing, sheets as thin as 20 gage (0.032 in) are used. Items that are fabricated of brake-formed brass are from 14- or 12-gage (0.0640 or 0.0808 in) metal.

Brass and bronze are joined with mechanical fasteners, adhesives, or by brazing or soldering. Mechanical fasteners include screws, bolts, rivets, and various types of clips in compatible alloys. In most cases the appearance of metalwork is improved if mechanical fasteners are concealed. If the installation makes it impossible to conceal fasteners, their type, size, and location should be given careful consideration based on the final installed position.

Adhesives are used for laminating sheets onto backing material or to join smaller pieces to other materials when exposed fasteners would be objectionable. Unless some additional mechanical fastening device can be incorporated into a detail, adhesive bonding should not be used alone where the metal has to support forces other than its own weight.

Brass can be joined by brazing, soldering, or welding as discussed in the earlier section on joining metals. Of the three methods, brazing is most often used for joining brass for architectural purposes. If possible, brazed joints should be concealed because the filler metal does not exactly match the brass.

Perforated Metal

Perforated metal is sheet metal that has been punched with a regular pattern of holes. Standard perforations include round and square holes as well as slots in a wide range of patterns, hole sizes, and hole spacings. For interior applications, perforated metals are used for space dividers, railing guards, shelving, furniture, supply air and return air grills, coverings for acoustical panels, custom light fixtures, or any specialty fabrication that can be constructed with sheet metal.

Architectural Mesh

Architectural mesh is a specialty metal that is most often used for elevator cab interiors, but it can be creatively applied in other architectural applications such as wall panels and door facings. Architectural mesh is formed by "weaving" thin strips of metal or heavy wire and then grinding off a portion of one face to reveal a highly textured but relatively flat surface. The final surface appearance depends on the type of weave, the type of metal used, and how much is ground off. Stainless steel and brass are the most commonly used materials.

Figure 24.5 Expansion Joint Cover Assemblies

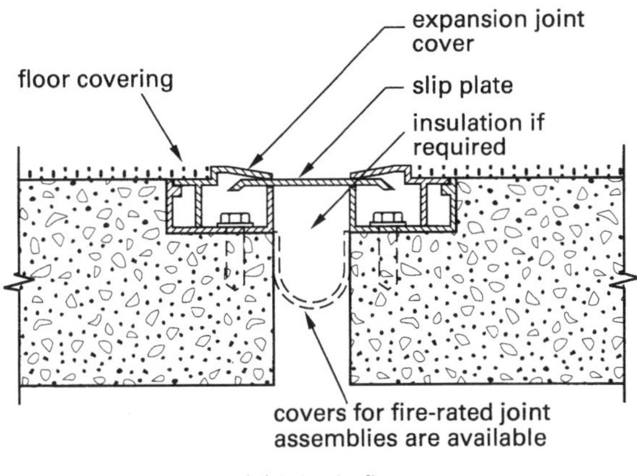

(a) joint in floor

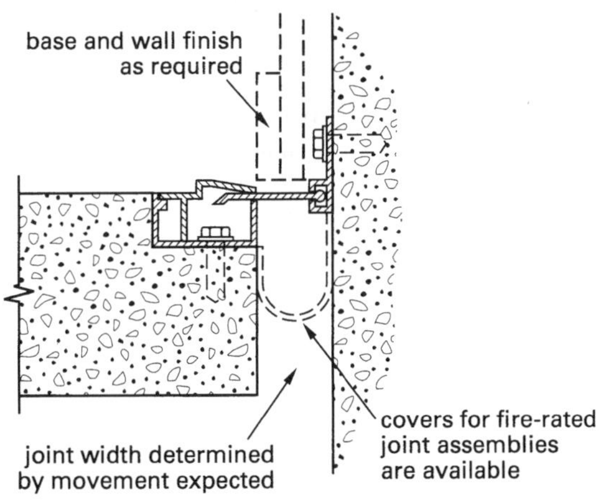

(b) joint at wall

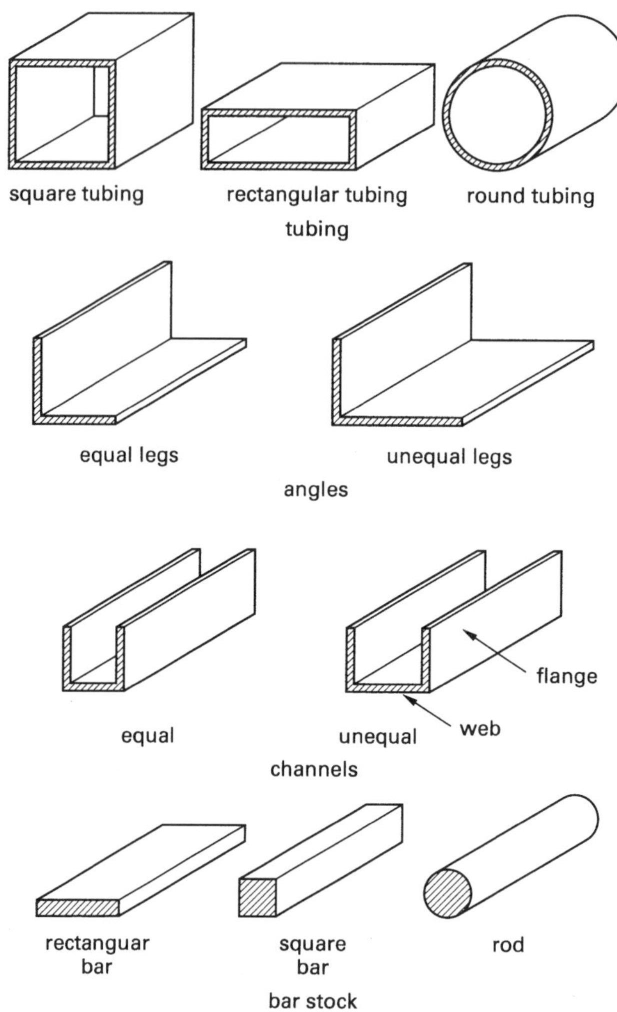

Figure 24.6
Standard Brass and Bronze Shapes

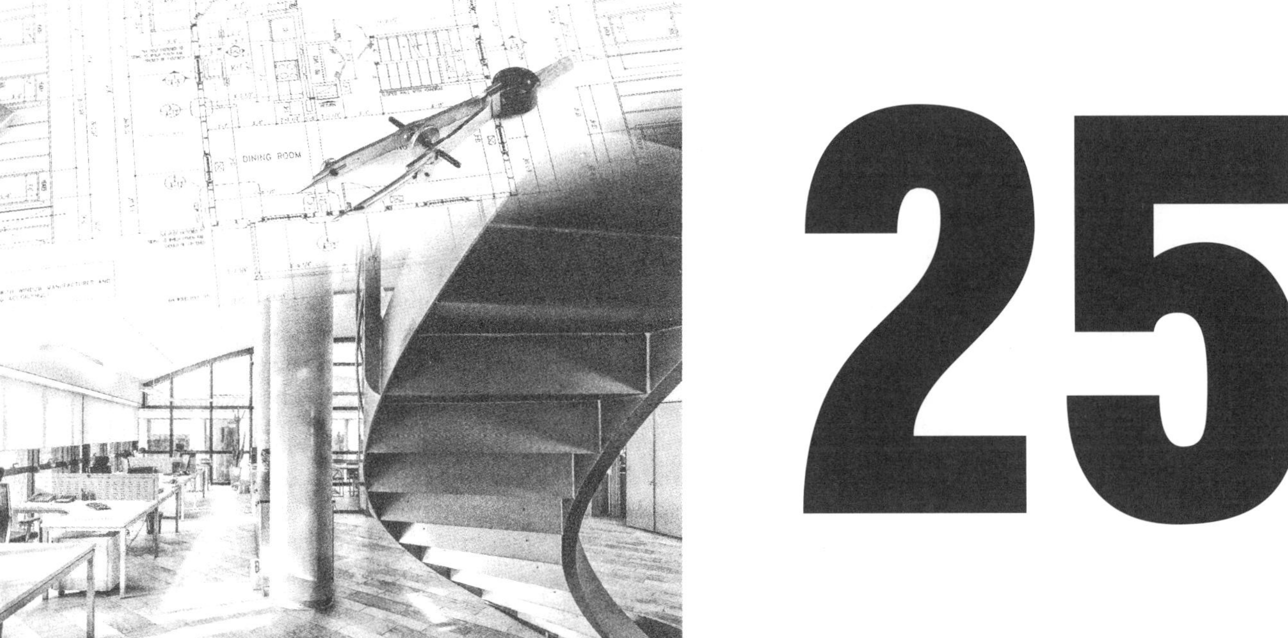

25

STRUCTURAL AND ROUGH CARPENTRY

There are two broad categories of wood use in construction: rough carpentry and finish carpentry. *Rough carpentry* includes the structural framing, sheathing, blocking, and miscellaneous pieces necessary to prepare the building for finish work. Most rough carpentry is hidden once construction is complete, but exposed lumber such as heavy timber beams, glued-laminated members, and outdoor deck frames is considered rough carpentry.

As the name implies, *finish carpentry* includes the exposed, finished pieces of lumber necessary to complete a job, including such things as window and door trim, base, wood paneling, cabinets, and shelving. Finish carpentry work is normally done on the job site, but it also includes architectural woodwork, which is the fabrication of wood items in a manufacturing plant. Finish carpentry and architectural woodwork are reviewed in Chap. 40.

This chapter includes a general review of wood as a structural material. However, methods for calculating sizes of members and fasteners are not included.

When discussing wood as a construction material, several terms are often used interchangeably, but there are distinctions. *Wood* is the fibrous substance forming the trunk, stems, and branches of the tree. *Lumber* is the product of sawing, planing, and otherwise preparing wood to be used as construction members. *Timber* is lumber with a 5 in minimum sectional dimension.

CHARACTERISTICS OF LUMBER

Lumber is a very versatile building material and has many advantages—it is plentiful, relatively low in cost, easy to shape and assemble, has good thermal insulating qualities, and is aesthetically pleasing. As a natural material, however, it lacks the uniform appearance and strength that manufactured materials have. Also, because of its cellular structure, it is susceptible to dimensional changes when its moisture content changes.

These disadvantages can be overcome with some of the manufactured wood products available. A few examples of these products are plywood, glued-laminated timber, and plywood web joists.

Types and Species

There are two general classifications of wood: softwood and hardwood. These terms have nothing to do with the actual hardness of the wood, but refer to whether the wood comes from a coniferous tree or a deciduous tree. *Conifers* (softwood) are cone-bearing, needle-leaved trees that hold their foliage in the winter, such as fir, spruce, and pine. Deciduous (hardwood) trees are broad-leaved trees that lose their leaves in the winter, such as oak, walnut, and maple. Softwoods are used for structural and rough carpentry because of their greater availability and lower cost. Finish carpentry and architectural woodwork utilize both hardwoods and softwoods.

There are literally hundreds of species of softwood and hardwood available throughout the world. However, only a few are used in the United States for rough carpentry, primarily due to local availability and cost. For example, southern pine is used in the southeastern portion of the United States, whereas Douglas fir or Douglas fir-larch is used in the western region. Other commonly used species for rough carpentry include hem-fir, eastern white pine, and hemlock. Redwood and cedar are commonly used for exterior applications where resistance to moisture is required.

Strength

The strength of lumber is dependent on the direction of the load relative to the direction of the wood's grain. Lumber is strongest when the load is parallel to the direction of the grain, such as with a compressive load on a wood column. Wood can resist slightly less tensile stress parallel to the grain and even less when compressive forces are perpendicular to the grain.

Wood is weakest when horizontal shear force is induced, which occurs when bending forces are applied to a beam and the fibers tend to slip apart parallel to the grain. Allowable forces used in structural calculations are lowest for horizontal shear, and this quite often governs the design of bending members.

Defects

Because wood is a natural material, there are several types of defects that can be present in lumber. There are also many types of defects that can occur during manufacture. These affect the strength, appearance, and use of lumber and are reflected in how an individual piece of lumber is graded. Figure 25.1 shows some of the more common wood defects.

- *Knots* are the most common natural defect. A knot is a branch or limb embedded in the tree that is cut through in the process of lumber manufacture. Knots are classified according to quality, size, and occurrence. There are over 10 different types of knots.
- A *check* is a separation of the wood fibers occurring across or through the annual growth rings, a result of improper seasoning.
- A *pitch pocket* is an open area between growth rings that contains resin.
- A *shake* is a lengthwise separation of the wood that usually occurs between or through the annual growth rings.
- A *split* is similar to a check except that the separation extends completely through a piece of lumber, usually at the ends.
- A *wane* is the presence of bark or absence of wood from any cause on the edge or corner of a piece of lumber.

Warping is a common manufacturing defect. A *warp* is any variation from a true or plane surface and is usually caused by the natural shrinkage characteristics of wood and uneven drying during processing. A *bow* is a deviation parallel to the length of the lumber in line with the lumber's flat side. A *crook* is a deviation parallel to the length of the lumber perpendicular to the flat side of the piece. A *cup* is a deviation from true plane along the width of the board.

Figure 25.1 Common Wood Defects

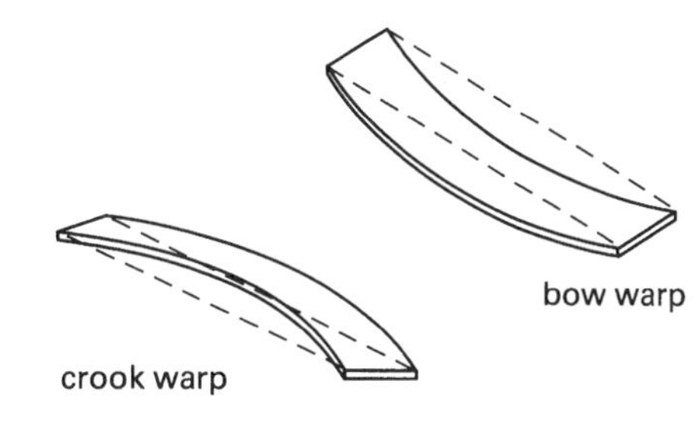

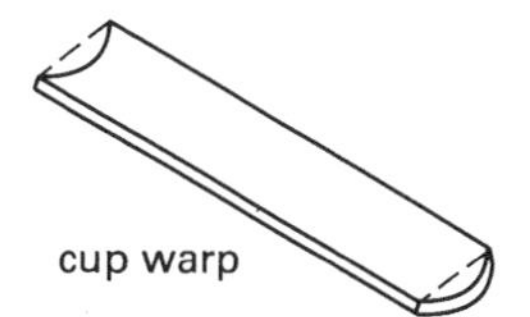

Grading

Because a log yields lumber of varying quality, the individual sawn pieces must be categorized to allow selection of boards that are best suited for a particular purpose. For structural lumber, the primary concern is the amount of stress that a grade of lumber of a specific species can carry. For finish lumber, the primary concern is the appearance of the wood and how it accepts stain, paint, and other finishes. Load-carrying ability is affected by such things as size and number of knots, splits, and other defects.

Grading of lumber used for structural and rough carpentry purposes is done under standard rules established by several agencies certified by the American Lumber Standards Committee. The grading is done at the sawmill, either by visual inspection or machine, if the lumber is to be used for structural purposes. The resulting allowable stress values are published in tables that are used when making structural calculations.

There are two primary classifications of softwood lumber: "yard lumber," used for structural purposes and rough framing, and "factory and shop lumber," used for making door frames, windows, and finish items.

Yard Lumber

Yard lumber is further classified as boards, dimension, and timber, as shown in Fig. 25.2. Dimension lumber and timber are the two classifications used for structural purposes, and these are further classified into groups based on nominal size and use. With this system the same grade of lumber in a species may have different allowable stresses depending on which category it is in. This can be confusing, but it is critical in selecting the correct allowable stress for a particular design condition.

Figure 25.2 Yard Lumber Types

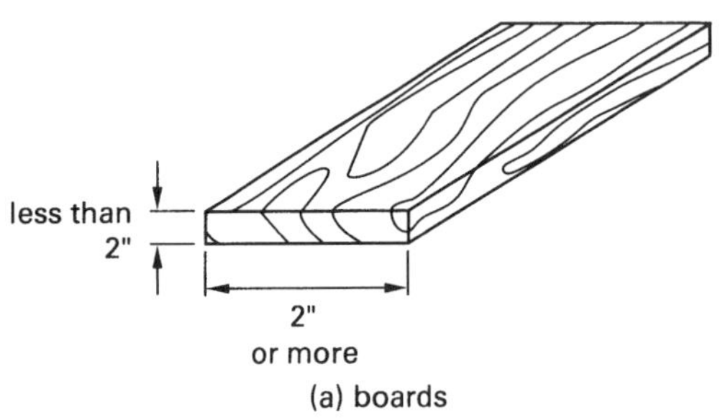

(a) boards

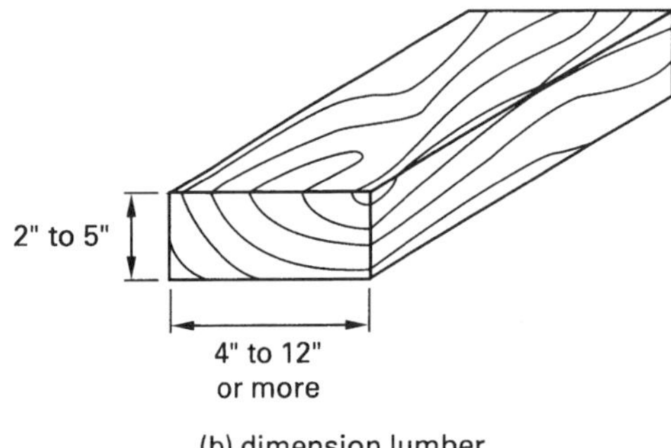

(b) dimension lumber

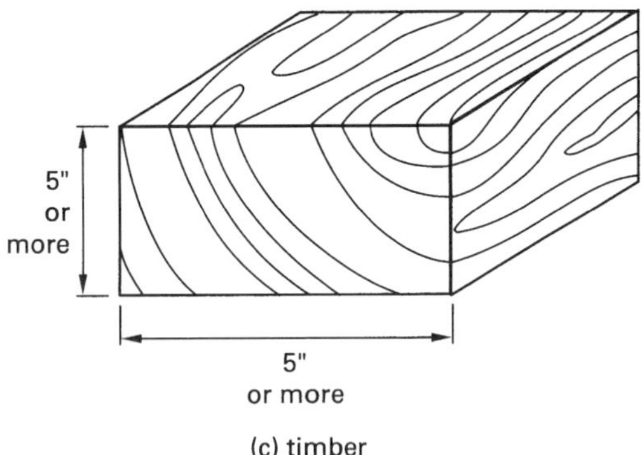

(c) timber

The five size groups (based on nominal dimensions) are as follows.

- 2 in to 4 in thick, 2 in to 4 in wide. This includes members such as 2 × 2s.
- 2 in to 4 in thick, 4 in wide. This is the category for 2 × 4s, which are usually subdivided into grades of construction, standard, and utility.
- 2 in to 4 in thick, 5 in wide and wider. This includes wood members such as 2 × 6s, 2 × 8s, and the like, but not 2 × 4s.
- *beams and stringers* are defined as members 5 in wide and wider having a depth of at least 2 in greater than the width.
- *posts and timbers* are defined as members 5 in by 5 in and larger with a depth not more than 2 in greater than the width.

These five size categories are further subdivided into smaller groups such as select structural, no. 1, no. 2, and so on. The exact nomenclature and method of subdivision vary with each grading agency and the wood species.

Machine-stress-rated lumber is based on grade designations that depend on the allowable bending stress and modulus of elasticity of the wood.

Factory and Shop Lumber

Factory and shop lumber for boards (less than 1 in nominal thickness) is graded according to defects that affect the appearance and use of the wood. Exact classifications vary with the grading agency and the species of lumber, but in general factory and shop lumber is divided into select and common grades. The three select grade categories are B & Better, C Select, and D Select, with B & Better being the best and free of knots.

Common grades available include no. 1, no. 2, no. 3, no. 4, and no. 5—no. 1 common being the best. The individual grades are determined by the size and character of the knots.

Dimensioning

Lumber for rough carpentry is referred to by its nominal dimension in inches, such as 2 × 4 or 2 × 10. However, after surfacing at the mill and drying, its actual dimension is somewhat less. Table 25.1 gives the actual dimensions for various nominal sizes of sawn lumber.

Lumber is ordered and priced by the *board foot.* This is a measure of a quantity of lumber equal to a piece 12 in wide by 12 in long by 1 in thick. Nominal sizes are used so an actual sized piece of lumber $^3/_4$ in thick, $11^1/_4$ in wide, and 2 ft long contains 2 board feet.

Table 25.1 Nominal and Actual Sizes of Lumber

nominal size	standard dressed size (in, width × depth)
1 × 2	$^3/_4 \times 1^1/_2$
1 × 4	$^3/_4 \times 3^1/_2$
1 × 6	$^3/_4 \times 5^1/_2$
1 × 8	$^3/_4 \times 7^1/_4$
2 × 2	$1^1/_2 \times 1^1/_2$
2 × 4	$1^1/_2 \times 3^1/_2$
2 × 6	$1^1/_2 \times 5^1/_2$
2 × 8	$1^1/_2 \times 7^1/_4$
2 × 10	$1^1/_2 \times 9^1/_4$
2 × 12	$1^1/_2 \times 11^1/_4$
4 × 4	$3^1/_2 \times 3^1/_2$
4 × 6	$3^1/_2 \times 5^1/_2$
4 × 8	$3^1/_2 \times 7^1/_4$
4 × 10	$3^1/_2 \times 9^1/_4$
4 × 12	$3^1/_2 \times 11^1/_4$
4 × 14	$3^1/_2 \times 13^1/_4$
6 × 6	$5^1/_2 \times 5^1/_2$
6 × 8	$5^1/_2 \times 7^1/_2$
6 × 10	$5^1/_2 \times 9^1/_2$

Moisture Content

Moisture content is defined as the weight of water in wood as a fraction of the weight of oven-dry wood. It is an important variable because it affects the amount of shrinkage, weight, and strength of the lumber, as well as the withdrawal resistance of nails.

Moisture exists in wood both in the individual cell cavities and bound chemically within cell walls. When the cell walls are completely saturated but no water exists in the cell cavities, the wood is said to have reached its *fiber saturation point.* This point averages about 30% moisture content in all woods. Above this point the wood is dimensionally stable, but as the wood dries below this point it begins to shrink.

When wood is used for structural framing and other construction purposes, it tends to absorb or lose moisture in response to the temperature and humidity of the surrounding air. As it loses moisture it shrinks, and as it gains moisture it swells. Ideally, the moisture content of wood when it is installed should be the same as the prevailing humidity to which it will be exposed. However, this is seldom possible so lumber needs to be seasoned, either by air drying or kiln drying, to reduce the moisture content to acceptable levels.

For the wood to be considered dry lumber, its moisture content cannot exceed 19%. To be grademarked "kiln dry," its moisture content cannot exceed 15%. Design values found in structural tables assume that the maximum moisture content will not exceed 19%. If it does, the allowable stresses must be decreased slightly.

Wood shrinks most in the direction perpendicular to the grain and very little parallel to the grain. When considered perpendicular to the grain, wood shrinks most in the direction of the annual growth rings (tangentially) and about half as much across the rings (radially). See Fig. 25.3. The position in the log where a piece of lumber is cut also affects the wood's shrinkage characteristics.

In detailing wood, an allowance must be made for the wood's shrinking and swelling during use, regardless of its initial moisture content. Of particular importance is the accumulated change in dimension of a series of wood members placed one on top of the next. The shrinkage of an individual member may not be significant, but the total shrinkage of several pieces may result in problems such as sagging floors, cracked plaster, distortion of door openings, and nail pops in gypsum board walls.

Figure 25.3
Wood Shrinkage

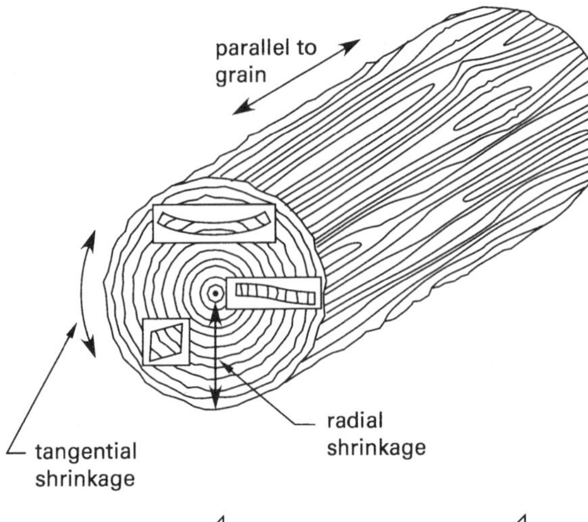

Figure 25.4
Light Frame Construction

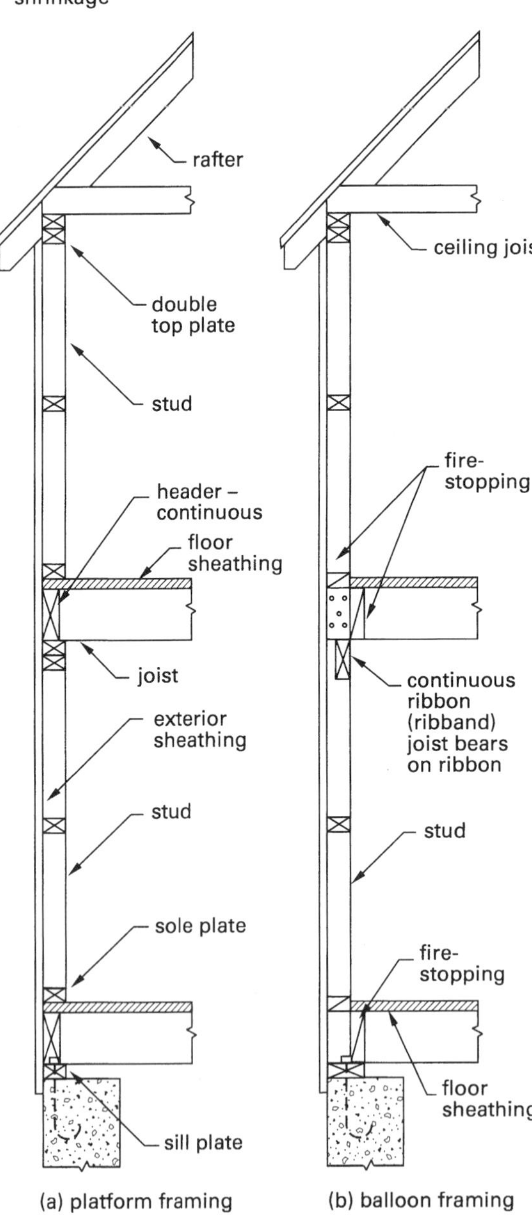

FRAMING

Framing is the assembly of lumber and timber components to construct a building. Because of code restrictions, structural limitations, and construction techniques, most wood construction is limited to small to moderate-sized buildings. This section discusses light frame construction; the next section reviews heavy timber construction used for larger structures.

Light Frame Construction

Light frame construction uses small, closely spaced members such as 2×4 or 2×6 studs for walls and partitions and nominal 2 in thick members for floor and roof joists. Beams may be built-up sections of nominal 2 in lumber, or heavy timber or steel.

Two systems of wall framing include the platform frame (also called *western framing*) and the balloon frame. The essential difference is that the platform frame uses separate studs for each floor of the building, with the top plates, floor joists, and floor framing of the second level being constructed before the second-floor wall studs are erected. The balloon frame uses continuous wall studs from foundation to second-floor ceiling. Figure 25.4 shows the two types of framing systems.

One advantage of the platform frame is that each floor can be completed and used for constructing the next floor, and shorter studs cost less. The advantage of the balloon frame is that vertical shrinkage is minimized because most of the construction is parallel to the direction of the grain where wood shrinkage is the least.

When wood joists are framed into masonry walls instead of wood stud walls, they must rest on metal hangers attached to wood ledger strips anchored to the masonry or be fire cut, as shown in Fig. 25.5. A fire cut is required to prevent the masonry from being pushed up and out if the wood member should collapse during a fire.

Framing Openings

Openings in wood construction are required for doors, windows, stairs, and similar conditions. Because light frame construction consists of many small, closely spaced members carrying the loads, eliminating any of these studs or joists affects the structural integrity of the building. As a result, framing of openings must be capable of transferring loads from one cut member

Project Planning

to other members. Two typical methods of framing vertical and horizontal openings are shown in Fig. 25.6. The size of header over a window opening depends on the span and usually consists of a double 2 in wide member (commonly expressed as 2×) bearing on studs at either side of the opening.

Plywood

Plywood consists of sheets of thin veneer glued together to form a rigid panel. Sheets are made in standard 4 ft by 8 ft sizes in thicknesses of $^1/_4$, $^3/_8$, $^1/_2$, $^5/_8$, and $^3/_4$ in. These are the most readily available, although other panel sizes and thicknesses are available.

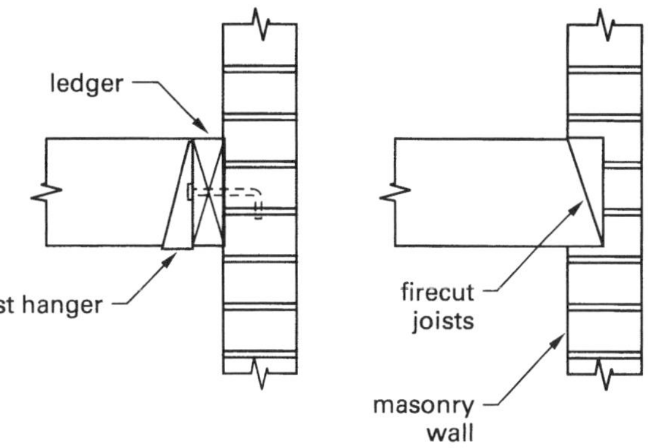

Figure 25.5 Wood Framing into Masonry

Plywood is graded in two ways. The first is by span rating and is used for most structural applications, including sheathing. The span rating is a measure of the strength and stiffness of the plywood parallel to the face grain. The rating consists of two numbers, such as $^{32}/_{24}$. The first number gives the maximum spacing in inches for roof supports under average loading conditions, and the second number gives the maximum spacing in inches for floor supports under average residential loading. These spacings are allowed if the face grain is perpendicular to the direction of the supports and if the panels are continuous over three supports.

Plywood for structural uses is also classified according to the species of wood used. There are five groups. Structural I plywood is made only from woods in group 1; Structural II can be made from woods in groups 1, 2, and 3.

The other way plywood is graded is by the quality of the face veneer. Veneer grades are classified by the letters N, A, B, C, and D. *N grade* is intended for a natural finish and is made from all heartwood or all sapwood. It is free from defects but is only available on special order. *A grade* is smooth and paintable with few knots or other defects and is the best grade commonly available. *B grade* allows for plugged knotholes but has a smooth surface. *C grade* allows small knotholes and some splits, and *D grade* allows for larger knotholes. Plywood should be specified with exterior glue for outdoor locations.

Special types of plywood are also produced. These include patterned panels for exterior finish siding, marine plywood that has special glues, and overlaid plywood with a surface of resin-impregnated paper to provide a smooth surface.

Sheathing and Miscellaneous Wood Framing Members

Sheathing is thin panel material attached to framing to provide lateral support, increase rigidity, and provide a base for applying exterior finishes. For structural purposes, sheathing most often consists of plywood or particleboard nailed to the wood studs or joists. In situations where lateral stability is not critical, insulating sheathing may be used.

Particleboard is composed of small wood particles, fibers, or chips of various sizes mixed together in a binder and formed under pressure into a panel. Like plywood, it is available in several thicknesses in 4 ft by 8 ft sheets and is available in low-, medium-, and high-density forms. Particleboard is generally preferred for backing and framing of finish carpentry and architectural woodwork because it is less expensive and more dimensionally stable than plywood.

Oriented strand board (OSB) is an engineered panel product manufactured from precision-cut wood strands a maximum of 4 in long and 0.0027 in thick. The strands are arranged in layers at right angles to one another, much like plywood, and bonded with resin waterproof glue under heat and pressure. OSB is available in several thicknesses and sizes from standard 4 ft by 8 ft size to much larger sizes, up to 8 ft by 28 ft. The primary strength of OSB panels is along the orientation of the chips on the face layer, which is generally parallel to the length of the panel. Although OSB is more susceptible to delamination than is plywood, it is still acceptable for use as sheathing with short-term weather exposure because of the waterproof glue used.

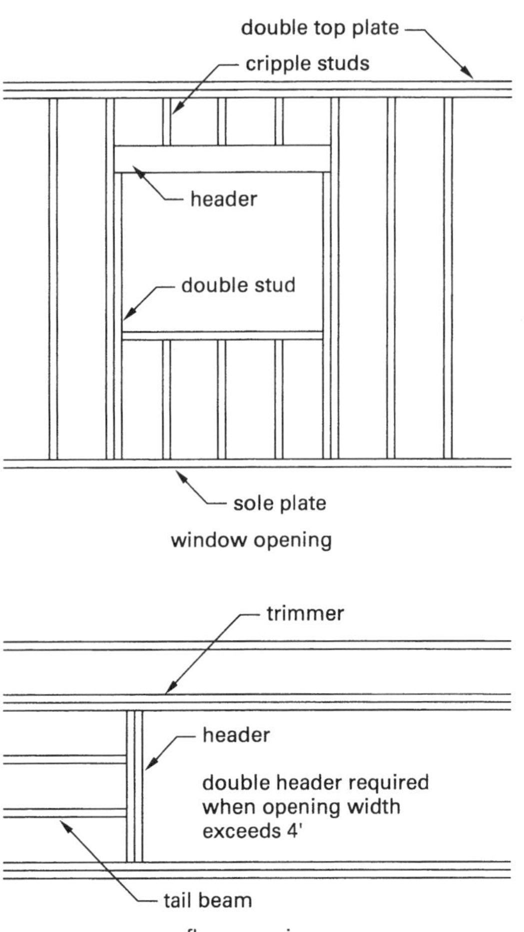

Figure 25.6 Framing for Openings

Medium-density fiberboard (MDF) is a panel product made from wood particles reduced to fibers in a moderate-pressure steam vessel and then combined with a resin and bonded together under heat and pressure. It is the most dimensionally stable of the mat-formed panel products. MDF has a smooth, uniform, and dense surface that makes it useful for painting, thin overlay materials, veneers, and high-pressure decorative laminate.

Hardboard is a panel product composed of inter-felted fibers consolidated under heat and pressure to a density of 31 lbm/ft^3 or more. It is available sanded on one or both sides and either tempered or untempered. Tempered hardboard has a greater hardness, stiffness, and weight than the untempered type.

Blocking is wood framing installed between main structural members such as studs or joists to provide extra rigidity or to provide a base for nailing other materials. For example, short pieces of lumber are often placed perpendicular to joists under the locations of interior partitions. Edge blocking is also placed at the intersection of wall and ceiling framing to provide a nailing base for the application of gypsum wallboard.

Bridging is bracing between joists that prevents the joist from buckling under load. Bridging may be solid wood blocking, 1 × 3 (actual $^3/_4$ in by $2^1/_2$ in) wood cross members, or metal cross bridging. It is installed at intervals not exceeding 8 ft unless both the top and bottom edges of the joists are supported for their entire length.

Firestops are barriers installed in concealed spaces of combustible construction to prevent the spread of fire caused by drafts. Allowable materials include nominal 2 in thick wood members, gypsum board, or mineral wool. In most cases, wood blocking is used. The building code specifies where and when firestops must be installed, but in general firestopping is used in concealed spaces between floors, between a floor and ceiling or attic space, between floors under stairs, and in vertical openings around vents, chimneys, and ducts between floors.

ENGINEERED WOOD PRODUCTS

Engineered wood products include a wide range of components that are either constructed of standard wood elements (such as factory-built trusses made from 2 × 4s) or that use waste products or smaller pieces of wood to create new construction components (such as laminated veneer lumber). In some cases, wood products are used in conjunction with other materials, such as metal fasteners or insulation. Engineered wood products have the following advantages.

- better use of natural resources
- an improved product without typical wood defects
- increased strength for a given size compared with standard wood products
- consistent size and strength

Plywood Web Joists

Plywood web joists are like wood I-beams. They are fabricated with a plywood or an oriented strand board web piece fitted into grooves of chord members made of solid wood or laminated veneer lumber. They are manufactured in the same depths as standard solid wood joists and deeper. For the same depth they have a much higher load-carrying capacity than do wood joists, and they make very efficient use of wood products and only require wood from second- or third-growth timber forests. Other advantages include minimal shrinkage, ease of handling, and uniformity of size and shape. See Fig. 25.7(a).

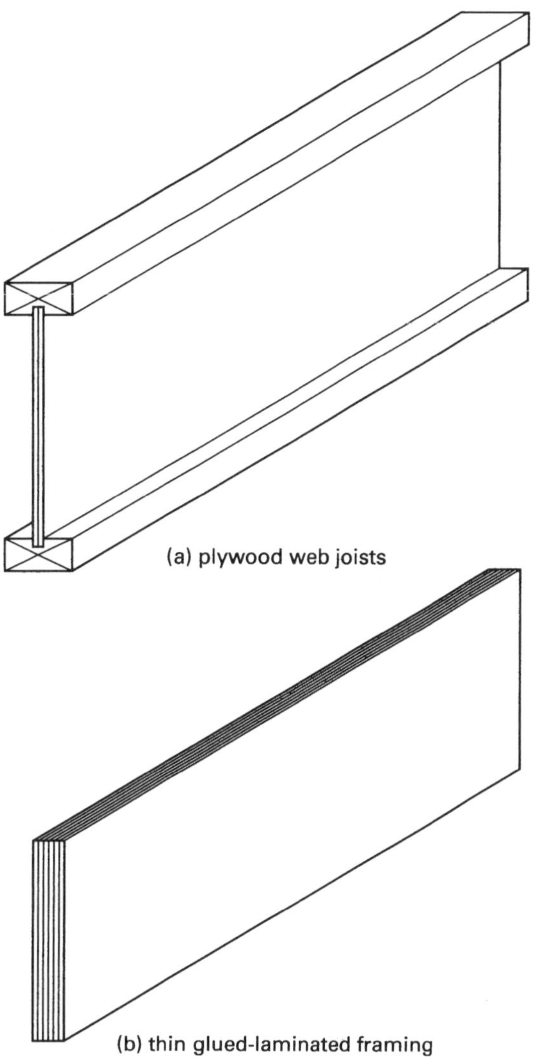

Figure 25.7
Prefabricated Structural Wood

Laminated Veneer Lumber

Laminated veneer lumber, sometimes called *thin glued-laminated framing* or *structural composite lumber*, is fabricated by gluing thin veneers of lumber together to build up a strong, rigid, dimensionally stable framing member that can be used like solid framing lumber. See Fig. 25.7(b). Laminated veneer lumber can be used for headers or beams and in place of studs.

Trusses

Wood trusses are factory-made assemblies consisting of relatively small wood members (normally 2 × 4s or 2 × 6s) held together with toothed plate connectors. They are available for residential and light commercial construction and can be fabricated with parallel top and bottom chords for floor framing or with sloped upper chords for roof framing. Common spacing is 24 in on center. Depending on the depth of the truss and loading, floor trusses can span up to about 40 ft, and roof trusses can span up to about 70 ft. Some of the common types of trusses are shown in Fig. 25.8.

Structural Insulated Panels (SIPs)

A *structural insulated panel* (SIP) is a composite building unit consisting of two outer skins bonded to an inner core of rigid insulating material. Most SIP panels are composed of $^7/_{16}$ in oriented strand board (OSB) facings with a core of molded expanded polystyrene (EPS). Other facings may include plywood, aluminum, cement board, and gypsum wallboard. However, not all units with other facings have undergone testing for building code approval. Other core materials include extruded polystyrene (XPS), urethane foam, and even compressed straw. CFC gases previously used to produce the insulation have been replaced with environmentally friendly processes.

SIPs are available in thicknesses from $4^1/_2$ in to $12^1/_4$ in and sizes from 4 ft by 8 ft up to 9 ft by 28 ft. Larger sizes are also possible from some manufacturers. Custom sizes are available and are normally used to speed construction and avoid waste. They are used for residential and light commercial construction and can be used for walls, floors, and roofs.

Figure 25.8
Types of Trusses

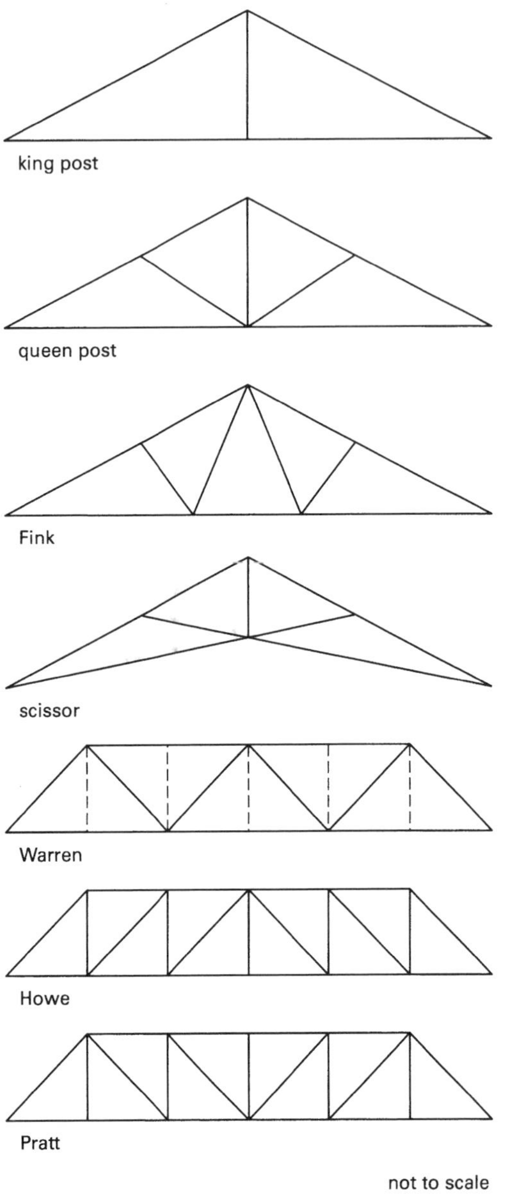

SIPs have the following advantages.

- decreased construction time (about one-third less than for stick-built buildings)
- improved insulation value with no thermal bridges (whole-wall R-values of R14 for a $3^1/_2$ in core vs. R9.6 for 2×4 studs with fiberglass insulation)
- reduced air infiltration
- stronger than conventional stud and sheathing construction
- very flat walls for subsequent finishes
- dimensional stability

Because of their composite construction, SIPs have strength in compression, bending, shear, and uplift. The erection of SIPs is accomplished by slipping the SIPs over wood plates attached to the floor. Wood splines at the vertical joints are used to fasten one panel to the next. Panels come with vertical and horizontal chases for wiring. Additional space can be made for piping or other electrical equipment by simply using a saw or hot wire to cut away the required insulation.

As a green product, SIPs require less wood than do conventional houses, use renewable resources for the facings, improve thermal performance, and reduce construction waste. Some manufactures recycle cutouts, trimmings, and EPS foam. The foam cores and water-based adhesives used have no formaldehyde content and are inert plastics. The amount of formaldehyde emitted by the OSB is less than 0.1 part per million (ppm), which is well below acceptable levels established by the U.S. Department of Housing and Urban Development.

Common coordination concerns include detailing a vapor barrier on the inside of the panel, providing seismic anchors where required, and detailing termite shields in geographical areas where they are required.

Composite Decking

Composite decking, or *wood-plastic composite*, is a mixture of small wood fibers (or wood flour) and plastic that is formed into planks used for exterior decks and railings. Colorants, stabilizers, and fungicides may be added. The exact mixture proportions depend on the manufacturer but are typically 50 percent wood and 50 percent plastic (polyethylene).

Composite decking generally lasts longer than wood and is easier to maintain. It is strong, durable, splinter-free, and typically made of recycled materials that may qualify for LEED credits. However, depending on sun exposure, composite decking can be hot underfoot, especially if a dark color is used.

Cross-Laminated Timber

Cross-laminated timber (CLT) is a wood product manufactured by layering dimension lumber at right angles to form a thick structural panel. Like plywood, CLT is formed from odd numbers of layers, typically three, five, or seven. Unlike plywood, the layers are made not from veneers, but from thicker pieces of wood. Panels are custom-manufactured and range from 2 ft to 10 ft wide, and up to 50 ft long. Thicknesses are engineered for each project.

Because of their composition, CLTs are very strong. They resist axial, bending, and racking loads and provide diaphragm action for lateral loads. Spans up to 25 ft can be achieved without intermediate supports. CLTs are manufactured under controlled conditions with precut openings for reduced construction time on job sites. Made of small-diameter timber, they are environmentally sustainable, with no job site waste.

HEAVY TIMBER CONSTRUCTION

Heavy timber construction consists of exterior walls of noncombustible masonry or concrete and interior columns, girders, beams, and planking manufactured of large solid or laminated timbers. The *Uniform Building Code* requires that interior columns be at least 8 × 8 in nominal size and that beams and girders supporting floors be at least 6 in wide and 10 in deep. Girders framed into masonry walls must be fire cut similar to the joists shown in Fig. 25.5. Floor decking must be at least 3 in in nominal thickness with no concealed spaces below. Roof decking must have at least a 2 in nominal thickness.

Due to the expense and limited availability of large, solid timbers, new heavy timber construction is most typically built with glued-laminated members.

Glued-Laminated Construction

Glued-laminated wood members, or *glulams* as they are usually called, are built up from a number of individual pieces of lumber glued together and finished under factory conditions for use as beams, columns, purlins, and other structural components. Glulams are used where larger wood members are required for heavy loads or long spans and simple sawn timber pieces are not available or cannot meet the strength requirements. Glulam construction is also used where unusual structural shapes are required and appearance is a consideration. In addition to being fabricated in simple rectangular shapes, glulam members can be formed into arches, tapered forms, and pitched shapes.

Glulam members are manufactured in standard widths and depths. In most cases, $1\frac{1}{2}$ in actual depth pieces are used, so the overall depth is some multiple of $1\frac{1}{2}$, depending on how many laminations are used. If a tight curve must be formed, $\frac{3}{4}$ in thick pieces are used. Standard actual widths are $3\frac{1}{8}$, $5\frac{1}{8}$, $6\frac{3}{4}$, $8\frac{3}{4}$, $10\frac{3}{4}$, and $12\frac{1}{4}$ in. See Fig. 25.9.

This is because individual pieces can be selected free from certain defects and seasoned to the proper moisture content, and the entire manufacturing process is conducted under carefully controlled conditions. The allowable stresses for glulam construction are higher than those for solid, sawn timber. Although glulam beams are usually loaded in the direction perpendicular to the laminations, they can be loaded in either direction to suit the requirements of the design.

For structural purposes, glulams are designated by size and a commonly used symbol that specifies the stress rating. Glulams are available in three appearance grades: industrial, architectural, and premium. These do not affect the structural properties but only designate the final look and finishing of the member. Industrial grade is used where appearance is not a primary concern, whereas premium is used where the finest appearance is important. Architectural grade is used where appearance is a factor but where the best grade is not required.

Planking

Wood planking, or *decking* as it is often called, is solid or laminated timber that spans beams. It is available in nominal thicknesses of 2, 3, 4, and 5 in with actual sizes varying with the manufacturer and whether the piece is solid or laminated. All planking has some type of tongue-and-groove edging so the pieces fit solidly together and load can be distributed among adjacent pieces. Unlike sheathing, planking is intended to span greater distances between beams rather than between closely spaced joists. Common spans range from 4 ft to 20 ft, depending on the planking thickness and loads carried.

Figure 25.9 Glued-Laminated Beams

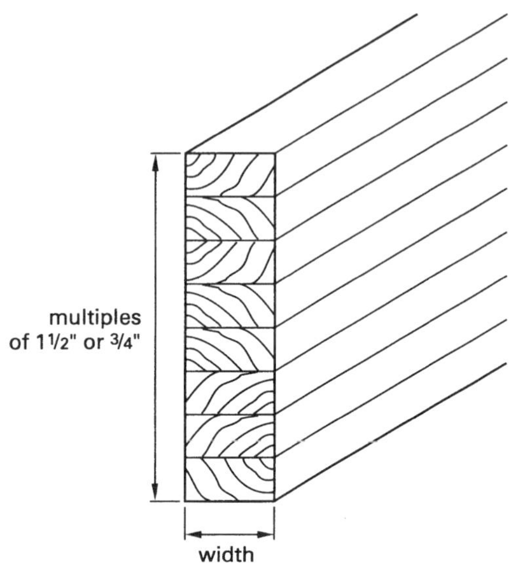

nominal	actual
4″	3 1/8″
6″	5 1/8″
8″	6 3/4″
10″	8 3/4″
12″	10 3/4″
14″	12 1/4″

In addition to satisfying the code requirements for heavy timber construction, planking has the advantages of easy installation, attractive appearance, and efficient use of material, because the planking serves as floor structure, finish floor, and finish ceiling below. Its primary disadvantage is that there is no place to conceal insulation, electrical conduit, and mechanical services.

FASTENERS

There are many types of fasteners used for carpentry, including nails, screws, bolts, and fabricated metal fasteners.

Nails

Although they are the weakest of wood connectors, nails are the most commonly used connectors in light frame construction. The types used most frequently for structural applications include common wire nails, box nails, and common wire spikes. *Wire nails* range in size from six penny (6d) to sixty penny (60d). *Box nails* range from 6d to 40d—6d nails are 2 in in length, and 60d nails are 6 in long. Common wire spikes range from 10d (3 in long) to $8\frac{1}{2}$ in long and $\frac{3}{8}$ in diameter. For the same pennyweight, box nails have the smallest diameter, common wire nails the next largest diameter, and wire spikes the greatest diameter.

For engineered applications, that is, where each nailed joint is specifically designed, there are tables of values giving the allowable withdrawal resistance and lateral load (shear) resistance for different sizes and penetrations of nails depending on the type of wood used. The more typical situation of most nailed wood construction is simply to use nailing schedules found in the building code. These give the minimum size, number, and penetration of nails for specific applications such as nailing studs to sole plates, joists to headers, and so forth.

There are several orientations that nails (as well as screws and lag screws) can have with wood members, which affect the holding power of the fastener. The preferable orientation is to have the fastener loaded laterally in side grain where the holding power is the greatest. The least desirable orientation is to have the nail or fastener parallel to the grain.

Screws

Wood screws are available in sizes from no. 0 (0.060 in shank diameter) to no. 24 (0.372 in shank diameter) and in lengths from $\frac{1}{4}$ in to 5 in. The most common types are flat head and round head. Because screws have a threaded design, they offer better holding power and can be removed and replaced more easily than nails. As with nails, screws are best used laterally loaded in side grain rather than in withdrawal from side grain or end grain.

Lead holes, slightly smaller than the diameter of the screw, must be drilled into the wood to permit the proper insertion of the screw and to prevent splitting of the wood.

A lag screw is threaded with a pointed end like a wood screw but has a head like a bolt. It is inserted by drilling lead holes and screwing the fastener into the wood with a wrench. A washer is used between the head and the wood.

Sizes range from $1/4$ in to $1^1/4$ in in diameter and from 1 in to 16 in in length. Diameters are measured at the nonthreaded shank portion of the screw.

Bolts

Bolts are one of the most common forms of wood connectors for joints of moderate to heavy loading. Bolt sizes range from $1/2$ in to 1 in in diameter and from $1/2$ in to 6 in in length. Washers must be used under the head and nut of the bolt to prevent crushing the wood and to distribute the load.

The design requirements for bolted joints are a little more complicated than those for screwed or nailed joints. The allowable design values and the spacing of bolts are affected by such variables as the thicknesses of the main and side members, the ratio of bolt length in the main member to the bolt diameter, and the number of members joined.

Metal Fasteners

Because wood is such a common building material, there are dozens of types of special fasteners and connectors especially designed to make assembly easy, fast, and structurally sound. Hardware is available for both standard sizes of wood members and special members such as wood truss joists. Some of the common types of connection hardware are shown in Fig. 25.10.

In addition to the lightweight connectors shown in Fig. 25.10, there are special timber connectors used for heavy timber construction and for assembling wood trusses. Two of the most common types are split rings and shear plates. Split rings are either $2^1/2$ in or 4 in in diameter and are cut through in one place in the circumference to form a tongue and slot. The ring is beveled from the central portion toward the edges. Grooves are cut in each piece of the wood members to be joined so that half the ring is in each section. The members are held together with a bolt concentric with the ring, as shown in Fig. 25.11(a).

Shear plates are either $2^5/8$ in or 4 in in diameter and are flat plates with a flange extending from the face of the plate. There is a hole in the middle through which either a $3/4$ in or $7/8$ in bolt is placed to hold the two members together. Shear plates are inserted in precut grooves in a piece of wood so that the plate is flush with one surface. (See Fig. 25.11(b).) Because of this configuration, shear plate connections can hold together either two pieces of wood or one piece of wood and a steel plate.

Split ring connectors and shear plates can transfer larger loads than can bolts or screws alone and are often used in connecting truss members. Shear plates are particularly suited for constructions that must be disassembled. Gang nail connectors are used in trusses also.

WOOD TREATMENT

As a natural material, wood is relatively durable if kept dry. Some woods, such as redwood, have naturally occurring resins that make them resistant to moisture and insect attack. However, most wood is subject to damage and decay from a number of sources and must be protected. The most common sources of attack and damage include fungi when moisture is present, insects such as termites and marine borers, and fire.

Preservatives may be applied by brushing, dipping, or pressure treatment. The most effective method is pressure treatment because the preservative is forced deep into the cells of the wood. For some applications such as marine use and protection from some insects, pressure treatment is the only satisfactory method to specify.

There are three basic types of wood preservatives: creosote, oil-borne preservatives, and waterborne preservatives. *Creosote* is a distillate of coal tar and is effective protection against insects. It is insoluble in water and is relatively easy to apply. Creosote is used mainly to protect railroad ties, marine timbers, and roadway guard posts. It is not used in building applications.

Figure 25.10 Special Connection Hardware

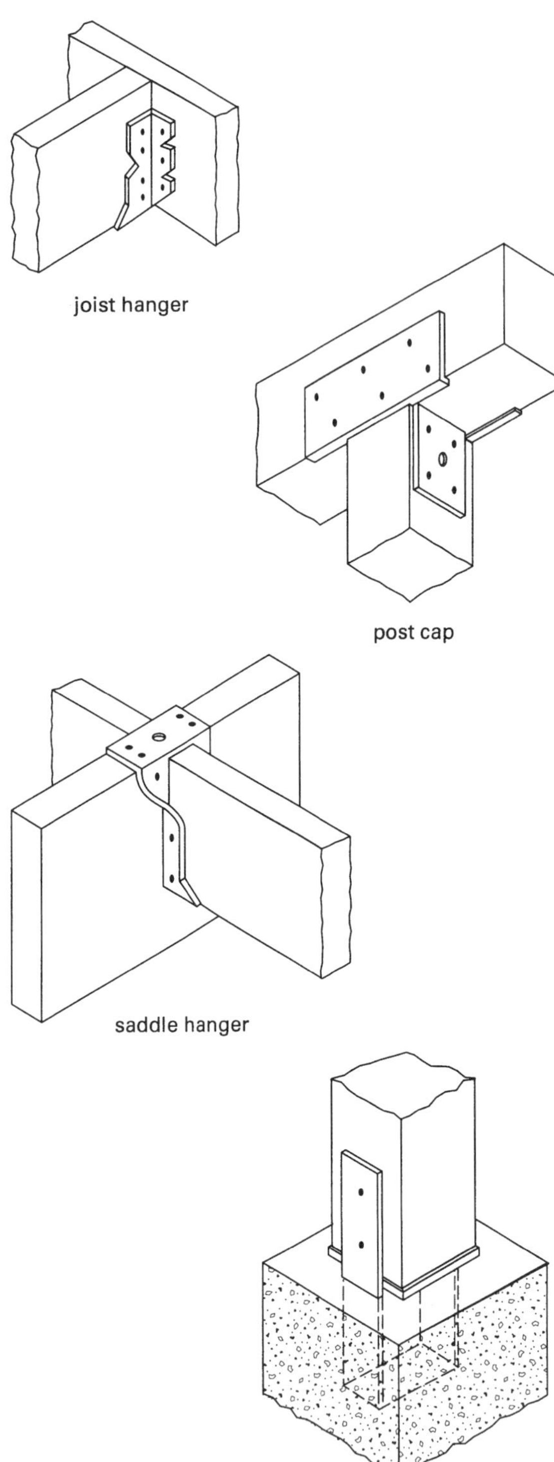

Oil-borne preservatives include *pentachlorophenol* (*penta*). This preservative is used to treat utility poles and cross arms, fresh water pilings, and bridge timbers. It is applied by brushing, dipping, or pressure treating. Penta is generally not used in building applications; however, it is sometimes used on glue-laminated beams supporting long spans in sports arenas and over swimming pools, and for similar applications.

Waterborne preservatives are the type most commonly used in residential, commercial, and industrial buildings. The types used include *ammoniacal copper quaternary* (ACQ), also called alkaline copper quat, copper azole, and sodium borate (SBX), and variations of these three basic types. These types of treatments are clean, odorless, and nonstaining, and they leave the wood paintable. They provide protection against termites and decay. Work is continuing to develop preservatives that are totally free of metals.

Two other chemicals that have traditionally been used are chromated copper arsenate (CCA) and ammoniacal copper zinc arsenate (ACZA). However, these have been shown to be harmful to health and the environment because of their arsenic content. Chromated copper arsenate was phased out for residential and general consumer use by the Environmental Protection Agency on December 31, 2003. Evidence had shown that arsenic could leach out of the treated wood and that disposal by burning could release toxic substances.

ACQ and copper azole are more corrosive than is CCA to fasteners and some flashing. Fasteners and connecters compatible with the chemical preservative used should be specified. Fasteners should be type 304 or 316 stainless steel or hot-dip galvanized products with a minimum G90 coating; that is, 0.90 oz/ft^2. Aluminum flashing should not be used with wood treated with these preservatives. Preservatives with borates will leach out of wood when exposed to moisture, so applications with borates are limited to areas protected from moisture and not in contact with the ground. When cuts are made to treated wood, the exposed areas should be treated with a copper naphthenate solution containing at least 2% copper.

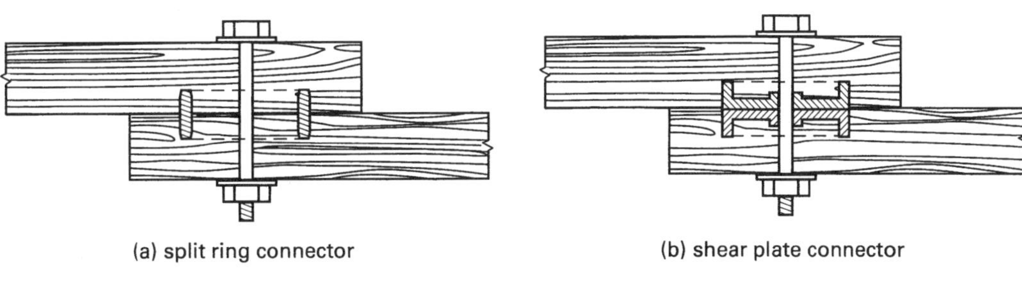

Figure 25.11 Timber Connectors

Example 25.1

Which of the following woods must be treated for resistance to decay when used in an exterior application?

(A) cedar

(B) spruce

(C) redwood

(D) cypress

Solution

Spruce trees are not inherently resistant to decay, but the heartwood of cedar, redwood, and cypress all possess a natural resistance that makes them a good choice for use in exterior applications such as siding, shingles or shakes, and decking. The outer rings of these species do not possess the same decay-resistant qualities, so it is important to specify that only heartwood may be used when decay resistance is of concern. These woods are considerably more expensive than other species that are more commonly used for construction such as pine, hemlock, fir, and spruce.

Species that are not inherently decay resistant must be chemically treated to protect them from rotting when exposed to moisture. Waterborne salts are pressure-impregnated into the wood to prevent decay, often for as long as 30 years. After a waiting period, salt-treated wood can be painted or stained.

The answer is (B).

WOOD FRAMING DETAILING

There is a growing emphasis on energy efficiency and sustainability in regard to the use of wood resources. Wood framing and ways to minimize the use of wood are discussed in this section. Sustainability issues with wood are also discussed in Chap. 13.

Energy-Efficient Detailing

As with other types of construction, careful attention should be paid to insulation and to controlling air infiltration when detailing the various parts of wood frame residential and light commercial construction. Both the *International Energy Conservation Code* and the *International Residential Code* give performance and prescriptive requirements for both.

When detailing wood frame construction, the weather barrier concepts discussed in Chap. 27 apply. There are several ways this can be accomplished. Figure 25.12 illustrates one possible way these principles can be applied in residential construction.

Figure 25.12 shows an ideal configuration in which structural sheathing (e.g., plywood or oriented strand board) is applied to the wood studs and provides a firm base for the house wrap or other *air barrier* or *water resistant barrier* (WRB). Rigid insulation is applied over this to protect the WRB against wind loading, to provide insulation as required by the climate and applicable building codes, and to prevent thermal bridges. This is in addition to insulation installed in the stud cavity.

Figure 25.12
Weather Barriers

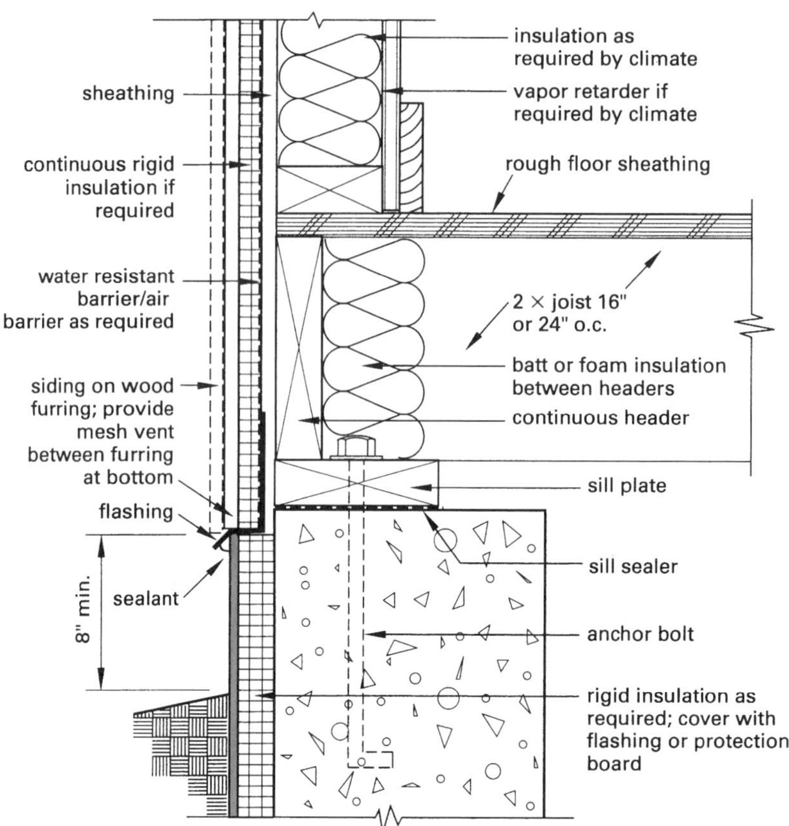

Vertical wood furring is applied using appropriate fasteners that can penetrate the insulation and sheathing and anchor to the wood studs as required by code. This creates an air space that creates a pressure equalized rain screen. Then, exterior cladding is applied. Figure 25.12 also shows required flashing at the base of the cladding assembly and insulation for the crawl space or basement wall.

Alternately, the exterior cladding can be applied without an air space using the appropriate fasteners to affix the cladding to the studs.

Another method to detail this type of wall is to use insulating sheathing applied directly to the wood studs and cover the exterior with a WRB or air barrier as required by the climate. The exterior cladding is then applied using appropriate fasteners that can penetrate the insulation to the wood studs.

In all cases, the WRB and interior vapor retarder (if any) must be chosen to provide the correct permeance rating for the climate and specific construction materials (see Chap. 27). Some way is needed for the interior wall to dry, either to the exterior or to the interior. If the exterior cladding is made of an absorptive material, such as brick veneer or stucco, there can be a high inward vapor drive due to solar radiation heating up the wet cladding and thus creating a high pressure difference between the cladding and the interior of the building. The air barrier must also be continuous at all changes in plane, at the roof, and around door and window openings.

The permeance of the rigid insulation may also affect the selection of the WRB. While either material may be vapor permeable, both together may become vapor impermeable. Increasing the thickness of continuous insulation may also affect the permeance. For example, a 1 in thickness of expanded polystyrene (XPS) insulation may be semi-permeable, while a 2 in thickness will be semi-impermeable, making it a class II vapor retarder instead of a class III vapor retarder. See Chap. 27 for a discussion of permeance and IBC classifications of vapor retarders.

Advanced House Framing

Advanced house framing is a method of building wood-frame residential and light commercial buildings to reduce the amount of lumber used and the waste that is generated. This method of building saves lumber resources and improves energy efficiency by reducing thermal bridging and replacing lumber with insulation while maintaining the structural integrity of the building. Engineered lumber can also be used with advanced house framing.

Advanced house framing techniques include

- using 24 in spacing instead of 16 in spacing for studs, joists, and roof rafters when allowed by code. This should be done in conjunction with in-line framing of the roof rafters, second-floor studs, and first-floor studs.
- using single top plates instead of double top plates when allowed by code
- using two-stud corner framing and drywall clips instead of three-stud framing
- covering openings with insulated headers sized for the load
- using a single stud at window openings with header hangers to support the header instead of the shorter jack studs, as shown in Fig. 25.6
- eliminating headers in non-load-bearing walls
- using ladder blocking instead of three-stud framing at the intersection of exterior walls with interior walls

The acceptability of all these techniques is contingent on the approval of the local building official.

26

FINISH CARPENTRY AND ARCHITECTURAL WOODWORK

Project Planning

Finish carpentry is the final exposed-wood construction done on the job site. It is usually nonstructural in nature. This class of work includes exterior wood siding, interior trim, door and window framing, stair framing, shelving and cabinetry, paneling, and similar finish items.

Although finish carpentry overlaps somewhat with architectural woodwork, the latter term refers to finish lumber items fabricated in a manufacturing plant and brought to the job site for installation. Architectural woodwork items normally include fine finished cabinetry, wall paneling, custom doors, and other items that can be better made under controlled factory conditions.

FINISH CARPENTRY

Wood Species and Grading

As stated in Chap. 39, wood is classified as softwood or hardwood. *Softwoods* are those cut from coniferous trees, and *hardwoods* are those coming from deciduous trees. Finish carpentry employs both. Lower cost interior trim is usually made from the better grades of pine and fir, but when appearance is important, hardwoods such as oak, mahogany, or birch are used. Hardwoods are used almost exclusively for architectural woodwork because of their superior appearance and durability.

There are hundreds of domestic and imported wood species available for finish carpentry and architectural woodwork. However, because of cost and availability, only a few are generally used for finish carpentry and several dozen are used for architectural woodwork. Some of the common hardwood species include red and white oak, ash, walnut, cherry, mahogany, birch, poplar, and maple.

Finish carpentry lumber is graded differently than are architectural woodwork and structural lumber. The grading varies slightly from species to species, but in general the Western Wood Products Association (WWPA) classifies finish lumber into selects, finish, paneling, and commons, along with grades for siding and what the WWPA terms alternate boards. Selects are divided into B & Better (the best grade in this category), C Select, and D Select. Finish is subdivided into superior, prime, and E grades. Western red cedar, redwood, and a few other domestic species have their own grading rules. These grades are summarized in Table 26.1.

Table 26.1 Selected Appearance Grades of Western Lumber

grade category	grades	description
selects	B & Better	Highest quality of select grade lumber available, with many pieces absolutely clear and free of defects.
	C Select	Appearance only slightly less than B & Better. Recommended for high-quality interior trim and cabinet work with natural stain or enamel finishes.
	D Select	Allows more defects than C Select grade but is suitable where finish requirements are less exacting.
finish	Superior; Superior VG	Highest quality of finish grade lumber available, with many pieces absolutely clear. Used for high quality trim and cabinet work where natural, stain, or enamel finishes are used and the finest appearance is required. Can be specified as VG for vertical grain.
	Prime; Prime VG	Allows slightly more defects than Superior, but can be used where finishing requirements are less exacting. Can be specified as VG for vertical grain.
	E	Boards in this grade can be cut in such a way as to produce pieces of Prime or Superior grades. E grade boards must contain two-thirds or more of such cuttings 2 in or wider and 16 in or longer.
paneling	any select or finish grade	C Select or any other grade can be used to produce paneling.
	selected 2 common for knotty paneling	Grade reserved for knotty paneling made from no. 2 Common grade boards (not shown in this table).

Note: Additional grades are available, but they are commonly used for other architectural purposes.

In addition to these grades, finish lumber may be specified as heartwood or sapwood. *Heartwood* comes from the center of the tree and *sapwood* from the perimeter. In some species, such as redwood, there is a marked color variance and resistance to decay between the two types of lumber. In some circumstances it is important to differentiate between the two.

For many types of softwood trim there is another category called *fingerjointed.* This is not really a grade but a method of manufacturing lengths of trim from shorter pieces of lumber. The ends of the short pieces are cut with finger-like projections, glued, and joined together. Fingerjointed material is less expensive than continuous molding but is only appropriate for a paint finish where the joints will be covered.

Lumber Cutting

The way lumber is cut from a log determines the final appearance of the grain pattern. There are three ways boards (also called *solid stock*) are cut from a log. Thin veneers are sliced in similar ways, but these are discussed in the next section on architectural woodwork. The three methods used are plain sawing (also called *flat sawing*), quartersawing, and rift sawing. These methods are illustrated in Fig. 26.1.

Plain sawing makes the most efficient use of the log and is the least expensive of the three methods. Because the wood is cut with various orientations to the grain of the tree, plain sawing results in a finished surface with the characteristic cathedral pattern shown in Fig. 26.1.

Quarter sawing is produced by cutting the log into quarters and then sawing perpendicular to a diameter line. Because the saw cut is more or less perpendicular to the grain, the resulting grain pattern is more uniformly vertical. Not only does this result in a different appearance than plain sawing, but quartersawn boards also tend to twist and cup less, shrink less in width, hold paint better, and have fewer defects.

As illustrated in Fig. 26.1, quartersawn boards cut from the edges of the log do not have the grain exactly at a 90° angle to the saw cut as do those in the middle. For an even more consistent vertical grain, *rift sawing* is used. With this method, the saw cuts from a quartered log are always made radially to the center of the tree. Because the log must be shifted after each cut and because there is a great deal of waste, rift cutting is more expensive than quartersawing.

Because of the limited availability of some species of wood and the expense of making certain cuts, not all types of lumber cutting are available in all species. In some cases, for a particular species, a veneer cut (discussed in the next section) will be available, but not the corresponding solid stock cut. The availability of cuts in the desired species should be verified before specifications are written.

Figure 26.1
Methods of Cutting Boards and Resultant Appearances

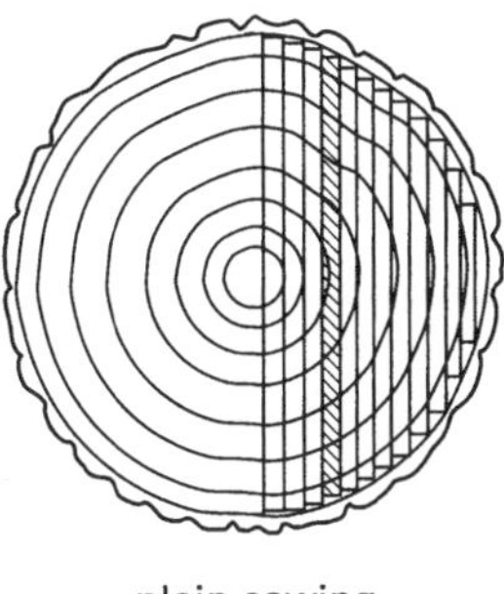

plain sawing

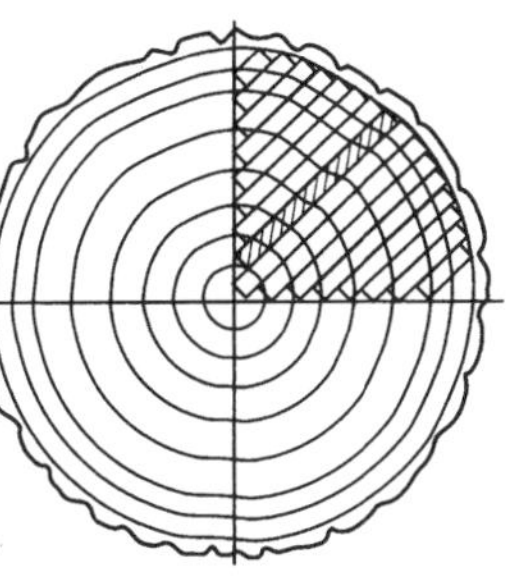

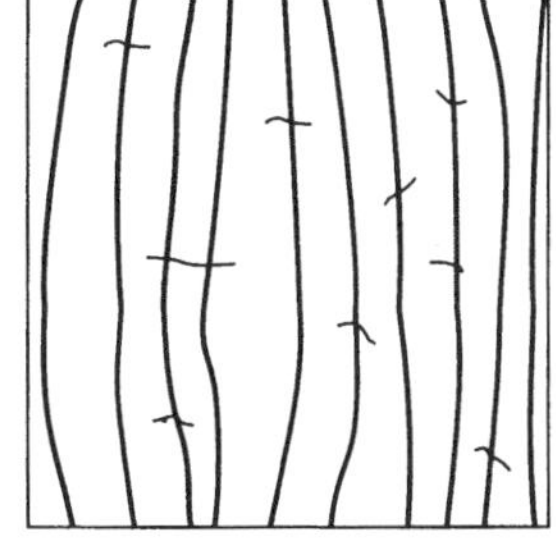

quarter sawing

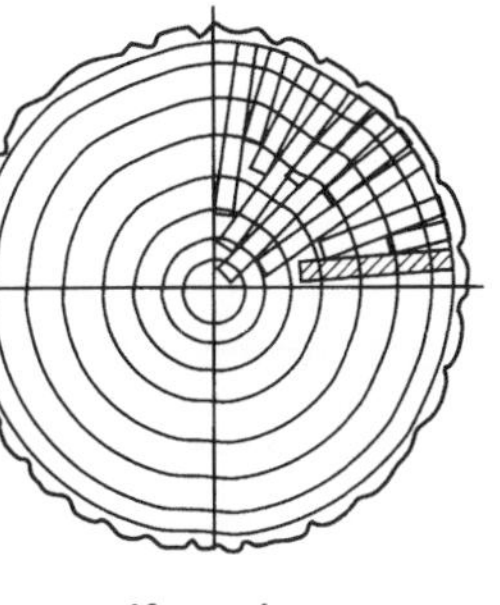

rift sawing

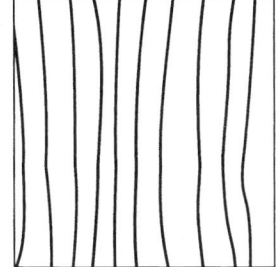

Figure 26.2
Wood Siding

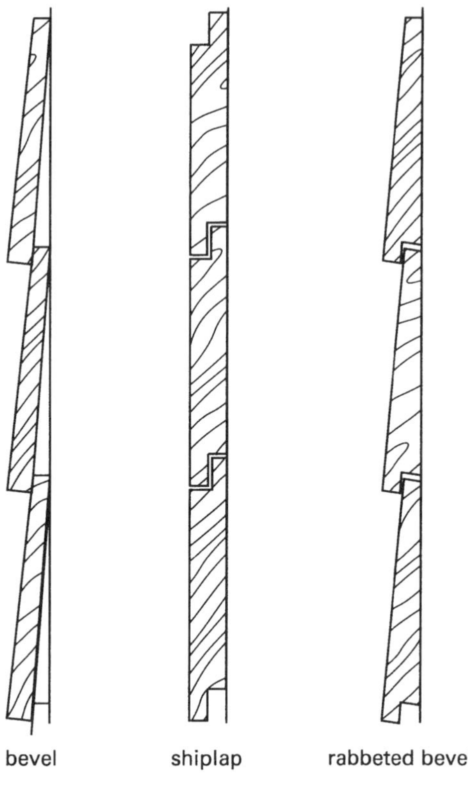

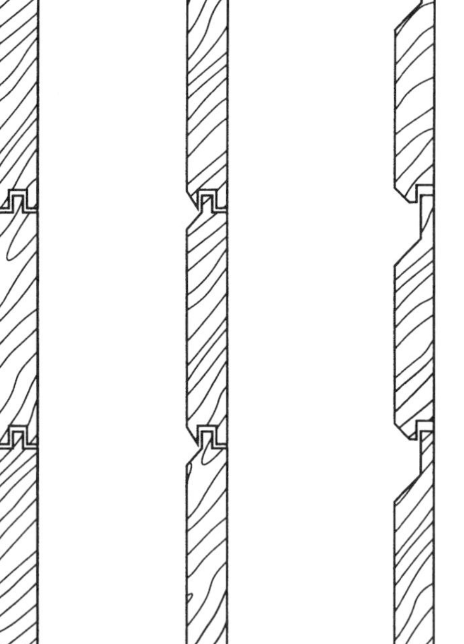

Wood Siding

Wood siding consists of individual boards applied horizontally, diagonally, or vertically. When the siding is applied over wood sheathing (either plywood or particleboard), a layer of building paper is placed over the sheathing to minimize air infiltration and improve the water resistance of the wall. When the siding is applied over fiberboard or insulating sheathing, an air infiltration barrier of high-density polyethylene is often used under the siding. This allows moisture vapor to pass through but minimizes air leakage.

Wood siding is milled from redwood, cedar, Douglas fir, pine, and several other species. Some, such as redwood and cypress, are naturally resistant to moisture and require less protection than varieties like pine. Siding comes in several shapes, as shown in Fig. 26.2. All are milled to allow one board to overlap the next lower board.

Wood Stairs and Trim

The construction of wood stairs is considered a finish carpentry item although most utilitarian and decorative stairs are fabricated in a millshop. Stairs can range from simple utilitarian assemblies to elaborate, ornate, crafted works. A simple form of stair construction is shown in Fig. 26.3 with the primary construction elements identified.

Interior and exterior trim is used to finish off the joints between dissimilar materials, close construction gaps between building elements, and provide decorative treatment. Simple, rectangular shapes are used for a great deal of construction trim, but there are dozens of standard, shaped molding pieces used for particular applications. Some of the more common types of interior trim are shown in Fig. 26.4.

More ornate molding sections can be built by using a combination of standard shapes or by having a millshop make a cutting blade that is used to shape special profiles.

ARCHITECTURAL WOODWORK

Architectural woodwork is custom, shop-fabricated lumber components used for interior finish construction, which includes cabinetry, paneling, custom doors and frames, shelving, custom furniture, fine stairs, and special interior trim. Architectural woodwork makes it possible to produce superior finish carpentry items because most of the work is done under carefully controlled factory conditions with machinery and finishing techniques that could never be duplicated on a job site.

Lumber for architectural woodwork and the quality of constructed woodwork items are graded differently than rough carpentry or finish carpentry. Standards for architectural woodwork are set by the Architectural Woodwork Institute (AWI) and are published in AWI's *Architectural Woodwork Standards* booklet.

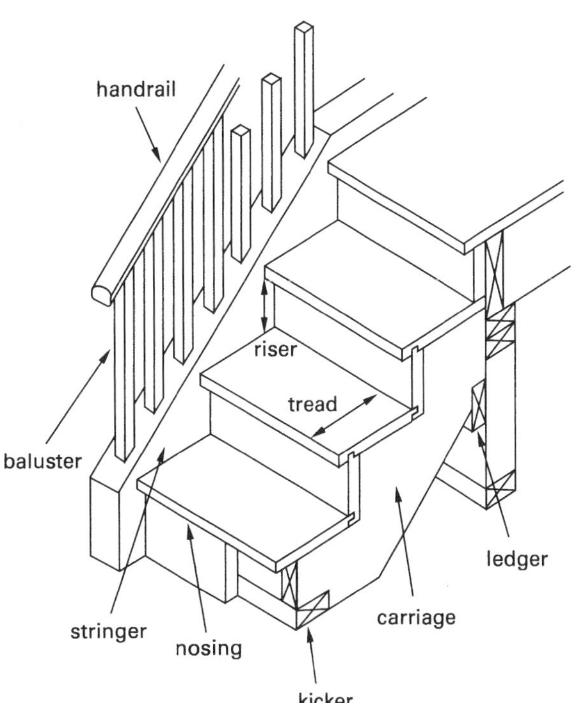

Figure 26.3 Typical Stair Construction

Lumber is classed as Grade I, II, and III and is based on the percentage of a board that can be used by cutting out defects. There are also limitations on the types of defects that are allowed in any grade.

Construction standards, tolerances, and the finished appearance of completed components are specified as premium, custom, and economy grades. These grades apply to doors, cabinets, paneling, and other woodwork items. For example, the maximum gap between a cabinet door and frame is $^{3}/_{32}$ in for premium grade, $^{1}/_{8}$ in for custom grade, and $^{5}/_{32}$ in for economy grade. A complete description for each item in each grade is given in the *Architectural Woodwork Standards* booklet.

Lumber and Veneers for Architectural Woodwork

Architects have a wider selection of solid stock and veneer for use in woodwork than for finish carpentry. Material comes from both domestic and foreign sources and varies widely in availability and cost.

Because of the limited availability of many hardwood species, most architectural woodwork is made from veneer stock. A *veneer* is a thin slice of wood cut from a log (as described in the next section) and glued to a backing of particleboard or plywood, normally $^{3}/_{4}$ in thick.

Refer to Chap. 13 for more information on certified wood products and alternates to standard veneers.

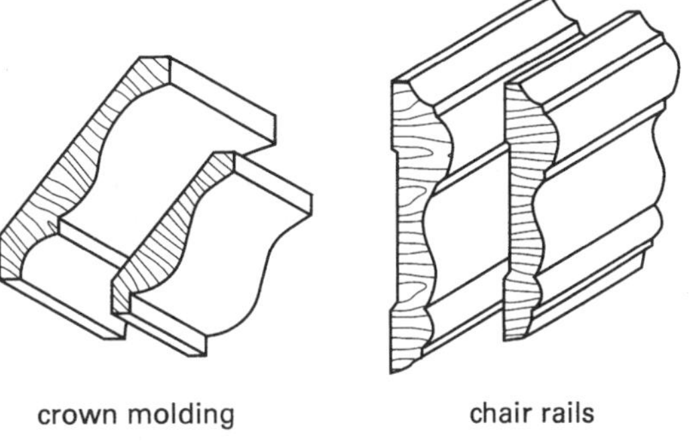

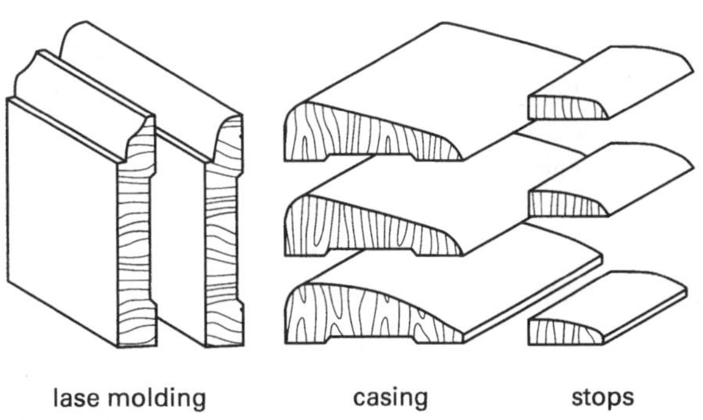

Figure 26.4 Interior Trim

Types of Veneer Cuts

Just as with solid stock, the way veneer is cut from a log affects its final appearance. There are five principal methods of cutting veneers, as shown in Fig. 26.5. Plain slicing and quarter slicing are accomplished the same way as cutting solid stock, except the resulting pieces are much thinner. Quarter slicing produces a more straight-grained pattern than does plain slicing because the cutting knife strikes the growth rings at approximately a 90° angle.

Project Planning

Figure 26.5
Veneer Cuts and Appearance

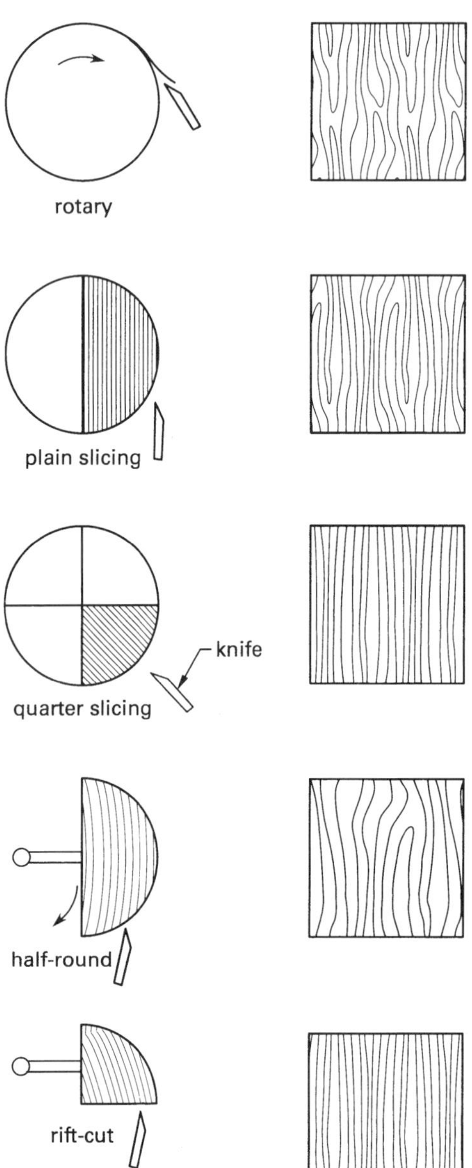

With *rotary slicing*, the log is mounted on a lathe and turned against a knife, which peels off a continuous layer of veneer. This produces a very pronounced grain pattern that is often undesirable in fine quality wood finishes, although it does produce the most veneer with the least waste.

Half-round slicing is similar to rotary slicing, but the log is cut in half and the veneer is cut slightly across the annular growth rings. This results in a pronounced grain pattern showing characteristics of both rotary-sliced and plain-sliced veneers.

Rift slicing is accomplished by quartering a log and cutting at about a 15° angle to the growth rings. Like quarter slicing, it results in a straight-grain pattern and is often used with oak to eliminate the appearance of markings perpendicular to the direction of the grain. These markings in oak are caused by *medullary rays*, which are radial cells extending from the center of the tree to its circumference.

Because the width of a piece of veneer is limited by the diameter of log or portion of log from which it is cut, several veneers must be put together on a backing panel to make up the needed size of a finished piece. The individual veneers come from the same piece of log, which is called a *flitch*. The word "flitch" is sometimes also used to describe the particular sequence in which the veneers are taken off the log as it is cut. The method of matching veneers is discussed in the following sections.

Joinery Details

Various types of joints are used for woodwork construction to increase the strength of the joint and improve the appearance by eliminating mechanical fasteners such as screws. With the availability of high-strength adhesives, screws and other mechanical fasteners are seldom needed for the majority of the work produced in the shop. Field attachment, however, often requires the use of blind nailing or other concealed fastening to maintain the quality look of the work. Some of the common joints used in both woodwork and finish carpentry are shown in Fig. 26.6.

Cabinetwork

Architectural woodwork cabinets are built in the shop as complete assemblies and are simply set in place and attached to surrounding construction at the job site. There are several methods of detailing door and drawer fronts on cabinets, but the construction of the cabinet frames is fairly standard, as shown in Fig. 26.7.

Countertops are built separately from base cabinets and put in place in the field. This is because the countertops are built in single lengths that are much longer than any individual base cabinet. Building and installing the countertops separately also gives the installers the ability to precisely fit the countertop to the wall. This is most commonly done with a scribe piece on top of the backsplash or the back of the countertop. A *scribe piece* is an oversized piece of plastic laminate or wood that can be trimmed in the field to follow any minor irregularities of the wall. As with other woodwork components, there are hundreds of possible configurations to countertops including variations in width, materials, front edge shape and size, and backsplash shape and size. Some of the more common configurations are shown in Fig. 26.8. Figure 26.9 shows typical plastic laminate countertop edge treatments.

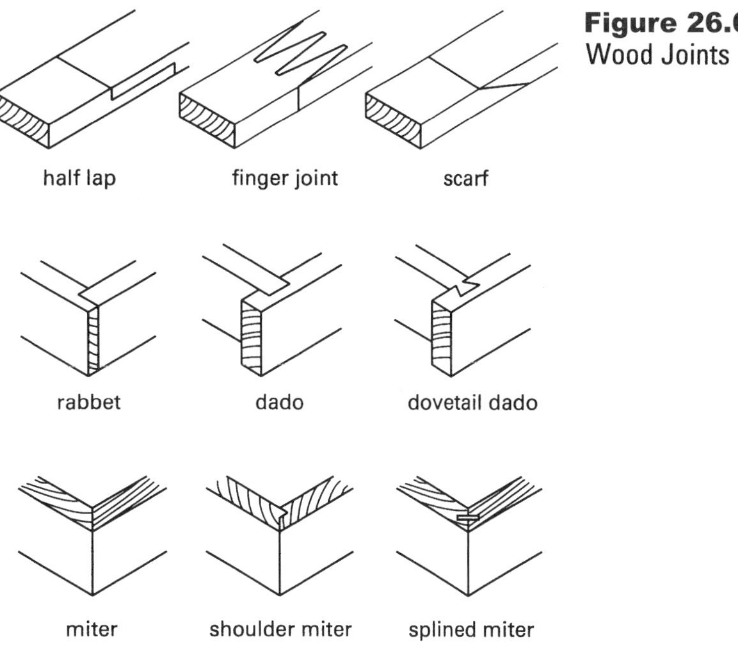

Figure 26.6
Wood Joints

For both base and upper cabinets there are four basic categories of door and drawer front construction: flush, flush overlay, reveal overlay, and lipped overlay. These are shown in Fig. 26.10.

With *flush* construction, the face of a drawer or door is installed flush with the face frame. The primary disadvantage with this type of construction is its expense because of the extra care required to fit and align the doors and drawers within the frame. Another disadvantage is that, with use, the doors and drawers may sag. This results in a nonuniform spacing between fronts and may cause some doors and drawers to bind against the frame.

With *flush overlay* construction, the fronts of the doors and drawers overlap the face frame of the cabinet. Edges of adjacent door or drawer fronts are separated only enough to allow operation without touching, usually about $\frac{1}{8}$ in or less. Only doors and drawers are visible, and they are all flush with each other. As with flush construction, the millshop must take great care in aligning and fitting the doors and drawers so that the gap between them is uniform.

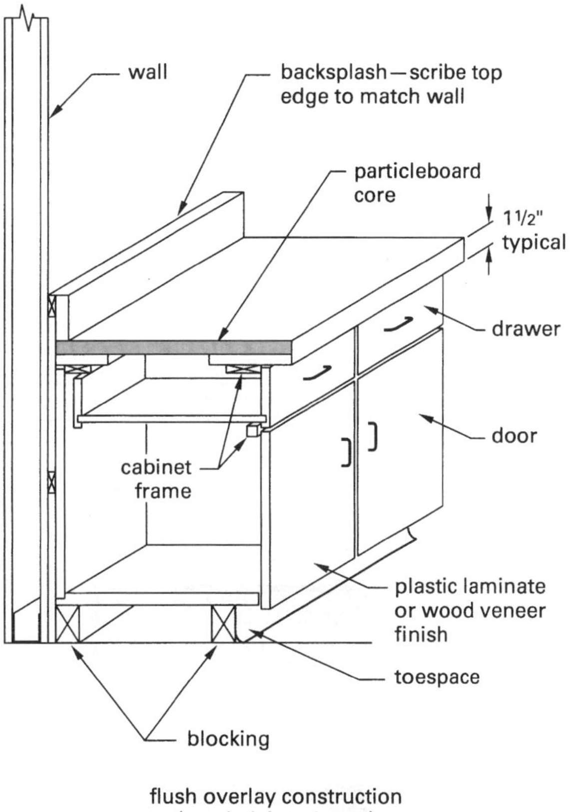

Figure 26.7
Typical Wood Cabinet

wall
backsplash—scribe top edge to match wall
particleboard core
$1\frac{1}{2}$" typical
drawer
door
cabinet frame
plastic laminate or wood veneer finish
toespace
blocking

flush overlay construction
(no shelving shown)

With *reveal overlay* construction, the edges of adjacent doors and door fronts are separated enough to reveal the face frame behind. This construction is less expensive than flush overlay construction because minor misalignments and sagging are not as noticeable. A variation is the *lipped overlay* construction in which part of the door or drawer overlaps the frame and covers the joint between the two pieces. See Fig. 26.10(d).

Project Planning

Figure 26.8 Typical Countertop Details

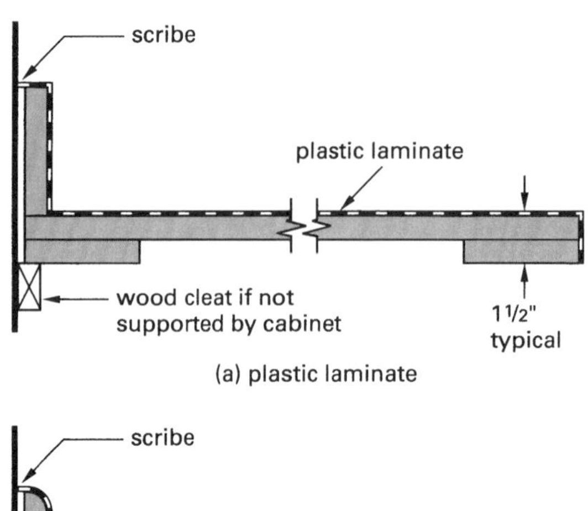

(a) plastic laminate

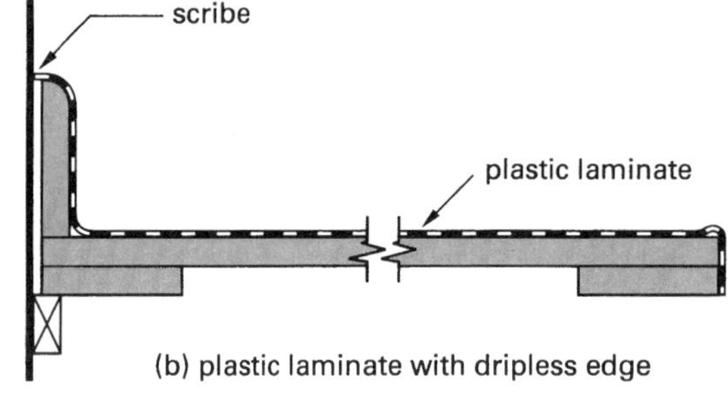

(b) plastic laminate with dripless edge

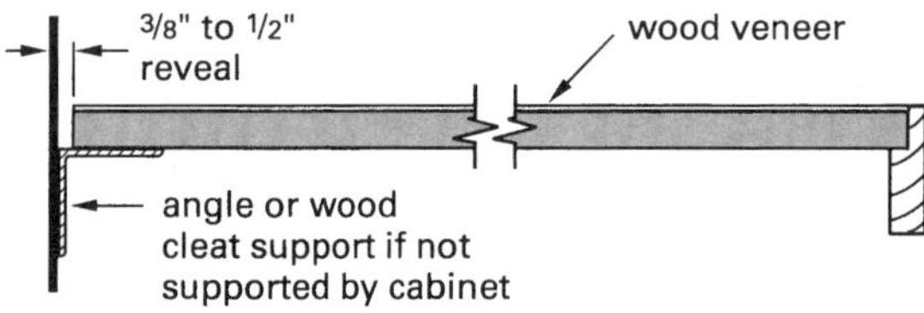

(c) hardwood veneer

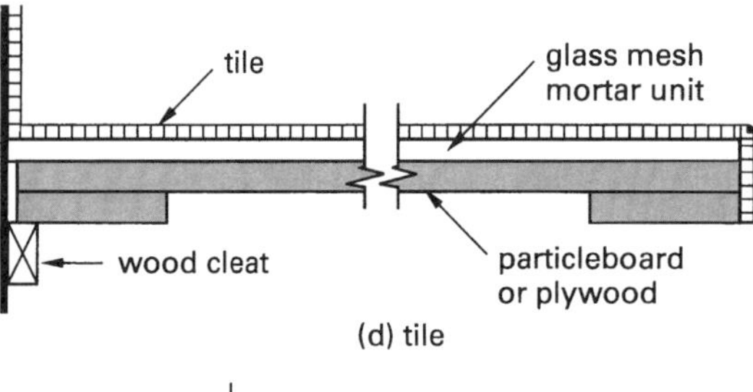

(d) tile

Upper cabinets are very similar in construction to base cabinets. The most notable exceptions are that they are not as deep as base cabinets, and some design and detailing consideration must be given to the undersides of upper cabinets because they are visible. In addition, there must be some way to securely anchor the cabinet to the wall. In residential construction, the cabinet is attached to the wall by screwing through the cabinet back and wall finish into the wood studs. In commercial construction where metal studs are used, wood blocking is required in the stud cavity behind the wall finish. This blocking is installed as the studs are being erected and is attached to them with screws. The blocking provides a solid base for attaching the cabinets to the wall. Figure 26.11 shows a typical upper cabinet detail.

Flush Paneling

Architectural woodwork paneling includes flush or raised panel constructions used to cover vertical surfaces. As mentioned before, large, flat areas like paneling are built of thin wood veneers glued to backing panels of particleboard or plywood.

In addition to the way the veneer is cut, there are several methods of matching adjacent pieces of veneer and veneer panels in a room that affect the final appearance of the job. The three considerations, in increasing order of scale, are matching between adjacent veneer leaves, matching veneers within a panel, and matching panels within a room.

Figure 26.9 High-Pressure Decorative Laminate (HPDL) Edge Treatments

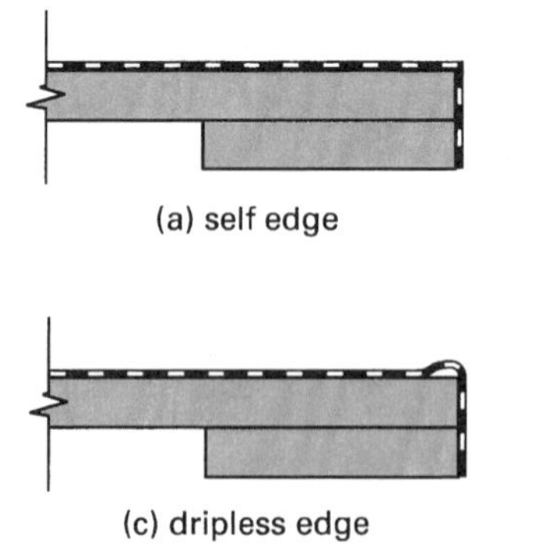

(a) self edge

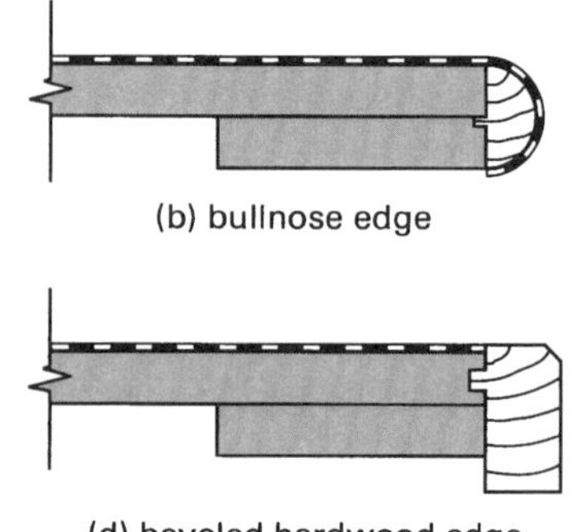

(b) bullnose edge

(c) dripless edge

(d) beveled hardwood edge

Figure 26.10
Types of Cabinet Door Framing

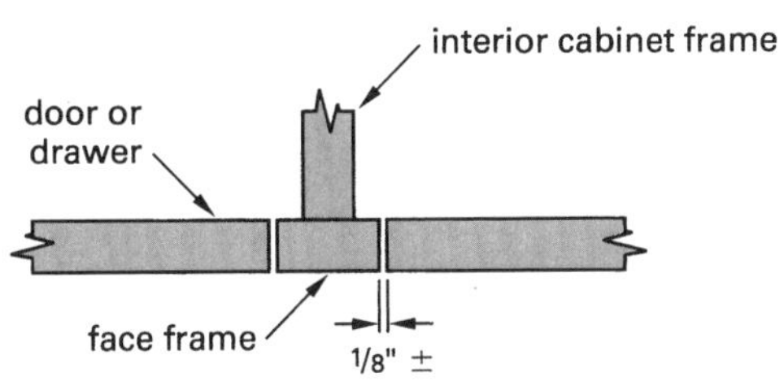

(a) flush construction

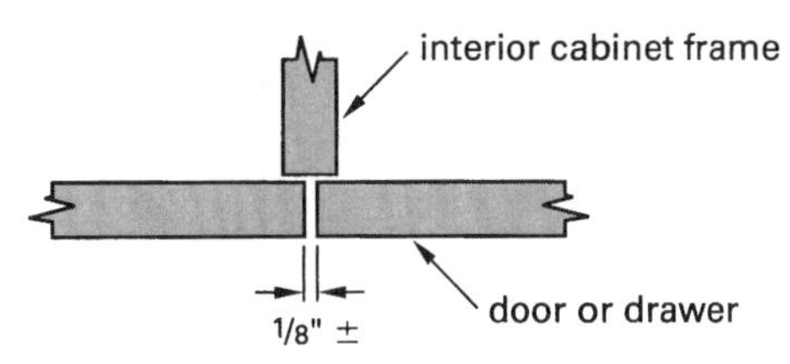

(b) flush overlay construction

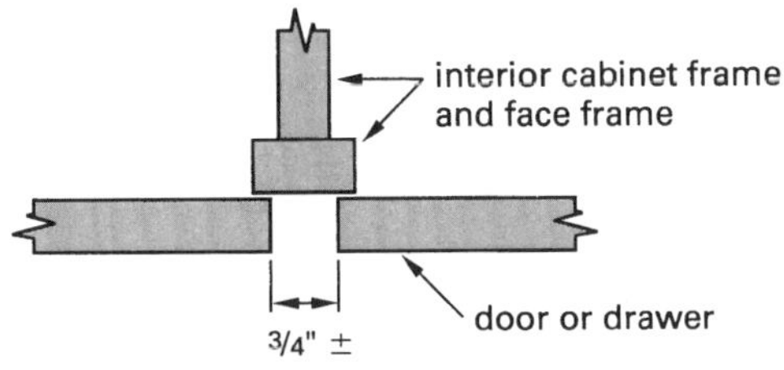

(c) reveal overlay construction

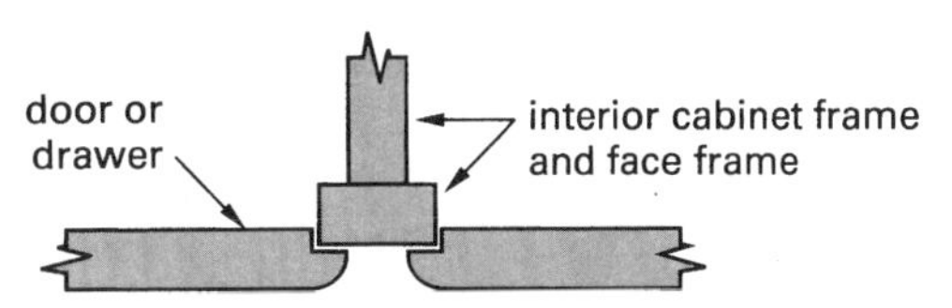

(d) lipped overlay construction

Figure 26.11
Typical Upper Cabinet

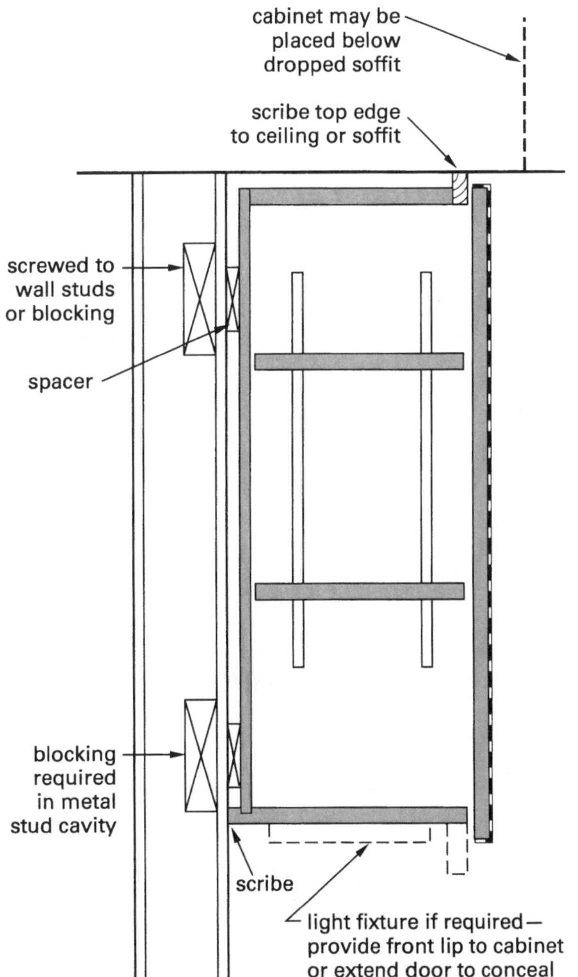

Matching adjacent veneer leaves may be done in three ways, as shown in Fig. 26.12. *Bookmatching* is the most common. As the veneers are sliced off the log, every other piece is turned over so that adjacent leaves form a symmetrical grain pattern. With *slip matching*, consecutive pieces are placed side by side with the same face sides being exposed. *Random matching* places veneers in no particular sequence, and even veneers from different flitches may be used.

Veneers must be glued to rigid panels to make installation possible. The method of doing this is the next consideration in specifying paneling. If the veneers are bookmatched, there are three ways, shown in Fig. 26.13, of matching veneers within a panel. A *running match* simply alternates bookmatched veneer pieces regardless of their width or how many must be used to complete a panel. Any portion left over from the last leaf of one panel is used as the starting piece for the next. In a *balance match*, veneer pieces are trimmed to equal widths; there may be an odd or even number of veneer pieces in each panel. A *center match* has an even number of veneer leaves of uniform width so that there is symmetry about a veneer joint in the center of the panel.

There are also three ways panels can be assembled within a room to complete a project (see Fig. 26.14). The first and least expensive is called *warehouse matching*. Premanufactured panels, normally 4 ft wide by 8 ft or 10 ft long are assembled from a single flitch that yields from six to twelve panels. They are field cut to fit around doors, windows, and other obstructions, resulting in some loss of grain continuity.

Figure 26.12
Veneer Matching

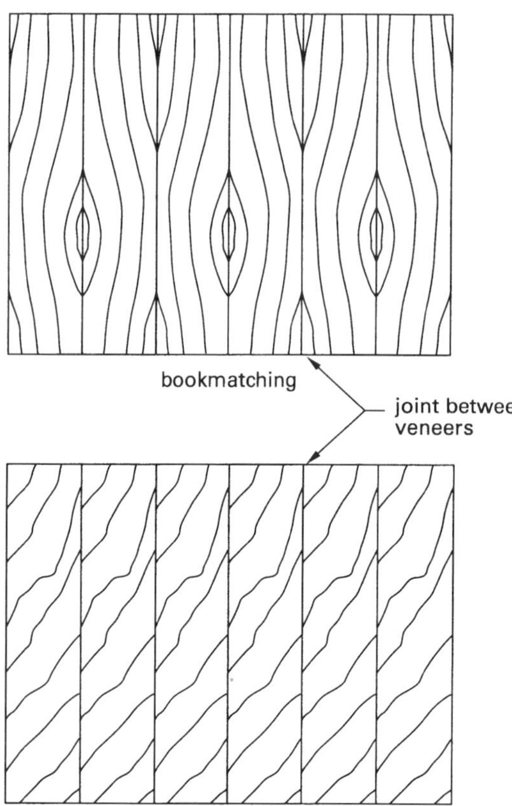

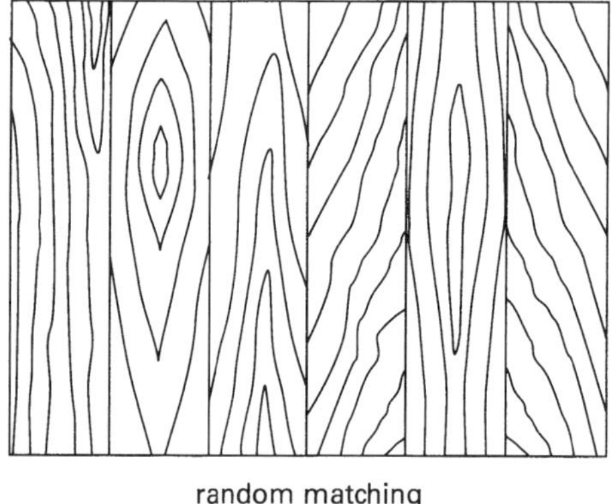

The second method, called *sequence matching*, uses panels of uniform width manufactured for a specific job and with the veneers arranged in sequence. If some panels must be trimmed to fit around doors or other obstructions, there is a moderate loss of grain continuity.

The third and most expensive method is called *blueprint matching*. The panels are manufactured to precisely fit the room and line up with every obstruction so that grain continuity is not interrupted. Veneers from the same flitch are matched over doors, cabinets, and other items covered with paneling.

Joints of flush paneling may be constructed in a number of ways depending on the finish appearance desired, as shown in Fig. 26.15. Paneling is hung on a wall with either steel Z-clips or wood cleats cut at an angle to allow the individual panels to be slipped over the hanger, which is anchored to the wall structure.

Stile and Rail Paneling

Stile and rail panel construction consists of a frame of solid wood that contains individual panels. Along with various types of molding and matching doors, raised panel construction is used to detail a traditional wood-paneled room interior (see Fig. 26.16). Traditionally, the panels were also made from solid wood, but it is more common for the panels to be veneered.

As shown in Fig. 26.17, the vertical frame pieces are called the *stiles*, and the horizontal members are the *rails*. The panels are held in place with grooves cut in the sides of the frames or with individual molding pieces, called sticking. The panels are set in the molding loosely to allow the panel to expand and contract with changes in the moisture content.

Stile and rail paneling may be hung on walls with wood cleats or metal Z-clips as with flush paneling, but if extensive molding is used the panels can be screwed to wood grounds behind the paneling and the fasteners concealed with the molding. Individual panels are joined with dowels or splines to keep the edges flush.

Laminates

A common finishing material used with architectural woodwork is *high-pressure decorative laminate* (HPDL). This is a thin sheet material made by impregnating several layers of kraft paper with phenolic resins and overlaying the paper with a patterned or colored sheet and a layer of melamine resin. The entire assembly is placed in a hot press under high pressure where the various layers fuse together. Plastic laminates are used for countertops, wall paneling, cabinets, shelving, and furniture.

Because laminates are very thin, they must be adhered to panel substrates such as plywood or particleboard. Smaller pieces can be glued to solid pieces of lumber. There are several types and thicknesses of plastic laminate, the most common being a general-purpose type that is 0.050 in thick. It is used for both vertical and horizontal applications. A post-forming type, 0.040 in thick, is manufactured so it can be heated and bent to a small radius.

When plastic laminate is applied to large surfaces of paneling, it must be balanced with a backing sheet to inhibit moisture absorption and to attain structural balance so that the panel does not warp.

There are several types of high-pressure decorative laminates manufactured for specific purposes. Although these generally cost more, they fill specific needs for some construction.

- *Colorthrough laminates.* These laminates are manufactured with decorative papers throughout the thickness so that the resulting sheet is a solid color. This eliminates the dark line visible at the edges of sheets when they are trimmed.
- *Fire-rated laminates.* These finishes comply with Class 1 or A ratings as long as the appropriate substrates and adhesives are selected.
- *Chemical-resistant laminates.* Special formulation of the laminate materials give these products additional resistance to strong chemicals found in laboratories, medical facilities, and photographic studios. They are available in horizontal as well as vertical thicknesses and can be post-formed for curved surfaces.
- *Static-dissipative laminates.* For areas where static control is required, such as in hospital operating rooms, electronic manufacturing plants, and computer rooms, these laminates provide a conductive layer in the sheet. When connected to suitable grounding they prevent the buildup of static charges and continuously channel them away.

Figure 26.13
Panel Matching Veneers

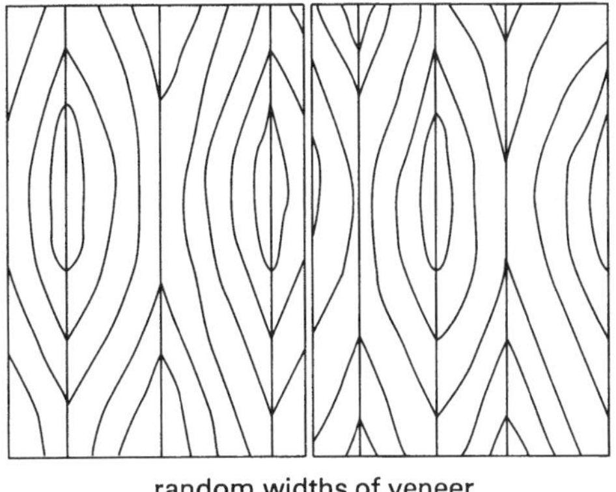

random widths of veneer
running match

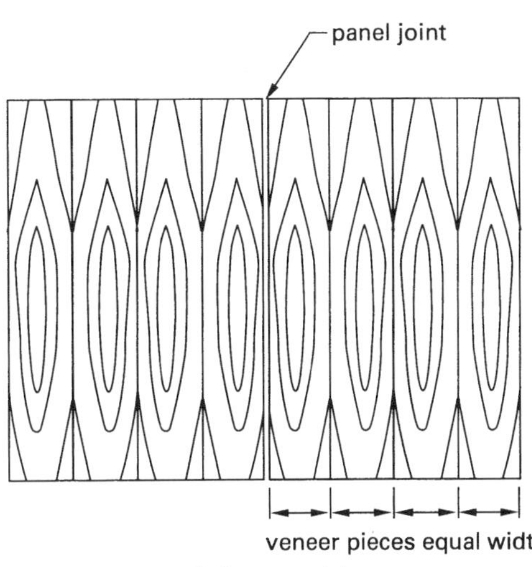

balance match

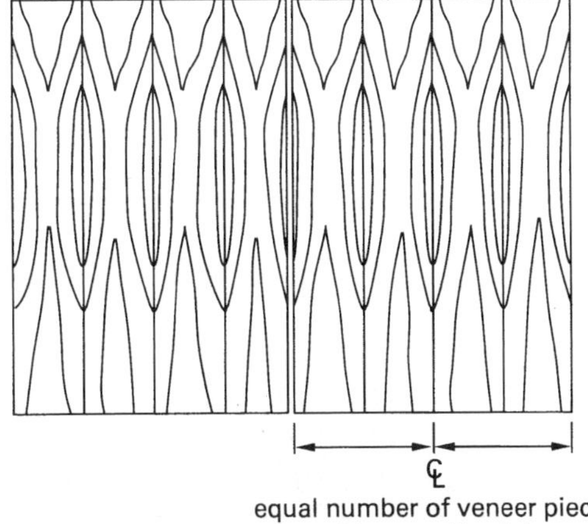

center match

- *Metal-faced laminates.* A limited number of metal finishes are available. They do not have the same wear resistance as real metal, so they should only be used on vertical surfaces subject to little abuse. They can be fabricated with standard woodworking equipment and cost much less than real metal. However, it is difficult to fabricate small, detailed items with finely crafted edges.

- *Natural wood laminates.* Thin veneers of actual wood are bonded to the standard type of laminate kraft papers and resins with this product. The laminate can be specified to provide untreated wood ready for finishing or with a protective layer of melamine resin.

Figure 26.14
Matching Panels Within a Room

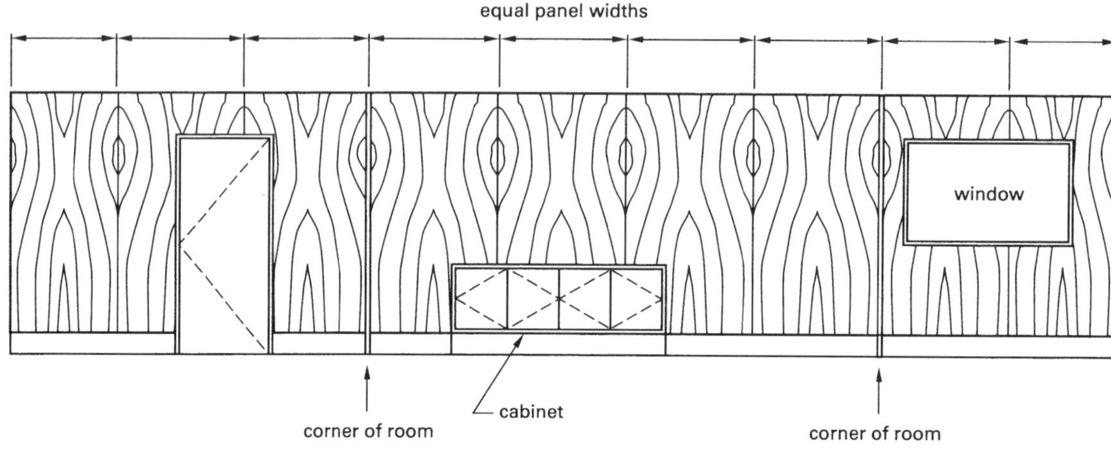

warehouse match

some loss of grain continuity

sequence match

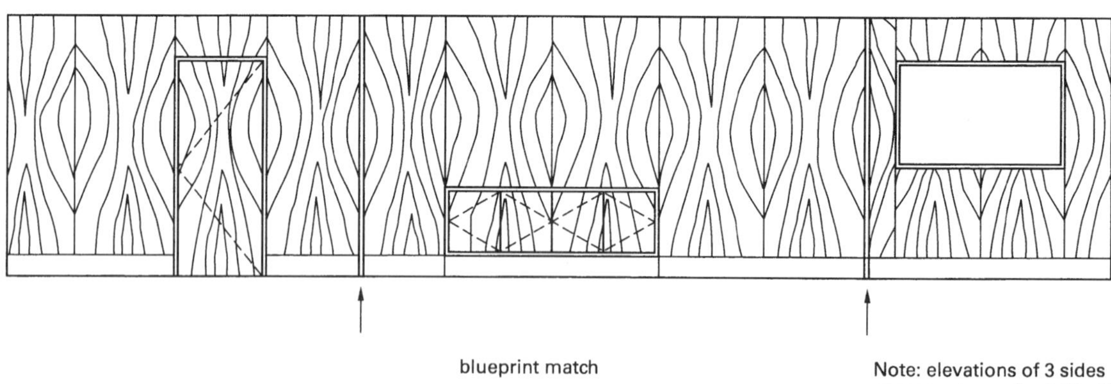

blueprint match

Note: elevations of 3 sides of room shown "unfolded"

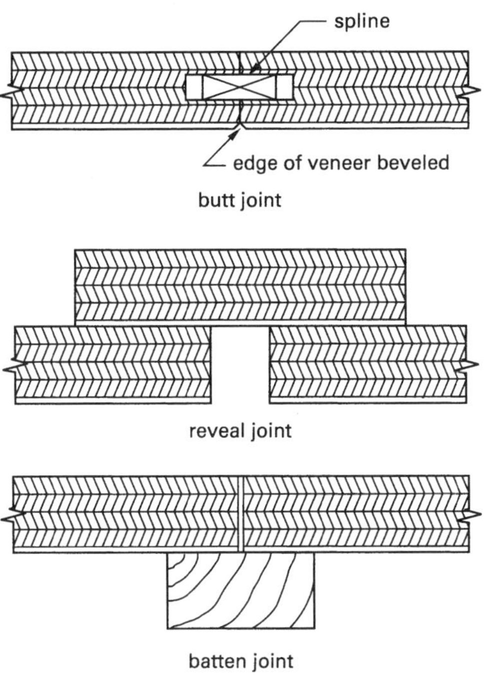

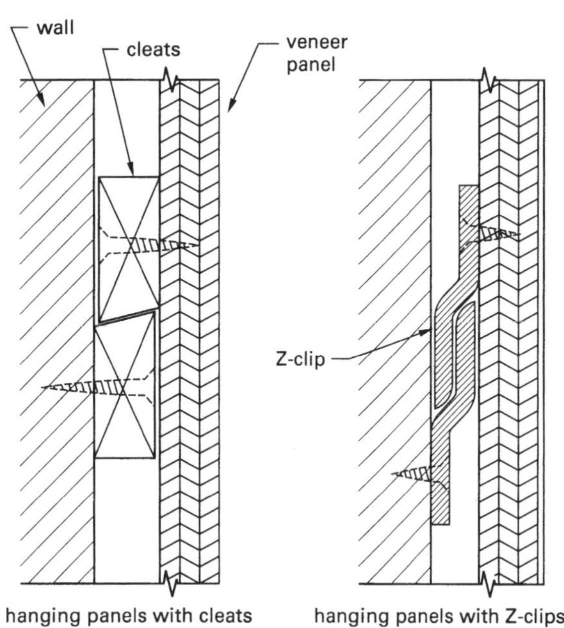

Figure 26.15
Flush Panel Joints

Another type of laminate product is *thermoset decorative paneling*. It is made by pressing a decorative overlay from a thermoset polyester or melamine resin-impregnated saturated sheet onto a cellulosic substrate such as particleboard or medium-density fiberboard. This paneling differs from high-pressure decorative laminates in that its decorative surface is fused to the substrate of particleboard. (In contrast, the decorative surface of high-pressure laminates is a thin veneer that must be adhesive-bonded to another substrate.) Because the process is usually done with pressures lower than HPDLs, these products are sometimes called "low-pressure laminates" or melamine. The manufacturers that produce thermoset decorative panels form the American Laminators Association (ALA) and use the trade name Permalam® to identify these types of panels.

Because the decorative surface is part of the substrate, the potential problem of delamination is eliminated and the panels come ready to be fabricated. Generally, the cost of thermoset panels is less than HPDL in many cases. However, there are several disadvantages to thermoset decorative panels. The choices of colors, textures, and grades are limited. Thermoset panels cannot be post-formed for curves, and they should not be used for high-wear horizontal surfaces such as countertops. Only a limited number of Class I or A fire-rated panels is available from a few manufacturers. Thermoset panels are typically used for furniture, fixtures, and kitchen cabinets or where resistance to heavy use is not required.

Standing and Running Trim

Standing and running trim are similar to standard molding sections applied as finish carpentry items. Unlike moldings, however, standing and running trim are custom-fabricated to meet the requirements of a specific project.

Standing trim is woodwork of a fixed length, intended to be installed as a single piece of wood. Examples include door frame trim, door stops, window casings, and similar items. *Running trim* is woodwork of a continuing length that must be installed in several pieces fitted end to end, such as base molding, cornices, chair rails, and soffits. *Rails* are gripping or protection surfaces on corridor walls of hospitals and the like and guard rails at glass openings.

The *profile* of trim, or its *cross-sectional shape*, can be identical to the many standard shapes available in premanufactured molding, or custom profiles can be milled.

Figure 26.16 Stile and Rail Panel Construction

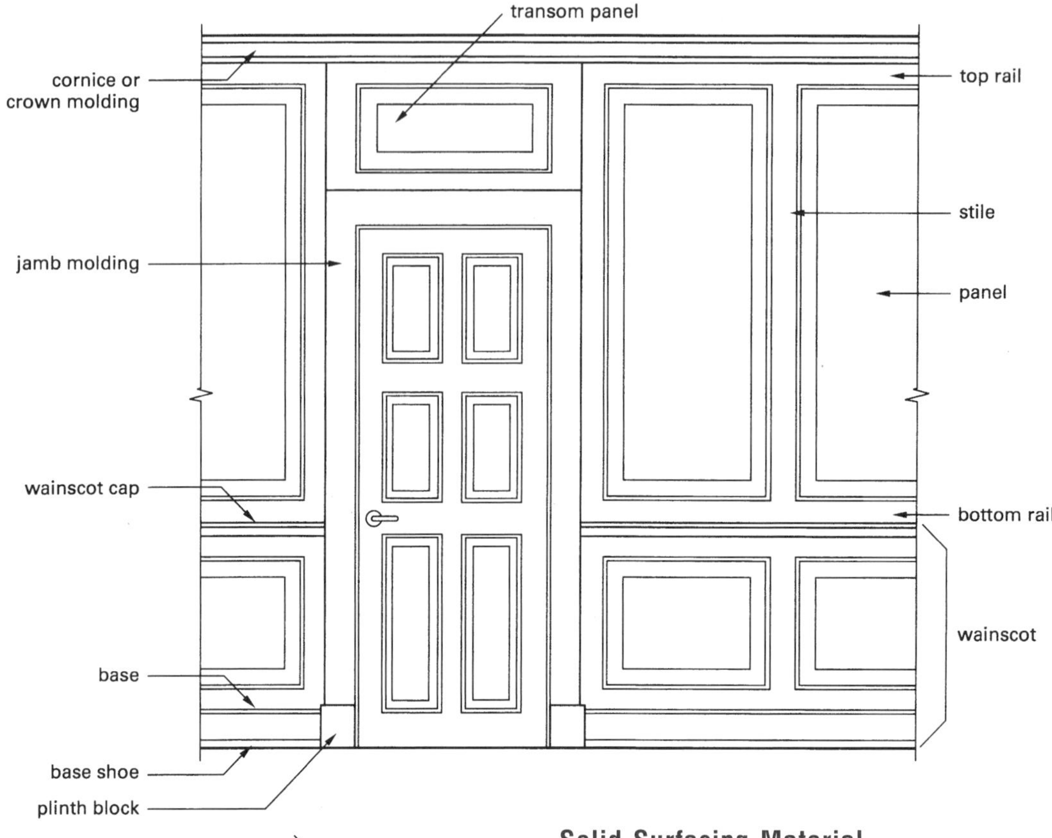

Figure 26.17 Stile and Rail Components

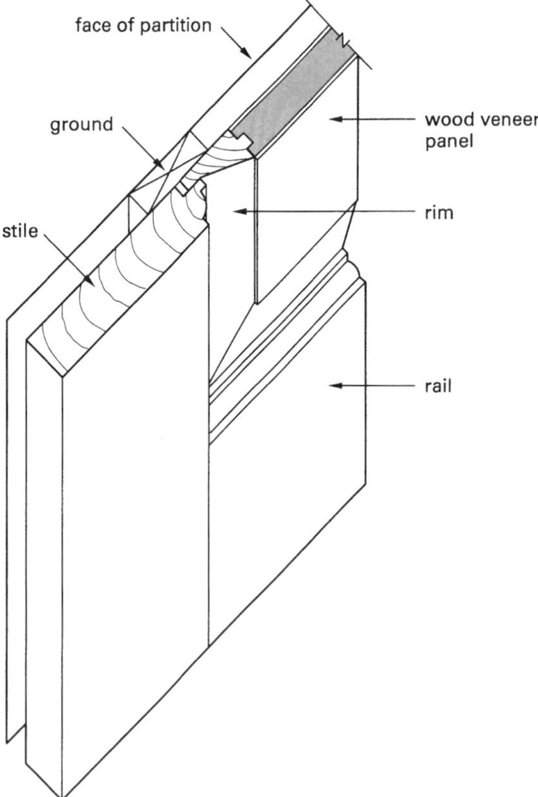

Solid Surfacing Material

Solid surfacing is a generic term for homogeneous, polymer-based surfacing materials. It can be formed into thick, flat sheets, or into shapes. It is frequently used for kitchen and bath countertops, sinks, toilet partitions, bars, and other areas where high-pressure plastic laminate might otherwise be used. It is available in a wide variety of colors and patterns. Standard thickness for countertops is $^3/_4$ in. Because the color is integral throughout the thickness of the material, scratches, dents, stains, and other types of minor damage can be sanded out or cleaned with a household abrasive cleanser. Because many of the available patterns resemble stone, it is often used as a lower cost, lighter weight substitute for stone tops.

Solid surfacing materials are easily fabricated and installed with normal woodworking tools. Edges can even be routed for decorative effects. When two pieces must be butted together, a two-part epoxy or liquid form of the material is used for a seamless appearance.

Moisture Content and Shrinkage

Shrinkage and swelling of lumber in architectural woodwork is not as much of a problem as for rough and finish carpentry because of the improved manufacturing methods available in the shop and the fact that solid stock and veneer can be dried or acclimated to a particular region.

However, some general guidelines should be followed. For most of the United States, the optimum moisture content of architectural woodwork for interior applications is from 5% to 10%. The relative humidity necessary to maintain this optimum level is from 25% to 55%. In the more humid southern coastal areas, the optimum moisture content is from 8% to 13%, and in the dry Southwest the corresponding values are from 4% to 9%.

Code Requirements

The various model building codes set limits on the flame-spread ratings of interior finishes based on the occupancy of the building and the use area within the building. In general, most of the model building codes regulate the use of woodwork as a wall or ceiling finish, but do not regulate the use of wood in furniture, cabinets, or trim. This includes cabinets attached to the structure.

Interior finish is defined in the IBC (and similarly in other model codes) as wall and ceiling finish including wainscoting, paneling, or other finish applied structurally or for decoration, acoustical correction, surface insulation, or similar purposes. Requirements do not apply to *trim*, which is defined as picture molds, chair rails, baseboards, and handrails; to doors and windows or their frames; or to materials that are less than $^1/_{28}$ in thick cemented to the surface of walls or ceilings.

As discussed in Chap. 14, there are three flame-spread groupings. In the IBC these are A, B, and C, corresponding to flame-spread ratings of 0-25, 26-75, and 76-200, respectively.

Different wood species have different flame-spread ratings, but very few have ratings less than 75, so wood is generally considered a Class C material unless it is treated with a fire retardant. However, treating often darkens the wood and makes it difficult to finish.

FINISHES

Finish is used on woodwork to protect it from moisture, chemicals, and contact and to enhance its appearance. Woodwork can either be field finished or factory finished. Because more control can be achieved with a factory finish this is the preferred method, although minor cabinet and trim work is often field finished in single-family residential and small commercial construction. For high-quality woodwork, field finishing is generally limited to minor touch-up and repair.

Prior to finishing, the wood must be sanded properly and filled, if desired. On many open-grain woods such as oak, mahogany, and teak, a filler should be applied prior to finishing to give a more uniform appearance to the woodwork, but it is not required. Other types of surface preparation are also possible depending on the aesthetic effect desired. The wood may be bleached to lighten it or to provide uniformity of color. Wood may also be mechanically or physically distressed to give it an antique or aged appearance. Shading or toning can also be used to change the color of the wood and subsequent finishing operations.

Opaque Finishes

Opaque finishes include lacquer, varnish, polyurethane, and polyester. They should only be used on closed-grain woods where solid stock is used and on medium-density fiberboard where sheet materials are used.

Lacquer is a coating material with a high nitrocellulose content modified with resins and plasticizers dissolved in a volatile solvent. Catalyzed lacquers contain an extra ingredient that speeds drying time and gives the finish additional hardness.

Varnish is a material consisting of various types of resinous materials dissolved in one of several types of volatile liquids. Conversion varnish is produced with alkyd and urea formaldehyde resins. When a high solids content is specified, the finish becomes opaque.

Polyurethane is a synthetic finish that gives a very hard, durable finish. Although difficult to repair or refinish, polyurethane finishes offer superior resistance to water, to many commercial and household chemicals, and to abrasion. Opaque polyurethanes are available in sheens from dull satin to full gloss.

Polyesters are another type of synthetic finish that give the hardest, most durable finish possible. Opaque polyesters can be colored and are available only in a full-gloss sheen. Like polyurethanes, polyester finishes are very difficult to repair and refinish outside the shop, but they give very durable finishes with as much as 80% the hardness of glass.

Transparent Finishes

Transparent finishes include lacquer, varnish, vinyl, penetrating oils, polyurethane, and polyester.

Standard lacquers are easy to apply, can be repaired easily, and are relatively low in cost. However, they do not provide the chemical and wear resistance of some of the other finishes. Catalyzed lacquers for transparent finishes are more difficult to repair and refinish, but they are more durable and resistant to commercial and household chemicals. A special water-reducible acrylic lacquer is available if local regulations prohibit the use of other types of lacquers.

Conversion varnish has many of the same advantages of lacquer but can often be applied with fewer coats.

Catalyzed vinyl yields a surface that has the most chemical resistance of the standard finishes of lacquer, varnish, and vinyl. Vinyl is also very resistant to scratching, abrasion, and other mechanical damage.

Penetrating oil finishes are one of the traditional wood finishes. They are easily applied and give a rich look to wood, but they require re-oiling periodically and tend to darken with age. An oil-finish look can be achieved with a catalyzed vinyl.

As with the opaque finishes, both polyurethane and polyester provide the most durable transparent finishes possible. They are the most expensive of the finishing systems and require skilled applicators. Transparent polyurethanes are available in sheens from dull to full gloss, whereas polyesters are available only in full gloss.

Stains

Prior to applying the final finish, wood may be stained to modify its color. The two types of stains are water-based and solvent-based. Water-based stains yield a uniform color but raise the grain. Solvent-based stains dry quickly and do not raise the grain but are less uniform. Both are penetrating finishes and cannot be easily removed.

27 MOISTURE PROTECTION AND THERMAL INSULATION

Project Planning

Water leakage and temperature transmission are two of the most troublesome technical problems an architect must solve. Water can leak into a building from every direction, from underground moisture and groundwater, and from precipitation on the roof and exterior walls. It can find its way into a building through a surface material such as roofing or a basement slab or through joints and penetrations between materials. Moisture can also be generated within a building from cooking, showering, or simple human habitation. The architect must try to prevent this moisture from permeating the structure, and, if it does, allow a way for it to migrate out.

Insulation is essential in controlling heat flow both into and out of the building and must be properly specified and detailed to minimize energy use while providing a comfortable interior environment.

This chapter discusses the methods and materials used to protect a building from moisture and to control heat loss and heat gain.

DAMPPROOFING

Dampproofing is the control of moisture that is not under hydrostatic pressure. Although the term can apply to water-repellent coatings used on walls above grade, it more typically refers to coatings and other treatments used on slabs and foundation walls below grade to protect them from vapor diffusion.

Dampproofing should not be used on elements below the water table; these call for waterproofing. Dampproofing coatings are always applied on the *positive side*, or wet side, of the element and are generally applied by sprayer, brush, roller, or trowel.

Methods of dampproofing include the following.

- *admixtures.* Various admixtures can be added to concrete to make it water repellent, such as the salts of fatty acids, mineral oil, and powdered iron. These may reduce the strength of the concrete, but they make it much less permeable to water.
- *bituminous coatings.* These are asphalt or coal-tar pitch materials applied to the exterior side of the foundation wall. They can be brushed or sprayed on, can be applied either hot or cold (depending on the type), and should be applied to smooth surfaces. These coatings will not seal cracks that develop after they are applied.
- *cementitious coatings.* One or two coats of portland cement mortar can be troweled over the surface of masonry or concrete foundation walls. Mortar coatings are often used over very rough walls to provide a smooth surface for the installation of other dampproofing materials, but they can also be used by themselves. Powdered iron is often added as an admixture to the mortar. As the iron oxidizes it expands, countering the shrinkage of the material and making a tighter seal.
- *membranes.* These include built-up layers of hot- or cold-applied asphalt felts or membranes of butyl, polyvinyl chloride, and other synthetic materials. Membranes are typically used for waterproofing walls subject to hydrostatic pressure because their cost and the difficulty of applying them is not usually warranted for simple dampproofing.
- *plastics.* Silicone and polyurethane coatings are available, but they are usually reserved for above-grade dampproofing.

Example 27.1

Which of the following would be most appropriate for dampproofing on above-grade concrete wall with a moderately rough surface?

(A) cementitious coating

(B) bituminous coating

(C) synthetic rubber

(D) silicone coating

Solution

Silicone coatings would provide the best coverage for rough walls because they can be sprayed, painted, or rolled on. If the wall was below grade, the correct choice would be a cementitious coating or a bituminous coating.

The answer is (D).

WATERPROOFING

Waterproofing is the control of moisture and water that is subject to hydrostatic pressure. This may include protecting parts of structures that are below the water table. Waterproofing is a more difficult technical problem than dampproofing because of the effect of the water pressure and the need to create a continuous seal over walls, slabs, and joints in the structure.

Waterproofing can be placed in one of three positions: on the positive side, negative side, or blind side. In *positive side waterproofing*, the most common, the waterproofing material is placed on the side of the element exposed to water—the exterior of a foundation wall, for example—after the element is in place. Backfilling is done after the wall is waterproofed; the backfill should be placed in lifts so that it is well compacted and will not settle in the future.

Negative side waterproofing is also applied after the element is in place, but to the side of the element that is not exposed to water, such as the interior of a foundation wall. *Blind side waterproofing* is applied before the element is in place, such as on a shored excavation against which a concrete foundation wall will be poured.

There are four basic types of applied waterproofing materials.

- *Sheet membranes* are built-up layers of bituminous saturated felts similar to roofing, or single-ply membranes of synthetic materials such as butyl, polyvinyl chloride, and other proprietary products. Sheet membranes may be loosely applied and attached to nailing strips, but more effective systems are adhered to the foundation on the positive side.
- *Fluid-applied systems* include modified asphalts, urethanes, and other synthetics. These are applied in liquid form to provide a continuous, seamless membrane. These systems are applied on the positive side.
- *Cementitious systems* consist of portland cement, sand, and some type of waterproofing agent. Most common is a system that includes metal oxides. Cementitious systems can be applied either on the positive or negative side, but locating them on the positive side is more effective; negative side applications should be used only as a backup for positive side waterproofing.
- *Bentonite systems* use an assembly of bentonite clay inside kraft paper packages or plastic liners in panel form. The bentonite expands in the presence of moisture, thereby preventing water from getting past. These systems are often combined with geotextile fabrics and can be used as both blind side and positive side waterproofing.

Membranes and fluid-applied systems should be protected from damage during construction and backfilling operations by placing protection board over the waterproofing prior to backfilling. The protection board may consist of asphalt-impregnated glass fiber mats, extruded polystyrene (XPS) rigid board insulation suitable for use below grade, or some other proprietary product with or without an integral drainage mat.

In addition to the waterproofing and protection board, a foundation waterproofing system may include a geotextile or drainage board to relieve hydrostatic pressure against the wall insulation, as called for by the climate zone and local code requirements.

Another type of product is *crystalline waterproofing*, which uses a proprietary mix of chemicals. During concrete hydration, the mixture comes in contact with water and expands to fill the pores, capillaries, and micro-cracks in the concrete with a nonsoluble crystalline formation. This process both waterproofs the concrete and provides protection from alkali aggregate reactions, chloride penetration, and carbonation (the corrosive effect that softens the surface layers of concrete). The process will continue after the concrete has cured if more moisture is introduced, essentially making the concrete self-healing should new cracks develop. This type of waterproofing can be applied to the surface on either the positive or negative side of the concrete by brushing or spraying, or it can be added to the concrete as an admixture at the batch plant.

To relieve water pressure and carry away accumulated water that drains down the wall, drain pipe or tile may be set in gravel at the level of the footing or slightly below the basement slab. This is especially important if a heavy concentration of water is expected. Perforated PVC pipe, 4 in or 6 in in diameter, is often used. The pipe should be sloped to an exterior drain if the site topography allows, or directed to a sump pump. The gravel around the pipe should be separated from the backfill with a layer of geotextile fabric, which keeps sediment from the backfill from clogging the gravel drainage system. Figure 27.1 shows a typical installation of a waterproofed slab and foundation wall.

Figure 27.1
Waterproofed Wall and Slab

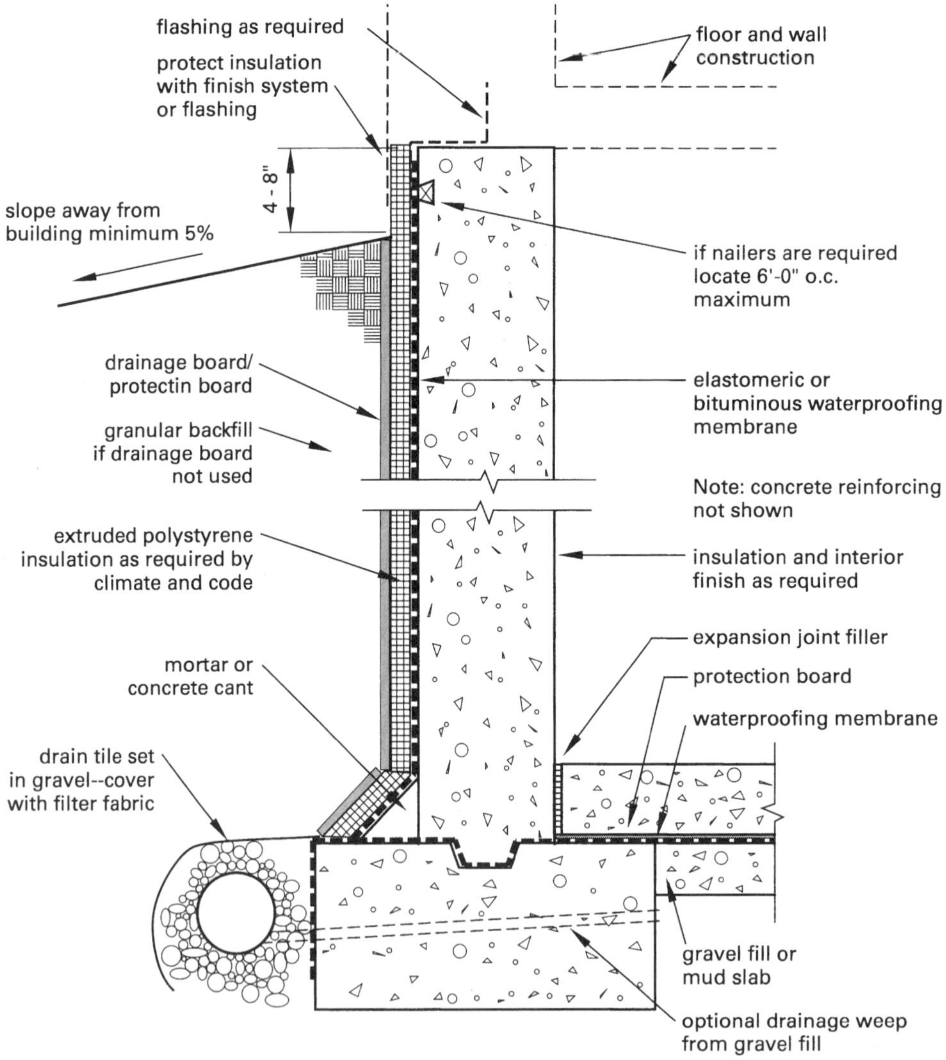

Joints in waterproofed walls are particularly subject to leakage. In concrete walls, *waterstops* are used to seal construction joints. Waterstops are continuous extrusions of rubber or neoprene, often with a dumbbell or ribbed profile. Half of the waterstop is placed in the form during the first pour of concrete, and the other half is allowed extend into the second pour. Waterstops are manufactured with a variety of profiles suited for different conditions, such as the degree and type of movement the joint may experience.

Good construction practice also includes extending the waterproofing up to the building moisture barrier and facade flashing, and protecting the waterproofing from ultraviolet radiation and damage with the building finish system or with flashing.

A positive slope should be created away from the building to minimize water penetration around the foundation. The *International Residential Code* requires a slope of no less than $^1/_2$ in per foot for at least 6 ft from the exterior wall. It is important to keep trees and plantings with deep roots away from perimeter drainage systems. A tree should be planted no closer to the building than its eventual height, to prevent roots from clogging drains or interfering with the foundation wall.

WEATHER BARRIER CONCEPTS

The exterior enclosure of a building must provide weather protection against rain and snow, water vapor, air infiltration, and temperature differentials. The ways in which these elements enter the building vary, as do the methods for preventing or reducing their effects. Before developing details, the architect should understand exactly what protection is needed and evaluate which of the general approaches to solving the problems best fits the project conditions. (See Fig. 27.2.)

What types of construction details should be created during design development to provide protection from weather and climate can depend on many factors, including

- the climatic zone in which the building is located
- the individual microclimate surrounding the building
- environmental conditions required inside the building
- the type of structure and exposed cladding being used
- expected building movement
- other detailing considerations of cost, desired appearance, security, acoustics, fire resistance, durability, and similar parameters

Moisture generated inside a building can also be problematic if there is no way to exhaust it at the source or provide for its diffusion to the exterior.

Climate Zones

The amount of insulation and the type and position of air barriers and water or vapor barriers in the exterior enclosure depend largely on the climate zone in which the project is located. The *International Energy Conservation Code* (IECC) and ANSI/ASHRAE/IESNA Standard 90.1 define eight climate zones in the United States. The hottest zone includes all of Hawaii and the southern tip of Florida; the coldest includes much of Alaska. Each climate zone is divided further into up to four subzones based on moisture: moist, dry, marine, and warm-humid. (See Fig. 9.2 and Table 9.2.) An appendix of Standard 90.1 gives a county-by-county listing of climate zones in the United States as well as information on climate regions of other countries.

Water Barriers

Water barriers are the first line of defense against water penetration into a building. Water barriers can include the exterior surfaces of walls, waterproof membranes within walls, roofing, below-grade waterproofing, drips, and flashing. These surfaces shed as much water as possible out of and away from the building or to drainage lines.

Historically, building walls employed the *barrier concept*, in which the exterior walls, joint sealants, and other components prevent water and water vapor from penetrating by forming a continuous barrier exposed to the weather. However, leaks, wind-driven rain, and other forces, as well as construction defects, often let water penetrate through this barrier. If the wall assembly is not properly detailed to allow this water to exit the wall cavity, problems will arise from moisture in the wall.

Figure 27.2 Determining Needs for Protection

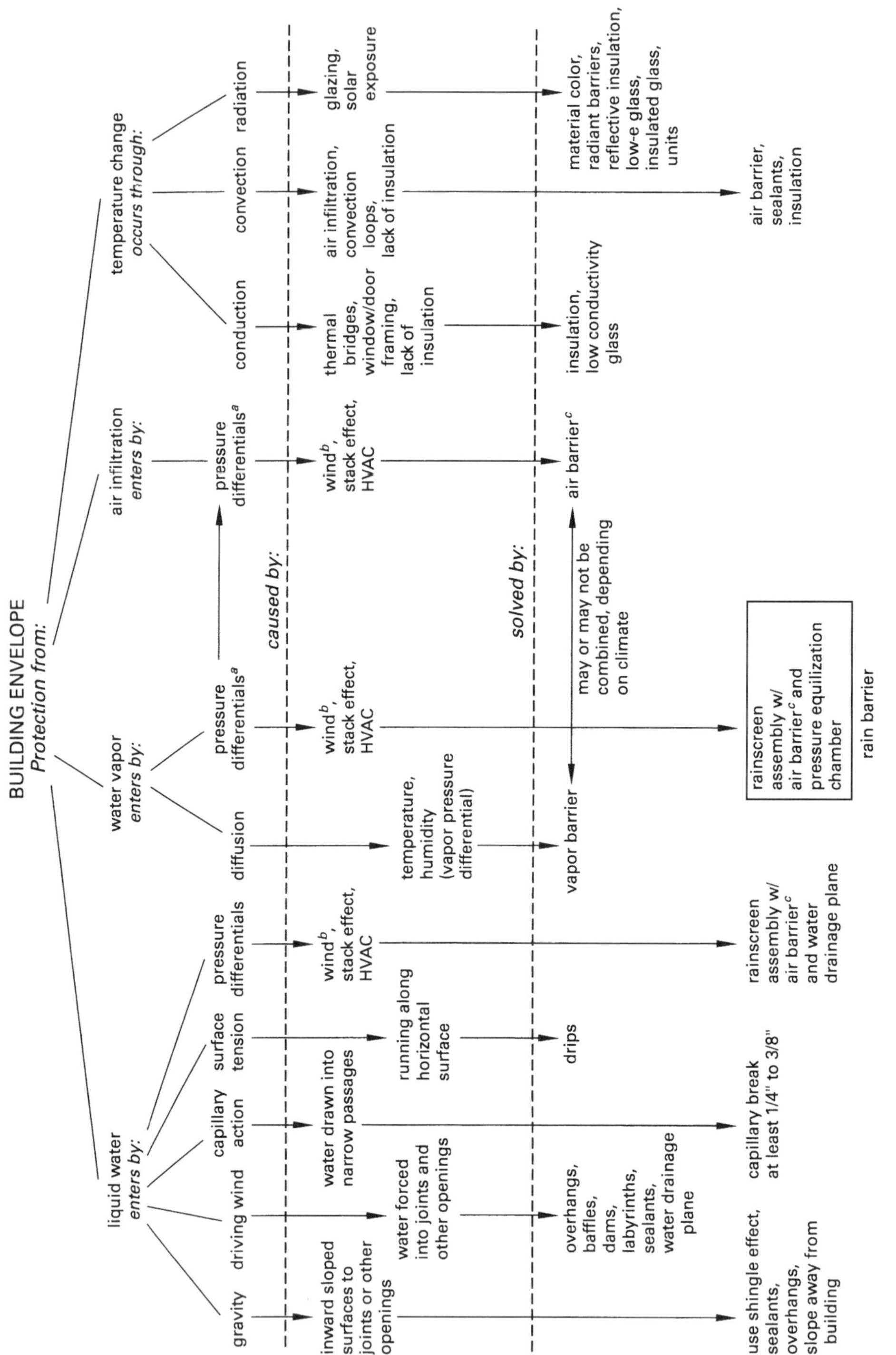

Contemporary cladding systems typically employ the *rain screen system*, in which the exposed surface provides protection from the elements, but is used in conjunction with an air space behind it and a watertight membrane and/or air barrier inside the air space. The air space is vented to the outside so that the pressure is equal on both sides of the rain screen. This minimizes the movement of water due to pressure differentials caused by wind or other forces. Any moisture that does penetrate the rain screen is prevented from entering the backup wall with a vapor barrier and flashing, and is drained down the air space and out through weep holes. Other openings in the rain screen allow excess water vapor to evaporate. Types of rain screen systems are discussed in more detail later in this section.

Vapor Retarders

A *vapor retarder* is a material used to slow the transmission or diffusion of water vapor between spaces. Vapor retarders are not themselves insulation, but they play an important role in preserving the effectiveness of other insulating materials.

Water vapor can enter a building by diffusion through materials or by air movement, or by both. (Air movement and air barriers are discussed in Chap. 12.) Moreover, water vapor is produced inside all buildings by human respiration and perspiration, cooking, and other activities that involve water. In addition, there is always a certain amount of humidity present in the air.

Warm air can hold more water than cold air. If air gets colder while the amount of water in that air stays constant, then the air's relative humidity will rise until it reaches 100%. At this point, the amount of water in the air is equal to the maximum amount of water that air at that temperature can hold. This is known as the *dew point*, the point at which water condenses from the vapor.

Vapor diffusion is the slow movement of water molecules through vapor-permeable materials. Warm, moist air tends to migrate into areas of cooler, drier air. Differences in temperature and relative humidity indoors and outdoors lead to differences in vapor pressure, and this causes the diffusion. In buildings, this can cause problems when the warm, moist air cools, reaches its dew point, and condenses. The condensation of moisture within a wall can degrade insulation and other building materials, promote rust, and support mold growth.

To prevent vapor migration, vapor retarders are used. These may be made of plastic sheeting (polyethylene), aluminum foil, self-adhering sheet membranes, or fluid-applied membranes. Vapor retarders may also function as air barriers if it is appropriate to place them in the same position within the wall as discussed in Chap. 12.

Different materials have different permeance ratings. As discussed in Chap. 12, *permeance* is the property of a material that prevents water vapor from diffusing through it. The basic unit of permeance is the *perm*. In customary U.S. units, a perm is one grain of moisture per hour per square foot per inch of mercury difference in vapor pressure, or 1 $gr/hr\text{-}ft^2\text{-}in\ Hg$. Table 27.1 gives perm ratings and their corresponding terminology.

Table 27.1 Perm Rating Terminology

perm rating	term
less than 0.1	vapor impermeable
0.1 to 1	semi-impermeable
1 to 10	semipermeable
10 or over	permeable

Anything less than 1 perm is considered to be a vapor retarder (or less accurately called a vapor barrier).

The ideal position of vapor retarders within a wall assembly will vary depending on the climate. (See Fig. 9.2 for the climatic zone map.) Their position must also be considered in conjunction with the location of the air barrier.

For example, in cold areas (generally, climate regions 5, 6, 7, and 8), warm, moist interior air will tend to migrate toward the cooler, drier air outdoors. This will lead to water vapor condensing inside the insulation cavity or elsewhere inside the wall. To prevent this, impermeable vapor retarders should be placed on the warmer inside of the insulation. Also, a *vapor-permeable* air barrier should be placed outside the insulation to prevent air infiltration while allowing any accumulated moisture to dry out. In most cases, the air barrier is placed outside the sheathing for support, protection, and ease of construction.

In air-conditioned buildings in hot, humid climates (generally, climatic regions 1, 2, 3A below the warm-humid line, and 3C), vapor retarders should be placed on the warmer outside of the insulation to prevent the moist, warm air outside the building from migrating to the cooler, dehumidified interior spaces. In these climate regions, the vapor retarder should also serve as air barrier; that is, the air barrier should be *vapor-impermeable.*

In mixed climatic regions (generally, climate zones 4, some parts of 5 and some parts of 3A, 3B, 3C, and 4B), a vapor-permeable air barrier should be placed outside the insulation, and no vapor retarders should be used. This allows any vapor or condensation to pass through the wall in either direction.

The *International Building Code* (IBC) requirements for vapor retarders reflect these principles. The IBC defines three classes of vapor retarders. Class I has a perm rating less than or equal to 0.1, which makes it vapor impermeable (a real vapor barrier). Class II materials have a perm rating greater than 0.1 and less than or equal to 1.0, making them semi-impermeable. Class III materials, such as latex or enamel paint, have a perm rating of more than 1.0 and less than or equal to 10.0, making them permeable.

The ideal position of vapor retarders within a wall assembly will vary depending on the climate. Their position must also be considered in conjunction with the location of the air barrier.

Based on the climate zone, the IBC states where vapor retarders of each class may and may not be placed or requires that a dew point analysis be performed. In climate zones 1 and 2, Class I and Class II retarders cannot be placed on the interior side of frame walls. In climate zones 3 and 4, Class I retarders cannot be placed on the interior side of frame walls. This keeps warm, moist air from the exterior from being trapped in the wall and condensing.

However, in climate zones 5, 6, 7, 8, and Marine 4, Class I and II retarders must be provided on the interior side of frame walls. Class III retarders are permitted only where one of several combinations of cladding material and insulated sheathing given in an IBC table are specified. This provision prevents situations in which the properties of the wall materials, along with the installation of a vapor retarder, would effectively place vapor retarders on both sides of the wall and trap moisture in the wall. When foam plastic insulated sheathing is installed on the exterior side of the wall and creates an effective vapor retarder, only a Class III material can be used on the interior so that any moisture in the wall can escape back into the interior of the building.

For mixed climates, the suggestions and requirements given above are general guidelines only. The local climate, interior environmental conditions, and specific building materials being used should be reviewed by the designer to determine the best use and placement of air and vapor barriers. Available computer programs can give a detailed analysis of heat and vapor transmission for a specific climatic region throughout the year and for specific interior environmental conditions through a proposed wall design.

Analysis can also be done manually using a *dew point analysis*, in which a temperature gradient line is developed from outside to inside based on the R-values (temperature resistance) of the individual building materials in a specific condition. This analysis will allow the designer to find the point in the wall where the interior temperature of the wall and the dew point meet, and to locate the vapor barrier appropriately.

Air Barriers

In addition to vapor retarders, air barriers are an important part of an energy-efficient building design to prevent infiltration, entry of pollutants, and the migration of moisture. Refer to Chap. 12 for more information on air barriers.

Example 27.2

Which material has the lowest perm rating?

(A) 10 mil (0.25) polyethylene

(B) gypsum wallboard

(C) 1 mil (0.025) aluminum foil

(D) exterior oil paint

Solution

Vapor retarders are selected based on their perm ratings. The best vapor retarders have the lowest ratings. This problem is essentially asking which of the listed materials is the best vapor retarder, and the answer is option C, aluminum foil, with a perm rating of zero. Polyethylene is the next best, with a perm rating of 0.03. Three coats of exterior oil paint have a perm rating of 1.6 to 3.0. Gypsum wallboard allows the most moisture to pass through, with a perm rating of 50.

The answer is (C).

DETAILING CONSIDERATIONS

There are two basic approaches for creating a weather-resistant exterior wall. One approach uses a barrier system, and the other uses the rain screen principle. The rain screen wall is generally preferred. If detailed and executed properly, water penetration is virtually eliminated, even with minor imperfections in construction and as the building ages. In contrast, a barrier wall system must be built perfectly and maintained with no leaks over the life of the building to function well.

In a *barrier wall system*, the exterior cladding serves as the exterior finish, protects the building from the elements, and serves to prevent water, snow, and condensation from entering the building. A solid, multi-wythe masonry wall or an exterior insulation and finish system (EIFS) applied directly to the structural wall are examples of barrier wall systems. In both cases, if any part of the wall has small cracks or other defects, gravity-driven or wind-driven water can seep into the structure or the interior of the building. Recognizing this problem, most EIFS manufacturers offer systems that include drainage planes and a secondary weather-resistant barrier.

In a *rain screen wall*, the exterior cladding is separated from the waterproof and airtight barriers with an air space cavity. The exterior cladding serves as the finish and protects the remainder of the wall from the gross effects of the weather. A drainage plane of a water-resistant barrier (WRB) applied on the outside of the insulation prevents any moisture that penetrates the cladding from entering the building and directs it back to the exterior with flashing, weep holes, or other openings at the bottom of the cavity. Insulation is located inside the drainage plane. The moisture barrier may either be air permeable or impermeable, depending on the climate, interior environmental conditions, and other factors.

If a rain screen wall is detailed and executed properly, water penetration is virtually eliminated, even with minor imperfections in construction and as the building ages.

There are two basic types of rain screen walls. One is drained and back-ventilated, and the true rain screen is pressure-equalized. In the drained type, the exterior cladding does not prevent water from penetrating due to pressure differentials between the exterior of the building and the air cavity. In a pressure-equalized rain screen, the air cavity is vented enough to equalize the pressure on both sides of the exterior cladding to reduce the amount of wind-driven water into the cavity and onto the drainage plane; a continuous air barrier is required. In addition to an air barrier, a pressure-equalized design subdivides the air cavity into separate compartments so air does not flow from high-pressure areas to low-pressure areas as the wind pressure varies across the building.

Figure 27.3 shows two basic configurations of a well-designed exterior cladding system using the rain screen principle. These are not construction drawings but show the essential components and their position in the wall.

Figure 27.3(a) illustrates an exterior wall with the insulation in the stud cavity. Figure 27.3(b) shows the insulation applied to the outboard side of the structural wall. If the structural wall is formed with wood or metal studs, the stud cavity may also be insulated.

Figure 27.3
Exterior Cladding System

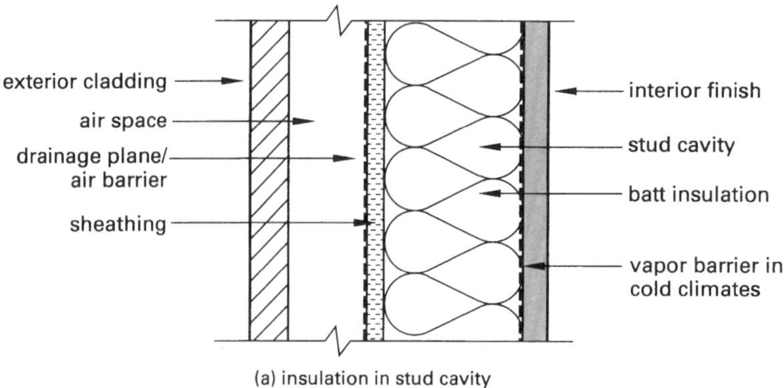

(a) insulation in stud cavity

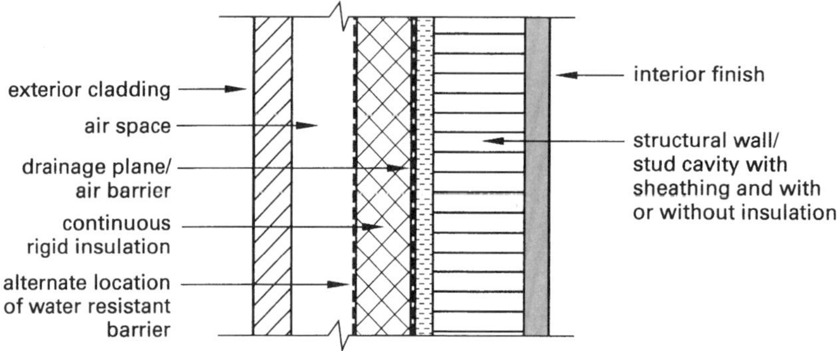

(b) insulation outboard of structural wall

Placing the WRB drainage plane on the outside of the sheathing, as shown in Fig. 27.3(a), with an insulated stud cavity makes construction easy and is one of the most common for residential construction. However, the drainage plane/air barrier is subject to damage during construction and the location of the insulation will create thermal bridges at the studs. Because of this, building codes and energy codes require continuous insulation to prevent thermal bridging. If a vapor retarder is used on the warm side of the insulation, the drainage plane/air barrier must be vapor permeable.

With the WRB drainage plane placed on the warm side of the insulation, as shown in Fig. 27.3(b), it is protected from temperature extremes and construction damage. The insulation is continuous and prevents thermal bridging at studs or other construction elements. Because the insulation is exposed to moisture in the air space, it must be a water-resistant material, such as extruded polystyrene or closed-cell spray polyurethane. Alternatively, the drainage plane with a WRB can be placed on the exterior side of the continuous insulation or be integral with the insulation.

Whatever the exact details are of the wall construction, if the assembly integrates combustible claddings, veneers, water-resistant barriers, and/or foam plastic insulations (which nearly all do), building codes require that, for Types I-IV commercial construction of two stories or more, the wall must meet the requirements of NFPA 285, *Standard Fire Test Method for Evaluation of Fire Propagation Characteristics of Exterior Non-Load-Bearing Wall Assemblies Containing Combustible Components.* Only specific combinations of materials have been tested for compliance with this requirement, and usually these test assemblies are comprised of products from one manufacturer. When designing the exterior wall assembly, particularly in a project where the architect may not have control over the brands of products provided, it is important to specify and verify that the products selected will together pass the test.

Additional detailing considerations include the following.

- The air barrier must be fully supported and continuous to be effective.
- Connections between the structural wall and the cladding should not allow water to travel across the air space. Built-in drips or clips on the connections should be specified. Manufacturers make connections for types of cladding that can span the insulation and air gap distance from structural wall to

the cladding while providing drips and gasketing to prevent the penetration of the WRB or air barrier.

- Eliminate air movement and ventilation on the conditioned side of the insulation.
- Only one vapor retarder should be used to allow the wall structure to dry through vapor diffusion, either to the outside or the inside.
- Consider the use of vinyl wallcovering on the inside face of exterior walls in hot-humid climates. If a vapor barrier is not placed on the warm side of the insulation, water vapor may condense behind the wallcovering and cause mold growth. Vapor-permeable paint or other permeable finish materials should be considered.
- In cold and mixed climate regions where vapor transmission from the interior to the exterior is a problem, vapor can travel from outside to inside when the cladding is absorptive (such as with masonry) and the wall is heated through solar radiation.
- Eliminate or minimize thermal shortcuts through thermal insulation. High-conductivity materials, such as metal window framing or metal studs, can greatly reduce the effectiveness of insulation. Specify brick ties and other cladding fasteners that are designed with a thermal break.
- If a radiant barrier is used, it must have an air space on the warm side to be effective.

Figure 27.4 shows a representative detail of one type of rain screen wall that incorporates the guidelines given above. It shows the head section of a window in a brick veneer wall with a steel stud backup. Exact details would vary with the type of building structure, the type and configuration of the window, and the interior finish details. The steel lintel shown is a loose lintel, meaning it spans from one side of the opening to the other and supports only the brick above the opening. Continuous relieving angles are anchored to the structure of the building with clip angles and the space between the back of the angle and the continuous insulation is filled with sprayed polyurethane foam insulation to seal all gaps and odd spaces around the clip angles. Alternatively, a block of rigid insulation could be used as shown in this detail, although it is not as good as sprayed insulation because it cannot be cut and fitted well enough to fill all the gaps in this part of the detail. Some important features of the detail include the following.

- The air space is 2 in as recommended, but it may be $1\frac{1}{2}$ in if space is tight.
- The air barrier should be carried down to the window framing and be sealed to the framing to provide a continuous air barrier plane.
- A strip of self-adhering waterproofing membrane should be lapped over the edge of the metal flashing.
- Cavity drainage mesh should be used at the bottom of the air space to catch mortar droppings.
- The metal flashing should include turned up end dams.
- The space between the top of the window assembly and the steel angle should be filled with a compressible insulation. If a spray-applied polyurethane foam insulation is used, remember that it must be covered with an appropriate thermal barrier on the inside of the building.
- If required by the climate, a vapor barrier would be used on the warm side of the insulation. If the ceiling was higher than the window, gypsum wallboard would be added to the steel studs.
- Any window frame should include thermal breaks and other seals as needed to maintain a continuous air barrier plane. The interior of the frame should be insulated if possible.

BUILDING INSULATION

Insulation is used to control unwanted heat flow, which can be from a warm building to a cold exterior or from a hot climate into a habitable space. Selecting and detailing insulation for buildings requires understanding of the processes of heat gain and heat loss because different kinds of insulation are used to control these factors. The architect must also understand the factors involved with water and air infiltration to develop a complete barrier system between the outside and inside of the building.

Figure 27.4
Detail of Rain Screen Wall

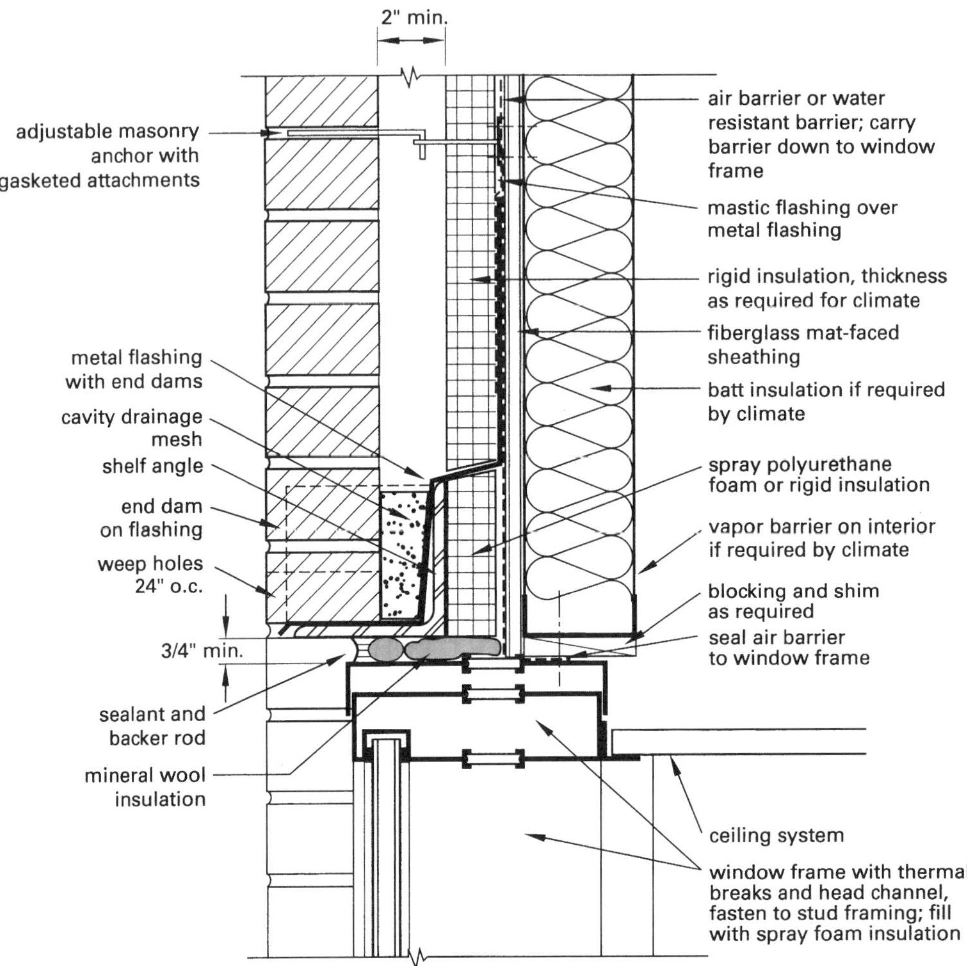

Methods of Heat Transfer

Heat is transferred in three ways.

- *Conduction* is the flow of heat within a material or between materials without displacement of the particles of the material.
- *Convection* is the transfer of heat within a fluid, either gas or liquid, by the movement of the fluid from an area of higher temperature to an area of lower temperature.
- *Radiation* is the transfer of heat energy through electromagnetic waves from one surface to a colder surface.

The best insulation is a vacuum; the next best is air that is kept absolutely motionless in a space between two materials. In reality, neither of these occurs perfectly, because convection currents carry warm air in one part of the space to the cooler parts of the space where heat is transferred by conduction. Most insulation products are designed to create air pockets small enough to prevent convection, but large enough to prevent the direct transfer of heat by conduction between the insulating materials.

Measuring Thermal Resistance

Thermal resistance is described with several terms, as outlined in Chap. 16. The quantity of heat used measure transfer is the *British thermal unit* (Btu), which is the amount of heat required to raise the temperature of 1 lbm of water by 1°F. The basic unit of conductance is a material's *k*-value, or *conductivity*. This is the number of Btus per hour that pass through 1 ft^2 of homogeneous material 1 in thick when the temperature differential is 1°F. When the material is more than 1 in thick, the unit is *conductance*, or the *C*-value.

The term more commonly used when discussing insulation is the *R*-value, or *resistance* of a material. Resistance is the number of hours needed for 1 Btu to pass through 1 ft^2 of a material of a given thickness when the temperature differential is 1°F. Resistance is the reciprocal of conductance. The lower a material's *k*-value or *C*-value, the better its insulating qualities, and higher *R*-values indicate a better insulating value.

Another rating method for foam insulation products is *long-term thermal resistance* (LTTR). It has been found that the thermal resistance of foam insulation changes over time due to changes in cell gas composition caused by the diffusion of air into the foam cells and the diffusion of blowing agents out of the cells. This is sometimes called *thermal drift*. LTTR is the thermal resistance value of a closed-cell foam insulation product measured after storage for five years under prescribed laboratory conditions. This has been shown to be the equivalent to the time-weighted average resistance value over a 15-year service condition. Standard test methods apply to polyisocyanurate, extruded polystyrene, and sprayed polyurethane. The LTTR value is the one that should be used for heat transfer calculations and is the one commonly found in insulation product literature.

TYPES OF BUILDING INSULATION

The following sections describe several types of insulation used to control heat transfer by conduction, convection, and radiation. Types of insulation and their *R*-values are shown in Table 27.2. Also included are *R*-values for some common materials for comparison.

Loose-Fill Insulation

Loose-fill insulation is produced as shreds, granules, or nodules and can be poured or blown into spaces to be insulated. Loose-fill insulation is used in places where it is difficult to install other types of insulation, such as in the cells of concrete block walls, plumbing chases, and attics. It is also widely used in retrofit applications because it can be blown into wall and ceiling cavities where other types of insulation cannot be installed without great difficulty.

This type of insulation can be made from a variety of materials: mineral wool, cellulose, cotton, fiberglass, perlite, and vermiculite. All loose-fill insulation will settle after installation. Cellulose settles about 20%, while rock wool and fiberglass only settle about 2% to 4%. Care must also be taken when installing thick layers in ceilings because too heavy of a load will cause ceiling drywall to sag. For example, the use of cellulose or rock wool is not recommended in ceilings with $1^1/_2$ in wallboard on 24 in centers. All loose-fill insulations require installation of a vapor retarder or vapor barrier.

Mineral wool is a generic term for two types of product: rock wool and slag wool. *Rock wool* is manufactured by melting basalt or other rocks in a high-temperature furnace and then spinning the molten material into long fibers. Binding agents and other materials are added through various manufacturing processes to give the desired properties. *Slag wool* is manufactured from iron ore blast furnace slag using similar production methods. Slag wool accounts for about 80% of the products produced by the mineral wool industry. It is formed into batts, blankets, and loose-fill material, and is used in applications similar to those of fiberglass.

The EPA recommends that rock wool insulation contain at least 50% recovered material. Most manufacturers use from 50% to 95% recycled material, with about 75% postindustrial content being average.

Cellulose insulation is made from 80% to 100% recycled paper combined with a fire-retardant additive. For loose-fill applications, a binder is added to prevent settling. Cellulose is used for loose-fill attic insulation as well as dry blown-in and wet-spray applications.

Table 27.2
R-Values for Insulation

insulation type	*R*-value/in (ft^2-hr-°F/Btu)
loose fill	
cellulose	3.2–3.8
fiberglass	2.2–2.7
perlite	2.3–2.7
rock wool	3.0–3.3
vermiculite	2.1
batts	
fiberglass, low density	3.1–3.5
fiberglass high density	4.3
mineral wool	3.5
boards	
polyisocyanurate	5.6–7.7 (LTTR)*
polyurethane (2.0 lbm/ft^3)	6.5 (LTTR)
expanded polystyrene	3.8–4.4 (LTTR)
extruded polystyrene	5.0 (LTTR)
sprayed foam	
polyurethane	5.0–7.0
polyicynene	3.6–4.0
soy-based polyurethane	3.7
sprayed fiber	
cellulose	3.5
fiberglass	3.0
rock wool	2.7
straw (loose)	1.4–2.0
straw bales	2.4–3.0
structural insulated panels	4.0–6.0
autoclaved aerated concrete	1.1
common building materials	
air, vertical, still with two reflective surfaces	1.39
brick	0.12–0.10
concrete	0.10–0.05
wood, Douglas fir-larch	1.06–0.99

Source: U.S. Department of Energy, Office of Energy Efficiency and Renewable Energy
*LTTR: long-term thermal resistance

The high recycled content of cellulose insulation and its low embodied energy are its main environmental benefits. There have been concerns about the dust generated during installation and the possible toxicity of some types of fire retardant treatments. However, with proper installation methods, detailing to isolate the insulation from interior spaces, and proper ventilation systems, dust and fibers are not a problem. A low-dust cellulose is available, and some manufacturers offer products that use only all-borate fire retardants, which are considered nontoxic.

Cotton insulation is made from pre-consumer recycled cotton denim scrap material with a small amount of polyester added for binding and stability. It is made in both loose-fill and batt forms. Low-toxicity borates are added as a fire retardant. Cotton insulation has a very high recycled content and requires very little energy to manufacture. Cotton batts have an *R*-value from 3.0 to 3.5 per inch.

Fiberglass insulation is produced by melting sand and recycled glass and spinning the product into thin fibers, which are held together with a binder. Fiberglass is sometimes used as loose fill, but is more commonly formed into batts, with or without a paper facing. In batt form, the insulation is placed between studs, between floor or roof joists, and in other cavities.

Fiberglass commonly contains about 30% recycled glass, and up to 90% recycled content is possible. There has been some concern that the fibers may be carcinogenic, but no long-term damage has been demonstrated. A small amount of formaldehyde is typically used in the binder, which has also raised concern; formaldehyde-free fiberglass is available.

Perlite insulation is an expanded form of a naturally occurring siliceous volcanic rock. It is manufactured in various densities from 2 lbm/ft^3 to 15 lbm/ft^3 and in different forms, including loose-fill insulation, board insulation, aggregate in lightweight concrete, and as a component in acoustical ceiling tiles. Its most common form is as loose fill used in hollow concrete unit masonry walls and between masonry walls. It is also used as insulation under floating concrete floors.

Vermiculite is a hydrated laminar magnesium-aluminum-iron silicate. When heated during processing, it forms small wormlike pieces. Although it is a fairly good insulating material, some vermiculite may contain asbestos. See Chap. 13 for information on vermiculite as a hazardous material.

Batt Insulation

Batt insulation consists of fibrous material placed on or within a kraft paper carrier. This material is usually mineral fiber or glass fiber. In addition to providing a means of installation and holding the insulation in place, the kraft paper also serves as a vapor retarder. Some batt insulation also comes with a reflective surface. Batts that have a flame-resistant facing are available for use in basement walls where the insulation will be left exposed.

Batts come in standard widths designed to fit within stud and joist spacings of 16 in or 24 in on center. It is either friction fitted or attached by stapling the paper flanges to the studs. Various thicknesses are available to suit the size of the cavity and the *R*-value needed.

Plastic fiber insulation, or polyester, is made from recycled plastic (PET) milk bottles and formed into batts similar to high-density fiberglass. It has about 50% recycled content but is fairly energy-intensive to manufacture. Polyester batts have an *R*-value of about 3.7 per inch, similar to fiberglass.

Board Insulation

Board insulation is made from a variety of organic or inorganic materials formed into rigid boards. Organic board insulation is made from wood, cane fiber, or straw sandwiched between coatings of bituminous material, paper, foil, or other materials. Rigid boards can also be made with perlite or cork. However, organic board insulation has given way to inorganic plastics, which have much higher insulating values—about two to three times greater than most other insulating materials of the same thickness. Inorganic board insulation is made from molded expanded polystyrene, extruded expanded polystyrene, polyisocyanurate, or polyurethane.

Originally polystyrene foams, polyisocyanurate, and polyurethane foams were made with CFCs as the blowing agent. CFCs were phased out in 1996 and replaced, in many instances, with HCFCs. However, HCFCs also cause depletion of the ozone layer. Under provisions of the Clean Air Act of 1990, the production and importation into the United States of many HCFCs with the greatest ozone depletion potential was banned, effective January 1, 2003. This included HCFC-141b. Two blowing agents often used as replacements are hydrocarbon (HC) and carbon dioxide (CO_2).

Expanded polystyrene (EPS) is a closed-cell material manufactured by mixing unexpanded polystyrene beads containing liquid pentane and a blowing agent. The mixture is heated to expand the beads, which are then injected into a mold to form a foam block. EPS (or *beadboard* as it is sometimes called) is manufactured in various densities for roofing and wall insulation. These densities range from 0.7 lbm/ft^3 to 3.0 lbm/ft^3, with 1.0 lbm/ft^3 being the density most commonly used for insulation. The spaces between the beads can absorb water, so a vapor retarder is needed if moisture migration is a concern.

Polystyrene is manufactured from petrochemicals. Polystyrene has more embodied energy per insulating unit than polyisocyanurate, fiberglass, cellulose, and mineral wool. However, it is manufactured without ozone-depleting chemicals and continues to be a flexible insulation product with a high *R*-value. It can be made with recycled material, though this is uncommon.

Extruded polystyrene (XPS) is a closed-cell material manufactured by mixing polystyrene pellets with various chemicals and then introducing a blowing agent. The resulting mass is forced through an extruder, where atmospheric pressure causes the mass to expand. Densities range from 1.4 lbm/ft^3 to 3.0 lbm/ft^3. Although more expensive than EPS, XPS foams have a higher insulative value per unit thickness and a higher compressive strength than EPS. XPS is used for residential sheathing and wall, foundation, and roof insulation. Because of its superior resistance to water absorption, XPS is the only insulation recommended for protected membrane roof systems and below-grade insulation.

Polystyrene has more embodied energy per insulating unit than polyisocyanurate, fiberglass, cellulose, and mineral wool.

The advantages of XPS are countered by some environmental disadvantages. Petroleum products are needed for its manufacture, and the blowing agent contains ozone-depleting chemicals and can outgas styrene monomer. The blowing agent most used, HCFC-14b, is hydrochlorofluorocarbon based, and the United States and other countries began phasing out its production and importation in 2010. Some European manufacturers have switched to other blowing agents. Polystyrene can be recycled, but few manufacturers do this.

Polyisocyanurate insulation (commonly referred to as *polyiso*) is manufactured by combining liquid isocyanate and polyol with catalysts and additives. A blowing agent expands the material into a closed-cell structure, which is then laminated between engineered facing materials. Polyisocyanurate insulation can also be blown in place. It is used in rigid boards for above-grade applications in roof and wall assemblies. Because it can readily absorb moisture, it is not suitable for below-grade uses except on the inside of foundation walls.

Like polystyrene, polyisocyanurate requires petroleum products in its manufacture. However, the hydrocarbon-based blowing agent used to expand it has no ozone depletion potential and no global warming potential. Polyisocyanurate also makes use of recycled materials, including PET from beverage bottles. The EPA recommends that polyisocyanurate rigid foam insulation contain at least 9% recovered material.

Polyurethane is a closed-cell foam made to a density of 2 lbm/ft^3. Most polyurethane foams are made without the use of HCFCs and have an *R*-value ranging from 6.5 ft^2-hr-°F/Btu to 7 ft^2-hr-°F/Btu. These types of foam boards are more expensive than the other foam boards.

Sprayed Foam Insulation

Sprayed foam insulation uses polyurethane or polyicynene as the base material. The components of the foam are delivered in two separate tanks and are mixed at the spray head, at which time they react immediately and expand to produce low-density foam that adheres to the cavity. Sprayed foam has an excellent *R*-value with the added advantages of conforming to the shape of the cavity and sealing all cracks and openings thoroughly.

Spray polyurethane insulation is a foam plastic that is applied in the liquid state. It rapidly expands to 30 to 50 times its original volume and cures to a solid form. The foam's density, amount of expansion, and water-resistant properties can vary by adjusting the proportions of the component materials. As the material foams, it expands to fill all spaces and acts as an effective air barrier. Polyurethane insulation is also made in rigid foam boards, which can be laminated with a variety of facings.

Spray polyurethane is available in either closed-cell or open-cell form. Closed-cell foams have higher densities and higher *R*-values, but some manufacturers still use an ozone-depleting blowing agent. Open-cell foams have lower *R*-values and lower densities, but the blowing agent is water and carbon dioxide, which make them more environmentally friendly.

While petrochemicals are required to manufacture polyurethane insulation, and some offgassing occurs, these insulation products are relatively sustainable when considering their high insulating and air-sealing properties.

Low-density foam is used to insulate open wall cavities, but because the foam expands so much, it must be sheared to be flush with the face of the wall studs before finish materials are applied. High-density foams are often used for roof insulation and can effectively cover gaps and roof structure to prevent thermal bridging, while providing a base with high compressive strength for the roofing material.

While petrochemicals are required to manufacture polyurethane insulation, and some offgassing occurs, these insulation products are relatively sustainable when considering their high insulating and air-sealing properties. The EPA recommends that polyurethane foam-in-place insulation contain at least 5% recovered material.

Icynene is a brand name for a water-based, HCFC-free, low-density, open-cell polyurethane insulation. When sprayed into open wall or ceiling cavities, it expands to about 100 times its original volume and cures to a soft foam. It adheres to other building materials and maintains its *R*-value over time. A different formulation is available that can be used in closed cavities for retrofitting. This formulation expands less only in the area of least resistance to prevent damage to walls and structure while filling the cavity.

Cementitious foam insulation, made by one manufacturer, consists of magnesium oxychloride cement, water, compressed air, and an expanding agent. The insulation is sprayed into closed cavities such as walls and concrete masonry units. It is fireproof, mold resistant, and nontoxic and contains no flame retardants, formaldehyde, or other VOCs. It has an *R*-value of 3.9 hr-ft2-°F/Btu and its manufacturer has claimed it could have an *R*-value even higher.

The IBC requires spray-applied foam insulation products to be separated from the interior of the building with an approved thermal barrier, such as $^1/_2$ in thick gypsum wallboard.

Sprayed Fiber Insulation

Sprayed fiber insulation consists of fibers of cellulose, glass, or rock wool mixed with an adhesive and a small amount of water to activate the adhesive. As with sprayed foam insulation, sprayed fiber insulation completely fills the cavities where it is installed and does a better job of filling voids than batt insulation. Because the adhesive binds the fibers to each other and to the cavity walls, this type of insulation does not settle as loose-fill types do. However, because of the moisture in the spray mixture, sprayed fiber insulation must be allowed to dry thoroughly before being enclosed with gypsum wallboard or other finishes. This can take from a few days to several weeks, depending on the type of insulation, its moisture content, and the humidity when it was applied.

Cellulose is the most commonly used type of sprayed fiber insulation. Fibers from recycled cardboard and newspaper are combined with a fire retardant. Fiberglass sprayed-on insulation is also known as a *blow-in-blanket system* (BIBS) and is the second most common type of sprayed fiber. It does not prevent air infiltration as well as sprayed cellulose does. Rock wool is commonly used for commercial building thermal insulation as well as fireproofing.

Radiant Barriers and Reflective Insulation

A *radiant barrier* is a single sheet of highly reflective material, usually aluminum, that faces an open air space. It reduces the passage of thermal radiation, most often by blocking summer heat gain, but sometimes to help retain winter heat. To block heat gain, a radiant barrier is placed on the outside of conventional thermal insulation, such as on top of attic insulation. Heat radiated from the hot roof deck is reflected back toward the roof, reducing the heat that would normally strike the top of the thermal insulation. To block heat loss, the reflective barrier would have to face the heated side of the insulation. When a radiant barrier is combined with a backing of insulation it is called *reflective insulation.*

Reflective surfaces have two properties that make them good for insulation. The first is *reflectivity* (also called *reflectance*), which is a measure of how much radiant heat is reflected by the material. This is a number between zero and one; sometimes it is given as a percentage between 0% and 100%. When a material has a reflectivity of 0.8, it means that 80% of the radiant energy striking the material is reflected. The second property is *emissivity* (also called *emittance*), which is a measure of how much energy is emitted. All materials give off, or emit, energy by thermal radiation as a result of their temperature. Emissivity is also measured on a scale of zero to one. For opaque materials, the sum of the reflectivity and the emissivity is one.

To be effective radiant barriers must have a minimum reflectivity of 0.9 and a maximum emissivity of 0.1, and they must face a ventilated air space. Some radiant barriers are manufactured with corrugations or folds that automatically provide air space.

Insulated Concrete Forms

Insulated concrete forms (ICF) are systems of interlocking foam insulation blocks or panels that serve as forms for pouring concrete walls and that remain in place after the concrete has cured. The foam greatly increases the insulation value of the wall, serves as a backing for gypsum wallboard finish on the inside, and provides a base for sheathing and exterior finish on the outside. Building codes require that a fire-resistant material be used to cover the inside layer of foam; generally $^1/_2$ in drywall is acceptable. Although ICFs are typically used for foundation walls, they can be used for the entire wall structure from the footings to the roof.

The foam used for the blocks is typically extruded polystyrene (XPS) and comes in a variety of configurations, from preformed interlocking blocks to large panels that are held in place with plastic ties. Reinforcing steel is installed before the concrete is poured.

Structural Insulated Panels

Structural insulated panels (SIPs) are composite building units consisting of two outer skins bonded to an inner core of rigid insulating material, most commonly expanded polystyrene (EPS). Approximate R-values for SIPs (including OSB on each side) range from *R*-17 for a $3^5/_8$ in core to *R*-34 for a $7^3/_8$ in core. Refer to Chap. 25 for more information on SIPs.

Sustainability Issues

As with other building materials, the sustainability of insulation involves consideration of its raw material acquisition, manufacture, use in place, and disposal or recycling potential. However, its primary purpose of slowing the transfer of heat is the most important environmental consideration. The long-term energy savings provided by insulation generally outweigh the disadvantages that any particular product may have.

From the standpoint of sustainability, no insulation material is perfect; each has advantages and disadvantages. When other factors are considered—including required *R*-value, physical form, cost, water resistance, installation method, combustibility, vapor permeance, and others—the best insulation for the application may not be the most environmentally sound. Insulation technology is constantly changing, however, and many of the environmentally detrimental aspects of insulation are being overcome with new materials and manufacturing techniques. Refer to Chap. 13 for a discussion of other sustainability issues.

SHINGLES AND ROOFING TILE

Shingles and tiles are two of the oldest types of roofing materials. They both consist of small, individual pieces of material placed in an overlapping fashion on a sloped surface in order to shed water.

Types of Roofs

Roofs are classified according to their shape. Some of the more common types are illustrated in Fig. 27.5, along with the common terms used to describe the various parts.

The slope of a roof is designated by its *pitch*, which is the ratio of *rise* (change in height) to *run* (change in horizontal distance). The rise is given first, and 12 (the number of inches in a foot) is used as the run. For example, a roof with a 5:12 pitch rises 5 in vertically for every foot (12 in) of horizontal distance.

Not all roofing materials are appropriate for all pitches, although the exact pitch for a material used may affect how the roofing is detailed and installed. For example, low-slope roofs for asphalt shingles require a double layer of roofing felt over the entire surface of the roof rather than the normal single layer. Some general guidelines are given in Table 27.3. When describing size, estimating, and ordering roofing materials, roofing area is referred to in squares. A square is equal to 100 ft^2.

Shingles

Shingles are small units, rectangular or in other shapes, that are intended to shed water rather than form a watertight seal. Asphalt or fiberglass shingles are made from a composition of felt, asphalt or fiberglass, mineral stabilizers, and mineral granules. They are available in a variety of colors and shapes and are laid over an asphalt-impregnated roofing felt that is nailed to solid wood sheathing.

Most wood shingles are manufactured from cedar, and they are available in a variety of grades, with no. 1, blue label, being the best. Some wood shingles have smooth, sawn surfaces; those that are manufactured by hand splitting, creating a rough, irregular surface, are also called *shakes*.

A typical installation is shown in Fig. 27.6. Wood shingles are laid over spaced sheathing so that they can breathe without a buildup of moisture.

Wood shingles are laid so that only a certain portion of each shingle is visible. The visible portion is called the *exposure*, and its dimension will vary with the pitch of the roof. The edges of shingles are staggered so that joints do not coincide. 30 lbm asphalt felt is used as an underlayment.

Roofing Tile

Roofing tile may be made from slate, clay, or concrete. Because each type of tile is heavy (10 lbm/ft^2 or more), the roof structure must be sized accordingly. Tile should be used only on roofs with slopes of 4 in/ft or greater.

Slate tile is made by splitting quarried slate into rectangular pieces from 6 in to 14 in wide and from 16 in to 24 in long. Slate tile is about $^1/_4$ in thick. It is laid over 30 lbm asphalt-saturated roofing felt on wood or nailable concrete decking. Slate tiles are laid like shingles, with sides and ends overlapping, and are attached with copper or galvanized nails driven through prepunched holes in the slate. Slate is a very expensive roofing material, but it is fire resistant and very durable; most slate roofs last over 100 years.

Clay tile, available in many colors, patterns, and textures, is made from the same clay as brick and can be formed into various shapes. Like slate, it is laid on roofing felt over a sloped wood or nailable deck and is attached by nailing through prepunched holes. Like slate, clay tile is expensive, but very durable, fire resistant, and attractive. Some of the available shapes are shown in Fig. 27.7.

Concrete tile, manufactured from portland cement and fine aggregates, is available in several styles, some flat and others formed to look like clay or slate tiles. It is also available in several colors. Concrete tile is less expensive than clay tile, but it is still durable and fire resistant.

PREFORMED ROOFING AND SIDING

Sheet Metal Roofing

Sheet metal roofing is durable and attractive, and it can conform to a wide variety of roof shapes. Its disadvantages include high cost and the difficulty of installing it properly.

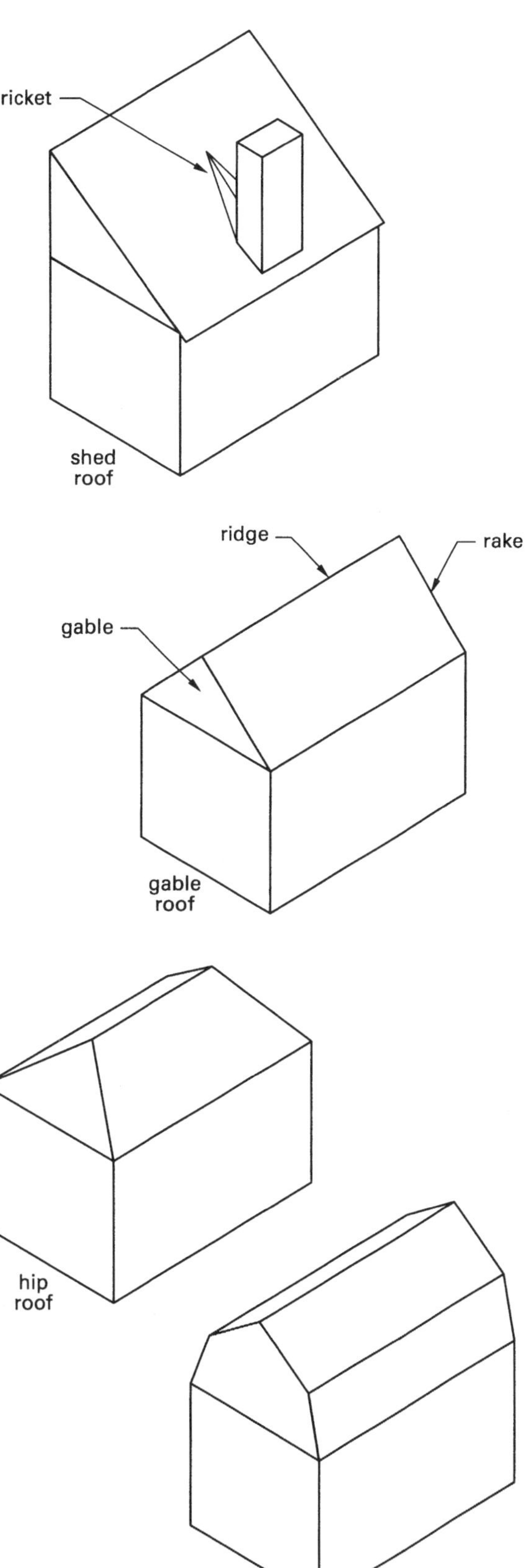

Figure 27.5
Roof Types

Project Planning

Table 27.3
Recommended Slopes for Roofing

roofing type	slope—vertical rise (in/ft) min.	max.
asphalt shingles, low slopes	2	4
asphalt shingles, normal	4	12
asphalt roll roofing	1	4
wood shingles	4	—
clay tile	4	—
slate tile	4	—
metal roofing	3	—
built-up roofing	1/4	1
single-ply membranes (varies with type and method of attachment)	1/4	6

Figure 27.6
Wood Shingle Installation

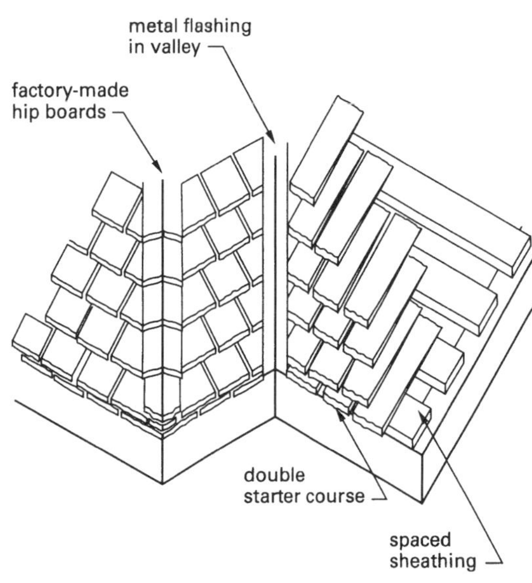

Figure 27.7
Clay Roofing Tile Profiles

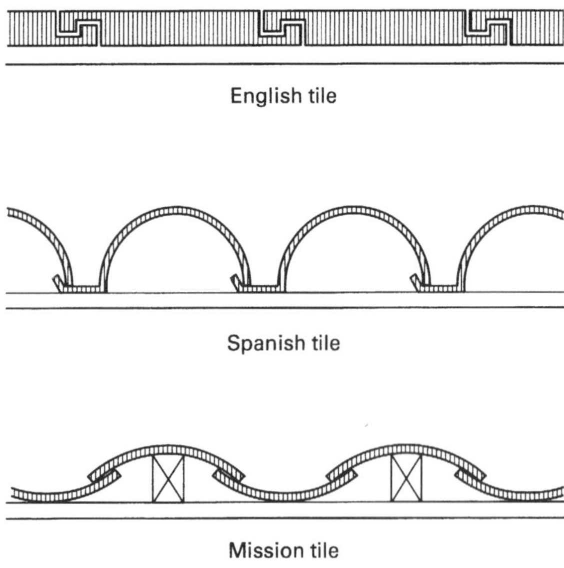

Metals commonly used for roofing include copper, galvanized iron, aluminum, and terneplate. *Terneplate* is steel sheet that has been coated to resist corrosion; the coating is of *terne*, an alloy of tin and either lead or zinc. Lead has been used in terne since the early nineteenth century, but it has largely been replaced by zinc since the late 1990s because of environmental concerns. Terne-coated stainless steel is also available.

Copper is a popular roofing material because of its long life and the attractive green patina that forms after a few years of weathering. A wide variety of necessary roofing accessories, such as gutters, flashing, and downspouts, are also available in copper.

Other metals that are sometimes used for roofing include uncoated stainless steel, aluminum, zinc, tin, and lead. Stainless steel is expensive but very durable and maintenance free.

Sheet metal roofs are made of individual sheets of metal joined with interlocking joints that are fabricated in the field. Because these metals have high coefficients of expansion, these joints and other parts of the roofing system must be designed to allow for expansion and contraction. The minimum slope for metal roofs is 3 in/ft.

Most metal roofs are installed over asphalt roofing felt, which is laid on top of wood or nailable concrete decking. However, tin can react with asphalt, so for roofs of tin or terneplate, the asphalt felt is replaced with rosin-sized paper.

In most cases, standing seams are made parallel to the slope of the roof and crimped tight. Flat seams are made perpendicular the standing seams and soldered. These connect two pieces of metal along the slope of the roof, as shown in Fig. 27.8.

The roofing is held to the sheathing or decking with metal cleats attached the roof and spaced about 12 in apart. Continuous cleats are often used at the eaves, rakes (gable ends), and flashing. In all cases, cleats, nails, and other fasteners must be of the same type of metal as the roofing material to avoid galvanic action.

Preformed Roof and Wall Panels

Preformed panels for roofs and walls can be simple, shaped pieces of corrugated or fluted metal, or assemblies of two finished metal faces with insulation between them. These panels are self-supporting and span intermediate supports; roof panels span purlins, and wall panels span horizontal girts.

The simpler panels are available in standard widths and lengths. These are assembled by lapping one corrugation at the edges and overlapping the ends. Common widths include 24 in, 30 in, and 36 in; other widths are available.

The sandwich assemblies are fabricated in lengths to match the requirements of the particular job. They are joined with interlocking edges and a weather seal. When used as wall panels in one-story buildings, they usually reach from the foundation to the roof framing.two panels must be placed end to end, they are butt-jointed with flashing between.

Preformed panels are available made from aluminum, galvanized steel, or porcelain enameled steel. They are attached to framing with screws, clips, or proprietary fasteners. They are durable, easy and quick to install, and do not require on-site finishing. For industrial buildings and some other types of structures, a sandwich panel can serve as the interior finish as well as the exterior finish if local and energy codes are satisfied. Preformed panels are most economical when used on large, flat, unbroken expanses of walls or roofs.

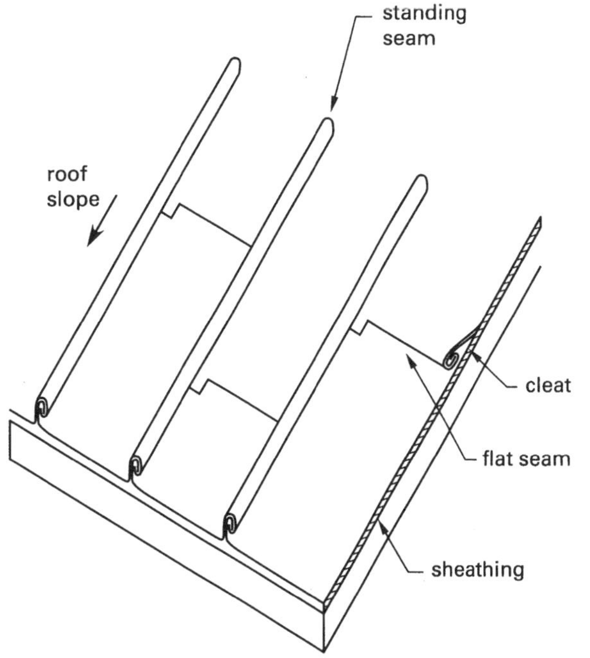

Figure 27.8 Standing Seam Metal Roof

MEMBRANE ROOFING

Membrane roofing includes solid, membrane-like materials that are applied in thin sheets to nearly flat roofs, as well as products applied in liquid form that can be used with any roof slope. Although some manufacturers claim that their products are suitable for completely flat roofs, every roof should have at least a $^1/_4$ in/ft slope over its entire surface with the slopes directing water to the roof drainage system, in order to avoid standing water and the possibility of ponding. Steeper slopes (up to $^1/_2$:12) may be recommended in certain areas or at crickets to direct water around obstructions or penetrations in the roof.

Ponding occurs when standing water causes a flat roof to deflect, allowing water to collect. This causes more deflection, which allows even more water to collect. The process continues until the roof fails.

Common types of membrane roofing include

- built-up bituminous roofing
- single-ply roofing
- elastic liquid roofing

Built-Up Bituminous Roofing

Built-up roofing consists of several overlapping layers of bituminous-saturated roofing felts cemented together with roofing cement. The bituminous material can be either asphalt or coal-tar pitch. The basic construction of such a roof is illustrated in Fig. 27.9.

A built-up roof can be installed over either a nailable or a non-nailable deck. For a nailable deck, a base sheet of unsaturated felt is nailed to the deck and covered with a coating of roofing cement. For a non-nailable deck, the base sheet is omitted and a base coat of roofing cement is applied.

Project Planning

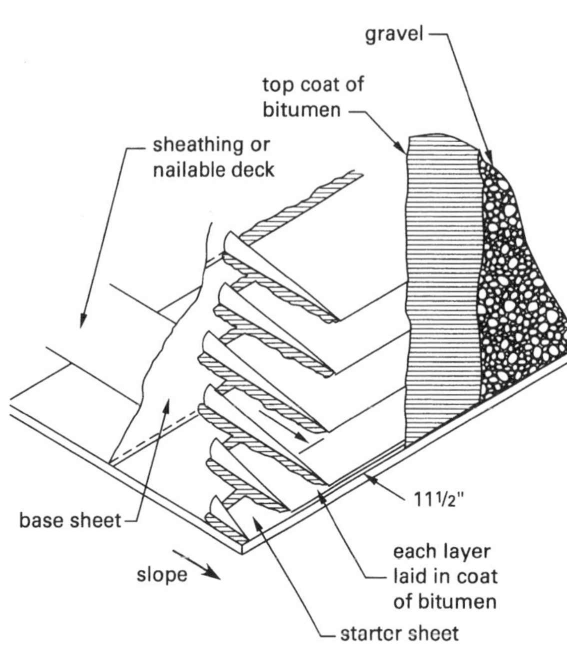

Figure 27.9
Three-Ply Built-Up Roof

Three to five layers of saturated roofing felt are then laid on top of each other, each layer bedded in roofing cement so that felt does not touch felt. The number of layers is determined by the type of deck used and the length of guarantee period desired. Five-ply roofs provide the most protection. A final coating of bituminous material is placed over the entire roof and covered with gravel or crushed slag. The gravel protects the roofing from sunlight and other effects of weathering.

A variation of the built-up roof is the *inverted membrane roof.* The built-up roof is placed on the structural decking and rigid, closed-cell insulation is placed on top of the membrane rather than under it. The insulation is held down with gravel ballast. This type of construction protects the membrane from the effects of expansion and contraction, drying, ultraviolet rays, and foot traffic, all of which can cause leaks.

Construction Details for Built-Up Roofing

As with any roof, a built-up roof must be designed to provide for positive drainage. The minimum roof slope should be $^1/_4$ in/ft. Nearly flat membrane roofs may be drained to interior drains, perimeter drains, or gutters on the low side of the roof.

Crickets should be used to provide positive drainage in all directions. A *cricket* is a saddle-shaped projection on a sloping roof used to divert water around an obstacle such as a chimney. When a roof is surrounded on four sides with a parapet or walls, there should be *scuppers* (also called *overflow drains*) through the parapet, positioned with their low edges slightly above the top of the roof to provide a secondary means of drainage should the primary drains become clogged. Crickets and scuppers are usually required by building codes.

At the intersection of the roof and any vertical surface such as a wall or parapet, continuous flashing must be provided. For built-up roofs, this intersection should be eased with a triangular cant strip so the felts do not have to be bent at a 90° angle and to provide positive drainage away from the joint. See Fig. 27.10. Single-ply elastomeric roofs can use flashing bent at a 90° angle.

When objects project through a roof, or when roof-mounted equipment needs to be supported, the intersection of the roofing and these projections must be waterproofed. One traditional way to do this is to provide a *pitch pan,* a small metal enclosure around the projection that is filled with bituminous material. The pitch pan, however, is usually not recommended because of its tendency to leak. Projections should be treated like other joints and installed with cant strips and flashing. Roof-mounted equipment should be placed on wood curbs that are likewise flashed.

Single-Ply Roofing

The quality of a built-up roofing system is largely dependent on proper installation, which is labor intensive. For this reason, single-ply roofing has come into widespread use. *Single-ply roofing* is a single-membrane layer of any of various types of materials. Although this layer must be applied carefully, there are fewer installation problems than with built-up roofing. Single-ply roofing is also more resistant to limited building movement and the damaging effects of the weather.

There are several types of single-ply membranes. *Modified bitumens* are sheets about 50 mils thick that are composed of *bitumen,* a chemical additive to enhance the elastic properties of the bitumen, and a reinforcing fabric to add tensile strength. The bitumen sheet is laid over insulation, or over an insulating deck with a separator sheet between the deck and the membrane. The separator sheets allow the roof to move independently of the structure, and some are designed to allow water vapor from the building to escape to the perimeter of the roof. To anchor the membrane and protect it from ultraviolet degradation, the surface is covered with gravel ballast.

The quality of a built-up roofing systems is largely dependent on proper installation, which is labor intensive. For this reason, single-ply roofing has come into widespread use.

Other types of membranes fall into two categories: thermoset plastics and thermoplastics. When *thermoset plastics* are cured by being subjected to heat, they harden into a permanent shape. Once they have set, if they are heated they will char rather than melt again, so they cannot be remolded. On the other hand, *thermoplastic materials*, also called *thermoplastics*, can be repeatedly softened by heating and hardened by cooling, so they can be remolded. Thermoset roofing materials include EPDM and CSPE. Thermoplastic roofing materials include PVC and TPO, as well as various hybrid blends.

Ethylene propylene diene monomer (EPDM) roofing is a thermoset plastic membrane manufactured in thicknesses of 0.045 in and 0.060 in. It has excellent resistance to weathering, heat, and fatigue, but is only available in black. Because it is a thermoset material, seams of EPDM roofing must be sealed with adhesive or pressure-sensitive tape. EPDM can be installed loose and covered with ballast, fully adhered with adhesive, mechanically fastened, or used in a protected membrane roof system. EPDM is one of the most common types of single-ply membrane roofing materials.

Chlorosulfonated polyethylene (CSPE), trademarked as Hypalon, is highly resistant to weathering and is available in white. As a roofing material, it is applied fully adhered. However, CSPE roofing has generally been superseded by PVC and TPO roofing.

Polyvinyl chloride (PVC) roofing is a thermoplastic membrane manufactured in thicknesses of 0.048 in, 0.060 in, and 0.072 in. PVC membranes have excellent resistance to weathering (including hail), are easy to install, and are relatively inexpensive. PVC tends to be more resistant to animal fats and other types of oils than other membranes. It loses flexibility over time, so many manufacturers add a resin called *ketone ethylene ester* (KEE), trademarked as Elvaloy, to the material; this helps maintain flexibility permanently. Seams are heat welded. PVC can be installed loose and covered with ballast, fully adhered with adhesive, mechanically fastened, or used as a part of a protected membrane roof system. It is available in white, tan, or gray. However, as mentioned in Chap. 13, PVC can cause environmental problems during manufacture and disposal.

Thermoplastic polyolefin (TPO) roofing is a type of single-ply membrane made with a blend of polypropylene and ethylene propylene. It can be installed loose and covered with ballast, fully adhered with adhesive, mechanically fastened, or used as a part of a protected membrane roof system. The mechanically attached system is used where high wind uplift is a concern and for reroofing applications. It is available in 45 mil, 60 mil, and 80 mil thicknesses. It has a lower installation cost than EPDM and can be ordered in a variety of colors, but white, tan, and gray are the most common.

Both PVC and TPO roofing materials are available in white, making them good choices for cool roof systems that minimize heat transfer into a building and the subsequent energy needed to cool it, as well as for minimizing the heat island effect. The *heat island effect* is the unnatural buildup of heat around buildings, especially in urban areas. Some jurisdictions such as California require the use of cool roofs to minimize interior heat gain and save energy. They can also help a building gain LEED credits. A new, white PVC or TPO roof will reflect approximately 78% of the radiant energy striking it, compared with about 6% for a black EPDM roof. This is ideal for climates where cooling demand outweighs heating demand. In northern areas of the country, however, where heating takes precedence over cooling, a white roof isn't necessarily the most energy efficient option.

Because PVC and TPO membranes are thermoplastics, they can be recycled for roofing, but thermoset membranes such as EPDM cannot be reused for roofing. To be recycled, EPDM roofing must be chopped up and mixed with another material to make another product, such as rubber flooring.

Figure 27.10 Metal Flashing Details

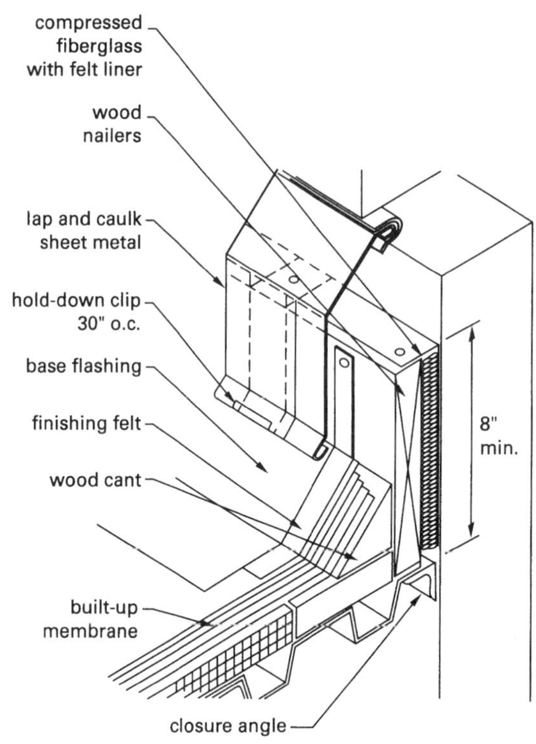

(a) metal flashing at parapet

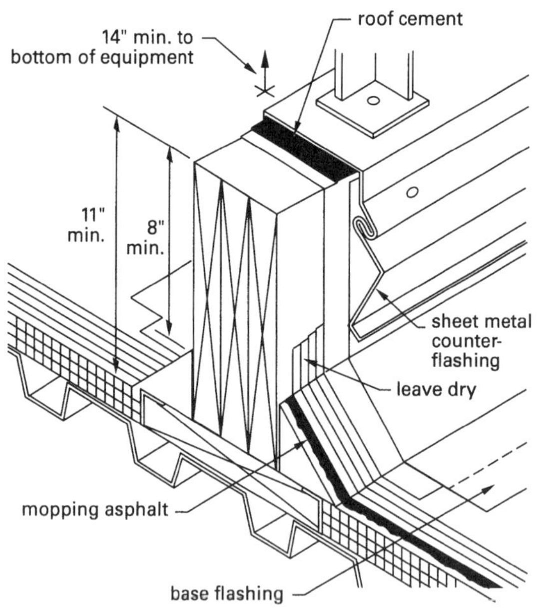

(b) metal flashing at equipment support

The commonly used single-ply membranes are available with or without reinforcing. The reinforcing is typically polyester fibers, but some products use glass fiber reinforcing. Reinforced membranes have more dimensional stability and tear strength than nonreinforced membranes, and they have better puncture and wind load resistance. Reinforcing also helps the roofing lie flat for easier seaming. Reinforced membranes are good choices where high wind conditions exist and where heavy foot traffic is expected. Reinforced membranes are required where the roof is fully adhered or mechanically attached. Nonreinforced membranes have a higher elongation factor, which is good for accommodating substrate movement and to bridge small gaps in the substrate. Nonreinforced membranes are less expensive and are suitable for loose-laid and ballasted roof systems and where larger sheets are wanted.

Elastic Liquid Roofing

Liquid-applied roofingmaterials include butyl, Neoprene, Hypalon, and other products. They are applied in liquid form in one or two coats by brushing or spraying and are air-cured to form an elastic, waterproof surface. Liquid-applied membranes are also used for below-grade waterproofing on foundation walls, tanks, and pools, and for similar applications. These products are particularly well-suited for roofs with complex shapes, such as thin-shell concrete domes.

FLASHING

Flashing prevents water penetration and directs any water that does get into construction back to the outside. Flashing is made of galvanized steel, stainless steel, aluminum, copper, plastic, and elastomeric materials. Material selection depends on the other metals or materials with which it comes in contact, the configuration of the joint, the durability desired, and the cost.

Flashing protects joints wherever water penetration is expected or where two dissimilar surfaces meet at an angle. This may include where roofs intersect parapets, above windows, above steel lintels supporting masonry, between butt joints of preformed siding, and elsewhere.

Figure 27.10 shows some common metal flashing details, and Fig. 27.11 illustrates flashing for single-ply roofing installations. A masonry flashing detail is shown in Fig. 23.5. In all cases, the flashing detail should allow joint movement without compromising the integrity of the flashing connection.

ROOF ACCESSORIES

Roof accessories include items needed to form a complete installation in addition to the roofing itself or flashing. Roof accessories include expansion joints, copings, roof hatches, smoke vents, and similar fabrications.

Expansion joints are needed in buildings to allow for movement caused by temperature changes in materials and differential movement between building sections. They are placed at frequent intervals in long buildings: about every 100 ft to 150 ft in masonry buildings, and about every 200 ft in concrete buildings. Expansion joints should also be located where the wall direction changes in T-, L-, and U-shaped buildings, and where a low building portion abuts a higher, heavier section.

Expansion joints are particularly important in roofs because of the extremes of temperature changes and because joints in the roof are exposed to the most severe weathering conditions. Figure 27.12 shows some typical roof expansion joints. Refer to Chap. 22 and Chap. 23 for a discussion of joints for concrete and masonry structures.

Smoke vents allow smoke to escape in the event of a fire. Exact requirements for smoke vent locations and sizes are given in the various model building codes, but in general these vents must be located in hazardous occupancies, in certain business occupancies over 50,000 ft^2, over stages, and above elevator shafts. Vents are designed to release automatically in the event of fire, usually by being spring loaded and connected to a fusible link.

Roof hatches allow access to the roof for maintenance personnel and are reached by means of ladders. *Copings* are protective caps, either metal or stone or other material, placed over parapets, pilasters, or other room penetrations to shed water.

CAULKING AND SEALANTS

Sealants are flexible materials used to close joints between materials. (*Caulking*, sometimes spelled *calking*, is often used to designate low-performance sealants employed where little movement is expected, such as between a wood window frame and an exterior wall.) A sealant must be capable of adhering to the materials on both sides of the joint while remaining elastic and weatherproof.

There are several types of sealants, each with slightly different properties and uses under various conditions. Sealants are classified as low, intermediate, and high performance, depending on the maximum amount of joint movement they can tolerate.

- low: ±5%
- intermediate: ±12.5%
- high: 25% or more

The width and depth of a sealant are important to its proper performance (see Fig. 27.13). The width is determined by the expected joint movement, the movement capability of the sealant, construction tolerances, and the temperature at which the sealant is applied. Joint movement may be caused by such factors as thermal expansion and contraction, moisture absorption of the materials being sealed (brick, for example), and the various forms of structural movement. Construction tolerances may include manufacturing, fabrication, and erection tolerances. Detailing a joint either too wide or too narrow for the movement capability of the joint can cause it to fail.

Figure 27.11 Elastomeric Flashing Details

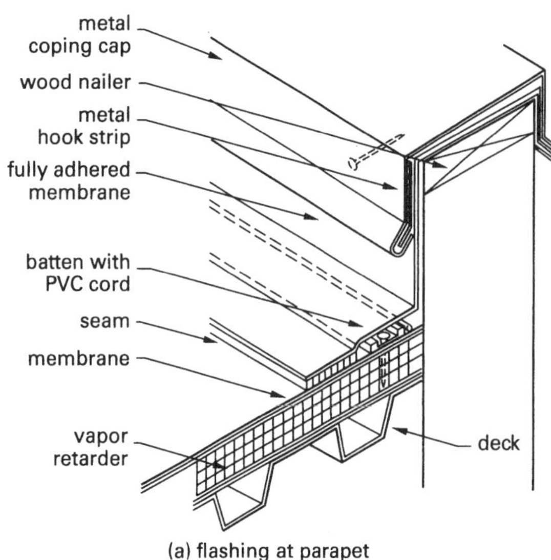

(a) flashing at parapet

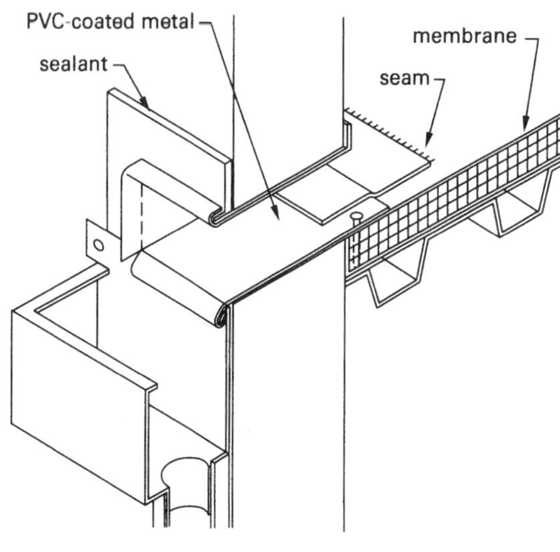

(b) flashing at scupper

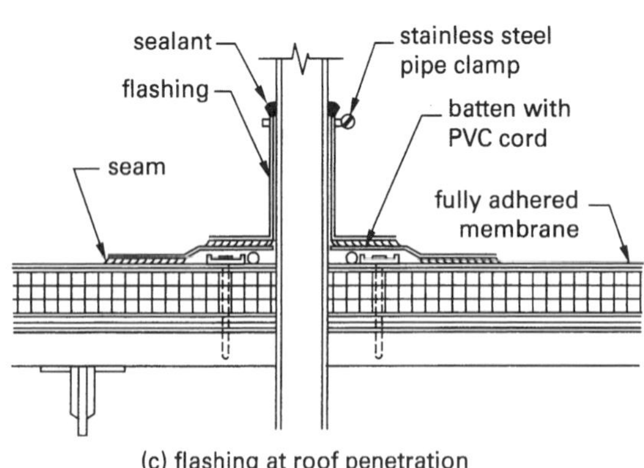

(c) flashing at roof penetration

The depth of the joint should be equal to the width for joints up to $\frac{1}{2}$ in wide; for joints from $\frac{1}{2}$ in to 1 in, the depth should be one-half the width. For wider joints, the sealant depth should not be greater than one-half the width, or as recommended by the manufacturer. Joint fillers are used behind the sealant to control the depth of the sealant. Table 27.4 lists some of the common sealant types and their properties.

EXTERIOR INSULATION AND FINISH SYSTEMS

An *exterior insulation and finish system* (EIFS) is a cladding assembly consisting of a wet-applied cementitious finish over a rigid insulation board that is attached to building sheathing. Although portland cement stucco is included in these types of finish systems, the coating consists of various types of polymers (usually acrylics) or a mixture of cement and polymers. The exact formulation of an EIFS varies with each manufacturer, but there are three classifications.

- Class PB: polymer based
- Class PM: polymer modified
- Class MB: mineral based

A polymer-based (PB) system uses expanded polystyrene insulation. The base coat is applied directly to the insulation with an embedded fiberglass mesh and has a high percentage of polymeric binder, which gives the system a great deal of flexibility. The finish coat consists of acrylic polymer, sand, pigments, and other additives.

A variation of the polymer-based system is the high-impact PB system, which is like the PB system but includes a heavy-duty fiberglass mesh and an additional layer of base coat.

A polymer-modified (PM) system uses extruded polystyrene insulation that is mechanically fastened to the building sheathing and structure along with the reinforcing mesh. The base coats of PM systems are thicker, from $^3/_{16}$ in to $^3/_8$ in, and include a higher percentage of portland cement than PB systems. As a result, control joints are needed in PM systems to limit cracking. These joints should be located from 10 ft to 12 ft apart with no section exceeding 150 ft^2 in area. The finish coat, like that of a PB system, consists of acrylic polymer, sand, pigments, and other additives. PM systems are more resistant to impact than standard PB systems, and the extruded polystyrene is more resistant to water penetration and has a higher thermal resistance than the expanded polystyrene.

A mineral-based (MB) system uses portland cement stucco in the traditional manner.

EIFS claddings were first developed as a barrier wall system that relied on the integrity of the exterior surface for moisture protection. Construction imperfections and minor cracks allowed water penetration and degradation of underlying materials, leading to a series of failures and associated lawsuits in the 1990s. Since that time, manufacturers have improved EIFS cladding by developing proprietary systems that use the rain screen principle to minimize the problem and, as a result, the use of EIFS systems is permitted under the IBC provided that it complies with code requirements. The modern products can also be used to provide continuous insulation on the outside of the sheathing, as well as serve as the exterior finish.

Figure 27.12
Expansion Joints

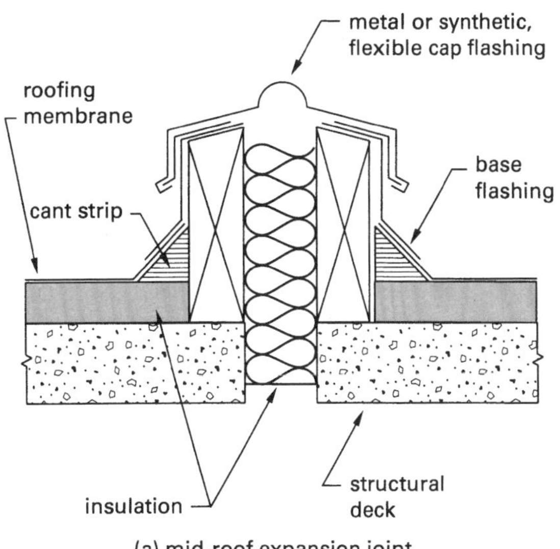

(a) mid-roof expansion joint

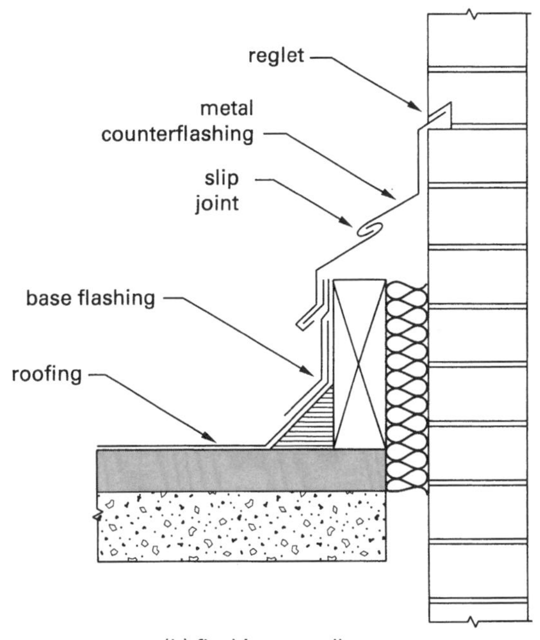

(b) flashing at wall

Figure 27.13
Typical Joint with Sealant

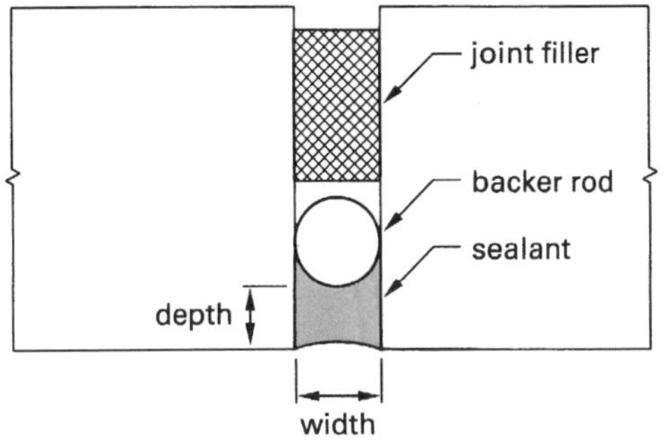

Project Planning

Table 27.4 Comparative Properties of Sealants

	sealant types								
	butyl	acrylic, water base	acrylic, solvent base	polysulfide, one part	polysulfide, two part	polyurethane, one part	polyurethane, two part	silicone	notes
recommended maximum joint movement (%)	7.5-10	12.5-25	12.5	25	25	25	50	50-100	(a)
life expectancy (years)	5-15	5-10	10-20	10-20	10-20	10-20+	10-20+	20+	
maximum joint width (in)	$\frac{3}{4}$	$\frac{3}{8}$	$\frac{3}{4}$	$\frac{3}{4}$	1	$\frac{3}{4}$	1-2	$\frac{3}{4}$	(b)
adhesion to:									
wood	•	•	•	•	•	•	•	•	(c)
metal	•	•	•	•	•	•	•	•	(c)
masonry/concrete	•	•	•	•	•	•	•	•	(c, g)
glass	•	•	•	•	•	•	•	•	(c)
plastic	•	•	•					•	
curing time (days)	120	5	14	14+	7	7+	3-50	2-14	(d, e)
shore A hardness	20-40	30-35	30-50	30-55	25-55	25-55	25-60	15-40	
self-leveling available	n/a		•	•	•		•	•	
non-sag available	n/a	•	•	•	•	•	•	•	
paintable?	No	Yes	Yes	Yes	Yes	Yes	Yes	No	(f)
resistance to: (see legend)									
ultraviolet	1-2	2-3	3-4	2	2-3	3	3	5	
cut/tear	2	1-2	1	3	3	4-5	4-5	1-2	
abrasion	2	1-2	1-2	1	1	3	3	1	
weathering	4-5	3-4	3-4	3	3	3-4	3-4	4-5	
oil/grease	1-2	2	3	3	3	3	3	2	
compression	2-3	1-2	1	2	2	4	4	4-5	
extension	1	1-2	1	1-2	1-2	4-5	4-5	4-5	

(a)Some high performance silicones have movement capabilities up to 200% extension and 75% compression. Verify with the manufacturer.
(b) Figures given are conservative. Verify manufacturers' literature for specific recommendations.
(c) Primer may be required.
(d) Cure time for low and medium modulus silicones to a tack-free condition is about 2 hours.
(e) Silicone sealants can be applied over a wide temperature range.
(f) Some silicones are field tintable or come in a variety of colors.
(g) Silicones may stain stone and masonry. Verify primer requirements and other limitations with the manufacturer.

Legend:
1 = Poor
2 = Fair
3 = Good
4 = Very good
5 = Excellent

DOORS, WINDOWS AND GLAZING

With the materials and construction systems available, doors and windows no longer serve simply to provide passage between spaces or admit light. Openings can be selectively designed and specified to fulfill particular functions. For example, a window can admit light but also reduce sound transmission while providing security. A door passage can be designed as an unobtrusive, clear opening while still providing fire protection in the event of an emergency.

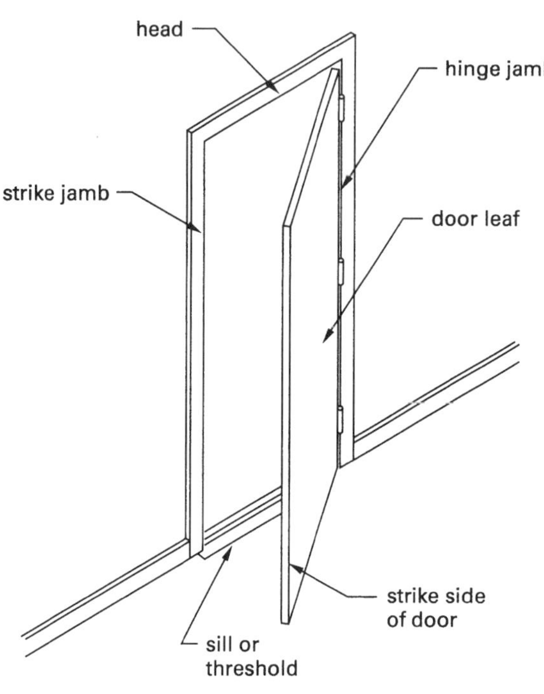

Figure 28.1
Parts of a Door

DOOR OPENINGS

Both metal doors and wood doors can control passage, provide visual and aural privacy, maintain security, supply fire resistance and weather protection, control light, and serve as radiation shielding. When selecting the most appropriate type of door, it is important to understand what kinds of control are needed. Considerations of durability, cost, appearance, ease of use, method of construction, and availability are also important.

There are three major components of a door system: the door itself, the frame, and the hardware. Each must be coordinated with the other components and be appropriate for the circumstances and the design intent. The common parts of a door opening are illustrated in Fig. 28.1. To differentiate the two jambs, the side where the hinge or pivot is installed is called the *hinge jamb*, and the jamb where the door closes is called the *strike side* or *strike jamb*.

The standard method of referring to the way a door swings is called the *door hand* or the *handing* of a door. Specifiers, hardware suppliers, and manufacturers use handing to indicate exactly what kind of hardware must be supplied for a specific opening. Some hardware will only work on a door that swings a particular way because of the way the strike side of the door is beveled. Hardware that can work on any hand of door is called *reversible* or *nonhanded*.

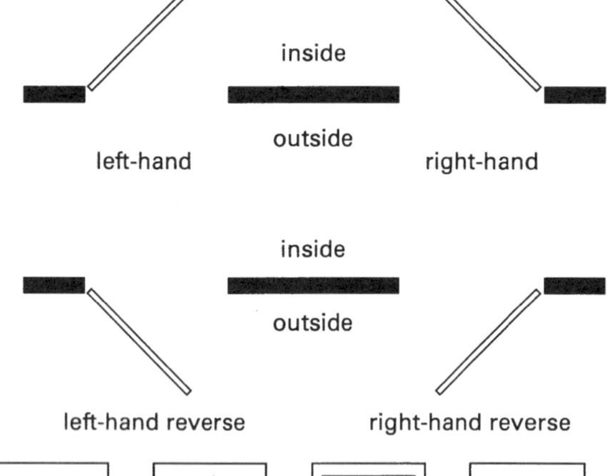

Figure 28.2
Door Handing

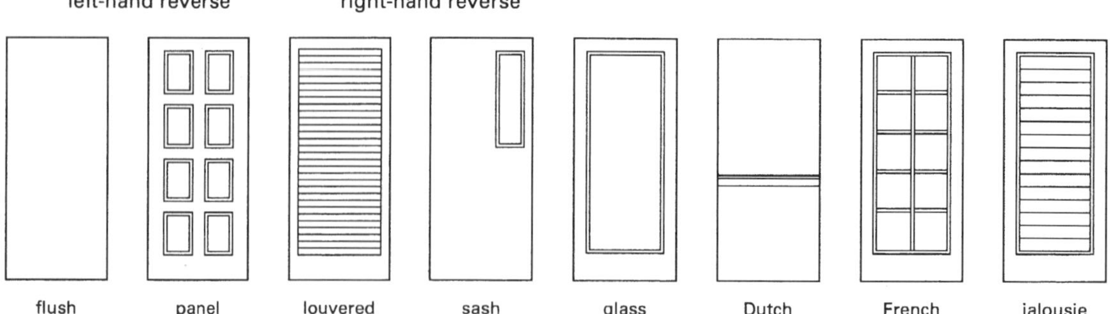

Figure 28.3
Types of Swinging Doors

The hand of a door is determined from outside the door, as shown in Fig. 28.2. The exterior of a building is considered the outside, as are the hallway and lobby sides of a room door. situations where the distinction is not clear, the outside is considered to be the side of the door where the hinge is not visible.

When standing on the outside looking at the door, if the door hinges on the left and swings away from the viewer, it is a *left-hand door.* If it hinges on the right and swings away from the viewer, it is a *right-hand door.* If the door swings toward the viewer, it is considered a *left-hand reverse* or a *right-hand reverse,* depending on the location of the hinge or pivot.

A door can be classified by the function it serves, its operation, and the material from which it is made. Each type of classification is useful in selecting the best door for a particular situation. Figure 28.3 illustrates some of the common types of swinging doors, and Table 28.4 shows doors classified by type of operation. Fig. 28.4 summarizes some of the advantages and disadvantages of various door types.

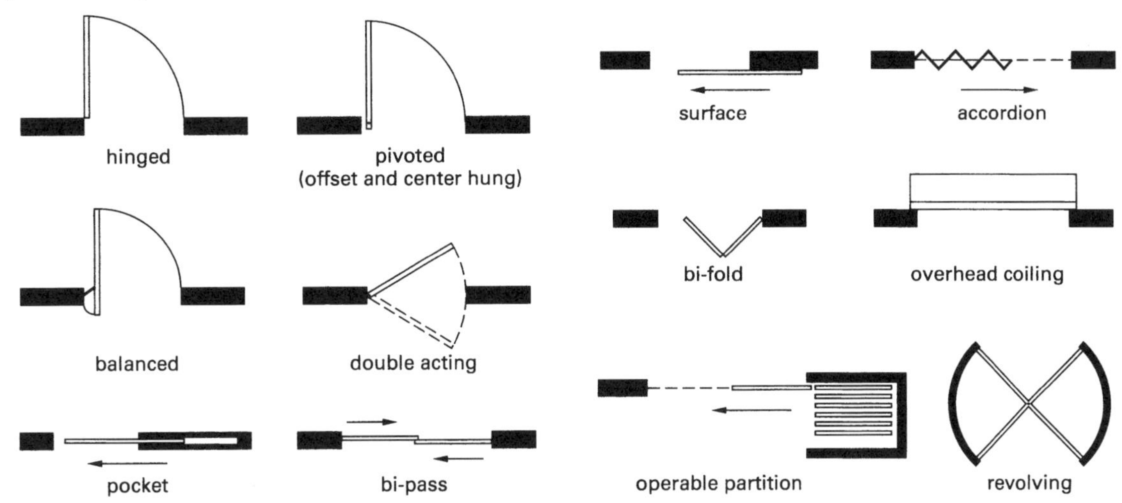

Figure 28.4 Door Classification by Operation

METAL DOORS AND FRAMES

Types of Metal Doors

The three most common types of metal doors are flush, sash, and louvered.

- A *flush door* has a single, smooth surface on each side.
- A *sash door* contains one or more glass lites.
- A *louvered door* has an opening with metal slats to provide ventilation.

Paneled steel doors, which resemble wood panel doors, are available with insulated cores for residential use. They offer energy conservation and durability in addition to a more traditional appearance.

Metal doors are commonly available in steel, stainless steel, aluminum, and bronze, and many other materials are available on special order. The most common material is steel with a painted finish.

Construction

Steel doors, commonly referred to as *hollow metal doors,* are constructed with faces of cold-rolled sheet steel. The most common thicknesses are 18-gage and 14-gage, although 20-gage is available for light-duty doors. 16-gage is also available. The steel faces are attached to a core of honeycomb kraft paper, steel ribs, hardboard, or other materials. The edges are made of steel channels, with the locations for hardware reinforced with heavier-gage steel. Mineral wool or other materials can be used to provide sound-deadening qualities, if needed.

Sizes

Although metal doors can be custom made in almost any practical size, standard widths are 2 ft 0 in, 2 ft 4 in, 2 ft 6 in, 2 ft 8 in, 3 ft 0 in, 3 ft 4 in, 3 ft 6 in, 3 ft 8 in, and 4 ft 0 in. Standard heights are 6 ft 8 in, 7 ft 0 in, and 8 ft 0 in. The standard thickness is $1^3/_4$ in.

Table 28.1
Door Type Advantages and Disadvantages

door operation type	advantages	disadvantages
swinging		
hinged	ease of use and installation inexpensive can be fire-rated wide variety of hinge styles	appearance of hinges sometimes undesirable
offset pivoted	ease of use closer can be part of pivot can be fire rated can accommodate very heavy doors minimal hardware appearance	more expensive than hinges floor closers require solid flooring and adequate thickness to accommodate closer
center-hung pivoted	ease of use closer can be part of pivot allows door to swing both ways support hardware fully concealed can be fire rated can accommodate very heavy doors	more expensive than hinges floor closers require solid flooring and adequate thickness to accommodate closer height limitations required to avoid bowing
balanced	little effort required to operate clear width reduced when open	expensive
double acting	easy operation both ways	cannot be used as exit door dangerous unless glass lite provided
sliding		
pocket sliding	no operating space required	awkward for frequent use difficult to seal against light or sound susceptible to sticking cannot be used as exit door
bi-pass sliding	no operating space required	awkward for frequent use difficult to seal cannot be used as exit door
surface sliding	no operating space required	appearance of hardware cannot be used as exit door
folding		
bi-fold	minimum operating space	awkward to use cannot be used as exit door
accordion folding	useful for subdividing space inexpensive	poor as a sound barrier cannot be used as exit door limited finishes and colors available
moveable		
operable partition	good for very large openings good sound barrier wide choice of finishes	expensive cannot be used as exit door
overhead coiling	automatic closing of large openings for security or fire separation	visible when door closed requires large space for housing cannot be used as exit door
revolving	accommodates large numbers prevents air infiltration types available for darkrooms	only appropriate for entrance doors requires large space; expensive cannot be used as exit door

Frames

Steel door frames, which can be used for either steel doors or wood doors, are made from sheet steel bent into the shape needed for the door installation. Frames are made from 12-, 14-, or 16-gage steel, depending on location and use. The frame is mortised for the installation of hinges and door strikes and is reinforced at these points with heavier-gage steel. Two of the most common frame profiles are shown in Fig. 28.5, along with some standard dimensions and the terminology used to describe the parts.

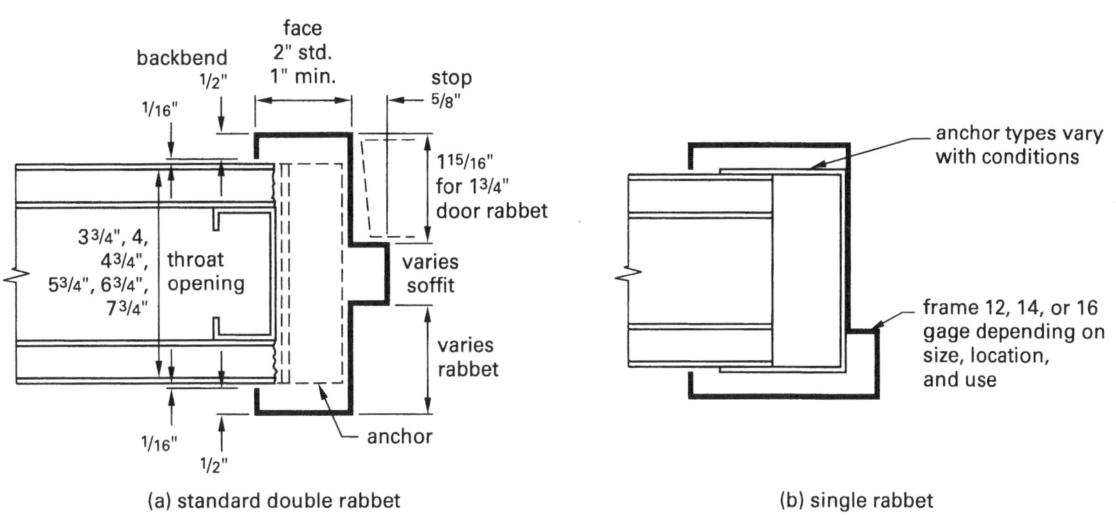

(a) standard double rabbet
(b) single rabbet

Figure 28.5
Standard Steel Door Frames

Various types of anchoring devices are used inside the frame to attach it to gypsum board, masonry, concrete, and other materials. Where a fire rating over 20 minutes is required, steel frames are used almost exclusively, although some specialty wood frames are available with higher ratings.

Steel frames are manufactured in three styles.

- one-piece, welded frames
- knock-down (KD) frames, with the two jamb sections and the head section shipped to the job site as separate pieces
- slip-on frames

A one-piece frame must be set in place before the partition is constructed, while a knock-down frame or a slip-on frame can be set after the gypsum wallboard partition is built. Slip-on frames are not available with welded corners and should be avoided if the appearance of the joint is objectionable.

Aluminum frames are used for both aluminum doors and wood doors. They are constructed of extruded sections and, as a consequence, can have thinner face dimensions and more elaborate shapes than are possible with bent steel.

Steel frames are painted, either in the shop or on site. Aluminum frames can be anodized with the standard anodized colors or they can be factory-coated with baked acrylic paint or other finishes in a variety of colors.

WOOD DOORS AND FRAMES

Wood doors are the most common doors for both residential and commercial construction. They are available in a variety of styles, sizes, finishes, and methods of operation.

Types of Wood Doors

Wood doors can be classed according their operation, as shown in Fig. 28.4. *Swinging doors* are the most common type. They function by being hinged or pivoted on one side. They are relatively inexpensive, easy to install, and can accommodate a large volume of traffic. Double-acting doors swing in both directions when mounted on pivot hardware or special double-acting hinges.

Pocket sliding doors are mounted on a top track and move horizontally into a pocket built into the wall. They are good for areas with limited space, but they are awkward to operate, and latching and sealing are difficult.

Bi-pass sliding doors also travel on a top or bottom rail and are often used for closet doors where space is limited. Bi-folding and multi-folding doors are also used for closets and other large openings where full access needs to be provided when the doors are open.

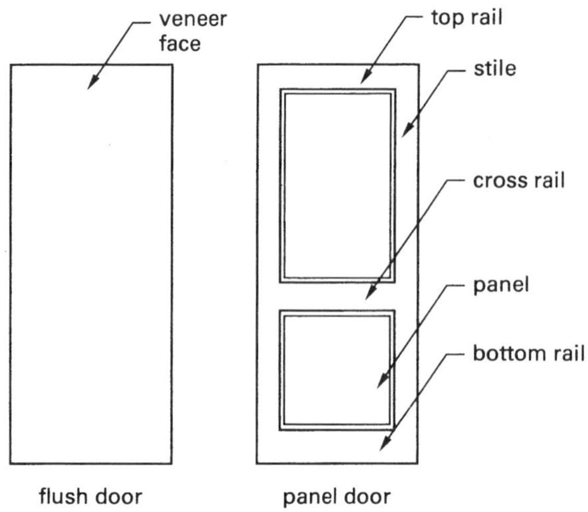

Figure 28.6
Types of Wood Doors

The two main types of wood doors are the flush door and the panel door. See Fig. 28.6. A *flush door* consists of thin, flat veneer laminated various types of cores as described. A *panel door* consists of solid vertical stiles and horizontal rails that serve as a frame for flat or raised panels.

Construction

Wood doors are either hollow core or solid core. *Hollow-core doors* are made of one or three plies of veneer on each side of a cellular cardboard interior. The stile-and-rails frame inside is made of solid wood, with larger blocks of solid wood where the locksets or latchsets are installed. Hollow-core doors are used in interior applications where only light use is expected and where cost is a consideration. They have no fire-resistance properties and poor acoustical properties.

Solid-core doors are made with a variety of core types depending on the functional requirements of the door. Cores may be particleboard, stave core (solid blocks of wood), or mineral core for fire-rated doors. Solid-core doors are used for their fire-resistance properties, as acoustical barriers, for security, and for their superior durability. Solid-core doors may have a fire rating from 20 minutes to $1\frac{1}{2}$ hours. Mineral-core doors are used when fire ratings of 45 minutes, 1 hour, or $1\frac{1}{2}$ hours are required.

The veneer for a wood door can be made from any available hardwood species using rotary-cut, plain-sliced, quarter-sliced, or rift-cut methods, just as with wood panels. The veneers can be bookmatched, slip matched, or random matched; bookmatching is the most common. Plastic laminate faces are available, as are hardboard veneers suitable for painting.

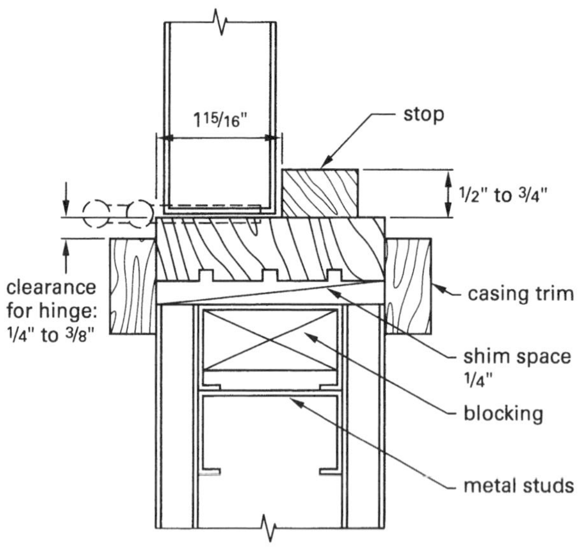

Figure 28.7
Standard Wood Door Frame

Sizes

Like metal doors, wood doors can be custom made any size, but the standard widths are 2 ft 0 in, 2 ft 4 in, 2 ft 6 in, 2 ft 8 in, 3 ft 0 in, and 3 ft 4 in. Standard heights are 6 ft 8 in and 7 ft 0 in, but taller doors, often used in commercial construction, are available. Hollow-core doors are $1\frac{3}{8}$ in thick, and solid-core doors are $1\frac{3}{4}$ in thick; doors $2\frac{1}{4}$ in thick are available for large, exterior doors and acoustical doors.

Frames

Frames for wood doors are made from wood, steel (hollow metal), and aluminum. A common wood frame jamb is illustrated in Fig. 28.7. Although the stop and casing are shown here as rectangular pieces, several different profiles of trim are available.

Which type of frame to use for a wood door depends on a few factors.

- appearance desired
- type of partition in which the opening is being installed
- fire-rating requirements

- security needed
- durability desired

For example, wood frames may be used in 20-, 30-, and 45-minute fire door assemblies, but a 1-hour-rated door must be installed in a rated metal frame. Solid-core wood doors are typically installed in hollow metal frames when durability and sound attenuation are needed.

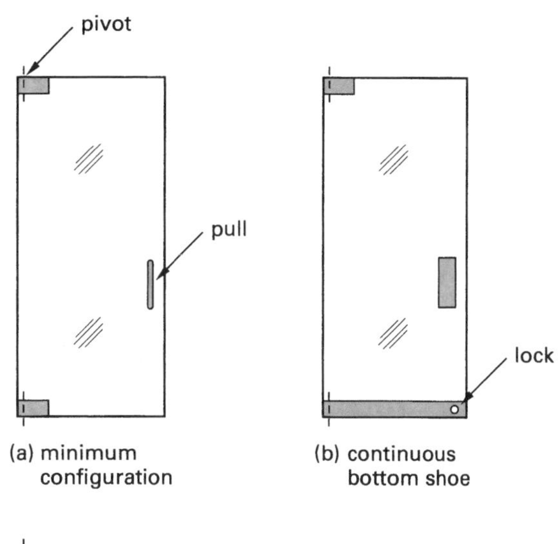

Figure 28.8 Standard Glass Door Configurations

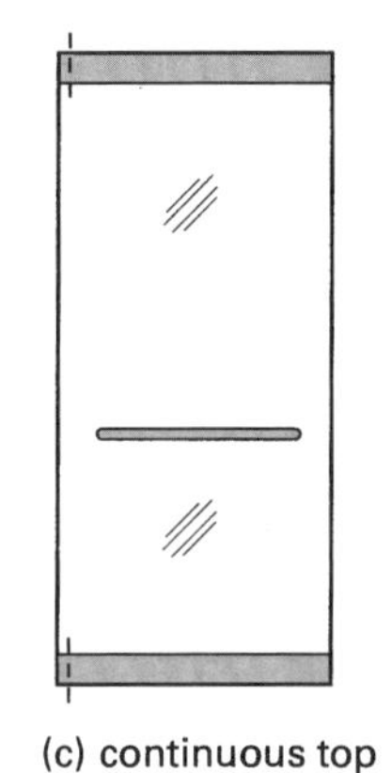

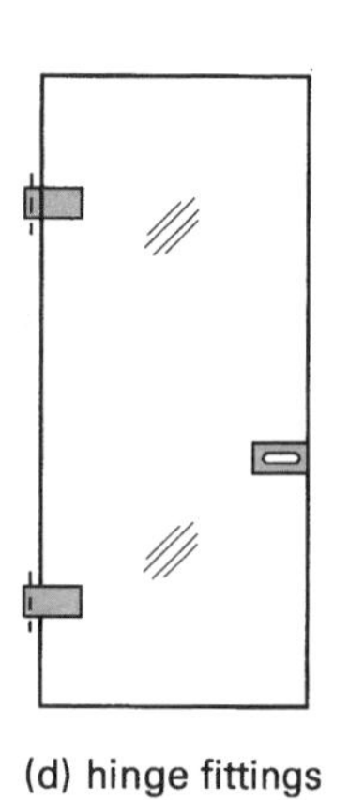

GLASS DOORS

Glass doors (sometimes called *all-glass doors*) are constructed primarily of glass with fittings to hold the pivots and other hardware. Their strength depends on the glass rather than the framing. They are different from sash doors in that a sash door has a frame around all four sides of the door.

Components

A glass door is generally constructed of tempered glass $1/2$ in or $3/4$ in thick, with fittings and operating hardware as required by the installation. Common door sizes are 36 in wide and 7 ft 0 in high, although many architects prefer to specify glass doors at the same height as that of the ceiling.

Some of the typical configurations are shown in Fig. 28.8. The minimum hardware needed is a door pull and a corner fitting at the top and bottom to hold the pivots. In lieu of corner fittings, some manufacturers provide hinge fittings that clamp on the glass and support the door in much the same way as a standard hinged door. If a lock is needed, the bottom fitting may be continuous across the door to allow the installation of a dead bolt. Some architects prefer continuous fittings (sometimes called *shoes*) on both the top and bottom.

Because a full glass door poses potential hazards and must have extra strength, the glass must be tempered. Any holes, notches, or other modifications must be made before the glass is tempered.

Standard Assemblies

Glass doors can be used alone and set within a wall opening with or without a frame, or they can be installed between glass sidelights. If glass sidelights are used, the same type of fitting used on the door generally supports the sidelights. Although jamb frames of aluminum, wood, or ornamental metal can be used, they are not necessary, and the glass sidelights can be butted directly to the partition or held away a fraction of an inch.

Building Code Requirements for All-Glass Doors

Because all-glass doors cannot be fire rated, they cannot be used where a protected opening is required in a fire-rated partition. When they are allowed, and they are serving as exit doors, the type of hardware used must conform to the requirements of the local building code. Some codes and local amendments are more restrictive than others, but most prohibit the use of a simple deadbolt in the bottom rail fitting for an exit door. Instead, special *panic hardware* is available that allows the door to be locked from the outside (and operated with card keys or keypads, if needed), while still allowing the door to be unlatched and opened from the inside in a single operation without any special knowledge or effort. See Fig. 28.9.

Figure 28.9
Glass Door Panic Hardware

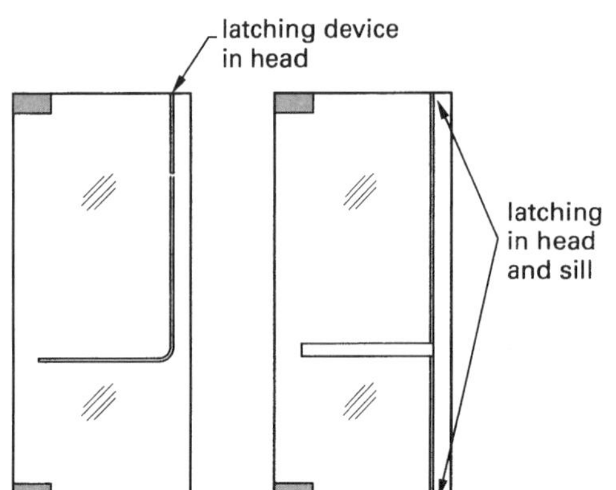

SPECIAL DOORS

Special doors have a wide variety of applications where a special closing assembly is needed. Common types of special doors include

- revolving doors
- overhead coiling doors
- sectional overhead doors

A *revolving door* is an assembly of three or four leaves connected at a central point that rotates within an enclosure. Revolving doors are used to control air infiltration and to allow large numbers of people pass in and out. They are made of glass framed with aluminum, bronze, or other metals. In most cases, revolving doors are not counted in determining the total exit width from a building and do not count as required exits. Some revolving doors are available with collapsing leaves that will fold open if a crowd of people is pushing against them.

An *overhead coiling door* is made from thin slats of metal that roll up into an enclosure above the head of the opening. Overhead coiling doors are used as doors for large openings, such as industrial doors and garage doors, or as fire separations for large openings. They can be connected to fusible links so that they automatically close in the event of fire.

Sectional overhead doors also close large openings and are typically used for industrial buildings and garages. The door is made from individual sections of wood or metal that hinge as the door opens.

Other common types of special doors include blast-resistant doors, sound-retardant doors, hangar doors, folding doors used to divide rooms, security doors, and cold-storage doors.

HARDWARE

Hardware includes weather stripping, electrical locking devices, window operators, and the various types of finish hardware normally found on interior and exterior doors. (Cabinet, curtain, and drapery hardware are discussed in conjunction with those items.)

Functions of Hardware

Hardware is a vital part of any door opening assembly. In general, hardware can be grouped according to the function it serves.

- *hanging the door:* hinges, pivots, and combination pivots and closers
- *operating the door:* handles, latchsets, push plates, and pull bars
- *closing the door:* door closers and combination pivots and closers
- *locking the door:* locksets, dead bolts, flush bolts, electric locks, and other special devices
- *sealing the door:* weather stripping, sound seals, and smoke seals
- *protecting the door:* kick plates, corner protection, and similar materials

Hinges

Hinging is the most common method of attaching a door to its frame. Hinges are also referred as *butt hinges* because they are usually attached to the butt edge of a door. A hinge consists of two *leaves*, with an odd number of *knuckles* on one leaf and an even number of knuckles on the other. The knuckles interlace and are attached with a pin. The pin and knuckles form the *barrel* of the hinge, which is finished with a *tip*.

There are four basic types of hinges, shown in Fig. 28.10.

Full-mortise hinges are the most common type. A full-mortise hinge has both leaves fully mortised into the frame and edge of the door. A *half-mortise hinge* has one leaf surface-applied to the frame and the other leaf mortised into the edge of the door. A *half-surface hinge* has one leaf mounted on the face of the door and the other leaf mortised into the frame. The leaves of a *full-surface hinge* are applied to the faces of both the door and frame. The type of hinge used depends on whether either the door or frame cannot be mortised. For example, a half-mortise hinge may be bolted or welded to a heavy steel frame.

There are also special types of hinges. *Raised barrel hinges* are used when there is not room for the barrel to extend past the trim. The barrel is offset to allow one leaf to be mortised into the frame. *Swing clear hinges* have a special shape that allows the door to swing 90° so that the full opening of the doorway is available. These are often used in health care facilities or for accessible openings. See Fig. 28.11. Without a swing clear hinge, standard hardware decreases the opening width by the thickness of the door when it is open 90°.

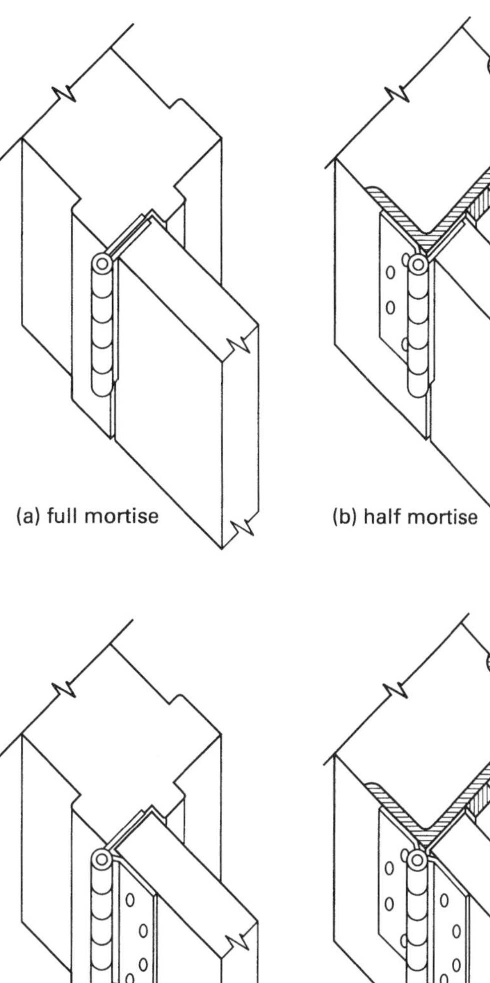

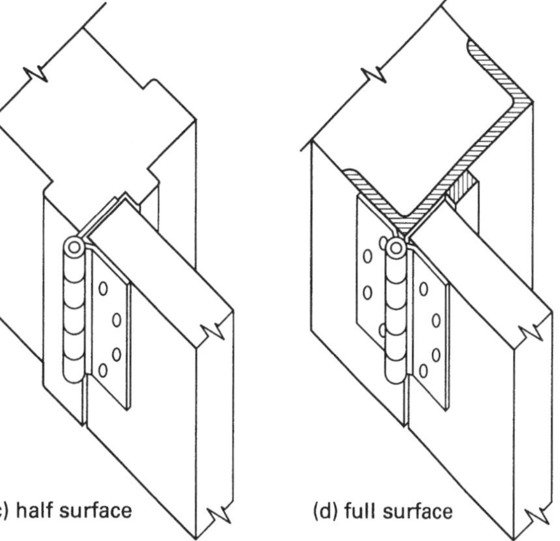

Figure 28.10 Common Hinge Types

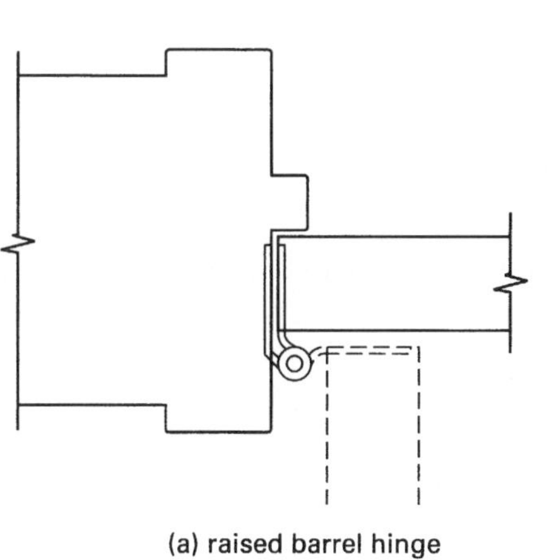

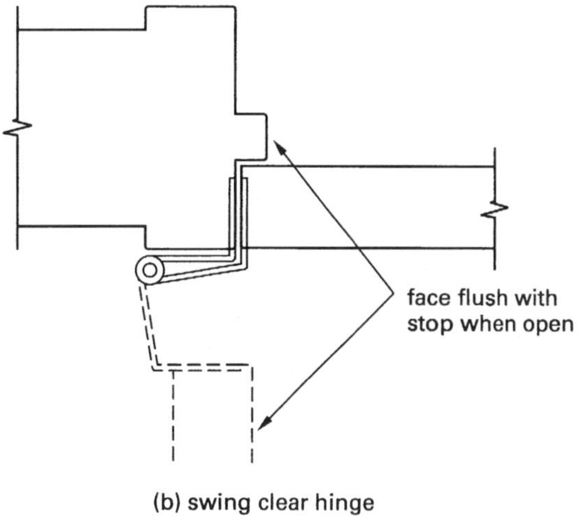

Figure 28.11 Special Hinge Types

Hinges are available with or without ball bearings and in three weights. Which type to use depends on the weight of the door and frequency of use. *Low-frequency doors*, such as residential doors, can use standard-weight, plain-bearing hinges. Most commercial applications need standard-weight, ball-bearing hinges. *High-frequency applications*, such as office building entrances, theaters, and so forth, need heavy-weight, ball-bearing hinges. In addition, ball-bearing hinges are required for fire-rated assemblies and on all doors with closers.

The size and number of hinges required per door depends on a number of factors. The size is given by two numbers such as 4 × 4½ The first number is the length of the barrel in inches, and the second number is the width, which is the dimension in inches when the hinge is open.

The width of the hinge is determined by the width of the door and the clearance needed around jamb trim. A guideline is that the width of the hinge equals twice the door thickness, plus trim projection, minus in. If a fraction falls between standard sizes, use the next larger size. Common hinge widths for 1¾ in doors are 4 in and 4½ in.

The length of the hinge is determined by the door thickness and the door width, as shown in Table 28.2.

Table 28.2
Hinge Heights

door thickness (in)	door width (in)	height of hinge (in)
¾ to 1⅛	≤ 24	2½
1⅜	≤ 32	3½
1⅜	>32–37	4
1¾	≤ 36	4½
1¾	>36–48	5
1¾	>48	6
2, 2¼, 2½	≤ 42	5 (heavy weight)
2, 2¼, 2½	>42	6 (heavy weight)

The number of hinges is determined by the height of the door. Numbers of hinges are commonly referred to in pairs of hinges. Doors up to 60 in high require two hinges (one pair). Doors from 60 in to 90 in require three hinges pair), and doors 90 in to 120 in require four hinges (two pair).

Latchsets and Locksets

Latchsets and locksets are devices that hold a door in the closed position. A *latchset* holds the door in place but has no provision for locking. A beveled latch extends from the face of the door edge and automatically engages the strike mounted in the frame when the door is closed. A *lockset* also has a special mechanism that allows the door be locked with a key, thumb turn, or electronic device.

There are four types of latches and locks: mortise, preassembled, bored, and interconnected. These are shown in Fig. 28.12. Another type, the integral lock, is no longer produced in the United States, but is still found in older buildings.

A *mortise lock* or *mortise latch* is installed in a rectangular area cut out of the door. It is generally more secure than a bored lock and offers a wider variety of locking options. Mortise locks allow the use of a dead bolt and a latch bolt, both of which can be retracted with a single operation. A variety of knob and lever handle designs can be used with the basic mechanism.

Preassembled locks and latches (also called *unit locks*) come from the factory as a complete unit. They are slid into a notch made in the edge of the door and require little adjustment. Preassembled locks are often found in older buildings but seldom installed in new buildings.

Bored locks and latches (also called *cylindrical locks or latches*) are installed by boring holes through the face of the door and from the edge of the door to the other bored opening. They are relatively easy install and are less expensive than mortise locks, but they offer fewer operating functions. They are generally used in residential and small commercial projects.

Interconnected locks have a cylindrical lock and a dead bolt. The two locks are interconnected so that a single action of turning a knob or lever handle on the inside releases both bolts.

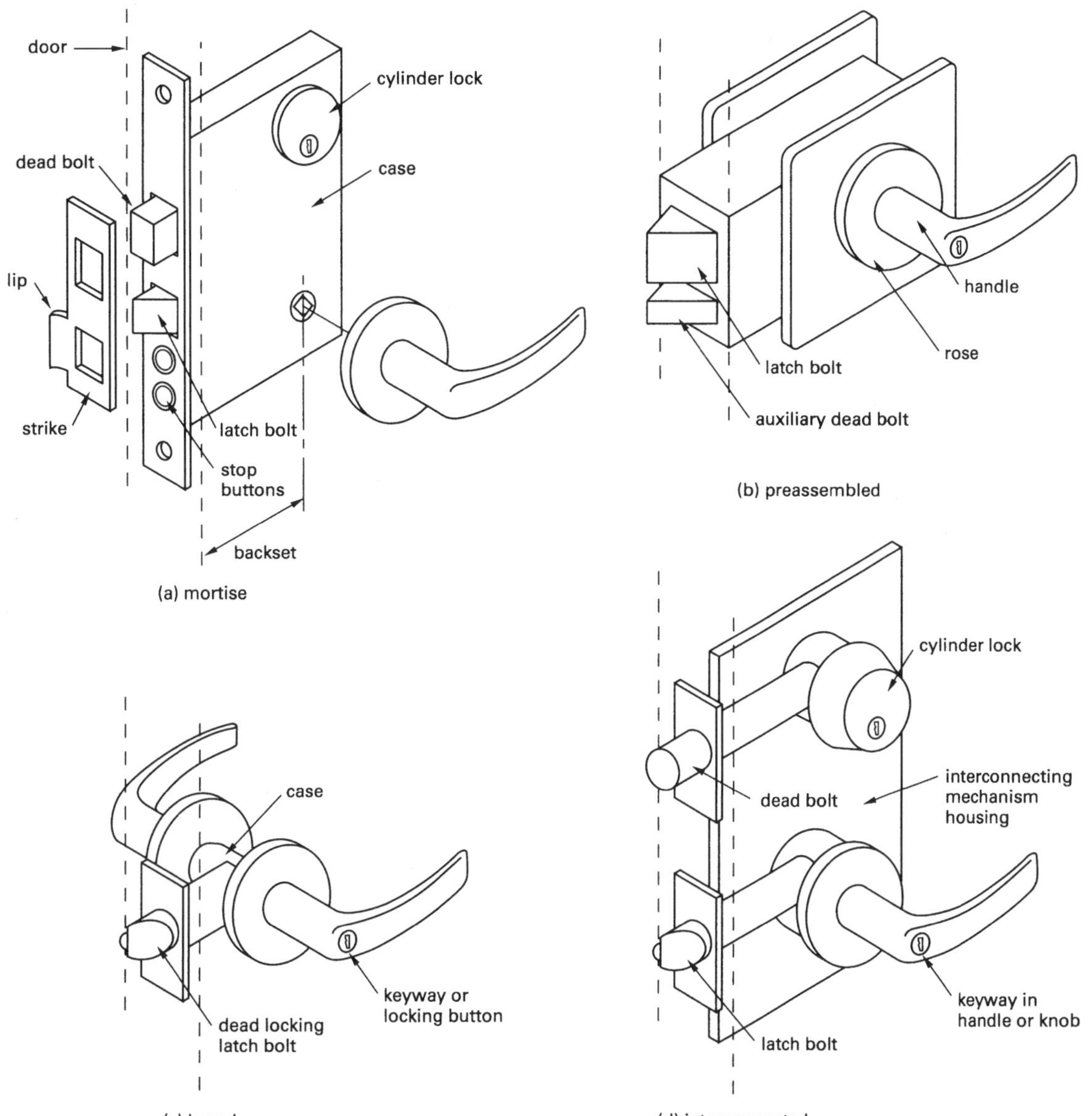

Figure 28.12
Types of Locksets

With all types of latches and locks, either a doorknob or lever handle may be used to operate the latching device. In most cases, a lever handle is required to meet requirements for accessibility.

The distance from the edge of the door to the center line of the doorknob or pivot of a lever handle is called the *backset*. Standard backsets are $2^3/_4$ in and 5 in, although others are available on special order.

Other Types of Hardware

- *Pivots* provide an alternative method of hanging doors where the visual appearance of hinges is objectionable or where a frameless door design may make it impossible use hinges. Pivots may be center hung or offset and are mounted in the floor and head of the door. See Fig. 28.13. For large or heavy doors, an intermediate pivot is often needed for offset-hung doors only. Center-hung pivots allow the door to swing in either direction and can be completely concealed, but they allow only a 90° swing. Offset pivots allow the door to swing 180°.
- *Panic hardware* is used where required by the building code for safe egress during a panic situation. Push bars extending across the width of the door operate vertical rods that disengage latches at the top and bottom. The vertical rods can be surface mounted or concealed. When panic hardware is listed (such as with UL) for use on fire door assemblies, it is called *fire exit hardware.*

Figure 28.13
Door Pivots

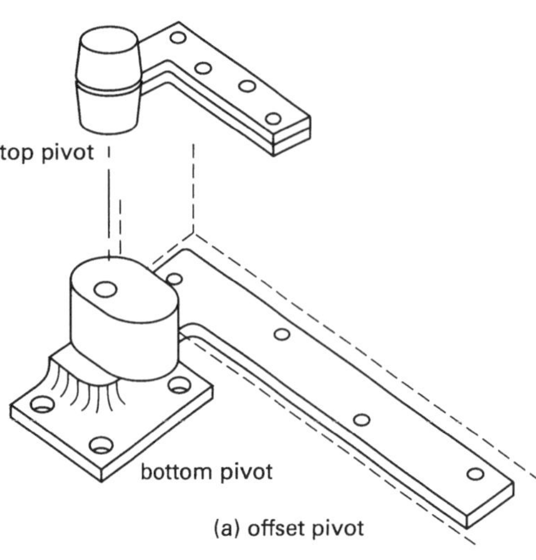

(a) offset pivot

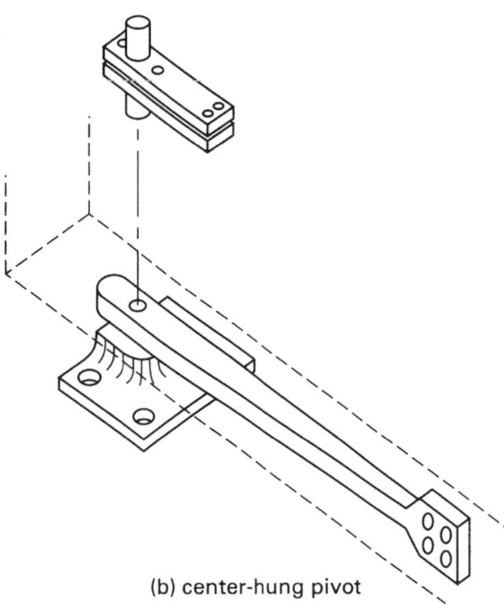
(b) center-hung pivot

- *Push plates and pull bars* are used to operate a door that does not require automatic latching. They are also used on doors to toilet rooms and commercial kitchens.
- *Closers* are pneumatic devices that automatically return a door to its closed position after it is opened. They also control the distance a door can be opened and thereby protect the door and surrounding construction from damage. Closers can be surface mounted on the door or head frame or concealed in the frame or door. Selection of a closer depends on the type, size, and weight of the door, the frequency of operation, the visual appearance desired, and the door height clearance required. Closers can also be integral with pivots mounted in the floor or ceiling, either center hung or offset.
- Closers are available with built-in fire and smoke detectors, so that a door may be held open during normal operation but will close when smoke is sensed. Exit doors must have closers, but most codes allow them to be held in an open position if they close automatically on the activation of a smoke detector or other approved fire signal.
- *Door stops and bumpers* should be provided to keep a door or its hardware from damaging adjacent construction. Closers will do this to some extent, but floor stops or wall bumpers provide more protection. These devices are small metal fabrications with rubber bumpers attached. See Fig. 28.14.
- *Astragals* are vertical moldings or wooden strips used between double doors to seal the opening, act as a door stop, or provide extra security when the doors are closed. Astragals may be fixed or removable to allow for a wide opening when moving furniture.
- A *coordinator* is a device used with double doors that are rabbeted or that have an astragal on the active leaf. The coordinator is mounted in or on the head of the frame, coordinating the closing sequence of the two doors so that they close completely, rather than having the leaf with the astragal close first, preventing the other leaf from closing completely.
- *Flush bolts* are used on the inactive leaf of a pair of doors to lock the doors. They may be surface mounted or mortised into the edge of the door. The active leaf then closes to the locked inactive leaf, but both can be opened when needed. Flush bolts are not allowed on exit doors.
- *Automatic door bottoms* are devices that are mortised or surface applied to the bottom of the door to provide a sound or light seal. When the door is open, the seal is up; as the door closes a plunger strikes the jamb and forces the seal down.

- *Weather stripping* is used along the edges and bottoms of doors to provide a tight seal against water and air infiltration. Various types of door seals are used to provide light and sound protection on interior doors, as well as seal against the passage of smoke around fire doors. Different types of neoprene, felt, metal, vinyl, and other materials are used.
- *Thresholds* are used where floor materials change at a door line, where weather stripping is required, where a hard surface is required for an automatic door bottom, or where minor changes in floor level occur.

Figure 28.14 Miscellaneous Door Hardware

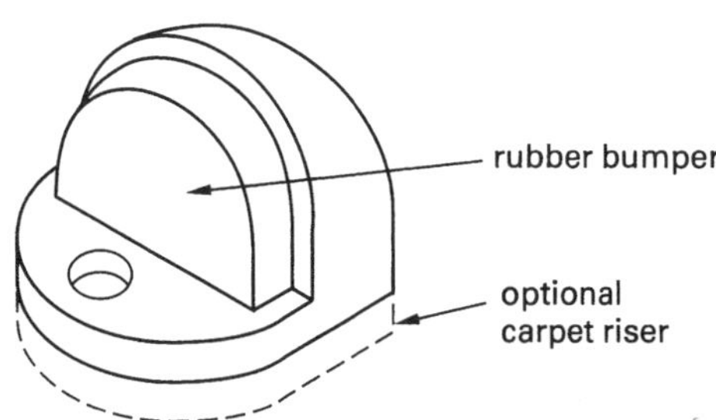

(a) dome floor stop

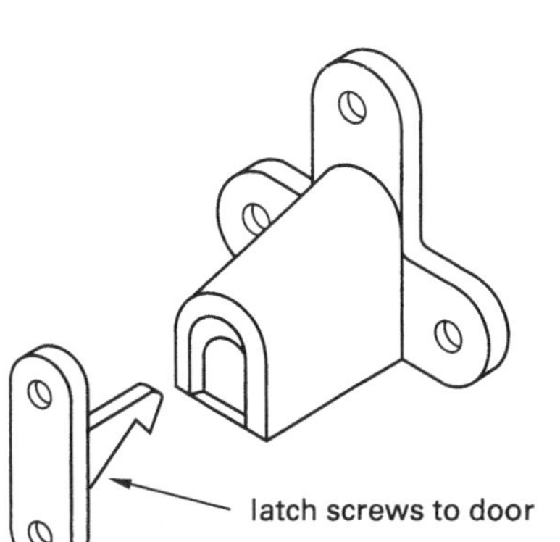

(b) combination stop and hold open

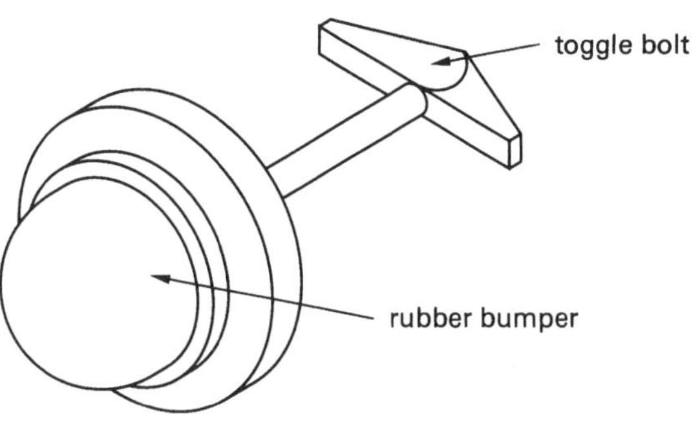

(c) wall bumper

Electronic Hardware

Electronic hardware for doors includes devices that control or monitor door openings using electric or electromechanical means. Local building codes must be consulted because some electronic hardware items do not qualify as allowable exit devices. If an exit door is electronically locked and controlled from the outside, most codes require that exiting be possible from the inside through a purely mechanical action on the locking device—that is, one that does not depend on any power supply or deactivation of the lock on the inside by the person exiting. Following are some of the most common types of electronic hardware.

- An *electric lock* maintains a mortise or bored lockset in the locked position until a signal is activated by a regulating device. Regulating devices can include wall switches, pushbuttons, card readers, key switches, computerized controls, automatic time devices, security consoles, and other sophisticated control devices. Electric locks also can be specified so that they open automatically if there is a power failure. In either case, the inside knob or handle mechanically unlatches the door for exiting at any time.

  A variation of the electric lock is the *electric latch*. This device is normally in a position to hold the latchbolt of the lock so that the door cannot be opened. On activation, the electric latch pivots, allowing the door to be opened. From the inside, the mechanical operation of the knob or handle retracts the latch, allowing exit regardless of the position of the electric latch. Electric latches have the advantage of not requiring any power to be run to the door; all wiring is done in the door jamb. Electric locks require the use of electric hinges or other power-transfer devices to make the low-voltage wiring connections from the door frame to the mechanism in the door.

- *Electric bolts* are separate from the operating hardware of a door. They can be mounted in the strike jamb or head of a door. In the locked position, a bolt extends from the unit into a strike in the door. A pushbutton, card reader, or other regulating device activates a solenoid that retracts the bolt. Fail-safe units are available that open when there is a power failure. Electric bolts are generally not allowed on exit doors because there is no sure way to mechanically open the door if the bolt does not retract.

- *Key card readers* and *key fob readers* are regulating devices that can read a magnetic code on a small plastic card or fob when it is inserted into the reader or is within a certain distance of the reader. If the reader detects a valid code, the switch is activated and the door is unlocked. The reader can also send a signal to a central monitoring computer that keeps track of whose card or fob was used to open which door and when the entry was made. The central computer can control the times of day when a door can be opened by particular cards or fobs. The reader is usually mounted on the partition near the door it controls, but it can also be part of the lockset, as is typically the case in hotels.
- An alternative to the card reader is the *keypad*, into which a coded number must be entered to gain access. A keypad can be a separate unit mounted near the door or it can be part of the door knob or lever.
- Like a closer activated by a smoke detector, a *magnetic hold-open device* allows a door to be held in an open position and then closed automatically in case of fire. An electromagnet mounted on a wall or on the floor contacts a metal plate attached to the door. When activated by a central alarm signal, a smoke detector, or a power failure, the electromagnet releases and the door closes.

Finishes

Hardware is available in a variety of finishes. The choice of hardware depends primarily on the appearance desired but also on its ability to withstand use and weathering. The finish is applied over a base metal from which the hardware is made. For most hardware items this is not important, but for hinges and other operating hardware it can be significant.

There are five basic metals: steel, stainless steel, bronze, brass, and aluminum. Fire-rated doors must have steel or stainless steel hinges. Hardware in corrosive environments may require stainless steel or bronze base metals with compatible surface finishes.

Hardware finishes have been standardized and given numerical designations by the federal government (U.S. numbers) and the Builders Hardware Manufacturers Association (BHMA numbers). These are listed in Table 28.3.

Table 28.3
Hardware Finishes

BHMA no.	U.S. no.	BHMA finish description
605	US3	bright brass, clear coated
606	US4	satin brass, clear coated
611	US9	bright bronze, clear coated
612	US10	satin bronze, clear coated
613	US10B	satin bronze, dark oxidized
618	US14	bright nickel, clear coated
619	US15	satin nickel-plated, clear coated
622	US19	flat black
623	US20	light oxidized, statuary bronze, clear coated
624	US20A	dark statuary bronze, clear coated
625	US26	bright chromium plate
626	US26D	satin chromium plate
627	US27	satin aluminum, clear coated
628	US28	satin aluminum, clear anodized
629	US32	bright stainless steel
630	US32D	satin stainless steel

One specialty type of hardware finish is a *bactericidal copper alloy*. This copper-based finish will kill several types of bacteria on contact, making it ideal for hospitals, nursing homes, and other types of health care facilities. It can be used on door handles, door pulls, push plates, grab bars, switch plates, and other hardware items that people touch frequently. Although only certain alloys meet the EPA requirements for bactericidal properties, they can be made of rose bronze, silicon bronze, or white bronze in matte or brushed finishes.

BUILDING CODE REQUIREMENTS FOR DOORS AND HARDWARE

The requirements fall into three major categories.

- exiting requirements
- requirements for fire-rated assemblies
- access requirements

Many of the exit door requirements are reviewed in Chap. 14. Additional regulations specifically related to doors and hardware are included here.

Building codes regulate the circumstances under which a door must provide fire protection. If a partition must have a fire rating, the openings in that partition must also be fire rated. Typical places where fire-rated doors are required include openings in stairways, in fire-rated corridors, in occupancy separation walls, and in certain hazardous locations.

The codes consider the fire door assembly to be not just the door but the entire unit of door, frame, and hardware. Every part of the assembly must be rated to make an approved opening. Doors, frames, and hardware are tested by Underwriters Laboratories (UL) and Factory Mutual (FM) according to standard ASTM and NFPA tests. If the door meets the requirements of the standard fire test, a small metal label is attached to the edge of the door, indicating its class and hourly rating. Thus, a fire-rated door is also called a *labeled door.*

Doors are rated according to the time they can withstand the standard fire test and according to the rating of assembly in which they can be installed. A few of the time ratings are summarized in Table 28.4, and range from 20 minutes to 3 hours. Refer to Table 14.2 and Table 14.3 for a complete listing.

Table 28.4
Fire Door Classifications

use of partition	rating of partition or wall (hours)	required door assembly rating (hours)
exit access corridors	1	0.33
fire partitions	1	$\frac{3}{4}$
fire barriers (1-hour)		
shaft and exit enclosure walls	1	1
other fire barriers	1	$\frac{3}{4}$
fire walls and fire barriers having a required fire-resistance rating greater than 1 hour	4	3
	3	3
	2	$1\frac{1}{2}$
	$1\frac{1}{2}$	$1\frac{1}{2}$
exterior walls	3	$1\frac{1}{2}$
	2	$1\frac{1}{2}$
	1	$\frac{3}{4}$

The standard test for doors is NFPA 252. This test is described in Chap. 8.

All hardware on fire doors must be tested and approved for use on fire exits. Fire doors must be operable from the inside without the use of any special knowledge or effort. This provision prohibits the use of devices such as combination locks, thumb-turn locks, and multiple locks. Some occupants in a building may not be familiar with these or similar devices and may find them too difficult to operate during panic conditions or when visibility is low. The code provides for some exceptions such as in residential units, places of detention, and a few other situations.

For certain occupancies, such as educational and assembly with an occupant load over 50, panic hardware is required. This is hardware that unlatches the door when pressure is applied against a horizontal bar rather than requiring a turning motion as with a level handle or doorknob. Panic hardware may also be required in some electrical rooms depending on the equipment housed within.

Fire doors must be self-closing or automatic closing. A *self-closing door* simply has a closer or other device that returns it to the closed position after someone passes through. *Automatic closing doors* are those that are normally held open, but that automatically close on activation of a smoke detector, fire alarm system, or other approved device.

Whenever a fire door is closed, it must be secured with an active latch bolt. This secures the door during a fire, preventing fire and gas pressure from pushing the door open.

Operating devices, including door handles, pulls, latches, and locks, must be installed on the door a minimum of 34 in and a maximum of 48 in above the finished floor. The only exception is that locks used only for security purposes and not used for normal operation can be at any height.

The requirements for glazing in fire door assemblies vary depending on what type of wall or partition the door is located in. When glass is installed in fire door assemblies, it must be wire glass set in metal frames, or special fire-protection-rated glass. The size of the glass is limited in area and maximum dimensions as shown in Table 28.2 and Table 28.3. Wire glass is considered by the IBC to have a fire rating of 45 minutes. Other types of fire-protection-rated glazing and fire-resistance-rated glazing may be used in lieu of wire glass if they conform to the size limitations of NFPA 80, *Standard for Fire Doors and Other Opening Protectives.*

Additional requirements based on the IBC are listed here. Verify exact requirements with the model code used in the area where the work is being done.

- A fire-rated door assembly must have a label attached to the door and frame.
- A fire door must be self-latching.
- All hardware used must be UL listed.
- A fire door must be self-closing. In some cases the code permits the door to be held open if the hold-open or closer is connected to an approved smoke or fire detector.
- A fire door must use steel hinges of the ball-bearing type.
- If a pair of doors is used, astragals or other required hardware must also be used.
- Glass (if permitted) must conform in maximum area and construction to requirements of the local code. It must be wire glass or fire-rated glass and set in a steel frame with the glass stop made of steel.
- Louvers must conform to UL requirements for maximum size and construction.

Accessibility requirements for doors and hardware include the following.

- Minimum width, clear of hardware, of an opened door must be 32 in.
- There must be adequate maneuvering clearance in front of and on the latch side of the door to operate it.
- There must be a minimum of 48 in between two doors in a series when they are open 90°.
- The maximum opening force required for various types of doors is specified by the code.
- Handles and latches must have a shape that is easy to grasp and use. This usually means lever handles or push-pull-type mechanisms.
- Thresholds with a change in level may have a vertical edge up to $^1/_4$ in high, but must be beveled with a slope of 1:2 for heights from $^1/_4$ in to $^1/_2$ in.

WINDOWS

A *window* is an opening in a wall used to provide viewing, light transmission, solar heat (when desired), and ventilation. The standard nomenclature of a window is shown in Fig. 28.15, and the types of windows are illustrated in Fig. 28.16.

Metal Windows

Metal windows are made of aluminum, steel, or bronze. Aluminum is the most common because of its light weight, low cost, strength, and resistance to corrosion. A variety of finishes can be applied in the factory to make aluminum windows compatible with almost any building.

Two disadvantages of aluminum are its susceptibility to galvanic action and its high heat conduction. However, both of these can be controlled. Galvanic action can be minimized or eliminated with the proper selection of fasteners and flashing. Heat transmission and condensation can be prevented by specifying aluminum frames with *thermal breaks*, nonmetallic elements in the frame that connect the exterior and interior portions of a window.

Steel windows are fabricated from small sections of hot- or cold-rolled steel. Because of steel's greater strength, frame sections are small compared with aluminum sections. Steel windows are more expensive and are used where high strength, high security, and a minimum profile size are needed. They can be shop painted, or the steel can be *bonderized*, given a coating that improves the adhesion of site-applied paint.

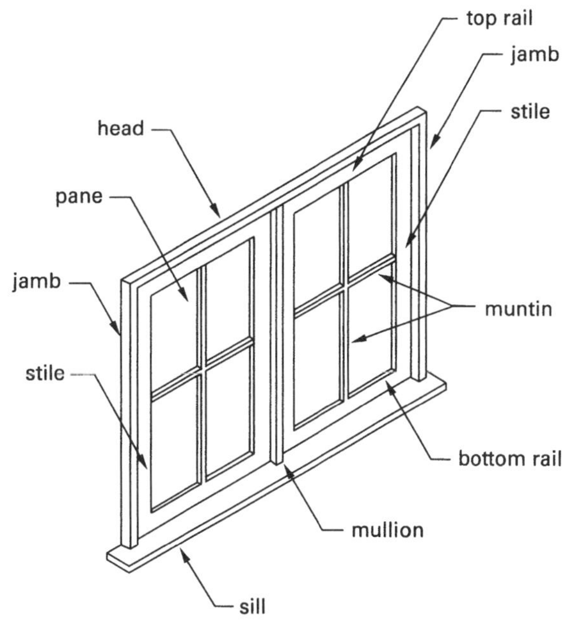

Figure 28.15 Parts of a Window

Wood Windows

Wood windows are popular because of the variety of types and sizes available, their appearance, their ease of installation, and their good insulating properties. These windows are delivered to the job site as complete manufactured units, including the exterior trim. They are placed in a rough opening and secured to the framing. Installation of interior trim finishes the window opening.

Common types of wood windows include *fixed sash*, *double hung*, *casement*, and *horizontal pivoted*, either awning or hopper types. Horizontal sliding units are also available, usually made of pine and fir, although other species such as redwood and cypress are occasionally used.

Many manufacturers provide clad wood windows. The exterior, exposed wood members are covered with a thin layer of steel or vinyl to minimize maintenance, and the interior portions are left exposed for painting or other types of wood finish.

Single-strength or double-strength glass is used for glazing windows. Most building codes require glazing to be insulated glass.

Skylights

Skylights are glazed openings in roofs that allow light (and ventilation, if operable) to penetrate the interior. Skylights may be glazed with glass or plastic. If plastic is used it must adhere to building code restrictions on location and maximum size. If glazed with glass, the glass must be laminated or wire glass. tempered or annealed glass is used, it must be protected from above and below with wire screening. These restrictions prevent injury to someone below if the glass breaks and falls.

A skylight should be mounted on curbs to raise the bottom edge above the roof surface, especially if the roof has a low slope. Because condensation of water vapor in a building can be a problem, a condensate gutter and weep holes in the skylight frame should allow collected water to drain to the outside.

Storefronts

Storefronts consist of extruded metal frames (usually aluminum), glass panels, doors, hardware, and miscellaneous fittings designed to be installed as one coordinated system. Storefront systems are used in one-story applications where the glass and its framing are supported within an opening rather than continuously supported across several floors as with curtain wall construction.

Advantages of storefront systems include

- ease of construction
- single-source supplying
- lightweight, coordinated elements
- relatively low cost
- a range of styles, finishes, and sizes from which to choose

GLASS AND GLAZING

Glass is the term for the actual material. Clear glass is a mixture of silica sand and small amounts of alkaline salts such as lime, potash, and soda. *Glazing* refers to the process of installing glass in the framing as well as the process of installing the framing itself; it can also refer to glass that has been installed through this process.

Types of Glass

In selecting the type of glass to be used, several factors must be considered: the amount of light to be transmitted, the degree of transparency, strength and security, sound isolation, insulating qualities, cost, availability, and special qualities such as radiation shielding. Refer to Chap. 12 for a discussion of energy-efficient glazing. Following are some common types of glass available.

Float Glass

Most of the glass produced in the United States is *float glass* Float glass is made by pouring molten glass on a bed of molten tin and allowing it to cool, forming a smooth, flat surface. It is also called *annealed glass.*

Heat-Strengthened Glass

Heat-strengthened glass is produced by heating glass to about 1100°F and slowly cooling it. Heat-strengthened glass has about twice the strength of annealed glass of the same thickness. This type of glass is used where the surface is subject to solar-induced thermal stresses and cyclic wind-loading.

Tempered Glass

Tempered glass is produced by subjecting annealed glass to a special heat treatment in which it is heated to about 1150°F and then quickly cooled. The process sets up compressive stresses on the outer surfaces and tensile stresses inside the glass. This glass is about four times stronger than annealed glass of the same thickness. Tempered glass is available in thicknesses from $^1/_8$ in to $^7/_8$ in.

In addition to its extra strength for normal glazing, tempered glass is considered safety glass, so it can be used in hazardous locations (discussed later in this section). If it breaks, it falls into thousands of very small pieces instead of creating dangerous, jagged shards.

Laminated Glass

Laminated glass consists of two or more pieces of glass bonded together by an interlayer of polyvinyl butyral resin. When laminated glass is broken, the interlayer holds the pieces together even though the glass itself may be severely cracked. This type of glass is used where very strong glazing is needed. It can be bullet resistant and provides high security against intentional or accidental breakage. Like tempered glass, it is considered safety glazing and can be used in hazardous locations.

Laminated glass is also used where sound control is desired. In addition to the sound control provided by the extra thickness of the glass, the interlayer has a damping effect on the otherwise rigid material. This glass is available in thicknesses from $^{13}/_{64}$ in to 3 in.

Tinted Glass

Tinted glass (also called *heat-absorbing glass*) is produced by adding various colorants to the glass material. The standard colors are bronze, gray, green, and blue. The purpose of tinted glass is to reduce the solar transmittance of the glass, which reduces the air conditioning load on the building, the brightness of the interior, and fading of fabrics and carpeting. Because tinted glass absorbs heat, it should not be used where portions of it are in direct sun and portions are shaded. The differential expansion and contraction (thermal load) will crack the glass. Because of this phenomenon, tinted glass is often heat strengthened or tempered.

One of the important variables for tinted glass, as well as other glass materials and sun blocking devices, is the *shading coefficient* (SC). This is the ratio of the solar heat gain through a particular glazing product to the solar heat gain through an unshaded $^1/_8$ in thick clear, double-strength glass under the same set of conditions. It is used when calculating heat gain. However, the shading coefficient is a value that represents the glazing only, not the frame or spacer effects. The *solar heat gain coefficient* (SHGC) of a window must also be taken into account. The SHGC is the ratio of the solar heat gain through glazing or a window compared to the total solar radiation incident on the glazing or window. It is expressed as a value between zero and one.

Although tinted glass can reduce heat gain and heat loss through windows, it also reduces the amount of visible light transmitted into the building.

Low-Iron Glass

Iron oxide gives a light green cast to ordinary clear float glass. *Low-iron glass* has a reduced amount of iron oxide, which gives it exceptional clarity, optimal light transmission, and excellent color transmission.

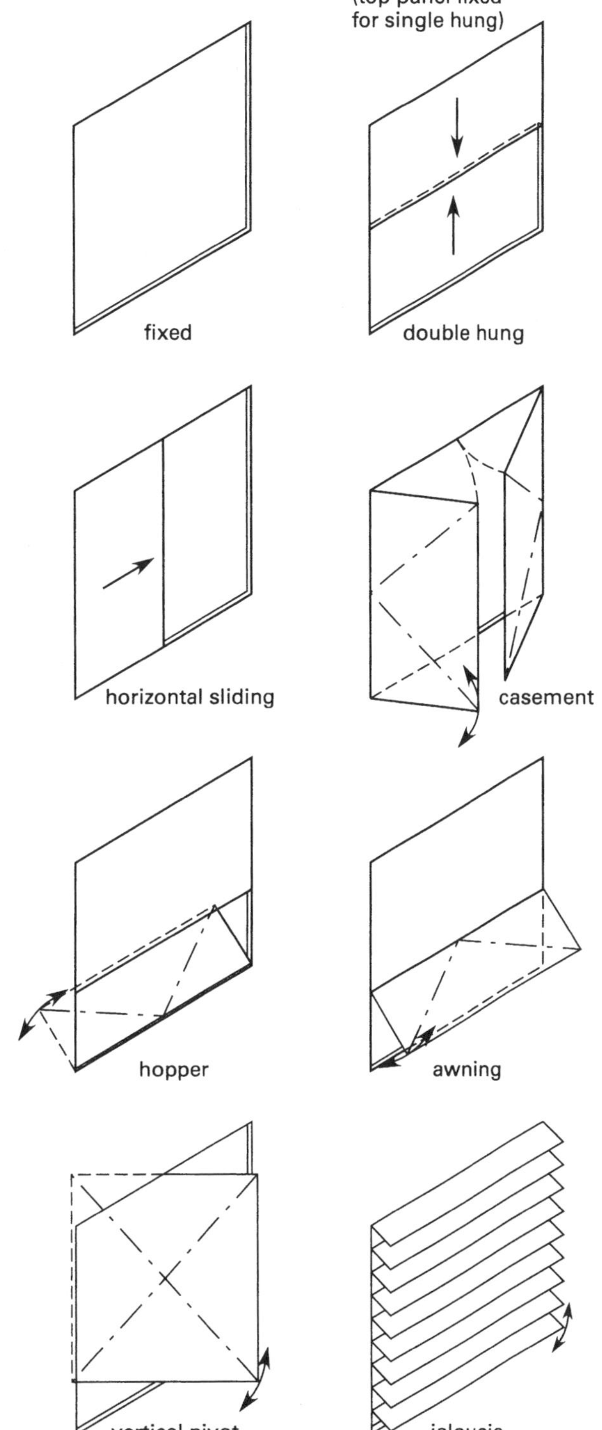

Figure 28.16 Types of Windows

Reflective Glass

Reflective glass is clear or tinted glass coated with an extremely thin layer of metal or metallic oxide. In insulating units, this reflective layer is placed on the inside of the exterior lite of glass. Its primary purpose is to save energy by reflecting solar radiation. In addition to this, the exterior of a building with reflective glass has a mirror-like surface that may have a desired aesthetic effect. Reflective coatings come in silver, copper, golden, and earth-tone shades that can be combined with the available colors of tinted glass.

Insulating Glass

Insulating glass is fabricated of two or three sheets of glass separated by a hermetically sealed air space of $^1/_4$ in to $^1/_2$ in. Insulating glass has a much lower *U*-value than that of single-thickness glass and is used almost exclusively in regions where heat loss is a problem. Insulating glass can be made with heat-strengthened, tempered, reflective, tinted, and laminated glass.

Patterned Glass

Patterned glass is made by passing a sheet of glass through rollers on which the desired pattern is etched on one or both sides. Vision through the panel is diffused but not totally obscured; the degree of diffusion depends on the pattern and depth of etch.

Wire Glass

Wire glass has a mesh of wire embedded in the middle of the sheet. The surface can be either smooth or patterned. Wire glass is used primarily in fire-rated assemblies of 45 minutes or less if it is not in a hazardous location. Despite the use of wire, it is not as strong as other common glass types and can present a hazard when broken. Wire glass cannot be tempered and does not qualify as safety glazing for hazardous locations.

Spandrel Glass

Spandrel glass is an opaque strip of glass that conceals the floor and ceiling structure in curtain wall construction. It is manufactured by permanently fusing a ceramic frit color to the back of heat-strengthened or tempered glass. It is normally manufactured and installed as a single sheet with insulation behind.

Low-Emissivity Glass

Low-emissivity glass, sometimes called *low-ε glass*, selectively reflects and transmits certain wavelengths of the electromagnetic spectrum. It is manufactured by placing an atomically thin coating of metal or metal oxide on the surface of a piece of glass or a thin film. Low-emissivity glass works by transmitting visible light and shortwave solar radiation but reflecting long-wave heat radiation from the air and warm objects.

In a cold climate, low-emissivity glass admits solar heat gain during the day but prevents the built-up heat inside the building from escaping at night. In the summer, the same glass will reflect much of the ambient long-wave infrared heat away from the glass. In warm climates, low-emissivity glass can be combined with tinted or reflective glass to prevent even more heat from being transmitted to the interior of the building.

Low-emissivity glass is used in insulated units where, placed on the interior surface of the inside lite, it reflects building heat back to the inside before it crosses the air gap. Low-emissivity glass can also be made by suspending a thin layer of film in the center of the air gap, creating two air spaces. This is even more efficient than directly applying the coating to the glass, although glass made through this process is more easily damaged.

Energy-Efficient Glazing

There are many *energy-efficient glazing* products available that can reduce heat loss and/or heat gain through windows, thereby reducing the energy needed to maintain a comfortable indoor temperature, without reducing the amount of visible light transmitted. Some improve upon older technologies while others are new and experimental technologies. Refer to Chap. 12 for a more detailed discussion of these products and how they are used.

Electrochromic Glazing

Electrochromic glazing is a general term for a type of glazing that changes from opaque to transparent with the application of an electric current. When the current is on, the glass is transparent; when current is off, the glass darkens or turns milky white, depending on its type.

There are three distinct types of this glazing, only one of which is technically known as electrochromic glazing. The other two types are more properly referred to as *suspended particle device* (SPD) and *polymer-dispersed liquid crystal film*. All three depend on the application of a low electric current to keep them clear, but they have slightly different characteristics.

- *Electrochromic glazing* uses an inorganic ceramic thin-film coating on glass and can be manufactured to range from transparent to heavily darkened (tinted). However, it is never opaque, so it cannot be used as privacy glass. It is intended for control of light, ultraviolet energy, and solar heat gain. The amount of tinting is not just an on or off condition; it can be controlled with a simple rheostat switch.
- *Suspended particle device glazing (SPD glazing)* uses a proprietary system in which light-absorbing microscopic particles are dispersed within a liquid suspension film, which is then sandwiched between two pieces of transparent conductive material. The appearance of the product can range from clear to partially darkened to totally opaque, so it can be used for privacy as well as for light control and energy conservation. It can also be controlled with a rheostat.
- *Polymer-dispersed liquid crystal film glazing* is created by placing the polymer film between two pieces of glass. The transparency can range from transparent to cloudy white. In its translucent state it offers total visual privacy but still allows a significant amount of light to pass through so it cannot be used for exterior light control. All types of electrochromic glazing are expensive, but the first two types offer the potential for significant energy savings, in the range of 20% to 30%.

Fire-Rated Glazing

In addition to wire glass, there are four other types of glazing that can be used in fire-rated openings.

The first is a clear ceramic that has a higher impact resistance than wire glass and a low expansion coefficient. It is available with a 1-hour rating in sizes up to 1296 in^2 and with a 3-hour rating in sizes up to 100 in^2. Although some forms of ceramic glass do not meet safety glazing requirements, there are laminated assemblies that are rated up to 2 hours and are rated for impact safety.

The second type is a special, tempered fire-protective glass. It is rated at a maximum of 30 minutes because it cannot pass the hose-stream test, but it does meet the impact safety standards of both ANSI and 16 CFR 1201.

The third type consists of two or three layers of tempered glass with a clear polymer gel between them. Under normal conditions, the glass is transparent, but when subjected to fire, the gel foams and turns opaque, slowing the passage of heat. This product is available with 30-minute, 60-minute, and 90-minute ratings, depending on the thickness and number of glass panes used. There are restrictions on the maximum size of lites and the type of permitted framing.

The fourth type of glazing is glass block. Since not all glass block is rated, it must be specifically tested for use in fire-rated openings and approved by the local authority having jurisdiction.

Installation of Glass

There are several ways glass can be framed. Some of the more common ones are shown in Fig. 28.17. The traditional way is to place the glass in a rabbeted frame, hold it temporarily with *glazier points* (small triangular pieces of metal), and face putty the glass in place, as shown in Fig. 28.17(a). This method is labor intensive, and the putty dries and cracks with time and must be replaced often.

Although this method may still be used for single-panes of glass on small residential jobs or for replacement work on older houses, it has been largely replaced with other methods. The glazing putty has been replaced with glazing compounds of various types that are applied like caulking and with *glazing tape*, a semirigid, formed material that is placed between the frame and the glass. See Fig. 28.17(b).

Glazing stops are required for most installations. These are removable pieces of framing that allow the glass to be installed and removed easily if it must be replaced. *Structural glazing gaskets* are also used. They are fairly rigid strips of neoprene specifically designed to hold glass. Figure 28.17(d) shows an application in a concrete reglet, but they can also be attached to metal frames. Once the glass is inserted, a compression strip is forced into a slot, which tightens the grip on the glass.

Figure 28.17 Methods of Glazing

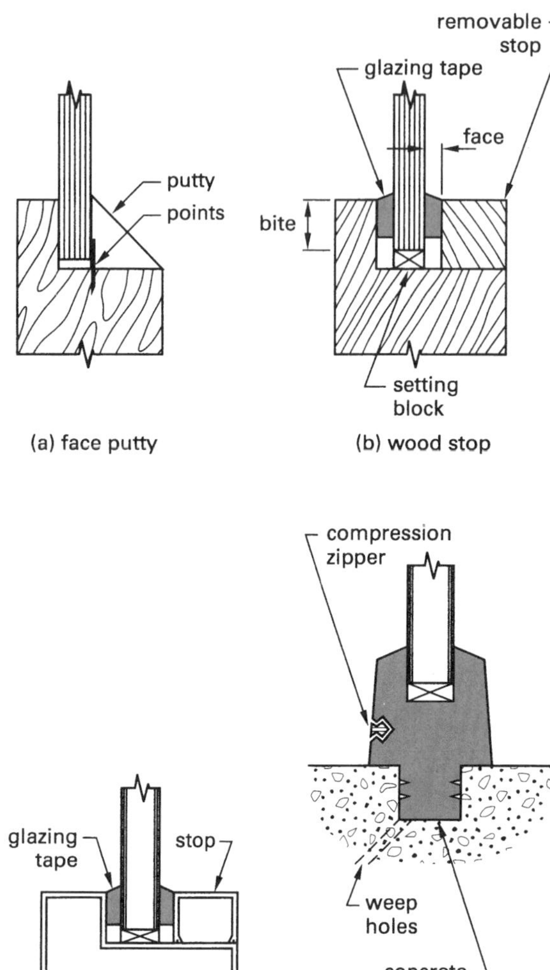

In all glazing installations, the glass should be placed on semirigid setting blocks of neoprene or other compatible elastomeric material. These prevent direct contact between the glass and frame and allow both to expand, contract, and move without putting excessive stress on the glass.

Two important dimensions when installing exterior glazing are the *face dimension* and the *bite*, as illustrated in Fig. 28.17(b). Because glass is subject to wind loading and deflects, effectively pulling out of the frame, the bite must be sufficiently deep to hold the glass in place.

Some glazing installations may also be made with a *frameless glazing system*. With this method, the glass is supported at the top and bottom, and the edges are simply butt-jointed and sealed with silicone sealant. With structural glazing systems, the vertical and horizontal framing members are entirely behind the glass (on the interior of the building) and the glass is attached to it with silicone sealant. From the exterior, the installation presents a smooth, uniform appearance, broken only by the thin, butt-jointed glass units.

As an alternative, a special type of foam tape may be used to attach glass to framing. *Acrylic foam structural glazing tape* is a two-sided, pressure-sensitive, closed-cell acrylic foam used to bind a wide variety of dissimilar materials. In addition to its use in the glazing industry, it can replace liquid adhesives, screws, rivets, spot welds and other mechanical fasteners for attaching metal panels to framing and for other interior and exterior applications.

Another type of framing system uses *spider fittings* that support the glass with clamps installed through small round holes, typically at the corners of a panel. The fitting is attached to metal framing on the inside of the glass or to glass fins on the inside. Individual panels are butted together and the joints filled with silicone sealant. From the outside, the overall appearance is one of a single plane of glass, broken only by small metal caps over each fitting. Spider fittings can be used to support glazing vertically, horizontally, or at an angle. The framing can be engineered as required to support nearly any size opening or covering.

The required thickness of exterior glass depends on the size of the glazed unit and the wind loading. Tables in building codes give the minimum thicknesses for various types of glass according to these variables. The basic maximum allowable glass area is based on float glass and accounts for wind pressure and glass thickness. Also provided are adjustment factors by which the basic area is increased depending on other types of glass used. Tempered glass has the highest adjustment factor (4.00) of all the glass types. Heat-strengthened glass has an adjustment factor of 2.00, while the factor for laminated glass is only 0.75.

Building Code Requirements for Glazing

The IBC regulates three commonly used glazing situations: the sizing of glass for wind loading, limitation on glass in fire-rated assemblies, and safety glazing subject to human impact in hazardous locations. The codes specify the minimum thickness for glass depending on wind loading and the size of the glazed unit. The subject of maximum glass areas in fire doors was discussed earlier in the chapter. For glass used in fire-resistance-rated partitions, the IBC differentiates between two types of glazing: fire-protection-rated glazing and fire-resistance-rated glazing.

Fire-protection-rated glazing is $^1/_4$ in thick wired glass in steel frames or other types of glazing that meet the requirements of NFPA 257, *Standard on Fire Test for Window and Glass Block Assemblies.* Such glazing must have a 45-minute rating and is limited to 1-hour-rated fire partitions or fire barriers where the fire barrier is used to separate occupancies or to separate incidental use areas. The amount of such glazing is limited to 25% of the area of the common wall within any room using the glazing. This limitation applies to partitions separating two rooms as well as a partition separating a room and a corridor. Individual lights of fire-protection-rated glazing cannot exceed 1296 in^2 (9 ft^2) in area and any one dimension cannot be more than 54 in. The IBC accepts $^1/_4$ in wire glass as meeting the requirements for a 45-minute rating without specific testing, but other glazing must meet the NFPA 257 test requirements for a 45-minute rating.

Fire-resistance-rated glazing is glass or other glazing material that has been tested as part of a fire-resistance-rated wall assembly Glazing, according to ASTM E119. This glazing definition allows the use of special fire-rated glazing that can have fire resistive ratings up to $1^1/_2$ hours. Refer to the previous section in this chapter for a discussion on these types of glazing products. This type of glazing may be used in partitions that must have a rating higher than 1 hour, although the glazing must have the same rating as the partition in which it is used. There are no size limitations.

The IBC requires all fire-rated glazing to be labeled by the manufacturer according to a standard system. This label consists of one or two letters followed by the fire rating in minutes. For fire-rated glazing, the letters are D, H, and T.

- D means the glazing is for use in doors and has been tested in accordance with NFPA 252.
- H means the glazing meets the hose stream test.
- T means the glazing meets the temperature rise requirements.

For fire-protection-rated glazing, a designation of OH means the glazing is appropriate for fire window openings, including window, sidelite, and transom openings, and has been tested in accordance with NFPA 257 for both fire protection and the hose-stream requirements. A designation of W means the glazing is appropriate for use as a wall and has been tested in accordance with ASTM E119, including all the fire, hose stream, and temperature rise requirements. For example, if glazing were labeled "D-H-W-90," this would mean that the glazing is appropriate for use in a door or as a wall, meets the hose stream requirements, and has been tested for a 90-minute rating.

In order to prevent injuries from people accidentally walking into glass doors and similar glazing, codes require safety glazing in hazardous locations. Hazardous locations are those subject to human impact, such as glazing in doors, glass doors, shower and bath enclosures, and certain locations in walls. A composite drawing of some situations where safety glazing is and is not required by the IBC is shown in Fig. 28.18. *Safety glazing* is considered to be tempered or laminated glass that meets the test requirements of the *Code of Federal Regulations*, 16 CFR 1201, Safety Standard for Architectural Glazing Materials.

Plastic glazing and glazing not in doors or enclosures for hot tubs, whirlpools, saunas, steam rooms, bathtubs, and showers is allowed to be tested in accordance with ANSI Z97.1, *For Safety Glazing Materials Used in Buildings—Safety Performance Specifications and Methods of Test*, Class A. Mirrors and other glass panels mounted or hung on a surface with a continuous backing do not have to be safety glazing.

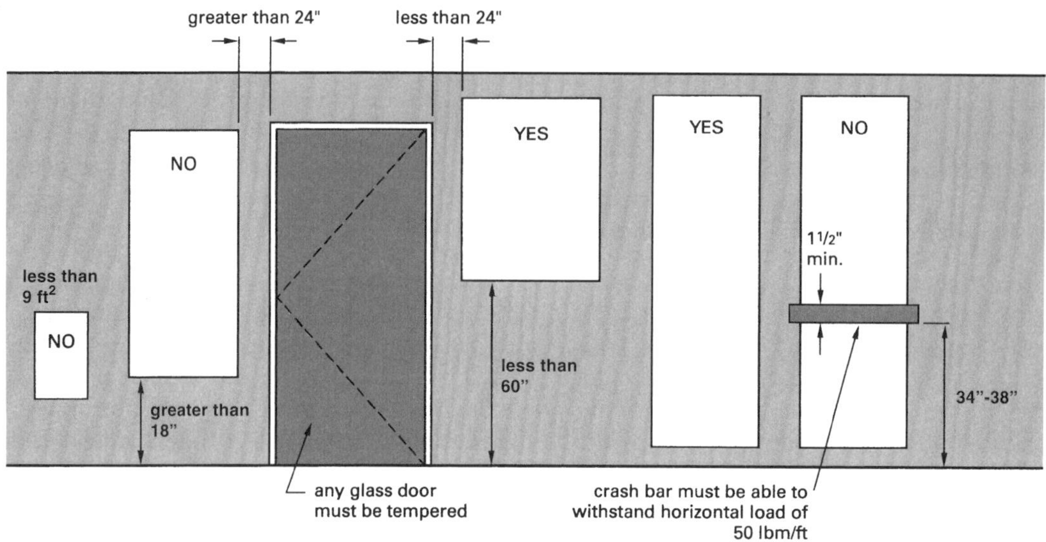

Figure 28.18
Selected Safety
Glazing Locations

CURTAIN WALL SYSTEMS

A *curtain wall* is an exterior wall system attached to the structural framework of a building that carries no load other than its own weight and the wind loading that it transfers to the structure. Curtain walls can be made of preformed metal panels, precast concrete, and prefabricated marble, granite, or masonry panels, but they are usually built of aluminum framing and glass panels. An *aluminum curtain wall* is a metal curtain wall comprised primarily of aluminum, glass, and opaque panels supported by a metal framework.

Curtain walls are categorized as standard, custom, or a combination of both. Standard curtain walls use components out of the catalog with little, if any, modification. Custom curtain walls are design specifically for one project. With each type, there are two classifications of systems. These are *stick systems* and unit, or *unitized systems.*

Figure 28.19 illustrates a stick system detail at the floor line in which mullions are installed first by attaching them to the building structure. Then the horizontal rails are placed, followed by the installation of the opaque spandrel panels and glazing.

Aluminum curtain walls can be designed in an almost unlimited number of ways. Figure 28.19 illustrates only some of the primary design considerations. Each manufacturer's product is slightly different, so final details are developed with the assistance of the manufacturer.

Unit systems are premanufactured in the factory, with the glass and spandrel panels already installed, and are attached to the building in one piece. These systems are the most common because much of the work can be completed in the factory under controlled conditions and they can be installed from the inside, without the need for scaffolding or extensive hoist work.

With both stick and unit systems, the vertical mullions are attached to the floors or beams at every floor. Attachment devices allow the vertical mullions to be adjusted in three dimensions to account for building frame tolerances and erection tolerances. This allows for a perfectly plumb and straight line for the entire height of the building. Because there is always a gap between the building structure and the back of the spandrel panel, *safing insulation* is used to provide a firestop between each floor.

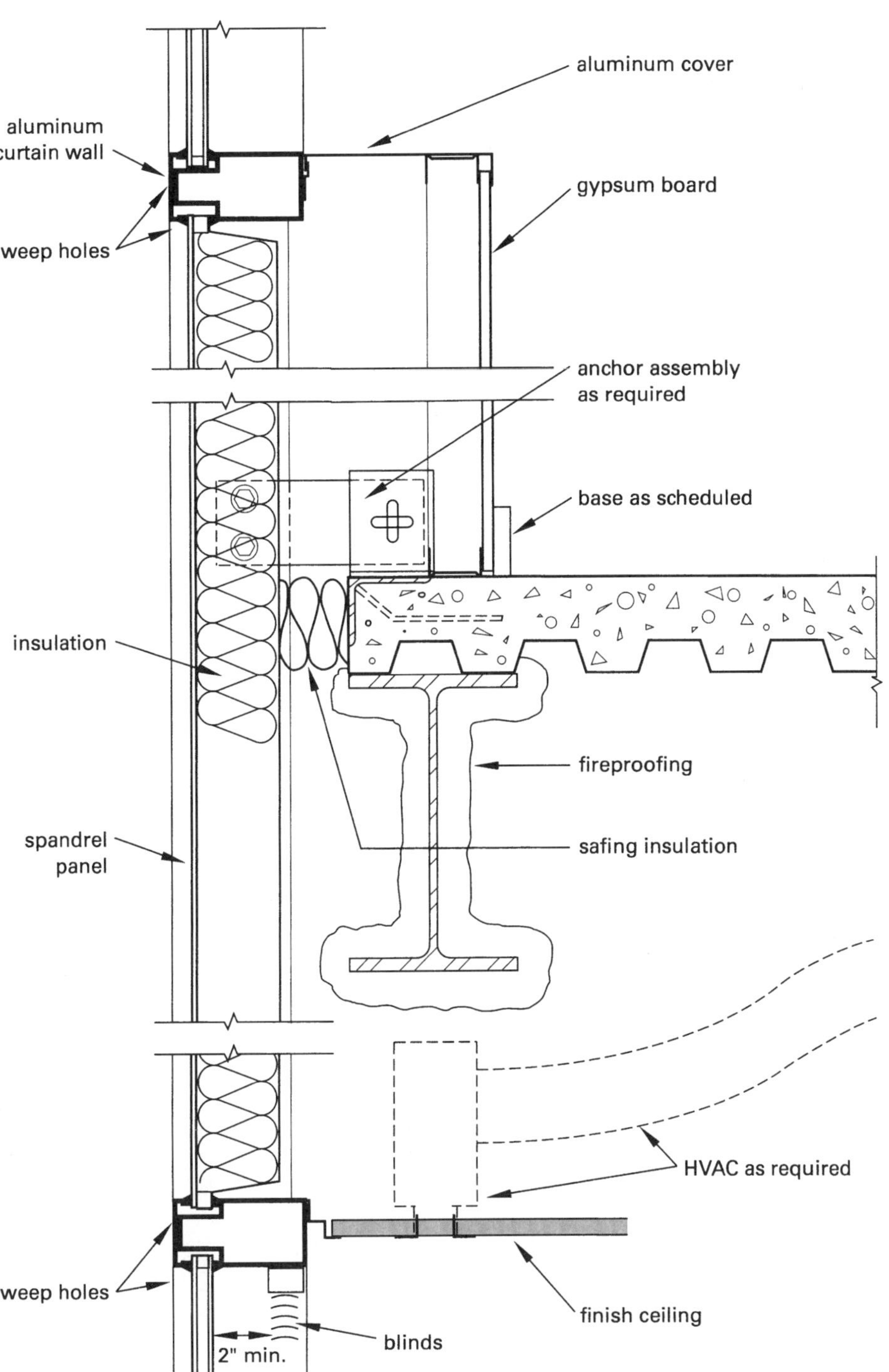

Figure 28.19
Stick System Detail

29

FINISH MATERIALS

LATH AND PLASTER

Plaster is a finish material made from cementing compounds (most often gypsum and lime), fine aggregates (sand, vermiculite, or perlite), and water. The most common cementing compound is *portland cement*, which is inexpensive and versatile. Plaster is used to form a smooth, level surface over base materials.

Some special varieties of plaster include the following.

- Vermiculite and perlite are used instead of sand when a lightweight, fire-resistant plaster is needed.
- A special process involving intense heat produces *Keene's cement*, a very hard plaster with a high resistance to abrasion and water penetration. Keene's cement is used in wet areas or on walls subject to scratching or other abuse.
- *Stucco* (also called *portland cement plaster*) is made from portland cement, lime, sand, and water. It is used for exterior applications of hard, water-resistant plaster, as a backing for tile walls, and as the preliminary coats for an application of Keene's cement.

There are two common methods of applying plaster. The first is on *metal lath* that is attached to metal or wood studs. Metal lath is available in several types: expanded diamond mesh, paper-backed diamond mesh, flat-rib lath, and high-rib lath (see Fig. 29.1). Expanded diamond lath is general purpose, used for both flat and curved surfaces. Paper-backed lath has an asphalt-impregnated paper applied to it and is used as a base for portland cement plaster under ceramic tile. Rib lath is more rigid due to the one-way, V-shaped ribs about 4 in on center, and it is used for ceilings and solid partitions.

Figure 29.1 Expanded Metal Lath

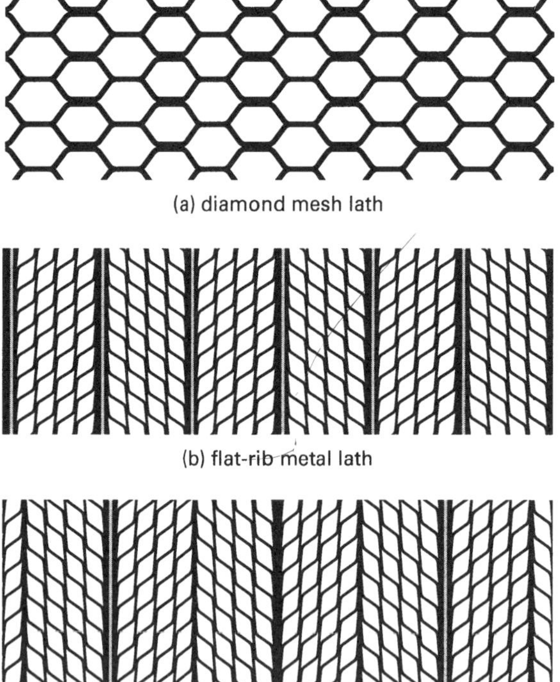

As the first coat of plaster covers the metal lath, it also flows into the openings in the surface, so that the plaster wraps around the metal and bonds with the lath as it dries. This first coat is called the *scratch coat*. In standard plastering, the scratch coat is followed by the *brown coat* and then the final *finish coat*. The scratch and brown coats are about $^1/_4$ in thick; the finish coat is about $^1/_8$ in thick. In *two-coat work*, the scratch and brown coats are combined.

The other common method of plastering uses *gypsum board lath* (also called *gypsum lath* or *rock lath*) instead of metal lath. This is a special gypsum product specifically designed for plastering. Gypsum lath comes in 16 in × 48 in boards (which are attached to the studs horizontally) and in 48 in × 96 in sheets. One or two coats of thin veneer plaster are applied over the boards. Veneer plastering requires fewer coats than the traditional method but still gives the appearance of a plastered wall; veneer plaster walls can be constructed to provide a 1- or 2-hour fire-rated partition.

Edges of plaster and stucco work must be finished with metal trim pieces. These provide a termination point for the work and serve as guides for the plasterers to maintain the required thickness. Common profiles of metal trim include the following.

- corner beads to protect outside corners
- casing beads to trim doors, windows, and other openings

- base screeds to finish plaster at the base of a room
- expansion joints to control cracking in the plaster or stucco surface

Stucco requires expansion joints at a minimum of every 10 ft or where it is likely to crack, such as at the corners of door and window openings.

In general, gypsum drywall systems have become more common for interiors than lath and plaster work because of drywall's lower cost and faster construction sequence. However, plaster is still used where curved shapes or hard, abrasion-resistant surfaces are needed. Stucco is still used for exterior applications, regardless of the surface form of the building.

GYPSUM WALLBOARD

Gypsum wallboard construction is one of the most common methods for building partitions in commercial and residential structures, since it is inexpensive and can satisfy most performance requirements. *Gypsum wallboard*, also known as *drywall* and trademarked as *Sheetrock*, is made of a gypsum plaster core sandwiched between sheets of paper or other materials.

The advantages of gypsum wallboard include the following.

- low installation cost
- quick and easy installation
- fire resistance
- sound control
- availability
- versatility (can be used for partitions, shaft enclosures, ceilings, etc.)
- ease of finishing and decorating
- ease of installation around doors, windows, and other openings

Gypsum Wallboard Materials

Gypsum wallboard is manufactured in panels 4 ft wide; standard lengths are 8 ft, 10 ft, 12 ft, and 14 ft. Special 1 in thick coreboard is manufactured in 2 ft widths for use in shaft enclosures. Contractors generally use the longest length of wallboard practical in order to minimize the number of joints, but the length used depends on the requirements of the job.

Standard gypsum wallboard is available in thicknesses of $^1/_4$ in, $^3/_8$ in, and $^5/_8$ in. There is also a $^3/_4$ in thick product that carries a 2-hour fire rating. This allows a 2-hour-rated partition to be constructed with a single layer of gypsum wallboard, without resorting to a standard two-ply application.

The thickness of the wallboard used depends on the particular application, the spacing of the framing, and the building code requirements. For most commercial and high-quality residential work, $^5/_8$ in thick wallboard is used. A $^1/_2$ in thickness is commonly used in residential projects and for some commercial applications such as furred walls.

Other applications require different wallboard thicknesses. For example, a $^3/_8$ in thickness is used in some double-layer applications or when wallboard is applied over other finished walls in remodeling work. A thickness of $^1/_4$ in is used for forming curved surfaces and for providing new finishes over old wall and ceiling surfaces. Double-layer applications are used when additional fire resistance is required or for extra acoustical benefits.

Gypsum wallboard is available with square edges, tapered edges, and tongue-and-groove edges. The tapered edge is the most commonly used because the slight taper makes it possible to apply joint compound and tape without showing a bulge in the finished surface.

Special varieties of gypsum wallboard include

- Type X, for fire-rated partitions
- foil-backed, for vapor barriers
- backing board, for use as a base for tile
- water-resistant, for moist conditions
- abuse-resistant, for high-traffic areas
- mold-resistant, which uses inorganic facings instead of paper
- predecorated with vinyl wall covering

Gypsum board faced with fiberglass mat is often used as exterior sheathing over studs and as a backing for water-resistant barriers.

Gypsum board can be applied to wood or metal framing with nails or screws, or to concrete or masonry walls with mastic. The joints are finished by embedding paper or fiberglass tape in a special joint compound and allowing it to dry. Additional layers of joint compound are added and sanded smooth after each application to give the wall surface a smooth finish. After this, the surface can be left smooth for the application of other wall coverings or covered with one of several types of textured finishes.

Because gypsum wallboard is produced in such large quantities, its manufacture, use, and disposal have a noticeable effect on the environment. Since the 1950s, gypsum wallboard manufacturers have been using recycled paper to create the surfaces of wallboard. In addition, some manufacturers use recycled newspaper mixed with gypsum as the core material; this yields a product that is more rigid than standard wallboard yet still maintains all the other advantages.

Because gypsum wallboard is produced in such large quantities, its manufacture, use, and disposal have a noticeable effect on the environment.

About half the gypsum used in wallboard in the United States is synthetic. Synthetic gypsum is chemically identical to natural, mined gypsum, but it is a by-product of various manufacturing, industrial, and chemical processes. The main source of synthetic gypsum in North America is *flue-gas desulfurization*, a process by which sulfur dioxide is removed from the exhaust gases of power plants and other industrial processes to prevent its release into the atmosphere. In this way, efficient use is made of refuse material that would otherwise have to be discarded.

A larger environmental concern involves the disposal of used gypsum wallboard, which cannot be reused for its original purpose after being ripped out of an old building or a renovation project. Some gypsum wallboard plants around the country will recycle old drywall, as long as it is free of screws, nails, asbestos, and lead paint. However, the cost of collecting, separating, and transporting the old wallboard is a disincentive for recycling.

Old wallboard can also be pulverized into pieces no larger than $^1/_2$ in and worked into the ground as a soil additive. Farmers in California and parts of Colorado use recycled gypsum as a soil conditioner for grapes, peas, and peanuts. If local and state regulations allow it, it is possible to work the gypsum directly into the soil around a job site, as long as the land has adequate drainage and aeration.

Framing

Gypsum wallboard framing for vertical construction can be either wood or metal. In residential construction, wood is generally used, in part because wood stud walls can double as load-bearing walls. Although metal framing could be used, residential contractors usually prefer wood.

In commercial construction, metal studs are commonly used because they are noncombustible, lightweight, non-shrinking, and easy to work with. Wood studs are occasionally used in smaller commercial projects when allowed by the building code.

Wood framing for gypsum wallboard partitions consists of 2 × 4 wood studs (actual size $1\frac{1}{2}$ in × $3\frac{1}{2}$ in) spaced 16 in or 24 in on center; 16 in spacing is more common, especially in residential construction. These spacings are used because they are even subdivisions of the 4 ft width and 8 ft, 10 ft, and 12 ft lengths of gypsum wallboard. For ceilings, the wallboard is generally attached directly to wood joists or ceiling rafters, which are also spaced 16 in on center.

Metal framing is light-gage, galvanized steel formed in a variety of sizes and shapes. Although metal stud partitions are usually non-load-bearing, they can be load-bearing if heavy-gage, structural steel studs are used.

Metal studs are available in several gages (thicknesses). The most common are 25 gage (0.0188 in), 22 gage (0.0284 in), and 20 gage (0.0344 in). 25 gage is used most often for studs and other metal framing. Heavier gages are used for very tall partitions, for partitions that must support unusual loads, and for framing door openings. For load-bearing partitions, exterior walls, and other heavy loading conditions, structural steel studs of 12-, 14-, 16-, or 18-gage thickness are used.

Metal studs are manufactured into a C shape with small flanges, as shown in Fig. 29.2. Openings are pre-punched along the length to allow for the passage of electrical conduit, small pipes, and other wiring. Metal studs are available in depths of $1\frac{5}{8}$ in, $2\frac{1}{2}$ in, $3\frac{5}{8}$ in, 4 in, and 6 in.

Metal studs are placed vertically and, like wood studs, are spaced either 16 in or 24 in on center. Because 24 in spacing is more economical and reduces construction time, it is common for most non-load-bearing commercial construction. Metal studs must be framed into runners at both the floor and ceiling, as shown in Fig. 29.2. The runners are C-shaped metal fabrications without a flange and have the same width as the studs. They are attached to the floor and upper support first, and then the studs are slipped into them and attached with self-tapping screws or a crimping device. Studs in other shapes are also available for special uses such as stairway shaft framing.

The depth of the stud depends on the height of the partition, the gage of the stud, the number of layers of wallboard, and the spacing of the studs. The most commonly used size is $2\frac{1}{2}$ in, which is sufficient for normal ceiling heights and slab-to-slab partitions and also allows enough room for electrical boxes and small pipes. Metal studs are normally spaced 16 in and 24 in on center with $\frac{1}{2}$ in or $\frac{5}{8}$ in thick gypsum board attached with screws.

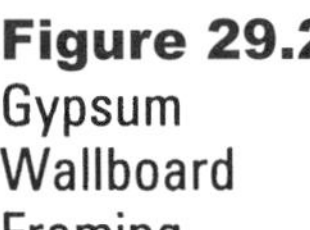

Figure 29.2 Gypsum Wallboard Framing

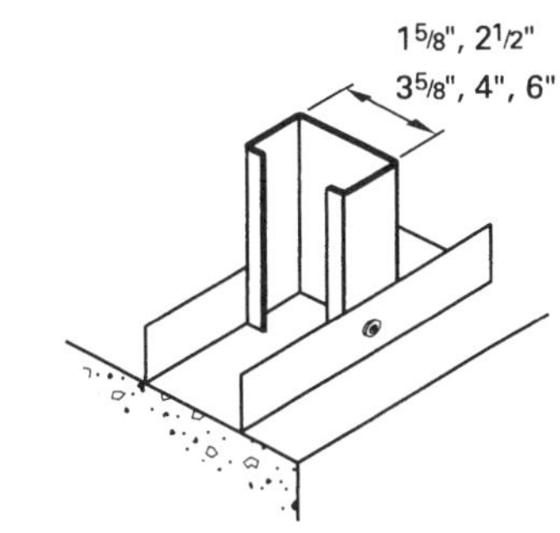

(a) typical stud and runner

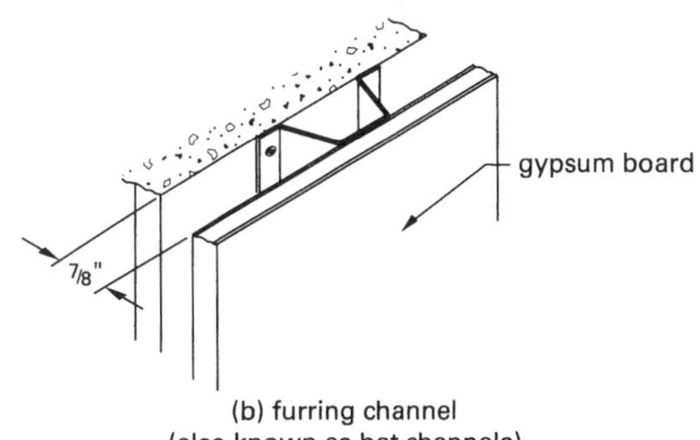

(b) furring channel
(also known as hat channels)

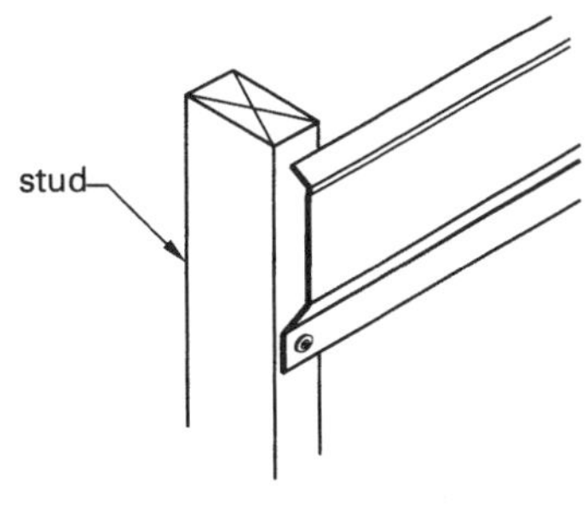

(c) resilient channel

Wallboard Trim

Like plaster walls, gypsum wallboard must have fabricated edging. This includes cornerbead, which is used for all exterior corners not otherwise protected, and various types of edge trim. These trim pieces are shown in Fig. 29.3 and are defined as follows.

- *LC bead:* edge trim requiring finishing with joint compound

- *L bead:* edge trim without a back flange; good for installation after the wallboard has been installed; requires finishing with joint compound
- *LK bead:* edge trim for use with a kerfed jamb; requires finishing with joint compound
- *U bead:* edge trim that does not require finishing with joint compound; has a noticeable edge; sometimes called *J metal* by contractors

Figure 29.3 Gypsum Wallboard Trim

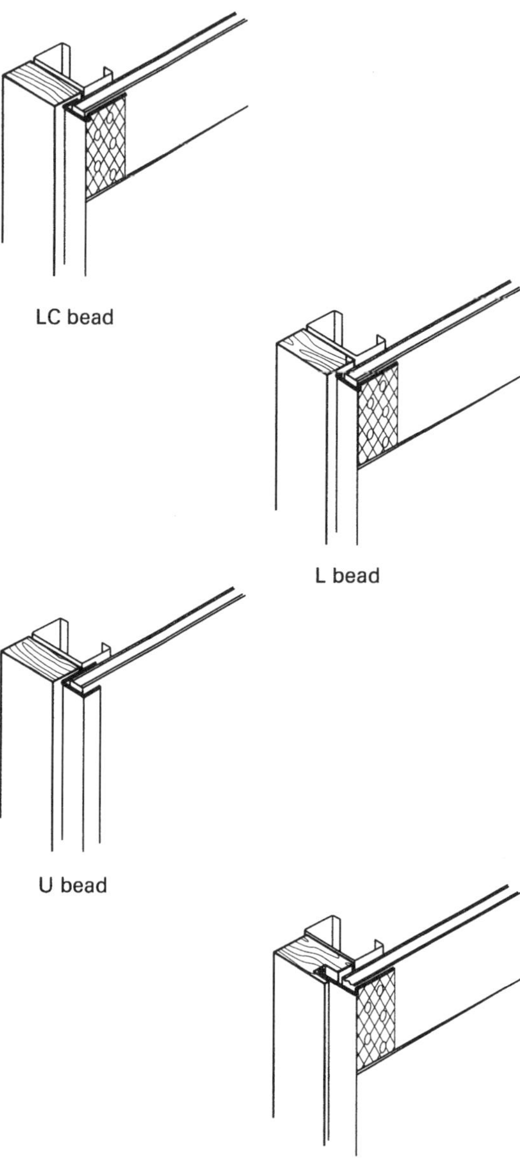

Two of the most common types of commercial gypsum wallboard construction on metal framing are shown in Fig. 29.4. A standard partition is built up only to the suspended ceiling, whereas a slab-to-slab partition is used when a complete fire-rated barrier must be constructed or when sound control is needed. By adding additional layers of Type X wallboard, fire-resistive ratings of 2 hours, 3 hours, and 4 hours can be obtained.

Gypsum wallboard is also used for ceilings and to provide fire protection for columns, stairways, and elevator shafts. It can be used as a base for finishing by attaching it to furring installed over other walls.

Glass-Reinforced Gypsum

Glass-reinforced gypsum (GRG) designates a broad class of products manufactured from a high-strength, high-density gypsum reinforced with continuous-filament glass fibers or chopped glass fibers. It is also known as *fiberglass-reinforced gypsum* (FRG) and *glass-fiber-reinforced gypsum* (GFRG).

GRG products are used for decorative elements such as column covers, arches, coffered ceilings, ornate moldings, light troughs, and trim. They are premanufactured products made by pouring GRG into molds. After setting, the products are shipped to the job site for installation and final finishing. They can be finished with any kind of material that can be put on plaster or gypsum wallboard. An unlimited variety of shapes can be manufactured using this process that would otherwise be too expensive or impossible to achieve with site-fabricated lath and plaster.

TILE

Tiles are small, flat finishing units made of clay or clay mixtures. The two primary types are ceramic tile and quarry tile. The advantages of tile include

- durability
- water resistance (if glazed)
- ease of installation

- ease of cleaning
- a wide choice of colors, sizes, and patterns
- fire resistance
- fade resistance
- ability to store heat for passive solar collection

Types of Tile

Ceramic tile is a surfacing unit, usually relatively thin in relation to facial area, made from clay or a mixture of clay and other ceramic materials. It may have either a glazed or unglazed face and is fired in the course of manufacture to a temperature sufficiently high to produce specific physical properties and characteristics.

Quarry tile is glazed or unglazed tile, usually with a facial area of 6 in^2 or more. It is made from natural clay or shale by the extrusion process.

Some of the common types of tile are glazed wall tile, unglazed tile, ceramic mosaic tile, paver tile, quarry tile (glazed or unglazed), abrasive tile, and antistatic tile. *Ceramic mosaic tile* is tile formed by the dust-pressed or extrusion method, is $^1/_4$ in to $^3/_8$ in thick, and has a facial area of less than 6 in^2. *Dust pressing* uses large presses to shape the tile out of relatively dry clay. The extrusion process uses machines to cut tiles from wetter and more malleable clay extruded through a die.

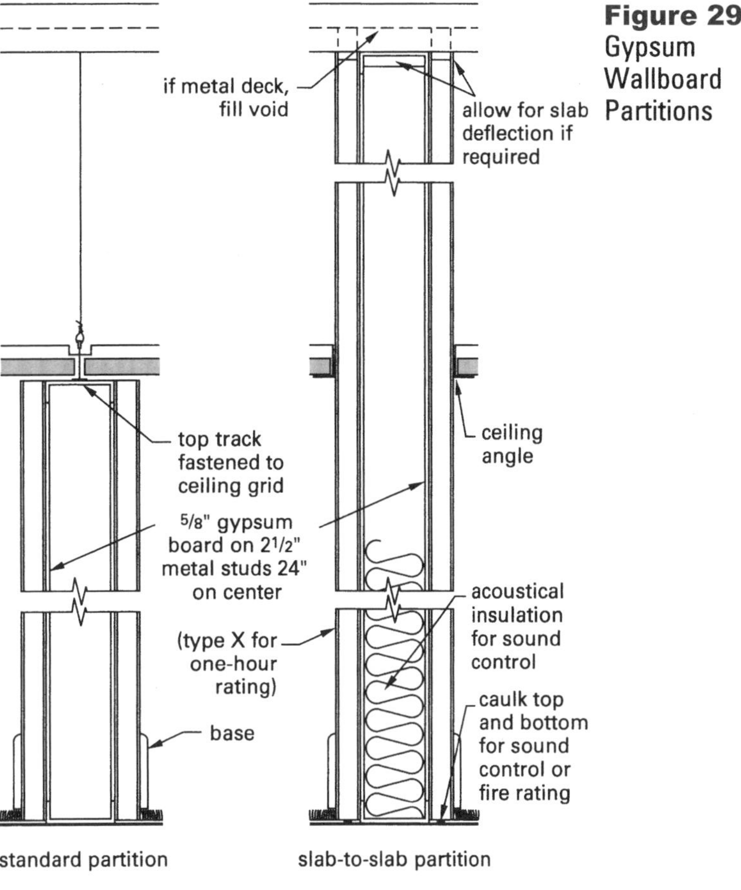

Figure 29.4 Gypsum Wallboard Partitions

Classification of Tile

The United States tile industry classifies tile based on size: under 6 in^2 is *mosaic tile*; 6 in^2 or larger is *wall tile*. Glazed and unglazed non-mosaic tile made by the extrusion method is *quarry tile*; glazed and unglazed tile 6 in^2 made by the dust-pressed method is called *paver tile*.

Tile is also classed according to its resistance to water absorption, as follows.

- *nonvitreous tile:* tile with water absorption of more than 7.0%
- *semivitreous tile:* tile with water absorption of more than 3.0% but not more than 7.0%
- *vitreous tile:* tile with water absorption of more than 0.5% but not more than 3.0%
- *impervious tile:* tile with water absorption of 0.5% or less

The classifications of abrasion resistance are as follows.

- Group I, light residential
- Group II, moderate residential
- Group III: maximum residential
- Group IV, highest abrasion resistance—commercial

Imported tile is classified differently from tile produced in the United States. European manufacturers classify tile according to its production method (either the dust-pressed or extrusion method), its degree of water absorption, its finish, and whether it is glazed or unglazed.

Tile Sizes and Shapes

Ceramic mosaic tile is available in standard nominal U.S. sizes of 1 in × 1 in and 2 in × 2 in with a nominal thickness of $^1/_4$ in. Some 2 in × 1 in tile is also available as well as tile in small hexagonal shapes. Glazed wall tile is manufactured in standard nominal sizes of $4^1/_4$ in × 4 in, 6 in × $4^1/_2$ in, and 6 in × 6 in with a nominal thickness of $^1/_4$ in or $^5/_{16}$ in. Individual manufacturers may produce other sizes as well.

Most manufacturers produce a complete line of trim pieces for ceramic tile installation. These include cove base, bullnose, inside and outside corners, and other shapes most often required. The standard trim shapes are illustrated in Fig. 29.5.

Figure 29.5
Ceramic Tile Shapes

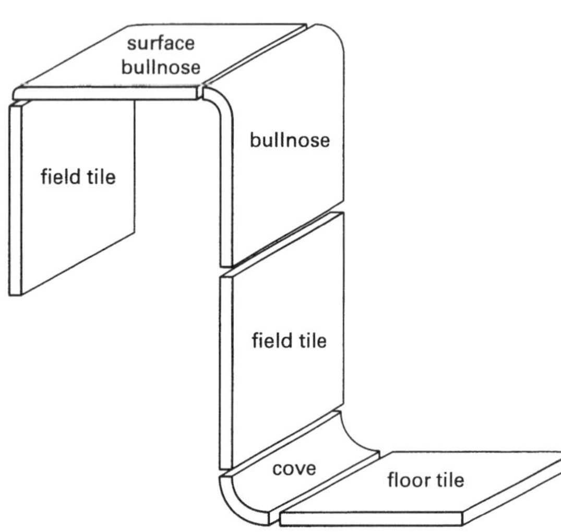

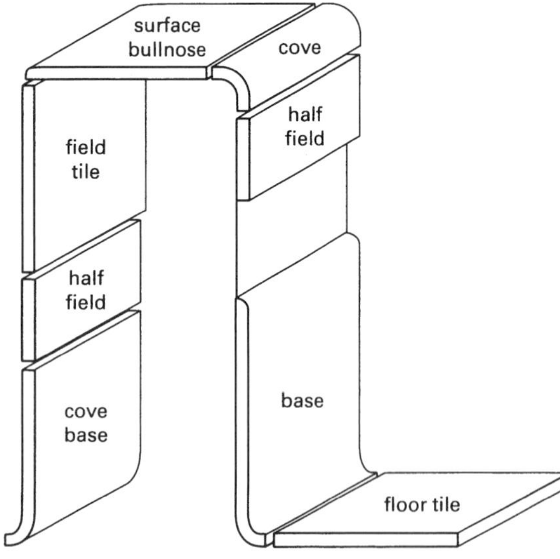

Quarry tile is available in nominal flat sizes of 3 in × 3 in, 4 in ×4 in, 6 in × 6 in, 8 in × 8 in, 8 in × 4 in, and 6 in × 3 in with a nominal thickness of $^1/_2$ in. Trim pieces are similar in shape to that of wall tile.

Tile Installation

Tile must be installed on solid, flat substrates capable of supporting the weight of the material. There are two ways of doing this: with a full-mortar bed or with thinset mortar.

The traditional method of installing floor tile is to lay it in a thick bed of mortar. The tile and reinforced mortar bed are separated from the structural floor with a cleavage membrane (15 lbm roofing felt or 4 mil polyethylene film) to allow the two floors to move independently. This system is used on floors where excessive deflection is expected and on precast and post-tensioned concrete floors. Because the mortar bed is reinforced with 2 in × 2 in, 16-gage welded wire fabric, the tile and bed are rigidly held together as a unit. In addition to providing for movement, the full-mortar bed allows for minor variations in floor level to be made up with the mortar (see Fig. 29.6).

The tile can be set on the mortar bed while the mortar is still plastic, or on a cured mortar bed using a second coat of dry-set or latex-portland cement mortar. If a waterproof floor is needed, a waterproof membrane can be used in place of the cleavage membrane. This is the preferred installation method for tile floors in commercial showers or where continuous wetting is present.

A thinset tile floor is laid on a substrate consisting of cementitious panels nailed to the subfloor. This substrate is commonly a glass-mesh mortar unit specifically manufactured for tile installation. The tile is laid on a thin coating of dry-set or latex-portland cement mortar with latex-portland cement grout. A standard sand and portland cement grout can also be used. When using the thinset tile installation method, the subfloor must be level, free from dirt and other contaminants, and able to support the extra weight of the tile. If a subfloor deflects or moves in some way, a thinset tile installation can develop cracks.

Tile on walls can be set with either the full mortar bed method or the thinset method. The full mortar bed method is typically used in commercial construction where extreme durability is needed and in continuously wet areas such as showers, laundries, pools, and tubs. For walls, instead of using welded wire fabric reinforcing, the base coat of portland cement plaster is attached to galvanized metal lath. For noncommercial construction, thinset methods are sometimes used in combination with waterproof cementitious backer boards.

Figure 29.6 Full Mortar Bed Ceramic Tile Installations

1-1/4" portland cement settling bed with reinforcing
cleavage membrane: 4 mil polyethylene or 15 lbm roofing felt
5/8" plywood
joists 16" o.c.

(a) on wood framing

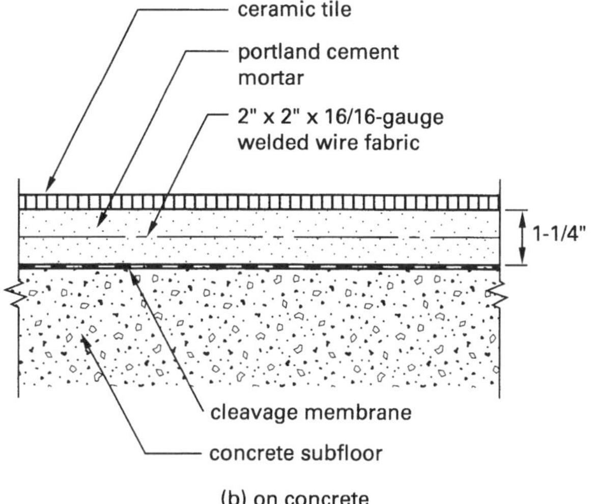

(b) on concrete

TERRAZZO

Terrazzo is a composite material used for floors, walls, stairs, and other construction elements. It consists of chips of marble, quartz, granite, or other suitable materials in a matrix that is cementitious, chemical, or a combination of both. This mixture is poured while still wet; once it is cured, the terrazzo is ground and polished to give a smooth, uniform surface with a visible texture. Terrazzo can be either poured in place or precast.

Terrazzo has many of the advantages of tile, including durability, water resistance, ease of cleaning, a wide choice of patterns and colors, and fire resistance. It can be installed on walls as well as floors.

Types of Terrazzo

There are four basic types of terrazzo. *Standard terrazzo* is the most common type, using small chips up to $^3/_8$ in. *Venetian terrazzo* uses chips larger than $^3/_8$ in. *Palladiana terrazzo* uses thin, random-fractured slabs of marble with standard terrazzo between them. *Rustic terrazzo* has the matrix depressed to expose the chips. Because any variety of chips and matrix colors can be combined, terrazzo has an unlimited number of finish options.

The most commonly used matrix is cementitious: a mixture of white portland cement, sand, and water. Modified cementitious matrices, created by mixing epoxy or polyacrylate with the portland cement, are used when additional chemical resistance or conductivity is needed or when the installation is thinset. Resinous matrices of epoxy or polyester are used for thinset applications. Conductive floors, which have black matrices due to their carbon black content, are used where static electricity buildup must be avoided.

Figure 29.7 Methods of Terrazzo Installation

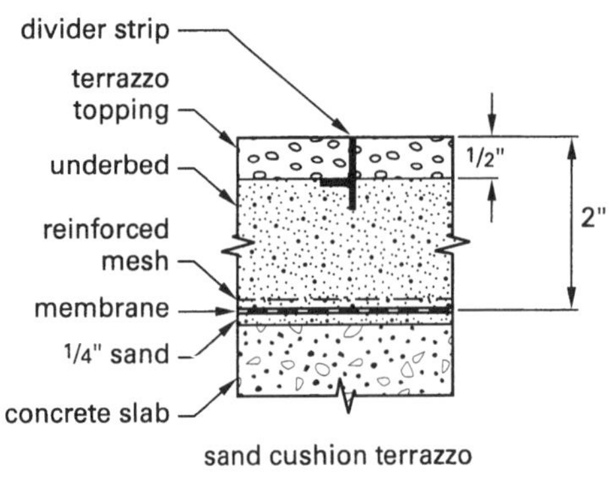

sand cushion terrazzo

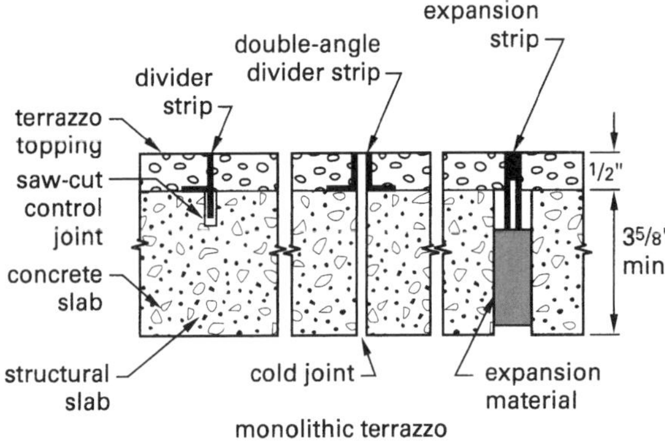

monolithic terrazzo

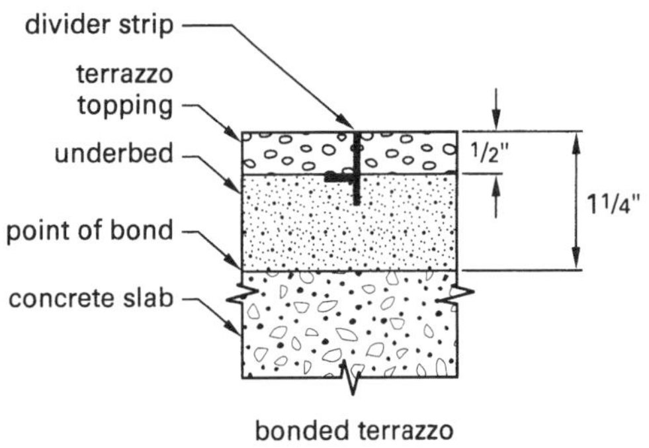

bonded terrazzo

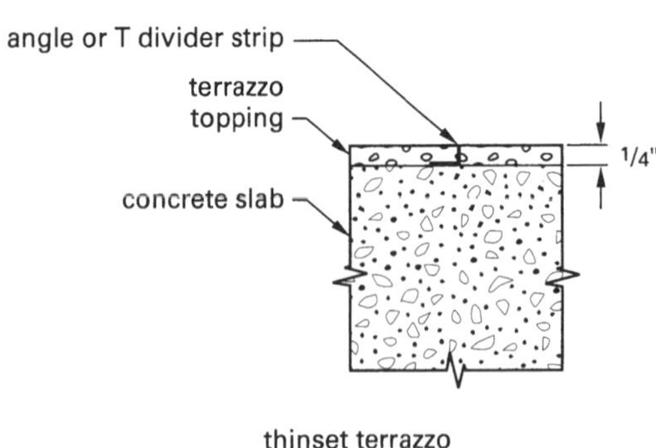

thinset terrazzo

Installation of Terrazzo

The four most common floor installations are shown in Fig. 29.7. The *sand cushion method* is the best way to avoid cracking, because the finish system is physically separated from the structural slab by a membrane. Because the underbed is reinforced, the terrazzo system can move independently of the structure. If floor movement or deflection is not expected, the *bonded method* can be used. Where the thickness of the installation is a problem, a *monolithic method* or *thinset method* can be used.

Terrazzo is generally finished to a smooth surface with an 80-grit stone grinder, but it can be ground with a rough, 24-grit grinder to achieve a more textured surface. Rustic terrazzo exposes some of the stone when the matrix is washed before it has set.

Terrazzo is also available as precast floor tiles in 12 in and 16 in squares. These are laid in a cement mortar like stone or ceramic tile.

STONE FINISHES

Stone is often used for interior finishes of walls and floors. Commonly used types include marble, granite, and, for flooring, slate. Interior veneer stone is about $^3/_4$ in to $^7/_8$ in thick and is attached to wall substrates with stainless steel wires or ties. These are anchored to the substrate and hold the stone by being set in holes or slots cut into the back or sides of the panel. Lumps of plaster of paris, called *spots*, are placed between the substrate and the back of the stone panel at each anchor to hold the slab in place and to allow for precise alignment before they set.

Anchoring stone inside a building is simpler than exterior stonework because there is no wind load, precipitation, or freezing and thawing to contend with, and panels are seldom stacked above each other so the weight of the panel can be carried by the floor. For high interior spaces many of the anchoring details are similar to those of exterior work, as shown in Fig. 29.7.

Thin stone tiles are also used for interior flooring and wall finishing. These are about $^3/_8$ in thick and come in sizes of 1 ft × 1 ft and 1 ft × 2 ft.

Stone can be installed as flooring in a number of ways, as illustrated in Fig. 29.8. Like terrazzo, stone floors are subject to cracking if bonded to a subfloor that deflects. To prevent this, a membrane is used so the subfloor and stone flooring can move separately. However, on rigid structures, stone may also be thinset.

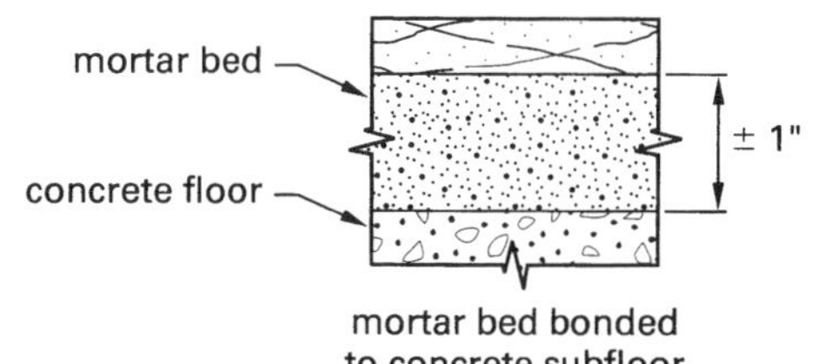

mortar bed bonded to concrete subfloor

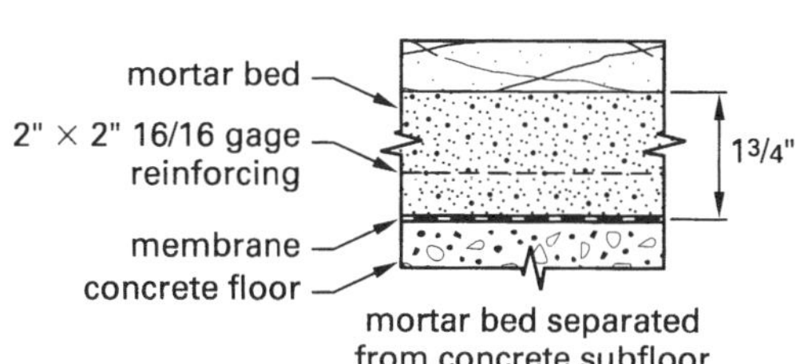

mortar bed separated from concrete subfloor

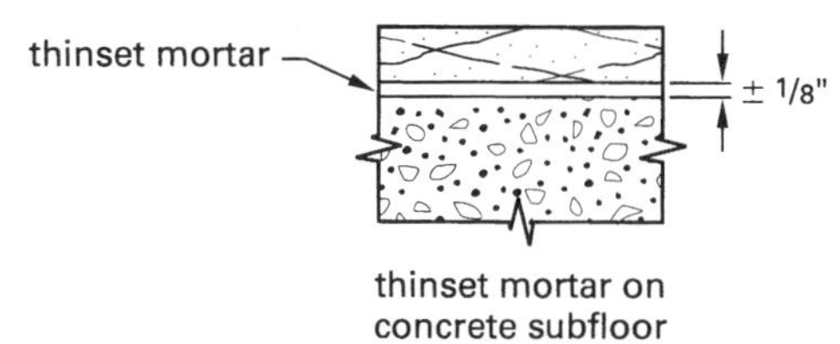

thinset mortar on concrete subfloor

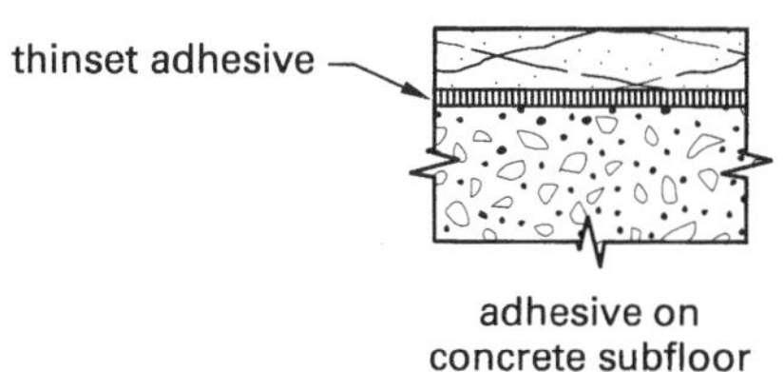

adhesive on concrete subfloor

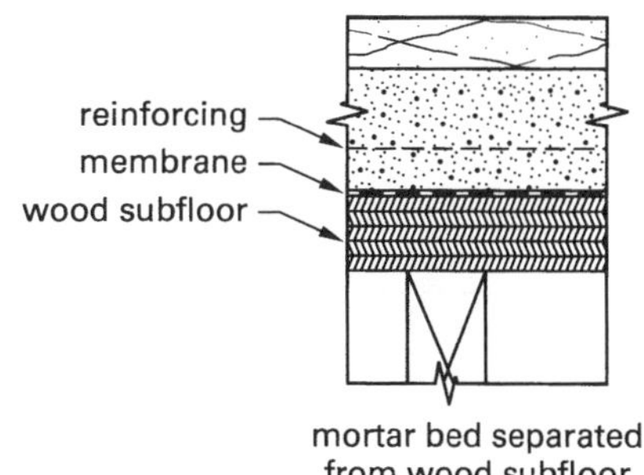

mortar bed separated from wood subfloor

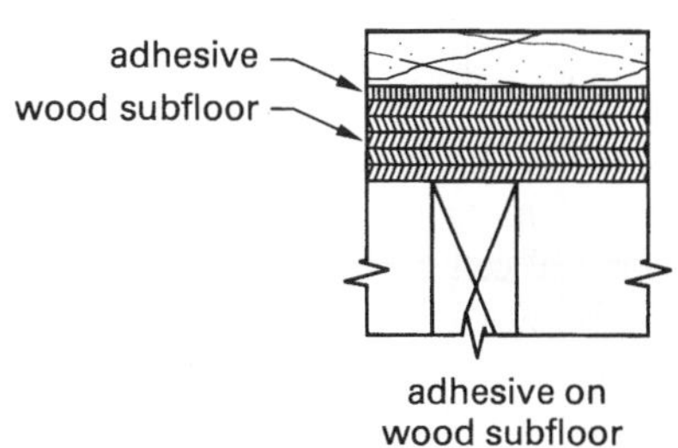

adhesive on wood subfloor

Figure 29.8 Stone Flooring Installation Methods

ACOUSTICAL TREATMENT

The three most common acoustical treatments for ordinary construction are

- ceilings
- special acoustical wall panels
- carpeting

Special devices used in auditoriums and similar spaces are not discussed in this book.

Acoustical Ceilings

In contemporary commercial construction, the ceiling is most often constructed separate from the rest of the structure. This allows a smooth, flat ceiling surface for partition attachment, lights, and acoustical treatment. The space above the ceiling but under the floor above, called the *plenum*, can be used for mechanical systems, wiring, and other services.

An *acoustical ceiling* consists of thin panels of wood fiber, mineral fiber, or glass fiber set in a support grid of metal framing that is suspended by wires from the structure above. This panels, called *acoustical ceiling tiles*, are manufactured with varying degrees of recycled content using newsprint, perlite, and ground-up pieces of old tiles. The recycled content of a set of tiles may range from 50% to 90%. The tiles are perforated or fissured in various ways to absorb sound. While acoustical ceilings absorb sound, they do not prevent sound transmission to any appreciable extent.

Acoustical ceiling tiles and the metal supporting grid are available in a variety of sizes and configurations. The most common type is the *lay-in system*, in which tiles are laid on top of an exposed T-shaped grid system. A variation of this is the *tegular grid system*, which uses tiles with rabbeted edges, as shown in Fig. 29.9(b). (See Fig. 29.9(a).) Systems in which the grid is completely concealed are also available, as shown in Fig. 29.9(c). These systems use 1 ft × 1 ft or 1 ft × 2 ft tile sizes. A typical lay-in acoustical system is shown in Fig. 29.10.

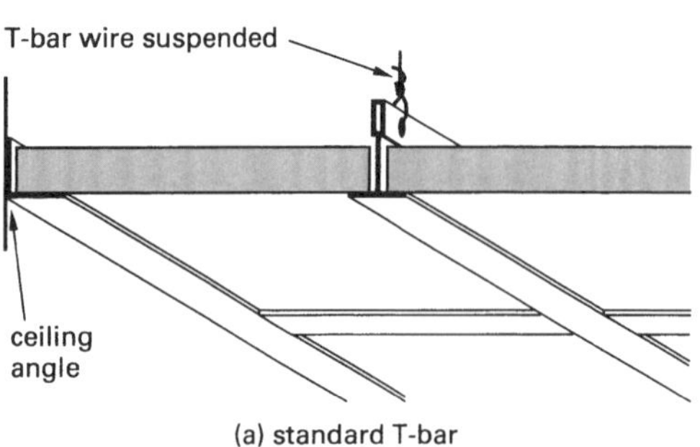

(a) standard T-bar

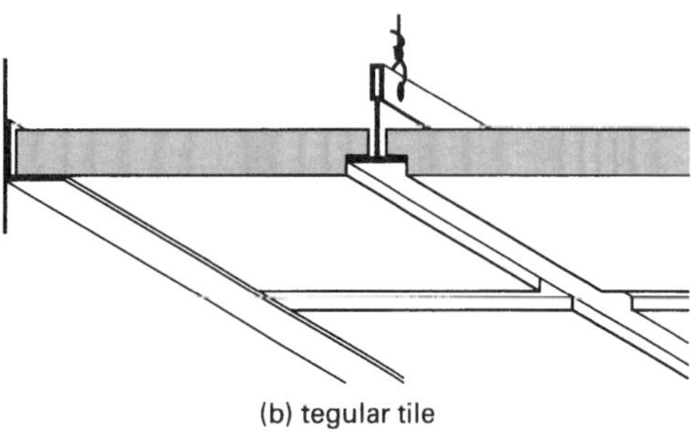
(b) tegular tile

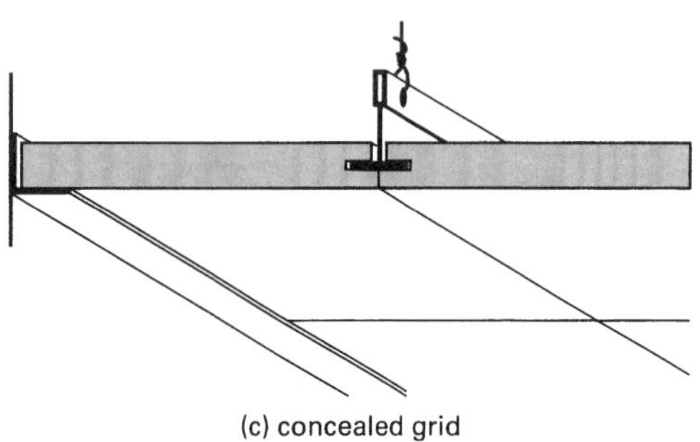
(c) concealed grid

Figure 29.9 Standard Acoustical Ceiling Systems

The most common tile and grid sizes for lay-in acoustical ceiling systems are 24 in × 24 in and 24 in × 48 in. A 20 in × 60 in size is also available for use in buildings with a 5 ft working module, so three panels fit within one 60 in grid. This allows office partitions to be laid out on the 5 ft module lines without interfering with HVAC registers and with special 20 in × 48 in light fixtures located in the center of a module.

Other types of suspended systems that provide acoustical properties are also available. These include metal strip ceilings, wood grids, and fabric-covered acoustical batts. They all serve to absorb rather than reflect sound, in order to reduce the noise level within a space.

Because suspended acoustical ceilings serve many purposes in addition to acoustical control, many elements must be coordinated in their selection and detailing. These include

- recessed lights
- ductwork
- sprinklers
- fire alarm speakers
- smoke detectors and similar items
- drapery pockets and other recessed fixtures

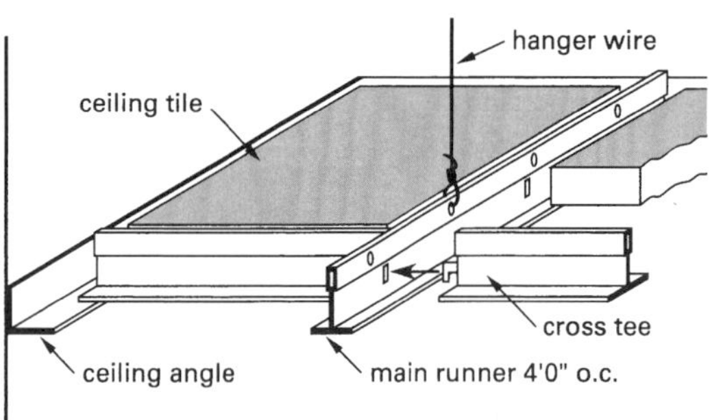

Figure 29.10 Lay-In Suspended Acoustical Ceiling

In many cases, the space above a suspended ceiling is used as a *return air plenum*. Return air grilles are set in the grid, and return air is allowed to pass through the grilles, through the ceiling space, and back to a central return air duct or shaft that connects to the HVAC system. In this case, the *International Mechanical Code* (IMC) requires that no combustible material be placed above the ceiling and that all plastic wiring be run in metal conduit. The IMC allows wiring used for telephone, computer, low-voltage lighting, and signal systems to be exposed if it is listed and labeled as plenum rated and installed in accordance with NFPA 70.

Suspended ceilings may be fire-rated or not. If they are fire-rated, it means that they are part of a complete rated floor-ceiling or roof-ceiling assembly. Suspended ceiling systems by themselves cannot be rated. Rated acoustical ceiling systems consist of rated mineral tiles and rated grid systems, the latter of which include hold-down clips to keep the tiles in place and expansion slots to allow the grid to expand if subjected to heat.

Acoustical Wall Panels

Sound-absorbent panels can be purchased or constructed for use in spaces that require acoustical treatment in addition to acoustical ceilings and carpeting. These are made from a sound-absorbent material such as fiberglass and are covered with a permeable material such as a loose-weave fabric. The acoustical material must be at least 1 in thick in order to be effective.

Seismic Restraint for Suspended Ceilings

Approximately half of the United States is considered to be at risk for seismic activity.

For human safety, a structure—and the ceiling and items attached to it, such as light fixtures—should not collapse during an earthquake. In high-risk areas, *seismic restraints*, which are structural elements designed to keep nonstructural elements in place during earthquakes, are required for ceilings and ceiling mounted items. The *International Building Code* (IBC) may also specify restraint requirements for various interior components, including

- nonstructural walls and partitions
- cabinets
- access floors
- sprinkler pipes
- bookcases

Refer to Chap. 45 for more information on earthquake design.

The IBC requires that every structure be assigned a *seismic design category*, which is determined by three factors: the soil conditions where the structure is located, the risk (or occupancy) category, and the geographical location of the structure. Soil is classified as one of the following.

- A: hard rock
- B: rock
- C: very dense soil and soft rock
- D: stiff soil (used as a default when soil conditions are unknown)
- E: soft soil
- F: special soil

There are four *risk* (or *occupancy*) *categories* given in the IBC.

- I: miscellaneous structures
- II: standard occupancy structures
- III: hazardous structures
- IV: essential structures

Each of these risk categories is assigned an importance factor from 1.00 to 1.50 depending on how important it is for the structures in those categories to remain undamaged after a major earthquake. Hospitals, fire stations, and power-generating stations, for example, are in risk category IV and have an importance factor of 1.50, while minor storage facilities, small office buildings, and retail stores may be in risk category I or II and have importance factors of 1.00.

The geographical location of a structure is determined based on detailed maps given in IBC Sec. 1613. (Detailed maps are available from the United States Geological Survey.) These maps give the ground motion of the maximum (worst case) considered earthquake, which is expressed as a percentage of the gravitational acceleration at various time intervals. Complex formulas use the percentage of gravitational acceleration for a given area to determine the area's seismic design category and aid in designing any structure to be constructed in the area.

Because determining the seismic design category is a complex process involving soil analysis, it must be done by a structural engineer. The IBC requires that the seismic design category be given on the construction documents. Most often it appears on the cover sheet of the structural engineering drawings or in the specifications. For a recently constructed structure, the seismic design category may also be available from the building architect or the local building department.

There are six seismic design categories, labeled A (least restrictive) through F (most restrictive). Buildings in categories A and B do not require any special design details. Seismic design categories E and F are subject to the most stringent requirements for earthquake design, including ceiling detailing. Seismic design category C has many of the same detailing requirements as D, E, and F, but is less stringent.

Because determining the seismic design category is a complex process involving soil analysis, it must be done by a structural engineer.

The areas with the greatest seismic risk are California, parts of Utah, Idaho, Montana, a small area near the border between North and South Carolina, and the area around the junction of Arkansas, Tennessee, Missouri, and Kentucky. Parts of Alaska and Hawaii are also at a high risk.

A building in risk category III or IV that is built on soft soil may be assigned to a high seismic design category even if it is in an area of relatively low seismic activity. If a project site is in or near an area of high seismic activity, or if it involves a structure in risk category III or IV; the architect should verify the exact seismic design category of the building and obtain specific design requirements for ceilings and other interior components from the local authority having jurisdiction. If necessary, the services of a qualified structural engineer should be obtained.

The type of detailing required for suspended ceilings is determined by the seismic design category of the building. No special seismic design is required for

- structures in seismic design category A or B
- ceilings with areas less than 144 ft^2
- gypsum wallboard suspension systems
- plaster and lath ceilings

Two publications give guidance for designing a ceiling when seismic conditions must be considered. Both are published by the Ceilings and Interior Systems Construction Association (CISCA). In seismic design category C, a suspended ceiling may be designed in accordance with CISCA 0-2, *Recommendations for Direct-Hung Acoustical Tile and Lay-in Panel Ceilings, Seismic Zones 0-2*. For seismic design categories D, E, and F, useful guidance can be found in CISCA 3-4, *Guidelines for Seismic Restraint for Direct-hung Suspended Ceiling Assemblies, Seismic Zones 3-4*. The titles refer to older seismic zones of the United States that are no longer commonly used.

The detailed provisions of seismic design of architectural components can be found in ASCE/SEI 7, *Minimum Design Loads for Buildings and Other Structures*, published by the American Society of Civil Engineers (ASCE).

Local ceiling system installation companies and ceiling manufacturers can provide valuable information for specific seismic design requirements. Table 29.1 summarizes some of the more important requirements for seismic design categories C through F, and the following descriptions provide detailed requirements. The requirements in Table 29.1 are based on IBC requirements for generic ceiling systems. However, several ceiling grid manufacturers have developed proprietary wall attachment clips, expansion joint clips, and other devices tested and approved for use. Each manufacturer is responsible for having its products tested by an approved testing laboratory according to the requirements of the IBC and applicable ASTM standards.

Table 29.1
Summary of Ceiling Seismic Design Requirements

system component	category C	categories D, E, and F
vertical hanger wire, 12 gauge at 48 in o.c.	required	required
main tee classification	intermediate or heavy-duty	heavy-duty
minimum intersection strength limits	60 lbf	180 lbf
grid end/wall clearance	min. $^3/_8$ in	min. $^3/_4$ in
perimeter closure width (ceiling angle)	min. $^7/_8$ in (or use perimeter wires)	min. 2 in
grid connection to perimeter attached on two adjacent walls[a]	not permitted	required
horizontal restraint (splay wires or rigid pacing) within 2 in of intersection and splayed 90° apart at 45° angles	not required	required
compression posts (struts) at 12 ft o.c. in both directions, starting 6 ft from walls	not required	required
splay bracing connection strength 200 lbf or the design load, whichever is greater	not required	required
partition attachment	allowed only if ceiling is able to move laterally	bracing independent of ceiling splay bracing
seismic separation joint	not required (or full-height partition)	required for areas greater than 2500 ft^2
rigid bracing for ceiling plane elevation changes	not required	required
light fixtures mechanically attached to grid or directly to structure[b]	required	required
sprinkler heads and other penetration clearance	min. $^3/_8$ in on all sides	min. 2 in diameter opening or a swing joint
cable trays and electrical conduit independently supported and braced	not required	required

[a]Alternate methods are approved that use perimeter clips, which modify these basic requirements.

[b]The exact type of light fixture support depends on the type of fixture and its weight. Refer to ceiling manufacturer's suggestions for support methods.

For structures in seismic design categories D, E, and F, the ceiling cannot be used to provide lateral support for partitions. Instead, the partitions must be braced with detailing similar to that shown in Fig. 29.11.

For seismic design category C, partitions may be attached to the ceiling grid if the ceiling is able move laterally. Perimeter attachment varies with the design category. For seismic design category C, the grid must not be attached to the perimeter trim. Instead, a minimum gap of $^3/_8$ in is required between the ends of the grid and the wall angle, which must be a minimum of $^7/_8$ in wide (see Fig. 29.12). For seismic design categories D, E, and F, the grid must be attached on two adjacent sides of the room and not attached on the opposite sides. The minimum gap is $^3/_4$ in, with a minimum ceiling angle dimension of 2 in. In both cases, spacer bars must be used to prevent the grid from

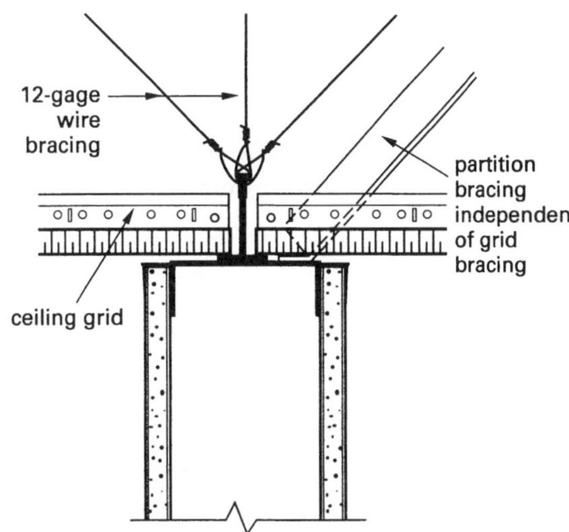
12-gage wire bracing
partition bracing independent of grid bracing
ceiling grid
Note: All components and connections must be designed to resist design loads applied perpendicular to the face of the partition.

Figure 29.11
Partition Bracing for Seismic Risk Areas

separating, and hanger wires must be installed no more than 8 in from the wall. In lieu of these provisions, manufacturers' proprietary clips that allow the grid to move perpendicular to the wall without moving laterally are available.

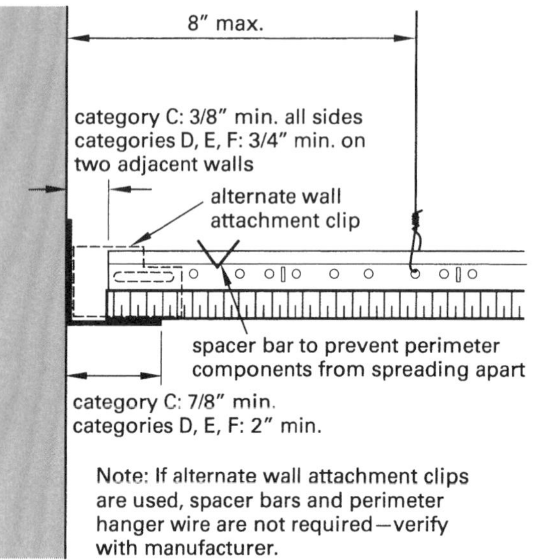

Figure 29.12 Detail of Runners at Perimeter Partition

In the field of the grid, vertical 12-gage hanger wires are required at 48 in on center. In seismic design categories D, E, and F, lateral bracing is also required at 12 ft on center with rigid compression struts to prevent excessive movement of the ceiling, as shown in Fig. 29.13.

For more information on seismic restraint for suspended ceilings, refer to USG's website at usg.com.

WOOD FLOORING

Wood flooring offers a wide variety of appearances while providing a surface that is durable, wear resistant, and comfortable. It can be laid in dozens of different patterns and is available in a variety of the following attributes.

- types of flooring: wood and engineered
- grades
- species
- finishes
- methods of installation

When using wood flooring in construction, it is important to consider and test the concrete underneath for its moisture content, as this can affect the longevity, quality, and appearance of the wood.

Types of Wood Flooring

There are four basic types of wood flooring: strip flooring, plank flooring, block flooring, and solid block flooring. See Fig. 29.14.

Strip flooring, one of the most common wood flooring types, consists of thin strips from $^3/_8$ in to $^{25}/_{32}$ in thick, of varying lengths, with tongue-and-groove edges. Most strip flooring is $2^1/_4$ in wide, but $1^1/_2$ in wide strips are also available. Strip flooring is used for residential and commercial wood floors for its appearance, warmth underfoot, durability, and resiliency.

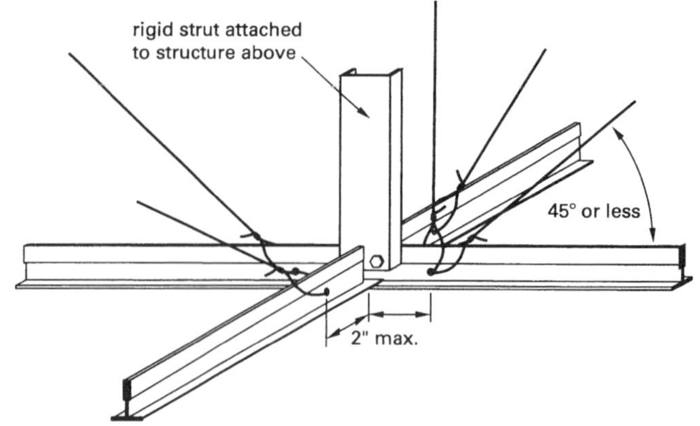

Figure 29.13 Ceiling Grid Bracing

Project Planning

Plank flooring comes in the same thicknesses as strip flooring but is from 3¼ in to in 8 wide. It is laid in random lengths with the end joints staggered. Plank flooring is used primarily in residential applications where a larger scale is desired or to emulate wider, historic planking.

Block flooring is made of preassembled wood flooring in two configurations. *Unit block flooring* is standard strip flooring assembled into a unit held together with steel or wood splines. *Laminated block flooring* is made with from three to five plies of cross-laminated wood veneer. Both types of block flooring are from ⅜ in to $^{25}/_{32}$ in thick, in varying lengths, depending on the manufacturer. Unit and laminated block flooring can be laid in any pattern, but herringbone is one of the most common.

Solid block flooring is made from solid end-grain blocks. These are solid pieces of wood 2 in, 2½ in, 3 in, and 4 in thick laid on end with adhesive. Solid block floors are very durable and resistant to oils, mild chemicals, and indentation. They are used for industrial floors or other heavy-duty commercial applications.

Wood floors are also available for special uses. *Resilient floors* are wood strip floors laid on one of three types of systems described in the next section. They provide extra buoyancy for uses such as dance and theater floors. *Relocatable floors* are systems of modular units, usually 2 ft × 2 ft, which can be quickly installed and dismantled. They are used for athletic and institutional floors where the type of flooring needs to be changed frequently.

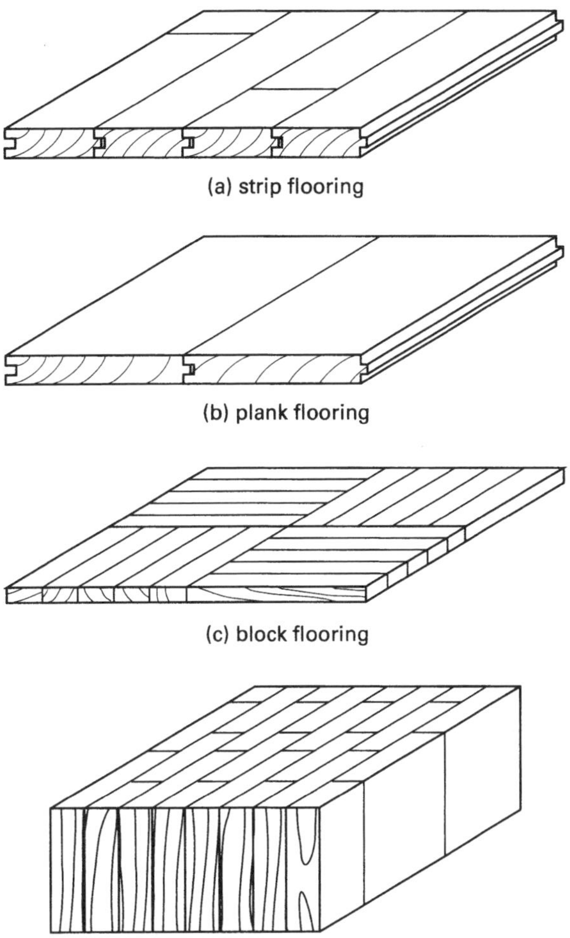

Figure 29.14
Types of Wood Flooring

(a) strip flooring

(b) plank flooring

(c) block flooring

(d) solid block flooring

Types of Engineered Flooring

Engineered flooring, including the laminated block flooring previously described, is available either unfinished or prefinished. Engineered wood flooring consists of three, five, or seven layers of wood veneer, each oriented at 90° to the adjacent layers, like plywood. The top layer is the finished wood species.

Because engineered wood floors are more dimensionally stable than solid wood, they shrink and swell less with changes in moisture. Some types of engineered floors are glued directly to a stable concrete or wood subfloor, while others consist of separate strips glued to each other along the edges but laid loose over thin foam padding, allowing the finish floor to move independently of the subfloor. This installation is often referred to as a *floating floor*.

Prefinished engineered flooring is dimensionally stable and can be installed more quickly than standard strip flooring. However, because of the thin layer of finish flooring, it cannot be sanded and refinished as solid flooring can, which reduces its overall lifespan. Because the top layer is bonded to the backing layer and cannot contract when it dries, engineered wood floors may not perform as well as solid wood floors in extremely dry climates unless indoor humidity is carefully controlled.

Parquet flooring is made of preassembled units of several small, thin slats of wood in a variety of patterns and available finished or unfinished. Some manufacturers make parquet with a cellular foam resilient backing with a factory-applied adhesive for residential "peel and stick" applications. Commercial applications use non-backed units that are field finished. Parquet flooring is usually sold for mastic application in 12 in squares that are $^{5}/_{16}$ in thick, although some manufacturers make other sizes. Parquet flooring is easier and less expensive to install than other types of flooring and can be installed in a wide range of designs.

Laminate flooring uses a variation of plastic laminate material that is composed of a clear wearing sheet over a melamine-impregnated decorative printed sheet, with core layers of phenolic-impregnated kraft paper. These sheets are laminated to a high-density fiberboard core under heat and pressure and covered with a water-resistant backing sheet. The decorative printed sheet can be made to resemble natural wood, tile, or stone, or can be printed in solid colors or even have photographic-quality images in it. Laminate flooring is available in planks (similar to wood-strip flooring but a little wider), square tiles, or rectangular blocks about $^{5}/_{6}$ in thick. It is normally laid on a cushioned foam underlayment with the tongue-and-groove edges glued together. When laminate flooring is laid over a concrete floor, a vapor barrier is needed.

Laminate flooring is hard, durable, and resistant to staining. It is a popular choice when a less expensive alternative to other types of flooring is needed. It can be used in most residential and light commercial locations, but it is not recommended for restrooms or other wet areas.

Grades of Wood Flooring

Wood flooring is graded differently from other wood products. Grading rules are set by the various trade associations, including the following.

- National Oak Flooring Manufacturers' Association
- Maple Flooring Manufacturers' Association
- Southern Pine Inspection Bureau
- West Coast Lumber Inspection Bureau
- Western Wood Products Association

Unfinished oak flooring is graded as clear, select, no. 1 common, and no. 2 common. Clear is the best grade with the most uniform color. Plain sawn is standard, but quarter sawn is available on special order. Lengths of pieces are $1^{1}/_{4}$ ft and up, with the average length being $3^{3}/_{4}$ ft.

Beech, birch, and maple are available in first, second, and third grades along with some combination grades.

Species of Wood Flooring

Wood flooring is made from both hardwood and softwood, with the hardwoods predominating. Standard hardwoods used are red oak, white oak, maple, birch, beech, pecan, mahogany, and walnut. Softwoods used are yellow pine, fir, and western hemlock, among others. In addition to these commonly used wood species, many both domestic and imported can be used for flooring. Of those available, however, only two qualify as sustainable products: bamboo and palm wood.

Bamboo is a fast-growing grass that reaches maturity in three to four years. It can be used for flooring as well as for veneer and paneling. It can be obtained from managed forests where it is grown on steep slopes and in hill lands where other forms of agriculture are difficult to propagate.

Bamboo flooring is available in $1^{1}/_{2}$ in and $^{3}/_{4}$ in thick strips about 3 in wide or wider, depending on the manufacturer. It is milled with tongue-and-groove edges, so it can be installed like standard wood-strip flooring. It can be installed by nailing or with an adhesive. Bamboo is almost as hard and twice as stable as red oak and maple. It is available in a natural color or a darker, amber color and is prefinished with a durable polyurethane coating.

Palm wood comes from coconut palms and is a by-product of commercial coconut plantations. Palm wood flooring is available in $^3/_4$ in × 3 in wide strips with tongue-and-groove edges like those of standard strip flooring. It is harder and more stable than maple, red oak, and white oak. The flooring ranges from medium- to dark-red mahogany in color and is prefinished with polyurethane.

Wood Flooring Finishes

Wood strip and plank flooring are usually installed unfinished for field sanding, staining, and finishing. Block flooring may come unfinished or prefinished. However, field finishing can create scheduling and environmental problems. Once the flooring is installed it may take several days to sand, finish, and allow the finish to dry before other construction operations can proceed. Sanding creates dust and the finishing process can release fumes.

Several types of finishes are available for wood floors. One of the most common is water-based urethane. It produces a durable, quick-drying finish that satisfies environmental regulations for limited volatile organic compound (VOC) content. It dries clear and inhibits color changes in certain woods. In addition, water-based urethane is the best choice for exotic woods that contain oils and chemical compounds that adversely react with some types of solvent-based finishes.

Oil-modified polyurethane also produces a durable finish, but it may be slower drying, contain an unacceptable VOC content, and darken some woods. However, some manufacturers have reformulated their oil-modified products to comply with VOC regulations.

Other finishes include moisture-cured urethanes and acid-cured (Swedish) finishes. Both provide an extremely durable cover but produce a strong, unpleasant odor during application.

Much of the wood flooring in newer installations comes with a factory finish. Prefinished wood floors reduce total installation time and eliminate the need for on-site sanding and wet finishing. Prefinished floors are generally more durable, with a urethane finish that is baked on with ultraviolet light under controlled conditions. Because prefinished flooring has no protection at the joint lines, a topcoat may be applied if the flooring will be installed in an area subject to liquid spills. The manufacturer should be consulted to verify the topcoat is compatible with the factory finish.

Installation of Wood Flooring

Wood flooring must be installed over a suitable base that can be nailed. Because wood swells if it gets damp, provisions must be made to prevent moisture from seeping up from below and to allow for expansion of the completed floor.

Figure 29.15 Wood Flooring Installation

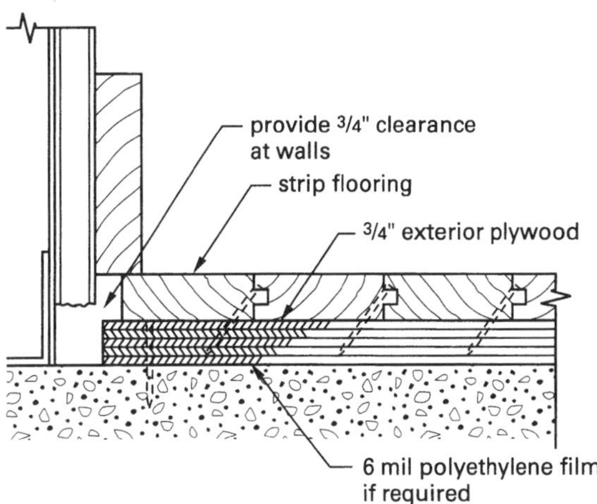

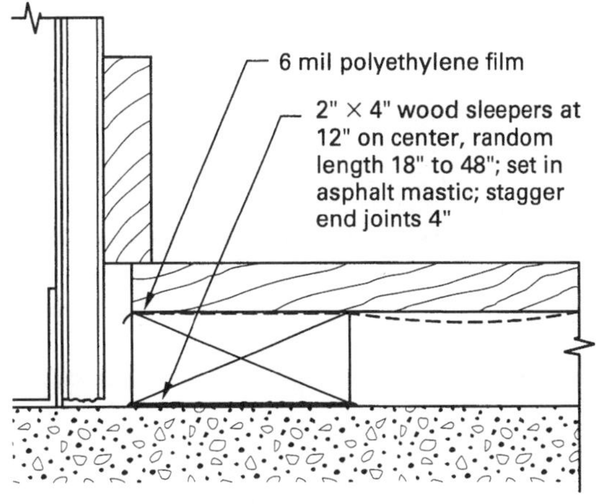

wood strip flooring over concrete

Strip flooring is installed by blind nailing through the tongue.

Figure 29.15 shows two methods of installing wood flooring over a concrete subfloor. In the first method, a sheet of $^3/_4$ in plywood is attached to the concrete to provide the nailable base. A layer of polyethylene film is laid down first if moisture may be a problem.

In the second method, the wood flooring is laid on wood sleepers. This method of installation not only produces a more resilient floor that is more comfortable under foot, but it also provides an air space so that any excess moisture can escape. In both instances, a gap of at least $^3/_4$ in is left at the perimeter to allow for expansion and is concealed by the wood base.

Figure 29.16 shows the typical installation over wood framing with a plywood subfloor. A layer of 15 lbm asphalt felt may be laid to prevent squeaking and to act as a vapor barrier.

Figure 29.16
Wood Flooring on Wood Framing

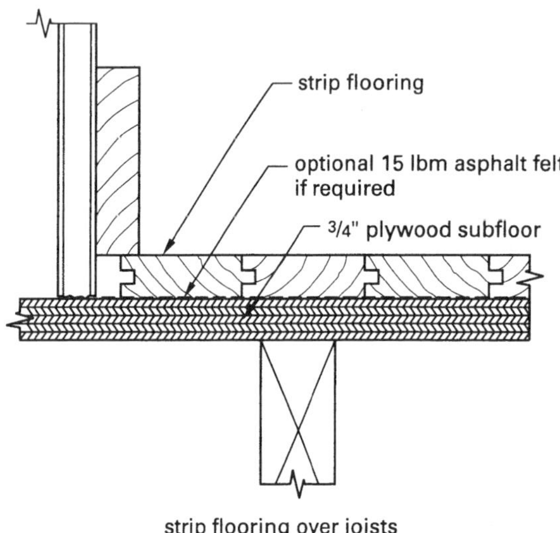

Resilient pads are also used in place of sleepers for strip flooring installation. These provide an even more resilient floor and are often used for dance floors and gymnasium floors.

Testing Concrete for Moisture Content

Regardless of what type of wood flooring is used, the substrate must be dry during installation and remain dry for the life of the floor. The National Wood Flooring Association (NWFA) recommends that moisture content of the wood floor substrate be within 4% of the area's average environmental conditions. Dry substrates are also important for successful application of resilient flooring. The alkalinity of the concrete should be acceptable for successful installation of wood and resilient flooring. Refer to Chap. 22 for a discussion of testing concrete for moisture content and alkalinity.

Example 29.1

Which of the following types of wood floors would be the LEAST appropriate for a commercial office?

(A) block

(B) parquet

(C) resilient

(D) strip

Solution

Resilient wood floors are commonly used for theater stages, dance floors, and gymnasiums. They provide extra bounce and resiliency for these types of uses.

The answer is (C).

RESILIENT FLOORING

Resilient flooring is a generic term describing several types of composition materials made from various resins, fibers, plasticizers, and fillers and formed under heat and pressure to produce a thin material in either sheets or tiles. Resilient flooring is applied to a subfloor of concrete, plywood, or other smooth underlayment with mastic. Some types may only be installed above grade, while others may be placed below, on, or above grade. The types of resilient flooring include vinyl, vinyl composition, rubber, cork, vinyl-faced cork, and asphalt.

Resilient flooring is available in tiles or in sheet form. Sheet flooring has several advantages over tile. Although it is more difficult to install, it provides a floor with fewer seams, which makes the floor easier to clean, more hygienic, and more resistant to moisture spills. Some types of sheet flooring also allow what few seams that do exist to be sealed.

Vinyl Flooring

Vinyl tile is the common term for flooring based on polyvinyl chloride. PVC is durable and resistant indentation, abrasion, grease, water, alkalis, and some acids. Vinyl comes in a variety of colors and patterns and is easy to install. It can be used below grade, on grade, or above grade and must be installed over a clean, dry, smooth surface.

Vinyl tiles are generally 12 in squares, although some are available in 9 in squares and other sizes. Both $^1/_{16}$ in and $^1/_8$ in thicknesses are available, but for commercial use and better residential floors, the $^1/_8$ in thickness is preferred.

Solid sheet vinyl, like solid vinyl tile, is a homogeneous non-layered construction of PVC with color and pattern extending through the entire thickness. It is very durable and resistant to indentation and rolling wheeled traffic. Because the seams can be sealed with heat welding or solvent welding, it is an excellent floor for health care facilities, clean rooms, and industrial flooring. Homogeneous vinyl is slightly more expensive than composition vinyl.

Vinyl Composition Flooring

Vinyl composition tile is similar to vinyl tile but includes various type of fillers that decrease the percentage of PVC. Although composition tile costs less than homogeneous vinyl, it has less flexibility and abrasion resistance. Because of this, through-grain types are preferred; on through-grain tiles, the color and pattern extend uniformly through the tile thickness. Vinyl composition tile is usually applied with mastic, but for residential applications peel-and-stick types are available, as well as tile with an attached foam backing for greater resilience.

Rubber Flooring

Rubber flooring is made from synthetic rubber and offers excellent resistance deformation under loads while providing a very comfortable, quiet, resilient floor. Rubber, however, is not very resistant to oils or grease, is hard to clean, and can be damaged by indentation of small objects. This flooring is available with a smooth surface or with a patterned, raised surface, which allows water and dirt to lie below the wearing surface. This helps prevent slipping or excessive abrasion. Rubber flooring is available in tiles or sheet form in several sizes and thicknesses.

Rubber sheet flooring has the same properties as rubber tile, but with fewer seams. The decorative types of flooring with raised patterns are usually specified in sheet form.

Linoleum Flooring

Linoleum is one of the traditional types of sheet flooring. It is composed of oxidized linseed oil or other binders, pigments, and fillers applied over a backing of burlap or asphalt-saturated felt. Linoleum is available as plain, battleship linoleum (which is a single color), or inlaid linoleum (which consists of multicolored patterns that extend through the thickness the backing). Linoleum has very good abrasion and grease resistance, but it has limited resistance to alkalis. A light gage is used for residential floors and a heavy gage for commercial floors. Linoleum is a good choice for sustainable flooring because it is made from natural, renewable products.

Cork Flooring

Available in tile form, *cork flooring* is used where acoustical control or resilience is desired. It is not resistant to staining, moisture, heavy loads, or concentrated foot traffic. It should only be used above grade and must be sealed and waxed to protect the surface.

Cork is a renewable resource. Cork is harvested by stripping bark tissue from certain trees; the trees live and can be harvested again in approximately nine years. In addition, the cork industry helps preserve forests. Portugal, which produces about half of the world's cork, regulates harvesting and has made it illegal to cut down cork-producing trees.

Cork is available in tile and plank forms and is used where acoustical control or a high degree of resilience is desired. Tiles are commonly 12 in square and either $^3/_{16}$ in or $^5/_{16}$ in thick. Planks are 12 in wide and 3 ft long and consist of cork that is laminated to tongue-and-groove medium-density fiberboard.

Preparation of Substractes

Regardless of the type of resilient flooring used, preparation of the subfloor is essential to a successful installation. Because moisture is the cause of most problems, concrete floors must be dry at the time of installation. For new concrete floors, it may take 6 to 12 weeks for the slab to thoroughly cure and dry. If there is any doubt about its dryness, the slab should be tested for moisture. Refer to Chap. 22 for a description of some methods of testing concrete floors for moisture.

A slab below grade or on grade should have a vapor barrier below it to prevent moisture from migrating from below. The concrete must be free of any curing compounds, sealers, and hardeners that will interfere with the adhesive that will be used to bond the flooring. The slab must also be free of solvents, grease, oil, and similar compounds. The surface should be smooth and level within $^1/_8$ in over 10 ft, with no abrupt transitions or depressions. Construction and control joints should be filled and leveled with a latex patching compound.

Wood subflooring should be smooth, with all boards securely fastened. Underlayment of plywood, hardboard, or particleboard is generally recommended. The board should be underlayment grade, at least $^1/_4$ in thick, and securely glued and nailed, with the joints staggered. The joints should be sanded and filled, if necessary, with all nails driven flush. Grade-level wood floors should be over a well-ventilated crawl space with a vapor barrier placed on the earth in the crawl space. Resilient floors may be installed over existing wood floors if the existing floorboards are smooth and tight and if all ridges are sanded. However, underlayment is preferred, as any imperfections in the surface below may telegraph through the finish material.

Example 29.2

Which of the following flooring types has the highest resilience?

(A) asphalt

(B) cork

(C) linoleum

(D) vinyl composition

Solution

Cork is a very resilient material. Its resilience is similar to that of rubber tile.

Asphalt tile, which is seldom used, has the lowest resilience. Linoleum and vinyl composition tile have low to moderate resilience.

The answer is (B).

SEAMLESS FLOORING

Seamless flooring is a mixture of a resinous matrix, fillers, and decorative materials applied in a liquid or viscous form that cures to a hard, seamless surface. Depending on the type of matrix and specific mixture, the flooring is either poured or troweled onto a subfloor. Some products are self-leveling, while others must be worked to a level surface. For instance, after epoxy terrazzo cures, it is ground to a smooth surface.

Seamless flooring is high-performance flooring used where there is a need for special characteristics such as extreme hardness, ease of cleaning, and high resistance to water, stains, and chemicals. It is used for industrial floors, commercial kitchens and food preparation plants, factories, clean rooms, laboratories, hospitals, correctional facilities, and parking garages.

Seamless flooring is applied in thicknesses from $^1/_{16}$ in to $1^1/_2$ in, depending on the type of product. Seamless flooring is applied over a suitable base of concrete or wood subflooring with the material turned up at the walls to form an integral cove base.

STATIC-FREE FLOORING

Static-free flooring, sometimes referred to as *anti-static flooring,* is a type of flooring capable of conducting electrostatic discharge to ground. *Electrostatic discharge* (ESD) is the spontaneous transfer of electric current. ESD is the cause of the shock a person may receive from walking on one surface and touching another.

Static-free flooring is used where ESD could damage sensitive electronic equipment or cause an explosion, such as semiconductor manufacturing facilities, computer rooms, telephone call centers, operating rooms, magnetic resonance imaging (MRI) suites, explosive manufacturing factories, and chemical processing plants.

There are two subtypes of static-free flooring, *conductive* and *static-dissipative.* These are defined by their electrical resistance. Conductive flooring has a resistance between $2.5 \times 10^4\ \Omega$ and $1.0 \times 10^6\ \Omega$. Static-dissipative flooring is more resistive, having a resistance between $1.0 \times 10^6\ \Omega$ and less than $1.0 \times 10^9\ \Omega$. Although less common, there is also super conductive flooring with a resistance between $1.0\ \Omega$ and $1.0 \times 10^4\ \Omega$.

The type of resistive flooring used depends on the application and the needs of the user. For example, super conductive flooring is used in munitions plants, conductive flooring is used in telecommunications installations with extremely sensitive equipment, and static dissipative flooring is used computer rooms and other areas with less sensitive equipment.

Static-free flooring is available in a variety of types, including carpeting, vinyl, rubber, high-pressure laminates, and epoxy. Flooring should be selected based on its electrical resistance properties as well as durability, appearance, resistance to loads, maintainability, and cost. When choosing the type of static-free flooring, it is important to determine if the user has special requirements related to footwear, grounding straps, and other aspects of the working environments. For example, some flooring types do not work well with most standard footwear.

Electrically conductive rubber flooring is considered one of the best types of static-free flooring because it meets all industry standards and it works with any type of footwear. Although more expensive than other types of flooring, rubber is durable, comfortable underfoot, dampens noise, and is easy to maintain.

ESD vinyl is available as solid or composition tiles, although solid vinyl does not need periodic wax or polish to work. It is also relatively inexpensive and can sustain heavy loads. ESD carpet is available as sheet goods or carpet tile. In both products, conductive fibers are woven into the yarn. Carpet tiles are often preferred because they can be

Flooring should be selected based on its electrical resistance properties as well as durability, appearance, resistance to loads, maintainability, and cost.

Project Planning

easily replaced if damaged. However, carpet stains easily, it is not suitable for rolling loads, and some types of ESD carpet are too conductive for many uses such as telecommunication facilities and offices.

Epoxy seamless flooring is durable, easy to clean, and can withstand heavy loads. It is also available in a variety of solid and multiple colors. However, it will not prevent static unless users wear special static-control footwear.

Regardless of what type of flooring is used, grounding is required. *Grounding* is the connection of electrical wiring to an earth ground or electrical ground. This is generally accomplished by placing copper strips under the flooring and connecting the strips to an earth ground, such as a steel structure, or to an electrical ground, which is part of the electrical system. In most cases, one grounding strip is recommended for every 1000 ft^2 of concrete on grade and for every 500 ft^2 of suspended concrete slabs. However, the exact number and configuration of grounding strips may vary depending on the requirements of the equipment and protection required.

CARPET

Carpet is a very versatile flooring material. It is attractive, quiet, easy to install, and needs less maintenance than many other types of flooring. If its material and construction are properly specified, it is appropriate for many interior uses. Carpet is made from several fibers and combinations of fibers including wool, nylon, acrylic, polyester, and polypropylene.

Wool is a natural material that is very durable and resilient, has superior appearance characteristics, and is easy to clean and maintain. Unfortunately, it is also one of the most expensive carpet fibers.

Nylon is an economical carpet material that is very strong and wear resistant. It has a high resistance to stains and crushing, can be dyed with a wide variety of colors, and cleans easily. However, its appearance can be less appealing than that of other fibers. Because of its many advantages, including cost, nylon is the most widely used fiber for both residential and commercial carpet.

Acrylic has moderate durability and a more wool-like appearance than nylon. It is easy to maintain and has a fair crush resistance.

The properties of *polyester* are similar to those of acrylic. However, polyester fibers are more likely to show wear patterns or crush over time.

Polypropylene (or *olefin*) is used for indoor-outdoor carpet. It has good durability and resistance to abrasion and fading, but it is less attractive than other carpet types and has poor resiliency.

Carpet can be manufactured by tufting, weaving, needlepunching, or fusion bonding.

- *Tufting* is the most common way of producing carpet and is done by inserting pile yarns through a woven backing. The tops of the yarns are then cut for cut pile carpet or left as is for level loop carpet.
- *Weaving* interlaces warp and weft yarns in the traditional manner, a method that produces an attractive, durable product, but is the most expensive method of manufacturing carpet.
- *Needlepunching* pulls fibers through a backing with barbed needles; it produces carpet with limited variation in texture and accounts for a very small percentage of the total carpet market.
- *Fusion bonding* embeds fabric in a synthetic backing; it is used to produce carpet tiles as well as other carpet types.

The appearance and durability of carpet is affected by the amount of yarn in a given area, how tightly that yarn is packed, and the height of the yarn. The *pitch* of a carpet is the number of warp lines of yarn in a 27 in width. The *stitch* is the number of lengthwise tufts in 1 in. The higher the pitch and stitch numbers, the denser the carpet will be. The *pile height* is the height of the fiber from the surface of the backing to the top of the pile. Generally, shorter and more tightly packed fibers result in a more durable carpet.

An important part of carpet installation is the *carpet cushion*, sometimes called *padding*. Cushion is not appropriate for all carpet installations (such as direct glue-down installation), nor is it required, but it is beneficial in most cases. Cushioning extends the life of the carpet, increases resiliency and comfort, helps sound absorption, lessens impact noise, and improves thermal qualities in some situations.

Common cushion materials include sponge rubber, felt, urethane, and foam rubber.

- *Sponge rubber* is made from natural or synthetic rubber and other chemicals and fillers with a facing on the top side. It is available in flat sheets or a waffled configuration.
- *Felt* is available in four forms: hair, fiber, combination, and rubberized. *Hair felt* is composed of animal hair. *Fiber felt* is composed entirely of non-animal fibers; synthetic fibers are often used. *Combination felt* is a mixture of animal hair and other fibers. *Rubberized felt* is any of the other three types with a rubberized coating on one side.
- *Urethane* is manufactured in three different ways to produce prime, densified, or bonded sheets, each of which has a different range of densities. Thickness ranges from $^1/_4$ in to $^3/_4$ in.
- *Foam rubber* is commonly applied as an integral backing to some carpet. It is natural or synthetic latex rubber with additives.

Carpet may be installed as a solid rolled sheet or as tiles. *Carpet tiles* are individual pieces of carpet, typically 18 in or 24 in square, that are applied to the floor with pressure-sensitive adhesive. Because of their modular design, damaged or worn carpet tiles can be replaced without removing the entire floor covering. Carpet tiles are generally specified for commercial installations over raised flooring systems, in areas where maintenance may be a problem, where frequent changes in room layout are expected, or where flat, undercarpet electrical and telephone cabling is used.

Carpet Flammability

Carpet flammability is measured and regulated in building codes in two ways. One way is to limit the carpet's ability to burn and to sustain a fire if it is the first item ignited; the other way is to limit the carpet's flammability when subjected to the heat and flame of a fully developed fire.

To prevent carpeting from igniting and spreading fire when exposed to something like a dropped match, current federal law requires all carpet manufactured and sold in the United States to meet the requirements of ASTM Standard D2859, *Standard Test Method for Ignition Characteristics of Finished Textile Floor Covering Materials*. This is more commonly known as the *methenamine pill test*, or simply the *pill test*. It is also known by its earlier designation, DOC FF-1. In this test, a methenamine tablet is ignited in the center of a carpet sample held in place with a metal plate with an 8 in diameter hole. If the carpet burns to within 1 in of the metal plate, the sample fails.

To limit the degree to which carpeting can sustain fire, the IBC requires the *flooring radiant panel test*, NFPA 253 (which is discussed in the section on finishes in Chap. 14). Refer to Chap. 13 for more information on the sustainability aspects of carpet.

Carpet Installation

Carpet is installed in one of three ways: direct glue-down, stretched-in, or double glue-down. In *direct glue-down* installation, the carpet is attached to the floor with adhesive. The carpet may be installed with an integral cushion. Direct glue-down installations resist shifting in heavy traffic areas and support wheeled traffic better than the stretched-in method. The direct glue-down method is also faster and less expensive to install than stretched carpet. However, glue-down installation without cushioning does not last as long because of the increased wear on the carpet. It is also harder underfoot. Because direct glue-down installation requires a low-pile carpet, the choice of textures and construction methods is limited.

A *stretched-in* installation uses tackless strips attached around the perimeter of the room. These plywood strips have embedded sharp points that face toward the walls. Carpet cushion is either stapled to wood floors or glued concrete floors after the tackless strips are in place. The carpet is then stretched against the strips, which hold the carpet in place.

Double glue-down uses a high-density cushion glued to the subfloor. Once the glue is dry, the carpet is glued to the cushion. This method combines the advantages of both stretched-in and direct glue-down installations. It is good for high traffic areas but is not as good as direct glue-down for rolling wheeled traffic.

PAINTING

Paint is a generic term for a thin coating used to protect and decorate the surface to which it is applied. Paints are composed of four components: the binder, pigments, liquid (or carrier), and additives. The binder and pigments together are often called the *solids.*

The *binder* gives the paint film integrity and holds the particles of pigment together. is the component that most determines the quality of the paint, including its durability, flexibility, color retention, gloss, and resistance to peeling, scrubbing, and staining.

The *pigments* are the finely ground, natural or synthetic, insoluble materials that give paint its color and hiding power. The primary pigment is titanium dioxide, which is white. Other colorants are added to produce the desired shade. Extenders may be added to the pigment to reduce the total amount of titanium dioxide, but this results in a lower quality paint. Extenders include clay, silica, silicates, calcium carbonate, and zinc oxide. Without any pigment, the binder would dry to a clear, glossy film like a varnish. As pigment is added, the gloss is reduced. Paint with a low ratio of pigment to binder yields a gloss finish, while a high ratio of pigment to binder gives a flat finish.

The *liquid* keeps the paint fluid so that it can be applied before it dries. The liquid evaporates after application, leaving a dry film of binder and pigments. In latex paints, the liquid is water; in oil-based paints, the liquid is typically mineral spirits.

Additives are mixed into the paint to impart certain attributes. *Mildewcides* are added to inhibit mildew from growing on the paint and are especially useful for exterior, kitchen, and bathroom coatings. *Rheology modifiers* affect the thickness or viscosity of the paint to make it easier to apply and more resistant to spattering and sagging. *Surfactants* help wet the surface as the paint is applied and keep the paint from separating or becoming too thick to use. *Defoamers* break bubbles when paint is applied and are useful when painting with a roller. While most of these chemicals are added into the paint during manufacturing, a number of available products can be mixed into the paint at the project site, such as nonskid floor finish or other textures, mildewcides, or extenders that slow drying time.

Paints are broadly classified into solvent-based and water-based types. *Solvent-based paints* are manufactured with binders containing or dissolved in organic solvents. *Water-based paints* have binders that are either soluble or dispersed in water. Epoxy, polyurethane, and other specialty coatings use special chemicals as binders to impart unique qualities to the coating that are not found in standard solvent or water-based paints.

Solvent-Based Paint

Clear, solvent-based coatings include varnishes, shellac, silicone, and urethane. When a small amount of pigment is added, the coating becomes a *stain*, which gives color to the surface but allows the appearance of the underlying material to show through. Stains are most often used on wood, but can also be used on concrete. Clear coatings can be used for interior applications because it is not necessary to have a pigment to protect the surface, as is usually required for exterior applications.

Oil paints use a drying or curing oil as a binder. In the past, linseed oil was standard, but other organic oils have been used. Synthetic, alkyd resin is used as the drying oil. An *alkyd* is a chemical compound made from vegetable oils and synthetic resins. Oil paints are durable but have a strong odor when applied and must be cleaned up with a solvent, such as mineral spirits. In addition, they cannot be applied to damp surfaces or on surfaces that may become damp from behind. Although the oxidizing process by which oil paints dry produces a hard paint surface, it can cause paint to yellow and crack or chip as it ages, which is particularly apparent when using white or light colored paints.

Water-Based Paint

Latex paints are water-based paints that use either vinyl chloride (also called polyvinyl acetate, PVA) or acrylic resins as binders. Acrylic latex is superior to vinyl latex in its durability, hiding power, and resistance to bleeding of underlying stains. Both types are relatively free from odor, can be used indoors as well as outdoors, and can be thinned with water.

Epoxy Paint

Epoxy is used as a very durable binder for resistance to corrosion and chemicals. Epoxies also resist abrasion and adhere strongly to concrete, metal, and wood. Epoxy is considered a high-performance coating and requires skilled applicators. Special ventilation is usually required for on-site application of epoxy because the fumes it gives off are noxious.

Polyurethane Paint

Polyurethane is considered another high-performance coating for its superior resistance to abrasion, grease, alcohol, water, and fuel. Interior applications most often include clear coverings for wood floors and clear or pigmented paint for anti-graffiti coatings. Polyurethane paint is sometimes used for strictly aesthetic appeal because it can have a very high gloss finish with an almost glasslike sheen.

Application

Successful application of coatings depends not only on the correct selection for the intended use, but also the surface preparation of the substrate, the primer used, and the method of application. Surfaces must be clean, dry, and free from grease, oils, and other foreign materials. Application can be done by brushing, rolling, or spraying. The amount of coating material to be applied is specified as either *wet film thickness* or *dry film thickness* (WFT or DFT) in mils (thousandths of an inch) for each coat needed. The coating should be applied under dry conditions when the temperature is between 55°F and 85°F.

If a semigloss or gloss paint is specified for gypsum wallboard partitions, the entire surface of the partition should receive a skim coat of joint compound to provide a uniform surface for the paint (level 5 gypsum board finish). If this is not done, the difference between the paper facing of the wallboard and the joint compound over joints and screws may become visible.

Paint Gloss

Most water-based and solvent-based paints are available in several surface finishes, which are referred to as *glosses*. The type of gloss is determined by the amount of light reflected from a surface according to a standard test method. Gloss and semigloss paints are chosen for their washability and shiny appearance. However, gloss paints tend to emphasize defects in the surfaces on which they are applied. Satin or matte finish paints provide a dull luster while still retaining some washability. Flat paints hide surface imperfections but are not as washable as glossier finishes.

Environmental Considerations

When recommending paint removal and specifying paint, the architect should be aware of two important environmental and safety considerations: the presence of lead-based paint in existing buildings and the use of volatile organic compounds in coating products.

Lead-Based Paint

Lead-based paint can be a problem in older homes and child-occupied facilities. Often in remodeling projects, existing paint must be removed. If the building was constructed before 1978, it may have lead-based paint. Such paint is dangerous if ingested by children or other occupants when it flakes off or is released as dust during construction activities.

Federal law requires that any contractor (other than homeowners working in their own residences) conducting activities with lead-based paint be certified, and that lead-based paint be removed from some types of residential occupancies and from all child-occupied facilities by a certified company using approved methods for removal and disposal. These requirements can considerably increase the cost of repainting. Sometimes covering the wall with a new layer of gypsum wallboard or simply repainting is an acceptable alternative.

Volatile Organic Compounds

Volatile organic compounds (VOCs) are hydrocarbon solvents used in paints, stains, and other products. They are released into the air during the application of coatings and react with nitrous oxides and sunlight to form ozone, the same byproduct produced by automotive exhaust and other pollutants. VOCs in paint and other coatings can also cause short-term health effects in sensitive building occupants, such as headache, membrane irritation, nausea, dizziness, or respiratory problems.

As required by the Clean Air Act of 1970, the Environmental Protection Agency (EPA) issued a regulation in 1999 that requires the amount of VOCs in paint and other coatings to be reduced. The amount of reduction depends on the coating and gloss types. The EPA regulation applies to all 50 states, the District of Columbia, and U.S. territories. Some state and local jurisdictions, such as California, have VOC regulations even stricter than the federal rule.

For most interior projects, specifying VOC-compliant paint is not a problem because architects can choose water-based products, which are generally environmentally friendly. In addition, manufacturers offer flat, nonflat, and multicolor wall paints, as well as many floor coverings, stains, and sealers with acceptable VOC levels. Refer to Chap. 13 for more information on sustainability and coatings.

COLOR

Color is one of the dominant perceptions of the physical world and one of the most powerful tools for architectural and interior design. The perception of color is one of the most complex physical and psychological phenomena, which makes it difficult to understand and use effectively. An emotional response to color depends on a variety of factors: the color and quality of light in the space, cultural references, gender, association with certain product brands, and the meanings that the color has in a society (for example, red means stop, green means go). The way colors are used in a space can affect the way that people behave. This section describes some fundamentals of color and its use.

Color Basics

Color is a physical property of visible light. Visible light is part of the larger electromagnetic spectrum, which also includes other radiation like X rays and infrared light. Each color is differentiated by its wavelength. Red has the longest wavelength of the visible spectrum, while violet has the shortest wavelength. The eye and brain perceive variations in these wavelengths to give the sensation of color.

When colors created with light are mixed, the wavelengths of both colors are present in the resulting light. For this reason, colors created with light are called *additive colors.* red light is added to green light, the resulting light contains wavelengths of both colors, and this combination stimulates the eye in a similar way that yellow light stimulates it; therefore the eye perceives yellow light. When all the colors of light are present in equal amounts, we perceive white light.

The color of a physical object, on the other hand, is conveyed by the wavelengths of light that the object absorbs, or subtracts, from the light that strikes it. When white light strikes a blue object, the object absorbs the wavelengths of light except that of blue light, which is reflected to the eye. For this reason, colors created with pigments are called *subtractive colors.* When all the colors of a pigment are present in equal amounts, we perceive no color, or black. When pigments are mixed in unequal amounts, they absorb various wavelengths of the light striking them, and the wavelengths that remain in the reflected light determine the color perceived.

The three *primary colors of light* are red, green, and blue. In various combinations and quantities, these three colors can create the other colors. They produce white light when combined equally. The three *primary colors of pigment* are yellow, red, and blue. (The primary colors used in printing are cyan, magenta, and yellow, along with black.) Theoretically, all other colors can be produced by mixing various proportions of the primaries. This arrangement is typically shown on a circle known as the color wheel, illustrated in Fig. 29.17.

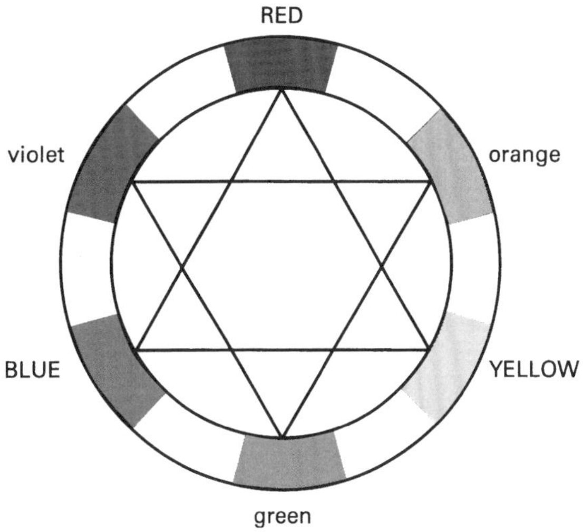

RED
violet
orange
BLUE
YELLOW
green

Figure 29.17
Brewster Color Wheel

This figure may be seen in color at **www.ppi2pass.com/ARRM/figures**.

Color has three basic qualities: hue, value, and intensity (or chroma). The *hue* is the attribute by which colors are distinguished from each other; for example, the hue of blue is different from the hue of red. The *value* describes the degree of lightness or darkness of color in relation white and black. The *intensity* (or *chroma*) of a color is defined by the degree of purity of the hue when compared with a neutral gray of the same value. These basic qualities of color are represented diagrammatically in Fig. 29.18. When white is added to a hue, its value is raised and a *tint* is created. When black is added, its value is lowered and a *shade* is created. Adding gray of the same value to a hue creates a *tone*. A tone can also be created by adding the color's *complement*, the hue of the color opposite it on the color wheel.

Color Systems

Many systems have been developed to describe and quantify color. Some focus on light and some focus on pigments, while still others try to define color strictly in mathematical terms. For most interior design purposes, it is necessary to be familiar with at least two of the commonly used systems: the Brewster system and the Munsell system.

The *Brewster color system*, also known as the *Prang color system*, is the familiar color wheel that organizes color pigments by their relationship with the three *primary colors* of red, blue, and yellow. See Fig. 29.17. In this case, primary means that these colors cannot be mixed from other pigments. Mixing pairs of primary colors in equal amounts produces the *secondary colors* of violet, orange, and green. When a primary color is mixed in equal amounts with an adjacent secondary color, a *tertiary color* is created.

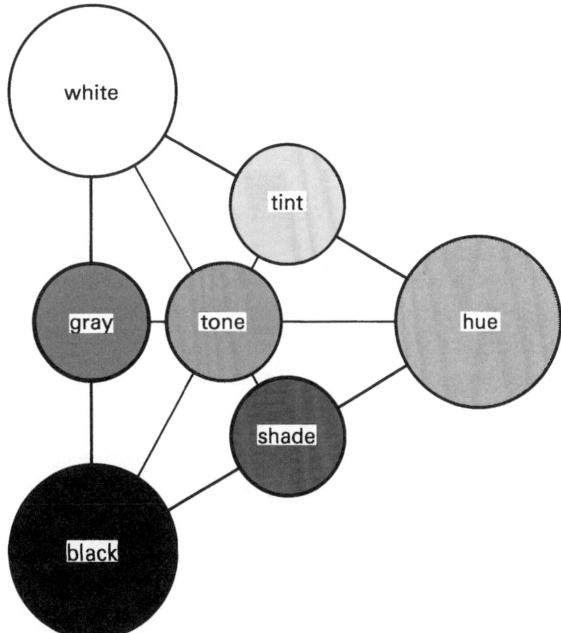

Figure 29.18
Modifying Values of a Hue

This figure may be seen in color at **www.ppi2pass.com/ARRM/figures**.

The *Munsell color system* defines color more precisely than the color wheel. It uses three scales in three dimensions to specify the values of hue, value, and chroma (intensity). Figure 29.19 shows these scales. There are five principal hues (yellow, green, blue, purple, and red), each designated by a single letter (Y, G, B, P, and R), and five intermediate hues, each halfway between two principal hues and designated by two letters (YR, GY, BG, PB, and RP). These ten hues are arranged in a circle.

Project Planning

Figure 29.19
Munsell Color System

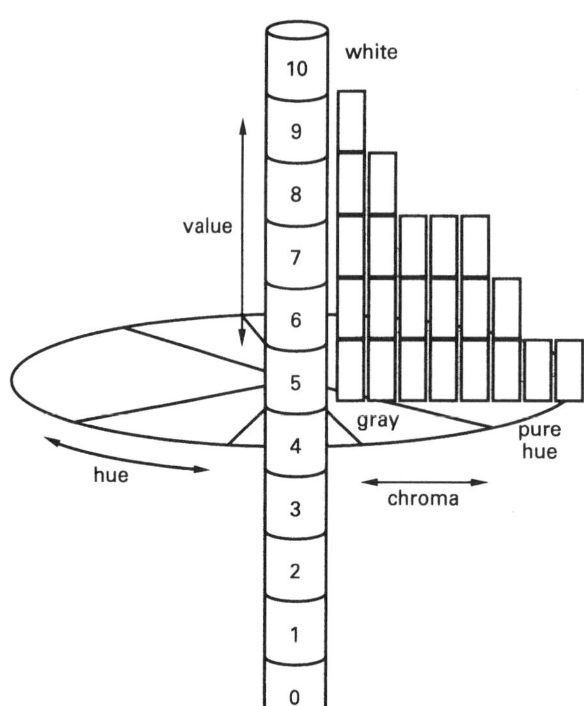

To create designations for hues that lie between the principal and intermediate hues, each hue is identified with a number from 1 to 10 to indicate its position on the color wheel and the letter designation of its nearest principal or intermediate hue. The principal and intermediate hues are given the designation 5. Thus, 5GY and 5G designate green-yellow and green, respectively. Additional subdivisions can be identified if required.

Value (the degree of lightness or darkness) is represented by the axis through the center of the circle. The steps along this axis consist of nine neutral grays plus white and black. White is at the top of the scale and is given a value of 10, and black is at the bottom with a value of 0.

Chroma is indicated by distance from the axis. Colors that are furthest from the axis have the highest chromas; these are the hues at their purest and most saturated. Moving toward the center, colors are closer to a neutral gray.

To indicate the value and chroma of a color, the numbers are written after the hue, so that 5G 6/4 is the principal hue green with value 6 and chroma 4. A neutral gray (with no hue) is designated with the letter N, so that 1N is a very dark gray and 5N is a middle gray.

Effects of Adjacent Colors and Light

As with any other aspect of design, a single color does not exist in isolation. It affects and is affected by the colors around it and by the color of the light that strikes it. Two colors affect each other when seen together in many ways. Some of the most common examples follow.

- *Complementary colors* (those opposite each other on the color wheel) reinforce each other. This phenomenon manifests itself in several ways. When someone stares at one color for some time and then looks at a white surface, an afterimage of the color's complement is seen. In addition, the color of an object will suggest or induce its complement in the surrounding background. When two complementary colors are seen adjacent to each other, each appears to heighten the other's saturation. When a small area of one color is placed against a background of its complementary color, the small area of color becomes more intense.
- When two noncomplementary colors are placed together, each appears to tint the other with its own complement. The two colors will appear to be further apart on the color wheel than they actually are.
- Two primary colors seen together will tend to appear tinted with the third primary.
- A light color placed against a darker background will appear lighter than it is, while a dark color against a lighter background will appear darker. Figure 29.20 shows an identical value placed against two contrasting backgrounds. This phenomenon is known as *simultaneous contrast.*
- A background color will tend to absorb the same color in a second, non-complementary color placed over it. For example, an orange spot on a red background will appear more yellow than it is because the red background "absorbs" some of the red in the spot.
- A neutral gray will appear warm when placed on a blue background and cool when placed on a red background.

One of the most important aspects of color interaction is how light affects the appearance of a color. Most light is perceived by the human eye as white, but in fact every light source produces some wavelengths more than others, so every light contains some colors more than others. For instance, incandescent light is very yellow, while midday sunlight is predominantly blue. Light from a cool white fluorescent lamp has much blue and green light in it, while light from a warm white fluorescent lamp contains much yellow and orange.

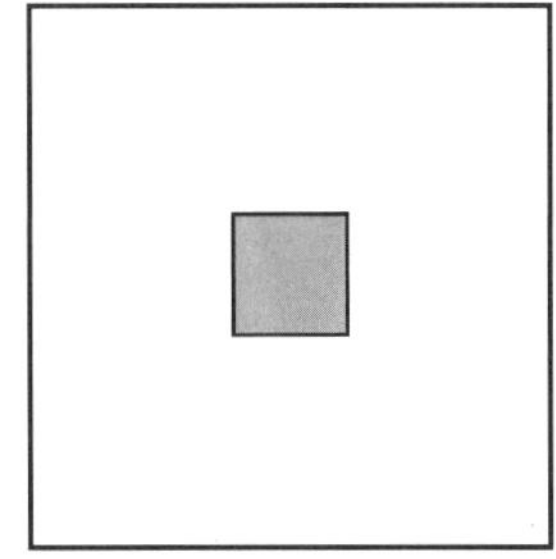

Figure 29.20 Simultaneous Contrast

In general, when light contains a strong component of a particular hue, the light will intensify colors with similar hues and neutralize colors of complementary hues. For example, a red object seen under incandescent light will appear more intensely red and vibrant, while a blue object of the same value will appear washed out and muddy. The same blue object, however, would be rendered closer to its actual color if seen under midday light or under a cool white fluorescent light. The amount of light also affects color. Dim lighting reduces a color's value and chroma. Strong lighting can either intensify a hue or make it appear washed out. For all these reasons, color selections should be made under the same type of lighting that will exist in the final building installation.

30 BUILDING CONFIGURATION AND BUDGETING

After completing the programming and analysis, the architect must plan the site, apply the relevant codes and regulations, and determine the building systems and materials that will be used. But these activities cannot be done separately; the architect must synthesize and integrate these, along with project context, environmental requirements, and cost considerations, into a single, logical design process. This chapter discusses how to do this, focusing on these areas.

- building configuration
- building systems
- environmental context
- costs and budgeting

The design process usually results in several design alternatives; from these alternatives, the single option that best satisfies the goals and needs of the client is selected. The final choice may also integrate ideas from a variety of concepts that the architect has developed.

These activities are part of the phase of work commonly known as *design development.*

BUILDING CONFIGURATION

Determining a building configuration requires the simultaneous application of program requirements and other design considerations, including basic methods of organizing space, circulation patterns, evidence-based design, social and cultural influences, historic precedent, and design theory.

Programming Information

The building program should provide the designer with a complete list of required spaces with their adjacencies and the floor area required for each. As mentioned in Chap. 10, the program includes the basic facts the designer needs to know about the project objectives, along with individual space needs, climatic influences, building code requirements, expansion plans, and money available for construction, among others. Along with site design information, these factors are integrated into the basic building configuration using organizing concepts and circulation systems during design development, as discussed in the rest of this section.

Design Considerations

A well-written program will do more than give a basic list of space and adjacency requirements. It will also state a number of general concepts that have been developed as a response to the goals and needs of the client.

These *programmatic concepts* are statements about functional solutions to the client's performance requirements. They differ from later *design concepts* because no attempt at a physical solution is made during programming; programmatic concepts guide the later development of design concepts.

For example, a programmatic concept might be that the facility should be easily expandable by 20% every three years. Exactly how this would happen in a particular building (where the additions would be constructed, how systems would be sized to allow for future expansion, and so on) would be developed as a design concept. For example, a possible design concept would be a linear building that can be extended by an addition to one wing.

Refer to Chap. 10 for more information on programmatic concepts. The rest of this section outlines some common design considerations that may be suggested during programming and schematic design, and which must be developed during design development.

Organization Concepts

How the physical environment will be organized is most often influenced by the functional needs of the particular type of building. However, the client's goal, the site, the desired symbolism, and other factors may also influence the organization pattern.

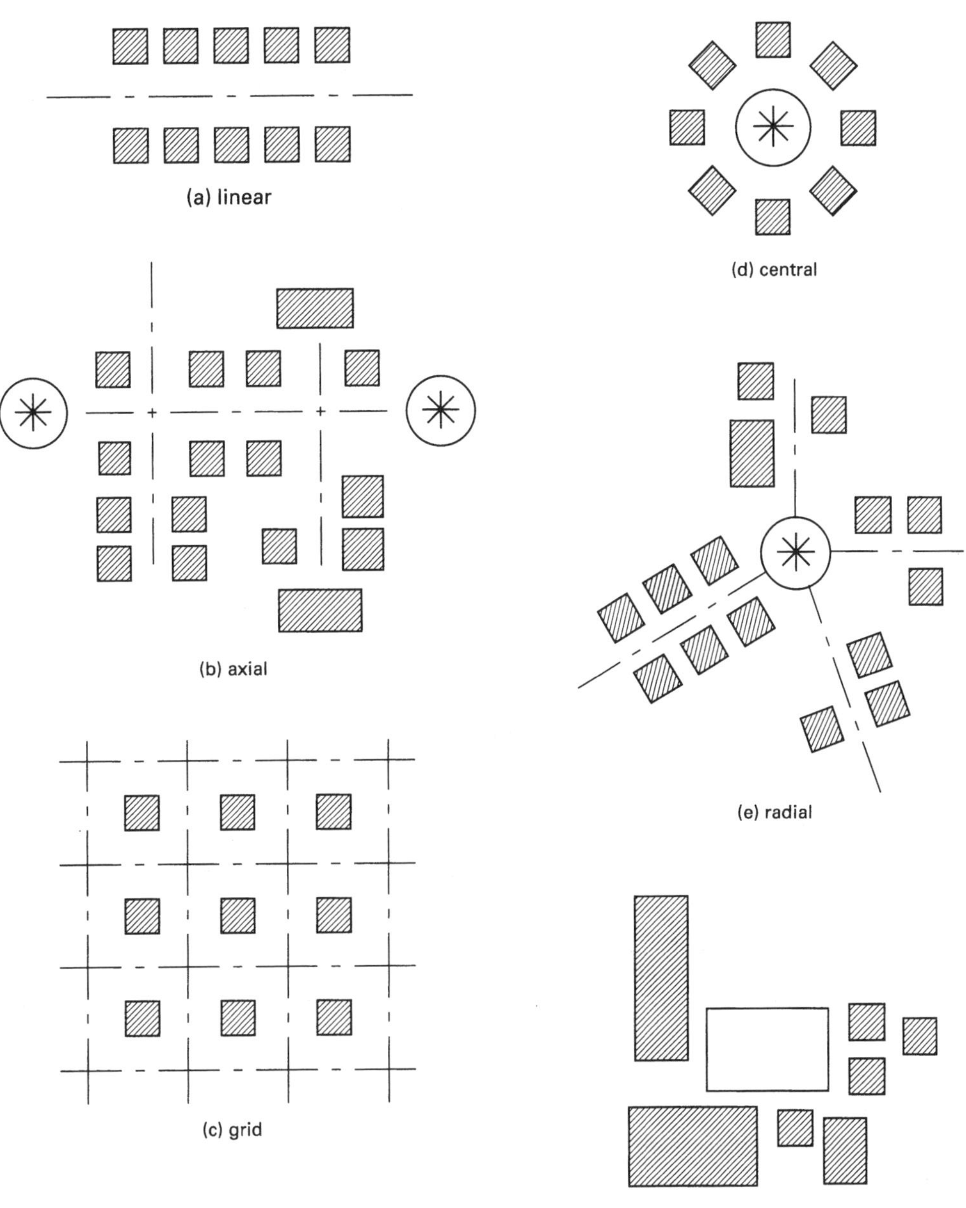

Figure 30.1 Organization Concepts

There are six basic organization concepts: linear, axial, grid, central, radial, and clustered. These are shown diagrammatically in Fig. 30.1.

A *linear organization* consists of a series of spaces or buildings placed in a single line. The spaces or buildings can be identical, or they can be of different sizes and shapes, but they always relate to a unifying line, usually a path of circulation.

A linear organization is very adaptable: it can be straight, bent, or curved to meet the requirements of the client, the site, solar orientation, or the construction process. With a linear organization, it is easy to integrate a structural grid and mechanical system distribution in an economical layout. It is easily expandable and can be built in a modular configuration if desired.

In an *axial organization*, spaces or buildings are placed along two or more major linear segments. These primary axes may be at right angles to each other or at some other angle, and there may be additional, secondary paths growing out of the primary axes. Like linear organization, axial organization can be an economical approach with a simple structural grid and compact mechanical distribution.

A *grid organization* consists of two sets of regularly spaced parallel lines, each set perpendicular to the other. This creates a strong and flexible pattern. Within a grid, portions can be subtracted, added, or modified. The size of the grid can be changed to create spaces of different sizes or to define special areas.

However, a grid can become monotonous and confusing if not used well. Because a grid system is generally defined by circulation paths, it is more appropriately used for very large buildings and building complexes where a great deal of circulation is needed. A grid organization has the same structural, mechanical, and cost advantages as linear and axial organizations.

A *central organization* is based on one primary space or point about which secondary elements are placed. This is a formal method of organizing spaces or buildings, which places emphasis on the central space. The spaces or rooms around the central focus can be arranged in a radial pattern as shown in Fig. 30.1, or at right angles to each other. There may also be more rooms on one side of the central space than another. Structural systems may be overlaid in an economical grid pattern, or they may follow a radial configuration, which may increase cost. With this type of layout, mechanical system distribution may be more extensive, and possibly more expensive. Central organizations are often used in conjunction with axial or linear plans.

When more than one linear organization extends from the same central point, they become a *radial organization*. This kind of plan has a central focus, and it extends outward to connect with other spaces. A radial organization can be circular or assume other shapes. While a radial organization suggests a strong building form, the integration of structural and mechanical systems may be more costly than with other organization concepts.

A *clustered organization* is a loose composition of spaces or buildings either related around a path, axis, or central space, or simply grouped together. The general impression is one of informality. Clusters are very adaptable to the requirements for different sizes of spaces, and they are easy to add to without disrupting the overall composition. Depending on the exact layout, a clustered organization can use an economical, varying structural grid, and a central or distributed mechanical system.

Circulation Patterns

Circulation patterns organize spaces, buildings, and groups of buildings. They are vital to the efficient organization of a structure and provide the strongest orientation within an environment. Paths of circulation provide the means to move people, products, and services.

Circulation is directly related to the organizational pattern of a building, but it does not necessarily mimic it. For example, a major circulation path may cut diagonally across a grid pattern. Typically there is a hierarchy of paths. Major routes connect major spaces, or they can become spaces themselves and have secondary paths branching from them. Different sizes and types of circulation are important for accommodating varying capacities and for providing means of orientation for the people who use them.

The circulation patterns for different functions may need to be separated. In a government building, for example, one set of corridors used by the public may be separate from an internal set of corridors used by workers. A detention facility may have a secure passage used for moving prisoners that is separate from other areas of public movement. A busy shopping center needs one circulation system for shoppers to use and another for the delivery of goods.

Establishing and maintaining a simple, efficient, and coherent circulation scheme is crucial to a successful building design. A common mistake in planning a building is to let the adjacency requirements take over the design, and only then to connect the spaces with a circulation path as an afterthought. This can create a maze of awkward corridors that decreases efficiency and produces dead-end corridors and other exiting problems.

All circulation paths are linear by nature, but there are some common variations, many of which are similar to the organizational patterns described in the previous section. Because circulation is an important aspect of a successful building, it is important to have a good mental picture of the various circulation concepts and the advantages and disadvantages of each. Five basic patterns are shown in Fig. 30.2, along with a hypothetical structural grid on top of them to illustrate how some patterns are better suited to integration of structure, adjacencies, and circulation system than others. Also, mechanical services can easily follow a logical circulation system.

Figure 30.2
Circulation Patterns

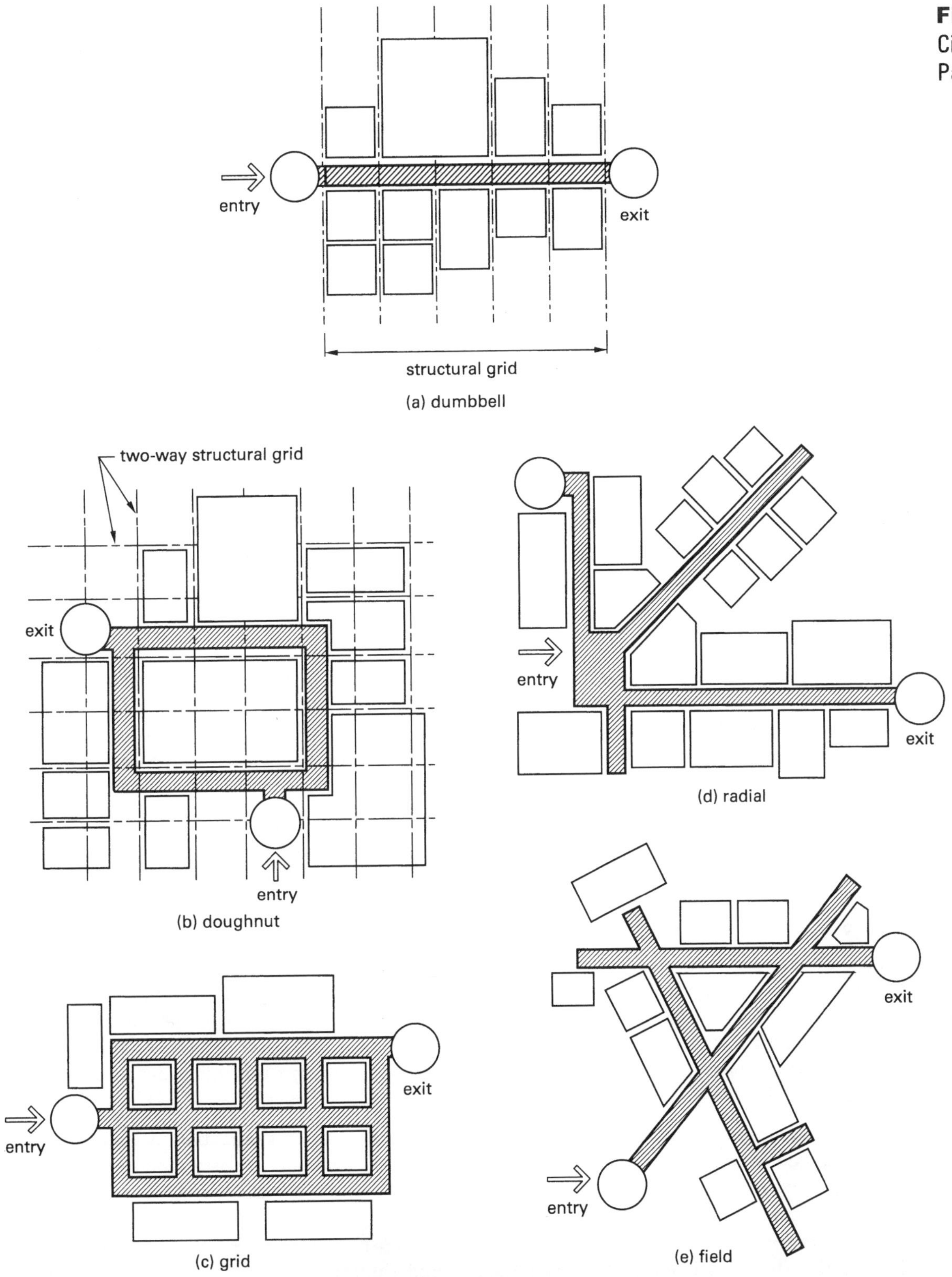

(a) dumbbell

(b) doughnut

(c) grid

(d) radial

(e) field

The *linear dumbbell layout* is the simplest and one of the most flexible circulation patterns. Spaces are laid out along a straight path, or spine, that connects major elements at each end. These major elements are usually the entrance to the building at one end and an exit at the other, but it is also possible for the primary entrance to occur anywhere along the spine, with exits at both ends. Site constraints may restrict the length of the spine, but even if there is no room on the site for a long, linear building, the path can be bent at a right angle.

This layout establishes a regular, one-way structural grid perpendicular to the direction of the path. A two-way structural grid can also be used with this layout. Spaces are laid out along the spine as needed, and spaces of various sizes can be accommodated by extending their length in the direction perpendicular to the spine. Eliminating a line or two of structure allows for the planning of a large, open space or the integration of a long-span structural system. This layout is also useful for integrating mechanical distribution systems along the spine.

The double-loaded corridor makes the building very efficient. This layout works well for a single-story building, as well as for a multistory building in which plumbing, mechanical, and other services can be economically stacked.

A doughnut configuration provides a double-loaded corridor and automatically forms a continuous exit route.

When the circulation pattern is made into a complete loop, the result is a *doughnut configuration*. This is also a very efficient building planning concept because it provides a double-loaded corridor and automatically forms a continuous exit route. Building entrances, exits, and stairways can be placed wherever needed. Spaces that do not need exterior exposure can be placed in the middle. Spaces of many different sizes can be accommodated on the perimeter because they can be expanded outward, just as with the dumbbell layout. A simple structural grid can be coordinated with the space layout as needed. A doughnut pattern is good for square or rectangular sites and for buildings both compact and large, whether single story or multistory.

A *grid layout* is often used for very large buildings, such as hospitals, where access must be provided to many internal spaces. A grid layout is seldom appropriate for a small building, however, where it leads to inefficient use of space, with single spaces surrounded by corridors.

A *radial layout* is oriented around one major space with paths extending from this central area. A large site is needed for a radial layout, so this pattern is more appropriate for large buildings and building complexes. It is more difficult to establish a simple structural system with this pattern unless the circulation paths extend from the central space at 90° angles. Each corridor longer than 20 ft must have an exit at its outer end.

A *field layout* consists of a network of paths with no strong direction. Major paths connect with secondary routes that extend from them. Orientation within a field pattern is difficult, as is integrating a logical structural system and mechanical services.

Flexibility

Depending on the requirements in the program, flexibility is a design consideration that involves a variety of concepts. *Expansibility* is the capacity of a building to be enlarged or added onto as needs change or growth occurs. *Convertibility* allows an existing building or space to be changed according to a new use. For example, a school gymnasium may be converted into classroom space in a second phase of construction. *Versatility* means the ability to use the same space for a variety of uses in order to make maximum use of limited space.

If a program requires flexibility, the designer must determine what type of organizational and structural system is required. Expansibility may suggest one type of organizational and structural system, while convertibility may require a completely different approach. The key is to find a harmonious compromise that suits the needs of the project and the owner.

Environmental Design Research and Evidence-Based Design

Environmental design research focuses on the interaction between humans and their environment. It aims at using scientific research, rather than anecdotal evidence or personal philosophies, as a rational basis for design decisions.

The challenge is that the interaction between humans and buildings is extremely complex, while scientific research must usually examine only one variable at a time, so that the effect of changing that variable can be measured without influence from other variables. For example, seating preferences can be studied scientifically by bringing people into a controlled environment, asking them to sit in a number of chairs that differ in only one aspect (the angle of the back, perhaps, or the thickness of the seat cushion), and then asking them to rate the chairs according to comfort. If the study is well conducted and the number of people is large enough, the results would be statistically valid. However, if the same chairs were placed in a real, uncontrolled environment and preferences were measured by observation, the reason for the preference would not be clear. Variables apart from comfort that would factor into a person's preference include

- design of the chair (color, size, shape)
- type of environment (library, school, waiting room)
- position of the chair in the room (near a window or door)
- separation from other people

If a particular chair was found to be preferable in one research environment, could that information be appropriately used in the decision to use the same chair for a different environment?

In spite of the difficulties inherent in applying it to building design, environmental design research should not be dismissed. Concepts such as territoriality and personal space, described in Chap. 7, have been shown to be useful in most situations. Furthermore, if the design project is especially important and the client's budget allows it, the architect can perform the necessary research before proceeding with design. The research can be as simple as a literature review of past work done on the subject of interest or as complex as performing original investigations specifically targeted to the project.

A more recent variation on this concept is *evidence-based design* (EBD), which bases design decisions on credible research that links one or more environmental elements with a desired outcome. For example, research has shown that patients in hospitals who have visual and physical access to nature recover faster, have less stress, and require less pain medication. This suggests that the design of hospitals should include large windows opening to natural views, easily accessible gardens, and artwork depicting nature. Much of the work on EBD has been within the context of the health care industry, but it is also applied to educational facilities and office design. With EBD the research may take the form of literature searches, observations of existing facilities, interviews and questionnaires with users and facility managers, and post-occupancy evaluations.

Social and Cultural Influences

Though architecture has a theoretical basis, it also reflects what the culture and society think is important. In the United States, for example, most single-family residential design is connected to the agrarian roots of the country, the ideal house still being one that is located on a farm or estate and surrounded by open space—even though the amount of open space has shrunk greatly as land costs have risen and land has become more scarce. Furthermore, the social idea of status is represented by increasing the size of a house as much as possible, often at the expense of better materials or more detailing. Inside, most home design reflects our culture's idea of privacy (separate bedrooms), hierarchy (master bedroom larger than the others), and methods of entertaining (a great room or formal living room separate from the family room).

In commercial design, cultural ideas about status and hierarchy are often reflected in the design of office space. The highest-ranking company officials get the larger corner offices or a private office with a view, while lower-echelon workers are placed in cubicles in an open plan.

Some of the social and cultural beliefs that often influence architecture are listed next. Many of these are common to all cultures in all time periods, although the physical response may be different depending on the society or culture. Refer to Chap. 7 for additional social influences on architecture.

- *political conditions:* Prevailing political attitudes and policies may affect design thinking. For example, the movement toward sustainability and "green" architecture promoted by environmental awareness, and the political recognition of this value, encouraged a response by architects.
- *economic conditions:* The state of the economy is often reflected in architecture. Prosperous times may promote lavish design (within the limits of the client's budget). A building can be an expression of a company or client's wealth or success. Uncertain or less prosperous conditions may promote austere or inward-looking design. The "cocooning" movement of the 1990s was partially a result of uncertain economic times. The rising cost of energy encourages sustainable and energy-conserving design.
- *cultural attitudes:* The prevailing cultural views of the family—shared values, religion, fashion, leisure pursuits, sports, and the like—may influence a design response. Current trends in fashion and consumer goods regarding color, material use, and industrial design often reach into the realms of architecture.
- *symbolism:* The physical environment holds a great deal of symbolism for people. For some, a house designed and furnished in early American style symbolizes the idea of home. For others, a bank of classical design with a large, impressive lobby symbolizes strength and security.
- *regionalism:* Regionalism reflects the local geographic area. Most architects and users of architecture believe that each geographic area is unique and that design should reflect that fact; therefore, buildings in Florida should be different than those in the Pacific Northwest.

As with theories of perception, cultural and social backgrounds affect the response to design. In the case of a small-scale design such as a residence, these factors can be gauged simply by interviewing the client. It is more difficult in the case of a public building or space, where the users of the building will come from many different cultures and social backgrounds and will have their individual tastes and preferences. In most cases, the best the architect can do is to make a prediction about the most likely cultural forces acting on a design problem. In some cases, environmental design research can assist the architect in making choices, but this does not replace the architect's understanding of the prevailing culture and social norms of the society in which the architect works.

Historic Precedent

A common approach to design theory throughout the ages has been to base current design on ideas and styles of the past. The new design approach can be an almost exact duplicate of a past style, such as with the classical revival style popular from the late 18th to mid-19th centuries in America, or based on a reaction against the ideals of the previous age, such as with the post-modern movement of the 1970s.

Historic precedent plays a large part in the response to architecture, regardless of the philosophy of the architect. Many clients insist that their house look like a New England saltbox or a Victorian cottage because that is their image of what a house should look like or what they grew up in; this comes regardless of any design theory that suggests it should look like something else, with planning, materials, and accessories more appropriate to the current time.

Historical precedent can be a valuable contribution to design theory by suggesting how past designs solved certain problems or represented particular ideals. These solutions or representations can then be applied to current design problems.

For example, the flowing curves of the art nouveau style or the organic architecture of Frank Lloyd Wright responded to the desire for connection with the earth and with natural forms. Although the forms of art nouveau and Wright do not have to be recreated, the lesson of the importance of the human-nature connection can be used to guide design decisions. For other designs, the strong axial and symmetric organization of religious and governmental buildings used throughout history can still be employed without creating duplicates of cathedrals or Greek temples.

Design Theory

Although there are many definitions, in general a *theory* is a mental construct of how and why things happen, which is often used to predict future events or actions. In the context of architecture, a *design theory* is a way to direct design, based on a system of beliefs or philosophy.

Theory is the fundamental beginning of design. Each designer brings a unique quality to the creative and problem-solving process. For example, the personal philosophies and theories explored by Mies van der Rohe, Le Corbusier, and Frank Lloyd Wright produced vastly different buildings, even though all three architects produced similar building types during approximately the same time period. (Differences in countries of birth only accounted for a small portion of the differences among their designs.)

It is important to understand that theory is not style. For example, southwestern is a style and includes the use of courtyards as semiprivate space. The belief that enclosed outdoor space should mediate between public and private space is part of a theory of the public/private continuum in architecture. The use of courtyards in southwestern building has a historic and cultural precedence as a way of providing safety and outdoor space within the confines of a walled compound. This approach to public/private space is quite different from the semiprivate front porch and front yard typical of many other parts of the United States.

Theory can be developed in many ways and based on many factors, including the following.

- the designer's personal worldview
- historic precedent
- environmental design research
- functional needs
- how humans perceive their environment
- a particular process of design

Most designers base their design theories on several of these influences.

BUILDING SYSTEMS

As an architect develops a design for a building, decisions about building systems should be made along with decisions about siting, space arrangements, and overall building form. Putting off decisions about systems until after the form and space arrangements have been finalized can result in solutions that are expensive, awkward, and inefficient.

Structural Systems

In most cases, structural systems are a secondary factor in the building design; the size, general shape, and space arrangements are determined, and those decisions suggest the structural materials and systems that will provide the most efficient and economical solution.

Ideally, as the programmatic requirements are resolved into a building form, the following factors should be considered when integrating structural systems into the project design.

- length of the required spans
- special structural requirements like seismic loads
- efficiency and cost
- time
- fire protection
- material availability
- unique construction requirements

The dimensions of required spaces are one of the most common determinants of a structural system. For example, a mid-rise, speculative office building would best be served by a simple post-and-beam steel structural system with spans in the range of 30 ft to 40 ft. This system allows for a flexible layout of office spaces, works with any parking areas provided below the building, facilitates integration of mechanical and electrical systems, and is quick, easy, and cost efficient to build. A warehouse is best structured with exterior bearing walls and interior columns to provide an open space with minimal obstructions. The bearing walls serve both to support the structure and provide a solid, secure, fire-resistant exterior. Refer to Chap. 18 for more information on typical spans for various structural systems.

Special structural requirements may include

- seismic loads
- unusual wind loading
- heavy snow loads
- extremely long spans

In some cases, these may result in a design where the structural response dominates the appearance of the building, such as diagonal bracing on a building's exterior. Consultation with a structural engineer early in the design process can inspire a concept that expresses the building's structure.

Cost and efficiency of a structural system usually go hand in hand. For a given span, which is usually determined by the building type, some structural systems and materials are more appropriate than others. For example, a flat plate concrete system would not be efficient for the spans needed for a big box retail store and would cost more than long-span open-web joists supported by steel columns. In many cases, the difference in cost between two or more structural systems is fairly close, and a detailed cost analysis can determine the best choice.

Time is often an important factor because of limitations dictated by the overall construction schedule, climate, or cost. A client's required move-in date or financing may dictate a reduced construction schedule. A shorter construction time almost always results in a reduced cost. The climate at the site can sometimes be a factor, requiring the structural system and the entire building to be completed in a short building season.

Cost and efficiency of a structural system usually go hand in hand.

Fire protection is sometimes the secondary consideration. The fire protection strategy suggests the most appropriate structural system. Although steel and other construction assemblies can be made fire resistant, concrete and masonry offer the advantage of inherent fire protection along with strength, acoustical control, and security in one material, which can have implications for speed of construction and cost. For example, a concrete and masonry apartment building could provide a fire-resistant frame and exterior wall without additional fireproofing, while at the same time providing acoustical separation between floors and the exterior.

Material availability refers to what types of structural materials are available in the geographic region of the project. In most cases this is not a major consideration, as most materials can be shipped anywhere in the country. However, some geographic regions may have one material that is less expensive and easier to obtain than others, which can support the local economy and result in project savings. For example, lumber may be more readily available and cost less in the northwest than in some other parts of the United States.

Unique construction requirements may include

- a restricted site that forces the use of small components and just-in-time delivery
- climatic restrictions that suggest as much prefabrication as possible

- limited availability of skilled workers in a particular trade, making it necessary to use one material instead of another

In some cases, the structure is the main influence on the building form. For large, signature projects such as an airport terminal, the structural system may become the major determinant of the building's form. Structural systems often dominate long-span buildings such as sports arenas and auditoriums. In such a case, the architect must work with the structural engineer to develop the solution that best satisfies aesthetic goals and well as cost and efficiency.

Refer to Chap. 11 for more information on the selection of structural systems.

Mechanical Systems

One of the first steps in integrating mechanical systems into a building design should be to decide whether the systems will be active or passive. An active system involves a physical element, such as a boiler, that supplies the building with energy needs. A passive system typically relies on natural energy sources, with building elements designed to make use of those sources effectively so that the needs of the occupants are met. For example, when daylighting is used as a passive lighting system, the natural light of the sun is modified and controlled through space layout, glazing, baffles, and other building elements, so that the lighting needs of the occupants are met. In most cases, buildings use a combination of active and passive systems. For example, an office building may rely on a central heating plant, but use windows for daylighting and ventilation.

Passive systems require more careful integration with the building design from the earliest stages of design, while active systems can usually be hidden within the structure. Some of the environmental resources that can be used to inform building design and layout are discussed in Chap. 17. For example, the goal of using daylighting for a high-rise may suggest a long, narrow building form.

Active mechanical systems are typically hidden from view and can be designed to fit any building configuration, but they should be integrated into the overall building form for greatest efficiency and lowest cost. This includes secondary spaces such as toilet and mechanical rooms, as well as service runs for ductwork and piping.

One of the firt steps in integrating mechanical systems into a building design should be to decide whether the systems will be active or passive.

Depending on the type of mechanical system, mechanical rooms should be located to minimize lengths of vertical chases, duct runs, and piping. This is especially true with all-air systems, which require return-air, supply-air, and large ductwork; in many cases the plenum can be used as a return air space leading back to a central collection point. An air-water system requires substantially smaller ductwork. An all-water system may require space for large piping. Refer to Chap. 17 for more information on mechanical system types. Mechanical rooms need easy access to the outside for servicing, as well as provisions for fresh-air intakes and exhaust. Exhaust outlets should not be placed near fresh-air intakes.

Toilet rooms should be located to satisfy adjacency requirements as stated in the program, or in an area that has easy access to the entire floor. Toilet rooms should be back-to-back to share a common plumbing wall and should be located near other plumbing in the building, if possible. In multistory buildings, toilet rooms should be stacked for greatest efficiency.

Depending on the particular layout of the building, space for major ductwork and piping can follow the path of major circulation routes. Early collaboration with mechanical, electrical, and structural engineers minimizes later problems when ductwork sizes and the type of mechanical system to be used are discussed and decided. These factors can influence structural layout, floor-to-floor heights, and vertical chase sizes and locations.

The type of air distribution system planned also affects the integration of mechanical systems with other components of the building. The commonly used above-ceiling distribution requires a network of ductwork, air supply diffusers or registers, and the necessary vertical space above the ceiling to accommodate them, as well as return air ducts; the plenum may be used for return air instead. This space, and any additional ceiling height required for effective daylighting, can result in a significant increase in floor-to-floor height.

The ductwork must also be coordinated with the space required by sprinkler and plumbing piping, electrical service, and other data and signal systems. A displacement ventilation system—sometimes called an underfloor air distribution system—has many advantages but requires a raised flooring system, additional space, and must be planned in the early stages of building design. See Chap. 17 for more information on displacement ventilation systems.

Lighting and Other Systems

In most cases, artificial lighting requires little integration with the overall project design and building program. This integration typically occurs at the detail level considering things such as visual tasks to be illuminated, ceiling type, ceiling height, interior finishes, and the like. However, if daylighting is planned, the use of artificial lighting may require more consideration. More task lighting than ambient lighting may be needed, and more sophisticated lighting controls will be needed to realize the energy-saving aspects of daylighting. Refer to Chap. 32 for more information on lighting design and Chap. 12 for daylighting.

Electrical, telephone, and data equipment are easy to integrate with a project design due to their relatively small size (compared with mechanical equipment). Exceptions to this include rooms for large service switches and switches and electrical rooms for large buildings that require access to the exterior for installation, servicing, and ventilation of transformers. Data centers require specialized design for the amount of equipment they contain.

ENVIRONMENTAL CONTEXT

The architect's task during design development is to select and prioritize which site-specific constraints and opportunities identified during programming and analysis (discussed in Chap. 7) are to be integrated into the final site planning and building form. These were discussed in Chap. 12 and should form the basis for building design and site development. As the exact layout of the building and its materials and systems are determined, the architect should make sure that the following features have been taken into account.

- *neighborhood context*, including design style, massing, fenestration patterns, scale, points of connection, contribution to image (edge, path, etc.), defensible space (site security), and views
- *climate*, including solar orientation and wind patterns
- *topography*, including the best places for building siting, parking, entry points, and service
- *transportation*, including how people get to the site and building with pedestrian access, bus stops, and other transportation; site and building entrances; driveway entrances; parking and other services
- *sustainability concepts,* as described in Chap. 7 and Chap. 13
- *drainage*, including modification of contours, location of retention ponds, and coordination with surrounding drainage patterns
- *utilities*, including the location of the closest sanitary and storm sewers, water supply, electrical service, and communication lines
- *geology*, including soil reports than indicate the best place for foundations, drainage requirements, and other geological factors
- *landscaping*, including existing trees and shrubbery, as well as any water features, rock outcroppings, and other natural features
- *site acoustics*, as described in Chap. 12, which could affect the design of the new building

COSTS AND BUDGETING

Refining the Construction Budget

As a project progresses, the budget must be refined and updated. Some of the methods of developing a preliminary budget during the programming process are discussed in Chap. 10, along with the various elements that influence cost beyond the construction costs. The broader issues of financing and land costs than can affect the budget are also discussed in Chap. 10.

Design development refines the size, configuration, and exact design of the project, including materials, structure, and building systems. The architect is, therefore, in a better position to assign costs to the various components of the site and building and compare these with the original project budget at this time than during the programming phase. In addition, the architect can perform a life-cycle cost analysis for various parts of the building to determine whether an alternative is more expensive initially but will cost less over time. Value engineering can also be used to fine-tune individual components or systems to see whether a less expensive way exists to accomplish the same function or goal.

There are three general methods of refining a project budget.

- parameter method
- matrix costing
- unit cost method

The first, the *parameter method*, is typically used during the design development phase and early stages of construction document production. It involves an expanded itemization of construction quantities and assignment of unit costs to these quantities. For example, instead of using one conglomerated sum for floor finishes, the cost is broken down into carpeting, vinyl tile, wood strip flooring, unfinished concrete, and so forth. Using an estimated cost per square foot, the cost of each type of flooring can be estimated based on the area.

With this type of estimation, it is possible to evaluate the cost implications of each building component and to make decisions concerning both quantity and quality in order to meet the original budget estimate. If floor finishes are over budget, the architect and the client can review the parameter estimate and decide to replace some wood flooring with less expensive carpeting. Similar decisions can be made concerning any of the parameters in the budget.

Profit is calculated as a percentage of the total of labor, materials, equipment, and overhead. This is one of the most variable parts of a budget.

Parameter line items are based on commonly used units that relate to the construction element under study. For instance, a gypsum board partition would have an assigned cost per square foot or linear foot of completed partitions of a particular construction type rather than separate costs for metal studs, gypsum board, screws, and finishing. Single-layer gypsum board partitions, 1-hour rated walls, 2-hour rated walls, and other partition types would have their own separate costs.

The second way to compare and evaluate alternative construction components is with *matrix costing*. With this technique, a matrix is drawn showing the various alternatives along one side and the individual elements that combine to produce the total cost of the alternatives on the other side. For example, in evaluating alternatives for workstations, all the factors that lead to the final cost could be compared. These factors might include the cost of custom-built versus pre-manufactured workstations, task lighting that could be planned with custom-built units versus higher-wattage ambient lighting, and so on.

Two additional components of construction cost are the contractor's overhead and profit. Overhead can be divided into general overhead and project overhead. *General overhead* is the cost to run a contracting business and involves office rent, secretarial help, heat, and other recurring costs. *Project overhead* is the money it takes to complete a particular job, not including labor, materials, or equipment. This includes temporary offices, telephone/data service, sanitary facilities, trash removal, insurance, permits, and temporary utilities. The total overhead costs, including both general and project expenses, can range from about 10% to 20% of the total costs for labor, materials, and equipment.

The last item added to an estimate, profit is calculated as a percentage of the total of labor, materials, equipment, and overhead. This is one of the most variable parts of a budget. Profit depends on the type of project, its size, the amount of risk involved, how much money the contractor wants to make, the general market conditions, and whether or not the job is being bid.

During difficult economic conditions, a contractor may drastically cut the profit margin to get the job and keep the workforce employed. If the contract is being negotiated with only one contractor, the profit percentage will be much higher. In most cases, profit will range from 5% to 20% of the total cost of the job. Overall, overhead and profit can total 15% to 40% of construction cost.

The third method of estimating costs is the *unit cost method*. The project is broken down into its individual building components and the labor needed to install them. Contractors typically use this method of estimating when they are determining a bid or negotiated price for the project. It is the most accurate method, but it can only be used when the construction drawings and specifications are complete or mostly complete and all the requirements of the project are known. The estimate should include

- material and labor costs
- cost of equipment, fees, and services necessary to complete the project
- the contractor's overhead and profit

When subcontractors or vendors will be performing work, the fixed prices of the subcontractors are added to the general contractor's costs.

Cost Information

One of the most difficult aspects of developing project budgets is obtaining current, reliable prices for the kinds of construction units being used.

A great many cost books are commercially produced and published each year. These books list costs in different ways: some are very detailed, giving the cost for labor and materials for individual construction items, while others list parameter costs and subsystem costs. The same data are often integrated into cost estimating software, which can help the architect prepare the needed projections. The detailed price listings are of little use to architects because they are too specific and make comparison of alternative systems difficult. However, the information on typical system costs can be used to develop a quick comparison of alternatives under consideration.

There are also cost-estimating services and software that require only general information from the architect about the project, location, size, major materials, and so forth. The computer service then applies its current price database to the information and produces a cost budget.

Commercially available cost information, however, is the average of many past construction projects from around the country. Local variations and particular conditions may affect the value of their use on a specific project. Many architects also work closely with general contractors to develop realistic budgets.

Geographical location and inflation must be accounted for in developing any project budget. These variables can be adjusted by using cost indexes that are published in sources like the major architectural and construction trade magazines. Using a base year as index 1000 for selected cities around the country, for example, new indexes are calculated each year that reflect the increase in costs (both material and labor) for that year.

These indexes can be used to apply costs from one part of the country to another and to escalate past costs to the expected midpoint of construction of the project being budgeted.

Example 30.1

The cost index in city A is 1257, and the cost index in city B is 1308. The expected construction cost for a building in city A is \$1,250,000. What will be the approximate expected cost for the same building if constructed in city B?

(A) \$1,100,000

(B) \$1,200,000

(C) \$1,300,000

(D) \$1,400,000

Solution

The ratio of expected costs in the two cities is estimated to be equal to the ratio of cost indices.

$$\frac{C_{\text{city A}}}{C_{\text{city B}}} = \frac{I_{\text{city A}}}{I_{\text{city B}}}$$

$$C_{\text{city B}} = \frac{C_{\text{city A}} I_{\text{city B}}}{I_{\text{city A}}} = \frac{(\$1,250,000)(1308)}{1257}$$

$$= \$1,300,716 \quad (\$1,300,000)$$

The answer is (C).

Life-Cycle Cost Analysis

Life-cycle cost analysis (LCCA) is a method for determining the total cost of a building, building component, or system. It takes into account the initial cost of a considered element or system, as well as the cost of financing, operation, maintenance, and disposal. Any residual value of the component value is subtracted from the other costs. The costs are estimated over a length of time called the study period. The duration of the study period varies with the needs of the client and the useful life of the material or system. For example, investors in a building may be interested in comparing various alternative materials over the expected investment time frame, while a city government may be interested in a longer time frame representing the expected life of the building. All future costs are discounted back to a common time, usually the base date, to account for the *time value of money* (TVM). The *discount rate* is used to convert future costs to their equivalent present values.

Using LCCA allows two or more alternatives to be evaluated and their total costs to be compared. This is especially useful when evaluating energy conservation measures in which one design alternative has a higher initial cost but a lower overall cost because of energy savings. Some of the specific costs involved in an LCCA of a building element include the following.

- *initial costs*, which include the costs of acquiring and installing the element
- *operational costs* for electricity, water, and other utilities
- *maintenance costs* for the element over the length of the study period, including any repair costs
- *replacement costs*, if any, during the length of the study period
- *finance costs* required during the length of the study period
- *taxes*, if any, for initial costs and operating costs
- *residual value*, the remaining value of the element at the end of the study period, which may be based on resale value, salvage value, value in place, or scrap value

The first six costs in this list are estimated, discounted to their present values, and added together. Any residual value is discounted to its present value and then subtracted from the previous total to get the final life-cycle cost of the element.

A life-cycle cost analysis is not the same as a life-cycle assessment (LCA), described in Chap. 13. An LCA analyzes the environmental impact of a product or building system over the entire life of the product or system.

Value Engineering

Value engineering (VE), or *value analysis* as it is sometimes called, is the process of analyzing a particular material, assembly, system, or even an entire design to see whether the same functional requirements can be met in a less expensive way, or whether a product or system of higher quality can be found for the same cost. The value engineering process uses a team approach that involves the client, the architect, engineers, contractors, and others on the design team.

Informally, value engineering can be performed by any group with a view toward improving function with a decrease in cost. Formally, VE follows a specific process as defined by the Society of American Value Engineers (SAVE). This process consists of six phases.

1. Gather information to better understand the project.
2. Perform functional analysis to understand and clarify the required functions.
3. Generate alternatives on how to accomplish the required functions.
4. Synthesize ideas and select the ones that are feasible for development into value improvements.
5. Select the best alternative for improving value.
6. Present the recommendations to the project stakeholders.

The suggestions that result from the VE process should be considered carefully, to avoid reducing costs by reducing quality.

Value engineering can be performed during any phase of a project, but the earlier it is applied, the more useful it is. For architectural projects, VE is best applied during the schematic design and design development phases. By this point, many decisions will have been made, but it is still early enough to make modifications.

DIVISION 5: PROJECT DEVELOPMENT & DOCUMENTATION

Chapter

31

INTEGRATION OF BUILDING SYSTEMS

During project development, the architect must work with the mechanical engineer to integrate the building's mechanical system with its other systems. Many aspects of the building must be coordinated with the mechanical system, including the

- capacity needed from the building's heating, ventilation, and air conditioning (HVAC) system
- location and amount of space needed for the mechanical equipment room and other equipment areas
- size and distribution of ductwork through the building
- location and appearance of terminal units like fan coils and induction boxes
- choice of return air methods (either ducted or above a suspended ceiling)
- means of air supply and location of air supply diffusers
- locations and appearances of air intakes or exhaust grills on the exterior of the building

In addition, the mechanical system may have to be integrated with whatever fire protection and smoke control methods are required for the building. Fire protection systems and signal and alarm systems are discussed later in this chapter and in Chap. 32.

HVAC SYSTEM SIZING AND INTEGRATION

Calculating the size of an HVAC system involves

- knowing the needed capacity of the heating and cooling equipment
- determining the size of the mechanical spaces needed to house the equipment
- figuring out the space and layout needed for the distribution system of pipes and ducts

The mechanical engineer determines the exact size and layout of the mechanical systems, but the architect best understands the context that the systems must work within, based on the overall building design and the needs of the client.

System Capacity

In determining how large an HVAC system must be, the most important factors to consider are the total heat gains and losses that the building will experience in the most extreme conditions. The procedures used for calculating these are discussed in Chap. 16. Equipment is then selected so that the system will have the capacity needed to offset these gains or losses.

In some cases, the cooling equipment chosen will be slightly undersized in order to keep initial costs low, with the knowledge that some occasional minor extremes in indoor design temperature will be tolerated.

Active heating and cooling equipment is often used in combination with one or more passive heating or cooling systems such as solar heating, ground-source heat pumps, and natural ventilation. When the active and passive systems are used together and controlled with the building's automation system, it is often possible to reduce the size of the active equipment, ductwork, and piping. Refer to Chap. 12 and Chap. 17 for more information on alternative energy sources and energy conservation measures that can be used with standard HVAC systems.

Mechanical Spaces

During the schematic and design development phases of planning, the architect estimates how much space to allocate for mechanical equipment and where to locate the mechanical spaces. This must be decided in conjunction with determining how air and water will be distributed throughout the building.

Variables Affecting Space Requirements

There are five major variables that influence the space needed for mechanical equipment.

- scope of the system (local, centralized, or district)
- type of HVAC system
- building size
- building type
- passive systems use

The first variable that must be considered is whether the system will be local, centralized, or district. A *local system* generally serves just one zone and is typically used for small buildings or for specific areas of a building. A residential furnace is an example of a local system; a window-mounted air conditioner is another. When more than one zone must be served in a small or moderate-size building, it is possible to use several local systems, such as commercial gas-fired heaters, for different areas of the building.

A *centralized system* serves several zones from one location. Centralized systems are most common in commercial and institutional buildings of moderate to large size. Boilers, chillers, pumps, and air handling equipment are located in one room, with conditioned air or water distributed throughout the building. In very large buildings, or for reasons of efficiency, there can be several centralized systems in one building.

In a *district system*, the heating and/or cooling for several buildings is served by a single plant. For example, a central steam plant on a college campus may provide heat for all the buildings; within each building, air or water is heated and distributed throughout the building.

Of the three, a centralized system needs the most space within the building. A district system needs less space because the generation of heat or cooling takes place elsewhere. Local systems, by their very nature, need the least space.

The use of passive energy systems can reduce – or in some cases even eliminate – the capacity needed from the equipment.

The second variable is the type of HVAC system selected. This will usually be an all-air, all-water, or air-water system. An *all-air system* needs the most space, both because of the size of the air handling units and because large ductwork is needed to distribute air throughout the building and return it to the central plant. An *all-water system* needs the least amount of space, because water pipes are smaller than air ducts and because there are no supply air ducts; ventilation is provided through the wall at each fan coil unit. An *air-water system* falls between the other two types because there are generally no return air ducts; when return air is needed, it is collected in plenums rather than in separate ducts.

There are also *electric systems* and *direct expansion systems*, which are small, simple systems and generally limited to small buildings and buildings using only localized heating and cooling. All these types of systems are discussed in greater depth in Chap. 17.

The third variable is the size of the building, which affects the volume of heating and cooling needed. For a larger building, the equipment and distribution system must have greater capacities, so more space is needed for them.

The fourth variable is building type. Laboratories and hospitals generally need more space for mechanical equipment than offices or apartments, because individual control is needed in many spaces and because special provisions for ventilation and positive pressure are needed in some rooms. Offices, schools, and retail establishments fall somewhere in between in terms of space needed.

The fifth variable is the extent to which passive energy systems are used and integrated with the active systems. For example, in spring and fall, solar heating may be used, with active systems serving only as a backup, while active heating may be needed in winter. The use of passive energy systems can affect the size of equipment needed, because passive systems reduce—or in some cases even eliminate—the capacity needed from the equipment.

Preliminary Sizing

In a medium to large building using an all-air or air-water system, the mechanical room should have a floor area equal to 3% to 10% of the total building area being served. This includes space for boilers, chillers, fans, fuel (if needed), and related pumps and piping. An all-water system will need a mechanical room with a floor area of about 1% to 3% of the total area. The low end of the range applies to building types such as apartments and hotels, while the high end of the range applies to buildings with complex mechanical services, such as laboratories. Offices, stores, schools, and theaters fall in the middle of this range.

Where cooling towers are needed, they are generally sized at approximately 0.2% to 1% of the building area served, and they are located on the roof or outside the building. A boiler needs to be housed in a room that is at least slightly more than twice the boiler's length, so that the boiler's tubes can be removed and replaced. A height of 12 ft to 18 ft is generally needed in an equipment room. Chillers may be located in a separate room, but more often they will be located in the same room as the boilers. There are usually at least two boilers, so that one can operate while the other is being serviced. The space needed for chimneys for the boilers ranges from about 4 ft^2 for small buildings to about 36 ft^2 for large buildings.

Air Handling Units and Fan Rooms

An all-air or air-water system will include an *air handling unit* (AHU). The AHU uses water from the boilers and chillers to heat or cool the air. In most cases the AHU is purchased and placed as a ready-to-use assembly. For large or complex buildings, the AHU may be custom designed and built.

The AHU is located in the *fan room.* The ideal location for the fan room is next to an exterior wall, but it can also be placed further inside the building as long as fresh air and exhaust air can be carried in and out by ductwork. Fan room equipment also includes fans, filters, humidifiers, preheat coils for cold climates, return air ducts, outside air intakes, and exhaust ports, as well as dampers and a mixing box to control the mixing of fresh air, return air, and exhaust air. This equipment is heavy, noisy, and produces vibrations, which the architect should consider when placing the fan room. Multiple fan rooms are often used to accommodate multiple building uses, seasonal changes, or zoning requirements.

Integration with Building Design

One of the first decisions that the architect must make in conjunction with the mechanical engineer is the location of the mechanical equipment room or rooms, based on the architect's estimate of the area needed. Decisions concerning conditioned air and/or water distribution are made in parallel. For small or low-rise buildings, the mechanical equipment is usually best located in the basement or on the ground floor. Boilers and chillers are heavy, noisy pieces of equipment, so they should be separated from sensitive areas of the building, and they are best located on lower levels to minimize structural requirements.

Boilers and chillers are heavy, noisy pieces of equipment, so they should be separated from sensitive areas of the building, and they are best located on lower levers.

In a high-rise building, the mechanical equipment rooms may be located in the basement along with a primary fan room that distributes air upward. Alternatively, boilers and chillers may be located in the basement with smaller fan rooms located on each floor. As an added advantage, this arrangement allows greater smoke control in case of fire. The air supply to the floor of the fire can be switched off, and return air from that floor can be exhausted to the outside; at the same time, the dampers on the floors above and below the fire can be switched on to provide full pressurization, preventing the spread of smoke. Mechanical equipment may also be located on the roof or in a mechanical penthouse, but noise control and structural support must be considered.

The mechanical room should be located next to an outside wall to allow for the intake of combustion air, and near a service door or removable panel large enough for the replacement of boilers and other equipment. The room should also be located near the chimney.

Ductwork Distribution and Sizing

In an all-air or air-water system, there must be supply ductwork running from the AHU to each terminal unit and supply air diffuser. Ductwork can occupy a significant amount of space, so a logical, simple, and direct route must be planned and coordinated with the other building systems. Either round or rectangular ducts can be used. Round ducts are more efficient and maintain air pressure better, but rectangular ducts often make better use of the space available above ceilings and in vertical duct chases.

For mid- and high-rise buildings, the architect may consider locating the main vertical supply duct (along with the main vertical return duct) in a chase in the core of the building, completely concealing it. At each floor, main trunk ducts extend from the vertical supply duct. Alternatively, one or more vertical ducts can be placed at the perimeter of the building with branch ducts feeding inward. The enclosures for the vertical ducts can be featured as a main architectural element on the exterior of the building; however, this also reduces the area available for external windows. If it is not possible or desirable to locate windows along an external wall—for example, if the building is placed directly adjacent to another building—duct work can be placed in this area instead, freeing up space elsewhere.

The main horizontal trunk ducts should follow the paths of building circulation systems because these must serve every space just as corridors do. The ductwork can be located above corridor ceilings or between or under structural beams. Some structural systems, such as open-web steel joists, make it possible for ductwork to run both parallel and perpendicular to the direction of the structure. If the floor-to-floor dimension must be minimized, the architect can coordinate with the structural engineer and the mechanical engineer to design and detail girders and beams with openings to allow major ductwork to penetrate steel framing.

In any air duct, there is some amount of friction between the moving air and the duct walls, fittings, registers, and other components. This friction creates resistance to the flow of air. The amount of pressure that must be applied to overcome this frictional resistance and cause the air to flow through the system is called the *static head* (or *static pressure*) and is measured in inches of water.

The architect should place fan rooms at locations in the building that will minimize the length of ductwork needed. The longer the ductwork, the more friction there is in the system, and the larger the ducts or fans (or both) must be to overcome it. Increasing the size of the ducts keeps the pressure lower, but means more space is needed for the ducts; increasing the size of the fans raises the pressure, but results in higher initial costs, higher operating costs, and more noise created by the fans and by the air moving through the system.

For the preliminary sizing of low-pressure duct space, allow a cross-sectional area of about 10 ft^2 to 20 ft^2 for every 10,000 ft^2 of floor space served. This figure includes both supply and return ducts, and it applies to both vertical and main horizontal duct runs. A system of high-pressure supply ducts will take up less space.

COORDINATION OF MECHANICAL SYSTEMS WITH PROJECT DESIGN DETAILS

Although the mechanical engineer designs the HVAC system and sizes the ductwork, the architect must coordinate with the engineer regarding the location of the mechanical rooms, available space, and location for ductwork and chases. Ceiling design and other details must also be coordinated.

Ducts, Pipes, and Mixing Boxes

In most commercial construction, horizontal ducts are run in the plenum, and vertical ducts are run within their own chases. A *chase* is a fully enclosed shaft that contains only ducts or piping.

Figure 31.1
Ceiling Diffusers

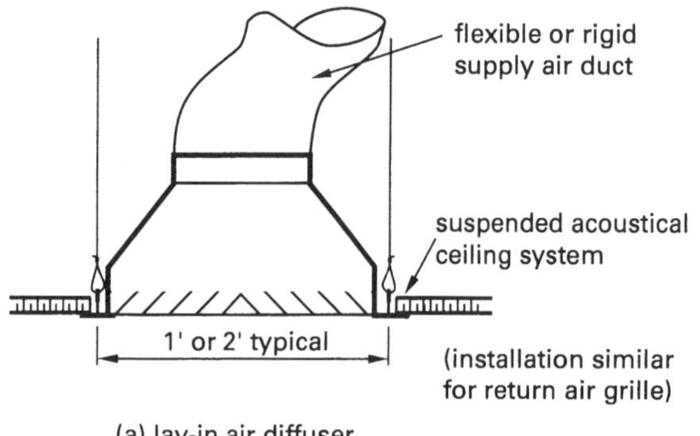

(a) lay-in air diffuser

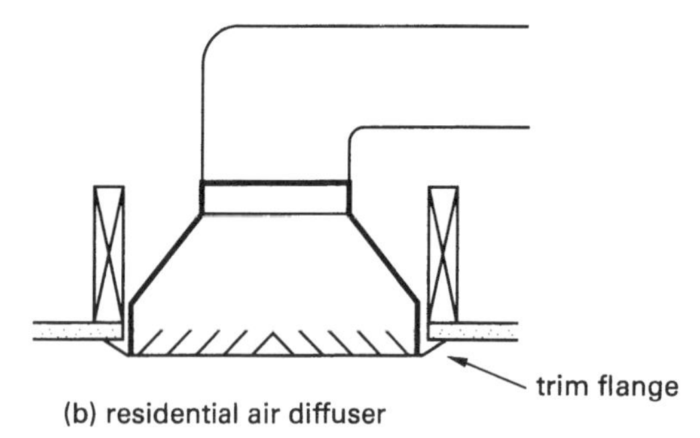

(b) residential air diffuser

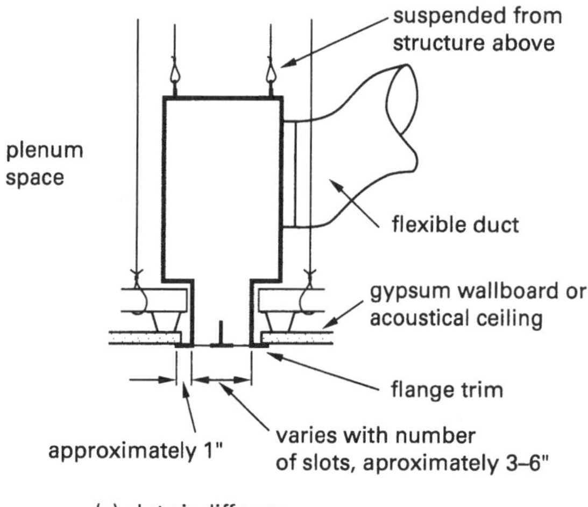

(c) slot air diffuser

Large horizontal ducts can occupy most of the vertical distance between a suspended ceiling and the structure above. In this situation, it can be difficult and sometimes impossible to recess light fixtures below the ducts. This is particularly true with standard line-voltage recessed incandescent downlights, which use vertical space. Sometimes it is possible to substitute smaller, low-voltage or low-clearance light fixtures to fit within the low space below a duct.

Mixing boxes must be considered as well, as they are also located in the plenum. A *mixing box* controls the air that flows into a space from the main air supply line. Responding to signals from a thermostat, the mixing box adjusts the air's quantity and/or temperature while reducing the air's velocity and the noise it makes. Depending on the type and capacity of the system, a mixing box can range in size from 6 in to 18 in high, 24 in to 60 in long, and 14 in to 66 in wide.

In a *terminal reheat system*, cool air enters the mixing box at a fixed temperature, and the mixing box contains a hot water coil that can add heat as needed. Terminal reheat systems can be identified easily by the air ducts and copper pipes leading into the mixing boxes.

In a *dual-duct system*, the mixing box receives cool air and hot air from two separate ducts; it mixes the air to obtain the needed temperature and distributes the air to ducts that serve individual rooms or spaces.

In a *variable air volume system* (*VAV system*), the control device is called a *VAV box* (or *VAV terminal unit*). The VAV box receives air at a constant temperature and varies the airflow rate as needed to maintain the desired temperature. One duct leads in and one or more lead out, attached to registers mounted in the ceiling. A VAV box is typically placed above the ceiling within or near the space it serves.

For new construction projects, the architect can inform the mechanical engineer where lights and other equipment are planned above the ceiling, and the engineer can locate the mechanical equipment to accord with the architect's plan. In remodeling work, however, existing mixing boxes may be difficult and expensive to move, due to their size and their connection with ductwork and thermostats, and they may restrict where the architect can place light fixtures and other recessed ceiling items.

The architect should verify the size and location of ductwork, mixing boxes, and piping before locating light fixtures and other recessed ceiling items. This information should be coordinated with the mechanical engineer during the design development and construction drawing phases. If the architect is considering the relocation of existing HVAC equipment or piping as part of a remodeling project, the architect should discuss the effects this will have on cost, scheduling, and heating and cooling with the mechanical engineer, contractor, and client.

The plenum above a suspended ceiling is not the only possible location for the ductwork and equipment. The architect can also use *access flooring*, which is a false floor of individual panels raised above the structural floor with pedestals. Although access flooring is more commonly used to run electrical, communication, and computer wiring, it can also be used for some types of HVAC ductwork that serve individual workstations, such as a displacement ventilation system (see Chap. 17). Refer to Chap. 29 for more information on access flooring.

In residential construction, small ducts and plumbing pipes are typically run within the walls and between floor joists or in crawl spaces or attics. Occasionally, larger horizontal ducts in a house must be run below the floor joists and a dropped ceiling or furred-down space must be built to conceal them.

Air Supply

Air supply diffusers vary with the needs of the HVAC system, the type of wall or ceiling in which they are mounted, and the appearance that is desired. Some of the more common types are shown in Fig. 31.1. Their finished appearance as viewed from below is shown in Fig. 31.2.

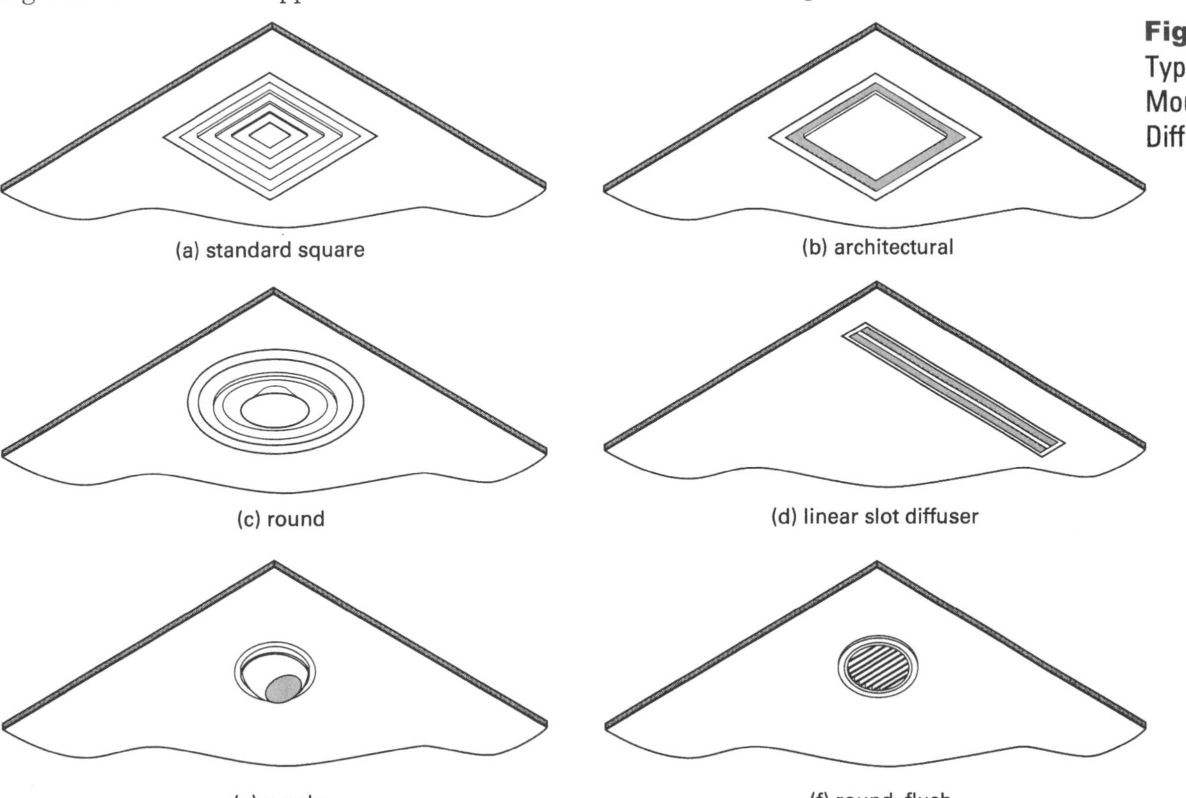

Figure 31.2 Types of Ceiling-Mounted Air Diffusers

In suspended acoustical ceilings, square air diffusers are commonly used because they are inexpensive and easy to install. They are typically 1 ft or 2 ft square and fit into standard ceiling grids as shown in Fig. 31.1(a). Similar types are available for gypsum wallboard and plaster ceilings; these usually have trim flanges that snap onto the diffuser and cover the rough cut opening in the ceiling, as shown in Fig. 31.1(b). (See also Fig. 31.2.)

Slot air diffusers can be used when the appearance of the air distribution device needs to be minimized or when the available space does not allow a square diffuser. As shown in Fig. 31.1(c), these diffusers are long and narrow and contain two to eight slots, resulting in a finished opening of about 3 in to 8 in in width. The diffusers can be purchased in any length and used for either supply or return air. Air is supplied by a flexible round duct attached to the side of a box in the ceiling as long as the slots. Slot air diffusers are most often used with wallboard ceilings to provide a trim, unobtrusive method of distributing air, but they are also available for suspended acoustical ceilings and gypsum wallboard and plaster ceilings. They efficiently and uniformly supply air along a window line.

Plenums

A *plenum* is the space between a suspended ceiling and the structural floor or roof. In most buildings, the plenum is used as a space for ductwork, sprinkler piping, plumbing piping, wiring, signal systems, speakers, and recessed lighting. While the plenum is a convenient location to place and conceal these services, it makes more economic sense, especially in mid- and high-rise buildings, to minimize the height of the plenum so as to reduce the floor-to-floor height. Adding just a few inches to each floor's height will also add costs for vertical structure, elevators, and exterior cladding.

If the architect decides to expose the services rather than use a suspended ceiling system, keeping within the dimensions suggested in this section will be less important.

The architect should coordinate with the structural, mechanical, and electrical engineers to determine how deep the plenum needs to be. The plenum can be thought of as consisting of a number of levels. The uppermost level is defined by the structure of the building itself. Steel structures require deep girders and intersecting beams with a few inches for fireproofing. For concrete structures, the space needed can vary depending on the framing method.

The plenum can be thought of as consisting of a number of levels.

The mechanical ducts, mixing boxes, and other HVAC equipment are usually located just below structural members; the depth needed for this layer of the plenum is usually determined by the depth of the largest duct that runs below the deepest steel girder or concrete beam. Large trunk ducts can sometimes pass through openings in large girders, if the architect coordinates this with the structural engineer and mechanical engineer. Smaller branch ducts to service individual areas may then need between 12 in and 16 in of space. Hanger supports may also increase the depth of space needed.

Sprinkler and plumbing piping are usually located below the ductwork. This layer may need 4 in to 6 in. More space may be needed if the sprinkler system is complex or if there are a large number of plumbing drains and supply lines.

The lowest layer of plenum space is used for recessed luminaires; the amount of additional space needed depends on the choice of fixtures. This can range from 9 in to 12 in for compact fluorescent downlights to 4 in to 5 in for standard fluorescent fixtures; more recent options such as LED lighting and improved compact fluorescent luminaires can reduce this further. If space is at a premium, the architect may consider semi-recessed fixtures or surface or suspended luminaires.

Finally, the depth of the suspended ceiling itself also must be provided for; this is usually about 2 in unless a specialty system is used.

In much commercial construction, the plenum is used as a return air space. In such cases, building codes prohibit the use of exposed combustible materials within the plenum, because smoke in this area can spread quickly to other parts of the building. Most electrical wiring is coated with plastic that gives off a great deal of thick, toxic smoke if it burns, so if it is run through a plenum of this sort, it must be contained within steel conduits. For telephone and communication, plenum-rated wiring is available coated with a flame-resistant, low-smoking material such as Teflon.

If required by the local authority, fire-rated dividers must be installed in the plenum to limit the horizontal spread of fire and smoke. Normally such dividers are simply an extension of a fire-rated partition.

Access to Above-Ceiling Equipment

Building codes (and common sense) require that there be access to components of mechanical and electrical systems such as valves, fire dampers, heating coils, mechanical equipment, electrical junction boxes, communication junction boxes, and similar devices that may need service and modification. If these components are located above a suspended acoustical ceiling, they can be reached by removing a ceiling tile. Gypsum wallboard ceilings or partitions require access doors for anything that might need to be inspected, adjusted, or repaired. *Access doors* are small steel doors with frames that are opened through use of a thumb latch or key. If required, access doors are available as a fire-rated assembly.

Thermostats

The locations of thermostats are normally determined by the mechanical engineer. They are placed away from exterior walls, heat sources, or other areas that may adversely affect their operation. They are normally located 48 in above the floor, but the mounting height should be coordinated with light switches and other nearby wall-mounted control devices. The placement must also be within the maximum allowable reach distances for accessibility. This may lower the thermostat's height to 44 in when an obstruction extends from 20 in to 25 in from the wall where the thermostat is located.

Coordination with Ceiling Items

The architect must coordinate the location of supply and return air diffusers with other ceiling items such as lights, sprinkler heads, smoke detectors, and speakers, so that the ceiling is as well planned as possible. The mechanical engineer must verify that the desired locations do not adversely affect the operation of the HVAC system. Air supply registers should be placed near windows and other sources of heat loss or heat gain, while return air grilles should be placed away from the supply points to provide good heat and air circulation throughout the space.

Window Coverings

Window coverings can affect the heating and air conditioning load in a space and may interfere with supply air diffusers or other heating units near the window. The mechanical engineer checks the proposed type, size, and mounting of window coverings to verify that they will not create a problem with the HVAC system. Commercial construction standards, for example, require a space of at least 2 in between the glass and any window covering to avoid excessive heat buildup, which might cause the glass to crack or break. Automated shades may need additional space in the ceiling or at the edges for operation.

Acoustic Separation

Mechanical and electrical services often present a challenge to maintaining acoustic separation, especially in offices and spaces with similar uses. Ducts, convectors, and piping run continuously along an exterior wall, while partitions intersect the exterior wall at regular intervals, and all this affects the acoustics of a building. Special detailing or construction may be needed to create a continuous sound seal around the floor and ceiling, above the ceiling, and along the perimeter wall. For example, joints between the wallboard and all pipe and duct penetrations above the ceiling should be sealed with acoustical sealant.

WATER SUPPLY DESIGN AND INTEGRATION

A water supply system has many parts that must be considered before implementation. Each of the following will be discussed in turn.

- types of supply systems
- components and materials
- system design
- irrigation systems
- hot water supply

Water Pressure and Static Head

When water is supplied from a city main or from a pressure tank accompanying a private well, it comes from the pipe at a certain pressure. In city mains, water pressure is about 50 psi. For a building's water supply system to work, this water pressure must be reduced by the friction in the system and still be high enough to operate fixtures. A flush valve, for example, needs 10 psi to 20 psi to operate properly; a shower needs about 12 psi.

In a column of water, pressure increases in proportion to depth. It is often convenient to express water pressure in terms of the height of a column of water; when pressure is expressed as a unit of length in this way, it is often called *static head.* For example, a column of water 1 ft high exerts a pressure of 0.433 psi at its base, so a pressure of 0.433 psi is equivalent to 1 ft of static head; 0.433 psi is also the pressure needed to raise water by 1 ft. Similarly, 1 psi is equivalent to 2.3 ft of static head; 1 psi of pressure will raise water 2.3 ft.

Example 31.1

Water enters a supply system from a water main with a pressure of 45 lbf/in^2. Ignoring loss due to friction, the pressure available to operate a fixture located 40 ft higher than the main is

(A) 28 psi

(B) 31 psi

(C) 35 psi

(D) 38 psi

Solution

The pressure loss between the main and the fixture is equivalent to 40 ft of static head. Use a conversion factor of 0.433 psi per foot of static head.

$$p_{\text{loss}} = (40 \text{ ft})\left(0.433 \frac{\frac{\text{lbf}}{\text{in}^2}}{\text{ft}}\right) = 17.32 \text{ lbf/in}^2$$

Ignoring friction loss, the water pressure at the fixture is

$$45 \frac{\text{lbf}}{\text{in}^2} - 17.32 \frac{\text{lbf}}{\text{in}^2} = 27.68 \text{ lbf/in}^2 \quad (28 \text{ psi})$$

The answer is (A).

Supply Systems

There are two primary types of water supply systems: upfeed and downfeed. The choice between the two is usually based on the height of the building and the pressure needed to operate the fixtures.

An *upfeed system* uses pressure in the water main to directly supply the fixtures. See Fig. 31.3. Because there is always some friction in the system and some pressure must be available to work the highest fixtures, the practical limit on building height with an upfeed system is about 40 ft to 60 ft.

If the building is too tall for an upfeed system, a *downfeed system* is most often used. In a downfeed system, water from the main is pumped to storage tanks near the top of the building (or near the top of the part of it served by the system) and flows to the fixtures by gravity. See Fig. 31.4. The pressure at any fixture or point in the system can be determined by the vertical distance from the outlet of the tank to the fixture, using the equivalency of 0.433 psi for every foot of height.

The height of the zone that can be served by a downfeed system is limited by the maximum allowable pressure on the fixtures at the bottom of the zone, allowing for friction loss in the piping. Depending on the fixture and manufacturer, this maximum pressure is from 45 psi to 60 psi. Therefore, the maximum height of a zone is 60 psi/(0.433 psi/ft), or about 138 ft. Beyond this, pressure-reducing valves are needed.

Another concern is the water pressure at the fixtures near the top of a downfeed system, because a minimum pressure is needed to make fixtures work properly. For example, if a flush toilet needs 15 psi, then the toilet must be lower than the water tank by at least 15 psi/(0.433 psi/ft), or about 34.6 ft. In fact, the difference in height should be slightly greater than this to overcome friction loss in the piping.

In some cases, the lower floors of a high-rise building are served by an upfeed system and the upper floors are served by a downfeed system.

Another type of supply system that can be used for medium-size buildings is the *direct upfeed pumping system*, or *tankless system*. Several pumps are used together and controlled by a pressure sensor. When demand is light, only one pump operates to supply the needed pressure. When the demand increases, the pressure drop is detected by the pressure sensor, and another pump is signaled to start.

Components and Materials

A water supply system consists of piping, fittings, valves, and other specialized components. Piping can be made of copper, steel, plastic, or brass. Copper is the most commonly used because of its corrosion resistance, strength, low friction loss, and small outside diameter.

Copper pipe is available in three grades: K, L, and M. Type K has the thickest walls and comes in straight lengths (hard temper) or in coils (soft temper). It is used for underground supply pipe where greater strength is needed. Type L has thinner walls than Type K and also comes in straight lengths or coils. It is the grade most commonly used for most of the plumbing system in a building. Type M is the thinnest of the three types and is available in straight lengths (hard temper) only. It is only used where low pressure is involved, such as branch supply lines, chilled water systems, exposed lines in heating systems, and drainage piping. Drain-waste-vent (DWV) copper is also used for applications that are not subject to pressure, but it is rarely used. Copper pipe is joined by heating it with a flame and then soldering it.

Figure 31.3
Upfeed System

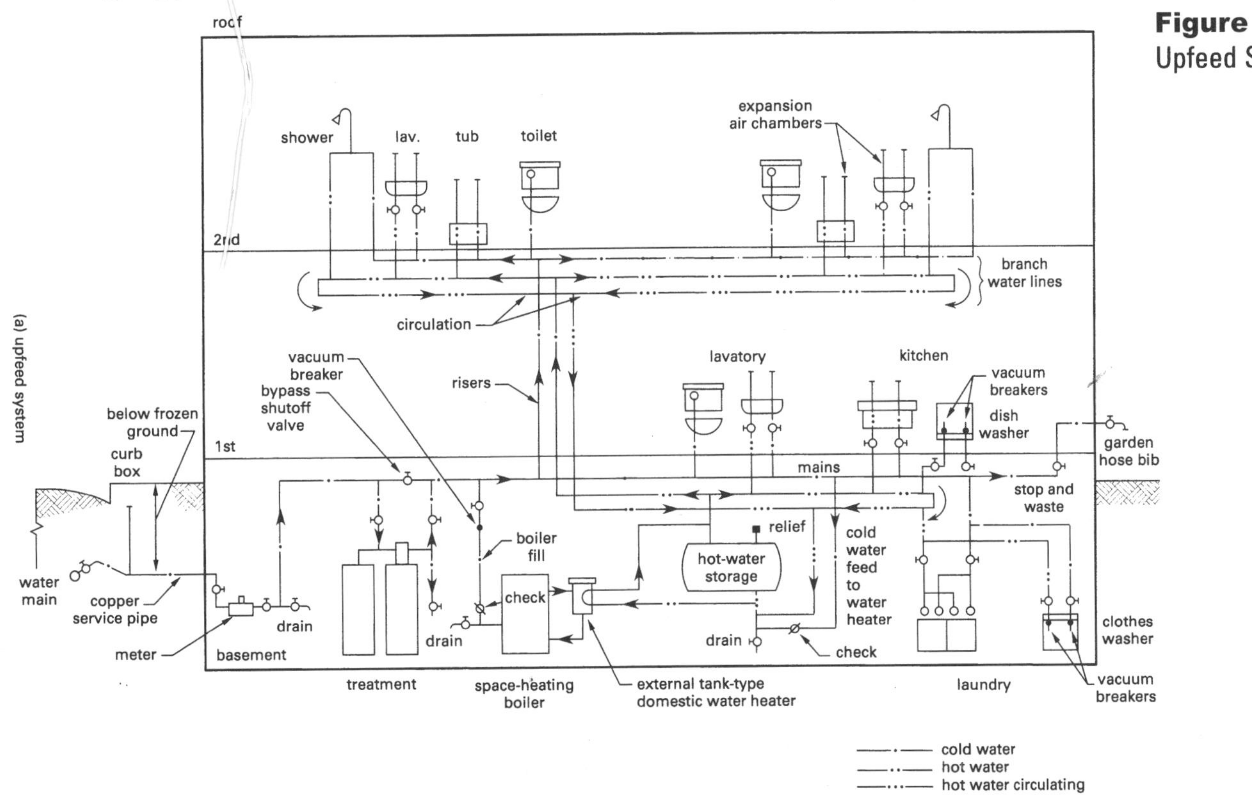

Figure 31.4
Downfeed System

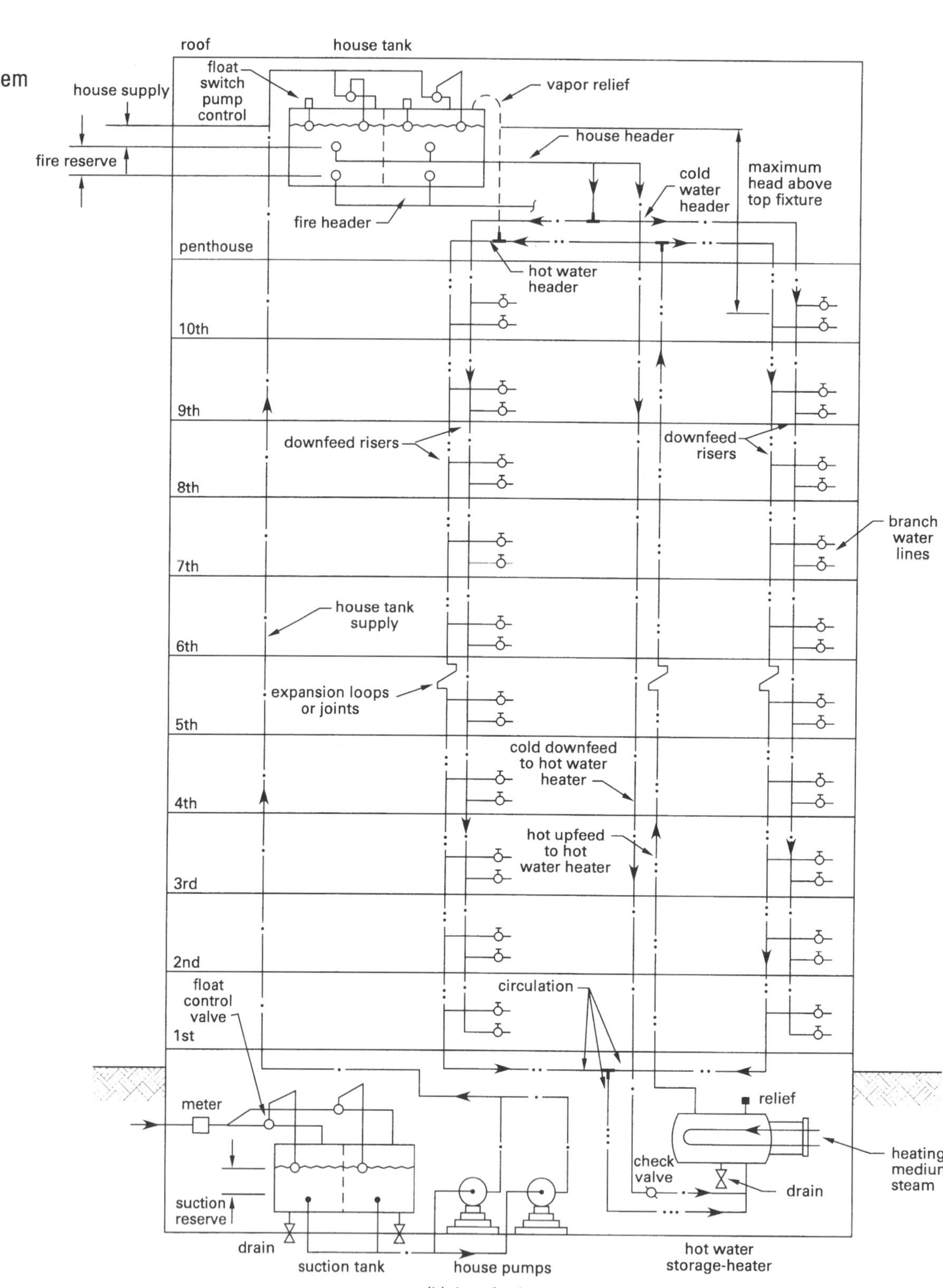

(b) downfeed system

Steel or galvanized steel pipe can be used where the water is not corrosive, but these materials are more difficult to assemble because of their screw fittings. Steel pipe is available in different wall thicknesses that are indicated by schedule numbers. Schedule 40 pipe is the most commonly used.

Plastic pipe is also suitable for supply piping, although some codes restrict its use. Local codes should be consulted to determine what type of plastic pipe may be used and in what types of buildings; some kinds of pipe are allowed in Type III, IV, and V buildings, but are not allowed in certain locations in Type I and II buildings. Types of plastic used for supply piping include acrylonitrile butadiene styrene (ABS), chlorinated polyvinyl chloride (CPVC), polyethylene (PE), and cross-linked polyethylene (PEX). ABS and PE types are allowed for water service only as pipe installed underground and outside. CPVC and PEX are typically used indoors as water service and distribution piping. Table 31.1 gives a summary of the types of plastic pipe in use.

Table 31.1 Plastic Pipe Types and Uses

abbreviation	name	uses	rigidity	connections
ABS	acrylonitrile butadiene styrene	drainage	rigid	hub and clamps, solvent
CPVC	chlorinated polyvinyl chloride	hot and cold supply, sprinklers	rigid	solvent welded, heat fused
HDPE	high-density polyethylene	exterior water supply	rigid/flexible	heat fused, solvent welded
PE	polyethylene	water supply, irrigation sprinklers, exterior drainage	flexible	expansion fittings, compressing, crimping
PEX-AL-PEX	cross-linked polyethylene-aluminum	water supply, compressed air and gas	flexible	expansion fittings, compressing, crimping
PP	polypropylene	industrial supply and waste for chemical resistance and high heat	rigid	compression, solvent weld
PVC	polyvinyl chloride	cold water supply only, drainage	rigid	solvent welded, threaded for schedule 80

Plastic pipe has many advantages over rigid copper or steel piping. It is lightweight, corrosion resistant, and flexible, and it can be installed quickly and easily without soldering or use of a flame. However, many plastics are flammable and will emit smoke and toxic gas if burned. Also, plastics are manufactured from petroleum products.

A relatively new pipe material is cross-linked polyethylene (PEX). PEX is manufactured as continuous flexible tubing suitable for use in both hot and cold water supply lines under pressure as well as for hydronic heating. Because it is stored on spools and cut to length, a single piece can be run from each fixture directly back to a manifold that connects to the main hot or cold supply piping. This avoids the need for fittings and makes installation faster. PEX has other advantages as well.

- *flexibility.* Can be run around corners and around obstructions in walls and ceilings.
- *light weight.* Easier to ship, handle, and install than rigid pipe.
- *low thermal conductivity.* Conserves energy.
- *resistance to freezing.* Less prone to breakage if a building loses heat.
- *resistance to scale buildup.* Scale buildup reduces water flow.
- *economy.* Less expensive to install than rigid piping or other types of plastic.
- *less noise.* Eliminates water hammer and lets water flow quietly.

Figure 31.5
Pipe Fittings

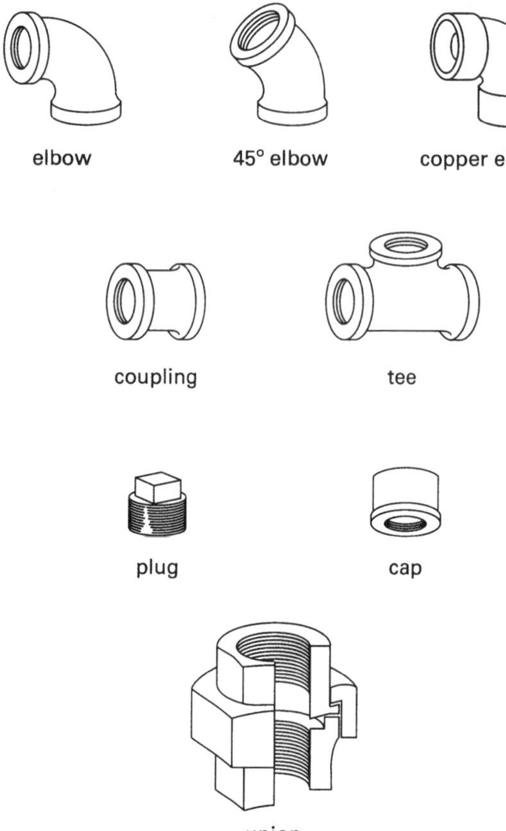

PEX is more environmentally friendly than copper, even though copper is highly recyclable, because of copper's environmentally intensive extraction and manufacturing processes. PEX is also more environmentally friendly than CPVC, because the manufacturing process for CPVC is toxic, the solvents used in joining CPVC pipe are hazardous, and CPVC can release toxins when burned.

Supply piping is connected with a variety of fittings, valves, and other components to form a complete system. Fittings connect pipes where lengths must be joined, where a change in direction occurs, where three pipes join, or where a change in size occurs. Figure 31.5 shows some common fittings for rigid piping.

A *union* is a special fitting that connects two rigid sections of pipe and that can be easily unscrewed to allow for repairs or additions to the piping system. Unions are also used between piping and devices that may need to be replaced, such as water heaters. Adapters are also available that allow two different piping materials to be joined.

Fittings for steel and brass pipe are made from malleable iron, cast iron, or brass, and are threaded to receive the threaded pipe. Pipe compound or pipe tape is used to produce a watertight seal when the pipe and fitting are joined. Copper and plastic fittings are slightly larger than the pipe, to allow them to be slipped in. Copper joints are sealed by soldering, sometimes called sweating, and plastic pipes are sealed by using a solvent that "melts" the plastic together. PEX connections are made by compression and crimping using a special tool.

The connections between small-diameter pipes connecting bath and kitchen fixtures to supply line valves are often made with compression fittings. To make these types of connections, a flare nut is slipped over the copper tubing. Then, the copper end is flared slightly and fit onto a mating flange on the valve or faucet. The flare nut is then screwed onto the threads of the valve or faucet fitting, compressing the flanged tubing tightly against the mating flange.

Valves are used to control water flow. They are located at risers, horizontal branch lines, and pipe connections to fixtures and equipment, such as water heaters and sinks. Valves allow selective shutdown of the system for repairs without affecting the entire building. Four common valve types are shown in Fig. 31.6.

A *gate valve* seats a metal wedge against two metal parts of the valve. It is used where control is either completely on or off. Because there are no turns, it has a low friction loss.

A *globe valve* is used where water flow is variably and frequently controlled, such as with faucets or hose bibbs. A handle operates a stem that compresses a washer against a metal seat. Because the water must make two 90° turns, the friction loss in this type of valve is high.

A *check valve* works automatically and allows water flow in only one direction where, for example, backflow might contaminate a potable water supply.

For water control in sinks and lavatories, a single-handle faucet, which is a kind of *angle valve*, is most commonly used. One handle controls both the hot and cold water supply and mixes the water to suit the temperature needs of the user. There are also valves that control temperature to prevent scalding and restrict flow to conserve water available.

Other types of plumbing components include air chambers, shock absorbers, pressure reducers, pressure relief valves, and flow restrictors. Air chambers and shock absorbers are used to prevent *water hammer*. This is the noise caused when a valve or faucet is closed quickly, causing the water moving in the system to stop abruptly and the pipes to rattle. An *air chamber* is a length of pipe installed above the connection to the faucet that cushions the surge of water. A *shock absorber* performs the same function with a manufactured expansion device.

Pressure reducers, sometimes called *pressure regulators*, are needed on fixtures if the supply pressure is too high, over about 60 psi. Most fixtures need only from 5 psi to 15 psi to operate, and higher pressures can cause excessive wear on the fixture.

Pressure relief valves are safety devices designed to open when pressure exceeds a predetermined maximum. They are used on water heaters and similar equipment where excessively high pressures could cause damage or explosion.

A *flow restrictor* is a device to reduce the amount of water that comes out of a tap or other fixture. Flow restrictors are used on shower heads and sinks to limit water use.

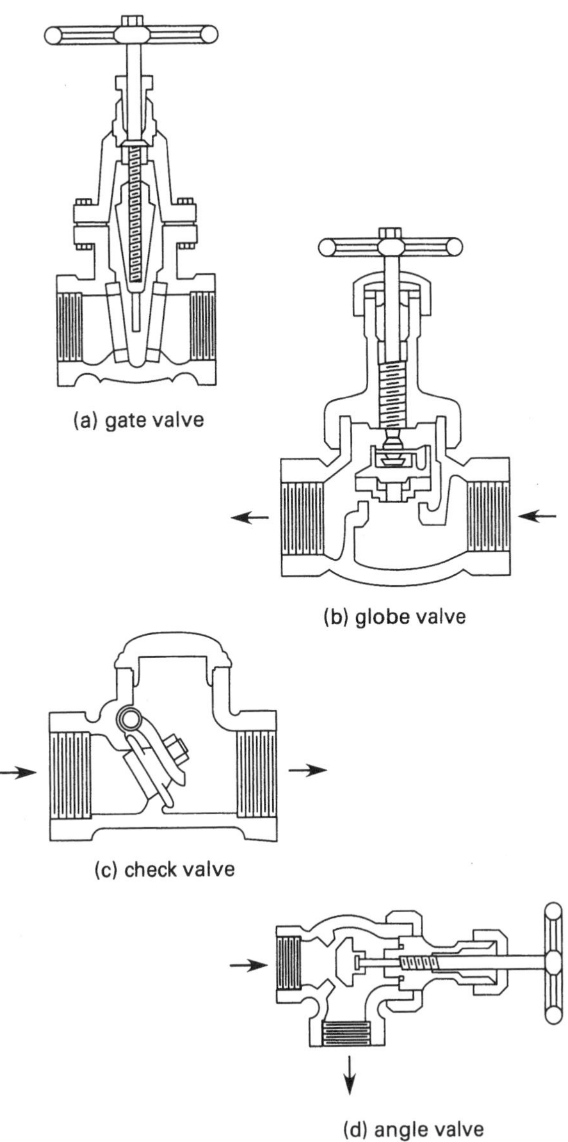

Figure 31.6
Valves

Product Development

System Design

Designing a plumbing system involves sizing the pipes and laying out the needed fittings, valves, and other components. The mechanical engineer does this, but the architect should be familiar with the general principles.

After the various pressure losses are deducted from the available pressure at the water main, there must still be adequate pressure at the most remote fixture. To put this another way, the pressure needed at the most remote fixture added to all pressure losses must not exceed the water main pressure.

The minimum pressures typically needed for various kinds of fixtures can be found in Table 31.2. The pressure loss from rises in elevation is found by multiplying the total rise in feet by 0.433 psi/ft. The water main pressure can be provided by the local water company. What remains is to ascertain the pressure losses through the piping and the water meter, which is most often a process of trial and error.

Table 31.2
Minimum Flow Pressure for Various Fixtures

fixture supply outlet serving	flow rate[a] (gpm)	flow pressure (psi)
bathtub, balanced-pressure, thermostatic or combination balanced-pressure/thermostatic mixing valve	4	20
bidet, thermostatic mixing valve	2	20
combination fixture	4	8
dishwasher, residential	2.75	8
drinking fountain	0.75	8
laundry tray	4	8
lavatory, private	0.8	8
lavatory, private, mixing valve	0.8	8
lavatory, public	0.4	8
shower	2.5	8
shower, balanced-pressure, thermostatic or combination balanced-pressure/thermostatic mixing valve	2.5[b]	20
sillcock, hose bibb	5	8
sink, residential	1.75	8
sink, service	3	8
urinal, valve	12	25
water closet, blow out, flushometer valve	25	45
water closet, flushometer tank	1.6	20
water closet, siphonic, flushometer valve	25	35
water closet, tank, close coupled	3	20
water closet, tank, one piece	6	20

[a]For additional requirements for flow rates and quantities, see *International Plumbing Code.*
[b]Where the shower mixing valve manufacturer indicates a lower flow rating for the mixing valve, the lower value shall be applied.

Pressure loss in pipes depends on the diameter of the pipe and on the flow rate, which is typically measured in gallons per minute. The pressure loss is due to friction within the pipe, and friction is greater for smaller diameters and for greater flow rates. If two pipes are carrying water at the same flow rate, the pipe with the smaller diameter has more friction. If two pipes have the same diameter, the pipe with the greater flow rate has more friction.

Demand Load

The *demand load* of the system (sometimes called *maximum possible flow*) is the flow rate that would be needed if every fixture in the system were in use at the same time. This is found by adding up the load values for all the fixtures. The load value for a fixture is measured in *water supply fixture units* (wsfu or fu); a *fixture unit* is a unit flow rate approximately equal to 1 ft^3/min. Load values for various kinds of fixtures have been established and are listed in Table 31.3.

Table 31.3
Load Values Assigned to Fixtures

fixture	occupancy	type of supply control	load values, in water supply fixture units (fu) cold	hot	total
bathroom group	private	flush tank	2.7	1.5	3.6
bathroom group	private	flush valve	6.0	3.0	8.0
bathtub	private	faucet	1.0	1.0	1.4
bathtub	public	faucet	3.0	3.0	4.0
bidet	private	faucet	1.5	1.5	2.0
combination fixture	private	faucet	2.25	2.25	3.0
dishwashing machine	private	automatic		1.4	1.4
drinking fountain	offices, etc.	$^3/_8$″ valve	0.25		0.25
kitchen sink	private	faucet	1.0	1.0	1.4
kitchen sink	hotel, restaurant	faucet	3.0	3.0	4.0
laundry trays (1 to 3)	private	faucet	1.0	1.0	1.4
lavatory	private	faucet	0.5	0.5	0.7
lavatory	public	faucet	1.5	1.5	2.0
service sink	offices, etc.	faucet	2.25	2.25	3.0
shower head	public	mixing valve	3.0	3.0	4.0
shower head	private	mixing valve	1.0	1.0	1.4
urinal	public	1″ flush valve	10.0		10.0
urinal	public	$^3/_4$″ flush valve	5.0		5.0
urinal	public	flush tank	3.0		3.0
washing machine (8 lbm)	private	automatic	1.0	1.0	1.4
washing machine (8 lbm)	public	automatic	2.25	2.25	3.0
washing machine (15 lbm)	public	automatic	3.0	3.0	4.0
water closet	private	flush valve	6.0		6.0
water closet	private	flush tank	2.2		2.2
water closet	public	flush valve	10.0		10.0
water closet	public	flush tank	5.0		5.0
water closet	public or private	flushometer tank	2.0		2.0

For fixtures not listed, loads should be assumed by comparing the fixture to one listed using water in similar quantities and at similar rates. The assigned loads for fixtures with both hot and cold water supplies are given for separate hot and cold water loads and for total load, the separate hot and cold water loads being three-fourths of the total load for the fixture in each case.

From *International Plumbing Code 2015,* © 2015, International Code Council, Inc. Reprinted with permission. All rights reserved. www.iccsafe.org

Example 31.2

The plumbing fixtures in a small office building consist of five flush-valve toilets, two $^3/_4$ in flush-valve urinals, four lavatories, two service sinks, and a drinking fountain. What is the demand load for cold water?

(A) 71 fu

(B) 75 fu

(C) 78 fu

(D) 82 fu

Product Development

Solution

From Table 31.3, find the cold water load values (in water supply fixture units) for the individual fixtures. An office building is a public occupancy.

$$\begin{aligned}
&\text{five flush-value toilets (water closets): } (5)(10.0\text{ fu}) = 50.0\text{ fu}\\
&\text{two } {}^3\!/_4\text{ in flush-valve urinals: } (2)(5.0\text{ fu}) = 10.0\text{ fu}\\
&\text{four lavatories: } (4)(2.0\text{ fu}) = 8.0\text{ fu}\\
&\text{two service sinks: } (2)(3.0\text{ fu}) = 6.0\text{ fu}\\
&\text{one drinking fountain: } (1)(0.25\text{ fu}) = 0.25\text{ fu}
\end{aligned}$$

The demand load is

$$50\text{ fu} + 10\text{ fu} + 8\text{ fu} + 6\text{ fu} + 0.25\text{ fu} = 74.25 \quad (75\text{ fu})$$

This is the minimum flow rate that the system must accommodate, so round up to 75 fu.

The answer is (B).

Probable Demand

Most plumbing fixtures are in operation only intermittently and for short periods. Designing a water supply system large enough to handle the demand load would be needlessly expensive, because it is unlikely that all the fixtures in a building will ever be in use at the same time. The value actually needed to design the water supply system, then, is the *probable demand* (sometimes called *peak demand, maximum probable flow,* or *maximum expected flow*), the maximum flow rate that can be expected under typical conditions. To find the probable demand, tables and graphs are available that relate the demand load (in fixture units) to the probable demand (in gallons per minute). These tables and graphs give two sets of values, one for systems that mostly use flush tank toilets and one for systems that mostly use flush valve toilets, which use more water.

Table 31.4 shows a portion of the table used in the *International Plumbing Code* (IPC) for estimating demand. These values show that the probable demand does not increase in direct proportion to increases in the demand load. This is because as the number of fixtures in a system increases, the percentage of them that are likely to be used at the same time becomes lower.

Example 31.3

The plumbing fixtures in a small office building consist of five flush-valve toilets, two $^3/_4$ in flush-valve urinals, four lavatories, two service sinks, and a drinking fountain. What is the probable demand?

(A) 30 gpm

(B) 40 gpm

(C) 50 gpm

(D) 60 gpm

Solution

Interpolating in Table 31.4, for a supply system that uses flush valve toilets, a demand load of 75 fu corresponds to a probable demand of approximately 60.0 gpm.

The answer is (D).

Table 31.4
Table for Estimating Demand

supply systems predominantly for flush tanks			supply systems predominantly for flush valves		
load	demand		load	demand	
(fu)	(gal/min)	(ft^3/min)	(fu)	(gal/min)	(ft^3/min)
1	3.0	0.041	—	—	—
2	5.0	0.068	—	—	—
3	6.5	0.869	—	—	—
4	8.0	1.069	—	—	—
5	9.4	1.257	5	15.0	2.005
6	10.7	1.430	6	17.4	2.326
7	11.8	1.577	7	19.8	2.646
8	12.8	1.711	8	22.2	2.968
9	13.7	1.831	9	24.6	3.289
10	14.6	1.952	10	27.0	3.609
11	15.4	2.059	11	27.8	3.716
12	16.0	2.139	12	28.6	3.823
13	16.5	2.206	13	29.4	3.930
14	17.0	2.273	14	30.2	4.037
15	17.5	2.339	15	31.0	4.144
16	18.0	2.906	16	31.8	4.241
17	18.4	2.460	17	32.6	4.358
18	18.8	2.513	18	33.4	4.465
19	19.2	2.567	19	34.2	4.572
20	19.6	2.620	20	35.0	4.679
25	21.5	2.874	25	38.0	5.080
30	23.3	3.115	30	42.0	5.614
35	24.9	3.329	35	44.0	5.882
40	26.3	3.516	40	46.0	6.149
45	27.7	3.703	45	48.0	6.417
50	29.1	3.891	50	50.0	6.684
60	32.0	4.278	60	54.0	7.219
70	35.0	4.679	70	58.0	7.753
80	38.0	5.080	80	61.2	8.181
90	41.0	5.481	90	64.3	8.596
100	43.5	5.815	100	67.5	9.023
120	48.0	6.417	120	73.0	9.759
140	52.5	7.0182	140	77.0	10.293
160	57.0	7.620	160	81.0	10.828
180	61.0	8.154	180	85.5	11.430
200	65.0	8.689	200	90.0	12.031
225	70.0	9.357	225	95.5	12.766
250	75.0	10.026	250	101.0	13.502

Product Development

Sizing the Pipe

Once the probable demand is known, this value can be used with a chart that shows how flow rate, pipe size, pressure loss due to friction, and velocity are related. Charts are available for different types of pipe. One such chart is shown in Fig. 31.7.

This information is used to select the smallest diameter of pipe that will handle the needed flow rate without losing so much pressure that the fixtures will not operate. The smallest possible diameter is the most economical choice because cost increases with pipe size.

To use the chart, find the probable demand in gallons per minute, and then read across to the intersection with one of the pipe diameter lines. If necessary, assume a pipe size at first, and then determine the total friction loss. If the total friction loss is too great, select a larger pipe size and perform the calculation again.

Figure 31.7
Flow Chart for Type L Copper Pipe

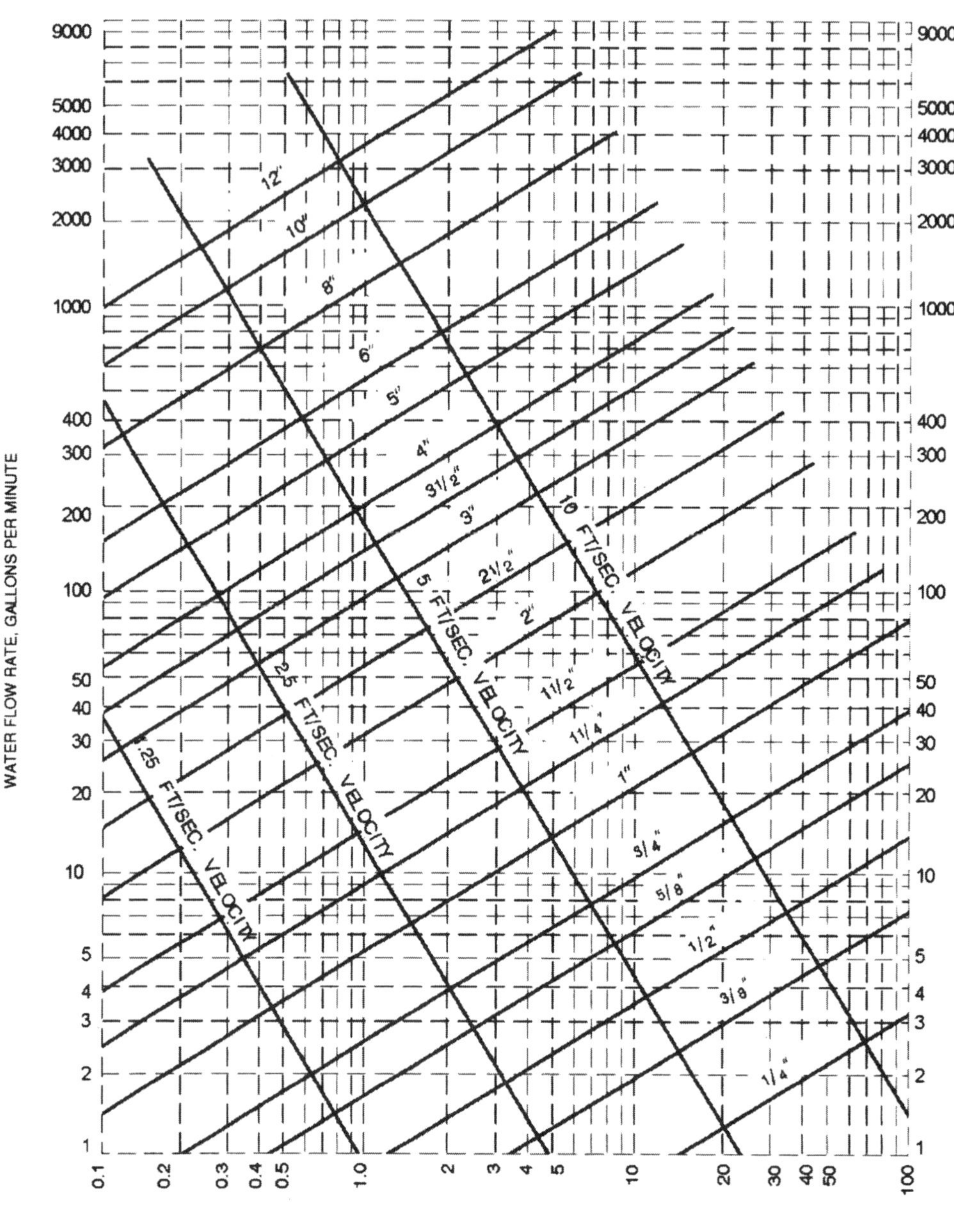

Note: Fluid velocities in excess of 5 to 8 feet/second are not usually recommended.

This chart applies to smooth new copper tubing with recessed (streamline) solder joints and to the actual sizes of types indicated on the diagram.

From *International Plumbing Code 2015*, © 2015, International Code Council, Inc.

Velocity must be also considered. At more than about 10 ft/sec, the water flowing is too noisy for most situations; in sound-sensitive situations, anything more than about 6 ft/sec may be too noisy.

For the situation in Ex. 31.2, if a $1\frac{1}{2}$ in pipe is used for a flow rate of 60 gpm, the velocity will be 10 ft/sec and the pressure loss will be about 12 psi per 100 ft. Both of these are relatively high, which suggests that at least a 2 in pipe should be used instead.

The total pressure loss from friction is the sum of the friction losses in the piping, the fittings, and the meter. The losses in the piping and fittings are calculated together. First, calculate the total length of piping from the meter to the fixture under consideration.

Next, each fitting is converted to its *equivalent length*, the length of pipe that would exhibit the same loss, with the aid of a table that gives equivalent lengths for fittings of various types and diameters. Table 31.5 is one such table.

Table 31.5 Allowance in Equivalent Lengths of Pipe for Friction Loss in Valves and Threaded Fittings (feet)

	pipe size (in)							
fitting or valve size	$1/2$	$3/4$	1	$1\frac{1}{4}$	$1\frac{1}{2}$	2	$2\frac{1}{2}$	3
45-degree elbow	1.2	1.5	1.8	2.4	3.0	4.0	5.0	6.0
90-degree elbow	2.0	2.5	3.0	4.0	5.0	7.0	8.0	10.0
tee, run	0.6	0.8	0.9	1.2	1.5	2.0	2.5	3.0
tee, branch	3.0	4.0	5.0	6.0	7.0	10.0	12.0	15.0
gate valve	0.4	0.5	0.6	0.8	1.0	1.3	1.6	2.0
balancing value	0.8	1.1	1.5	1.9	2.2	3.0	3.7	4.5
plug-type cock	0.8	1.1	1.5	1.9	2.2	3.0	3.7	4.5
check valve, swing	5.6	8.4	11.2	14.0	16.8	22.4	28.0	33.6
globe valve	15.0	20.0	25.0	35.0	45.0	55.0	65.0	80.0
angle valve	8.0	12.0	15.0	18.0	22.0	28.0	34.0	40.0

If the plumbing system has not been completely laid out, it may be necessary to estimate the number and locations of fittings.

Add the equivalent lengths of the fittings to the length of the piping and multiply their sum by the rate of pressure loss given in the chart. For example, if the piping is 54 ft long, the equivalent lengths of the fittings add up to 6 ft, and the rate of pressure loss is 8 psi per 100 ft, then the total friction loss in the piping and fittings is

$$(54\ \text{ft} + 6\ \text{ft})\left(\frac{8\ \frac{\text{lbf}}{\text{in}^2}}{100\ \text{ft}}\right) = 4.8\ \text{psi}$$

The final step is to calculate the pressure loss through the water meter. Charts that relate pressure loss to meter size and flow rate in gallons per minute are also available for this. When the supply main is $1\frac{1}{2}$ in or greater, the meter is typically one pipe size smaller than the main.

Thermal Expansion

One important part of plumbing design in large buildings is allowance for the expansion of piping. This is especially important in high-rise buildings that use long lengths of piping. For example, a 100 ft length of copper pipe can expand well over $1/2$ in with a temperature increase of 60°F. PVC pipe expands 3.5 times more than copper pipe. Figure 31.7 shows two common methods of providing for expansion. There are also in-line expansion fittings that do not require the extra space required by those in Fig. 31.8.

Irrigation Systems

Irrigation is needed for most landscape plantings, whether to encourage establishment of young plants or to provide additional water when there is not enough rain. However, to reduce potable water use and plan more sustainable buildings, irrigation must be designed efficiently or significantly reduced.

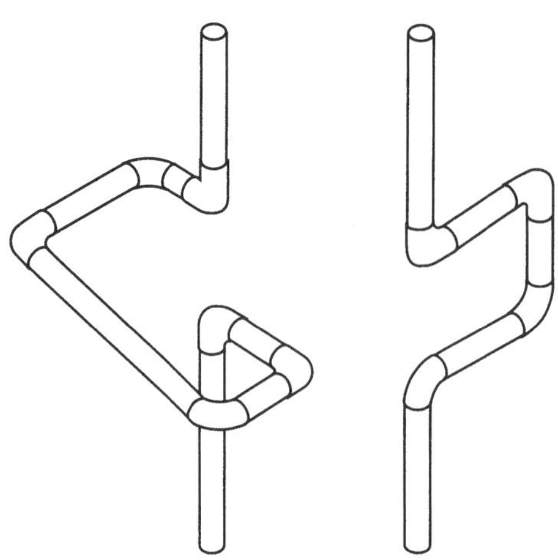

Figure 31.8
Expansion Sections for Hot Water Piping

This can be done in two ways: by landscaping with native plants that need little or no supplemental watering, and by using efficient irrigation systems. A building project can receive two to four points in the LEED rating system by incorporating water-efficient landscaping. The architect and the landscape designer coordinate to determine the most effective and efficient use of landscaping, as well as of other site features (sometimes called *hardscaping*) such as plazas, walks, and parking areas.

The simplest way to reduce the need for irrigation is to use plants that can grow with the climate's natural precipitation. In every climate, including in desert regions, it is possible to incorporate local, climate-appropriate plants into the design concept for the site. Even if the need for irrigation can't always be eliminated entirely, it can be limited to certain areas, and the rest of the site can be planted with plants that need little or no additional water.

If supplemental irrigation is used, it should be designed as efficiently as possible. Timers can be used to limit sprinkler watering to early mornings or evenings, which will reduce evaporation. Rain sensors can be installed to stop the watering when there is rain. A *tensiometer* measures the moisture content of the soil at the plant's root zone and can be used so that no more water is used than needed. For small trees, shrubs, and individual plants, a *drip irrigation system* is more efficient than sprinklers. This type of system slowly releases water at the soil level, only in the area of the plants, and can also be controlled with timers and rain sensors.

Hot Water Supply

Hot water is supplied by a tank-type water heater or boiler, in which the water is heated with gas, oil, electricity, or steam. In residences and small buildings, a single supply pipe runs from the heater to the fixtures. This minimizes the cost of piping but can result in long waits for hot water when the fixture has not been turned on for a while. The water cools in the pipes and must be run until fresh hot water travels from the heater to the fixture.

This problem can be solved with a two-pipe circulating system. All fixtures are connected to both a supply pipe and a return pipe. The natural convection in the system keeps the water slowly circulating; hot water rises to the uppermost fixtures and cools as it falls down to the water heater to be reheated. When a circulating system is used in long, low buildings or buildings where natural convection may not provide enough circulation, pumps must be used.

The size of the water heater is based on the total daily and peak hourly hot water demands of the building. The demand in a peak hour can range from 0.4 gal per person for an office building to 12 gal per unit for a small apartment building. The peak hourly demand is used because at certain times of the day, such as mornings and evenings, it is likely that most occupants will want hot water at the same time. For residences and small buildings, the capacity available to meet the peak hourly demand will be determined by the size of the water heater. For large buildings, a separate storage tank is needed in order to meet demand, while a smaller boiler actually heats the water.

In addition to storage capacity, the *recovery rate* of a water heater is important. This is the number of gallons per hour of cold water that can be heated to the desired temperature.

Hot water piping is sized much as cold water piping is, except that the demand load is calculated from only those fixtures that use hot water; toilets and urinals are excluded from this calculation. To get the hot water demand load, add the hot water load values from Table 31.3 for those fixtures that use hot water. Once the demand load is found, use Table 31.4 as before to find the probable demand, and Table 31.5 to select the pipe diameter. In no case can the pipe size be less than the minimum size given in the plumbing codes.

Water heaters are set to keep the water at the highest temperature that is needed at the point of use. Recommended point-of-use temperatures range from 95°F for therapeutic baths to 180°F for commercial and institutional laundries and sanitizing rinses for commercial dishwashers. Other common temperatures include 105°F for washing hands, 110°F for showers and baths, and 140°F for residential dishwashing and laundry. Above about 110°F, water becomes uncomfortable to the touch.

Water heaters are available in several configurations and use different heating methods as diagrammed in Fig. 31.9. There are two basic kinds of heating methods, direct and indirect. *Direct heating* brings the water into contact with surfaces heated directly by flame, hot gases, electricity, or solar radiation. This is the method used for the typical residential tank-type water heater. *Indirect heating* uses another medium to transfer the heat from its source to the surfaces that are in contact with the water. For example, in commercial applications where central steam is available, the steam can be piped into tubes within a tank that holds the domestic hot water.

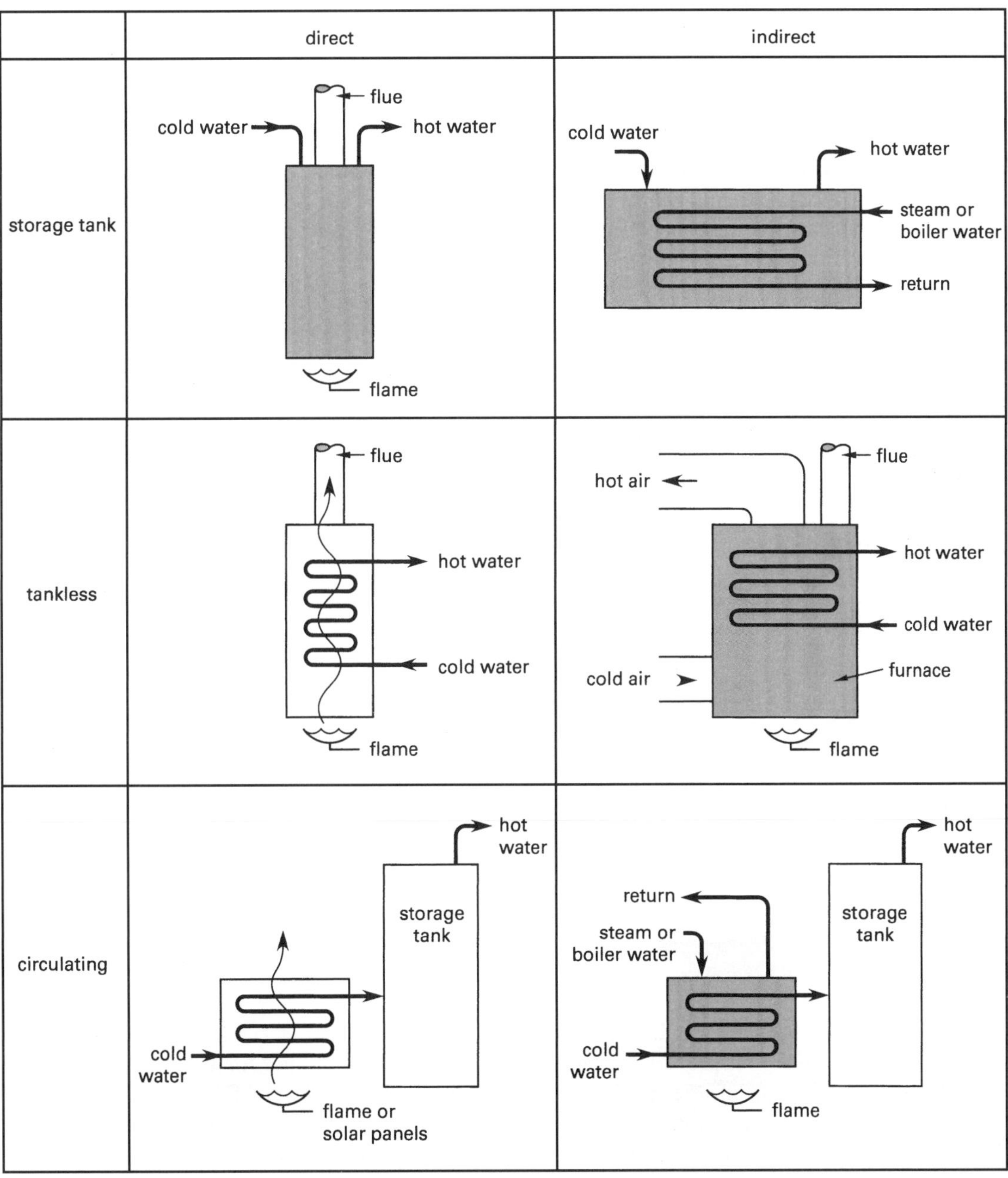

Figure 31.9
Water Heater Types

There are three basic types of heating systems: storage tank, tankless, and circulating. Diagrams of these types of units using both direct and indirect heating are shown in Fig. 31.9. In a *storage tank system*, the same tank is used both to heat the water and to store it for use. In a *tankless system*, water is quickly heated as it is needed and immediately sent to where it is needed. A common form of this is the electric instantaneous water heater, in which a high-capacity electric coil heats water quickly whenever the hot water faucet is turned on; this sort of heater is often used in locations where it is impractical or uneconomical to pipe hot water continuously, such as a remote sink in a residence. In a *circulating system*, the water is heated in one place and then moved to a separate tank for storage until needed. This method is commonly used in solar-powered water heating systems and in many commercial applications.

In some cases it is impractical or inefficient to use an indirect, tankless system. For example, water for a residence could be heated in the same furnace or boiler that heats air for space heating; however, the heating plant would then have to work throughout the summer. In a case like this, the heating plant can be used for supplemental water heating, to reduce the load on another source of heat that is used for water heating only. Tankless systems are also often impractical when a high flow rate and high temperature rise are both needed, such as for clothes washing or bathtubs.

SANITARY DRAINAGE AND VENTING

There are two types of drainage, which can be considered separately. *Sanitary drainage* includes any drainage that may include food or human waste, whereas *storm drainage* involves only runoff from roof drains, landscaped areas, and the like.

The main advantage of separating the two is that storm drainage does not have to be treated. A second advantage is that if the two were disposed of together, the drainage from an unexpectedly large storm could overload the disposal system and cause sewage to back up into a building. This section will discuss sanitary drainage only.

Sanitary drainage is sometimes divided further. *Blackwater* is wastewater from toilets, which contains human waste, and *graywater* is all other wastewater, such as that from sinks and dishwashers. (However, some graywater, such as that from showers and clothes washers, may still contain traces of human waste.) This distinction is made because graywater can sometimes be reused with little or no treatment for irrigation, flushing toilets, and other purposes, whereas blackwater needs more extensive treatment before reuse or disposal.

Drainage Systems

A drainage system is designed to safely carry away sewage to a private or municipal disposal system. It consists of the following parts.

- trap
- drainage piping
- vent
- air gap
- vacuum breaker
- stack
- drain
- sewer

With few exceptions, *traps* are located at every fixture and are designed to catch and hold a quantity of water, which forms a seal that prevents sewage system gases from entering the building. Some fixtures such as toilets have traps as an integral part of their design. Where adjacent fixtures are connected, as with a double kitchen sink, additional traps need not be installed. Traps are usually installed within 2 ft of the fixture but may be installed at slightly greater distances depending on the size of the pipe. A house trap is sometimes installed at the point where the house drain leaves the building, but this is not always mandatory.

Traps are connected to the actual drainage piping, but they must also be connected to *vents*, which are pipes that lead from the drainage system to the outside air, typically through an opening in the roof. Vents serve two primary purposes. First, they allow built-up sewage gases to escape instead of bubbling through the water in the traps. Second, they allow pressure in the system to equalize so that waste being discharged does not create a siphon that drains the water out of the traps.

Air gaps are also used as safety features in sanitary drainage systems. If an outlet for potable water, such as the outlet of a faucet, were below the overflow level of a sink or tub, wastewater in the sink or tub could be siphoned back into the potable water supply lines. To prevent this, faucets are always mounted with their outlets at least 2 in above the highest possible level of wastewater.

On fixtures where the water supply is below the rim of the fixture (on a flush valve toilet, for example), a device called a *vacuum breaker* is used to prevent siphonage by closing when backward water pressure is present.

Figure 31.10 shows a simplified diagram of a typical drainage and vent system. From the trap, sewage travels through fixture branch lines to a *stack*, a vertical pipe that carries wastewater down to the bottom of the building. If the stack carries wastewater that includes human waste from toilets, it is called a *soil stack*; otherwise it is called a *waste stack*.

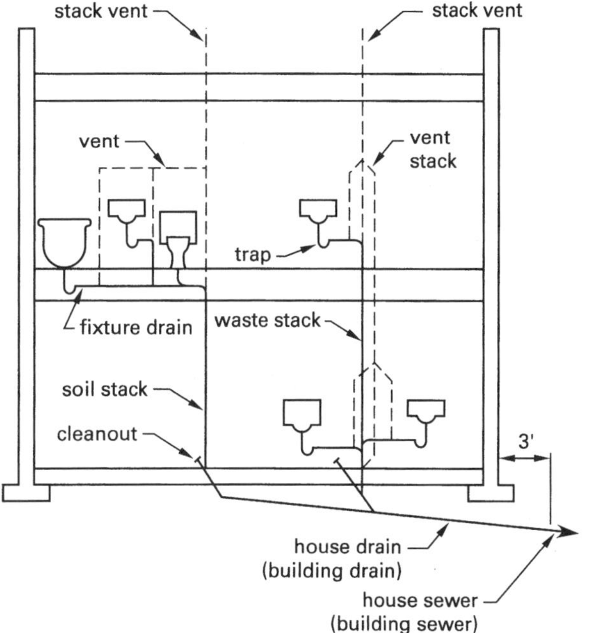

Figure 31.10 Drainage and Vent System

Each soil stack and waste stack must continue upward, extend through an opening in the roof, and be open to the outside air. That portion of a stack that is higher than any connection to a fixture is called a *stack vent.*

Each vent from an individual fixture must also be open to the exterior. Vents in a one-story building or on the top floor of a multistory building are typically connected to the stack vent at the top of the stack that serves those fixtures. In a multistory building, vents from fixtures on lower floors are typically connected to a *vent stack* that runs parallel to the soil or waste stack. When the vent stack reaches the top floor, it either connects to the stack vent or continues up through the roof.

All stacks are connected to a horizontal drain at the bottom of the building. Within the building and to a point 3 ft outside the building, this is called the *house drain* (also known as the *building drain*). From a point 3 ft outside the building to the main sewer line or private disposal system, the horizontal pipe is called the *house sewer* (also known as the *building sewer*). *Cleanouts* are provided where stack connect with the house drain to allow for maintenance. Cleanouts are also required outside the building for maintenance of the house sewer.

Horizontal drains must be sloped to allow for gravity drainage. The minimum slope for branch lines of house drains and sewers is typically $^1/_4$ in per foot, but for pipes larger than 3 in, $^1/_8$ in per foot is sometimes allowed. Changes in direction must be made with easy bends rather than right-angle fittings.

Materials and Components

Piping designed for drainage systems is called *drain, waste, and vent (DWV) pipe.* DWV pipe is available in copper, cast iron, and plastic. Plastic is the most common because it is less expensive than metal piping and its installation requires less labor. Polyvinyl chloride (PVC) and acrylonitrile butadiene styrene (ABS) plastics are suitable for DWV systems.

Copper and plastic piping are joined in the same way as they are for supply water piping. Cast-iron piping can be connected either with hub-and-spigot joints or with hubless joints. In a hub-and-spigot fitting, the end of one pipe is slipped into the enlarged hub of another pipe, and the joint is sealed with a gasket. A hubless joint uses a gasket held in place with a stainless steel retaining clamp. Cast-iron pipe is required for the house sewer and is also often used elsewhere to reduce noise.

Occasionally, vitrified clay pipe is used for building sewers if allowed by the local code. This sort of pipe is seldom used in new construction because tree roots can grow into the pipe joints, but it is sometimes found in older buildings.

Other components of a drainage system may include the following.

Backflow preventers such as *backwater valves*, keep wastewater from reversing flow and backing up into fixtures, which could contaminate the water supply or cause the basement to flood. Backflow can occur when there is wastewater in the system at a higher elevation than some fixtures, such as in a multistory building, or when wastewater is under higher pressure than the supply water, such as from thermal expansion.

When plumbing fixtures must be below the level of the house drain and house sewer, a *sump pit* and *sump pump* (sometimes called an *ejector pump*) are installed. This combination collects the sewage and pumps it to a higher level where it can flow by gravity into the sewer.

Floor drains collect water in shower rooms or in places where overflow is likely. Because some floor drains are seldom used, special care must be taken so that the water seal does not evaporate and allow sewer gases to penetrate the building. The traps of floor drains are usually required to have deeper seals than other types of traps.

Interceptors collect foreign matter at the source instead of allowing it to enter the sewer system. Some common types are grease traps, plaster traps, and lubricating oil traps. They should be designed to allow foreign matter to be cleaned out periodically. Interceptors are of no use in trapping toxic liquids.

System Design

The sizing of drainage pipes, like the sizing of water supply pipes, is based on flow rate expressed in fixture units. However, many fixtures have different load values for water supply and drainage. Drainage flow rate is expressed in *drainage fixture units* (dfu). For example, the drainage load of a lavatory is 1 dfu, and a public water closet has a drainage load of 6 dfu.

There are also certain minimum sizes of trap arms for individual fixtures: a single lavatory must have at least a $1^1/_4$ in drain and a single toilet must have at least a 3 in trap arm. The minimum size for a vent is $1^1/_4$ in. These values are given in tables in the plumbing code.

Design of a drainage system begins with the individual fixtures and branch lines and proceeds to the sizing of stacks and building drains. Tables in the plumbing code give the maximum number of fixture units and the maximum vertical and horizontal lengths of piping based on pipe diameter. It is then a simple matter to accumulate fixture units served by a particular stack or drain and increase the size as needed as more fixtures are added to it.

The plumbing code states the minimum sizes and lengths of vents based on fixture units connected, and gives the maximum horizontal distance of trap arms based on size.

LOCATING PLUMBING FIXTURES

During schematic design and design development, the architect should give careful consideration to the locations of toilet rooms, kitchens, and other spaces that need plumbing fixtures. Because of the cost of plumbing and the need for sloping drainage pipes, fixtures should be located as close to main plumbing lines as possible. These mains include horizontal lines and risers that run continuously through a multistory building.

Drains must generally slope at least $1/4$ in/ft, but a slope of $1/8$ in/ft is allowed for pipes larger than 3 in. If a pipe must be concealed within a floor space, the required slope and the size of the pipe itself will limit the distance from the fixture to a connection with a riser. Figure 31.11 illustrates these principles.

The maximum distance between a fixture and a vertical or horizontal waste line usually depends on the space available to maintain a $1/4$ in/ft slope, especially when the vent is located adjacent to the fixture. However, there are some instances when there is no wall or other construction directly behind the fixture in which to conceal vertical piping (for example, a sink in a peninsula cabinet). The vent must be located reasonably close to the fixture's trap. Plumbing codes limit the maximum distance from a trap to the nearest vent. The distance depends on the size of the pipe and ranges from 5 ft for a $1^1/_4$ in trap to 16 ft for a 4 in trap.

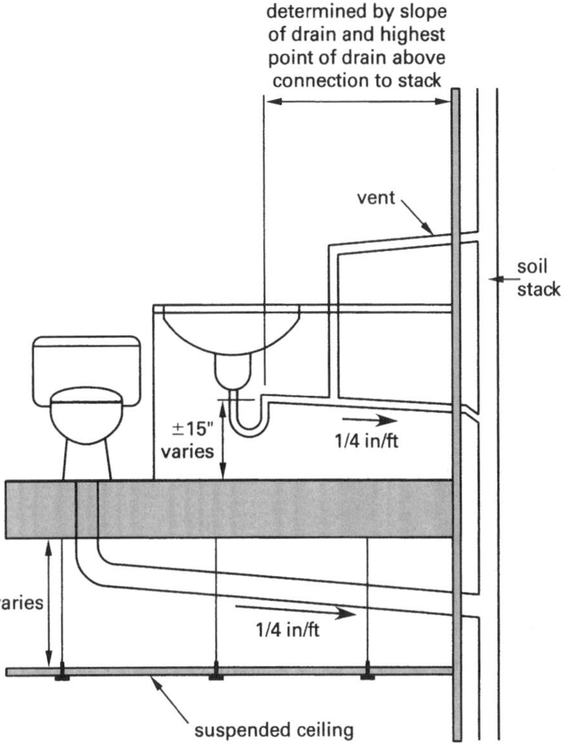

Figure 31.11 Planning for Drainage Lines

An island sink in the middle of a room may be vented in one of three ways. *Island fixture venting* connects directly above the waste line where the trap arm discharges. The vent is carried up above the bottom of the sink and then looped horizontally and downward below the floor line. Below the floor line the vent pipe runs horizontally to the nearest vent stack. An *air admittance valve* (AAV) can be placed above the vertical waste line in the island to vent the sink. When this type of venting is allowed by local codes, it is simpler than running a separate vent. Alternatively, a combination *waste and vent layout* may be used. In any of the methods used to vent an island sink, the detailing of cabinetry will likely involve leaving room for the extra plumbing. The local authority having jurisdiction must be consulted to confirm which venting methods may or may not be used.

In commercial buildings, most plumbing is concentrated in one area near the core where it serves the toilet rooms, drinking fountains, and similar fixtures. To provide service to sinks, private toilets, and the like, *wet columns* are sometimes included in the building. These are areas where hot and cold supply and drainage risers are located, usually at a structural column. Individual tenants can easily tap into these lines, if desired, without having to connect to more remote plumbing.

If extensive plumbing work is needed, pipes may not fit within the space provided by standard partitions. A soil stack from a toilet, for example, usually requires pipe with an inside diameter of at least 3 in. In some instances, however, 4 in pipe is required. In this case, either thicker partitions or plumbing chases are required.

A *chase wall* consists of two rows of studs separated by several inches, the exact dimension being determined by the largest pipe or duct that has to be concealed. Only the finish side of each row of studs is covered with wallboard. Chase walls are commonly used between back-to-back-commercial toilet rooms where extensive plumbing work as well as sink carriers and toilet carriers are needed.

A *sink carrier* is a steel framework inside a chase wall that carries the weight of wall-mounted sinks; a *toilet carrier* similarly supports wall-mounted toilets. In most cases, a chase wall with fixtures on one side should be about 12 in thick, and a chase wall with fixtures on both sides should be about 16 in thick. These dimensions provide enough space for supply and waste piping as well as the sink and toilet carriers.

WASTE DISPOSAL AND TREATMENT

After sewage leaves a building, it is transported through the house sewer to either a municipal collection system or a private disposal system.

A private disposal system generally consists of a septic tank and a leaching field. The *septic tank* collects the sewage and allows the solid matter to settle to the bottom. The liquid portion, called the *effluent*, then drains into the distribution system, where it seeps into the ground. See Fig. 31.12.

The size of septic tank needed is determined by the amount of daily flow. For residences this is usually based on the number of bedrooms and baths. For larger installations, it is based on the calculated sewage flow in gallons per day.

Figure 31.12 Private Sewage Disposal

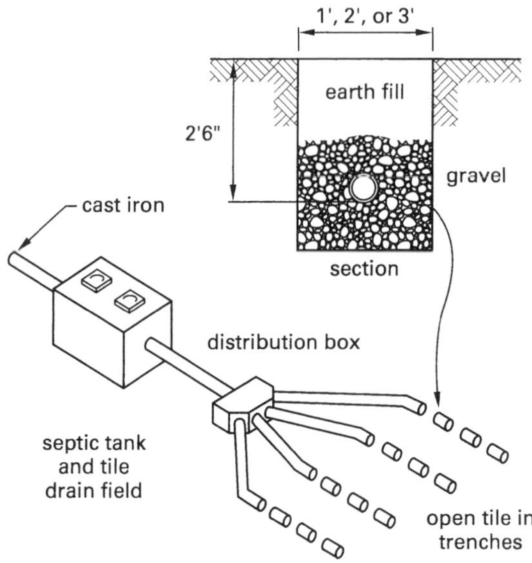

The size and length of the leaching field system are based on the ability of the soil to absorb the effluent. A *leaching field* is an area where effluent seeps from the drain tiles into the soil. This is determined by a *percolation test*, which measures the amount of time it takes water in a test hole to drop 1 in. Tables are available that give the minimum length of piping in leaching fields based on percolation and volume handled.

Septic tanks and leaching fields can potentially contaminate supplies of potable water, mainly wells. For this reason, plumbing codes prescribe minimum required distances between various parts of the system and other features of the site such as wells, property lines, rivers, and buildings. For example, there must be a minimum of 100 ft between a leaching field and a well, 50 ft between a septic tank and a well, and 10 ft between a leaching field and a building.

Where sewage is transported from a building to public sewer lines, the building sewer connects to a line in the street or other public right of way. From there, branch lines connect to larger main lines that eventually reach a sewage treatment facility. Access holes are provided for maintenance and inspection of the lines. They are located at every change in direction and at intervals of 150 ft.

Another method of treating wastewater is with *waste stabilization ponds* (WSP). These ponds are typically 4 ft to 8 ft deep and act as holding basins for secondary wastewater treatment. The wastewater is directed through a series of ponds, sitting in each pond for between three weeks and six months; the process takes longer in colder locations. In the ponds, sewage decomposes biologically through aerobic and anaerobic processes.

One type of WSP system is the *advanced integrated wastewater pond system* (AIWPS). As the wastewater makes its way through the four separate ponds in the system, it is exposed to different conditions to encourage the breakdown and removal of organic matter. The first pond is a *facultative pond*, in which the wastewater is exposed to aerobic activity near the surface and anaerobic activity near the bottom. The anaerobic activity ferments and consumes sludge, while the aerobic activity oxidizes gases that rise from the fermentation.

The second pond contains a high level of algae, which produce oxygen that promotes further aerobic activity, breaking down dissolved organic matter. Next is a *settling pond* in which more than half the algae settle out. Finally, the water rests in a *maturation pond* to allow pathogenic bacteria of human origin to die. The effluent can then be used for agricultural or landscape irrigation.

STORM DRAINAGE

Water drainage from rain and melted snow should be kept separate from sanitary drainage, to avoid overloading the sanitary drainage system and causing sewage to back up. In sparsely populated areas, storm drainage soaks into the ground or finds its way to rivers and lakes. In more populated areas that have a higher percentage of pervious surfaces such as roofs, paved streets, and parking lots, artificial systems are needed to carry away stormwater safely.

Private Systems

There are several ways water can be drained from a private home. The first and simplest consists of collecting water from the roof in roof drains or gutters and leaders and letting it run onto the ground surrounding the house, where it soaks in. Splash blocks and other devices carry the water far enough from the building to prevent water from seeping into the foundation or eroding soil around the base of the building. Some communities require that roof drains connect directly to the public storm sewer system.

If this is not adequate, drywells can be connected to the drain leaders with underground pipes. A *drywell* is a large, porous, underground container where water collects and seeps into the soil. If the capacity of the drywell is not adequate or the ground is not sufficiently porous, a *drain field*, similar to a leaching field, can be used.

The building should also be graded to divert water away from the foundation. It is good practice to slope the land at least $^1/_2$ in per foot away from the building's foundation.

Municipal Systems

A municipal storm sewer system is laid out in a manner similar to the sanitary sewage system, collecting runoff from street gutters, catch basins, and individual taps from private buildings and land developments. The system carries the water by gravity to natural drainage areas such as rivers, lakes, or oceans.

In some areas the potential volume of runoff from a storm may be too great for the storm system to handle. In this case, building regulations may require the inclusion of a retention pond in a site plan. A *retention pond* is designed to contain the maximum expected runoff and then slowly release the water to the storm sewer system. Retention ponds may have a small outlet at one end, such as a dam or drain to a low point in the middle of the pond, where a catch basin, or grate, covers the entrance to a pipe. This pipe transports the water to a storm sewer system or other natural drainage area.

Drains, Gutters, and Downspout Sizing

The sizes of horizontal drain pipes, gutters, and downspouts are determined based on the area of the roof or paved area drained and the maximum hourly rainfall. See Fig. 31.13. For gutters and horizontal piping, the slope of the pipe is also a factor; lower slopes require a greater size. Gutter slopes range from $^1/_6$ in/ft to $^1/_2$ in/ft.

Typical rainfall rates for a specific area are available from the local weather service or from published maps of the United States and Canada, which are in the *International Plumbing Code.* When calculating the roof area of a sloped roof, the *projected area* is used. This is the horizontal area defined by the edges of the roof without regard to the slope. Tables are available that give the minimum required diameter of gutter or roof leader based on maximum hourly rainfall rate, roof area, and proposed slope of gutter.

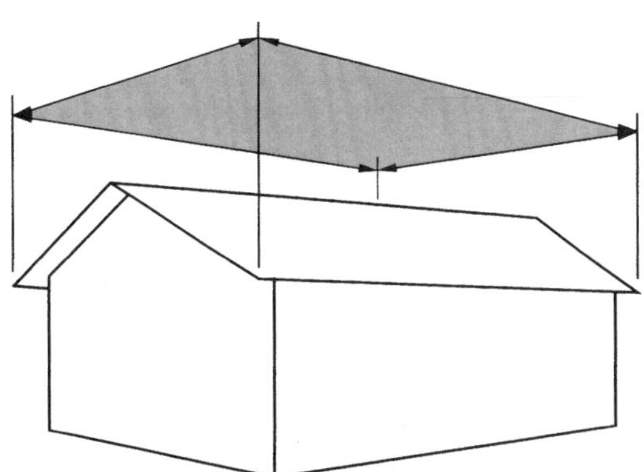

Figure 31.13 Sizing of Horizontal Drain Pipes, Gutters, and Downspouts

32 INTEGRATION OF SPECIALTY SYSTEMS

FIRE PROTECTION AND LIFE SAFETY

In the areas of fire protection and life safety in buildings, there are three major objectives: the protection of life, the protection of property, and the restoration and continued use of the building after the fire. (Life safety also aims to protect people during emergencies other than fire, such as earthquakes, floods, terrorist threats, and similar disasters. These, though, are beyond the scope of this book, and this section focuses on life safety during building fires.)

Fire protection in buildings has several aspects that the architect should be familiar with.

- *preventing fires:* This includes limiting the use of combustible building and finishing materials and avoiding hazardous situations. (This is covered in Chap. 8 and Chap. 14.)
- *early fire detection and alarm:* Sufficient warning must be given so that occupants can leave the building safely and so that fire fighting can start before the fire has spread.
- *planning for the quick exiting of occupants:* Occupants should have a safe exit route from anywhere in the building. (This is covered in Chap. 14.)
- *containing the fire:* This is achieved through choice of building materials, compartmentation, and smoke control.
- *suppressing the fire:* This is achieved through sprinkler systems, standpipes, and other methods.

Detection, containment, and suppression are discussed in this section.

Compartmentation

Compartmentation is a fundamental concept in fire and life safety. By containing a fire and limiting its spread, building occupants can escape and other parts of the building can be protected from fire damage. In a high-rise building, where it may not be practical to evacuate immediately, compartmentation can be used to create places of refuge where occupants can wait until the fire is extinguished or they can exit safely. Compartmentation also provides time for fire suppression to begin, whether by automatic sprinklers or by fire fighting personnel.

Compartmentation has been integral to building codes for a long time. Codes require fire separation between different occupancies, between use areas and exits, and between parts of a building when the maximum allowable area is exceeded. Separation is required both horizontally with fire-resistive floor-ceiling assemblies and vertically with fire-rated walls. Any openings through fire assemblies must also provide protection from the spread of fire and smoke. These topics are covered in Chap. 14.

On a larger scale, compartmentation also applies to an entire building, so that fire does not spread to adjacent structures. For this reason building codes require certain fire ratings for exterior walls, limit the locations of buildings on a piece of property, and either limit the size of exterior openings or require their protection when a building is near other structures or property lines. These requirements are also covered in Chap. 14.

On a smaller scale, load-bearing structural members are isolated to protect them from the effects of fire and prevent structural collapse. In addition, concealed areas above ceilings, in attics, in chase walls, and under floors are limited in size, because a fire in these parts is especially difficult to detect and extinguish. Firestops in stud spaces between the first and second floors of a house are an important example of this kind of small-scale compartmentation.

Smoke Control

Most deaths and injuries in fires occur not from flames and heat exposure but from inhaling smoke and other gases. For this reason, *smoke control* is one of the most important aspects of fire protection.

Smoke is particularly troublesome because it can move rapidly through a building, well beyond the location of the fire. There are several reasons for this. A fire causes large differences in air temperature and thus air pressure, and this in turn can cause smoke-filled air to circulate by natural convection. In multistory buildings, especially tall ones, the air pressure differences can create a strong *stack effect* that pulls smoke rapidly upward from one floor to the next through vertical penetrations such as stairways, elevator shafts, mechanical shafts, and atriums. HVAC systems can distribute smoke a great distance from its original source.

Smoke is particularly troublesome because it can move rapidly through a building, well beyond the location of the fire.

Several approaches can be used to control smoke. These include containment, exhaust, and—to a lesser degree—dilution. The same compartmentation that is used to contain fires is also used to contain the spread of smoke. Devices such as smoke dampers, fire dampers, gaskets on fire doors, and automatic-closing fire doors can seal openings in fire walls. By containing smoke to one area of the building, places of refuge can be established.

Containment alone is not enough. Because smoke is so deadly, it must be removed from a building as quickly as possible, through use of passive or active smoke control systems. This keeps the smoke out of refuge areas, removes toxic smoke and gases, makes it easier to fight the fire, and helps control the path of the fire.

A *passive smoke control system* is one with a series of smoke barriers arranged to limit the migration of smoke. An *active smoke control system* is an engineered system that uses mechanical fans to produce pressure differentials across smoke barriers or to establish airflows to limit and direct smoke movement.

Passive smoke barriers can be partitions, doors with smoke seals, or curtain boards. A *curtain board,* also called a *draft stop,* is a vertical panel made from fire-resistive materials that is attached to the ceiling immediately adjacent to an opening. The curtain board is secured tightly against the ceiling, so that no smoke can pass between them, and hangs a minimum of 18 in. Because smoke rises, the curtain board restricts the passage of smoke and flame during a fire's initial stages. Curtain boards are commonly used in vented buildings and around escalator enclosures in conjunction with closely spaced sprinklers to protect floor openings.

The *International Building Code* (IBC) requires that automatic smoke and heat vents be installed in one-story buildings of Group F and S occupancies over 50,000 ft^2 and in Group H occupancies over 15,000 ft^2 in a single-floor area. This kind of vent contains a *fusible link*, a small piece of wire that melts at a certain temperature and acts as a switch to open a vent, sprinkler head, or other fire-prevention system element. The IBC also requires that smoke vents be provided above stages that are more than 1000 ft^2 in area and in atriums, among other areas.

The concept of active smoke control combined with compartmentation is illustrated in Fig. 32.1, which shows a diagrammatic plan of one floor of a high-rise building. A *high-rise* is defined as any building with occupied floor area more than 75 ft above the lowest level of fire department vehicle access. High-rises require special consideration because a fire may be beyond the reach of outside fire fighting equipment, because evacuation takes longer, and because of the increased potential for a strong stack effect pulling smoke and gases upward.

When a fire activates an alarm, several events take place. All doors that connect the fire zone to other zones and that are connected to automatic closing devices are closed, such as the doors to the elevator lobby in Fig. 32.1. Supply air and return air ducts in the fire zone are shut down, and a vent that exhausts to outside air is turned on. This creates a negative pressure in the fire zone. In an adjacent refuge zone, return and exhaust air ducts are closed, and supply air is forced in. This creates a slight positive pressure in the refuge zone and helps keep smoke from entering, even if the doors are opened momentarily.

Figure 32.1
Smoke Control in High-Rise Buildings

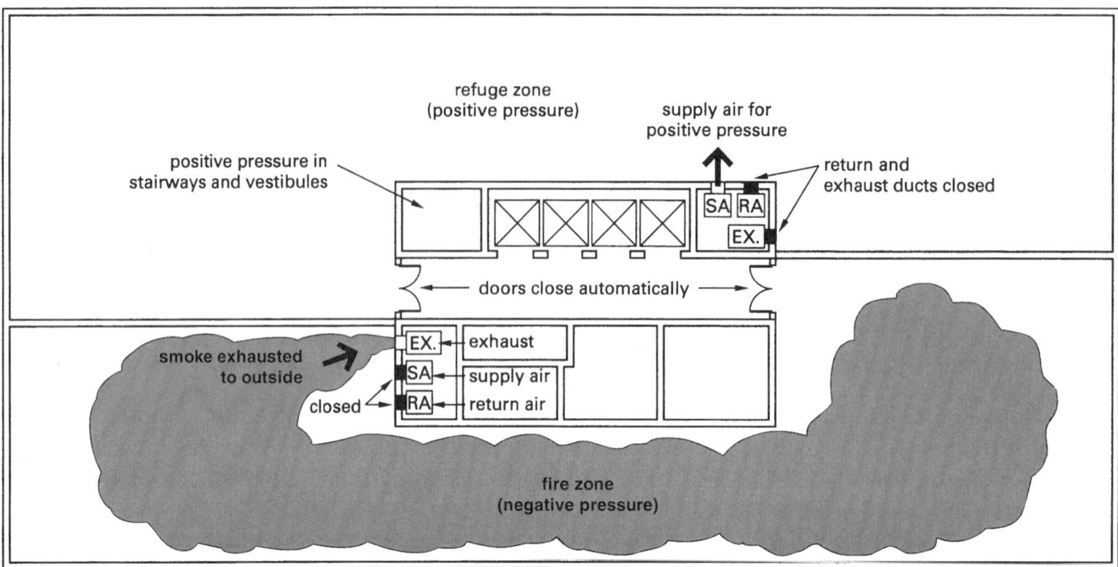

Stairways are pressurized to prevent smoke from entering. Vestibules are pressurized at a level slightly higher than that of the fire zone but slightly less than that of the stairway. This arrangement provides a double protection of the stairway and also keeps smoke out of the vestibules, where the areas of refuge for wheelchair occupants are located and where the standpipe connections and fire department communication devices are located. This system of protection for stairways replaces the "smoke-proof enclosures" of previous codes.

Similar systems can be used for other building types, such as large shopping malls, buildings with atriums, and large industrial buildings. The building code prescribes where smoke control must be installed and whether it must be active or passive.

Sprinkler Systems

Fire sprinkler systems have become common in new construction, both because building codes increasingly require them and because owners and insurance companies have become aware that sprinklers can minimize property damage and improve life safety. The IBC requires sprinklers in buildings over 75 ft high and in hotels.

There are four types of sprinkler systems: wet pipe, dry pipe, pre-action, and deluge. *Wet pipe systems* are the most common. A wet pipe system is kept filled with water at all times; when the temperature reaches the trigger point at any sprinkler, the system responds immediately. The trigger point is typically between 135°F to 170°F; the exact trigger point is generally chosen depending on the normal temperature at the ceiling. Fusible links are available for a range of temperatures. In most wet pipe systems, flow detectors are placed on every zone of sprinkler piping. When a sprinkler head opens, the detector senses the movement of water and sends a signal to an annunciator panel or fire control center so that firefighters know where the fire is.

Dry pipe systems are used in areas subject to freezing. The pipes are filled with compressed air or nitrogen until one or more heads are activated, allowing water to flow. Alternately, a dry pipe system can be activated by a valve connected to a fire alarm.

Pre-action systems are similar to dry-pipe systems, except that water is allowed into the system before any sprinkler head has opened. At the same time, an alarm is activated. The sprinkler head does not open immediately; there is a short delay that allows firefighters to respond. This sort of system is used where water damage is a concern. The early alarm allows the fire to be put out before any sprinkler head opens.

Deluge systems activate all the sprinkler heads in an area at once, regardless of where the fire is detected. All the sprinkler heads are kept open, and the pipes are kept empty. When an alarm is activated, valves automatically open, releasing water into the pipes and flooding the space. Deluge systems are used in high-hazard areas where a fire is likely to spread rapidly.

In tall buildings, water for a sprinkler system can be supplied either from a tank near the top of the building or zone (just as water is supplied to fixtures) or from pumps connected to an emergency power supply. If a tank is used, it is sized to supply water over a certain percentage of sprinklers for a certain length of time, until firefighters can arrive; the percentage and the length of time are determined by the relevant building codes.

A *siamese connection*, also called a *splitter*, is a wye-shaped pipe fitting installed close to the ground on the exterior of the building. A siamese connection allows two fire hoses at the same location to connect to the standpipes and sprinkler system of a building.

Deluge systems are used in high-hazard areas where a fire is likely to spread rapidly.

Specific requirements for installation of fire sprinkler systems are governed by each local building code, but most codes refer to NFPA 13, *Standard for the Installation of Sprinkler Systems*, published by the National Fire Protection Association (NFPA). This standard classifies buildings into three levels of fire hazard: light, ordinary, and extra. Each hazard classification is further divided into groups. The hazard classification determines the required spacing of sprinklers and other regulations.

Light hazard occupancies include the common types of uses that most architects deal with.

- residences
- offices
- hospitals
- schools
- museums
- retail space
- auditoriums
- restaurants
- other institutions

In these occupancies, there must be one sprinkler for each 225 ft^2 of floor area, provided that the design of the system is hydraulically calculated; otherwise, there must be one sprinkler per 200 ft^2. Most sprinkler systems for commercial buildings are hydraulically designed, either by the fire protection engineer or the fire protection contractor, so the maximum coverage area of 225 ft^2 is typically used in light hazard occupancies. For open-wood joist ceilings, the allowable coverage area drops to130 ft^2.

Maximum spacing between sprinkler heads is 15 ft for the 225 ft^2 coverage requirement, with the maximum distance from a wall being one-half the required spacing.

The minimum distance from a partition to the nearest sprinkler is 4 in. A sprinkler near a vertical obstruction, such as a column, that is more than 4 in wide and as much as 24 in deep must be located at a distance at least three times the maximum dimension of the obstruction. When beams, dropped ceilings, or other obstructions project below the main ceiling where the sprinklers are located, sprinklers must be located a certain distance away from the projection so that the water stream is not deflected.

When sprinklers are installed in rooms with modular furniture systems, free-standing partitions, privacy curtains, or room dividers, there must be a minimum distance between the sprinkler and the top of the obstruction. This ranges from 6 in when the vertical dimensions is 3 in or less, to 30 in when the vertical distance is 18 in or more.

When the architect is not designing the sprinkler system, he or she may suggest the locations of sprinkler heads to coordinate with other ceiling-mounted items.

Sprinkler Heads

Several styles of sprinkler heads are available, including upright, sidewall, and pendant. *Upright heads* sit above the sprinkler pipe and are used where plumbing is exposed and ceilings are high and unfinished.

Sidewall heads are used for corridors and small rooms where a single row of sprinklers can provide adequate coverage. Sidewall heads also can be plumbed from the walls instead of from the ceiling, which makes them useful for remodeling work.

A *pendant head* is located below the sprinkler pipe, and there are several variations. One of the most common is fully exposed below the ceiling. A *recessed head* is partially recessed above the ceiling, with its deflector below the ceiling. A *flush head* has only its thermosensitive element below the ceiling. A *concealed head* has a smooth cover that is flush with the ceiling. When there is a fire, the cover falls away and the sprinkler head activates.

Every sprinkler head must be kept closed until activated by high temperature. Older sprinkler heads use a fusible metal link designed to melt at a particular temperature, releasing the plug that holds back the water. Newer sprinkler heads use a fragile glass bulb that contains colored liquid and an air bubble; when the liquid reaches a particular temperature, it expands enough to break the bulb, releasing the plug. The color of the liquid indicates at what temperature the head is designed to activate.

There are different types of sprinklers; which one is used depends on the level of hazard, the specific type of occupancy, and the contents of the space being protected. *Standard residential sprinklers* are fast-response devices sensitive to both heat and smoldering. *Quick-response sprinklers* are more sensitive to heat than standard sprinklers, so it takes less time for the device to reach the temperature needed to open the sprinkler. *Early-suppression fast-response* (ESFR) sprinklers spray water at high pressure and at a higher rate of flow than most sprinklers, and are for use in more hazardous locations. While most sprinklers are designed to keep a fire from spreading until the fire department arrives to extinguish it, ESFR sprinklers are designed to extinguish the fire while it is small. In addition to spraying greater amounts of water under high pressure, ESFR sprinkler heads are more sensitive to heat and produce large droplets that penetrate plumes of fire.

Quick-response early-suppression (QRES) sprinklers are similar to ESFR sprinklers, but have smaller orifices and are designed for light-hazard occupancies. *Extended coverage* (EC) sprinklers cover a larger area per head than most sprinklers, but they may be used only in light-hazard occupancies and under smooth, flat ceilings.

Standpipes

Standpipes are vertical pipes to which fire hoses can be connected; they run the height of a building and provide water outlets at each floor. They are located within stairways or, in the case of pressurized enclosures, within vestibules.

IBC Sec. 905 defines three classes of standpipes. Class I is a dry-standpipe system that is not directly connected to a water supply and is equipped with $2\frac{1}{2}$ in outlets for use by fire department personnel. Class II is a wet-standpipe system directly connected to a water supply and equipped with $1\frac{1}{2}$ in outlets and hoses intended for use by building occupants. Class III is a combination system directly connected to a water supply and equipped with both $1\frac{1}{2}$ in and $2\frac{1}{2}$ in outlets.

IBC Sec. 905.3 defines where each class of standpipe is required. With a few exceptions, Class III standpipes are required in all buildings where the floor level of the highest story is more than 30 ft above the lowest level of fire department vehicle access, or where the floor level of the lowest story is more than 30 ft below the highest level of fire department access. The exceptions are buildings and basements equipped throughout with automatic sprinkler systems, open parking garages where the highest floor is not more than 150 ft above the lowest level of fire department access, and open parking garages subject to freezing temperatures. In these cases, Class I standpipes may be used.

Class I standpipe systems are required in non-sprinklered Group A buildings with occupant loads greater than 1000 persons, in covered and open mall buildings, in underground buildings, and on stages with areas greater than 1000 ft^2. If a stage is located in a building or area that is equipped throughout with an automatic sprinkler system, however, Class II standpipes may be used as prescribed by the IBC.

For Class I and III standpipe systems, hose connections must be provided at the following locations.

- on each side of the wall adjacent to the opening of a horizontal exit
- in every exit passageway, at the entrance from the exit passageway to other areas of the building
- in every required stairway, at each floor level above and below grade and at each intermediate landing between floors
- in covered mall buildings, adjacent to each exterior public entrance and adjacent to each entrance from an exit passageway or exit corridor to the mall
- in open mall buildings, adjacent to each public entrance at the perimeter
- on roofs with slopes less than 4:12

In the first two cases, a hose connection is not required if the floor area is reachable by a 30 ft hose stream from a nozzle attached to 100 ft of hose.

Where the most remote portion of a non-sprinklered floor is more than 150 ft from a hose connection, or where the most remote portion of a sprinklered floor is more than 200 ft from a hose connection, the local code official may require that additional hose connections be provided.

Water is supplied to the standpipe in two ways: from storage tanks and through siamese connections at ground level. Like a sprinkler system, standpipes can be either dry or wet. In a wet system, standpipes are filled with water at all times and are connected to a tank of water at the top of the building that provides a supply of water for immediate use. Once firefighters arrive, water is pumped from fire hydrants through the fire truck pumps to the standpipes. In a dry system, there is no water standing in the pipe. In the event of a fire, water must be charged with pumps in the building or by the fire department through siamese connections.

Other Extinguishing Agents

Although sprinkler systems are the most common type of automatic extinguishing system, other systems are available.

Portable fire extinguishers are helpful for stopping small fires in the early stages of development. There are four general classes of extinguisher, lettered A through D, which correspond to four fire types. Class A fires stem from ordinary combustibles such as paper, wood, and cloth; extinguishers for these fires contain water or water-based agents. Class B fires arise from flammable liquids such as gasoline, solvents, and paints; their extinguishers use chemicals like carbon dioxide, foam, and halogenated agents to smother flames. Class C fires are those that affect electrical equipment, and their corresponding extinguishers contain nonconductive agents. Class D fires involve combustible metals; extinguishers for these use dry powder extinguishing agents that will both absorb heat and smother the flames, such as sodium chloride or graphite.

Each type of fire must be fought with a suitable extinguisher. Combination extinguishers are available that can be used with type A, B, and C fires. When a room's contents, such as a computer installation, could be damaged by water, another extinguishing agent may be used. Alternative extinguishing agents include carbon dioxide, clean-agent gases, and various types of foam.

The IBC Sec. 906 requires that extinguishers be mounted in accessible and conspicuous locations, within 75 ft of all building areas, so that they can be employed easily by the building's occupants. Extinguishers are also required near cooking equipment, in areas where flammable or combustible liquids are stored or used, and in special-hazard areas.

A number of *halogenated gases* (or *halons*) can be used to quickly extinguish a fire by chemically interfering with combustion. A halon is created by replacing some of the hydrogen atoms in a hydrocarbon with atoms of fluorine or bromine. Halons were once commonly used in fire suppression systems, but these gases contain chlorofluorocarbons (CFCs) that can damage the earth's ozone layer, and the production of halons was banned in the United States in 1994. Existing supplies of halons may be recycled and reused. Halon fire-protection systems are suited to areas containing electronic equipment that would be damaged by water, but measures must be taken to prevent leakage to the outside, which makes such systems expensive.

Hydrochlorofluorocarbons (HCFCs) and hydrofluorocarbons (HFCs) have been used as substitutes for halons, but these gases also deplete the ozone layer. Their production is being phased out and will be eliminated in the United States and many other countries by 2020.

Another type of extinguishing agent is a building material that acts passively in reaction to a fire. *Intumescent materials* respond to fire by expanding rapidly, insulating the surface they protect and filling gaps to prevent the passage of fire, heat, and smoke. These materials are available in several forms such as strips, caulk, paint, and spreadable putty. For example, intumescent paint can add fire resistance to wood that would normally be flammable. A strip of intumescent material placed along the edge of one of a pair of fire doors will expand and seal the crack, substituting for an astragal that would otherwise be required.

LIGHTING DESIGN

Lighting design is both an art and a science. There must be sufficient light for the tasks and activities taking place while avoiding glare and other discomfort, but the lighting should also enhance the architectural design of the space or landscaping. Lighting must also be designed so as to minimize energy use, work with the HVAC design, and be cost efficient.

Figure 32.2
Candlepower Distribution Curve

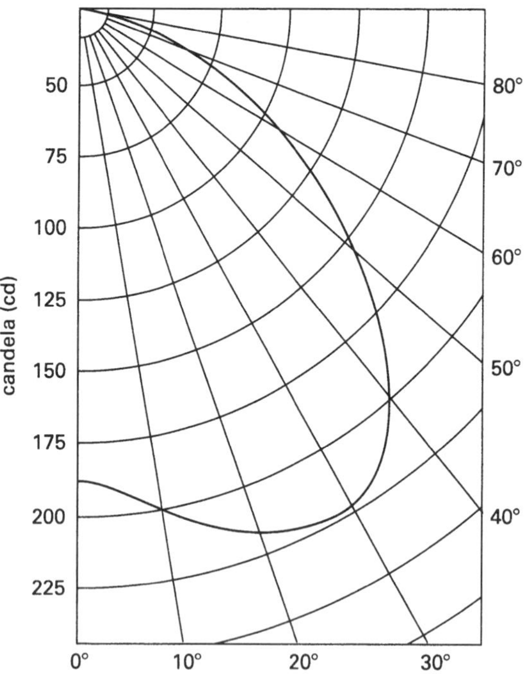

Lighting design is dependent on the *luminaires*, or fixtures, that are available to provide light. Thousands of different types of luminaires are available from hundreds of manufacturers, using many different types of lamps and satisfying a wide range of needs.

A basic element of every luminaire is the way it delivers light to the space. This can be shown graphically with a *candlepower distribution curve*, which shows how much light is output at every angle from the luminaire. A typical curve is shown in Fig. 32.2. This example is for a downlight luminaire (either square or round), for which the distribution is the same at all angles, so only one curve is shown. In contrast, a rectangular fluorescent luminaire typically distributes light differently in the directions parallel to the fixture and perpendicular to the fixture, so the candlepower distribution graph would have two slightly different curves. In some cases, three curves are shown, the third being the distribution at a 45° angle to the fixture.

Lighting Systems

Lighting systems come in several varieties. The International Commission on Illumination (abbreviated as CIE for *Commission internationale de l'eclairage*) classifies lighting systems based on the proportion of upward and downward light distribution. Lighting systems are broadly described as direct, semi-direct, direct-indirect, general diffuse, semi-indirect, and indirect. These terms can refer to an entire lighting installation or to individual luminaires. See Fig. 32.3.

Direct lighting focuses 90% to 100% of its light output downward on the task. A recessed fluorescent luminaire is an example of direct lighting. *Semi-direct lighting* casts 60% to 90% of its light down, and the other 10% to 40% toward the ceiling. Semi-direct fixtures are surface mounted or suspended from the ceiling. *Direct-indirect lighting* provides equal amounts of light up and down. *General diffuse lighting* provides from 40% to 60% downward and the rest upward. *Semi-indirect lighting* provides from 10% to 40% downward and the rest upward. *Indirect lighting* throws from 90% to 100% of its light up toward a reflective ceiling to illuminate the room by reflection, while no more than 10% is directed downward.

Another common kind of system is *task-ambient lighting*. This approach to lighting design recognizes that it is inefficient to illuminate an entire room to a level needed only for individual tasks scattered around the room. Instead, a general background level of illumination is provided, and separate light fixtures are available for increasing the light levels at individual workstations. These separate fixtures can be desk lamps, directed spotlights, or more fixtures mounted near the tasks needing more illumination. In addition to being more energy efficient and responsive to individual lighting needs, task-ambient systems usually create a more pleasant work environment.

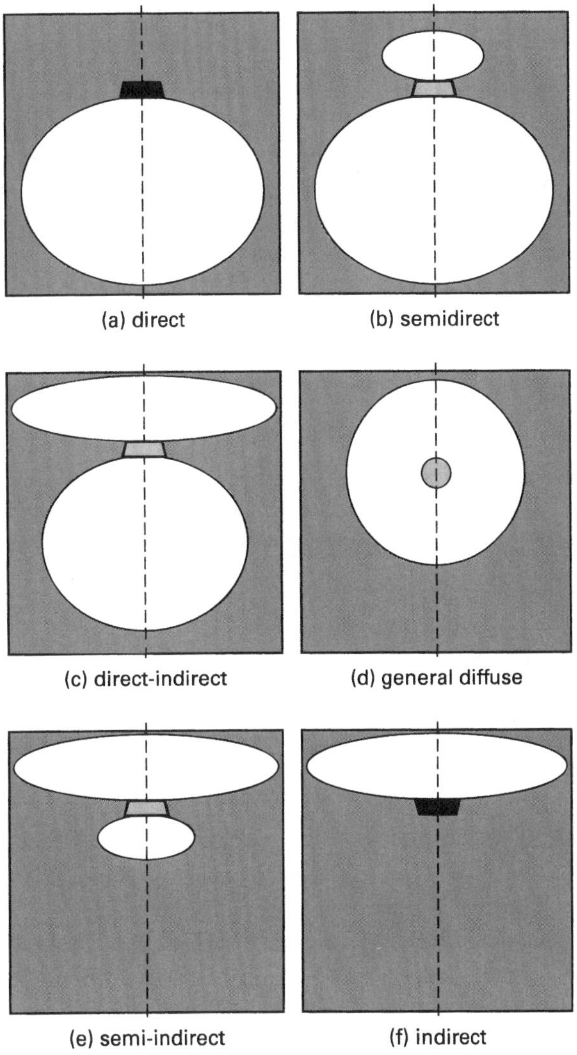

(a) direct

(b) semidirect

(c) direct-indirect

(d) general diffuse

(e) semi-indirect

(f) indirect

Figure 32.3
Lighting Systems

Luminaire Types

Several general types of luminaires are available for lighting design.

- surface mounted
- recessed
- suspended
- wall mounted
- furniture mounted
- freestanding fixtures
- decorative or accessory lighting

Surface-mounted fixtures are among the most commonly used types for residential and commercial buildings. The luminaire is attached directly to the finished surface of the ceiling, directing all or most of the light into the room. Surface-mounted fixtures are used where there is not sufficient space above the ceiling to recess a fixture, or where fixtures are added after the ceiling has been constructed.

Recessed fixtures are used in both residential and commercial construction and include a variety of types of fixtures that use incandescent, fluorescent, and LED lamps. Recessed fixtures can be general downlights for overall illumination, or they can be wall washers that aim light in one direction only. Continuous, narrow strips of fluorescent or LED luminaires can also be recessed next to a wall to wash the wall uniformly with light. When the entire ceiling is made up of lighting, a luminous ceiling is formed.

Luminaires dropped below the level of the ceiling are called *suspended fixtures*. These include track lighting, pendant lights, indirect systems, chandeliers, and other types of specialty lights that use LED, incandescent, or fluorescent lamps. Suspended mounting is needed for indirect lighting systems. The fixture must be located far enough below the ceiling to allow for the proper spread of light to bounce off the surface. Suspended mounting is also useful in a high-ceilinged room when the architect needs to get the source of light closer to the task area.

Wall-mounted luminaires can provide indirect, direct-indirect, or direct lighting. Wall sconces direct most of the light toward the ceiling and are used for general illumination. Various types of adjustable and non-adjustable direct lighting fixtures are available that serve as task lighting, such as bed lamps. Cove lighting can be mounted on a wall near the ceiling; it will indirectly light either the ceiling or the wall depending on how it is shielded.

Furniture-mounted lighting is common with task-ambient systems. Individual lights are built into the furniture above the work surface to provide sufficient task illumination, and uplighting is provided by lights either built into the upper portions of the furniture or designed as freestanding elements.

Freestanding light fixtures include items such as floor lamps. These are available in thousands of different styles and sizes and can be custom designed and manufactured if needed. A *torchère* is a freestanding light that directs most of its output to the ceiling. For task-ambient lighting systems, freestanding kiosks contain high-wattage lights that provide indirect lighting by illuminating the ceiling.

Accessory lighting includes table lights, reading lamps, and fixtures that are intended for strictly decorative lighting rather than for task or ambient lighting.

Quality of Light

Lighting design involves the selection of appropriate luminaires, lamps, and fixture arrangements to provide the correct quantity of light. The quality of light, however, is just as important. Color quality depends on the color of the light source and how the light interacts with objects. (The topics of glare and contrast are discussed in Chap. 19.)

Figure 32.4
Spectral Energy Distribution Curve

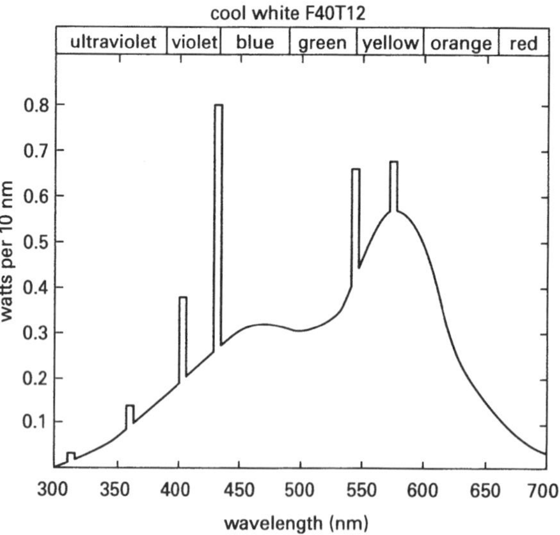

Every lamp has a characteristic *spectral energy distribution* (SED). This is a measure of the energy output at different wavelengths, or colors. One such energy distribution curve is shown in Fig. 32.4. The curve shown is typical of fluorescent and HID lamps, with a continuous curve interrupted by sharp peaks at certain points. Daylight and incandescent light have continuous spectrum light without any sharp peaks. The distribution curves of LED lamps vary with the particular type of lamp and how it is controlled.

The *color temperature* of a light source is the temperature in kelvins to which a black body radiator would have to be heated to produce light of the same dominant color. Lower color temperatures, such as 3100K, correspond to relatively warm colors like that of a warm white fluorescent light. Higher color temperatures, such as 5000K to 6000K, are cool colors with a high percentage of blue. A daylight fluorescent lamp has a color temperature of 6500K, for example.

Light sources are also rated with a number known as the *color rendering index* (CRI). This is a measure of how closely the perceived colors of an object illuminated with a test light source match the colors of the object when it is illuminated with daylight of the same color temperature. The maximum CRI rating is 100; a light source with a rating of 85 or more is excellent.

The use of the CRI system is problematic for LED sources, even though manufacturers provide CRI ratings for them. This is because of the method by which white light is produced and because different types of LEDs produce different colors, among other reasons. The CIE has proposed the development of a new color rendering index for LEDs.

It is important to know the color characteristics of a light source when designing a lighting system, as the color of the light can affect how colors of objects are perceived. A lamp whose light contains a high complement of blue and violet, for example, will make red finishes and furniture appear dull and washed out. Where color appearance is important, finishes and materials should be selected under the same lighting as will be used in the finished space.

Lighting Calculations

The quantity of light in a space can be found through lighting calculations. These calculations can be complex because illumination is a result of several variables.

For point sources of light, the illumination on a surface varies directly with the luminous intensity of the source, and inversely with the square of the distance between the source and the point. If the surface is perpendicular to the direction of the source, the illumination can be found with the formula

$$E = \frac{I}{d^2} \quad 32.1$$

In Eq. 32.1, E is illumination (in foot-candles), I is candlepower (in candelas), and d is distance from the source to the surface (in feet).

For surfaces that are not perpendicular to the source, Eq. 32.1 must be adjusted to account for the angle from the vertical, θ, as shown in Fig. 32.5. h is the height of the light source, and r is the horizontal distance from the source to the point. The formula for finding the illumination on the horizontal surface is

$$E = \frac{I\cos\theta}{d^2} \quad 32.2$$

For spaces with several luminaires, other methods are used to calculate the illumination on the work surface or, if the desired illumination level is known, to determine the number of luminaires needed. One of the most common approaches is the *zonal cavity method.* This procedure takes into account several variables.

- lumen output of the lamps used
- number of lamps in each luminaire
- portion of the light that reaches the work surface
- amount of light lost due to various factors

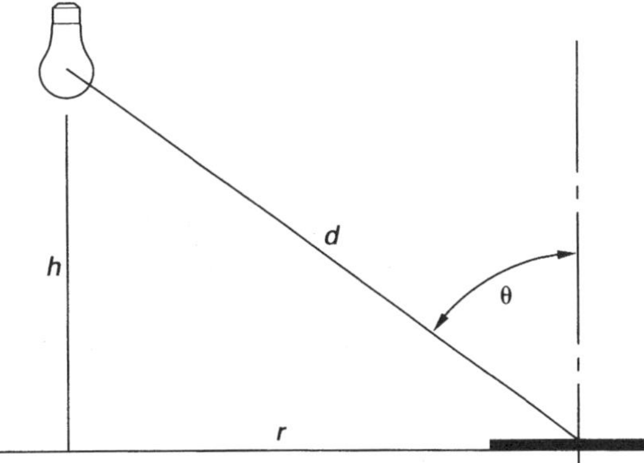

Figure 32.5 Illumination at an Angle from a Point Source

The efficiency of a luminaire in a particular space is represented by its *coefficient of utilization* (CU). The CU, which is a number between zero and 1.00, is the fraction of the total light from a luminaire that reaches the work surface. The CU depends not only on the design of the light fixture itself but on the characteristics of the room in which the fixture is placed, including the room size and surface reflectances. Manufacturers publish tables that give the CU for each of their luminaires under various conditions.

The amount of light from the lamp that is lost is represented by the *light loss factor* (LLF). The LLF, which is a number between zero and 1.00, is the fraction of the total light from a luminaire that is lost due to a number of factors, including *lamp lumen depreciation* (LLD), which is light loss due to the age of the lamp, and *luminaire dirt depreciation* (LDD), which is light loss due to accumulated dirt. Additional factors include lamp burnout, room surface dirt, the operating voltage of the lamps, and the ambient operating temperature of the lamps.

Equation 32.3 can be used to calculate the number of luminaires needed in a room to maintain a given illumination level.

$$N_{\text{luminaires}} = \frac{EA}{N_{\text{lamps}} N_{\text{lumens}} (\text{CU})(\text{LLF})} \qquad 32.3$$

In Eq. 32.3, E is the desired level of illumination (in foot-candles, fc), A is the area of the room (in square feet), N_{lamps} is the number of lamps per luminaire, and N_{lumens} is the number of lumens per lamp.

For complex spaces, manual calculation can be time consuming and error prone, so other tools have been developed to make evaluation and design more efficient. One is the *isolux chart* (sometimes called an *isofootcandle chart*), a diagram showing lines of equal illumination produced by a specific luminaire from a particular manufacturer. The chart is produced by constructing and analyzing full-scale mock-ups of the luminaire or by computer simulation. If several fixtures are used, they can be moved around on a floor plan, and the illumination levels can be added to determine the total illumination at any given point.

Lighting design by computer is accurate and fast, and it allows the designer to try out many more alternatives than would be possible with manual calculations. In addition, computer-based design gives more information than is common with manual calculation.

The coefficient of utilization takes into account the characteristics of both the luminaire and the room it is used in, but the efficacy of a luminaire can also be evaluated by itself. The *luminaire efficacy rating* (LER), also called *luminous efficacy* or simply *efficacy*, is the ratio of the luminaire's light output to its input power, typically expressed in lumens per watt. In practical terms, the LER measures how efficiently a particular luminaire can produce visible light from electricity. It takes into account the luminaire's efficiency and lumen output, as well as the total power it uses, including the power required by the ballast. The LER is calculated using Eq. 32.4.

$$\text{LER} = \frac{(\text{EFF})(\text{TLL})(\text{BF})}{W} \qquad 32.4$$

In Eq. 32.4, EFF is the luminaire's *efficiency* expressed as a two-place decimal fraction; this is a measure, based on photometric testing, of how efficiently the luminaire distributes light. TLL is the *total lamp lumens*, the number of lamps multiplied by the rated lumens output of each lamp. BF is the *ballast factor* expressed as a two-place decimal fraction. W is the total power input expressed in watts.

The LER applies to five different types of fluorescent luminaires, high-intensity discharge luminaires, and commercial downlights. When comparing one luminaire with another, only similar types should be compared. The five types of fluorescent lights are

- fluorescent lensed (FL)
- fluorescent parabolic (FP)
- fluorescent wraparound (FW)
- fluorescent industrial (FI)
- fluorescent strip light (FS)

Energy Conservation

Nearly all building code jurisdictions in the United States require energy conservation measures for electricity use in buildings. The jurisdictions may adopt the *International Energy Conservation Code* (IECC), ANSI/ASHRAE/IESNA Standard 90.1, or some other standard. The IECC itself adopts, by reference, Standard 90.1, *Energy Standard for Buildings Except Low-Rise Residential Buildings.* The LEED rating system also gives points for optimizing energy performance.

In addition to setting requirements for switching and other lighting controls, as discussed in Chap. 17, Standard 90.1 limits the total amount of power that can be used for lighting. The architect and electrical engineer may comply with the requirements through one of three methods.

- building area method
- space-by-space method
- energy cost budget method

The *building area method* limits the total power used in a building by giving a maximum allowable power in watts per square foot of building area, based on the building type. This maximum is the *lighting power density* (LPD) and varies with the type of facility. In Standard 90.1, these values are listed in a simple table. The LPDs given for various facilities are based on the lighting needed for the tasks in the space.

For example, a courthouse is allowed 1.2 W/ft^2 while a hotel is allowed 1.0 W/ft^2. The gross lighted floor area of the building is multiplied by the LPD. If there are different area types in the building, the area of each type is multiplied by the appropriate LPD to get the *lighting power allowance* (LPA) for that area. The LPAs for the individual areas are then added together to determine the total LPA for the building. Trade-offs are permitted, so if one area uses less power, the unused allowance can be assigned to another area.

The *space-by-space method* assigns LPDs to common space types. The designer must determine the gross area of each space type in the building and multiply each area by the allowable wattage per square foot. For example, a dining area for a hotel is allowed 1.3 W/ft^2 while a family dining area is allowed 2.1 W/ft^2. The LPAs for all areas are added to arrive at a total LPD for the building.

In the space-by-space method, additional lighting power is allowed for certain functions. This includes an increase of 1.0 W/ft^2 for decorative lighting in the space used. Decorative lighting includes things such as chandeliers, wall sconces, and lighting for art or exhibits. When lighting is installed in retail spaces specifically highlight merchandise, an additional allowance of 1000 W is given, plus an allowance per unit area that ranges from 1.0 W/ft^2 to 4.2 W/ft^2, depending on what type of merchandise is being displayed.

Standard 90.1 gives LPDs for various exterior applications for use with both the building area method and the space-by-space method. Both these methods provide for many exceptions to the LPA, as long as the lighting is controlled by an independent control device. Some of these exceptions include

- exhibit displays for museums, monuments, and galleries
- lighting that is integral to equipment and instrumentation installed by the manufacturer
- lighting for medical and dental procedures
- open and glass-enclosed refrigerator and freezer cases
- equipment for food warming and food preparation
- growth and maintenance of plants
- areas specifically designed for the visually impaired
- retail display windows, provided that the display is enclosed by ceiling-height partitions
- interior spaces specifically designated as registered interior historic landmarks

Product Development

- lighting that is an integral part of advertising or directional signage
- exit signs (however, internally illuminated exit signs cannot exceed 5 W per face)
- demonstration systems used in selling or teaching about lighting equipment
- theatrical, stage, film, and video production
- television broadcasting in sports activity areas
- casino gaming areas
- furniture-mounted supplemental task lighting controlled by automatic shutoff

The *energy cost budget method* is used to determine the energy cost budget for a specific building design. The budget is calculated by means of a computer simulation of hourly energy use over the course of a year by use of appropriate climatic data, approved building envelope design, comparisons to a baseline building, and other aspects as defined in Standard 90.1. In this method, LPAs are only one aspect of the building's total energy use. The designer can make trade-offs between energy needs for lighting and energy needs for other building systems.

Although it is a complex procedure, the energy cost budget method is the only way to deal with unique designs, renewable energy, high-efficiency equipment, and other unique aspects of a building's design. This method is also used to verify compliance with LEED requirements. However, any building that proves compliance with Standard 90.1 by this method must still meet the requirements of all sections of the standard.

Another energy conservation measure is *lighting system tuning*, which is adjustment of the lighting installation after construction is complete. It is common for many changes to be made in the lighting design between its first execution and when the client is ready to move in. During tuning, lamps are replaced with lower or higher wattage units, adjustable luminaries are aimed for their optimal positions, ballasts are adjusted for maximum efficiency, and switches are replaced with dimmer controls or time-out units.

Emergency Lighting

The IBC, *National Electrical Code*, and *Life Safety Code* all include requirements for emergency lighting. Because the requirements of each jurisdiction differ, the local codes in force must be reviewed. Generally, however, all codes require that in the event of a power failure, sufficient lighting be available to safely evacuate building occupants.

Emergency and standby power systems are required to provide electricity for

- emergency egress illumination
- exit signs
- smoke control systems
- horizontal sliding doors
- means of egress elevators

In some occupancies, voice communication systems and other items must also be powered. The power systems may include batteries, generators, or both.

Building codes require that the means of egress path be illuminated whenever the building is occupied. In the event of a power failure, the emergency power system must provide illumination to

- exit access corridors and aisles in rooms and spaces required to have two or more exits
- exit access corridors and exit stairways in buildings required to have two or more exits
- interior exit discharge elements when permitted, such as building lobbies where 50% of the exit capacity may egress through the ground-floor lobby

The means of egress illumination level must be a minimum of 1 fc measured at the floor level and must be maintained for not less than 90 minutes.

With some exceptions, exit signs are required at exits and exit access doors, positioned in such a way that no point in an exit access corridor is more than 100 ft from an exit sign. Directional exit signs are required at corridor intersections or where a corridor changes direction so that it is always evident to the occupants where the exits are. Exit signs may be either externally or internally illuminated. If the sign is externally illuminated, the minimum light level cannot be less than 5 fc. Internally illuminated signs must be lit at all times and must be UL listed and labeled. Illuminated exit signs, whether illuminated internally or externally, must be connected to an emergency power circuit.

Self-luminous and photoluminescent exit signs may be used if approved by the local jurisdiction. *Self-luminous* exit signs are "glow in the dark" and do not need external power or batteries. They are illuminated by tritium, which is a self-luminous isotope of hydrogen. *Photoluminescent* exit signs are charged with energy absorbed from the ambient lighting during normal building operation. When the ambient lighting is gone, the signs give off the stored energy and glow in the dark, but their glow slowly dims as the darkness continues. In some jurisdictions and in some buildings, like hotels, photoluminescent markings are required in stairways and along the egress path.

In Group R-1 occupancies (hotels and motels), floor-level exit signs must be provided in addition to standard-height exit signs. Floor-level exit signs must be mounted so that the bottom of the sign is no less than 10 in and no more than 12 in above the floor level. Signs must be flush mounted to the door or wall, and when mounted in the wall the edge must be within 4 in of the door frame on the latch side. Floor-level exit signs must be internally illuminated, self-luminous, or photoluminescent.

SIGNAL AND SAFETY ALARM SYSTEMS

Contemporary buildings contain complex networks of signal and communication systems. These low-voltage circuits connect various types of devices that make it possible for the building to function properly and protect the occupants. In addition to communication systems such as telephone and data lines, automation systems control the mechanical, electrical, and security systems for the building from one central station and continuously monitor their operation.

Because telephone and communication systems are low-voltage systems, the requirements for conduit and other protection may not be quite as stringent as those for standard voltage power. In many cases, an outlet box is provided at the connections in the wall and the wire is run within the walls and ceiling spaces without conduit. In some commercial construction, however, all cable is required to be protected in conduit. Special plenum-rated cable is available that does not require conduit, but it is more expensive than standard cable.

The architect's or engineer's drawings usually show telephone and communication systems on the same plan as the power outlets. If the system is complex, communication system outlet locations may be shown on a separate plan for clarity. This plan may include the locations for telephone and data jacks, communication systems, public address speakers, card readers, and buzzers or intercom systems. The location of power outlets is also shown on the electrical engineer's drawings; these drawings, as well as the requirements of other communications contractors, must be coordinated with the architect's drawings. Circuiting, wire sizes, and connections to central equipment are usually determined by the electrical engineer as well, or by the contractor responsible for installing the equipment.

Communication Systems

Communication systems include telephone systems, intercom systems, paging and sound systems, television, closed circuit television (CCTV), and computer systems, as well as local area networks (LANs) that allow the sharing of data on several computers within one building or in a complex of buildings.

Telephone and computer systems are the most prevalent type of communication system. In most buildings, main telephone lines enter the structure in a main cable and connect to the *terminal room*, sometimes called the *equipment room*, where they are split into riser cables located in *riser shafts*. These are generally located near the core and connect telephone equipment rooms on each floor. From these equipment rooms, the lines branch out to serve individual spaces.

Since the proliferation of separate telephone companies each tenant space needs its own equipment room.

The main terminal room contains the cable splice boxes, cabinets, termination of conduit entering the building from various utility companies, and other equipment needed to connect the main cables to the building's distribution network. For multistory buildings, this room is often located near the other vertical shafts at the core of the building, so risers can take off directly from this room. In smaller buildings this room is usually located near other building service spaces.

Riser shafts provide space for cabling to serve each floor's *riser closets*, or *apparatus closets*. In the past, each floor would have one telephone equipment room that contained relay panels and other equipment. Since the proliferation of separate telephone companies, however, each tenant space in a large building needs its own equipment room. The size of the room depends on the type of equipment used and the number of telephone and communication lines connected, but it generally ranges from 20 ft^2 to 30 ft^2. The architect should verify the size needed with the equipment suppliers and coordinate with the electrical engineer to provide the necessary lighting, ventilation, and power in these rooms.

Other types of communication systems are typically wired as the building is constructed. Cabling terminates at electrical boxes in the wall or floor with a jack into which individual equipment can be connected. Most signal cabling is run in metal conduit, like electrical cable, unless the local building code allows it to be exposed. Conduit protects the cable and prevents it from burning in a fire and giving off dangerous gases. There may be additional requirements for fiber optic cabling.

Building Automation Systems

If the building has a building automation system (BAS), then a separate space is needed for the control center, which contains computers, monitors, display devices, and one or more workstations for supervisory personnel. The BAS usually contains controls for HVAC systems, energy management, lighting, life safety, security, and elevator operation. The size of the control center depends on the size of the building, the complexity of the system, and what types of building services are monitored and controlled from this location. The control center is usually located near the mechanical service rooms in the basement or main floor of the building, often adjacent to the building lobby.

Security Systems

Security systems include methods for detecting intruders, preventing entry, controlling access to secure areas, and notifying authorities in the event of unauthorized entry or other emergencies. The types of hardware and electronic devices that are used depend on the nature of the threat, the level of security desired, and the amount of money that can be devoted to the system. Two important areas of security are

- intrusion detection
- access control

In both areas, when an intrusion is detected the *notification system* triggers an alarm signal. This signal can activate an audible alarm such as a bell or horn, turn on lights, alert an attendant at a central control station, or be relayed over phone lines to a central security service. Combinations of any or all these notifications are possible. If an office building has a central station, a building tenant may be able to connect the security system that serves the leased space with the central station. When a central station is notified, the alarms are automatically recorded in the system.

Intrusion Detection

Intrusion detection devices can be classified into three types.

- perimeter protection
- area or room protection
- object protection

Perimeter protection devices secure the entry points to a space or building. Entry points include doors, windows, skylights, and even ducts, tunnels, and other service entrances. The following are some common types of perimeter protection equipment.

- *Magnetic contacts* are used on doors and windows either to sound an alarm when the contact is broken (when the door or window is opened) or to send a signal to a central monitoring and control station. Magnetic contacts can be surface mounted, recessed into the door and frame, or concealed in special hinges.
- *Glass break detectors* sense when a window has been broken or cut. These devices use either metallic foil or a small vibration detector mounted on the glass.
- *Window screens* in which fine wires are embedded can set off alarms when cut or broken.
- *Photoelectric cells* detect when an emitted beam of electrons has been broken, either by either a door opening or by a person passing through an opening. These devices can be surface mounted, but they are more secure and look better if provisions are made to recess them in a partition or other construction.

Area or room protection devices detect when someone passes within the device's field of coverage. These devices can warn of unauthorized entry even when perimeter sensors have not been activated. Area intrusion devices include the following.

- *Photoelectric beams* send a pulsed infrared beam across a space. If the beam is broken, the device can sound an alarm or send a signal to a monitoring station. Photoelectric beams can be focused in large and small areas alike.
- *Infrared detectors* sense sources of infrared radiation, such as the human body, that exceed normal room radiation. These devices are unobtrusive, but they must have a clear field of view of the area they are protecting.
- *Audio detectors* are triggered by unusual sounds. When the normal level of noise is exceeded, an alarm is sounded. Microphones can also be used to continuously monitor all sounds in a space through a speaker at a central monitoring station.
- *Pressure sensors* detect weight on a floor or other surface. Sensor mats can be separate fixtures laid over the existing floor finish, or they can be placed under carpet or other building materials.
- *Ultrasonic detectors* emit sound waves at very high frequencies. When the waves are interrupted, an alarm signal is activated. The range of ultrasonic detectors varies depending on the specific equipment, but can be used in spaces as large as about 50 ft by 200 ft.
- *Microwave detectors* emit microwave radiation and sense interruptions in the radiation field. Their use is limited in interior construction, however, because microwave radiation can penetrate most building materials and can be reflected by metal.

Object protection is used to sense movement or tampering with individual objects such as safes, artwork, file cabinets, and other equipment. *Capacitance proximity detectors* sense touch on metal objects, *vibration detectors* sense a disturbance of an object, and *infrared motion detectors* can determine if the space around an object is violated.

Access Control

Access control devices restrict access to secure areas. The simplest access control device is the traditional mechanical lock. High-security locksets are available that provide additional security through the use of key types that are difficult to duplicate, special tumbler mechanisms, and long-throw dead bolts.

Because access and duplication of keys can be a problem even for the most secure mechanical lock, various types of electronic locks are available. Electronic locks not only selectively control access better than keys, but they can monitor who enters and exits a door and record when the access was made.

Any time that an automated lock is mounted on a door that is a part of the means of egress, the door must open in the direction of egress at all times, without use of special equipment or knowledge.

Card readers are common electronic access control devices. When a valid card is passed through or near the reader, a coded magnetic strip or electronic code on the card unlocks the door. Card readers are connected to a central monitoring computer that keeps a log of whose card was used to open a door and when the door was opened. A card reader system can be programmed to limit cards to certain doors, certain hours during the day, and certain days of the week. If a card is lost or stolen, its access code can be quickly and easily removed from the system.

Numbered keypads unlock a door when the user enters the correct numerical code. Although numbered keypads, like card readers, eliminate the key control problem of standard locksets, they do not provide the same programming flexibility. They are not connected to a central station, so may not offer the ability to track or monitor individuals.

Card readers and other devices control the operation of the locking mechanisms, of which there are several types. One type is the *electric lock*, which retracts the bolt when activated from the secure side of the door. From the inside, the lock can be opened by pressing a button or switch or by mechanical retraction of the bolt with the lever handle. Electric locks need an electric hinge or other power transfer device to carry the low-voltage wiring from the control device to the door and then to the lock.

An *electric strike* replaces the standard door strike and consists of a movable mechanism that is mortised into the frame. The latch bolt is fixed from the secure side of the door. On activation, the electric strike retracts, allowing the door to be opened. On the inside, the latch bolt can be retracted by mechanical means with the lever handle.

A door can also be secured with an *electromagnetic lock*. When activated, the lock holds the door closed with a powerful magnetic force. Card readers, keypads, buttons, or other devices deactivate the electromagnet. These can be designed to open on activation of a fire alarm or power failure.

A *biometric device* can recognize a voice or a biological feature such as the iris or retina of the eye, a hand, or a fingerprint, providing a counterfeit-proof method of identification. These devices are expensive but may be worth the cost when a very high level of security is needed.

Fire Detection and Alarms

There are five basic types of fire detection devices. They are useful for detection at different stages of a developing fire, from the incipient stage (where no visible flame, smoke, or noticeable heat has yet been produced) to the final heat stage.

A fire can smolder and produce smoke long before it reaches the flame stage.

The first type is the *ionization detector*, which responds to combustion-ionized particles rather than to smoke. Because these devices detect particles from a smoldering fire before it bursts into flames, they are considered early warning detectors. Ionization detectors are not appropriate where fires may produce a lot of smoke but few particles.

Another early warning device is the *gas-sensing detector*. This type of unit detects combustion gases that are not normally present in the air. These devices are often used in combination with ionization detectors so that both gases and particulate matter can be sensed.

Photoelectric detectors detect the next stage of a developing fire. This kind of device contains a light beam that is obscured by smoke. Photoelectric detectors are useful where potential fires may produce a great deal of smoke before bursting into flames. Variations of photoelectric detectors include *projected beam smoke detectors*, *scattered-light photoelectric detectors*, and *laser beam detectors*.

Two types of detectors are triggered in the final heat stage of a fire; neither can provide an early warning of smoldering fires. *Flame detectors* respond to infrared or ultraviolet radiation given off by flames. *Rise-of-temperature detectors* sense the presence of heat and can be set to trip an alarm when a particular temperature is reached in the room. The major disadvantage with both of these devices is that flames must usually be present before the alarm temperature is reached. By that time it may be too late, because a fire can smolder and produce deadly smoke long before it reaches the flame stage.

A combination of fire detection devices is usually needed, depending on the type of space in which they are placed. For example, an ionization device will not operate properly where air currents or other circumstances prevent the products of combustion from entering the device.

The building code states the required types and locations of fire detectors. Detectors are generally required near fire doors, in exit corridors, in individual hotel rooms, in bedrooms, and in places of public assembly. They are also often required in main supply and return air ducts. Codes usually require them in other spaces based on a given area coverage. Carbon monoxide alarms are required in Group I and R occupancies located in a building containing a fuel-burning appliance or in a building that has an attached garage.

Fire detectors can be wired so that when activated they will trigger a general audible alarm as well as visual alarm lights for the deaf. They can also activate a central monitoring station or notify a municipal fire station. In large buildings with a central station, the detection of a fire also activates fire dampers, exhaust systems, the closing of fire doors, and other preventive measures as the alarm is transmitted to fire officials.

SOUND CONTROL

Acoustics are a necessary consideration for nearly all building types. The architect can begin to integrate basic acoustical concepts during the design development and construction document phases. The plan must incorporate

- room noise and acoustics
- sound transmission
- speech privacy
- impact noise
- mechanical noise

Control of Room Noise

There are three main ways that sound can be controlled within a space: reducing the level of the sound source, modifying the absorption in the space, and introducing nonintrusive background sound to mask the unwanted sound.

Reducing the level of the sound source is not always possible. If the sound is coming from people talking within the room or from a piece of machinery that must remain in the room, for example, options may be limited. If the noise is from outside or from an adjacent room, however, the sound insulation of the enclosing walls can be improved. Sometimes a noisy machine can be enclosed or modified to reduce its sound output.

Modifying the absorption of the space by adding absorptive materials can achieve some noise reduction. This approach is most useful when the problem room has a large percentage of hard, reflective surfaces.

Figure 32.6
Noise Reduction

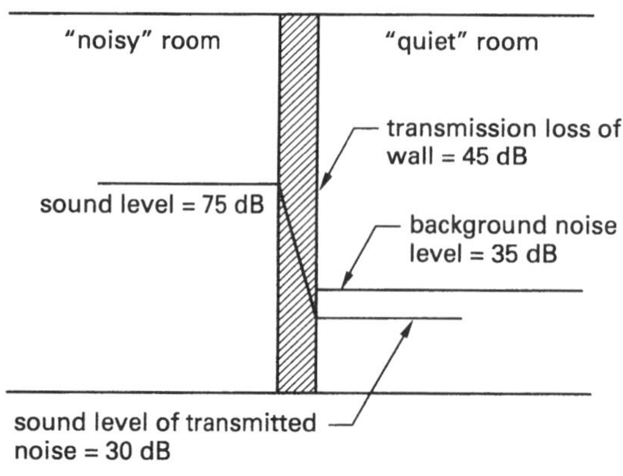

If transmitted sound level is below the background level, the sound is not perceptible.

In most cases, introducing nonintrusive background sound is desirable because it can mask unwanted noise. Some amount of background noise is always present. This may come from the steady hum of HVAC systems, business machines, traffic, conversation, or other sources.

In an office, for example, if a partition has a sound transmission classification (STC) rating of 45, the sound level on one side of the partition is 75 dB, and the background noise on the other side of the partition is 35 dB, the sound coming through the wall from the noisier side will probably not be heard on the quieter side. See Fig. 32.6. If the background noise level is decreased to 25 dB, then the sound through the wall will be heard.

Ordinary, random background noise need not be relied on, however. Carefully controlled sound—often called *white noise*, *random noise*, or *acoustical perfume*—can be introduced into a space. Speakers can be placed in the ceiling of a space and connected to a sound generator that produces a continuous, ignorable sound at particular levels across the frequency spectrum. The sound generator can be tuned to produce the frequencies and sound levels most useful for masking the undesired sounds. White noise is often used in open offices to provide speech privacy and to help mask office machine noise.

Figure 32.7
Details for Low-Frequency Sound Absorption

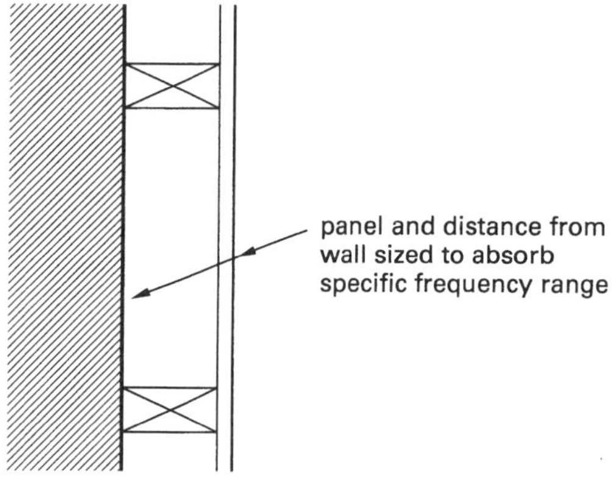

(a) vibrating panel

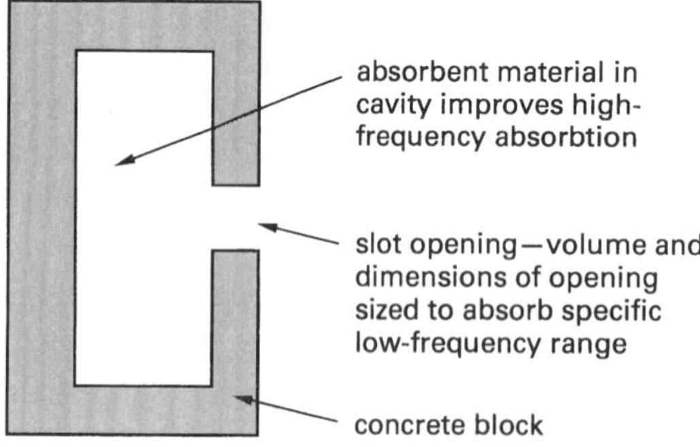

(b) volume resonator (Helmholtz resonator)

Room noise can also be reduced by adding absorption in the space, through the installation of some type of acoustic panels or upholstered walls. However, these types of panels are effective only for higher frequency noise and for speech. Controlling low-frequency and very high-frequency sounds within a room requires construction elements that can trap the longer, low-frequency wavelengths or control the very short high-frequency wavelengths.

Low-frequency control usually requires thicker partitions or more space for detailing that absorbs low-frequency sound. Two typical examples of this kind of detailing are panel resonators and cavity resonators. See Fig. 32.7. A *panel resonator* is an open box mounted on the face of a wall, or constructed as a part of a wall assembly, which absorbs low-frequency energy while reflecting mid- and high-frequency energy. This is sometimes referred to as a *bass trap*.

A *cavity resonator* (also called a *Helmholtz resonator*) consists of a large air space with a small opening. As sound strikes the resonator, the air mass inside the construction resonates at a particular frequency where the absorption is very high. However, the amount of absorption above and below the frequency in question drops off rapidly. A common type of cavity resonator is a concrete block wall constructed of special masonry units with narrow slits opening into the cavity of the block.

Control of Sound Transmission

As mentioned in Chap. 19, control of sound transmission through a barrier depends mainly on the mass of the barrier and to a lesser extent its stiffness. Walls and floors are generally rated with their STC values; the higher the STC rating, the better the barrier is in reducing transmitted sound. Manufacturers' literature, testing laboratories, and reference literature typically give the transmission loss at different frequencies.

In addition to the construction of the barrier itself, other variables are important for the control of sound transmission. See Fig. 32.8.

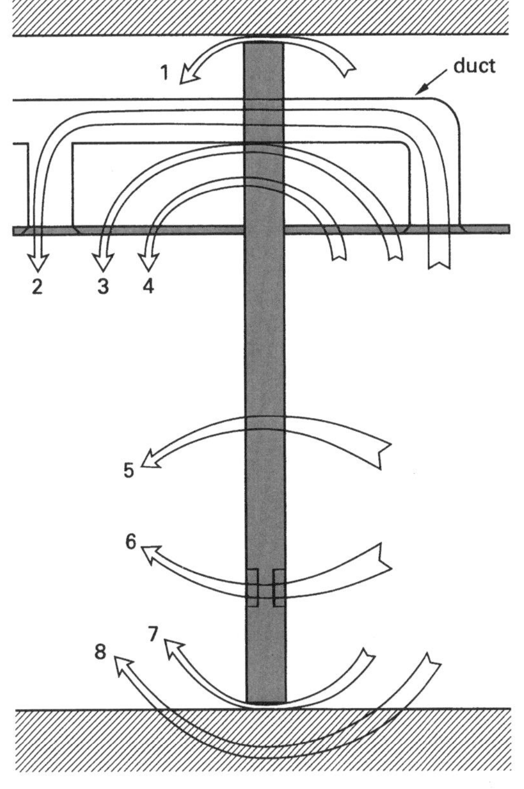

Figure 32.8
Potential Sources of Sound Leaks Through Partitions

Gaps in the barrier must be sealed. Edges at the floor, ceiling, and intersecting walls should be caulked. Pipes, ducts, and similar penetrations of the barrier provide paths for both airborne sound and mechanical vibration and should be avoided; if they are unavoidable, they should not be rigidly connected to the barrier and any gaps should be sealed and caulked. Electrical outlets on opposite sides of the barrier should not be placed back to back; rather, they should be staggered in separate stud spaces and caulked.

Doors and windows in the barrier should be avoided or given special treatment. Any construction with a lower STC rating than the barrier itself will decrease the overall rating of the barrier. A door placed in an otherwise well-built sound wall is a common problem and can be dealt with in several ways. The perimeter of the door should be completely sealed, with weather-stripping specifically designed for sound sealing at the jamb and head, and with a threshold or automatic door bottom at the sill. The door itself should be as heavy as possible, preferably a solid-core wood door. Often, two doors are used, separated by a small air gap. See Fig. 32.9.

Interior glass lights can be designed with laminated glass set in resilient framing. Laminated glass provides more mass, and the plastic interlayer improves the damping characteristics of the barrier. If more transmission loss is needed, two or more layers can be installed with an air gap between them. See Fig. 32.10.

Air conditioning ducts, plenum spaces above ceilings, hallways, and pairs of open windows in adjacent rooms can all serve as *flanking paths* for sound to travel along; flanking paths should be eliminated or treated appropriately. Unusual sound conditions or frequencies should be given special consideration and design. Low-frequency rumbling and high-frequency sounds often cannot be stopped, even with a wall with a high STC rating.

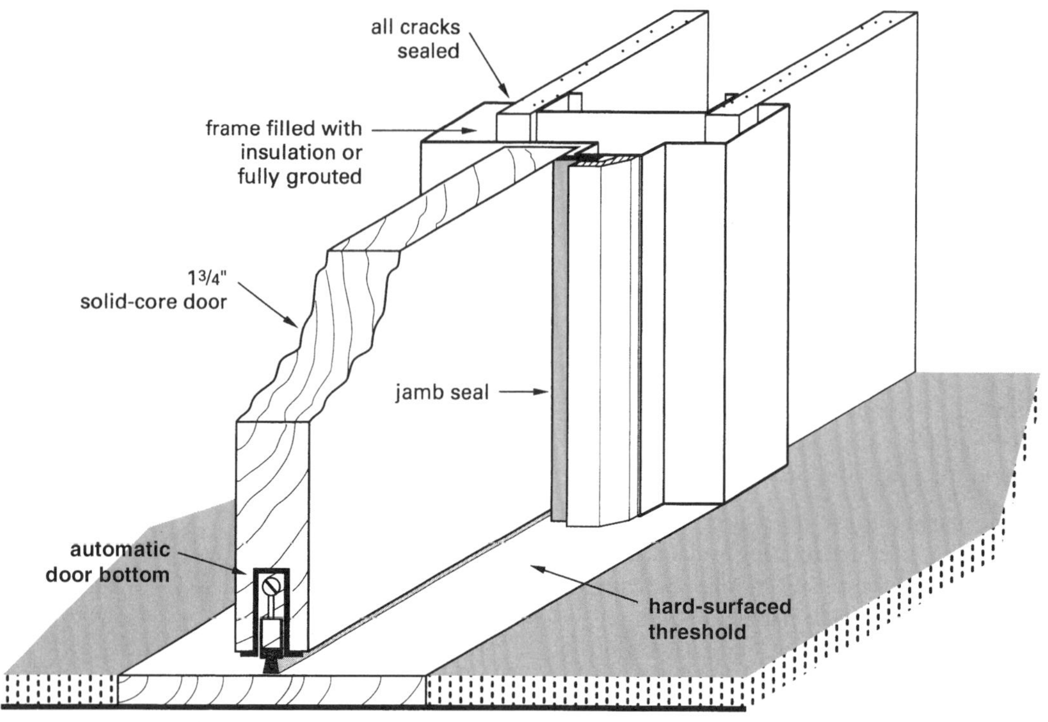

Figure 32.9 Principles of Acoustic Control for Doors

Speech Privacy

In many architectural situations, the utmost acoustical concern is not to eliminate all noise or to design a room for music, but to provide for a certain level of privacy in a specific space while still allowing people to talk at a normal level. When there is *speech privacy*, conversations may be heard by others as unintelligible background sound, but they cannot easily be understood.

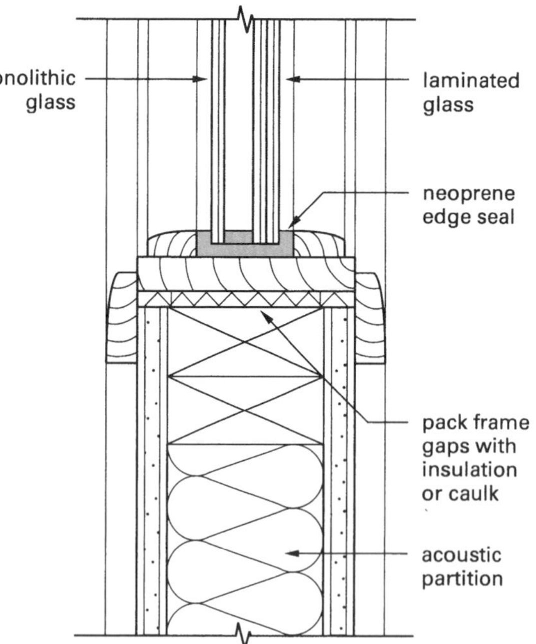

Figure 32.10 Glazing Assembly for Sound Control

Speech privacy, however, is subjective and depends on circumstances. People involved in highly confidential conversations need greater privacy than those conducting normal, nonconfidential business in an open office. Some people are more annoyed by nearby conversations than others.

Speech privacy is of great concern in office planning, especially in open office planning. Because speech privacy in open offices depends on the complex interaction of many variables, two measures are used to evaluate open office acoustics: the articulation class (AC) and the articulation index (AI). (These two measures have largely replaced the older *noise isolation class* (NIC) and *speech privacy potential* (SPP) classifications as industry standards.)

The *articulation class* (AC) gives a rating of system component performance and does not account for masking sound. The *articulation index* (AI) measures the performance of all the elements of a particular configuration working together: ceiling absorption, space dividers, furniture, light fixtures, partitions, background masking systems, and HVAC systems. It is used to objectively test speech privacy of open office spaces, either in the actual space or in a laboratory mock-up of the space.

The AI is used to compare the relative privacy between pairs of workstations or areas, to evaluate how changes in open office components affect speech privacy, and to measure speech privacy objectively for correlation with subjective responses. The AI predicts the intelligibility of speech for a group of talkers and listeners; the result of the test is a number rating between zero and one, with zero being complete privacy and one being no privacy at all, with each individual spoken word understood.

Confidential speech privacy exists when speech cannot be understood; it occurs when the AI is at or below 0.05. *Normal speech privacy* means that concentrated effort is needed to understand intruding speech; it occurs when the AI is between 0.05 and 0.20. At an AI above 0.20, speech becomes readily understood. At an AI above 0.30, privacy no longer exists.

Both the articulation index and the articulation class are intended only for open office situations. However, the articulation index can be adapted for other open-plan environments such as schools and can be applied to measure speech privacy between enclosed and open spaces and between two enclosed rooms.

Another way to evaluate sound design conditions and predict the intelligibility of speech is with the *speech interference level* (SIL). The SIL, in decibels, is the average of the sound pressure levels (above a reference pressure level) of the interfering noise in the four one-octave bands centered on the frequencies of 500, 1000, 2000, and 4000 Hz. The SIL is a useful measure of the effect of background noise on spoken communications, such as is described in Table 32.1. Charts and graphs have also been developed that relate the SIL to various types of communications at different distances.

Table 32.1
Effect of SIL on Communication

speech interference level (dB)	effect on communication
30–40	communication in normal voice possible
40–50	communication in normal voice satisfactory at 3 ft to 6 ft need to raise voice at 6 ft to 13 ft telephone use satisfactory
50–60	communication in normal voice satisfactory at 1 ft to 2 ft need to raise voice at 3 ft to 6 ft telephone use slightly difficult
60–70	communication with raised voice satisfactory at 1 ft to 2 ft telephone use difficult
70–80	communication slightly difficult with raised voice satisfactory at 1 ft to 2 ft communication slightly difficult with shouting at 3 ft to 6 ft telephone use very difficult
80–85	communication slightly difficult with shouting at 1 ft to 2 ft telephone use unsatisfactory

In areas divided by full-height partitions, speech privacy is achieved by sound loss through the partitions and, to a lesser extent, by the proper use of sound-absorbing surfaces. In open areas, such as an open-plan office, speech privacy is more difficult to achieve. There are five important factors in designing for speech privacy in an open area. All of these must be present to achieve an optimal acoustical environment.

- The ceiling must be highly absorptive. The idea is to create a "clear sky" condition so that sounds are not reflected from their source to other parts of the environment.
- There must be space dividers that reduce the transmission of sound from one space to the adjacent space. To minimize sound reflections, each divider should consist of absorptive surfaces placed over a solid liner (septum).
- Other surfaces such as the floor, furniture, windows, and light fixtures must be designed or arranged to minimize sound reflections. A window, for example, can provide a clear path for reflected noise around a partial height partition.
- If possible, activities should be distanced from each other to take advantage of the normal attenuation of sound with distance.

- There must be a properly designed background masking system. the right number of sound-absorbing surfaces is provided, the surfaces will absorb all sounds in the space, not just the unwanted sounds. Background sound must then be reintroduced to maintain the right balance between speech sound and the background noise. This is referred to as the *signal-to-noise ratio.* Speech privacy will be compromised if the signal-to-noise ratio is too great, as a result of either loud talking or minimal background noise.

Control of Impact Noise

Impact noise is the sound resulting from direct contact of an object with a sound barrier. It can occur on any surface, but it occurs most often on a floor and ceiling assembly, where it can be caused by footfalls, shuffled furniture, and dropped objects.

Impact noise is quantified by the *impact insulation class* (IIC), a numerical rating of a building floor's effect on sound performance. A floor and ceiling assembly is analyzed in accordance with a standardized test that covers 16 third-octave bands, and the results are compared with a reference plot much as noise criteria ratings are established. The higher the IIC rating, the better the floor reduces impact sounds in the test frequency range.

The IIC value of a floor can be increased in several ways.

- adding carpet
- providing a resilient suspended ceiling below
- floating a finished floor on resilient pads over the structural floor
- providing sound-absorbing material in the air space between the floor and the finished ceiling

Control of Mechanical Noise

Mechanical noise is similar to impact noise in that the cause is due to direct contact with a building element. However, mechanical noise occurs when a vibrating device is in continuous direct contact with the building structure. There are several ways mechanical noise can be transmitted.

- Rigidly attached equipment can vibrate the building structure or pipes, which in turn radiate sound into occupied spaces.
- The airborne noise of equipment can be transmitted through walls and floors to occupied spaces.
- Noise can be transmitted through ductwork.
- The movement of air or water through ducts and pipes can cause undesirable noise. This is especially true of high-velocity air systems or situations where the air or water changes velocity rapidly.

Depending on the circumstances, mechanical noise can be controlled in several ways.

- Mechanical equipment should be mounted on springs or resilient pads (isolators).
- Connections between equipment and ducts and pipes should be made with flexible connectors.
- Where noise control is integral, ducts should be lined or provided with mufflers.
- Where possible, noise-producing equipment should be located away from quiet, occupied spaces.
- Walls, ceilings, and floors of mechanical rooms should be designed to lessen airborne noise.
- Mechanical and plumbing systems should be designed to minimize high-velocity flow and sudden changes in fluid velocity.

ROOM ACOUSTICS

Reflection, Diffusion, and Diffraction

Reflection is the return of sound waves from a surface. If the dimension of a surface is at least four times the wavelength of a sound striking it, the angle of incidence will equal the angle of reflection. See Fig. 32.11(a).

Wavelength varies with frequency as shown by Eq. 19.1 in Chap. 19. For example, Table 32.2 gives the wavelengths that are associated with various frequencies for sound traveling at a velocity of 1130 ft/sec. For example, a 1000 Hz sound has a wavelength of about 1.1 ft. In Fig. 32.11(a), if the length of the sound reflecting surface is about 4.4 ft or greater, the angle of incidence of a sound with a frequency of 1000 Hz or greater will equal the angle of reflection.

Reflection can be useful for amplifying sound in lecture rooms and concert halls and for directing sound where it is wanted. It can be annoying, however, if it produces echoes, which occur when a reflected sound reaches a listener more than about $\frac{1}{17}$ sec after the direct sound. For sound traveling at 1130 ft/sec can echo will occur whenever the reflected sound path exceeds the direct sound path by 70 ft or more.

Diffusion is the random distribution of sound from a surface. It occurs when the depth of the surface dimension equals the wavelength of the sound striking it. See Fig. 32.11(b).

Diffraction is the bending of sound waves around an object or through an opening. Diffraction explains why sounds can be heard around corners and why even small holes in partitions allow so much sound to be heard. Refer to Chap. 12 for a discussion of diffraction around site barriers.

Figure 32.11 Reflection and Diffusion Based on Wavelength

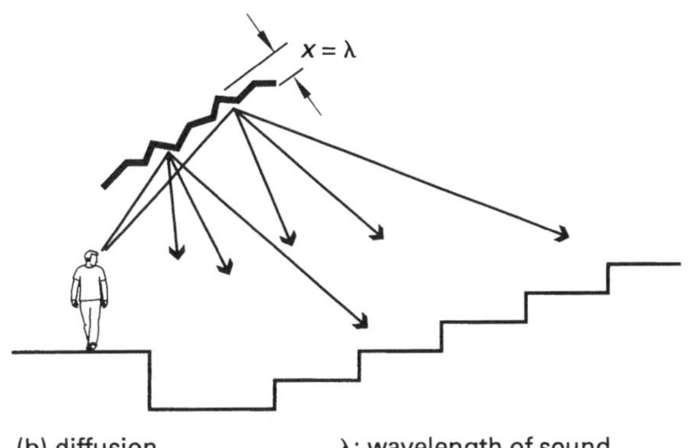

Table 32.2 Wavelengths Based on Frequency

frequency (Hz)	wavelength (ft)
50	23.0
100	11.0
250	4.5
500	2.25
1000	1.13
2000	0.57
5000	0.23
10,000	0.11

Room Geometry and Planning Concepts

The floor plan layout and the size and shape of a room itself can affect the acoustical performance of a building in many ways. In addition to designing walls and floors to lessen sound transmission and provide proper sound absorption, use the following suggestions to help minimize acoustical problems.

- Plan similar use areas next to each other. For example, in an apartment complex it is better to place bedrooms in adjacent units next to each other than to place a bedroom next to the adjacent unit's kitchen. This concept is applicable to vertical organization as well as horizontal (plan) organization.
- Use buffer spaces such as closets and hallways to separate noise-producing spaces whenever possible. For example, plan closets in a common wall between bedrooms.

- Locate noise-producing areas such as mechanical rooms, laundries, and playrooms away from quiet areas.
- Stagger the locations of doorways in halls and other areas to avoid giving a straight-line path for noise.
- Locate operable windows as far from each other as possible.
- If possible, locate furniture and other potential noise-producing objects away from walls between spaces.
- To reduce sound transmission between two rooms, minimize the area of the common wall.
- Avoid room shapes that reflect or focus sound. Barrel-vaulted hallways and circular rooms, for example, produce undesirable focused sounds. Rooms that focus sound also deprive some listeners of useful reflections.
- Avoid giving small rooms parallel facing walls with hard surfaces. Repeated echoes, called *flutter echoes*, can be generated that are perceived as a high-frequency buzzing sound. This is why small music practice rooms have splayed walls. Standing waves can also be produced in a small room, when a steady tone is introduced such that the distance between parallel walls is a multiple of one-half the wavelength.

33

LOADS ON BUILDINGS

Nomenclature

A	area of floor or roof	ft^2
A_t	tributary roof area supported by a structural member	ft^2
A_T	tributary floor area supported by a structural member	ft^2
D	dead load	lbf/ft^2
E	earthquake or seismic load	lbf/ft^2
f_1	floor live load occupancy combination factor	–
f_2	snow load roof shape combination factor	–
F	load due to fluids with well-defined pressures and maximum heights	lbf/ft^2
F	roof slope	in/ft
h	depth of retaining wall	ft
H	load due to lateral earth pressures, ground water pressure, or pressure of bulk materials	lbf/ft^2
K_{LL}	live load element factor	–
L	floor live load	lbf/ft^2
L_O	unreduced floor live load	lbf/ft^2
L_r	roof live load	–
p	direct wind pressure	lbf/ft^2
p	maximum soil pressure on retaining wall	lbf/ft^2
P	lateral soil force	lbf/ft^2
q	lateral soil pressure	lbf/ft^2
r	rate of reduction of live load	–
R	allowable reduction of floor live load	%
R	rain load	lbf/ft^2
R_1	roof area reduction factor	–
R_2	roof slope reduction factor	–
S	snow load	lbf/ft^2
v	wind velocity	mi/hr
w	uniform total load	lbf/ft^2
W	wind load	lbf/ft^2
ω	wind load coefficient	–

Determining the loads acting on buildings is basic to structural analysis and design. An accurate determination of loads is necessary to design a safe building and satisfy building code requirements while not requiring a more costly structure than necessary. The probable magnitudes of building loads have been determined over a long period of time based on successful experience and the statistical probability that a particular situation will result in a given load. They are also based on the worst-case situation. For example, the common live load for residences of 40 psf is highly unlikely to occur on every square foot in a house, but it provides an allowance for safety and unusual circumstances.

Table 33.1
Weights of Some Common Building Materials

material	weight or density
asphalt shingles	2 psf
brick, 4" wall	40 psf
built-up roofing, 5-ply	6 psf
concrete block, 8" heavy aggregate	55 psf
concrete, reinforced	150 pcf
concrete slab, per inch of thickness	12.5 psf
curtain wall, aluminum and glass, average	15 psf
earth, moist and packed	100 pcf
glass, 1/4"	3.3 psf
granite	170 pcf
gypsum wallboard, 1/2"	1.8 psf
hardwood floor, 7/8"	2.5 psf
marble	165 pcf
partition, 2 × 4 with 1/2" gypsum board each side	8 psf
partition, metal stud with 5/8" gypsum board	6 psf
plaster, 1/2"	4.5 psf
plywood, 1/2"	1.5 psf
quarry tile, 1/2"	5.8 psf
steel decking	2.5 psf
suspended acoustical ceiling	1 psf
terrazzo, 2 1/2" sand cushion	27 psf
water	62 pcf
wood joists and subfloor, 2 × 10, 16" o.c.	6 psf

Typically, loads are defined by building codes and by common practice. Codes, for example, give live load requirements, wind values, and earthquake values. Standard published tables provide accepted weights of building materials for dead load calculations. Occasionally, special situations may require custom load determination such as when building models are tested in a wind tunnel. Most loads on buildings are static, and those that are dynamic, such as wind, are assumed to have a static effect on the building structure so calculations are easier.

There are many types of loads on buildings. This chapter provides an overview of what the different types are, how they are determined, and their effects on buildings and architectural design. More detailed information concerning building code requirements is given in Chap. 17, while specific calculation procedures for lateral loads due to wind and earthquakes are described in Chap. 44 and Chap. 45, respectively.

Product Development

GRAVITY LOADS

Dead Loads

Dead loads are the *vertical loads* due to the weight of a building and any permanent equipment. These include such things as beams, exterior and interior walls, floors, and mechanical equipment. Dead loads of structural elements cannot always be readily determined because the weight depends on the size, which in turn depends on the weight to be supported. Initially, the weight of the structure must be assumed in order to make a preliminary calculation of the size of the structural member. Then the actual weight can be used for checking the calculation.

Most dead loads are easily calculated from published lists of building material weights found in standard reference sources. Some common weights are given in Table 33.1. In addition to these, the *International Building Code* (IBC) requires that floors in office buildings and other buildings with live loads of 80 psf or less where partition locations are subject to change be designed to support a minimum partition load of 20 psf. This partition load is considered part of the live load.

Example 33.1

Find the uniform load on a typical interior beam supporting the floor shown. Do not include the weight of the beam.

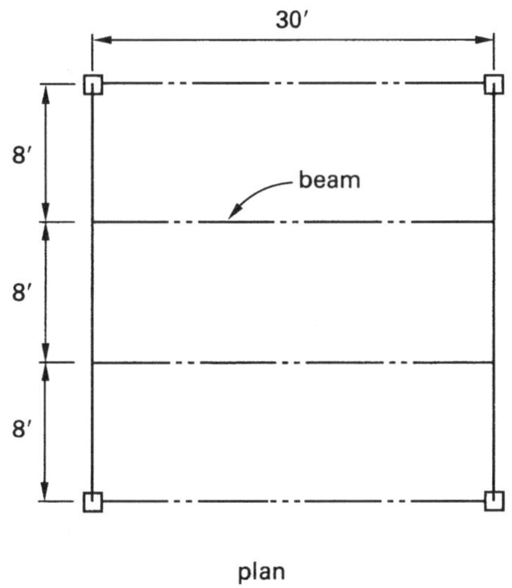

plan

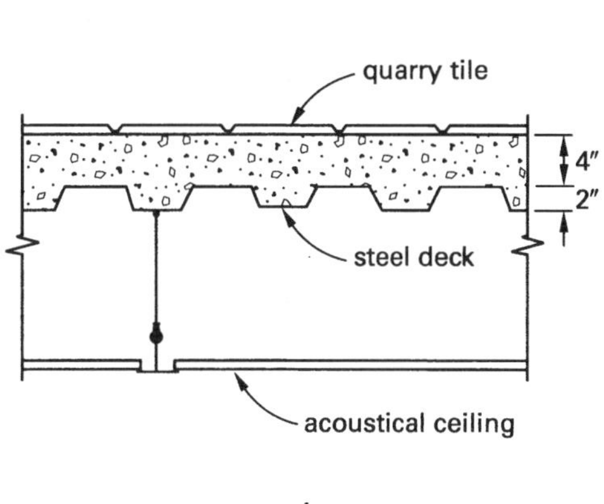

section

(A) 504 lbf/ft

(B) 528 lbf/ft

(C) 552 lbf/ft

(D) 576 lbf/ft

Solution

From Table 33.1, determine the weight per square foot of the materials comprising the floor. Since the concrete is on a fluted steel deck, take the average thickness of 5 in.

Therefore, the total weight of the floor is

quarry tile	5.8 psf	
concrete	62.5 psf	(5 × 12.5 psf)
steel deck	2.5 psf	
suspended ceiling	1.0 psf	
total	71.8 psf	

Product Development

In practice, this is rounded to the nearest whole number, or 72 psf. The beams are eight feet apart, so each beam supports a portion of the floor four feet wide on either side of the beam, or eight feet wide in all. Each foot of the beam supports eight square feet of floor, so the uniform load on the beam is $(8\ \text{ft}^2)(72\ \text{lbf/ft}^2)$ per foot, or 576 lbf/ft.

The answer is (D).

Live Loads

Live loads are those imposed on a building by the building's particular use and occupancy and are generally considered movable or temporary. People, furniture, and movable equipment are examples of live loads. Wind, earthquake, and snow loads are not considered live loads. Snow load is often considered a special type of transient load because it is so variable. To determine snow loads, local building officials or building codes must be consulted.

Live loads are established by the building code for different occupancies. Table 33.2 gives the uniform live loads from the IBC. Roofs must also be designed for uniform live loads or any special snow loads. The snow load specification is primarily covered in ASCE/SEI Standard 7, *Minimum Design Loads for Buildings and Other Structures* (ASCE/SEI 7). The code also specifies requirements for special loads such as cranes, elevators, and fire sprinkler structural supports.

The code also requires that floors be designed to support concentrated loads if the specified load on an otherwise unloaded floor would produce stresses greater than those caused by the uniform load. The concentrated load is assumed to be located on any space $2\frac{1}{2}$ ft square. The concentrated load requirements are given in the last column in Table 33.2.

The IBC allows for the live load to be reduced in most cases. The live load may not be reduced for any public assembly occupancy with a live load less than or equal to 100 psf or for any member supporting one floor of a parking garage or with a live load exceeding 100 psf. The reduced live load is given by the following formula.

$$L = L_O\left(0.25 + \frac{15}{\sqrt{K_{LL}A_T}}\right) \qquad 33.1$$

The value of L_O is the uniform live load from Table 33.2, and the value of K_{LL} is given in Table 33.3. The final value of L must not be less than $0.5L_O$ for members supporting one floor or $0.4L_O$ for members supporting more than one floor. In addition, L must not be less than $0.8L_O$ for members supporting more than one floor with a live load exceeding 100 psf or in parking garages.

The IBC allows for an alternate method to calculate live load reduction. This reduction method applies to members supporting more than 150 ft^2. The reduction may not be used for public assembly occupancy or live loads exceeding 100 psf.

The allowable percentage reduction from the load values shown in Table 33.2 is given by the following formula.

$$R = r(A - 150) \qquad 33.2$$

The *rate of reduction*, r, is equal to 0.08, and the tributary area uses the variable A. There are a few limitations, however. The reduction cannot exceed 40% for horizontal members or 60% for vertical members, nor can the reduction exceed the percentage determined by the following formula.

$$R = 23.1\left(1 + \frac{D}{L_O}\right) \qquad 33.3$$

Table 33.2 Minimum Uniformly Distributed Live Loads, L_O, and Minimum Concentrated Live Loads[g]

occupancy or use	uniform load (psf)	concentrated load (lbf)
2. access floor systems		
office use	50	2000
computer use	100	2000
3. armories and drill rooms	150[m]	–
4. assembly areas		
fixed seats (fastened to floor)	60[m]	–
lobbies	100[m]	–
movable seats	100[m]	–
stage floors	150[m]	–
follow spot, projections, and control rooms	50	–
platforms (assembly)	100[m]	–
other assembly areas	100[m]	–
7. cornices	60	–
8. corridors		
first floor	100	–
other floors	Same as occupancy served except as indicated	–
14. garages (passenger vehicles only) trucks and buses	40[m] See Sec. 1607.7	Note[a] See Sec. 1607.7
17. hospitals		
operating rooms, laboratories	60	1000
patient rooms	40	1000
corridors above first floor	80	1000
19. libraries		
reading rooms	60	1000
stack rooms	150[b,m]	1000
corridors above first floor	80	1000
20. manufacturing		
light	125[m]	2000
heavy	250[m]	3000
21. marquees, except one- and two-family dwellings	75	–
22. office buildings		
file and computer rooms shall be designed for heavier loads based on anticipated occupancy	–	–
lobbies and first-floor corridors	100	2000
offices	50	2000
corridors above first floor	80	2000
25. residential		
one- and two-family dwellings uninhabitable attics without storage[i]	10	
uninhabitable attics with storage[i,j,k]	20	–
habitable attics and sleeping areas[k]	30	
canopies, including marquees	20	
all other areas	40	
hotels and multifamily dwellings private rooms and corridors serving them	40	
public rooms and corridors serving them	100	
27. schools		
classrooms	40	1000
corridors above first floor	80	1000
first-floor corridors	100	1000
30. stairs and exits		
one- and two-family dwellings	40	300[f]
all other	100	300[f]
31. storage warehouses (shall be designed for heavier loads if required for anticipated storage)		–
light	125[m]	
heavy	250[m]	
32. stores (retail)		
first floor	100	1000
upper floors	75	1000
wholesale, all floors	125	1000
34. walkways and elevated platforms (other than exitways)	60	–

[a]Floors in garages or portions of buildings used for the storage of motor vehicles shall be designed for the uniformly distributed live loads of this table or the following concentrated loads: (1) for garages restricted to passenger vehicles accommodating not more than nine passengers, 3000 lbf acting on an area of 4.5 in by 4.5 in; (2) for mechanical parking structures without slab or deck that are used for storing passenger vehicles only, 2250 lbf per wheel.

[b]The loading applies to stack room floors that support nonmobile, double-faced library bookstacks, subject to the following limitations.

1. The nominal bookstack unit height shall not exceed 90 in;
2. The nominal shelf depth shall not exceed 12 in for each face; and
3. Parallel rows of double-faced bookstacks shall be separated by aisles not less than 36 in wide.

[c]Design in accordance with ICC 300.

[d]Other uniform loads in accordance with an approved method containing provisions for truck losdings shall be considered where appropriate.

[f]The minimum concentrated load on stair treads shall be applied on an area of 2 inches by 2 inches. This load need not be assumed to act concurrently with the uniform load.

[g]Where snow loads occur that are in excess of the design conditions, the structure shall be designed to support the loads due to the increased loads caused by drift buildup or a greater snow design determined by the building official (see Sec. 1608).

[i](N/A)

[j](N/A)

[k](N/A)

[m](N/A)

Note: Some rows/columns not pertinent to this text have been omitted by PPI.

Product Development

Example 33.2

What live load should be used to design an interior beam that supports 225 ft^2 of office space, a live load of 50 psf, and a dead load of 72 psf? Calculate and compare both code methods.

(A) 25 psf

(B) 34 psf

(C) 47 psf

(D) 64 psf

Solution

Since the live load is less than 100 psf and the office is not a public assembly space or a parking garage, a reduction is permitted by either method. For each method, first determine the reduction, and then check against the limitations. Since this is an interior beam, the value of K_{LL} from Table 33.3 is 2.

$$\begin{aligned} L &= L_O\left(0.25 + \frac{15}{\sqrt{K_{\text{LL}}A_T}}\right) \\ &= \left(50\ \frac{\text{lbf}}{\text{ft}^2}\right)\left(0.25 + \frac{15}{\sqrt{(2)(225\ \text{ft}^2)}}\right) \\ &= 47.86\ \text{psf} \end{aligned}$$

The limiting load is $0.5L_O = (0.5)(50\ \text{psf}) = 25$ psf, which is less than the calculated value. Use 47.86 psf. The alternate reduction yields a similar result.

$$\begin{aligned} R &= r(A - 150) \\ &= (0.08)(225\ \text{ft}^2 - 150) \\ &= 6\% \end{aligned}$$

The limiting reduction is 40% for horizontal members, and it cannot exceed the percentage determined by the following formula.

$$\begin{aligned} R &= 23.1\left(1 + \frac{D}{L_O}\right) \\ &= (23.1)\left(1 + \frac{72\ \frac{\text{lbf}}{\text{ft}^2}}{50\ \frac{\text{lbf}}{\text{ft}^2}}\right) \\ &= 56.36\% \end{aligned}$$

Of the three values, 6% is the least, so the reduced live load will be 50 psf − (0.06)(50 psf), or 47 psf.

The answer is (C).

Minimum roof live loads are prescribed by the code and act on a horizontal projected area. This *roof live load*, L_r, is given by the following formula, with a minimum value of 12 psf.

$$L_r = 20R_1R_2 \quad 33.4$$

The value of R_1 is based on the *tributary area*, A_t, of the member. If A_t does not exceed 200 ft^2, R_1 is 1.0. If A_t exceeds 600 ft^2, R_1 is 0.6. For values of A_t between these two limits the following equation is used.

$$R_1 = 1.2 - 0.001A_t \quad 33.5$$

Table 33.3 Live Loads Element Factor, K_{LL}

element	K_{LL}
interior columns	4
exterior columns without cantilever slabs	4
edge columns with cantilever slabs	3
corner columns with cantilever slabs	2
edge beams without cantilever slabs	2
interior beams	2
all other members not identified above including	
edge beams with cantilever slabs	
cantilever beams	
one-way slabs	
two-way slabs	1
members without provisions for continuous shear transfer normal to their span	

From *2015 International Building Code*, www.iccsafe.org

The value of R_2 is based on the *roof slope*, F, in inches of rise per foot of run. If F does not exceed 4 in/ft, R_2 is 1.0. If F exceeds 12 in/ft, R_2 is 0.6. For values of F between these two limits the following equation is used.

$$R_2 = 1.2 - 0.05F \quad 33.6$$

Example 33.3

What roof live load should be used to design a column that supports 450 ft^2 of a roof with a slope of 5 in of rise per foot of run? Calculate the reduction factors for tributary area and slope, and then find the design roof live load.

(A) 6.35 psf

(B) 9.53 psf

(C) 14.3 psf

(D) 21.5 psf

Solution

$$\begin{aligned} R_1 &= 1.2 - 0.001A_t \\ &= 1.2 - (0.001)(450) \\ &= 0.75 \end{aligned}$$

$$\begin{aligned} R_2 &= 1.2 - 0.05F \\ &= 1.2 - (0.5)(5) \\ &= 0.95 \end{aligned}$$

$$\begin{aligned} L_r &= 20R_1R_2 \\ &= \left(20\ \frac{\text{lbf}}{\text{ft}^2}\right)(0.75)(0.95) \\ &= 14.25 \text{ psf} \quad (14.3 \text{ psf}) \end{aligned}$$

Product Development

Since the calculated roof live load is greater than the minimum value of 12 psf, use 14.3 psf.

The answer is (C).

Load Combinations

It is generally agreed that when calculating the load on a building, all sources will not act at full values at once. For example, full snow load will not be present when full wind load exists because the wind will blow some of the snow away. The IBC recognizes this and requires that several combinations of load be calculated to find the most critical case. In addition some structural materials are designed using strength design while others use allowable stress design. The difference in these two methods is discussed in the appropriate structural material chapter.

The basic load combinations per IBC Sec. 1605.2.1 using strength design or load and resistance factor design are as follows.

- $1.4(D+F)$
- $1.2(D+F)+1.6(L+H)+0.5(L_r \text{ or } S \text{ or } R)$
- $1.2(D+F)+1.6(L_r \text{ or } S \text{ or } R)+1.6H+(f_1L \text{ or } 0.5W)$
- $1.2(D+F)+1.0W+f_1L+1.6H+0.5(L_r \text{ or } S \text{ or } R)$
- $1.2(D+F)+1.0E+f_1L+1.6H+f_2S$
- $0.9D+1.0W+1.6H$
- $0.9(D+F)+1.0E+1.6H$

The value of f_1 is 1.0 for floors in places of public assembly, parking garages, and where the live load exceeds 100 psf. For any other cases a value of 0.5 may be used for f_1. The value of f_2 is 0.7 for roof configurations that do not shed snow off the structure (such as saw tooth). For any other cases a value of 0.2 may be used for f_2.

The American Concrete Institute's *Building Code Requirements for Structural Concrete* give requirements that allow for a slightly different set of factors.

The basic load combinations per IBC Sec. 1605.3.1 using allowable stress design are as follows.

- $D+F$
- $D+H+F+L$
- $D+H+F+L_r \text{ or } S \text{ or } R$
- $D+H+F+0.75L+0.75(L_r \text{ or } S \text{ or } R)$
- $D+H+F+(0.6W \text{ or } 0.7E)$
- $D+H+F+0.75(0.6W)+0.75L+0.75(L_r \text{ or } S \text{ or } R)$
- $D+H+F+0.75(0.7E)+0.75L+0.75S$
- $0.6D+0.6W+H$
- $0.6(D+F)+0.7E+H$

Alternate basic load combinations per IBC Sec. 1605.3.2 using allowable stress design are as follows.

- $D+L+(L_r \text{ or } S \text{ or } R)$
- $D+L+0.6\omega W$
- $D+L+0.6\omega W+S/2$

- $D + L + S + 0.6\omega W/2$
- $D + L + S + E/1.4$
- $0.9D + E/1.4$

The coefficient ω is taken as 1.3 in some cases as defined in IBC Sec. 1605.3.2, and as 1.0 otherwise.

LATERAL LOADS

Wind

Wind loading on buildings is a dynamic process. That is, the pressures, directions, and timing are constantly changing. For purposes of calculation, however, wind is considered a static force. There are several variables that affect wind loading. The first is the *wind velocity* itself. The pressure on a building varies as the square of the velocity according to the following formula.

$$\ell_c = 0.00256\mathrm{v}_{\mathrm{mph}}^2 \qquad 33.7$$

The second variable is the *height* of the wind above the ground. Since wind acts as any fluid where a surface causes friction and slows the fluid, wind velocity is lower near the ground and increases with height. Wind speed values are taken at a standard height of 33 ft above the ground, so adjustments must be made when calculating pressure at different elevations.

A third variable is the nature of the building's *surroundings*. Other buildings, trees, and topography affect how the wind will finally strike the structure under consideration. Buildings in large, open areas are subject to more wind force than those in protected areas. The surroundings are taken into account along with multiplying factors found in the building codes.

Finally, there are factors like the size, shape, and surface texture of the building. Some buildings allow the wind to flow around them, while others channel or focus the wind.

A building subjected to wind forces responds in several ways. These are shown diagrammatically in Fig. 33.1. There is, of course, positive pressure on the windward side of the building. On the leeward side and roof there is often a negative pressure, or suction. In addition to these, there are local areas where wind pressure is greater such as building corners, overhangs, parapets, and other projections. For complex buildings, wind tunnel tests may need to be performed. For some rectangular buildings not exceeding a height of 60 ft, simplified wind calculations are allowed. However, the code specifies an analytical method for most buildings. This analytical method is described in detail in Chap. 22.

Of particular interest to architects are building shapes and design features that may exacerbate wind problems. These include things such as closely spaced buildings or small openings at ground level that cause normally acceptable wind speeds to increase to unacceptable levels. Because wind is a fluid, forcing a given volume at a given speed into a smaller area causes the speed to increase. There have been instances, for example, where localized winds are so great that entry doors cannot be opened or an otherwise pleasant outdoor plaza is unusable.

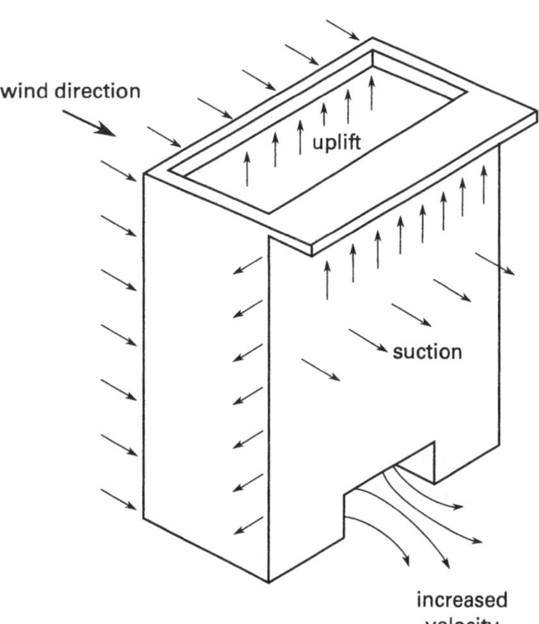

Figure 33.1 Forces on a Building Due to Wind

Other potential problems include *building drift*, which is the distance a building moves from side to side in the wind. This is particularly of concern in very tall buildings where the drift may be several feet. Generally, a building should be designed to be stiff enough that the maximum drift does not exceed $^1/_{500}$ of the height of the building.

Earthquake

Like wind, an earthquake produces dynamic loads on a building. During an earthquake, the ground moves both vertically and laterally, but the lateral movement is usually most significant and the vertical movement is normally ignored.

For some tall buildings or structures with complex shapes or unusual conditions, a *dynamic structural analysis* is required. With this method, a computer is used to model the building and earthquakes to study the response of the structure and what forces are developed. In most cases, however, building codes allow a static analysis of the loads produced, greatly simplifying the structural design.

With the *static analysis method*, the total horizontal shear at the base of the building is calculated according to a standard formula. Then, this total lateral force is distributed to the various floors of the building so the designer knows what force the structure must resist. Chapter 45 discusses calculation of earthquake loads in more detail.

MISCELLANEOUS LOADS

Dynamic Loads

When a load is applied suddenly or changes rapidly, it is called a *dynamic load.* When a force is only applied suddenly, it is often called an *impact load.* Examples of dynamic loads are automobiles moving in a parking garage, elevators traveling in a shaft, or a helicopter landing on the roof of a building. Dynamic loads do not occur on every building but are important to analyze and design for. The IBC specifies minimum requirements for many of these types of loads. In many cases, a dynamic load is treated as a static load value multiplied by an impact factor.

A unique type of dynamic load is a *resonant load.* This is a rhythmic application of a force to a structure with the same fundamental period as the structure itself. The *fundamental period* is the time it takes the structure to complete one full oscillation, such as a complete swing from side to side in a tall building in the wind or one up-and-down bounce of a floor. Resonant loads are usually small compared to other types of loads but slowly build over time as the load repeatedly amplifies the motion of the structure. The principle of resonant loading is what makes it possible for a few people to overturn a heavy car by bouncing it on its springs in time with the fundamental period of the springs. The rocking motion of the car eventually is great enough that a final push makes the car overturn.

Resonant loads can affect an entire structure. One example is repeated gusts of wind on a tall building or on portions of a building. A common problem is a vibrating machine attached to a floor that has the same period as the machine's vibrations. In such a situation, the floor can be subjected to forces larger than it was designed for. The problem can be alleviated by placing the machine on resilient pads or springs to dampen the vibration, or by stiffening the floor to change its fundamental period.

Occasionally, a tuned dynamic damper is placed at the top of tall buildings to dampen the effects of wind sway. This is a very heavy mass attached to the sides of the building with springs of the same period as the building. As the building oscillates in one direction, the spring-mounted mass moves in the opposite direction, effectively counteracting the action of the wind. With this approach, costly wind bracing normally required to stiffen the entire building can be minimized.

Temperature-Induced Loads

All materials expand when they are heated and contract when they are cooled. The amount of the change is dependent on the material and is expressed as the *coefficient of expansion* measured in inches per inch per degree Fahrenheit. Some materials, like wood, have a low coefficient of expansion while others, like plastic, have a high value. If a material is restrained so it cannot move and is then subjected to a temperature change, a load is introduced on the material in addition to any other applied loads.

In the worst case, temperature-induced loads can so overload a structural member that failure may occur. Most often, however, failing to account for temperature-induced loads causes other types of failures such as tight-fitting glass breaking when a metal frame contracts, or masonry walls cracking when expansion joints are not provided. In nearly all cases, the solution is fairly simple: the material or assembly of materials must be allowed to expand and contract for the expected distance. This is fairly easy to calculate, and detailed methods are described in Chap. 34.

Soil Loads

Retaining walls are required to resist the lateral pressure of the retained material in accordance with accepted engineering practice. Table 33.4 gives the minimum lateral pressures to be used in the design of retaining walls, as specified by the IBC. This is in addition to any surcharge such as vertical loads near the top of the wall or other lateral loads. In addition, retaining walls must be designed to resist sliding by at least 1.5 times the lateral force and resist overturning by at least 1.5 times the overturning moment.

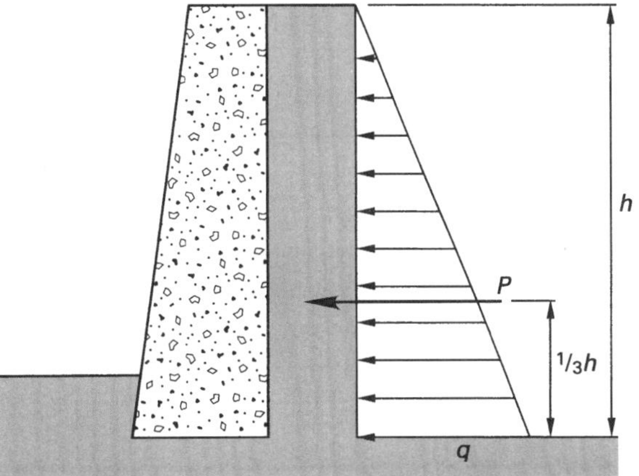

Figure 33.2
Load from Soil on Retaining Wall

To calculate the pressure at the bottom of the wall, p, simply multiply the design lateral soil pressure, q, by the depth of the wall, h, to get pounds per square foot. The active pressure specified in the table is used for free-draining backfill, while the passive pressure is used for other cases. Since the pressure varies uniformly from zero at the very top of the wall, where no earth is retained, to a maximum at the bottom, the total horizontal load per linear foot acting on the wall is found by calculating the area of the triangular distribution or the maximum earth pressure at the bottom times the height divided by two (see Fig. 33.2).

$$P = P_{\text{max}}\left(\frac{h}{2}\right) \qquad 33.8$$

Example 33.4

A retaining wall 8 ft high is retaining free-draining silty sand. From Table 33.4, an active pressure of 45 psf/ft may be used for the silty sand. What is the total horizontal load exerted on the wall?

(A) 650 plf

(B) 850 plf

(C) 1110 plf

(D) 1440 plf

Solution

The pressure at the bottom is (8 ft)(45 psf/ft), or 360 psf. The total horizontal load is (360 psf/2)(8 ft), or 1440 lbm/ft.

It will be shown that this total load acts at the centroid of a triangle, or one-third the distance from the base. Retaining wall design is discussed in more detail in Chap. 21.

The answer is (D).

Table 33.4
Soil Lateral Loads

description of backfill material[c]	unified soil classification	design lateral soil pressure[a] (psf/ft of depth)	
		active pressure	at-rest pressure
well-graded, clean gravels; gravel-sand mixes	GW	30	60
poorly graded clean gravels; gravel-sand mixes	GP	30	60
silty gravels, poorly graded gravel-sand mixes	GM	40	60
clayey gravels, poorly graded gravel-and-clay mixes	GC	45	60
well-graded, clean sands; gravelly sand mixes	SW	30	60
poorly graded clean sands; sand-gravel mixes	SP	30	60
silty sands, poorly graded sand-silt mixes	SM	45	60
sand-silt clay mix with plastic fines	SM-SC	45	100
clayey sands, poorly graded sand-clay mixes	SC	60	100
inorganic silts and clayey silts	ML	45	100
mixture of inorganic silt and clay	ML-CL	60	100
inorganic clays of low to medium plasticity	CL	60	100
organic silts and silt clays, low plasticity	OL	Note b	Note b
inorganic clayey silts, elastic silts	MH	Note b	Note b
inorganic clays of high plasticity	CH	Note b	Note b
organic clays and silty clays	OH	Note b	Note b

[a]Design lateral soil loads are given for moist conditions for the specified soils at their optimum densities. Actual field conditions shall govern. Submerged or saturated soil pressures shall include the weight of the buoyant soil plus the hydrostatic loads.

[b]Unsuitable as backfill material.

[c]The definition and classification of soil materials shall be in accordance with ASTM D 2487.

Water Loads

Loads from water can occur in many situations: in water tanks, in swimming pools, and against retaining walls holding back groundwater. The load developed from water and other fluids is equal to the unit weight of the fluid in pounds per cubic foot multiplied by its depth. For water, the specific weight is about 62 lbf/ft^3. The water force exerted on structures is called *hydrostatic pressure.*

34 STRUCTURAL FUNDAMENTALS

Nomenclature

A	area	in^2 or ft^2
b	base of rectangular section	in
d	depth of rectangular section	in
d	diameter	in
d	distance between axes	in
e	total deformation (strain)	in
E	modulus of elasticity	lbf/in^2
f	stress	lbf/in^2
F	force	lbf
I	moment of inertia	in^4
I_n	moment of inertia about a new axis	in^4
I_x	moment of inertia of area about neutral x-axis	in^4
L	original length	in
P	total force	lbf
r	radius	in
R	reaction force	lbf
T	temperature	°F
W	weight	lbf
α	coefficient of linear expansion	in/in-°F
ε	strain	decimal
θ	angle	deg

STATICS AND FORCES

Statics

Statics is the branch of mechanics that deals with bodies in a state of equilibrium. *Equilibrium* is said to exist when the resultant of any number of forces acting on a body is zero. For example, a 10 lbm object on the ground is acted on by gravity to the magnitude of 10 lbf. The ground, in turn, exerts an upward force of 10 lbf and the object is in equilibrium.

Three fundamental principles of equilibrium apply to buildings.

- The sum of all vertical forces acting on a body must equal zero (as in the preceding simple example).
- The sum of all horizontal forces acting on a body must equal zero.
- The sum of all the moments acting on a body must equal zero.

Forces

A *force* is any action applied to an object. In architecture, external forces are called *loads* and result from the weights of such things as people, wind, snow, or building materials. The internal structure of a building material must resist external loads with internal forces of their own that are equal in magnitude and of opposite sign. These external loads are called *stresses.* The structural design of buildings is primarily concerned with selecting the size, configuration, and material of components to resist, with a reasonable margin of safety, external forces acting on them.

A force has both direction and magnitude and as such is called a *vector quantity.* Direction is shown by using a line with an arrowhead, and magnitude is indicated by establishing a convenient scale. For example, at a scale of 1 in equals 2000 lbf, a line 2 in long represents a force of 4000 lbf. An 8000 lbf force would, therefore, be shown with a line 4 in long.

The line of action of a force is a line concurrent with the force vector. A force acting anywhere along the line of action can be considered equal or unchanged as long as the direction and magnitude do not change. This is the principle of *transmissibility.*

There are several types of forces.

- *Collinear forces* are those whose vectors lie along the same straight line. See Fig. 34.1(a). Structural members subjected to collinear forces such as tension or compression are said to be two-force members.
- *Concurrent forces* are those whose lines of action meet at a common point. See Fig. 34.1(b).

- *Nonconcurrent forces* have lines of action that do not pass through a common point. See Fig. 34.1(c). A special case of this type that is commonly found in architectural applications is a parallel force system, such as a type that may be acting on a beam. See Fig. 34.1(d).
- *Coplanar forces* are forces whose lines of action all lie within the same plane. Noncoplanar forces do not lie within the same plane.
- *Structural forces* in buildings can be any combination of these types. For example, a truss is a collection of sets of concurrent-coplanar forces, while a space frame is an example of a combination of sets of concurrent-noncoplanar forces.

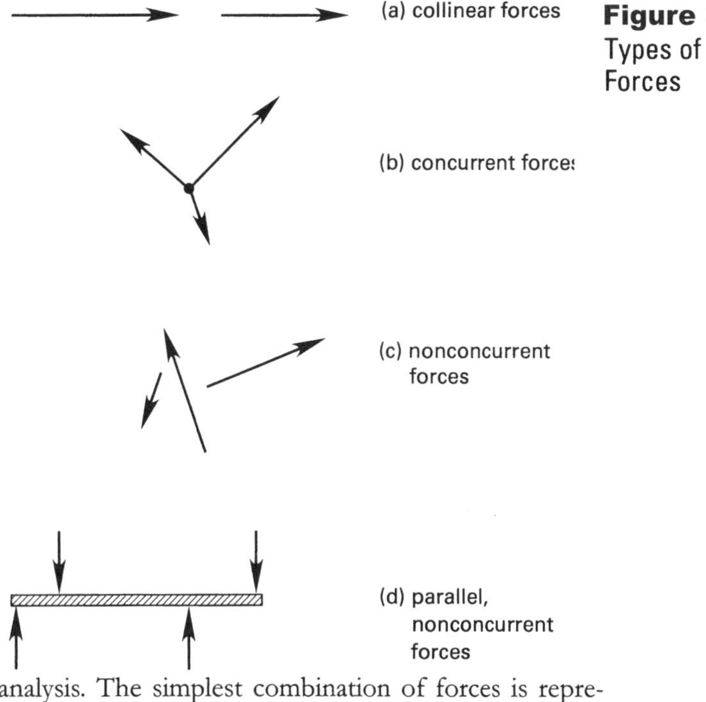

Figure 34.1 Types of Forces

It is often necessary to add two or more concurrent forces or to break down a single force into its components for purposes of structural analysis. The simplest combination of forces is represented by collinear forces. The magnitudes of the forces are added directly in the same direction of force. See Fig. 34.2.

With concurrent and nonconcurrent forces, the effect of the direction of the force must be taken into account. The methods used to find resultant forces or to break down a force into its components will be discussed in the Structural Analysis section in this chapter.

1000 lbf + 1800 lbf = 2800 lbf

Figure 34.2 Addition of Collinear Forces

Stresses

Stress is the internal resistance to an external force. There are three basic types of stress: tension, compression, and shear. Tension and compression stresses are known as *normal stresses.* All stresses consist of these basic types or some combination thereof.

Tension is stress in which the particles of the member tend to pull apart under load.

Compression is stress in which the particles of the member are pushed together and the member tends to shorten.

Shear is stress in which the particles of a member slide past each other.

With tension and compression, the force acts *perpendicular* to the area of the material resisting the force. With shear, the force acts *parallel* to the area resisting the force.

For these three conditions, stress is expressed as force per unit area and is determined by dividing the total force applied to the total area.

$$f = \frac{P}{A} \qquad 34.1$$

Example 34.1

A balcony is partially supported from structure above by a steel rod with a $1^1/_4$ in diameter. The load on the rod is 10,000 lbf. What is the stress in the rod?

Solution

The radius of the rod is

$$r = \frac{d}{2} = \frac{1.25 \text{ in}}{2} = 0.625 \text{ in}$$

The area of the rod is

$$A = \pi r^2 = \pi(0.625 \text{ in})^2 = 1.23 \text{ in}^2$$

From Eq. 34.1, the stress is

$$f = \frac{P}{A} = \frac{10{,}000 \text{ lbf}}{1.23 \text{ in}^2} = 8130 \text{ psi}$$

Other types of stresses consist of torsion, bending, and combined stresses. *Torsion* is a type of shear in which a member is twisted. *Bending* is a combination of tension and compression like the type that occurs in beams. This will be discussed in more detail in Chap. 34. *Combined loads* can occur in many situations. For example, a column resisting loads from above and lateral wind loads is subjected to both compression and bending.

Thermal Stress

When a material is subjected to a change in temperature, it expands if heated or contracts if cooled. For an unrestrained material, the general formula is

$$e = \alpha L \Delta T \qquad 34.2$$

Some coefficients of common materials are shown in Table 34.1.

Table 34.1
Coefficients of Linear Expansion

material	coefficient (in/in-°F)
aluminum	0.0000128
brick	0.0000034
bronze	0.0000101
concrete	0.0000055
glass	0.0000051
marble	0.0000045
plastic, acrylic	0.0000450
structural steel	0.0000065
wood, fir parallel to grain	0.0000021

If the material is restrained at both ends, a change in temperature causes an internal thermal stress. The formula for this stress is

$$f = E\alpha \Delta T \qquad 34.3$$

The stress is independent of the cross-sectional area of the member if there are no other loads being applied to the member while it is undergoing thermal stress.

Strain and Deformation

As a force is applied to a material, the material changes size. For example, a tensile force causes a rod to elongate and narrow, while a compressive force causes a material to shorten and widen. *Strain* is the deformation of a material caused by external forces. It is the ratio of the total change in length of a material to its original length. As a formula, it is represented as

$$\varepsilon = \frac{e}{L} \qquad 34.4$$

As a force is applied to a material, the deformation (strain) is directly proportional to the stress, up to a certain point. This is known as *Hooke's law*, named after Robert Hooke, the British mathematician and physicist who first discovered it. This relationship is shown graphically in Fig. 34.3. At a certain point, however, the material will begin to change length at a faster ratio than the applied force. This point is called the *elastic limit*. At any stress up to the elastic limit, the material will return to its original size if the force is removed. Above the elastic limit there will be permanent deformation, even if the force is removed.

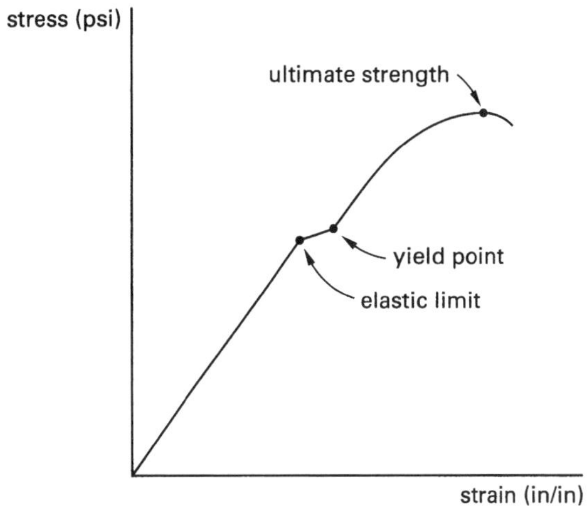

Figure 34.3 Hypothetical Stress-Strain Graph

With some materials there is also a point, slightly above the elastic limit, called the *yield point*. This is the point at which the material continues to deform with very little increase in load. Some materials, such as wood, have poorly defined elastic limits and no yield points.

Table 34.2 Modulus of Elasticity of Some Common Building Materials*

material	modulus of elasticity (psi)
structural steel (soft)	29,000,000
brass	15,000,000
aluminum	10,000,000
concrete (3000 psi)	3,200,000
lumber (Douglas fir-larch)	1,700,000
lumber (western cedar)	900,000

*These are representative values only. Exact values depend on such things as the alloy of the metal, mix of concrete, or species and grade of lumber.

If the load is continually increased, the material will ultimately rupture. The unit stress just before this occurs is called the *ultimate strength* of the material.

Although the entire range of a material's stress/strain relationship is interesting from a theoretical point of view, the most important portion from a practical standpoint is where the stress and strain are directly proportional, up to the elastic limit. Sound engineering practices and limitations set by building codes establish the working stresses to be used in calculations at some point below the yield point.

Every material has a characteristic ratio of stress to strain. This is called the *modulus of elasticity*, E, which is a measure of a material's resistance to deformation, or its stiffness. It can be expressed as the following formula.

$$E = \frac{f}{\varepsilon} \qquad 34.5$$

Since stress was defined as total force divided by total area, $f = P/A$ (Eq. 34.1), and strain was defined as total strain divided by original length, $\varepsilon = e/L$ (Eq. 34.4), the equation can be rewritten as follows.

$$E = \frac{\frac{P}{A}}{\frac{e}{L}} = \frac{PL}{Ae} \qquad 34.6$$

This equation can also be used to find the total strain (deformation) of a material under a given load by rearranging the values.

$$e = \frac{PL}{AE} \qquad 34.7$$

Example 34.2

If a load of 12,000 lbf is applied to a 3 ft long, 4 × 4 Douglas fir no. 2 wood column, how much will it compress? The modulus of elasticity for Douglas fir no. 2 is 1,700,000 psi.

Solution

The actual area of a 4 × 4 is $3\frac{1}{2}$ in by $3\frac{1}{2}$ in, or 12.25 in^2. The change in length is, therefore,

$$e = \frac{PL}{AE} = \frac{(12{,}000\ \text{lbf})(3\ \text{ft})\left(12\ \frac{\text{in}}{\text{ft}}\right)}{(12.25\ \text{in}^2)\left(1{,}700{,}000\ \frac{\text{lbf}}{\text{in}^2}\right)} = 0.021\ \text{in}$$

Some representative values of E for various materials are given in Table 34.2 to show how they vary with material type. Actual values of E to be used in calculations should be derived from building codes or accepted tables of values.

Figure 34.4 Moments in Equilibrium

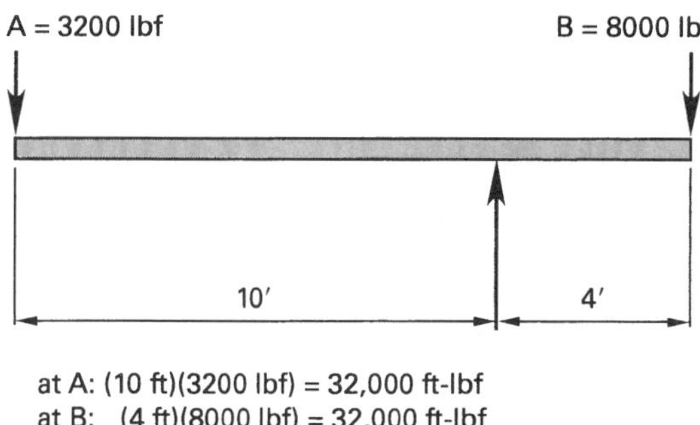

Moment

Moment is a special condition of a force applied to a structure. A *moment* is the tendency of a force to cause rotation about a point. As such, it is the product of the force times the perpendicular distance to the point about which it is acting. The units are in foot-pounds, inch-pounds, or kip-feet. Figure 34.4 illustrates a simple condition of moments where two downward forces are balancing a lever on one pivot point. Even though the forces are of unequal value, they balance the lever because the distances from the pivot point result in equal moments.

Understanding the concept of moments is important in structural design because in a system in equilibrium the algebraic sum of moments about any point is zero. This concept allows an architect to analyze structures, determine support reactions, and design structural systems. When dealing with moments, it is necessary to be consistent with the values given to moments based on the directions in which they act. If a force tends to cause a clockwise rotation, the moment is said to be *positive*. If it tends to cause a counterclockwise rotation, the moment is said to be *negative*. This is a purely arbitrary convention and could be reversed, as long as the calculations are kept consistent.

Example 34.3

Consider a simply supported beam with two concentrated loads at the locations shown. Determine the reactions of the two supports, ignoring the weight of the beam itself.

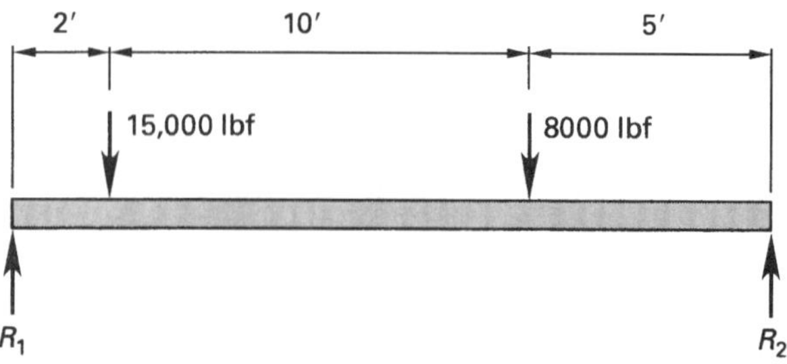

Solution

Since there are two unknowns, R_1 and R_2, select one of these points as the pivot point about which to make calculations. This eliminates one of the variables because the distance the force acts from the pivot point is zero, so the moment will be zero also. Select R_1 as the first point.

Since the algebraic sum of moments about point R_1 is zero, the formula is as follows.

About R_1,

$$(15{,}000\ \text{lbf})(2\ \text{ft}) + (8000\ \text{lbf})(12\ \text{ft}) - R_2(17\ \text{ft}) = 0\ \text{ft-lbf}$$

The two concentrated loads tend to cause rotation in a clockwise direction (positive), while the reaction of the other beam support tends to cause a counterclockwise rotation (negative) about point R_1.

Solving for R_2 gives 7412 lbf.

Since one of the principles of equilibrium is that the sum of all vertical forces equals zero, R_1 and R_2 (upward) must equal the loads (downward). Therefore,

$$R_1 = 15{,}000\ \text{lbf} + 8000\ \text{lbf} - 7412\ \text{lbf} = 15{,}588\ \text{lbf}$$

However, you can use the same procedure of summing moments about reaction R_2 to find R_1 another way.

About R_2,

$$R_1(17\ \text{ft}) - (15{,}000\ \text{lbf})(15\ \text{ft}) - (8000\ \text{lbf})(5\ \text{ft}) = 0\ \text{ft-lbf}$$

$$R_1 = 15{,}588\ \text{lbf}$$

Moments on beams will be discussed in more detail in Chap. 35.

PROPERTIES OF SECTIONS

Regardless of material, all structural sections used to support building loads have certain properties. These properties affect how efficiently the sections can resist a load and how they are designed. The most common properties are *area*, *centroid*, *statical moment*, *moment of inertia*, *section modulus*, and *radius of gyration*. The area of a section is self-explanatory and its use in calculating stress has already been shown.

Centroid

In all solid bodies, there is a point at which the mass of the body can be considered concentrated. This is the *center of gravity*. Although technically a flat area cannot have a center of gravity because it has no mass, the point on a plane surface that corresponds to the center of gravity is called the *centroid*. In symmetrical sections, such as a rectangular wood beam or round bar, the centroid is located in the geometric center of the area as shown in Fig. 34.5.

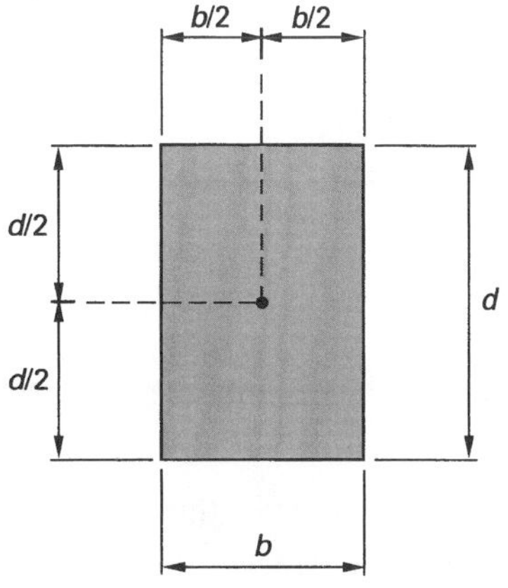

Figure 34.5
Centroid of a Symmetrical Area

Product Development

Figure 34.6 Centroids for Some Common Shapes

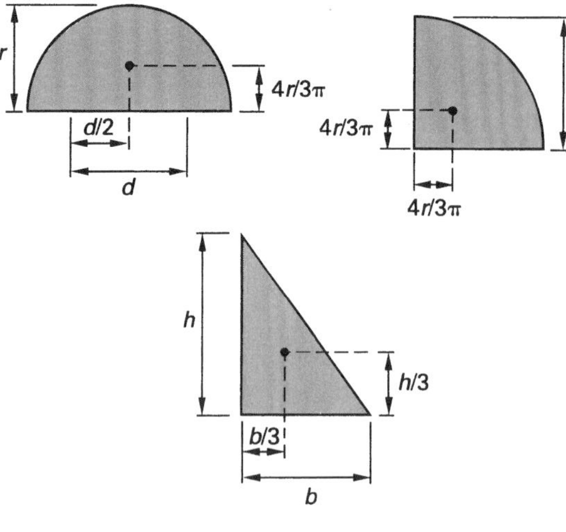

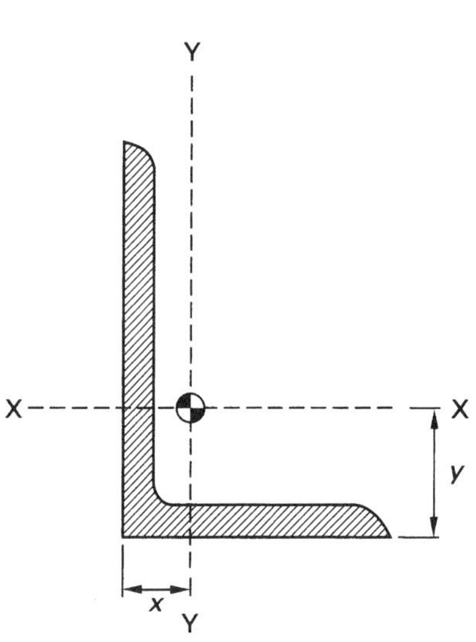

The locations of centroids have been computed for simple nonsymmetrical areas (see Fig. 34.6).

Manufacturers of structural members also include the location of centroids as part of their published data. Figure 34.7 illustrates one example of a steel section as found in the American Institute of Steel Construction *Steel Construction Manual.*

Statical Moment

To find the centroid of unsymmetrical areas, the statical moment must be used. The statical moment of a plane area with respect to an axis is the product of the area times the perpendicular distance from the centroid of the area to the axis. If a complex unsymmetrical area is divided into two or more simple parts, the statical moment of the entire area is equal to the sum of the statical moments of the parts.

Figure 34.7 Centroidal Axes of Steel Angle with Unequal Legs

Example 34.4

Locate the centroid of the area shown.

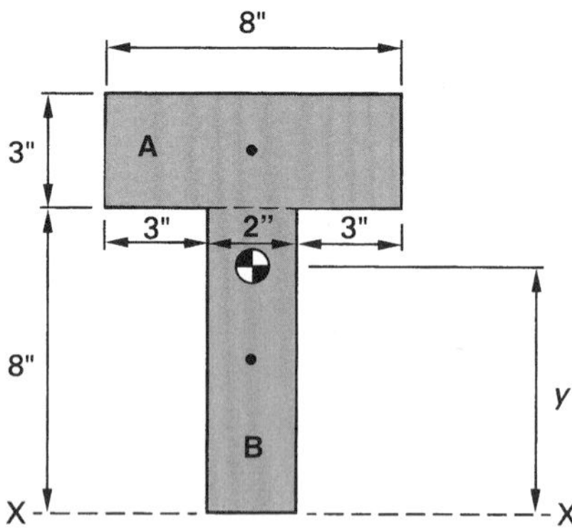

Solution

Select any convenient axis. In this case, use the X-X axis at the base of the object. Let y equal the distance from the axis to the centroid of the entire object. Divide the area into two rectangular sections, A and B, each having its centroid in the geometric center of its respective area.

The sum of the statical moments of the parts equals the statical moment of the entire section—all about the axis X-X. The distance from X-X to the centroid of area A is 9.5 in, and the distance to the centroid of area B is 4 in.

$$(9.5\text{ in})(24\text{ in}^2) + (4\text{ in})(16\text{ in}^2) = y(24\text{ in}^2 + 16\text{ in}^2)$$
$$y = 7.3\text{ in}$$

Since this object is symmetrical about the vertical, or Y-Y axis, the centroid will be in the center of the object between the right and left edges.

Moment of Inertia

Another important property of structural sections is the *moment of inertia*. In general terms, this is a measure of the *bending stiffness* of a structural member's cross-sectional shape, similar to how the modulus of elasticity is a measure of the stiffness of the material of a structural member.

In more exact terms, the moment of inertia about a certain axis of a section is the summation of all the infinitely small areas of the section multiplied by the square of the distance from the axis to each of these areas. Its common designation is I, and its units are inches to the fourth power. It is most common to use the neutral axis (axis passing through the centroid) as the axis of reference, but the moment of inertia about an axis through the base of a figure is also useful when calculating I for unsymmetrical sections. See Fig. 34.8.

The derivation of the moment of inertia for a section is done with calculus, but I for common shapes can be calculated with simple equations that have been derived with calculus. In addition, most manufacturers of structural shapes give the value of the moment of inertia with respect to both vertical and horizontal axes passing through the centroid. For example, the tables of structural steel shapes give the value I for both the X-X and Y-Y centroidal axes.

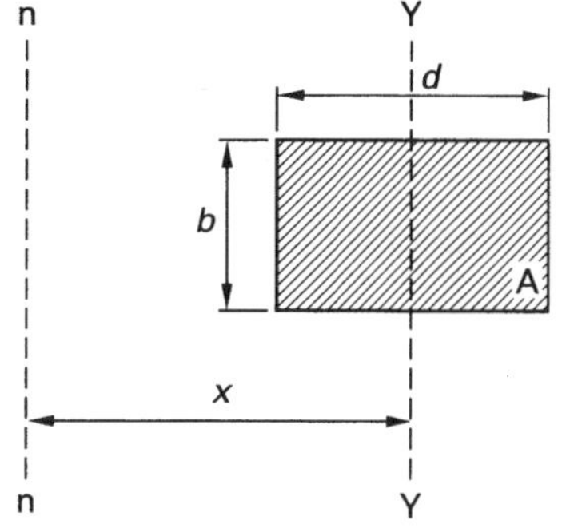

Figure 34.8
Transfer of Moment of Inertia

For rectangular sections, the moment of inertia about the centroidal axis parallel to the base is

$$I = \frac{bd^3}{12} \qquad 34.8$$

The moment of inertia about an axis through the base of a rectangular section is

$$I = \frac{bd^3}{3} \qquad 34.9$$

Example 34.5

Find the moment of inertia of a solid wood beam 6 in wide and 13½ in deep.

Solution

$$I = \frac{bd^3}{12} = \frac{(6\text{ in})(13.5\text{ in})^3}{12}$$
$$= 1230\text{ in}^4$$

Product Development

In order to find the moment of inertia for composite areas, transfer the moment of inertia of each section about its centroid to a new axis, typically the centroid of the composite section. The general formula for doing this, as illustrated in Fig. 34.8, is

$$I_n = I_X + Ax^2 \quad (34.10)$$

$$I_n = I_X + Ad^2 \quad (34.11)$$

The transferred moments of inertia of the various sections are then added to get the moment of inertia for the entire section.

The moment of inertia is dependent on the area of a section and the distance of the area from the neutral axis, but from that statement the moment of inertia is the summation of the areas times the square of the distances of those areas from the neutral axis. From Eq. 34.8 and Eq. 34.9, it is evident that a beam's depth has a greater bearing on the beam's resistance to bending than its width or total area. This explains why a board placed on edge between two supports is much stronger than the same board placed on its side.

There are two other important properties of sections: the *section modulus* and the *radius of gyration*. However, these are more appropriately discussed in Chap. 13. Section modulus will be explained in the sections on beams and the theory of bending, while radius of gyration will be discussed in the section on columns.

Example 34.6

Using the same composite section as shown in Ex. 34.4, calculate the moment of inertia.

Solution

The first step is to locate the centroid of the object. This was done in the previous example problem and was found to be 7.3 in above the base.

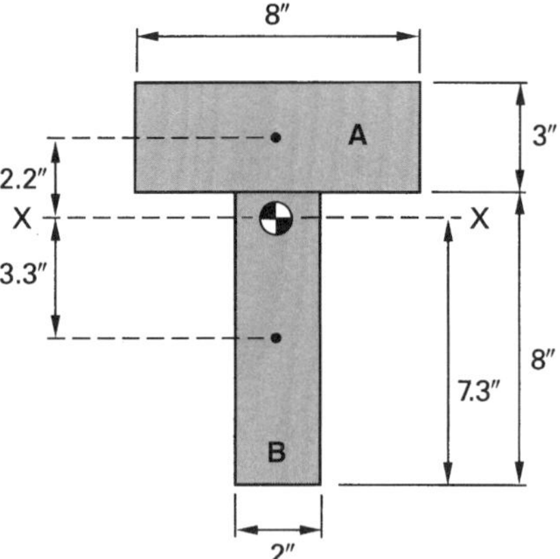

The next task is to transfer the individual moments of inertia about this centroidal axis and add them. To do this, it is helpful to set up a table so all the figures and calculations can be seen easily. This is an especially useful technique when dealing with several individual areas.

The moments of inertia of areas A and B are found with Eq. 34.8, and are denoted I_o to express the fact that these are the moments of inertia about an axis passing through the centroid of the elementary figure. y is the distance from the centroidal axis to the axes of areas A and B.

Performing the calculations yields

area	I_o (in^4)	A (in^2)	y (in)	Ay^2 (in^4)	$I_o + Ay^2$ (in^4)
A	18.00	24.00	2.200	116.2	134.2
B	85.33	16.00	3.300	174.3	259.6
					$I_x = 393.8\ in^4$

STRUCTURAL ANALYSIS

Resultant Forces

There are times when it is desirable to combine two or more concurrent forces into one force such that the one force produces the same effect on a body as the concurrent forces. This single force is called the *resultant*. If the forces are collinear, as described previously in this chapter, the resultant is simply the sum of the forces, with forces acting upward or to the right considered positive and forces acting downward or to the left considered negative. For example, in Fig. 34.9 the three forces are added to get the resultant.

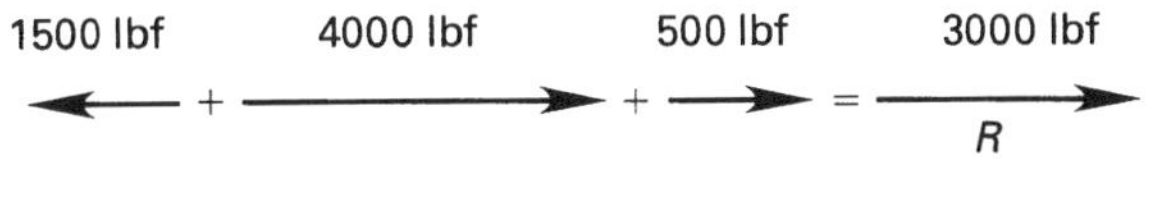

Figure 34.9 Resultant of Collinear Forces

For concurrent forces (forces whose lines of action pass through a common point), both the magnitude and direction must be taken into account. Consider the two forces shown in Fig. 34.10(a). The resultant of these forces can be found graphically or algebraically.

To find it graphically, draw the lines of force to any convenient scale, such as 1 in equals 100 lbf, and in the direction they are acting as shown in Fig. 34.10(b). Then draw a line parallel to each force, starting with the head of the force vector, to form a parallelogram. Connect the point of concurrence to the opposite corner of the parallelogram with a line. This is the resultant whose magnitude and direction can be found by scaling the length of it and measuring its angle.

To find the resultant algebraically, sketch a force triangle as shown in Fig. 34.10(c). Since the forces are in equilibrium, the triangle must close. The resultant will then be the third side of the triangle. Both the magnitude and direction can be solved with trigonometry using the law of cosines and sines, or the Pythagorean theorem for a right triangle.

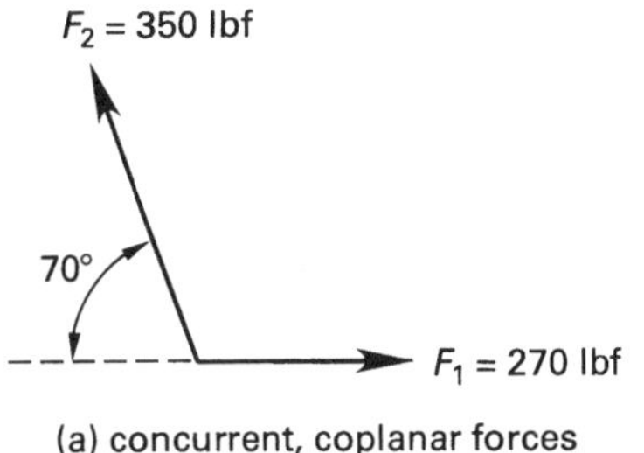

(a) concurrent, coplanar forces

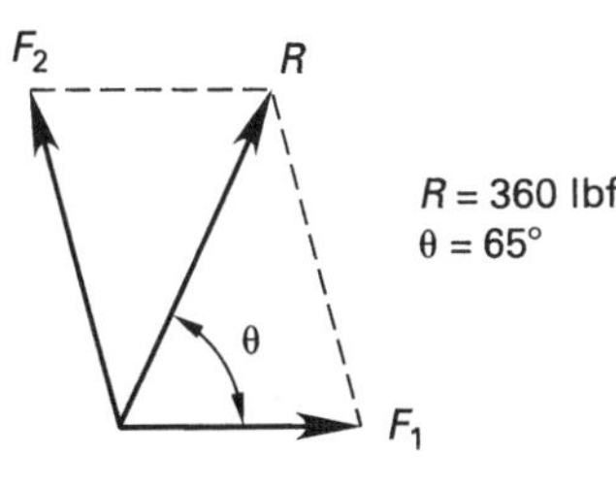

(b) graphic solution

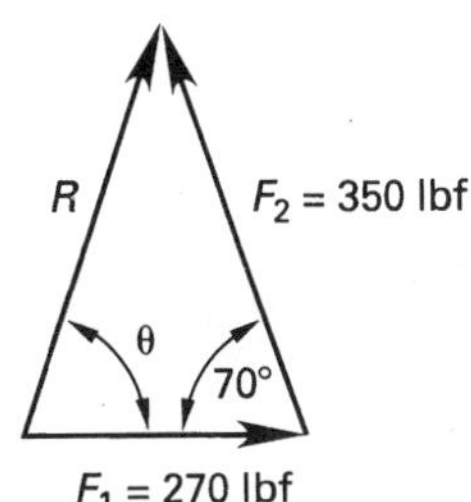

(c) algebraic solution

Figure 34.10 Finding the Resultant of Concurrent Coplanar Forces

Product Development

Figure 34.11
Law of Cosines

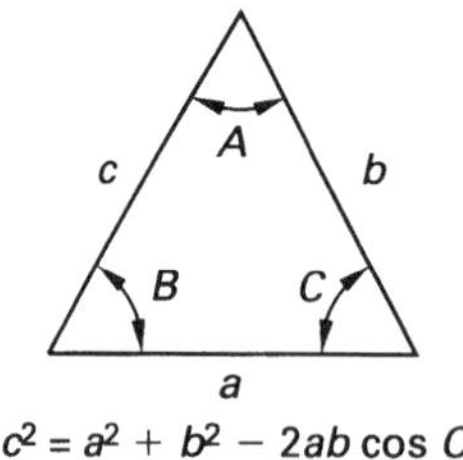

To find the magnitude of the resultant, use the law of cosines. From Fig. 34.11,

$$
\begin{aligned}
c^2 &= a^2 + b^2 - 2ab\cos C \\
R^2 &= (350\ \text{lbf})^2 + (270\ \text{lbf})^2 \\
&\quad -(2)(350\ \text{lbf})(270\ \text{lbf})\cos 70^\circ \\
R &= 361.6\ \text{lbf}
\end{aligned}
$$

To find the direction of the resultant, use the law of sines.

$$
\begin{aligned}
\frac{a}{\sin A} &= \frac{b}{\sin B} = \frac{c}{\sin C} \\
\frac{F_2}{\sin\theta} &= \frac{R}{\sin 70^\circ}
\end{aligned}
$$

$$
\begin{aligned}
\sin\theta &= \frac{F_2 \sin 70^\circ}{R} = \frac{(350\ \text{lbf})\sin 70^\circ}{361.6\ \text{lbf}} = 0.9095 \\
\theta &= \arcsin 0.9095 = 65.4^\circ
\end{aligned}
$$

Components of a Force

Just as a resultant can be found for two or more forces, so can a single force be resolved into two components. This method is often required when analyzing loads on a sloped surface (a roof, for example) and is necessary to find the horizontal and vertical reactions. As with finding resultant forces, both graphic and algebraic solutions are possible.

Example 34.7

Consider the diagonal force shown. What would be the vertical and horizontal reactions necessary to resist this force?

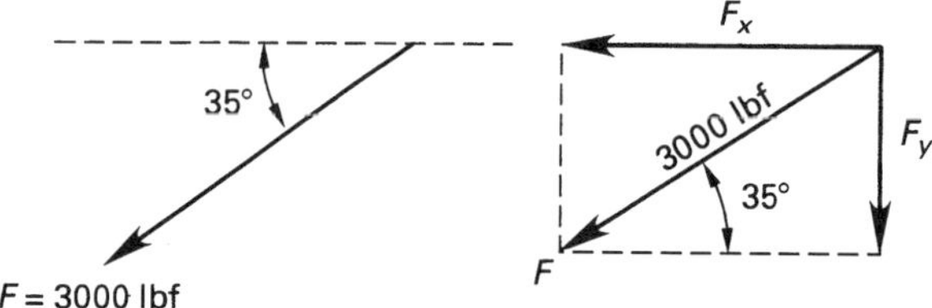

The reactions to the force would be equal in magnitude but opposite in direction to the vertical and horizontal components of the force. To solve the problem algebraically, construct a right triangle with the 3000 lbf force as the hypotenuse and the legs of the triangle as the horizontal and vertical forces.

Then,

$$
\begin{aligned}
\sin 35^\circ &= \frac{F_y}{3000\ \text{lbf}} \\
F_y &= 1721\ \text{lbf}
\end{aligned}
$$

$$
\begin{aligned}
\cos 35^\circ &= \frac{F_x}{3000\ \text{lbf}} \\
F_x &= 2457\ \text{lbf}
\end{aligned}
$$

The same solution could be obtained by drawing the triangle to scale and measuring the legs of the triangle, although this method is not as accurate.

Three or more forces can be resolved by resolving each one into its horizontal and vertical components, summing these components (taking care to be consistent with positive and negative signs), and then finding the resultant of the horizontal and vertical components with the Pythagorean theorem.

Free-Body Diagrams

In analyzing structures it is sometimes convenient to extract a portion of the structure and represent the forces acting on it with force vectors. The portion then under study is called a *free-body diagram* to which the principles of equilibrium can be applied.

Consider the simple structure shown in Fig. 34.12(a) with a single load of 3000 lbf applied at the end. Find the load in member BC.

Take member BC as a free body as shown in Fig. 34.12(b). There are three forces acting on this member: the vertical load of 3000 lbf, the force in member BC (compression), and the force through member AB (tension). Since these forces act through a common point, and since the structure is in equilibrium, construct a force triangle with the force vectors as the sides of the triangle as shown in Fig. 34.12(c).

The angle, θ, can be determined from $\arctan {}^5\!/_8 = 32°$.

Then, the force, F, in member BC is found from

$$\sin 32° = \frac{3000\ \text{lbf}}{F}$$
$$F = 5661\ \text{lbf}$$

Knowing the force in member BC, it is possible to find the horizontal and vertical components of the force using the methods described in the previous section.

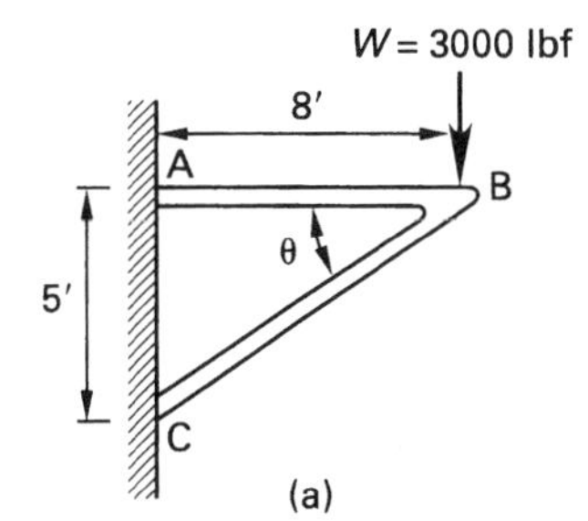

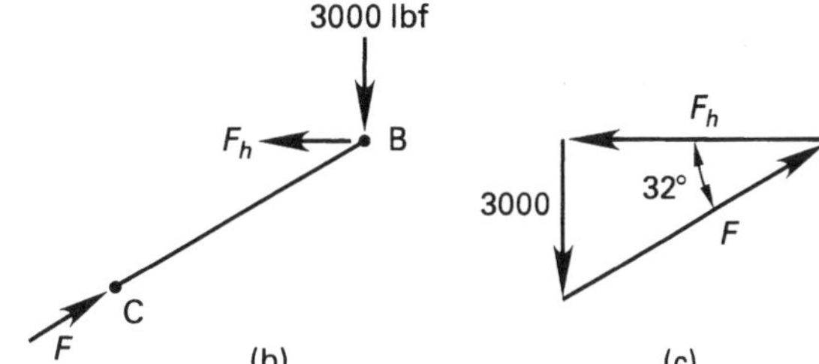

Figure 34.12
Free-Body Diagrams

Product Development

35

BEAMS AND COLUMNS

Product Development

Nomenclature

A	area	in^2	P	concentrated load	lbf
b	width of beam	in	Q	statical moment about neutral axis of the area above the plane under consideration	in^3
c	distance from extreme fiber in bending to neutral axis	in	r	radius of gyration	in
d	depth of beam	in	S	section modulus	in^3
E	modulus of elasticity	lbf/in^2	v_b	horizontal shear stress	lbf/in^2
f	allowable fiber stress in bending	lbf/in^2	V	vertical shearing force	lbf
f_b	extreme fiber stress in bending	lbf/in^2	w	uniformly distributed load	lbf/in
F_a	allowable axial stress	lbf/in^2	W	total uniformly distributed load	lbf
I	moment of inertia	in^4	x	distance along a beam length	ft
L	length	in	σ	axial stress	lbf/in^2
M	bending moment	in-lbf			

BEAMS

Basic Principles

When a simply supported beam is subjected to a load, it deflects as shown in the exaggerated diagram in Fig. 35.1(a).

Figure 35.1
Behavior of Simply Supported Beam Under Load

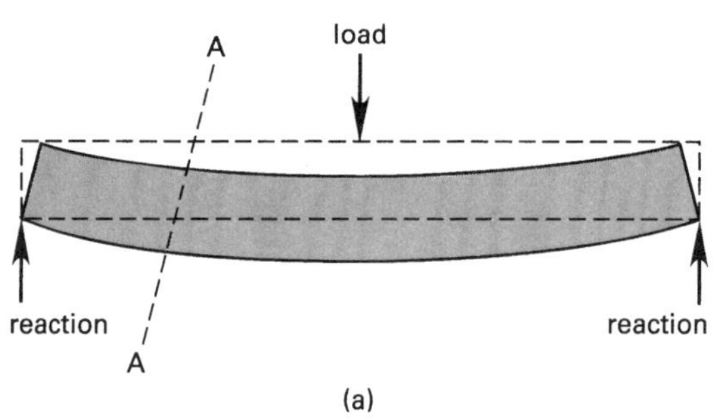

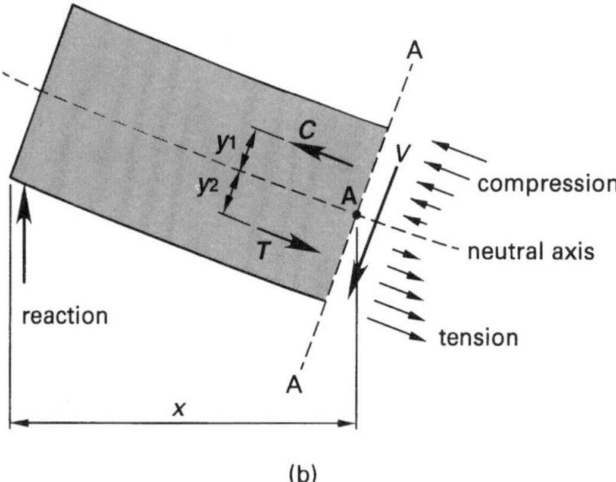

In order for this to happen, the top of the beam compresses and the bottom of the beam stretches, which causes compressive stresses to develop in the top half of the beam and tension stresses to develop in the bottom half. At the neutral axis, or centroid, which is in the geometric center of the beam if it is rectangular or symmetrical, the beam does not change length so no compressive or tension stresses are developed.

The actions occurring in the beam can be seen more clearly by taking an enlarged section of the beam to the left of an arbitrary cut as shown in Fig. 35.1(b).

In this diagram there are only three forces acting on the section: the reaction of the support, the compressive forces in the top of the beam, and the tensile forces in the bottom of the beam. If the beam is in equilibrium as discussed in Chap. 12, then all the moment forces must cancel out; those acting in a clockwise rotation must equal those acting in a counterclockwise rotation. Therefore, taking moments about point A in Fig. 35.1(b),

$$Rx = Cy_1 + Ty_2 \quad 35.1$$

$$Rx = Cy_1 + Ty_2 \quad 35.2$$

This formula represents the basic theory of bending: the internal resisting moments at any point in a beam must equal the bending moments produced by the external loads on the beam.

As shown in Fig. 35.1(b), the moment increases as the distance from the reaction increases or as the distance from the neutral axis increases (assuming the loads stay the same). Therefore, in the case of a simply supported beam, the maximum moment occurs at the center of the span and the beam is subjected to its highest bending stresses at the extreme top and bottom fibers. (*Fibers* is the general term, regardless of the beam's material.)

Therefore, in order for a beam to support loads, the material, size, and shape of the beam must be selected to sustain the resisting moments at the point on the beam where the moment is greatest. There must be some way to relate the bending moments to the actual properties of a real beam. Although the derivation will not be given, the final formula is simple.

$$\frac{M}{f_b} = \frac{I}{c} \qquad 35.3$$

Theoretically, Eq. 35.3 can be used to design a beam to resist bending forces, but it gets a little cumbersome with steel sections and unusual shapes. There is another property of every structural section that simplifies the formula even further. This is the *section modulus*, which is the ratio of the beam's moment of inertia to the distance from the neutral axis to the outermost part of the section (extreme fiber).

$$S = \frac{I}{c} \qquad 35.4$$

Substituting the value of S with Eq. 35.3 gives

$$S = \frac{M}{f_b} \qquad 35.5$$

Knowing only the maximum moment on a beam caused by a particular loading condition and the maximum allowable fiber stress (given in tables and building codes), the required section modulus can be calculated. The minimum required section to support the bending loads can be found from reference tables or manufacturers' tables. For example, the *Steel Construction Manual* published by the American Institute of Steel Construction (AISC) gives the section modulus for all beam sections. How this formula is used will be illustrated in the sample question.

Another fundamental type of stress in beams is *shear*. This is the tendency of two adjacent portions of the beam to slide past each other in a vertical direction. See Fig. 35.2(a).

There is also *horizontal shear*, which is the tendency of two adjacent portions of a beam to slide past each other in the direction parallel to the length of the beam. This tendency can readily be seen by considering that the top portions of a beam tend to compress and the bottom portions tend to stretch. See Fig. 35.2(b).

The general equation for finding horizontal shear stress is

$$v_h = \frac{VQ}{Ib} \qquad 35.6$$

Q is the statical moment discussed in Chap. 12.

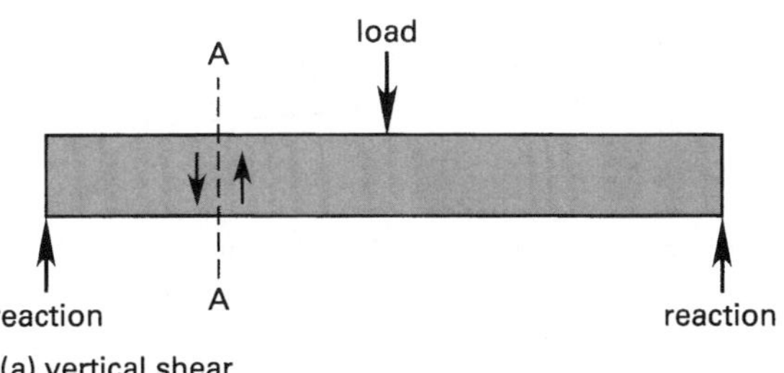

(a) vertical shear

A

A

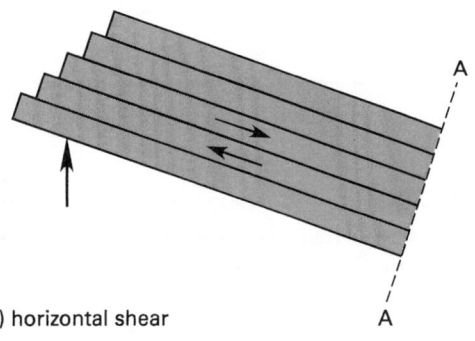

(b) horizontal shear

Figure 35.2
Shear Forces in Beams

For rectangular sections, the horizontal shear stress at middepth of the beam, where the stress is a maximum, is given by

$$v_h = \frac{3V}{2bd} \quad \text{[at neutral axis of beam]} \qquad 35.7$$

This formula is obtained by substituting applicable terms in for the specific case of a rectangular beam. Usually, horizontal shear is not a problem except in wood beams where the horizontal fibers of the wood make an ideal place for the beam to split and shear in this direction.

Another important aspect of the behavior of beams is their tendency to deflect under the action of external loads. Although beam deflection usually does not control the selection of beam size (as does bending or horizontal shear stress), it is an important factor that must be calculated. In some cases, it can be the controlling factor in determining beam size. Even though a large deflection will usually not lead to a structural collapse, excessive deflection can cause finish materials to crack, pull partitions away from the floor or ceiling, crush full-height walls, and result in a bouncy floor structure.

Figure 35.3
Types of Beams

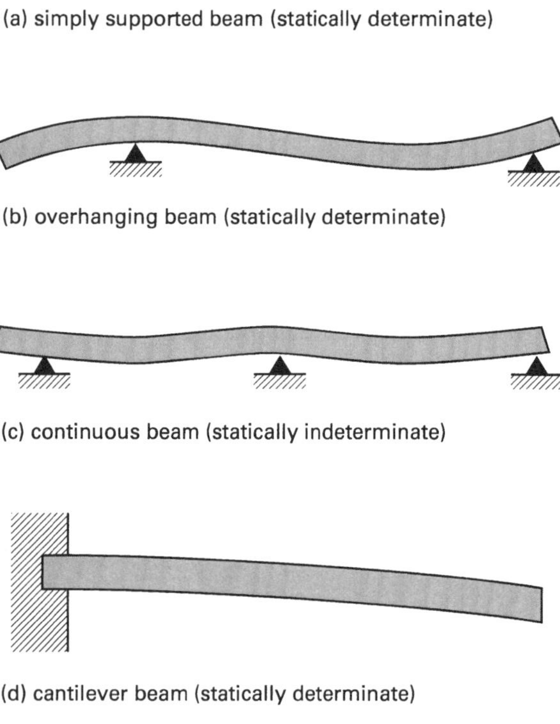

Types of Beams

There are several basic types of beams. These are shown in Fig. 35.3, with their typical deflections under load shown exaggerated.

The simply supported, overhanging, and continuous beam all have ends that are free to rotate as the load is applied. The cantilever and fixed-end beams have one or both sides restrained against rotation. A continuous beam is one that is held up by more than two supports. Of course, there are many variations of these types, such as an overhanging beam with one end fixed, but these are the most typical situations.

There are also two typical kinds of loads on building structures: *concentrated load* and *uniformly distributed load*. Graphic representations of these loads are shown in Fig. 35.4. A concentrated load is shown with an arrow and designated P, and a uniformly distributed load is shown as w pounds per linear foot or W for the total load. Loads may either be expressed in pounds or kips (1 kip is 1000 pounds). The resultant of uniformly distributed loads is at the center of the loads. This principle is particularly useful when summing moments of partial uniform loads.

It is worth noting that simply supported, overhanging, and cantilever beams are *statically determinate*. This means that the reactions can be found using the equations of equilibrium. That is, the summation of horizontal, vertical, and moment forces equals zero as described in Chap. 12. Continuous and fixed-end beams are statically indeterminate, and other, more complex calculation methods are required to find reactions in these types of beams. The ARE will deal primarily with determinate beams, so only these types will be described in this section.

One of the basic requirements for the structural design of a beam is to determine the stresses due to bending moment and vertical shear caused by the particular loading conditions. Before these are determined, however, the reactions of the supports must be calculated. The method of doing this for statically determinate beams was introduced in Chap. 12 but will be briefly reviewed.

Remember the three basic principles of equilibrium.

- The sum of all vertical forces acting on a body equals zero.
- The sum of all horizontal forces acting on a body equals zero.
- The sum of all moments acting on a body or the moment of all forces about a point on the body equals zero.

Figure 35.4
Types of Loads

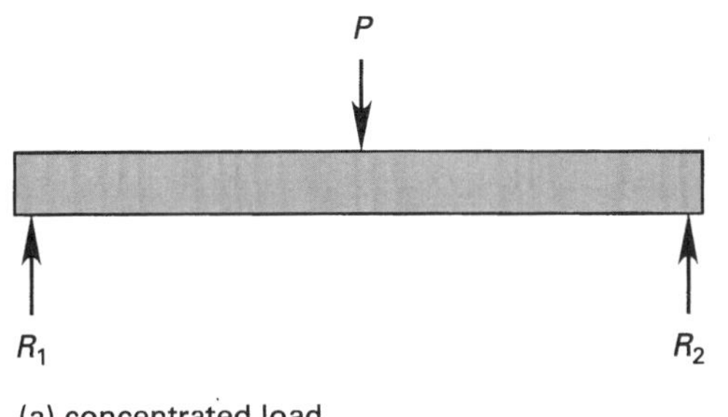

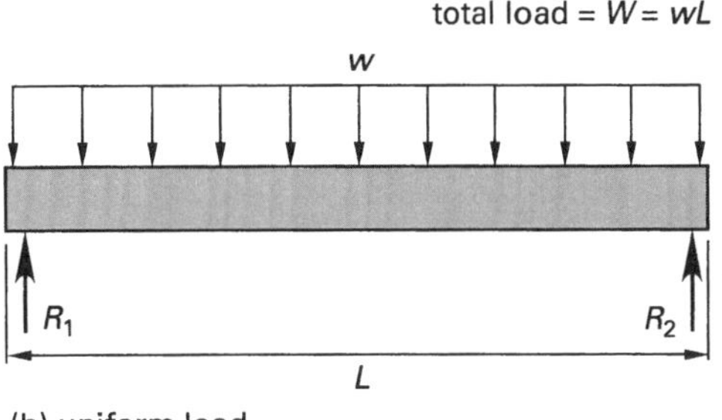

Additionally, as a matter of convention, if a force tends to cause a clockwise rotation, the resulting moment is said to be positive; if it tends to cause a counterclockwise rotation, it is said to be negative.

Example 35.1

Find the approximate reactions of the beam shown.

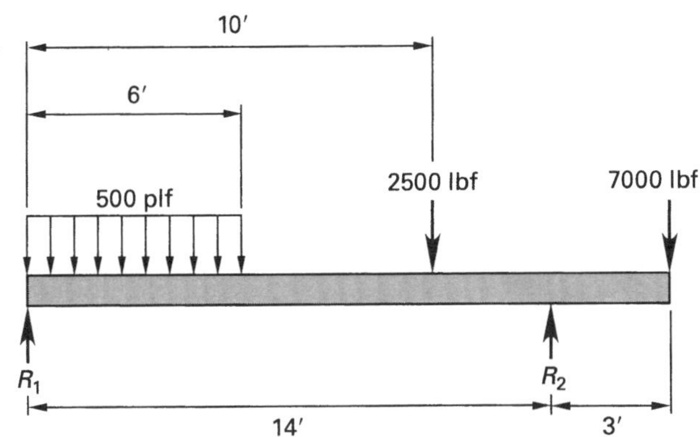

(A) $R_1 = 8000$ lbf, $R_2 = 2000$ lbf

(B) $R_1 = 9000$ lbf, $R_2 = 3600$ lbf

(C) $R_1 = 9500$ lbf, $R_2 = 500$ lbf

(D) $R_1 = 11{,}000$ lbf, $R_2 = 1600$ lbf

Solution

Sum the moments about R_1 to eliminate one of the unknowns. Each of the three loads tends to cause a clockwise rotation about point R_1, so these will be positive numbers; the resisting reaction, R_2, will tend to cause a counterclockwise rotation, so this will be negative. The moment sum of the loads and the

Product Development

resisting reaction must be zero. The total load of the uniform load is taken to act at its center, or 3 ft from R_1.

$$(3\text{ ft})\left(\left(500\ \frac{\text{lbf}}{\text{ft}}\right)(6\text{ ft})\right) + (2500\text{ lbf})(10\text{ ft}) + (7000\text{ lbf})(17\text{ ft}) - (14\text{ ft})R_2 = 0\text{ ft-lbf}$$

$$R_2 = 10{,}929\text{ lbf}\quad(11{,}000\text{ lbf})$$

Since the summation of all vertical forces must also be equal, the reaction R_1 can be found by subtracting 10,929 lbf from the total of all loads acting on the beam, or

$$\left(\left(500\ \frac{\text{lbf}}{\text{ft}}\right)(6\text{ ft}) + 2500\text{ lbf} + 7000\text{ lbf}\right) - 10{,}929\text{ lbf} = 1571\text{ lbf}\quad(1600\text{ lbf})$$

The same answer for R_1 can be found by summing moments about reaction R_2.

Once all the loads and reactions are known, shear and moment diagrams can be drawn. These are graphic representations of the value of the shear and moment at all points on the beam.

Although it is not critical to know the values at every point on the beam, there are certain important points that are of interest in designing the beam—mainly where the shear and moment are at their maximum values and where they are zero.

The answer is (D).

Shear Diagrams

A shear diagram is a graphic representation of the values of the *vertical shear* anywhere along a beam. To find the values, take a section at any point and algebraically sum the reactions and loads to the left of the section. The same answer can be found by taking values to the right of the section, but the convention for both shear and moment is to work from left to right. Also by convention, upward forces are considered positive and downward forces are considered negative. The standard designation for shear is V.

Figure 35.5
Shear Diagram of Uniformly Loaded Beam

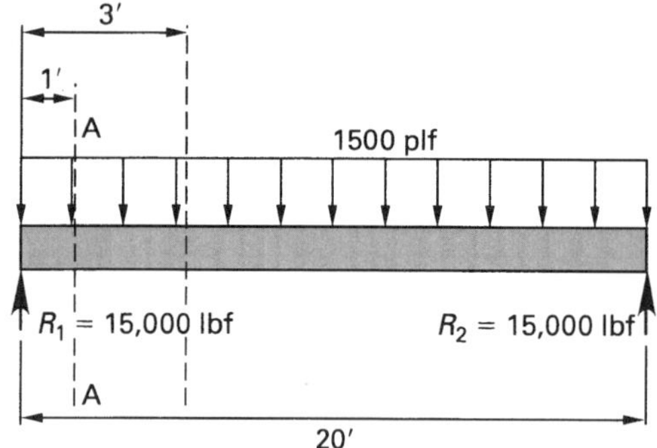

(a) beam loading and reactions

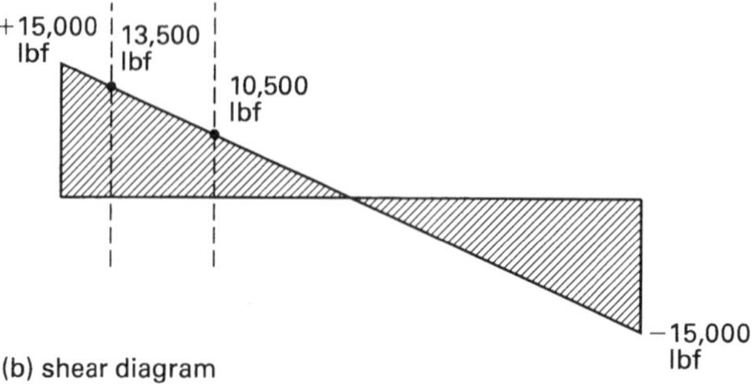

(b) shear diagram

Example 35.2

What is the vertical shear at points 4 ft and 10 ft to the right of reaction R_1 as shown?

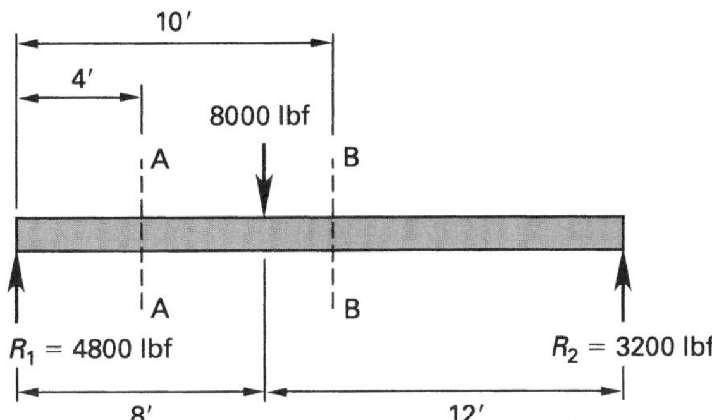

(a) beam loading and reactions

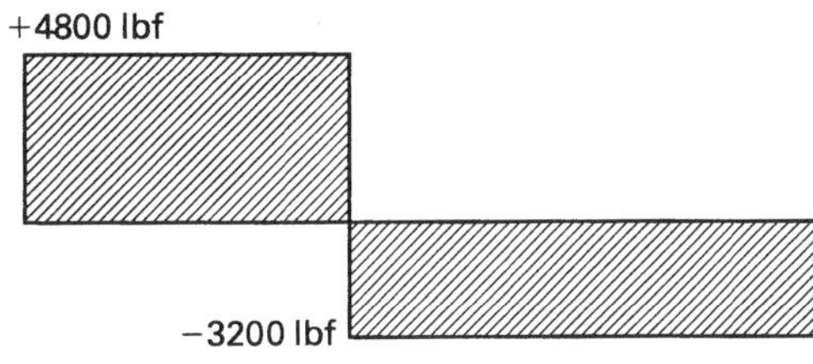

(b) shear diagram

Solution

First, compute the reaction using the summation of moments as discussed previously. R_1 is 4800 lbf, and R_2 is 3200 lbf.

Consider the point 4 ft from the left reaction marked as A-A in the sketch. At this point there is only the reaction of 4800 lbf acting in an upward direction, so the shear is 4800 lbf. At the point 10 ft from the reaction there are two forces to the left of the section, the reaction of +4800 lbf and the load of −8000 lbf, for a net shear of −3200 lbf. Notice that this is exactly the same as the reaction R_2. This makes sense because there are no other loads and reactions, so the summation of all vertical loads must equal zero as dictated by the principles of equilibrium.

To draw the shear diagram of a beam, first draw the beam and its loads to scale as shown in the upper portion of the sketch. Below the beam sketch, draw a horizontal line the same length as the beam and decide on a convenient vertical scale to represent the loading. Beginning from the left, the values of the shear are plotted above and below this line: the positive values above and the negative values below. The lower portion of the sketch shows the shear diagram for the beam.

Notice two things about the shear diagram. First, when there are no intervening loads between a reaction and a load (or between two loads), the portion of the shear diagram between them is a horizontal line. Second, a concentrated load or reaction causes the shear diagram to change abruptly in the vertical direction. Knowing these two facts makes it easy to draw a shear diagram by calculating shear at a few points and then just connecting the lines.

A uniformly distributed load creates a sightly different looking shear diagram. Consider the same beam loaded with a uniform load of 1500 plf. See Fig. 35.5. The total load is (1500 plf)(20 ft), or 30,000 lbf, which is equally distributed between the two reactions. Just at the left reaction R_1, the only force is the reaction of +15,000 lbf. Beginning here, for the remainder of the beam, the uniform load acts in a downward direction. At a point 1 ft from the reaction, the shear is 15,000 lbf − (1 ft)(1500 plf) = 13,500 lbf. At a point 3 ft from the reaction, the shear is 15,000 lbf − (3 ft)(1500 plf), or 10,500 lbf. At the midpoint of the span, the shear is zero and begins to be a negative value because the accumulating load is larger than the reaction R_1. At reaction R_2, the positive value of the reaction brings the shear back to zero, which is consistent with the principles of equilibrium.

A uniform load creates a shear diagram with a uniformly sloping line. In the case of the example shown in Fig. 35.5, simply calculate the shears at the reactions, plot the one on the left as positive and the one on the right as negative, and connect the two points with a straight line. If the diagram is drawn to scale, it is possible to find the shear at any point by simply scaling the drawing. For a more exact value, use the principle of similar triangles to find the shear at any distance along the beam.

A shear diagram provides two important pieces of information vital to designing a beam: the *maximum shear* and the point on the beam where the value of shear is zero (where maximum moment occurs and where the beam has its greatest tendency to fail in bending). In the case of Ex. 35.2, the maximum shear is 4800 lbf; in Fig. 35.5, the maximum is 15,000 lbf.

Figure 35.6
Relationship of Shear and Moment Diagrams

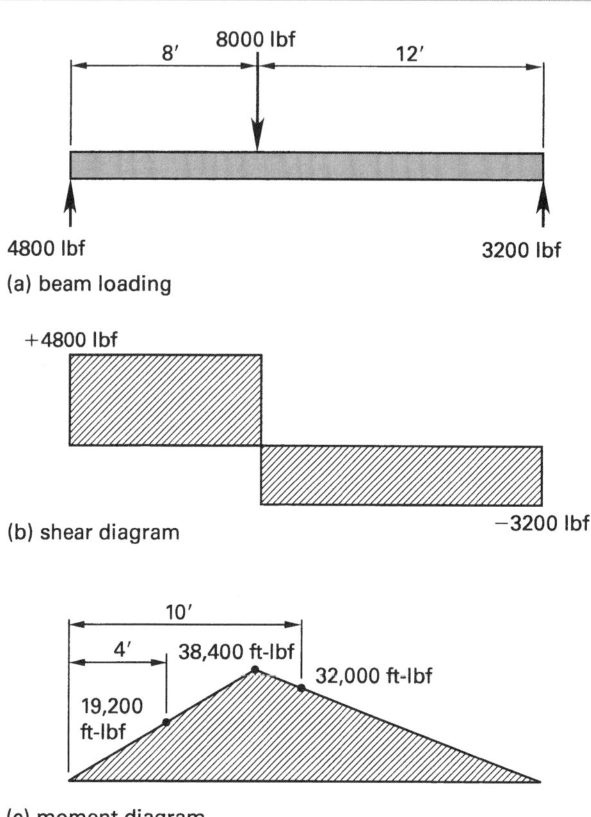

Moment Diagrams

A *moment diagram* is a graphic representation of the moment at all points along a beam. To find the moment at any point, remember that the bending moment is the algebraic sum of the moments of the forces to the left of the section under consideration and that moment is the value of force times distance. As mentioned in Chap. 12, moments tending to cause a clockwise rotation are considered positive, and those causing a counterclockwise rotation are considered negative.

Example 35.3

Using the same beam and loading as shown in Ex. 35.2, find the moments at sections A-A and B-B.

Solution

To visualize the situation a little easier, draw free-body diagrams of the two conditions. See the accompanying illustration. Of course, the moment at the reaction is zero since the moment arm distance is zero. At point A-A, 4 ft from the left reaction, the moment is

$$(4\ \text{ft})(4800\ \text{lbf}) = 19{,}200\ \text{ft-lbf}$$

At point B-B, the moment is

$$(4800 \text{ lbf})(10 \text{ ft}) - (8000 \text{ lbf})(2 \text{ ft}) = 32{,}000 \text{ ft-lbf}$$

Because the maximum moment occurs where the shear diagram crosses zero, it is wise to calculate moment at this point also. From the shear diagram shown in Ex. 35.2, this is the point where the concentrated load occurs. The moment just to the left of this point is (4800 lbf)(8 ft), or 38,400 ft-lbf. Just to the right of this point the concentrated load begins to act in a counterclockwise rotation, so the moment begins to decrease from the maximum until it is again zero at the righthand support.

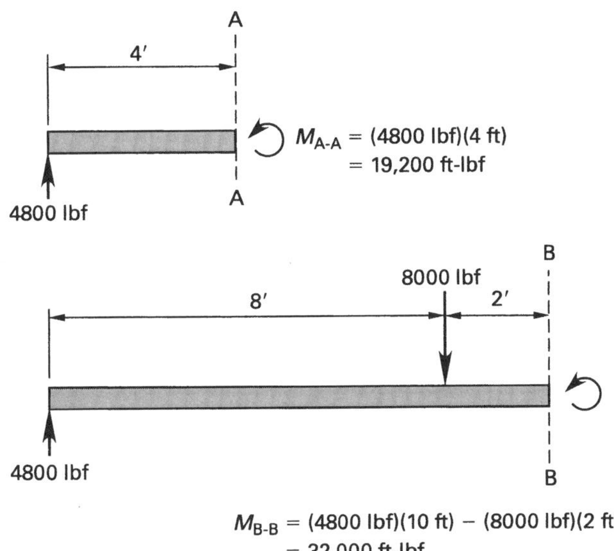

To draw the moment diagram, calculate moments at several points and connect them with a line in a way similar to drawing the shear diagram. This is shown in Fig. 35.6 along with the beam loading and shear diagrams from Ex. 35.2 repeated to show the relationship between the three drawings. Positive moment is shown above the base line, and negative moment (if any) is shown below the line. Negative moment will be illustrated in a later example.

As with shear diagrams, notice some important facts about the moment diagram. First, the *maximum moment* does occur where the shear diagram passes through zero, and this is indicated by the highest point of the moment diagram. Second, when the shear diagram is a constant horizontal line between two concentrated loads or reactions, the moment diagram between these two points is a straight, constant sloped line. Third, where the shear changes abruptly as shown by a vertical line, the slope of the line representing moment also changes abruptly.

Also note, as in the next example, that when there is a uniformly distributed load and the shear diagram is a sloped line, the moment diagram will be composed of one or more parabolic curves.

Example 35.4

Draw the moment diagram of the example previously shown in Fig. 35.5.

Solution

Since the distance of the moment arm at each reaction is zero, the moment at these two points will also be zero. Start with the maximum moment as it will occur where the shear diagram passes through zero. The moment is

$$\begin{aligned} M &= (15{,}000 \text{ lbf})(10 \text{ ft}) - \left(1500 \ \frac{\text{lbf}}{\text{ft}}\right)(10 \text{ ft})(5 \text{ ft}) \\ &= 75{,}000 \text{ ft-lbf} \end{aligned}$$

Therefore, the moment diagram is as follows. The beam loading, reactions, and shear diagrams are repeated in the sketch for convenience, along with the moment diagram to illustrate the relationship among the three.

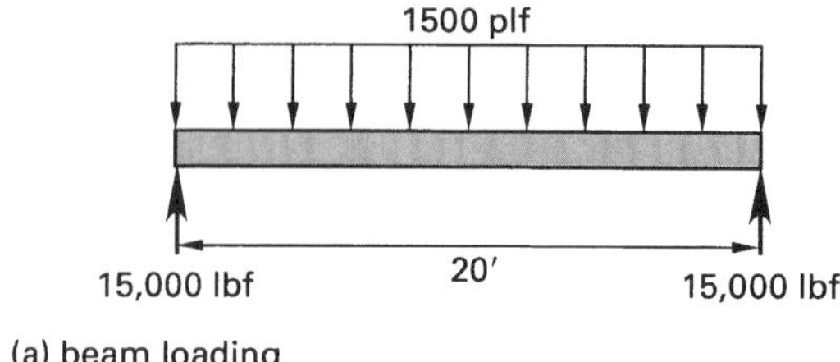

(a) beam loading

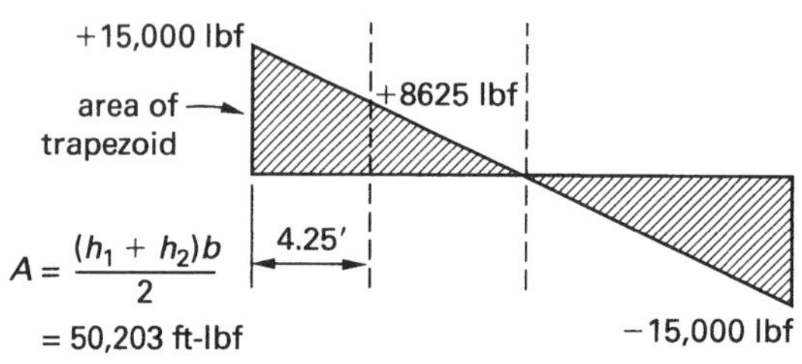

(b) shear diagram

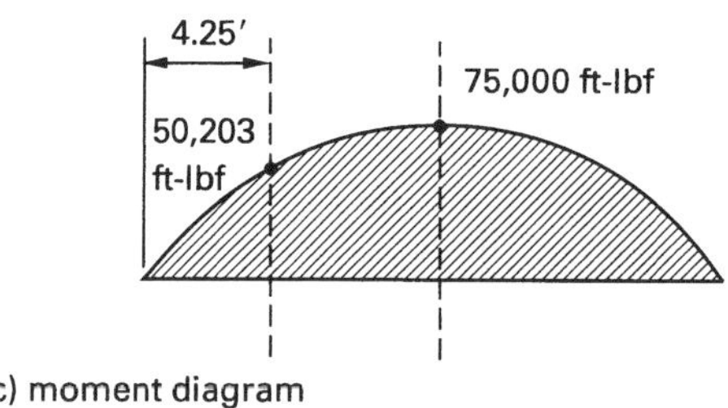

(c) moment diagram

When calculating moments due to uniform loads, remember that the moments' resultant is at the center of the loads and therefore the moment of those loads is calculated as if the total load were concentrated at the midpoints of the loads. This is why the uniform load on the beam is multiplied by 5 ft in the preceding calculation. It is recorded as a negative number because it tends to cause a counterclockwise rotation about the center of the beam where moments are taken.

To find other points of the moment diagram curve it is possible to calculate several moments and connect the points with a smooth curve, but the curve of a moment diagram of a uniformly loaded beam is parabolic so this is usually not necessary.

Note one final interesting point. The area of the shear diagram between two points along the beam is numerically equal to the change in moment of the beam between the same two points. Thus, at the midpoint of the beam as shown in the sketch, the area of the triangle is (15,000)(10)/2, or 75,000 ft-lbf, exactly the same as calculating it with moment arms. Since the shear diagram is drawn to scale in pound units in the vertical direction and foot units in the horizontal direction, the result is in foot-pounds.

In the example shown in the sketch, finding the moment at a point 4.25 ft from the left reaction would involve finding the area of the trapezoid with a height of 4.25 ft, the larger base of 15,000 lbf, and the smaller base of 8625 lbf. This latter figure can easily be found by the law of proportions of similar triangles.

Example 35.5

Find the reactions and draw the shear and moment diagrams of the beam shown.

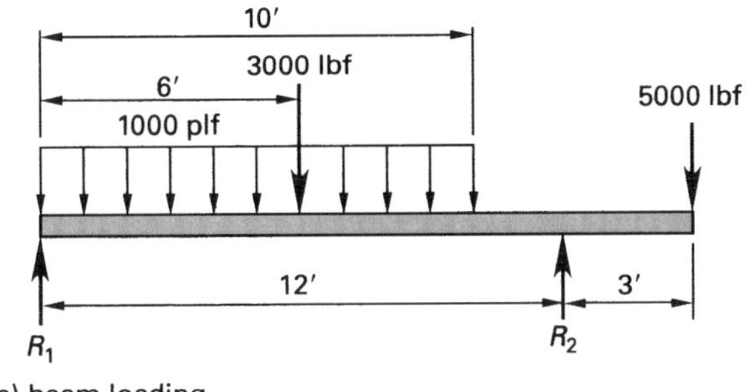

(a) beam loading

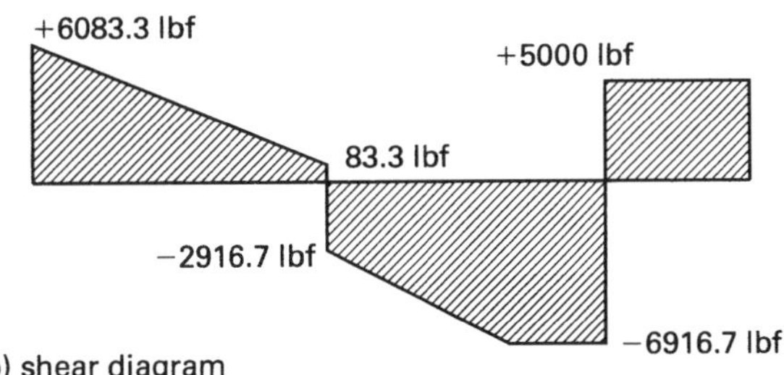

(b) shear diagram

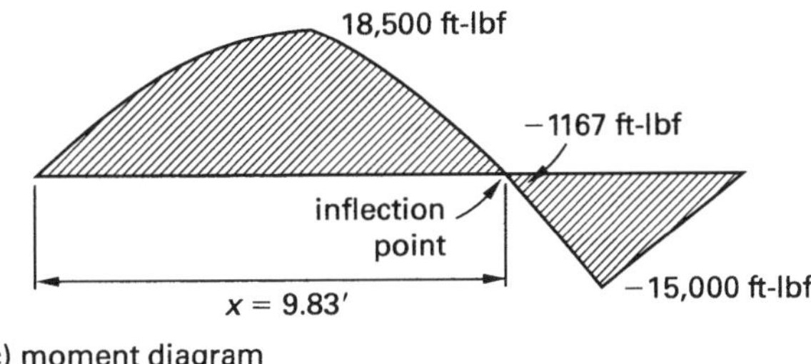

(c) moment diagram

Solution

This example is more complicated than previous ones and illustrates negative moment and combinations of load types.

First, find the reactions. As before, find the sum of moments about one of the reactions and set them equal to zero. About reaction R_1, the equation is

$$\begin{aligned}\left(1000\ \frac{\text{lbf}}{\text{ft}}\right)(10\ \text{ft})(5\ \text{ft}) + (3000\ \text{lbf})(6\ \text{ft})& \\ -R_2(12\ \text{ft}) + (5000\ \text{lbf})(15\ \text{ft}) &= 0 \\ 50{,}000\ \frac{\text{lbf}}{\text{ft}} + 18{,}000\ \frac{\text{lbf}}{\text{ft}} + 75{,}000\ \frac{\text{lbf}}{\text{ft}} &= R_2(12\ \text{ft}) \\ R_2 &= 11{,}916.7\ \text{lbf}\end{aligned}$$

R_1 is the difference between the total load and R_2, or 6083.3 lbf.

Next, find the vertical shears and draw the shear diagram.

Starting with the left reaction, the shear is 6083.3 lbf in the upward direction. The shear just to the left of the 3000 lbf load is the sum of the loads and reactions, so at this point it is

$$V = 6083.3 \text{ lbf} - \left(1000 \, \frac{\text{lbf}}{\text{ft}}\right)(6 \text{ ft}) = 83.3 \text{ lbf}$$

At the 3000 lbf load, the shear is

$$\begin{aligned} V &= 6083.3 \text{ lbf} - \left(1000 \, \frac{\text{lbf}}{\text{ft}}\right)(6 \text{ ft}) \\ &\quad -3000 \text{ lbf} = -2916.7 \text{ lbf} \end{aligned}$$

Since the load between R_1 and the 3000 lbf load is uniformly distributed, the two points connect with a sloped line as shown in the sketch. The shear at the end of the uniform load is found in the same way. From this point to the reaction R_2 there are no loads or reactions (ignoring the weight of the beam), so the line is horizontal. At the support, reaction R_2, the load changes abruptly in the magnitude of the reaction, or 11,916.7 lbf, which is added to the negative shear of 6916.7 lbf, giving a net value of +5000 lbf.

No other loads are encountered until the 5000 lbf load at the end of the overhang. Since it is in the downward direction, it is negative and brings the shear to zero at the end of the beam, which is the expected result because of the principles of equilibrium.

Finally, calculate and draw the moment diagram. In this example there are two points where the shear diagram crosses zero, so there will be two maximum moments: one positive, as in a simply supported beam, and one negative. A negative moment simply means that the beam is bending upward above a support instead of downward because of the way the loads are applied. Both moment values need to be calculated to determine which one is the greater of the two because it is not always clear from visual inspection. The highest value is the one that must be used to design the beam.

There are two ways to find the moments. One way is to draw free-body diagrams at each point of interest and take the moments about that point as was done in previous examples.

Another, sometimes simpler way is to find the area of the shear diagram between points of interest.

To find the maximum moment at the 3000 lbf load, find the area of the trapezoid with the bases of 6083.3 lbf and 83.3 lbf and the height of 6 ft.

$$\begin{aligned} A &= \tfrac{1}{2}(b_1 + b_2)h \\ &= \left(\frac{1}{2}\right)(6083.3 \text{ lbf} + 83.3 \text{ lbf})(6 \text{ ft}) \\ &= 18{,}500 \text{ ft-lbf} \end{aligned}$$

To find the moment 10 ft to the right of reaction, R_1, find the area of the trapezoid from the 3000 lbf load to the end of the uniform load and subtract it from the previous moment. This is because this area is below the baseline of the shear diagram and is negative.

$$A = \left(\frac{1}{2}\right)(2916.7 \text{ lbf} + 6916.7 \text{ lbf})(4 \text{ ft}) = 19{,}667 \text{ ft-lbf}$$

The moment is, therefore,

$$18{,}500 \text{ ft-lbf} - 19{,}667 \text{ ft-lbf} = -1167 \text{ ft-lbf}$$

Next, find the area of the rectangle from the end of the uniform load to the reaction R_2 (13,833 ft-lbf) and subtract this from the last value. The maximum negative moment is then 15,000 ft-lbf.

Connect the points just found. The lines connecting points below a sloped line in the shear diagram will be sections of parabolas, and the lines below horizontal lines in the shear diagram will be straight sloped lines as shown in the moment diagram of the sketch.

Notice that the slopes of the parabolas change abruptly where the concentrated load of 3000 lbf occurs. Also notice that the curve of the moment diagram between the 6 ft point and 10 ft point crosses the zero line a little to the left of the 10 ft point. Where this occurs in a moment diagram is called the *inflection point.* Knowing where this point occurs is often important in designing beams. For instance, the inflection point is where reinforcing rods in concrete beams are bent to change from carrying positive moment to negative moment. In this example, the inflection point just happens to be very close to the end of the uniform load, but it can occur anywhere depending on the distribution of loads.

To find the inflection point, let the distance from reaction R_1 be x. Then, knowing the moment at this point is zero, draw a free-body diagram cut at this point, sum the moments to the left of this point, and set those moments equal to zero.

$$\begin{aligned}(6083\ \text{lbf})x - \left(1000\ \frac{\text{lbf}}{\text{ft}}\right)x\left(\frac{x}{2}\right)& \\ -(3000\ \text{lbf})(x - 6\ \text{ft}) &= 0\ \text{ft-lbf}\end{aligned}$$

This reduces to the quadratic equation.

$$\left(500\ \frac{\text{lbf}}{\text{ft}}\right)x^2 - (3083\ \text{lbf})x - 18{,}000\ \text{ft-lbf} = 0\ \text{ft-lbf}$$

Using the general formula for the solution of a quadratic equation.

$$\begin{aligned}x &= \frac{-b \pm \sqrt{b^2 - 4ac}}{2a} \\ &= \frac{-(-3083\ \text{lbf}) \pm \sqrt{\begin{array}{c}(-3083\ \text{lbf}) - (4)\left(500\ \frac{\text{lbf}}{\text{ft}}\right) \\ \times(-18{,}000\ \text{ft-lbf})\end{array}}}{(2)\left(500\ \frac{\text{lbf}}{\text{ft}}\right)} \\ &= 9.83\ \text{ft}\end{aligned}$$

Deflection

Deflection is the change in vertical position of a beam due to a load. The amount of deflection depends on the load, the beam length, the moment of inertia of the beam, and the beam's modulus of elasticity. Generally, the amount of *allowable deflection* is limited by building code requirements or practical requirements such as how much a beam can deflect before ceiling surfaces begin to crack or before the spring of the floor becomes annoying to occupants.

In many cases, the deflection due to live load is limited to $1/360$ of the beam's span, whereas the deflection due to total load (dead load plus live load) is usually limited to $1/240$ of the beam's span. If there are two or more loads on a beam, such as a uniform load and concentrated load, the deflections caused by the loads individually are added to find total deflection.

Deriving the formulas for beam deflection under various loads is a complex mathematical process. However, standard formulas for deflection as well as shear and moment are given in reference sources such as the AISC *Steel Construction Manual.* These apply to beams of any material. A few of the more common loading situations with accompanying formulas are given in Fig. 35.7.

Figure 35.7
Static Formulas for Some Common Loads

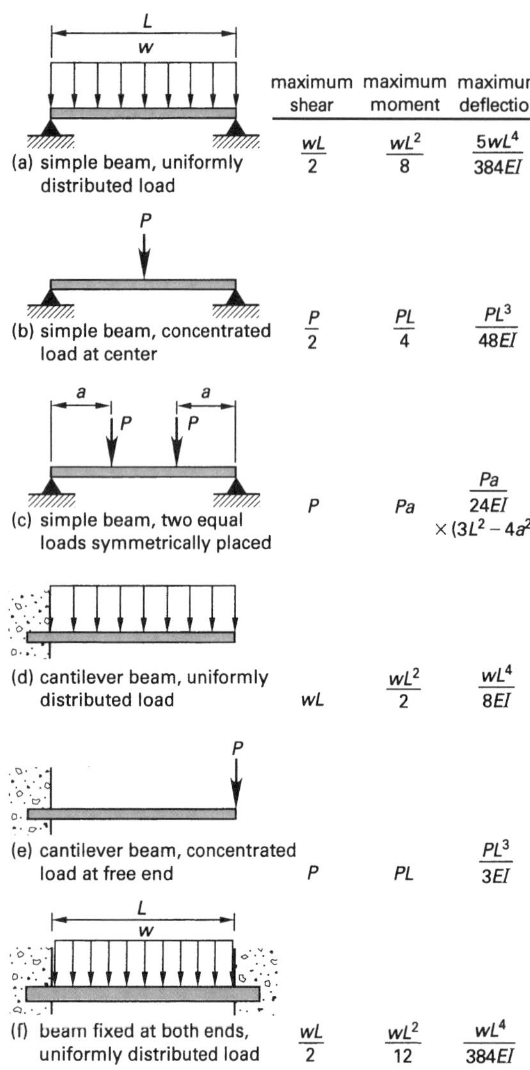

L
w
maximum shear
maximum moment
maximum deflection
(a) simple beam, uniformly distributed load
wL/2
wL²/8
5wL⁴/384EI
P
(b) simple beam, concentrated load at center
P/2
PL/4
PL³/48EI
a
a
P
P
(c) simple beam, two equal loads symmetrically placed
P
Pa
Pa/24EI × (3L² − 4a²)
(d) cantilever beam, uniformly distributed load
wL
wL²/2
wL⁴/8EI
P
(e) cantilever beam, concentrated load at free end
P
PL
PL³/3EI
L
w
(f) beam fixed at both ends, uniformly distributed load
wL/2
wL²/12
wL⁴/384EI

COLUMNS

Basic Principles

Although columns resist axial compressive forces, there are other considerations that must be taken into account. The first is the tendency of a long, slender column to *buckle* under a load. Even though the column's material and size can withstand the load according to Eq. 35.8, the column will fail in buckling under a much smaller load.

$$F_a = \frac{P}{A} \qquad 35.8$$

The second consideration is the *combined loading* that occurs on many columns. This can be due to the normal compressive force plus lateral load, such as wind, on the column. Combined loading can also be induced by an eccentric compressive load, one that is applied off the centroidal axis of the column. In this case, the column acts a little like a beam standing on end with one face in compression and the other in tension. The compressive forces due to the eccentric load add to the normal compressive stresses on one side and subtract from the normal compressive stresses on the other. The *flexural stress* caused by eccentricity is given by the flexure formula (see Eq. 35.3).

$$f = \frac{Mc}{I} \qquad 35.9$$

Because of the inexact nature of how columns respond to loads, various column formulas have been developed and adopted for different conditions and for various materials. These have been established through experience and are standardized in building codes. The methods for designing columns in different materials will be discussed in the individual chapters on specific structural materials. This chapter focuses on the general principles of column design.

Radius of Gyration

The ability of a column to withstand a load is dependent on the column's length, cross-sectional shape and area, and moment of inertia. There is a convenient way to combine the properties of area and moment of inertia that is useful in column design. This is called the *radius of gyration* and is expressed with the following formula.

$$r = \sqrt{\frac{I}{A}} \qquad 35.10$$

For nonsymmetric sections, such as rectangular columns, there are two radii of gyration, one for each axis. The one of greater interest in column design is the lesser radius of gyration since it is in this axis that a column will fail by buckling. For example, a 4 × 8 wood column will bend under a load parallel to the 4 in dimension before it will bend in the other dimension.

Slenderness Ratio

The slenderness ratio is the most important factor in column design and is equal to

$$\text{slenderness ratio} = \frac{L}{r} \qquad 35.11$$

The slenderness ratio is used in a basic equation that applies to all columns and gives the maximum stress a column can resist without buckling. It is called *Euler's equation* and predicts the actual load just prior to failure.

$$\frac{P}{A} = \frac{\pi^2 E}{\left(\frac{L}{r}\right)^2} \quad \text{[Euler's equation]} \qquad 35.12$$

However, because various materials behave differently, end conditions vary, and slenderness ratios affect loads, this equation is theoretical and not used without modification in actual column design. For simple wood column design, for example, the thinnest dimension of the column is used in place of the least radius of gyration.

Example 35.6

A 4 × 6 structural steel column is 9 ft 6 in long. The colum's least radius of gyration is 1.21 in. What is approximately the column's slenderness ratio?

(A) 94

(B) 113

(C) 135

(D) 162

Solution

The slenderness ratio is

$$\frac{L}{r} = \frac{(9.5 \text{ ft})\left(12 \ \frac{\text{in}}{\text{ft}}\right)}{1.21 \text{ in}} = 94.2 \quad (94)$$

The answer is (A).

Categories of Columns

Compression members are categorized into three groups based on their slenderness ratios: *short compressive members*, *intermediate columns*, and *slender columns*. For short compressive members, the basic stress formula $\sigma = P/A$ holds true (that is, column buckling is not a problem). For slender columns, Euler's equation generally holds true, modified to account for safety factors and end conditions. For intermediate columns, there are several formulas that attempt to predict column behavior. Building codes and sound engineering practices give the formulas used in actual design for various materials. These will be discussed in later chapters on specific materials.

End Conditions

The method by which the ends of a column are restrained affects the column's load-carrying capacity. These methods are shown diagrammatically in Fig. 35.8. The end of any column may be in one of four states: it may be fixed against both rotation and movement from side to side (translation), it may be able to rotate but not translate, it may be able to move from side to side but not rotate, or it may be free to both rotate and translate.

The strongest type of column is one that is fixed against both rotation and translation; the weakest is one that is free to move at one end. Column formulas generally assume a condition in which both ends are fixed in translation but free to rotate. When other conditions exist, the load-carrying capacity is increased or decreased so the allowable stress must be increased or decreased or the slenderness ratio increased. For example, for steel columns, a factor, K, is used to multiply by the actual length to give an effective length. The theoretical K-values are listed in Fig. 35.8, but more conservative recommended values are often used. For steel design these are discussed in Chap. 41.

Figure 35.8
End Conditions for Columns

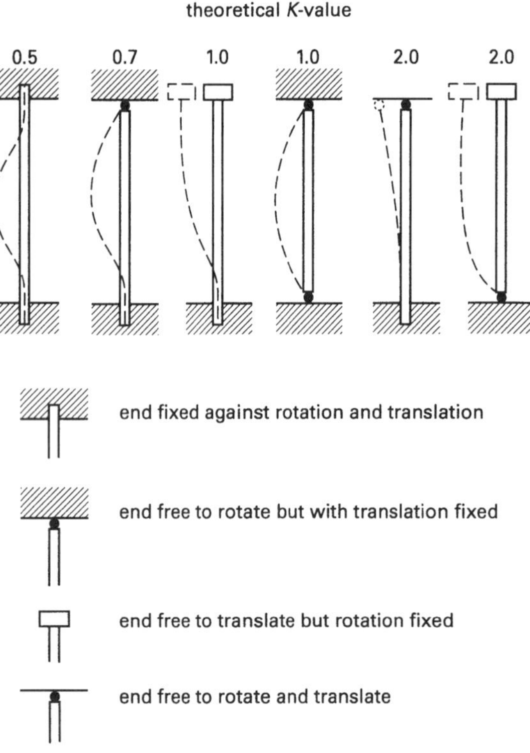

36

TRUSSES

BASIC PRINCIPLES

A *truss* is a structure generally composed of straight members to form a number of triangles with the connections arranged so that the stresses in the members are either in tension or compression. Trusses are very efficient structures and are used as an economical method of spanning long distances. Typical depth-to-span ratios range from 1:10 to 1:20, with flat trusses requiring less overall depth than pitched trusses. Spans generally range from 40 ft to 200 ft. However, some wood-trussed rafters are used to span shorter distances.

Figure 36.1
Types of Trusses

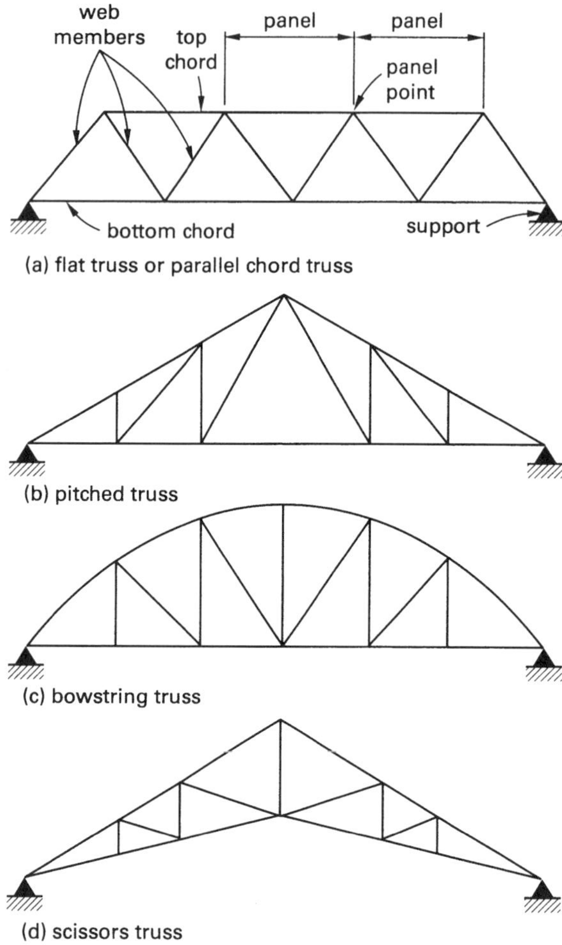

Some typical truss types are shown in Fig. 36.1 with nomenclature of the various parts. Generally, roof loads on a truss are transferred from the decking to purlins, which are attached to the truss at the panel points to avoid putting any bending stresses in the top chord of the truss. If concentrated loads are placed between panel points or uniform loads are applied directly to the top chords, the member must be designed for the axial loading as well as for bending.

Trusses act much like beams in that there is usually compression in the top chords and tension in the bottom chords, with the web members being either in compression or tension, depending on the loading and type of truss used. Like a beam, the forces in a parallel chord truss increase toward the center. In a bowstring truss, on the other hand, the chord forces remain fairly constant because the truss depth varies from a minimum at the supports to a maximum in the center.

In designing a trussed roof, trusses are placed from 10 ft to 40 ft on center, depending on the loads and the spanning capabilities of the purlins. In residential and light commercial construction, trussed rafters made of 2 × 4 or 2 × 6 members are often placed 2 ft on center. Open-web steel joists are usually placed 2 ft to 3 ft on center for floor construction and 4 ft to 6 ft on center for roof construction, depending on the spanning capabilities of the roof deck. Since trusses are thin and deep and subject to buckling, they must be laterally supported with bridging along the bottom chord. In some cases, diagonal bracing is required along the top chords of pitched roofs if the roof deck is not adequate to act as a diaphragm.

Individual truss members are designed as columns if they are in compression. If in tension, they must have adequate net area (after deducting for the area of fasteners) to resist the unit tensile stress allowed by the material being used. If concentrated loads or uniform loads are placed on any chord member between the panel points, the member must also be designed to resist bending stresses.

As with columns, the effective length of chord members in compression is important; that is, Kl in which K is determined by the restraint of the ends of the members. For steel trusses, K is usually taken as 1.0 so the effective length is the same as the actual length. Also for steel trusses, the ratio of length to least radius of gyration, l/r, should not exceed 120 for main members and 200 for secondary and bracing members.

When designing steel trusses with double angles as is usually the case, allowable concentric loads and other properties for various double-angle combinations can be found in the American Institute of Steel Construction *Steel Construction Manual* (*AISC Manual*). Given the compressive load, the length of the member, and the strength of the steel, the size and thickness of a double-angle combination can be determined.

For members in tension, the net area must be determined. This is the actual area of the member less the area of bolt holes, which is taken to be $\frac{1}{8}$ in larger than the diameter of the bolt.

Regardless of material, truss members should be designed so they are concentric; that is, so the member is symmetric on both sides of the centroid axis in the plane of the truss. To accomplish this, steel truss members are often built with two angles back-to-back separated by $\frac{3}{8}$ in or $\frac{1}{2}$ in gusset plates, with tee sections, or with wide flange sections. See Fig. 36.2.

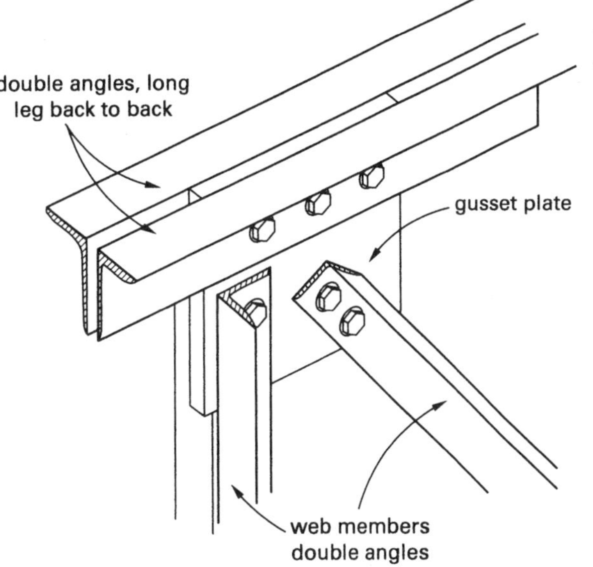

Figure 36.2 Typical Steel Truss Construction

With light loads, bars or rods can be used for tension members. Wood trusses are often constructed with web members between double top and bottom chord members or with all members in the same plane connected with steel gusset plates. See Fig. 36.3.

The centroidal axes of all intersecting members must also meet at a point to avoid eccentric loading. For steel members composed of angles, it is standard practice to have the gage lines rather than the centroidal axes meet at a common point as shown in Fig. 36.4. The *gage line* is a standard dimension from the corner edge of an angle to the centerline of the bolt hole or holes. Its value depends on the size of the angle, and the standard dimensions are published in the *AISC Manual*.

TRUSS ANALYSIS

The first step in designing a truss is to determine the loads in the various members. Before reviewing the methods to do this, there are some general guidelines to know for truss analysis.

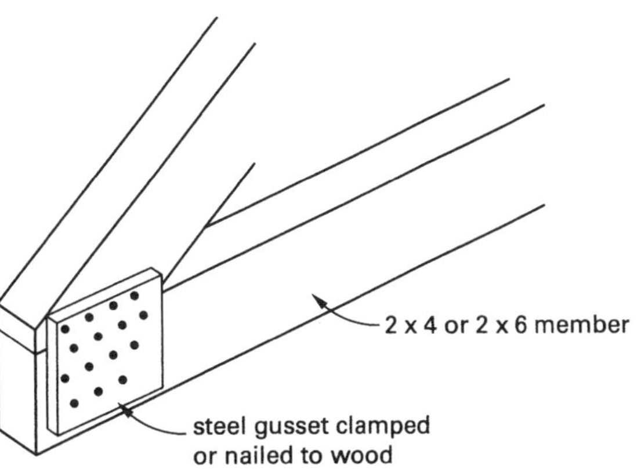

Figure 36.3 Typical Wood Trussed Rafter Construction

- The sum of vertical forces at any point equals zero.
- The sum of horizontal forces at any point equals zero.
- The sum of the moments about any point equals zero.
- Forces in each member are shown by an arrow away from a joint or cut section if in tension and toward a joint or cut section if in compression.
- Forces acting upward or to the right are considered positive (+). Forces acting downward or to the left are considered negative (−).
- All forces should be indicated acting in their known direction. If the direction is unknown when beginning the analysis, show the force in tension, acting away from the joint or cut section. If the calculation of the force is negative, this indicates that the direction is reversed.
- For analysis, trusses are assumed to have pivoting or rolling supports to avoid other stresses at these points.

Product Development

Figure 36.4
Alignment of Lines of Force in a Truss

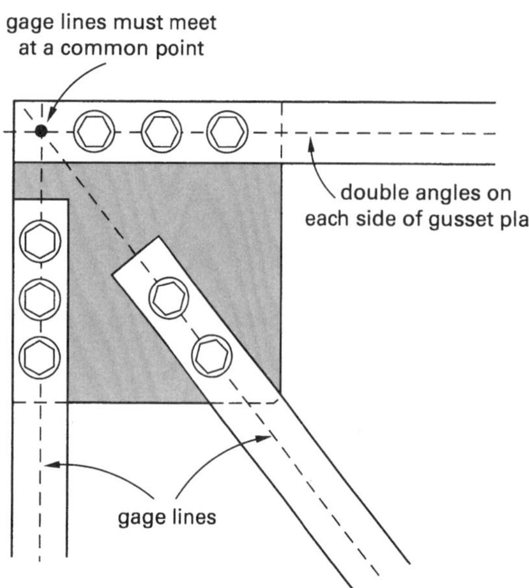

Since truss analysis often involves resolving forces into their horizontal and vertical components and finding the resultant of two forces, the following guidelines will be helpful. See Fig. 36.5.

The x-component of a force (horizontal) is equal to the force times the cosine of the angle the force vector makes with the x-axis.

$$F_x = F \cos a \tag{36.1}$$

The y-component of a force (vertical) is equal to the force times the cosine of the angle the force vector makes with the y-axis.

$$F_y = F \cos b \tag{36.2}$$

Also note that the x- and y-axes can be tilted to any convenient angle if required by the problem.

There are three methods that can be used to determine the forces in truss members: the *method of joints*, the *method of sections*, and the *graphic method*. The method of joints is useful in determining the forces in all the members or when only the forces in members near the supports need to be calculated. The method of sections is convenient when it is only necessary to find the forces in a few members, particularly ones that are not at or near the supports. The graphic method is useful for complex trusses and avoids all the calculation inherent in analytic solutions but, of course, is not as accurate.

Figure 36.5
Determining Horizontal and Vertical Truss Components

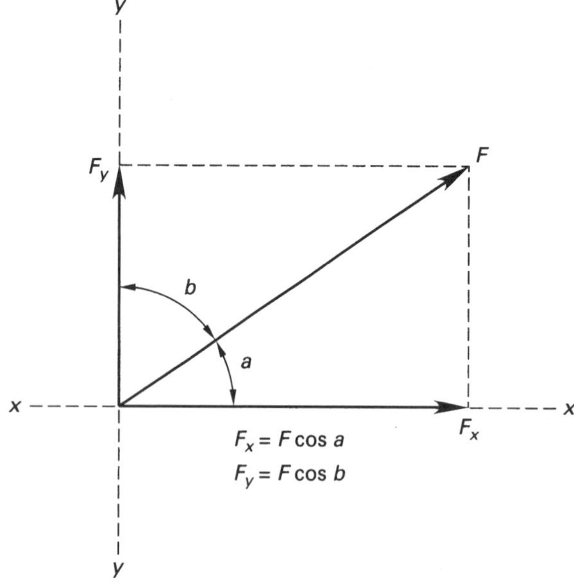

Method of Joints

With this method, each joint is considered separately as a free-body diagram to which the equations of equilibrium are applied. Starting from one support, the force in each member is determined, joint by joint, until all have been calculated.

Example 36.1

Consider the simple truss shown in the sketch. Find the forces in the members using the method of joints. Neglect the weight of the structure.

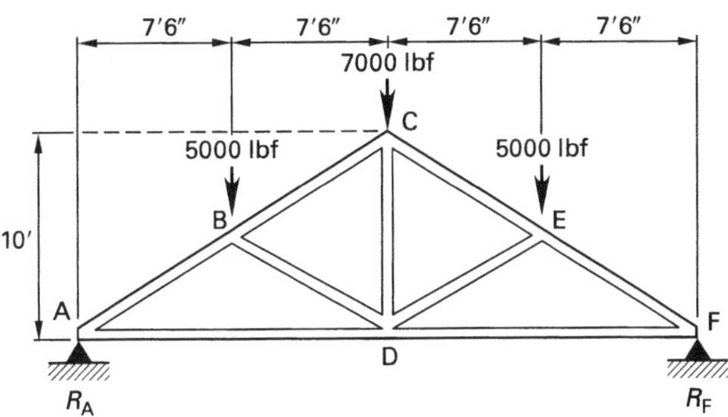

Solution

First, find the reactions. Since the loads are symmetric, $R_A = R_F = (0.5)(17{,}000 \text{ lbf}) = 8500$ lbf. If the loads were not symmetric, the reactions could be found by taking the moments about one reaction and setting the moments equal to zero.

Next, start with joint A at reaction R_A, and draw this joint as a free-body diagram as shown.

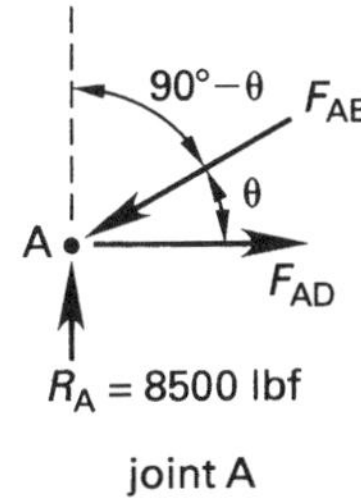

joint A

The direction of the reaction is known (upward), and the types of forces in the top chord and bottom chord can be assumed to be in compression and tension, respectively. Therefore, using the labeling convention, show force F_{AB} with an arrow toward the joint and force F_{AD} with an arrow away from the joint. Calculate the angle between member AB and AD.

$$\tan\theta = \frac{10 \text{ ft}}{15 \text{ ft}}$$
$$\theta = 33.7°$$

The complement of this angle is 56.3°.

Since the sum of vertical forces at any point equals zero, and since the vertical component of F_{AB} equals the force times the cosine of the angle with the y-axis (Eq. 36.2), then,

$$8500 \text{ lbf} - F_{AB}\cos 56.3° = 0$$

Remember, the reaction force is positive since it is acting upward, and the y-component of F_{AB} is negative since it is acting downward. Force F_{AD} has no vertical component.

Solve for F_{AB}

$$F_{AB} = \frac{8500 \text{ lbf}}{\cos 56.3°} = 15{,}320 \text{ lbf (compression)}$$

Since the answer is positive, the assumption that the force AB is in compression is correct.

The force in member AD is found in a similar way, knowing that the sum of the horizontal forces also equals zero.

$$F_{AD} - F_{AB}\cos 33.7^\circ = 0$$
$$F_{AD} = 12{,}746 \text{ lbf (tension)}$$

Consider joint B as a free-body diagram as shown.

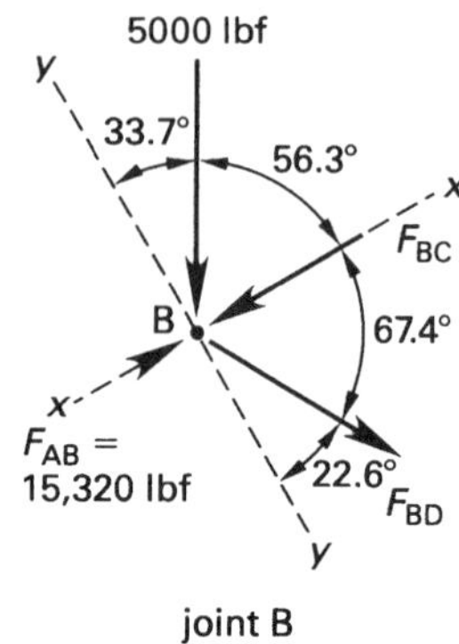

joint B

Since the direction of the force in member BD is not clear, assume it is in tension and draw it with the arrow away from the joint. (Actually, since the 5000 lbf load is acting down, there must be a force acting upward to counteract this, so member BD would have to be in compression. For purposes of illustration, however, assume it is in tension.)

In this case, tilt the x- and y-axes so the x-axis aligns with the top chord of the truss. The angles between the x- and y-axes and the forces can easily be determined by trigonometry and are shown in the joint B sketch. With the axes tilted, force F_{BC} has no vertical component in this free-body diagram, so force F_{BD} can be found easily.

$$(-5000 \text{ lbf})\cos 33.7^\circ - F_{BD}\cos 22.6^\circ = 0$$

(Since both forces are acting downward, they are both negative values.)

$$F_{BD} = -4506 \text{ lbf}$$

The negative number indicates that the assumption that member BD was in tension is incorrect; it is in compression.

Find the force in BC knowing that the sum of forces in the x-direction equals zero.

$$15{,}320 \text{ lbf} - (5000 \text{ lbf})\cos 56.3^\circ - F_{BC} - (4506 \text{ lbf})\cos 67.4^\circ = 0$$
$$F_{BC} = 10{,}814 \text{ lbf (compression)}$$

Finally, draw joint C as a free-body diagram.

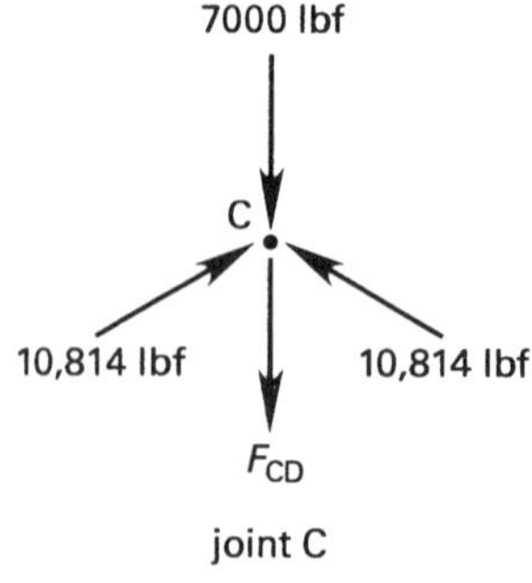

joint C

Product Development

The sum of the forces in the y-direction is zero, so,

$$(10{,}814\ \text{lbf})\cos 56.3^\circ - 7000\ \text{lbf} + (10{,}814\ \text{lbf})\cos 56.3^\circ - F_{\text{CD}} = 0$$
$$F_{\text{CD}} = 5000\ \text{lbf (tension)}$$

Since the truss and loading are symmetric, the forces in the right half are identical to those in the left half.

Method of Sections

With this method, a portion of the truss is cut through three members, one of which is the member under analysis. The cut section is then drawn as a free-body diagram, and the force in the members is found by taking moments about the various points knowing that $\Sigma M = 0$. It is also possible to use the equations $\Sigma F_x = 0$ and $\Sigma F_y = 0$ when there is more than one unknown, but this is not usually necessary if the center of moment was selected in such a way as to eliminate two unknowns.

Example 36.2

Using the same truss as shown in Ex. 36.1, determine the forces in members BD and BC using the method of sections.

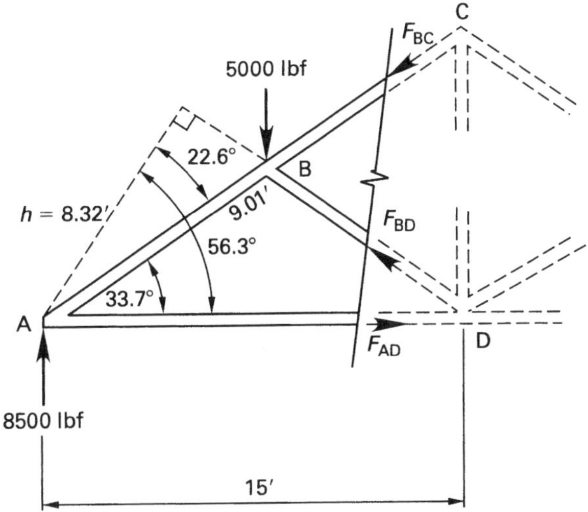

First, solve for the reactions as in the previous problem. These were determined to be 8500 lbf at each reaction.

Next, cut a section through the two members under analysis as shown in the sketch. In this free-body diagram there are five forces acting: two that are known and three that are unknown. To find the force in member BD, take moments about point A. Selecting this point eliminates the unknowns of F_{BC} and F_{AD} because their lines of action pass through the point so their moment is zero. This leaves only F_{BD} acting about A.

Remember, by convention, moments acting in a clockwise direction are positive and those acting in a counterclockwise direction are negative.

Before taking moments, find the dimension of the moment arm of BD, a line passing through A perpendicular to BD. With some simple trigonometry, the length of AB is found to be 9.01 ft and the angle between AB and the moment arm of BD is found to be 22.6°. Then,

$$\cos 22.6^\circ = \frac{h}{9.01\ \text{ft}}$$
$$h = 8.32\ \text{ft}$$

Product Development

Then, the sum of moments about A equals zero, or

$$(5000 \text{ lbf})(7.5 \text{ ft}) - F_{BD}(8.32 \text{ ft}) = 0$$
$$F_{BD} = 4507 \text{ lbf}$$

This is the same value (within 1 lbf) that was calculated by the method of joints in the previous example.

Find the value of F_{BC}. In this case, to eliminate two unknowns, take moments about point D. This is acceptable even though it is outside the free-body diagram because the equation of moment equilibrium holds at any point in the truss. The moment arm from D perpendicular to BC must be found. It is the same dimension as the previous moment arm calculated: 8.32 ft. Then, the sum of moments about joint D is

$$(8500 \text{ lbf})(15 \text{ ft}) - (5000 \text{ lbf})(7.5 \text{ ft}) - F_{BC}(8.32 \text{ ft}) = 0 \text{ lbf-ft}$$
$$F_{BC} = 10{,}817 \text{ lbf}$$

In both cases, the answer is a positive number, indicating that the original assumption of direction of force (compression) is correct. If either answer were negative, it would simply mean that the assumption was incorrect and the arrow or arrows should be reversed. (This answer is within 3 lbf of that found by the method of joints, allowing for some minor inaccuracies due to rounding off when calculating the length of moment arms.)

Graphic Method

Finding forces in truss members with graphics is a quick method and is particularly suited for complex trusses. However, its accuracy depends on the scale selected and the accuracy with which the diagram is drawn. A truss is analyzed graphically by drawing a stress diagram. This is a carefully drawn diagram, to scale, showing all the force polygons for each joint on one drawing.

When developing a stress diagram there are a few things to keep in mind.

- Since the truss is in equilibrium, the force polygon of each joint must close.
- When developing the force polygon for a joint, work in a clockwise direction around the joint. Do this consistently for every joint.
- To determine whether a member is in compression or tension, trace the rays of the force polygon. Imagine that the ray was transposed onto the truss diagram. If the direction of the ray is toward the joint, the member is in compression. If it is away from the joint, the member is in tension.
- There will be as many sides to each force polygon as there are truss members and forces entering a joint.

Example 36.3

Consider the same truss as used in the previous two examples. Draw a diagram of the truss, and allow room below to draw the stress diagram. Label the spaces between each load and reaction with a letter of the alphabet, A, B, C, and so on. Number each triangle of the truss. Then, each load or reaction can be identified with a two-letter combination, and each structural member can be identified with a letter/number combination.

Begin the diagram by drawing a force polygon of the loads and reactions. In the sketch, start with reaction AB. With a convenient scale, in this case 1 in = 3000 lbf, draw a line parallel to the reaction in the truss drawing (in this case vertical) to a scale of 8500 lbf. Working clockwise, the next load is the 5000 lbf load BC. Draw a line downward, parallel to a scale of 5000 lbf. Continue until you are back at point A. Since the loads and reactions are all vertical, the force polygon is a straight line, but it does close on itself.

Next, draw a force polygon for the joint at the left reaction, AB1. The load AB is already drawn, so working clockwise, draw a line parallel to B1 from point B on the stress diagram. Then, draw a line representing member 1A horizontally from point A. Where these two lines intersect is point 1. To determine the type of force, trace the lines of the polygon beginning with point A. AB is the reaction and is acting upward. B1 runs down and to the left toward point 1, which in the truss drawing is toward the joint, so B1 must be in compression. From point 1, line 1A runs to the right, which in the truss drawing is away from the joint, so 1A must be in tension.

Study joint BC21. Since lines 1B and BC have already been drawn, start with point C and draw a line parallel with C2. From point 1, draw a line parallel with member 12. Where these intersect is point 2, and the force polygon closes. Measuring line 12 and C2 to scale gives the magnitude of the forces in these members.

Continue the procedure until all joints have been solved. A tabulation of the forces is given in the sketch. Compare these values with those found by the method of joints and sections in the previous examples.

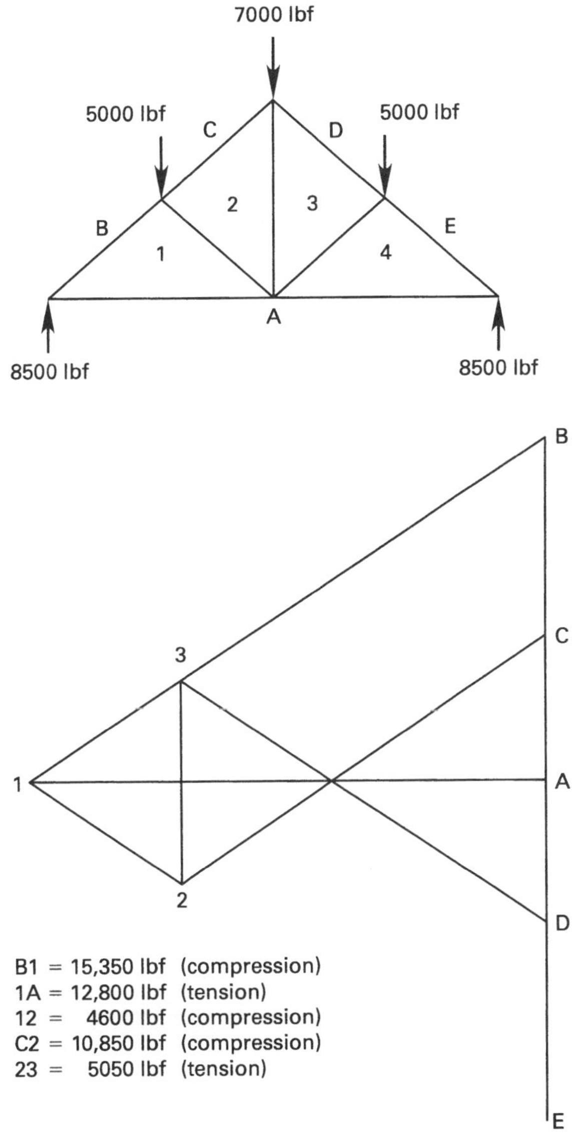

Product Development

37

FOUNDATIONS

Nomenclature

a	depth of rectangular stress block	in	l_d	development length	in
A_s	area of steel	in^2	L	actual live load	lbf
b_w	width of footing	ft	M_u	ultimate moment	ft-lbf/ft
B	bearing capacity of soil	lbf/ft^2	p	earth pressure	lbf/ft^2
C_o	coefficient of earth pressure	–	P	load	lbf/ft
d	effective depth—distance from top of footing to centroid of reinforcing steel	in	q_s	design soil pressure	lbf/ft^2
			U	required ultimate strength load	lbf
d_b	diameter of reinforcing steel	in	v	actual shear	lbf/ft
D	actual dead load	lbf	V	shear	lbf/ft
	specified compressive strength	lbf/in^2	V_c	maximum allowable shear	lbf/ft
f_c'	design strength of concrete	lbf/in^2	w	width of foundation wall	in
			W	unit weight of soil behind retaining wall	lbf/ft^3
f_y	specified yield strength of reinforcing steel	lbf/in^2	x	distance from face of foundation wall to edge of footing	ft
h	height of retaining wall from below grade	ft	ϕ	strength reduction factor (LRFD)	–

The *foundation* is the part of the building that transmits all the gravity and lateral loads to the underlying soil. Selection and design of foundations depends on two primary elements: the required strength of the foundation to transmit the loads on it, and the ability of the soil to sustain the loads without excessive total settlement or differential settlement among different parts of the foundation. Soil properties are discussed in Chap. 21.

FOUNDATION SYSTEMS

Foundations can be categorized into two broad divisions: *spread footings* and *pile* or *caisson foundations.* Spread footings do just what their name implies—they spread the load from the structure and the foundation walls over a large area, so the load-carrying capacity of the soil is not exceeded and settlement is minimized. Pile and caisson foundations (often referred to as piers) distribute the load from the building to the ends of the piles, which often bear on bedrock, or to the surrounding soil in contact with the pile through skin friction, or a combination of both.

Spread Footings

There are several types of spread footings. These are shown in Fig. 37.1. One of the most common is the *wall footing* that is placed under a continuous foundation wall that in turn supports a bearing wall. Both the footing and foundation are reinforced (except where very small loads are supported), and the joint between the footing and foundation wall is strengthened with a keyed joint (see Fig. 37.1(a)).

The *independent column footing* is similar in concept but supports only one column. The footing is usually square but may be rectangular if the column is rectangular or if there is not enough room to form a square footing.

The required size of both wall and independent column footings is found by dividing the total load on the footing by the load-carrying capacity of the soil. A safety factor is often used as well. For wall footings, design is on a linear foot basis.

Combined footings support two or more columns in situations where the columns are spaced too closely together for separate ones, or where one column is so close to the property line that a symmetrically loaded footing could not be poured. If the two columns are far apart, a variation of the combined footing is used for economy. This is the *strap footing* or *cantilever footing* (see Fig. 37.1(d)), which uses a concrete strap beam to distribute the column loads to each footing to equalize the soil pressures on each footing. The beam itself is poured on compressible material so it does not bear on the soil. Strap footings are also used where the exterior column is next to the property line but the footing cannot extend beyond the property line.

A *mat* or *raft foundation* (see Fig. 37.1(e)) is used when soil bearing is low or where loads are heavy in relation to soil pressures. With this type of foundation, one large footing is designed as a two-way slab and supports the columns above it. Walls or beams above the foundation are sometimes used to give added stiffness to the mat.

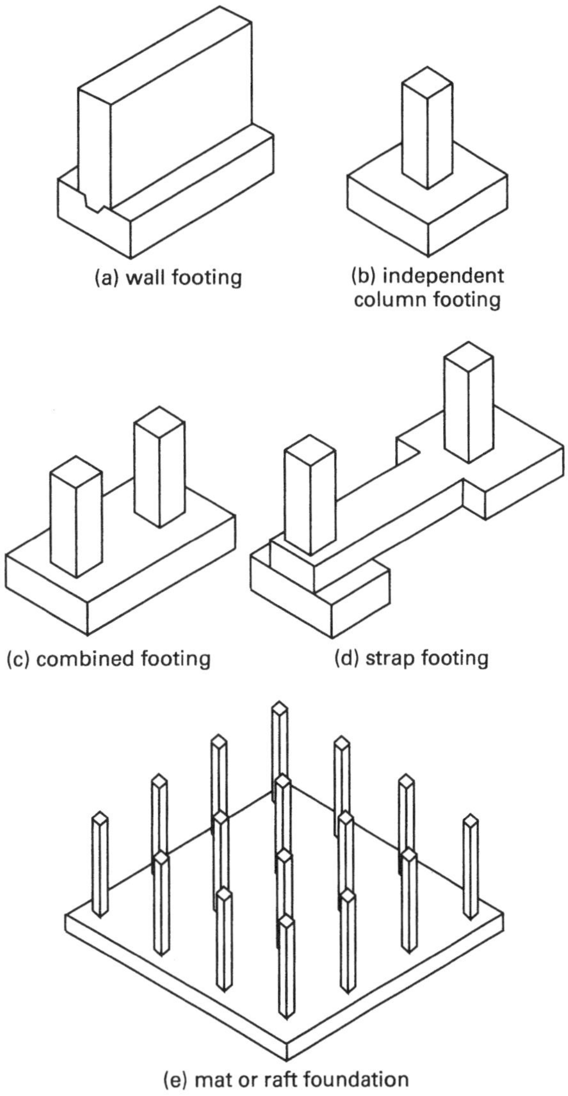

Figure 37.1
Types of Spread Footings

(a) wall footing

(b) independent column footing

(c) combined footing

(d) strap footing

(e) mat or raft foundation

Pile Foundations

When soil near grade level is unsuitable for spread footings, pile foundations are used. These transmit building loads through the unsuitable soil to a more secure bearing with end bearing or side friction. Piles are either driven or drilled. Driven piles may be of timber, steel, or precast concrete and are placed with pile-driving hammers powered with drop hammers, compressed air, or diesel engines. Drilled piles or caissons are usually called *piers*. Some common types of piles are shown in Fig. 37.2.

Drilled piers are formed by drilling out a hole to the required depth and then filling it with concrete. If the soil is soft, a metal lining is used to keep the soil from caving in during drilling. It is removed as the concrete is poured or may be left in. If the soil pressure is not sufficient for a drilled pier of normal dimensions, the bottom is "belled" out to increase the surface area for bearing (see Fig. 37.2).

Piles are usually placed in groups or in a line under a bearing wall with the loads from the building transferred to them with pile caps. See Fig. 37.3(a). The piles are embedded from 4 in to 6 in into the pile cap, which is designed and reinforced to safely transmit the loads and resist shear and moment stresses as they develop. When two or more piles are used to support one column, the centroid of the pile group is designed to coincide with the center of gravity of the column load.

One type of pile foundation system frequently used is the *grade beam*. See Fig. 37.3(b). With this system, piles are driven or drilled in line at regular intervals and connected with a continuous grade beam. The grade beam is designed and reinforced to transfer the loads from the building wall to the piles.

This system is often used where expansive soils or clay, such as bentonite, are encountered near the surface. In this case, the grade beams are poured on carton forms that support the concrete during pouring but do not transmit any upward pressures from the soil when they expand because they disintegrate and form a void shortly thereafter.

Designing Footings

There are three primary factors to investigate when designing footings. The first is the *unit loading*, so that the allowable bearing pressure of the soil is not exceeded and differential settlement in various parts of the structure is eliminated as much as possible. The other two are *shear* and *bending*. There are two kinds of shear failure. A footing fails in punching or two-way shear when the column or wall load punches through the footing. A footing can also fail in flexural shear or diagonal tension the same as regular beams. Footings fail in bending when the lower surface cracks under flexural loading.

Figure 37.2
Pile Types

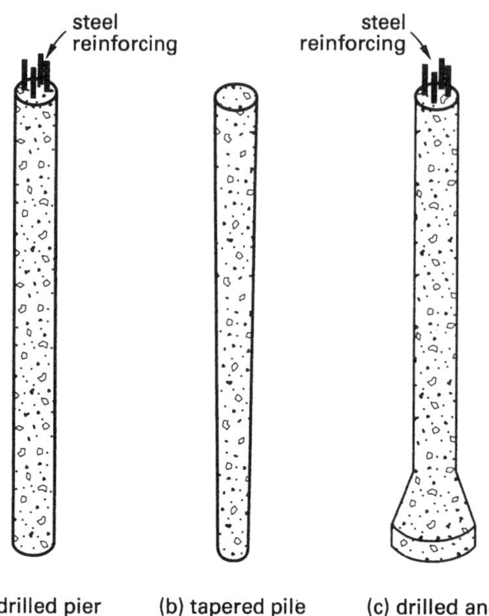

Simple spread footings act much like inverted beams with the upward soil pressure being a continuous load that is resisted by the downward column load (although in reality, the column load is the action, and the upward pressure is the reaction). See Fig. 37.4. This tends to cause bending in the upward direction, which induces compression near the top of the footing and tension near the bottom of the footing. If the tension is great enough, tension reinforcing must be added near the bottom of the footing.

The area of a spread footing is determined by dividing the total wall or column load on it plus its own weight plus any soil on top of the footing by the allowable soil bearing pressure. Then, the footing itself is designed for shear, moment, and other loads with factored loads as required by ACI 318, *Building Code Requirements for Structural Concrete* published by the American Concrete Institute (ACI). These, in effect, are safety factors to make sure the footing is of sufficient size and design to resist all loads.

Figure 37.3
Pile Caps

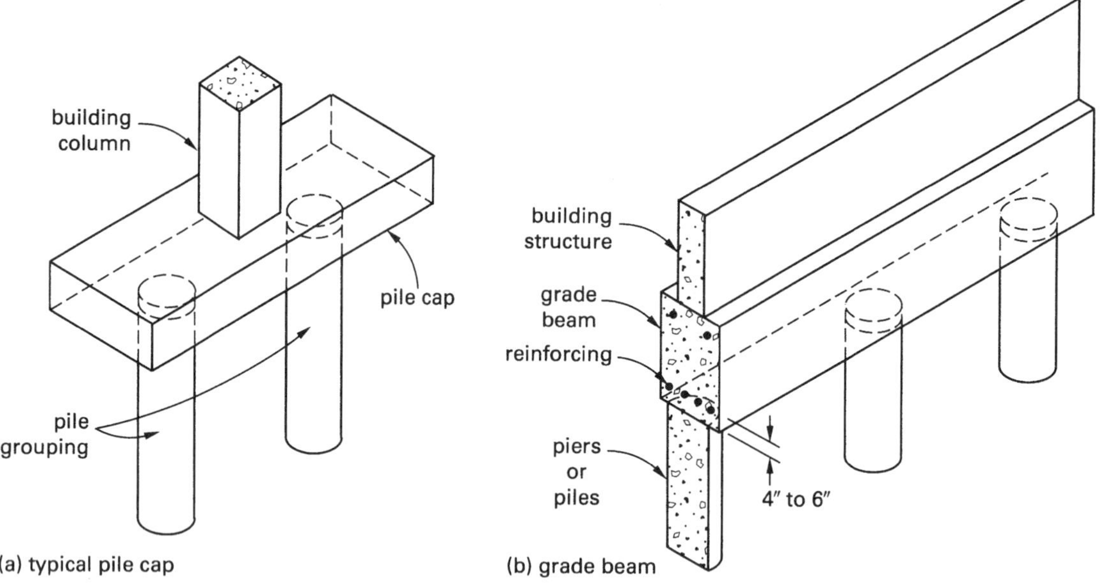

There are various formulas to take into account combinations of live loads, dead loads, wind, earthquake, earth pressure, fluids, impact loads, and settlement, creep, and temperature change effects.

For foundations, the following formula is used.

$$U = 1.2D + 1.6L \tag{37.1}$$

The two most basic kinds of spread footings are the wall footing and the independent column footing (see Fig. 37.1(a) and Fig. 37.1(b)). Each behaves a little differently, and each is designed based on slightly different conditions.

When designing wall footings, there are two critical sections that must be investigated. These are at the face of the wall where bending moment is greatest, and at a distance, d, from the face of the wall in wall footings where flexural shear is of most concern. These sections are shown in Fig. 37.5(a) and Fig. 37.5(b). However, the critical two-way shear section for column footings is distance $d/2$ from the face of the wall. See Fig. 37.6.

d is the distance from the top of the footing to the centroid of the reinforcing steel, called the *effective depth* of the footing since the concrete below the steel does not contribute any structural properties. The distance, d, for masonry and concrete foundation walls is a little different as shown in the two sketches. For concrete walls, it is measured from the face of the wall.

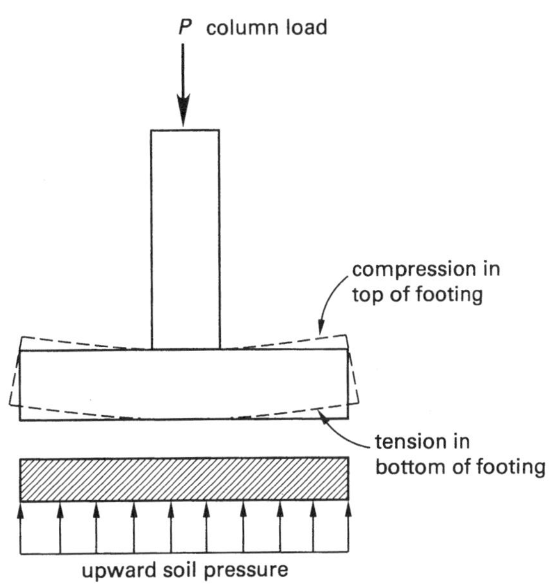

Figure 37.4 Load Action on Simple Spread Footings

For lightly loaded walls where the total width of the footing is not too great, the bending action is not as critical as the shear that must be resisted by the thickness of the footing. Generally, it is not economical to provide tension reinforcement in wall footings, so the width and thickness are designed to resist the wall load and shear forces using only the strength of unreinforced concrete. Usually, however, longitudinal reinforcing is included (parallel to the length of the wall) for temperature reinforcing and to help the footing span any intermittent, weaker soil conditions.

Where heavy loads or weak soil conditions are present, the width of the footing may become great enough to require tension reinforcement. In most cases, however, maximum allowable flexural shear governs the design depth of wall footings.

Individual column footings are subject to two-way action, much like flat slabs near columns, as well as one-way shear. Because of this, both types of shear must be calculated, and the depth of the footing must be designed to resist these shear forces. When both are calculated, the greater shear value is used for design.

Fig. 37.6 shows the two locations where shear must be calculated. For one-way shear at distance d from the face of the column, the factored soil design pressure is calculated over the rectangular area indicated as abcd in Fig. 37.6. For two-way shear, the soil design pressure is calculated over the area outside the square efgh indicated in Fig. 37.6.

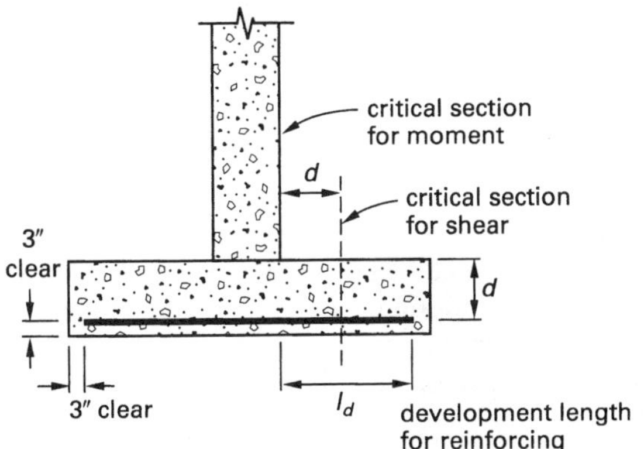

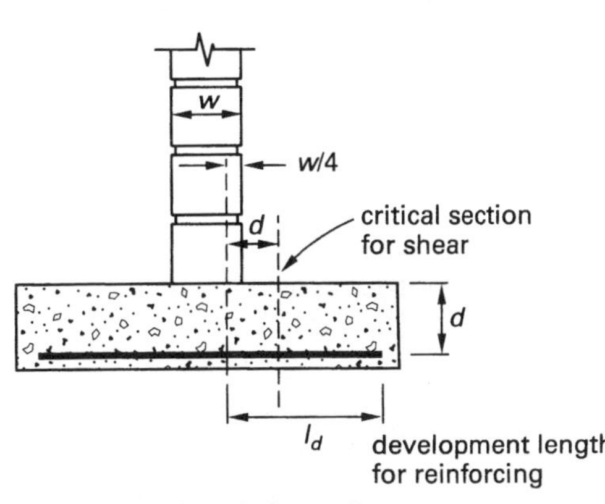

Figure 37.5 Critical Sections for Wall Footings

In addition, bottom reinforcing in both directions is usually required to resist the moment forces at the face of the column.

Figure 37.6
Individual Column Footings

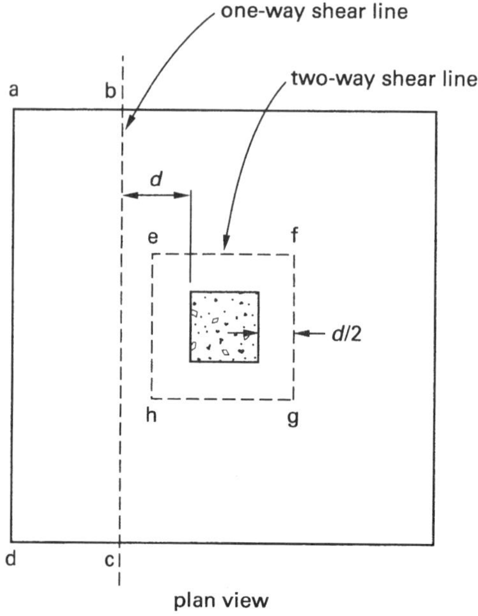

Example 37.1

Find the required depth, width, and transverse reinforcing for the footing shown. The bottom of the footing is 5 ft below grade and carries a load per linear foot of 14,000 lbf dead load, including the wall weight, and 7000 lbf live load on a 12 in wide foundation wall. The concrete strength is 3000 psi, and the steel yield point is 60,000 psi. Soil tests have shown the allowable soil bearing pressure to be 3500 psf.

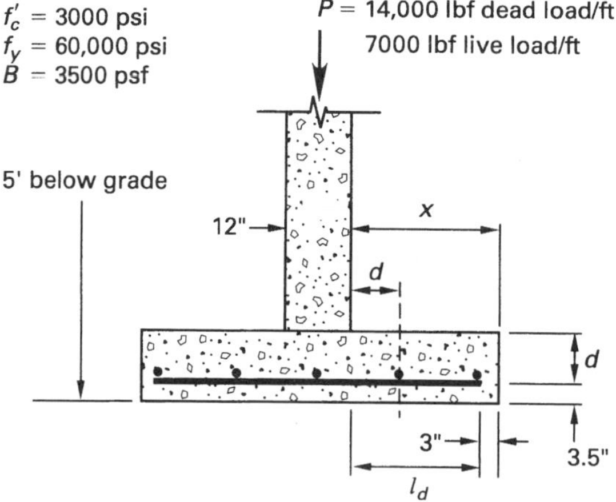

Solution

Step 1. In the design, consider a 1 ft long section of wall and footing. To find the width of the footing, divide the total load plus an allowance for the weight of the footing and an allowance for the soil on top of the footing by the allowable soil bearing pressure. Estimate the footing width as 7 ft and its depth as 12 in. With concrete weighing about 150 lbf/ft^3, a 1 ft long section of footing weighs 1050 lbf. Soil weighs about 100 psf, so the soil weight is 4 ft times 100, or 400 psf, or 1200 lbm for the 3 ft section on either side of the foundation wall.

Product Development

So, the width of the footing should be

$$b_w = \frac{14{,}000\ \frac{\text{lbf}}{\text{ft}} + 7000\ \frac{\text{lbf}}{\text{ft}} + 1050\ \frac{\text{lbf}}{\text{ft}} + 2400\ \frac{\text{lbf}}{\text{ft}}}{3500\ \frac{\text{lbf}}{\text{ft}^2}}$$
$$= 6.99 \text{ ft}$$

Use a 7 ft wide footing.

Step 2. To begin the design of the footing, ACI 318 requires the design soil pressure to be calculated based on factored loads according to Eq. 37.1.

$$\begin{aligned} U &= 1.2D + 1.6L \\ &= (1.2)\left(14{,}000\ \frac{\text{lbf}}{\text{ft}}\right) + (1.6)\left(7000\ \frac{\text{lbf}}{\text{ft}}\right) \\ &= 28{,}000 \text{ plf} \end{aligned}$$

Note that this excludes the weight of the footing and the soil above the footing because they do not contribute to producing moment or shear in the footing.

The design soil pressure is then equal to the factored design load divided by the area.

$$q_s = \frac{28{,}000 \text{ plf}}{7 \text{ ft}} = 4000 \text{ psf}$$

Step 3. Assuming a footing depth of 12 in, check the flexural shear at the critical section since flexural shear almost always governs footing design. This section is at a distance, d (the effective depth of the footing), from the face of the wall (see Fig. 37.5). The distance is from the top of the footing to the centroid of reinforcing steel. Since ACI 318 requires a 3 in clear dimension from steel to the bottom of a footing cast against the earth, use this plus an allowance (guess at this point) of $1/2$ in for one-half the diameter of reinforcing steel. The rebars will probably be less than no. 8s, but this gives an easy number of $3\frac{1}{2}$ in to work with. Distance, d, is then 12 in − 3.5 in, or 8.5 in, or 0.708 ft.

Shear at this point is the distance to the end of the footing times the design soil pressure. Remember, this is a 1 ft long section of wall, so units are in feet and pounds per foot.

$$\begin{aligned} V &= (x - d)q_s \\ &= (3 \text{ ft} - 0.708 \text{ ft})\left(4000\ \frac{\text{lbf}}{\text{ft}^2}\right) \end{aligned}$$

(0.708 is $8\frac{1}{2}$ in converted to a fraction of a foot.)

$$V = 9168 \text{ plf}$$

ACI 318 limits one-way shear on plain or reinforced sections to a maximum of

$$\begin{aligned} V_c &= \phi 2\sqrt{f_c'}\, b_w d \\ &= (0.75)(2)\sqrt{3000\ \frac{\text{lbf}}{\text{in}^2}}\,(12 \text{ in})(8.5 \text{ in}) \\ &= 8380 \text{ lbf/ft} \end{aligned} \qquad 37.2$$

The actual shear of 9168 lbf is more than the allowable of 8380 lbf, so the section needs to be revised.

Product Development

Try a 14 in deep footing with d = 14 in − 3.5 in, or 10.5 in.

$$\begin{aligned} V_c &= (0.75)(2)\sqrt{3000\ \frac{\text{lbf}}{\text{in}^2}}(12\ \text{in})(10.5\ \text{in}) \\ &= 10{,}350\ \text{lbf/ft} \end{aligned}$$

A 14 in thick footing will work since the allowable shear is more than the actual shear of

$$\begin{aligned} v = (x-d)q_s &= (3\ \text{ft} - 0.875\ \text{ft})\left(4000\ \frac{\text{lbf}}{\text{ft}^2}\right) \\ &= 8500\ \text{plf} \end{aligned}$$

Step 4. Find the moment at the face of the wall. The leg of the footing acts as an inverted cantilevered beam, so the moment is

$$M_u = \frac{q_s l^2}{2} = \frac{\left(4000\ \frac{\text{lbf}}{\text{ft}^2}\right)(3\ \text{ft})^2}{2} = 18{,}000\ \text{ft-lbf/ft}$$

Step 5. Find the area of the steel required according to Eq. 37.3.

$$A_s = \frac{M_u}{\phi f_y\left(d - \frac{a}{2}\right)} \qquad 37.3$$

a is the depth of rectangular stress block determined by

$$a = \frac{A_s f_y}{0.85 f_c' b} \qquad 37.4$$

Since steel area is not known, assume a value for a. Try 1 in to begin with. For shear, the strength reduction factor, ϕ, is 0.75.

The strength reduction factor, ϕ, is 0.90 for flexure members.

$$\begin{aligned} A_s &= \frac{M_u}{\phi f_y\left(d - \frac{a}{2}\right)} \\ &= \frac{\left(18{,}000\ \frac{\text{ft-lbf}}{\text{ft}}\right)\left(12\ \frac{\text{in}}{\text{ft}}\right)}{(0.90)\left(60{,}000\ \frac{\text{lbf}}{\text{in}^2}\right)\left(10.5\ \text{in} - \frac{1\ \text{in}}{2}\right)} \\ &= 0.40\ \text{in}^2/\text{ft of footing} \end{aligned}$$

There are several possible combinations of bar sizes and spacings that will satisfy this requirement. Number 5 bars at 9 in on center gives a steel area of 0.41 in^2/ft, so use this.

Check to see that the value of a is less than that used in the assumption by using Eq. 37.4.

$$a = \frac{A_s f_y}{0.85 f_c' b} = \frac{\left(0.41\ \frac{\text{in}^2}{\text{ft}}\right)\left(60{,}000\ \frac{\text{lbf}}{\text{in}^2}\right)}{(0.85)\left(3000\ \frac{\text{lbf}}{\text{in}^2}\right)\left(12\ \frac{\text{in}}{\text{ft}}\right)} = 0.80\ \text{in}$$

This is less than the 1 in assumed in finding the area of steel, so this will work.

Step 6. Find the development length required for the steel. This is the minimum length required to develop a sufficient bond between the steel and the concrete. It is measured from the face of the wall to the end of the steel as shown in Fig. 37.5 and is found by

$$l_d = \left(\frac{f_y \Psi_t \Psi_e}{25\lambda \sqrt{f_c'}} \right) d_b \qquad 37.5$$

This equation assumes adequate concrete cover and bar spacing under normal conditions with $\Psi_t = \Psi_e = 1.0$.

The area of a no. 5 bar is 0.31 in^2, and its diameter is 0.625 in.

$$\begin{aligned} l_d &= \left(\frac{f_y \Psi_t \Psi_e}{25\lambda \sqrt{f_c'}} \right) d_b \\ &= \left(\frac{\left(60{,}000\ \frac{\text{lbf}}{\text{in}^2}\right)(1.0)(1.0)}{(25)(1.0)\sqrt{3000\ \frac{\text{lbf}}{\text{in}^2}}} \right)(0.625\ \text{in}) \\ &= 27.39\ \text{in} \end{aligned}$$

The minimum length is 12 in, so 27.39 in governs. Since the actual length is 36 in − 3 in, or 33 in, there is sufficient length of steel.

Step 7. Find the longitudinal temperature reinforcement required.

ACI 318 requires at least 0.0018 times the area of the section to be steel, so

$$A_s = (0.0018)(12\ \text{in})(14\ \text{in}) = 0.3024\ \text{in}^2$$

For example, a no. 4 reinforcing bar has a cross–sectional area of 0.20 in^2 (see Table 42.1), so no. 4 bars at 7 in on center will provide (0.20 in^2/7 in) = 0.34 in^2/ft of steel.

RETAINING WALLS

Retaining walls are used to hold back soil or other material when the desired change in elevation between two points is greater than can be achieved by letting the soil rest at its normal angle of repose.

Types of Retaining Walls

There are three types of retaining walls: the gravity wall, the cantilever wall, and the counterfort wall. See Fig. 37.7. The *gravity wall* resists the forces on it by its own weight and by soil pressure and soil friction against its surface opposite to the earth forces. It is commonly used for low retaining walls up to about 10 ft where the forces on it are not too great.

The *cantilever wall* is the most common type and is constructed of reinforced concrete. This type resists forces by the weight of the structure as well as by the weight of the soil on the heel of the base slab. It is often constructed with a key projecting from the bottom of the slab to increase the wall's resistance to sliding as shown in Fig. 37.7(b). Occasionally, the toe is omitted if the wall is next to a property line or some other obstruction. Since the arm, heel, and toe act as cantilevered slabs, the thickness and reinforcement increase with increased length because of the larger moments developed.

Because of this, cantilevered walls are economically limited to about 20 ft to 25 ft in height.

For walls higher than 20 ft to 25 ft, the *counterfort wall* is used. This is similar to the cantilevered wall, but with counterforts placed at distances equal to or a little larger than one-half the height. The counterforts are simply reinforced concrete webs that act as diagonal bracing for the wall.

Figure 37.7
Types of Retaining Walls

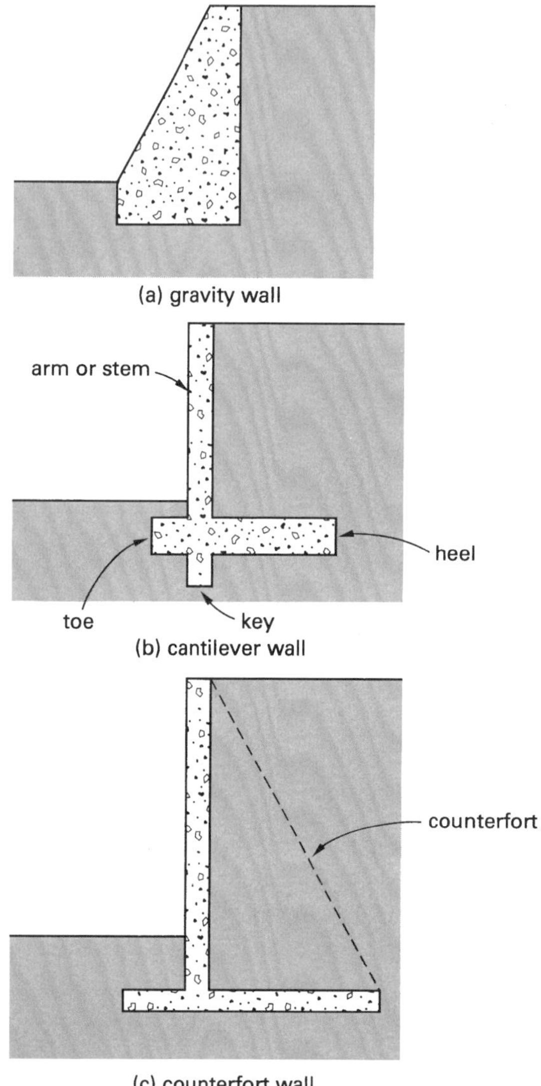

Forces on Retaining Walls

In the simplest case, the force on a retaining wall results entirely from the pressure of the earth retained acting in a horizontal direction to the wall. The earth pressure increases proportionally with the depth from the surface, ranging from zero at ground level to a maximum at the lowest depth of the wall in a triangular distribution pattern. See Fig. 37.8.

The earth pressure at any point is given by Eq. 37.6.

$$p = C_o W h \tag{37.6}$$

The coefficient of earth pressure, C_o, depends on the soil type and the method of backfilling and compacting it. The value may range from 0.4 for uncompacted soils like sands and gravels to 1.0 for cohesive, compacted soils. In many situations, the formula is simplified so that C_o is eliminated and the weight of the soil is considered to be equivalent to a fluid weighing 30 lbf/ft^3. Therefore, the pressure at any point is

$$p = 30h \tag{37.7}$$

Figure 37.8
Forces Acting on a Retaining Wall

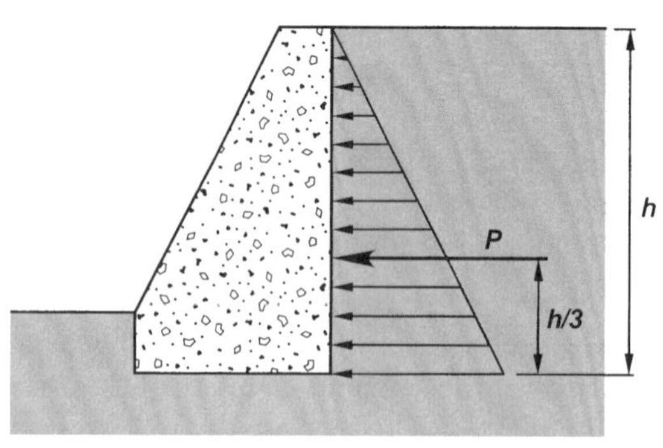

In the situation shown in Fig. 37.8, since the pressure acts in a triangular form, the total lateral load against the wall can be assumed to be acting through the centroid of the triangle, or one-third the distance from the base. To find the total load, multiply the pressure at the base of the wall by the area of the triangle, $\frac{1}{2}h$. The formula for this is

$$P = (C_o W h)\left(\frac{1}{2}h\right) = \frac{1}{2}C_o W h^2 \tag{37.8}$$

Or, if using the 30 lbf/ft^3 assumption for the equivalent weight of the soil, the formula reduces to

$$P = 15h^2 \tag{37.9}$$

Example 37.2

Assuming the soil has an equivalent fluid weight of 30 psf per foot of height, what is the total earth pressure load on a retaining wall 9.5 ft high?

Solution

The total load acts at a point 9.5 ft/3, or 3.17 ft above the base. From Eq. 37.9, the load is

$$P = \left(15\ \frac{\text{lbf}}{\text{ft}^3}\right)(9.5\ \text{ft})^2 = 1354\ \text{plf}$$

Additional forces may act on retaining walls. The earth being retained may slope upward from the top of the wall, resulting in the total force acting through the centroid of the pressure triangle, but in a direction parallel to the slope of the soil. Additional loads, called surcharges, may result from driveways or other forces being imposed on the soil next to the wall. If the ground behind the wall becomes wet, there is additional pressure resulting from the water that must be added to the soil pressure.

Design Considerations

A retaining wall may fail in two ways: It may fail as a whole by overturning or by sliding, or its individual components may fail, such as when the arm or stem breaks due to excessive movement. In order to prevent failure by overturning or sliding, the resisting moment or forces that resist sliding are generally considered sufficient if there is a safety factor of 1.5. For example, the total dead load of the wall plus the weight of the earth backfill acting on the footing of a cantilevered retaining wall should be at least 1.5 times the overturning moment caused by earth pressure to be safe. See Fig. 37.9(a). To prevent sliding, the friction between the footing and surrounding soil and the earth pressure in front of the toe (and key, if any) must be 1.5 times the pressures tending to cause the wall to slide. See Fig. 37.9(b).

Figure 37.9 Resisting Forces on Retaining Walls

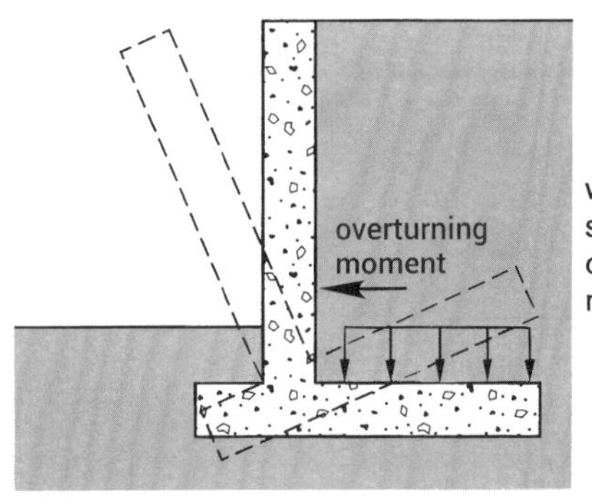

(a) overturning

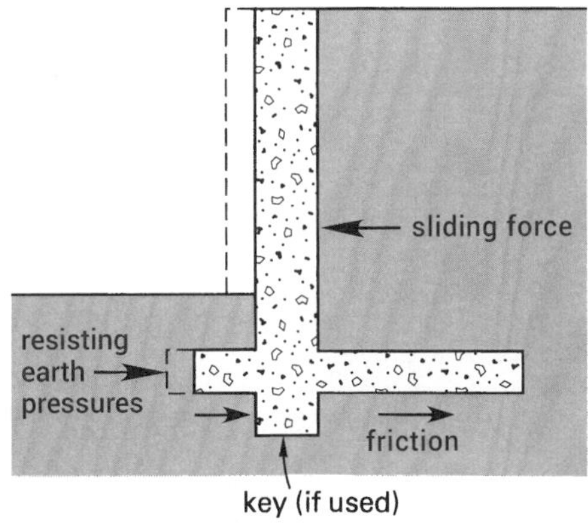

(b) sliding

To prevent failure of individual components, the thickness, width, and reinforcing of the retaining wall must be designed to resist the moment and shear forces induced by soil pressures, surcharges, and any hydrostatic pressures.

Retaining walls should be designed to eliminate or reduce the buildup of water behind them. This can be accomplished by providing weep holes near the bottom of the wall and by providing a layer of gravel next to the back of the wall. In some cases, it is necessary to install a drain tile above the heel of the wall to carry away excess water.

38

CONNECTIONS

Product Development

Nomenclature

F_c	unit stress in compression perpendicular to the grain	lbf/in^2
F_g	design value for end grain in bearing parallel to grain	lbf/in^2
F_n	compressive normal stress at inclination θ with the direction of grain	lbf/in^2
F_p	allowable bearing stress	lbf/in^2
F_t	allowable tensile stress	lbf/in^2
F_u	minimum tensile strength of steel or fastener	lbf/in^2
F_v	allowable shear stress	lbf/in^2
F_y	specified minimum yield stress of steel	lbf/in^2
G	specific gravity	–
P	tensile load	lbf
t	thickness	in
Z	nominal lateral design value for single fastener connection	lbf
θ	angle between the direction of grain and direction of load normal to face considered	deg

The majority of structural failures occur in the connections of members, not in the members themselves. Either the incorrect types of connectors are used, or the connectors are undersized, too few in number, or improperly installed. It is therefore important for ARE candidates to have a good understanding of the various types of connectors and how they are used.

WOOD CONNECTIONS

There are several variables that affect the design of wood connections. The first, of course, is the load-carrying capacity of the connector itself. Nails and screws, for example, carry relatively light loads, while timber connectors can carry large loads. Other variables that apply to all connections include the species of wood, the type of load, the condition of the wood, the service conditions, whether or not the wood is fire-retardant-treated, and the angle of the load to the grain. Additional design considerations are the critical net section, the type of shear the joint is subjected to, the spacing of the connectors, and the end and edge distances to connectors.

Species of Wood

The species and density of wood affect the holding power of connectors. Species are classified into four groups. There is one grouping for timber connectors, such as split ring connectors and shear plates, and another grouping for lag screws, nails, spikes, wood screws and metal plate connector loads. The four groups for timber connectors are designated Groups A, B, C, and D, while the grouping for other connectors are designated Groups I, II, III, and IV. Tables that give the allowable loads for connectors have separate columns for each group. Design values for connectors in a particular species apply to all grades of that species unless otherwise noted in the tables.

Type of Load

The design values for connectors can be adjusted for the duration of loading just as wood members can be (see Chap. 40). This is because wood can carry greater maximum loads for short durations than for long durations. The tables of allowable connector loads are for a normal duration of 10 years. For other conditions, the allowable values can be multiplied by the following factors.

- 0.90 for permanent loading over 10 years
- 1.15 for two months' duration (snow loading, for example)
- 1.25 for seven days' duration
- 1.60 for wind or earthquake loads
- 2.00 for impact loads

Condition of Wood

Tabulated design values found in building codes and elsewhere are for fastenings in wood seasoned to a moisture content of 19% or less. This is adequate for most use, but partially seasoned or wet wood (either at the time of fabrication or in service) reduces the holding power of the connector.

Service Conditions

Service conditions refer to the environment in which the wood joint will be used. These conditions can either be dry, wet, exposed to weather, or subject to wetting and drying. Any service conditions other than dry or continuously wet reduce the holding power of the connector.

Fire-Retardant Treatment

Wood that has been fire-retardant-treated does not hold connectors as well as wood that has not been treated. The *International Building Code* (IBC) and *National Design Specification for Wood Construction ASD/LRFD* (NDS) both specify that allowable design values for treated wood be obtained from the manufacturer.

Angle of Load

One of the most important variables affecting allowable loads carried by connectors is the angle of the load to the grain, which is defined as the angle between the direction of load acting on the member and the longitudinal axis of the member. Wood connectors can carry more load parallel to the grain than perpendicular to it, so tables of design values include both. If the load is acting other than parallel or perpendicular to the grain, it must be calculated using the *Hankinson formula* or by using one of the graphs that gives the same results.

The Hankinson formula gives the compressive normal stress at angle θ.

$$F_n = \frac{F_g F_c}{F_g \sin^2\theta + F_c \cos^2\theta} \tag{38.1}$$

Example 38.1

A 2 × 6 truss member bears on a 4 × 6 member at an angle of 40°. Both pieces of lumber are select structural Douglas fir ($F_g = 1400$ psi and $F_c = 625$ psi). What is the allowable unit compressive stress for the connection?

Solution

Using the Hankinson formula,

$$\begin{aligned} F_n &= \frac{F_g F_c}{F_g \sin^2\theta + F_c \cos^2\theta} = \frac{\left(1400\ \frac{\text{lbf}}{\text{in}^2}\right)\left(625\ \frac{\text{lbf}}{\text{in}^2}\right)}{\left(1400\ \frac{\text{lbf}}{\text{in}^2}\right)\sin^2 40^\circ + \left(625\ \frac{\text{lbf}}{\text{in}^2}\right)\cos^2 40^\circ} \\ &= 926\ \text{psi} \end{aligned}$$

Critical Net Section

When a wood member is drilled for one of the many types of connectors (except for nails and screws), there is a decrease in area of wood to carry the imposed load. The section where the most wood has been removed is called the *critical net section*. Once the size of the drilled area is known, the member must be checked for load-carrying capacity at this section. It may be necessary to increase the size of the member just to compensate for this decrease in area. See Fig. 38.1(a).

Type of Shear

Connectors such as bolts and lag screws can be in single shear, double shear, or multiple shear as shown in Fig. 38.1(b). The type of shear condition and the relative thickness of each piece to the others are especially important when designing bolted connections.

Connector Spacing

Connector spacing is the distance between centers of connectors measured along a line joining their centers as shown in Fig. 38.1(c). Minimum spacing is given for various types of connectors in building codes and in the NDS.

End and Edge Distances to Connectors

End distance is the distance measured parallel to the grain from the center of the connector to the square-cut end of the member. Edge distance is the distance from the edge of the member to the center of the connector closest to the edge of the member measured perpendicular to the edge. See Fig. 38.1(c).

For loading perpendicular to the grain, a distinction is made between the loaded and unloaded edges. The loaded edge is the edge toward which the fastener load acts, and the unloaded edge is the edge opposite from this. Minimum values for these distances are given in tables of allowable loads for the various types of connectors.

Figure 38.1
Wood Connector Design Variables

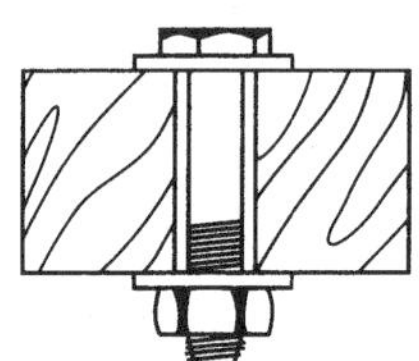

(a) critical net area

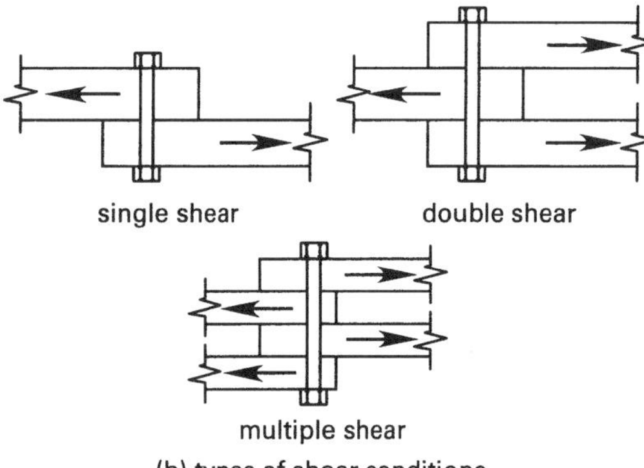

single shear

double shear

multiple shear

(b) types of shear conditions

end distance for vertical member

spacing

end distance for horizontal member

unloaded edge distance

spacing

load

loaded edge distance for horizontal member

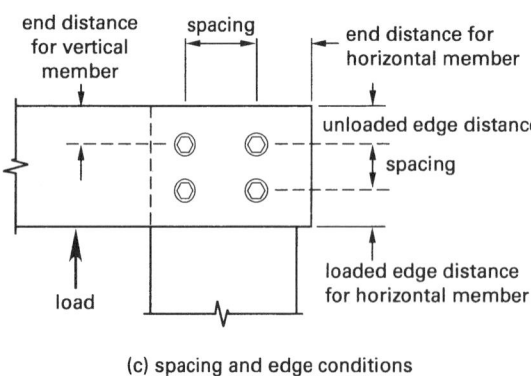

(c) spacing and edge conditions

Nails

Although they are the weakest of wood connectors, nails are the most common for light frame construction. The types used most frequently for structural applications include common wire nails, box nails, and common wire spikes. Wire nails range in size from six penny (6d) to sixty penny (60d). Box nails range from 6d to 40d. 6d nails are 2 in long, while 60d nails are 6 in long. Common wire spikes range from 10d (3 in long) to $8^1/_2$ in long and $^3/_8$ in diameter. For the same pennyweight, box nails have the smallest diameter, common wire nails have the next largest diameter, and wire spikes have the greatest diameter.

For engineered applications, that is, where each nailed joint is specifically designed, there are tables of values giving the allowable withdrawal resistance and lateral load (shear) resistance for different sizes and penetrations of nails depending on the type of wood used. The typical situation of most nailed wood construction is to simply use nailing schedules found in the building code. These give the minimum size, number, and penetration of nails for specific applications such as nailing studs to sole plates, joists to headers, and so forth.

There are several orientations that nails, screws, and lag screws have with wood members. These are shown in Fig. 38.2 and affect the holding power of the fastener. The preferable orientation is to have the fastener loaded laterally in side grain where the holding power is the greatest. If one of the pieces is metal rather than wood, allowable values may be increased by 25%. For nails, the design values for shear are the same regardless of the angle of load to grain.

Fasteners may also be driven or screwed so that there is withdrawal from side grain. Fasteners loaded in withdrawal from end grain are not allowed by building codes.

Screws

Wood screws used for structural purposes are available in sizes from no. 6 (0.138 in shank diameter) to no. 24 (0.372 in shank diameter) in lengths up to 5 in. The most common types are flat head and round head. As with nails, design tables give withdrawal and lateral load values for screws of different sizes, penetrations, and types of wood in which they are used. Also like nails, screws are best used laterally loaded in side grain rather than in withdrawal from side grain. Withdrawal from end is not permitted.

Design values given in the tables are for a penetration into the main member of approximately seven diameters. In no case should the penetration be less than four diameters. Like nails, design values can be increased by 25% if a metal side plate is used.

Lead holes must be drilled into the wood to permit the proper insertion of the wood screw. The recommended size of the lead hole depends on the species group of the wood being used and whether the screw is in lateral resistance or withdrawal resistance. Soap or other lubricant may be used to facilitate insertion.

Figure 38.2 Orientation of Wood Fasteners

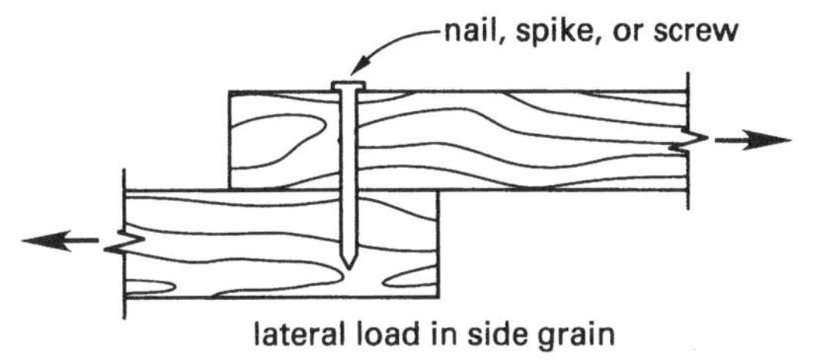

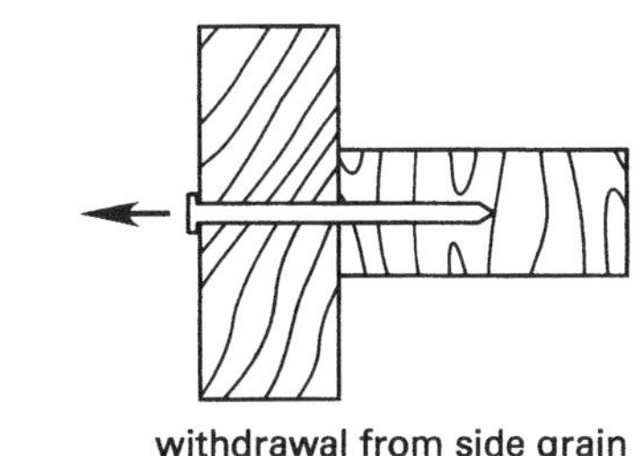

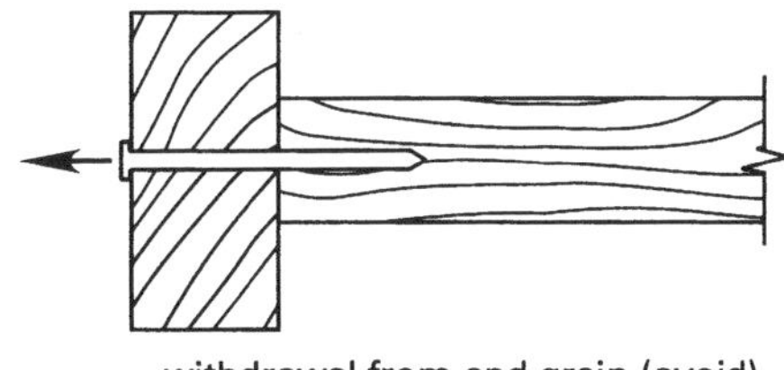

Lag Screws

A lag screw is threaded with a pointed end like a wood screw but has a head like a bolt. It is inserted by drilling lead holes and screwing the fastener into the wood with a wrench. A washer is used between the head and the wood. Lag screws are also called *lag bolts.*

Sizes range from $^1/_4$ in to $1^1/_4$ in diameters and from 1 in to 12 in lengths. Diameters are measured at the nonthreaded shank portion of the screw.

The design values for lateral loading and withdrawal resistance depend on the species group, the angle of load to grain, the diameter of the lag screw, the thickness of the side member, and the length of the screw. These variables are summarized in allowable load tables for loading parallel and perpendicular to the grain. Unlike nails and spikes, if the load is other than at a 0° or 90° angle, the design value must be determined from the Hankinson formula. Spacings, end distances, and edge distance for lag screw joints are the same as for bolts of the same diameter as the shank of the lag screw.

Bolts

Bolts are one of the most common forms of wood connectors for joints of moderate to heavy loading. The design requirements for bolted joints are a little more complicated than those for screwed or nailed joints. Variables such as the thicknesses of the main and side members, ratio of bolt length in main member to bolt diameter, and the number of members joined affect the allowable design values and the spacing of the bolts.

Figure 38.3
Typical Bolted Connection Conditions

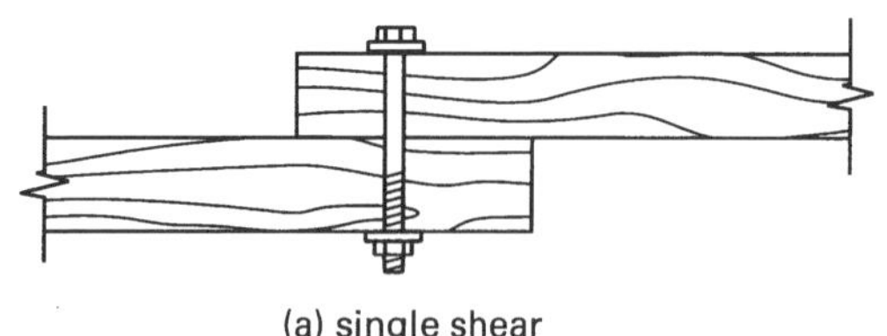

(a) single shear

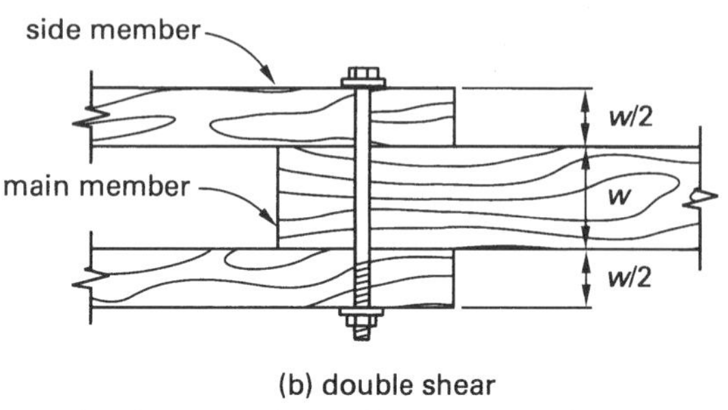

(b) double shear

The two typical conditions are joints in single shear and double shear as illustrated in Fig. 38.3.

Design values given in tables are usually for conditions where the side members in double shear joints are one-half the thickness of the main member. If a value is given for only double shear joints, values for single shear joints of members of equal widths are taken as one-half the values for double shear joints. Table 38.1 and Table 38.2 give bolt design values for single and double shear, respectively.

When $^1/_4$ in steel plates are used for side members, the design values are found in tables like Table 38.1 and Table 38.2. The values must be reduced by 60% if separate side plates are not used for each row of bolts parallel to the grain or if the wood will not be dry at fabrication and service. Similar adjustments to the tabulated design values are required if adequate bolt spacing is not provided or if multiple bolts are placed in a line parallel to the load.

If loading is at an angle to the grain, the Hankinson formula must be used to determine allowable loading on a bolt. When side member dimensions vary from those shown in Fig. 38.3(b) or the bolt grouping consists of rows of multiple bolts, procedures for modifying the design values are given in the NDS.

Example 38.2

A nominal 4 × 6 southern pine beam is to be supported by two 2 × 6 members acting as a spaced column as shown in the illustration. The minimum spacing and edge distances for $^1/_2$ in bolts are shown. Assume that all normal conditions apply to the beam. How many $^1/_2$ in bolts will be required to safely carry a load of 1500 lbf?

Solution

This is a double shear connection, and Table 38.2 is appropriate. Look under the column labeled "main member." Since the length of the bolt in the main member is $3^1/_2$ in (4 in nominal width), use that row and the portion of the row labeled $1^1/_2$ in in the side members and $^1/_2$ in bolt diameter. Select the lower of the values under southern pine for $Z_{\|} = 1320$ lbf and $Z_m = 940$ lbf. This value is 940 lbf. Two bolts will allow for a load of (940 lbf)(2), or 1880 lbf, which is well above the 1500 lbf required.

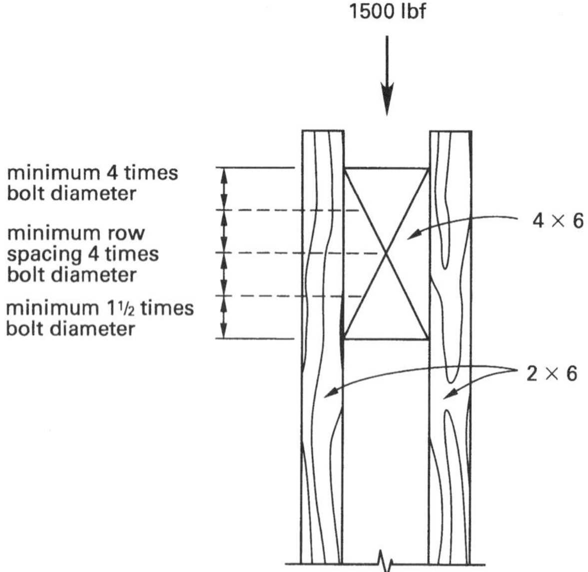

Using the spacing and edge distances given in the illustration, there must be a spacing of 2 in, a top distance of 2 in, and a bottom distance of 3/4 in, for a total of 4 3/4 in, within the total actual depth of 5 1/2 in of a 4 × 6 member.

Table 38.1 Bolt Lateral Design Values (Z) for Single Shear (Two Member) Connections[a,b] (for sawn lumber or SCL with both members of identical specific gravity)

thickness (in)		bolt diameter, D (in)	$G = 0.55$ mixed maple southern pine (lbf)				$G = 0.50$ Douglas fir-larch (lbf)				$G = 0.46$ Douglas fir (S) hem-fir (N) (lbf)			
main member, t_m	side member, t_s		$Z_{\|\|}$	$Z_{s\perp}$	$Z_{m\perp}$	$Z_{\perp}$	$Z_{\|\|}$	$Z_{s\perp}$	$Z_{m\perp}$	$Z_{\perp}$	$Z_{\|\|}$	$Z_{s\perp}$	$Z_{m\perp}$	$Z_{\perp}$
1 1/2	1 1/2	1/2	530	330	330	250	480	300	300	220	440	270	270	190
		5/8	660	400	400	280	600	360	360	240	560	320	320	220
		3/4	800	460	460	310	720	420	420	270	670	380	380	240
		7/8	930	520	520	330	850	470	470	290	780	420	420	250
		1	1060	580	580	350	970	530	530	310	890	480	480	280
3 1/2	1 1/2	1/2	660	400	470	360	610	370	430	330	580	340	400	310
		5/8	940	560	620	500	880	520	540	460	830	470	490	410
		3/4	1270	660	690	580	1200	590	610	510	1140	520	550	450
		7/8	1680	720	770	630	1590	630	680	550	1470	550	600	480
		1	2010	770	830	670	1830	680	740	590	1680	600	660	520
	3 1/2	1/2	750	520	520	460	720	490	490	430	690	460	460	410
		5/8	1170	780	780	650	1120	700	700	560	1070	650	650	500
		3/4	1690	960	960	710	1610	870	870	630	1540	800	800	560
		7/8	2170	1160	1160	780	1970	1060	1060	680	1810	980	980	590
		1	2480	1360	1360	820	2260	1230	1230	720	2070	1110	1110	640
5 1/2	1 1/2	5/8	940	560	640	500	880	520	590	460	830	470	560	430
		3/4	1270	660	850	660	1200	590	790	590	1140	520	740	520
		7/8	1680	720	1090	720	1590	630	980	630	1520	550	860	550
		1	2150	770	1190	770	2050	680	1060	680	1930	600	940	600
	3 1/2	5/8	1170	780	780	680	1120	700	730	630	1070	650	690	580
		3/4	1690	960	1090	850	1610	870	1030	780	1540	800	970	710
		7/8	2300	1160	1410	1020	2190	1060	1260	910	2060	980	1130	790
		1	2870	1390	1550	1100	2660	1290	1390	970	2500	1210	1250	860
7 1/2	1 1/2	5/8	940	560	640	500	880	520	590	460	830	470	560	430
		3/4	1270	660	850	660	1200	590	790	590	1140	520	740	520
		7/8	1680	720	1090	720	1590	630	1010	630	1520	550	950	550
		1	2150	770	1350	770	2050	680	1270	680	1930	600	1190	600
	3 1/2	5/8	1170	780	780	680	1120	700	730	630	1070	650	690	580
		3/4	1690	960	1090	850	1610	870	1030	780	1540	800	970	710
		7/8	2300	1160	1450	1020	2190	1060	1350	930	2060	980	1280	850
		1	2870	1390	1830	1210	2660	1290	1630	1110	2500	1210	1470	1030

[a]Tabulated lateral design values (Z) for bolted connections shall be multiplied by all applicable adjustment factors (see NDS Table 11.3.1).

[b]Tabulated lateral design values (Z) are for "full diameter" bolts (see NDS Appendix L1) with bolt bending yield (F_{yb}) of 45,000 psi.

Note: Some rows/columns not pertinent to this text have been omitted by PPI.

Table 38.2 Bolt Lateral Design Values (Z) for Double Shear (Three Member) Connections[a,b] (for sawn lumber or SCL with both members of identical specific gravity)

thickness (in) main member, t_m	thickness (in) side member, t_s	bolt diameter, D (in)	$G = 0.55$ mixed maple southern pine (lbf) $Z_{\|\|}$	$Z_{s\perp}$	$Z_{m\perp}$	$G = 0.50$ Douglas fir-larch (lbf) $Z_{\|\|}$	$Z_{s\perp}$	$Z_{m\perp}$	$G = 0.46$ Douglas fir (S) hem-fir (N) (lbf) $Z_{\|\|}$	$Z_{s\perp}$	$Z_{m\perp}$
1½	1½	½	1150	800	550	1050	730	470	970	680	420
		⅝	1440	1130	610	1310	1040	530	1210	940	470
		¾	1730	1330	660	1580	1170	590	1450	1040	520
		⅞	2020	1440	720	1840	1260	630	1690	1100	550
		1	2310	1530	770	2100	1350	680	1930	1200	600
3½	1½	½	1320	800	940	1230	730	860	1160	680	810
		⅝	1870	1130	1290	1760	1040	1190	1660	940	1090
		¾	2550	1330	1550	2400	1170	1370	2280	1040	1210
		⅞	3360	1440	1680	3180	1260	1470	3030	1100	1290
		1	4310	1530	1790	4090	1350	1580	3860	1200	1400
	3½	½	1500	1040	1040	1430	970	970	1370	920	920
		⅝	2340	1560	1420	2240	1410	1230	2150	1290	1090
		¾	3380	1910	1550	3220	1750	1370	3090	1610	1210
		⅞	4600	2330	1680	4290	2130	1470	3940	1960	1290
		1	5380	2780	1790	4900	2580	1580	4510	2410	1400
5½	1½	⅝	1870	1130	1290	1760	1040	1190	1660	940	1110
		¾	2550	1330	1690	2400	1170	1580	2280	1040	1480
		⅞	3360	1440	2170	3180	1260	2030	3030	1100	1900
		1	4310	1530	2700	4090	1350	2480	3860	1200	2200
	3½	⅝	2340	1560	1560	2240	1410	1460	2150	1290	1390
		¾	3380	1910	2180	3220	1750	2050	3090	1610	1900
		⅞	4600	2330	2650	4390	2130	2310	4130	1960	2020
		1	5740	2780	2810	5330	2580	2480	4990	2410	2200
7½	1½	⅝	1870	1130	1290	1760	1040	1190	1660	940	1110
		¾	2550	1330	1690	2400	1170	1580	2280	1040	1480
		⅞	3360	1440	2170	3180	1260	2030	3030	1100	1900
		1	4310	1530	2700	4090	1350	2530	3860	1200	2390
	3½	⅝	2340	1560	1560	2240	1410	1460	2150	1290	1390
		¾	3380	1910	2180	3220	1750	2050	3090	1610	1940
		⅞	4600	2330	2890	4390	2130	2720	4130	1960	2560
		1	5740	2780	3680	5330	2580	3380	4990	2410	3000

[a]Tabulated lateral design values (Z) for bolted connections shall be multiplied by all applicable adjustment factors (see NDS Table 10.3.1).

[b]Tabulated lateral design values (Z) are for "full diameter" bolts (see NDS Appendix L) with bending yield (F_{yb}) of 45,000 psi.

Note: Some rows/columns not pertinent to this text have been omitted by PPI.

Timber Connectors

There are two types of timber connectors: split rings and shear plates. *Split rings* have either a 2½ in or 4 in diameter and are cut through in one place in the circumference to form a tongue and slot. The ring is beveled from the central portion toward the edges. Grooves are cut in each piece of the wood members to be joined so that half the ring is in each section. The members are held together with a bolt concentric with the ring as shown in Fig. 38.4(a).

Shear plates have either a $2\frac{5}{8}$ in or 4 in diameter and are flat plates with a flange extending from the face of the plate. There is a hole in the middle through which either a $\frac{3}{4}$ in or $\frac{7}{8}$ in bolt is placed to hold the two members together. Shear plates are inserted in precut grooves in a piece of wood so that the plate is flush with one surface. See Fig. 38.4(b). Because of this configuration, shear plate connections can hold together either two pieces of wood or one piece of wood and a steel plate.

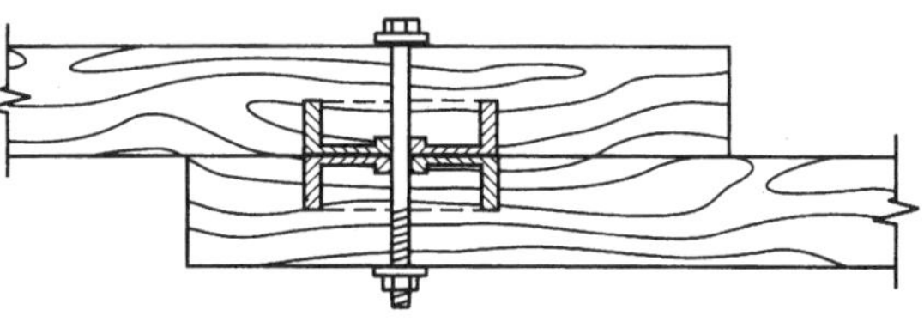

(a) split ring connector

(b) shear plate connector

Figure 38.4 Timber Connectors

Split ring connectors and shear plates can transfer larger loads than bolts or screws alone and are often used in connecting truss members. Shear plates are particularly suited for constructions that must be disassembled. Tables of design values for loads, spacing, and end and edge distances are published by the National Forest Products Association.

Miscellaneous Connection Hardware

Because wood is such a common building material, there are dozens of types of special connectors especially designed to make assembly easy, fast, and structurally sound. Hardware is available for standard sizes of wood members as well as for special members like wood truss joists. Manufacturers publish allowable design values for each of their pieces. Some of the common types of connection hardware are shown in Fig. 38.5.

STEEL CONNECTIONS

Bolting and *welding* are the two most common methods in use for making steel connections. *Riveting* was once widely used but has been generally replaced with bolting because bolting is less expensive and does not take such a large crew of skilled workers to accomplish.

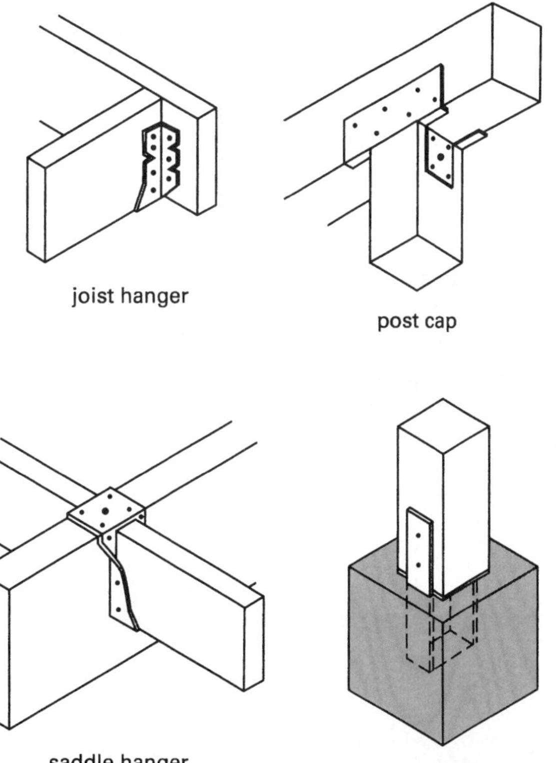

Figure 38.5 Special Connection Hardware

Bolts

There are two types of bolted connections: bearing type and slip-critical. *Bearing-type connections* resist the shear load on the bolt through friction between surfaces but may also produce direct bearing between the steel being fastened and the sides of the bolts. This is due to the fact that bolt holes are slightly larger than the bolts, and under load the two pieces of steel being connected may shift until they are bearing against the bolt.

Slip-critical connections are those where any amount of slip would be detrimental to the serviceability of the structure, such as joints subject to fatigue loading or joints with oversized holes. With slip-critical joints, the entire load is carried by friction.

Bolts are further classified as to whether the bolt threads are included or excluded from the shear plane. This affects the strength of the connection because there is less area to resist the load through the threaded portion. See Fig. 38.6. Like wood connections, bolts may be either single shear or double shear.

There are three basic types of bolts used in modern steel construction. Bolts designated with the American Society of Testing and Materials (ASTM) number A307 are called *unfinished bolts* and have the lowest load-carrying capacity. They are used only for bearing-type connections. Bolts designated A325 and A490 are *high-strength bolts* and may be used in bearing-type connections but must be used in slip-critical connections. In slip-critical connections, the nuts are tightened to develop a high tensile stress in the bolt, thus causing the connected members to develop a high friction between them that resists the shear.

Figure 38.6 Location of Bolt Threads in Relation to Shear Plane

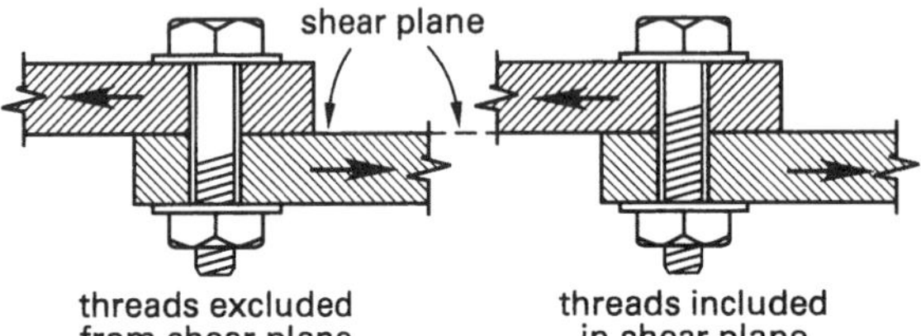

Bolts range in diameter from $^5/_8$ in to $1^1/_2$ in in $^5/_8$ in increments, but the most typically used diameters are $^3/_4$ in and $^7/_8$ in. Bolts are installed with a washer under the head and nut. In addition to the ASTM designations, there are standard codes for the conditions of use.

- SC: slip-critical connection
- N: bearing-type connection with threads included in the shear plane
- X: bearing-type connection with threads excluded from the shear plane
- S: bolt in single shear
- D: bolt in double shear

The American Institute of Steel Construction *Steel Construction Manual* (*AISC Manual*) gives the allowable loads for various types of connectors in both shear and bearing. For bearing connections, different values are given based on the minimum tensile strength of the base material of the connected part. For A36 steel, this value is 58 ksi. The maximum allowable bearing stress between the bolt and the side of the hole is given by the equation

$$F_p = 1.2F_u \quad 38.2$$

The allowable loads for shear are given in Table 38.3, and the allowable loads for bearing based on bolt spacing are given in Table 38.4. Similar tables for bearing strength are given in the *Steel Construction Manual* based on bolt edge distance. To use the tables, the bolt's diameter and designation must be known, as well as the type of hole being used, the connection type, and the loading condition. Procedures for using these tables will be shown in following examples.

Table 38.3
Available Shear Strength of Bolts

Available Shear Strength of Bolts, kips

Nominal Bolt Diameter, *d*, in.					5/8		3/4		7/8		1	
Nominal Bolt Area, in.^{2}					0.307		0.442		0.601		0.785	
ASTM Desig.	Thread Cond.	F_{nv}/Ω (ksi)	ϕF_{nv} (ksi)	Load-ing	r_n/Ω	ϕr_n	r_n/Ω	ϕr_n	r_n/Ω	ϕr_n	r_n/Ω	ϕr_n
		ASD	LRFD		ASD	LRFD	ASD	LRFD	ASD	LRFD	ASD	LRFD
Group A	N	27.0	40.5	S	8.29	12.4	11.9	17.9	16.2	24.3	21.2	31.8
				D	16.6	24.9	23.9	35.8	32.5	48.7	42.4	63.6
	X	34.0	51.0	S	10.4	15.7	15.0	22.5	20.4	30.7	26.7	40.0
				D	20.9	31.3	30.1	45.1	40.9	61.3	53.4	80.1
Group B	N	34.0	51.0	S	10.4	15.7	15.0	22.5	20.4	30.7	26.7	40.0
				D	20.9	31.3	30.1	45.1	40.9	61.3	53.4	80.1
	X	42.0	63.0	S	12.9	19.3	18.6	27.8	25.2	37.9	33.0	49.5
				D	25.8	38.7	37.1	55.7	50.5	75.7	65.9	98.9
A307	–	13.5	20.3	S	4.14	6.23	5.97	8.97	8.11	12.2	10.6	15.9
				D	8.29	12.5	11.9	17.9	16.2	24.4	21.2	31.9

Nominal Bolt Diameter, *d*, in.					1 1/8		1 1/4		1 3/8		1 1/2	
Nominal Bolt Area, in.^{2}					0.994		0.442		1.48		1.77	
ASTM Desig.	Thread Cond.	F_{nv}/Ω (ksi)	ϕF_{nv} (ksi)	Load-ing	r_n/Ω	ϕr_n	r_n/Ω	ϕr_n	r_n/Ω	ϕr_n	r_n/Ω	ϕr_n
		ASD	LRFD		ASD	LRFD	ASD	LRFD	ASD	LRFD	ASD	LRFD
Group A	N	27.0	40.5	S	26.8	40.3	33.2	49.8	40.0	59.9	47.8	71.7
				D	53.7	80.5	66.4	99.6	79.9	120	95.6	143
	X	34.0	51.0	S	33.8	50.7	41.8	62.7	50.3	75.5	60.2	90.3
				D	67.6	101	83.6	125	101	151	120	181
Group B	N	34.0	51.0	S	33.8	50.7	41.8	62.7	50.3	75.5	60.2	90.3
				D	67.6	101	83.6	125	101	151	120	181
	X	42.0	63.0	S	41.7	62.6	51.7	77.5	62.2	93.2	74.3	112
				D	83.5	125	103	155	124	186	149	223
A307	–	13.5	20.3	S	13.4	20.2	16.6	25.0	20.0	30.0	23.9	35.9
				D	26.8	40.4	33.2	49.9	40.0	60.1	47.8	71.9
ASD	LRFD	For end loaded connections greater than 38 in., see AISC *Specification* Table J3.2 footnote b.										
Ω = 2.00	ϕ = 0.75											

From *Steel Construction Manual,* © 2011, American Institute of Steel Construction, Inc.

Product Development

Table 38.4
Available Bearing Strength at Bolt Holes Based on Bolt Spacing

Available Bearing Strength at Bolt Holes Based on Bolt Spacing

kips/in. thickness

Hole Type	Bolt Spacing, s, in.	F_u, ksi	Nominal Bolt Diameter, d, in.							
			5/8		3/4		7/8		1	
			r_n/Ω	ϕr_n	r_n/Ω	ϕr_n	r_n/Ω	ϕr_n	r_n/Ω	ϕr_n
			ASD	LRFD	ASD	LRFD	ASD	LRFD	ASD	LRFD
STD SSLT	$2^2/_3\ d_b$	58	34.1	51.1	41.3	62.0	48.6	72.9	55.8	83.7
		65	38.2	57.3	46.3	69.5	54.4	81.7	62.6	93.8
	3 in.	58	43.5	65.3	52.2	78.3	60.9	91.4	67.4	101
		65	48.8	73.1	58.5	87.8	68.3	102	75.5	113
SSLP	$2^2/_3\ d_b$	58	27.6	41.3	34.8	52.2	42.1	63.1	47.1	70.7
		65	30.9	46.3	39.0	58.5	47.1	70.7	52.8	79.2
	3 in.	58	43.5	65.3	52.2	78.3	60.9	91.4	58.7	88.1
		65	48.8	73.1	58.5	87.8	68.3	102	65.8	98.7
OVS	$2^2/_3\ d_b$	58	29.7	44.6	37.0	55.5	44.2	66.3	49.3	74.0
		65	33.3	50.0	41.4	62.2	49.6	74.3	55.3	82.9
	3 in.	58	43.5	65.3	52.2	78.3	60.9	91.4	60.9	91.4
		65	48.8	73.1	58.5	87.8	68.3	102	68.3	102
LSLP	$2^2/_3\ d_b$	58	3.62	5.44	4.35	6.53	5.08	7.61	5.80	8.70
		65	4.03	6.09	4.88	7.31	5.69	8.53	6.50	9.75
	3 in.	58	43.5	65.3	39.2	58.7	28.3	42.4	17.4	26.1
		65	48.8	73.1	43.9	65.8	31.7	47.5	19.5	29.3
LSLT	$2^2/_3\ d_b$	58	28.4	42.6	34.4	51.7	40.5	60.7	46.5	69.8
		65	31.8	47.7	38.6	57.9	45.5	68.0	52.1	78.2
	3 in.	58	36.3	54.4	43.5	65.3	50.8	76.1	56.2	84.3
		65	40.6	60.9	48.8	73.1	56.9	85.3	63.0	94.5
STD, SSLT SSLP, OVS, LSLP	$s \geq s_{full}$	58	43.5	65.3	52.2	78.3	60.9	91.4	69.6	104
		65	48.8	73.1	58.5	87.8	68.3	102	78.0	117
LSLT	$s \geq s_{full}$	58	36.3	54.4	43.5	65.3	50.8	76.1	58.0	87.0
		65	40.6	60.9	48.8	73.1	56.9	85.3	65.0	97.5
Spacing for full bearing strength s_{full}[a], in.		STD, SSLT, LSLT	$1^{15}/_{16}$		$2^5/_{16}$		$2^{11}/_{16}$		$3^1/_{16}$	
		OVS	$2^1/_{16}$		$2^7/_{16}$		$2^{13}/_{16}$		$3^1/_4$	
		SSLP	$2^1/_8$		$2^1/_2$		$2^7/_8$		$3^5/_{16}$	
		LSLP	$2^{13}/_{16}$		$3^3/_8$		$3^{15}/_{16}$		$4^1/_2$	
Minimum Spacing[a] = $2^2/_3 d$, in.			$1^{11}/_{16}$		2		$2^5/_{16}$		$2^{11}/_{16}$	

STD = standard hole
SSLT = short-slotted hole oriented transverse to the line of force
SSLP = short-slotted hole oriented parallel to the line of force
OVS = oversized hole
LSLP = long-slotted hole oriented parallel to the line of force
LSLT = long-slotted hole oriented transverse to the line of force

ASD	LRFD
$\Omega = 2.00$	$\phi = 0.75$

Note: Spacing indicated is from the center of the hole or slot to the center of the adjacent hole or slot in the line of force. Hole deformation is considered. When hole deformation is not considered, see AISC *Specification* Section J3.10.

[a] Decimal value has been rounded to the nearest sixteenth of an inch.

From *Steel Construction Manual*, © 2011, American Institute of Steel Construction, Inc.

There are several types of holes for bolted connections. *Standard round holes* are $^1/_{16}$ in larger than the diameter of the bolt. Other kinds of holes may be used with high-strength bolts having $^5/_8$ in and larger diameters.

Oversized holes may have nominal diameters up to $^3/_{16}$ in larger than bolts $^7/_8$ in and less in diameter, $^1/_4$ in larger than 1 in bolts, and $^5/_{16}$ in larger than bolts $1^1/_8$ in and greater in diameter. These holes may only be used in slip-critical connections.

Short slotted holes are $^1/_{16}$ in wider than the bolt diameter and have a length that does not exceed the oversized hole dimensions by more than $^1/_{16}$ in. They may be used in either bearing or slip-critical connections, but if used in bearing, the slots have to be perpendicular to the direction of the load.

Long slotted holes are $^1/_{16}$ in wider than the bolt diameter and a have length not exceeding $2^1/_2$ times the bolt diameter. They may be used in slip-critical connections without regard to direction of load, but must be perpendicular to the load direction in bearing-type connections.

Slotted holes are used where some amount of adjustment is needed. Long slotted holes can only be used in one of the connected parts of a joint. The other part must use standard round holes or be welded.

In addition to the load-carrying capacities of the bolts, the effect of reducing the cross-sectional area of the members must be checked. Figure 38.7 shows a typical example of this. In this case, a beam is framed into a girder with an angle welded to the girder and bolted to the beam. With a load applied to the beam, there is a tendency for the web of the beam to tear where the area of the web has been reduced by the bolt holes. This area is known as the *net area.* As shown, there is both shear failure parallel to the load and tension failure perpendicular to the load.

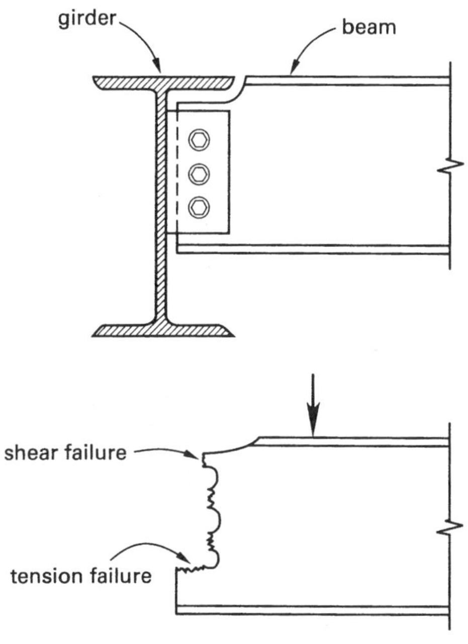

Figure 38.7
Tearing Failures at Bolted Connection

The *AISC Manual* limits the allowable stress on the net tension area to

$$F_t = 0.50F_u \qquad 38.3$$

The allowable stress on the net shear area is limited to

$$F_v = 0.30F_u \qquad 38.4$$

For A36 steel, $F_u = 58$ ksi and $F_y = 36$ ksi.

The total tearing force is the sum required to cause both forms of failure.

The stress on net tension area must be compared with the allowable stress on the gross section, which is

$$F_t = 0.60F_y \qquad 38.5$$

Product Development

Example 38.3

A $\frac{3}{8}$ in A36 steel plate is suspended from a $\frac{1}{2}$ in plate with three $\frac{3}{4}$ in A325 bolts in standard holes spaced as shown. The threads are excluded from the shear plane, and the connection is bearing type. Assuming full bearing capacity, what is the maximum load-carrying capacity of the $\frac{3}{8}$ in plate?

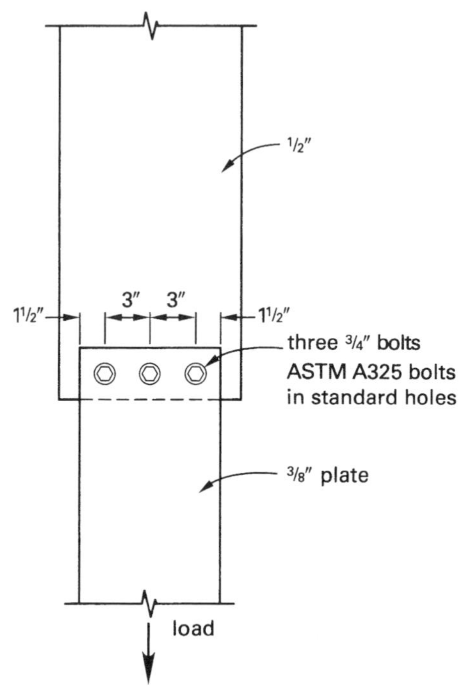

Solution

First, check the shear capacity of the bolts. From Table 38.3, one bolt can carry a load of 13.3 kips, or three bolts can carry (3)(13.3 kips), or 39.9 kips.

Next, check bearing capacity. The thinner material governs, which is $\frac{3}{8}$ in. In Table 38.4, read from the STD and $s > s_{\text{full}}$ row under the $\frac{3}{4}$ in diameter column (with $F_u = 58$ and ASD). The available strength is 52.2 kips/in thickness. Multiply this value by the $\frac{3}{8}$ in thickness to get 19.6 kips. Three bolts will then carry (3)(19.6 kips) = 58 kips.

Finally, determine the maximum stress on the net section through the holes. Once again, the thinner material is the most critical component. The allowable unit stress is

$$F_t = 0.50F_u = (0.50)(58 \text{ kips}) = 29 \text{ ksi}$$

The diameter of each hole is $\frac{1}{8}$ in larger than the bolt for net sections, $\frac{1}{8}$ or $\frac{7}{8}$ in, which is 0.875 in. The net width of the $\frac{3}{8}$ in plate is

$$9 \text{ in} - (3)(0.875 \text{ in}) = 6.375 \text{ in}$$

The allowable load on the net section is

$$P = (6.375 \text{ in})(0.375 \text{ in})\left(29 \ \frac{\text{kips}}{\text{in}^2}\right) = 69.33 \text{ kips}$$

The allowable stress on the gross section is

$$P = (0.6)\left(36 \ \frac{\text{kips}}{\text{in}^2}\right)(9 \text{ in})(0.375 \text{ in}) = 72.9 \text{ kips}$$

From these four loads, the minimum governs, which is the shear capacity of the bolts, or 39.9 kips.

There are many kinds of framed connections depending on the type of connector being used, the size and shape of the connected members, and the magnitude of the loads that must be transferred. Figure 38.8 illustrates some of the more typical kinds of steel connections. In most cases, the angle used to connect one piece with another is welded to one member in the shop and bolted to the other member during field erection. Slotted holes are sometimes used to allow for minor field adjustments.

If the top flange of one beam needs to be flush with another, the web is coped as shown in Fig. 38.8(b).

Simple beam-to-column connections are often made as illustrated in Fig. 38.8(c). The seat angle carries most of the gravity load, and the clip angle is used to provide stability from rotation. If a moment connection is required, a detail similar to Fig. 38.8(d) is used, although welding is more suitable for moment connections. For tubes and round columns, a single plate can be welded to the column and connected with beams as shown in Fig. 38.8(f). When the loads are heavy, some engineers prefer to slot the column and run the shear plate through, welding it at the front and back of the column.

Since connecting beams to columns and other beams with angles and bolts is such a common method of steel framing, the *AISC Manual* gives tables of allowable loads for various types and diameters of bolts and lengths and thicknesses of angles.

One of the important considerations in bolted steel connections, just as in wood connections, is the spacing of bolts and the edge distance from the last bolt to the edge of the member. The *AISC Manual* specifies minimum dimensions. The absolute minimum spacing is $2\frac{2}{3}$ times the diameter of the bolt being used, with 3 times the diameter being the preferred dimension. Many times, a dimension of 3 in is used for all sizes of bolts up to 1 in diameter.

The required edge distance varies with the diameter of the bolt being used: at the edges of plates, shapes, or bars, the dimension is 1 in for a $\frac{3}{4}$ in bolt and 1.25 in for a 1 in bolt. To simplify detailing and tabulated values, a dimension of 1.25 in is often used for all bolts having a diameter up to 1 in.

Figure 38.8 Typical Steel Framing Connections

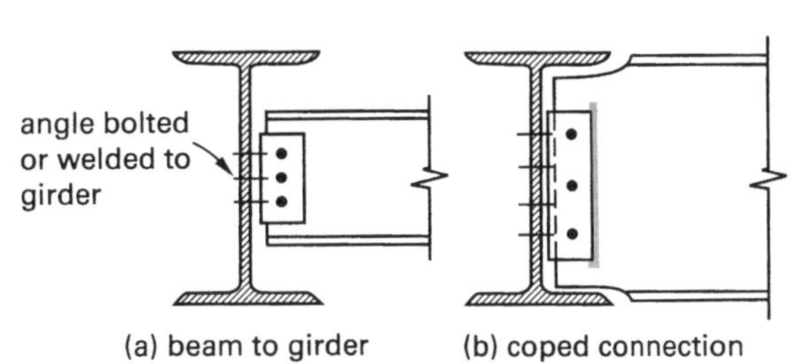

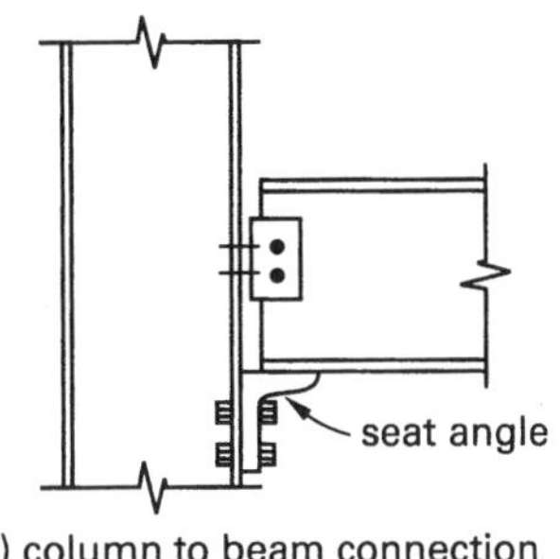

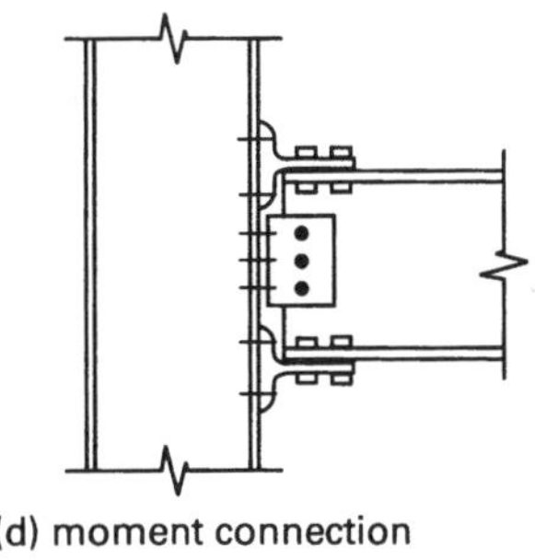

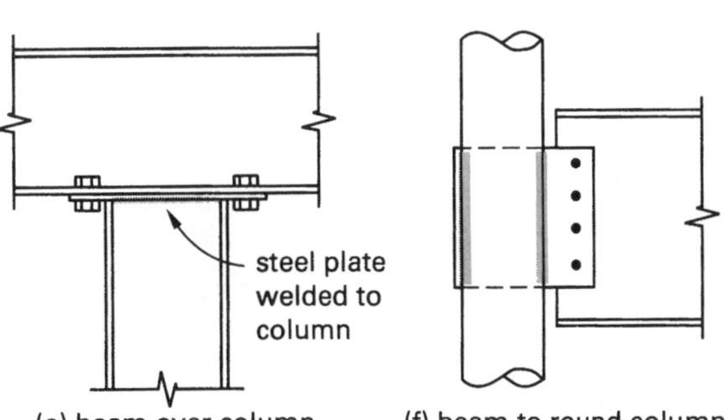

Welds

Welded connections are quite frequently used in lieu of bolts for several reasons.

- The gross cross section of the members can be used instead of the net section.
- Construction is often more efficient because there are no angles, bolts, or washers to deal with and no clearance problems with wrenches.
- Welding is more practical for moment connections.

Figure 38.9
Types of Welded Connections

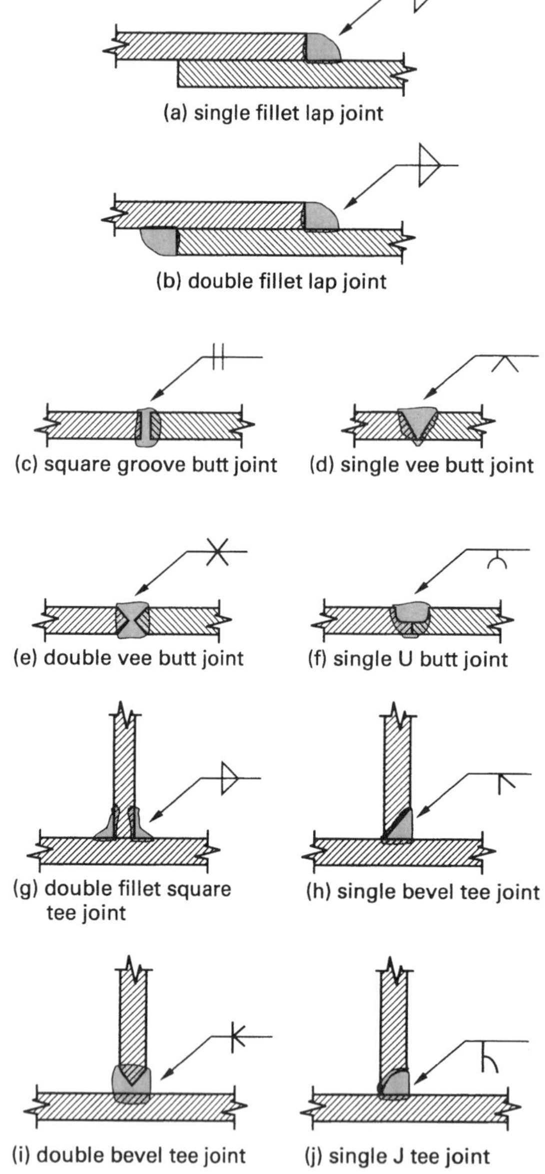

Since members must be held in place until welding is completed, welding is often used in combination with bolting. Connection angles and other pieces are welded to one member in the shop with the outreach leg punched or slotted for field connection with bolts.

There are several types of welding processes, but the one most commonly used in building construction is the *electric arc process.* One electrode from the power source is attached to the steel members being joined, and the other electrode is the welding rod the welder holds in his or her hand. The intense heat generated by the electric arc formed when the welding rod is brought close to the members causes some of the base metal and the end of the electrode to melt into the joint, so the material of the electrode and both pieces of the joint are fused together. *Penetration* refers to the depth from the surface of the base metal to the point where fusion stops.

Two types of electrodes are in common use: the E60 and the E70. The allowable shear stress for E60 electrodes is 18 kips per square inch (ksi), and for E70 electrodes it is 21 ksi.

There are many types of welds. Which one to use depends on the configuration of the joint, the magnitude and direction of the load, the cost of preparing the joint, and what the erection process will be. The three most common types of welded joints are the *lap*, the *butt*, and the *tee.* Some of the common welding conditions for these joints are shown in Fig. 38.9 along with the standard welding symbol used on drawings. In addition to the welds shown, plug or slot welds are frequently used to join two pieces. In these welds, a hole is cut or punched in one of the members, and the area is filled with the weld.

The fillet weld is one of the most common types. In section, its form is an isosceles triangle with the two equal legs of the triangle being the size of the weld. The perpendicular distance from the 90° corner to the hypotenuse of the triangle is called the *throat.* See Fig. 38.10(a). Because the angles are 45°, the dimension of the throat is 0.707 times the leg dimension.

For a butt joint, the throat dimension is the thickness of the material if both pieces are the same thickness, or the size of the thinner of two materials if they are unequal as shown in Fig. 38.10(b).

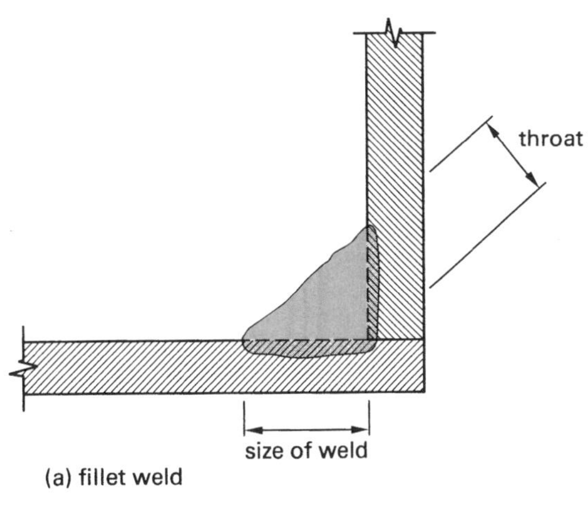

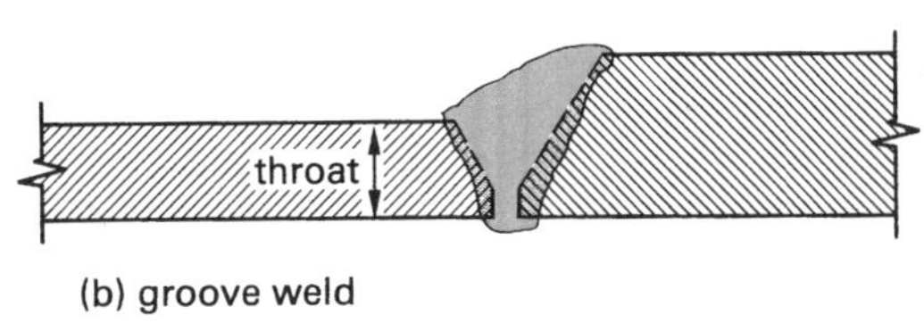

Figure 38.10 Weld Dimensions

There are common symbols used for welding. These are listed in the *AISC Manual.* A few are reproduced in Fig. 38.11(a). The full range of symbols gives information regarding the type, size, location, finish, welding process, angle for grooves, and other information. To indicate information about a weld, a horizontal line is connected to an arrowhead line that points to the weld. This is shown in Fig. 38.11(b).

The type of weld is indicated with one of the standard symbols and placed below the line if the weld is on the side near the arrow and above the line if it is on the side away from the arrow. If the members are to be welded on both sides, the symbol is repeated above and below the line. Other data placed with the weld symbol are the size, length of weld, and spacing, in that order, reading from left to right. Field welds are indicated with a flag placed at the junction of the horizontal line and the arrowhead line and pointing toward the tail of the reference line. A circle at the same point indicates that the weld should be made all around. The perpendicular legs of the fillet, bevel, J, and flare bevel welds must be at the left.

Designing a welded joint requires knowledge of the load to be resisted and the allowable stress in the weld. For fillet welds, the stress is considered as shear on the throat regardless of the direction of the load. For butt welds, the allowable stress is the same as for the base metal. As previously mentioned, the allowable stress for fillet welds of E60 electrodes is 18 ksi, and for E70 electrodes it is 21 ksi. These stresses apply to A36 steel. For any size fillet weld it is possible to multiply the size by 0.707 and by the allowable stress to get the allowable working strength per linear inch of weld, but these values have been tabulated for quicker calculations. The allowable strengths are listed in Table 38.5.

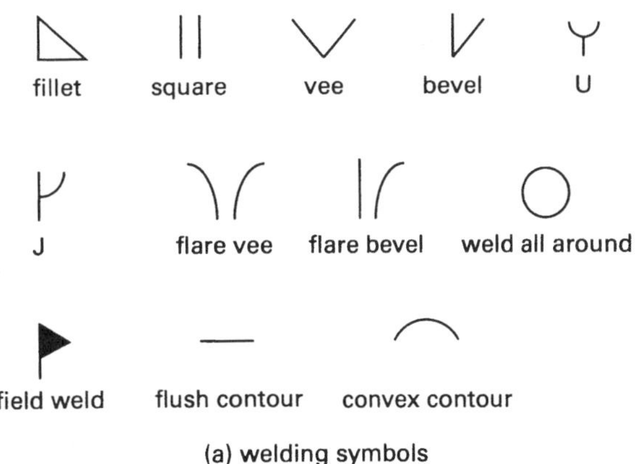

weld all around
field weld
1/4
3@4
length of weld and spacing
weld symbol
size of weld

(b) typical welding symbol

Figure 38.11 Welding Symbols

Product Development

Table 38.5
Allowable Working Strengths of Fillet Welds

size of weld (in)	allowable load (kips/in)	
	E60 electrodes	E70 electrodes
$^3/_{16}$	2.4	2.8
$^1/_4$	3.2	3.7
$^5/_{16}$	4.0	4.6
$^3/_8$	4.8	5.6
$^1/_2$	6.4	7.4
$^5/_8$	8.0	9.3
$^3/_4$	9.5	11.1

From *Steel Construction Manual*, © 2014, American Institute of Steel Construction, Inc.

Table 38.6
Minimum Size of Fillet Welds

material thickness of the thicker part joined (in)	minimum size of fillet weld (in)
to $^1/_4$ inclusive	$^1/_8$
over $^1/_4$ to $^1/_2$	$^3/_{16}$
over $^1/_2$ to $^3/_4$	$^1/_4$
over $^3/_4$	$^5/_{16}$

From *Steel Construction Manual*, © 2014, American Institute of Steel Construction, Inc.

In addition to knowing the allowable stresses, some *AISC Manual* provisions apply to weld design. The following are some of the requirements.

- The maximum size of a fillet weld is $^1/_{16}$ in less than the nominal thickness of the material being joined if it is $^1/_4$ in thick or more. If the material is less than $^1/_4$ in thick, the maximum size is the same as the material.
- The minimum size of fillet welds is shown in Table 38.6.
- The minimum length of fillet welds must not be less than 4 times the weld size plus $^1/_4$ in for starting and stopping the arc.
- For two or more welds parallel to each other, the length must be at least equal to the perpendicular distance between them.
- For intermittent welds, the length must be at least $1^1/_2$ in.

Product Development

Example 38.4

An A36 steel bar, $^3/_8 \times 4$, is welded to a tube section with E70 electrodes as shown. What is the maximum load-carrying capacity if the maximum size of weld is used?

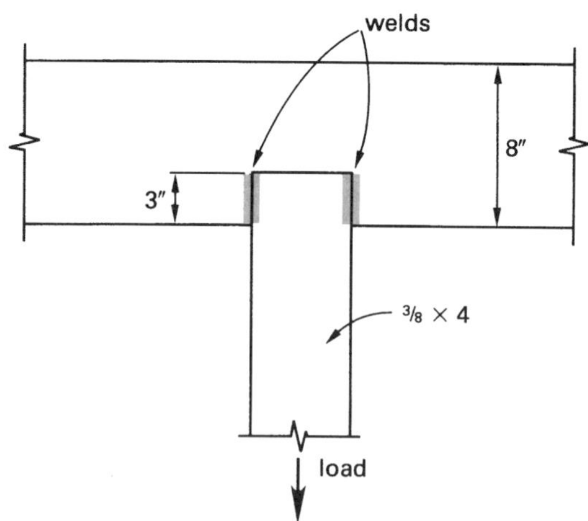

Solution

Since the maximum weld size is $1/16$ in less than the member being joined, a weld of $5/16$ in will be used. From Table 38.5, the allowable load is 4.6 kips/in. The total load is therefore

$$(2)(3\text{ in})\left(4.6\ \frac{\text{kips}}{\text{in}}\right) = 27.6\text{ kips}$$

Example 38.5

A $3 \times 3 \times 3 \times 1/4$ angle (area of 1.44 in^2) is to be welded to a gusset plate to serve as a tension member as shown. If A36 steel and E60 electrodes are used, what are the required size and length of weld on both sides of the angle if the full load-carrying capacity of the angle is to be developed?

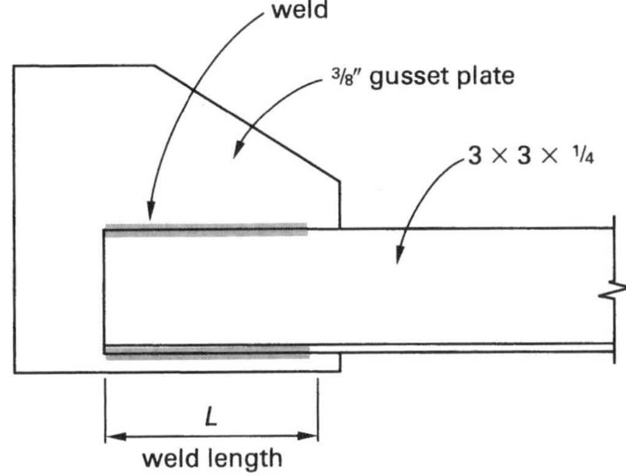

Solution

First, the maximum allowable capacity of the angle must be determined. The allowable unit stress is 0.60 times the minimum yield point of steel (Eq. 38.5). The total maximum capacity is the unit stress times the area of the angle.

$$P = 0.60F_yA = (0.60)\left(36\ \frac{\text{kips}}{\text{in}^2}\right)(1.44\text{ in}^2) = 31.1\text{ kips}$$

For a $1/4$ in angle, the maximum size of weld is $3/16$ in which, from Table 38.5, has a load-carrying capacity of 2.4 kips/in with E60 electrodes. The total length of weld is

$$\frac{31.1\text{ kips}}{2.4\ \frac{\text{kips}}{\text{in}}} = 12.96\text{ in}$$

Round up to 13 in. Since the welding will be on both sides of the angle, each weld should be at least $6\frac{1}{2}$ in long.

Figure 38.12
Concrete Joints Tied with Rebars

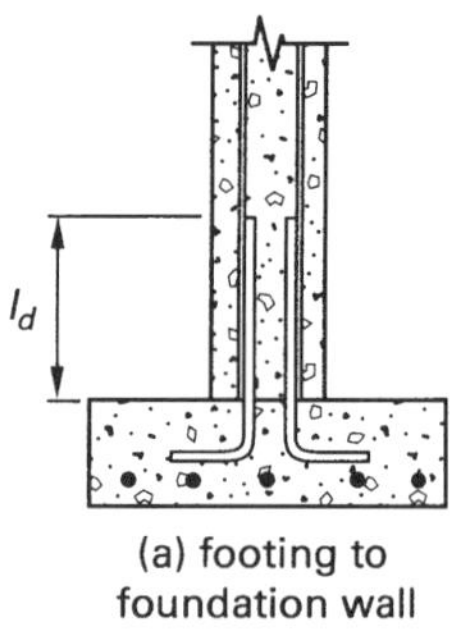

(a) footing to foundation wall

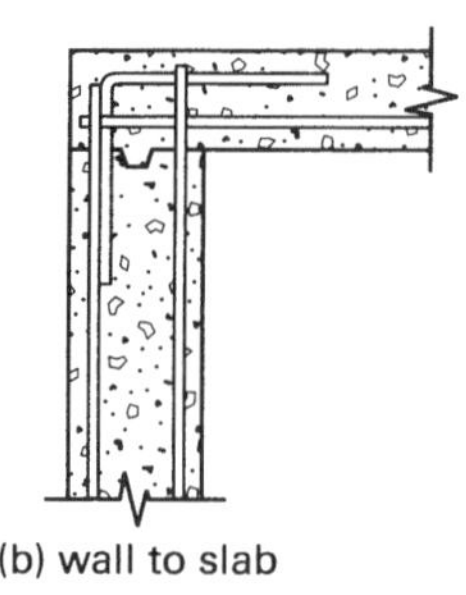

(b) wall to slab

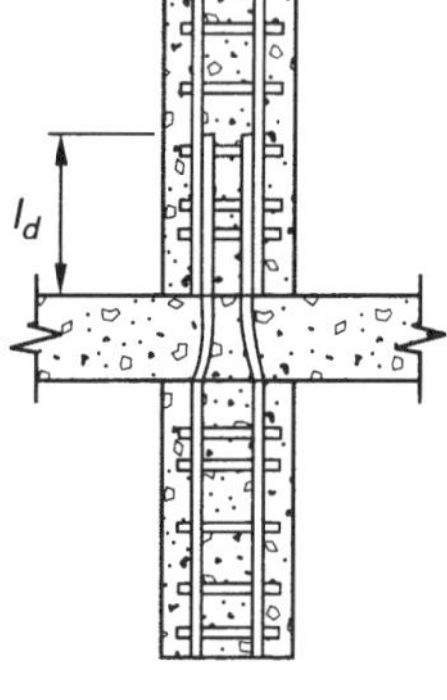

(c) column to column

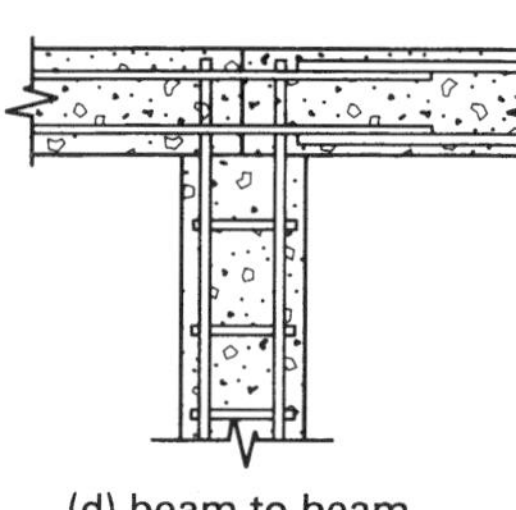

(d) beam to beam

CONCRETE CONNECTIONS

In most cast-in-place concrete construction there are generally no connectors as with wood or steel. Different pours of concrete are tied together with reinforcing bars or with keyed sections. For precast concrete construction, however, there must be some way of rigidly attaching one piece to another. This is accomplished with weld plates.

Rebars and Keyed Sections

The most typical type of cast-in-place concrete joint is one where the reinforcing bars are allowed to extend past the formwork to become part of the next pour. Continuity is achieved through the bonding of the two pours of concrete with the rebars that extend through the joint. These types of joints are found in many situations: footing to foundation wall, walls to slabs, beams to beams, columns to beams, and several others. When the reinforcing is only for the purpose of tying two pours of concrete together rather than transmitting large loads, they are called *dowels*. Some typical conditions are shown in Fig. 38.12. The length of the dowels or extensions of rebar from one section of concrete to the next is determined by the minimum development length required to transmit the loads or by ACI 318.

Keyed sections are used either alone or with rebars to provide a stronger joint between two pours of concrete. Keyed sections are often used in footings and floor slabs as shown in Fig. 38.13.

Figure 38.13
Keyed Concrete Connections

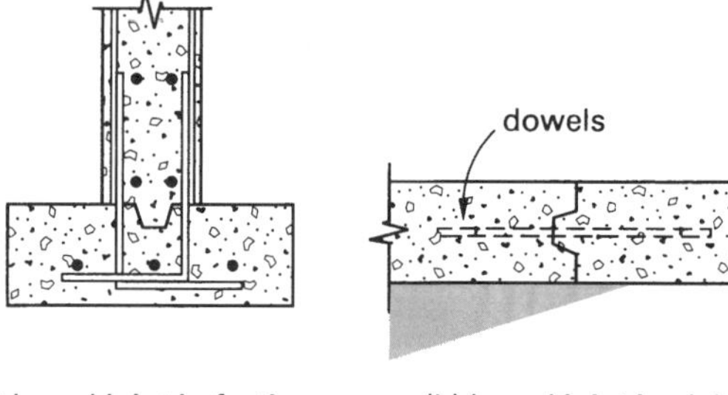

(a) keyed joint in footing (b) keyed joint in slab

Weld Plates

Because precast structures are built in sections, there must be some way to transmit horizontal, vertical, and moment forces from one piece to the next. This is usually accomplished by casting weld plates, angles, and other types of steel pieces into the concrete members at the factory. At the site, the members are placed in position, and corresponding plates are welded together. When allowance must be made for horizontal movement due to temperature changes, concrete shrinkage, and the like, precast members often bear on elastomeric pads rather than being rigidly fastened. Figure 38.14 shows two of the many possible types of precast connections.

Shear Connectors

Shear connectors are not really connectors in the usual sense, but are used to tie steel and concrete together in composite sections so forces are transmitted from one to the other. They are available in diameters of $^5/_8$ in, $^3/_4$ in, and $^7/_8$ in. One of the typical applications of shear connectors is with concrete slab/steel beam composite sections as shown in Fig. 38.15. The connectors are welded to the top of the steel beam in the fabricating shop at a fairly close spacing, which is determined by engineering calculations to transmit the forces created by the applied loads.

When the beam is erected, forms are placed and the concrete is poured around the connectors (along with any tensile and temperature steel). The enlarged head of the connector is provided to give extra bearing surface. These are often called *headed anchor studs* and abbreviated HAS on the drawings.

Figure 38.15 shows a single row of studs, but two rows may be used if required. Metal decking instead of removable forms is often used for forming the concrete.

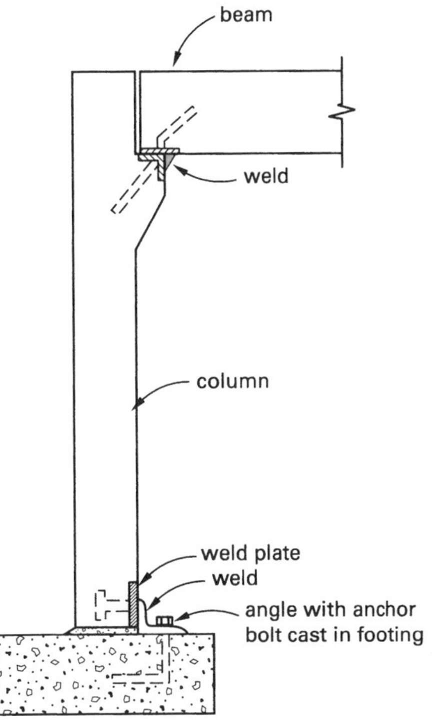

Figure 38.14 Precast Concrete Connections

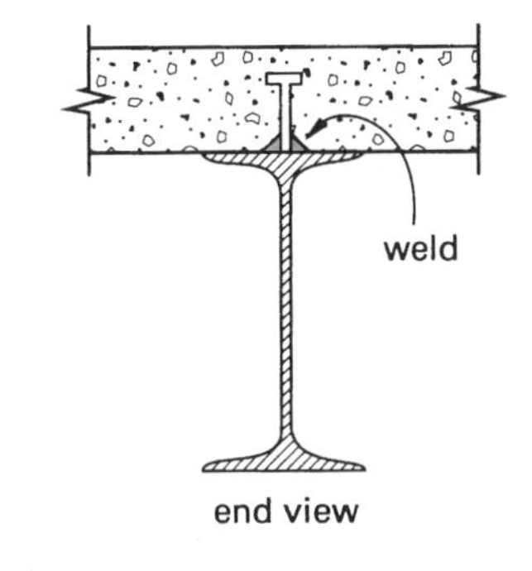

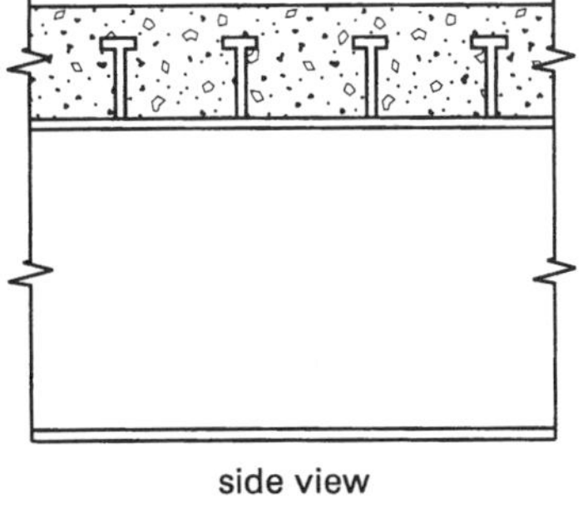

Figure 38.15 Shear Connectors

Product Development

39 BUILDING CODE REQUIREMENTS ON STRUCTURAL DESIGN

Nomenclature

C_F	size factor	–	F_v	allowable shear stress	lbf/in²
d	depth of beam	in	F_y	specified minimum yield stress of the type of steel being used	lbf/in²
D	dead load	lbf/ft²	L	live load	lbf/ft²
E	earthquake or seismic load	lbf/ft²	L_r	roof live load	–
f_1	floor live load occupancy combination factor	–	R	rain load	lbf/ft²
f_2	snow load roof shape combination factor	–	S	snow load	lbf/ft²
f_c'	compressive strength	lbf/in²	W	wind load	lbf/ft²
F_b	allowable bending stress	lbf/in²	ω	wind load coefficient	–
F_t	allowable axial tensile stress	lbf/in²	Ω	safety factor (ASD)	–

Building code provisions related to structural design deal with how loads must be determined, what stresses are allowed in structural members, formulas for designing members of various materials, and miscellaneous requirements for construction. This chapter provides an overview of the requirements with which the candidate should be familiar. Specific provisions and calculation methods are presented in other chapters. Loads on buildings are covered in Chap. 33, wind loading and calculation methods in Chap. 44, and seismic design methods are reviewed in Chap. 45. The code provisions outlined are based on the *International Building Code* (IBC).

ALLOWABLE STRESSES

The IBC establishes basic allowable stresses for various types of construction materials. The design of any structural member must be such that these stresses are not exceeded. Although some provisions of the code are extremely complex (such as with concrete), this section outlines some of the more important provisions to be familiar with.

Wood

Tables 4A, 4B, 4C, 4D, 4E, 5A, 5B, and 5C of the *National Design Specification for Wood Construction* (NDS) give allowable unit stresses in structural lumber and glued-laminated timber. Examples of these tables are shown in Chap. 18. These include allowable stresses for extreme fiber in bending, tension parallel to the grain, horizontal shear, and compression perpendicular and parallel to the grain. The stresses given are for normal loading and must be adjusted according to various conditions of use as follows.

Repetitive use: A factor (C_r) equal to 1.15 is used when several beam members, such as joists or rafters, are used together. In order to use the repetitive factor C_r, the members cannot be over 4 in thick (nominal), cannot be spaced more than 24 in on center, and must be joined by transverse load-distributing elements (such as bridging or decking), and there must be at least three members in a group.

Duration of load: The amount of stress a wood member can withstand is dependent on the time during which the load producing the stress acts. This relation of strength to duration of load is shown graphically in Fig. 39.1. Allowable design loads are based on what is called *normal duration of load*, which is assumed to be 10 years. For duration of loads shorter than this, the allowable stress may be increased according to the following percentages.

- 15% for two months' duration, as for snow
- 25% for seven days' duration, as for roof loads
- 60% for wind or earthquake loads
- 100% for impact loads

If a structural member is fully stressed to the maximum allowable stress for more than 10 years under conditions of maximum design load, the allowable stress cannot exceed 90% of those listed in the tables.

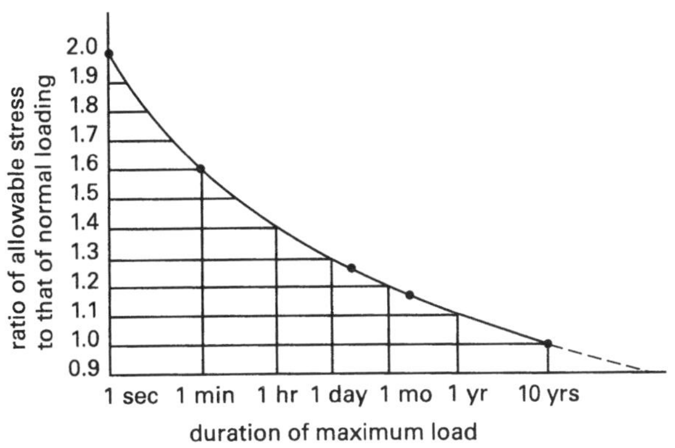

Figure 39.1 Relation of Strength to Duration of Load for Wood Structural Members

Fire-retardant treatment: The NDS states that the effect of fire retardant chemical treatments on strength must be considered. Allowable design values, including connection design values, for lumber and structural glued-laminated timber pressure treated with fire-retardant chemicals must be obtained from the company providing the treatment and redrying service.

Size factor adjustment: Design values for bending, tension, and compression parallel to the grain for visually graded dimension lumber 2 in to 4 in thick must be multiplied by size factors given at the beginning of NDS Tables 4A, 4B, 4C, and 4E. When the depth of a rectangular sawn bending member 5 in or thicker exceeds 12 in, the bending design values, F_b, must be multiplied by a size factor determined by Eq. 39.1.

$$C_F = \left(\frac{12}{d}\right)^{1/9} \tag{39.1}$$

There is also a slenderness factor adjustment for unsupported beams. However, most wood members are supported either with bridging or with continuous decking material, so this adjustment is not usually required.

Steel

Using the ASD method of design, the allowable stress for a steel member is expressed as the yield stress of the steel divided by a safety factor, Ω. This factor varies with the type of stress the member is under (shear, compression, bending, or tension) and with conditions such as unsupported lengths and geometry of the section. Some of the more common code requirements for allowable stress are as follows.

For tension on the gross area, $\Omega = 1.67$.

$$F_t = F_y/\Omega = 0.60F_y \tag{39.2}$$

For tension on the net effective area, $\Omega = 2.00$.

$$F_t = F_u/\Omega = 0.50F_u \tag{39.3}$$

For shear on gross sections, $\Omega = 1.50$.

$$F_v = 0.6F_y/\Omega = 0.40F_y \tag{39.4}$$

At beam end connections where the top flange is coped, and similar conditions where failure might occur along a plane through the fasteners, $\Omega = 2.00$.

$$F_v = 0.6F_u/\Omega = 0.30F_u \tag{39.5}$$

Product Development

For bending where the beam is laterally supported and the section meets the requirements of a compact section and is loaded in the plane of the minor axis, $\Omega = 1.67$.

$$F_b = F_y/\Omega = 0.60F_y \quad (39.6)$$

For bending where the beam is not a compact section but where it is supported laterally, the stress will be less.

Allowable stresses for bolts, rivets, and threaded parts are based on the type of load placed on them and are given as values in kips per square inch based on the ASTM designation of the fastener or as a fraction of the minimum tensile strength of the type of fastener. These are shown in Table 38.2 and Table 38.3 in Chap. 38.

Allowable stresses for welds are based either on the yield strength of the base metal or on the nominal tensile strength of the weld metal. The allowable stress is then multiplied by the area of the weld. IBC Chap. 22 and the AISC *Steel Construction Manual* both describe the requirements for welds in great detail. Table 38.6 in Chap. 38 summarizes the allowable working strengths for welds of various sizes.

Concrete

Building code requirements for reinforced concrete are very complex and detailed and cover all aspects of formwork, reinforcing, mixing, placing, and curing. IBC Chap. 19 concerns concrete construction. It contains specific requirements too numerous to mention here. In addition, it makes reference to ACI 318, as well as to other ACI publications.

The candidate is not expected to know all the code provisions for concrete design, but to have a general understanding of the more important limitations. Two of the most important concepts are the safety factors of increased ultimate load above the calculated dead and live loads, and the strength reduction factor. These are discussed in detail in Chap. 42 along with other code requirements.

Concrete construction is based on the specified compressive strength, f_c', expressed in pounds per square inch. Many of the formulas for concrete design use this as a part of the equation.

Because concrete is a highly variable material, the IBC goes to great lengths to specify how concrete is to be mixed and then how quality control is to be maintained. This is to ensure that a building is actually constructed of concrete that meets or exceeds the original design strength.

The IBC requires that samples for strength tests are taken for each class of concrete placed. Samples must be taken not less than once per day, nor less than once for each 150 yd^3 of concrete, nor less than once for each 5000 ft^2 of surface area for slabs or wall. The average of all sets of three consecutive strength tests must equal or exceed f_c', and no individual test can be less than 500 psi below the f_c' value.

CONSTRUCTION REQUIREMENTS

In addition to allowable stresses and other requirements related to structural calculations, the IBC places many restrictions on how various materials may be used. The following sections outline some of the more important ones with which ARE candidates should be familiar.

Wood

Since the structural integrity of wood is dependent on such factors as moisture, fire, insect attack, and connections, the IBC goes to great lengths to specify wood construction techniques. Be familiar with the following requirements.

- The bottom of wood joists must be at least 18 in above exposed ground, and the bottom of wood girders must be at least 12 in above ground, unless they are treated or made of a species with a natural resistance to decay.
- Ends of wood girders entering masonry or concrete walls must be provided with a $\frac{1}{2}$ in airspace on top, sides, and end, unless the wood is of natural resistance to decay or it is treated.

- Foundation plates and sills must be treated or made of foundation redwood.
- Under-floor areas such as crawl spaces must be ventilated with openings having a net area of not less than 1 ft^2 for each 150 ft^2 of under-floor area, and they must be placed to provide cross ventilation.
- Wood used for construction of permanent structures located nearer than 6 in to earth must be treated or wood of natural resistance to decay.
- All wood used as structural members must be protected from exposure to the weather and water with approved protection.
- Fire stops are required in walls at the ceiling and floor levels and at 10 ft intervals both vertical and horizontal.
- Fire stops are required at interconnections between concealed vertical and horizontal spaces such as soffits and dropped ceilings.
- Fire stops are required in concealed spaces in stairway construction and in vertical openings between floors and the roof that could afford a passage for fire.

Steel

Two provisions in the IBC relate to an important consideration in steel design. The first requires that roof systems without sufficient slope for drainage be investigated to ensure stability under ponding conditions. This is to prevent failure when an amount of water collects on a roof causing it to deflect, which allows a further accumulation of water, which leads to further deflection.

The second provision requires that horizontal framing members be designed for deflection criteria and ponding requirements. It also requires that trusses longer than 80 ft be cambered for the dead load deflection.

Concrete

In addition to allowable stresses, the IBC and ACI 318 set forth highly detailed requirements for other aspects of concrete use. In addition to those mentioned in Chap. 42, some of the more important ones include the following.

- Construction loads cannot be supported nor any shoring removed until the concrete has sufficient strength to safely support its weight and loads placed on it. However, some formwork can be removed if the structure in combination with remaining formwork can support the loads.
- There are limitations on the amount and placement of conduits and other pipes embedded in concrete so as not to decrease the load-resisting area. Aluminum conduits cannot be embedded unless effectively coated or covered to prevent aluminum-concrete reaction or electrolytic action between steel and aluminum. Pipes carrying fluids or gases must be pressure-tested prior to placement of concrete.
- The size and bending of reinforcement are clearly spelled out to ensure that a sufficient bond is developed between the concrete and steel and that all reinforcement acts together.
- Minimum concrete cover over reinforcing is specified. This is to protect the steel from rusting and to ensure proper bonding of the concrete to the steel. Concrete exposed to the weather or in direct contact with the ground requires more cover than do concrete members in a protected area.

FIREPROOFING

One of the primary purposes of any building code is to ensure that buildings are adequately protected from fire and that if a fire does occur, structural members are sufficiently protected. Chapter 6 of the IBC defines fire-resistance requirements for various building elements based on types of construction. Chapter 7 and Table 7-A of the IBC define the minimum protection of structural portions of a building based on time periods for various noncombustible insulating materials.

Although steel is noncombustible, it loses strength at high temperatures and must be protected with approved insulating materials, such as sprayed-on fireproofing or gypsum wallboard. The exception to this is for roof framing, other than the structural frame, that is more than 25 ft above the floor. This framing may be of unprotected noncombustible materials.

Wood framing, of course, is combustible but may be used in certain types of construction if adequately protected. A unique property of wood is that while it is combustible, thick pieces of wood exposed to fire will char but not immediately loose structural integrity. The IBC recognizes this by having a separate type of construction, Type IV, for heavy timber construction. In this type of construction, columns must be at least 8 in in any dimension, beams and girders must be at least 6 in wide and 10 in deep, and floor decking must be at least 3 in thick.

40

WOOD CONSTRUCTION

Nomenclature

A	area of a member	in^2
b	width of beam	in
C_D	load duration factor	–
C_F	size factor	–
C_{fu}	flat use factor	–
C_M	wet service factor	–
C_r	repetitive member factor	–
d	depth of beam	in
d'	depth of beam remaining at a notch	in
E	modulus of elasticity	lbf/in^2
f_v	actual unit stress in horizontal shear	lbf/in^2
F_b	design value for extreme fiber in bending	lbf/in^2
F_b'	allowable bending stress	lbf/in^2
F_c	design value for compression parallel to grain	lbf/in^2
F_c'	design value for compression parallel to grain, adjusted for l/d ratio	lbf/in^2
$F_{c\perp}$	design value for compression perpendicular to grain	lbf/in^2
F_t	design value for tension parallel to grain	lbf/in^2
F_v	design value for horizontal shear	lbf/in^2
I	moment of inertia	in^4
K_e	effective buckling length factor	–
L	span of bending member	ft
M	moment	in-lbf
S	section modulus	in^3
V	vertical shear	lbf
w	uniform load per foot	lbf/ft
Δ	deflection	in

PROPERTIES OF STRUCTURAL LUMBER

Sizes

Structural lumber is referred to by its nominal dimension in inches such as 2×4 or 2×10. However, after surfacing at the mill and drying, its actual dimension is somewhat less.

Table 40.1 gives the actual dimensions for various nominal sizes of sawn lumber. Also shown in Table 40.1 are the actual areas, section modulus, and moment of inertia, which are all based on the actual size. The majority of structural lumber used is surfaced and dried to the actual sizes listed in Table 40.1, so these are the values that must be used in structural calculations.

Grading

Since a log yields lumber of varying quality, the individual sawn pieces must be categorized to allow selection of the quality that best suits the purpose. For structural lumber, the primary concern is the amount of stress that a particular grade of lumber of a species will carry. The load-carrying ability is affected by such things as size and number of knots, splits, and other defects, as well as the direction of grain and the specific gravity of the wood.

Grading of structural lumber is done under standard rules established by several different agencies certified by the American Lumber Standards Committee. The grading is done at the sawmill either by visual inspection or by machine. The resulting allowable stress values are published in tables referred to as design values for visually graded structural lumber and design values for machine-stress-rated structural lumber.

Visually graded lumber is divided into categories based on nominal size, so the same grade of lumber in a species may have different allowable stresses depending on which category it is in. This can be confusing, but is critical in selecting the correct allowable stress for a particular design condition. For example, one of the most common categories is 2 in to 4 in thick, 5 in and wider. This includes wood members like 2×6s, 2×8s, and the like, but not 2×4s. 2×4 members are in two separate categories: 2 in to 4 in thick, 2 in to 4 in wide; and 2 in to 4 in thick, 4 in wide. The first category is based on structural grades, and the second category is based on appearance grades.

Table 40.1 Sectional Properties of Standard Dressed Lumber

nominal size	standard dressed size, $b \times d$ (in)	area, A (in^2)	moment of inertia, I (in^4)	section modulus, S (in^3)
2 × 3	$1\frac{1}{2} \times 2\frac{1}{2}$	3.750	1.953	1.563
2 × 4	$1\frac{1}{2} \times 3\frac{1}{2}$	5.250	5.359	3.063
2 × 6	$1\frac{1}{2} \times 5\frac{1}{2}$	8.250	20.797	7.563
2 × 8	$1\frac{1}{2} \times 7\frac{1}{4}$	10.875	47.635	13.141
2 × 10	$1\frac{1}{2} \times 9\frac{1}{4}$	13.875	98.932	21.391
2 × 12	$1\frac{1}{2} \times 11\frac{1}{4}$	16.875	177.979	31.641
4 × 4	$3\frac{1}{2} \times 3\frac{1}{2}$	12.250	12.505	7.146
4 × 6	$3\frac{1}{2} \times 5\frac{1}{2}$	19.250	48.526	17.646
4 × 8	$3\frac{1}{2} \times 7\frac{1}{4}$	25.375	111.148	30.661
4 × 10	$3\frac{1}{2} \times 9\frac{1}{4}$	32.375	230.840	49.911
4 × 12	$3\frac{1}{2} \times 11\frac{1}{4}$	39.375	415.283	73.828
4 × 14	$3\frac{1}{2} \times 13\frac{1}{4}$	46.375	678.475	102.411
6 × 6	$5\frac{1}{2} \times 5\frac{1}{2}$	30.250	76.255	27.729
6 × 8	$5\frac{1}{2} \times 7\frac{1}{2}$	41.250	193.359	51.563
6 × 10	$5\frac{1}{2} \times 9\frac{1}{2}$	52.250	392.963	82.729
6 × 12	$5\frac{1}{2} \times 11\frac{1}{2}$	63.250	697.068	121.229
6 × 14	$5\frac{1}{2} \times 12\frac{1}{2}$	74.250	1127.672	167.063
6 × 16	$5\frac{1}{2} \times 15\frac{1}{2}$	85.250	1706.776	220.229
8 × 8	$7\frac{1}{2} \times 7\frac{1}{2}$	56.250	263.672	70.313
8 × 10	$7\frac{1}{2} \times 9\frac{1}{2}$	71.250	535.859	112.813
8 × 12	$7\frac{1}{2} \times 11\frac{1}{2}$	86.250	950.547	165.313

There are also categories for beams and stringers, and posts and timbers. *Beams and stringers* are defined as members 5 in and wider, having a depth more than 2 in greater than the width. *Posts and timbers* are defined as members 5 in by 5 in and larger, with a depth not more than 2 in greater than the width.

Machine-stress-rated lumber is based on grade designations, which depend on the allowable bending stress and modulus of elasticity of the wood.

Design Values

For visually graded lumber, allowable design values are based on the species of wood, the size category, the grade, and the direction of loading. Different values are required based on the direction of loading because wood is not an isotropic material. The tables give values for extreme fiber stress in bending, F_b; tension parallel to the grain, F_t; horizontal shear, F_v; compression perpendicular to grain, $F_{c\perp}$; and compression parallel to grain, F_c. Table 40.2 shows a portion of a table of design values as published by the National Forest Products Association.

One additional variable for selecting the extreme fiber in bending stress is whether or not the member is being used alone or with other members such as a row of joists. In order to qualify for repetitive member use, there must be at least three members spaced not more than 24 in apart, and there must be some method to distribute the load among them such as bridging or sheathing.

As mentioned in Chap. 17, the amount of stress a wood member can withstand is also dependent on the length of time the load acts on the member. Design values given in the tables are based on what is considered a normal duration of loading—10 years.

However, for a shorter loading duration, the allowable unit stresses may be increased as follows.

- 15% for two months' duration, as for snow
- 25% for seven days' duration, as for roof loading
- 60% for wind or earthquake loading
- 100% for impact loads

Table 40.2 Design Values for Visually Graded Dimension Lumber (use with adjustment factors)*

species and commercial grade	size classification	bending, F_b	tension parallel to grain, F_t	shear parallel to grain, F_v	compression perpendicular to grain, $F_{c\perp}$	compression parallel to grain, F_c	modulus of elasticity, E	grading rules agency
beech-birch-hickory								
select structural		1450	850	195	715	1200	1,700,000	
no. 1		1050	600	195	715	950	1,600,000	
no. 2	2" & wider	1000	600	195	715	750	1,500,000	
no. 3		575	350	195	715	425	1,300,000	NELMA
stud	2" & wider	775	450	195	715	475	1,300,000	
construction		1150	675	195	715	1000	1,400,000	
standard	2"–4" wide	650	375	195	715	775	1,300,000	
utility		300	175	195	715	500	1,200,000	
cottonwood								
select structural		875	525	125	320	775	1,200,000	
no. 1		625	375	125	320	625	1,200,000	
no. 2	2" & wider	625	350	125	320	475	1,100,000	
no. 3		350	200	125	320	275	1,000,000	NSLB
stud	2" & wider	475	275	125	320	300	1,000,000	
construction		700	400	125	320	650	1,000,000	
standard	2"–4" wide	400	225	125	320	500	900,000	
utility		175	100	125	320	325	900,000	
Douglas fir-larch								
select structural		1500	1000	180	625	1700	1,900,000	
no. 1 & btr		1200	800	180	625	1550	1,800,000	
no. 1		1000	675	180	625	1500	1,700,000	
no. 2	2" & wider	900	575	180	625	1350	1,600,000	WCLIB
no. 3		525	325	180	625	775	1,400,000	WWPA
stud	2" & wider	700	450	180	625	850	1,400,000	
construction		1000	650	180	625	1650	1,500,000	
standard	2"–4" wide	575	375	180	625	1400	1,400,000	
utility		275	175	180	625	900	1,300,000	
Douglas fir-larch (north)								
select structural		1350	825	180	625	1900	1,900,000	
no. 1 & btr		1150	750	180	625	1800	1,800,000	
no. 1/no. 2	2" & wider	850	500	180	625	1400	1,600,000	
no. 3		475	300	180	625	825	1,400,000	NLGA
stud	2" & wider	650	400	180	625	900	1,400,000	
construction		950	575	180	625	1800	1,500,000	
standard	2"–4" wide	525	325	180	625	1450	1,400,000	
utility		250	150	180	625	950	1,300,000	
Douglas fir-south								
select structural		1350	900	180	520	1600	1,400,000	
no. 1		925	600	180	520	1450	1,300,000	
no. 2	2" & wider	850	525	180	520	1350	1,200,000	
no. 3		500	300	180	520	775	1,100,000	WWPA
stud	2" & wider	675	425	180	520	850	1,100,000	
construction		975	600	180	520	1650	1,200,000	
standard	2"–4" wide	550	350	180	520	1400	1,100,000	
utility		250	150	180	520	900	1,000,000	

*Design values for construction, standard, and utility grades are based on a 4 in nominal width, design values for stud grade are based on a 6 in nominal width, and design values for all other grades (select structural, no. 1 & btr, no. 1, no. 2, and no. 3) are based on a 12 in nominal width.

Reprinted with permission from *National Design Specification for Wood Construction,* © 2014, American Wood Council.

Adjustment Factors

Repetitive Member Factor, C_r

Bending design values, F_b, for dimension lumber 2 in to 4 in thick shall be multiplied by the repetitive member factor, $C_r = 1.15$ when such members are used as joists, truss chords, rafters, studs, planks, decking, or similar members that are in contact or spaced not more than 24 in on centers, are not less than 3 in number and are joined by floor, roof, or other load distributing elements adequate to support the design load.

Wet Service Factor, C_M

When dimension lumber is used where moisture content will exceed 19% for an extended time period, design values shall be multiplied by the appropriate wet service factors from Table 40.3.

Table 40.3 Wet Service Factors, C_M

F_b	F_t	F_v	$F_{c\perp}$	F_c	E
0.85*	1.0	0.97	0.67	0.8**	0.9

*when $F_bC_F \leq 1150$ psi, $C_M = 1.0$

**when $F_cC_F \leq 750$ psi, $C_M = 1.0$

Reprinted with permission from *National Design Specifications for Wood Construction*, © 2014, American Wood Council.

Flat Use Factor, C_{fu}

Bending design values adjusted by size factors are based on edgewise use (load applied to narrow face). When dimension lumber is used flatwise (load applied to wide face), the bending design value, F_b, shall also be multiplied by the flat use factors in Table 40.4.

Table 40.4 Flat Use Factors, C_{fu}

	thickness (breadth)	
width (depth)	2" & 3"	4"
2" & 3"	1.0	–
4"	1.1	1.0
5"	1.1	1.05
6"	1.15	1.05
8"	1.15	1.05
10" & wider	1.2	1.1

Reprinted with permission from *National Design Specifications for Wood Construction*, © 2014, American Wood Council.

Size Factor, C_F

Tabulated bending, tension and compression parallel to grain design values for dimensional lumber 2 in to 4 in thick are multiplied by the size factors in Table 40.5.

Table 40.5 Size Factors, C_F

		F_b		F_t	F_c
		thickness (breadth)			
grades	width (depth)	2" & 3"	4"		
select structural, no. 1 & btr, no. 1, no. 2, no. 3	2", 3" & 4"	1.5	1.5	1.5	1.15
	5"	1.4	1.4	1.4	1.1
	6"	1.3	1.3	1.3	1.1
	8"	1.2	1.3	1.2	1.05
	10"	1.1	1.2	1.1	1.0
	12"	1.0	1.1	1.0	1.0
	14" & wider	0.9	1.0	0.9	0.9
stud	2", 3" & 4"	1.1	1.1	1.1	1.05
	5" & 6"	1.0	1.0	1.0	1.0
	8" & wider	Use no. 3 grade tabulated design values and size factors.			
construction, standard	2", 3" & 4"	1.0	1.0	1.0	1.0
utility	4"	1.0	1.0	1.0	1.0
	2" & 3"	0.4	–	0.4	0.6

Reprinted with permission from *National Design Specifications for Wood Construction*, © 2014, American Wood Council.

Moisture Content

Moisture content is defined as the weight of water in wood as a fraction of the weight of oven-dry wood. Moisture content is an important variable because it affects the amount of shrinkage, weight, strength, and withdrawal resistance of nails.

Moisture exists in wood both in the individual cell cavities and bound chemically within cell walls. When the cell walls are completely saturated but no water exists in the cell cavities, the wood is said to have reached its *fiber saturation point.* This point averages about 30% moisture content in all woods. Above this point, the wood is dimensionally stable, but as the wood dries below this point it begins to shrink.

When wood is used for structural framing and other construction purposes, it tends to absorb or lose moisture in response to the temperature and humidity of the surrounding air. As it loses moisture it shrinks, and as it gains moisture it swells. Ideally, the moisture content of wood when it is installed should be the same as the prevailing humidity to which it will be exposed. However, this is seldom possible, so lumber needs to be dried—either air-dried or kiln-dried—to reduce the moisture content to acceptable levels.

To be considered dry lumber, moisture content cannot exceed 19%. To be grademarked *kiln dry*, the maximum moisture content permitted is 15%. Design values found in tables assume that the maximum moisture content will not exceed 19%. If it does, the allowable stresses must be decreased slightly.

Wood shrinks most in the direction perpendicular to the grain and very little parallel to the grain. Perpendicular to the grain wood shrinks most in the direction of the annual growth rings (tangentially) and about half as much across the rings (radially).

In developing wood details, an allowance must be made for the fact that wood will shrink and swell during use regardless of its initial moisture content. Of particular importance is the accumulated change in dimension of a series of wood members placed one on top of the next. The shrinkage of an individual member may not be significant, but the total shrinkage of several may result in problems such as sagging floors, cracked plaster, distortion of door openings, and nail pops in gypsum board walls.

WOOD BEAMS

The design of wood beams is a fairly simple procedure. First, the loads and stresses on the beam are determined as described in Chap. 35. This includes finding the support reactions, vertical shear forces, and bending moments. Then, the basic flexure formula is used to find the required section modulus needed to resist the bending moment. A beam size is then selected that has the required section modulus. Second, horizontal shear stresses are calculated and compared with the allowable horizontal shear for the species and grade of lumber being used. This is especially important because wood beams have a tendency to fail parallel to the grain where their strength is lowest. Finally, deflection is checked to see if it is within acceptable limits. This, too, is important because wood is not as stiff as steel or concrete. Even though a beam may be strong enough to resist bending moment, the deflection may be outside of tolerable limits.

Design for Bending

To design wood beams for bending, the basic flexure formula is used.

$$S = \frac{M}{F_b'} \tag{40.1}$$

The basic allowable extreme fiber stress in bending, F_b, is found in Table 40.2 or similar tables in the building code or other referenced sources, and the section modulus is found in Table 40.1. This value must be modified for many factors, including those shown in Table 40.2. For sawn lumber under major axis bending, the following formula is used.

$$F_b' = F_b C_D C_M C_t C_L C_F C_i C_r \tag{40.2}$$

The definitions of C_M, C_F, and C_r are given in Table 40.2. Values of C_D are used to include the duration of load. In any combination of loads the largest value of C_D is used. This corresponds to the shortest load duration. The durations of load factors are as follows.

- permanent duration, dead load = 0.90
- normal, 10-year duration, floor live load = 1.00
- two-month duration, snow load = 1.15
- seven-day duration, roof live load = 1.25
- 10-minute duration, wind or earthquake load = 1.60
- impact duration = 2.00

The other values are for special cases of high temperature, C_t; laterally unbraced beams, C_L; and incised members, C_i. For laterally braced beams under normal usage, these values, along with C_M, may all be taken as 1.0. The examples presented in this chapter will assume this is the case.

Example 40.1

A simply supported wood beam spans 12 ft and carries a combined dead and roof live load of 350 plf. If the beam is Douglas fir-larch, no. 2, what nominal size lumber should be used?

Solution

First, find the maximum bending moment. From Fig. 35.7, the moment for a uniformly loaded beam is $wL^2/8$. The moment is

$$\begin{aligned} M &= \frac{wL^2}{8} = \frac{\left(350\ \frac{\text{lbf}}{\text{ft}}\right)(12\ \text{ft})^2}{8} \\ &= 6300\ \text{ft-lbf} \end{aligned}$$

Using Table 40.2, find the column labeled “bending.” For Douglas fir-larch no. 2, the tabulated value of F_b is 900 psi. All appropriate adjustments must be made to this value. The load is due to dead and roof live load, so the value of C_D should be 1.25. Since the beam size is unknown, a value of C_F must be assumed. A reasonable assumption would be 1.1. The allowable bending stress is then found by multiplying the tabulated values by the appropriated factor, using Eq. 40.2.

$$\begin{aligned} F_b' &= C_D C_F F_b = (1.25)(1.1)\left(900\ \frac{\text{lbf}}{\text{in}^2}\right) \\ &= 1237\ \text{psi} \end{aligned}$$

The required section modulus is then found from the basic flexure formula, Eq. 40.1.

$$\begin{aligned} S &= \frac{M}{F_b'} = \frac{(6300\ \text{ft-lbf})\left(12\ \frac{\text{in}}{\text{ft}}\right)}{1237\ \frac{\text{lbf}}{\text{in}^2}} \\ &= 61.11\ \text{in}^3 \end{aligned}$$

Remember to multiply the moment by a factor of 12 to convert foot-pounds to inch-pounds.

Looking in Table 40.1, the smallest beam that will provide this section modulus is a 4 × 12 with an S of 73.828 in^3. A 6 × 10 would also provide the required value (82.729), but this has more area and, therefore, costs more than the 4 × 12. In addition, if a 6 in wide beam were used, a different value for F_b may have to be used in the beams and stringer category. The adjustment factors would also be different for a beam and stringer.

The assumed value for C_F of 1.1 is correct. This value is given in Table 40.2 for a no. 2 grade, 12 in wide and 4 in thick. The 4 × 12 is the most appropriate selection to support the load.

Example 40.2

What is the maximum moment-carrying capacity, in foot-pounds, of a 2×10 select structural Douglas fir-larch beam with applied dead and floor live load?

Solution

Rearranging Eq. 40.1 gives

$$M = SF_b'$$

The allowable tabulated unit stress, F_b, from Table 40.2 is 1500 psi, and the section modulus (from Table 40.1) of a 2 × 10 is 21.391 in^3. The load duration factor, C_D, for combined dead and floor live load is 1.0. The size factor, C_F, from Table 40.2 is 1.1.

$$\begin{aligned} F_b' &= C_D C_F C_b = (1.00)(1.1)\left(1500\ \frac{\text{lbf}}{\text{in}^2}\right) \\ &= 1650\ \text{psi} \end{aligned}$$

$$\begin{aligned} M &= SF_b' = \frac{(21.391\ \text{in}^3)\left(1650\ \frac{\text{lbf}}{\text{in}^2}\right)}{12\ \frac{\text{in}}{\text{ft}}} \\ &= 2941\ \text{ft-lbf} \end{aligned}$$

Sometimes, either the width or depth of a beam is established by some limiting factor (such as ceiling clearance), and the other dimension must be found. This is easy to calculate, recalling that the section modulus of a rectangular beam is

$$S = \frac{bd^2}{6} \qquad 40.3$$

Example 40.3

A wood beam spanning 10 ft must be designed to support a concentrated load of 2900 lbf in the center of the span, but there is only enough room for a nominal 8 in deep beam. If the beam can be dense select structural Douglas fir-larch with an allowable unit stress of 1900 psi, what beam width is necessary?

Solution

The moment of a beam with a concentrated load is $PL/4$ (from Fig. 35.7). The moment is

$$\begin{aligned} M &= \frac{PL}{4} = \frac{(2900\ \text{lbf})(10\ \text{ft})\left(12\ \frac{\text{in}}{\text{ft}}\right)}{4} \\ &= 87{,}000\ \text{in-lbf} \end{aligned}$$

The required modulus from Eq. 40.1 is

$$\begin{aligned} S &= \frac{M}{F_b'} = \frac{87{,}000 \text{ in-lbf}}{1900 \ \frac{\text{lbf}}{\text{in}^2}} \\ &= 45.79 \text{ in}^3 \end{aligned}$$

If there were no limitation on the depth of the beam, a 4 × 10 would work with a section modulus of 49.911. However, if the maximum depth is 7.5 in (the actual depth of a nominal 8 in beam and stringer), then the required section modulus, from Eq. 40.3, is

$$S = \frac{bd^2}{6}$$

Rearranging the formula to calculate width gives

$$\begin{aligned} b &= \frac{6S}{d^2} = \frac{(6)(45.79 \text{ in}^3)}{(7.5 \text{ in})^2} \\ &= 4.88 \text{ in} \end{aligned}$$

A nominal 6 in wide beam will work with an actual width of 5.50 in.

Example 40.4

A Douglas fir-larch no. 1 beam supports a roof with a dead load of 100 plf and a snow load of 150 plf. If the beam must span 8 ft, what is the most economical size to use?

Solution

For the snow load, a load duration factor of 1.15 is multiplied by the tabulated allowable stress. However, when there are loads of different durations on wood members, each load combination should be checked. For the dead load, a load duration of 0.9 is used. From Fig. 35.7, for a uniformly loaded beam, the moment due to dead loads is

$$\begin{aligned} M &= \frac{wL^2}{8} = \frac{\left(100 \ \frac{\text{lbf}}{\text{ft}}\right)(8 \text{ ft})^2\left(12 \ \frac{\text{in}}{\text{ft}}\right)}{8} \\ &= 9600 \text{ in-lbf} \end{aligned}$$

The moment due to dead load and snow load is

$$\begin{aligned} M &= \frac{\left(250 \ \frac{\text{lbf}}{\text{ft}}\right)(8 \text{ ft})^2\left(12 \ \frac{\text{in}}{\text{ft}}\right)}{8} \\ &= 24{,}000 \text{ in-lbf} \end{aligned}$$

Remember, the factor of 12 must be used to convert foot-pounds to inch-pounds.

Since the beam size is unknown, the size factor will be assumed to be 1.1. The tabulated bending stress from Table 40.2 for Douglas fir-larch no. 1 is 1000 psi. The required section modulus for dead load only is

$$\begin{aligned} S &= \frac{M}{F_b'} = \frac{M}{C_D C_F F_b} = \frac{9600 \text{ in-lbf}}{(0.9)(1.1)\left(1000 \ \frac{\text{lbf}}{\text{in}^2}\right)} \\ &= 9.70 \text{ in}^3 \end{aligned}$$

Product Development

The required section modulus for the combined load is

$$S = \frac{24{,}000 \text{ in-lbf}}{(1.15)(1.1)\left(1000 \ \frac{\text{lbf}}{\text{in}^2}\right)} = 18.97 \text{ in}^3$$

Use the greater of the calculated section moduli—a 2 × 10 with a section modulus of 21.391 in^3 (from Table 40.1). The assumed value for C_F of 1.1 is correct. This value is given in Table 40.2 for a no. 1 grade, 10 in wide and 2 in thick. The 2 × 10 is the most appropriate selection to support the loads.

Design for Horizontal Shear

Because it is easy for wood to shear along the lines of the grain, actual horizontal shear must always be checked against the allowable unit shear stress, F_v. This is especially important for short spans with large loads. Frequently, a beam that is sufficient in size to resist bending stresses must be made larger to resist horizontal shear stresses.

Because horizontal shear failure will always occur before vertical shear failure, it is not necessary to check for vertical shear except for beams notched at their supports.

For rectangular beams, the maximum unit horizontal shear stress is

$$f_v = \frac{3V}{2bd} \qquad 40.4$$

The basic allowable stress in shear, F_v, is found in Table 40.2, and the sizes are found in Table 40.1. This value must be modified for five factors, including those shown in Table 40.2. The following formula is used for allowable shear stress.

$$F_v' = F_v C_D C_M C_t C_i C_H \qquad 40.5$$

The values of C_D, C_M, C_t, and C_i are found in a manner similar to that for finding the values applied to bending stress. Values of C_H are omitted from Table 40.2. This value should only be used if the architect or engineer will verify the extent of cracking in the wood member.

When calculating the vertical shear, V, the loads within a distance from the supports equal to the depth of the member may be neglected.

Example 40.5

Check the beam found in Ex. 40.1 for horizontal shear.

Solution

The load is 350 plf for 12 ft, or 4200 lbf total. The vertical shear at each reaction is 2100 lbf. Subtract the load within a distance equal to the depth of the beam, 11¼ in.

$$V = 2100 \text{ lbf} - \left(\frac{11.25 \text{ in}}{12 \ \frac{\text{in}}{\text{ft}}}\right)\left(350 \ \frac{\text{lbf}}{\text{ft}}\right) = 1772 \text{ lbf}$$

The value of bd is the area, found in Table 40.1 to be 39.375 in^2.

The actual horizontal shear is found from Eq. 40.4.

$$f_v = \frac{3V}{2bd} = \frac{(3)(1772 \text{ lbf})}{(2)(39.375 \text{ in}^2)}$$
$$= 67.50 \text{ psi}$$

From Table 40.2, the allowable tabulated horizontal shear, F_v, is 180 psi for Douglas fir-larch no. 2. This must be multiplied times the duration of load factor of 1.25. The allowable shear stress, F_v', is 225 psi and is larger than the actual stress, so the beam is adequate to resist horizontal shear. If the actual value were greater than the allowable, a larger beam would be needed.

Design for Deflection

Since wood is not as stiff as steel or concrete, deflection is always a concern. Detrimental effects of deflection can include nail popping in gypsum ceilings, cracking of plaster, bouncy floors, and visible sagging. In many cases, a wood member can be selected that will satisfy bending requirements but will not satisfy deflection criteria. Therefore, the design of wood beams must always include a check for deflection.

The formulas for deflection are the same ones used for other materials and are outlined in Fig. 35.7. The criteria for maximum deflection is given in the *International Building Code* (IBC) and requires that two different conditions of loading be checked. The first limits deflection due to live load only to $L/360$ of the span. The second limits deflection due to live load and dead load for unseasoned wood to $L/240$ of the span. In both cases, the units of deflection will be the same as the units used for the value of L.

The IBC does allow a reduction by one-half of the dead load for the condition of the live load and dead load if seasoned wood is used. *Seasoned wood* is defined as wood with a moisture content of less than 16% at the time of installation and used under dry conditions. This is typically the case, but since wood will deflect under long-term use beyond its initial deflection, it is common practice to use the full value of dead load and live load when checking deflection against the $L/240$ criterion. This provides for the extra stiffness necessary to limit deflection under long-term loading.

The basic modulus of elasticity, E, is found in Table 40.2. This value must be modified for four factors, including those shown in Table 40.2. The following formula is used for allowable modulus of elasticity.

$$E' = EC_M C_t C_i C_T \qquad 40.6$$

The values of C_M, C_t, and C_i are found in a manner similar to that for finding the values applied to bending stress. Values of C_T only apply to small truss members in compression. All of these values are 1.0 under normal conditions.

Product Development

Example 40.6

Using the same beam found in Ex. 40.1, check to see that its deflection is within allowable limits. Assume that of the total load of 350 plf, dead load is 150 lbf and live load is 200 plf.

Solution

From Fig. 35.7, the deflection for a uniformly loaded beam is

$$\Delta = \frac{5wL^4}{384EI} \qquad 40.7$$

The modulus of elasticity of Douglas fir-larch no. 2 is 1,600,000 psi as found in Table 40.2, and the moment of inertia of a 4 × 12 is 415.283 in^4 as found in Table 40.1.

In this case, it is important to keep units consistent in order for the answer to be in inches. Remember that in Eq. 40.7, w is the load per unit length and L is the length. If L is in inches, the load must be in pounds per inch, not feet. For calculating the total dead and live load, 350 plf is 350/12, or 29.167 lbf/in. The beam length of 12 ft must be converted to inches and then raised to the fourth power.

$$\begin{aligned}\Delta &= \frac{(5)\left(29.167\ \frac{\text{lbf}}{\text{ft}}\right)\left((12\ \text{ft})\left(12\ \frac{\text{in}}{\text{ft}}\right)\right)^4}{(384)\left(1{,}600{,}000\ \frac{\text{lbf}}{\text{in}^2}\right)(415.283\ \text{in}^4)}\\ &= 0.25\ \text{in}\end{aligned}$$

Another way to arrive at the same answer is to remember that Eq. 40.7 can also take the form

$$\Delta = \frac{5WL^3}{384EI} \tag{40.8}$$

W is the total uniformly distributed load on the beam. The length still needs to be converted to inches and then raised to the third power, so the calculation is

$$\begin{aligned}\Delta &= \frac{5WL^3}{384EI} = \frac{(5)\left(\left(350\ \frac{\text{lbf}}{\text{ft}}\right)(12\ \text{ft})\right)\left((12\ \text{ft})\left(12\ \frac{\text{in}}{\text{ft}}\right)\right)^3}{(384)\left(1{,}600{,}000\ \frac{\text{lbf}}{\text{in}^2}\right)(415.283\ \text{in}^4)}\\ &= 0.25\ \text{in for dead and live loads}\end{aligned}$$

For deflection due to the live load only,

$$\begin{aligned}\Delta &= \frac{5WL^3}{384EI} = \frac{(5)\left(\left(200\ \frac{\text{lbf}}{\text{ft}}\right)(12\ \text{ft})\right)\left((12\ \text{ft})\left(12\ \frac{\text{in}}{\text{ft}}\right)\right)^3}{(384)\left(1{,}600{,}000\ \frac{\text{lbf}}{\text{in}^2}\right)(415.283\ \text{in}^4)}\\ &= 0.14\ \text{in}\end{aligned}$$

Next, determine the allowable deflection limits. For the live load only,

$$\frac{L}{360} = \frac{(12\ \text{ft})\left(12\ \frac{\text{in}}{\text{ft}}\right)}{360} = 0.40\ \text{in}$$

This is more than the actual deflection under the live load only of 0.14 in, so this is acceptable. For the total load,

$$\frac{L}{240} = \frac{(12\ \text{ft})\left(12\ \frac{\text{in}}{\text{ft}}\right)}{240} = 0.60\ \text{in}$$

This is also more than the actual deflection under the total load of 0.25 in, so the 4 × 12 beam is acceptable for deflection requirements.

MISCELLANEOUS PROVISIONS

Notched Beams

Notching of beams should be avoided, but if it is done, the IBC states that notches in sawn lumber bending members cannot exceed one-sixth the depth of the member and cannot be located in the middle third of the span. When the notches are at the supports as shown in Fig. 40.1, the depth cannot exceed one-fourth of the beam depth.

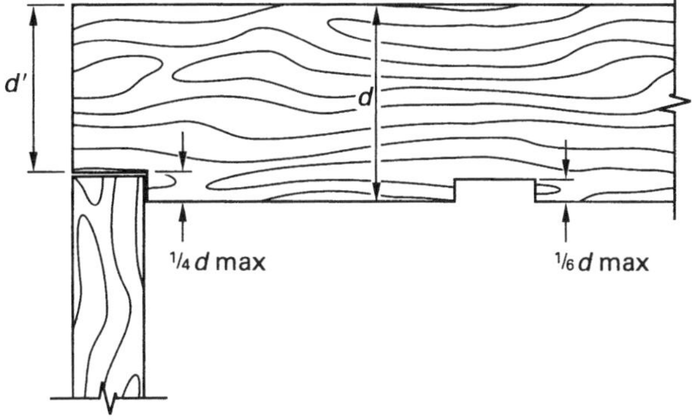

Figure 40.1 Notching of Beams

If beams are notched, the vertical shear cannot exceed the value determined by the formula

$$V = \left(\frac{2bd'F_v'}{3}\right)\left(\frac{d'}{d}\right) \quad \text{40.9}$$

Example 40.7

If the beam in Ex. 40.1 is notched 2 in, is it still an acceptable size?

Solution

The beam found in Ex. 40.1 is a 4×12, so its actual width is 3.5 in and its actual depth is 11.25 in. Subtracting 2 in from the depth gives a d' value of 9.25 in. From Ex. 40.5, the allowable horizontal shear for Douglas fir-larch no. 2 is 225 psi. Applying Eq. 40.9, the vertical shear is

$$\begin{aligned} V &= \left(\frac{2bd'F_v'}{3}\right)\left(\frac{d'}{d}\right) \\ &= \left(\frac{(2)(3.5 \text{ in})(9.25 \text{ in})\left(225 \ \frac{\text{lbf}}{\text{in}^2}\right)}{3}\right)\left(\frac{9.25 \text{ in}}{11.25 \text{ in}}\right) \\ &= 3993 \text{ lbf} \end{aligned}$$

From Ex. 40.5, the vertical shear at each reaction was found to be 2100 lbf, so this beam could be notched 2 in without exceeding the allowable vertical shear limitation.

Size Factor

As the depth of a beam increases, there is a slight decrease in bending strength. The IBC requires that the allowable unit stress in bending, F_b, be decreased by a size factor as determined by the formula

$$C_F = \left(\frac{12}{d}\right)^{1/9} \quad \text{40.10}$$

This applies only to rectangular sawn bending members that are visually graded timber or visually graded southern pine dimension lumber exceeding a depth of 12 in. Design values for bending, tension, and compression parallel to the grain for visually graded dimension lumber 2 in to 4 in thick, excluding southern pine, must be multiplied by size factors given at the beginning of NDS Tables 4A, 4B, 4C, and 4E. The size factor does not affect the allowable strength to any great amount. C_F for a 14 in deep beam, for example, is only 0.987, and for a 16 in deep beam, it is 0.972.

Lateral Support

When a wood beam is loaded in bending, there is a tendency for it to buckle laterally. The IBC provides that a decrease in allowable bending strength be made if certain conditions are not met. For the vast majority of wood construction, this is not required if proper lateral support is provided. This amounts to providing continuous support at the compression edge, such as with sheathing or subflooring, and providing restraint against rotation at the ends of the members and at intervals with bridging. Most wood construction meets these conditions, so adjustments are not required.

Bearing

The load on a wood beam compresses the fibers where the weight is concentrated at the supports. To determine the required bearing area, the total reaction load is divided by the allowable compression perpendicular to grain, $F_{c\perp}$, found in Table 40.2. For joists, the IBC states that there must be at least $1\frac{1}{2}$ in bearing on wood or metal, and at least 3 in bearing on masonry. Beams or girders supported on masonry must have at least 3 in of bearing surface.

Example 40.8

What is the required bearing area on a masonry wall for the beam selected in Ex. 40.1?

Solution

The total reaction of the beam is

$$R = \frac{\left(350\ \frac{\text{lbf}}{\text{ft}}\right)(12\ \text{ft})}{2} = 2100\ \text{lbf}$$

The required bearing area is

$$A = \frac{2100\ \text{lbf}}{625\ \frac{\text{lbf}}{\text{in}^2}} = 3.36\ \text{in}^2$$

Since the beam is $3\frac{1}{2}$ in wide, the required length of bearing is 3.36 in^2/3.5 in, or 0.96 in. However, since this is less than the code requirement of 3 in, 3 in must be used.

WOOD COLUMNS

As discussed in Chap. 35, columns have a tendency to buckle under a load, so even though a column may have enough cross-sectional area to resist the unit compressive forces, it may fail in buckling. For wood columns, the ratio of the column length to its width is just as important as it is for concrete and steel columns. However, for wood columns, the slenderness ratio is defined as the laterally unsupported length in in divided by the least dimension of the column. This is a little different than the length divided by the radius of gyration as discussed in Chap. 35, but the same principles apply.

Wood columns can be solid members of rectangular, round, or other shapes, or spaced columns built up from two or more individual solid members separated by blocking. Since almost all wood columns are solid rectangular sections, the method of design in this section will be limited to these types.

As mentioned in Chap. 35, the load-carrying capacity of a wood column depends on the way the ends of the column are fixed. For design, the *effective length* must be determined. This is the total unsupported length multiplied by an *effective buckling length factor*, *K*. These factors for various end conditions are shown in Fig. 40.2. Notice that this diagram is very similar to Fig. 35.8, but the values are slightly different.

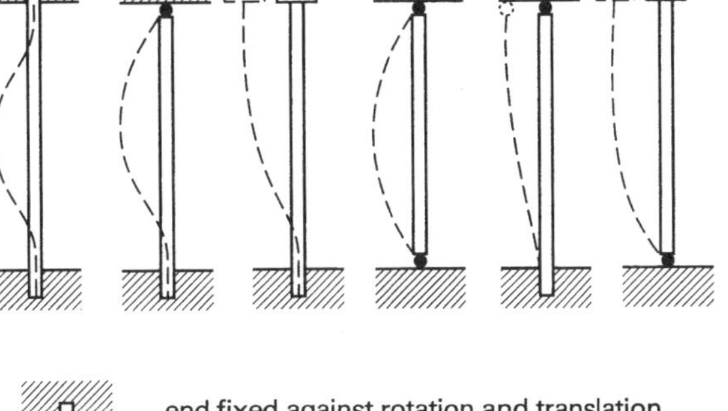

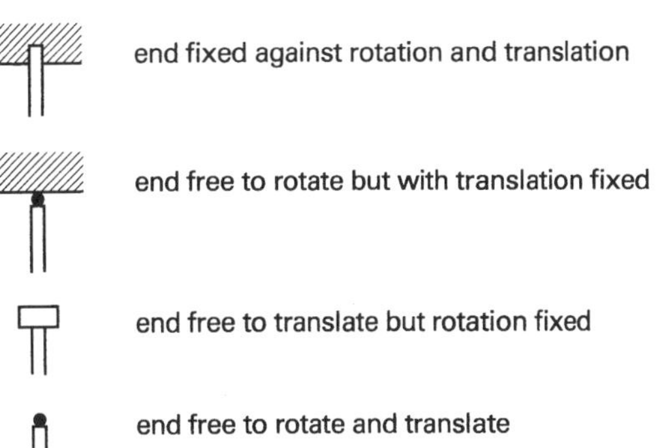

Figure 40.2 *K*-Values for Wood Columns

Because of the way most wood construction is detailed, columns are usually fixed in translation but free to rotate, so the *K*-value is taken as 1, and the effective length is taken as the actual unsupported length.

The allowable unit stress in pounds per square inch of cross-sectional area of square or rectangular solid columns is determined according to a complex formula that considers the effective length; whether the wood is visually graded or machine graded; and whether the wood is sawn lumber, round timber piles, or glued-laminated timber. Because of the complexity of the formula, it is unlikely that the test will ask for specific values to be calculated.

JOISTS

Joists are a very common type of wood construction. They are small, closely spaced members used to support floor, ceiling, and roof loads, and are usually lumber nominally 2 in wide by 6, 8, 10, and 12 in deep, spaced 12, 16, or 24 in on center. Of course, they are beams and can be designed using the methods described earlier in this section, but since they are used so frequently, their size and spacing is usually selected from tables. When they are designed as beams, the design value of F_b from Table 40.2 should be multiplied by the repetitive use factor, C_r, from Table 40.2. The design value is slightly larger for multiple member use than for single members.

Table 40.6 shows one joist table from the IBC. Similar tables are published by the National Forest Products Association, the Southern Forest Products Association, other trade groups, and reference sources. For a given joist size and spacing and a given modulus of elasticity, the table gives the maximum allowable span when the bending and deflection are the limiting factors. Most tables are established for typical floor and roof loads, so in unusual circumstances the required size and spacing will have to be calculated using the methods of beam design.

To use the table, either begin with a known span and lumber species and find the required size and spacing of joists, or begin with the span and joist design and determine what design values are required to satisfy the requirements. Then specify a lumber species and grade that have the design values needed. The design values are found in Table 40.2.

Table 40.6 Floor Joist Spans for Common Lumber Species (Residential Living Area, Live Load = 40 psf, $L/\Delta = 360$)

joist spacing (in)	species and grade		maximum floor joist spans (ft-in)							
			dead load = 10 psf				dead load = 20 psf			
			2 × 6	2 × 8	2 × 10	2 × 12	2 × 6	2 × 8	2 × 10	2 × 12
12	Douglas fir-larch	SS	11-4	15-0	19-1	23-3	11-4	15-0	19-1	23-3
	Douglas fir-larch	no. 1	10-11	14-5	18-5	22-0	10-11	14-2	17-4	20-1
	Douglas fir-larch	no. 2	10-9	14-2	17-9	20-7	10-6	13-3	16-3	18-10
	Douglas fir-larch	no. 3	8-8	11-0	13-5	15-7	7-11	10-0	12-3	14-3
	southern pine	SS	11-2	14-8	18-9	22-10	11-2	14-8	18-9	22-10
	southern pine	no. 1	10-9	14-2	18-0	21-11	10-9	14-2	16-11	20-1
	southern pine	no. 2	10-3	13-6	16-2	19-1	9-10	12-6	14-9	17-5
	southern pine	no. 3	8-1	10-3	12-6	14-9	7-5	9-5	11-5	13-6
16	Douglas fir-larch	SS	10-4	13-7	17-4	21-1	10-4	13-7	17-4	21-0
	Douglas fir-larch	no. 1	9-11	13-1	16-5	19-1	9-8	12-4	15-0	17-5
	Douglas fir-larch	no. 2	9-9	12-7	15-5	17-10	9-1	11-6	14-1	16-3
	Douglas fir-larch	no. 3	7-6	9-6	11-8	13-6	6-10	8-8	10-7	12-4
	southern pine	SS	10-2	13-4	17-0	20-9	10-2	13-4	17-0	20-9
	southern pine	no. 1	9-9	12-10	16-1	19-1	9-9	12-7	14-8	17-5
	southern pine	no. 2	9-4	11-10	14-0	16-6	8-6	10-10	12-10	15-1
	southern pine	no. 3	7-1	8-11	10-10	12-10	6-5	8-2	9-10	11-8
19.2	Douglas fir-larch	SS	9-8	12-10	16-4	19-10	9-8	12-10	16-4	19-2
	Douglas fir-larch	no. 1	9-4	12-4	15-0	17-5	8-10	11-3	13-8	15-11
	Douglas fir-larch	no. 2	9-1	11-6	14-1	16-3	8-3	10-6	12-10	14-10
	Douglas fir-larch	no. 3	6-10	8-8	10-7	12-4	6-3	7-11	9-8	11-3
	southern pine	SS	9-6	12-7	16-0	19-6	9-6	12-7	16-0	19-6
	southern pine	no. 1	9-2	12-1	14-8	17-5	9-0	11-5	13-5	15-11
	southern pine	no. 2	8-6	10-10	12-10	15-1	7-9	9-10	11-8	13-9
	southern pine	no. 3	6-5	8-2	9-10	11-8	5-11	7-5	9-0	10-8
24	Douglas fir-larch	SS	9-0	11-11	15-2	18-5	9-0	11-11	14-9	17-1
	Douglas fir-larch	no. 1	8-8	11-0	13-5	15-7	7-11	10-0	12-3	14-3
	Douglas fir-larch	no. 2	8-1	10-3	12-7	14-7	7-5	9-5	11-6	13-4
	Douglas fir-larch	no. 3	6-2	7-9	9-6	11-0	5-7	7-1	8-8	10-1
	southern pine	SS	8-10	11-8	14-11	18-1	8-10	11-8	14-11	18-1
	southern pine	no. 1	8-6	11-3	13-1	15-7	8-1	10-3	12-0	14-13
	southern pine	no. 2	7-7	9-8	11-5	13-6	7-0	8-10	10-5	12-4
	southern pine	no. 3	5-9	7-3	8-10	10-5	5-3	6-8	8-1	19-6

Check sources for availability of lumber in lengths greater than 20 ft.

Note: Some rows/columns not pertinent to this text have been omitted by PPI.

Example 40.9

A floor must be designed to support a live load of 40 psf and a dead load of 20 psf. The joists will span 13 ft. If the most readily available grade of wood joist is Douglas fir-larch no. 2, what size and spacing is required?

Solution

Table 40.6 gives span values based on lumber species, joist spacing, dead load, and joist size for a live load of 40 psf. For Douglas fir-larch no. 2 joists spaced 12 in on center, the first size that will carry 20 psf of dead load for at least a 13 ft span is a 2×8. These 2×8 joists spaced 12 in on center will span 13 ft 3 in as indicated in Table 40.6. Additionally, 2×10 joists spaced 16 in on center will span 14 ft 1 in. A 24 in spacing would require 2×12 joists.

GLUED-LAMINATED CONSTRUCTION

Glued-laminated wood members consist of a number of individual pieces of lumber glued together and finished under factory conditions for use as beams, columns, purlins, and other structural uses. Glued-laminated construction, or *glulam* as it is usually referred to, is used when larger wood members are required for heavy loads or long spans and simple sawn timber pieces are not available or cannot meet the strength requirements. Glulam construction is also used where unusual structural shapes are required and appearance is a consideration. In addition to being fabricated in simple rectangular shapes, glulam members can be formed into arches, tapered forms, and pitched shapes.

Glulam members are manufactured in standard sizes of width and depth. In most cases, $1\frac{1}{2}$ in actual depth pieces are used, so the overall depth is some multiple of $1\frac{1}{2}$ depending on how many laminations are used. $\frac{3}{4}$ in thick pieces are used if a tight curve must be formed. Standard widths and depths are shown in Fig. 40.3.

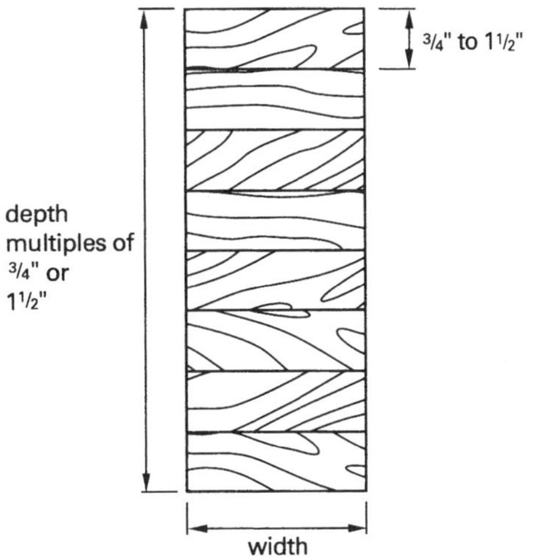

Because individual pieces can be selected free from certain defects and seasoned to the proper moisture content, and the entire manufacturing process is conducted under carefully controlled conditions, the allowable stresses for glulam construction are higher than for solid, sawn lumber. Although glulam beams are usually loaded in the direction perpendicular to the laminations, they can be loaded in either direction to suit the requirements of the design. Tables of design values give allowable stresses about both axes.

depth multiples of 3/4" or 1 1/2"

3/4" to 1 1/2"

width

nominal	actual
4"	3 1/8"
6"	5 1/8"
8"	6 3/4"
10"	8 3/4"
12"	10 3/4"
14"	12 1/4"

Figure 40.3 Glued-Laminated Beam

For structural purposes, glulams are designated by size and a commonly used symbol that specifies its stress rating. For design purposes, glulams are available in three appearance grades: *industrial*, *architectural*, and *premium*. These do not affect the structural properties but only designate the final look and finishing of the member. Industrial is used where appearance is not a primary concern, while premium is used where the finest appearance is important. Architectural grade is used where appearance is a factor but the best grade is not required.

PLANKING

Wood planking, or *decking* as it is often called, is solid or laminated lumber laid on its face spanning between beams. Planking is available in nominal thicknesses of 2, 3, 4, and 5 in with actual sizes varying with manufacturer and whether the piece is solid or laminated. All planking has some type of tongue-and-groove edging, so the pieces fit solidly together and load can be distributed among adjacent pieces.

The allowable span depends on the thickness of the planking and load to be supported, and ranges from 4 ft to 20 ft. Planking is often used in heavy timber construction with glued-laminated beams and purlins. Planking has the advantages of easy installation, attractive appearance, and efficient use of material since the planking serves as floor structure, finish floor, and finish ceiling below. Its primary disadvantages are that there is no place to put additional insulation or conceal mechanical and electrical services.

41 STEEL CONSTRUCTION

Nomenclature

A	cross-sectional area	in^2
BF	factor used in calculating flexural strength (Eq. 41.3)	–
d	actual depth of beam	in
E	modulus of elasticity	lbf/in^2
f_b	computed bending stress	lbf/in^2
f_v	shear stress	lbf/in^2
F_{cr}	allowable axial buckling stress	lbf/in^2
F_y	specified minimum yield stress of the type of steel being used	lbf/in^2
I	moment of inertia	in^4
K	effective length factor	–
l	unbraced span or column length	ft
L	span or column length	ft
L_b	unbraced length of bending compression flange	ft
L_p	maximum unbraced length of the compression flange at which the allowable bending strength may be taken at M_p	ft
L_r	maximum unbraced length of the compression flange at which the allowable bending strength may be taken	ft
M	moment	ft-lbf
M_n	nominal resisting moment	ft-lbf
M_p	maximum bending strength permitted in a member in the absence of axial force	ft-lbf
P_n	allowable tensile strength	lbf
r	governing radius of gyration	in
t_w	thickness of web	in
V	maximum web shear	lbf
V_n	allowable shear strength	lbf
w	weight per foot	lbf
Z	plastic section modulus	in^3
Δ	deflection	in

There are currently two accepted methods of structural steel design in the United States: the *allowable stress design* (ASD) method and the *load and resistance factor design* (LRFD) method. The use of either method is allowed by the *International Building Code* (IBC), but the IBC is based on the ASD method. The material in this chapter is also based on the ASD method.

PROPERTIES OF STRUCTURAL STEEL

Steel is one of the most widely used structural materials because of its many advantages, which include high strength, ductility, uniformity of manufacture, variety of shapes and sizes, and ease and speed of erection. Steel has a high strength-to-weight ratio. This makes it possible to reduce a building's dead load and to minimize the space taken up by structural elements. In addition, steel has a high modulus of elasticity, which means it is very stiff.

Ductility is a property that allows steel to withstand excessive deformations, due to high tensile stresses, without failure. This property makes steel useful for earthquake-resistant structures.

Because steel is manufactured under carefully controlled conditions, the composition, size, and strength of steel members can be uniformly predicted. Unlike concrete structures, structures made of steel do not have to be overdesigned to allow for unpredictable variations in manufacturing or erection.

The variety of available sizes and shapes of steel also allows the designer to select a member that is the most efficient for the job and that is not larger than it needs to be. These properties make possible a wide range of cost-efficient structures.

Finally, because most of the cutting and preparation of members can occur in the fabricating plant, steel structures can be erected very quickly and easily, thus reducing overall construction time.

In spite of its advantages, however, steel does have negative properties that must be allowed for. Most notable are its reduction in strength when subjected to fire and its tendency to corrode in the presence of moisture. Steel itself does not burn, but it deforms at high temperatures. As a result, steel must be protected with fire-resistant materials such as sprayed-on cementitious material or gypsum board, or it must be encased in concrete.

As with any ferrous material, steel will rust and otherwise corrode if not protected. This can be accomplished by including alloys in the steel to protect it (e.g., stainless steel), or by covering it with paint or other protective coatings.

Types and Composition of Steel

Steel is composed primarily of iron with small amounts of carbon and other elements that are part of the alloy, either as impurities left over from manufacturing or deliberately added to impart certain desired qualities to the alloy. In *medium-carbon steel* used in construction, these other elements include manganese (from 0.5% to 1.0%), silicon (from 0.25% to 0.75%), and smaller amounts of phosphorus and sulfur. Phosphorus and sulfur in excessive amounts are harmful in that they affect weldability and make steel brittle, but sulfur is difficult to remove completely, and a very small amount of phosphorus improves strength and hardness.

The percentage of carbon present affects the strength and ductility of steel. As carbon is added, the strength increases but the ductility decreases. Percentages of carbon range from about 0.15% for very mild steel to 0.70% for high-carbon steel. Standard structural steel has from 0.20% to 0.50% carbon.

The most common type of steel for structural use is ASTM A992, which means that the steel is manufactured according to ASTM International specification number A992. The yield point for this steel is 50 kips per square inch (ksi). Other high-strength steels include A242, A440, A441, and A572 steel, which have yield points of 46 ksi or 50 ksi.

Shapes and Size of Structural Steel

Structural steel comes in a variety of shapes, sizes, and weights. This gives the designer a great deal of flexibility in selecting an economical member that is geometrically correct for any given situation. Figure 41.1 shows the most common shapes of structural steel.

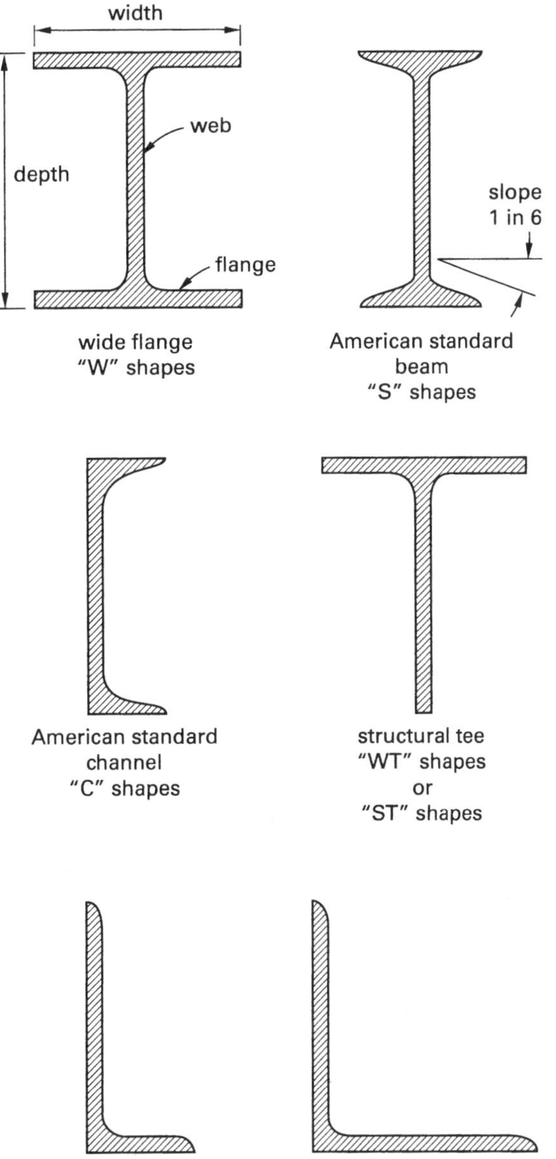

Figure 41.1 Structural Steel Shapes

Wide-flange members are H-shaped sections used for both beams and columns. They are called "wide flange" because the width of the flange is greater than that of standard I-beams. The outside and inside faces of the flanges are parallel. Many of the wide-flange shapes are particularly suited for columns because the width of the flange is very nearly equal to the depth of the section, so they have about the same rigidity in both axes. 14 in deep wide-flange sections are often used for columns in high-rise multistory structures. In low-rise and mid-rise multistory buildings, usually the smallest column used is an 8 in deep wide flange.

Wide-flange sections are designated with the letter W followed by the nominal depth in inches and the weight in pounds per linear foot (plf). For example, a W18 × 86 is a wide flange nominally 18 in deep and weighing 86 plf. Because of the way these sections are rolled in the mill, the actual depth varies slightly from the nominal depth.

American standard I-beams have a relatively narrow flange width in relation to their depth, and the inside face of the flanges have a slope of $16\frac{2}{3}\%$, or $\frac{1}{6}$. Unlike wide-flange members, the actual depth of an

I-beam in any size group is also its nominal depth. Heavier sections are made by adding thickness to the flanges on the inside face only. The designation of depth and weight per foot for these sections is preceded with the letter S. These sections are usually used for beams only.

American standard channel sections have a flange on one side of the web only and are designated with the letter C followed by the depth and the weight per foot. Like the American standard I-beams, the depth is constant for any size group. Extra weight is added by increasing the thickness of the web and the inside face of the flanges. Channel sections are typically used to frame openings, to form stair stringers, and in other applications where a flush side is required. They are seldom used by themselves as beams or columns because they tend to buckle due to their asymmetrical shape.

Structural tees are made by cutting either a wide-flange section or I-beam in half. If cut from a wide-flange section, a tee is given the prefix designation WT, and if cut from an American standard I-beam, it is given the designation ST. A WT9 × 65, for example, is cut from a W18 × 130. Because they are symmetrical about one axis and have an open flange, tees are often used for chords of steel trusses.

Steel angles are available with either equal or unequal legs. They are designated by the letter L followed by the lengths of the two legs and their thickness. Angles are used in pairs for members for steel trusses or singly as lintels in a variety of applications. They are also used for miscellaneous bracing of other structural members.

Table 41.1 Standard Designations for Structural Shapes

shape	example
wide-flange shapes	W12 × 22
American standard beams	S12 × 35
miscellaneous shapes	M12 × 11.8
American standard channels	C15 × 40
miscellaneous channels	MC12 × 35
angles, equal legs	L3 × 3 × 3/8
angles, unequal legs	L4 × 3 × 1/2
structural tees—cut from wide flange shapes	WT7 × 15
structural tees—cut from American standard beams	ST9 × 35
plates	PL10" × 1/2" × 0'10"
structural tubing, square	HSS8 × 8 × 3/8
pipe	pipe 4 std.

Square tube sections, *rectangular tube sections*, and *round pipe* are also available. These are often used for light columns and as members of large trusses or space frames. Structural tubing of various sizes is available in several different wall thicknesses, while structural pipe is available in standard weight, extra strong, and double-extra strong. Each of the three weights has a standard wall thickness depending on the size. Pipe is designated by its nominal diameter, but the actual outside dimension is slightly larger, while the size designation for square or rectangular tubing refers to its actual outside dimensions.

Finally, steel is available in bars and plates. A *bar* is considered any rectangular section 6 in or less in width with a thickness of 0.203 in or greater, or a section 6 in to 8 in in width with a thickness of 0.230 or greater.

A *plate* is considered any section over 8 in wide with a thickness of 0.230 in and over, or a section over 48 in wide with a thickness of 0.180 in and over.

Table 41.1 gives examples of the standard designations for structural steel shapes.

Allowable Stresses

Allowable unit stresses for structural steel are expressed as percentages of the minimum specified yield point of the grade of steel used. For A992 steel, the yield point is 50 ksi. The percentages used depend on the type of stress, the condition of use, and other factors. Allowable strengths are established by the American Institute of Steel Construction (AISC) and are commonly adopted by reference by model codes such as the IBC and by local codes. Table 41.2 summarizes some of the more common AISC values for 50 ksi steel.

Table 41.2 Selected Allowable Strengths for 50 ksi Steel

type of stress and condition	strength nomenclature	AISC safety factor	stress value for A992 steel (ksi)
bending			
tension and compression on extreme fibers of laterally supported compact sections symmetrical about and loaded in the plane of their minor axes	M_p	1.67	30
compression on axially loaded compact section	P_n	$F_{cr}/1.67$	varies
shear on gross sections	V_n	$0.60F_y/1.50$	20
tension			
on net section	P_n	$F_y/1.67$	30
on effective net area, except at pinholes	P_n	$F_u/2.00$	29

STEEL BEAMS

The design of steel beams involves finding the lightest weight section (and therefore the least expensive) that will resist bending and shear forces within allowable limits of stress, and one that will not have excessive deflection for the condition of use. Beam design can be accomplished either through the use of the standard formulas for flexure, shear, and deflection, or by using tables in the *Steel Construction Manual* published by the AISC. Both methods will be reviewed in the following sections.

Lateral Support and Compact Sections

Before proceeding with methods for steel beam design, gain a firm understanding of two important concepts: lateral support and compact sections. When a simply supported beam is subjected to a load, the top flange is in compression and the bottom flange is in tension. At the compression flange, there is a tendency for the beam to buckle under load, just as a column can buckle under an axial load. For overhanging beams, when the bottom flange is in compression the same potential problem exists.

To resist this tendency, either the compression flange needs to be supported or the beam needs to be made larger. In many cases, steel beams are automatically laterally supported because of standard construction methods. This occurs with beams supporting steel decking welded to the beams, beams with the top flange embedded in a concrete slab, or composite construction. In some instances, a girder is only supported laterally with intermittent beams.

If a beam is continuously supported or supported at intervals no greater than L_p, the full allowable strength of M_p may be used. If the support is greater than L_p but not greater than L_r, then the allowable strength must be reduced to the value in Eq. 41.3. The values of L_p and L_r are given in tables in the *AISC Manual* and will be illustrated in later example problems.

Sections are determined to be either *compact* or *noncompact* based on the yield strength of the steel and the width-to-thickness ratios of the web and flanges. If a section is noncompact, a lower allowable bending stress must be used. Identification of noncompact sections and the reduced stresses are incorporated into the design tables in the *AISC Manual.*

Design for Bending

There are two approaches to designing steel beams: with the flexure formula as discussed in Chap. 35 and with the tables found in the *AISC Manual.* Both will be discussed next.

The basic flexure formula is

$$Z = \frac{M}{F_y} \qquad 41.1$$

This formula from Chap. 35 is the same for steel design, except that the AISC uses the nomenclature M_n for the allowable moment strength instead of f_b, which it reserves for computed bending stress.

Product Development

The basic formula is used in two forms either to select a beam by finding the required section plastic modulus, Z, or to calculate the maximum resisting moment, M, when a beam is being analyzed. These two forms are Eq. 41.1 and Eq. 41.2.

$$M_n = ZF_y \tag{41.2}$$

The following equation is used when the unbraced length of the compression flanges is between L_p and L_r. The values are given in Table 41.4.

$$M_n = M_p - \text{BF}(L_b - L_p) \tag{41.3}$$

Moments are calculated using the static formulas for various types of loading conditions as shown in Fig. 35.7, or by using the methods described in Chap. 35 with shear and moment diagrams, or with the summation of moments method.

It is important to keep the units consistent. It is typical in steel design to use the units of kips (thousands of pounds) instead of pounds, and feet instead of inches. However, allowable stresses are often listed in kips per square inch, so it is often necessary to convert between inch-kips and foot-kips. In addition, many of the tables used in the *AISC Manual* are in kips while problems are often given in pounds. The best way to avoid difficulty is to adopt a consistent procedure of using kips and feet in all problems. If a problem is stated in pounds or inches, the first step should be to convert the units. The following example problems will illustrate this point.

Example 41.1

An A992 steel beam that is laterally supported is to span 26 ft, supporting a uniform load of 1500 plf not including its own weight. What is the most economical wide-flange section that can be used?

Solution

The weight of a beam can be accounted for in one of two ways. Either assume a weight and add it to the load and then calculate moment, or ignore it, solve the problem to find the actual weight of the beam, and then recheck the work. Since the weight of a steel beam is usually a very small percentage of the total load, it can usually be ignored for preliminary calculations. For example, the heaviest wide-flange section used for a beam is a W44 × 335, so the most additional weight possible is 0.335 klf.

Find the maximum moment, ignoring the weight of the beam.

From Fig. 35.7, the formula for moment is

$$M = \frac{wL^2}{8}$$

Converting 1500 plf to 1.5 klf,

$$M = \frac{\left(1.5\ \frac{\text{kips}}{\text{ft}}\right)(26\ \text{ft})^2}{8} = 127\ \text{ft-kips}$$

For A992 steel, the allowable bending stress is 30 ksi (Table 41.2). Use Eq. 41.1 to find the required section modulus.

$$Z = \frac{(127\ \text{ft-kips})\left(12\ \frac{\text{in}}{\text{ft}}\right)}{30\ \frac{\text{kips}}{\text{in}^2}} = 50.8\ \text{in}^3$$

Product Development

The value of 127 ft-kips had to be converted to inch-kips to work with the value of 30 ksi and yield an answer in cubic inches for the section modulus.

To find the most economical section (the lightest weight), look in the various AISC tables showing properties of sections (Table 41.3, for example), or look in the section modulus table in the *AISC Manual.* A portion of this table is reproduced in Table 41.4. This table lists the various sections in the order of descending section modulus value with the lightest member in a group shown in boldface type. For this problem, the lightest section that satisfies the required section modulus is a W16 × 31 with a Z of 54.0 in^3.

Table 41.4 also lists the maximum resisting moment that the beam can carry and the length limits, L_p and L_r, for unsupported sections. The columns on the right are for calculating M_n. The maximum moment this beam can resist, assuming L_b is less than L_p, is 135 ft-kips. If an additional 40 lbf (0.040 kips) of beam weight is added to the load and the moment is recalculated, the resulting moment is 130.1 ft-kips. This is less than the maximum allowable of 135 ft-kips, and the selection is okay.

The other way to select the beam is to use the Maximum Total Uniform Load tables in the *AISC Manual.* One page is reproduced in Table 41.5. These tables make it very easy to calculate allowable loads for a given size beam, select a beam for a given span and loading, find deflections and shear values, and check for unbraced lengths. The tables take into account the weight of the beams, but these should be deducted to determine the net load that the beam will support.

The tables are for uniformly loaded beams, but they can be used for concentrated loads by using the table of concentrated load equivalents in the *AISC Manual,* which give factors for converting concentrated loads to uniform loads. In Table 41.5, the notation L_p is used to denote the maximum unbraced length of the compression flange, in feet, for which the allowable loads for compact symmetrical shapes are calculated with an allowable strength of M_p. The tables are not applicable for beams with an unbraced length greater than L_r.

For relatively short spans, the allowable loads for beams may be limited by the shear stress in the web instead of by the maximum bending stress. Loads above the heavy line in the tables are limited by the maximum allowable web shear.

When the spacing of lateral bracing exceeds L_p, but is less than L_r, the tabulated loads must be reduced by the ratio of M_p to the value of M_n as derived from Eq. 41.3.

Example 41.2

An A992 beam, fully laterally supported, spans 20 ft and carries a uniform load of 2700 plf. If there is only space for a 12 in deep beam, what size section should be used? If the beam is only laterally supported at its third points, could the same beam be used?

Solution

2700 plf is 2.7 klf, so the total load on the beam is 2.7 klf times 20 ft, or 54.0 kips.

From Table 41.5, the lightest 12 in section that can support 54.0 kips is a W12 × 40 (which has a uniform load value of 56.9 kips).

If the beam is only supported at its third points (every 6.67 ft), this distance is less than the L_p value for a W12 × 40 (6.85 ft, from Table 41.5). Because the unsupported length is less than 6.85 ft, the beam is adequate. Therefore, this beam is acceptable.

Table 41.3
Properties of Wide Flange Shapes

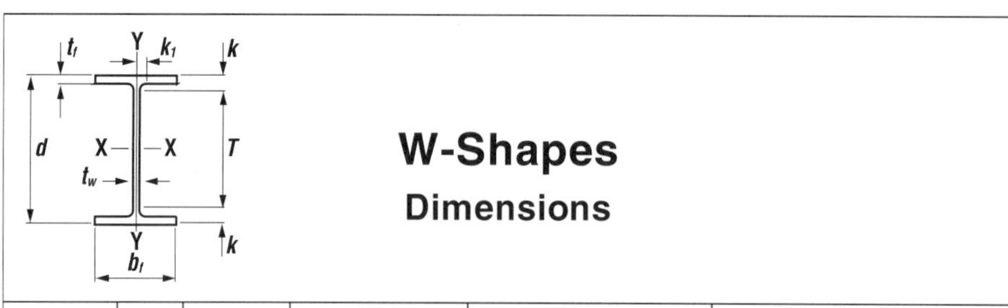

Shape	Area, A	Depth, d		Web Thickness, t_w		$\frac{t_w}{2}$	Flange Width, b_f		Flange Thickness, t_f		Distance k k_{des}	k k_{det}	k_1	T	Workable Gage
	in.²	in.		in.		in.	in.		in.		in.	in.	in.	in.	in.
W12x58	17.0	12.2	12 1/4	0.360	3/8	3/16	10.0	10	0.640	5/8	1.24	1 1/2	15/16	9 1/4	5 1/2
x53	15.6	12.1	12	0.345	3/8	3/16	10.0	10	0.575	9/16	1.18	1 3/8	15/16	9 1/4	5 1/2
W12x50	14.6	12.2	12 1/4	0.370	3/8	3/16	8.08	8 1/8	0.640	5/8	1.14	1 1/2	15/16	9 1/4	5 1/2
x45	13.1	12.1	12	0.335	5/16	3/16	8.05	8	0.575	9/16	1.08	1 3/8	15/16	↓	↓
x40	11.7	11.9	12	0.295	5/16	3/16	8.01	8	0.515	1/2	1.02	1 3/8	7/8	↓	↓
W12x35[c]	10.3	12.5	12 1/2	0.300	5/16	3/16	6.56	6 1/2	0.520	1/2	0.820	1 3/16	3/4	10 1/8	3 1/2
x30[c]	8.79	12.3	12 3/8	0.260	1/4	1/8	6.52	6 1/2	0.440	7/16	0.740	1 1/8	3/4	↓	↓
x26[c]	7.65	12.2	12 1/4	0.230	1/4	1/8	6.49	6 1/2	0.380	3/8	0.680	1 1/16	3/4	↓	↓
W12x22[c]	6.48	12.3	12 1/4	0.260	1/4	1/8	4.03	4	0.425	7/16	0.725	15/16	5/8	10 3/8	2 1/4[g]
x19[c]	5.57	12.2	12 1/8	0.235	1/4	1/8	4.01	4	0.350	3/8	0.650	7/8	9/16	↓	↓
x16[c]	4.71	12.0	12	0.220	1/4	1/8	3.99	4	0.265	1/4	0.565	13/16	9/16	↓	↓
x14[c,v]	4.16	11.9	11 7/8	0.200	3/16	1/8	3.97	4	0.225	1/4	0.525	3/4	9/16	↓	↓
W10x112	32.9	11.4	11 3/8	0.755	3/4	3/8	10.4	10 3/8	1.25	1 1/4	1.75	1 15/16	1	7 1/2	5 1/2
x100	29.3	11.1	11 1/8	0.680	11/16	3/8	10.3	10 3/8	1.12	1 1/8	1.62	1 13/16	1	↓	↓
x88	26.0	10.8	10 7/8	0.605	5/8	5/16	10.3	10 1/4	0.990	1	1.49	1 11/16	15/16	↓	↓
x77	22.7	10.6	10 5/8	0.530	1/2	1/4	10.2	10 1/4	0.870	7/8	1.37	1 9/16	7/8	↓	↓
x68	19.9	10.4	10 3/8	0.470	1/2	1/4	10.1	10 1/8	0.770	3/4	1.27	1 7/16	7/8	↓	↓
x60	17.7	10.2	10 1/4	0.420	7/16	1/4	10.1	10 1/8	0.680	11/16	1.18	1 3/8	13/16	↓	↓
x54	15.8	10.1	10 1/8	0.370	3/8	3/16	10.0	10	0.615	5/8	1.12	1 5/16	13/16	↓	↓
x49	14.4	10.0	10	0.340	5/16	3/16	10.0	10	0.560	9/16	1.06	1 1/4	13/16	↓	↓
W10x45	13.3	10.1	10 1/8	0.350	3/8	3/16	8.02	8	0.620	5/8	1.12	1 5/16	13/16	7 1/2	5 1/2
x49	11.5	9.92	9 7/8	0.315	5/16	3/16	7.99	8	0.530	1/2	1.03	1 3/16	13/16	↓	↓
x33	9.71	9.73	9 3/4	0.290	5/16	3/16	7.96	8	0.435	7/16	0.935	1 1/8	3/4	↓	↓
W10x30	8.84	10.5	10 1/2	0.300	5/16	3/16	5.81	5 3/4	0.510	1/2	0.810	1 1/8	11/16	8 1/4	2 3/4[g]
x26	7.61	10.3	10 3/8	0.260	1/4	1/8	5.77	5 3/4	0.440	7/16	0.740	1 1/16	11/16	↓	↓
x22[c]	6.49	10.2	10 1/8	0.240	1/4	1/8	5.75	5 3/4	0.360	3/8	0.660	15/16	5/8	↓	↓
W10x19	5.62	10.2	10 1/4	0.250	1/4	1/8	4.02	4	0.395	3/8	0.695	15/16	5/8	8 3/8	2 1/4[g]
x17[c]	4.99	10.1	10 1/8	0.240	1/4	1/8	4.01	4	0.330	5/16	0.630	7/8	9/16	↓	↓
x15[c]	4.41	9.99	10	0.230	1/4	1/8	4.00	4	0.270	1/4	0.570	13/16	9/16	↓	↓
x12[c,f]	3.54	9.87	9 7/8	0.190	3/16	1/8	3.96	4	0.210	3/16	0.510	3/4	9/16	↓	↓

[c] Shape is slender for compression with F_y = 50 ksi.
[f] Shape exceeds compact limit for flexure with F_y = 50 ksi.
[g] The actual size, combination and orientation of fastener components should be compare with the geometry of the cross section to ensure compatibility.
[v] Shape does not meet the h/t_w limit for shear in AISC Specification Section G2.1(a) with F_y = 50 ksi.

Product Development

Table 41.3 (continued)

(continued)
W-Shapes
Properties

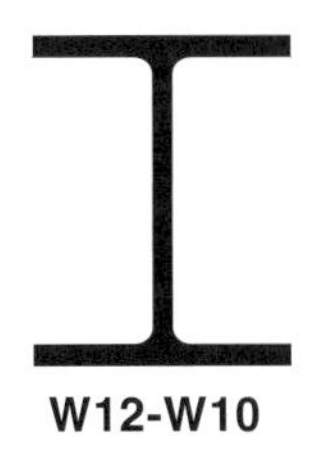

W12-W10

Nominal Wt.	Compact Section Criteria		Axis X-X				Axis Y-Y				r_{ts}	h_o	Torsional Properties	
	$\frac{b_f}{2t_f}$	$\frac{h}{t_w}$	I	S	r	Z	I	S	r	Z			J	C_w
lb/ft			in.^{4}	in.^{3}	in.	in.^{3}	in.^{4}	in.^{3}	in.	in.^{3}	in.	in.	in.^{4}	in.^{6}
58	7.82	27.0	475	78.0	5.28	86.4	107	21.4	2.51	32.5	2.81	11.6	2.10	3570
53	8.69	28.1	425	70.6	5.23	77.9	95.8	19.2	2.48	29.1	2.79	11.5	1.58	3160
50	6.31	26.8	391	64.2	5.18	71.9	56.3	13.9	1.96	21.3	2.25	11.6	1.71	1880
45	7.00	29.6	348	57.7	5.15	64.2	50.0	12.4	1.95	19.0	2.23	11.5	1.26	1650
40	7.77	33.6	307	51.5	5.13	57.0	44.1	11.0	1.94	16.8	2.21	11.4	0.906	1440
35	6.31	36.2	285	45.6	5.25	51.2	24.5	7.47	1.54	11.5	1.79	12.0	0.741	879
30	7.41	41.8	238	38.6	5.21	43.1	20.3	6.24	1.52	9.56	1.77	11.9	0.457	720
26	8.54	47.2	204	33.4	5.17	37.2	17.3	5.34	1.51	8.17	1.75	11.8	0.300	607
22	4.74	41.8	156	25.4	4.91	29.3	4.66	2.31	0.848	3.66	1.04	11.9	0.293	164
19	5.72	46.2	130	21.3	4.82	24.7	3.76	1.88	0.822	2.98	1.02	11.9	0.180	131
16	7.53	49.4	103	17.1	4.67	20.1	2.82	1.41	0.773	2.26	0.983	11.7	0.103	96.9
14	8.82	54.3	88.6	14.9	4.62	17.4	2.36	1.19	0.753	1.90	0.960	11.7	0.0704	80.4
112	4.17	10.4	716	126	4.66	147	236	45.3	2.68	69.2	3.08	10.2	15.1	6020
100	4.62	11.6	623	112	4.60	130	207	40.0	2.65	61.0	3.04	10.0	10.9	5150
88	5.18	13.0	534	98.5	4.54	113	179	34.8	2.63	53.1	2.99	9.81	7.53	4330
77	5.86	14.8	455	85.9	4.49	97.6	154	30.1	2.60	45.9	2.95	9.73	5.11	3630
68	6.58	16.7	394	75.7	4.44	85.3	134	26.4	2.59	40.1	2.92	9.63	3.56	3100
60	7.41	18.7	341	66.7	4.39	74.6	116	23.0	2.57	35.0	2.88	9.52	2.48	2640
54	8.15	21.2	303	60.0	4.37	66.6	103	20.6	2.56	31.3	2.85	9.49	1.82	2320
49	8.93	23.1	272	54.6	4.35	60.4	93.4	18.7	2.54	28.3	2.81	9.44	1.39	2070
45	6.47	22.5	248	49.1	4.32	54.9	53.4	13.3	2.01	20.3	2.27	9.48	1.51	1200
39	7.53	25.0	209	42.1	4.27	46.8	45.0	11.3	1.98	17.2	2.24	9.39	0.976	922
33	9.15	27.1	171	35.0	4.19	38.8	36.6	9.20	1.94	14.0	2.20	9.30	0.583	791
30	5.70	29.5	170	32.4	4.38	36.6	16.7	5.75	1.37	8.84	1.60	10.0	0.622	414
26	6.56	34.0	144	27.9	4.35	31.3	14.1	4.89	1.36	7.50	1.58	9.86	0.402	345
22	7.99	36.9	118	23.2	4.27	26.0	11.4	3.97	1.33	6.10	1.55	9.84	0.239	275
19	5.09	35.4	96.3	18.8	4.14	21.6	4.29	2.14	0.874	3.35	1.06	9.81	0.233	104
17	6.09	36.9	81.9	16.2	4.05	18.7	3.56	1.78	0.845	2.80	1.04	9.77	0.156	85.1
15	7.41	38.5	68.9	13.8	3.95	16.0	2.89	1.45	0.810	2.30	1.01	9.72	0.104	68.3
12	9.43	46.6	53.8	10.9	3.90	12.6	2.18	1.10	0.785	1.74	0.983	9.66	0.0547	60.9

Table 41.4
Section Modulus and Moment of Resistance of Selected Structural Shapes

Z_x **W-Shapes** F_y = 50 ksi

Selection by Z_x

Shape	Z_x	M_{px}/Ω_b	$\phi_b M_{px}$	M_{rx}/Ω_b	$\phi_b M_{rx}$	BF/Ω_b	$\phi_b BF$	L_p	L_r	L_x	V_{nx}/Ω_v	$\phi_v V_{nx}$
		kip-ft	kip-ft	kip-ft	kip-ft	kips	kips				kips	kips
	in.^{3}	ASD	LRFD	ASD	LRFD	ASD	LRFD	ft	ft	in.^{4}	ASD	LRFD
W18x35	66.5	166	249	101	151	8.14	12.3	4.31	12.3	510	106	159
W12x45	64.2	160	241	101	151	3.80	5.80	6.89	22.4	348	81.1	122
W16x36	64.0	160	240	98.7	148	6.24	9.36	5.37	15.2	448	93.8	141
W14x38	61.5	153	231	95.4	143	5.37	8.20	5.47	16.2	385	87.4	131
W10x39	60.4	151	227	95.4	143	2.46	3.71	8.97	31.6	272	68.0	102
W8x58	59.8	149	224	90.8	137	1.70	2.55	7.42	41.6	228	89.3	134
W12x40	57.0	142	214	89.9	135	3.66	5.54	6.85	21.1	307	70.2	105
W10x45	54.9	137	206	85.8	129	2.59	3.89	7.10	26.9	248	70.7	106
W14x34	54.6	136	205	84.9	128	5.01	7.55	5.40	15.6	340	79.8	120
W16x31	54.0	135	203	82.4	124	6.86	10.3	4.13	11.8	375	87.5	131
W12x35	51.2	128	192	79.6	120	4.34	6.45	5.44	16.6	285	75.0	113
W8x48	49.0	122	184	75.4	113	1.67	2.55	7.35	35.2	184	68.0	102
W14x30	47.3	118	177	73.4	110	4.63	6.95	5.26	14.9	291	74.5	112
W10x39	46.8	117	176	73.5	111	2.53	3.78	6.99	24.2	209	62.4	93.7
W16x26[v]	44.2	110	166	67.1	101	5.93	8.98	3.96	11.2	301	70.5	106
W12x30	43.0	108	162	67.4	101	3.97	5.96	5.37	15.6	238	64.0	95.9
W14x26	40.2	100	151	61.7	92.7	5.33	8.11	3.81	11.0	245	70.9	106
W8x40	39.8	99.3	149	62.0	93.2	1.64	2.46	7.21	29.9	146	59.4	89.1
W10x33	38.8	96.8	146	61.1	91.9	2.39	3.62	6.85	21.8	171	56.4	84.7
W12x26	37.2	92.8	140	58.3	87.7	3.61	5.46	5.33	14.9	204	56.1	84.2
W10x30	36.6	91.3	137	56.6	85.1	3.08	4.61	4.84	16.1	170	63.0	94.5
W8x35	34.7	86.6	130	54.5	81.9	1.62	2.43	7.17	27.0	127	50.3	75.5
W14x22	33.2	82.8	125	50.6	76.1	4.78	7.27	3.67	10.4	199	63.0	94.5
W10x26	31.3	78.1	117	48.7	73.2	2.91	4.34	4.80	14.9	144	53.6	80.3
W8x31[f]	30.4	75.8	114	48.0	72.2	1.58	2.37	7.18	24.8	110	45.6	68.4
W12x22	29.3	73.1	110	44.4	66.7	4.68	7.06	3.00	9.13	156	64.0	95.9
W8x28	27.2	67.9	102	42.4	63.8	1.67	2.50	5.78	21.0	98.0	45.9	68.9
W10x22	26.0	64.9	97.5	40.5	60.9	2.68	4.02	4.70	13.8	118	49.0	73.4
W12x19	24.7	61.6	92.6	37.2	55.9	4.27	6.43	2.90	8.61	130	57.3	86.0
W8x24	23.1	57.6	86.6	36.5	54.9	1.60	2.40	5.69	18.9	82.7	38.9	58.3
W10x19	21.6	53.9	81.0	32.8	49.4	3.18	4.76	3.09	9.73	96.3	51.0	76.5
W8x21	20.4	50.9	76.5	31.8	47.8	1.85	2.77	4.45	14.8	75.3	41.1	62.1

ASD	LRFD
$\Omega_b = 1.67$	$\phi_b = 0.90$
$\Omega_v = 1.50$	$\phi_v = 1.00$

[f] Shape exceeds compact limit for flexure with F_y = 50 ksi.

[v] Shape does not meet the h/tw limit for shear in AISC Specification Section G2.1(a) with F_y = 50 ksi; therefore, ϕ_v = 0.90 and Ω_v = 1.67.

From *Steel Construction Manual*, 14th Ed.,

Table 41.4 (continued)

F_y = 50 ksi

(continued)

W-Shapes

Selection by Z_x

Z_x

Shape	Z_x	M_{px}/Ω_b	$\phi_b M_{px}$	M_{rx}/Ω_b	$\phi_b M_{rx}$	BF/Ω_b	$\phi_b BF$	L_p	L_r	I_x	V_{nx}/Ω_v	$\phi_v V_{nx}$
		kip-ft	kip-ft	kip-ft	kip-ft	kips	kips				kips	kips
	in.³	ASD	LRFD	ASD	LRFD	ASD	LRFD	ft	ft	in.⁴	ASD	LRFD
W12x16	**20.1**	**50.1**	**75.4**	**29.9**	**44.9**	**3.80**	**5.73**	**2.73**	**8.05**	**103**	**52.8**	**79.2**
W10x17	18.7	46.7	70.1	28.3	42.5	2.90	4.47	2.98	9.16	81.9	48.5	72.7
W12x24[v]	**17.4**	**43.4**	**65.3**	**26.0**	**39.1**	**3.43**	**5.17**	**2.66**	**7.73**	**88.6**	**42.8**	**64.3**
W8x18	17.0	42.4	63.8	26.5	39.9	1.74	2.61	4.34	13.5	61.9	37.4	56.2
W10x15	16.0	39.9	60.0	24.1	36.2	2.75	4.14	2.86	8.61	68.9	46.0	68.9
W8x15	13.6	33.9	51.0	20.6	31.0	1.90	2.85	3.09	10.1	48.0	39.7	59.6
W10x12[f]	**12.6**	**31.2**	**46.9**	**19.0**	**28.6**	**2.36**	**3.53**	**2.87**	**8.05**	**53.8**	**37.5**	**56.3**
W8x13	11.4	28.4	42.8	17.3	26.0	1.76	2.67	2.98	9.27	39.6	36.8	55.1
W8x10[f]	**8.87**	**21.9**	**32.9**	**13.6**	**20.5**	**1.54**	**2.30**	**3.14**	**8.52**	**30.8**	**26.8**	**40.2**

ASD	LRFD
$\Omega_b = 1.67$	$\phi_b = 0.90$
$\Omega_b = 1.50$	$\phi_b = 1.00$

[f] Shape exceeds compact limit for flexure with F_y = 50ksi.
[v] Shape does not meet the h/t_w limit for shear in AISC *Specification* Section G2.1(a) with F_y = 50 ksi; therefore, ϕ_v = 0.90 and Ω_v = 1.67.

Product Development

Table 41.5
Maximum Total Uniform Load

F_y = 50 ksi

Maximum Total Uniform Load, kips

W Shapes

W12

Shape		W12x											
		53		50		45		40		35		30	
Design		ASD	LRFD	ASD	LRFD	ASD	LRFD	ASD	LRFD	ASD	LRFD	ASD	LRFD
Span, ft	6									**150**	225	**128**	193
	7			**180**	271	**162**	242			**146**	219	**123**	185
	8			**179**	270	**160**	241	**141**	211	**128**	192	**108**	162
	9	**166**	250	**159**	240	**142**	214	**126**	190	**114**	171	**95.6**	144
	10	**155**	234	**144**	216	**128**	193	**114**	171	**102**	154	**86.0**	129
	11	**141**	212	**130**	196	**116**	175	**103**	155	**92.9**	140	**78.2**	118
	12	**130**	195	**120**	180	**107**	161	**94.8**	143	**85.2**	128	**71.7**	108
	13	**120**	180	**110**	166	**98.6**	148	**87.5**	132	**78.6**	118	**66.2**	99.5
	14	**111**	167	**103**	154	**91.5**	138	**81.3**	122	**73.0**	110	**61.4**	92.4
	15	**104**	156	**95.7**	144	**85.4**	128	**75.8**	114	**68.1**	102	**57.4**	86.2
	16	**97.2**	146	**89.7**	135	**80.1**	120	**71.1**	107	**63.9**	96.0	**53.8**	80.8
	17	**91.5**	137	**84.4**	127	**75.4**	113	**66.9**	101	**60.1**	90.4	**50.6**	76.1
	18	**86.4**	130	**79.7**	120	**71.2**	107	**63.2**	95.0	**56.8**	85.3	**47.8**	71.8
	19	**81.8**	123	**75.5**	114	**67.4**	101	**59.9**	90.0	**53.8**	80.8	**45.3**	68.1
	20	**77.7**	117	**71.8**	108	**64.1**	69.3	**56.9**	85.5	**51.1**	76.8	**43.0**	64.7
	21	**74.0**	111	**68.3**	103	**61.0**	91.7	**54.2**	81.4	**48.7**	73.1	**41.0**	61.6
	22	**70.7**	106	**65.2**	98.0	**58.2**	87.5	**51.7**	77.7	**46.5**	69.8	**39.1**	58.8
	23	**67.6**	102	**62.4**	93.8	**55.7**	83.7	**49.5**	74.3	**44.4**	66.8	**37.4**	56.2
	24	**64.8**	97.4	**59.8**	89.9	**53.4**	80.3	**47.4**	71.3	**42.6**	64.0	**35.8**	53.9
	25	**62.2**	93.5	**57.4**	86.3	**51.3**	77.0	**45.5**	68.4	**40.9**	61.4	**34.4**	51.7
	26	**59.8**	89.9	**55.2**	83.0	**49.3**	74.1	**43.8**	65.8	**39.3**	59.1	**33.1**	49.7
	27	**57.6**	86.6	**53.2**	79.9	**47.5**	71.3	**42.1**	63.3	**37.9**	56.9	**31.9**	47.9
	28	**55.5**	83.5	**51.3**	77.0	**45.8**	68.8	**40.6**	61.1	**36.5**	54.9	**30.7**	46.2
	29	**53.6**	80.6	**49.5**	74.4	**44.2**	66.4	**39.2**	59.0	**35.2**	53.0	**29.7**	44.6
	30	**51.8**	77.9	**47.8**	71.9	**42.7**	64.2			**34.1**	51.2	**28.7**	43.1
	31									**33.0**	49.5		
Beam Properties													
W_c/Ω_b	$\phi_b W_c$, kip-ft	1550	2340	1440	2160	1280	1930	1140	1710	1020	1540	860	1290
W_p/Ω_b	$\phi_b M_p$, kip-ft	194	292	179	270	160	240	142	240	128	192	108	162
W_r/Ω_b	$\phi_b M_r$, kip-ft	123	185	112	169	101	151	89.9	135	79.6	120	67.4	101
BF	BF, kips	3.65	5.48	3.97	5.97	3.83	5.75	3.66	5.50	4.28	6.43	3.92	5.89
V_n/Ω_v	$\phi_v V_n$, kips	83.2	125	90.2	135	80.8	121	70.4	106	75.0	113	64.2	96.3
Z_x, in.^{3}		77.9		71.9		64.2		57.0		51.2		43.1	
L_p, ft		8.76		6.92		6.89		6.85		5.44		5.37	
L_r, ft		28.2		23.9		22.4		21.1		16.7		15.6	

ASD	LRFD	
Ω_b = 1.67	ϕ_b = 0.90	Note: For beams laterally unsupported, see Table 3-10.
Ω_v = 1.50	ϕ_v = 1.00	Available strength tabulated above heavy line is limited by available shear strength.

Product Development

Example 41.3

A W12 × 45 beam of A992 steel spans 21 ft. What is the maximum load per foot this beam can carry?

Solution

From Table 41.5 for a W12 × 45 beam, the total allowable load for a 21 ft span is 61 kips. Dividing by 21, the allowable load per foot is

$$w = \frac{61 \text{ kips}}{21 \text{ ft}} = 2.9 \text{ kips/ft}$$

Design for Shear

In most cases, shear is not a factor when designing steel beams. The section selected to resist the required bending stresses is typically more than adequate to resist shear. However, shear should be checked, especially for short, heavily loaded beams or beams with heavy loads near the supports. In these cases, shear may govern the design of the beam.

Because shearing stresses are not distributed evenly over the cross section and are zero at the extreme fibers, the flanges are discounted in calculating resistance to shear; only the area of the web is used. The unit shearing stress is given by the formula

$$f_v = \frac{V}{dt_w} \qquad 41.4$$

Example 41.4

Check the shear in the beam in Ex. 41.2.

Solution

Since the total load on the beam is 54.0 kips, the maximum vertical shear at one support is one-half this, or 27.0 kips. From Table 41.3 for a W12 × 40 beam, the actual depth is 11.90 in, and the web thickness is 0.295 in. The actual unit shear stress is

$$\begin{aligned} f_v &= \frac{27.0 \text{ kips}}{(11.90 \text{ in})(0.295 \text{ in})} \\ &= 7.69 \text{ ksi} \end{aligned}$$

From Table 41.2, the allowable shear on gross sections is 20 ksi. The area of the web is (11.90 in)(0.295 in), or 3.51 in^2. The allowable shear force is

$$V = \left(20 \frac{\text{kips}}{\text{in}^2}\right)(3.51 \text{ in}^2) = 70.2 \text{ kips}$$

This allowable shear can also be found at the bottom of Table 41.5 under the row labeled V. In this case it is rounded to 70.4 kips.

Design for Deflection

Steel beams need to be checked for deflection. Although a beam may be sufficient to resist bending stresses, it may sag enough to be objectionable or create problems such as cracking of finished ceilings or ponding of water on a roof. The maximum allowable deflection is determined partly by codes and partly by design judgment. For example, the AISC limits the live load deflection of beams supporting plaster ceilings to $1/360$ of the span.

Deflection can be calculated in one of two ways: by using the deflection formulas for various static loads as given in Fig. 35.7 and in the *AISC Manual*, or by using tables. Both methods are presented.

Example 41.5

Find the actual deflection of the W12 × 40 beam used in Ex. 41.2.

Solution

Using the formula for maximum deflection of a uniformly loaded beam as given in Fig. 35.7,

$$\Delta = \frac{5wl^4}{384EI}$$

All units must be consistent. In this example, all feet must be converted to inches. Since the load in Ex. 41.2 is 2700 plf and the weight of the beam is 40 plf, the total load is 2740 plf, or 228.3 lbf/in (2740 lfb/ft divided by 12 in/ft). The span must also be converted to inches. From Table 41.3, the moment of inertia for a W12 × 40 beam is 307 in^4. The modulus of elasticity for steel is 29,000,000 psi.

$$\Delta = \frac{(5)\left(228.3\ \frac{\text{lbf}}{\text{in}}\right)\left((20\ \text{ft})\left(12\ \frac{\text{in}}{\text{ft}}\right)\right)^4}{(384)\left(29{,}000{,}000\ \frac{\text{lbf}}{\text{in}^2}\right)(307\ \text{in}^4)} = 1.108\ \text{in}$$

If deflection were limited to $^1/_{360}$ of the span, the maximum allowable deflection would be

$$\Delta_{\text{max}} = \frac{(20\ \text{ft})\left(12\ \frac{\text{in}}{\text{ft}}\right)}{360} = 0.67\ \text{in}$$

The actual deflection in this example is more than the maximum, so the selected beam would be inadequate in deflection.

Product Development

STEEL COLUMNS

As with columns of any material, the amount of load a steel column can support depends not only on its area and allowable unit stress, but also the unbraced length of the column. As discussed in Chap. 35, columns of moderate to long length tend to fail first by buckling under load. The properties of a column that resist buckling are the area and the moment of inertia. These are mathematically combined into a single value, the radius of gyration. For a nonsymmetrical column, the radius of gyration is different for each axis. Review the section on columns in Chap. 35 for a further explanation.

The effect of a column's unbraced length and radius of gyration is combined in the slenderness ratio, which is defined for steel columns as the ratio of a column's length in inches to the radius of gyration.

$$\text{slenderness ratio} = \frac{l}{r} \qquad 41.5$$

In general, the greater the slenderness ratio, the greater the tendency for the column to fail under buckling, and therefore the smaller the load the column can carry. Because most steel columns are not symmetrical about both axes (such as with a wide-flange shape), the least radius of gyration governs for design purposes because it is about this axis that the column will fail first. The radii of gyration, r, about both axes are given in the *AISC Manual*, and some representative values are shown in Table 41.3.

Ideally, for the most efficient column, the radius of gyration should be the same in each direction such as with a pipe column or a square tube column. For light to moderate loads, these types of sections are often used as columns for this reason. However, they are not appropriate for heavy loads and where many beam connections must be made. Wide-flange sections are most often used because the radius of gyration in the Y-Y axis is close to the radius of gyration in the X-X axis. There are special wide-flange sections specifically manufactured to provide nearly symmetrical columns with large load-carrying capacities. Most of these are 12 in and 14 in in nominal depth.

The allowable axial compressive stress, F_a, in steel columns depends on the slenderness ratio and the allowable yield stress of steel. The exact value of the allowable stress is calculated with several rather complex equations based on the Euler equation. The specific equation to be used depends on the slenderness ratio of the column. Once the allowable stress is determined, the basic equation for axial loading can be used.

$$P_n = F_{cr}A \qquad 41.6$$

End Conditions

There is one additional variable that affects steel column design: the method in which the ends of the columns are fixed. Column ends can be in one of four states: They can be fixed against both rotation and translation (side-to-side movement) such as with a column embedded in concrete or with a moment-resisting connection. They can be fixed in rotation but free in translation. They can be fixed in translation but free to rotate. Finally, they can be free to both rotate and move side to side like the top of a flagpole.

How the ends are fixed affects the ability of a column to resist axial loads, so the AISC introduces an *effective length factor*, K, to modify the unbraced length of a column when calculating the slenderness ratio. Multiplying the K-value by the actual unbraced length gives the effective length of the column. The entire formula for slenderness ratio then becomes

$$\text{slenderness ratio} = \frac{Kl}{r} \qquad 41.7$$

Values for the various end conditions are given in Fig. 41.2. For most building conditions, the value of K is taken as 1.0.

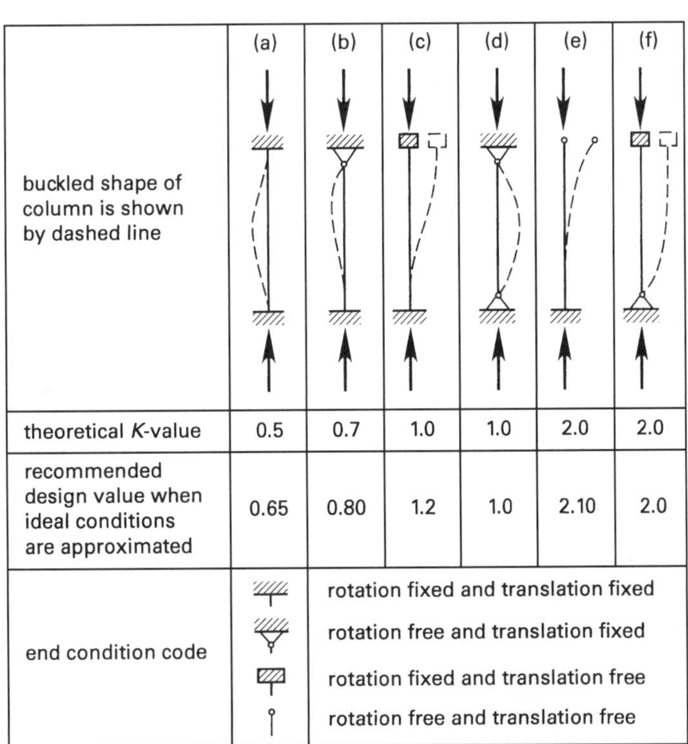

	(a)	(b)	(c)	(d)	(e)	(f)
buckled shape of column is shown by dashed line						
theoretical *K*-value	0.5	0.7	1.0	1.0	2.0	2.0
recommended design value when ideal conditions are approximated	0.65	0.80	1.2	1.0	2.10	2.0

end condition code	
(fixed-support symbol)	rotation fixed and translation fixed
(pinned-support symbol)	rotation free and translation fixed
(box symbol)	rotation fixed and translation free
(open-circle symbol)	rotation free and translation free

Figure 41.2
K-Values for Various End Conditions

Example 41.6

A W12 × 50 column 13 ft high is fixed at the top and bottom in both rotation and translation. What is the effective slenderness ratio?

Solution

From Table 41.3, the radius of gyration for a W12 × 50 section is 5.18 in the X-X axis and 1.96 in the Y-Y axis. Figure 41.2 gives the recommended K-value for fixed top and bottom ends as 0.65. The slenderness ratio is

$$\frac{Kl}{r} = \frac{(0.65)(13\ \text{ft})\left(12\ \frac{\text{in}}{\text{ft}}\right)}{1.96\ \text{in}} = 51.7$$

The length must be converted to inches and the least radius of gyration must be used.

Design for Axial Compression

As with most steel design, calculation can be done with formulas or with tables in the *AISC Manual*. Both are discussed next. Even though the column formulas to determine allowable axial stress are complicated, the *AISC Manual* has tabulated allowable stress values based on the slenderness ratio and the allowable yield stress of the steel being used. One page of these tables is shown in Table 41.6 for Kl/r values of 1 to 200. Kl/r values over 200 are not allowed.

Example 41.7

A W12 × 26 column of A992 steel has an unsupported length of 18 ft. If it is free to rotate but fixed in translation at both ends, what is the column's maximum load-carrying capacity?

Solution

From Table 41.3, a W12 × 26 section has an area of 7.65 in^2 and a least radius of gyration of 1.51 in.

The K-value for this type of column is 1.0, so the slenderness ratio is

$$\frac{Kl}{r} = \frac{(1.0)(18\ \text{ft})\left(12\ \frac{\text{in}}{\text{ft}}\right)}{1.51\ \text{in}} = 143$$

From Table 41.6, the allowable axial stress, F_a, is 7.35 ksi. Using Eq. 41.6, the maximum load is then

$$\begin{aligned} P_n &= F_{cr}A = \left(7.35\ \frac{\text{kips}}{\text{in}^2}\right)(7.65\ \text{in}^2) \\ &= 56.23\ \text{kips} \end{aligned}$$

The other design method involves the use of tables of allowable column loads in the *AISC Manual*. These give allowable axial loads in kips for various wide flange shapes, pipe columns, and square structural tubing of steel with yield values for both ASD and LRFD. Table 41.7 shows one page of the AISC tables. The loads are arranged according to effective length, Kl. For wide-flange sections, the values are calculated with respect to the minor axis.

Table 41.6
Available Critical Stress for Compression Members

Available Critical Stress for Compression Members

	F_y = 35 ksi			F_y = 36 ksi			F_y = 42 ksi			F_y = 46 ksi			F_y = 50 ksi	
$\frac{KL}{r}$	F_{cr}/Ω_c ksi ASD	$\Phi_c F_{cr}$ ksi LRFD	$\frac{KL}{r}$	F_{cr}/Ω_c ksi ASD	$\Phi_c F_{cr}$ ksi LRFD	$\frac{KL}{r}$	F_{cr}/Ω_c ksi ASD	$\Phi_c F_{cr}$ ksi LRFD	$\frac{KL}{r}$	F_{cr}/Ω_c ksi ASD	$\Phi_c F_{cr}$ ksi LRFD	$\frac{KL}{r}$	F_{cr}/Ω_c ksi ASD	$\Phi_c F_{cr}$ ksi LRFD
121	9.91	14.9	121	10.0	15.0	121	10.2	15.4	121	10.3	15.4	121	10.3	15.4
122	9.79	14.7	122	9.85	14.8	122	10.1	15.2	122	10.1	15.2	122	10.1	15.2
123	9.67	14.5	123	9.72	14.6	123	9.93	14.9	123	9.94	14.9	123	9.94	14.9
124	9.55	14.3	124	9.59	14.4	124	9.78	14.7	124	9.78	14.7	124	9.78	14.7
125	9.43	14.2	125	9.47	14.2	125	9.62	14.5	125	9.62	14.5	125	9.62	14.5
126	9.31	14.0	126	9.35	14.0	126	9.47	14.2	126	9.47	14.2	126	9.47	14.2
127	9.19	13.8	127	9.22	13.9	127	9.32	14.0	127	9.32	14.0	127	9.32	14.0
128	9.07	13.6	128	9.10	13.7	128	9.17	13.8	128	9.17	13.8	128	9.17	13.8
129	8.95	13.4	129	8.98	13.5	129	9.03	13.6	129	9.03	13.6	129	9.03	13.6
130	8.83	13.3	130	8.86	13.3	130	8.89	13.4	130	8.89	13.4	130	8.89	13.4
131	8.71	13.1	131	8.73	13.1	131	8.76	13.2	131	8.76	13.2	131	8.76	13.2
132	8.60	12.9	132	8.61	12.9	132	8.63	13.0	132	8.63	13.0	132	8.63	13.0
133	8.48	12.7	133	8.49	12.8	133	8.50	12.8	133	8.50	12.8	133	8.50	12.8
134	8.37	12.6	134	8.37	12.6	134	8.37	12.6	134	8.37	12.6	134	8.37	12.6
135	8.25	12.4	135	8.25	12.4	135	8.25	12.4	135	8.25	12.4	135	8.25	12.4
136	8.13	12.2	135	8.13	12.2	135	8.13	12.2	135	8.13	12.2	135	8.13	12.2
137	8.01	12.0	137	8.01	12.0	137	8.01	12.0	137	8.01	12.0	137	8.01	12.0
138	7.89	11.9	138	7.89	11.9	138	7.89	11.9	138	7.89	11.9	138	7.89	11.9
139	7.78	11.7	139	7.78	11.7	139	7.78	11.7	139	7.78	11.7	139	7.78	11.7
140	7.67	11.5	140	7.67	11.5	140	7.76	11.5	140	7.76	11.5	140	7.76	11.5
141	7.56	11.4	141	7.56	11.4	141	7.56	11.4	141	7.56	11.4	141	7.56	11.4
142	7.45	11.2	142	7.45	11.2	142	7.45	11.2	142	7.45	11.2	142	7.45	11.2
143	7.35	11.0	143	7.35	11.0	143	7.35	11.0	143	7.35	11.0	143	7.35	11.0
144	7.25	10.9	144	7.25	10.9	144	7.25	10.9	144	7.25	10.9	144	7.25	10.9
145	7.15	10.7	145	7.15	10.7	145	7.15	10.7	145	7.15	10.7	145	7.15	10.7
146	7.05	10.6	146	7.05	10.6	146	7.05	10.6	146	7.05	10.6	146	7.05	10.6
147	6.96	10.5	147	6.96	10.5	147	6.96	10.5	147	6.96	10.5	147	6.96	10.5
148	6.86	10.3	148	6.86	10.3	148	6.86	10.3	148	6.86	10.3	148	6.86	10.3
149	6.77	10.2	149	6.77	10.2	149	6.77	10.2	149	6.77	10.2	149	6.77	10.2
150	6.68	10.0	150	6.68	10.0	150	6.68	10.0	150	6.68	10.0	150	6.68	10.0
151	6.59	9.91	151	6.59	9.91	151	6.59	9.91	151	6.59	9.91	151	6.59	9.91
152	6.51	9.78	152	6.51	9.78	152	6.51	9.78	152	6.51	9.78	152	6.51	9.78
153	6.42	9.65	153	6.42	9.65	153	6.42	9.65	153	6.42	9.65	153	6.42	9.65
154	6.34	9.53	154	6.34	9.53	154	6.34	9.53	154	6.34	9.53	154	6.34	9.53
155	6.26	9.40	155	6.26	9.40	155	6.26	9.40	155	6.26	9.40	155	6.26	9.40
156	6.18	9.28	156	6.18	9.28	156	6.18	9.28	156	6.18	9.28	156	6.18	9.28
157	6.10	9.17	157	6.10	9.17	157	6.10	9.17	157	6.10	9.17	157	6.10	9.17
158	6.02	9.05	158	6.02	9.05	158	6.02	9.05	158	6.02	9.05	158	6.02	9.05
159	5.95	8.94	159	5.95	8.94	159	5.95	8.94	159	5.95	8.94	159	5.95	8.94
160	5.87	8.82	160	5.87	8.82	160	5.87	8.82	160	5.87	8.82	160	5.87	8.82

ASD	LRFD
Ω_c = 1.67	Φ_c = 0.90

Product Development

Table 41.7
Available Strength in Axial Compression

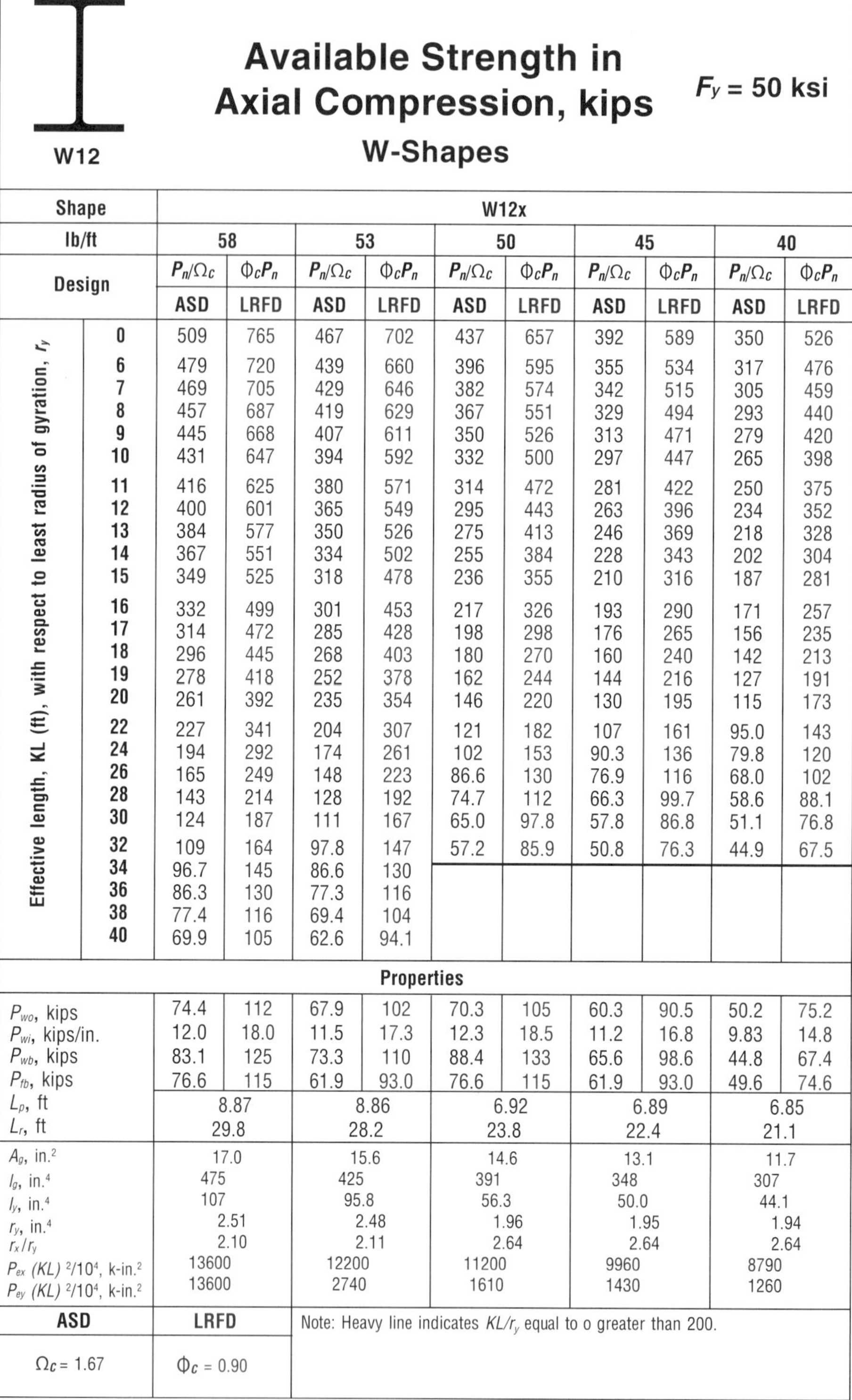

W12

Available Strength in Axial Compression, kips

W-Shapes

F_y = 50 ksi

Shape		W12x									
lb/ft		58		53		50		45		40	
Design		P_n/Ω_c	$\phi_c P_n$	P_n/Ω_c	$\phi_c P_n$	P_n/Ω_c	$\phi_c P_n$	P_n/Ω_c	$\phi_c P_n$	P_n/Ω_c	$\phi_c P_n$
		ASD	LRFD	ASD	LRFD	ASD	LRFD	ASD	LRFD	ASD	LRFD
Effective length, KL (ft), with respect to least radius of gyration, r_y	0	509	765	467	702	437	657	392	589	350	526
	6	479	720	439	660	396	595	355	534	317	476
	7	469	705	429	646	382	574	342	515	305	459
	8	457	687	419	629	367	551	329	494	293	440
	9	445	668	407	611	350	526	313	471	279	420
	10	431	647	394	592	332	500	297	447	265	398
	11	416	625	380	571	314	472	281	422	250	375
	12	400	601	365	549	295	443	263	396	234	352
	13	384	577	350	526	275	413	246	369	218	328
	14	367	551	334	502	255	384	228	343	202	304
	15	349	525	318	478	236	355	210	316	187	281
	16	332	499	301	453	217	326	193	290	171	257
	17	314	472	285	428	198	298	176	265	156	235
	18	296	445	268	403	180	270	160	240	142	213
	19	278	418	252	378	162	244	144	216	127	191
	20	261	392	235	354	146	220	130	195	115	173
	22	227	341	204	307	121	182	107	161	95.0	143
	24	194	292	174	261	102	153	90.3	136	79.8	120
	26	165	249	148	223	86.6	130	76.9	116	68.0	102
	28	143	214	128	192	74.7	112	66.3	99.7	58.6	88.1
	30	124	187	111	167	65.0	97.8	57.8	86.8	51.1	76.8
	32	109	164	97.8	147	57.2	85.9	50.8	76.3	44.9	67.5
	34	96.7	145	86.6	130						
	36	86.3	130	77.3	116						
	38	77.4	116	69.4	104						
	40	69.9	105	62.6	94.1						
Properties											
P_{wo}, kips		74.4	112	67.9	102	70.3	105	60.3	90.5	50.2	75.2
P_{wi}, kips/in.		12.0	18.0	11.5	17.3	12.3	18.5	11.2	16.8	9.83	14.8
P_{wb}, kips		83.1	125	73.3	110	88.4	133	65.6	98.6	44.8	67.4
P_{fb}, kips		76.6	115	61.9	93.0	76.6	115	61.9	93.0	49.6	74.6
L_p, ft		8.87		8.86		6.92		6.89		6.85	
L_r, ft		29.8		28.2		23.8		22.4		21.1	
A_g, in.^{2}		17.0		15.6		14.6		13.1		11.7	
I_x, in.^{4}		475		425		391		348		307	
I_y, in.^{4}		107		95.8		56.3		50.0		44.1	
r_y, in.^{4}		2.51		2.48		1.96		1.95		1.94	
r_x/r_y		2.10		2.11		2.64		2.64		2.64	
$P_{ex}(KL)^2/10^4$, k-in.^{2}		13600		12200		11200		9960		8790	
$P_{ey}(KL)^2/10^4$, k-in.^{2}		13600		2740		1610		1430		1260	

ASD	LRFD	
Ω_c = 1.67	ϕ_c = 0.90	Note: Heavy line indicates KL/r_y equal to o greater than 200.

From *Steel Construction Manual*, 14th Ed., © 2011, American Institute of Steel Construction, Inc.

Product Development

Example 41.8

Select the lightest 12 in wide-flange shape of A992 steel to support a concentric axial load of 250 kips if the unbraced length is 12 ft and the K-value is 1.0.

Solution

In Table 41.7, find the row for Kl equal to 12. Look in the ASD columns for the allowable loads for various sections.

W12 × 58	401 kips
W12 × 53	364 kips
W12 × 50	294 kips
W12 × 45	264 kips
W12 × 40	234 kips

The W12 × 45 is the lightest section with an allowable load greater than 250 kips, so this is the best choice.

The same design procedures apply for columns of allowable loads for round pipe and rectangular tube columns.

BUILT-UP SECTIONS

There are many times when standard rolled sections are inadequate or uneconomical to support heavy loads or exceptionally long spans. In these cases, special built-up sections can be fabricated to meet the special needs of the structure. One of the most typical is a *plate girder section*, which consists of a steel plate as a web and steel plates welded to it for flanges. It is similar to a wide-flange or I-section in shape but is much heavier. These can easily be fabricated deeper than the maximum 44 in deep rolled section available in the United States.

Because the web of a plate girder is thin relative to the girder's depth, it must usually be reinforced with vertical stiffeners to prevent buckling. These are usually angle sections welded to the web perpendicular to the depth of the section as shown in Fig. 41.1.

Another common built-up section is a *standard rolled section* with cover plates welded to the top and bottom flanges to provide additional cross-sectional area where the bending moment is the greatest. This combines the advantages of using a standard section with minimizing total weight of the beam. Cover plates can also be welded to columns to provide extra cross-sectional area or to equalize the radius of gyration in one axis with that of the other axis.

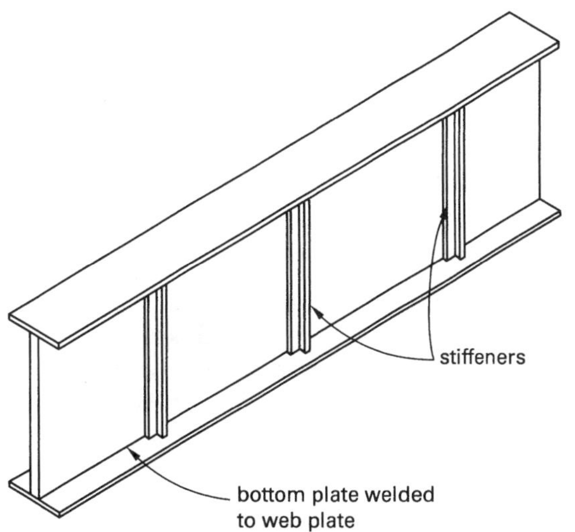

Figure 41.3 Plate Girder

OPEN-WEB STEEL JOISTS

Open-web steel joists are standardized, shop-fabricated trusses with webs that comprise linear members and with chords that are typically parallel. However, some types have top chords that are pitched for roof drainage. See Fig. 41.4.

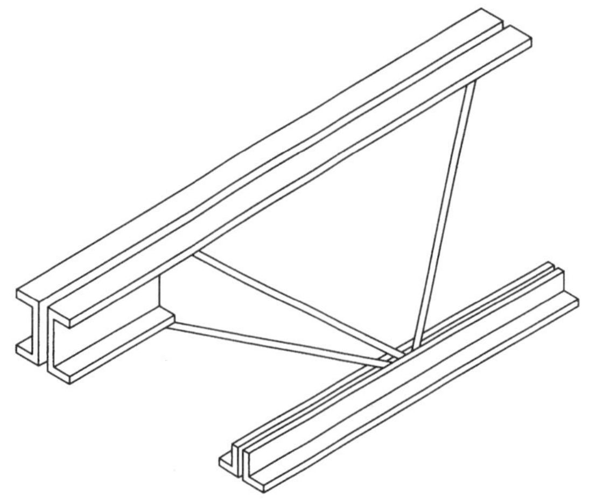

Figure 41.4 Open-Web Steel Joist

There are three standard series of open-web joists: the *K-series*, *LH-series*, and *DLH-series*, with properties as summarized in Table 41.8. The standard depths in the K-series are multiples of 2 in, and the standard depths in the LH- and DLH-series are multiples of 4 in; LH-series joists are also available with a depth of 18 in. The standard designation for an open-web joist consists of the depth, the series designation, and the particular type of chord used. For example, a 36LH13 joist is a 36 in deep joist of the LH-series with a number 13 chord type. Within any size group, the chord type number increases as the load-carrying capacity of that depth joist increases.

Open-web steel joists have many advantages for spanning medium to long distances. They are lightweight and efficient structural members, easy and quick to erect, and the open webbing allows for ductwork and other building services to be run through the joists rather than under them. In addition, a variety of floor decking types can be used, from wood systems to steel and concrete deck systems. They can easily be supported by steel beams, masonry or concrete bearing walls, or heavier open-web joist girders.

Table 41.8 Open-Web Steel Joist Series

series	name	span limits (ft)	depths in series (in)
K	standard	8 to 60	8 to 30
LH	long span	25 to 96	18 to 48
DLH	deep long span	89 to 144	52 to 72

Because open-web joists are deep and slender, they are subject to buckling and must be laterally supported both at the top and bottom chords. All the tables are based on the assumption that there is continuous lateral support at the top chord. The Steel Joist Institute gives minimum requirements for horizontal or diagonal bridging based on the span length and chord size.

Exact configurations of open-web joists vary with manufacturers, but certain standards have been established by the Steel Joist Institute, which also publishes standard load tables for design purposes. The design tables give the load-carrying capacities in pounds per linear foot of the various joist designations based on span. In the tables, two numbers are given: The top number gives the total safe uniformly distributed load-carrying capacity. The bottom number gives the live load per linear foot of joist, which will produce an approximate deflection of $^1/_{360}$ of the span. Live loads that will produce a deflection of $^1/_{240}$ of the span may be obtained by multiplying the bottom number by 1.5.

When using the tables, both the total load and live load must be determined so both of the allowable load numbers can be compared with actual loads. To use the tables, determine the span in feet and the live load and total load per linear foot. Look at the row of the required span in the table, and read across until a load equal to or greater than the required total load is reached. Then look at the bottom number to determine if the allowable live load is greater than the actual live load. If either of these conditions is not met, look for a heavier joist in the same depth group or use a deeper section.

A portion of the design tables for the K-series is shown in Table 41.9. For the K-series, there is also an economy table that lists the various sections in order of increasing weight, so it is easier to select the most economical section in this series.

Example 41.9

Open-web joists spaced 2 ft on center span 30 ft. They support a dead load of 50 psf including an allowance for their own weight and a live load of 60 psf. If the maximum allowable deflection due to live load is $^1/_{360}$ of the span, what is the most economical section to use?

Solution

First, the load must be converted to load per linear foot of joist. Since the joists are 2 ft on center, the dead load is (50 psf)(2 ft), or 100 plf, and the live load is (60 psf)(2 ft), or 120 plf, for a total load of 220 plf.

Looking in Table 41.9 across the row of 30 ft spans, there is an 18K4 that will support 245 lbf total load and 144 lbf live load. There is also a 20K3 that will support 227 lbf total load and 153 lbf live load. Both of these will work, but looking at the weight per foot it can be seen that the first section weighs 7.2 plf, and the second section weighs 6.7 plf. Therefore, the 20K3 is the more economical section. (There is also a 16K5 joist that will work, but it is not shown in Table 41.9.)

Table 41.9 Standard Load Table for Open-Web Steel Joists, K-Series (ASD)
(based on a maximum allowable tensile stress of 50,000 psi; loads in pounds per linear foot)

STANDARD LOAD TABLE FOR OPEN WEB STEEL JOISTS, K-SERIES
Based on a 50 ksi Maximum Yield Strength - Loads Shown In Pounds Per Linear Foot (plf)

Joist Designation	18K3	18K4	18K5	18K6	18K7	18K9	18K10	20K3	20K4	20K5	20K6	20K7	20K9	20K10	22K4	22K5	22K6	22K7	22K9	22K10	22K11
Depth (In.)	18	18	18	18	18	18	18	20	20	20	20	20	20	20	22	22	22	22	22	22	22
Approx. Wt. (lbs./ft.)	6.4	7.2	7.7	8.4	8.9	10.1	11.6	6.5	7.2	7.7	8.4	8.9	10.1	11.6	7.3	7.7	8.5	9.0	10.2	11.7	11.9
Span (ft) ↓																					
18	550 550	550 550	550 550	550 550	550 550	550 550	550 550														
19	514 494	550 523	550 523	550 523	550 523	550 523	550 523	550 550	550 550	550 550	550 550	550 550	550 550	550 550							
20	463 423	550 490	550 490	550 490	550 490	550 490	550 490	517 517	550 550	550 550	550 550	550 550	550 550	550 550							
21	420 364	506 426	550 460	550 460	550 460	550 460	550 460	468 453	550 520	550 520	550 520	550 520	550 520	550 520	550 550	550 550	550 550	550 550	550 550	550 550	550 550
22	382 316	460 370	518 414	550 438	550 438	550 438	550 438	426 393	514 461	550 490	550 490	550 490	550 490	550 490	550 548	550 548	550 548	550 548	550 548	550 548	550 548
23	349 276	420 323	473 362	516 393	550 418	550 418	550 418	389 344	469 402	529 451	550 468	550 468	550 468	550 468	518 491	550 518	550 518	550 518	550 518	550 518	550 518
24	320 242	385 284	434 318	473 345	526 382	550 396	550 396	357 302	430 353	485 396	528 430	550 448	550 448	550 448	475 431	536 483	550 495	550 495	550 495	550 495	550 495
25	294 214	355 250	400 281	435 305	485 337	550 377	550 377	329 266	396 312	446 350	486 380	541 421	550 426	550 426	438 381	493 427	537 464	550 474	550 474	550 474	550 474
26	272 190	328 222	369 249	402 271	448 299	538 354	550 361	304 236	366 277	412 310	449 337	500 373	550 405	550 405	404 338	455 379	496 411	550 454	550 454	550 454	550 454
27	252 169	303 198	342 222	372 241	415 267	498 315	550 347	281 211	339 247	382 277	416 301	463 333	550 389	550 389	374 301	422 337	459 367	512 406	550 432	550 432	550 432
28	234 151	282 177	318 199	346 216	385 239	463 282	548 331	261 189	315 221	355 248	386 269	430 298	517 353	550 375	348 270	392 302	427 328	475 364	550 413	550 413	550 413
29	218 136	263 159	296 179	322 194	359 215	431 254	511 298	243 170	293 199	330 223	360 242	401 268	482 317	550 359	324 242	365 272	398 295	443 327	532 387	550 399	550 399
30	203 123	245 144	276 161	301 175	335 194	402 229	477 269	227 153	274 179	308 201	336 218	374 242	374 286	533 336	302 219	341 245	371 266	413 295	497 349	550 385	550 385
31	190 111	229 130	258 146	281 158	313 175	376 207	446 243	212 138	256 162	289 182	314 198	350 219	421 259	499 304	283 198	319 222	347 241	387 267	465 316	550 369	550 369
32	178 101	215 118	242 132	264 144	294 159	353 188	418 221	199 126	240 147	271 165	295 179	328 199	395 235	468 276	265 180	299 201	326 219	363 242	436 287	517 337	549 355
33	168 92	202 108	228 121	248 131	249 145	332 171	393 201	187 114	226 134	254 150	277 163	309 181	371 214	440 251	249 164	281 183	306 199	341 221	410 261	486 307	532 334
34	158 84	190 98	214 110	233 120	260 132	312 156	370 184	176 105	212 122	239 137	261 149	290 165	349 195	414 229	235 149	265 167	288 182	321 202	386 239	458 280	516 314
35	149 77	179 90	202 101	220 110	245 121	294 143	349 168	166 96	200 112	226 126	246 137	274 151	329 179	390 210	221 137	249 153	272 167	303 185	364 219	432 257	494 292
36	141 70	169 82	191 92	208 101	232 111	278 132	330 154	157 88	189 103	213 115	232 125	259 139	311 164	369 193	209 126	236 141	257 153	286 169	344 201	408 236	467 269
37								148 81	179 95	202 106	220 115	245 128	294 151	349 178	198 116	223 130	243 141	271 156	325 185	386 217	442 247
38								141 74	170 87	191 98	208 106	232 118	279 139	331 164	187 107	211 119	230 130	256 144	308 170	366 200	419 228
39								133 69	161 81	181 90	198 98	220 109	265 129	314 151	178 98	200 110	218 120	243 133	292 157	347 185	397 211
40								127 64	153 75	172 84	188 91	209 101	251 119	298 140	169 91	190 102	207 111	231 123	278 146	330 171	377 195
41															161 85	181 95	197 103	220 114	264 135	314 159	359 181
42															153 79	173 88	188 96	209 106	252 126	299 148	342 168
43															146 73	165 82	179 89	200 99	240 117	285 138	326 157
44															139 68	157 76	171 83	191 92	229 109	272 128	311 146

From *Standard Specifications, Load Tables, and Weight Tables for Steel Joists and Joist Girders*, © 2010, Association of Steel Distributors. Reproduced with permission.

42

CONCRETE CONSTRUCTION

Nomenclature

a	height of rectangular stress block	in
A_s	area of steel reinforcing	in^2
A_v	area of web reinforcement	in^2
b	width of beam	in
b_w	width of beam web, rectangular or T-beam	in
C	resultant of compressive forces	lbf
d	effective depth of beam	in
d_b	diameter of reinforcing bar	in
D	calculated dead load	lbf/ft^2, lbf/ft
E	earthquake or seismic load	lbf/ft^2, lbf/ft^2
f'_c	design strength of concrete	lbf/in^2
f_{ct}	average splitting tensile strength of lightweight concrete	lbf/in^2
f_y	yield strength of steel	lbf/in^2
l_d	minimum development length	in
L	calculated live load	lbf/ft^2, lbf/ft
M_u	ultimate moment capacity	ft-lbf
s	spacing of web reinforcement	in
T	resultant of tension forces	lbf
U	factored load	lbf/ft^2, lbf/ft
V_c	design shear strength of concrete	lbf
V_u	required shear strength	lbf
W	wind load	lbf/ft^2, lbf/ft
β_c	distance from top of beam to resultant of compressive force	in
β_1	constant for finding percentage of steel	–
λ	lightweight aggregate factor	–
ρ_b	percentage of steel for balanced design	decimal
ρ	percentage of steel	decimal
ρ_{max}	maximum allowable percentage of steel	decimal
ρ_{min}	minimum allowable percentage of steel	decimal
ϕ	strength reduction factor	–
Φ_e	coating factor	–
Φ_t	reinforcement location factor	–

Structural design of concrete is more complicated than design with steel or wood because there are more variables and the choices depend on the experience and trained judgment of the designer. In modern construction, concrete is always reinforced. (See Chap. 22 for information about reinforcement bars and other forms of reinforcement for concrete.) This results in a nonhomogeneous section with two materials of differing strengths and in structural shapes that are not symmetrical about the neutral axis. Because of these facts, concrete design is an iterative process; certain design assumptions have to be made and then tested to see if they work. If not, the assumption must be changed and new calculations made.

The strength design method is used for concrete. Although the working stress method is still allowed by some building inspection departments in some instances, it has generally been supplanted by the newer procedure. The *Building Code Requirements for Structural Concrete* (ACI 318), published by the American Concrete Institute (ACI), is based on the strength design method.

This chapter will discuss some of the basic principles of structural reinforced concrete design and show how to make some common, fairly simple design calculations.

CONCRETE MATERIALS AND PLACEMENT

Composition of Concrete

Concrete is a combination of cement, aggregates, and water mixed in the proper portions and allowed to cure to form a hard, durable material. As a construction material, it is a mixture of portland cement, sand, gravel, and water. In addition, *admixtures* are used to impart particular qualities to the mix. Since the strength of concrete depends on the materials and their proportions, it is important to understand the relationship between the constituent parts.

Cement is the binding agent in concrete. It chemically interacts with water to form a paste that binds the other aggregate particles together in a solid mass. *Portland cement* is a finely powdered material manufactured primarily from limestones and clays or shales. It is supplied in bulk or in 94 lbm bags containing one cubic foot.

Although water is required for hydration (the chemical hardening of concrete) and to make it possible to mix the concrete and place it into forms, too much water can decrease concrete's strength. This is because excess water not used in the chemical process remains in the paste and causes pores to form, which cannot resist compressive forces. Generally, for complete hydration to occur, an amount of water equal to 25% of the weight of the cement is required. An extra 10% to 15% or more is required to make a workable mix. The water itself must be potable, or drinkable, to ensure that it is free of any foreign matter that could interfere with adhesion of the aggregates to the cement paste.

For most concrete mixes, the minimum *water-cement ratio* is about 0.35 to 0.40 by weight. Based on the weight of water, this works out to about 4 to 4.5 gallons of water per 94 lbm sack of cement. Because of the way water and cement interact, the water-cement ratio is the most critical factor in determining the strength of concrete. For a given mix, there should be just enough water to give a workable mix without being excessive.

The water-cement ratio is the most critical factor in the determining the strength of concrete.

Aggregates consist of coarse and fine aggregates. *Fine aggregates* are those that pass through a no. 4 sieve (one with four openings per linear inch). Since cement is the most expensive component of concrete, the best mix is one that uses a combination of aggregate sizes that fill most of the volume with a minimum amount of cement while still achieving the desired strength. Typically, aggregates occupy about 70% to 75% of the total volume of the concrete.

Generally, aggregates are sand and gravel, but others are used. Materials such as expanded clays, slags, and shales are used for lightweight structural concrete. Pumice or cinders are used for insulating concretes. While standard reinforced stone concrete weighs about 150 lbm/ft^3, lightweight mixes can range from 50 lbm/ft^3 for insulating concretes to 120 lbm/ft^3 for lightweight reinforced structural concrete.

The size of *coarse aggregates* is determined by the size of the forms and the spacing between the reinforcing. In most instances, it should not be larger than three-fourths of the smallest distance between reinforcing bars, nor larger than one-fifth of the smallest dimension of forms, nor more than one-third of the depth of slabs.

Several methods are used to specify the proportions of the concrete mix. One is to define the ratio of cement to sand to gravel by weight using three numbers such as 1:2:4, which means 1 part cement, 2 parts sand, and 4 parts gravel. In addition, the amount of water must also be specified. Another method is to specify the weight of materials, including water, per 94 lbm bag of cement. Yet another method is to define the weight of the materials needed to make up one cubic yard of concrete. This is useful for large batch quantities.

The strength of the final mix is specified by the compressive strength of the concrete after it has cured and hardened for 28 days—this is known as the *design strength of concrete.* Typical specified design strengths, indicated with the symbol f_c', are 2000 psi, 3000 psi (one of the most common), and 4000 psi. Higher strengths up to 12,000 psi are available for special applications, but these are more expensive than the standard mixes.

Admixtures

Admixtures are chemicals and other materials added to concrete to impart certain qualities. Admixtures are used to speed hydration, retard hardening, improve workability, add color, and improve durability, and for a variety of other purposes. The following are some of the more common admixtures.

Air-entraining agents form tiny dispersed bubbles in the concrete. These agents increase the concrete's workability and durability and improve its resistance to freezing and thawing cycles. They also help reduce segregation of the components during placing of the mix into forms.

Accelerators speed up the hydration of the cement so the concrete achieves strength faster. This allows for faster construction and reduces the length of time needed for protection in cold weather.

Plasticizers are used to reduce the amount of water needed while maintaining the consistency needed for correct placement and compaction. Reducing the water, of course, makes it possible to mix higher-strength concrete.

Reinforcing Steel

Because concrete's tensile strength is low, concrete is often reinforced with steel to increase its resistance to bedding and other tensile stresses. Concrete also has low ductility (that is, it is brittle), so that when a concrete beam or slab fails, it can shatter suddenly and with little or no warning.

For this reason, it is desirable that the amount of steel reinforcement be kept low enough that the steel will yield before the concrete fails. When this is the case, the concrete is said to be *under-reinforced.* An under-reinforced concrete beam will bend before the concrete fails, giving a visible warning of possible danger.

The cross-sectional areas and other dimensional properties of the standard reinforcing bars are given in Table 42.1, along with the amount of reinforcement given by various combinations of bars and spacings.

Table 42.1 Properties of Reinforcing Bars

dimensional properties of individual bars

bar no.	diameter	area (in^2)	perimeter (in)	weight (lbm/ft)
3	0.375	0.11	1.18	0.376
4	0.500	0.20	1.57	0.668
5	0.625	0.31	1.96	1.043
6	0.750	0.44	2.36	1.502
7	0.875	0.60	2.75	2.044
8	1.000	0.79	3.14	2.670
9	1.128	1.00	3.54	3.400
10	1.270	1.27	3.99	4.303
11	1.410	1.56	4.43	5.313
14	1.693	2.25	5.32	7.650
18	2.257	4.00	7.09	13.600

areas of bars in reinforced concrete (in^2/ft)

spacing	bar size								
(in)	3	4	5	6	7	8	9	10	11
3	0.44	0.80	1.24	1.76	2.40	3.16	4.00	5.08	6.25
$3\frac{1}{2}$	0.38	0.69	1.06	1.51	2.06	2.71	3.43	4.35	5.35
4	0.33	0.60	0.93	1.32	1.80	2.37	3.00	3.81	4.68
$4\frac{1}{2}$	0.29	0.53	0.83	1.17	1.60	2.11	2.67	3.39	4.16
5	0.26	0.48	0.74	1.06	1.44	1.90	2.40	3.05	3.74
$5\frac{1}{2}$	0.24	0.44	0.68	0.96	1.31	1.72	2.18	2.77	3.40
6	0.22	0.40	0.62	0.88	1.20	1.58	2.00	2.54	3.12
$6\frac{1}{2}$	0.20	0.37	0.57	0.81	1.11	1.46	1.85	2.34	2.88
7	0.19	0.34	0.53	0.75	1.03	1.35	1.71	2.18	2.67
$7\frac{1}{2}$	0.18	0.32	0.50	0.70	0.96	1.26	1.60	2.03	2.50
8	0.17	0.30	0.46	0.66	0.90	1.18	1.50	1.90	2.34
9	0.15	0.27	0.41	0.59	0.80	1.05	1.33	1.69	2.08
10	0.13	0.24	0.37	0.53	0.72	0.94	1.20	1.52	1.87
12	0.11	0.20	0.31	0.44	0.60	0.79	1.00	1.27	1.56

Placing and Curing

Two important parts of the entire process of concrete design and construction are getting the concrete to the forms and ensuring that it is allowed to cure properly. Transporting the material from the truck or mixer actually involves several steps. First it must be conveyed to the formwork. This is done with bottom-dump buckets, by pumping, or in small buggies or wheelbarrows.

Then the concrete must be placed in the formwork in such a way as to avoid segregation, which is the separation of the aggregates, water, and sand from each other because of their inherent dissimilarity. Dropping concrete long distances from the conveying device to the forms is one of the typical ways segregation can occur. Excessive lateral movement of the concrete in forms or slab work is another practice that should be minimized.

Finally, the concrete must be compacted to make sure the wet material has flowed around all the forms and rebars, that it has made complete contact with the steel, and to prevent *honeycombing*, which is the formation of air pockets within the concrete and next to the forms. For small jobs, hand compaction can be used. More typically, various types of vibrators are used.

Since concrete hardens and gains strength by curing through chemical reaction between the water and the cement rather than by drying, it is critical that the proper conditions of moisture and temperature be maintained for at least seven days and up to two weeks for critical work. If concrete dries out too fast, it can lose strength—up to 30% or more in some instances. With high-early-strength cements, of course, the time can be reduced. This is because concrete gains about 70% of its strength during the first week of curing, and final 28-day design strength depends on the initial curing conditions.

There are many techniques for maintaining proper moisture levels, including covering with plastic, using sealing compound, or continually sprinkling the surfaces with water.

Concrete must also be kept from freezing while curing or it will also lose strength, sometimes as much as half. Since concrete produces heat while it cures (known as *heat of hydration*), it is often sufficient to cover the fresh material with insulated plastic sheets for a few days. In very cold conditions, external heat may need to be supplied or other construction techniques employed.

Testing Concrete

Because there are so many variables in concrete construction, the material must be continually tested at various stages to maintain quality. There are three tests that the architect must be familiar with: the *slump test*, the *cylinder test*, and the *core cylinder test*.

The slump test measures the consistency of the concrete, usually at the job site. In this test, concrete is placed in a 12 in high truncated cone, 8 in at the base and 4 in at the top. It is compacted by hand with a rod, and then the mold is removed from the concrete and placed next to it. The distance the concrete slumps from the original 12 in height is then measured in inches. The amount of slump desired depends on how the concrete is going to be used, but is typically in the range of 2 in to 6 in. Too great a slump indicates excessive water in the mix, and a very small slump indicates the mixture will be too difficult to place properly.

The cylinder test measures compressive strength. As the concrete is being placed, samples are put in cylinder molds, 6 in in diameter and 12 in high, and are moist-cured for 28 days at which time they are laboratory-tested according to standardized procedures. The compressive strength in pounds per square inch is calculated and compared with the value used in the design of the structure. Almost always, cylinders are tested at seven days when their strength is about 60% to 70% of the 28-day strength.

There are three tests that the architect must be familiar with: the slump test, the cylinder test, and the core cylinder test.

The core cylinder test is used when a portion of the structure is in place and cured, but needs to be tested. Usually, if regular cylinder tests do not come up to the specified design strength, core cylinder tests are requested by the architect or structural engineer. A cylinder is drilled out of the concrete and then tested in the laboratory to determine its compressive strength. Drilled core cylinders are about $2\frac{1}{2}$ in in diameter, and their length varies depending on the location they are drilled from, but usually they are about 6 in long.

SAFETY FACTORS

Because of the many variables with reinforced concrete and the loads applied to concrete structures, there are two fundamental ways that safety provisions are built into ACI 318. The first is the recognition that the structure should be designed to support the loads that would cause it to fail. However, since these are not known with certainty, load factors are applied to the calculated loads to increase them to values that in all probability would never be reached, but which represent an acceptable factor of safety.

ACI 318 gives a variety of load factor formulas to account for various combinations of dead loads, live loads, wind, earthquake, earth pressure, fluids, impact, settlement, creep, shrinkage, and temperature change effects. The most basic load combination is

$$U = 1.2D + 1.6L \tag{42.1}$$

This formula accounts for the concept that dead loads can be calculated with more accuracy than live loads, so the dead load needs to be increased less than the potential live load. Other formulas are used for other loading situations.

Table 42.2 Strength Reduction Factors

type of loading	strength reduction factor, ϕ
flexure and axial tension (tension controls)	0.90
shear and torsion	0.75
bearing on concrete	0.65
spirally reinforced columns	0.75
tied columns	0.65

The second safety provision is known as the *strength reduction factor*, commonly symbolized by the Greek letter ϕ. The calculated strength of each member is reduced by multiplying it by ϕ. This factor is always less than one, but varies to reflect the limitations on how accurately strength can be calculated for different kinds of structural members, the quality control achievable with concrete, and the importance of various kinds of structural members. For example, columns are more important than beams in preventing catastrophic collapse, so ϕ generally has lower values for columns than for beams. The strength reduction factors for various types of loading are given in Table 42.2.

This combination of load factors and strength reduction factors is designed to reduce the probability of failure to about 1 in 100,000.

CONCRETE BEAMS

Candidates for the ARE need to have a general understanding of the particular requirements of reinforced concrete construction and how it differs from building with other materials such as steel or timber. Since beams are one of the many common uses of concrete, they will be used to illustrate some of the unique aspects of concrete design.

Basic Concepts of Design

Concrete design is complex because of the many variables involved. Some of these variables include the strength of concrete, the strength of the reinforcing steel, the amount of reinforcing used, and the size of the member. In addition, building code conditions change depending on the type of structural member being designed, its condition of use, and the strength of the basic materials.

Because of the many combinations possible with these variables, there is usually no single structural solution to a concrete design problem. Many combinations of design elements can support the same loading conditions. In most cases, concrete design is an iterative process where the designer must make some assumptions to start the process, work through the calculations, and then check the results against code requirements and cost efficiency. If the initial assumptions yield a less than optimum result, they are modified and new calculations are made. Fortunately, design aids such as graphs, tables, and computers make the process easier than it once was.

As discussed in Chap. 35, when a load is applied to a simply supported rectangular beam there are compression forces in the top half and tension forces in the lower half. If the beam is constructed from a homogeneous material such as timber, the neutral axis is at the center of the beam where no compression or tension forces exist. These forces increase in proportion to the distance from the neutral axis until they reach their maximum value at the extreme fibers of the beam.

In a simply supported concrete beam, the same general action occurs. However, because the beam is nonhomogeneous, that is, composed of two materials, concrete and steel, the neutral axis is not at the midpoint of the beam's depth. In fact, the location of the neutral axis changes as the load on the beam is increased.

In concrete design, it is assumed that the concrete resists only compressive forces and the reinforcing steel resists only the tension forces. Because of this assumption, none of the concrete on the tension side (lower side) of the beam below the centroid of the steel is assumed to have any structural value—it only serves to protect the steel from moisture and fire. Therefore, the *effective depth of the beam*, commonly referred to as d in formulas, is the distance from the top of the beam to the centroid of the steel. See Fig. 42.1.

In order to resist bending moments in a beam, the internal compressive and tension forces form a couple with the resultant of the tension forces, T, at the centroid of the steel and the resultant of the compressive forces, C, at some fraction of the distance from the top of the beam to the neutral axis, β_c. See Fig. 42.1(a). The shape of the distribution of the compressive forces varies considerably, with one of the many possible shapes shown in Fig. 42.1(a). However, the stress distribution curve can be replaced with a more regular shape in which the resultant C acts in the same position.

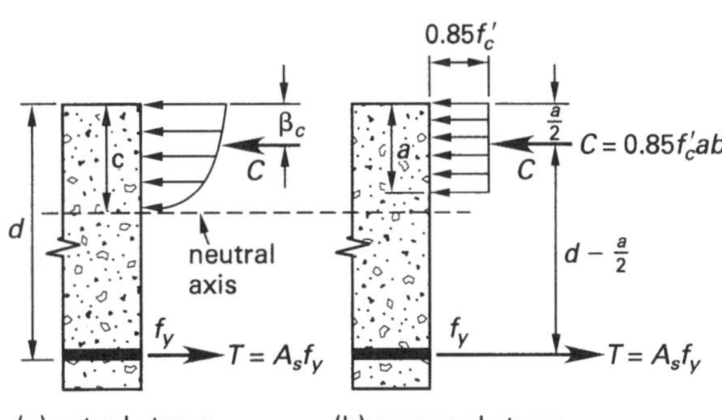

Figure 42.1 Stress Distribution in Concrete Beams

The assumed distribution pattern that is used is called the *Whitney stress block* as shown in Fig. 42.1(b), and although its resultant still acts at a distance β_c from the top of the beam, its height is somewhat less than the distance to the neutral axis and is referred to as a, while its width is the width of the beam, or b. Through extensive testing of concrete beams it has been determined that the compressive force that a beam can resist is

$$C = 0.85 f_c' ab \qquad 42.2$$

The 0.85 value is a stress intensity factor that has been determined through testing to be independent of f_c'.

The tensile force, T, that a beam can resist is simply the strength of the steel, f_y, times the area of the steel, A_s.

$$T = f_y A_s \qquad 42.3$$

These two values of T and C, shown in the preceding formulas, give the forces in the steel and concrete just as the beam is about to fail. This is part of the current theoretical approach to concrete design known as the *strength method*. In order to resist the bending moment caused by a load, the values of T and C created in the beam will be equal but, of course, will act in opposite directions.

However, if a beam was designed to resist equal values of T and C, the concrete would be designed to fail (crush) at the same time the steel failed (yielded). This is what is known as balanced design. This is not desirable since concrete fails by crushing without warning, and rather explosively, resulting in immediate collapse of the member. Steel, on the other hand, fails in a concrete beam more slowly, giving advance warning with excessive cracking of the concrete on the tension side and excessive deflection.

Therefore, current building codes require that the reinforcing steel should fail before the concrete crushes so building occupants have some advance warning.

To ensure that the steel will fail before the concrete, the beam must actually be under-reinforced. First, the amount of steel reinforcement needed for balanced design (that is, that will cause the steel and the concrete to fail simultaneously) is found. This amount of steel, ρ_b, is expressed as a percentage of the total cross-sectional area.

$$\rho_b = \frac{A_s}{bd} \tag{42.4}$$

Then, ACI 318 Sec. 10.3.5 (see also Sec. R10.3.5) requires that the minimum amount of steel that can be used is approximately (and slightly less than) three-fourths of ρ_b.

$$\rho_{\text{max}} \approx 0.75\rho_b \tag{42.5}$$

The precise value of the maximum steel area is based on a steel strain of 0.004. This value will vary depending on the strength of the steel.

The formula for finding the percentage of steel for a balanced design is given by

$$\rho_b = 0.85\beta_1\left(\frac{f_c'}{f_y}\right)\left(\frac{87{,}000}{87{,}000 + f_y}\right) \tag{42.6}$$

β_1 is a constant that is 0.85 for concrete with strength equal to or less than 4000 psi.

There are, however, limits to the minimum amount of steel. ACI 318 sets this minimum at

$$\rho_{\text{min}} = \frac{200}{f_y} \leq \frac{3\sqrt{f_c'}}{f_y} \tag{42.7}$$

Even though the steel may be designed to yield first, the actual design cannot be based on the assumption that the resisting forces, T and C, will be reached under the expected design load. Factors of safety must be included. These are the load factors and the strength reduction factor, ϕ, as discussed in the previous section. The idea is to find out what the design of the beam must be at failure under increased loads, which will likely never be reached, and at a reduced strength, which is probably less than what the designed member will actually provide.

Design for Flexure

Since the design of simple concrete members can be complex and time consuming, it is unlikely that problems will be given on the test that require detailed calculations. However, this section shows how to design a simple concrete beam to illustrate the iterative process and how the formulas are used.

For design, a few additional formulas are needed. The moment-carrying capacity of a beam is given by the formula

$$M_u = \phi A_s f_y\left(d - \frac{a}{2}\right) \tag{42.8}$$

ϕ is 0.90 for flexure.

In Eq. 42.8, a is found with the formula

$$a = \frac{A_s f_y}{0.85 f_c' b} \tag{42.9}$$

With substitutions, and using the percentage of steel instead of the area, Eq. 42.8 can be rewritten as follows.

$$M_u = \phi\rho f_y bd^2\left(1-(0.59)\left(\frac{\rho f_y}{f'_c}\right)\right) \qquad 42.10$$

Example 42.1

Design a reinforced concrete beam to support a live load of 3.4 klf and a dead load of 1.5 klf. The beam is simply supported and 20 ft long. Concrete strength is 4000 psi, and steel strength is f_y = 60,000 psi.

Solution

Step 1. Determine the factored load from Eq. 42.1.

$$\begin{aligned} U &= 1.2D + 1.6L = (1.2)\left(1.5\ \frac{\text{kips}}{\text{ft}}\right) + (1.6)\left(3.4\ \frac{\text{kips}}{\text{ft}}\right) \\ &= 7.24\ \text{ft} \end{aligned}$$

Step 2. Determine the amount to be carried.

$$\begin{aligned} M_u &= \frac{wl^2}{8} = \frac{\left(7.24\ \frac{\text{kip}}{\text{ft}}\right)(20\ \text{ft})^2\left(12\ \frac{\text{in}}{\text{ft}}\right)}{8} \\ &= 4344\ \text{in-kips} \end{aligned}$$

Step 3. At this point, there are three unknowns: the beam width, beam depth, and steel area. Using the formulas previously given, assume a value for one or two unknowns and find the others. Since there are minimum and maximum guidelines for finding the percentage of steel, begin with that.

From Eq. 42.4, the balanced steel percentage is

$$\begin{aligned} \rho_b &= (0.85)(0.85)\left(\frac{4000\ \frac{\text{lbf}}{\text{in}^2}}{60{,}000\ \frac{\text{lbf}}{\text{in}^2}}\right)\left(\frac{87{,}000\ \frac{\text{lbf}}{\text{in}^2}}{87{,}000\ \frac{\text{lbf}}{\text{in}^2} + 60{,}000\ \frac{\text{lbf}}{\text{in}^2}}\right) \\ &= 0.0285 \\ &= 0.0214 \end{aligned}$$

The maximum percentage allowed is $0.75\rho_b$.

$$\rho_{\text{max}} \approx (0.75)(0.0285) \approx 0.0214$$

This percentage can be used to design an adequate beam but will result in a beam that is shallower than necessary since the steel is at its maximum. If there are no functional or architectural needs for a shallow beam, reducing the steel percentage and increasing the beam depth generally results in a more economical design and may reduce deflection. For economy of material, a concrete beam with a depth 2 to 3 times the width is desirable.

The minimum steel percentage is $\rho_{\text{min}} = 200/f_y$, or 0.0033. As a starting point, try a percentage of 0.0180, which is a little less than ρ_{max} calculated above.

Step 4. Find the dimensions of the beam using the assumed steel percentage and Eq. 42.10. With this formula, assume a beam width and solve for d, the effective depth. Or, solve for the quantity bd^2 to

Product Development

more easily try different width-to-depth proportions. Reduce pounds per square inch to kips per square inch to keep units consistent.

$$M_u = \phi \rho f_y b d^2 \left(1 - (0.59)\left(\frac{\rho f_y}{f_c'}\right)\right)$$

$$4344 \text{ in-kips} = (0.90)(0.0180)\left(60 \ \frac{\text{kips}}{\text{in}^2}\right) b d^2 \times \left(1 - (0.59)\left((0.0180)\left(\frac{60 \text{ kips}}{4 \text{ in}^2}\right)\right)\right)$$

$$b d^2 = 5316 \text{ in}^3$$

Assume a $b = 12$ in wide beam. Then,

$$d = \sqrt{\frac{bd^2}{b}} = \sqrt{\frac{5316 \text{ in}^3}{12 \text{ in}}} = 21.05 \text{ in}$$

Round up to 22 in. With a cover below the centroid of the steel of about 2½ in, this will give an overall beam depth of 24½ in minimum. At this point, such a beam would seem reasonable.

Step 5. Find the actual area of steel using the minimum dimensions.

$$A_s = \rho b d = (0.0180)(12 \text{ in})(21.05 \text{ in}) = 4.55 \text{ in}^2$$

Using Table 42.1, six no. 8 bars will give exactly 4.74 in^2, or five no. 9 bars will give 5.00 in^2.

Unfortunately, this number of bars will not fit in a single layer in a 12 in wide beam. This is because of the minimum cover and spacing requirement of ACI 318, which requires a minimum of 1½ in clear between the steel and exterior of concrete in beams and columns. It also requires a minimum clear dimension of one inch or one bar diameter (whichever is greater) between bars to allow proper placement of the concrete. For a 12 in beam (assuming no. 4 bars for shear reinforcement) the clearance requirements leave a width of only 8 in for the tension steel. This only leaves room for four no. 8 bars; an additional 3 in would be needed to accommodate six no. 8 bars. Actually, the beam would probably be made 16 in wide rather than 15 in, because widths are usually multiples of 2 in.

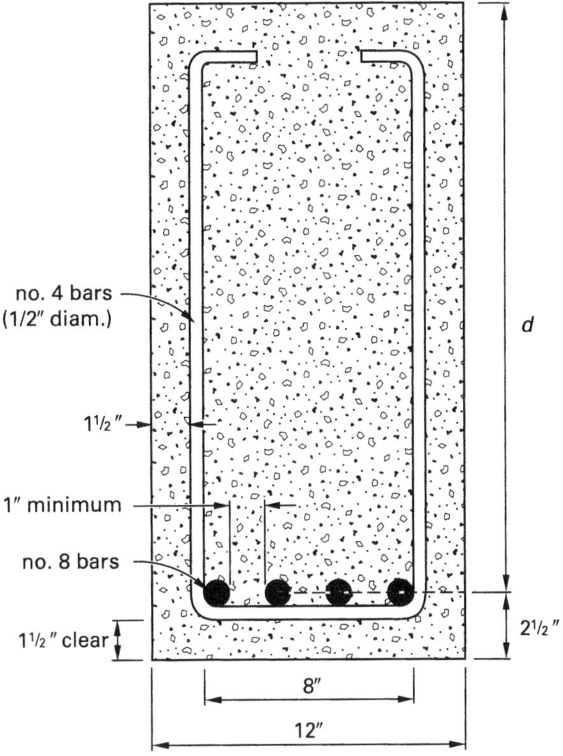

Either the beam must be increased in width, or the percentage of steel must be reduced. It would be more economical to reduce the steel percentage and increase the depth of the beam, so try a new percentage of 0.0130 and recalculate.

$$4344 \text{ in-kips} = (0.90)(0.0130)\left(60\ \frac{\text{kips}}{\text{in}^2}\right)bd^2\left(1-(0.59)\left((0.0130)\left(\frac{60\ \frac{\text{kips}}{\text{in}^2}}{4\ \frac{\text{kips}}{\text{in}^2}}\right)\right)\right)$$

$$bd^2 = 6993 \text{ in}^3$$

Since at this point it is known that the width of the beam is important simply to accommodate the steel, try a width of 14 in this time.

$$\begin{aligned}(14 \text{ in})d^2 &= 7611 \text{ in}^3\\ d &= 22.35 \text{ in}\end{aligned}$$

Rounding up to $22\frac{1}{2}$ in and assuming a cover of $2\frac{1}{2}$ gives a total beam depth of 25 in. A 14 × 25 beam seems reasonable, so use this.

Find the actual area of steel with this new size and new assumed percentage of steel.

$$A_s = (0.0130)(14 \text{ in})(22.5 \text{ in}) = 4.09 \text{ in}^2$$

This can be satisfied with four no. 10 bars ($A = 5.08 \text{ in}^2$) or five no. 9 bars ($A = 5.00 \text{ in}^2$). However, once again, five bars will not quite fit in a 14 in wide beam (required minimum width 14.15 in), so use four no. 10 bars in a 14 × 25 beam.

Product Development

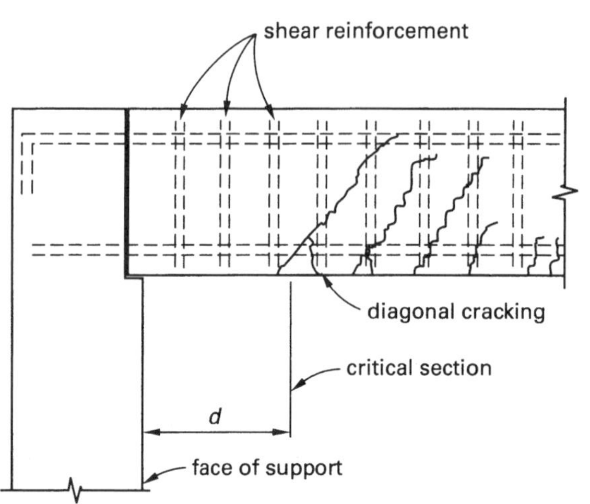

Figure 42.2 Typical Shear Cracking Pattern Near End of Beam

Shear

In the previous section, only stresses due to bending were discussed. However, forces caused by shear can also be significant and must be checked and provided for with additional reinforcement if the concrete itself is not capable of resisting them. It is especially important that concrete beams be adequately designed for shear, because, like compressive failure, shear collapse occurs suddenly and without warning.

Actually, what is commonly referred to as shear stress is really *diagonal tension stress* caused by the combination of shear and longitudinal flexural stress. The result is a characteristic diagonal cracking of the concrete beam in the areas of high shear forces, usually close to the beam supports as shown in Fig. 42.2.

When calculating for shear forces, the critical section is usually taken at the distance, d, from the support. This is because the reactions from the supports or from a monolithic column introduce vertical compression into the beam, which mitigates excessive shear in that area.

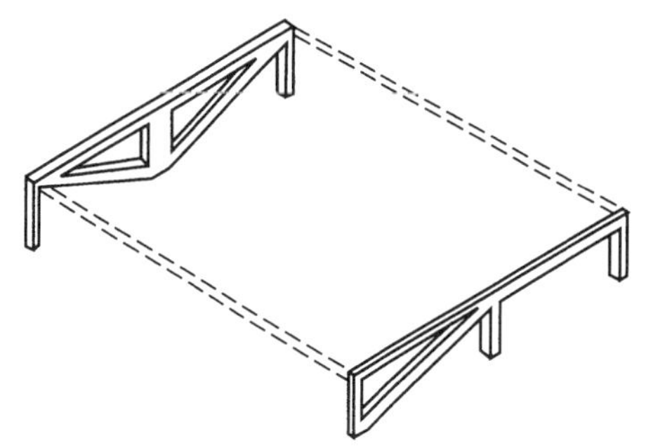

(a) single-story braced frame

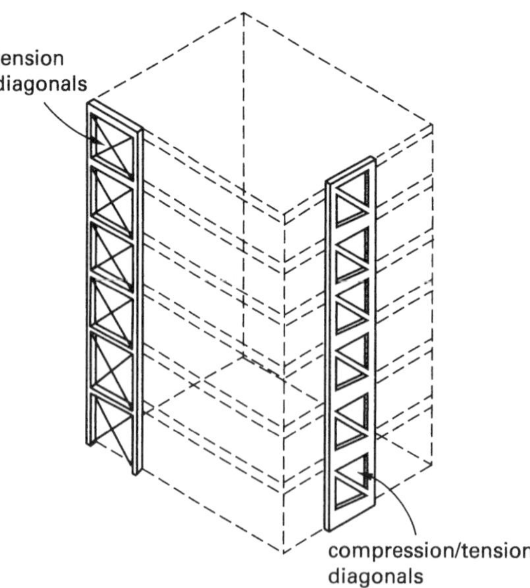

(b) multistory braced frame

Figure 42.3 Methods of Providing Web Reinforcement

There are two ways shear reinforcement, correctly called *web reinforcement*, is provided for. One way is to bend up some of the tension steel near the supports at a 45° angle as shown in Fig. 42.3(a). This is possible since most of the tension steel is required in the center of the beam where the moment is the greatest. The other, more common way, is to use vertical stirrups as shown in Fig. 42.3(b). These are small diameter bars (usually no. 3, no. 4, or no. 5 bars) that form a U-shaped cage around the tension steel.

The theories behind shear and diagonal tension in beams are still not completely understood. Exact, rational-analysis formulas do not exist. The existing formulas are based on tests, experience, and some mathematical analysis, and can become quite complicated.

The following formulas are a few of the basic ones with which ARE candidates should be familiar.

$$V_c = 2\sqrt{f_c'}\,b_w d \tag{42.11}$$

Product Development

The minimum area of web reinforcement required by the ACI 318 is given by the formula

$$A_v = 50\left(\frac{b_w s}{f_y}\right) \tag{42.12}$$

This formula must be used if the required shear strength, V_u, is more than one-half of the shear capacity, which is V_c times the strength reduction factor, ϕ. For shear, ϕ is 0.75.

To design the area of steel required for vertical stirrups the following formula is used.

$$s = \frac{\phi A_v f_y d}{V_u - \phi V_c} \tag{42.13}$$

Compression Steel

In most reinforced concrete construction, reinforcement is added to the top side of a beam, compression side of a beam, or some other section. Such beams are often called *doubly reinforced beams.* There are several reasons for this. First, the concrete alone may not be able to resist the compressive forces. This is especially true if the concrete is of low strength or if the cross-sectional area is small in proportion to the applied loads. Second, compression steel reduces long-term deflections caused by concrete creep. Third, steel in the compression zone may simply be used to support stirrups before the concrete is poured. Finally, it may be included to provide for expected or unexpected negative moment in a member normally stressed with only positive moment. This can happen when an imposed load on one portion of a continuous span causes an adjacent unloaded span to bend upward.

If the member is designed for compression, the steel must be restrained to prevent its buckling outward just as with a column. Lateral ties are used for this purpose and must encircle the compression and tension steel on all four sides and be spaced for the entire length of the member. The shear reinforcement can serve part of this purpose, but instead of being U-shaped bars, it must continue across the top of the compression reinforcement to form a secure tie.

Development Length and Reinforcement Anchorage

In order for concrete reinforcement to do its job, there must be a firm bond between the two materials so that they act together to resist loads. As mentioned earlier, this is accomplished by mechanical bonding due to the deformations of the rebars and through chemical bonding between the two materials. One of the primary requirements for safety is that there is a sufficient length of steel bar from any point of stress to the end of the bar to develop the necessary bond.

The required tension development length is primarily dependent on the strength of concrete, the strength of steel, the size of bar, the amount of concrete surrounding the bar, and the amount of transverse reinforcement surround the bar. ACI 318 allows the development length to be calculated by two separate means. Both methods include the dependent factors, but one is more detailed in calculation. The first method will be presented, as it is more simply applied.

The choice of which equation to use is based on the amount of concrete clear cover on the bar, the clear spacing between bars, and whether the transverse reinforcing is at least minimum in terms of stirrups or ties. Case I may be used if either of the following conditions applies. First the clear cover is not less than the bar diameter, and the clear spacing is not less than two times the bar diameter. Second, the clear cover is not less than the bar diameter, the clear spacing is not less than the bar diameter, and the transverse reinforcing meets the minimum for ties or stirrups. Case II applies if neither of the Case I conditions are met.

The following are the tension development length equations for each case.

Case I for no. 6 bars and smaller:

$$l_d = \left(\frac{f_y \Psi_t \Psi_e \lambda}{25\sqrt{f'_c}}\right) d_b \tag{42.14}$$

Product Development

for no. 7 bars and larger:
$$l_d = \left(\frac{f_y \Psi_t \Psi_e \lambda}{20\sqrt{f_c'}} \right) d_b \qquad 42.15$$

Case II for no. 6 bars and smaller:
$$l_d = \left(\frac{f_y \Psi_t \Psi_e \lambda}{50\sqrt{f_c'}} \right) d_b \qquad 42.16$$

for no. 7 bars and larger:
$$l_d = \left(\frac{3f_y \Psi_t \Psi_e \lambda}{40\sqrt{f_c'}} \right) d_b \qquad 42.17$$

However, ACI 318 requires that the length not be less than 12 in.

The variables of Ψ_t, Ψ_e, and λ are used to account for bar location, coating, and lightweight concrete, respectively. The values of each are as follows.

Ψ_t = reinforcement location factor
= 0.75 for horizontal reinforcement with more than 12 in of fresh concrete placed below the bar
= 1.0 for other reinforcement
Ψ_e = coating factor
= 1.5 for epoxy-coated bars with clear cover < $3d_b$ and clear spacing < $6d_b$
= 1.2 all other epoxy-coated bars
= 1.0 for uncoated reinforcement

However, the product $\Psi_t\Psi_e$ need not exceed 1.7.

λ = lightweight aggregate factor
= 0.75 for lightweight aggregate used and f_{ct} (splitting tensile strength) is not specified
= 1.0 for normal weight
= as follows if f_{ct} is specified, but not less than 1.0

$$\lambda = 6.7\left(\frac{\sqrt{f_c'}}{f_{ct}} \right) \leq 1.0 \qquad 42.18$$

Deflections

Although concrete may seem to be a very stiff material and not subject to much deflection, this is not the case. This is true because the strength design method of design, and higher strength concretes and steels, both result in smaller structural members that are less stiff than in the past.

Controlling deflection in concrete structures is important to avoid cracking partitions, glass, and other building components attached to the concrete, to avoid sagging of roofs and subsequent ponding of water, and to prevent noticeable deflection of visible members.

As with other aspects of concrete design, predicting deflection is not as easy as it is with homogeneous materials such as steel and wood. Design is further complicated by the fact that concrete has two phases of deflection: *immediate deflection* caused by normal dead and live loads, and *long-term deflection* caused by shrinkage and creep. Long-term deflection may be two or more times the initial deflection.

There are formulas and procedures that give the approximate initial and long-term deflections. These deflections can then be compared with deflection limitations in ACI 318 for various types of members and conditions of deflection. These limitations are expressed in terms of fractions of the total span. See Table 42.3.

Table 42.3 Maximum Computed Deflections

member	deflection to be considered	deflection limitation
flat roofs not supporting or attached to nonstructural elements likely to be damaged by large deflections	immediate deflection due to maximum of L_r, S, and R	$\frac{\ell^a}{180}$
floors not supporting or attached to nonstructural elements likely to be damaged by large deflections	immediate deflection due to live load L	$\frac{\ell}{360}$
roof or floor construction supporting or attached to nonstructural elements likely to be damaged by large deflections	that part of the total deflection occurring after attachment of nonstructural elements (sum of the long-time deflection due to all sustained loads and the immediate deflection due to any additional live load)[c]	$\frac{\ell^b}{480}$
roof or floor construction supporting or attached to nonstructural elements not likely to be damaged by large deflections		$\frac{\ell^d}{240}$

[a]Limit not intended to safeguard against ponding. Ponding should be checked by suitable calculations of deflection, including added deflections due to ponded water, and considering long-time effects of all sustained loads, camber, construction tolerances, and reliability of provisions for drainage.

[b]Limit may be exceeded if adequate measures are taken to prevent damage to supported or attached elements.

[c]Long-time deflection shall be determined in accordance with ACI Sec. 9.5.2.5 or 9.5.4.2 but may be reduced by amount of deflection calculated to occur before attachment of nonstructural elements. This amount shall be determined on basis of accepted engineering data relating to time-deflection characteristics of members similar to those being considered.

[d]But not greater than tolerance provided for nonstructural elements. Limit may be exceeded if camber is provided so that total deflection minus camber does not exceed limit.

From *ACI 318-14: Building Code Requirements for Structural Concrete*, © 2014, reprinted with permission from the American Concrete Institute.

If certain conditions are met, ACI 318 gives minimum depths of members in the form of span-to-depth ratios for various conditions. These are shown in Table 42.4.

Continuity

Since continuity is such a typical condition in concrete construction, ARE candidates should be familiar with its basic principles. *Continuity* is an extension of a structural member over one or more supports. An example of a continuous member is placing a 30 ft steel beam over four supports, each 10 ft on center. Since concrete is typically poured in forms extending across several columns (or a slab extending over several beams), concrete structures are inherently continuous. Concrete structures are typically continuous in the vertical direction as well as in the horizontal direction.

Table 42.4 Minimum Thickness of Solid Nonprestressed One-way Slabs

support condition	minimum h
simply supported	$\ell/20$
one end continous	$\ell/24$
both ends continuous	$\ell/28$
cantilever	$\ell/10$

Expressions applicable for normal-weight and f_y = 60,000 psi. For other cases, minimum h shall be modified in accordance with 7.3.1.1 through 7.3.1.1.3, as appropriate.

From *ACI 318-14: Building Code Requirements for Structural Concrete*, © 2014, reprinted with permission from the American Concrete Institute.

Product Development

Table 42.5
Minimum Depth of Nonprestressed Beams

support condition	minimum h^*
simply supported	$\ell/16$
one end continous	$\ell/18.5$
both ends continuous	$\ell/21$
cantilever	$\ell/8$

*Expressions applicable for normalweight and f_y = 60,000 psi. For other cases, minimum h shall be modified in accordance with 9.3.1.1 through 9.3.1.1.3, as appropriate.

A portion of an exaggerated concrete structure is shown in Fig. 42.4(a) with deflections due to vertical load also shown exaggerated. In the midspans of the beams, there is positive moment as discussed in Chap. 35. Over the center column support, however, the loads tend to cause the beam to bend upward with negative moment, while at the outer columns, the beam is fixed.

Figure 42.4
Continuity in Concrete Construction

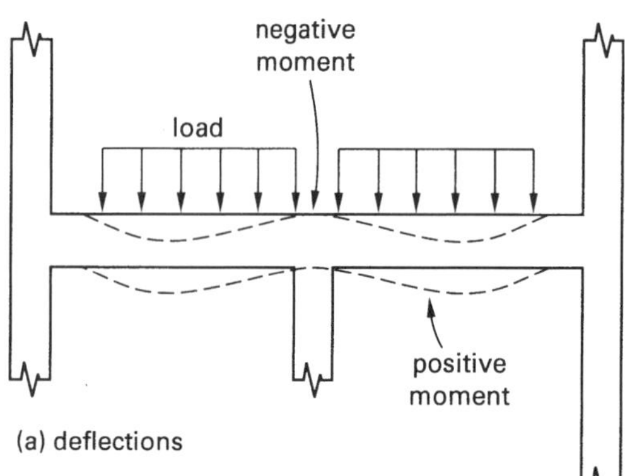

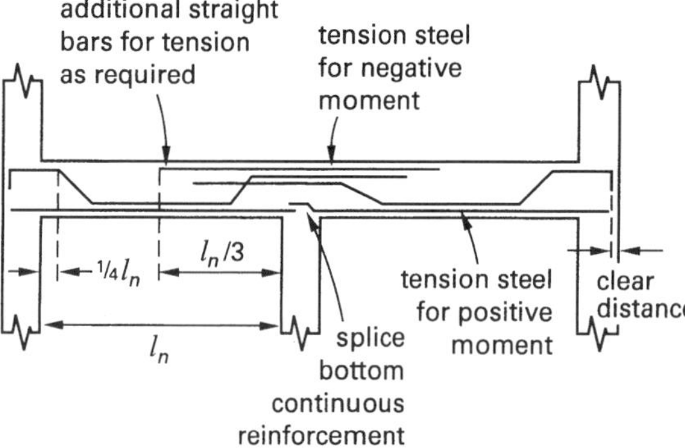

(b) reinforcement pattern
(stirrups and column reinforcement not shown)

Continuous beams and columns are statically indeterminate, meaning that they cannot be solved with the principles or equations of equilibrium discussed in Chap. 35. A few of the typical conditions for shear, moment, and deflection for beams are shown in Fig. 35.7. Continuous beams are more efficient than simply supported beams because the maximum moment for a given load and span is less than the moment for the corresponding simple beam. This is because the loads in adjacent spans effectively counteract each other to a certain extent.

For concrete structures, the negative moment causes the top of the beam to experience tension rather than the usual compression, so reinforcing steel must be added to counteract the forces just as in the bottom of a simply supported beam. In some cases, straight rebars are added over the supports to act as tension reinforcement. In other cases, some of the bottom tension steel is bent upward at the point of inflection to serve as negative reinforcement. See Fig. 42.4.

T-Beams

Since floor and roof slabs are always poured with the beams that support them, the two elements act integrally, with a portion of the slab acting as the top portion of the beam. In effect, then, what looks like a simple rectangular beam becomes a T-beam with a part of the slab resisting compressive forces. The horizontal portion is called the *flange*, and the vertical portion below the flange is called the *web* or *stem*. For an isolated T-section, the entire top flange acts in compression. However, for stems that are in the middle of slabs or edge beams, the effective flange width is smaller than what is actually available. The various conditions are shown in Fig. 42.5. ACI 318 limits the effective flange widths as shown in Fig. 42.5.

For isolated beams, the flange thickness shall not be less than one-half the width of the web, and the total flange width shall not be more than four times the web width. See Fig. 42.5(a).

For symmetrical T-beams (such as interior beams poured with the slab), the smallest of three conditions determines the effective width. This width shall not exceed one-fourth of the span of the beam, nor shall the overhanging slab width on either side of the beam web exceed eight times the thickness of the slab, nor shall it exceed one-half the clear distance to the next beam. See Fig. 42.5(b).

For edge beams, the effective overhanging slab portion shall not exceed $1/12$ the span of the beam, nor shall the overhanging slab exceed six times the thickness of the slab, nor shall it exceed one-half the clear distance to the next beam. See Fig. 42.5(c).

If the neutral axis is equal to or less than the slab thickness, the section is designed as though it were a solid beam with a width equal to the effective width of the flange. If the neutral axis is in the web, special T-beam analysis is required.

CONCRETE SLABS

As part of a structural system of columns and beams, slabs can either span (structurally) in one direction or two directions. The former is called a *one-way slab* and the latter is called a *two-way slab.*

In a one-way slab, reinforcement is run in one direction perpendicular to the beams supporting the slab. Two-way slabs have rebars in both directions and are more efficient because the applied loads are distributed in all directions. However, in order for two-way slabs to work as intended, the column bays supporting them should be square or nearly square. When the ratio of length to width of one slab bay approaches 2:1, the slab begins to act as a one-way slab regardless of the reinforcement or edge supports.

One-way slabs need extra reinforcement to counteract the effects of shrinkage and temperature changes. Often called *temperature steel,* the minimum amount of reinforcement is set by ACI code by percentage as tension steel is, but in no case can the rebars be placed farther apart than five times the slab thickness or more than 18 in. The minimum steel ratio, based on gross concrete area, is 0.0018 for $f_y = 60$ ksi or 0.0020 for $f_y = 40$ ksi or 50 ksi.

Figure 42.5
T-Beams

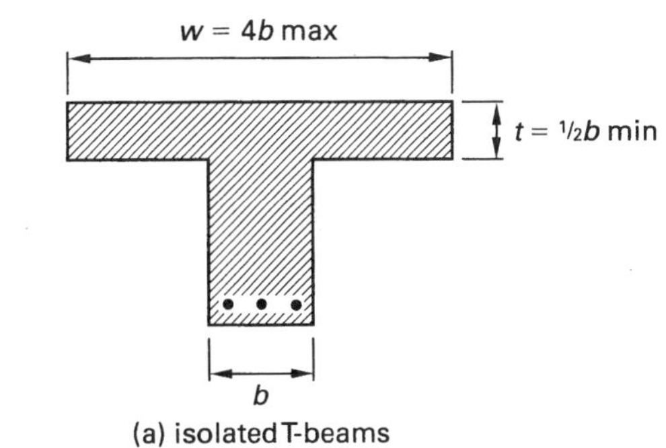

(a) isolated T-beams

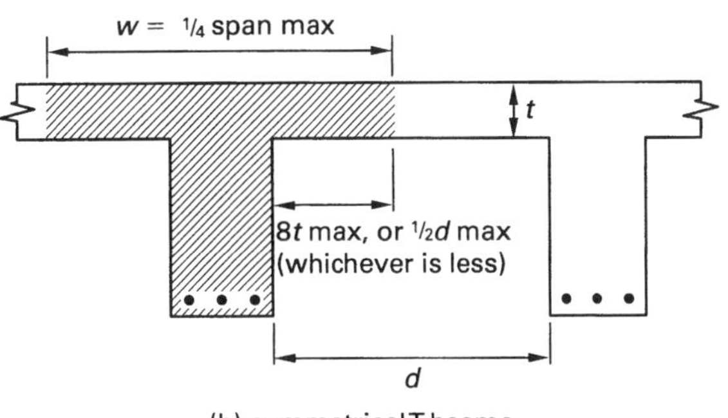

(b) symmetrical T-beams

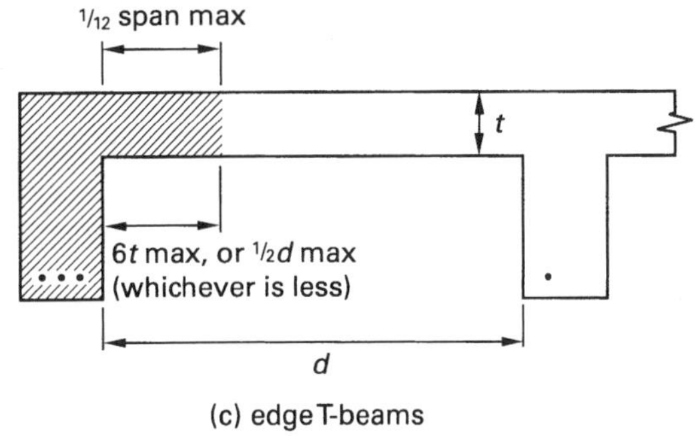

(c) edge T-beams

CONCRETE COLUMNS

Columns are the most typical of several types of concrete compressive members, including arch ribs, compressive members of trusses, and portions of rigid frames. The design of concrete compressive members is complex, especially when eccentric loading is involved or when the member supports both axial and bending stresses. This section will cover the basics of the two most typical types of concrete compressive members: *tied columns* and *spiral columns.* Composite compressive members, which consist of concrete reinforced with structural steel shapes, are sometimes used, but are not included here.

As with other types of columns, one of the primary considerations in design is the effect of buckling of the column caused by the axial load. The overall size of concrete columns usually results in length-to-width ratios of from 8 to 12, so slenderness is often not a critical consideration. However, since the steel reinforcement is very slender, it tends to fail by buckling and pushing out the concrete cover at the faces of the column. To prevent this, lateral ties are required, either as individual tied bars or a continuous spiral as discussed in the next two sections. Ties also hold the longitudinal steel in place before the concrete is poured. If columns are slender, either by design or by using higher strength concretes and reinforcement, then special calculations are required.

ACI 318 limits the percentage of longitudinal steel to from 0.01 minimum to 0.08 maximum of the gross concrete cross section. It further requires there be at least four bars for tied columns and six for spiral columns. One reason for a limited percentage of steel is that large numbers of bars create a congested column form and make proper placing of the concrete difficult.

Figure 42.6
Concrete Columns

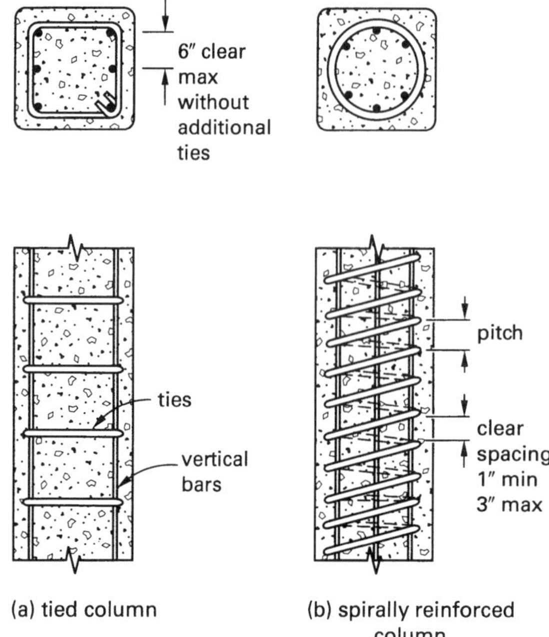

Tied Columns

Tied columns consist of vertical steel running parallel to the length of the column near its faces, with lateral reinforcement consisting of individual rebars tied to the vertical reinforcement at regular intervals. See Fig. 42.6(a).
ACI 318 requires that the lateral ties be at least no. 3 rebars for longitudinal bars up to no. 10 and at least no. 4 rebars for no. 11, no. 14, and no. 18 bars. No. 4 rebars must also be used for bundled reinforcement. Tied columns are most often used for square or rectangular shapes.

The spacing of the ties cannot exceed 16 diameters of vertical bars, 48 diameters of tie bars, or the least dimension of the column. The ties must be arranged so that every corner and alternate vertical bar has lateral support in both directions. No bar can be more than 6 in clear from such a laterally supported bar.

The strength reduction factor, ϕ, is 0.65 for tied columns.

Spiral Columns

Spiral columns have a continuous spiral of steel in lieu of individual lateral ties as shown in Fig. 42.6(b). The spiral must be at least $^3/_8$ in in diameter, and the clear spacing between turns cannot be less than 1 in or more than 3 in. The distance between the center lines of the turns is called the *pitch of the spiral*. Figure 42.6 shows a square spiral column, but they may also be round.

The strength reduction factor, ϕ, for spiral columns is 0.75, reflecting the fact that spiral columns are slightly stronger than tied columns of the same size and reinforcement. Another important difference to note is that spiral columns are more ductile, meaning that they fail in a gradual manner with the outer covering of concrete spalling before the column fails. Tied columns tend to fail suddenly without warning.

PRESTRESSED CONCRETE

Prestressed concrete consists of members that have internal stresses applied to them before they are subjected to service loads. The prestressing consists of compressive forces applied where normally the member would be in tension, which effectively eliminates or greatly reduces tensile forces that the member is not capable of carrying. In addition to making a more efficient and economical structural section, prestressing reduces cracking and deflection, increases shear strength, and allows longer spans and greater loads. Prestressing is accomplished in one of two ways: *pretensioning* or *post-tensioning*.

Precast, Pretensioned

With this system, concrete members are produced in a precasting plant. High-strength pretensioning stranded cable or wire is draped in forms according to the required stress pattern needed, and a tensile force is applied. The concrete is then poured and allowed to cure. Once cured, the cables are cut, and the resulting compressive force is transmitted to the concrete through the bond between cable and concrete.

Post-tensioned

For post-tensioning, hollow sleeves or conduit are placed in the forms on the site, and concrete is poured around them. Within the conduit is the prestressing steel, called *tendons*, which are stressed with hydraulic jacks or other means after the concrete has cured. In some cases, the space between the tendons and the conduit is grouted. The resulting stress is transferred to the concrete through end plates in the concrete member.

43

WALL CONSTRUCTION

Nomenclature

A_g	gross area of concrete wall	in^2	h'	effective wall height (Kh)	in
A_s	area of reinforcing	in^2	K	effective length factor	–
f'_c	specified compressive strength of concrete	lbf/in^2	l_c	vertical distance between supports	in
f'_m	compressive strength of masonry at 28 days	lbf/in^2	P_n	nominal axial load strength	lbf
			r	radius of gyration	in
F_a	allowable average axial compressive stress for centroidally applied axial load	lbf/in^2	t	effective thickness of wythe or wall	in
			ϕ	strength reduction factor (0.70 for concrete bearing walls)	–
h	height of wall	in			

The two primary classifications of walls are *load-bearing* and *non-load-bearing.* Load-bearing walls support their own weight in addition to vertical and lateral loads. They can be further classified into *vertical load-bearing walls*, *shear walls*, and *retaining walls.* Vertical load-bearing walls support the weight of other walls above, in addition to floor and roof loads. Shear walls are structural walls that resist lateral loads acting in the plane of the wall. Retaining walls, as discussed in Chap. 37, are structural walls that resist the movement of soil.

Non-load-bearing walls support only their own weight and are used to enclose a building or to divide space within a building. When used for a building enclosure, they do serve to transfer wind forces to the primary structural frame. A non-load-bearing exterior wall is called a *curtain wall.*

Although the primary focus of this chapter is the structural design of walls, there are other considerations in selecting the optimum wall for a particular circumstance. In addition to load-carrying ability, a wall must provide for openings, keep out the weather, be cost effective, satisfy the aesthetic requirement of the job, resist heat loss and gain, and be easy to maintain. The architect must exercise judgment in selecting the wall system to best satisfy all the requirements of a project.

Product Development

MASONRY WALLS

There are many varieties of masonry walls, both non-load-bearing and load-bearing, consisting of single or multiple wythes, either reinforced or unreinforced. A *wythe* is a continuous vertical section of a wall one masonry unit in thickness. For structural purposes, the two primary masonry materials are brick and concrete block.

Table 43.1 Compressive Strength of Clay Masonry

net area compressive strength of clay masonry units (psi)		net area compressive strength of masonry (psi)
Type M or S mortar	Type N mortar	
1700	2100	1000
3350	4150	1500
4950	6200	2000
6600	8250	2500
8250	10,300	3000
9900	–	3500
13,200	–	4000

From *Building Code Requirements and Specification for Masonry Structures, the Masonry Standards Joint Committee* (MSJC), © 2013, The Masonry Society. Reproduced with permission.

Masonry walls can be engineered or designed by empirical requirements given in building codes and generally accepted rules of thumb. The model codes differ in some areas concerning requirements for masonry walls; the ones in this book are based on the *Building Code Requirements and Specification for Masonry Structures* (MSJC). Requirements also vary depending on which seismic zone the building is in. Structures in zones subject to more frequent and severe earthquakes, of course, require additional reinforcement, and there are limitations on the types of mortar and masonry units that can be used.

The specified compressive stress in masonry walls depends on the strength of the masonry unit as well as the strength of the mortar. Because the quality of a masonry wall is highly dependent on the workmanship, the formulas for allowable stress given by the building code assume that special inspection will be made during the construction of the wall. If this inspection is not made, the allowable stresses must be reduced by one-half.

The compressive strength of a masonry wall, f_m', can be based on tests of actual wall samples; on field experience based on similar mortar, masonry, and construction combinations; or on assumed values given in the MSJC. Table 43.1 and Table 43.2 give the assumed designed strength of clay and concrete masonry, respectively, for three mortar types.

The allowable axial compressive stress for reinforced and unreinforced walls is determined by the following formula.

Table 43.2 Compressive Strength of Concrete Masonry

net area of compressive strength of concrete masonry, psi	net area compressive strength of concrete masonry units, psi	
	Type M or S mortar	Type N mortar
1700		1900
1900	1900	2350
2000	2000	2650
2250	2600	3400
2500	3250	4350
2750	3900	
3000	4500	

For units of less than 4 in. nominal height, use 85 percent of the values listed.

$$F_a = 0.25f_m'\left(1 - \left(\frac{h'}{140r}\right)^2\right) \quad \left[\text{where } \frac{h'}{r} \leq 99\right] \qquad 43.1$$

$$F_a = 0.25f_m'\left(\frac{70r}{h'}\right) \quad \left[\text{where } \frac{h'}{r} > 99\right] \qquad 43.2$$

As indicated in this formula, the allowable stress is determined not only by the masonry strength but also by the slenderness ratio of the wall, just as with column design. There are five basic types of masonry walls: veneered, single-wythe, reinforced hollow unit masonry, cavity, and reinforced grouted masonry. These are illustrated in Fig. 43.1.

A *veneered wall* is a non-load-bearing wall having a facing of a single wythe of masonry, usually brick, anchored to a backing. The masonry is primarily for decorative and weatherproofing purposes such as a brick veneer wall over a wood stud backing wall.

Product Development

Single-Wythe Walls

A *single wythe* consists of a single unit of unreinforced masonry that can act as either a bearing or non-loadbearing wall. Since it is unreinforced vertically, there are limits to the amount of load that can bear on this type of wall, and building codes limit the maximum ratio of unsupported height or length to thickness. For solid masonry walls or bearing partitions designed according to the IBC, the ratio cannot exceed 20. For hollow masonry or cavity walls, the ratio cannot exceed 18.

Example 43.1

What is the maximum unsupported height for a solid brick wall 8 in thick?

Solution

The nominal thickness, t, of the wall is used in the calculation, so the maximum height is (8 in)(20), or 160 in, or 13 ft 4 in.

Even though single-wythe walls are not reinforced vertically, they must have a minimum amount of horizontal reinforcement, just as multi-wythe walls must. The most commonly used reinforcements are prefabricated assemblies consisting of minimum nine-gage steel laid every 16 in. See Fig. 43.2.

Figure 43.1 Masonry Wall Types

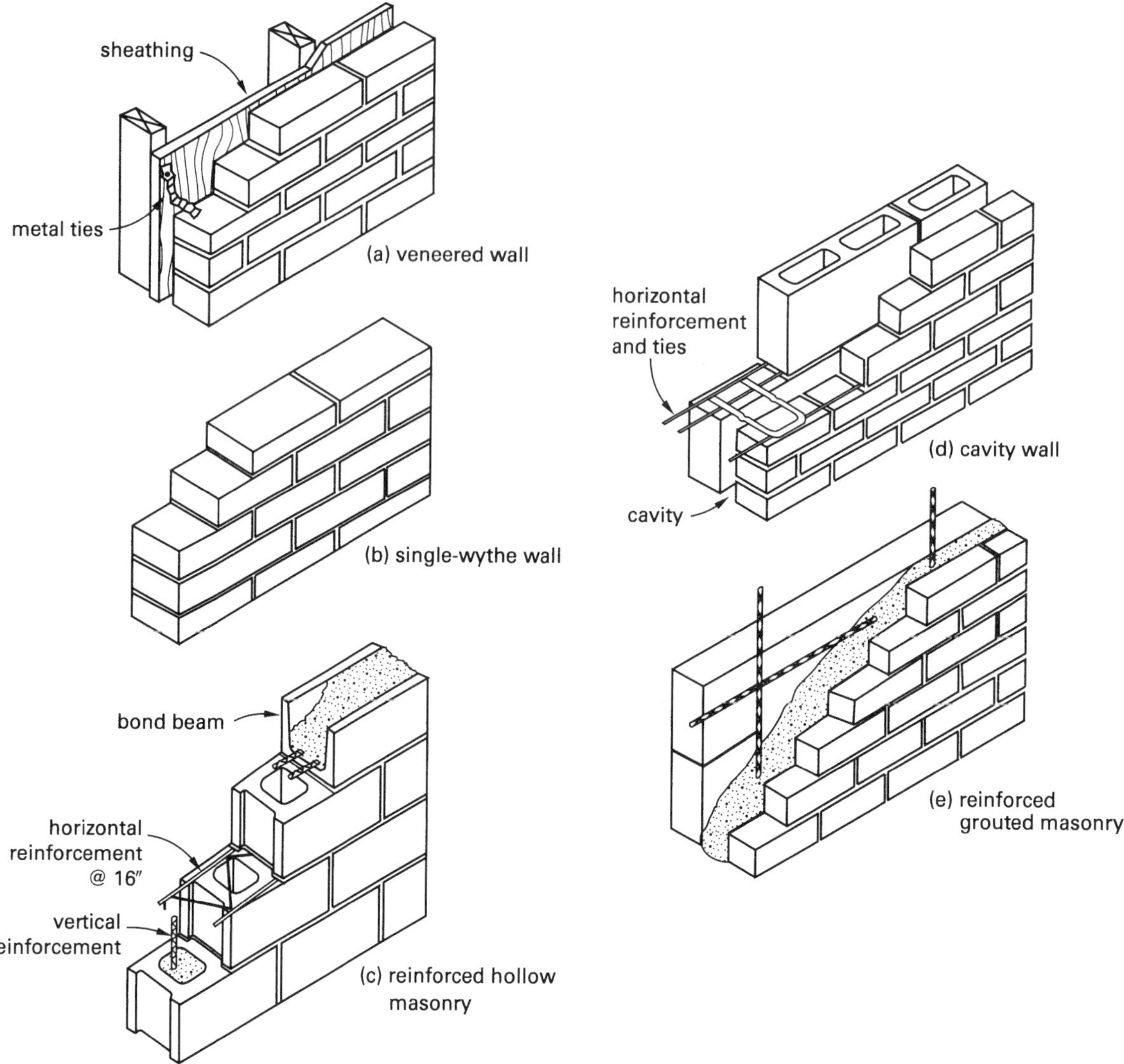

Reinforced Hollow Unit Masonry

This type of wall construction consists of a single wythe of concrete block with vertical reinforcing rods placed in the cells of the block, which are filled with grout. See Fig. 43.1(c). Grout may be placed in every cell or just in those cells containing the reinforcing. Since concrete block is based on an 8 in module, the spacing of the vertical reinforcing bars is a multiple of 8 in.

Horizontal reinforcement is provided by prefabricated units as shown in Fig. 43.2. When additional horizontal reinforcement is needed over openings or at the top of the wall, a U-shaped block, called a *bond beam*, is used with rebar placed in the bottom and filled with grout. The minimum nominal thickness of a reinforced masonry bearing wall is 6 in.

Cavity Walls

Cavity walls consist of two wythes of masonry, separated by an air space normally 2 in wide. See Fig. 43.1(d). Cavity walls have the advantages of providing extra protection against water penetration and additional insulation value because of the air. The cavity is often filled with insulation to enhance the insulation value of the wall. Both wythes may be of the same masonry type, or they may be mixed. A common type of cavity wall is a backing of 4 in or 8 in concrete block with an exterior wythe of brick.

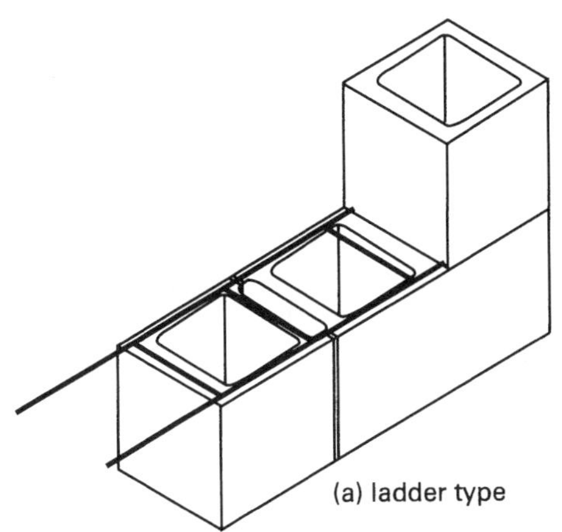

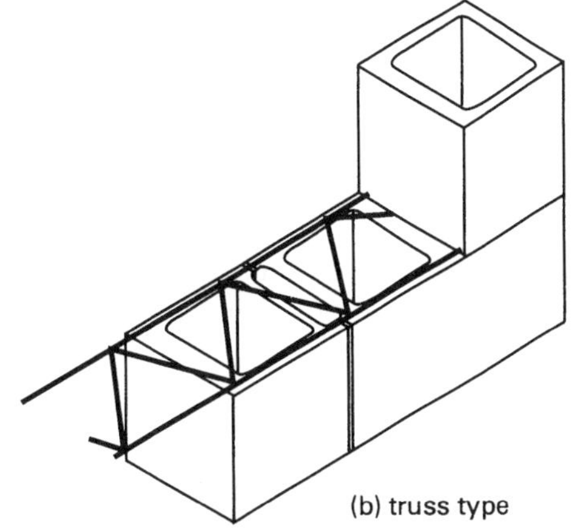

Figure 43.2 Horizontal Joint Reinforcement

The wythes of a cavity wall must be tied together with a corrosion-resistant metal tie at least 3/16 in in diameter for every 4½ ft^2 of wall area, or with other approved horizontal joint reinforcement as shown in Fig. 43.2. Metal ties are normally spaced every 16 in vertically.

Example 43.2

What is the maximum unsupported height for a cavity wall consisting of a 4 in brick facing and an 8 in concrete block wall separated by a 1 in space?

Solution

In computing the ratio for cavity walls, the thickness is the sum of the nominal thicknesses of the wythes. The maximum height is (4 in + 8 in)(18), or 216 in, or 18 ft.

Reinforced Grouted Masonry

Reinforced grouted masonry is used where additional load-carrying capacity is required, for lateral loads such as wind or earthquake. Reinforcing bars are installed in the cavity of the wall, and then the cavity is filled with grout. See Fig. 43.1(e).

Reinforcement is usually installed both vertically and horizontally, especially in seismic design categories E and F where it is required. For these seismic zones, the code requires that the sum of the areas of horizontal and vertical reinforcement be at least 0.002 times the gross cross-sectional area of the wall, and that the minimum area of reinforcement in either direction be at least 0.0007 times the gross cross-sectional area of the wall. The spacing of the reinforcement cannot exceed 4 ft and must have at least a 3/8 in diameter.

Example 43.3

What reinforcing should be provided for a masonry cavity wall consisting of an 8 in concrete block backup wythe separated by a 2 in space from a 4 in brick facing wythe?

Solution

The IBC defines the gross cross-sectional area as that encompassed by the outer periphery of any section, so the actual width of the above wall assembly is the sum of the actual width of the block (7 5/8 in) plus the cavity plus the actual width of the brick (3 5/8 in), or a total of 13.25 in.

The required horizontal and vertical reinforcing per foot of height or length is

$$\begin{aligned} A_s &= (0.0007)(13.25\text{ in})\left(12\ \frac{\text{in}}{\text{ft}}\right) \\ &= 0.1113\text{ in}^2/\text{ft} \end{aligned}$$

The minimum sum of vertical and horizontal reinforcing is

$$\begin{aligned} A_s &= (0.002)(13.25\ \text{in})\left(12\ \frac{\text{in}}{\text{ft}}\right) \\ &= 0.318\ \text{in}^2/\text{ft} \end{aligned}$$

When deciding on the size and spacing of the reinforcing bars, use standard bar sizes while minimizing the amount of steel used (and therefore the cost) and the number of bars placed (more bars placed generally increases the labor cost). The area of rebars is given in Table 42.1.

Decide on horizontal reinforcing first. 0.1113 in^2/ft means a minimum steel area of (0.1113 in^2/ft)(4), or 0.445 in^2 per 4 ft (48 in) of height. One option is to use a no. 7 bar every 4 ft (area = 0.60 in^2), but this size bar would be heavy and awkward to place and make it difficult to grout the cavity. Try a spacing of 16 in instead, or three bars per 4 ft of height. The steel area needed is

$$\frac{0.45\ \text{in}^2}{3} = 0.15\ \text{in}^2$$

A no. 4 bar ($A = 0.20$ in^2) spaced every 16 in would work.

Next, determine the size and spacing of vertical reinforcement. The total area required per 4 ft length is (0.318 in^2/ft)(4 ft), less the actual area of the horizontal reinforcement.

$$\left(0.318\ \frac{\text{in}^2}{\text{ft}}\right)(4\ \text{ft}) - (0.20\ \text{in}^2)(3) = 0.672\ \text{in}^2$$

Once again, try a spacing of 16 in. Each bar would need a minimum area of 0.672 in^2/3, or 0.224 in^2. A no. 4 bar spaced every 16 in will not work, but a no. 5 bar spaced every 16 in would be satisfactory.

The grout used for reinforced masonry walls is a mixture of portland cement, hydrated lime, and aggregate. It may either be fine grout or course grout. Course grout has a higher percentage of larger aggregates.

A wall may be grouted in one of two ways. The first is called *low-lift grouting*, which is accomplished by laying up no more than 8 in of masonry and then placing the grout. The second method is *high-lift grouting*. A larger portion of the wall, no more than 6 ft in height, is laid up and the reinforcing placed. Grout is then pumped into the cavity and mechanically vibrated to ensure that all voids are filled.

The building code specifies the minimum clear dimensions of the cavity less the width of horizontal reinforcing based on the height of the grout pour and whether fine or course grout is used. For low-lift grouting with fine grout, the minimum grout space is $^3/_4$ in plus the width of the reinforcing. For coarse grout, it is $1^1/_2$ in. Mortar projections must be kept to a minimum of $^1/_2$ in, and the cavity space must be kept clear of loose mortar and other foreign material.

Openings

Regardless of the type of lintel used to span an opening, there is always arch action over an opening, provided the masonry has a running bond. This is shown diagrammatically in Fig. 43.3. Unless a concentrated load or a floor load is near the top of the opening, the lintel only carries the weight of the wall above the opening in a triangular area defined by a 45° angle from each side of the opening. If a floor line is within a distance equal to the top of this imaginary triangle, the lintel carries the weight of the wall and the weight of the floor load as wide as the opening.

Openings in masonry walls may be spanned with masonry arches, steel lintels, precast reinforced concrete lintels, or precast masonry lintels reinforced with rebars and filled with grout. See Fig. 43.4.

Steel lintels are often used because they are inexpensive and simple to install and the size and thickness can be varied to suit the span of the opening. Lintels should bear on each end of the supporting masonry such that the bearing capacity is not exceeded, but in no case should the bearing length be less than 6 in.

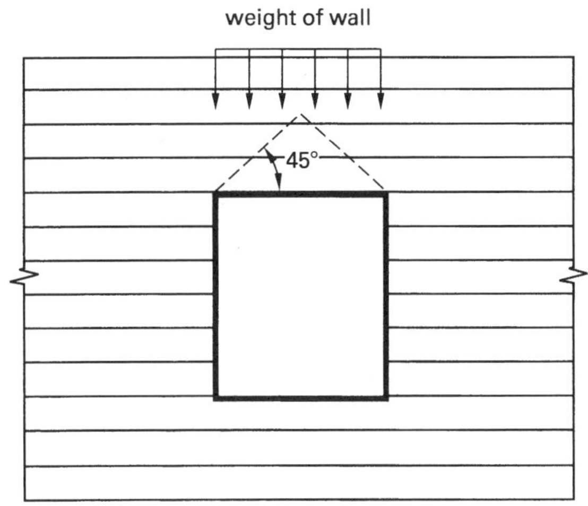

Figure 43.3 Arch Action in a Masonry Wall over an Opening

STUD WALLS

Stud wall systems are one of the most common types of structural systems for residential and light commercial buildings. Stud walls are relatively small members, closely spaced and tied together with exterior and interior sheathing. The sheathing is necessary to brace the small members against buckling and to resist lateral loads.

Stud wall systems have many advantages. They are easy to erect by a small construction crew, relatively inexpensive, and lightweight; their materials are readily available; they are adaptable to a variety of designs; and the space between the studs can be used for insulation and electrical service.

Stud wall systems allow for many types of exterior finish materials such as wood or aluminum siding, stucco, and brick veneer.

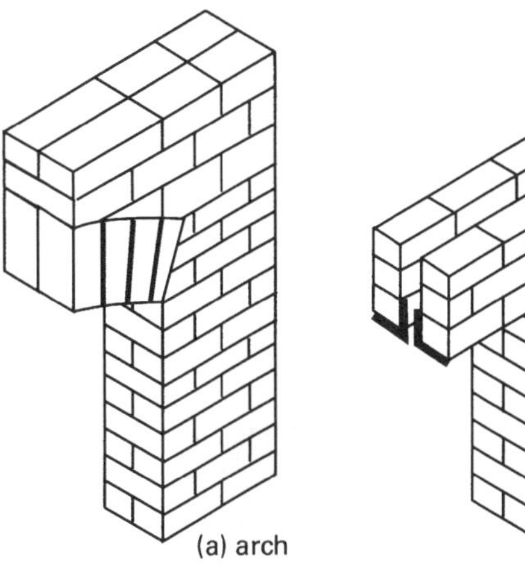

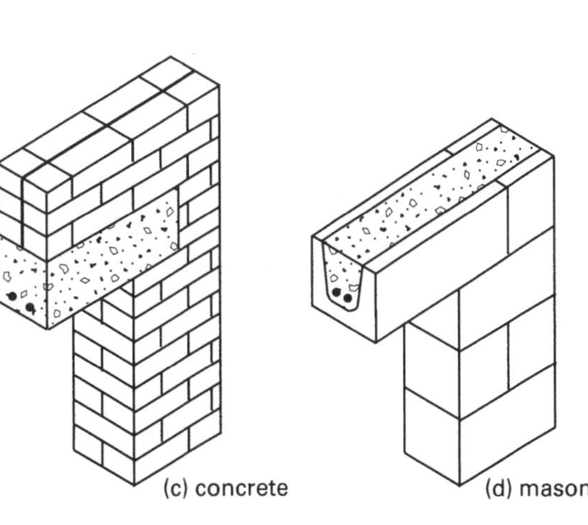

Figure 43.4 Masonry Lintels

Wood Studs

Wood studs are the most common type of material used for stud wall systems. They are typically 2×4 members spaced 16 in or 24 in on center, covered with plywood or particle board sheathing on the exterior and gypsum board on the interior. 2×4 and 2×6 studs can be used for bearing walls up to 10 ft high. If the studs support one floor, roof, and ceiling, the maximum spacing is 16 in for 2×4s and 24 in for 2×6s.

The most common type of wood stud construction is *platform framing* as illustrated in Fig. 43.5. With this method, wood studs one story high are placed on a sole plate at the bottom and spanned with a double top plate at the ceiling level. The second floor joists bear on the top plate and, when the second floor sheathing is in place, serve as a platform on which to erect the second-story stud walls.

The other method of stud construction is *balloon framing*, in which the studs run the full height from the first floor to the top of the second floor. The second-floor joists bear on a continuous 1 × 4 ribbon let into the studs, and are also nailed into the sides of the studs. This method of construction is seldom used, although its advantage is that it minimizes the overall shrinkage of the vertical dimension of the wall because the majority of the lumber is oriented parallel to the grain of the wood.

Product Development

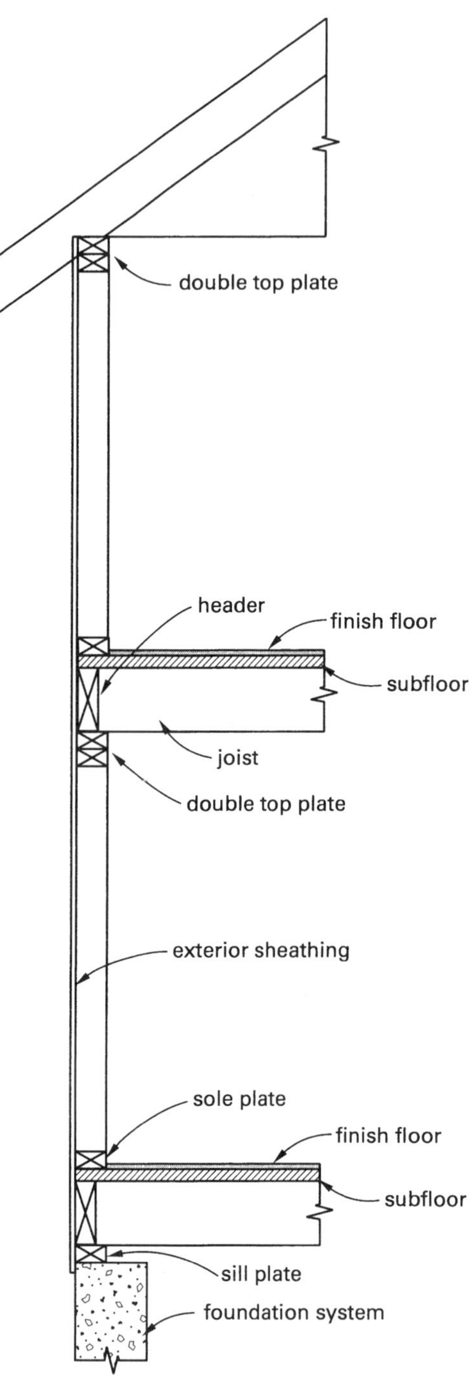

Figure 43.5 Platform Construction

Metal Studs

Metal stud systems are similar in concept to wood stud systems except that light-gage C-shaped metal members are used instead of wood. Standard sizes of exterior metal studs are $3\frac{1}{2}$, $3\frac{5}{8}$, 4, and 6 in in depth, in thicknesses of 14, 16, and 18 gage. Deeper studs are also available. Metal studs are usually placed 24 in on center rather than 16 in. If the entire building is being framed in light-gage metal, floor joists and rafters are constructed of steel members as well.

Metal stud wall systems may be used with other structural framing systems. For example, a building may have a steel or concrete primary structural frame with light-gage steel studs used for nonbearing exterior and interior walls. The exterior stud walls are then faced with brick, siding, tile, or some other weatherproof finish material.

Openings

Openings in stud walls are framed in the same material as the stud wall itself. Openings in wood stud walls are spanned with headers consisting of nominal 2 in thick lumber placed on edge as shown in Fig. 43.6. The width of the header depends on the width of the opening. Double 2×4s can be used on openings up to 3 ft, 2×6s can be used on openings up to 4 ft, and 2×8s can be used on openings up to 5 ft.

The headers are supported by short studs that are doubled next to the full-height studs and next to the space above and below the opening framed with cripple studs. Openings in metal stud walls are framed in a similar manner.

CONCRETE WALLS

Concrete walls are ideal where high strength, durability, and fire resistance are required. Although concrete walls can be designed just as bearing walls, they usually also act as shear walls and sometimes as deep beams spanning between footings. Having them serve more than one function makes more efficient use of the material and labor required for their construction.

Building codes and the American Concrete Institute detail the many requirements that concrete bearing walls must meet, and like other aspects of concrete construction, they are quite complicated and depend on iterative design processes. However, the following guidelines are a useful summary.

Cast-in-Place

When certain conditions are met, the IBC allows an empirical design method to be used. With this method, the design axial load strength can be computed with the formula

$$\phi P_n = 0.55\phi f_c' A_g \left(1 - \left(\frac{Kl_c}{32t}\right)^2\right) \qquad 43.3$$

The effective length factor, K, is taken as 0.8 for walls restrained against rotation at the top or bottom or both, and as 1.0 for walls unrestrained against rotation at both ends. The strength reduction factor, ϕ, is taken as 0.7 for walls in compression. Additional loads such as seismic and wind loading may require extra reinforcing.

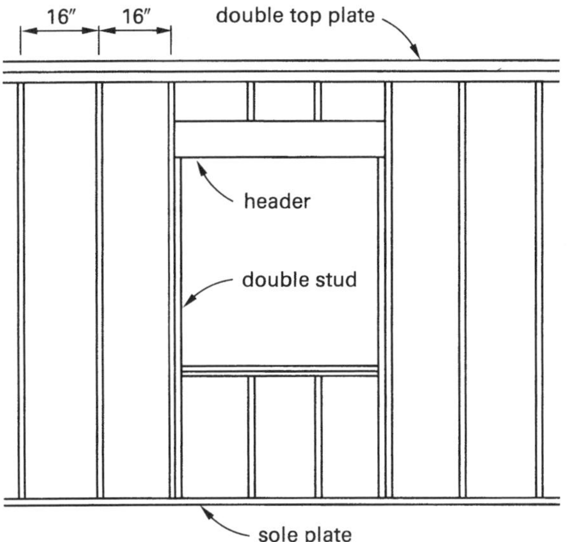

Figure 43.6 Typical Wood Stud Wall Framing

The conditions that must be met in order to use Eq. 43.3 include the following.

- Walls must be anchored to intersecting elements such as floors, roofs, columns, and intersecting walls and footings.
- The minimum ratio of vertical reinforcement area to gross concrete area must be 0.0012 for deformed bars not larger than no. 5 with a yield strength of not less than 60 ksi. For other bars, the ratio is 0.0015.
- The minimum ratio of horizontal reinforcement area to gross concrete area must be 0.0020 for deformed bars not larger than no. 5 with a yield strength of not less than 60 ksi. For other bars, the ratio is 0.0025.
- Walls more than 10 in thick, except basement walls, must have the reinforcement placed in two layers with the layer next to the exterior face containing not less than one-half and not more than two-thirds of the total reinforcement required.
- Reinforcement cannot be spaced farther apart than three times the wall thickness, or 18 in.
- Not less than two no. 5 bars must be provided around all window and door openings, and these must be extended past the corners of the openings not less than 24 in.
- The minimum thickness of bearing walls cannot be less than $1/25$ of the unsupported height or length, whichever is shorter, nor less than 4 in.
- The resultant of the loads must fall within the middle one-third of the wall thickness to avoid eccentricity.

Precast Concrete Walls

Precast bearing walls are required to be designed in the same way as cast-in-place walls, including the effects of temperature and shrinkage. Often, extra reinforcing is needed simply to protect the integrity of the panels against the stresses of transportation and erection.

Precast walls are an economical way to enclose a building and provide for bearing if there is sufficient repetition in the panel sizes and configurations to make mass production possible. Rather than serving as a bearing member, precast walls are often nonbearing and attached to a structural framework of steel or precast concrete.

Figure 43.7
Precast Concrete Wall Panel Connections

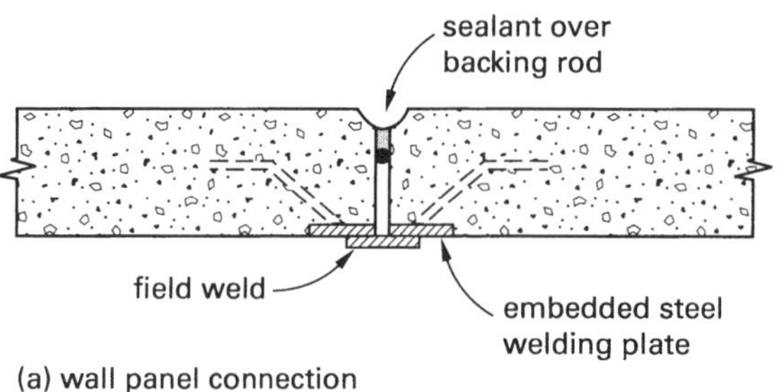

(a) wall panel connection

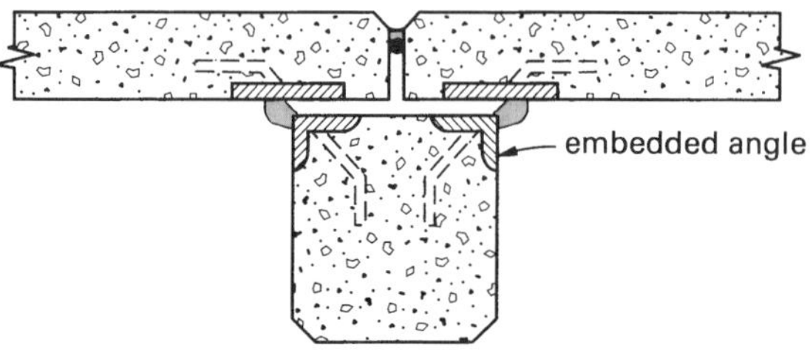

(b) connection to column

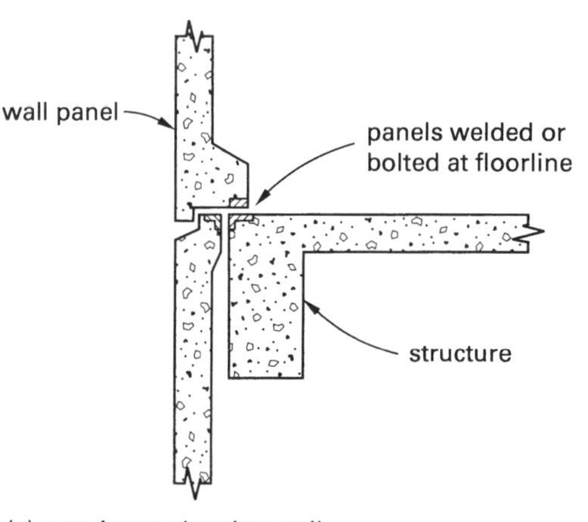

(c) exterior nonbearing walls

Precast bearing walls are most often connected by field welding steel plates that have been cast into the panel at the precasting plant. Figure 43.7 illustrates some of the typical connections used.

BUILDING ENVELOPE

The design of the walls that enclose a building is one of the most difficult detailing problems in building construction because not only does the exterior wall have to be structurally sound, but it must also accommodate various kinds of movement that occur in all structures. In addition, connections between the cladding and the structure must be designed to allow for on-site adjustments during erection, so the final wall will be within proper tolerances. These requirements exist whether the exterior wall is bearing or nonbearing. However, this section will only discuss the attachment of nonbearing exterior cladding to the primary structural frame.

Attachment to Structural Members

Exterior cladding and its attachment to the primary structural frame must resist three basic types of loads: the *dead load* of the wall system itself, *horizontal wind loads*, and *seismic loads*.

The method of providing dead load support depends on the material used and the structural frame. For example, heavy materials, such as brick and concrete block used in one- or two-story buildings, usually rest directly on the foundation. In taller buildings, the load must be carried at intermediate floor levels because the strength of a panel or portion of a wall is not sufficient to carry any weight beyond its own dead load.

Figure 43.8 illustrates a typical method of supporting masonry in a multistory building. In this case, the weight of the masonry is carried on a continuous steel angle bolted to the structural frame. Horizontal ties provide for attachment of the exterior wall to the frame and help in the transfer of wind loads as well. The attachment of veneer stone is accomplished in a similar manner, although individual details are somewhat different.

Precast concrete panels are also attached at every floor or every other floor using various combinations of embedded steel angles and plates that are field-welded or bolted together as shown in Fig. 43.7(c).

With metal curtain wall systems, the provision for both dead loads and wind load is made with various types of clip attachments of the curtain wall system to the structural frame. There are many possible ways this can be accomplished depending on the type of curtain wall system, its fabrication, the loads that must be resisted, and the type and configuration of the primary structural frame, as well as other variables.

Product Development

In most cases, some type of steel anchor is firmly attached to the structure at floor and column lines. The support system for the curtain wall is then attached to these anchors using shims and slotted bolt holes to provide for precise alignment of the exterior wall. One system of this type is shown in Fig. 43.9.

In resisting wind loading, the cladding must maintain its own structural integrity and transfer the wind loads to the structural frame. Wind can either produce a positive or negative load on a component. Quite often, the suction on an exterior wall can be greater than the inward pressure caused by wind. In most cases, however, nonbearing exterior walls are designed to span between supports, so intermediate connections for the transfer of wind loads are not required. One exception is brick masonry, which may require intermittent horizontal ties because of its low flexural strength.

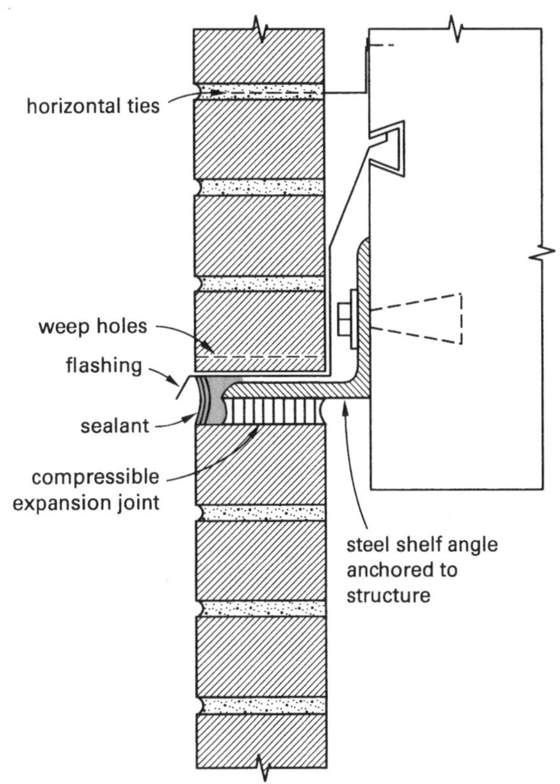

Figure 43.8 Typical Attachment of Brick Facing at Intermediate Floor

Nonbearing, exterior wall systems in areas of frequent seismic activity must be designed primarily to maintain their integrity and connection to the building to avoid injury caused by falling debris. Although it is desirable to provide for movement and absorption of energy during an earthquake to avoid cracking and damage of the wall material, this is usually not practical for severe earthquakes. Instead, connections and joints should accommodate movement to avoid buildup of stresses that could dislocate the wall from the structure.

The design of curtain wall systems is especially important in resisting seismic loads. Of course, the panels must withstand the force of an earthquake, but most of the load is concentrated in the connections to the primary structural system. In severe earthquake zones, additional connections may be required above those needed for gravity and wind loading. Much of the earthquake energy in a curtain wall system can be dissipated by providing joints that can move slightly in several directions with such details as slip joints or flexible bushings between bolt and steel members.

To minimize the possibility of damage to nonbearing panels during an earthquake, the panels should be anchored vertically at column lines and horizontally at floor lines. It is at these points where the seismic forces are concentrated, so curtain wall panels should not span across these points.

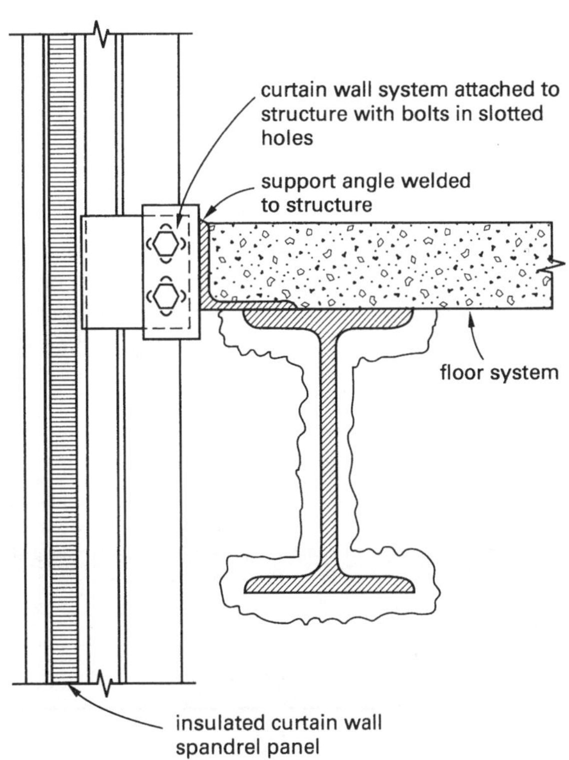

Figure 43.9 Typical Attachment of Curtain Wall

Product Development

Movement

All buildings move. There are a variety of causes of building movement, and the exterior walls must accommodate all of them. Movement can be a result of wind loads, temperature changes, moisture, earthquakes, differential movement of building materials, and deflection of the structure, both immediate and long term.

Building materials expand and contract with changes in temperature as noted in Chap. 33. The amount of movement is dependent on the material's coefficient of thermal expansion and length. An aluminum curtain wall system will change dimension to a much greater degree than a masonry wall.

Moisture can cause some material to change size to such an extent that if the change is not accounted for, damage can occur. Wood, of course, swells when wet, so siding or a structure exposed to the weather must be protected with coatings, or an allowance must be made for the amount of movement expected. Even changes in humidity levels can cause wood members to expand and contract.

Differential movement of materials is another important concern. Brick will swell and expand at a different rate than a concrete block backing wall. Metal windows will move in response to wind and temperature changes more than the concrete wall they are anchored to. An aluminum curtain wall will change size much more than the steel frame it is attached to. These examples are just a few of the many situations where differential movement can cause problems.

The deflection of both the structure and the attached exterior wall is often overlooked. For example, a masonry wall laid up to the underside of a beam or floor can buckle under dead loading or long-term deflection. There should always be some method of providing for this kind of movement. The compressible expansion joint shown in Fig. 43.8, for example, allows for minor deflection of the steel angle above as well as provides for expansion of the brick below.

The methods of dealing with all the types of building movement mentioned in this chapter are varied, depending on the material and the type and amount of movement expected. Following are a few general guidelines.

First, there must be *through-building expansion joints* to accommodate large-scale movement of portions of the entire building. These are needed in large buildings where there is a change in height, structural system, or major materials, or where differential movement might be expected between various parts of the building. For example, a parking structure connected to an office tower would probably require a building expansion joint between the two structures.

Second, there must be *through-wall expansion joints* to allow for movement in wall sections caused by temperature, moisture, differential movement, and other forces. These are usually made by separating the materials structurally, but providing for weatherproofing.

One example of a vertical masonry expansion joint is shown in Fig. 43.10. The individual brick walls are securely anchored to the concrete structural frame, but the joint allows each to move independently in the direction parallel to the wall. The dovetail anchors allow for minor movement in the direction perpendicular to the wall. The joint filler and sealant accommodate expansion and contraction while providing a tight seal.

Figure 43.10
Typical Horizontal Attachment of Masonry to Primary Structure

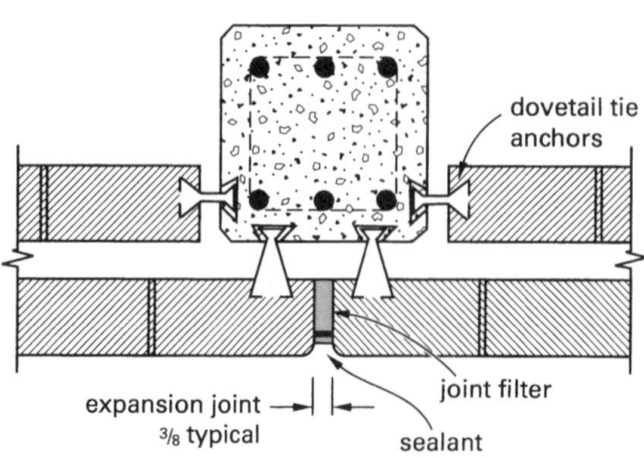

Third, *construction joints* must be used to separate one type of material from another. These joints allow for differential movement as well as provide for clearance when one building component is installed within another. For example, the caulked joint between a wood door frame and a brick wall allows the frame to shrink and swell and allows the brick to move slightly without causing damage to either material.

44 LATERAL FORCES—WIND

Nomenclature

C	chord force	lbf	M	diaphragm moment	ft-lbf
d	depth of building	ft	P	design wind pressure	lbf/ft^2
f	load on individual building element	lbf/ft	v	unit shear stress	lbf/ft
L	length of building	ft	V_s	total shear	lbf

BASIC PRINCIPLES

Wind is air in motion. The movement of the atmosphere is caused by differences in the temperature of air over various parts of the globe. These temperature differences are produced by the uneven absorption and reradiation of heat from the sun as it strikes the air, water vapor, and different earth surfaces.

As warm air rises near the equator, it forms jet streams that move toward the colder, denser air of the polar regions. Some of the air descends in the temperate regions, forming high pressure systems, and then splits, some of it moving north and south closer to the earth. On a global scale, the winds caused by these temperature differences are further affected by the rotation of the earth, resulting in a worldwide wind pattern that is generally predictable from season to season.

On a smaller scale, wind is affected by topography and local climatic conditions. For example, the shores of the Great Lakes have unusual winds, unlike the surrounding country, as do the areas along the eastern front range of the Rocky Mountains in Colorado.

The Effect of Wind on Buildings

The primary effects of wind on buildings are the lateral forces it places on the exterior cladding and lateral forces on the entire structure. As mentioned in Chap. 33, wind can cause a direct, positive pressure as well as a suction, or negative pressure. The exact location of the negative pressure depends on the configuration of the building but most often occurs on the leeward side and frequently occurs on the sides parallel to the wind direction. See Fig. 44.1. It also occurs on the roof, whether flat or sloped.

Smaller, localized areas on a building are also subject to specific pressures that can exceed the pressure on the main body of the structure. This occurs at the building corners, under eaves, on parapets, and elsewhere.

A building's shape or the locations of several buildings in a group can be subject to unusual wind forces that may not affect the structural design as much as the comfort of people and use of the building. Figure 44.1, for example, shows the funneling effect of a small opening. Similar conditions can be produced by two or more buildings placed near one another. The high-speed, localized winds produced can make outdoor plazas and building entries unpleasant at best and unusable at worst. In many cases, wind tunnel testing is required to determine the precise nature of wind around buildings.

Figure 44.1 Forces on a Building Due to Wind

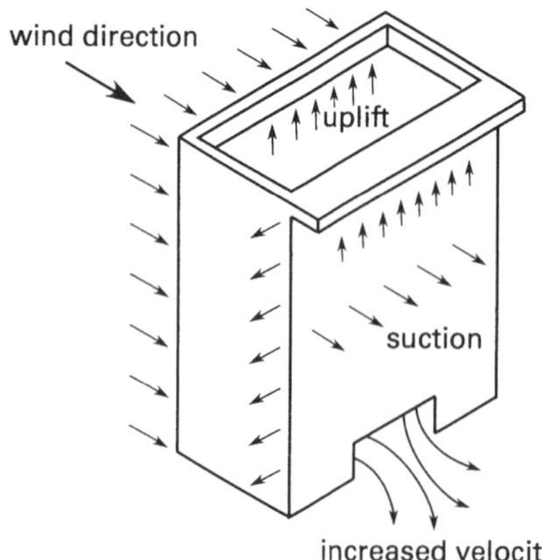

Another effect of concern to architects is the drift, or lateral displacement, of a building when subjected to wind forces. Excessive drift can damage brittle or tightly attached exterior materials and can affect the comfort of the occupants near the top of a tall building, and so it must be minimized. Maximum drift should be limited to $^1/_{500}$ of the building's height, and drift between adjacent stories should be limited to 0.0025 times the story height.

Wind can cause a potentially damaging dynamic load on a building, called a *resonant load* or *oscillating load*, and can result in the building oscillating side to side perpendicular to the direction of the wind. Dynamic loads can also be induced when repeated gusts of wind strike a building at the same rate as the fundamental period of the building. The *fundamental period* is the time it takes the structure to complete one full swing from side to side. The

American Society of Civil Engineers standard ASCE/SEI 7, *Minimum Design Loads for Buildings and Other Structures*, recognizes these potential problems and requires that structures sensitive to dynamic effects be designed in accordance with approved national standards, which usually means wind tunnel testing.

Wind Measurement

Wind speed is measured in several different forms. One of the most common methods is called the *fastest-mile wind*. This is the average speed of a column of air 1 mile long that passes over a given point. Using this method eliminates the effect of sudden, short-term gusts. This type of wind speed is measured with an anemometer.

The value used in designing buildings and other structures is the *three-second peak gust wind*. This is the maximum 3 sec peak gust speed recorded at 33 ft above the ground. The ASCE/SEI 7 wind speed corresponds to an ultimate wind speed that would occur approximately every 700 years. The basic wind speeds used for determining wind pressures on buildings are given in the code. Because friction against the ground affects wind speed, in order to establish some uniformity in measurement and reporting, the values shown are taken at 10 m above the ground. Linear interpolation between wind speed contours is acceptable.

Some areas on the map in the code are designated as special wind regions. These are locales where topography and conditions are so variable that wind speeds are determined by local records and experience or are individually set by the building official.

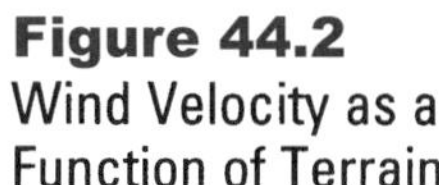

Figure 44.2
Wind Velocity as a Function of Terrain

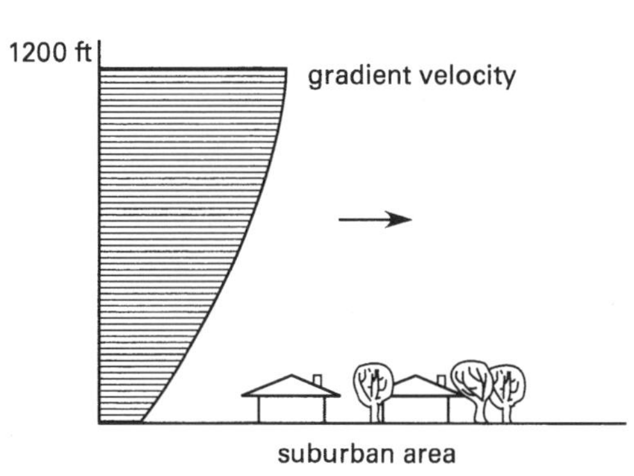

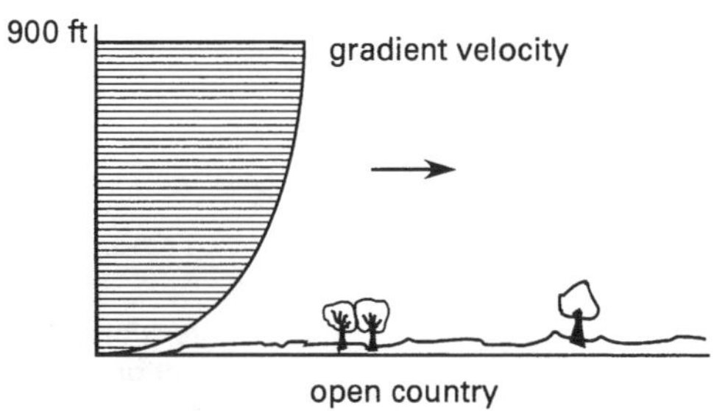

Variables Affecting Wind Loading

One of the primary factors affecting wind speed is the friction caused by the ground. Since wind acts like water or any other fluid, its speed is reduced when it is in contact with or near other surfaces. There are three basic surface conditions for the purpose of building design: *open country*, *suburban areas*, and *metropolitan areas*. Open country results in the most severe wind conditions because there is nothing to slow the movement of air.

In each of three cases, wind speed is slowest right at ground level and gradually increases with height until its gradient height is reached. *Gradient height* is that height above which the friction from the ground and other obstructions no longer affects wind speed. This height is 900 ft for open country, 1200 ft for suburban areas, and 1500 ft for metropolitan areas. See Fig. 44.2.

Below the gradient height, wind speed can be calculated at any given elevation according to a formula that includes the factors of wind pressure at 10 m elevation, a velocity pressure coefficient, and a gust response factor. However, for most building design purposes, ASCE/SEI 7 simplifies the effects of height and surface exposure into one factor.

Product Development

Surrounding buildings also affect the wind speed, by either reducing it with shielding effects or increasing it by funneling it between narrow openings. ASCE/SEI 7 does not allow for any reduction in wind pressure due to the shielding effect of adjacent structures. However, if wind tunnel tests are conducted on a model of a proposed building, any increases in wind pressure on the building due to adjacent conditions would be taken into account.

DESIGN OF WIND-RESISTING STRUCTURES

Once the wind forces have been calculated for the various surfaces and components of a building, their distribution to the structural elements must be determined, and then suitable sizes and connections of the structure must be designed to resist the wind forces. Before reviewing some of the specific design methods, it is necessary to understand the basics of lateral load distribution and some of the concepts of shape and framing methods used to resist both wind and earthquake forces.

Figure 44.3 Diaphragm Loading

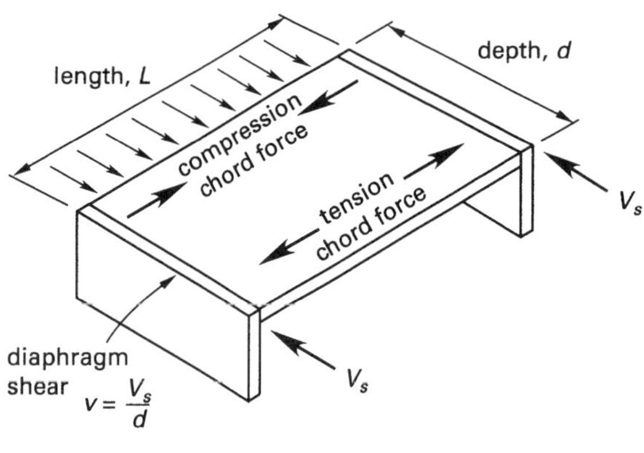

(a) diaphragm loads

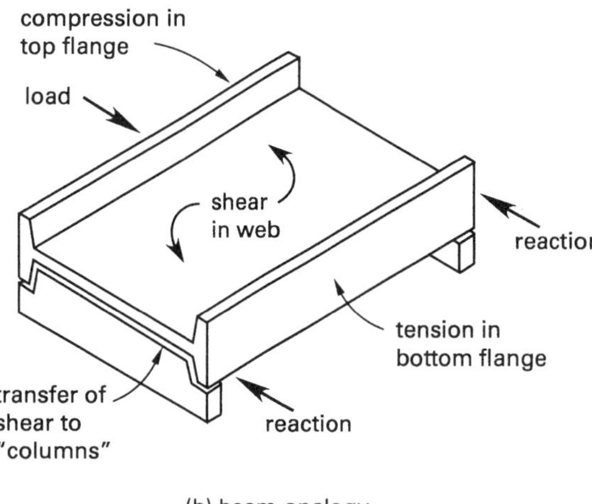

(b) beam analogy

Lateral Force Distribution

When wind strikes the sides of a building, the pressures are transferred through the exterior cladding to the points of connections with the floors and roof. The horizontal surfaces of floors and roof act as diaphragms to transfer the forces to the lateral-force-resisting elements, which can be the side walls of the building, interior walls, or the structural frame. Walls designed to carry lateral loads are called *shear walls* because they transfer the horizontal shear to the foundations of the building. Column and beam lines designed to carry wind loads are called *bents*. Figure 44.3 shows a simplified diagram of the transfer of lateral forces using shear walls.

It is helpful to conceptualize the diaphragm as a beam laid on its side, viewing the floor or roof as the web of the beam and the windward and leeward edges as the top and bottom flanges of the beam. The beam spans between the two end walls (or intermediate shear walls), which can be imagined as columns that carry the load to the foundations. Just as with a beam, there is compression in the top (the side facing the wind) and tension in the bottom (the side away from the wind). These edges, called the *chords*, will be discussed in more detail in a later section.

When designing a building to resist lateral forces, all of these components must be examined: the shear in the diaphragm, the chord forces, the shear walls, and all of the connections.

Example 44.1

A one-story office building 13 ft high, 150 ft long, and 75 ft wide with a flat roof has two 75 ft end walls acting as shear walls. Assuming the wind force is applied perpendicular to the length of the building, determine the total force each shear wall must resist and the stress per linear foot along the shear walls that the roof diaphragm must transfer to the shear walls.

Solution

The building and a wall section are shown diagrammatically in the following figures. The wind load on the roof results from the wind pressure from the midpoint of the wall to the top of the roof.

The wind pressure was calculated to be 6.83 psf on the windward side of the building. Because the structure is less than 60 ft high, the negative pressure on the leeward side must be included. These pressures are also shown in the following figure showing the wall section. The load per foot of length on the roof is the pressure multiplied by one-half the height of the building.

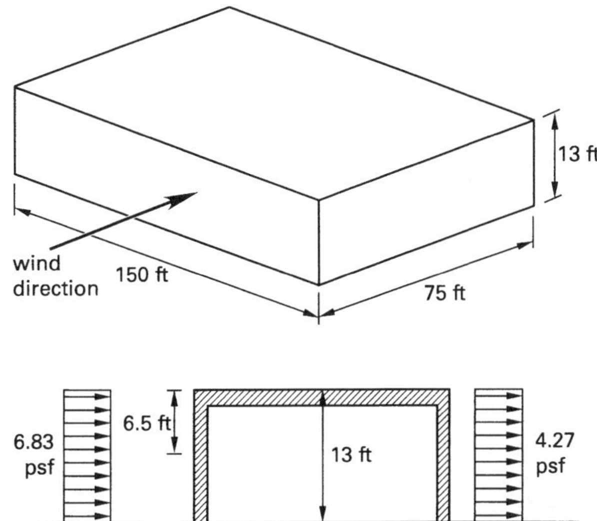

building section

Windward roof load is calculated as follows.

$$\left(6.83\ \frac{\text{lbf}}{\text{ft}^2}\right)(6.5\ \text{ft}) = 44.4\ \text{plf}$$

Leeward roof load is calculated as follows.

$$\left(4.27\ \frac{\text{lbf}}{\text{ft}^2}\right)(6.5\ \text{ft}) = 27.8\ \text{plf}$$

This is a total of 72.2 plf.

The total shear force each wall must resist is found by taking the total load per foot times the length of the building and dividing by two because there are only two walls.

$$\begin{aligned} V_s &= \frac{fL}{2} \\ &= \frac{\left(72.2\ \frac{\text{lbf}}{\text{ft}}\right)(150\ \text{ft})}{2} \\ &= 5415\ \text{lbf} \end{aligned}$$

The unit shear stress is the total shear distributed along the depth of the building.

$$\begin{aligned} v &= \frac{V_s}{d} = \frac{5415\ \text{lbf}}{75\ \text{ft}} \\ &= 72.2\ \text{plf} \end{aligned}$$

Building Shape and Framing Methods

Some building shapes and framing systems are more resistant to wind forces than others. The first consideration in designing a structure to resist wind is the plan shape of the building. Rectangular shapes have a tendency to block more wind than round and tapered shapes, but they are also usually more functional in terms of space planning and are generally less expensive to construct.

Rectangular shapes, however, do allow for some adjustment in planning to make them more efficient. Consider the two building shapes shown diagrammatically in Fig. 44.4 with the wind coming from an assumed direction. Building A is rectangular in plan, while building B is square in plan. Both buildings have the same height and floor area, but building B is more efficient in resisting wind for two reasons.

Figure 44.4
Effect of Building Shape on Efficiency

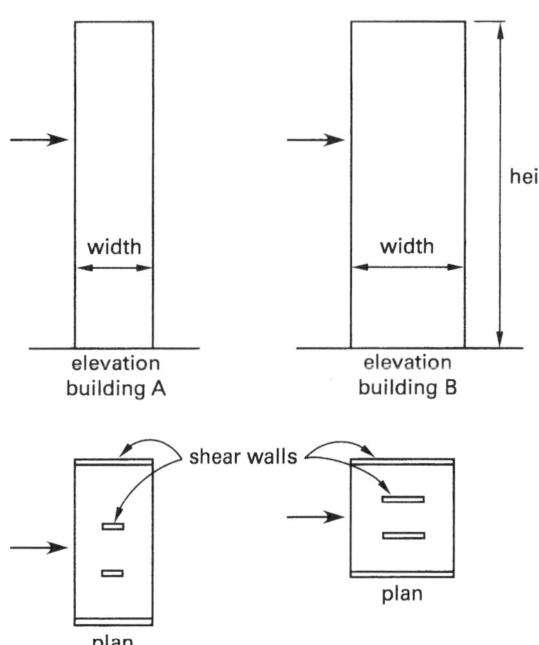

First, the surface area of building B facing the wind is less than that of building A, so the total force on the structural system will be less. Secondly, building B's increased width allows for deeper shear walls and a reduction in the height-to-width ratio. Since shear walls act as beams cantilevered out of the ground, the deeper section is more efficient and requires less structural material to resist the forces.

However, if the length-to-width ratio is increased enough, the basic rigidity in the long dimension will distribute the wind forces among the normal structural elements enough so that special wind bracing will not be required; it will only be necessary in the short dimension.

Framing methods are the second consideration that determines a building's inherent resistance to lateral loads. The illustrations in Fig. 44.5 show some of the basic types of steel framing systems that are used to resist both wind and earthquake loads.

The simplest is the *moment-resisting frame*. See Fig. 44.5(a). With this system, moment-resisting connections are used between columns and beams as discussed in the section on connections. The connections may consist of simple welded joints or may include small brackets when larger loads are involved. This system is useful for low-rise buildings and high-rise buildings under 30 stories. Above this height, the wind loads cannot be efficiently resisted without additional types of bracing.

Knee bracing, as shown in Fig. 44.5(b), is an economical way to provide rigidity to a steel frame, whether it is a one-story industrial building or a large high-rise. The bracing struts are usually short enough that they can be concealed above a suspended ceiling if appearance is a concern.

Two of the most common types of lateral bracing for tall structures are the *X-brace* and the *K-brace* or *chevron brace*. See Fig. 44.5(c) and Fig. 44.5(d). They are usually placed in a central set of bays in a building's structural framework and act as vertical trusses cantilevered out of the ground. The diagonal members can be designed primarily as tension members to minimize their size. With this approach, it is assumed that when the wind loads the building from one side, one of the braces is in tension and the other is not stressed. When the building is loaded from the opposite side, the stresses in the diagonal members reverse. Although both systems are very efficient, the K-bracing system results in less horizontal drift because the diagonal members are shorter and, therefore, elongate less under stress.

The *portal frame* system illustrated in Fig. 44.5(e) is composed of trusses at each floor level with knee braces connecting the truss to the columns. It is not used very much unless the trusses are also used to support the vertical loads of the floor system or the roof of a one-story building.

As lateral loads increase and buildings become taller, the *framed tube* system (see Fig. 44.5(f)) is often used. This system creates a large, hollow tube cantilevered from the ground. It is built of closely spaced exterior columns and beams that are rigidly connected to form a very efficient, stiff structure.

The *trussed tube* concept shown in Fig. 44.5(g) uses a combination of rigid frame and diagonal braces on the exterior wall. The X-braces span from 5 to 10 floors and result in a structure very resistant to lateral loads. For additional strength and reduced drift, the exterior walls can be sloped slightly like the John Hancock Tower in Chicago.

Finally, a steel frame can be used in conjunction with concrete *shear walls* as shown in Fig. 44.5(h). The steel frame carries most of the vertical loads while the concrete shear walls transmit the lateral forces to the foundation. This system is frequently used because the concrete shear walls can easily be a part of the core of the building, enclosing elevators, stairways, and mechanical duct space. For added efficiency, the shape of the concrete walls can be varied to suit the structural needs of the building, forming H- or T-shaped sections so there is rigidity in both directions.

There are many variations to these basic types of framing systems. The bundled tube concept used for the Sears Tower in Chicago, for example, extends the framed tube idea by grouping nine tubes together. Other systems include belt trusses at intermediate floors and buildings with tapered profiles.

Framing systems for concrete structures follow some of the same approaches as steel with a few variations owing to the nature of the material.

Rigid frame structures can be built out of concrete, but moment-resisting connections between columns and beams are not as easy to make, so these building systems are limited to 20 to 30 stories.

For greater resistance, rigid frames are combined with concrete shear walls that are designed to take the majority of the lateral forces. Frame walls can also be used with shear walls so the two act together in resisting wind and earthquake loads.

Figure 44.5
Framing Systems to Resist Lateral Loads

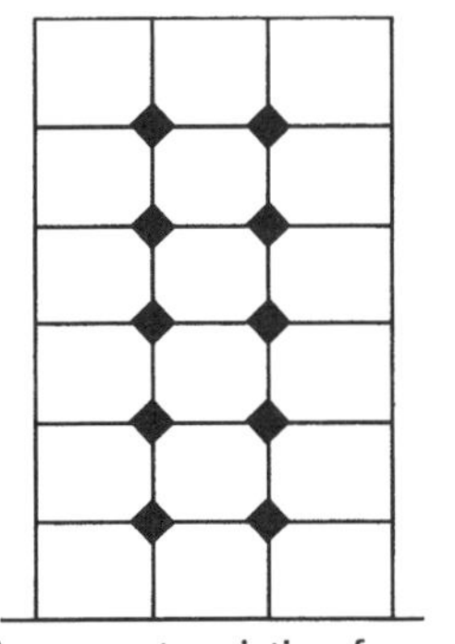
(a) moment-resisting frame

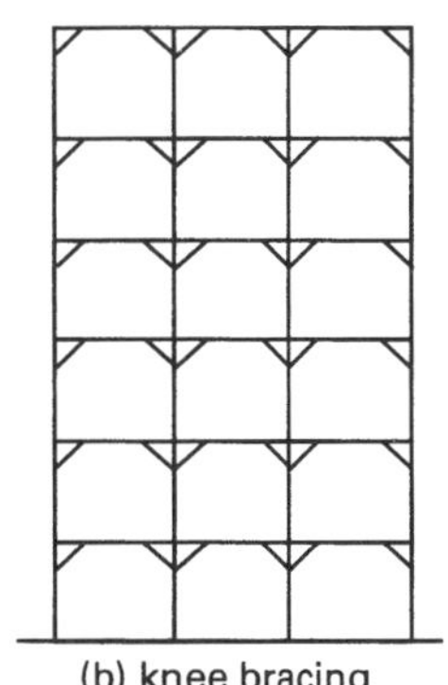
(b) knee bracing

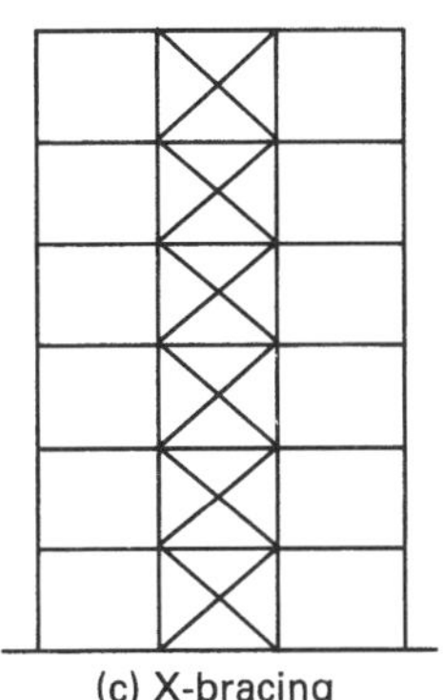
(c) X-bracing

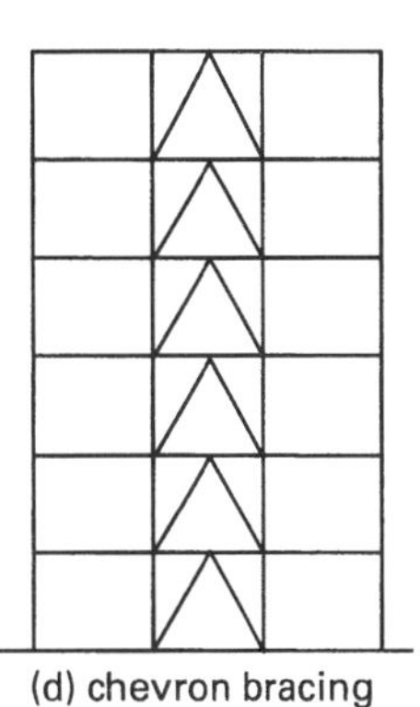
(d) chevron bracing

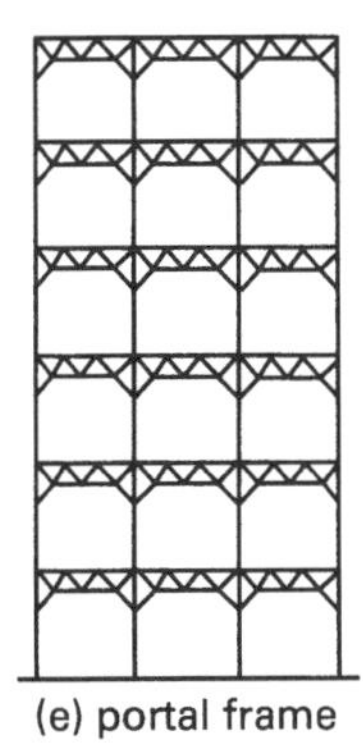
(e) portal frame

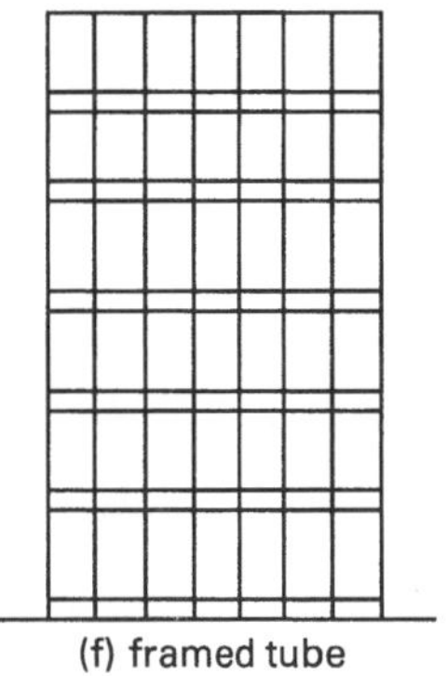
(f) framed tube

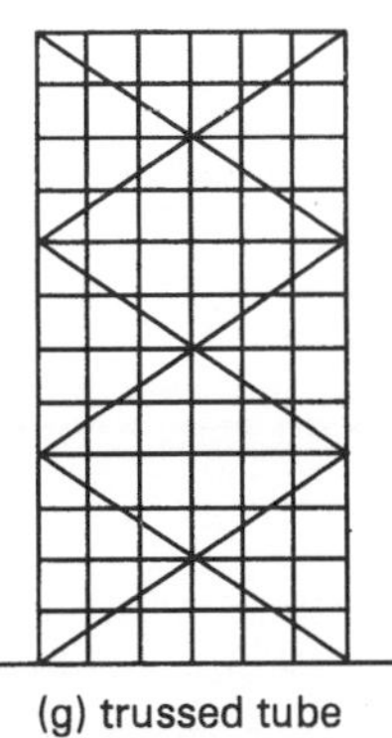
(g) trussed tube

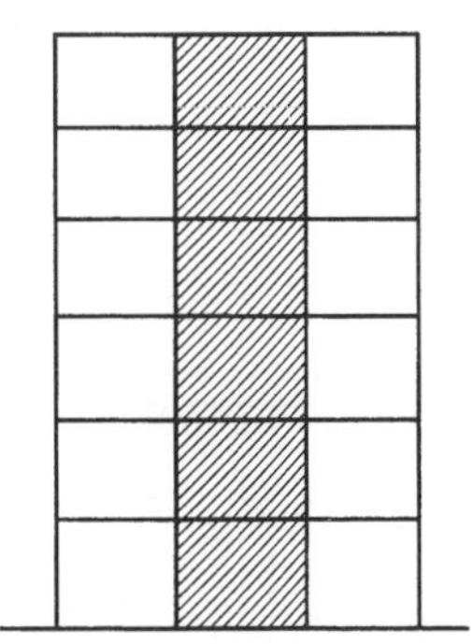
(h) shear walls

Product Development

Framed tubes can be built out of concrete as well as steel. Like steel structures, these are buildings with closely spaced exterior columns rigidly connected with the beams. Such a building also acts as a large tube cantilevered from the ground. When this idea is extended, the system becomes a tube-within-a-tube system where an additional tube of closely spaced interior columns is attached to the exterior grouping with a rigid floor at each level. This is one of the most efficient kinds of high-rise concrete structures, exemplified by Water Tower Place in Chicago.

Diaphragm Design

A diaphragm must be able to resist the lateral loads placed on it without excessive deformation or failure. It must be designed to act as a unit so the forces can be transferred to the shear walls. Horizontal diaphragms can be constructed of plywood, particleboard, concrete, steel decking, and combinations of these materials. Each material or combination has its own load-carrying capacity as a diaphragm member.

Chord Force

As shown in Fig. 44.3, wind loading along a floor or roof of a building produces a compression and tension force in the diaphragm, just like in the top and bottom flanges of a beam. This force, distributed along the depth of the diaphragm, is known as the *chord force* and is used to determine the kind of connection that is needed between the diaphragm and the shear walls in order to transfer the lateral load.

Since the diaphragm acts like a simple, uniformly loaded beam when it is between two shear walls, the chord force can be found by first determining the moment at the edges of the diaphragm using the formula: $wl^2/8$. Then, the chord force is the moment divided by the depth of the diaphragm.

$$C = \frac{M}{d} \qquad 44.1$$

Example 44.2

Find the chord force for the roof in Ex. 44.1.

Solution

As calculated in Ex. 44.1, the total force on the roof is 72.2 plf, the length of the building is 150 ft, and the building depth is 75 ft.

The moment is

$$\begin{aligned} M &= \frac{\left(72.2\ \frac{\text{lbf}}{\text{ft}}\right)(150\ \text{ft})^2}{8} \\ &= 203{,}060\ \text{ft-lbf} \end{aligned}$$

The chord force, using Eq. 44.1, is

$$\begin{aligned} C &= \frac{203{,}060\ \text{ft-lbf}}{75\ \text{ft}} \\ &= 2707\ \text{lbf} \end{aligned}$$

Shear Walls and Overturning

Once the wind forces have been transferred through the diaphragm and chords into the shear wall, the shear wall must transfer the forces to the foundation. In addition, the shear walls and the entire building must resist the tendency for the structure to overturn due to the moment caused by the lateral force. Finally, the shear wall must be attached to the foundation and footings in such a way as to prevent the entire building from sliding, and the footings and foundation system must be designed to resist the additional loads (caused by the overturning moment), which are added to the simple vertical forces of dead and live loads.

The methods of analysis and design for shear walls are complex and beyond the scope of this book, but the following example will illustrate some of the basic principles.

Example 44.3

Considering the same hypothetical building discussed in the previous examples, assuming the shear walls are constructed of 8 in lightweight aggregate concrete block (35 psf) with 30% open area for windows, find the total shear forces in one of the end walls and the overturning moment.

Solution

The figure shows the loads on the shear wall. The load on the roof is the load per linear foot times the length divided by 2.

$$f = \frac{\left(72.2\ \frac{\text{lbf}}{\text{ft}}\right)(150\ \text{ft})}{2} = 5415\ \text{lbf}$$

These are the loads that would be used to design the structure of the shear wall, regardless of what material was used.

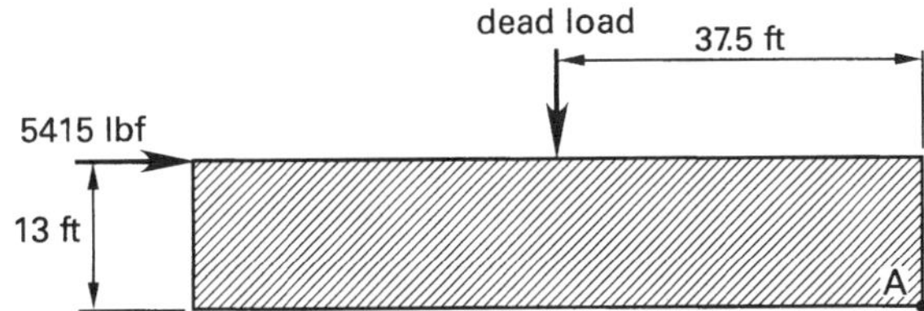

The overturning moment is important to calculate because the building code requires that the resisting moment developed by the dead load on the shear wall be 1.5 times the overturning moment caused by the wind. In this example, the overturning moment is the force at the roof multiplied by the length of the moment arm.

$$\begin{aligned} M &= (5415\ \text{lbf})(13\ \text{ft}) \\ &= 70{,}395\ \text{ft-lbf} \end{aligned}$$

The required dead load moment must be

$$(1.5)(70{,}395\ \text{ft-lbf}) = 105{,}590\ \text{ft-lbf}$$

The actual weight of the wall allowing for 30% void is

$$(75\ \text{ft})(13\ \text{ft})\left(35\ \frac{\text{lbf}}{\text{ft}^2}\right)(0.7) = 23{,}887\ \text{lbf}$$

This weight is assumed to act at the midpoint of the wall, so the moment arm is 37.5 ft. The resisting moment is

$$\begin{aligned} M &= (23{,}887\ \text{lbf})(37.5\ \text{ft}) \\ &= 895{,}781\ \text{ft-lbf} \end{aligned}$$

This is more than adequate to resist the wind overturning moment without using special anchors attaching the walls to the foundation.

Drift

Drift is the lateral displacement of a building caused by a lateral load from a true vertical line. For wind loading, the local code governs. It is generally accepted that the drift of one story relative to an adjacent story may not exceed 0.0025 times the story height, and some municipalities enforce more stringent limits. In the previous example, if the story height is 13 ft, the maximum drift is

$$(0.0025)(13\ \text{ft})\left(12\ \frac{\text{in}}{\text{ft}}\right) = 0.39\ \text{in}$$

Connections

Connections are a critical part of any structural frame that resists lateral loads. These include connections of curtain wall to frame, beams to columns, diaphragm to shear wall, and primary structural frame to the foundation, among others. Moment-resisting connections are fairly common because they occur somewhere in practically any structure designed for lateral forces. Four of the more common types of connections used in steel framed buildings are shown in Fig. 44.6. In all connections, the resisting moment increases with increased distance between the centroids of the top and bottom portions of the connection.

Figure 44.6 Beam-to-Column Connections

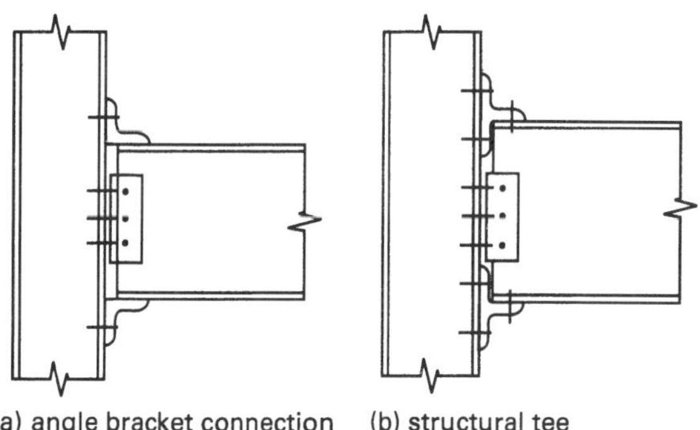

(a) angle bracket connection (b) structural tee

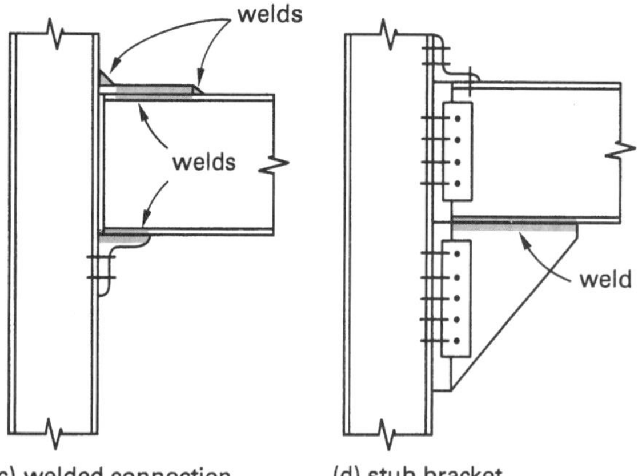

(c) welded connection (d) stub bracket

One type of connection that has little moment resistance is the angle bracket connection, shown in Fig. 44.6(a). This is a typical steel frame semirigid connection. Because the angles are relatively flexible, very little moment can be transferred from beam to column. The structural tee connection shown in Fig. 44.6(b) is sometimes used instead. The increased rigidity of the structural tees can provide a moment-resisting joint.

In order to minimize the number of pieces and ensure a good moment-resisting joint, beams and columns are often welded as shown in Fig. 44.6(c). There is usually an angle seat to hold the beam in place during erection and to carry the shear loads, but the welded plates transfer the moment.

For an even more rigid connection, a small stub bracket as shown in Fig. 44.6(d) can be used. The triangular shape is structurally efficient and usually can be concealed by the finish column cover or within a suspended ceiling. There are many variations of this connection detail; usually, it includes a combination of bolted and welded joints.

45

LATERAL FORCES—EARTHQUAKES

Nomenclature

R	response modification coefficient	–
S_{D1}	design spectral response at period of 1 sec	–
S_{DS}	design spectral response at short period	–
T	building fundamental period of vibration	sec
T_s	ratio of S_{D1}/S_{DS}	sec
V	total design lateral force or base shear	lbf

Although a great deal has been learned about earthquakes and their effects on buildings during the last 50 years, seismic design is still an inexact science. Because seismic design deals with dynamic forces rather than static forces, and because of the many variables involved, it is often difficult to precisely predict the performance of a building in an earthquake and provide the best possible design to resist the resulting lateral forces.

Another difficulty with seismic design is that the forces produced by an earthquake are so great that no building can economically and reasonably be designed to completely resist all loads in a major earthquake without damage. Building codes and analytical methods of design are, therefore, a compromise between what could resist all earthquakes and what is reasonable. Because of this, the current approach in designing earthquake-resistant structures is that they should first of all not collapse during major seismic activity. Additionally, the components of buildings should not cause other damage or personal injury even though they may be structurally damaged themselves. Finally, structures should be able to withstand minor earthquakes without significant damage.

The analytic methods of analysis and design of earthquake-resistant structures are complex, even with the equivalent lateral force method allowed by the *International Building Code* (IBC). However, a great deal of resistance is provided by the basic configuration and structural system of a building. The design of buildings for earthquake loads requires an early and close collaboration between the architect and engineer to arrive at the optimum structural design while still satisfying the functional and aesthetic needs of the client.

This chapter will discuss some of the basic principles of earthquakes and the primary design and planning guidelines. In addition, a basic review of the static analysis method will be presented along with some simplified problems to help explain the design concepts. However, the complete and detailed design of earthquake-resistant structures is a complex procedure and beyond the scope of this book.

BASIC PRINCIPLES

The IBC provides for several methods of design for seismic forces. These may be categorized into three types of procedures: simplified analysis, equivalent lateral force, and dynamic analysis. The equivalent lateral force method treats the seismic loads as equivalent lateral loads acting on various levels of the building. The total base shear is calculated and then distributed along the height of the building. The dynamic method uses a computer to mathematically model the building so the response of the structure can be studied at each moment in time using an actual or simulated earthquake accelerogram.

The IBC is specific about which analysis method may or must be used. The use of each method is based on the seismic design category and the seismic use group of the structure. These will be discussed in later sections. The simplified analysis can only be used in seismic design category A and in category B for three-story light-framed buildings and other two-story buildings of use group 1. Any structure may be designed using one of the dynamic methods of analysis. The equivalent lateral force method may be used for buildings in seismic design categories A, B, and C. In the following cases, it may also be used for buildings in seismic design categories D, E, and F.

- regular structures with $T < 3.5T_s$
- irregular structures with $T < 3.5T_s$ and having only plan irregularities 2, 3, 4, or 5 or vertical irregularities 4 or 5

All other structures must be designed using a dynamic method of analysis.

Characteristics of Earthquakes

Earthquakes are caused by the slippage of adjacent plates of the earth's crust and the subsequent release of energy in the form of ground waves. Seismology is based on the science of plate tectonics, which proposes that the earth is composed of several very large plates of hard crust many miles thick, riding on a layer of molten rock closer to the earth's core. These plates are slowly moving relative to one another, and over time tremendous stress is built up by friction. Occasionally the two plates slip, releasing the energy we know as earthquakes. One of the best-known boundaries between two plates occurs between the Pacific plate and the North American plate along the coast of California. Earthquakes also occur in midplates, but the exact mechanism, other than fault slippage, is not fully understood.

The plates slip where the stress is at a maximum, usually several miles below the surface of the earth, at a location called the *hypocenter* of the earthquake. The term heard more often is the *epicenter*, which is the point on the earth's surface directly above the hypocenter.

The modified Mercalli intensity scale is a measure of an earthquake's intensity. It is an entirely subjective rating based on the observed damage to structures and other physical effects.

When an earthquake occurs, complex actions are set up. One result is the development of waves that ultimately produce the shaking experienced in a building. There are three types of waves: *P* or *pressure waves*, *S* or *shear waves*, and *surface waves* Pressure waves cause a relatively small movement in the direction of wave travel. Shear waves produce a sideways or up-and-down motion that shakes the ground in three directions. These are the waves that cause the most damage to buildings. Surface waves travel at or near the surface and can cause both vertical and horizontal earth movement.

The ground movement can be measured in three ways: by acceleration, velocity, and displacement. All three occur over time, with most earthquakes lasting only a few seconds. It is the acceleration of the ground that induces forces on a structure.

The interaction of the various waves and ground movement is complex. Not only does the earth move in three directions, but each direction has a different, random acceleration and amplitude. In addition, the movement reverses, creating a vibrating action. Even though there is vertical movement, the IBC allows these forces to be neglected under certain types of seismic design. The weight of a structure is usually enough to resist vertical forces. It is side-to-side movement that causes the most damage.

Measurement of Earthquakes

Earthquake strength is commonly measured in two ways: with the Richter scale and with the modified Mercalli intensity scale. The *Richter scale* measures magnitude as an indirect measure of released energy based on instrument recordings according to certain defined procedures. The scale runs from zero at the low end and is open at the upper end, although the largest earthquake ever recorded had a Richter magnitude of nine.

The scale is logarithmic; each whole number value on the scale represents a tenfold increase in amplitude. In terms of energy released, each scale number represents about 32 times the amount of energy below it.

The *modified Mercalli intensity scale* is a measure of an earthquake's intensity. It is an entirely subjective rating based on the observed damage to structures and other physical effects. The scale ranges from I to XII, with the upper rating being the most severe. Each scale includes a verbal description of the effects and damage of an earthquake.

The modified Mercalli scale is imprecise because it depends on people's observations, but it does provide information on how an earthquake affects structures and how the same earthquake affects areas at different distances from the epicenter, both of which cannot be accounted for with the Richter scale.

Unfortunately for building design, neither scale is useful. This is because neither provides any information on the acceleration or duration of an earthquake, both of which are critical in the analysis and design of structures. However, they are used for risk analysis and determination of seismic zones.

Objective, quantified data useful for building design is provided by the *strong motion accelerograph*. This device measures the acceleration of the ground or a building. The IBC requires that in seismic design categories D, E, and F every building over 6 stories with an aggregate floor area of 60,000 ft^2 or more, and every building over 10 stories regardless of floor area, be provided with not less than three accelerographs. These must be placed in the basement, midportion, and near the top of the building. Some jurisdictions may have additional requirements.

The records obtained by these instruments provide valuable data for research and design of similar buildings in the same geographical area. The acceleration they measure is usually expressed as a fraction of the acceleration of gravity, g, which is 32.2 ft/sec^2. Thus, an earthquake may be recorded as having an acceleration of $0.55g$.

Seismic Design Categories

Based on seismic records, experience, and research, some areas of the United States are determined to have a greater probability of earthquakes than others, and some areas have more severe earthquakes (areas where two major plates abut, for example). This is taken into account by dividing the country into different zones that represent estimates of future earthquake occurrence and strength.

Figure 45.1 Building Motion During an Earthquake

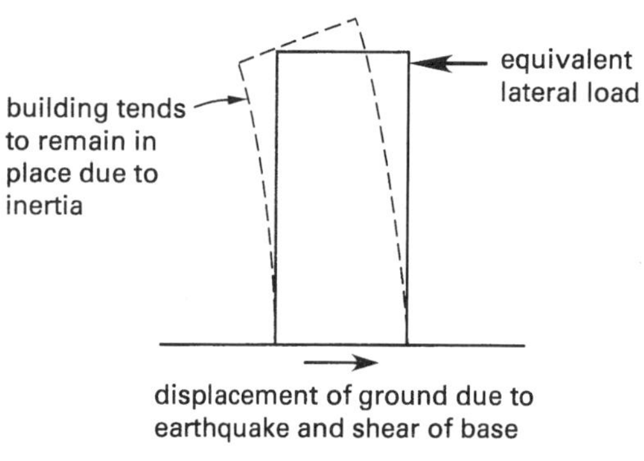
equivalent lateral load
building tends to remain in place due to inertia
displacement of ground due to earthquake and shear of base

(a) response of a building to earthquake

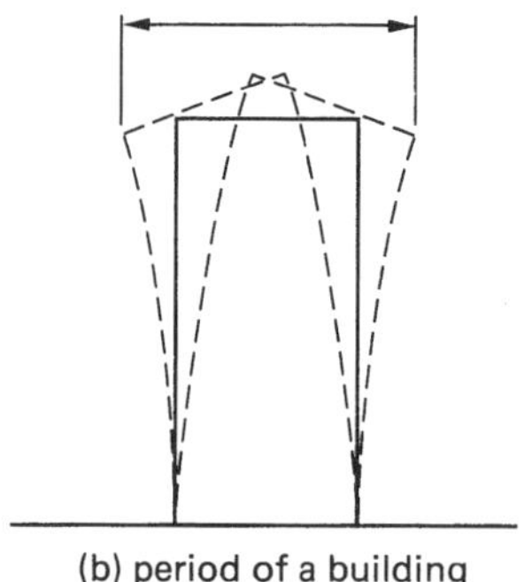
period is time for one complete oscillation of the building

(b) period of a building

The Effect of Earthquakes on Buildings

When an earthquake occurs, the first response of a building is to not move at all due to the inertia of the structure's mass. Almost instantaneously, however, the acceleration of the ground causes the building to move sideways at the base, causing a lateral load on the building and a shear force at the base, as though forces were being applied in opposite directions. See Fig. 45.1. As the direction of the acceleration changes, the building begins to vibrate back and forth.

Theoretically, the force on the building can be found by using Newton's law, which states that force equals mass times acceleration. Since the acceleration is established by the given earthquake, the greater the mass of the building, the greater the force acting on it. However, the acceleration of the building depends on another property of the structure—its natural period.

If a building is deflected by a lateral force such as the wind or an earthquake, it moves from side to side. The period is the time in seconds it takes for a building to complete one full side-to-side oscillation. See Fig. 45.1. The period is dependent on the mass and the stiffness of the building.

In a theoretical, completely stiff building, there is no movement, and the natural period is zero. The acceleration of such an infinitely rigid building is the same as the ground. As the building becomes more flexible, its period increases and the corresponding acceleration decreases. As mentioned previously, as the acceleration decreases, so does the force on the building. Therefore, flexible, long-period buildings have less lateral force induced, and stiff, short-period buildings have more lateral force induced.

As the building moves, the forces applied to it are either transmitted through the structure to the foundation, absorbed by the building components, or released in other ways such as collapse of structural elements.

The goal of seismic design is to build a structure that can safely transfer the loads to the foundation and back to the ground and absorb some of the energy present rather than suffering damage.

The ability of a structure to absorb some of the energy is known as *ductility*, which occurs when the building deflects in the inelastic range without failing or collapsing. The elastic limit, as discussed in Chap. 34 , is the limit beyond which the structure sustains permanent deformation. The greater the ductility of a building, the greater is its capacity to absorb energy.

Ductility varies with the material. Steel is a very ductile material because of its ability to deform under a load above the elastic limit without collapsing. Concrete and masonry, on the other hand, are brittle materials. When they are stressed beyond the elastic limit, they break suddenly and without warning. Concrete can be made more ductile with reinforcement, but at a higher cost.

STRUCTURAL SYSTEMS TO RESIST LATERAL LOADS

The IBC specifies the types of structural systems used to resist seismic loads. The code requires that structural systems be classified as one of the types listed in IBC. In addition to outlining the various types of structural systems, this table gives the R factor used in calculations and the maximum height of each type of structural system. There are four broad categories of systems.

Figure 45.2
Shear Walls

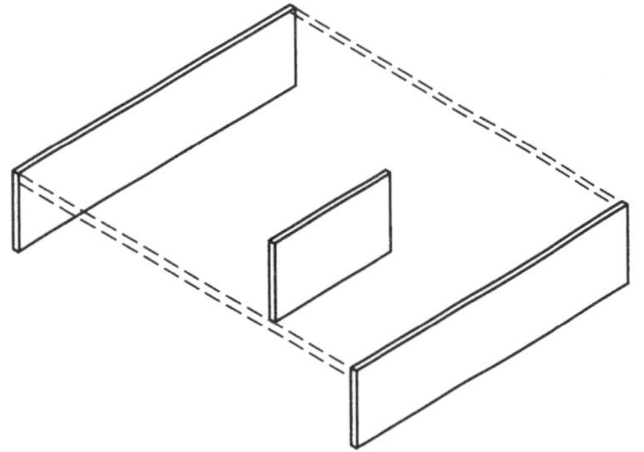

(a) end shear walls and interior shear wall

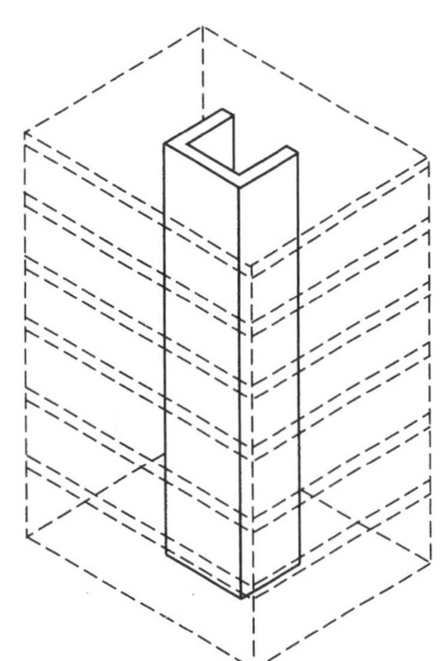

(b) interior shear walls for bracing in two directions

Bearing Wall System

A bearing wall system is a structural system without a complete vertical load-carrying space frame in which the lateral loads are resisted by shear walls or braced frames. Bearing walls or bracing systems provide support for all or most gravity loads. Remember that a space frame is defined as a three-dimensional structural system, without bearing walls, that is comprised of members interconnected such that it functions as a complete, self-contained unit.

A *shear wall* is a vertical structural element that resists lateral forces in the plane of the wall through shear and bending. Such a wall acts as a beam cantilevered out of the ground or foundation, and just as with a beam, part of its strength derives from its depth. Figure 45.2 shows two examples of a shear wall, one in a simple one-story building and another in a multistory building.

In Fig. 45.2(a), the shear walls are oriented in one direction, so only lateral forces in this direction can be resisted. The roof serves as the horizontal diaphragm and must also be designed to resist the lateral loads and transfer them to the shear walls.

Figure 45.2(a) also shows an important aspect of shear walls in particular and vertical elements in general. This is the aspect of symmetry that has a bearing on whether torsional effects will be produced. The shear walls in Fig. 45.2(a) show the shear walls symmetrical in the plane of loading. Torsion will be discussed in a later section.

Figure 45.2(b) illustrates a common use of shear walls at the interior of a multistory building. Because walls enclosing stairways, elevator shafts, and mechanical chases are mostly solid and run the entire height of the building, they are often used for shear walls. Although not as efficient from a strictly structural point of view, interior shear walls do leave the exterior of the building open for windows.

Notice that in Fig. 45.2(b) there are shear walls in both directions, which is a more realistic situation because both wind and earthquake forces need to be resisted in both directions. In this diagram, the two shear walls are symmetrical in one direction, but the single shear wall produces a nonsymmetric condition in the other since it is off center. Shear walls do not need to be symmetrical in a building, but symmetry is preferred to avoid torsional effects.

Figure 45.3
Braced Frames

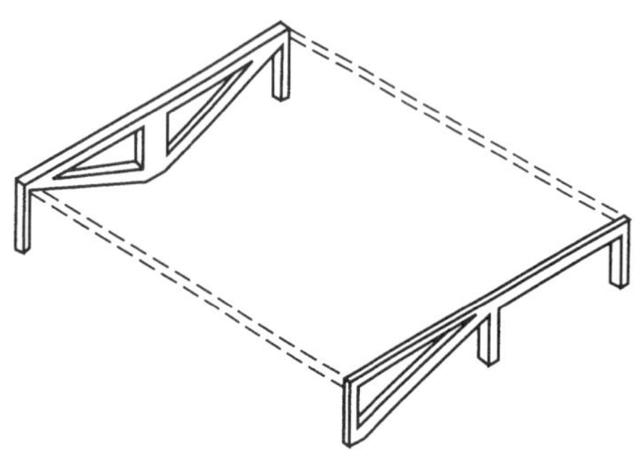

(a) single-story braced frame

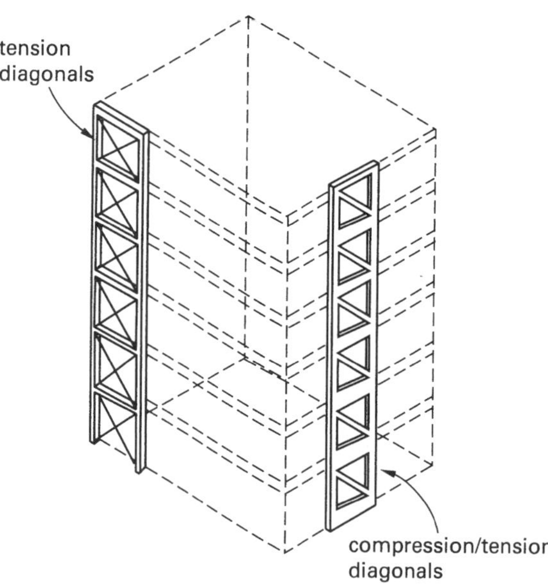

(b) multistory braced frame

Shear walls can be constructed from a variety of materials, but the most common are plywood on wood framing for residential and small commercial buildings, and concrete for larger buildings. Reinforced masonry walls can also be used. Shear walls may have openings in them, but the calculations are more difficult, and a wall's ability to resist lateral loads is reduced depending on the percentage of open area.

Building Frame Systems

A *building frame system* is an essentially complete space frame that provides support for gravity loads in which the lateral loads are resisted by shear walls or braced frames. A *braced frame* is a truss system of the concentric or eccentric type in which the lateral forces are resisted through axial stresses in the members. Just as with a truss, the braced frame depends on diagonal members to provide a load path for lateral forces from each building element to the foundation. Figure 45.3 shows a simple one-story braced frame. At one end of the building two bays are braced, and at the other end only one bay is braced. As with Fig. 45.2, this building is only braced in one direction and uses compression braces because the diagonal member may be either in tension or compression, depending on which way the force is applied.

Figure 45.3 shows two methods of bracing a multistory building. A single diagonal compression member in one bay can be used to brace against lateral loads coming from either direction. Alternately, tension diagonals can be used to accomplish the same result, but they must be run both ways to account for the load coming from either direction.

Braced framing can be placed on the exterior or interior of a building and may be placed in one structural bay or several. In a trussed tube building, the diagonals span between several floors of the building. Obviously, a braced frame can present design problems for windows and doorways, but it is a very efficient and rigid lateral force resisting system.

Moment-Resisting Frame Systems

Moment-resisting frames carry lateral loads primarily by flexure in the members and joints. Joints are designed and constructed so they are theoretically completely rigid, and therefore any lateral deflection of the frame occurs from the bending of columns and beams. The IBC differentiates between three types of moment-resisting frames.

The first type is the special moment-resisting frame, which must be specifically detailed to provide ductile behavior and comply with the provisions of Chap. 19 and Chap. 22 (Concrete and Steel) of the IBC.

The second type is the intermediate moment-resisting frame, which has fewer restrictive requirements than special moment-resisting frames. These cannot be used in seismic design category D, E, or F; however, steel intermediate moment-resisting frames up to 35 ft high may be used in category D.

The third type is the ordinary moment-resisting frame. This is a steel or concrete moment-resisting frame that does not meet the special detailing requirements for ductile behavior. Ordinary steel frames may be used only in seismic design categories A, B, and C, while ordinary concrete frames can be used only in categories A or B.

Moment-resisting frames are more flexible than shear wall structures or braced frames; the horizontal deflection, or drift, is greater. Adjacent buildings cannot be located too close to each other, and special attention must be paid to the eccentricity developed in columns, which increases the column bending stresses.

Two types of moment-resisting frames are shown in Fig. 45.4.

Figure 45.4 Moment-Resisting Frames

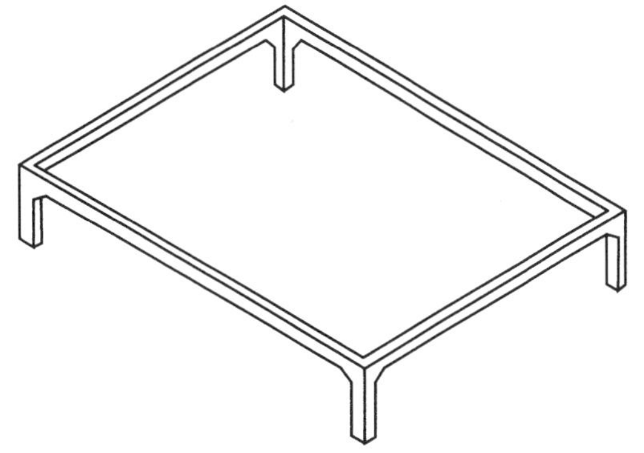

(a) single-story frame

(b) multistory frame

Dual Systems

A *dual system* is a structural system in which an essentially complete frame provides support for gravity loads, and resistance to lateral loads is provided by a specially detailed moment-resisting frame and shear walls or braced frames. The moment-resisting frame must be capable of resisting at least 25% of the base shear, and the two systems must be designed to resist the total lateral load in proportion to their relative rigidities. The moment-resisting frame may be either steel or concrete. Other types of dual systems include the use of eccentrically braced frames and shear wall-frame interactive systems.

Horizontal Elements

In all lateral-force-resisting systems, there must be a way to transmit lateral forces to the vertical resisting elements. This is done with several types of structures, the most common of which is the *diaphragm*. As discussed in Chap. 44, a diaphragm acts as a horizontal beam resisting forces with shear and bending action. Refer to Fig. 44.3.

Figure 45.5
Diaphragm Load Distribution

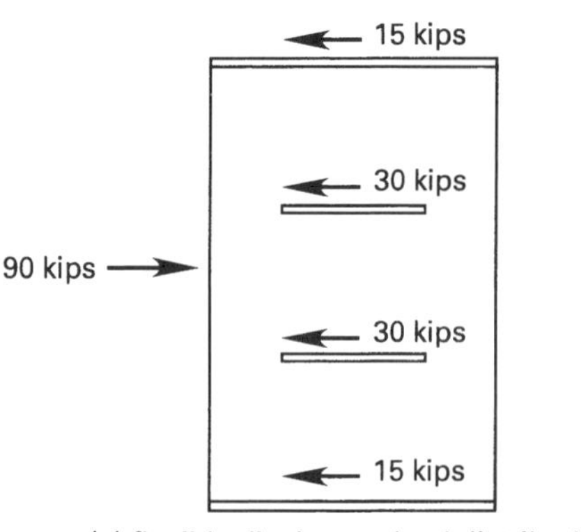

(a) flexible diaphragm load distribution

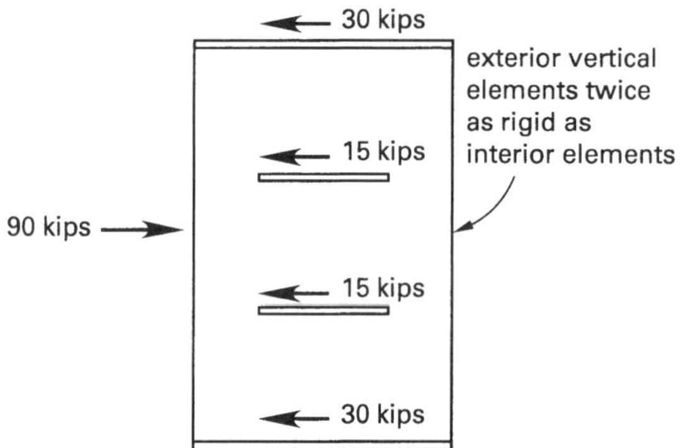

(b) rigid diaphragm load distribution

Other types of horizontal elements include horizontal trussed frames and horizontal moment-resisting frames. There are two types of diaphragms: flexible and rigid. Although no horizontal element is completely flexible or rigid, a distinction is made between the two types because the type affects the way in which lateral forces are distributed.

A *flexible diaphragm* is one that has a maximum lateral deformation more than two times the average story drift of that story. This deformation can be determined by comparing the midpoint in-plane deflection of the diaphragm with the story drift of the adjoining vertical resisting elements under equivalent tributary load. The lateral load is distributed according to tributary areas as shown in Fig. 45.5(a).

With a *rigid diaphragm*, the shear forces transmitted from the diaphragm to the vertical elements will be in proportion to the relative stiffness of the vertical elements (assuming there is no torsion). See Fig. 45.5(b). If the end walls in the diagram are twice as stiff as the interior walls, then one-third of the load is distributed to each end wall and one-third is distributed to the two interior walls and equally divided between them. Figure 45.5(b) shows symmetrically placed shear walls, so the distribution is equal. However, if the vertical resisting elements are asymmetric, the shearing forces are unequal.

Concrete floors are considered rigid diaphragms, as are steel and concrete composite deck construction. Steel decks may be either flexible or rigid, depending on the details of their construction. Wood decks are considered flexible diaphragms.

BUILDING CONFIGURATION

In recent years, there has been increased emphasis on the importance of a building's configuration in resisting seismic forces. Early decisions concerning size, shape, arrangement, and location of major elements can have a significant influence on the performance of a structure. Since the design professional plays a large role in these early decisions, it is imperative that the architect thoroughly understand the concepts involved.

Building configuration refers to the overall building size and shape and the size and arrangement of the primary structural frame, as well as the size and location of the nonstructural components of the building that may affect its structural performance. Significant nonstructural components include such things as heavy nonbearing partitions, exterior cladding, and large weights like equipment or swimming pools.

In ASCE/SEI 7, elements that constitute both horizontal and vertical irregularities are specifically defined, so it is clear which structures must be designed with the dynamic method and which structures may be designed using the static analysis method.

The code states that all buildings must be classified as either regular or irregular. Whether a building is regular or not helps determine if the static method may be used. Irregular structures generally require design by the dynamic method (with exceptions mentioned in the Basic Principles section), and additional detailed design requirements are imposed depending on what type of irregularity exists.

The following sections describe some of the important aspects of building configuration.

Torsion

Lateral forces on a portion of a building are assumed to be uniformly distributed and can be resolved into a single line of action acting on a building. In a similar way, the shear reaction forces produced by the vertical resisting elements can be resolved into a single line of action. For symmetric buildings with vertical resisting elements of equal rigidity, these lines of action pass through the same point as shown diagrammatically in Fig. 45.6(a).

If the shear walls or other vertical elements are not symmetric or are of unequal rigidity, the resultant of their shear resisting forces, the center of rigidity, does not coincide with the applied lateral force. This is shown in Fig. 45.6(b). Since the forces are acting in opposite directions with an eccentricity, torsion force is developed, which is in addition to the lateral load alone.

When the force on a vertical element caused by the eccentricity acts in the same direction as the force caused by the lateral load directly, the forces must be added. However, when the torsional force acts in the opposite direction, one force cannot be subtracted from the other.

The IBC requires that even in symmetrical buildings a certain amount of accidental torsion be planned for. This accounts for the fact that the positions of loads in an occupied building cannot be known for certain. The code requires that the mass at each level is assumed to be displaced from the calculated center of mass in each direction by a distance equal to 5% of the building dimension at that level perpendicular to the direction of the force under consideration. For example, for a building 50 ft wide and 100 ft long, the center of mass for forces acting perpendicular to the 100 ft dimension is offset 5 ft. For forces acting in the other direction, the center of mass is offset $2\frac{1}{2}$ ft.

The importance of understanding the concept of torsion will become apparent in the following sections.

Figure 45.6
Development of Torsion

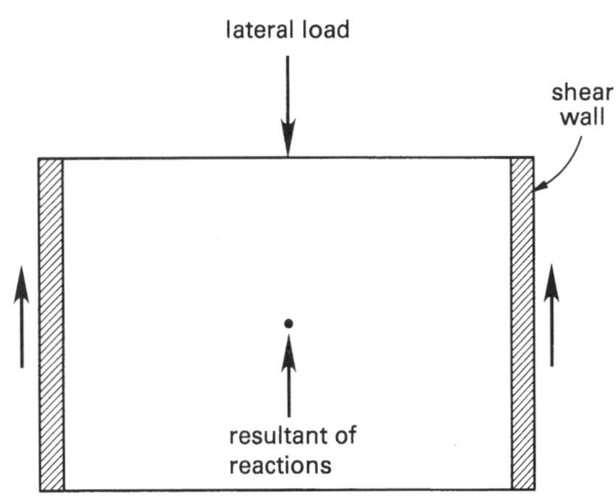

(a) symmetric building

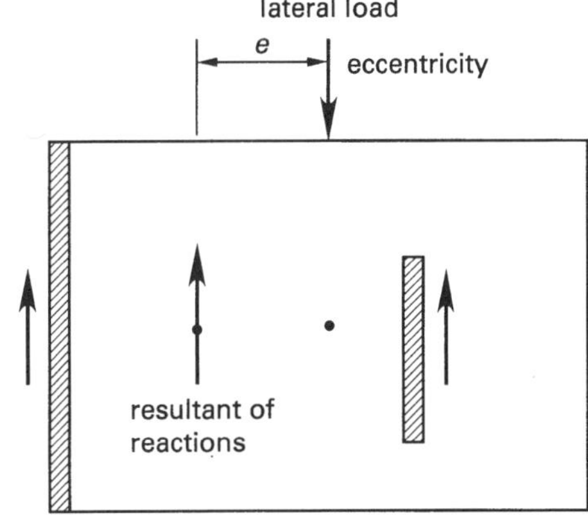

(b) nonsymmetric vertical load-resisting elements

Plan Shape

Irregularities in plan shape can create torsion and concentrations of stress, both of which should be avoided whenever possible. One of the most common and troublesome plan shapes is the reentrant corner. Figure 45.7(a) shows some common varieties of this shape. During an earthquake, the ground motion causes the structure to move in such a way that stress concentrations are developed at the inside corners. See Fig. 45.7(a).

Figure 45.7 Problem Plan Shapes

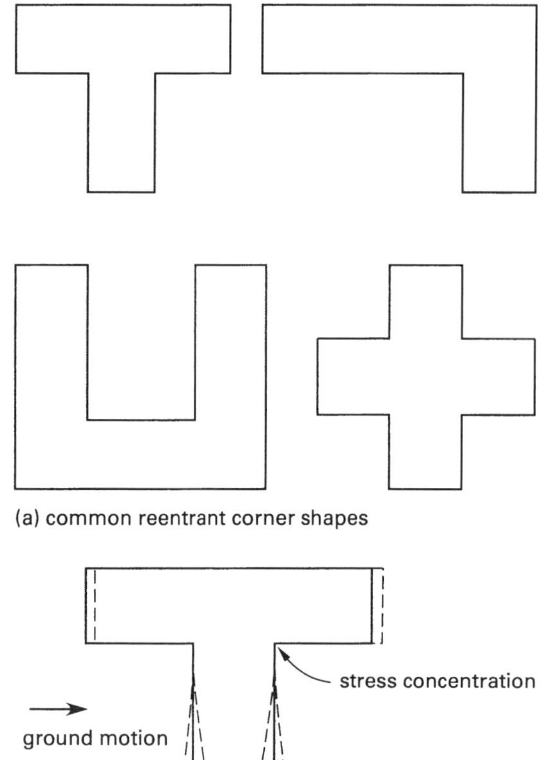

In addition, since the center of mass and the center of rigidity do not coincide, there is an eccentricity established that results in a twisting of the entire structure as discussed in the previous section and shown in Fig. 45.6(b).

Of course, building shape is often dictated by the site, the program, or other requirements beyond the control of the architect or engineer. In the cases where such shapes are unavoidable, there are ways to minimize the problem. The portions of the building can be separated with a seismic joint, they can be tied together across the connection, or the inside corner can be splayed. These design approaches are shown in Fig. 45.8.

A second common problem that arises with building plans is a variation in the stiffness and strength of the perimeter. Even though a building may be symmetric, the distribution of mass and lateral resisting elements may place the centers of mass and rigidity in such a way that torsion is developed. One example of this is shown diagrammatically in Fig. 45.9, where a building has rigid shear walls on three sides but is open in the front.

During an earthquake, the open end of the building acts as a cantilevered beam causing lateral displacement and torsion. There are four possible ways to alleviate the problem. These are shown in Fig. 45.9.

In the first instance, a rigid frame can be constructed with symmetric rigidity, and then the cladding can be made nonstructural. Secondly, a strong, moment-resisting or braced frame can be added that has a stiffness similar to the other walls. Third, shear walls can be added to the front if this does not compromise the function of the building. Finally, for small buildings, the structure can simply be designed to resist the expected torsion forces.

Figure 45.8 Solutions to Reentrant Corners

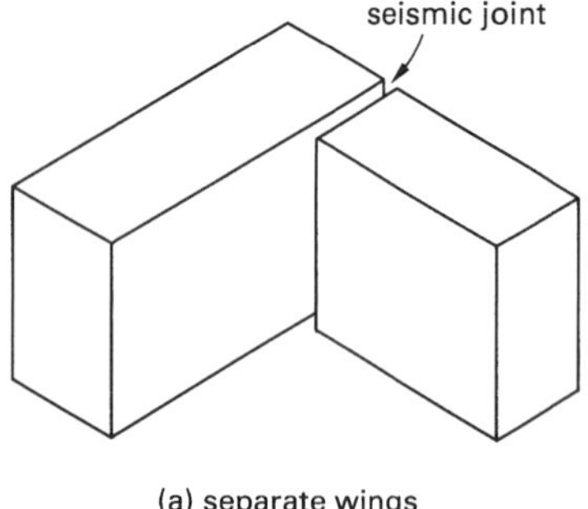

(a) separate wings

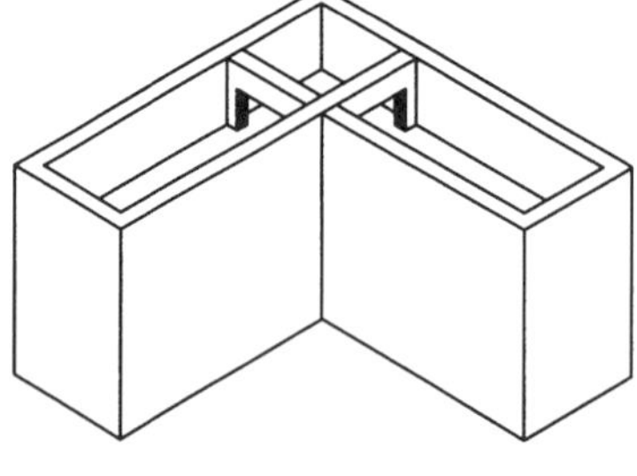

(b) provide strong connection

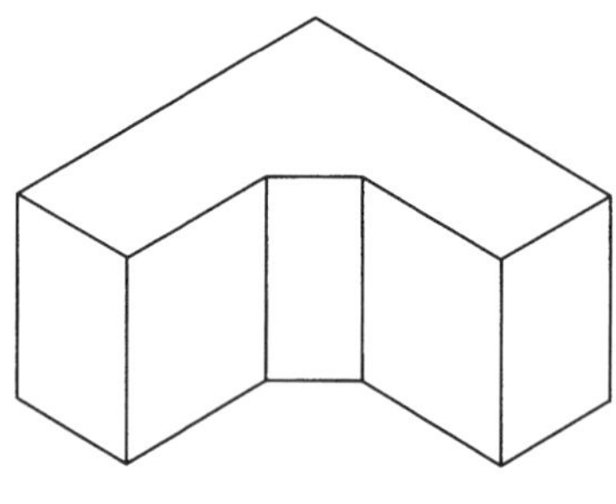

(c) splay corner

Figure 45.9
Variation in Perimeter Stiffness

movement during earthquake

nonstructural cladding

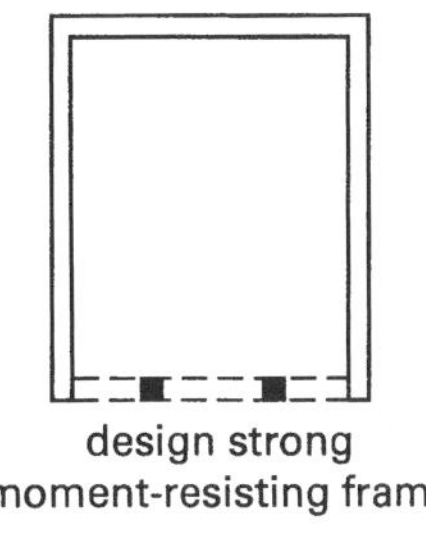
design strong moment-resisting frame

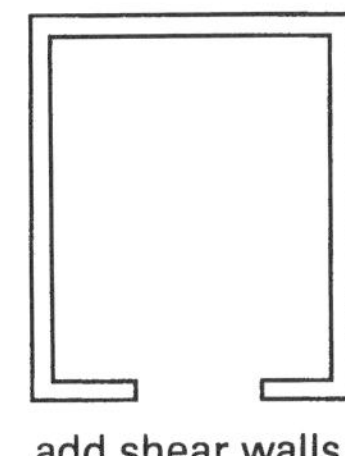
add shear walls

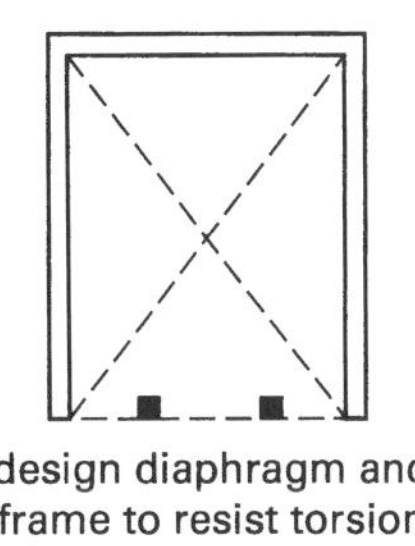
design diaphragm and frame to resist torsion

(a) open ended building plan

(b) four ways to alleviate lateral displacement

Elevation Design

The ideal elevation from a seismic design standpoint is one that is regular, symmetrical, continuous, and matches the other elevations in configuration and seismic resistance. Setbacks and offsets should be avoided for the same reason as reentrant corners in a plan should be avoided—to avoid areas of stress concentration. Of course, perfect symmetry is not always possible due to the functional and aesthetic requirements of the building, but there are two basic configurations that should (and can) be avoided by the architect early in the design process.

The first problem configuration is a discontinuous shear wall. This is a major mistake and should never happen. Discontinuities can occur when a shear wall is given a large opening, stops short of the foundation, or is altered in some other way. Since the entire purpose of a shear wall is to carry lateral loads to the foundation and act as a beam cantilevered out of the foundation, any interruption of this is counterproductive. Of course, small openings like doors and small windows can be placed in shear walls if proper reinforcement is provided.

Two common examples of discontinuous shear walls are shown in Fig. 45.10. In the first, the shear wall is stopped at the second floor level and supported by columns. This is often done to open up the first floor, but it creates a situation where stress concentrations are so great that even extra reinforcing cannot always resist the build-up of stress.

The second example, shown in Fig. 45.10(b), is also a common design feature where the second floor and floors above are cantilevered slightly from the first floor shear wall. Even though the shear wall continues, the offset also creates an undesirable situation because the direct load path for the lateral loads is interrupted, and the floor structure has to carry the transfer of forces from one shear wall to the next.

In all cases of discontinuous shear walls, the solution is simple: shear walls should run continuously to the foundation.

Another serious problem with building configuration is the soft story. This occurs when the ground floor is weaker than the floors above. Although a soft story can occur at any floor, it is most serious at grade level because this is where the lateral loads are the greatest. The discontinuous shear wall discussed in the previous section is a special case of the soft story. Others can occur when all columns do not extend to the ground or when the first story is high compared with the other floors of the structure. See Fig. 45.11.

Product Development

Figure 45.10
Discontinuous Shear Walls

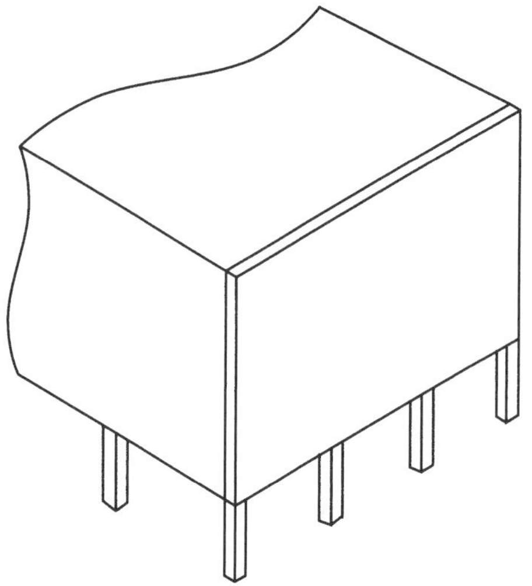

(a) shear wall to column transition

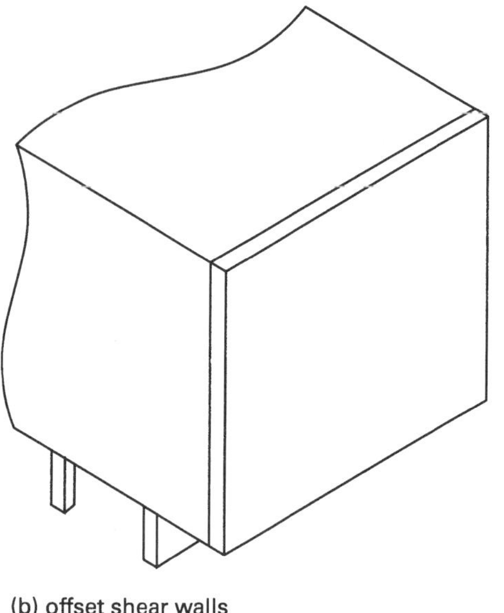

(b) offset shear walls

A *soft story* can also be created when there is heavy exterior cladding above the first story and the ground level is open. Of course, there are usually valid reasons for all of these situations to occur. For example, a hotel may need a high first story but shorter floors above for the guest rooms.

When earthquake loads occur, the forces and deformations are concentrated at the weak floor instead of being uniformly distributed among all the floors and structural members.

There are several ways to solve the problem of a soft story. The first, of course, is to eliminate it and try to work the architectural solution around the extra columns or lower height. If height is critical, extra columns can be added at the first floor. Another solution is to add extra horizontal and diagonal bracing. Finally, the framing of the upper stories can be made the same as the first story. The entire structure then has a uniform stiffness. Lighter, intermediate floors can be added above the first between the larger bays so they do not affect the behavior of the primary structural system.

ADDITIONAL CONSIDERATIONS

Overturning Moment

Because the inertial force created by an earthquake acts through the center of mass of a building, there is a tendency for the moment created by this force acting above the base to overturn the structure. This overturning force must be counteracted in some way. Normally, the dead weight of the building, also acting through the center of mass, is sufficient to resist the overturning force, but it must always be checked. However, only 90% of the dead load may be used to resist uplift. Figure 45.12 shows these two forces and the resulting moments diagrammatically.

Drift

Drift is the lateral movement of a building under the influence of earthquake- or wind-induced vibrations. Story drift is the displacement of one level relative to the level above or below. ASCE/SEI 7 gives stringent limitations on story drift. These limits are more stringent for the higher seismic use groups. For example, the value for a normal frame structure is 0.02 times the story height for use group I and 0.01 times the story height for use group III.

Drift as a limiting factor is important in order to ensure that exterior facades do not break off or crack excessively. When two buildings or portions of buildings are isolated by a seismic joint, they must be separated by at least the sum of the drifts to avoid pounding during an earthquake.

Figure 45.11 Soft First Stories

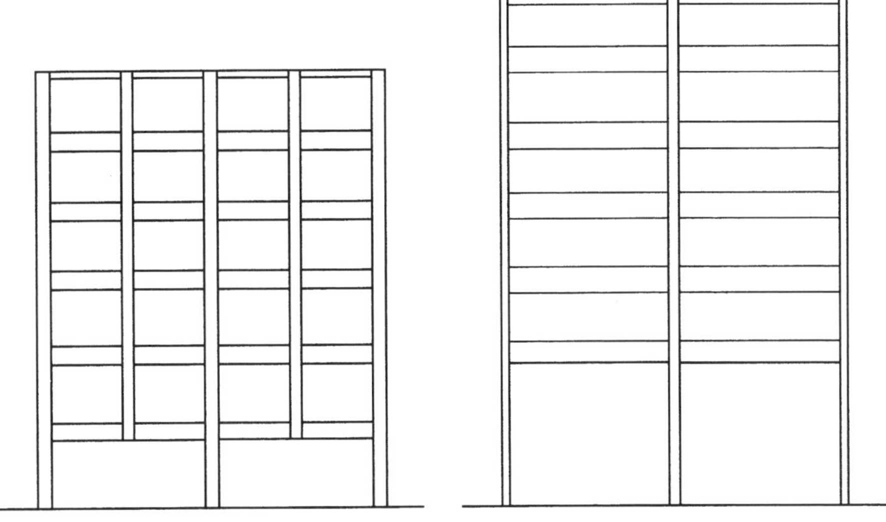

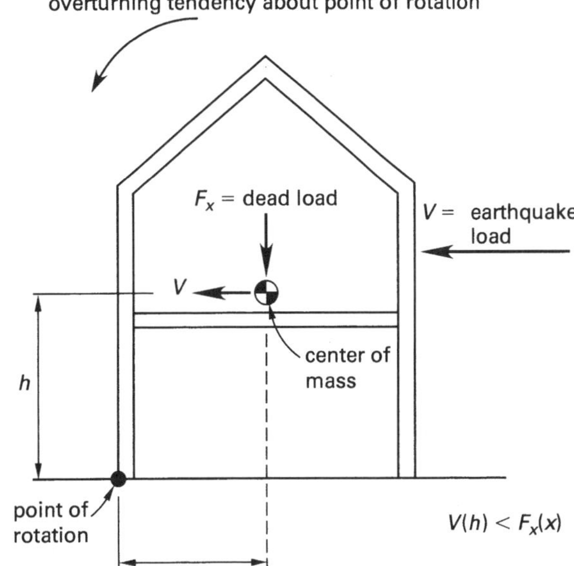

Figure 45.12 Overturning Moment

46

CONSTRUCTION DOCUMENTATION

Construction documentation includes the construction drawings and the project manual, which contains the technical specifications. The construction drawings and project manual are considered *instruments of professional service* and are legal documents, as they are part of the contract for a project. This chapter covers construction drawings; the project manual is covered in Chap. 47.

Construction drawings, sometimes called *working drawings*, represent the architect's final decisions concerning design, building methods, and construction technology. They must show the technically correct ways of meeting the many functional requirements of the design, from keeping water out to distributing electricity to providing safe finishes. They must also clearly communicate this information to the contractor, material suppliers, and other people involved with the project.

This chapter reviews how design decisions are translated into construction drawings in the following ways.

- planning the appropriate methods of documenting the project
- determining the content of the drawings
- applying criteria involved in developing construction details
- applying industry standards for documentation
- organizing the content and layout of drawings
- coordinating the architect's drawings with the consultant's drawings
- determining how project changes should be documented

PLANNING CONSTRUCTION DOCUMENTATION

When beginning to prepare construction documents, one of the first decisions the architect must make is what tools and methods to use to best organize and communicate the needed information.

Traditionally, this consists of a set of two-dimensional drawings on paper that describe the overall configuration of the project, giving dimensions, details, general notes, and schedules itemizing individual elements such as doors and windows. The architect develops a combination of plans, elevations, and sections to provide (with the specifications) all the information the contractor needs to build the project.

Before the advent of computers, architectural drawings were drawn by hand on vellum or Mylar and reproduced by large-format printing. As design and computer technology evolved, drawings have come to be more often prepared with the help of *computer aided drafting* (CAD) programs, which have become powerful tools for creating and modifying technical drawings; drawings are reproduced using high-quality computer printers called *plotters*. The development of *building information modeling* (BIM) software has enabled architects to document their designs with three-dimensional computer models.

Whatever production method is selected, the architect must determine how to organize the content and layout of the drawings and specifications to communicate the project's intent and its requirements. When deciding on which strategy to use, the architect should seek a balance of efficiency, accuracy, and cost.

Building Information Modeling

In traditional drafting, whether prepared manually or with CAD software, a drawing is a two-dimensional representation of a project's three-dimensional physical aspects. Building information modeling (BIM) is a method of designing, documenting, and managing a facility with the use of a three-dimensional computer model of the building and site. As a project develops, more detail is added to the model and shared with all members of the project team through computer networking. Because all the information about the building is in one model, individual drawings such as floor plans, elevations, and details can be produced easily with the appropriate commands. Three-dimensional renderings can also be produced. BIM can be used for a wide range of tasks, ranging from relatively simple 3-D visualization to complex automation of many design and construction tasks.

A model created by BIM is considered a "smart" model because it is more than just a representation; each individual object such as a door or a partition has information attached to it, which means the model can be used as a database. Thus, the model is useful in creating estimates of materials, door schedules, cost estimates, and the like. Because the model is three-dimensional and dimensionally accurate, the software can detect interferences, such as a conflict between a structural beam and HVAC ductwork, and this can prevent problems when the job is under construction. A BIM model can also be used to aid in structural design, run energy simulations, complete solar analyses, and do daylighting studies using a variety of available software. Once the building is completed, the BIM model can serve as a facility management tool. BIM is also valuable when a building is being designed and constructed with integrated project delivery. Refer to Chap. 3 for a discussion of integrated project delivery.

A firm considering using BIM must balance the increasing requirements for computer power and memory against the cost as well as the management needed for coordinating all the users of the model to determine if it offers a cost effective solution.

Each individual object such as a door or a partition has information attached to it, which means the model can be used as a database.

BIM can be used for 3-D *visualization* and for initial development of design ideas. As the model is developed, it is easy to view components not only in two dimensions but also as three-dimensional models that can be rotated, zoomed, and animated. Simple monochromatic scenes or more elaborate and detailed full-color renderings can be created. The ideas come together and become a single, tangible object that can be manipulated to suit the needs of the project as changes arise.

Closely related to visualization is the idea of *documentation*. A BIM model can be used to create the traditional, two-dimensional drawings of plans, elevations, sections, and details. In most cases the model also carries information about all the component parts, so it can be used to create specifications, cost estimates, schedules, and material lists. Normally both the visualization and documentation levels of BIM are used.

A BIM model can be used as the basis for running *simulations* such as energy studies, structural reviews, and similar predictive analyses. The data from the BIM model can be exported to third-party software to produce these studies. BIM can also be used to run *integrated analyses* that combine several types of studies or disciplines at once. One of the most common and useful examples of this type of analysis is clash detection, where the model can determine if there are any spatial conflicts between architectural, structural, and HVAC elements.

At its highest level, BIM can be used for *automation* of design and construction tasks. For very complex buildings, for example, the BIM information can be used to fabricate structural steel or complex cladding systems. The architect can also use parametric tools to develop several design options to analyze and compare their attributes. One promising use of BIM is building code checking, either by the architect or by the building department.

Standard of Care

Whatever method is used, the construction drawings should be produced as accurately as possible. Errors and omissions can cause problems with pricing, construction, and performance; they can also lead to litigation. If there are inaccuracies in the drawings, the architect will have to respond to *requests for information* (RFIs) during bidding or construction, which can include additional drawing time for which the architect is not compensated.

It is important to remember, however, that the drawings, like much of the architect's work, are not expected to be perfect; legally, the drawings must be produced with the standard of care that a prudent architect would use, given the same or similar facts and circumstances, in the same locale. This means that some minor errors are allowed in the drawings; it does not, however, ensure that the architect will never end up in court with expert witnesses expressing their opinions on what the standard of care should have been in a specific circumstance.

CONTENT OF CONSTRUCTION DRAWINGS

Types of Construction Drawings

Drawings should show the general configurations, sizes, shapes, and locations of the components of construction. General notes accompany the illustrations and are used to explain materials, construction requirements, and dimensions.

Figure 46.1 through Fig. 46.8 show various types of construction plans for the same portion of a building. Figure 46.9 through Fig. 46.13 show some of the standard symbols used on construction drawings. Detailed requirements for material quality, workmanship, and other items are contained in the technical specifications of the project manual. The following are brief descriptions of some of the more common items that should be included with the architectural drawings. (This list is by no means comprehensive.)

- *site plan:* Vicinity map, property description, property line locations with dimensions and bearings, location of existing utilities, benchmarks, existing structures, new building location, landscaping, site improvements, fencing, roads, streets, right of way, drainage, and limit of the work of the contract.

  A *benchmark* is a fixed elevation point from which all other elevations on the site and building are referenced. A benchmark may be an official surveying marker, if one exists on or near the site, or simply a nearby object that is fixed, such as the top of a manhole cover. The surveyor uses benchmarks to lay out the vertical dimensions of the site and building and to check the accuracy of the building construction.

  In most architectural projects, the first floor of the building is arbitrarily set at an elevation of 100 ft for the purposes of developing the construction drawings. This allows foundation and basement elevations to be positive numbers, while elevations above the first floor are larger than 100 ft. Used in this way, the first floor becomes a *datum*, or plane of reference from which other elevations are taken. A vertical plane may also be a datum, and other horizontal dimensions may be referenced from it.

  The site plan also shows surveying *control points* used for horizontal measurement. These are fixed points established by the surveyor, and they usually consist of a primary system and a secondary system. The primary system is tied to the official control system of the jurisdiction (national, municipal, or other higher-order coordinate system), and it normally covers the entire site. The corner points of the site are also related to the higher-order coordinate system. Two or three primary control points are indicated on the site plan so that dimensions can be checked and for ease of reference as the building is constructed. The secondary system is the grid reference system that is used for the building construction itself, typically based on the centerlines of the building's structural grid or the faces of major structural walls.

- *floor plans:* Building configuration with all walls and dimensions shown, structural grid center lines, grade elevations at the building line, existing construction to remain unchanged, references to other details and elevations, room names and numbers, door swings and door numbers, window numbers, floor material indications, control and expansion joint locations, plumbing fixtures, built-in fixtures, stairs, special equipment, vertical transportation, and notes as needed to explain items on the plan (see Fig. 46.1).

- *roof plans:* Roof outline, overall dimensions, dimensions of setbacks, slope of roof, roof drainage system, reference to other drawing details, roof materials, penetrations through the roof, and roof-mounted equipment.

- *reflected ceiling plans:* Partitions extending to and through the ceiling; ceiling material and grid lines; ceiling height notes; changes in ceiling heights; locations of all lights (including exit lights), diffusers, access panels, speakers, and other equipment and ceiling penetrations; and expansion joints (see Fig. 46.2).

- *exterior elevations:* Structural grid center lines, vertical dimensions that include floor-to-floor heights and opening heights, references to other details, floor lines, elevations of major elements, grade lines, foundation lines (dashed), material indications and notes, symbols for window schedule, gutters and downspouts, signs and other building graphics, and all other openings including windows and doors.
- *building sections:* Vertical dimensions, elevations of the tops of structural components and finish floor lines, general material indications, footings and foundations; references to other details, ceiling lines, and major mechanical services.
- *wall sections:* Dimensions to grid centerlines, face of wall dimensions to other components, vertical dimensions from foundations to parapet relating all elements to top of structural elements, material indications with notes, all connection methods, mechanical and electrical elements shown schematically, roof construction, floor construction, and foundation construction.
- *interior elevations:* Vertical dimensions to critical elements, references to other details, openings in walls, wall finishes, built-in items, and locations of switches, thermostats, and other wall-mounted equipment such as light fixtures.
- *schedules:* Common schedules found on most drawings include room finish schedule and key, door schedule, window schedule, and hardware schedule. Other details that can be communicated in a schedule are louvers, architectural woodwork, piling, and equipment schedules.
- *structural drawings:* Footing and foundation plans, rebar layout, framing plans, major structural sections, detail sections, pier reinforcing schedules, and connection details.

  Based on information provided by the structural engineer, the architect uses the exact sizes of structural members to coordinate construction details and ensure that sufficient space is provided for construction, clearances, tolerances, fireproofing, and finishes. Generally, only the overall outline of piers, footings, foundation walls, structural walls, and framing is shown on the architectural drawings; these elements are more thoroughly documented on the structural drawings. Elevations for tops of beams, structural walls, and floors are shown on both sets of drawings. (See Fig. 46.3.)
- *mechanical and plumbing drawings:* Location of mechanical equipment; layout of ductwork, pipes, fixtures, and other major components; plumbing isometrics; details of mechanical room layout; details, such as ductwork connections and pipe support; and equipment schedules.

  Mechanical and plumbing items are shown on the architectural drawings only where they interface with other construction. Examples include the locations of grilles and registers on the reflected ceiling plan, the locations of sprinkler heads on the reflected ceiling plan, plumbing fixtures, ducts and piping when part of an architectural section or detail, and other situations where coordination with other construction elements is important. Because of the obvious potential for conflicts when different offices complete different drawings, coordination between the architect and the consulting engineers is very important. This is an area where BIM is especially useful. (See Fig. 46.4 and Fig. 46.5.)
- *electrical drawings:* Power plans, lighting plans, telecommunication and data plans, signal and security system plans, one-line diagrams, and transformer, equipment, and fixture schedules.

  The number of electrical plans needed will vary depending on the complexity of the project. For simple projects, all telecommunication and signal work may be shown on the power plan; in other cases, a separate plan is developed for each system. (See Fig. 46.6.)

  The electrical drawings contain information concerning the circuiting of lighting and power outlets, including the number and size of conductors in each conduit, the sizes of conduits, and home runs to panel boxes. A *home run* is a graphic indication (an arrowhead and the numbers of the circuits) that the line on the drawing connecting lights or outlets is connected to particular circuit breakers in a particular electrical panel box. This graphic device is used so that the entire line does not have to be drawn to the panel box, thereby avoiding clutter on the drawing.

  As with mechanical and plumbing work, electrical elements shown on the architectural drawings are indicated for coordination and location only. Where the location of power outlets is significant, the architectural drawings may include a separate power and telephone plan with exact dimensions.

The locations of luminaires are also shown on the architect's reflected ceiling plan so they can be coordinated with other ceiling-mounted equipment and architectural features. Usually, no other electrical information is given on these drawings. However, in some cases, the architect may want to show the locations of switches on the reflected ceiling plan. Compare the electrical engineer's power plan shown in Fig. 46.6, the architect's telephone/power plan shown in Fig. 46.7, and the architect's reflected ceiling plan shown in Fig. 46.2.

Figure 46.1 Construction Floor Plan

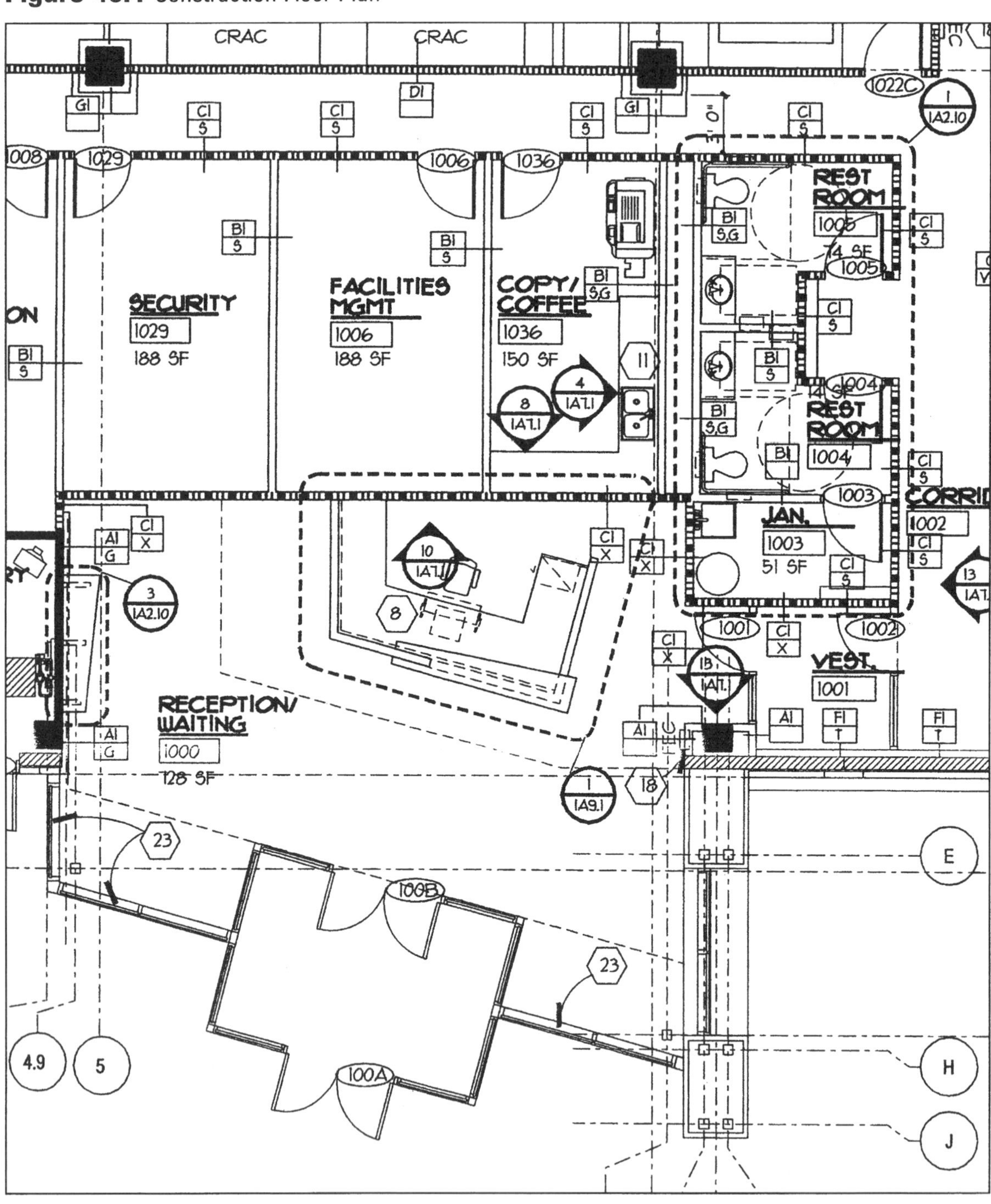

Figure 46.2 Reflected Ceiling Plan

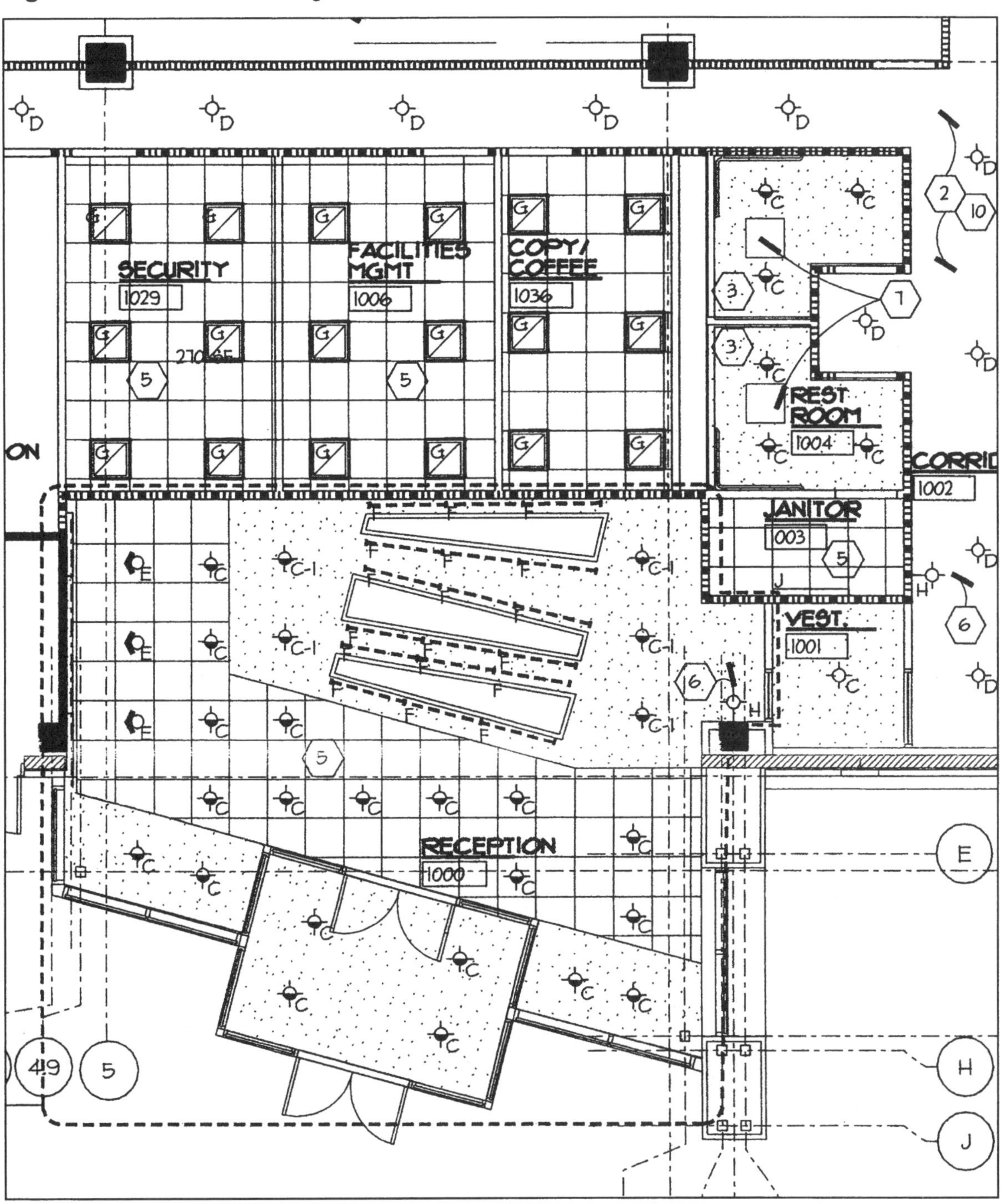

Figure 46.3 Structural Plan

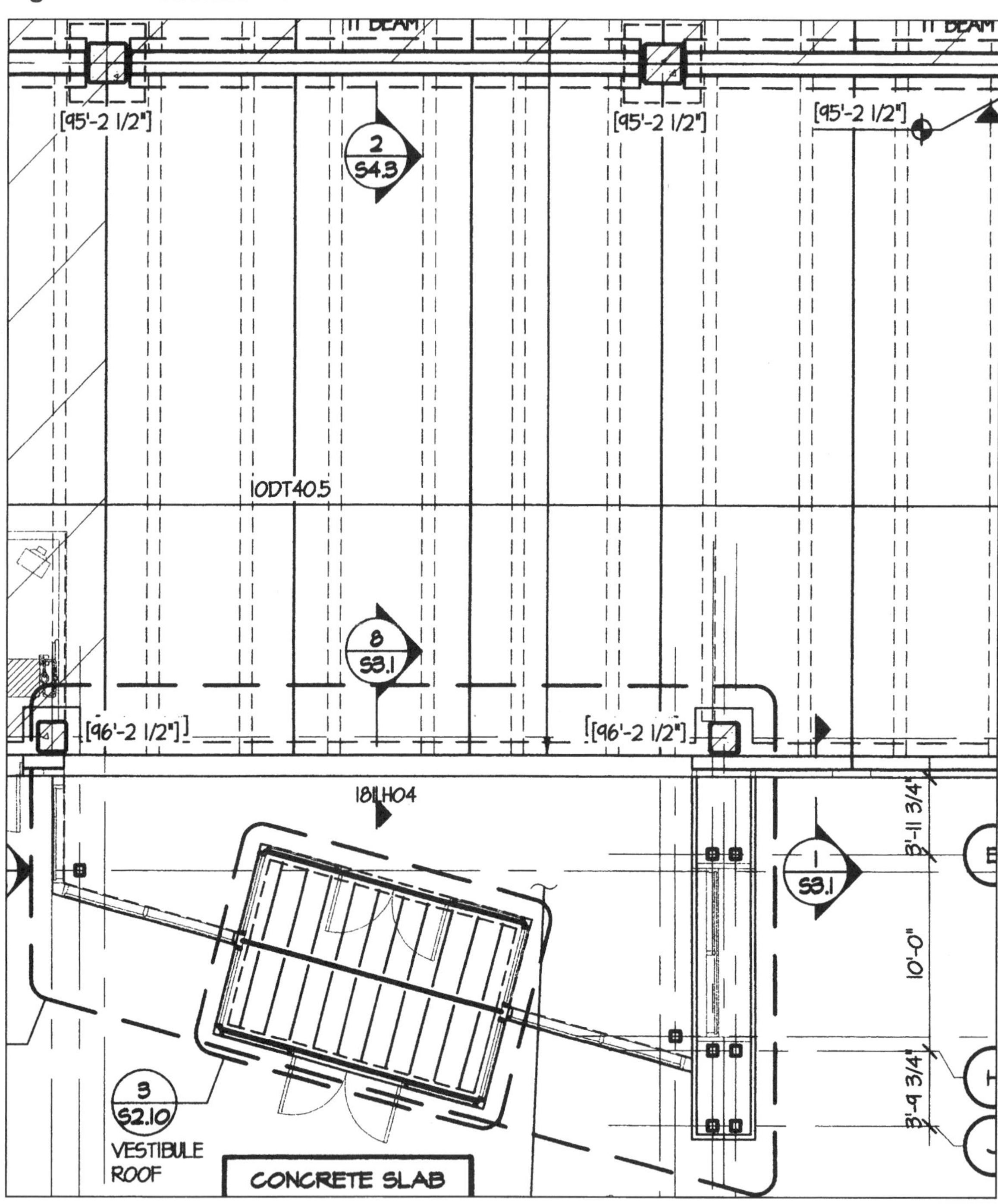

Product Development

Figure 46.4 Mechanical Plan

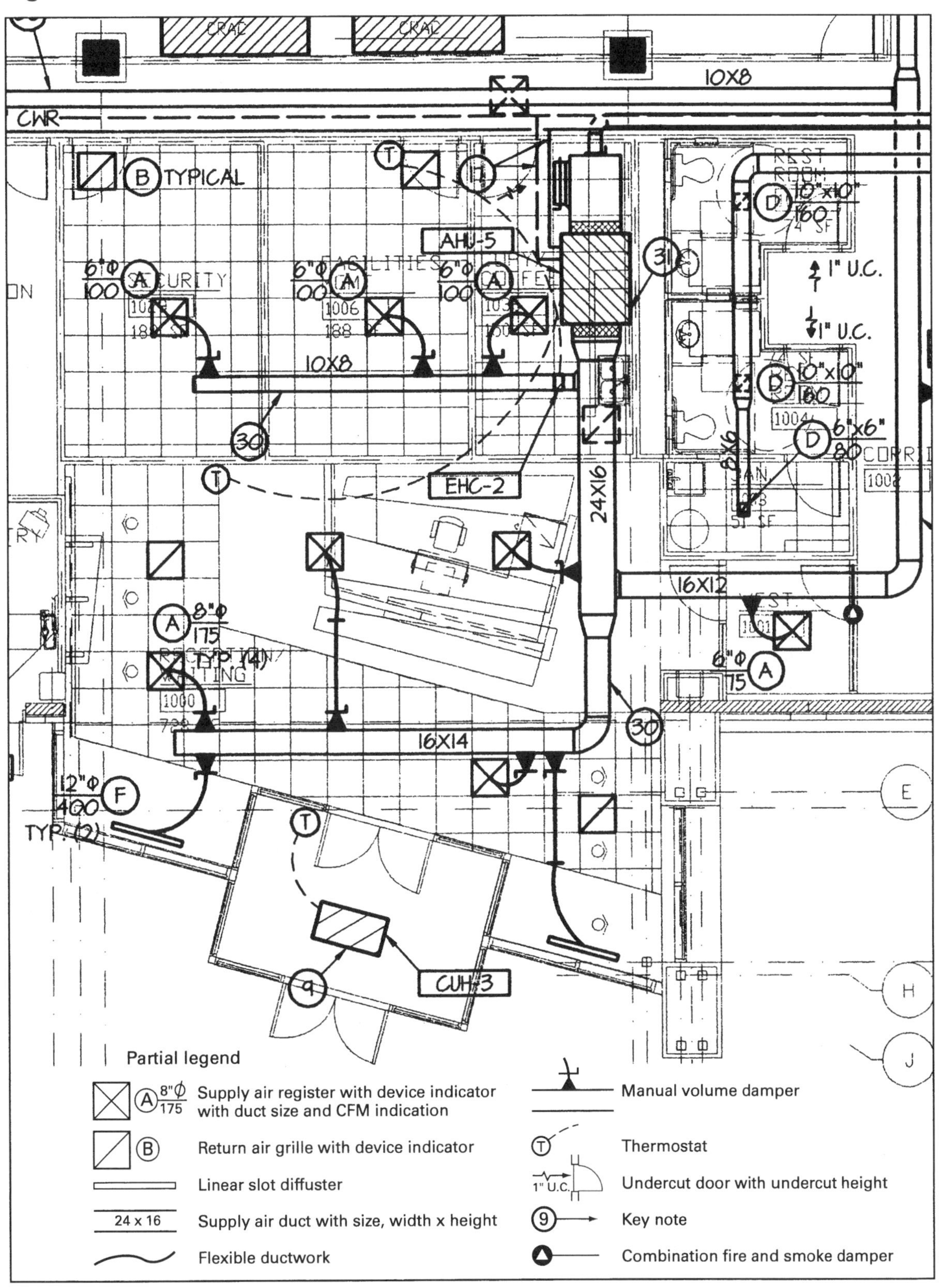
CRAC
CRAC
10X8
CWR
B TYPICAL
T
H
AHU-5
31
REST ROOM
D 10"x10" 160
1" U.C.
1" U.C.
6"Φ 100 A SECURITY 1002 188 SF
6"Φ 100 A FACILITIES MGM 1006 188
6"Φ 100 A STAFF 1003
10X8
D 10"x10" 160
1004
D 6"x6" 80
CORRI 1008
30
T
EHC-2
24X16
8X6
JAN. 51 SF
16X12
A 8"Φ 175
RECEPTION/WAITING 1000
TYP (4)
6"Φ 75 A
VEST. 1001
30
16X14
12"Φ 400 F
TYP. (2)
T
E
CUH-3
9
H
J
Partial legend
A 8"Φ 175 Supply air register with device indicator with duct size and CFM indication
B Return air grille with device indicator
Linear slot diffuster
24 x 16 Supply air duct with size, width x height
Flexible ductwork
Manual volume damper
T Thermostat
1" U.C. Undercut door with undercut height
9 Key note
Combination fire and smoke damper

Product Development

Figure 46.5 Plumbing Plan

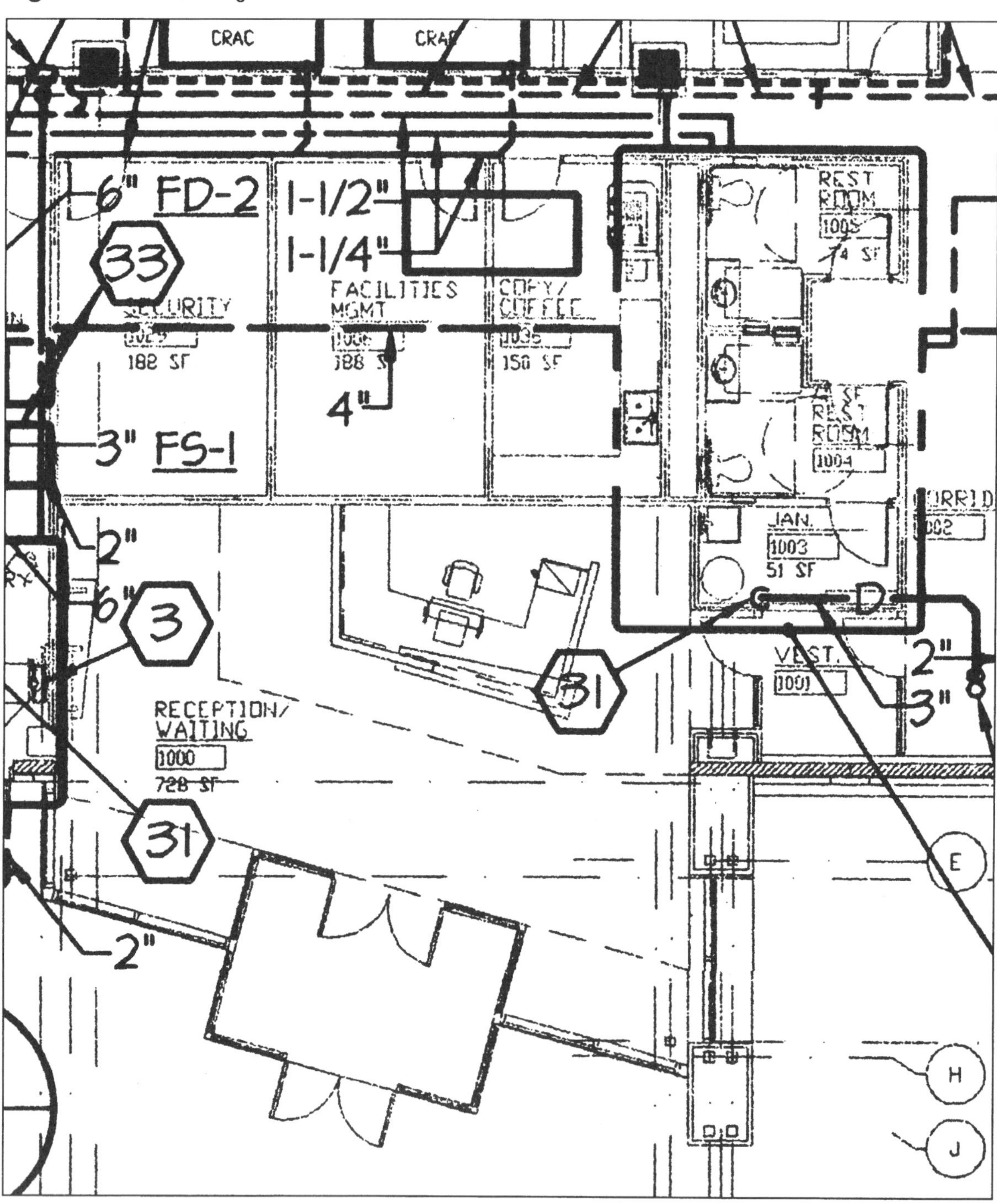

Figure 46.6 Power Plan

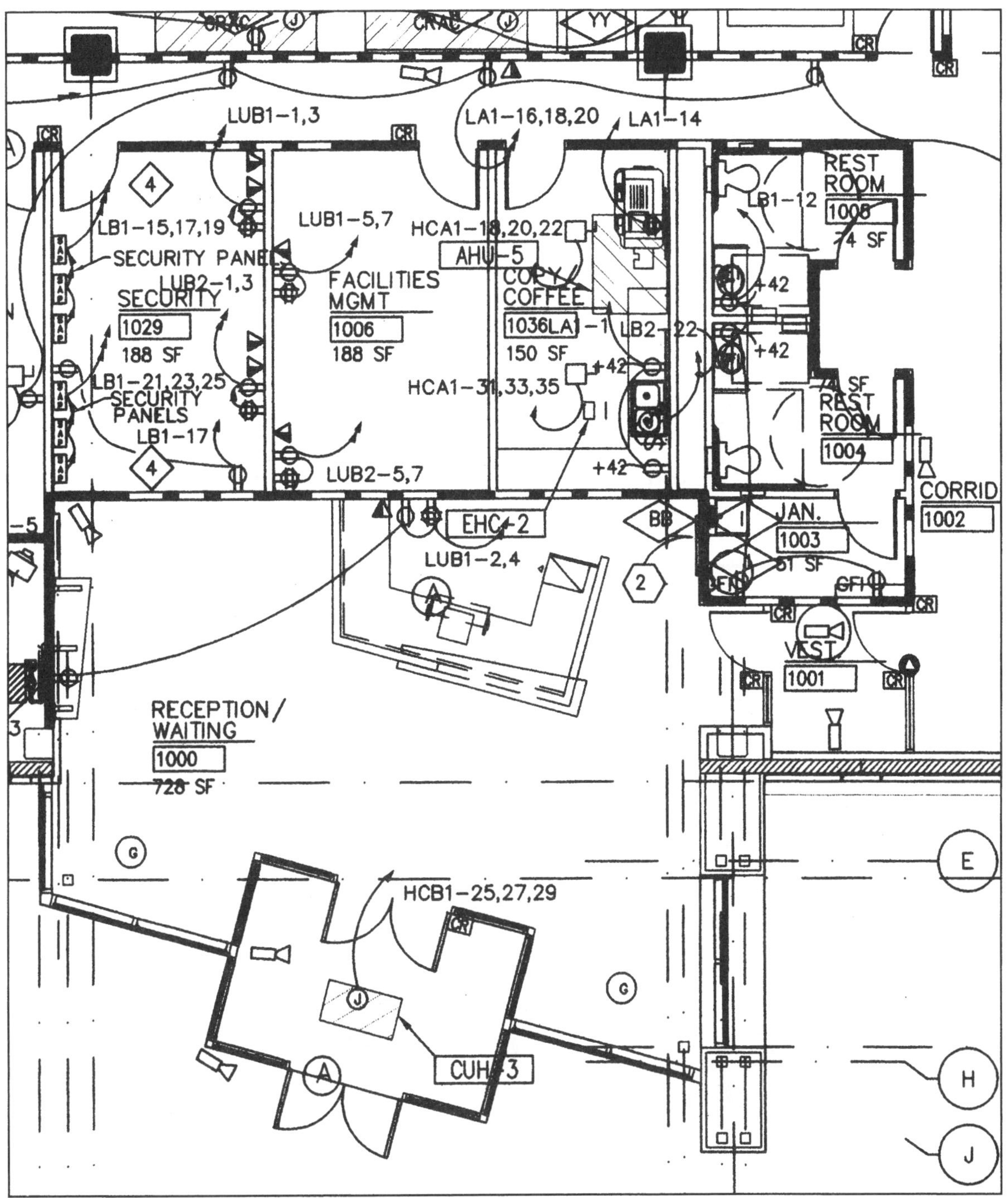

Product Development

Figure 46.7 Telephone/Electrical Plan

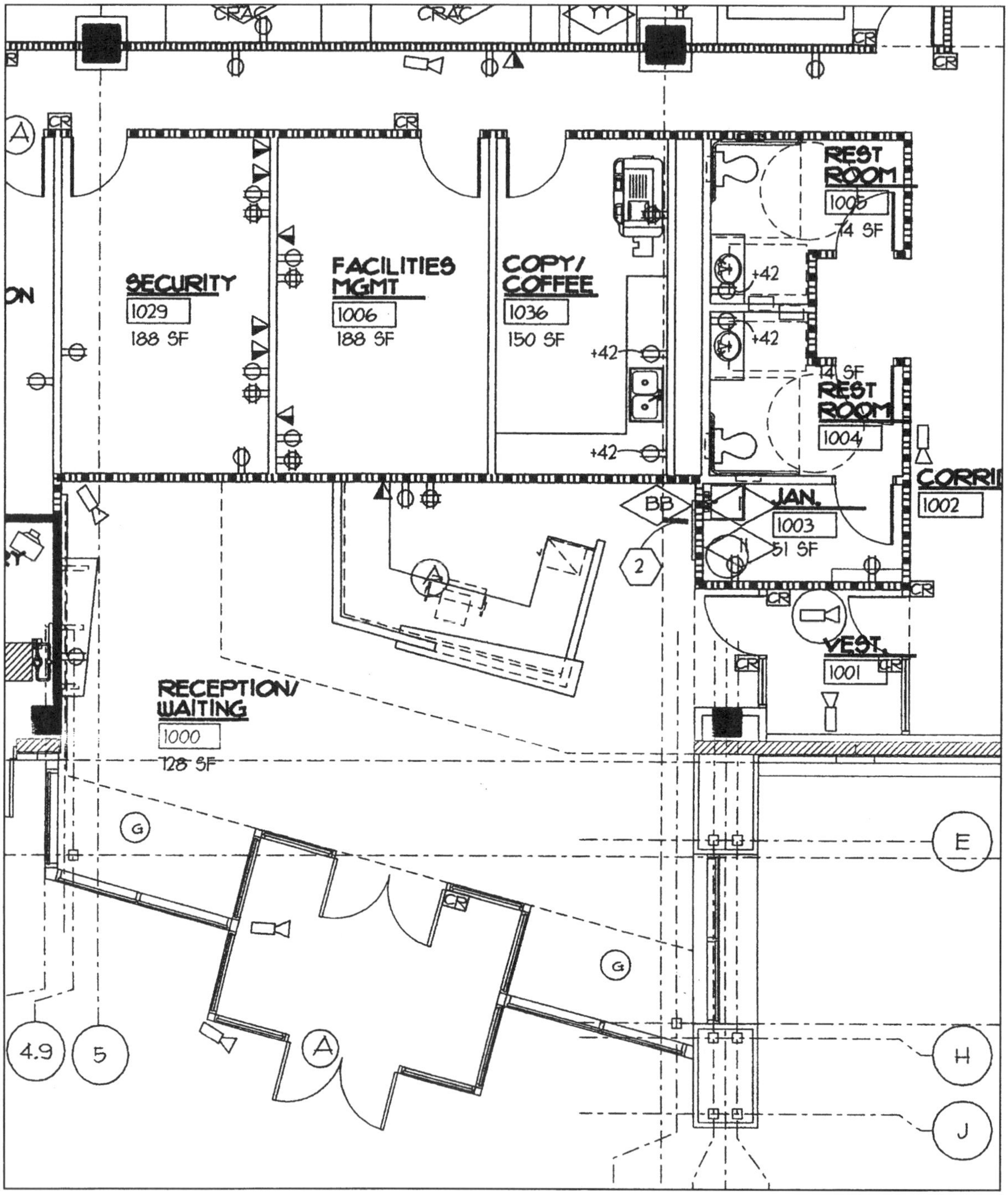

SECURITY
1029
188 SF
FACILITIES MGMT
1006
188 SF
COPY/ COFFEE
1036
150 SF
REST ROOM
1005
74 SF
REST ROOM
1004
74 SF
JAN.
1003
51 SF
CORRI
1002
VEST.
1001
RECEPTION/ WAITING
1000
728 SF

Figure 46.8 Lighting Plan

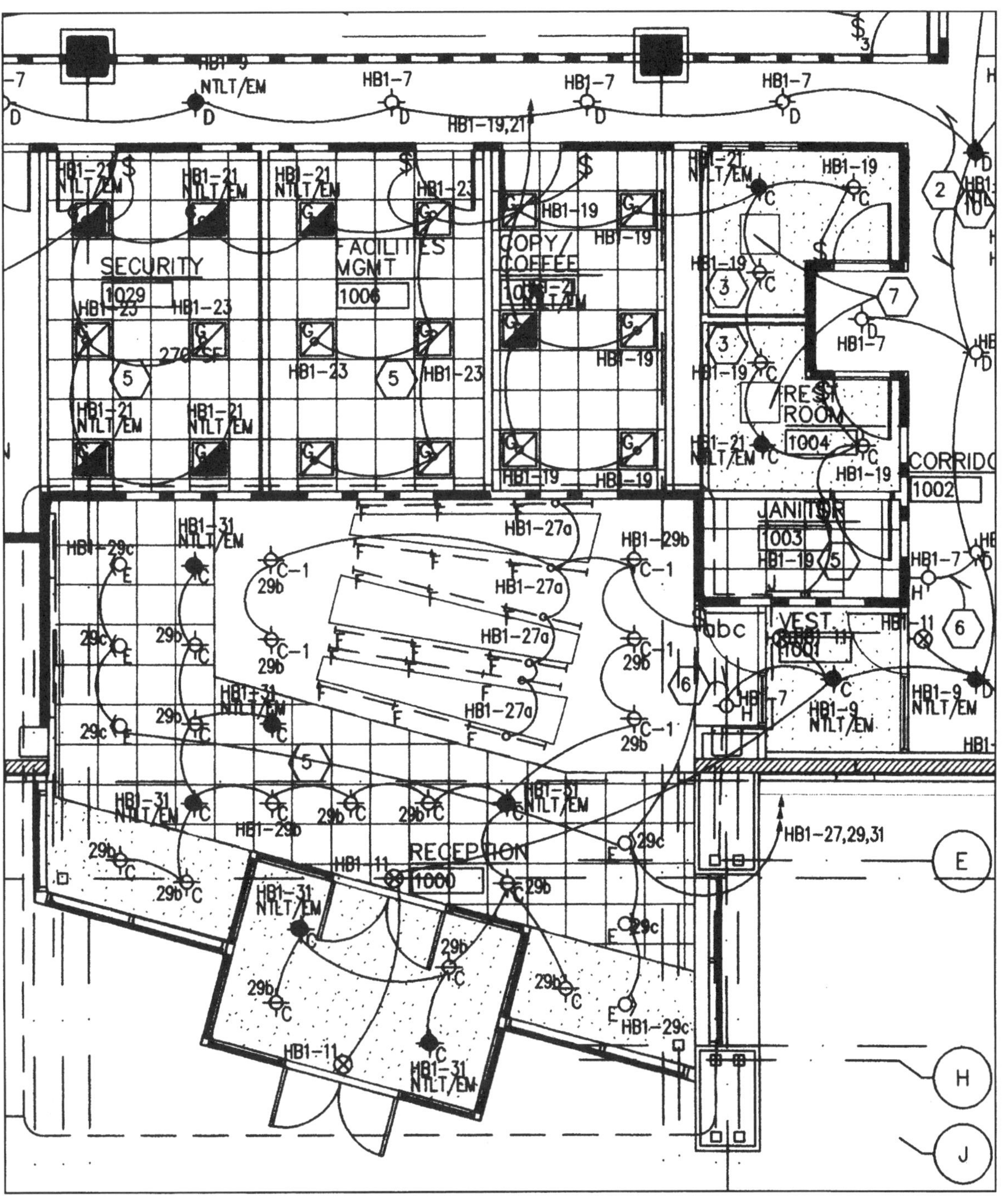

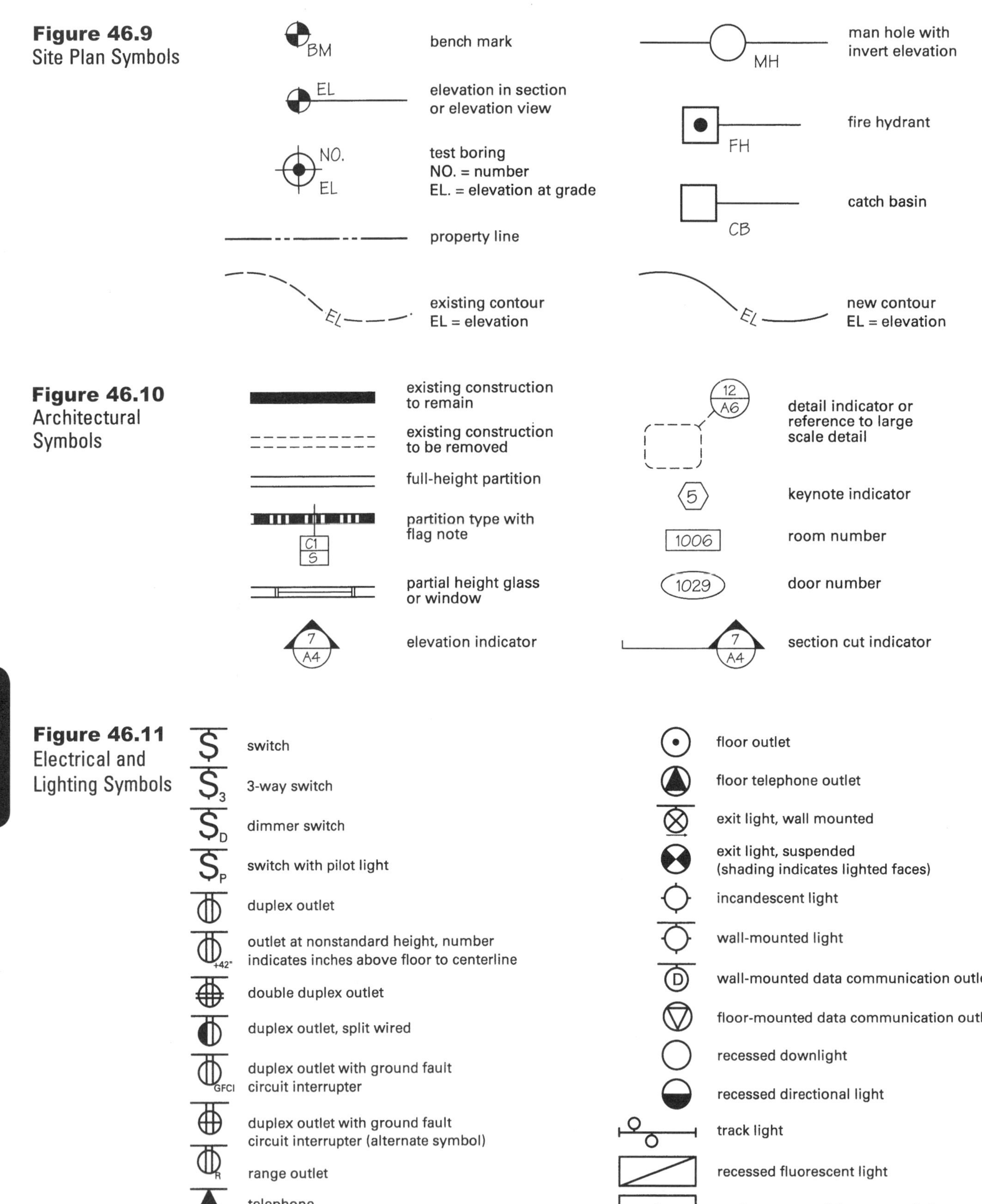

Figure 46.9 Site Plan Symbols

Figure 46.10 Architectural Symbols

Figure 46.11 Electrical and Lighting Symbols

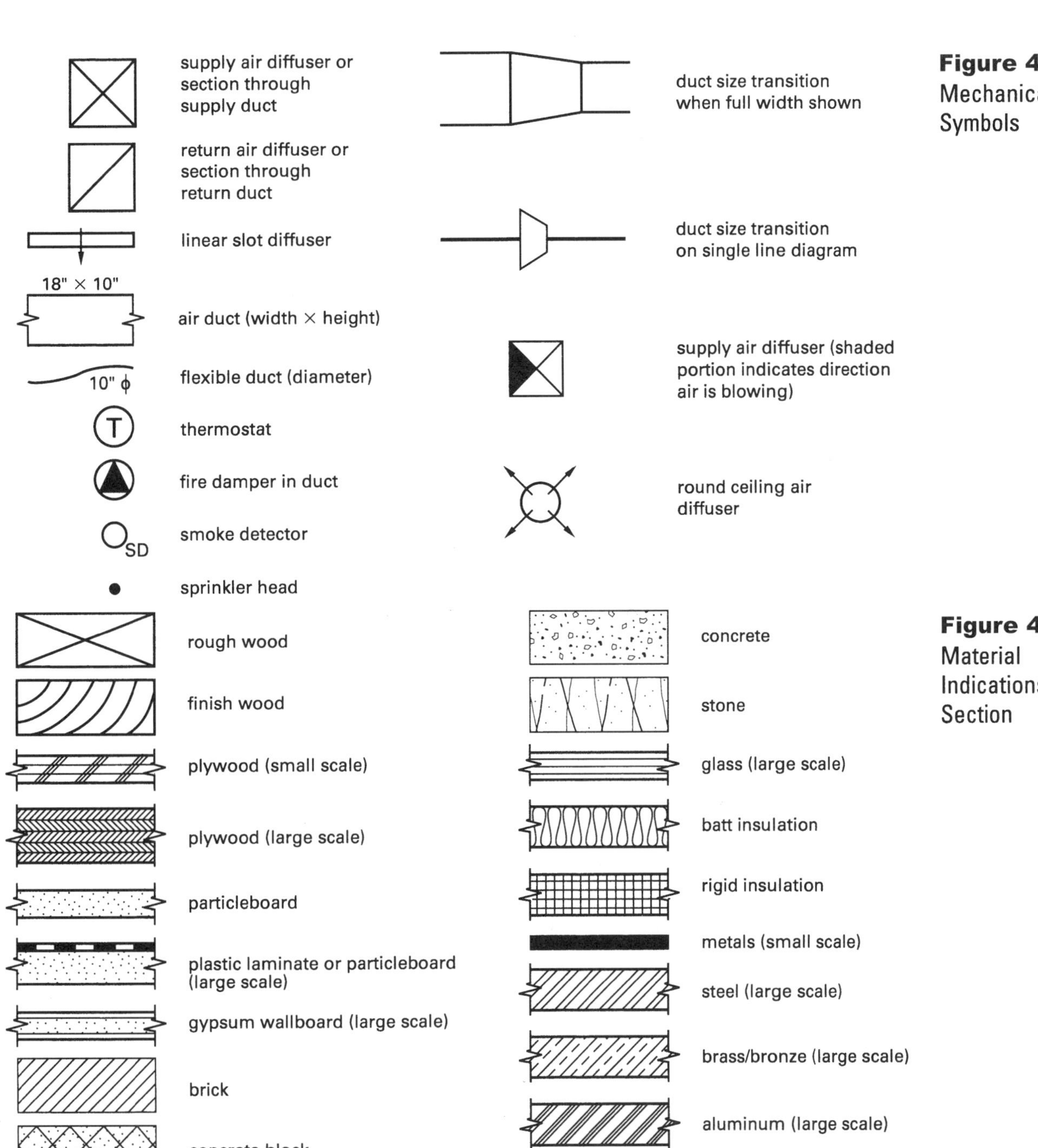
supply air diffuser or section through supply duct
return air diffuser or section through return duct
linear slot diffuser
18" × 10"
air duct (width × height)
10" ϕ
flexible duct (diameter)
T
thermostat
fire damper in duct
SD
smoke detector
sprinkler head
duct size transition when full width shown
duct size transition on single line diagram
supply air diffuser (shaded portion indicates direction air is blowing)
round ceiling air diffuser
rough wood
finish wood
plywood (small scale)
plywood (large scale)
particleboard
plastic laminate or particleboard (large scale)
gypsum wallboard (large scale)
brick
concrete block
concrete
stone
glass (large scale)
batt insulation
rigid insulation
metals (small scale)
steel (large scale)
brass/bronze (large scale)
aluminum (large scale)

Figure 46.12 Mechanical Symbols

Figure 46.13 Material Indications in Section

In addition to these overall views of the construction, the drawings should include corresponding details for all portions of the work.

Information Required by Building Departments

Building codes require that certain information appear on the set of construction documents submitted for plan review. The exact list of required information varies from one jurisdiction to another, but the IBC requires the following.

- In general, construction documents must indicate with sufficient clarity the locations, nature, and extent of the proposed work and how it will conform to the code. This normally includes standard drawings such as floor plans, elevations, sections, and details for architectural, structural, mechanical, electrical, and other specialty construction, as well as applicable schedules and written specifications.
- A site plan must be included to show the size and location of new construction and existing structures on the site, including distances from lot lines, established street grades, and the proposed finished grades. An accurate boundary survey must be shown.
- The drawings must show all means of egress. The number of occupants to be accommodated on every floor and in all rooms and spaces must be indicated.
- The exterior wall envelope must be shown in sufficient detail to determine compliance with code provisions.
- Fire protection shop drawings may have to be submitted to show conformance with the code.
- Structural calculations are usually required to be submitted.

The local authority having jurisdiction may want to see listed on the first sheet of the drawings some or all of the following information.

- names and addresses of all design professionals responsible for the work
- street address or legal description of the property
- square footage of the building
- building type and occupancy group or groups
- occupant load calculations
- the valuation of new construction represented by the plans and specifications

In addition to the above information, the *International Energy Conservation Code* (IECC) requires the following information to be included on the construction documents.

- insulation materials and their *R*-values
- fenestration *U*-factors and solar heat gain coefficients (SHGCs)
- area-weighted *U*-factor and SHGC calculations
- mechanical system design criteria
- mechanical and service water heating system and equipment types, sizes, and efficiencies
- economizer description
- equipment and system controls
- fan motor horsepower and controls
- duct sealing, and insulation and location for ducts and pipes
- lighting fixture schedule with wattage and control narrative

- location of daylight zones on floor plans
- air sealing details
- the building's thermal envelope

DEVELOPING CONSTRUCTION DETAILS

In all buildings, the larger organization of spaces, structure, and materials must be designed and documented with the same thoroughness as the overall form, layout, and appearance of the building itself. The ways in which things are connected are the construction details that the architect must develop. Many of the details are worked out, at least preliminarily, during the design development phase of a project, but everything must be finalized during project development and documentation.

More specifically, a *detail* may be thought of as the manner in which an assembly of several parts is organized, connected, and attached or otherwise interfaced to adjacent parts of the building. A detail may be as simple as how a drawer is attached to a cabinet or as complex as the intersection of a curtain wall, roof, ceiling, structural beam, and parapet consisting among them of dozens of different materials in all.

Because of the complexity of most details, they are most often described on the construction documents with a section view. Sections are a type of orthographic drawing that can convey a lot of information, including relationships of the parts, dimensions, material notations, and explanatory notes. Details also document the implied connections to adjacent building parts, as well as references to other individual drawings. Other types of detail drawings often used are isometrics, large-scale elevations, and large-scale plan views.

The appropriate documentation of detailed building drawings must take into account common functional characteristics that are involved with almost every category of construction detail. The correctness of the assembly can be developed or evaluated based on these characteristics. For example, the intersection of a roof and a parapet must be designed to fulfill several functions, one of which is to drain water while avoiding leakage into the structure. This holds true regardless of the roofing material or the method of wall construction. Different materials may influence certain aspects of the detail, but the intersection will always need flashing and positive drainage, and material expansion and contraction must always be taken into account.

A detail may be as simple as how a drawer is attached to a cabinet or as complex as the intersection of a curtain wall, roof, ceiling, structural beam, and parapet.

The following characteristics should be considered in a construction assembly's design and documentation. Not all of them will relate to every detail.

Compatibility with Design Intent

All building design begins with the desire to satisfy the program requirements and the specific needs they bring. These needs and requirements must be balanced against practical constraints such as code requirements, cost, and material limitations.

There are many ways to design within these prescribed guidelines. Sometimes during the long process of design and detailing, however, the original design intent gets lost in the practicalities of solving functional problems and making changes.

A detail may work but not look like what the client and designer originally intended. For example, a client might have originally requested a simple, unobtrusive system of demountable partitions. After the process of material selection, cost analysis, and integration with other building systems is complete, the final product may satisfy the requirements of demountability, sound transmission, cost, and finish, but may not have the clean, simple look the client wants.

As a detail develops, the architect should constantly check it against its original purpose, performance requirements, and desired appearance. The architect must also evaluate the characteristics of specific products and assemblies. For instance, how well does an acoustical ceiling absorb sound? How slip resistant is a floor tile? Does the material meet applicable code requirements, and will it perform in the way the architect and owner intend? Answering these questions tests how well the product will do its intended job.

Structural Integrity

Structural integrity is the ability of a material or construction component to withstand the forces applied to it. These include not only the obvious natural forces of gravity, snow, wind, and seismic loading, but also other forces such as impact. Each acting force should be reviewed to verify that the design will perform as intended.

The following are some common forces that may act on an assembly or material.

- live and dead loads
- wind loads
- seismic loads
- hydrostatic pressure
- forces induced by building movement
- loads induced by human use (for example, the forces produced on a door jamb through the hinge from door operation)
- loads created by one material acting as the substrate for another
- forces caused by accidental or intentional abuse
- strength properties of a material or assembly that may be necessary to resist various forces including compression, tension, shear, torsion, rupture, hardness, and impact

Safety

The architect is responsible for protecting the health, safety, and welfare of the public through his or her designs and details. Be aware of safety concerns such as the following.

- *structural safety.* Will the material or detail physically collapse or otherwise fail, causing harm?
- *fire safety.* Is the material fire resistant enough for its intended use? Will it produce smoke or toxic fumes if burned? If it burns, will its failure lead to failure of adjacent construction?
- *safety with human contact.* Is there a potential for harm when people come in contact with the material or detail? For example, will sharp edges cut people, wet floors promote slipping, or poorly designed stairs cause falls?

Security

Security systems and strategies can provide protection against theft, vandalism, intentional physical harm, or a combination of all three. Common security concerns include

- residential and commercial burglary
- employee pilferage
- vandalism
- sabotage or theft of company records and property
- confinement of prisoners

- protection of personnel
- safety and confinement in psychiatric wards
- abduction
- terrorism (in extreme cases)

In addition to creating physical barriers, security strategies include methods for preventing entry, detecting intruders, controlling access to secure areas, and notification in the event of unauthorized entry or other emergencies. Refer to Chap. 32 for information on the many types of security devices.

The security consultant, equipment vendor, electrical engineering consultant, and contractor are responsible for designing and installing elements of security systems and providing the power they need to operate. However, the architect must coordinate the efforts of the design team so their work fits within the overall design and construction of the project. Important elements of security system coordination that may be included on the drawings and in the specifications include the following.

- Lighting needed for surveillance and deterrence should be compatible with the general ambient lighting whenever possible. The electrical engineer or lighting designer should know what types of cameras are used so that they can select the best lighting types. Lighting positions and details are shown on the architectural drawings, but detailed circuiting drawings are produced by the electrical engineer.
- The architect must provide adequate space and support for video cameras, monitors, access devices, controls, and other equipment and show these areas on the architectural drawings. The electrical and signal circuiting will be shown on the electrical drawings.
- Conduit must be shown on the electrical consultant's drawings to accommodate signal system wiring, electric lock wiring, telecommunication wiring, and other wiring that may be provided by a separate contractor.
- Speakers needed for public address and communication systems within secured areas should be shown on the architectural drawings and coordinated with other elements on the reflected ceiling plan.
- Power transfers for doors should be specified to meet the necessary level of security, but should be concealed whenever possible.

Durability and Maintainability

Building materials and construction details are subject to a wide range of abuses both from natural forces and from human use. They must be able to withstand this abuse to the greatest extent possible and be maintained and repaired throughout their lifetimes.

Exterior materials must have resistance to ultraviolet radiation, temperature changes, pollution, water, and atmospheric corrosion. Materials and details within human reach must be resistant to scratching, abrasion, impact, and marking. All details must be maintainable. Can a material be cleaned easily? How will it look if it is not regularly maintained? How costly will the maintenance be? Can part of a detail be easily replaced or repaired?

Code Requirements

All construction details and building components must satisfy the requirements of the local building code and other statutory regulations. Checking for code compliance should be an ongoing process while developing or reviewing construction drawings. Many of these requirements are discussed in other chapters, with reference to specific materials and areas of construction.

Construction Trade Sequence

All buildings integrate resources from a variety of trades and material suppliers. The best details are those that allow construction to proceed directly from one trade to another in a timely fashion. Labor is one of the biggest expenses of a building project, so anything that reduces the amount of labor needed (while remaining within the bounds of adequate craftsmanship) saves money. Detailing a building to allow for a clear division of the labor trades will reduce interference, potential conflicts, and the overlap of crews and efforts.

For example, in the construction of a standard partition, the drywallers first install the metal framing. Then the electricians and plumbers install conduit and piping. After that, the drywallers return, finish the wall, and leave, making way for the painters. If a partition is detailed in a way that requires deviation from this standard sequence, it will take longer to complete and be more costly.

Fabrication and Installation Methods

The architect should review all construction details to ensure that they do not present logistical problems. For example, the transportation available may limit the size and shape of assemblies. Swinging a steel beam into position and then tightening the bolts requires certain minimum clearances. Installing a door frame in an opening requires some shim space to allow for possible deviations in plumb of the rough door opening.

Tolerances

Each element of construction is built to be within a certain degree of closeness to perfection. The amount of variance that is allowable from a given line, dimension, or size is known as *tolerance*, and it must be accounted for in the detailing on the construction drawings. Some construction items such as woodwork have very small tolerances, sometimes as small as $^1/_{64}$ in, while other elements such as poured concrete footings may be oversized by as much as 2 in and still be acceptable.

Tolerances for many construction components have been established by various trade organizations. These are considered the accepted norms for the industry. If the architect asks for tolerances that are closer than industry norms, it will usually be necessary to use better materials, more time, more labor, or a combination of all three, which means a higher cost.

Details should allow for expected tolerances. For example, a finished wood-panel wall installed over cast concrete must have enough space for shimming and blocking so that the final wall surface can be plumb, because the rough structural wall may be out of plumb by as much as $^1/_4$ in over a 10 ft height.

Clearances

A *clearance* is a gap or space in the design that allows for the construction or installation of a material, construction element, or piece of equipment. Details must provide enough clearance to make construction possible. For example, shim space around doors and windows is provided so that the door or window unit can be slipped into the rough opening and then leveled and plumbed before being attached to the framing. Structural steel connections made with bolts must give enough clearance to allow the use of pneumatic impact wrenches.

Costs

The three biggest factors in the cost of building are materials, labor, and equipment. In addition there are the costs of overhead and contractor profit, which may change as the other costs fluctuate. In combination these represent the initial costs of the structure.

Beyond the initial construction costs, however, there are life-cycle costs that the architect and client must be aware of. An assembly with a low initial cost may be an expensive detail to maintain and ultimately replace. Refer to Chap. 13 and Chap. 30 for information on life-cycle cost analysis.

Cost control involves striking the proper balance between client needs, initial costs, and life-cycle costs. The client may want more than is affordable, or may ask for the lowest initial costs without realizing that inexpensive materials will cost more in the long run. On the other hand, if the building is a speculative venture, low initial costs may be acceptable to the developer regardless of the consequences. It is up to the architect to make sure that the client understands the choices and the ramifications of design and detailing decisions.

It is also important to keep in mind the cost of a portion of a building in proportion to the building's total cost. If the entire building is going to cost $2 million, it does not make sense to spend a great deal of time and worry over saving $100 on one detail. On the other hand, if extensive research and study on a typical wall detail of the same building can save $30,000, then it is reasonable to make the effort. It is also desirable to save a little money on an item that will be constructed or purchased in large quantities. If a hotel will have 2000 rooms, trimming just $100 from the cost of construction of one hotel room will add up to $200,000.

If the entire building is going to cost $2 million, it does not make sense to spend a great deal of time and worry over saving $100 on one detail.

Cost is directly related to the choice of materials, which depends on intended use, durability, strength, maintainability, and all the other considerations involved with designing a detail. Labor cost is largely determined by how much effort is needed to build a detail; in general, construction costs can be minimized by developing simple details that still satisfy all other criteria. Equipment costs involve the purchase or rental of specialized machinery needed to build the project. For example, prefabricated concrete components may need large, expensive cranes to set them in place, but this cost may be more than offset by the savings in formwork and time delays involved with cast-in-place concrete.

Material Availability

Construction is a geographically localized industry. Not only does the availability of labor vary with location, but many materials are found only in certain parts of the country. Any material can be shipped to another location, but the cost may not be justified. For example, specifying southern pine for rough framing in Oregon does not make sense when other species of wood that are harvested in the Pacific Northwest are just as suitable for building. Steel framing may be less expensive than concrete in parts of the country near steel mills, yet may be prohibitively expensive in other areas where concrete is more readily available.

Building Movement and Substrate Attachment

Because every detail consists of a number of components connected with each other, it is important to understand that one material must provide an appropriate base, or substrate, for the attachment of another.

This attachment may be done in one of three ways. The first is a rigid attachment, such as plaster fixed to lath: if one material moves, both move. The second attachment is rigid but adjustable for installation, such as a curtain wall anchored to a floor beam. The third type of attachment is flexible so that movement is allowed at a specific location and in a specific direction. An expansion joint in curtain wall or an uncoupling membrane specified under tile to prevent cracking will allow a certain amount of movement.

Each detail needs to include space for the attaching device as well as clearance for workers and equipment. Problems with incompatible materials must also be considered, such as possible galvanic action where metals meet or the deterioration of one material from water leakage through another. If the materials are chemically bonded with sealants, mastics, paint, or other coatings, the base material must be compatible with the coating or the joining material.

In every case, the detail must provide affordances for expected building movement as discussed in other chapters. Movement is inevitable, whether it is from live, dead, or lateral loading, temperature changes, water absorption, or other forces. How much movement will occur on a given detail varies, but movement is always present and must be considered as a part of the design.

Conformance to Industry Standards

Certain common methods of building are considered industry standards. These methods have been developed through practice and experience, from the recommendations of trade associations and testing organizations and from building codes. Each reinforced masonry wall, for example, should be built in a similar manner regardless of who designs it, who builds it, or what it is used for. The only things that should change to suit the particular needs of the building are the specifications as to materials, dimensions, and so on—things such as the finish, the size of reinforcing, and the type of mortar.

Conforming to these industry standards not only increases the likelihood that the detail will work, but also minimizes potential liability if something goes wrong. These standards or best practices have been tested in theory and in practice and represent the collective knowledge of experts in the industry. This does not mean that the architect should not try new design approaches or be creative in solving unusual technical problems, but only when necessary. Deviation from industry standards should only be considered

- after the performance requirements for the building assembly have been precisely defined and specified
- after the materials and construction techniques being proposed to meet these requirements have been thoroughly researched
- with careful analysis of how the construction might perform

The architect should provide information and make recommendations, but the final decision should be made by the client.

Resistance to Moisture and Weathering

Controlling moisture is one of the most troublesome areas of construction design and detailing, and one of the most prone to error. Specific methods of waterproofing are discussed in Chap. 27.

The architect should carefully review each detail that could be affected by moisture. This includes all roofing, exterior walls and wall penetrations, below-grade walls and slabs, pools, areas under and around showers and tubs, kitchens, mechanical rooms, and any other interior space where excess moisture might be present.

Some of the considerations are as follows.

- *the permeability of the material itself.* Can it resist moisture, or must it be protected with a coating or by some other mechanical means?
- *the durability of the material.* Will aging, building movement, and other forms of deterioration cause the material to crack or break up and allow water to penetrate?
- *aggravating circumstances.* Will other conditions cause a normally water-resistant detail to leak? An exterior material may normally shed water, yet leak when wind-driven rain is forced in.
- *joints.* Are joints constructed, flashed, and sealed so that water cannot enter? Will building movement damage the integrity of the joints?
- *capillary action.* Are tiny joints or holes that can admit water inherent in the material? Brick mortar joints are a perfect example of this. The wrong type of joint can crack imperceptibly and let water seep into the wall. A windowsill or coping without a drip edge can allow water to flow up the underside and into the structure.
- *outlets.* If water does get into the structure, as is normal in some situations, is there a way for it to drain back out? Weep holes in masonry walls and curtain walls allow this to happen. A *weep hole* is a small opening or outlet in a wall or at the bottom of a window member through which accumulated condensation and other water can drain to the exterior. For example, the small extension of metal framing at the lower portion of a skylight collects the condensation that forms inside the glass and allows the water to drip out.
- *sealants.* Have the proper types of sealants been selected for the type of material used and for the expected movement of the joint? Is the backup material correct, and is the sealant installed with the correct dimensions?

In addition to precipitation, other forms of weathering include ultraviolet degradation, freeze-thaw cycles, and atmospheric corrosion. Materials must be selected to withstand the expected conditions.

Thermal Resistance

The architect must investigate each detail's resistance to heat transfer, including both heat loss and heat gain. The prudent architect will not only check the resistance of insulation, but also look for breaks where the full thickness of the insulation is not present.

A *heat bridge* is formed when metals or other conductive materials are connected in a way that they span from the exterior face to the interior face of a wall. Exterior studs, pipes penetrating walls, and metal door frames are examples of areas where there may be a weakness in the insulation value of the exterior wall.

The architect should also look for paths by which air may infiltrate through the insulation. Penetrations in the exterior wall should be given careful attention when detailing to make sure that all gaps are sealed.

Sustainability

The architect should review details with an eye toward their environmental impact. Many of the criteria for evaluating the sustainability of building materials (as discussed in Chap. 13) can also be used as guidelines for detailing.

- Details should be designed to keep energy consumption as low as possible. Something as simple as adding insulation in a small gap can yield significant energy savings, especially if the detail is repeated dozens or hundreds of times in a building.
- The embodied energy of the materials in the detail should be as low as possible. This includes not just finish materials but also materials that are hidden, such as blocking and bracing. See Chap. 13 for a discussion of embodied energy.
- As many of the materials and components as possible should be made from renewable materials or have recycled content.
- As many of the materials and components as possible should come from local sources.
- Adhesives, cleaning compounds, and finishes should be low in volatile organic compounds (VOCs). For example, in some cases mechanical fasteners can be used instead of construction mastics. See Chap. 13 for a discussion of VOCs.
- If possible, the detail should be designed to allow for easy deconstruction, so that the individual components can be recycled.

Other Properties

There are many other properties of materials and construction details to review when developing or evaluating drawings. These include, when applicable, such things as acoustical properties, light reflection, abrasion resistance, resistance to termites and other insects, holding power of fasteners, resistance to fading, mildew resistance, color, and finish. No material will completely satisfy all criteria, but it is the architect's responsibility to find the best balance.

STANDARDS IN CONSTRUCTION DOCUMENTATION

Through much of the twentieth century, there were no widely accepted standards for the organization, layout, and production of construction drawings. Each architect's office developed its own methods, and, although drafting was beautifully done and work was well coordinated within each office, there were no agreements that extended beyond the walls of a single firm.

During the last decades of the twentieth century, the development and spread of computer-aided drafting brought with it new organizational issues, such as the need for standard conventions in file naming and layering. As architects and engineers began sharing digital files, it became evident that, to improve collaboration, consistent standards were needed for construction documents (as well as for specifications, as discussed in Chap. 47).

These concerns led to the development of the two standards that are used or closely emulated by most architectural firms, the United States National CAD Standard (NCS) and the National BIM Standard—United States (NBIMS-US).

United States National CAD Standard

The development of the NCS has been a joint effort of the National Institute of Building Sciences (NIBS), the American Institute of Architects (AIA), and the Construction Specifications Institute (CSI). The NCS consists of

- a foreword and administration notes
- CAD layer guidelines (contributed by the AIA)
- the Uniform Drawing System (UDS, originally developed by CSI in the 1990s)
- BIM implementation and plotting guidelines (contributed by the NIBS)

The Uniform Drawing System is a set of standards for organizing and presenting building design information, including guidelines for

- drawing set organization
- sheet organization
- schedule formats
- drafting conventions
- terms and abbreviations
- symbols
- notation
- code conventions

The intent of the NCS is to improve the efficiency of building design, construction, and management throughout the life cycle of a facility. Use of the NCS is voluntary, but it has been adopted by most government agencies and large organizations and by many prominent architectural firms.

National BIM Standard—United States

The NBIMS-US is a standard based on industry consensus and developed by the buildingSMART alliance, a council of the National Institute of Building Sciences. It is intended as a consistent method by which the various participants in a project create and use building information models.

While the NCS was created for paper-based drafting, the NBIMS-US sets standards for computer-based exchanges of information during the creation and operation of buildings and other facilities. However, the NCS remains important as a standard for construction drawings that are output from the BIM process. The latest version of the NCS has been aligned with the NBIMS-US to make this possible and makes electronic design data available throughout the life cycle of a building.

The following sections describe some components of construction drawing standards.

- organization, layout, and coordination of construction drawings
- project changes
- documentation

ORGANIZATION, LAYOUT, AND COORDINATION OF CONSTRUCTION DRAWINGS

Organization of the Construction Drawing Set

The Uniform Drawing System (UDS) described in the NCS is a standardized method of numbering and organizing construction drawings. When the UDS is being used, the drawing set is organized first by discipline and then by sheet type (as described later in this section). The disciplines are usually arranged in the following sequence as required by the project.

- general
- hazardous materials
- survey/mapping
- geotechnical
- civil
- landscape
- structural
- architectural
- interiors
- equipment
- fire protection
- plumbing
- process
- mechanical
- electrical
- distributed energy
- telecommunications
- resource
- other disciplines

When the UDS is not being used, the construction drawings are usually organized in the following sequence based on the order of construction.

- title and index sheet
- civil engineering drawings (if any)
- site drawings (landscape)
- architectural drawings
- demolition plan (if any)
- floor plans
- reflected ceiling plans
- roof plans
- exterior elevations
- interior elevations
- building sections

- wall sections
- exterior details
- interior details
- schedules
- structural drawings
- plumbing drawings
- mechanical drawings
- electrical drawings
- other consultants' drawings (kitchen equipment, acoustical design, and so on)

This is a typical order, but some firms vary the sequence of architectural drawings. The intent is to present the information in a logical sequence so that the contractors and others can find the information they need quickly and without confusion.

Sheet Numbering

A numbering system must be established so that drawings can be logically organized and referenced. Each drawing sheet in a set must have a unique number. There are several ways to accomplish this, depending on the size and complexity of the project, the number of drawings, and whether the UDS is being used.

In the UDS, each sheet is uniquely identified by a string of five characters. (See Fig. 46.14.) The first character is a letter of the alphabet, the second is either another letter or a hyphen, and the last three are digits.

The first character indicates the discipline. For example, A is used for architectural drawings, E for electrical, S for structural, T for telecommunications, and so on.

When the complexity of a project makes it desirable to identify and organize the drawings more specifically, the second character indicates a subcategory within the discipline. For example, within the telecommunications drawings, TA can be used for audiovisual systems, TN for data networks, and TY for security systems. If the two-letter designations already defined by the UDS do not meet the needs of a particular project, user-defined designations are allowed. When two-letter designations are not needed, the second character is a hyphen.

The third character is a digit that identifies the type of drawing.

- 0 for general
- 1 for plans
- 2 for elevations
- 3 for sections
- 4 for large-scale views
- 5 for details
- 6 for schedules and diagrams
- 7 and 8 for user-defined drawing types that don't fall into other categories
- 9 for 3-D representations

The last two characters form a two-digit number from 01 to 99 (00 is not allowed) that identifies the particular drawing. These numbers define how drawings of the same discipline and type are placed in sequence. Numbering starts with 01, but later numbers do not have to be consecutive, so that additional sheets can be inserted later during production of the drawing set. A suffix consisting of a hyphen and up to three alphanumeric characters may also be added; suffixes can be defined by the user, such as to identify supplemental drawings or different versions or revisions of the same drawing.

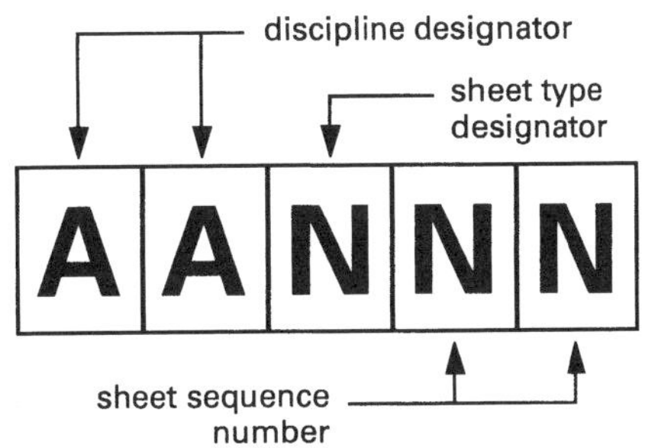

Figure 46.14
UDS Sheet Identification

If the UDS is not used, a similar method can be used. The simplest method uses only numbers, beginning with 1. Some firms also include the total number of sheets in the set, so that a set might be numbered 1 of 6, 2 of 6, and so on. This method is only acceptable for small projects, such as a residence, where there are no consultants' drawings.

For larger drawing sets where consultants are involved, numbers can be preceded with a capital letter to designate the discipline involved. In this case, drawings will be designated A1, A2, A3, ..., M1, M2, ..., E1, E2, and so on. The letters used for most architectural projects are as follows.

A	architectural
E	electrical
FP	fire protection
I	interiors
M	mechanical
S	structural

On some projects, HVAC and/or plumbing drawings are separated from other mechanical drawings and designated with H and P, respectively.

For larger projects, drawings within each discipline can be grouped by type. For example, floor plans can be group 1, reflected ceiling plans group 2, elevations group 3, and so on. Individual drawings within a group are designated by numbers following a decimal point; for example, a set of drawing could include A1.1, A1.2, A1.3, ..., A2.1, A2.2, ..., A3.1, A3.2, ... M1.1, M1.2, and so on. More sheets can be added at the end of any group without disrupting the numbers already assigned. This system is good for large commercial projects with several disciplines contributing to the drawing set.

For projects in high-rise buildings or large buildings with different sections or building complexes, the number can be preceded with the floor number or the building section number. For example, 54A1.3 can indicate a floor plan sheet (group 1) in the architectural series (A) on the 54th floor of a project. (Some firms prefer to keep the letter first, so that this sheet would be designated A54-1.3.) This system is useful for building owners and managers, as well as for design firms doing work on different floors in the same building.

Sheet Sizes

A firm will typically have one or two standard sheet sizes that it uses for its architectural drawings on all projects. The size or sizes will vary depending on several factors, including the typical size of the firm's projects, the filing system used, the capabilities of the firm's reproduction and plotting equipment, and the client's requirements. The determining factor is often the need to draw a floor plan on a single sheet without dividing the plan into sections.

In the architectural, interior design, and engineering industries, standard sheet sizes are used for manual drafting, CAD, and BIM. These standard sizes are based on three systems: architectural, ANSI (American National Standards Institute), and ISO (International Standards Organization). Each sheet size is given a letter designation. These are shown in Table 46.1.

Product Development

Table 46.1
Drawing Sheet Sizes

system and sheet sizes					
architectural		ANSI		ISO	
size (in)	mark	size (in)	ma-rk	size (mm (in))	mark
9 × 12	A	8.5 × 11	A	210 × 297 (8.3 × 11.7)	A4
12 × 18	B	11 × 17	B	297 × 420 (11.7 × 16.5)	A3
18 × 24	C	17 × 22	C	420 × 594 (16.5 × 23.4)	A2
24 × 36	D	22 × 34	D	594 × 841 (23.4 × 33.1)	A1
36 × 48	E	34 × 44	E	841 × 1189 (33.1 × 46.8)	A0
30 × 42	F	—	—	—	—

The ISO sizes are based on the SI system of units, commonly called the metric system. Although most firms in the United States use the architectural sizes, the U.S. federal government requires that its projects use the ANSI sizes. In other countries, the ISO sizes are generally used.

Sheet Organization and Layering

In most firms, individual sheets are organized in a consistent manner. Whatever method is used, a firm will use consistent sheet sizes. The title block is generally located along the right side of the drawing sheet. See Fig. 46.15.

Borderlines are typically used to confine the drawing within a set area. Borderlines were originally needed to allow for imperfections in reproducing drawings from originals; borderlines continue to be needed because some plotters cannot plot to the extreme edges of paper. Borderline width varies depending on the firm's preferences, client needs, and the limitations of plotting devices. Typically, the right, top, and bottom edges are $^1/_2$ in or $^3/_4$ in wide and the left, binding edge is about $1^1/_2$ in wide.

After the borderlines and title block are drawn, the remaining drawing area is organized on a module system as shown in 46.14. The exact size of the module depends on the firm's standards, the size of the drawing sheet, and how much of the sheet is allotted for the borderline width and the title block (usually drawn along the right side of the sheet). The typical drawing module is about 6 in square, but this dimension can vary to keep an even division of modules within the borderline. Drawings are developed to fit within one or more modules. For example, a small detail may require only one module, while a wall section may require a space one module wide and three modules high. A floor plan may require an entire sheet of modules.

This system allows for the development and easy use of standard or master details fit within the module. This system works with manual drafting, CAD, and BIM. A standard numbering system for the modules also makes it possible for individual drawings to be numbered early in the development of the construction drawings.

In a CAD system, information is placed on various *layers* of the drawing. *Layering* allows different kinds of information to be shown or hidden independently. In this way several drawings can be developed from one computer file of information, depending on which layers are shown. For example, a layer showing the partition layout can be used in both a floor plan and a reflected ceiling plan for the same space; other layers are shown or hidden depending on the kind of plan. Individual firms may develop their own layering systems, but most use the UDS CAD layering system or some variation of it.

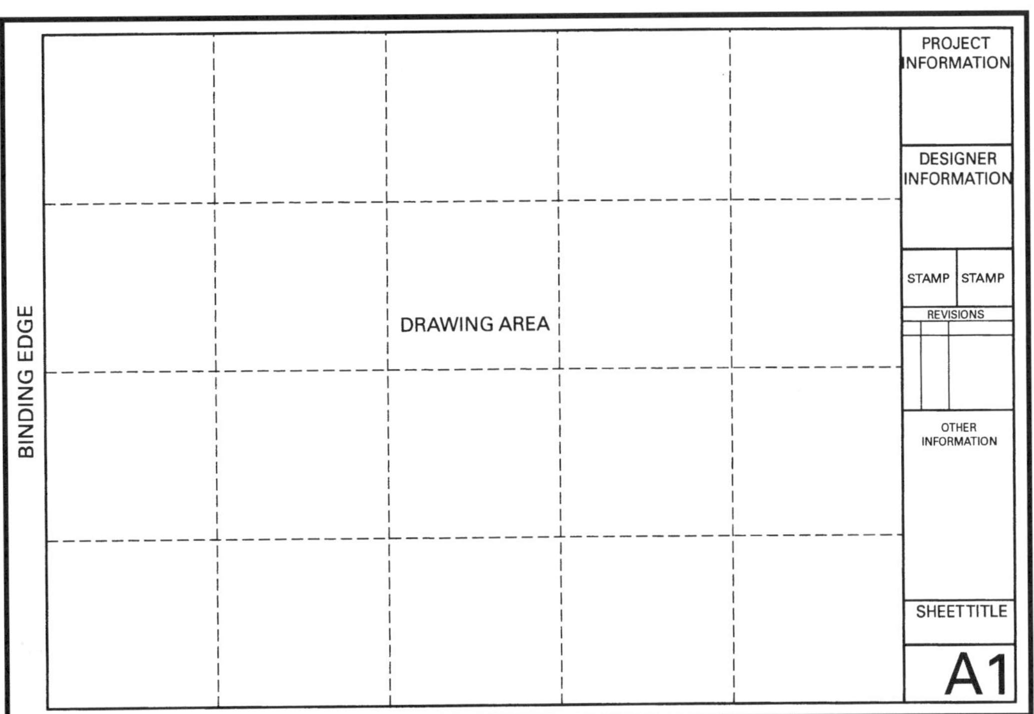

Figure 46.15 Drafting Sheet Layout

Title Blocks

Each sheet of the drawing set contains a *title block*, which gives identifying information about the drawing, such as the sheet number, sheet name, revision dates, and so on. The title block is placed along the full length of the right edge of the sheet. The information may either be oriented in the way the sheet is normally viewed or widthwise, along the short dimension of the sheet.

Most firms design their own title blocks with space for the information they want to include. Although the design and placement of title blocks varies from firm to firm, each firm standardizes its title block layout so that the same information will appear in the same place on every job a firm takes on.

Before the use of computers, standard title block sheets with borderlines were printed on vellum or polyester; the line work and information that did not change from job to job, such as the designer's name and address, were printed on each sheet. The use of CAD software for drawings allows the title block and borderlines to be kept in a single reference file that is used in all sheet files. In this way, the title block design has to be developed only once, which saves computer memory and allows all drawings to be updated at one time if the title block information changes.

The following is a list of the information that should appear on every title block. Optional information is also noted.

- *the designer's name, address, and phone number.* Other contact information, such as email address and website, is optional.
- *a logo or some special design.* This is optional.
- *consultants' names, addresses, and phone numbers.* Email addresses are sometimes also included. If the title block is too small, this information is listed on the title sheet for the set.
- *the project title and address.*
- *the owner's name and address..* This is optional if the owner desires it. Some owners don't want to be identified, while others want their logos to appear, too.
- *the project number or file number.* This number may be assigned by the designer for accounting and filing convenience, or may be a number assigned by the client.

- *space for professional stamps, if needed.* Provide a 2 in × 2 in space for each stamp.
- *revisions column.* This should include space for the revision number, date, and a brief note. There should be space for at least 10 revisions, and more is not uncommon.
- *sheet title.* This should be short, like Details or First Floor Plan.
- *sheet number.* In the lower right-hand corner, large and easy to see.
- *the words "drawn by," followed by a small space for initials.*
- *the words "checked by," followed by a small space for initials.*
- *the words "approved by" followed by a small space for the client's initials.* The space is optional, but it's a good idea to provide a space where the client can sign off on the drawings.
- *copyright notice.* This is optional, but a good idea. U.S. law no longer requires a notice, but if one is used, it must include the copyright symbol © or the word "copyright," the date of publication, and the name of the copyright owner. See United States Copyright Office Circular 3 for more information.
- *space for a key plan.* This is optional for interior work, but useful for very large projects. A *key plan* is a plan of a large building or complex of buildings, drawn at a very small scale to fit within the title block. The key plan, shaded or otherwise, is marked to show which part of the larger building a particular floor plan refers to. If a single, large floor plan must be divided over two or more sheets, *match lines* are also drawn to show where the parts of the plan join up.
- *scale.* This is optional, and a holdover from early drafting practices. Modern practice is to indicate the scale in the title of each drawing, because a single sheet often contains several drawings at different scales.
- *north arrow.* This is optional on sheets used for elevations or details. Some firms provide space for it when needed.
- *space for notes, legends, or keynotes.* This is optional but can be a good idea, provided that the firm uses these consistently and the drawing sheet is large enough to provide the space for them.

A *keynote* is an annotation, such as a special instruction or explanation, about a particular item in the drawing. Each keynote is numbered, and the same number is also placed on the drawing next to the item that the note refers to. This reduces the space needed for the drawing, especially when notes are lengthy or the same note refers to multiple items. The keynote number can also be coordinated with specification numbers. The annotations themselves are often located either in the title block or in a *note block* on the same sheet as the drawing.

Some firms find it useful to have a computer-generated date stamp automatically printed on each sheet, to note the time that a hard-copy print was plotted. This helps identify the latest version of a sheet that has been published.

Coordination with Consultants' Drawings

The architectural construction drawings are only a part of the entire set of contract documents, so they must be coordinated with other documents in the set. Thorough coordination is vital in avoiding errors, cost overruns, and scheduling delays, as well as in minimizing the architect's exposure to liability. Depending on how an individual firm is organized, the responsibility for coordination may fall to the project architect, project manager, or job captain; in any case, ongoing effort is needed during the design development and production phases.

On nearly every project, multiple consultants work with the architect. Small to medium jobs will have structural, mechanical, and electrical consultants at a minimum. Larger projects may have additional consultants in fire protection, civil engineering, landscape architecture, food service, elevators, curtain walls, and interior design, among others.

Each of these disciplines develops its own drawings, so coordination among everyone on the team is crucial. Although all consultants must be diligent in their efforts to work with others, the main responsibility for overall coordination is with the architect's firm. The project manager most often takes on this duty; in smaller firms or on smaller jobs, the project architect may be responsible for it.

Larger projects may be have additional consultants in fire protection, civil engineering, landscape architecture, and interior design, among others.

There are a number of ways to keep everyone up to date with drawings during the design and production of contract documents. Meetings should be held periodically (either face to face or electronically) to exchange information and alert everyone to the progress of the job. At these meetings, anyone may ask questions and raise issues that may affect the work of others.

Progress prints or electronic files should be exchanged between the architect and the consultants for ongoing comparison of the work being produced. Exchanging information electronically through PDF files that can be reviewed, marked up, and annotated is fast and minimizes paper use. Several technologies are available that can help with project management and PDF file exchange.

The project manager must notify all consultants of changes made as they occur. It is important that the architect documents how and when this information was transmitted to members of the project team. Finally, the architect must thoroughly check and coordinate the entire drawing set before issuing it for bidding or negotiation.

Coordination with the Specifications

Architectural drawings and specifications are complementary contract documents. They both give necessary information about the design of the project, and they should work together without duplication or overlap. Each component is incomplete without the other.

Specifications are part of the project manual and describe the following.

- types and quality of materials
- quality of workmanship
- methods of fabrication and installation
- general requirements related to the construction of the project

These are normally written after the production of the drawings has started and materials have been selected. Because the specifications may be written by someone other than the person developing the drawings, there must be close coordination within the architect's office. Preliminary information sharing, checking, and coordination of the specifications and the drawings are usually the responsibility of the project manager.

If a computer-aided master specification system is used, there may be a sheet of drawing coordination notes produced by the system for each section of the specifications. The people who are producing the drawings can use these to check their drawings against.

Many problems in coordination are related to materials. A material may be shown on the drawings but not be described in a specification section, or the drawings may indicate one material while the specifications indicate another. Refer to Chap. 47 for a further discussion of coordinating the specifications with the drawings.

PROJECT CHANGES AND DOCUMENTATION

The architect-client agreement documents a proposed scope of work for a project. The scope of work can be affected by changes, however, throughout the entire process of planning, designing, and documenting a project. These changes can come about due to a change in the owner's requirements, a revision of the budget, problems with material supplies, a change to code or administrative requirements, or any of a number of other reasons. A change in scope can also reflect the architect's research and the natural evolution of the design and information gathered through this process.

A minor change in scope can be explained by the architect and approved by the owner through phone calls or emails with the owner and consultants. When a proposed change is more extensive, however, or may require additional research and development, the architect needs to assess how the change will affect documentation and the project schedule and take appropriate action.

The architect's first step is to determine whether responding to the proposed change qualifies as a normal part of the work as specified in the contract, or whether it is an extra service for which the architect should receive additional compensation. If it is an additional service, the client should be notified of the proposed change, the reason for the change, who requested the change (if not the client), and whether there will be cost implications. The contract should be referenced to establish that the proposed work is an additional service. The requirements and procedures for doing this are itemized in the standard AIA contracts, including AIA Document B101, *Standard Form of Agreement Between Owner and Architect.* Refer to Chap. 5 for a discussion of additional services.

The architect may want to notify the client first, before spending time studying the proposed change in great detail, in case the client instructs the architect to ignore it. In some cases, though, such as an additional requirement imposed by a local authority having jurisdiction, the client may not be able to ignore it and the additional work must become a part of the project.

If the architect is directed to proceed, the next step is to estimate the potential cost of making the change. The architect should analyze the proposed change and estimate both the extent of the additional work and the extra charge for services.

The architect should also determine how the change will affect documentation. The following questions should be considered.

- What type of change is it? For example, is it additional construction, a change in materials, a modification of an existing detail design, or something else?
- Have the drawings that will be affected by the change already been started?
- How complex is the change?
- Will research be needed? If so, how much time will it take?
- How many drawings must be completed to communicate the change to the project team?
- Will new drawings by consultants be needed? If so, what will be their additional fees? How much more time will be needed to coordinate with the consultants? How much time will be needed to modify the architectural drawings to coordinate with the consultants' new drawings?
- Will new or modified specifications be needed?

Once the architect has determined the number, type, and complexity of the drawings needed, the architect can then estimate the time needed to complete them and multiply it by the hourly charge stated in the contract for additional services. The architect should then notify the owner by mail or email regarding the time and cost needed.

The architect should not proceed with creating new documentation until the owner gives written authorization in accordance with the contract. Once the client has authorized the change, the architect can inform others on the project team by email attachment, paper copies, or any of the available methods of electronic exchange mentioned earlier. Time and costs associated with changes should be invoiced separately as additional services.

47

THE PROJECT MANUAL AND SPECIFICATIONS

THE PROJECT MANUAL

The *project manual* is a bound book or series of volumes containing all contract and noncontract documents for a construction project other than the drawings. The project manual contains the technical specifications, as well as several other types of documents.

Organization of the Project Manual

The project manual is divided into four major parts.

- bidding requirements
- contract information, including the owner-contractor agreement, bond forms, and the like
- general and supplementary conditions of the contract
- technical specifications

The bidding requirements and supplements to bid forms are not part of the contract documents, but they are typically included in the project manual for reference.

A project manual might include some or all of the following.

- bidding requirements
  - invitation to bid
  - prequalification forms
  - instructions to bidders
  - additional information available to bidders (such as copies of geotechnical reports)
  - bid forms
- supplements to bid forms
  - bid security form
  - subcontractor list
  - substitution request form
  - request for information form
- contract forms
  - sample agreement (contract between owner and contractor)
  - sample performance bond
  - sample labor and materials payment bond
  - sample certificates of insurance and list of insurance requirements
- general and supplementary conditions
  - sample general conditions of the contract (such as AIA Document 201)
  - supplementary conditions
- technical specifications

Contracts, bidding documents, and general conditions of the contract are discussed in more detail in Chap. 5 and Chap. 49. This chapter focuses on the technical specifications.

SPECIFICATIONS

The specifications are part of the project manual and are legal documents. As such, they must be complete, accurate, unambiguous, and exact. Specifications communicate complex technical information in spare and specific language, which makes them difficult to write correctly. Fortunately, some standard methods and formats of preparing specifications are in general use. These will be described later in this section.

In addition, master specifications are available that can be used as starting documents. A *master specification* contains standardized text in an editable format; the text includes most of the requirements that apply to the products defined in a particular specification section. Master specifications are edited by deleting unnecessary portions, adding particular requirements for the specific job, making choices among alternates, and coordinating the requirements with other specification sections and other parts of the project manual.

The challenge in using a master specification template is knowing what to keep and what to delete, accurately describing the products to be used, not including or excluding something that would disqualify the desired product, and not allowing the use of something that does not meet the design intent. Master specifications are available in electronic format from various commercial sources, or they may be written in house.

There are also computer programs that can generate specifications through interactive question-and-answer sessions. Some programs can also be linked to some types of CAD and BIM software to help with coordination between the drawings and the specifications.

Master specifications, whether written and maintained by an individual office or purchased from a commercial source, must be carefully edited for each project to eliminate what is not needed, including provisions in Division 1. They must also be updated periodically to conform to new or updated reference standards, codes, products, and manufacturers.

- Master specifications and notes are excellent tools for information management. They can contain the institutional knowledge of a firm, the lessons learned over time about materials, products, and systems that work for the types of projects in which the firm typically engages.

Some of the master specifications available include

- *SpecText*, by ARCOM. This product is primarily used for infrastructure and civil engineering projects. (arcomnet.com/spectext)
- *MasterSpec* by ARCOM, under contract with the AIA. (arcomnet.com/masterspec)
- *SpecLink-E* by Buildings Systems Design, Inc., a subsidiary of the Construction Specifications Institute. (bsdsoftlink.com)

The Construction Criteria Base (CCB) is a library service of the Whole Building Design Guide (WBDG), a part of the National Institute of Building Sciences. The CCB publishes the *Unified Facilities Guide Specifications* (UFGS), which is used on nearly all government projects, as well as the NAVFAC Specifications and VA Specifications for military projects. Other regulations and design criteria applying to federal projects can be obtained through the CCB (wbdg.org/ccb).

Types of Specifications

There are two broad categories of specifications: prescriptive and performance. *Prescriptive specifications* (also called *closed specification*) specify brand names and tell the contractor exactly what product or material to use. *Performance specifications* (also called *open specifications*) tell what results the final construction assembly should achieve, but give the contractor room to decide how the results will be achieved. Most specifications fall somewhere between these two extremes.

The type of specification used will depend on several factors. Public projects almost always use performance specifications in order to encourage competitive bidding; when specific products are cited, the specification generally lists at least three product options. In other cases, it may be preferable to use a prescriptive specification to ensure that only one particular product is used.

Whether the job is bid or negotiated in a contract may also affect the choice. When the job is bid, allowing contractors as much choice as possible can result in the lowest price being found that meets the specification requirements.

The following types of specifications are the ones most commonly used.

Types of Prescriptive (Closed) Specifications

Proprietary specifications are the most restrictive in that they require use of a specific manufacturer's product. They give the architect complete control over what is installed.

A template for a particular product can often be obtained from the product's manufacturer, to assist the specifier in writing an accurate and comprehensive description; this is usually short and simple.

Proprietary specifications have some drawbacks. They do not allow for competitive bidding. They may force the contractor to use materials that are difficult or expensive to procure in a certain geographical area or that need long delivery times. The burden, then, is on the specifier to call out products that meet code requirements, are within the budget, and are technically correct.

A *base bid with alternates* is a type of specification that calls out a proprietary product but allows the substitution of other products that the contractor determines to be equal to the one stated. This can be risky because a contractor may substitute a less expensive item that is thought to be equal but actually does not have the same properties or aesthetic qualities as the product specified.

There are two variations of a base bid specification. The first lists several approved manufacturers of a product. The contractor is free to bid using any one listed. This satisfies the requirements for public work where at least three different manufacturers must be listed, but it puts the burden on the architect to make sure that all the listed products or manufacturers listed are in fact equal. Where the specified alternatives vary in dimension, attachment method, or interface with other products, the project details must be prepared in a way that will allow use of any of the listed products without additional work or cost.

The second variation is a base bid with "approved equal" language. This type of specification states that a particular product or an approved equal must be used. Substitutions must be proposed by the contractor during the bid phase. The submitted product is subject to review and approval by the architect before it can be incorporated into the bid. This gives the contractor some freedom in looking for lower-priced alternatives, but the work of finding these alternatives and providing information to prove that they are equal falls to the contractor.

The responsibility for fairly and accurately evaluating the proposed alternatives is placed on the architect or owner. This can be a large burden during a hectic bidding period, both on the architect and on the contractor who is waiting to know whether an alternative is approved. The specifications should clearly state how much lead time the contractor must give the architect and how alternatives will be evaluated. If an option is approved as equal, the architect should notify all bidders.

Types of Performance (Open) Specifications

A pure performance specification is a statement establishing the criteria and the results required of the item being specified. These requirements can be verified by measurement, test evaluation, or other types of assurance. The means of achieving the desired results are not specified; they are left up to the person trying to meet the specification.

This type of specification is often used when the specifier wants to encourage new ways of achieving a particular end result. For example, a movable partition system could be specified by stating its requirements for fire rating, acoustical properties, finish, maximum thickness, tolerances, required size, and all other required properties. It would then be up to the contractor and manufacturer to design and develop a system to satisfy these criteria.

Performance specifications are more difficult to write because the specifier must state all relevant criteria and give the methods that will be used for testing compliance. A product or system described with a performance specification will be unique and therefore may be more expensive; the specifier must be prepared for the effect this may have on costs.

The means of achieving the desired results are left up to the person trying to meet the specification.

A *descriptive specification* gives detailed written descriptions of the material or product and the workmanship required for its fabrication and installation. It does not mention trade names. In its purest form, a descriptive specification is difficult to write because the architect must include all the pertinent requirements for the construction and installation of the product.

A variation of the descriptive specification type is a *reference standard specification*. This describes a material, product, or process based on the performance of that material or assembly in comparison to reference standards set by an accepted authority or test method. For example, a product can be required to meet testing standards produced by organizations such as the American Society for Testing and Materials (ASTM), the American National Standards Institute (ANSI), and Underwriters Laboratories (UL). Reference can also be made to standards published by specific trade associations, such as the Architectural Woodwork Institute (AWI), the American Iron and Steel Institute (AISI), and the Gypsum Association.

For example, in specifying gypsum wallboard the architect can state that all gypsum wallboard products must meet the requirements of ASTM C1396. This recognized industry standard describes in great detail

- the properties of different types of gypsum wallboard
- how the wallboards are to be tested (which includes references to other ASTM tests)
- what performance requirements must be met for approval
- which types of materials are to be used for specific applications

Rather than repeat all these criteria in the specification, by citing ASTM C1396 the architect incorporates all the requirements of this document into the description of the desired product.

Reference standard specifications are fairly short and easy to write. Chances for errors are reduced and liability is minimized by using industry standards and recognized building methods. However, the architect must know what is in the standard; if the standard includes more provisions than are needed for the job, the architect must also understand how to refer to the appropriate part of the standard if it.

The type of specification required by a particular project depends, in part, on the method of contract that will be used. For example, a design-build contract may benefit from a specification that allows for choice of materials and systems to help meet budgetary and other restraints; because the contractor and designer are working together to achieve common goals, there may be less need for restrictive, tightly written requirements.

On the other hand, a standard design-bid-build contract for a government agency needs an open specification with detailed, specific, tightly controlled requirements for bidding. A tight specification may also be needed if the architect wants a specific manufacturers' product or a specific way of building something.

Organization of the Technical Sections

The material presented in the sections on technical specification has been standardized through general adoption of the MasterFormat system. This system was developed by the Construction Specifications Institute (CSI) and Construction Specifications Canada (CSC) to standardize the numbering and format of project-related information for use in specifying, cost estimating, and data filing.

The organization of the MasterFormat divisions is shown in Fig. 47.1. There are major subgroups, with individual divisions within each subgroup. Many divisions are reserved for future use to allow the system to grow as new materials and technologies emerge.

Figure 47.1
MasterFormat Divisions

Procurement and Contracting Requirements Group:
Division 00 – Procurement and Contracting Requirements

Specifications Group:

General Requirements Subgroup:
Division 01 – General Requirements

Facility Construction Subgroup:
Division 02 – Existing Conditions
Division 03 – Concrete
Division 04 – Masonry
Division 05 – Metals
Division 06 – Wood, Plastics, and Composites
Division 07 – Thermal and Moisture Protection
Division 08 – Openings
Division 09 – Finishes
Division 10 – Specialties
Division 11 – Equipment
Division 12 – Furnishings
Division 13 – Special Construction
Division 14 – Conveying Equipment
Division 15 – Reserved for future expansion
Division 16 – Reserved for future expansion
Division 17 – Reserved for future expansion
Division 18 – Reserved for future expansion
Division 19 – Reserved for future expansion

Facility Services Subgroup:
Division 20 – Reserved for future expansion
Division 21 – Fire Suppression
Division 22 – Plumbing
Division 23 – Heating, Ventilating, and Air Conditioning
Division 24 – Reserved for future expansion
Division 25 – Integrated Automation
Division 26 – Electrical
Division 27 – Communications
Division 28 – Electronic Safety and Security
Division 29 – Reserved for future expansion

Site and Infrastructure Subgroup:
Division 30 – Reserved for future expansion
Division 31 – Earthwork
Division 32 – Exterior Improvements
Division 33 – Utilities
Division 34 – Transportation
Division 35 – Waterway and Marine Construction
Division 36 – Reserved for future expansion
Division 37 – Reserved for future expansion
Division 38 – Reserved for future expansion
Division 39 – Reserved for future expansion

Process Equipment Subgroup:
Division 40 – Process Interconnections
Division 41 – Material Processing and Handling Equipment
Division 42 – Process Heating, Cooling, and Drying Equipment
Division 43 – Process Gas and Liquid Handling, Purification, and Storage Equipment
Division 44 – Pollution and Waste Control Equipment
Division 45 – Industry-Specific Manufacturing Equipment
Division 46 – Water and Wastewater Equipment
Division 47 – Reserved for future expansion
Division 48 – Electrical Power Generation
Division 49 – Reserved for future expansion

The MasterFormat system identifies each specification section with a six-digit number divided into three pairs; for example, a section pertaining to athletic wood flooring would be numbered 09 64 66. The first pair of numbers indicates the division number (with a leading zero if needed); in this example, the 09 indicates Division 09, Finishes. The next pair of numbers represents a section within that division; in this case, the 64 indicates wood flooring. The last pair of numbers represents a subsection within that section; in this case, the 66 indicates wood athletic flooring.

The hierarchy allows a specifier to be as precise as needed for the project. A very small project with only one kind of finish could number this part of the specification 09 00 00. A remodel in a private residence with multiple finishes but only one type of wood flooring could use the number 09 64 00 to identify the section of the specification that deals with wood flooring. A large, complex project with many types of wood flooring could use 09 64 66 for athletic wood flooring, 09 64 23 for wood parquet flooring, 09 64 33 for laminated wood flooring, and so on. In this way the information in the specification is kept organized in a standard sequence.

There may be questions on the ARE pertaining to MasterFormat sections and where information on a particular material is found. Know the titles of the divisions, especially those in the facility construction subgroup and the facility services subgroup, and become familiar with what is included in each one. Generally, only the first two numbers (representing the division) have to be remembered, even if the answer options give full six-digit numbers.

- *Division 00, Procurement and Contracting Requirements.* This division covers requirements for bidding and contracting, including bid solicitation, instructions to bidders, information available to bidders, bid forms, the agreement (contract), bonds and certificates, and general conditions of the contract, supplementary conditions, addenda, and modifications. These parts of the contract documents are discussed in Chap. 5.
- *Division 01, General Requirements.* This division covers requirements that apply to the entire project or all the individual technical sections. These include a summary of the work, how pricing and payment will be handled, alternates, value analysis, contract modification procedures, unit prices, construction progress documentation, submittal procedures (for samples, shop drawings, etc.), quality control, temporary facilities at the job site, product substitution procedures, owner-furnished items, special execution requirements, and final cleaning and protection of the work. Clients who have been involved with multiple construction projects will often provide their own Division 01 sections to the architect for use on the proposed project.

  Don't confuse General Requirements with General Conditions of the Contract for Construction, as discussed in Chap. 5. The procedures listed in Division 01 must be coordinated with the terms of the owner-architect and owner-contractor agreements used for the project to ensure that the same responsibilities are assigned to each party in both documents.
- *Division 02, Existing Conditions.* This division covers site remediation, site decontamination, subsurface investigation, surveying, and selective demolition, and other items related to existing conditions on a job site.
- *Division 03, Concrete.* This division covers forms, reinforcement, cast-in-place concrete, precast concrete, cementitious decks and underlayment, grouts, concrete restoration and cleaning, and all other aspects of concrete.
- *Division 04, Masonry.* This division covers brick, concrete block, stone, terra cotta, simulated masonry, glass block, masonry restoration and cleaning, and all other aspects of masonry.
- *Division 05, Metals.* This division covers all types of structural steel and other structural metals, ornamental metals, metal fabrications (metal stairs, ornamental ironwork, handrails, gratings, metal castings, and stair treads and nosings), as well as expansion joint covers and metal restoration and cleaning. (Light-gage metal framing for partitions is located in Division 09, Finishes.)
- *Division 06, Wood, Plastics, and Composites.* This division covers typical structural wood framing, rough carpentry, finish carpentry, and architectural woodwork. It also includes structural plastics, plastic fabrications, wood and plastic restoration and cleaning, and specialty composite materials. (Manufactured casework is in Division 12, Furnishings.)
- *Division 07, Thermal and Moisture Protection.* This division covers dampproofing and waterproofing, insulation, vapor retarders, air barriers, shingles, roof tiles, siding, membrane roofing, flashing, joint sealers, fire and smoke protection, and roofing specialties such as roof hatches, smoke vents, roof pavers, scuppers, and gravel stops.
- *Division 08, Openings.* This division covers metal doors and frames, wood doors and frames, specialty doors, storefronts, windows of all types, skylights, hardware, curtain walls, and glazing.
- *Division 09, Finishes.* This division covers all finish materials, including plaster and gypsum wallboard (including light-gage metal framing), floor and wall tile, terrazzo, all flooring materials, access flooring, acoustical ceilings, decorative ceilings, wall coverings, acoustical treatments, and paints and other coatings.
- *Division 10, Specialties.* This division covers a long list of accessory items such as visual display boards, toilet compartments, louvers, grilles, wall and corner guards, prebuilt fireplaces, flagpoles, signage, lockers, awnings, demountable partitions, storage shelving, exterior protection (such as sun screens and storm panels), and toilet and bath accessories.
- *Division 11, Equipment.* This division covers architectural equipment, including vaults and security items, teller and security equipment, church-related equipment, library equipment, theater and stage equipment,

musical equipment, mercantile equipment, checkroom equipment, vending machines, audiovisual equipment, loading dock equipment, detention equipment, athletic equipment, medical equipment, mortuary equipment, and equipment for laboratories, planetariums, observatories, and offices.

- *Division 12, Furnishings.* This division covers freestanding furniture and case goods, systems furniture, art, window treatments, accessories, fixed seating for theaters or auditoriums, and interior plants. (This division includes manufactured casework; custom casework is found in Division 06, Wood, Plastics, and Composites.)
- *Division 13, Special Construction.* This division covers structures created from unconventional materials (such as fabric, glass, and rammed earth), special-purpose rooms (such as clean rooms and planetariums), towers, geodesic domes, pre-engineered structures (such as metal building systems and conservatories), saunas, swimming pools, hot tubs, kennels, radiation protection (such as in X-ray rooms), control of sound and vibration, and seismic control.
- *Division 14, Conveying Equipment.* This division covers elevators, escalators, dumbwaiters, moving walks, and lifts.
- *Division 21, Fire Suppression.* This division covers detection equipment, alarms, standpipes, hoses, and all types of fire suppression systems, including wet-pipe, dry-pipe, deluge, carbon dioxide, foam, preaction, and dry chemical systems. (Construction materials used to create fire separation assemblies, such as doors, fire-stopping, and so on, are in their relevant divisions.)
- *Division 22, Plumbing.* This division covers piping, fixtures, equipment, pipe insulation, and gas and vacuum systems. It also includes specifications for the commissioning of these systems.
- *Division 23, Heating, Ventilating, and Air Conditioning.* This division covers heating and cooling equipment, cooling towers, ductwork, duct insulation and accessories, air filtration equipment, humidification equipment, and special ventilation equipment such as kitchen or laboratory fume hoods. It also includes specifications for the commissioning of these systems.
- *Division 25, Integrated Automation.* This division covers integrated automation systems, including energy monitoring and control, environmental control, and lighting control.
- *Division 26, Electrical.* This division covers electrical controls, wiring, electrical distribution (including substations, transformers, switchgear, meters, and circuit protection), low-voltage systems, generators, lightning protection, and lighting. It also includes specifications for the commissioning of these systems.
- *Division 27, Communications.* This division covers computer networks, cabling, and all kinds of communications systems, including data communications (including email and internet), voice communications, audiovisual communications, assisted listening, and healthcare communications.
- *Division 28, Electronic Safety and Security.* This division covers systems that monitor access to and conditions within the building, including intrusion detection, access control, video surveillance, fire detection, radiation detection, gas detection, fuel-oil detection, refrigerant detection, water detection, and mass notification.
- *Division 31, Earthwork.* This division covers modifications to the land, including site clearing, excavation, fill, grading, embankments, slope protection, soil and rock stabilization, soil treatment, erosion control, sedimentation control, shoring, underpinning, excavation support and protection, special foundation systems (such as piles, caissons, and aggregate piers) and tunneling. Most of the items in this division are below-grade work.
- *Division 32, Exterior Improvements.* This division covers above-grade site work, including paving, athletic and recreational surfacing (such as for playgrounds, baseball fields, and tennis courts), fences, gates, retaining walls, site furnishings, screening devices, wetlands, irrigation, and planting.
- *Division 33, Utilities.* This division covers water utilities (such as distribution, disinfection, and storage), wells, sanitary sewerage utilities (including piping, pumping stations, septic tanks, and on-site treatment facilities), storm drainage utilities (including piping, culverts, drains, pumps, subdrainage, ponds, and reservoirs), and communications utilities (including towers, cabling, and wireless

communication). It also includes specifications for distribution systems for fuel, hydronic energy, steam, and electricity.

Questions involving Divisions 10, 11, and 13 can be especially difficult because these divisions include a wide range of items. Following are some suggestions for understanding what they contain.

Division 10, Specialties, includes items that are *not* standard construction materials. For example, this division does not contain wallboard, flooring, finishes, or ceilings, because these are standard materials found in most buildings. Items in this division are typically relatively small, used as manufactured (rather than altered to fit or assembled on site), used in multiples, and not found in most buildings.

For example, visual display boards, lockers, and corner guards are included in Division 10.

For example, visual display boards, lockers, and corner guards are included in Division 10. They are relatively small in comparison to the building and its spaces, they are installed as manufactured, more than one is usually installed (more than one display board, more than one locker, and more than one corner guard), and they are not typically found in most buildings.

Division 11, Equipment, includes items that are indispensable to the basic functions of a building or a specific space within a building. For example, a checkout desk, study carrels, and a book depository can be found in virtually any library, whether a small community library or a specialty library within a law school.

Items in Division 11 are typically bound by electrical, mechanical, or structural requirements that must be considered and accommodated as the space is being designed. The size and configuration of these items may dictate the arrangement of a space. For example, the size and types of equipment in a commercial kitchen, the size and arrangement of the lanes in a bowling alley, and the vault, teller stations, and safe deposit boxes in a bank all affect the design of the spaces that will contain them. Equipment items in Division 11 are generally larger and more expensive than the specialty items in Division 10.

Items in Division 13, Special Construction, are typically much larger, so much so that a special construction item can be thought of as a building in its own right, whether it is a separate structure (such as a swimming pool, an air-supported structure, or an animal kennel) or virtually a building within a building (such as an athletic court, a seismic control system, or security vault). The building, room, or element can be either prefabricated or assembled on site, and can be either freestanding or integrated into another type of facility.

Technical Section Outline and Format

In addition to organizing the sections within the specification, the MasterFormat system establishes a standard way of organizing any particular section, called SectionFormat. All specifications complying with the MasterFormat guidelines are structured in the same way and are separated into three parts: Part 1, General; Part 2, Products; and Part 3, Execution. The specific articles within the parts vary depending on the type of material or product being specified.

Part 1, General, lists the general requirements for the section, such as the scope of the section, submittals required, quality assurance requirements, warranties, project conditions, and specifications for the delivery, storage, and handling of materials.

Part 2, Products, details the specifications for the materials and products themselves, including acceptable manufacturers (if applicable), standards and test methods to which the materials must conform, how items are to be fabricated, and similar concerns.

Part 3, Execution, tells how the products and materials are to be installed, applied, or otherwise put into place. This part also describes the examination and preparation required before installation, how quality control should be maintained in the field, and requirements for adjusting, cleaning, and protecting the finished work.

Figure 47.2 shows the SectionFormat outline, listing all the possible articles of each part.

Figure 47.2
SectionFormat Outline

PART 1 – GENERAL

SUMMARY
- Section Includes
- Products Furnished [or] Supplied But Not Installed Under This Section
- Products Installed But Not Furnished [or] Supplied Under This Section
- Related Requirements

PRICE AND PAYMENT PROCEDURES
- Allowances
- Unit Prices
- Alternates [or] Alternatives
- Measurement and Payment

REFERENCES
- Abbreviations and Acronyms
- Definitions
- Reference Standards

ADMINISTRATIVE REQUIREMENTS
- Coordination
- Preinstallation Meetings
- Sequencing
- Reference Standards

SUBMITTALS
ACTION SUBMITTALS / INFORMATIONAL SUBMITTALS
- Product Data
- Shop Drawings
- Samples
- Certificates
- Delegated Design Submittals
- Test and Evaluation Reports
- Manufacturers' Instructions
- Source Quality Control Submittals
- Field [or] Site Quality Control Submittals
- Manufacturer Reports
- Sustainable Design Submittals
- Special Procedures
- Submittals
- Qualification Statements

CLOSEOUT SUBMITTALS
- Maintenance Contracts
- Operation and Maintenance Data
- Bonds
- Warranty Documentation
- Record Documentation
- Sustainable Design Closeout Documentation
- Software

MAINTENANCE MATERIAL SUBMITTALS
- Spare Parts
- Extra Stock Materials
- Tools

QUALITY ASSURANCE
- Regulatory Agency Sustainability Approvals
- Qualifications
  - Manufacturers
  - Suppliers
  - Fabricators
  - Installers / Applicators / Erectors
  - Testing Agencies
  - Licensed Professionals
- Certifications
- Sustainability Standards Certifications
- Preconstruction Testing
- Field [or] Site Samples
- Mock-Ups

DELIVERY, STORAGE, AND HANDLING
- Delivery and Acceptance Requirements
- Storage and Handling Requirements
- Packaging Waste Management

FIELD [or] SITE CONDITIONS
- Ambient Conditions
- Existing Conditions

WARRANTY [or] BOND
- Manufacturer Warranty
- Special Warranty
- Extended Correction Period

PART 2 – PRODUCTS

OWNER-FURNISHED [or] OWNER-SUPPLIED PRODUCTS
- New Products
- Existing Products

[SYSTEMS] / [ASSEMBLIES] / [MANUFACTURED UNITS] / [EQUIPMENT] / [COMPONENTS] / [PRODUCT TYPES] / [MATERIALS] / [USER-DEFINED HEADING]

Manufacturers
- Manufacturer List
- Substitution Limitations
- Product Options

Description
- Regulatory Requirements
- Sustainability Characteristics
- Performance / Design Criteria
- Capacities

Operation
- Operators
- Controls
- Operation Sequences

Materials
Assembly [or] Fabrication
Factory Assembly
- Shop Fabrication
- Assembly [or] Fabrication Tolerances

Mixes
Finishes
- Primer Materials
- Finish Materials
- Shop Finishing Methods

ACCESSORIES
SOURCE QUALITY CONTROL
- Tests and Inspections
- Non-Conforming Work
- Manufacturer Services
- Coordination of Other Tests and Inspections

PART 3 – EXECUTION

INSTALLERS
- Installer List
- Substitution Limitations

EXAMINATION
- Verification of Conditions
- Preinstallation Testing
- Evaluation and Assessment

PREPARATION
- Protection of In-Place Conditions
- Surface Preparation
- Demolition / Removal

ERECTION / INSTALLATION / APPLICATION / [USER-DEFINED PROCESS]
- Special Techniques
- Interface with Other Work
- Systems Integration
- Tolerances

[REPAIR] / [RESTORATION]
RE-INSTALLATION
FIELD [or] SITE QUALITY CONTROL
- Field [or] Site Tests and Inspections
- Non-Conforming Work
- Manufacturer Services

SYSTEM STARTUP
ADJUSTING
CLEANING
- Waste Management

CLOSEOUT ACTIVITIES
- Demonstration
- Training

PROTECTION
MAINTENANCE
ATTACHMENTS
END OF SECTION
- Schedules
- Tables
- Illustrations

The Division Numbers and Titles used in this product are from MasterFormat™ 2014 Edition and the three part SectionFormat outline from SectionFormat™/PageFormat™ are published by the Construction Specifications Institute (CSI) and Construction Specifications Canada (CSC), and are used with permission from CSI, 2014.

The Construction Specifications Institute (CSI)
110 S. Union St., Suite 100
Alexandria, VA 22314
800-689-2900; 703-684-0300
CSINet URL: http://www.csinet.org

Specifying for Sustainability

The specifications for sustainable projects should clearly define related restrictions and requirements. The owner may expect compliance with his or her own sustainability guidelines, or the architect may seek LEED certification or recognition by another green building rating system for the project. Sustainability issues are addressed in both Division 01, General Requirements, and in all the individual technical sections that cover specific materials and construction elements.

Division 01, General Requirements

A separate specification section in Division 01 should apply to all the other specification sections and set the goals for sustainability and environmental quality as well as the general direction of the project. This section should advise the contractor of the design requirements used by the architect and design team in the preparation of the contract documents. These criteria can then be referenced if the contractor wants to propose substitutions or make enhancements.

The topics addressed in the general Division 01 specification section include the following.

- *a summary of the environmental goals of the project and the special requirements expected of the contractor.* This summary generally includes initiatives in three areas: resource-efficient materials and systems, energy conservation, and indoor air quality. The complexity of these goals is dictated by the project or the client's goals. If LEED certification is being sought, the individual credits required by LEED may be used to develop a list of requirements. Refer to Chap. 13 for information on LEED certification.
- *required submittals from the contractor and instructions for preparing the documentation.* The contractor may be required to include manufacturer's certificates of recycled content, certification of wood products as coming from an accredited certifier (refer to Chap. 35 for information on wood certification), material emission testing reports, cleaning product information, and other documentation as may be required for LEED certification. If this information is to be presented in a specific format, sample forms may be incorporated by reference.
- *required tests and procedures for testing materials to verify that they comply with the requirements.*
- *a list of hazardous materials and chemicals.* The architect should request that the contractor submit safety data sheets for all products that may contain hazardous materials. A *safety data sheet* (SDS) is a listing of product safety information prepared by manufacturers and marketers of products containing toxic chemicals. (This was formerly known as a *materials safety data sheet* or MSDS.) An SDS is formatted to comply with the Globally Harmonized System of Classification and Labeling of Chemicals (GHS), which is required for compliance with the Occupational Safety and Health Administration's (OSHA) Hazard Communication Standard.

  Information in an SDS is presented in sixteen standardized sections arranged in a particular order. In addition to stating the basic product components, the SDS must list the health effects of the material, protective equipment required for handling, procedures for handling leaks and spills, and guidelines for first aid, safe storage, and disposal. SDSs are intended for use by employers and emergency responders rather than by consumers, and are written in a way that will help those who may come into contact with the chemicals understand the hazards and handle these materials appropriately.
- *a list of terms and definitions with which the contractor may not be familiar.* These may be included in this section, or they may be found in individual sections if they apply only to one material (for example, "certified wood product").
- *a list of resources for product certification or sustainability that the contractor can reference.* This may include trade associations and specific regulatory agencies' names and addresses.
- *requirements for the packaging of materials with recycled products.*
- *requirements for construction activities to minimize pollution, dust, erosion, chemical emissions, spills, and water and moisture leaks.* This may include a no-smoking provision for the job site.

Individual Technical Sections

The individual technical sections of the specification should contain the sustainability requirements unique to each product, such as the following.

- the use of locally harvested or manufactured products
- minimum recycled content
- requirements for VOC content limits

Product Development

- energy efficiency
- cleaning and maintenance requirements
- certifications provided by a third party
- other material criteria mentioned in Chap. 13

This type of information would usually fit into the section's Part 1, General. For most green building projects, the sections affected will include concrete, rough carpentry, architectural woodwork, plastic products, doors, windows, gypsum wallboard, acoustical ceilings, carpeting, resilient flooring, ceramic tile, wood flooring, paints and coatings, and toilet partitions. Relevant information shall be included in other sections as needed.

Performance specifications are even more difficult to write if the sustainability information provided by manufacturers is incomplete.

In Part 2, Products, the architect can use several approaches to define the requirements. First, the architect can write a performance specification giving the requirements for minimum recycled content, maximum emissions of chemicals, and other criteria, as well as the testing standards by which the products must be evaluated. Performance specifications are difficult to write, but they can be even more difficult if the sustainability information provided by manufacturers is incomplete.

Another approach is to give a list of three to five approved products that the architect knows will satisfy the requirements of the specification section. This list can contain products that have the desired recycled content or are capable of being recycled, products that have low emissions of VOCs and other hazardous chemicals, and equipment that is low polluting. Along with this, a provision can be included to permit the contractor to submit a proposed substitution if the contractor can prove that the substitution meets the same requirements as the approved products.

This approach should be used with caution, however. It can put an additional burden on both the contractor and the architect during the bidding or negotiation phase, however, when limited time may be available for the preparation and consideration of substitution proposals.

The Construction Specifications Institute (CSI) has developed GreenFormat, a way for manufacturers to organize sustainable information associated with materials, products, systems, and technologies. Specifiers can use it to assist in comparisons of products. The various master specifications listed previously also contain sustainability-related information for individual products. Web sites that can assist in identifying and vetting sustainable products include the following.

- *BuildingGreen* is a subscription-based materials review and evaluation service at buildinggreen.com.
- *Pharos* focuses on materials health data at pharosproject.net.
- CADdetails' *SpecGREEN* lists sustainable products at caddetails.com

If only one particular product satisfies the sustainability, aesthetic, and functional requirements of the project, then a proprietary specification can be written. This is typically permitted only for private work, where the requirements for competitive bidding are not as strict as they are for public work. Even for private work, the number of proprietary specifications should be kept to a minimum.

Specification Writing Guidelines

Specifications are legal documents, so they must be complete, accurate, and unambiguous. The language must be precise. Some important things to remember include

- Know what the standards and test methods referred to include, and know what parts of them apply to your project. Make sure the specification references the most current editions.

- Specify either the desired result or the required product, but not both. For example, don't specify a particular type of brick and also specify that the brick must have certain characteristics according to a particular test method. If the specified brick doesn't meet the stated requirements, the specification will be impossible to comply with.
- Do not include standards that cannot be measured. For example, don't specify that the work should be done "in a first class manner." This could be subject to wide interpretation.
- Avoid exculpatory clauses. These are phrases that try to shift responsibility to the contractor or someone else in a broad, general way. For example, avoid saying that "the contractor shall be totally responsible for all ...." Unless the clause is generally accepted wording or makes sense in the context of the specification, legal opinion disapproves of such clauses—especially when they favor the person who wrote them.
- Avoid ambiguous words or phrases. For example, replace the combination *and/or* with one word or the other. Avoid the abbreviation *etc.*, which may be interpreted to include undesirable factors or to imply that a list may go on forever. The word *any* implies that the contractor has a choice; this is acceptable if the architect wants to allow a choice, but this is usually not the case.
- Keep the specifications as short as possible. Specification writing can be terse, even sometimes omitting words such as *all*, *the*, *an*, and *a*.
- Describe only one major idea in each paragraph. This makes reading easier, improves comprehension, and allows for changes of the specification.

Coordination with the Drawings

The drawings, technical specifications, and other parts of the project manual must be coordinated with each other to avoid conflicting requirements, duplications, omissions, and errors. AIA Document A201 states that the contract documents are complementary and that what is required by one is as binding as if it was required by all.

The drawings show the following aspects of the building.

- general configuration and layout
- size
- shape
- dimensions of construction

Drawings may also include general notes to explain the graphic representations.

The technical specifications, on the other hand, describe the quality of materials and workmanship required, along with general requirements for the execution of the work, standards, and other items that are more appropriately described in written rather than graphic form.

There are several areas of particular concern when coordinating the drawings and specifications.

First, the specifications should contain requirements for all the materials and construction elements indicated on the drawings. Conversely, specifications should not include any materials that are not on the drawings. One way to accomplish this is for the specifications writer and the project manager or job captain to use the same checklist. Phrases in the specifications such as "as indicated on the drawings" must each have a corresponding drawing indication.

Second, the terminology used in both documents should be the same. If the term *gypsum board* is used in the specifications, the term *drywall* should not be used on the drawings. The use of a keynoting system can help solve this problem. In this system, a number on the drawing refers to a corresponding number and associated term in a list elsewhere on the drawing. This makes it relatively easy to check terms on the drawings with those used in the specifications.

Third, each dimension or thickness should be indicated in only one place. If the same thickness of flashing is used everywhere, and this is included in the technical specifications, there is no need to note it on the drawings as well.

Fourth, notes on the drawings should not describe methods of installation or material qualities; these belong in the specifications.

Finally, the provisions in Division 01, General Requirements, should be carefully checked against the general conditions and other contracts that are being used for the project.

48 DETAILED REGULATORY AND COST REVIEWS

REVIEWING THE PROJECT FOR COMPLIANCE

By the time the construction documents are being produced, most of the broad building code requirements should have been satisfied. These include

- setting occupancies
- determining occupant load
- determining height and area limitations based on the proposed type of construction
- setting the locations of fire separation walls and floors
- organizing the egress system
- calculating loads and using that information to design the structural systems

Also by this time, the consultants should have identified and satisfied requirements for HVAC, plumbing, fire protection, and other building systems.

At this point, during the construction documents phase, the architect must review the design and all the details of the project to make sure all requirements have indeed been satisfied. These include building code, specialty regulatory, and accessibility requirements. Because there are so many requirements, it's often best to treat these as separate reviews, and they are covered separately in the next three sections.

Refer to Chap. 46 for a list of the required content of construction drawings. This list, along with the items discussed in this chapter, can be used as guide for checking the content of the drawings. Also refer to Chap. 46 for a list of information commonly required by building departments to include in the construction documents.

DETAILED BUILDING CODE REVIEW

The following list gives some of the major areas of concern in regard to compliance with building codes. This list is not meant to be comprehensive, however, and other items may need to be checked as well, depending on the project and the particular codes that apply to it. This list follows the chapter sequence of the *International Building Code.*

Types of Construction

- Verify that the primary structural frame and its enclosures are detailed to provide the required fire-resistance rating and that details have a corresponding UL number, if required by the authority having jurisdiction (AHJ).
- Verify that each rated partition and wall type is detailed to provide the required fire-resistance rating and that each assembly has a corresponding UL number, if required by the AHJ.
- Verify that each rated floor/ceiling and roof/ceiling assembly is detailed to provide the required fire-resistance rating and has a corresponding UL number, if required by the AHJ.
- Verify that combustible materials are used only where permitted.

Fire Protection

- Verify that exterior walls meet the requirements of fire resistance, projections, and allowable openings.
- Double-check which walls and partitions need to be fire walls, fire barriers, fire partitions, smoke barriers, and smoke partitions, and verify their detailing accordingly. Make sure that these are indicated on the plan and are continuous from floor to floor.
- Check the requirements for horizontal assemblies, vertical openings, and shaft enclosures, including allowable penetrations through them. Firestop systems at penetrations through rated walls should be detailed appropriately and should have a corresponding UL number, if required by the AHJ.

- Make sure that opening protectives, such as doors and glazing, have the required fire-resistive ratings and meet the detailed requirements for size, frame material, and marking.

Interior Finishes

- Verify that interior wall and ceiling finishes are of the appropriate classes to meet the requirements for the occupancy group and location in the building. Verify that all interiors finishes coordinate with the specifications.
- Verify that floor finishes comply with the code requirements for their locations (corridors, exit passageways, and so on). Confirm that substrates for finish materials are correctly detailed and specified.
- Make sure that decorative materials and trim meet requirements for flame spread and maximum area and that they coordinate with the specifications.

Fire Protection Systems

- Working with the fire protection engineer, make sure that the location of sprinklers coordinates with other ceiling-mounted fixtures such as lights and diffusers.
- Locate portable fire extinguishers to conform to code requirements.
- Make sure that fire alarms and detection devices are located where required and that they are coordinated with other ceiling-mounted fixtures.

Means of Egress

- Determine the required number of exits from each space, exit widths, maximum common paths of egress travel, and exit access travel distance. If these were calculated during design development, recheck them, as changes may have been made.
- Verify that the required exit and exit access doorways are located correctly.
- Make sure that an accessible means of egress is provided and all accessible egress components meet code requirements.
- Review all egress door designs and specifications for code compliance.
- Review stairway designs and details for compliance, including handrail and guard details.
- Double-check ramp slopes and ramp components for compliance with code and accessibility requirements.
- Check detailing of corridors and openings in corridors for compliance with accessibility requirements.

Interior Environment

- Working with the engineers, verify that ventilation and lighting requirements are satisfied. Pay particular attention to areas that may have special requirements, such as computer rooms and server rooms.
- If applicable, confirm that detailing of doors and walls meets acoustical value ratings.
- Verify that the correct number of plumbing fixtures have been provided based on occupant load calculations.
- Verify that toilets and bathrooms meet the minimum requirements for finishes and waterproofing.
- Verify that requirements for accessible fixtures and accessories have been met.

Energy Efficiency

- Verify that insulation and air barrier details are appropriate for the climate and that minimum *R*-values satisfy energy code requirements.

- Working with HVAC, electrical, and mechanical consultants, verify that the detailing for energy efficiency meets the requirements of the *International Energy Conservation Code.* Provide final design drawings for exterior wall assemblies, including R-values, and coordinate the types of glazing required on each elevation to meet energy efficiency goals.
- If required, perform energy performance calculations.

Exterior Walls

- Verify that exterior wall detailing provides the required weather protection, insulation, and air and vapor barriers.
- Working with structural consultants, verify that attachment details for cladding provide the necessary strength.
- Verify that exterior walls satisfy combustibility requirements.

Roof Assemblies

- Review all roof details for correct construction, drainage, flashing, and wind resistance.
- Verify that roof assemblies have the correct fire classifications.
- Make sure roof insulation meets the requirements of applicable energy codes.

Glass and Glazing

- Check all exterior glazing details and glass thicknesses for resistance to wind, snow, and seismic loads.
- Verify required locations for safety glazing.
- Review details for glass handrails and guards.

Plastic

- Review all plastics used in the building, including plastic glazing, and make sure they meet requirements for location, type, support, combustibility, and area limitations.

DETAILED SPECIALTY REGULATORY REVIEW

Many specialty regulatory agencies at the federal, state, and local levels have detailed guidelines or requirements for building and site design elements under their purview. Most of these agencies should be identified and contacted during programming as described in Chap. 8. Any written or online material the agency issues can be used as a checklist, or the requirements that are pertinent to the project can be compiled into a personalized checklist.

As described in Chap. 8, states may regulate environmental standards, energy codes, fabric flammability standards, rules for state government buildings, and rules for institutions such as nursing homes.

The most common types of local regulations are city or county zoning ordinances and city planning department requirements. Zoning is discussed in Chap. 8. City planning departments often have specific requirements about landscaping, view ordinances, traffic access, and the like. These regulatory departments should be contacted early in the design process to determine the requirements that will apply to the project.

Other state agencies or local regulations may govern specific uses such as restaurants, hospitals, and day care facilities. Restaurants, for example, are typically regulated by a city or state agency that provides its own requirements for design features such as ventilation, plumbing, fire protection, lighting, and finishes. The architect should determine which local agencies govern the design and operation of the appropriate building type and obtain a copy of their guidelines and requirements.

ACCESSIBILITY REVIEW

The following guidelines highlight some of the major areas to be aware of in regard to *accessibility*. Refer to Chap. 15 for a discussion of barrier-free design, and review the *ADA/ABA Guidelines*, the accessibility chapter of the *International Building Code*, and ICC/ANSI Standard A117.1, *Accessible and Usable Buildings and Facilities*, for a complete discussion of requirements.

- Review all site design details for conformance to accessibility requirements.
- Check zoning and scoping requirements, and confirm the minimum required numbers of accessible items such as parking spaces and seats.
- Make sure that the required number and design of accessible entrances are provided and that paths from accessible parking spaces to the building entrance satisfy all requirements. Check both paths of travel and cross slopes.
- Trace all accessible routes throughout the building to make sure they provide access to all required spaces.
- Verify minimum widths required for accessible routes, turning spaces, and openings.
- Check all accessible doorways for required width, hardware, and maneuvering clearances.
- Verify all requirements for toilet rooms, showers, and bathrooms. Refer to Chap. 15 for the detailed requirements.
- Check floor finishes and threshold details for conformance to accessibility requirements.
- Review ramp and stairway design details.
- Check for potential problems with protruding objects, especially wall-mounted light fixtures, fire extinguisher cabinets, and other accessories.
- Review the signage drawings for conformance and confirm that signs are provided in all required locations.

A firm can minimize or avoid many potential problems by developing standard sets of details for common elements such as toilet room layout and accessory placement, door swing clearances, stair design, typical mounting heights, ramp handrail details, and threshold details. Once these have been vetted, they can be used again on any project.

To avoid potential problems, do not detail to the required maximums or minimums. When a range of allowable dimensions is given, use the midpoint.

To avoid potential problems with tolerance issues, do not detail to the required maximums or minimums. When a range of allowable dimensions is given, use the midpoint of the range. In other cases, plan for slightly more space or a slightly gentler slope as appropriate. For example, instead of showing a 1:12 slope for ramps, use a 1:13 or 1:14 slope instead.

FINAL COST ESTIMATE REVIEW

Throughout the programming and design process, the architect should update the project cost estimates as required by the owner-architect agreement (AIA Document B101 or a similar document). These cost estimates can be used to track how the design decisions made have affected the final project cost.

In theory, by the time construction documents are being prepared, the cost estimate should be close to the final bid or negotiated amount. However, changes typically continue to be made after design development as the details of construction documents are being produced. It is often not until drawings are nearly complete that everything large or small that will affect the cost is fully known.

If the project uses the traditional design-bid-build method, it is important for the architect to have control of the project costs.

For these reasons, the architect must compare how the final project design in the detailed construction documents (including specifications) aligns with the most recent cost estimate. At this stage most of the evaluation focuses on construction and site-development costs and not the other costs described in Chap. 10 such as professional fees, land costs, and the like.

At this stage the architect can ask some basic questions to determine whether the cost of the final design may exceed earlier estimates. How much has the design changed since the latest construction cost estimate? Who performed the previous estimate? Was it accurate? Has the project increased in size, scope, or material qualities? Has the detailing gone beyond what was originally planned? The architect can also coordinate with the project consultants on doing their own cost-versus-design reviews. If the project is complex, the architect may choose to retain the services of a cost consultant for design-bid-build projects.

Beyond answering these basic questions and developing a general sense of the design's compliance with the project budget, the architect must understand how last-minute design efforts can affect the final construction cost. When the project is being awarded through a traditional design-bid-build method, the architect must be very careful not to overdesign and overdetail in the final stages and thereby exceed the projected budget.

Influence of Estimating Methods

The original cost estimate may include specific line item costs for various components or systems, as with the parameter method or the unit cost method described in Chap. 30. If so, it is relatively simple to look at each of these components or systems at the construction document phase, price them out as detailed, and compare each one with its original line item estimate. As design decisions are made and the construction drawings are developed, the architect can directly compare the amount, quality, and scope of individual items with the latest assumptions and estimates. In this way, the architect can continually evaluate whether the expected project costs are still on track.

However, if the original cost estimate was based on a system cost budget as shown in Table 10.5, or if it was developed using an even more general method like CSI's UniFormat and broad categories were used to develop a cost estimate, then quick checks are not as easy to make. For example, if the initial estimate includes an expected cost for interiors, but does not specify line items under that category, then in order to compare the final design against this original estimate, the architect must look at each interior component (partitions, flooring, ceilings, woodwork, and so on), assign a cost to each, and total them. In the first stages of a project, it is easier to prepare an estimate by system cost analysis, but it is more difficult to update this kind of estimate as the project evolves.

Influence of Project Delivery Methods

If the project uses the traditional design-bid-build method, it is important for the architect to have control of the project costs, because if the budget is exceeded, it is the architect who will have to work without compensation to revise the design. For this reason, some firms choose to perform cost reviews in house, using published construction cost data and cost-estimating software or a spreadsheet program.

However, if the company lacks the expertise or personnel to do a detailed cost review, an independent consultant can be retained. This is often a more efficient and economical approach. It allows the designers to focus on refining the design and producing the documents, and a cost estimator often has better local data, as well as contacts with contractors and suppliers to improve the accuracy of the estimate.

If a more collaborative project delivery method is being used—such as a negotiated contract, design-build, contract with a construction manager, or integrated project delivery—the architect may have additional resources available to help with preparing the cost review.

If the contract is to be negotiated, the architect can work with the contractor throughout the process of design development and construction document production, getting the contractor's opinion on whether the design is within the original budget.

In a design-build approach, whether led by the architect or the contractor, there is a continual review of design versus cost as the design process proceeds. Design-build projects may include a guaranteed maximum price.

If the project has a construction manager (CM), then he or she can prepare the cost analysis. This is true whether the CM is an independent consultant or an employee of the contractor. The CM is usually in the best position to evaluate construction costs based on the current state of the construction drawings. In addition, the CM has access to accurate cost data, experience in the geographical area where the project is to be built, relationships with subcontractors, and knowledge of the local labor market.

The CM will have been working with the architect and owner from the project's inception and should offer suggestions throughout the design process; this feedback helps the architect adjust the design to comply with the owner's original budget. If a guaranteed maximum price is called for as part of a construction manager as constructor contract, then the design and final cost must align.

If the project is completed using integrated project delivery (IPD), the contractor and everyone on the team carefully tracks project costs throughout the entire design process to meet the owner's budget. Subcontractors and suppliers who are part of the IPD process will have submitted their prices. As discussed in Chap. 49, relatively few subcontractors and vendors will be bidding or negotiating late in the process. The contractor may even provide a guaranteed maximum price to the owner.

Addressing Mismatches Between Cost and Design

In many owner-architect agreements, the architect commits to designing a project that will cost no more than the owner's budgeted amount. If the cost of the project exceeds the budget, the architect is obligated to redesign the project or portions of it and rebid the project to bring the cost down. This can result in substantial losses for the architect, who must provide these additional services without additional compensation.

One way that an architect can guard against budget overruns is to include a contingency in all cost projections. (This can be in addition to the construction contingency amount that the owner has established.) To do this, the architect works to design a project that is estimated to cost a little less than the stated project budget; 1% to 5% is a reasonable allowance, depending on the scope of the work. The stated budget, reduced by the contingency, becomes the architect's target budget, which offers a little bit of a cushion should the bids come in higher than expected.

If the final design does exceed the budget, there are a number of steps the architect can take.

First, elements can be cut from the design. This is usually the least desirable solution, as it compromises the original intent of the client and architect. When elements are cut, the owner has to accept losing features of the design, and the architect must commit more time and resources to revisions and rebidding. However, if a material or product is included but is not essential to the function or operation of the building, it may be possible to delete it without compromising the project. For example, the marble wall finish of a lobby may be changed to vinyl wall fabric, or a basement may be left unfinished. Usually, this approach comes down to reducing either quantity or quality, or finding a better price for the same thing.

Second, value engineering can be used. This involves finding a lower-cost alternative that will achieve the same results. Value engineering is best undertaken earlier in the design process, but it can be used during the production of construction documents when precise costs can be applied to alternatives. Value engineering is discussed in greater depth in Chap. 30.

This offers a little bit of a cushion should the bids come in higher than expected.

Third, if the architect is unsure of the cost of a building component and the project is being bid, "add alternates" or "deduct alternates" can be used in the bidding. These alternative options are listed on the bid form, and prices for them are solicited during the bidding process. If the bid price exceeds the budget, one or more of the “deduct alternates” can be incorporated into the project to reduce costs. If the budget exceeds the bid price, on the other hand, one of more of the “add alternates” can be incorporated in order to improve the project while staying within the budget.

The alternates should be items that can be added to the project or deleted from it without changing the base scope of work shown on the drawings, in order to prevent the need for revisions or additional work on the part of the architect. Alternates should not be used as a substitute for conscientious cost estimating, but they do allow the owner some flexibility in modifying the cost of the project after the bids have been received, without requiring revisions or rebidding. The use of alternates is discussed in greater depth in Chap. 49.

2
4.630
1
0,000
166.420
770
13
12
10

DIVISION 6: CONSTRUCTION & EVALUATION

49

PRECONSTRUCTION ACTIVITIES

Many of the architect's roles and responsibilities during preconstruction will vary with the type of project delivery system being used. There are five major types of project delivery systems (with some minor variations).

- design-bid-build (or design-award-build)
- construction manager as adviser
- construction manager as constructor
- design-build
- integrated project delivery

Methods of project delivery are discussed in detail in Chap. 3, and general responsibilities of the architect defined in owner-architect agreements are discussed in Chap. 5.

Regardless of the project delivery system, the architect's duties will also include assisting in the selection of a contractor and in controlling costs.

DESIGN-BID-BUILD (OR DESIGN-AWARD-BUILD) PROJECT DELIVERY

The traditional method of completing a project is through the *design-bid-build* method of delivery. The architect designs the project, completes construction drawings, writes specifications, and estimates costs. The contract for the architect's work is typically based on one of the standard AIA owner-architect agreements, and it references AIA Document A201, *General Conditions of the Contract for Construction*, or similar documents to establish the contractual relationships and responsibilities of the parties. With this type of delivery method, the architect's preconstruction responsibilities consist mainly of assisting with the bidding process.

The contract documents are put out to bid, and the successful bidder (usually the firm that has submitted the lowest cost) is awarded the contract. Once the owner-contractor agreement is signed, the contractor constructs the building while the architect provides construction administration services, for which the architect is compensated by the owner.

Competitive bidding is popular with owners because it usually results in the lowest construction cost. However, the bidding must be conducted within clearly defined guidelines that protect the owner from disreputable contractors and unethical bidding practices.

For most public agencies, open public bidding is mandatory. In some jurisdictions, contractors for publicly funded projects can be selected through a *value-based selection* (VBS) process that considers more than just the lowest cost, but also factors such as quality, schedule, and contractor personnel.

In contrast, *negotiation* is the process in which the owner, with the assistance of the architect, works out a final contract price with one contractor. The contractor with whom the owner negotiates may be selected in one of two ways. The owner may already know which contractor he or she wants to complete the project, having worked with the contractor before, through a referral, or by reputation.

Competitive bidding is popular with owners because it usually results in the lowest construction cost.

Alternatively, the owner may select several possible contractors to be considered for the job. Each contractor is interviewed, and one contractor is selected based on qualifications (and possibly a fee proposal).

At the owner's request, the architect may assist with organizing and may participate in the selection interviews and the negotiation process. During the negotiation process, the contractor may point out potential problems, make suggestions, or propose changes to the design or specifications to reduce the cost of the project. If the agreement is negotiated with a general contractor, the subcontracts may still be open to competitive bidding.

Bidding Procedures

Through many decades of practice, the bidding procedure has been standardized and codified in various industry association documents. Everyone involved with the process is expected to know the rules and expectations. This chapter reviews the common procedures and documents used during this phase of the design-bid-build project delivery process. The duties of the architect are given in AIA Document B101, *Standard Form of Agreement Between Owner and Architect*, and in similar agreements.

Prequalification of Bidders

Bidding may be open to any contractor, or it may be restricted to a list of contractors who have been prequalified by the owner. Prequalification is usually based on the following information submitted by contractors.

- financial qualifications
- personnel
- experience
- references
- size of firm
- bonding capability
- any special qualities that make them particularly suited for the project under consideration

When prequalification is allowed in public work, it is usually based on the financial assets and size of the firm. Refer to the section on contractor selection later in this chapter for more information on prequalification.

The purpose of prequalification of bidders is to consider proposals from only those contractors who meet certain standards of reliability, experience, financial stability, and performance. An owner contemplating the construction of a multimillion-dollar laboratory building would likely not review the bid of a contractor who specializes in hotels or in small residential projects. Once all contractors have established that their companies meet the minimum standards needed for the project, the owner is better able to review the contractors' bids based primarily on price, personnel, and completion time.

Advertising for Bids

There are two ways to notify prospective bidders. When any contractor is permitted to submit a bid, an *advertisement for bids* is published in one or more newspapers, trade journals, or online publications. When contractors must be prequalified, the owner may send each selected contractor an *invitation to bid.*

An advertisement for bids is usually written by the architect, and it is typically placed in newspapers or other publications by the architect or owner. It can also be delivered to a physical or online plan room, advertised on the owner's website, or sent to a construction trade association that can distribute the information to its membership through its communications channels.

An advertisement for bids should include the following information.

- the fact that a call for bids is being made
- the project name and location
- the names and addresses of the owner and architect
- a brief description of the project, including building type, size, principal construction materials and systems, and other pertinent information
- when and where bids are due
- how and where bidding documents can be obtained and the deposit required, if any

- where bid documents may be viewed
- the type and amount of bid bonds required
- the procedures for submitting bids
- whether or not the bids will be opened publicly
- other information as needed, such as the owner's right to waive irregularities of the bidding process or to accept bids other than the lowest

Advertising for bids is usually required for public work. These clients may have specific guidelines for the number of times the advertisement must run, publications to which it is to be submitted, and other administrative guidelines. Private work can also be publicly advertised if the bidding is open.

An invitation to bid is sent to prospective, prequalified bidders. The invitation contains the same information that would be included in an advertisement for bids. It may also include a set of drawings and specifications, or instructions for obtaining these from an online plan room. When the list of bidders is limited to prequalified firms, enough bidders should be invited to encourage price competition.

Availability of Bid Documents

Bid documents can be distributed in several ways. Traditionally they are made available in hard-copy format through the architect's office. Each bidder receives the required documents, including prints of the drawings, specifications, bidding documents, bid forms, and other items. It is general practice to require prospective bidders to put down a deposit on each set of documents; the deposit may be refunded when the documents are returned to the architect in usable condition. In some cases the documents are loaned with no deposit required. Extra sets of documents can be purchased by the contractor.

If there is a selected list of bidders, then bidders, subcontractors, and material suppliers can receive and review the documents in one of the following ways.

- The documents may be sent directly to the bidders at no charge.
- Documents may be put on file in a central plan room.
- Documents may be available for purchase at printing companies, plan rooms, or similar places.
- Electronic versions of the central plan room or documents may be available on a project website.

Substitutions

During bidding, many contractors request that substitutions be considered for some of the specified materials. This happens when a project has proprietary specifications or a very limited list of acceptable manufacturers. The conditions under which substitutions will be considered and the procedures for reviewing submissions are clearly defined in the instructions to bidders, outlined later in this chapter.

Addenda

An *addendum* is a written or graphic document, issued by the architect during the bid period prior to the execution of the contract, that modifies or interprets the bidding documents by addition, deletion, clarification, or correction. During the bidding process, questions arise that need answers, errors are discovered, substitutions are made, and the owner or architect decides to make changes. Addenda are the instruments with which to do this

When an addendum is issued, it is transmitted to all registered bidders no later than four or five days before receipt of bids to give the bidders ample opportunity to study it and modify their proposals accordingly.

Pre-bid Conference

On some projects it is advantageous to hold a pre-bid conference. This is a meeting during which the bidders can ask questions and the architect and owner can emphasize important conditions of the project. Pre-bid conferences are particularly useful for renovation or addition projects, as they give the bidders the opportunity to see the existing conditions. On very large projects, there may be separate conferences for mechanical subcontract bidders, electrical bidders, and so on. During these conferences, complete notes concerning the items discussed should be taken, and copies of the notes should be sent to all bidders whether or not they were in attendance. Answers to significant questions received at the pre-bid conference should be formalized in an addendum.

Bid Opening

For public work, bids generally must be opened and read publicly. If the project is owned by a private individual or entity, the owner may choose to open bids privately, at the owner's convenience, and share the bid results at a later time.

The instructions to bidders should state whether bids will be opened publicly or privately; if publicly, the instructions should also include the date, time, and place at which bids will be opened and read.

Unless modified by addenda, the bid opening time and the methods of submitting and receiving the bids should be strictly observed. AIA Document A701, *Instructions to Bidders* states that bids received after the time and date established for receipt of bids must be returned unopened, even if the late bid is delivered before any bids have been opened.

Most public bid openings are conducted by the architect with the owner and bidders present. The bids are read aloud, and the presence or absence of any required supporting documentation is noted. The architect usually prepares a bid log to note the base bid amount, the amounts of alternates (if any), whether receipt of addenda was acknowledged, and other pertinent information. This bid log should be made available to the bidders in both open and private bidding.

When all the bids have been read, the architect thanks everyone for submitting and states that the submissions will be evaluated and a decision of award made within a certain time, usually seven to ten days. The architect should not announce the apparent lowest bid at the bid opening.

Evaluation and Awarding of Bid

The architect and the owner evaluate the bids together. This can include checking references, confirming insurance, rejecting bids with incomplete documentation, and any other review the owner thinks is needed. The architect and owner do not look simply for the lowest proposed contract sum; they also review the prices quoted for alternates, substitutions, lists of proposed subcontractors, qualification statements, and the other documentation required by the instruction to bidders.

The owner has the right to reject any or all bids, including bids that are not accompanied by the required bid bond or other required documentation, and bids that are in any way incomplete or irregular.

If, after the bids have been opened, a bidder discovers and can support the claim that a clerical or mathematical error has been made, the bidder is usually allowed to withdraw the bid. If this proposal was the low bid, the next lowest bidder is accepted.

When the final decision has been made, it should be sent to all the bidders, not just the one to whom the project is awarded.

If all bids exceed the project budget, and the owner-architect agreement fixes a limit on construction, the owner may take one of four possible courses of action.

- The owner may rebid the project. This requires the architect to assist in the process a second time with no additional compensation. Rebidding a project without revising its scope or details, however, will seldom result in any significant reduction in cost unless the bidding marketplace is changing rapidly.
- The owner may authorize an increase in the construction cost and proceed with the project.
- The owner may work with the architect in revising the scope of the project to reduce construction cost. This requires the architect to redesign and revise the documents and then rebid the project with no additional compensation.
- The owner may abandon the project.

Alternates are often used as a flexible method of deleting or substituting alternative materials or construction elements to help reduce costs. Because the alternates are priced along with the base bid, the owner and architect can quickly estimate the ramifications of selecting certain alternates.

Bidding Documents

The architect usually prepares bidding documents using standard AIA forms or forms provided by the owner. Clients who engage in a great deal of building may develop their own forms and procedures, but they are typically similar in content to the AIA forms. If the architect is not familiar with the form or document that the client plans to use, the architect should review it carefully to confirm the responsibilities that may be assigned.

Although the bidding documents are bound into the project manual, they are not part of the contract documents.

The bidding documents usually include the following.

- the advertisement or invitation to bid
- instructions to bidders
- supplementary instructions to bidders (if any)
- bid forms
- bid security information
- performance bond, if required
- labor and material payment bond, if required

Other documents that are sometimes added are qualification forms, a proposed subcontractor list form, certificates of insurance, certificates of compliance with applicable laws and regulations, and additional information available to bidders, such as geotechnical data.

In addition to the bidding documents, the bidding package also includes the drawings, specifications, general and supplementary conditions of the contract, special conditions (if any), addenda issued prior to the receipt of bids, and the form of agreement between owner and contractor.

Advertisment for Bids or Invitation to Bid

These are discussed earlier in this chapter. The advertisement for bids or invitation to bid is printed and bound into the project manual with the other bidding documents.

Instructions to Bidders

The *instructions to bidders* outline the procedures and requirements that the bidders must follow in submitting bids, how the bids will be considered, and submittals required of the successful bidder. AIA Document A701, *Instructions to Bidders* is often used; other organizations produce similar forms.

Instructions to bidders normally include the following items. (If the AIA form is being used and additional requirements must be included, it is suggested that supplementary instructions to the bidders be written; do not modify or rewrite the AIA form.)

- *bidder's representations.* In making a bid, the bidder represents that the documents have been read and understood, the plans and specifications have been reviewed, and the site has been visited to familiarize the bidder with the conditions under which the work will take place. It is also implicit that the bidder understands that the bid is based on the materials, equipment, and systems required by the bidding documents, without exception.
- *bidding documents.* This article of the Instructions to Bidders states where the documents may be obtained, how many sets the bidders may have, and the amount of deposit, if any, required to obtain the documents. If the documents are returned to the architect in reusable condition within 10 days after receipt of bids, the deposit is usually returned. The cost of replacing any missing or damaged documents is deducted from the deposit. The bidder who is awarded the contract may keep the documents, and the bidder's deposit is returned. Bidding documents are not normally issued directly to sub-bidders unless specifically stated in the advertisement or invitation to bid.
- *interpretation or correction of bidding documents.* This article requires the contractor to carefully study the documents and examine the site and local conditions, and to report to the architect any errors, inconsistencies, or ambiguities discovered. If the bidders or sub-bidders need clarification or interpretation of any of the information in the bidding documents, they must make a written request to the architect at least seven days prior to the bid date. The architect must then issue any interpretations or corrections by an addendum, which is sent to all bidders. Bidders must acknowledge receipt of all addenda on the bid form.
- *substitutions.* The materials and products described on the drawings and specifications establish a standard for the work. If the bidder wants to propose a substitution, it must meet this standard. A bidder is required to submit a request for approval of a proposed substitution at least 10 days prior to the bid opening date. The request must include the name of the material or equipment for which the substitution is submitted, along with complete backup information about the proposed substitution. The bidder must prove the merit of the substitution. The architect then reviews the submission and may either reject it or approve it. If approved, the architect issues an addendum stating this fact and sends it to all the bidders. No substitutions can be considered after the contract award.
- *addenda.* According to the Instructions to Bidders, addenda must be transmitted to all bidders and made available for inspection wherever bidding documents are on file for that purpose. Addenda must be issued no later than four days prior to the date of bid opening. Addenda are discussed in more detail earlier in this chapter.
- *bidding procedures.* This article specifies how the bid form is to be completed, what kind of bid security will accompany the bid, and the procedure for submitting the bid. Bids are normally submitted in sealed envelopes, with the name of the party receiving the bid on the outside, along with the project name and the name of the entity submitting it. (Bid security is discussed later in this chapter.)
- *modification or withdrawal of bid.* Bids may not be modified after the designated bid time and date. Before that time, however, a bid may be modified or withdrawn by making notice in writing over the signature of the bidder. Writing over the signature confirms that the bid has been modified or withdrawn so that the original bid cannot be used. The person receiving bids must date- and time-stamp the request. Withdrawn bids can be resubmitted if they are in full conformance with the Instructions to Bidders.

- *consideration of bids.* The procedure for opening bids and reviewing them is explained in this article, including under what conditions bids may be rejected, how they will be evaluated, and conditions for award of the contract. The owner has the right to reject any or all bids and to accept alternates in any order or combination and to determine the low bidder on the basis of the sum of the base bid and alternates accepted.
- *post-bid information.* After the award of the bid, the contractor submitting the low bid must submit to the architect AIA Document A305, *Contractor's Qualification Statement*, unless it has already been submitted as part of the bidding process. The contractor must also furnish to the owner the following.
    - a summary of the work to be performed with the contractor's own forces
    - the names of the manufacturers, the products, and the supplier of the principal items proposed for the project
    - the names of persons or companies proposed to perform major portions of the work
- If requested by the successful bidder, the owner must furnish the bidder with reasonable evidence that the financial arrangements have been made to fulfill the owner's obligations. This must be done no later than seven days prior to the expiration of the time for withdrawal of bids.
- *performance bond* and *payment bond.* The required bonds and the time during which they must be delivered are outlined in this article. Normally, the cost of bonds is included in the bid price, unless the bonds are specifically required to be furnished after the receipt of bids and before execution of the contract. Performance and payment bonds are described in more detail later in this chapter.

Bid Forms

To ensure that all bids will be in an identical format, there should be a standardized form on which each bidder enters the required information. This makes it easier for the owner and architect to compare and evaluate the bids. The bid form should contain space for the amount of the base bid written in both numbers and words, the prices for any alternates or substitutions, the proposed unit prices (if any), and the number of calendar or work days in which the bidder proposes to complete the work. Space should be provided for the bidder to list and acknowledge receipt of any addenda. The bid form must be signed by someone legally empowered to bind the contractor to the owner in a contract and often includes a space for a corporate seal.

Bid Security

Bid security is required to ensure that the successful bidder will enter into a contract with the owner. Bid security may come in the form of a certified check, cashier's check, or bid bond. If the successful bidder does not enter into an agreement, the bid security may be retained to compensate for the difference between the low bid and the next lowest bidder. The amount of the bid security is either set as a fixed price or as a percentage of the bid; it is usually about 5% of the estimated cost of construction or the bid price.

Performance Bonds

A *performance bond* is a statement by a surety company that obligates complete construction of the project in the event that the contractor defaults on his or her obligations. If this happens, the surety company may complete construction by hiring another contractor, or it may simply supply additional money to the defaulting contractor to allow construction to proceed.

Performance bonds are usually mandatory on public work and are advisable on private work. The cost of the performance bond is paid by the owner and usually included in the amount of the construction price. The architect or owner must verify that the bond is written by a surety qualified to issue bonds in the particular state where the construction is to take place. Some states will not accept surplus-lines carriers who are based in a different state. In such cases the bond may be invalid.

Labor and Material Payment Bonds

Although a performance bond ensures the completion of the contract, it does not guarantee payment for labor and materials to suppliers, employees, or subcontractors by the defaulting contractor. As a result, if the general contractor defaults, subcontractors and material suppliers could file liens against the property or sue the owner to obtain compensation. Because of this, a labor and material payment bond is usually required along with a performance bond to protect the owner against these possibilities.

Example 49.1

With which kind of project delivery method are the architect's duties and responsibilities during preconstruction most limited?

(A) construction manager as adviser

(B) design-bid-build

(C) design-build

(D) integrated project delivery

Solution

When the integrated project delivery method is used, the architect's responsibilities are more limited than in the other three methods because the bidding or negotiation for large portions of the work has already been done. The architect is still responsible for working with permitting agencies to ensure code compliance, answering questions from subcontractors and vendors bidding for relatively small portions of the work, and reviewing prefabrication studies.

The answer is (D).

CONSTRUCTION MANAGER AS ADVISER

As described in Chap. 3, the owner may elect to use a construction manager (CM) to assist in project delivery. The CM can fulfill the following roles and duties.

- advising on constructability issues
- providing cost estimating
- establishing the project schedule
- managing the construction contracts
- making early material purchases of items with long lead times
- acting as a third-party adviser, working with the owner and architect on matters of constructability and cost
- acting as contractor, giving preconstruction advice, estimating cost, scheduling services, and construction services
- acting as agent, coordinating and assisting the activities of the owner, architect, and contractor

It is less common for the CM to act as agent than as adviser or constructor.

When the owner uses a CM as adviser, the responsibilities of the architect are governed by AIA Document B132, *Standard Form of Agreement Between Owner and Architect, Construction Manager as Adviser Edition*, which is used along with AIA Document A132, *Standard Form of Agreement Between Owner and Contractor, Construction Manager as Adviser Edition*, AIA Document A232, *General Conditions of the Contract for Construction, Construction Manager as Adviser Edition*, and other documents in this family. The owner has the option to retain a construction manager and complete the project with either one contractor or with multiple prime contractors. Under AIA Document B132, the roles and responsibilities of the architect during preconstruction are similar to those under the traditional design-bid-build project delivery method with the following exceptions.

The architect works with the CM during the design phases as the CM develops the cost and schedule of the project and advises on matters of constructability; providing cost estimates is not part of the architect's services under AIA Document B132. The architect submits a schedule of the design services for inclusion in the overall project schedule to the owner and CM. The architect also prepares schematic design documents and reviews them with the owner and CM, who uses these as a basis for a preliminary cost estimate. In developing a design that meets the owner's requirements, the architect must consider the owner's and CM's suggestions for alternative materials building systems, and other considerations based on the program and aesthetics. This process continues during the design development phase. The architect prepares and submits outline specifications that identify major materials and systems and establish their quality levels, and the CM adjusts the cost estimate to reflect this additional information.

If the CM's estimate of the cost of the work exceeds the owner's budget prior to the conclusion of design development, the architect must consult with the CM and make appropriate recommendations to the owner to adjust the project's size, quality, or budget. The owner must cooperate with the architect to make the necessary adjustments.

If the CM's estimate at the conclusion of design development exceeds the owner's budget, the owner has three options.

- give written approval to increase the budget for the project
- revise the project program, scope, or quality as required to reduce the cost
- implement any other mutually acceptable alternative

If the owner decides to revise the program, scope, or quality, the architect must incorporate the needed modifications in the construction documents phase to comply with the owner's budget without additional compensation. After the owner has approved the design development documents and made any adjustments in the project requirements and budget, the architect proceeds to complete the construction documents as with the traditional design-bid-build approach.

Once construction documents are completed the project can either be sent out for competitive bidding or the contract can be negotiated with a qualified contractor. If the project is bid, the roles and responsibilities of the architect are similar to those described in the previous section on design-bid-build projects. If the project is negotiated, the architect assists the owner and CM by facilitating the reproduction of proposal documents, participating in selection interviews with prospective contractors, and aiding in negotiations with prospective contractors. After the contractor is selected, the project proceeds through construction as with the traditional design-bid-build process, and the architect and CM provide construction administration services as defined in AIA Document A232 and discussed in Chap. 3.

The major differences between the CM as advisor and the CM as constructor, described later in this chapter, are that multiple prime contractors may be used, there is no guaranteed maximum price set by the CM, and bidding or negotiation is used to set the final cost of the project.

CONSTRUCTION MANAGER AS CONSTRUCTOR

When the owner chooses to hire a construction company that also provides construction management services, the responsibilities of the architect are generally governed by AIA Document B133, *Standard Form of Agreement Between Owner and Architect, Construction Manager as Constructor Edition.* AIA Document B133 is intended to be used with AIA Document A201, *General Conditions of the Contract for Construction.*

Under this agreement the roles and responsibilities of the architect during preconstruction are similar to those under the traditional design-bid-build project delivery method with a few exceptions. Most notably, the architect must work with the construction manager (CM) during the design phases as the CM develops the cost and schedule of the project and advises on matters of constructability; providing cost estimates is not part of the architect's services under AIA Document B133. The architect submits to the owner and CM a schedule of design services for inclusion in the overall project schedule. The architect also prepares schematic design documents and reviews them with the owner and CM; the CM uses these as a basis for beginning to establish a proposal or cost estimate.

In developing a design that meets the owner's requirements, the architect must consider the owner's and CM's suggestions for alternative materials, building systems, and other considerations based on the program and aesthetics. This process continues during the design development phase with the addition of outline specifications that identify major materials and systems and establish their quality levels.

If the CM's estimate of the cost of the work exceeds the owner's budget prior to the conclusion of design development, the architect must consult with the CM and make appropriate recommendations to the owner to adjust the project's size, quality, or budget. The owner must cooperate with the architect to make the needed adjustments.

If the CM's estimate at the conclusion of design development exceeds the owner's budget the owner has three options.

- The owner may give written approval to increase the budget for the project.
- The owner may revise the project program, scope, or quality as needed to reduce the cost.
- The owner may implement any other mutually acceptable alternative.

If the owner decides to revise the program, scope, or quality, then in the construction documents phase the architect must incorporate the modifications needed to comply with the owner's budget. The architect receives no additional compensation for this. After the owner has approved the design development documents and made any adjustments in the project requirements and budget, the architect proceeds to complete the construction documents as with the traditional design-bid-build approach.

Under the owner construction manager as constructor agreement, the basis of payment is the cost of the work plus a fee, either with or without a guaranteed maximum price. At a time mutually agreed on by the owner and CM, the CM prepares either a guaranteed maximum price proposal or a control estimate for the owner's review and acceptance. This can be anytime during one of the design phases. At this point, the architect assists the owner in reviewing the CM's proposal or estimate. During this review, the architect is not responsible for discovering errors and omissions or for the assumption of any of the CM's responsibilities, but if the architect discovers any inaccuracies the owner and CM should be promptly notified.

DESIGN-BUILD

When the owner uses a design-build approach to project delivery as described in Chap. 3, and the architect serves as a consultant to the design-builder, the responsibilities of the architect are governed by AIA Document B143, *Standard Form of Agreement Between Design-Builder and Architect.* Under this agreement, the roles and responsibilities of the architect during all phases of the project, including preconstruction activities, are defined in an exhibit to the agreement.

The design-builder, architect, and owner select services from a list which the architect will provide. For example, the architect may contract with the design-builder to provide design services only, while the design-builder provides construction procurement and construction administration services. In this case, the architect would have no roles or responsibilities related to bidding or negotiation. In contrast, if the architect and design-builder agree that the architect will provide construction procurement services, then the architect's duties would be the same as with a traditional design-bid-build approach.

If the proposed cost of the work for the architect's portion of the project exceeds the lowest bona fide bid or negotiated proposal, the design-builder has four options.

- The design-builder may give written approval of an increase in the budget for the architect's portion.
- The design-builder may authorize rebidding or renegotiation.
- The design-builder may terminate the agreement with the architect.

- The design-builder may cooperate in revising the project scope and quality as needed to reduce the cost of the work for the architect's portion of the project.

If the design-builder elects to use this last option, then the architect must modify the documents for which the architect is responsible, as directed by the design-builder, without additional compensation. If the design-builder is an architectural firm or a contracting firm with in-house architects, the design-build entity becomes responsible for preconstruction activities as well as all other services.

Example 49.2

In addition to making a base bid for a project as specified, each contractor is asked to state how much less his or her bid will be if eight large twin windows shown in the plans and elevations are replaced with smaller casement windows. This is an example of the use of

(A) add alternates

(B) allowances

(C) deduct alternates

(D) reduction

Solution

A request that the contractor supply, in addition to a base bid on the project as specified, a price for some variation, such as a change in materials or in some component of construction, is called an *alternate*. When the alternate will lead to a reduction in the bid, it is a *deduct alternate.*

The answer is (C).

INTEGRATED PROJECT DELIVERY

When the owner uses an integrated project delivery (IPD) approach as described in Chap. 3, the responsibilities of the architect are defined by various AIA documents depending on what type of approach is being used.

- transitional forms
- multi-party agreements
- a single purpose entity

If transitional forms are used, the main documents governing the architect's involvement during preconstruction are AIA Document B195, *Standard Form of Agreement Between Owner and Architect for Integrated Project Delivery* and AIA Document A295, *General Conditions of the Contract for Integrated Project Delivery.*

With any of these three approaches, the roles and responsibilities of the architect during preconstruction are fairly limited. In IPD terms, preconstruction is the phase that includes agency review and buyout.

Agency review includes the standard building code check by the authority having jurisdiction (AHJ) as well as any other reviews by permitting agencies. IPD encourages early involvement by permitting agencies. If building information modeling (BIM) data can be shared with the agency, this review is streamlined and may employ the use of electronic plan checking and analysis software. The architect's role during this phase is limited to working with agency representatives to ensure code compliance and coordinating any questions or communication issues related to the building information model.

Buyout is the process of selecting suppliers and finalizing prices from any remaining subcontractors and vendors that are not part of the IPD process. There is no major bidding or negotiating in the traditional sense because the prime contractor, major subcontractors, and major vendors have already been selected and have priced out their portion of the work. The architect may be required to answer questions from the remaining bidders and review prefabrication studies to ensure the integrity of the design intent. The architect may be also be involved in the remaining bidding or negotiation efforts, but the contractor and owner are generally responsible for finalizing these arrangements prior to the start of construction.

CONSTRACTOR SELECTION

The architect is often placed in the role of assisting with the selection of the contractor when the project is privately funded, or when the project is publicly funded and the local jurisdiction allows a value-based selection process, as mentioned previously. When the project delivery process for a public sector client is based strictly on the design-bid-build method, the contractor is commonly selected based solely on submission of the lowest bid.

In addition to cost, the architect should consider the following criteria when assisting with the selection of a contractor.

- previous experience in the project type being built
- references from past clients
- experience of personnel
- sufficient personnel to complete the project
- financial qualifications, including responsibility and past experience
- bonding capacity for types of bonds required
- ability to obtain the insurance required by the project
- history of past claims or other types of disputes
- history of work with subcontractors and vendors
- history of ability to complete jobs on time and on budget
- knowledge and experience with special construction methods, if required
- possession of special licensing or certification if required by the project

In addition to personally interviewing contractors the architect and owner can use AIA Document A305, *Contractor's Qualification Statement*, to gather the same information from a number of potential contractors. The contractor can use this document to provide a sworn, notarized statement with appropriate attachments to verify the contractor's capabilities.

COST CONTROL

The cost of a project is one of the most important concerns of the owner, and in the case of design-bid-build project delivery, the architect is obligated by contract to provide cost estimates and design a project to meet the owner's budget. Techniques for providing cost estimates during the various phases of a project and with different project delivery methods prior to preconstruction are discussed in Chap. 10 and Chap. 30.

Cost Control in Design-Bid-Build Project Delivery

With a design-bid-build project delivery method, the architect has limited ability to adjust project costs. Throughout the design process and up to completion of contract documents, the construction cost is only an estimate prepared by the architect or by a cost-estimating consultant on the architect's behalf. It is only with bidding or negotiation that the owner receives a firm price on the project. If the architect or cost consultant has been doing a reasonable job of tracking design changes and has a good idea of component costs, the bid price should be fairly close to the estimated amount.

The architect does not (and cannot) guarantee that the final construction cost will not vary from the estimate, because there are several variables that can affect the final bid price.

Bidding in the Marketplace

Bidding is a competitive activity. The price a contractor is willing to submit to an owner is dependent on the following variables.

- actual cost of subcontractor bids
- cost of the contractor's own labor and materials
- cost of equipment rental
- the contractor's indirect costs
- overhead
- profit

Bidding is also affected by the construction marketplace, which is itself competitive. For example, if the local economy is depressed, contractors, subcontractors, and material suppliers may be willing to lower prices or reduce profit margins in order to get work and stay in business. When work is plentiful, contractors are more selective about the jobs they choose to bid on and what profit allowance to put in their bids. They are not as concerned about reducing prices to get jobs.

Both the architect and owner should be sensitive to these types of market conditions. If there is some flexibility in the owner's schedule, it can be advantageous to either delay or accelerate design and bidding to match favorable market conditions.

Effects of Documents on Bids

One of the variables over which the architect and owner have control is the quality of the set of contract documents. What they contain and how they are put together, beyond the amount and quality of construction they represent, can affect the amount of bids they receive.

Poorly prepared drawings and specifications can raise questions in the mind of the contractor about what is specifically required, what may be implied or omitted. To cover possible unforeseen items, the contractor may add extra money in the bid to cover these unknowns. A complete and clearly coordinated set of documents gives the contractor confidence in the scope and quality of the work. The contractor can then bid with more confidence and include only those items shown. If a building information model is used and made available the contractor may have even more confidence, because BIM makes it possible to run coordination checks and find other problems before construction starts.

Alternates

An *alternate* is a request included in the bidding documents asking the contractor to supply a price for some type of variation from the base bid. This may be a change in materials or level of quality of a material, a deletion of some component, or the addition of some construction element. For example, the base bid may include carpet as a floor covering, whereas an alternate may be to substitute wood flooring for the carpet.

Alternates allow the owner some flexibility in modifying the cost of the project once the bids are in, by varying the quantity or quality of the project. Alternates also allow the owner to make certain decisions based on firm prices rather than on preliminary estimates. However, alternates seldom significantly lower the total cost of the project at bidding, because they generally represent a small percentage of the large cost items such as structure, mechanical systems, and cladding.

An alternate is called an*add alternate* if it adds to the base bid, and a *deduct alternate* if it reduces the base bid amount. Because alternates require more time for both the architect and bidders to prepare, they should be used carefully and should not replace conscientious cost estimating and reasonable design for the base bid amount.

When bids are evaluated, the selected alternates should be considered in deciding the lowest overall bid, but alternates should not be manipulated to favor one bidder over another.

Unit Prices

Unit prices are set costs for certain portions of work, based on an individual quantity. When required, they are listed on the bid form and provide a basis for determining the cost of changes to the contract. For example, if the full extent of paving is unknown at the time of bidding, a square-foot cost for asphalt paving may be requested. Even though the total cost may not yet be known, the unit costs of the bidders can be compared.

If unit prices are used when work is deleted from the contract, the amount of credit is usually less than the price for an additional quantity of the same item. Spaces should be provided in the bid form to add and deduct amounts when applicable.

Allowances

As described in Chap. 5, an *allowance* is a set amount of money estimated by the architect to cover a particular material or piece of equipment when the cost for that material or equipment cannot be determined precisely at the time of the bid or negotiated proposal. For bidding, an allowance provides a way to allocate some amount of money for an item in the bid, even if the exact quantity or quality of the item is not known. The allowance (or allowances) is stated in the appropriate section (or sections) of the specifications, so all bidders are using the same amount in their bids. The contractor must add to the allowance the cost for unloading, handling, and installing the item as well as costs for the contractor's overhead and profit. If the costs for the allowance are more or less than the original estimate, the contract sum is adjusted accordingly by change order.

Value Engineering

Value engineering (VE), or *value analysis*, can be used prior to bidding, or even after, but it is considered an additional service if the owner hires a value analysis consultant (per AIA Document B204). VE is best used earlier in the design process. See Chap. 30 for a discussion of VE.

Cost Control in Construction Management Project Delivery

When a project has a construction manager, the architect does not have direct responsibility for estimating or guaranteeing construction costs. Under AIA Document B133, the architect works with the CM to meet the project budget and considers requests for substitutions. The architect provides clarifications or interpretations regarding the drawings and specifications prior to the owner's acceptance of the GMP or control estimate. In addition, the architect assists the owner in reviewing the GMP or control estimate after the CM has provided these to the owner.

Cost Control in Design-Build Project Delivery

The extent to which the architect is involved in project cost control during preconstruction is based on the scope of services agreed to under the design-builder–architect agreement, AIA Document B143. It is possible that the architect will not have been contracted to provide any type of estimating services. However, AIA Document B143 may call for the architect to provide an evaluation of information furnished by the design-builder, including the budget for the cost of the work for the architect's portion of the project.

Alternatively, an estimate for the architect's portion of the work may need to be prepared. Under AIA Document B143, if the project is bid the architect may be required to provide assistance to the design-builder with bidding services. In this case, the architect would be providing services similar to those described by the design-bid-build approach.

The design-builder may be paid by the owner based on either a stipulated sum, the cost of the work plus fee, or the cost of the work plus fee with a guaranteed maximum price. If the design-builder contracts with an architect, the architect's work should align with the design-builder's cost commitment to the owner, because the two entities are working together throughout the design process. However, if the estimated cost for the architect's portion of the project exceeds the budget after construction documents are completed, the design-builder has four options, as previously outlined. If the design-builder chooses to revise the project scope and quality to reduce costs, the architect must modify the documents for which the architect is responsible without additional compensation.

Cost Control in Integrated Project Delivery

Under an integrated project delivery method, the architect has very little ability to adjust project costs during preconstruction. However, such adjustments are generally unnecessary because of the contractor's input and the method by which the design is developed. At this stage, the contractor has already provided the owner with a guaranteed maximum price after the owner's acceptance of the detailed design documents (design development documents in traditional terms). If changes or substitutions need to be made to maintain the GMP, the architect will incorporate these into the implementation documents (construction drawings and specifications).

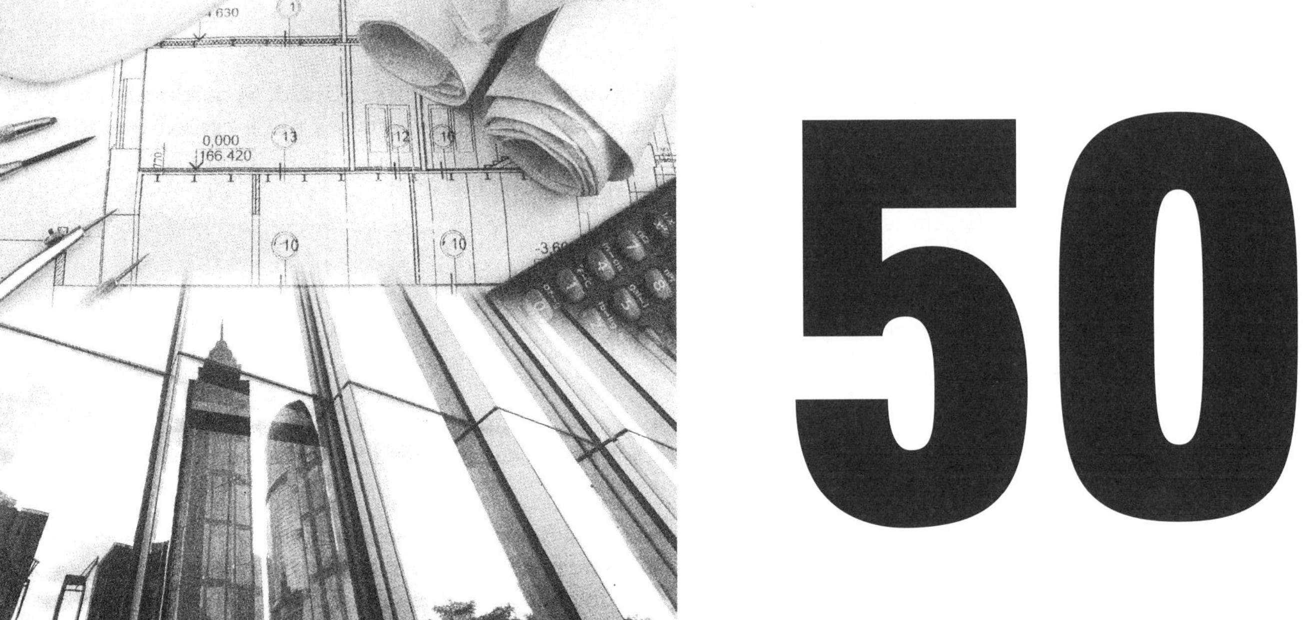

50

CONSTRUCTION ADMINISTRATION

Construction of the project is the culmination of a great deal of planning, design, documentation, and organization and one of the most important phases of project delivery. The architect should be closely involved with this phase of the project to the extent of his or her contractual responsibilities. During this phase, the architect is responsible for the following areas.

- project delivery methods and construction administration services
- meetings and administration activities
- construction observation
- managing requests for changes in the work and supplemental documentation
- submittals and applications for payment
- ensuring conformance with contract documents
- additional construction administration activities

PROJECT DELIVERY METHODS AND CONSTRUCTION ADMINISTRATION SERVICES

The extent of the architect's participation and responsibility is governed by contractual requirements, which, in turn, are dependent on the type of project delivery method being used. The roles and responsibilities of the architect described in this chapter are based on the traditional design-bid-build method of project delivery under AIA Document B101, *Standard Form of Agreement Between Owner and Architect*, and AIA Document A201, *General Conditions of the Contract for Construction*. See Chap. 5 for a discussion of the architect's duties enumerated in these two documents.

Variations of these responsibilities for other types of project delivery methods are briefly described in this section.

Construction Manager as Adviser

The architect's roles and responsibilities under AIA Document B132, *Standard Form of Agreement Between Owner and Architect, Construction Manager as Adviser Edition*, and AIA Document A232, *General Conditions of the Contract for Construction, Construction Manager as Adviser Edition*, are similar to those under a traditional delivery method, with some exceptions.

- The architect and construction manager (CM) jointly provide administration of the contract. AIA Document B132 requires that the architect "advise and consult with the owner and construction manager."
- The architect reports to the CM results of site visits, but the CM also has a representative at the site and reports to the architect any known deviation from the contract documents and schedule and any defects and deficiencies observed in the work.
- Unlike the traditional delivery method, the owner and contractor communicate through the CM with copies to the architect. Communications with the architect's consultants still go through the architect.
- Both the architect and CM have the authority to require inspections and testing and to reject work.
- Submittals are reviewed by both the CM and architect.
- The CM, not the architect, prepares change orders and construction change directives. Change orders must be signed by the CM as well as by the architect, owner, and contractor.
- The CM receives and reviews requests for information from the contractor and forwards each to the architect with the CM's recommendation. If necessary, the architect prepares and issues supplemental drawings and specifications in response to requests for information.

The architect remains the initial decision maker on claims between the owner and contractor.

Construction Manager as Constructor

When the project is being delivered with a CM as constructor method, the architect's roles and responsibilities are almost identical to those assigned with the traditional design-bid-build method. In this case the CM is really serving as the standard "contractor." In fact, AIA Document B133, *Standard Form of Agreement Between Owner and Architect, Construction Manager as Constructor Edition*, is intended to be used in conjunction with AIA Document A201, *General Conditions of the Contract for Construction.* There are three main differences to note.

- The architect must advise and consult with both the owner and construction manager during construction.
- Under AIA Document B101, the owner-architect agreement, the architect's start of construction phase services commences with the award of the contract for construction. Under AIA Document B133, however, the architect's responsibilities for the construction phase begins with the owner's acceptance of the CM's guaranteed maximum price (GMP) proposal, the owner's approval of the CM's control estimate, or the owner's issuance of a notice to proceed.
- Applications for payment are still submitted to the architect by the CM for the architect's review and signature. The CM issues the certificate for payment to the owner, but a more complex method is used to calculate the amount of each progress payment. This method is described in detail in AIA Document A133, *Standard Form of Agreement Between Owner and Construction Manager as Constructor.*

Design-Build

When the owner uses a design-build approach to project delivery as described in Chap. 3 and the architect serves as a consultant to the design-builder, the responsibilities of the architect are governed by AIA Document B143, *Standard Form of Agreement Between Design-Builder and Architect.* Under this agreement, the roles and responsibilities of the architect during all phases of the project, as well as construction administration activities, are defined in an exhibit to the agreement. The design-builder, architect, and owner select from a list of services that the architect will provide. These construction administration services may include the following. The exact language of each provision is essentially the same as the descriptions of the tasks included in AIA Documents B101 and A201.

- provide administration of the contract for construction between the design-builder and the contractor for the *architect's portion of the project.* This consists of all elements of the project designed or specified by the architect.
- review requests by the contractor for additional information about the contract documents and issue necessary supplemental drawings and specifications to clarify the requirements.
- make site visits on behalf of the design-builder to determine the progress of the job, to endeavor to guard the design-builder against defects, and to determine if the work is meeting the requirements of the contract documents. These site visits are to review and comment on the architect's portion of the project only.
- reject work that does not conform to the contract documents and, if necessary, require inspection or testing of the work.
- review the contractor's applications for payment and make recommendations for payment to the owner as needed.
- review and approve submittals for the architect's portion of the project.
- review and prepare proposed change orders and construction change directives.
- issue orders for a minor change in the work.
- make the substantial completion observations.
- process the final payment request.

- receive from the contractor and forward to the design-builder various documents, including the consent of surety for release of retainage, affidavits, receipts, releases, waivers of liens or bonds indemnifying the owner and design-builder against liens, written warranties, and other documents required by the contract documents.

When one or more services are selected, the architect provides the service in the same way as with a traditional design-bid-build project delivery method. See Chap. 5 for a more detailed discussion of these services.

If the architect is in the employ of the design-builder, then all services provided by the architect fall under the umbrella of services provided by the design-builder. These follow the traditional construction administration activities of the architect, but the architect isn't mentioned specifically. For example, periodic requests for payment are made by the design-builder directly to the owner instead of to the architect.

Integrated Project Delivery

With this type of project delivery method, once the project reaches the construction phase, the architect's roles and responsibilities are basically the same as those under AIA Document A201. This is true with transitional documents, a multi-party agreement, and a single purposc cntity (SPE) agreement. The architect's tasks in the construction administration phase focus on quality control and cost monitoring because so much of the design and coordination work has been done prior to this phase. In theory, there should be fewer on-site problems or requests for information because all parties have been involved in resolving issues during the detailed design and implementation documents phases.

MEETINGS AND ADMINISTRATIVE ACTIVITIES

One of the key elements of successful contract administration, and project management in general, is good communication. One of the most useful tools for facilitating communication between all team members is the face-to-face meeting. Two types of construction meetings are especially important: the preconstruction conference and the periodic project meeting.

Preconstruction Conference

The construction phase of a project should begin with a preconstruction conference. For a traditional design-bid-build project, the architect is responsible for organizing and conducting the meeting. The conference should be attended by the architect, owner, personnel from the contractor's office who will be responsible for the project (project manager, supervisors, etc.), major subcontractors, design consultants as required (structural, mechanical, electrical), and any other participants whose involvement the architect deems important.

The agenda should include the following

- how communications will be handled
- construction and submittal schedules
- access to the site and restrictions on site usage, including parking, security, and use of or provision of resources such as restrooms, electricity, temporary heat, phones, and space for a construction office or trailer
- insurance requirements
- submittal requirements
- procedure for requests for information
- changes in the work
- nonconforming work
- sustainability requirements

- site visits by the architect and others
- reporting required by the contractors
- tolerances required for critical elements
- separate contracts by the owner
- partial occupancy
- coordination among the contractors

Project Meetings

Project meetings may be organized by the architect, contractor, or owner, but they are typically organized by the architect. Project meetings should be attended by the architect, design consultants as required, the contractor or contractor's representatives, major subcontractors if required, and any specialty sub-subcontractors or vendors whose attendance is vital for the progress and successful completion of the work. The owner may be required to attend some of these meetings as well. The architect's project meetings are separate from any meetings the contractor may organize to coordinate the efforts of the contractor's personnel. The standard owner-architect agreement requires that the architect attend project meetings regardless of who organizes them.

CONSTRUCTION OBSERVATION

The architect visits the site at intervals appropriate to the stage of construction or as agreed to in the owner-architect agreement.

The purpose of the architect's observation is the following.

- to become generally familiar with the progress and quality of the work and to keep the owner informed
- to endeavor to guard the owner against defects and deficiencies in the work
- to determine if the work is progressing in such a way that it will be in accordance with the contract documents when completed

During the construction administration phase, lines of communication among the parties are established by the *General Conditions of the Contract for Construction*. During this time the owner and contractor must communicate through the architect, unless otherwise stated in the owner-architect agreement and the *General Conditions*. Communications between the contractor and design consultants should also be through the architect. Communications between the architect and the subcontractors and material suppliers should be through the contractor.

The number and timing of visits to a job site are left to the judgment of the architect, based on a few factors.

- the size and complexity of the project
- the type of construction contract being used
- the exact schedule of construction operations

During each site visit, the architect should make complete notes of the observations and include these in appropriate field reports. The form most commonly used for this is AIA Document G711, *Architect's Field Report*. Reports may be distributed in hard copy format or electronically.

A field report should include the following items.

- report name and the architect's project number (and a project number assigned by the owner or contractor, if applicable)
- field report number

- date and time of the observation, and the weather conditions at the site
- work currently in progress
- number of workers present at the site or an estimate of the number, if the project is large
- observations made, including any problems, which may include photographs documenting the conditions at the site
- an assessment of the conformance with the construction schedule and the estimated percentage of completion
- list of items to verify, and action or information needed from owner, contractor, or consultants
- list of any attachments, and the name of the person making the report

Copies of the field reports are sent to the contractor and to the owner, to keep everyone informed of the progress of the work. Unless otherwise agreed to in writing in the owner-architect agreement, the architect is not responsible for exhaustive or continuous on-site inspections, nor is the architect responsible for the contractor's failure to carry out the work, for the means, methods, or techniques of construction, or for safety precautions on the job.

Example 50.1

During construction, the architect is obligated to visit the site to keep the client informed about the progress and quality of the work. According to the basic provisions of AIA Document B101, these visits must occur

(A) every week

(B) every two weeks

(C) as appropriate to the stage of the contractor's operations

(D) only if they have been written into the agreement as additional services

Solution

Site visits are part of the basic services of contract administration, but no specific time interval for them is given in the contract. AIA Document B101 states that the architect shall visit the site at intervals appropriate to the stage of the contractor's operations or as agreed by the owner and architect.

The answer is (C).

Uncovering and Correction of Work

There are two situations where work may have to be uncovered. The first occurs when a portion of the work has been covered contrary to the architect's request or to specific requirements in the contract documents. In this case, the work must be uncovered for the architect's examination. The cost for uncovering and for replacing the construction is paid by the contractor. The second situation occurs when the architect has not specifically made a request to view a portion of the work and the work has already been covered. If the architect then requests that the work be uncovered and it is found that the work does conform to the contract documents, the owner must pay for the uncovering and replacement through a change order. If the work does not conform, it must be corrected and replaced, and the cost must be borne by the contractor. However, if the owner or a separate contractor caused the unsatisfactory work, the owner must pay the costs.

Example 50.2

An architect suspects that blocking has been installed in the wrong location and asks that a portion of the work be uncovered. When the drywall is removed, the blocking is found to be in the correct location. Who is responsible for paying for the removal and replacement of the portion of the wall?

(A) architect

(B) owner

(C) contractor

(D) architect and owner should split the cost

Solution

The owner is responsible for paying for uncovering and rebuilding the wall. Presumably, the architect requested that the drywall be removed because there was a reason to suspect that the construction was in error and the architect was protecting the owner's interests.

If the blocking had been in the wrong location, the contractor is responsible for the cost of uncovering and repairing the work.

The answer is (B).

Safety

The contractor is solely responsible for safety on the job site. If the architect volunteers suggestions or directions concerning construction means and techniques in regard to safety issues, the architect may also assume legal responsibility and be held liable for accidents or other problems.

If the architect observes an obvious safety violation, it should be called to the attention of both the contractor and owner and followed up with a notice in writing, but the architect should not suggest how the safety violation can be corrected. If the safety problem is not corrected, the architect should notify both the contractor and the owner in writing.

Field Tests

When tests and inspections are required by the contract documents, laws, regulations, or orders of public authorities (building departments), the contractor is responsible for making arrangements with testing agencies acceptable to the owner or with the appropriate public authorities. The contractor pays for the tests and must give the architect timely notice of when and where the test is to be made so that the architect can observe the procedure.

If the architect, owner, or public authorities require additional testing beyond what is required in the contract documents, the architect should instruct the contractor to make arrangements, but only after obtaining written authorization from the owner. In this case, the owner pays for the tests.

The architect should not suggest how the safety violation can be corrected.

Regardless of whether the tests were required originally by the contract documents, or later by the architect or public authorities, if a test shows that a portion of the work does not conform to the contract documents (including violating building codes or other laws), the contractor must pay all costs needed to correct the problem. This includes the cost of additional testing required and compensation for the architect's services related to the issue.

In some cases special inspections of portions of the work may be required by provisions of the IBC. These are inspections that are required of materials, installation, fabrication, erection, or placement of components requiring special expertise to ensure compliance with the construction documents and referenced standards. Examples include prefabricated items, steel, concrete, sprayed fire-resistant materials, or systems designed to address seismic requirements. According to the *International Building Code* (IBC) the architect is required to develop a Statement of Special Inspections and submit this to the code official for review and approval. The owner, or the architect as the owner's agent, must engage a qualified, independent special inspection firm (not the contractor) to do the work. The owner pays for the costs of these services and tests. The results of the inspections and test must be submitted to the code official for evaluation and approval.

Documentation and Communication

During all phases of the architect's service, but especially during the construction administration phase, the architect should maintain complete documentation of the progress of the job. This includes the following.

- the standard forms used to administer the contract, such as change orders, certificates of payment, and the like
- correspondence
- memoranda
- meeting notes
- emails
- telephone logs
- similar written or electronic material that records the daily who, what, why, when, and how of the project

All documentation should have a date and the project name and/or number on it. This kind of documentation is important to have on file in case disputes arise or the client objects to fee payments for extra services of the architect. Even conversations should be documented if they affect the project. Written or electronic notes of the conversation should be recorded and a copy sent to those affected by any decisions made during the conversation.

One valuable documentation and communication tool is the project website. This can either be a website developed specifically for the participants in a project to use to share information and communicate with each other, or it may be a feature of a project management software program. The information shared can be made available to all participants, or access can be restricted to designated people. Some project management software also provides tools to facilitate communication and documentation of discussion, decisions, and documents related to the project, such as RFI responses and submittals, as well as time and expense tracking for the architectural firm.

Conformance with Sustainability Requirements

When a project is completed under AIA Document B101 SP, *Standard Form of Agreement Between Owner and Architect, for use on a Sustainable Project*, AIA Document A201 SP, *General Conditions of the Contract for Construction, for use on a Sustainable Project*, and one of the owner-contractor agreements for sustainable projects, the contract documents contain one of more of the following.

- the owner's goals for sustainability
- the objective to achieve a green building rating system certification (LEED certification, for example)
- desired benefits to the environment to enhance the health and well-being of building occupants
- guidelines for improving energy efficiency

One of the contract documents is the *sustainability plan*, which describes the following.

- targeted sustainable measures
- implementation strategies
- the owner's, architect's, and contractor's roles and responsibilities associated with achieving the sustainable measures
- details about design reviews, testing, or metrics to verify achievement of each sustainable measure
- the documentation and format required

During the construction administration phase, the architect has the following responsibilities. Refer to Chap. 5 for a summary of the architect's responsibilities prior to the construction administration phase and other details of contract requirements when a project is completed using AIA sustainability project documents.

- The architect must advise and consult with the owner regarding the progress of the project toward achieving the sustainable measures. As part of the field reports prepared during regular site visits, the architect must notify the owner of any known deviations from the contract documents that might impact achievement of sustainable measures.
- If a proposed design or construction change that is needed to address a field condition might impact a sustainable measure or the sustainable objective, the architect must notify the owner.
- The architect must respond to the contractor's requests for information when the contractor asks the architect to describe how a product, material, or equipment was intended to satisfy the requirements of a sustainable measure.
- The architect must register the project with the certifying authority. Any fees paid by the architect to do so are deemed reimbursable expenses.
- The architect must collect the sustainability documentation from the owner and contractor, organize and manage the information and confirm that it is in an appropriate format, and submit the documentation to the certifying authority as required for the sustainability certification process.
- The architect must prepare and submit the application for certification to the certifying authority and, if needed, prepare responses to any additional questions or documentation required by the certifying authority.

Assuming the architect receives timely notice from the owner or certifying authority, the architect must prepare and file necessary documentation to appeal a ruling or interpretation denying a requirement to achieve a sustainability certification.

Accelerated Schedules

While many construction scheduling problems involve delays, there are some instances where the schedule is actually accelerated. There are three primary causes for this. With *directed acceleration*, the owner instructs the contractor to speed up and agrees to pay the additional costs associated with the change, which is directed through a change order. With *voluntary acceleration*, the contractor may decide to accelerate the work because the work has fallen behind the original schedule, the construction company is trying to finish early to collect a bonus, or they want to move personnel to another job. With *constructive acceleration*, a situation may occur that causes an excusable or unavoidable delay, such as caused by weather, deliveries, or change orders, but the extra time is neither requested by the contractor nor granted by the owner. The contractor must determine how to speed up the process to meet the project deadline. The contractor may choose to file a claim for damages if the extra time is warranted but not given and the contractor had to incur extra expenses to complete the work on time.

Example 50.3

Which of the following is the contractor NOT solely responsible for?

(A) field reports to the owner

(B) selection of subcontractors

(C) scaffolding

(D) reviewing claims of subcontractors

Solution

Scaffolding is part of the means of construction, which is the contractor's responsibility.

Field reports are the responsibility of the architect. Selection of subcontractors is subject to the approval of both the architect and the owner. If a subcontractor makes a claim to the contractor, the contractor in turn makes a claim to the owner that is reviewed by the architect.

The answer is (C).

CHANGES IN THE WORK AND SUPPLEMENTAL DOCUMENTATION

During construction, changes in the work are usually needed. They may be necessitated by errors discovered in the drawings, unforeseen site conditions, design changes requested by the client, rulings of building officials, and many other factors. During bidding and prior to contract award, changes are made by addenda. Any costs associated with changes made by addenda are included in the contractor's bid. During construction, changes in the work are accomplished in one of three ways.

- minor changes in the work
- construction change directives
- change orders

Minor Changes in the Work

When a change does not involve modification of the contract sum or time and is consistent with the contract documents, the architect may issue a written order directing the contractor to make a minor change. For example, moving a door opening over 6 in before the wall is framed would be a minor change; if this change was requested after the wall was framed, however, the modification would have time or cost implications and would be handled through a change order. AIA Document G710, *Architect's Supplemental Instructions*, may be used for this purpose, as discussed later in this section. The architect may issue an order for such a minor change without the approval of either the owner or contractor.

Construction Change Directives

When a change needs to be made right away to allow the project to proceed, but the owner and contractor cannot agree on a price or time revision, the architect may issue a *construction change directive.* This is a written order prepared by the architect directing a change in the work before the owner and contractor agree on an adjustment in contract cost, time, or both. AIA Document G714, *Construction Change Directive*, may be used for this purpose, as discussed later in this section.

The construction change directive gives the owner a way to unilaterally order changes to the contract without changing the terms of the contract. It is used in the absence of total agreement on the terms of a change order. The change in the work may involve additions, deletions, or other revisions. The construction change directive must be signed by both the architect and the owner, but does not have to be signed by the contractor.

In addition to describing the changes needed, the directive should include a proposed basis for determining the adjustment of cost or time or both. If the directive involves a cost adjustment, the architect's proposed basis of adjustment must be based on one of four methods.

- a lump sum, properly itemized and mutually accepted
- unit prices previously agreed to in the specifications
- costs to be determined by mutual agreement on a fixed or percentage fee
- as provided for in a subsequent clause as summarized in the following paragraph

Under provisions of the *General Conditions of the Contract*, the contractor must proceed with the work described in the construction change directive in a timely manner and advise the architect of the contractor's agreement or disagreement with the basis for cost and time adjustment. If the contractor agrees with the architect's proposal, the change is recorded as a change order. If the contractor disagrees, the architect determines the appropriate adjustment based on evaluation of reasonable expenditures for additional labor and materials required, and calculated savings for deleted work. In addition to the actual cost of the work, the architect must include costs related to workers' benefits, equipment rental, supplies, premiums for bonds and insurance, field supervision, permit fees, and reasonable contractor profit.

While the parties make a determination of the total cost of the construction change directive, the contractor's applications for payment may include a request for payment for work completed under the directive. The architect must make an interim determination whether the costs are justified and, if so, include them in the monthly certification for payment. The architect's interim determination adjusts the contract sum on the same basis as a change order.

Change Orders

A *change order* is a document authorizing a variation from the original contract documents that involves a change in contract price, contract time, or both. Technically, a change order is issued by the owner because the owner has the agreement with the contractor, but it is prepared by the architect. It must be approved by the owner, architect, and contractor.

Any of the three parties may suggest a change order, but most of the time, the architect submits a proposal request to the contractor. This request is accompanied by supporting drawings or other documents as required to fully describe the proposed change. The contractor submits a quotation of price and time change to the architect for review. The architect evaluates the proposal and recommends approval of, modifications to, or rejection of the proposal to the owner, who makes the final decision. If the specifics are acceptable to the owner, the formal change order document is prepared and signed by all three parties.

Supplemental Contract Documentation

Questions inevitably arise during construction, not only from the contractor but from the architect and the owner as well. These questions should not be asked in informal phone calls or emails; more formal documentation should be used.

One way to proceed formally is to use AIA Document G716, *Request for Information* (RFI). This is a standard form that the owner, architect, and contractor may use to request further information from one another during construction. The form provides a space for the requesting party to list the relevant drawing, specification, or submittal reviewed in attempting to find information. The response to the RFI may include text as well as drawings but is neither a specific or implied authorization for work that increases the cost or time of the project.

When a minor change in the work is needed, the architect should issue AIA Document G710, *Architect's Supplemental Instructions* (ASI). This is intended to allow the architect to perform his or her obligations as interpreter of the contract documents in accordance with the owner-architect agreement and the *General Conditions of the Contract*. An ASI is a means for the architect to address minor changes to the extent that AIA Document A201 authorizes, and may include both written instructions and drawings.

When the owner and contractor cannot agree on a proposed change in the contract sum and/or time, the architect may issue AIA Document G714, *Construction Change Directive.* This directs the contractor to make a change, with the change in cost or time to be decided later. The directive may include both written instruction and drawings.

SUBMITTALS

After the contract is awarded, the contractor is responsible for providing those *submittals* that are called for in the contract documents. These include the following.

- shop drawings
- samples
- product data
- documents related to sustainability issues, where applicable

Submittal requirements are listed in each specification section; the requested information may vary depending on the type of material under consideration. The submittals are sometimes prepared by the contractor, but most often they are prepared by subcontractors, vendors, and material suppliers and reviewed by the general contractor for coordination before they are submitted to the architect. Although all submittals show in detail how much of the work is going to be built and installed, they are not contract documents.

Shop drawings are drawings, diagrams, schedules, and other data prepared to show how a subcontractor or supplier proposes to supply and install work to conform to the requirements of the contract documents for this specific project. Shop drawings are usually very detailed, showing how portions of the work will be constructed, and may include drawings showing how the particular product or assembly will fit into the building.

A *sample* is a physical example of a portion of the work, intended to show exactly how a material, finish, or piece of equipment will look in the completed job. A collection of samples may also be submitted so that the architect can choose a color or finish when this choice is not specifically identified in the specifications. Samples become standards of appearance and workmanship by which the final work will be judged. *Product data* include brochures, charts, instructions, performance data, catalog pages, and other information that illustrate some portion of the work. These data are usually published by the product manufacturer and is less specific than the information included in shop drawings, since the same documents may be used for multiple projects. A *cut sheet* is a short-format summary of a material or product's properties and characteristics and is often included in the product data submission. If the standard published data includes products other than those proposed for incorporation into the work, the contractor should clearly indicate which products are being submitted.

When shop drawings and other submittals are prepared by subcontractors and material suppliers, they are sent to the general contractor, who is responsible for reviewing and approving them. By reviewing them, the contractor confirms that field measurements have been verified, materials have been checked, and other construction criteria have been coordinated. If there are any decisions required of the architect (such as selection of a color or finish), these items should be identified on the submittal. After this review the contractor must give the submittals to the architect in accordance with the submittal schedule approved by the architect or, in the absence of an approved submittal schedule, with reasonable promptness and in sequence so there is no delay in the work.

The architect reviews the submittals only to check for conformance with the information given and the design intent. The architect is not responsible for determining the accuracy of measurements and completeness of details, for verifying quantities, or for checking fabrication or installation procedures. The architect's review does not relieve the contractor of the responsibilities set down in the contract documents.

If the submittals require the review of one of the architect's consultants, the architect forwards them to the consultant, who returns the submittals to the architect after review. The architect then reviews them and returns them to the contractor, who returns them to the subcontractor or material supplier who prepared them. The architect may indicate that no exceptions are taken, that marked corrections should be made, that the submittals should be revised and resubmitted, or that they are rejected.

Firms usually stamp submittals (either with a rubber stamp and ink pad, or electronically) with series of check boxes indicating the possible responses and the date and initials of the reviewer. The architect can use the check boxes to indicate the action taken as a result of the review. The stamp generally includes a statement that the submittal has been reviewed for conformance to the design intent and requirements of the construction documents only, and states that the contractor is responsible for coordination or dimensions, quantities, and construction techniques.

The architect's review does not relieve the contractor of the responsibilities set down in the contract documents.

The architect may also include comments or questions for the contractor and indicate the responses to any questions posed by the contractor. It is possible that the response to such questions may necessitate a change to the project time or cost; if this is the case, the architect can request that the contractor submit an RFI on the issue, which can initiate the change order process as necessary.

The architect must review submittals in accordance with the submittal schedule prepared by the contractor and approved at the beginning of the project by the architect. In the absence of an approved submittal schedule, the submittals are approved with reasonable promptness while allowing sufficient time in the architect's professional judgment to permit adequate review.

The issue of time is generally dealt with in two ways. First, the *General Conditions of the Contract for Construction* require the contractor to prepare a construction schedule for the project, which must include a schedule of submittals that allows the architect a reasonable amount of time for review. Second, in the section on submittals in Division 01 of the specifications, the architect should indicate the procedure for making submittals, including the time that the contractor must allow for review. When establishing the construction schedule, the contractor factors in this review period requirement and allows for the possibility that submittals may not be approved and will require resubmission.

Submittals are generally marked in one of four ways, although the language used varies by firm.

- approved
- approved with changes
- revise and resubmit
- rejected

Marking a submittal "approved," "no exceptions taken," or "reviewed" implies that the product or assembly may be incorporated into the work as submitted and is in compliance with the requirements of the contract documents. Submittals may also be marked "approved with changes noted," "approved as noted," or "note markings." This means that if the changes indicated are made, the product or assembly may be used on the project. If submittals are marked in either of these ways they do not require resubmission by the contractor or additional review by the architect.

Submittals for items that do not comply with the contract requirements are marked "revise and resubmit" or "rejected." "Revise and resubmit" is usually used when the product may be suitable for use on the project but the information provided is inadequate for performing a thorough review, or when there are significant errors or conflicts in the submittals package. "Rejected" indicates that the product proposed does not comply with the contract requirements and may not be used on the project. If submittals are marked in either of these ways, they are returned to the contractor with comments, and the contractor must prepare additional or revised submittal data and submit it to the architect again.

Model specifications often designate submittals as action or informational submittals. An action submittal requires the architect's review and approval before the product may be used on the project. If the contractor proceeds without obtaining the architect's approval, the item is provided at the risk of the contractor, and if the properties of the item do not comply with the contract requirements, the contractor may be required to remove and replace it at the contractor's own expense. Informational submittals do not require a response from the architect.

According to the owner-architect agreement, the architect must keep a log of submittals as well as copies of the submittals. For each submittal, the log should include the submittal name or other identification and the date it was received by the architect. The log should also include the date the submittal was sent from the architect to the consultant (if necessary), the date it was returned to the architect by the consultant, and the date it was returned to the contractor. The action taken on each submittal should be noted.

Shop drawings and submittals are not a way for the architect to make changes in the design or refine details. Although minor corrections and changes can be made, the contractor may request a change order if the architect's modification of the shop drawings or samples results in an increase in project cost or time.

APPLICATIONS FOR PAYMENT

During the course of a job, the contractor is entitled to receive periodic payments, usually monthly, against the total contract sum. These payments reflect progress to date and allow the contractor to have a stream of income with which to pay for materials and compensate employees and subcontractors for services provided to date.

Under the *General Conditions of the Contract*, the architect is responsible for making sure that the amounts requested are consistent with the amount of work performed and the quantities of materials stored.

Intermediate Payments

In order to receive periodic payment, the contractor must submit to the architect a notarized application for payment at least 10 days before the date established for each payment in the owner-contractor agreement. This application should include the value of work—both labor and materials—completed up to the date of the application, in addition to the value of materials purchased and in acceptable storage but not yet incorporated into the work.

The actual time and money expended can be compared to the budgeted amounts to determine how the project is progressing.

In most cases, 'acceptable storage' means stored at the site. However, if approved in advance by the owner, payment can also be authorized for materials and equipment suitably stored off site at a location agreed to in writing. When the application for payment includes off-site storage, the amount must also include costs of applicable insurance, storage, and transportation to the site.

Certification of the application for payment requires confirmation by the architect that the work has progressed to the point indicated and that, to the best of the architect's knowledge, information, and belief, the quality of the work is in accordance with the contract documents. Certification is *not* a representation that the architect has

- made exhaustive on-site inspections
- reviewed construction methods, techniques, or procedures
- reviewed copies of requisitions received from subcontractors and material
- determined how and for what purpose the contractor has used money previously paid

Sometimes a subcontractor may want to know if the contractor has been paid for work performed by the subcontractor but has not received payment from the contractor. AIA Document 201, *General Conditions of the Contract for Construction* allows the architect to provide, upon request by the subcontractor, the percentages of completion or amounts applied for by the contractor.

The amount due to the contractor is based on the *schedule of values* that the contractor submits to the architect after the award of the contract. This allocates the total contract sum to various portions of work, such as site work, foundations, framing, and so forth. The contractor indicates the percentage of completion of each line item on the pay application. The difference between the quantities between one application for payment and the previous represents the amount of work completed during the payment period and the amount of money due to the contractor.

A project management technique that is often used to determine the schedule of values is the *earned value management* method (sometimes called *earned value analysis*). This technique attempts to predict both the time and money (or percentage of overall project budget) that is required to complete certain tasks. The actual time and money expended can be compared to the budgeted amounts to determine how the project is progressing.

If the application for payment is approved, the architect signs it and sends it to the owner for payment. An amount, called the *retainage*, is withheld from each application until the end of the job or another time during the work that is agreed on by both the contractor and the owner. This is usually about 10% of the total contract sum. The retainage gives the owner leverage in making sure the job is completed and can be used to provide money to satisfy lien claims. As the project nears satisfactory completion, the retainage amount may be reduced.

The architect may withhold all or a portion of the funds requested on applications for payment in order to protect the owner, if the architect cannot represent that the amount of work done or materials stored is in conformance with the application. The architect may also withhold payment for any of the following reasons.

- defective work not remedied
- third-party claims or evidence of probability of third-party claims
- known failure of the contractor to make payments to subcontractors (however, approval of an application for payment does not indicate that the architect has confirmed that the contractor is making such payments to subcontractors)
- reasonable evidence that the work cannot be completed for the unpaid balance of the contract sum
- damage to the owner or a separate contractor
- reasonable evidence that the work will not be completed on time and that the unpaid balance will not be sufficient to cover damages due to the delay
- repeated failure of the contractor to carry out the work in accordance with the contract documents.

Public projects that require the use of prevailing wage rates may require submission of payroll records with applications for payment.

Final Payment

After the final punch list inspection, the contractor notifies the architect in writing that the work is ready for final inspection and submits a final application for payment. If, after a final inspection, the architect determines that the work is complete and acceptable under the conditions of the contract documents, a final certificate for payment is issued to the owner. At this time, the withheld retainage may be released and paid to the contractor.

Before the certificate can be issued, however, the contractor must submit to the architect the following items.

- an affidavit stating that payrolls, materials, and other debts for which the owner might be responsible have been paid (AIA Document G706, *Contractor's Affidavit of Payment of Debts and Claims*, is often used)
- a certificate showing that insurance required by the contract documents to remain in force after final payment will not be canceled or allowed to expire without at least 30 days' written notice to the owner

- a written statement that the contractor knows of no reason that the insurance will not be renewable
- the consent of surety to final payment, if applicable (AIA Document G707, *Consent of Surety to Final Payment*, may be used for this purpose)
- any other data required by the owner that establishes evidence of payment of obligations, such as releases and waivers of liens

If final completion is delayed through no fault of the contractor, the owner may, with certification by the architect, make partial payment for that portion completed without terminating the contract.

NONCONFORMANCE WITH CONTRACT DOCUMENTS

During any project there are aspects of construction that do not conform to the contract documents. Elements may be missing, incorrectly installed, of the wrong type, or of a quality not meeting the requirements of the specifications. In most cases it is a minor problem, like a door being the wrong size. Sometimes it is a major problem, such as an incorrectly installed structural detail that could threaten building collapse.

Although the architect is not required to make exhaustive or continuous on-site inspections to check the quality or quantity of the work, if the architect notices something that deviates from the contract documents, the contractor and owner must be notified. Although the architect may make an informal verbal comment to the contractor when the deficiency is identified, this observation must be documented in writing in a field report; the format most commonly used is AIA Document G711. These reports are sent to the contractor, owner, and other designated parties. The nonconforming work should be tracked until it is corrected.

Ultimately, however, the architect is *not* responsible for the contractor's failure to perform the work in accordance with the requirements of the contract documents, as stated in AIA Document A201.

Rejecting Work

Under AIA Document A201, *General Conditions of the Contract*, the architect has the authority to reject work that does not conform to the contract documents. Because rejecting work will result in extra time and expense for the contractor, the reasons for rejection should be carefully documented, and the owner should be kept informed of the situation.

The architect has the authority to require inspection or testing of work when it is suspected that it does not conform to the contract requirements, whether or not such work is fabricated, installed, or completed. However, this action does not give rise to any duty or responsibility of the architect to the contractor, subcontractors, or anyone else performing portions of the work.

The contractor must promptly correct work rejected by the architect or work not conforming to the contract documents, whether discovered before or after substantial completion. The contractor pays for the cost of correcting such work.

As discussed in Chap. 5 describing the terms of AIA Document A201, if the contractor fails to correct work not in conformance with the contract documents, the owner may order the contractor to stop the work until the issue is resolved. The owner also has the right to carry out the work if the contractor fails to correctly do so and to charge these expenses to the contractor.

Accepting Nonconforming Work

At times, an element of the construction does not conform to the design intent or the requirements of the contract documents, yet may be determined to be acceptable in terms of appearance, functionality, and quality. For example, the contractor may apply a vinyl wall fabric from a different manufacturer than specified, but the product may be essentially the same color and weight and perform in the same way as the specified product.

Rather than rejecting the work and possibly delaying the project or causing other problems, the architect may accept it with the approval of the owner. The deviation should still be noted on the field report as required by contract. If the accepted product or work is determined to be less expensive that the specified product would have been, the owner has the right to request a credit for the difference. If the installed product or work is more expensive than the work required by the contract documents, and the error is the contractor's or the substitution was made without the owner's approval, the contractor will bear the cost.

There are also times when nonconforming work is not acceptable to the architect but acceptable to the owner. For example, the wood grain pattern on paneling may not be what the specifications called for, and the architect may object to the final appearance, but the owner does not view the difference as objectionable and is willing to accept it. In this case, the owner has the final authority to accept the deviation, but the architect, as required by contract, must note the difference as not conforming to the contract documents. On the certificate of substantial completion, the architect should note the difference as a nonconforming exception. The contractor must document the deviation on the as-built drawings as required by AIA Document A201 or a similar agreement.

Disputes and Claims

Disputes and claims are a part of any construction project, and these typically occur during the construction phase. The procedure to be followed if a claim or dispute arises is outlined in the *General Conditions of the Contract.*

A *claim* is a demand or assertion by the contractor or owner seeking payment of money, an extension of time, an adjustment or interpretation of the contract terms, or other relief from terms of the contract. Claims must be made by written notice to the other party and to the architect. They also must be initiated within 21 days from the occurrence of what prompted the claim or within 21 days after the person making the claim first recognized the problem. Whoever makes the claim must substantiate it with documentation or other evidence.

Claims are first referred to the initial decision maker (IDM). The IDM is usually the architect unless the owner and contractor agreed to name a third-party IDM in the owner-contractor agreement. (See Chap. 5 for a more detailed discussion of this.)

If the owner or contractor has a dispute or makes a claim, the IDM must take certain preliminary action within 10 days of receipt of the claim. Such action may include

- requesting additional supporting data from the claimant
- suggesting a compromise
- accepting the claim
- rejecting the claim
- advising the parties that the IDM is unable to resolve the claim because of a lack of sufficient information
- advising the parties that it would be inappropriate for the IDM to resolve the claim

In evaluating claims, the IDM may consult with or seek information from either party or from anyone with special knowledge or expertise relevant to the situation. The IDM can ask the owner to authorize the retention of experts at the owner's expense. If the IDM asks either the owner or the contractor to respond to a claim or provide additional information, that person must respond within 10 days and must either give the response or information, tell the IDM when the response will be furnished, or tell the IDM that no supporting data will be provided.

The approval or rejection of a claim by the IDM is final and binding on the parties but is subject to mediation and binding dispute resolution. A demand for mediation can be made by the claiming party at any time. Mediation is a condition precedent to arbitration, litigation, or the institution of other legal proceedings and these procedures are discussed later in this section.

Although claims can arise from a multitude of conditions, there are two that are especially common.

- *claims for additional time.* If the contractor feels that extra time is needed, the reasons for the request must be submitted and include an estimate of the cost. If weather conditions are the basis for the claim, the contractor must submit evidence that weather conditions were abnormal for the time period, could not have been reasonably anticipated, and had an adverse effect on the construction schedule; this evidence may be obtained from a source such as the National Weather Service.
- *claims for concealed or unknown conditions.* Sometimes there are surprises on the job site once construction begins. When this happens, the contractor may make a claim for additional time or money. However, to be valid, the unknown conditions must meet one of two criteria: (1) they must be subsurface in nature or otherwise physically concealed, causing the site to differ from what is shown on the contract documents, or (2) they must be of an unusual nature that is different from what would ordinarily be found as part of construction activities for the project type. For example, test borings may indicate a standard type of soil, and the contractor may budget for normal excavation. If a large boulder is discovered that requires blasting or special excavation techniques, the contractor would be entitled to extra money and possibly an extension of the contract time. According to the *General Conditions of the Contract,* claims of this type must be made within 21 days from first discovery.

Mediation and Arbitration

Mediation and *arbitration* are methods of resolving claims and disputes without the lengthy and costly procedure of litigation. Both methods make use of neutral third parties to help the parties reach a resolution. Mediation is not legally binding; arbitration is. Under the *General Conditions of the Contract,* if a dispute cannot be resolved by the IDM, the owner and contractor must try to resolve it through mediation before they may resort to a legally binding method such as arbitration or litigation. (See also Chap. 5.)

In mediation, a mediator facilitates a discussion between the parties using techniques in compliance with the Model Standards of Conduct for Mediators. The mediator defines and limits the issues, puts the issues in perspective, and sees that each side in the dispute hears and understands the opposing point of view. The mediator does not judge the case; the role of the mediator is to guide the parties toward reaching their own settlement.

Arbitration is a more formal process. Under the *General Conditions,* arbitration proceedings are conducted under the Construction Industry Arbitration Rules of the American Arbitration Association and any applicable state laws.

Under arbitration, the two parties agree to submit their claims to an arbitrator or a panel of three arbitrators and agree to abide by the arbitrator's or arbitrators' decision. The arbitrator or arbitration board is knowledgeable about the construction industry and listens to evidence, reviews documents, and hears witnesses before making a decision.

Arbitration has the advantages over litigation of speed, economy, and privacy. However, unlike a trial, there are no rules of evidence, and the decision cannot be appealed.

Example 50.4

A pressure test on plumbing supply piping required by the specifications reveals a leak in the system. According to AIA Document A201, the responsibility for fixing the leak and paying for a follow-up test rests with the

(A) owner

(B) contractor

(C) plumbing subcontractor

(D) owner and contractor jointly

Solution

AIA Document A201, Sec. 13.5.3, requires the contractor to be responsible for all costs made necessary by failures, including costs of repeated tests.

The answer is (B).

ADDITIONAL CONSTRUCTION ADMINISTRATION ACTIVITIES

In addition to the construction administration duties discussed in this chapter, the architect is responsible for completing the following project management tasks.

- verifying that the owner has received the required performance bonds and labor and material payment bonds
- verifying that the contractor issues acceptable certificates of insurance to the client
- establishing a site visit schedule based on contract and project requirements
- receiving the construction schedule from the contractor.
- receiving field reports from design consultants and forwarding copies to the client
- reviewing and approving design consultant's billings
- monitoring the contractor's progress against the construction schedule and notifying the client of any problems that may be identified
- monitoring the architect's fees expended and conformance to the architect's schedule
- monitoring allowances and contingencies
- maintaining all documentation of construction administration activities, including issuance of architect's supplemental instructions, responses to requests for information, construction change directives, and change orders
- verifying issuance of certificate of occupancy by the building official
- monitoring conformance to sustainability requirements and process reports, certificates, and other forms as required by the type of sustainability certification being used

51

PROJECT CLOSEOUT

The process by which a project is deemed complete must be executed with as much care as any of the project's earlier stages. There are also several important activities to be carried out after the project is completed.

- building commissioning
- project follow-up
- post-occupancy evaluation

PROJECT CLOSEOUT

Project closeout is the final portion of the construction administration phase. During this time the building work is completed, the structure is made ready for occupancy, and all remaining documentation is finalized.

One of the most important milestones of a project is the date of *substantial completion*. This is the point in the project at which the work is sufficiently complete in accordance with the contract documents so that the owner can occupy or utilize the work for its intended purpose. The date of substantial completion has many legal and administrative implications. For example, in many states, the statute of limitations for errors or omissions caused by the architect begins with the date of substantial completion.

The contractor's schedule for the project ends at the date of substantial completion. If there are early completion bonuses or liquidated damages involved, they are based on this date. The date of substantial completion also establishes responsibilities of the owner and contractor for security, maintenance, utilities, warranties, damage to the work, and insurance.

The architect then makes an inspection to determine whether the work (or a portion of it) is substantially complete.

As detailed in AIA Document A201, *General Conditions of the Contract for Construction*, the contractor begins closeout procedures by notifying the architect in writing and submitting a comprehensive list of items still to be completed or corrected. The architect then makes an inspection to determine whether the work (or a designated portion of it) is substantially complete and whether there are more items that need to be added to the list.

The list of items made by the architect as a result of the inspection is called the *punch list*. During this inspection for substantial completion, the architect notes work that needs to be completed and items that need to be corrected because they are not in accordance with the contract documents. The contractor must correct these items, after which another inspection is held.

If this second inspection determines the work to be substantially complete, the architect prepares a certificate of substantial completion that establishes the date of substantial completion. AIA Document G704, *Certificate of Substantial Completion*, may be used for this purpose. The architect should include a statement of time within which the contractor must correct or complete any remaining items, as well as a list of any nonconforming work that the owner has accepted. The certificate of substantial completion is submitted to both the owner and contractor, for their written acceptance of the responsibilities that the certificate assigns to them.

If, based on the site inspection, the architect determines that the work is not substantially complete, the architect notifies the contractor of work that must be completed before a certificate of substantial completion can be prepared. The owner may choose to move into and use the building (or part of it) while punch list work is still being corrected, or the owner may choose to wait until the entire project is complete.

After the contractor has completed all remaining work, the contractor notifies the architect in writing that the work is ready for a final inspection and acceptance. The contractor sends a final application for payment with this request, and the architect schedules and performs the final inspection. As a part of the work following the substantial completion date, the contractor must also complete final cleaning, instruct the owner or owner's representatives in the operation of systems and equipment, complete the keying for locks and turn keys over to the owner, and restore any items damaged by the contractor. If the specifications require the contractor to provide *attic stock*, or extra materials for future repairs, this material should be delivered and documented.

If the architect finds the work acceptable and in compliance with the contract requirements, the architect issues the final certificate for payment and the entire balance due to the contractor, including retainage, is due and payable. Final completion is documented by the architect's issuance of the final certificate for payment. (There is no AIA document published for this purpose; the *General Conditions* outline the necessary steps and documentation.) The architect's consultants may issue separate certificates of completion for their portions of the work, such as electrical, HVAC, and so forth.

Before authorizing final payment, the architect must receive the following documentation from the contractor.

- an affidavit that payrolls, bills for materials and equipment, and other project-related expenses have been paid
- a certificate proving that insurance required by the contract to remain in force after final payment is currently in effect
- a written statement that the contractor knows of no substantial reason that the insurance will not be renewed
- consent of surety to final payment, if applicable
- other data establishing payment or satisfaction of obligations arising out of the contract
- all warranties, maintenance contracts, operating instructions, certificates of inspection, and bonds
- all documentation required to be submitted with the application for final payment (as described above)
- a set of as-built drawings, if required by the owner-contractor agreement
- the certificate of occupancy as issued by the building department (this is part of the permit process originally paid for by the contractor)
- extra stock of materials as called for in the specifications

The architect's services may terminate when the final certificate for payment is issued, if so described in the owner-architect agreement. In AIA Document B101, *Standard Form of Agreement Between Owner and Architect*, and similar agreements, construction administration services provided by the architect beyond the date of substantial completion are considered an additional service.

Example 51.1

The punch list is created and maintained by the

(A) architect

(B) authority having jurisdiction

(C) contractor

(D) owner

Solution

The punch list is a list of items still needing completion. It is created and maintained by the architect.

The answer is (A).

BUILDING COMMISSIONING

Building commissioning is the process of planning, designing, installing, inspecting, testing, starting up, and adjusting building systems and then verifying and documenting that they operate as intended and meet the design criteria of the contract documents. Commissioning is an expansion of the traditional testing, adjusting, and balancing (TAB) that is commonly performed on mechanical systems, but with a greatly broadened scope.

The commissioning agent is ideally involved with the project throughout the design and construction process and provides post construction evaluation services. Building commissioning is often thought of as a quality control process for enhancing the delivery of a project; usually a third party, separate from the design team and the contractor, provides these services. Commissioning of the energy systems is a prerequisite for LEED certification.

The Commissioning Process

The extent of the building commissioning process varies with the size and function of the project and the amount of time and money the owner is willing to expend for these services. There are three basic stages of commissioning: determining performance requirements, planning the commissioning process, and performance and functional testing. The commissioning agent should participate in the project from the programming phase through post-occupancy and should document the whole process of commissioning.

Determining Performance Requirements

Building commissioning begins during the design phase, or even the pre-design phase, with the determination of which systems will be commissioned and what the criteria for acceptance will be, and the preparation of commissioning specifications to outline the requirements for subsequent phases. One of the documents developed during this stage is the *owner's project requirements* (OPR), which is a summary of the critical planning requirements and owner expectations. This statement can be extensive if the project is complex or includes multiple buildings, and it should be updated by the commissioning team as the project progresses. This stage of the commissioning process may take place in parallel with the overall programming phase of the project.

The OPR is developed into a *basis of design* (BOD) document during the design phase. The BOD explains how the OPR have been satisfied by the proposed design. While the OPR are broad statements regarding the performance of the building and its systems and energy efficiency goals, the BOD is a more technical document used for systems selections, integration, and sequence of operations.

Planning the Commissioning Process

Drafting a commissioning plan includes determining the scope of the commissioning activities, establishing a budget, setting a schedule, establishing a testing and inspection plan, developing specifications, determining special testing needs, and writing a commissioning plan. The commissioning plan is a written statement that may include

- introduction and description of the scope of the commissioning
- list of the systems and other elements to be commissioned
- responsibilities and identification of team members
- commissioning schedule
- commissioning protocols
- documentation required during the process
- test procedures and inspection plans
- construction checklists

Performance and Functional Testing

The most important part of the commissioning process occurs near the completion of the construction phase, when the various building systems and other elements slated for commissioning are started up and tested to determine whether they meet the design criteria. The contractor adjusts, corrects, and repairs incorrectly functioning equipment as needed to comply with the performance standards. The operation and maintenance of the building systems controls and equipment are demonstrated, and training is conducted for the building operators (owner).

During this phase, the commissioning agent generates a *commissioning report*; this report summarizes the results of the construction-phase commissioning tests and provides detailed operation and maintenance instructions for each of the systems. The commissioning agent also reviews the equipment manufacturers' product information and manuals and may include this documentation in a report to the owner.

Finally, commissioning activities and evaluation should continue into the post-occupancy phase. Ideally, this testing should occur one year after initial occupancy to verify that systems continue to operate as intended under normal occupancy and operating conditions. Adjustments and corrections should take place at this time if necessary. Ideally, the contractor's warranty should be coordinated with the commissioning activities so that the contractor can make any corrections under warranty.

Elements of Building Commissioning

Which building systems and construction elements require commissioning will depend on the complexity of the building and the needs of the owner. For example, a hospital will require more thorough commissioning of a greater number of types of systems than a small office building will. These elements may include some or all of the following.

- mechanical systems (including heating and cooling equipment, air handling equipment, distribution systems, pumps, sensors and controls, dampers, and cooling tower operation)
- electrical systems (including switchgear, controls, emergency generators, fire management systems, and safety systems)
- plumbing systems (including tanks, pumps, water heaters, compressors, and fixtures)
- fire suppression (sprinkler) systems (including standpipes, alarms, hose cabinets, and controls)
- fire management and life safety systems (including alarms and detectors, air handling equipment, smoke dampers, and building communications)
- energy efficiency and water efficiency
- vertical transportation systems (including elevator controls and escalators)
- telecommunication and computer networks
- exterior envelope
- accessibility
- security and safety
- survivability
- space functionality
- maintainability

The Commissioning Provider and Team

Because commissioning a large, complex building is an involved process, a knowledgeable person should be responsible for coordinating the efforts of everyone on the team. In most cases the *commissioning provider* (CxP, also known as the *commissioning agent* or CxA) should be an independent, third-party agent who specializes in this service and is hired by the owner. The CxP may also be a construction manager if the CM is serving as advisor and not part of the contractor's firm. Occasionally, an architectural or engineering firm may act as CxP, provided it has the expertise and can provide these services with objectivity. Architects may use AIA Document B211, *Standard Form of Architect's Services: Commissioning,* for contractual agreement to provide these services to the owner.

The following people should participate in building commissioning.

- commissioning provider
- architect
- mechanical, electrical, and plumbing engineers as well as other design consultants as appropriate
- general contractor
- various subcontractors providing elements of the systems to be commissioned, such as mechanical, electrical, fire protection, and so on
- owner, owner's operation personnel, and owner's maintenance personnel
- others directly involved with the construction process, including the owner's agent, code officials, and construction manager

Example 51.2

In most cases, the person responsible for coordinating the process of commissioning a large building should be

(A) the architect

(B) the constructor

(C) the owner

(D) a third-party agent

Solution

Commissioning a large building can be a complicated process, and in most cases it should be done by an independent, third-party agent.

The answer is (D).

PROJECT FOLLOW-UP AND ADDITIONAL SERVICES

In addition to the administrative tasks required by the contract documents, project closeout may include other activities that can benefit both the owner and the architect. Maintaining a good follow-up program has several advantages for the architect's firm.

- Helping an owner through the difficult period of a move creates a lasting good impression of the firm. Satisfied owners are good references for future projects and one of the most important components of any firm's marketing program.
- Continued follow-up makes it possible to maintain contacts within the owner's organization for future business development, either for expansion of the owner's building, work on other projects with which the owner may be involved, or for referrals to other organizations.
- Follow-up provides the opportunity for evaluation of a completed, occupied design. The knowledge gained should be placed in an office database and reused for future projects to continually upgrade the quality of the firm's services. This knowledge may include written notes, drawings of details that worked well (or didn't work), well-written specifications, photographs, and other information. However, this knowledge base should be maintained without reference to specific projects, to avoid liability issues.

Moving into a new building can be a difficult experience for an owner; both operational processes and personnel must adapt to a new situation. Even if the new building is an improvement over the old one, people can find it hard to make changes and get used to a new environment. Problems and complaints are often common during the first few weeks or months of occupancy, as furniture and equipment are installed, occupants begin using building elements, and the owner and owner's staff begin getting to know the building.

The architect can assist the owner with minor problems in a hand-holding capacity by forwarding problems to the appropriate persons, explaining new features of the building, suggesting modifications to how the building is used, and answering relevant questions from the occupants.

It is also helpful to both the client and the design firm to make follow-up visits at six-month and one-year intervals. At these visits, a representative of the firm can review maintenance problems, look for defects that should be repaired under the contractor's or manufacturer's warranties, and see how materials and other design decisions are withstanding the test of time.

These services should be expected when preparing the initial agreement, because AIA Document B101, *Standard Form of Agreement Between Owner and Architect*, provides that the owner may request that the architect, without additional compensation, conduct a meeting with the owner to review the facility operations and performance. This meeting must take place within one year of the date of substantial completion.

Additional follow-up activities may include

- verifying that all operating instructions, guarantees, maintenance guidelines, and other documentation required by contract have been forwarded to the client
- verifying that the owner has received all lien waivers
- photographing the project
- sending a gift to the client, to arrive in time for opening ceremonies, if any
- holding an in-house review of the project
- evaluating the performance of consultants on the project
- compiling information about schedule performance, design fees, and construction costs for in-house records
- completing a job history for office records and use by marketing staff
- filing all project-related documents, to be kept for the required retention period

POST-OCCUPANCY EVALUATION

A *post-occupancy evaluation* (POE) is a review of a completed project after the client has occupied it for some time, typically from three to six months. A POE is not a standard part of the architect's services, but can be incorporated by including it in the original list of services in one of the standard AIA owner-architect agreements, or by using AIA Document G802, *Amendment to the Professional Services Agreement.* A POE can also be contracted for separately after the project is complete. From the architect's standpoint, it may be preferable to use AIA Document G802 because any POE services are added to the original agreement; the statute of limitations thus begins on the date of substantial completion, rather than the much later date when the POE is completed.

Most often, the client will be unwilling to pay extra for a formal evaluation of a new building unless the client intends to construct additional, similar facilities. In most instances, then, a POE is an informal review undertaken at the architect's own expense and for the benefit of the architecture firm.

Regardless of how it is accomplished or who pays for it, a POE provides valuable information for the architect. As mentioned above, it is a good public relations effort, and it allows the architect to maintain contact with the client for marketing purposes. A POE can also be turned into a more rigorous and extensive research effort to provide the basis for evidence-based design as described in Chap. 30.

POEs are performed to provide answers to some or all of the following questions. These issues may also be considered as a part of a one-year walkthrough, if requested by the owner prior to the one-year date from substantial completion.

- Is the design image consistent with the owner's stated goals?
- Does the final design satisfy the original program requirements?
- Is adequate flexibility and expansibility provided, consistent with the owner's original needs?
- Are rooms and spaces of adequate size for their intended function?
- Were all required adjacencies provided?
- Are all site features working as intended?
- Have any structural problems been identified?
- Is the exterior envelope, including the roof, functioning as designed?
- Are construction details adequate for their use?
- Are materials and finishes holding up to use?
- Is the lighting adequate for all spaces?
- Are the HVAC systems functioning as designed?
- Are the plumbing fixtures working properly?
- Is the fire protection system working properly?
- Are the acoustics adequate?
- Were adequate power and communication networks provided?
- Are energy conservation systems and products performing satisfactorily?
- Are the actual users of the space satisfied with the performance of the building?
- Is the owner satisfied with the project?

In addition to evaluating the building itself, the architect should review in what ways the project delivery process worked and did not work, so that improvements can be made for future jobs. The firm should also review design processes, programming information, project management techniques, scheduling, fee allotment, specification and detailing methods, and construction documentation procedures.

Example 51.3

Which of the following statements about post-occupancy evaluations (POEs) is true?

(A) typically made three to six months after occupancy

(B) a standard part of an architect's services

(C) typically paid for by the client

(D) performed for the benefit of the client, not the architect

Solution

A post-occupancy evaluation is a review of a completed project, typically made three to six months after occupancy. However, it is not a standard part of an architect's services. It is most often performed at the architect's expense for the benefit of the architectural firm.

The answer is (A).

INDEX

B

C

E

G

H

INDEX - H

J

K

L

M

INDEX - L

P

INDEX - P

Q

R

S

INDEX - S

INDEX - S

U

INDEX - T

X

Y

INDEX - Y

Z